ADDITIONAL Praise for the *Global Handbook of Impact Investing*

"A society filled with justice and opportunity for each of us, in a sustainably cultivated natural world, can also result in profitable investment portfolios. Via impact investing, we can invest in equitable communities, beneficial banks, regenerative farms, climate, and equity-forward public schools, that boost well-being for families around the world. This global handbook provides investors innovative pathways that fund solutions for building a better world."

Kat Taylor, JD/MBA, Board Chair, Past CEO, Co-Founder, Beneficial State Bank; Board Chair, Community Development Bankers Association; Impact Investor

"With a decade left to meet the 17 Sustainable Development Goals by 2030, we need all forms of finance—public and private—to work together to develop new solutions for social and environmental crises, under stress as a result of COVID-19. This book is a must-read for anyone who believes that a greener and more sustainable world is the only way forward."

Hon. Jorge Moreira da Silva, Director, OECD Development Co-operation Directorate, former Minister of Environment, Energy & Spatial Planning for Portugal

"Communities and governments around the world are reeling from the triple whammy of COVID-19, the erosion of civil society, and failing economies. This book is a compelling antidote for institutional, philanthropic and family office investors who want to be part of the solution—a comprehensive guide to net positive investing, a viable and systems-level intervention that the world and investors need now."

Lisa Kleissner and Charly Kleissner, 100% Impact Investors; Founders, KL Felicitas Foundation; Founders, TONIIC and the "100% for Impact Investing Network"

"Impact investing is an emerging strand of finance, and yet its market is growing so fast, that makes it hard to picture this new age of finance in a global handbook. Elsa de Morais Sarmento and R. Paul Herman met the challenge, by taking on board an intrepid group of 50 academics and experts. They substituted the traditional parameters of labor, land, and networks with the new sustainable ones—people, planet, and trust—to build up a useful guide to the impact investment market, products, and risk management. An interesting read for anyone willing to approach finance with a responsible attitude."

Dr. Mario La Torre, Full Professor of Sustainable Finance and Impact Banking at Sapienza University of Rome; responsible for the Center for Positive Finance, Unitelma Sapienza

"Every global citizen needs access to healthy food, clean air and water, and affordable mobility—but how can we deliver this at scale and in an equitable way? Impact investors can accelerate solutions by committing global portfolios to investments that are specifically designed to address climate change and social equity. This global handbook shares how impact investors can realize financial, environmental, and social results through a variety of tools. There is no time like the present to mobilize more capital and more people to build a better future for all."

Dawn Lippert, MEM, Founder and CEO, Elemental Excelerator; Director, Innovation and Community, Emerson Collective; Founder, Women in Renewable Energy (WiRE)

"The awareness and allocations to Socially Responsible Investing (SRI) and Environmental, Social and Governance (ESG) have led to the discipline of impact investing globally. Impact investing requires new tools, new approaches, new organizations, and essentially, a whole new mindset, leading to an investment approach that moves us faster and closer towards a better, more sustainable world. Thus, training students, professionals, and leaders of the finance community is essential. This global handbook is a significant and meaningful contribution to achieving this goal."

Dr. Thierry Sibieude, Professor, ESSEC Business School, Chaired Professor in Social Innovation and Entrepreneurship

"Impact investing is a brilliant path forward for humanity, seeking to deliver the power of the capital markets to the world's biggest challenges. The *Global Handbook of Impact Investing* spurs hope with prescriptions for bolder action—including quantifiable outcomes for people and our planet—by those investors compelled to allocate their portfolios to pursue both measurable purpose and sustainable profit."

Eric Letsinger, MBA, Founder and CEO of Quantified Ventures

"An inclusive, resilient economy perpetuates the interests of markets, communities and the environment. To catalyze this shift to a more sustainable economic system requires unprecedented partnerships, policy changes, innovation, and investment. This global handbook captures the powerful role that impact investing plays in driving change, helping to reshape the global economy so that investors and society can accurately value natural, social and human capital."

Tazia Smith, CFA, Managing Director at Closed Loop Partners; co-founder of the IMP+ACT Alliance; former MD Deutsche Bank; former VP, Goldman Sachs

"The *Global Handbook of Impact Investing* should be a major tool in any problem solver's toolbelt. When done well, impact investing can increase one's asset base, complement philanthropy, and scale in a cost-effective way while creating measurable social impact. This global handbook explains how investors can improve the quality of life in local communities and global regions by embedding impact criteria in every financial allocation of capital."

Josh Cohen, Managing Partner, City Light Capital; Board Member, Impact Capital Managers; co-founder, The ImPact

"The *Global Handbook of Impact Investing* adds tremendous depth and breadth for investors with the goals of cleaner energy, higher quality of life for citizens, and well-functioning societies."

Hans Kobler, MBA, Founder and Managing Partner, Energy Impact Partners

Global Handbook
of Impact Investing

Global Handbook of Impact Investing

Solving Global Problems via Smarter Capital Markets Towards a More Sustainable Society

Edited by
Elsa De Morais Sarmento
Paul R. Herman

WILEY

For general information on our other products and services or for technical support, please contact our Customer Care Department within the United States at (800) 762-2974, outside the United States at (317) 572-3993, or fax (317) 572-4002.

Wiley publishes in a variety of print and electronic formats and by print-on-demand. Some material included with standard print versions of this book may not be included in e-books or in print-on-demand. If this book refers to media such as a CD or DVD that is not included in the version you purchased, you may download this material at http://booksupport.wiley.com. For more information about Wiley products, visit www.wiley.com.

Library of Congress Cataloging-in-Publication Data is available:

9781119690641 (hardback)
9781119691082 (ePDF)
9781119691136 (ePUB)

Cover Design: Wiley
Cover Image: © Wang An Qi/Shutterstock

SKY10022784_112020

From Elsa
Dedicated to my husband, António,
and my children, Inês, Francisco, and Sofia,
who enrich my life every day and provide me with
the greatest motivation to keep on challenging myself,
my parents, Cândido and Celestina, who gave me
the freedom to explore and dream,
to R. Paul Herman, for his support, and the authors
who embarked on this project,
for their trust and inspiration, which kept me going,
to all survivors, those who despite the many
obstacles they face in their daily lives,
find each morning the inner strength to endure and excel,
to all of you, making the world a better place.

From Paul
Dedicated to all the strong women of the world, and in my life, especially:
my wife and soul mate, Gayle; my mother, Alice; my sister, Mary;
my mother-in-law, Sue Ann; my Aunt Marilyn
and Aunt Lauretta, my cousin Cindy,
and the memories of my grandmothers, Mary and Martha;
and my co-editor, Elsa – and for
all of us seeking to build a better world,
via our actions every day, including
the power of our investment portfolios.

Contents

xi

**CHAPTER 8   Gender Lens Investing in the African Context   273
                Michael Z. Ngoasong, PhD and Richmond O.
                Lamptey, PhD**

**CHAPTER 9   The Evolution from Gender-Focused
                Microfinance to Gender Lens Investing in
                Latin America: The Case of Pro Mujer   303
                Angélica Rotondaro, PhD, Maria Cavalcanti,
                MBA, MS and Carmen Correa, BS**

CHAPTER 10   Inclusive Investing: Impact Meets Diversity,
                Equity, and Inclusion   333
                Julianne Zimmerman, MSci, Edward Dugger
                III, MPA-UP, and Shijiro Ochirbat, MBA, MPA

CHAPTER 11   Investing for Impact in Employee Retirement
                Plans   371
                Megan E. Morrice, MBA

Foreword

Most science fiction takes place decades or centuries in the future because the human brain is not adroit at exponential thinking. So, imagine an ambitious vignette. The year is 22,015 (yes, Twenty-Two Thousand Fifteen), and trillions of people have already lived and died on Earth, and many others have inhabited other planets. Your many-greats granddaughter, Anousheh, opens the tap in her home and fills a cup with perfectly pure drinking water. Her nuclear family – your descendants – don't live near running water, but they have a device on their home that captures and converts solar energy, gathers humidity from ambient air, cleans and mineralizes it, then pumps perfect drinking water to the family faucet. She wonders, "Where did this water come from?" and instantly understands, courtesy of her brain-machine's connection to general artificial intelligence (AI). A very successful company called Zero Mass Water pioneered the yielding-water-from-air technology twenty thousand years ago – more than 600 generations – in the year 2015.

Anousheh learned that Zero Mass Water's founder, Cody Friesen, a scientist and an entrepreneur, figured out how to convert electrical and thermal power in a modified psychrometric cycle to make optimal drinking water potentially available to all the world's people, somewhat akin to a dehumidifier for the sky. Since the early ages of humankind, men fought wars over access to water. Women and children walked kilometers along often perilous paths, risking their lives to fetch often non-potable water from distant sources. People transported water in non-compostable plastic containers all over the world, which alone accounted for 2% of all man-made carbon emissions. Zero Mass Water's breakthrough solution was to tap the abundant water in the air; people just needed an efficient way to capture it locally.

From 1900 to 2019, global average human lifespan more than doubled, from 32 to 72.6 years, and quality of life increased dramatically for most people.[1] Given that it is reasonable to expect that people will live

---

[1] Ourworldindata.org/life-expectancy; Hdr.undp.org/en/content/human-development-index-hdi.

increasingly higher-quality lives, I ascribe more moral weight to future generations because there will be many more of them (trillions), and because they should enjoy longer, higher-quality lives.[2] Earth should continue to be habitable for at least several hundred million years. If *Homo sapiens* (Latin for "wise human") can live up to the name and be wise enough to figure out a way to stick around at least that long, we should be able to flourish. Oxford University philosopher and effective altruist William MacAskill notes that it is plain to see that humans have made great moral progress over time, expanding our focus of moral concern in concentric circles out from ourselves, to our tribes, to nations, and to all people alive today. I agree with MacAskill and other philosophers such as Peter Singer,[3] Derek Parfit, Nick Bostrom, Toby Ord, and Nick Beckstead that now is the time to expand the circle again to include the more than 99% of people who will ever live: the trillions or quadrillions who will do so in the future.[4] As MacAskill and Singer note, just as we ought not ignore the plight of those who live in distant geographies, we should not ignore disenfranchised future generations, especially if acting in ways that help them in the future also helps us today.

Ascribing due moral worth to distant generations clarifies for those alive now that our actions will ripple across time in more dramatic ways than most of us actively contemplate. Indeed, for our descendants to thrive, markets must work better, and more sustainably. Given the scale and efficiency of capital markets, helping governments, companies, and people to align their values with their resources is critical to ensuring humanity can flourish. It is thus imperative that a new generation of investors seeking impact alongside financial returns – impact investors – is able to thrive.

I decided to invest in Zero Mass Water in 2017 for several reasons. First, 2.2 billion people – nearly one in three alive today – do not have access to clean drinking water.[5] Second, the water market is massive and the need for reliable, clean water is constant, and a top priority for biological, agricultural, industrial, and commercial purposes. Third, the founder is highly talented,

---

[2]More info at 80000hours.org/articles/future-generations/.

[3]Peter Singer planted the seed that grew into my interest in alignment of values and resources when I audited his Practical Ethics course while at university.

[4]Approximately 108 billion people have ever lived on Earth. See prb.org/howmany peoplehaveeverlivedonearth/. If we humans do not go extinct (most likely by annihilating ourselves), quadrillions of us should live in the hundreds of millions of years that Earth will remain habitable. Many more could colonize other planets.

[5]World Health Organization report: WHO.int/news-room/detail/18-06-2019-1-in-3-people-globally-do-not-have-access-to-safe-drinking-water-unicef-who.

driven, and mission-oriented. Fourth, like other great impact-oriented businesses, the core business model yields positive financial return and positive measurable impact in concert. Put another way, the financial return and the environmental impact are linearly correlated; each one enhances the other in a sustainable feedback loop. The venture could scale massively, making a significant contribution to sustainable economic growth, especially for those at the bottom of the pyramid. To the extent my dollars and support help Zero Mass Water improve the lives of people today and those who will live many years in the future, the small role I played will be one part of my personal legacy.

By helping to build the impact-investing movement, I seek to honor my family's traditions of capitalism and philanthropy, which both inform and are foundational to Impact Investing.[6] The traditional model of making money in one sector and then later donating some of it across other sectors is not the recipe for a sustainable form of market economics that will endure for many millennia. The impact-investing approach should ultimately prove more sustainable and just.

As a fifth-generation member of the Rockefeller family, I am predisposed to think about the meaning of legacy. I am humbled by my ancestors' outsized accomplishments, in only three generations, in capitalism (e.g. Standard Oil; Chase Bank; Rockefeller Center; early investments in Apple Computer, Inc., and Eastern Air Lines) and philanthropy (e.g. Rockefeller University; Population Council; Rockefeller Foundation; the University of Chicago; Grand Teton National Park; and donated land for the United Nations in New York City). Mine was a very privileged upbringing, but perhaps the privilege I appreciate the most was the consistent emphasis on long-term thinking, more easily afforded to those who need not worry about tomorrow's meal. My ancestors focused on education, cultural dialogue and understanding, medical research, preservation of land, institution building, and legacy – not of name, but of positive impact on people and planet.

Families with wealth, including family offices, play a unique role in the burgeoning Impact Investing market. As investors, business owners,

---

[6]Impact investments intend to generate financial return and measurable social or environmental benefits. The term started out more narrowly defined (e.g. focused on private equity, real assets, and private debt for their higher focus on "intentionality"), yet has spread to all asset classes as impact can be achieved and measured in every type of investment. "Impact investing" has become an umbrella term (similar to the way "Kleenex" can now reference all tissues, or "Google" for "Internet search," and historically "Xerox" for "copy"), generally synonymous with values-aligned investing across asset classes, strategies, sectors, geographies, and risk-return profiles.

donors, and stewards of wealth across generations, enterprising families are uniquely positioned to shift the cultures and practices of finance, business, and philanthropy. Families think and act on behalf of future generations, less distracted by the short-term, quarterly-results-oriented capitalism that makes long-term flourishing less likely. Families are committed to building for the long term, but they are also nimble and experimental. Families are indispensable investors in emerging concepts, companies, managers, and markets. Families lead some of the largest and most important enterprises in every sector and every market around the world, and they support the research, advocacy, and network building that creates vibrant market ecosystems. Families are also influential, which can be harmonized and leveraged in order to change the behavior of market-shaping institutions such as large banks.

Five family generations may feel lengthy to an American, but they are a mere blink of an eye compared with the Japanese royal family, who have been shaping Japanese legacy since 660 BCE. When Emperor Naruhito assumed the throne in October 2019, his family reached 126 generations and 2,679 years as monarchs. Shaping a nation as sublime and harmonious as Japan is an extremely impressive legacy, but even that accomplishment pales in comparison with the opportunity and responsibility currently facing the collective human family that has to safeguard future generations – to flourish amidst our interdependent ecology and economy. Growing sustainably and minimizing existential threats are two critical components of what leaders of the effective altruism movement espouse as the moral priority in the world today: to ensure a flourishing long-run future.[7] The sooner we figure out how to live sustainably and harmoniously, the more likely we will be able to build a just and verdant future.

A TOOL BELT FOR CHANGEMAKERS

Tools for effecting change include one's capital, time, knowledge, passion, influence, network, voice, and vote. If the ways each of us makes, spends, donates, and invests money have moral consequences, so too do the choices of whether to use or not to use those tools.[8] Ashoka founder

---

[7]Effective altruism is the project of using evidence and reason to figure out how to benefit others as much as possible, and taking action on that basis. More info at EffectiveAltruism.org.

[8]As philosopher Peter Singer has emphasized since 1972, being a bystander to preventable poverty, though an omission and not an act of commission, also has moral consequences. See Utilitarian.net/singer/by/1972----.htm.

Bill Drayton argues passionately that everyone can and should be a change-maker – someone who sees patterns, identifies problems and their potential solutions, organizes dynamic teams, leads collective action, and then continually adapts as situations change.[9] As individuals use more tools on their tool belts and effect change, however small at first, they feel a growth of agency.

Imagine a 20-something citizen who, purely for financial reasons, decides after a devastating nearby wildfire to invest her retirement savings with an environmental, social, and governance (ESG) lens (criteria to better determine the future financial performance of companies by measuring their sustainability and societal impact) to mitigate risk. Her decision alone makes it more likely she will learn more about ESG factors. As she learns about and reflects on the positive and negative effects of her investments, she becomes more likely to think more deeply about the 3% of her annual income she donates. But could she afford 5%, or even 10%? What are the causes she cares about most, and how can she learn about the most effective non-governmental organizations (NGOs) addressing those challenges? She is then more likely to consider her career, and how she can best align how she earns money with her values. Years later, she thinks again of the wildfire that encouraged her to alter the way she invests her retirement portfolio, suspecting that climate change would exacerbate wildfires and other natural disasters. She decides that, when she needs to purchase a car, she will purchase an electric vehicle instead of one with a combustion engine, and will decrease her consumption of meat, skewing more vegetarian than she had been growing up. When that goes well, she convinces her two roommates to try going vegan. She posts about their collective vegan efforts on a social media platform, influencing others' behavior, galvanizing their actions, and affecting culture. When someone replies to a post saying that she inspired him to learn more about factory farming and to become a vegan, she no longer suspected she had agency to effect change – she knew it.

Perhaps without knowing there was a label for it, she became a change-maker. She has not yet changed a system, but she recognized several problems, modified her personal behavior, and used several tools on her tool belt to effect change: her capital, her time, her career, and her influence. She formed a group and leveraged a technology platform to influence others.

---

[9]More info at Ashoka.org/en-us/focus/organizing-changemaking; NYTimes.com/2018/02/08/opinion/changemaker-social-entrepreneur.html; Ashoka.org/sites/default/files/atoms/files/innovations8.5x11final_0.pdf.

Incrementally, she incorporated her values with the way she invests, donates, earns, and spends money. Her behavior changes gave her the confidence to realize she had agency, and she continued down an impactful path. We all have experiences that shape our worldview, bit by bit. I, too, have made incremental progress in discovering where I may be able to pull levers to try to effect positive change.

MY TOOL BELT FOR EFFECTING CHANGE

I am an insignificant changemaker relative to others who, for example, have changed national policy. And relative to my ancestors, I do not have the financial resources to think of an idea, endow an institution, and hire a first-rate team. But through Impact Investing, I hope to contribute to positive impact through a regenerative process of building and reinvesting capital back into additional impactful investments. I seek to identify challenges that are important, solvable, and neglected, and address them with investment and philanthropic capital. Still relatively early in my career and journey, I am confident that I can apply my agency to effect change by thinking strategically about how to use various tools on my tool belt to change my own behavior (self), to influence people I know (small groups), and, I hope, to change culture and, perhaps, eventually, a system.

"Self" is what I control directly, and includes how I allocate my time and resources. I control how I earn, spend, donate, and invest capital. I vote. I try to influence others' thinking and behavior. I can decide and act quickly, but my impact may be limited unless I try to influence others within groups or via platforms.

I have additional influence within various communities of which I am a member, and their potential for effecting change is much greater than my own. Those groups include, among others: my nuclear family; the Rockefeller and Percy families; boards of directors, including the private foundation Rockefeller Brothers Fund; lesbian, gay, bisexual, transgender, and queer (LGBTQ) allies; New Yorkers; voters; and U.S. citizens. To mobilize group action among fellow impact investors, I co-founded in 2013 and currently chair The ImPact, a group of families who seek to align their values with their investments and learn from each other, cross-pollinate ideas and best practices, and co-invest in impactful opportunities.

Platforms benefit many people, most of whom I will never encounter. I work at Addepar, a company that is building a platform connecting people, data, and technology to fix broken parts of the financial industry, including robust reporting on impact in portfolios. Rockefeller Brothers Fund tracks its mission-aligned portfolio on The ImPact's data platform, which is powered by Addepar pro bono. The levers I can pull differ from those of every reader, but I explain them below in more detail in the hope that reading about one person's approach might prove helpful as you, the reader, consider the tools on your tool belt.

This synergy among my advocacy work, The ImPact, Rockefeller Brothers Fund (RBF), and Addepar enables me to use finite hours to fuller effect. Pursuing impact and aligning my values unifies my mission, time, and career choices. I have written down and regularly revisit my values (e.g. justice, integrity, effectiveness) and the causes I care about (e.g. democracy, sustainability, promoting science), and think actively about how to align each of those with my tool belt.

For example, from 2009 to 2018, I served on RBF's board of directors and investment committee. Founded in 1940 by my grandfather and his four brothers, RBF is a private foundation whose mission is to advance social change that contributes to a more just, sustainable, and peaceful world. About half of RBF's charitable giving fights climate change, so it seemed hypocritical that about 7% of our endowment (a then-typical percentage for endowments) was invested in fossil fuels – somewhat akin to a cancer-fighting foundation investing in tobacco companies. We decided to align our endowment and mission – a process that required leaving one outsourced chief investment office (OCIO) that commingled its clients' funds for another OCIO that treats our endowment as a controllable, customizable, separate account – and announced publicly that we would divest of fossil fuels.[10]

Believing oil companies to be overpriced, we decided to divest for financial reasons as well as for moral and philanthropic ones. Fortunately, we started divesting in spring 2014, when oil was USD $106 per barrel; oil's price subsequently fell precipitously for years. We embraced and capitalized on the irony that the source of RBF's endowment was oil money from our family's founding of Standard Oil. Indeed, the surname attached to the foundation and its historical ties to the fossil fuel industry helped increase the visibility and impact of our decision. The public announcement made waves and helped "fuel" the divest-invest movement.[11] We then invested

---

[10]More info at RBF.org/mission-aligned-investing and the case study section of TheImPact.org/library.

[11]See DivestInvest.org/.

the divested money in managers whose work aligns with our mission. Six years in, we are handily beating our initial benchmark.[12] Given that the foundation's goal is not merely to maximize the effectiveness of our grantmaking, but also to maximize the impact of the foundation as a whole, the endowment and the Rockefeller surname became helpful tools to pursue our mission.

As RBF began the journey of aligning mission and endowment, venture capitalist Josh Cohen and I decided there should be a safe space for impact investors to trade notes with one another. Thus, fifteen families co-founded The ImPact Pact (a play on words from The Giving Pledge, which in part inspired the model),[13] later shortened to The ImPact. I chair the board of this NGO's global membership community of families committed to aligning our assets with our values.

Everything The ImPact does is built on a foundation of peer-to-peer exchange: members make a pact to explore the impact of all of their investments, and to invest to create social benefit. Members share insights and opportunities with each other to convert interest in Impact Investing into action. We created the organization for the types of families who called RBF after our announcement about aligning mission and endowment with questions such as "Do you need to compromise returns? What works and what does not? Can we learn from your mistakes along the way?" Those families were intrigued by the idea of Impact Investing and even willing to get into the metaphorical raft, but could benefit from river guides who are also peers.

The ImPact was founded by families, for families. The ImPact enables families to realize their full potential as impact investors, market leaders, and ecosystem builders, working collaboratively to make "net positive impact" the standard, not the afterthought or exception. The ImPact's membership experience is designed to provide families with the relationships, knowledge, and opportunities they need to make more impact investments more effectively, which is our mission. Our collective purpose is to improve the probability and pace of solving social and environmental problems by increasing the flow of capital to investments that generate measurable impact. Our members work collectively to influence the behavior of

---

[12]See highlights at WashingtonPost.com/climate-environment/2020/05/09/rockefeller-heirs-big-oil-find-dumping-fossil-fuels-improved-bottom-line/ or details at RBF.org/investing-in-our-mission.

[13]The Giving Pledge (GivingPledge.org/) is a movement of billionaire philanthropists who commit to giving the majority of their wealth to philanthropy or charitable causes, either during their lifetimes or in their wills. One "takes a pledge" or "makes a pact."

institutions to raise standards for sustainable investment activity throughout the market.[14]

Given that the average person works for 80,000 hours, one's career is likely the most consequential tool for effecting change for most people.[15] Addepar is a financial technology company where I have been the Global Director of Family Offices for eight years. The first time I visited its Mountain View, California–based office in 2011, as a venture capitalist doing diligence on the company, I asked whether the software could hypothetically track impact metrics alongside financial returns for more comprehensive reporting. The response was, "Yeah, I suppose so." I joined Addepar as a full-time employee a few months later, before it had revenue, and the company has experienced dramatic growth. As of this writing in 2020, the platform tracks $2 trillion in assets among some of the world's largest wealth-management firms, the majority of them family offices.

Addepar brings together data, technology, and people, providing wealth managers with real-time portfolio reporting and insights required to make and implement better investment decisions. The company's aim is to get more assets flowing into more impactful investments and ideas, benefiting society as a whole. To align one's values and investments, one must first understand what one owns, then what that money is doing in the world.

Addepar-enabled transparency helps its clients, including members of The ImPact, to allocate capital more prudently. ImPact members can log into Addepar to see, all the way to the transaction level for individual securities, their impact portfolios, across asset classes, geographies, impact sectors, impact strategies, and return profiles. Product integrations, third-party data feeds, and member-uploaded impact metrics supplement members' understanding of what their money is doing in the world, in their native currency. Members can click on other members' anonymized portfolios to learn from one another on an individual basis, or from various collective views of all values-aligned investments made across The ImPact network.[16] From these network effects, cross-pollination of ideas, and tech-enabled transparency, members de-risk and inform investment decisions.

By leveraging technology to help people align their values and their investments, I seek symbiosis among the hats I wear, and try to build on family legacies in capitalism and philanthropy, which intersect at Impact Investing.

---

[14]More detail about The ImPact's theory of change at TheImPact.org/theory-of-change.

[15]The choice matters. Learn more about the opportunity to use one's career as the biggest tool on one's tool belt at 80000hours.org.

[16]Sharing is based on reciprocity, and members can choose the level of anonymity for their sharing view.

WHY CARE ABOUT IMPACT INVESTING?

The field of Impact Investing is relatively new, but has already garnered tremendous interest and momentum.[17] Despite the field's nascency, I find five reasons to care about Impact Investing to be most compelling:

1. **Scale and urgency:** For humanity to flourish for millions of years, we need innovation and cooperation among sectors – private, public, and civil society – to address seemingly intractable problems such as climate change; poverty; and access to basics, such as water, food, health care, education, and opportunity. Like mounting public debt, these challenges have compounding effects, so require urgent attention. The private sector's scale and efficiency can prove invaluable in addressing these challenges, for which we need to use more of the tools on our collective, societal tool belt. Fortunately, big challenges mean big opportunities to make money and positive impact, and frameworks like the United Nations Sustainable Development Goals help investors prioritize.

2. **Net risk-adjusted performance:** Financial performance and risk are inextricably linked. In the long term, social and environmental factors are major drivers of investment risk mitigation and success. Companies that proactively respond to factors such as climate change, economic inequality, and resource scarcity will outperform companies that do not, or lag behind their peers. Multiple peer-reviewed academic studies have already shown this to be the case.[18] Outperformance may come in the form of more calculated risk, reduced volatility, or business growth.

3. **Sustainable markets and representative governments:** Indirect, semi-hidden risks to the financial system such as excess leverage, misinformation, fraud, waste, abuse, and other inefficiencies contributed to the Great Recession of 2008. That, in turn, led to distrust of elites

---

[17]My former colleague Jed Emerson and others have been writing about Impact Investing's tenets for decades (BlendedValue.org/writings/), but the field became more organized after The Rockefeller Foundation formally coined the term "Impact Investing" in 2007, and the subsequent financial crisis that inspired many to rethink how business and markets should work: RockefellerFoundation.org/blog/bringing-scale-impact-investing-industry/.

[18]See Tandfonline.com/doi/full/10.1080/20430795.2015.1118917 and Harvard Professor George Serafeim's work: HBS.edu/faculty/Pages/profile.aspx?facId=15705.

and a great recession of democracy and cooperation, coupled with a rise of populism, xenophobic nationalism, and authoritarianism.[19] By contrast, Impact Investing makes market economies more sustainable and equitable, which increases the likelihood that participating governments will be of the people, by the people, and for the people. International cooperation among governments with fair rules and open markets eases the movement of ideas, money, goods, and people.[20] When markets work better, representative government works better, and vice versa.

4. **Major risk mitigation:** A robust rules-based international economic order better equips humanity to deal with potentially devastating risks, such as climate change and totalitarianism, and potential existential risks, such as nuclear annihilation, an engineered pandemic caused by pathogens that combine the worst traits of various viruses, and general AI "gone awry." These challenges are all worthy of our attention because they are important, solvable, and neglected.

5. **Ethics:** Technology, awareness, and a growing supply of financial products have made aligning values and investments increasingly easy to do, as well as beneficial to current and future generations. We ought to do so.

Given the deep dive into Impact Investing that is included in this *Global Handbook of Impact Investing*, I share here six high-level observations about the field:

- **Don't get bogged down in evolving terminology;** think of Impact Investing as a framework: impact investments intend to generate financial return and measurable social or environmental benefits.
- **Profit and purpose are not mutually exclusive;** business and commerce can be the expression of one's values, and positive impact can bolster recruiting, improve team culture, and drive profit.
- **All investments (and thus all companies) have both positive and negative impacts,** which can ultimately be viewed as "net positive" or "net negative" across a spectrum. Investing becomes more meaningful and interesting when you apply customizable technology and

---

[19]For a deeper dive into this fascinating topic, read Yuval Noah Harari's books *Sapiens* (2011) and *21 Lessons for the 21st Century* (2018), or his op-ed in *The Economist*: economist.com/open-future/2018/09/26/we-need-a-post-liberal-order-now.
[20]en.wikipedia.org/wiki/Liberal_international_economic_order.

insightful data to track what those impacts are, determine net effects on people and planet, and decide how they relate to your values and portfolio.

- **Impact investors are intentional about the value they invest to create,** and seek to account for the impacts – both positive and negative – of their investments. By rigorously incorporating social and environmental factors into investment decision-making, impact investors aim to minimize the harm, and maximize the good, that their investments actively create in the world.

- **Impact Investing can be an engine for global solutions, including addressing market failures,** to bring risk capital to opportunities that yield measurable social and environmental impact but that otherwise would not be funded by traditional markets and financial instruments.

- **Depending on the nature of the challenge one is trying to address, capital allocators can invest, donate, or both.**[21]

A GUIDE TO USING IMPACT INVESTING AS A TOOL

The editors and contributing authors of *The Global Handbook for Impact Investing* are world-class "river guides" to aligning values and investments. They discuss Impact Investing across geographies, asset classes, sectors, impact strategies and methodologies, stages, return profiles, and many other aspects of this exciting, growing field. As you read, please remember to:

- **Engage experts and advisors.** You need not figure this out on your own. Read this book. Join or form a group. Learn from impact-oriented investment professionals about how you can best align your values and your investments. If your current wealth advisor is not willing to learn, work instead with one who is more committed and more experienced.

- **Try to understand what your money is doing in the world.** How can you learn more about the impacts – both positive and negative – of

---

[21] For example, if one's aim is to reduce the number of drinking-and-driving-related fatalities, one may lobby government officials for policy changes, or support NGOs such as Mothers Against Drunk Driving, or invest in ride-sharing and self-driving-car companies. I strongly suspect for-profit solutions will ultimately prove most effective in reducing drinking-and-driving-related fatalities.

the assets you already own? Knowing what you own is a prerequisite to aligning values and investments.

- **Personalize your impact.** Rank by importance to you the values and the causes you care about. Assigning percentages to each, as uncomfortable as that may be, will help you prioritize and allocate in line with what matters to you.[22] What metrics are important to you?

- **Consider cost effectiveness.** Impact Investing is not a silver bullet. A sum of money can be invested in one of several for-profit, impact-oriented ventures, or it can be donated to NGOs whose cost effectiveness has been validated by independent evaluators. Robust analysis and evaluation of impact in Impact Investing, including contribution, attribution, and cost effectiveness, should help this young field grow.

- **Express your values through your tool belt.** Consider how you can best use each tool on your tool belt to effect change. How can you leverage self, groups, and platforms to make markets more sustainable for those alive today, and, more importantly, for future generations?

There are moral consequences of the ways we earn, spend, donate, and invest money. The more actively we consider the negative and positive impacts within each of those categories, the more likely we will be to behave in a way that allows the more than 99.9% of people who will ever live – our descendants – to flourish. Recognition of the hundreds of millions of years humans may be able to live on Earth should inform our perspective on the importance of sustainability, and how we address existential threats. We possess the creativity and the technology to act in a way that maximizes the positive – and minimizes the negative – ripple effects of our actions across time. If acting morally and living sustainably increase our own well-being and that of our descendants, we ought to do so, and with urgency.

Impact Investing is an invaluable tool to shape a more just and verdant future for all of us.[23] Everyone, regardless of their wealth, can align their values and their resources, influence groups, and potentially change cultures

---

[22]To ensure our charitable giving matches our priorities, my wife and I assign percentages to the causes we care about, and rank highly effective organizations within each category. Individuals who skip this more disciplined approach that foundations have been using for decades will likely find a surprisingly high percentage of their annual giving goes to friends who happened to ask instead of to their favorite causes. A similar approach can be applied to one's Impact Investing.

[23]To read a beautifully written "letter from a utopian future," go to nickbostrom.com/utopia.html.

and systems. Everyone can be a changemaker. The sooner and more successfully we do so, the more we will improve our lives and those of our descendants. The only thing bigger than our opportunity to leave a legacy that allows our children to flourish is the future itself.

By Justin Rockefeller
May 2020

Acknowledgments

Producing this *Global Handbook of Impact Investing,* covering the latest innovative ideas, engaging examples, and leading lessons, involved the efforts of many people. We share our deepest gratitude and thanks to:

- The 48 authors (not including ourselves as co-authors) of the 30 insightful chapters of the book. We are grateful to you for investing your time, intellect, wisdom, and for the sharing of experiences with us, to produce a "how-to guide" for all investors seeking to achieve both higher impact and profit.

- All the thoughtful partners and collaborators of the authors and editors, who inspired, informed, and spurred all of us toward innovative solutions. Iconic pioneers for us include Dr. Muhammad Yunus, winner of the Nobel Prize for Peace, which recognized that microfinance loans to women worldwide could "create the conditions under which peace can exist."

- Our supporting team, Lucia Gaia Pohlman, Srdana Pokrajac, and Isabel Alonso Gomes, who contributed to the clarity and readability of this book.

- Early supporters Isabella Massa and Tula Weis, for an earlier version of this project.

- The thoughtful, agile, and patient team at Wiley and Sons, Inc., especially during the COVID-19 pandemic. Thank you, Kevin Harreld, for partnering with us; Susan Cerra, for shepherding our manuscript to the finish line; Amy Handy, for ensuring readability and accuracy; and the marketing, design, and production teams.

- Our spouses (António for Elsa; Gayle for Paul) and families (kids, parents, and siblings) for their understanding, patience, and support during the long days, late nights, weekends, and holidays – especially during the confinement period of the pandemic.

- Each of you for reading, learning, experimenting, piloting, and pursuing a higher-impact portfolio across all asset classes, so that we can all build a better world together.

Let us know your feedback. We look forward to hearing of your implementations and innovations.

Elsa de Morais Sarmento and R. Paul Herman
Paris and San Francisco
May 31, 2020

About the Contributors

Editors and Co-Authors

Elsa de Morais Sarmento, MA, is an applied economist with experience in development finance, private sector development, and impact evaluation. She is an associate researcher at NOVAFRICA, Nova Business School of Management and Economics in Portugal. She has lectured for over a decade at several universities in Europe. She worked for the European Commission, World Bank, International Finance Corporation (IFC), African Development Bank, European Bank for Reconstruction and Development (EBRD), and United Nations agencies, among several other international organizations and national governments in 140 countries. She has published several articles and book chapters and edited *The Emerald Handbook of Public-Private Partnerships in Developing and Emerging Economies* (Emerald Publishing Limited 2017).

R. Paul Herman, BSci, is an investment manager and ratings provider for higher-impact portfolios for investors, advisors, and retirement plans. He is founder and CEO of HIP (Human Impact + Profit) Investor, which produces and licenses ratings of 129,000 stocks, bonds, and funds across all asset classes on ESG, impact, Sustainable Development Goals (SDG), and climate action. Herman authored *The HIP Investor: Make Bigger Profits by Building a Better World* (Wiley 2010), a how-to guide for investors seeking human impact and profit. He has advised corporations at McKinsey; improved corporates, nonprofits, and governments at CSC Index; funded social entrepreneurs at Ashoka.org; designed impact investing strategy at Omidyar.net; and started, scaled, and sold an impactful fintech firm. He is a graduate of the Wharton School of Finance at the University of Pennsylvania, and an MBA and MPA lecturer.

Chapter 1

Haifa Ben Abid, MPhil, leverages substantial experience of over 12 years in consulting in the private and nonprofit sectors, in banking, finance, and international development. She holds a master's degree in Finance and

Financial Risks Management from the Academy of Louvain and pursued a PhD in Economics and Management, with a focus on Impact Investing and development as research topics at the Doctoral School ULB-UMons-ULiège in Belgium. Haifa is very eager to deepen her work on Impact Investing and has followed many online courses and EVPA trainings related to the subject.

Chapter 2

Stoyan Tenev, PhD, is a senior manager for independent evaluations at the World Bank Group (WBG). His responsibilities include financial and private sector development operations of the WBG. He was previously a regional economist for the East Asia and Pacific Region of the International Finance Corporation.

Raghavan Narayanan, MBA, is a Senior Evaluation Officer at the World Bank Group (WBG). He manages thematic reviews and coordinates evaluation initiatives focused on the 2030 SDG agenda. Previously, he worked in think tanks, investment banks, and asset managers in major financial centers around the world. He has co-founded and exited successful startups in the technology sector.

Chapter 3

Lauryn Agnew, MBA, has more than three decades of experience in developing and implementing strategies in the institutional investment industry. She is the founder of the Bay Area Impact Investing Initiative (www.baiii .org), a model for Place-Based Impact Investing model portfolios across all asset classes. Through her company, Seal Cove Financial, she serves as a resource to nonprofit organizations for investment consulting services and provides fiduciary education and trustee training for public fund and nonprofit board and committee members. She has a BA degree in Economics from Whitman College (US) and an MBA in Finance from the University of Oregon.

Chapter 4

Kirstin Dougall, MFA, is a researcher at Presidio Graduate School in San Francisco and Stanford University, currently focused on social sustainability. She is interested in people management strategies that foster humane, high-performing organizations. Her wide-ranging expertise encompasses a diverse field of entrepreneurial start-ups, biotech, science writing, and cutting-edge medical research and development (R&D). She is also currently working with a Stanford research team exploring the development of gene therapies to cure pediatric diseases.

R. Paul Herman: see Editors.

Chapter 5

Rajen Makhijani, MBA, brings interdisciplinary approaches to pressing issues for leaders in business, politics, and development, as consultant, CXO coach, TEDx speaker, and award-nominated screenwriter, from India and Singapore. Rajen was Country Director for the University of Chicago's Tata Centre for Development, founder and Global Head of the Talent and Leadership practice at Dalberg, and helped build the Asia-Pacific leadership practices at McKinsey and Heidrick & Struggles. He serves impact investors, private equity, development finance institutions, the United Nations, Fortune 500, governments, and impact enterprises across Asia and Africa. He founded Leadership by Results to accelerate results-delivery through leadership and culture.

Chapter 6

Edward T. Jackson, OMC, EdD, is a Senior Research Fellow at the Carleton Centre for Community Innovation at Carleton University, Honorary Associate with the Institute of Development Studies (IDS), and president of E. T. Jackson and Associates Ltd. His research and consulting for foundations, development agencies, and financial institutions focus on field-building and evaluation in Impact Investing, blended finance, and gender lens investing in Africa, Asia, and the Caribbean.

Elsa de Morais Sarmento: see Editors.

Chapter 7

Kristin Hull, PhD, is a pioneer in the field of Impact Investing. She founded Nia Impact Capital, a Registered Investment Advisor, and is investment manager for the Nia Global Solutions strategy, focused on solutions for women, equality and climate action, leading the charge to "Change the Face of Finance"™ by hiring and training women and people of color in sustainable investing. She earned her PhD in Education from the University of California at Berkeley, a master's in Educational Research from Stanford University, and her BA and teaching credentials from Tufts University.

Chapter 8

Michael Z. Ngoasong, PhD, is a senior lecturer and director of Postgraduate Business Programs at Open University Business, United Kingdom. He is also a research associate at the School of Tourism and Hospitality, University of Johannesburg, South Africa. His research and consultancy activities focus on the area of women's entrepreneurship, informal microfinance institutions, digital entrepreneurship, and Impact Investing for inclusive development the African context. He holds a PhD in Science, Technology, and Society from the University of Nottingham in the UK. His thesis examines how global health partnerships shape national health policies and local practices for HIV/AIDS and malaria treatment and control in Cameroon.

Richmond O. Lamptey, PhD, is an early career academic and impact investment consultant. He recently completed a PhD in Business Studies from the Open University in the UK. His thesis examines the influence of bank-based and capital market-based impact investments on small and medium-sized enterprises in Ghana. He worked as graduate assistant for Ghana Centre for Impact Investing (2014–2016), associate partner for Novation Capital Ltd (2012–2013), and branch manager for National Investment Bank Ltd of Ghana. He is certified by the Project Management Institute (US) and Chartered Institute of Bankers (Ghana).

Chapter 9

Angélica Rotondaro, PhD, is the co-founder of Alimi Impact Ventures, an advisory firm that supports scaling up sustainable investing in Latin America and a board member of the Climate-Smart Institute, a think tank focused on pro-climate start-ups, with a strong element of technology and women entrepreneurs. She is a member of the World Economic Forum (WEF) Experts Platform, a senior lecturer at Insper, and associate researcher at the University of São Paulo's Center for Organizational Studies (Brazil). She holds a PhD in Organization Studies and Cultural Theory from the University of St. Gallen in Switzerland.

Maria Cavalcanti, MBA, MS, is president and CEO of Pro Mujer, and a recognized speaker on Impact Investing, women's empowerment, and financial inclusion. She co-founded and became the managing partner of FIRST Impact Investing, a private equity fund in Brazil. She served as Chief Strategy Officer for Fundación Avina and worked at Dell Inc. and A.T. Kearney. In 2019, she was named among Apolitical's Gender Equality Top 100. She has served on boards, including ANDE, NetHope, and FUNDES. She holds an

MBA from the University of Texas and an MS from Columbia University in New York.

Carmen Correa, BS, is Chief Operating Officer at Pro Mujer and holds over 25 years of experience developing Latin America's entrepreneurial ecosystem. Carmen created a new investment instrument at ANII in Uruguay and was responsible for the inclusive market regional strategy at Avina. She worked as Managing Director of Endeavor Uruguay, at the Inter-American Development Bank (IDB) in Washington, DC, and at the OAS in Uruguay. She co-leads the Southern Cone Task Force of the Global Steering Group on Impact Investment and serves on various international boards. Carmen holds a BS in Management from National-Louis University.

Chapter 10

Julianne Zimmerman, MSci, is the managing director of Reinventure Capital. Previously, she co-founded a seed-stage practice, where she invested in energy, water, food, and health. Julianne earned undergraduate degrees in literature and aero/astro engineering from MIT, MSci in aerospace engineering from the University of Maryland, and a Sustainability Management certificate from Presidio Graduate School in San Francisco. She was twice a NASA astronaut finalist. A frequent keynote, reviewer, and competition judge in the United States and abroad, she speaks and writes on innovation and systemic social, racial, and gender inequity. Julianne teaches Innovative Social Enterprises at Tufts University (USA).

Edward Dugger III, MBA-UP, is the president of Reinventure Capital and an inclusive investing pioneer with over 23 years' experience managing profitable and socially responsible investments. As president of UNC Partners (UNCP), he focused on investing in companies led by people of color. He is currently director and executive committee member of Boston Community Capital, one of the largest regulated Community Development Financial Institutions (CDFIs) in the United States; chair of Boston Community Ventures; and executive committee member of the Massachusetts Business Roundtable. He was previously executive committee member of the Federal Reserve Bank of Boston. He graduated from Harvard and Princeton University.

Shijiro Ochirbat, MBA, MPA, is an intern at Reinventure Capital. She participates in internal research, deal flow cultivation, and due diligence, contributing analytical insights regarding fundraising, investment, and impact assessment. She is an experienced strategist with a broad spectrum of industry and finance experience in governmental, international, and private organizations. Shijiro earned a bachelor's degree in accounting from the National University of Mongolia, an MBA from the University of Sydney (Australia), and an MPA from Harvard Kennedy School.

Chapter 11

Megan E. Morrice, MBA, is the Head of Operations for ValuesAdvisor, a matchmaking platform for clients to find advisors who specialize in sustainable investing. Megan previously led client and partnership development at HIP (Human Impact + Profit) Investor, a global leader in Impact Investing. Megan's professional background includes working as a financial advisor and as an investment wholesaler. Megan earned an MBA in Sustainable Management from Presidio Graduate School (USA), where she now is Adjunct Faculty member. She is passionate about helping individuals and organizations understand their financial options and align their money with their values.

Chapter 12

Umachander Balakumar, MSci, currently works within the product team of a leading alternative investment fintech company specializing in cloud-based customer relationship management (CRM) and portfolio management services. He focuses on building new portfolio management features, artificial intelligence (AI) capabilities, and advancing environmental, social, and governance (ESG) reporting capabilities. He earned his Master's of Science in financial analytics, with his undergraduate degree in psychology from the University of Michigan-Dearborn. The Max M. & Marjorie S. Fisher Foundation in Detroit introduced him to Impact Investing and HIP (Human Impact + Profit) Investor, where he began his impact career as an Impact Investing Analyst.

Chapter 13

Pauline Deschryver, MSci, MPA, is an expert in green finance, with a focus on sustainable infrastructure investment in emerging economies. She has worked for the French government on development finance, in strategy consulting for a firm specialized in fragile and post-conflict countries, and for Morgan Stanley on sustainable finance. Pauline is an alumna of Sciences Po Paris, HEC Paris, and the School of International and Public Affairs at

Columbia University in New York, with a major in development economics and energy and environmental policies.

Frederic de Mariz: see Chapter 30.

Chapter 14

Maria Basílio, PhD, is an adjunct professor at the Management Department from the Polytechnic Institute of Beja, Portugal. She holds a PhD in management from the Lisbon School of Economics and Management (ISEG), earning her MSc in management (Finance) from the Universidade Lusíada in Lisbon, Portugal. Since 1997, she has taught several finance and management accounting subjects. Her main research interests include public-private partnerships (PPPs), development finance, econometric models, risk, and performance analysis. She has authored several publications on PPPs, infrastructures and regional development, public performance, and related topics.

Chapter 15

Jyotsna (Jo) Puri, PhD, is the head of Green Climate Fund's Independent Evaluation Unit (IEU). She has 23 years' experience in evaluating research in agriculture, environment, health, and infrastructure related to poverty alleviation. She has worked for the World Bank, UNDP, UNEP, and the International Initiative of Impact Evaluation (3ie). She has published several books and written extensively. She is also adjunct professor at the School of International and Public Affairs, Columbia University, and research fellow at the Centre for Evaluation and Development (C4ED).

Aemal Khan, MA, is currently working with the Independent Evaluation Unit (IEU) of the Green Climate Fund (GCF) as an evaluation assistant. Aemal has more than five years of international development experience, mostly in the field of evaluations, data collection, analysis, and management. Before joining the IEU, Aemal worked with UNESCO, UNDP, and UN Pulse Lab Jakarta. He earned his MA degree in sustainable economic development from the University for Peace in Costa Rica.

Solomon Asfaw, PhD, is a Principal Evaluation Officer at the Green Climate Fund's Independent Evaluation Unit (IEU). He oversees impact evaluations, data systems, methods advice, and capacity support. His 15 years of work in international research and development include positions with the FAO as an economist and strategic program adviser, and with CGIAR as a regional scientist in impact evaluation and markets. His work has been published extensively across many economic and development journals. He holds a PhD in economics from the University of Hannover, Germany.

Chapter 16

Ana Pimenta, MEcon, is currently part of the social impact team at Santander Universities, responsible for its impact strategy and measurement. She is also an invited lecturer in several Impact Investing courses. She has more than 11 years of international experience in Impact Investing and consulting, private equity/venture capital, and corporate finance, mainly focused in education, renewable energy, and real estate. Ana holds a master's degree in economics from NOVA School of Business and Economics (Portugal). She is currently a PhD candidate at the Universidad Autónoma Madrid (Spain), developing her thesis in the social impact measurement field.

Elsa de Morais Sarmento: see Editors.

Chapter 17

Jane Reisman, PhD, connects the dots between Impact Measurement and Management in Impact Investing and the evaluation profession. As the founder of US-based evaluation firm ORS Impact, Jane developed a record of engaging in new frontiers and field building to optimize and scale impact. Her current work as a social impact advisor focuses on strengthening impact measurement and management, engaging with field leaders such as The Rockefeller Foundation, the GIIN, MacArthur Foundation, Mission Investors Exchange, the American Evaluation Association, the Impact Management Project, and the World Economic Forum.

Veronica Olazabal, MCRS, senior adviser and director at The Rockefeller Foundation, is an award-winning evaluator with a portfolio ranging over 15 years, four continents, and numerous global agencies, including the Master-Card Foundation. With a BA in Communications and an MCRS in Policy and Planning from Rutgers University (US), she serves on a number of funding and advisory boards, including the World Benchmarking Alliance. She has published on this topic in the *American Journal of Evaluation* and in the *Stanford Social Innovation Review*.

Chapter 18

Courtney Bolinson, MS, an independent consultant, is an experienced facilitator, systems thinker, and evaluator. She has worked with nonprofits, universities, government, and the private sector. She previously worked as the Impact Evaluation and Learning Manager for seed-stage impact investor Engineers Without Borders Canada and continues to design evaluations for impact investors, social enterprises, and gender lens investing projects. She holds two master's degrees, one in agricultural and applied economics and the other in agroecology, from the University of Wisconsin-Madison.

Donna M. Mertens, PhD, professor emeritus at Gallaudet University, specializes in research and evaluation methodologies designed to support social transformation. She has authored or co-authored many methodological books related to social and environmental justice and human rights, most recently the second edition of *Program Evaluation Theory and Practice* (Guilford Press, 2018); *Mixed Methods Design in Evaluation* (Sage Publications 2017), and the fifth edition of *Research and Evaluation in Education and Psychology* (Sage Publications 2019). She consulted with Engineers Without Borders Canada on a transformative evaluation of a seed-stage impact investment project in Africa.

Chapter 19

Mario Negre, PhD, is a senior researcher at the German Development Institute and consultant at the World Bank, where he worked as senior economist and co-directed the "Poverty and Shared Prosperity 2016: Taking on Inequality" report. He has also worked at the European Parliament. He holds a degree in Physics (University of Barcelona, Spain), an MA in Development Policies (University of Bremen, Germany), and a PhD in Development Economics (Jawharlal Nehru University, India).

Hannes Öhler, PhD, is a researcher at the German Development Institute. He worked at the University of Goettingen (Sweden), Heidelberg University (Germany), and University of Milano-Bicocca (Italy) in the past. He holds a degree in economics (University of Innsbruck, Austria) and a PhD in development economics (Heidelberg University, Germany).

Željko Bogetić, PhD, is a lead economist at the World Bank Group's Independent Evaluation Group (IEG), where he leads thematic and project evaluations on economic policy and budget support operations. He has published extensively on economic policy issues and served at the World Bank and the International Monetary Fund (IMF) for 30 years in a variety of economist and leadership roles in most world regions. He holds PhD and MA degrees in economics from the University of Connecticut.

Chapter 20

Maximilian Foedinger, MBA, MPA, was born in Austria. He holds a Master's of Advanced Studies in economics, an MBA, and an MPA. He specializes in topics related to innovation and export in an SME context. During his career, he implemented projects in over 31 different countries, mainly in Eastern Europe, CIS, and MENA region, on behalf of international donors, such as the European Union, ADA, EBRD, ETF, GIZ, USAID, and the World Bank. He is frequently invited to lecture in academic institutions, as well as conferences, like the Astana Economic Forum.

Elsa de Morais Sarmento: see Editors.

Chapter 21

Jean-Philippe de Schrevel, MBA, is the founder and managing partner of Bamboo Capital Partners. Previously, he co-founded BlueOrchard Finance in 2001. As a pioneer of the Impact Investing industry with over 20 years of experience, he has been at the forefront of investing in environmental and social causes in emerging and frontier markets. He holds an MA in economics from Université Notre-dame de la Paix, Namur, and an MBA from the Wharton School of Business at the University of Pennsylvania.

Chapter 22

Zhao Jianbo, PhD, graduated from the School of Economics and management of Tsinghua University in 2007 with a PhD in Management. He is currently an assistant professor at the Institute of Industrial Economics, Chinese Academy of Social Sciences. His research focuses on industrial economics, business models, venture capital in the New Industrial Revolution. Recently, he authored the book *The Rhythm of Change: The Strategic Innovation in the Era of Internet* (China Social Science Press 2017).

Chapter 23

Tanvi Kiran, PhD, is presently working as assistant professor of Health Economics in the Department of Community Medicine and School of

Public Health, Postgraduate Institute of Medical Education and Research (PGIMER), Chandigarh, India. Previously, she worked as University Grants Commission (UGC) Postdoctoral Fellow in the Department of Economics, Panjab University, Chandigarh, India. She has also taught the subjects of Research Methodology, Financial Markets, and Basic and Advanced Econometrics to both graduate and postgraduate students. Her areas of interest are in the fields of development economics, health economics, macroeconomics, and applied econometrics.

Shivam Dhawan, MA, is working as assistant professor in the Department of Economics, Desh Bandhu Gupta Government College Panipat, Haryana, India. He is also a registered candidate for a PhD program in the Department of Economics of Panjab University, Chandigarh, India. He was awarded a master's degree in economics in 2013 by Panjab University. After clearing the national-level competitive exam, he also was awarded a University Grants Commission Junior Research Fellowship (UGC-JRF).

Chapter 24

Robin Kipfer, MSci, is originally from Switzerland and currently employed in the Country Management at Danske Bank in Finland. Persuaded that business and sustainability can together generate a substantial and powerful strategic impact, he specialized in Impact Investing while working in India, when he conducted research for the Global Steering Group for Impact Investing (GSGII). He holds a master's degree from Hanken School of Economics (Finland) in International Strategy and Sustainability. During his studies, he received several awards for outstanding academic records and extracurricular engagement.

Chapter 25

Alessandro Rizzello, PhD, received his PhD from the University Magna Graecia of Catanzaro with a dissertation that focused on social Impact Investing and social impact bonds in the health care sector. Currently, he teaches Social and Sustainable Finance at the University Magna Graecia of Catanzaro, Italy. His research interests include social Impact Investing, social impact bonds, sustainable finance, and crowdfunding of social ventures. His working experience includes positions of head of the Budgetary and Financial Office in the Italian public administration. He earned his degree in esconomics from LUISS Guido Carli University, in Rome, Italy.

Elisabetta Scognamiglio, PhD, received her PhD from the University of Naples Federico II (Italy) with a dissertation which focused on the nature of risks in social impact bonds. Currently, she is project manager at Italia-Camp, since 2017, where her main activities are management and advisory on impact evaluation, strategy, and impact assessment processes. She also contributes to the LUISS course Integrated and Impact Reporting. Previously, she was a project manager for leading microfinance institutions.

Ludovica Testa, LM, graduated in economics at Luiss Guido Carli in Rome, Italy. She is currently an analyst within the ItaliaCamp team dedicated to impact assessment and measurement. She provided research contributions on issues related to impact measurement in research and development for several of ItaliaCamp's activities. She also contributed to the management of academic presentations on lessons focused on impact measurement and management, including training research groups and conferences.

Lorenzo Liotta, LLM, is head of the Impact and Financial Services business unit of Italiacamp. His division deals with social impact assessment projects and the planning of strategies for improving impact performance. He also coordinates the company's research team and the teaching activities carried out with Luiss Guido Carli University and other prestigious Italian universities. Previously, he held the role of assistant manager in KPMG Advisory S.p.A in Strategy and Public Policy.

Chapter 26

Vikram Raman, CA, MBA, is an experienced impact investment professional with 16 years of financial sector experience, including over 13 years of Impact Investing expertise. He has worked in leadership positions with Acumen, Unitus Capital, Grassroots Business Fund, and IIX Growth Fund. He has led investments and supported social enterprises in South and Southeast Asia across financial inclusion, affordable health care, agriculture, clean energy, livelihoods, and gender lens investing. Vikram holds an MBA in finance and strategy from the Indian School of Business and is a qualified chartered accountant (India).

Chapter 27

Richard Harrison, PhD, is professor of Entrepreneurship and Innovation and director of the Compassionate Leadership Initiative at University of Edinburgh Business School. He has a broad interest in the nature of the entrepreneurial process in social and corporate as well as new venture contexts and in the implications of research and theorizing for practice and public policy. He was the 2015 recipient of the UK Economic and Social Research Council Award for Outstanding Research Impact on Business, and 2018 recipient of the US Academy of Management award for Impact on Entrepreneurial Practice.

Suwen Chen, MBA, MSci, is a doctoral researcher at the University of Edinburgh Business School, studying Impact Investing and social entrepreneurship. Suwen has been advising social enterprises, investment firms, and charities on sustainability strategies. She is currently working with the United Nations Development Program (UNDP) on their Green Entrepreneurship Program. Her recent publications include the e-book *Invisible Hand with Visible Heart: Scottish Social Enterprises,* and two letters to the editor in the *Financial Times* on Impact Investing and artificial intelligence.

Chapter 28

Filipa Pires de Almeida, MSci, is a Research Fellow at the Center for Responsible Business and Leadership at Católica Lisbon School of Business and Economics (Portugal), exploring how companies can embrace sustainable strategies to leverage their competitive advantage. She is in charge of the Sustainable Development Goals (SDG) Task Force. She also mentors impact businesses worldwide and leads Social Innovation Bootcamps, powered by INSEAD, at IES-Social Business School (Portugal). She is currently a PhD candidate at Rotterdam School of Management with a thesis on how to advance SDGs as the new competitive advantage for the corporate world.

Marta Bicho, PhD, is an associate professor and Deputy Dean for Degree Programs at IPAM Lisboa; a Research Fellow at Instituto Universitário de Lisboa (ISCTE-IUL); and invited assistant professor at Católica Lisbon School of Business and Economics, Portugal. Marta earned her PhD in Marketing at ISCTE-IUL. Her research on corporate responsibility and hybrid organizations was published in the *Journal of the Academy of Marketing Science* and the *Journal of Small Business Management.* She mentors Social Entrepreneurship Projects at IES-Social Business School (powered by INSEAD).

Chapter 29

Trang Fernandez-Leenknecht, LLM, CAIA, is the president of Holistik, a Swiss-based wealth and pension planning firm. Her previous roles include director of Wealth Planning Switzerland in a leading sustainable bank, vice chairwoman of the Board, and member of the Investment Committee of a USD $1 billion pension fund. Currently, Trang co-chairs the Annual Conference on Smart Finance and Impact Investing of the United Nations and is a jury member at a global accelerator based in Boston for high-impact start-ups. Trang is an alumna of Oxford University and a CAIA charter holder.

Chapter 30

Frederic de Mariz, PhD, is adjunct professor of Financial Innovation and Impact Investing at Columbia University, SIPA (US), and head of the Financial Institutions Group for Latin America at UBS. He is a member of the Brazilian Private Equity Association, the Brazilian Banking Association, and was an advisor to several microfinance institutions. He published a number of academic articles and book chapters. He graduated from ESSEC (MBA), Sciences Po. (MA), Columbia University (MIA), and completed his PhD at University of São Paulo (Brazil).

Acronyms and Abbreviations

A

AAAA Addis Ababa Action Agenda
ABC Fund Agri-Business Capital Fund
ACSEP Asia Centre for Social Entrepreneurship and Philanthropy
ADB Asian Development Bank
AfDB Africa Development Bank
AGG Barclays Aggregate Index
AGRA Alliance for a Green Revolution in Africa
AI Artificial intelligence
AIMM Anticipated impact measurement and monitoring
ALP Action learning projects
ATM Automated teller machine
AUM Assets under management
AUSAID Australian Government's Overseas Aid Program
AWD African Women's Development Fund

B

B Corp Benefit Corporation
B2B Business-to-business
B2C Business-to-consumer
B2G Business-to-government
BA TOD Bay Area Transit Oriented Development
BACO Best alternative charitable option
BAIII Bay Area Impact Investing Initiative

BAMA Bay Area Medical Academy
BAMES Bay Area Model Equity Strategy
BART Bay Area Rapid Transit
BCG Boston Consulting Group
BCOM Bloomberg Commodity Index
BHAG Big hairy audacious goals
BOE Barrel of oil equivalent
BoP Base of the pyramid

C

CAD Canadian dollars
CBA Cost-benefit analysis
CBI Climate Bond Initiative
CBUS Construction and Building Unions Superannuation
CD Certificate of deposit
CDD Cooling degree day
CDFI Community development financial institution
CDP Carbon Disclosure Project
CDSB Climate Disclosure Standards Board
CEA Cost-effectiveness analysis
CEO Chief executive officer
CFI Center for Financial Inclusion
CFO Chief financial officer
CH_4 Methane
CIB Climate Impact Bonds
CNY Chinese yuan
CO_2 Carbon dioxide
CO_2e Carbon dioxide equivalent
COO Chief operating officer
CPF Country Partnership Framework
CPM Critical path method
CRB Center for Responsible Business & Leadership (Portugal)
CSA Corporate Sustainability Assessment

CSA Center for Sustainable Agriculture
CSR Corporate social responsibility
CWS Center for World Solidarity

D

DAF Donor-advised funds
DANIDA Danish International Development Agency
DB Defined benefit
DBFOM Develop, build, finance, operate, maintain
DBSA Development Bank of South Africa
DC Defined Contribution (or District of Columbia, USA)
DCED Donor Committee for Enterprise Development
DEI Diversity, equity, inclusion
DFA Development Finance Assessments
DFC Development Finance Corporation (formerly OPIC)
DFI Development Finance Institution
DIB Development Impact Bond
DJSI Dow Jones Sustainability Index
DLT Distributed Ledger Technology
DWM Department of Watershed Management (City of Atlanta)

E

EBITDA Earnings before interest, taxes, depreciation, and amortization
EBRD European Bank for Reconstruction and Development
EC European Commission
EE Energy efficiency
EFCS Employees first, customers second
EFQM European Foundation for Quality Management
EFSI European Fund for Strategic Investments
EIA Environmental impact assessment
EIB Environmental Impact Bonds
EIB European Investment Bank

EMS Emergency medical services
ERISA Employee Retirement Income Security Act
ERP Enterprise resource planning
ERR Economic rate of return
ESG Environmental, social, and governance
ETF Exchange Traded Fund
EU ECB European Central Bank
EVPA European Venture Philanthropy Association
EWB Engineers Without Borders

F

FAO Food and Agriculture Organization (United Nations)
FASB Financial Accounting Standards Board
FCAS Frequency Control Ancillary Service
FCF Free cash flow
FCT Fundação para a Ciência e a Tecnologia
FDI Foreign direct investment
FEA-USP Centre for Organization Studies of the School of Business and Economics, University of São Paulo
FGE Fourth generation evaluation
Fintech Financial technology
FP Funding proposal
FPA Foreign policy analytics
FPR Forward-looking performance review
FT Fair trade

G

GAAP Generally accepted accounting principles
GADCO Global agri-development company
GB Green bond
GBF Grassroots business fund
GBP Government, business, people

GBV Gender-based violence

GCF Green Climate Fund

GDP Gross domestic product

GER Gross enrollment ratio

GHG Greenhouse gas

GIIN Global Impact Investment Network

GIIRS Global Impact Investing Rating System

GISR Global Initiative for Sustainability Ratings

GIZ Deutsche Gesellschaft für Internationale Zusammenarbeit

GLI Gender lens investing

GLIMR Gender lens investing and market risk

GMV Gross merchandise value

GoM Government of Malawi

GP General partner

GRI Global Reporting Initiative

GSDS Growth and Sustainable Development Strategy

GSG Global Steering Group for Impact Investing

GSIA Global Sustainable Investment Alliance

GVC Global value chain

H

HAT Human African Trypanosomiasis

HBS Harvard Business School

HC ROI Human capital return on investment

HCM Human capital management

HCV Human capital value (or valuation)

HDD Heating degree day

HIO Hypothetical International Organization

HIP (Human Impact + Profit) Investor

HIT Housing Investment Trust

HLEG High-Level Expert Group on Sustainable Finance

HNW/UHNW High-net-worth/Ultra-high-net-worth individual

HRMS Human Resource Management Systems

HUD Housing and Urban Development

I

I&P Investisseurs & Partenaires
IAF Impact America Fund
IB Interpretive Bulletins
IBRD International Bank for Reconstruction and Development
ICMA International Capital Market Association
ICT Information Communication Technology
IDB Inter-American Development Bank
IDD Insurance Distribution Directive
IE Impact evaluation
IEG Independent Evaluation Group
IEN Intentional Endowments Network
IEU Independent Evaluation Unit
IFAD International Fund for Agricultural Development
IFC International Finance Corporation
IFRS International Finance Reporting Standards
IILA Impact Investing Latin America
IIRC International Integrated Reporting Council
IIRF International Integrated Reporting Framework
IIX Impact Investment Exchange Asia
ILO International Labor Organization
IMM Impact Measurement and Management
IMP Impact Management Project
INFF Integrated National Financing Frameworks
INR Indian rupees
IPA Innovations for Poverty Action
IPCC Intergovernmental Panel on Climate Change
IPO Initial public offering
IPPs Independent Power Producer
IPS Investment Policy Statement
IRIS Impact Reporting and Investment Standards
IRR Internal Rate of Return
ISA Income Share Agreements
ISO International Organization for Standardization

IV Instrumental Variable
IW Investing in Women Initiative
IWEF Ilu Women's Empowerment Fund
IYP Incredible Years Parenting

J

J-PAL Abdul Latif Jameel Poverty Action Lab
JV Joint venture

K

KPI Key performance indicators
KYC Know-Your-Customer policy

L

LAC Latin America and Caribbean
LAC Local advisory committee
LGBTQ Lesbian, gay, bisexual, transgender, and queer
LCA Life cycle assessment
LCCR Low-carbon, climate-resilient
LEAF Lawrencedale Agro Processing India
LEED Leadership in Energy and Environmental Design
LORTA Learning-Oriented Real-Time Impact Assessment
LP Limited partners
LPAC Limited Partner Advisory Committee

M

M&E Monitoring and evaluation
MBA Master's in business administration
MCC Millennium Challenge Corporation
MDB Multilateral Development Bank
MDG Millennium Development Goals

MDR Merchant discount rate
MFI Microfinance institution
MIC (Lower) Middle-income countries
MiFID Markets in Financial Instruments Directive
MiFID II Markets in Financial Instruments Directive II
MiFIR Markets in Financial Instruments Regulation
MIINT MBA Impact Investing Network & Training
MOA Ministry of Agriculture
MOF Ministry of Finance
MPT Modern Portfolio Theory
MRI Mission-related investment
MSIs Multi-stakeholder initiatives
MSME Micro, small, and medium enterprises
MSMRs Micro, small, and medium retailers
MST Multi-Systemic Therapy
MT Metric tons
MXN Mexican pesos

N

NCCLF Northern California Community Loan Fund
NEET Not in education, employment, or training
NEST UK's National Employment Saving Trust
NFC Near-field communication
NGFS Network for Greening the Financial System
NGO Non-governmental organization
NPA Net nonperforming assets
NPS Net promoter scores
NPV Net present value
NSF NEPAD Spanish Fund
NVG New Ventures Group

O

O&M Operations and maintenance
OAS Organization of American States

OECD Organization for Economic Cooperation and Development
OECD-DAC Organization for Economic Cooperation and Development Assistance Committee0
OGM Oil, gas, and mining
OPEC Organization of the Petroleum Exporting Countries
OPIC Overseas Private Investment Corporation
OZ Opportunity Zone

P

P&L Profit and loss
p.a. Per annum
P2G People to government
P2P Peer-to-peer
PBI Place-based investor
PBII Place-based impact investing
PbR Payment by results
PCV Pacific Community Ventures
PE Private equity
PERT Program evaluation and review rechnique
PFS Pay for success
POS Point of service
PPA Power purchase agreements
PPA Pension Provision Act
PPP Public-private partnership
PRI Principles for responsible investing
PRI Program-related investment
PRME Principles for Responsible Management Education
PSD Private sector development
PSF Private sector facility
PSIA Poverty social impact assessment (or analysis)

Q

QALY Quality-adjusted life year
QDIA Qualified default investment alternative

QOZ Qualified opportunity zones
QR Quick response

R

R&D Research and development
RAG Red, amber, and green
raiSE Singapore Centre for Social Enterprise
RBM Results-based management
RBP Results-based payments
RCT Randomized control trial
RDD Regression discontinuity design
REC Renewable energy credit
REDD+ Reducing emissions from deforestation and forest degradation
REDF Roberts Enterprise Development Fund
REITs Real estate investment trusts
RFIIM Rockefeller Foundation Impact Investment Management
RI Responsible investing
RIA Registered investment advisor
ROA Return on assets
ROC Return on capital
ROI Return on investment
ROIC Return on invested capital
ROTC Return on total capital
RRI Responsible research and innovation
RWA Risk-weighted assets
RWi Risk-weights

S

S&P Standard and Poor's
SAA Social accounting and auditing
SAA Strategic asset allocation
SASB Sustainability Accounting Standards Board

SBI Small Business Initiative Review
SBI Sustainable Business Initiative
SBT Science-based targets
SC Supply chain
SCBA Social cost-benefit analysis
SCGC Shenzhen Capital Group Company, Ltd.
SD Standard deviation
SDC Swiss Agency for Development and Cooperation
SDG (United Nations) Sustainable Development Goal
SDSN Sustainable Development Solutions Network
SE Social entrepreneurship
SEAD Social entrepreneurship accelerator
SEAF Small Enterprise Assistance Funds
SEB Scandinavian Individual Bank
SEC Securities and Exchange Commission
SEIF Social Enterprise Investment Fund
SF San Francisco
SHS Solar home systems
SIA Social impact assessment
SIB Social impact bond
SIDA Swedish International Development Agency
SIILK Sustainable & Impact Investing Learning & Knowledge Network
SMA Separately managed accounts
SME Small and medium enterprises
SNV Netherlands Development Organization
SOCAP Social capital markets
SPO Social purpose organization
SPY SPDR S&P 500 ETF Trust
SRI Socially responsible investing
SROI Social return on investment
SSE Social and solidarity economics
STEM Science, technology, engineering, and math
SVT Social Venture Technology Group

T

TBL Triple bottom line
TCFD Task Force on Climate-Related Financial Disclosures
TEA Total early-stage entrepreneurial activity
TEG Technical Expert Group
TFCD Task Force on Climate-Related Disclosures
TFSG Transition Finance Study Group
TIPS Treasury Inflation-Protected Securities
ToC Theory of Change
TOP Teen Outreach Program
TWC Total cost of workforce

U

UFA Universal financial access
UK United Kingdom
UK SIF UK Sustainable Investment and Finance Association
UN United Nations
UNCV UNC Ventures
UNDP United Nations Development Program
UNEP United Nations Environment Program
UNFCCC United Nations Framework Convention on Climate Change
UNGC United Nations Global Compact
UNIDO UN Industrial Development Organization
US United States
US DOL United States Department of Labor
US SIF US Forum for Sustainable and Responsible Investment
USAID United States Agency for International Development
USD United States dollar
UWC United World College
WSME Women-owned small and medium-sized enterprises

V

VBDO Association of Investors for Sustainable Development
VC Venture capital
VC Value chain
VCD Value chain development
VPO Venture Philanthropy Organization
VSLA Village Savings and Loan Association

W

WAMA Water Management Authority
WB World Bank
WBCSD World Business Council for Sustainable Development
WBG World Bank Group
WEF World Economic Forum
WEP Women's Empowerment Principles
WFP World Food Program
WHO World Health Organization
WIN-WIN Women Investing in Women Initiative
WLB Women's Livelihood Bond
WVL Women's Voice and Leadership
WWF Worldwide Fund

X, Y, Z

ZMD Z Meteorological Department
ZHL Ziqitza Healthcare Limited

Introduction

By Elsa de Morais Sarmento and R. Paul Herman

The longest rivers on every continent of the earth – the Nile in Africa, the Amazon in South America, the Yangtze in Asia, the Mississippi in North America, the Volga in Europe, the Murray-Darling in Australia, and the Onyx in Antarctica – support the essentials of life: supplying water, growing food, providing efficient transport, and enabling thriving communities.

Water is the source of life, and an essential element of everyday survival: to hydrate, wash, farm, and cool off.

Similarly, the source of life for the growth of organizations (business, governments, civil society) to seed ideas, grow ventures, and scale up is capital. For most of us, the term "capital" signifies monetary investments. That's what our balance sheets convey: assets equal liabilities plus equity. Thus, capital includes loans and bonds, plus equities and stocks.

Yet several types of capitals exist, beyond purely financial. Human capital, natural capital, and social capital are the three primary types. In more common terms, these are People, Planet, and Trust. In traditional economic terms, these are labor, land, and networks. All forms of capital, allocated by investors, and invested by money managers, can support thriving, sustainable communities that we all want to live in. Many of these goals are summarized in the 17 United Nations Sustainable Development Goals (SDGs) – such as no poverty, gender equality, and climate action, as well as peace and partnerships.

In this *Global Handbook of Impact Investing*, we showcase the full spectrum of capitals to be invested and allocated. "People are our most important asset" is a common theme espoused by Chief Executive Officers (CEOs). However, those essential assets are not on the balance sheet as an asset, but rather on the income statement as costs. For investors seeking impact, the value of people is critical, as no products can be invented and no customer served without human resources. Natural capital typically does not have a toll charge from the earth, only the extraction costs of paying people or transporting from mines or wells or farms. If investors paid the ecosystem

1

for its actual services to us, no business would be profitable. It is possible to harness social capital, and the networks of relationships can produce and strengthen multi-stakeholder initiatives, public-private partnerships, and value chains.

Investors seeking impact have the opportunity to ensure a full end-to-end system that is kept sustainable, responsible, and realizing positive impact. Whether "farm-to-fork" in agriculture and food systems, or "stone-to-phone" in mining rare earths to producing mobile devices, the most resilient portfolios take into the full systems view – and impact investors build these precepts into their investment policy, decision-making, and investment choices.

When investors understand that intangible value, which is the difference between market value and book value, is more than 80% of the stock market value of the S&P 500 index, according to Ocean Tomo Advisors,[1] then investment professionals can more fully see and embrace that current systems, views, and tools need to be expanded.

With that goal in mind, we have assembled authors who are innovators, pioneers, experts, and academics inside this *Global Handbook*, which draws heavily on their professional and personal experiences in this field, to build capacity and disseminate learning.

This volume aims to offer a view of how Impact Investing is already providing an integrated alternative toward the creation of more inclusive markets, fighting poverty through wealth creation, fostering regional national cohesion and work in favor of countries' competitiveness and inclusiveness objectives within the framework of SDGs. Impact Investing's innovative approach and tools have helped rethink and reshape an economy from which everyone can now benefit. This *Global Handbook* describes how Impact Investing has grown globally, how different frameworks are being created and evolving to measure impact, and what actions and strategies can be pursued toward positive impact and profit potential. Moreover, the *Global Handbook* offers targeted, practical advice and tools on how to engage as an impact investor, bearing in mind that many different types of impact investors pursue a variety of impact objectives and varying financial return targets. In addition, the Impact Investing community at large can lead policymakers and institutional actors toward smarter approaches that blend solutions across sectors and instruments.

The Global Handbook of Impact Investing is segmented into six parts. Part I explains "The Expanding Boundaries and Sophistication of the Impact

---

[1]See the latest numbers at https://www.oceantomo.com/intangible-asset-market-value-study/.

Investing Ecosystem." Part II delves into "The Value of People in Impact Investing." Part III explores "The Value of Nature, Climate, and Planet in Impact Investing." Part IV explains a spectrum of "Measuring and Reporting Impact: Approaches, Standards, Methods, and Tools." Part V highlights "The Call to Action: Impact Experiences from Around the Globe." Finally, Part VI looks forward to "Where Is the Future of Impact Investing Headed?"

To learn how the investment ecosystem is becoming more sophisticated in all types of impacts, Part I, "The Expanding Boundaries and Sophistication of the Impact Investing Ecosystem," informs the reader comprehensively on the field, discipline, and industry of Impact Investing. This part offers a characterization of the Impact Investing ecosystem and the drive toward social change and social impact creation, exploring the global Impact Investing phenomenon and why investors are increasingly leaning into Impact Investing and how it can make a difference.

The book's first chapter, "Impact Investing Frameworks Across All Asset Classes" by **Haifa Ben Abid, MPhil,** provides a literature review of the latest Impact Investing definitions, frameworks, and measurement systems. Chapter 2, "Investing for Impact: Socially Motivated Investors and Externalities" by **Raghavan Narayana, MBA,** and **Stoyan Tenev, PhD,** highlights new metrics of success, and the associated "hurdle rates" for sought-after environmental and social impacts, as well as traditional financial rates of return. Chapter 3, "Place-Based Impact Investing: Local and Regional Assets for Local and Regional Impact in Globally Diversified Portfolios" by **Lauryn Agnew, MBA,** encourages all investors to collaborate more actively across the entire "capital stack" (cash, loans, equity, real estate, and more) to ensure stronger, more resilient communities – and purposely to allocate locally, and regionally, not just globally.

Part II, "The Value of People in Impact Investing," describes how value is created from many sources that are known but typically ignored. As introduced earlier, people are a valuable asset and can be half the cost structure of an organization. Chapter 4, "How to Invest in Human Capital: Measuring and Integrating Human Capital Valuation to Realize Higher-Impact Portfolios" by **Kirstin Dougall, MFA,** and the book's co-editor **R. Paul Herman, BSci,** provides the analytics and guidance showing that the critical foundation of value creation starts with employees as innovators and leaders and explains how to invest in human capital, by measuring and integrating human capital to realize higher impact portfolios. While all investees are managed by CEOs and their teams, their highest potential is not always realized. Chapter 5, "Leadership by Results for Impact Investors and Investees" by **Rajen Makhijani, MBA,** profiles leadership types, offers assessment criteria that investment managers can use, and shows how a programmatic approach to "leadership by results" can unleash increased value.

Gender lens investing (GLI) is explained in four insightful chapters. In Chapter 6, "Gender Lens Investing: Co-Creating Critical Knowledge to Build a Credible, Durable Field," **Edward T. Jackson, OMC, EdD,** and co-editor **Elsa de Morais Sarmento, MA,** bring a global perspective to the critical success factors for this valuable approach implementable across asset classes, while also detailing cross-border programs for investing in women, such as those funded by Australia and operating in Indonesia, the Philippines, and Vietnam. In Chapter 7, "Investing with a Gender Lens: Uncovering Alpha Previously Overlooked," investment manager **Kristin Hull, PhD,** presents a systematic framework to build gender criteria into the investment policy statement, to track results in portfolio investees, and gender-focused investee examples in every asset class to consider for a gender-smart portfolio. In Chapter 8, "Gender Lens Investing in the African Context," **Michael Z. Ngoasong, PhD,** and **Richmond O. Lamptey, PhD,** profile the African landscape of GLI, with in-depth examples of microfinance organizations in Ghana and Cameroon, and strategies for explicit and implicit GLI strategies covering all regions of northern, southern, western, and eastern Africa. In Chapter 9, "The Evolution from Gender-Focused Microfinance to Gender Lens Investing in Latin America: The Case of Pro Mujer," **Angelica Rotondaro, PhD, Maria Cavalcanti, MBA, MS**, and **Carmen Correa, BSci,** examine GLI in Latin America, with a deep-dive into the first-hand experience of Pro Mujer and its expansion into additional financing vehicles for higher impact for women, ranging from Brazil to Colombia and Mexico.

Chapter 10, "Inclusive Investing: Impact Meets Diversity, Equity, and Inclusion (DEI)," provides a new framework for deepening the power from investing actively blending diversity and inclusion into the portfolio. **Julianne Zimmerman, MSci, Edward Dugger III, MPA-UP,** and **Shijiro Ochirbat, MBA, MPA**, illuminate the benefits of diversity in investment portfolios, while detailing three levels of investment analysis for impact investors to pursue across asset classes.

Chapter 11, "Investing for Impact in Employee Retirement Plans," taps the trillions invested for the future of billions of employees and citizens. **Megan Morrice, MBA,** illustrates how firms and nations of all sizes offering retirement plans can balance their fiduciary duty with opportunities for more sustainable investment fund choices, with examples from Australia's super-annuation program to the USA's 401(k) and 403(b) plans.

Part III, "The Value of Nature, Climate, and Planet in Impact Investing," illuminates how a portfolio can adapt to the energy revolution and climate action, as well as new financial instruments promoting transparency, performance, and accountability.

In Chapter 12, "Fossil-Fuel-Free Investing: Weaving a New Investment Paradigm," **Umachander Balakumar, MSci,** explores how to build a portfolio that drops the carbon-dioxide emissions intensity while remaining diversified, and highlights tools that can help investors go fossil-fuel-free. In Chapter 13, "The Role of Transition Finance Instruments in Bridging the Climate Finance Gap," **Pauline Deschryver, MSci,** and **Frederic de Mariz, PhD,** introduce a new financial instrument called "transition finance bonds" to build bridges to close the climate-finance gap.

The next two chapters showcase the increasing accountability that can be built into financial instruments. In Chapter 14, "Social Impact Bonds: Promises and Results," **Maria Basílio, PhD,** details how social impact bonds and environmental impact bonds align investor and issuer interests for positive improvements in people and planet, while compensating risky investor capital with appropriate returns. In Chapter 15, "Climate and Money: Dealing with 'Impact Washing' and a Case for Climate Impact Bonds," **Jyotsna Puri, PhD; Aemal Khan, MA;** and **Solomon Asfaw, PhD,** address the causes of potential cases of "impact washing," and also introduce a new financial instrument design of a "climate impact bond" with an even higher degree of impact measurement.

Part IV, "Measuring and Reporting Impact: Approaches, Standards, Methods, and Tools," brings the leading-edge thinking and how-to's of more rigorously quantifying the results of Impact Investing.

The following three chapters cover the next generation of impact measurement frameworks, offering the latest perspective for measuring, evaluating, and reporting impacts. In Chapter 16, "Measuring and Evaluating Social Impact in Impact Investing: An Overview of the Main Available Standards and Methods," **Ana Pimenta, MEcon,** and book co-editor **Elsa de Morais Sarmento, MA,** summarize the primary methods for evaluating impact, and which are appropriate for varying scenarios. In Chapter 17, "Impact Measurement and Management Techniques to Achieve Powerful Results," **Jane Reisman, PhD,** and **Veronica Olazabal, MCRS,** provide an in-depth look into impact measurement success factors and examples of the latest evaluation approaches used by leading foundations. In Chapter 18, "Transformative Evaluation and Impact Investing: A Fruitful Marriage," **Courtney Bolinson, MS,** and **Donna Mertens, PhD,** showcase "transformative evaluation" as a method to ensure that stakeholders of all types are purposely included in any impact measurement scorecard of results.

The next two chapters explore advanced tools for multisector Impact Investing, profiling the latest approaches to measuring impact with geolocation, and a fuller engagement with smaller firms in the supply chain. In Chapter 19, "Geospatial Analysis of Targeting of World Bank's Development Assistance in Mexico," **Mario Negre, PhD; Hannes Öhler, PhD; and Željko Bogetić, PhD,** apply scientific geospatial analysis to evaluate whether the lowest-income beneficiaries are receiving the full investment capital relative to their needs, and how these tools can be applicable to other impacts and geographies. In Chapter 20, "Evaluating the Impact of Portfolio Allocations to Large Firms Along the Value Chain to Develop Small and Medium-Sized Enterprises," **Maximilian Foedinger, MBA, MPA,** and co-editor **Elsa de Morais Sarmento, MA,** introduce a new measurement system to evaluate how small and medium-sized enterprises can be developed more methodically as part of the value chains and supply chains of larger enterprise borrowing from development banks, like the European Bank for Reconstruction and Development (EBRD).

This *Global Handbook* is intended for a wide audience of investors, experts, and academics – from Africa to Europe, from Australia to Asia, from South America to North America. Part V, "The Call to Action: Impact Experiences from Around the Globe," offers perspectives and experiences of successes, inspiring cases, and best practices from around the world.

In Chapter 21, "Two Decades of Front-Line Impact Investing," **Jean-Philippe de Schrevel, MBA,** shares his two decades of pioneering front-line experience and lessons learned as the founder of Bamboo Capital to fund and scale high-impact enterprises. In Chapter 22, "China's Rapidly Evolving Practice of Impact Investing: A Critical Perspective," **Jianbo Zhao, PhD,** details the multiple initiatives inside China to rapidly evolve Impact Investing along with the growing wealth of the country. In Chapter 23, "Impact Investing through Corporate Social Responsibility: The Indian Experience," **Tanvi Kiran, PhD,** and **Shivam Dhawan, MA,** examine India's corporate-social responsibility (CSR) mandate to collect 2% of all corporate profits to reinvest in multiple social and environmental initiatives. In Chapter 24, "What Drives Impact Investors? Benchmarking Developed and Developing Countries," **Robin Kipfer, MSci,** details the distinct interests of high-net-worth investors and venture capitalists in Finland and in India, and how investment goals and experiences align or diverge from the contrasting perspectives of developed and developing countries. In Chapter 25, "Understanding the Demand for Impact Investments: Insights from the

Italian Market," **Alessandro Rizzello, PhD; Elisabetta Scognamiglio, PhD; Ludovica Testa, LM;** and **Lorenzo Liotta, LLM,** report on 300-plus early-stage ventures based in Italy, and how those ventures are positioned and ready for impact investors to fund and scale them.

Part VI concludes this book with "Where Is the Future of Impact Investing Headed?"

Chapter 26, "The Importance of Scale in Social Enterprises: The Indian Case," by **Vikram Raman, CA, MBA,** explains how human capital is essential for scaling organizations and social enterprises to achieve maximum impact and reach.

The following three chapters investigate how to strengthen the foundations of the Impact Investing ecosystem and highlight how Impact Investing brings together pioneers and innovators that build a better world across sectors, from academia to multinational corporations to policymakers. In Chapter 27, "The Role of the Entrepreneurial University and Engaged Scholarship in Impact Investing Capacity Building," **Richard T. Harrison, PhD,** and **Suwen Chen, MBA,** bring a systems-level view of how universities can engage scholars and spur more entrepreneurial initiatives to properly train current students, enhance curricula, and bring the full power of academic institutions to the field of Impact Investing. In Chapter 28, "A Road Map for Implementing Impact Investing: The Case of Multinational Companies," **Filipa Pires de Almeida, MSc,** and **Marta Bicho, PhD,** present a roadmap for implementing impact in companies, specifically profiling Unilever, IKEA, and General Electric, and the new financial approaches to realize more impact. In Chapter 29, "Impact Investing and European Wealth Managers: Why Impact Investing Will Go Mainstream and Evolve to Suit European Investors," **Trang Fernandez-Leenknecht, CAIA, LLM,** examines in detail the new European standards and policies that will increase the level of fiduciary duty and suitability for any Impact Investing related to the European Union.

The final chapter looks at how extending Impact Investing to financial services for all expands the power of an impactful approach to the full suite of financial products and services. Chapter 30, "Fintech for Impact: How Can Financial Innovation Advance Inclusion?" by **Frederic de Mariz, PhD,** profiles how financial-technology (fintech) solutions and ventures can bring inclusivity to all seven billion citizens globally, including insurance and savings, to achieve higher impact in their lives.

This *Global Handbook* is intended for you – whether that means investor, family office, foundation, pension, endowment, retirement plan, development financial institution, multilateral bank, bilateral donor, donor-driven organization, NGO, civil society organization, academic institution, student, faculty, or other role. We have sought to bring you the latest insights and wisdom from around the world to inform and inspire you, the reader. We encourage you to share this content with your peers and decision makers. We look forward to your experimenting, testing, and piloting of these compelling approaches in your portfolios. We are curious to hear of your experiences in pursuing Impact Investing. We welcome your feedback on the book, and the lessons learned in your own portfolios.

Overall, we hope that you see that investing for impact is beneficial: by bringing a systems-level view; by integrating all capitals into your investment analyses; by measuring people, planet, and profit and evaluating versus high standards and peers; by engaging all your stakeholders and geographical networks; and by progressing forward into the future in a methodical manner.

We wish you stronger, more resilient investment portfolios that can achieve human impact and profit at the same time – just as our flowing rivers of capital contain many nutrients to enhance the well-being of people and planet across all continents.

Yours in impact,
Elsa de Morais Sarmento and R. Paul Herman
Paris and San Francisco
July 2020

CHAPTER 1

Impact Investing: Innovation or Rebranding?

Haifa Ben Abid, MPhil

Abstract

In recent years, individuals and organizations in both private and public sectors at national and international levels have been seeking lasting solutions to daunting global challenges, from climate change to unprecedented levels of youth unemployment. In their search, many have embraced Impact Investing as a new investment strategy that brings together the worlds of profit-making and social and environmental problem-solving. Despite the increasing interest in Impact Investing, scholarly work in the field remains scarce. While a myriad of practitioner contributions exist, a dearth of academic research on Impact Investing persists. Yet bodies of literature that have emerged over the years focus on the broader trend of "positive" investment classes that closely resemble Impact Investing, including socially responsible investments (SRI), social entrepreneurship, sustainable investments (related to environmental, social, and governance investments (ESG); microfinance; and ethical investments. A consensus on Impact Investing's definition eludes scholars and practitioners alike; likewise, debates

9

continue over how, and in what ways, Impact Investing represents a distinctive and innovative investment strategy that sets it apart from other forms of positive investment as well as institutional investment. This chapter intends to shed light on the concept of Impact Investing, providing greater conceptual clarity, encouraging the burgeoning interest in Impact Investing among scholars, and helping to foster research in this area by offering insights into Impact Investing's key features and actors, related practices, opportunities and challenges that together constitute the uniqueness of Impact Investing.

Keywords

Impact Investing; Social Impact Investment; Socially Responsible Investment; Microfinance; Social Entrepreneurship; Ethical Investment

INTRODUCTION

As a global community, we face daunting social and environmental problems, from persistently high levels of greenhouse gas emissions, defor- estation, and pollution, to increasingly frequent epidemics and rising youth unemployment, inadequate access to clean water, sanitation, and health care. Addressing such problems sustainably—both immediately and over the long term—will require trillions of dollars of funding. Against a back- drop of economic turbulence, austerity measures on public budgets, and a burgeoning youth population, a new investment strategy that brings together the worlds of profit-making and social and environmental problem-solving is garnering global attention: Impact Investing.

Emerging on a global scale over the past 20 years (Ormiston et al. 2015), *Impact Investing* refers to an investment strategy that intentionally aims to achieve both financial returns and positive social and environmental impacts (O'Donohoe et al. 2010; Rodin and Brandenberg 2014; Vecchi et al. 2016). According to its proponents, Impact Investing promises to offer an innovative way to bring the resources of the world's financial markets to its seemingly intractable problems (Clarkin and Cangioni 2016).

For years, Impact Investing has been met with enthusiasm by prac- titioners who have produced a vast array of studies and reports on the subject (Höchstädter and Scheck 2015; Vecchi et al. 2016). Likewise, it has become a priority issue on the agendas of governments and interna- tional, bilateral, and multilateral institutions alike. Yet it has received scant attention among scholars, with few studies published in academic books and peer-reviewed journals (Emerson and Spitzer 2007; Höchstädter and Scheck 2015; Moore et al. 2012; Nicholls 2010). The limited scholarly literature has left the field of Impact Investing with a substantial degree of ambiguity and lack of consensus regarding its definitions and terminology. Consequently, Impact Investing's distinctiveness from related forms of investing remains unclear. Similarly, Impact Investing's unique strategies, principles, practices, and objectives are often muddled (Clarkin and Cangioni 2016; Höchstädter and Scheck 2015).

This lack of clarity prompts the research question that forms the scope of this chapter: *Is Impact Investing truly a new concept and an innovative investment strategy, making its mark in a significant way?* That is, does it merely represent a rebranding of similar forms of alternative, socially conscious investment, such as socially responsible investment (SRI), venture philanthropy, social enterprise investment, or microfinance practices?

This chapter aims to present a better understanding of the concept of Impact Investing with the purpose of contributing to the existing knowledge base, encouraging further academic research, and supporting practitioners. To that end, this chapter examines existing works of scholars and practitioners who have contributed to discussions and debates regarding the foundations of Impact Investing, its definition, framework, opportunities, constraints, and empirical research.

The next section of this chapter presents the methods used to conduct a comprehensive literature review that produced three thematic discussions. The following section provides an overview of Impact Investing's origins, philosophy, and practices, with the aim of clarifying the concept of Impact Investing. The next section traces the growth of Impact Investing and the response from the world of investment. The following section explores the key features of Impact Investing in greater detail, highlighting what it shares with other forms of positive investing and what sets it apart. The conclusion outlines suggestions for future research directions in the field of Impact Investing.

METHODOLOGY

To assess the current state of the field of Impact Investing, a comprehensive review of the existing literature relevant to Impact Investing was conducted, utilizing content analysis techniques. The literature review utilized the approach provided by Cooper (1988, 1998), Cooper and Hedges (1994), and Hedges and Cooper (1994), which emphasizes two main elements of the literature review: (i) report, describe, and clarify existing primary research on impact investing; and (ii) summarize research findings. Given that the term *Impact Investing* is relatively new, the dearth of academic research, and the fact that the Impact Investing discourse is primarily driven by practitioners, the present study draws upon both academic and practitioner contributions (Höchstädter and Scheck 2015).

Keyword searches were conducted in Google, Google Scholar, and major scholarly databases, including ProQuest, Web of Science, EBSCO, Academic Search Complete, and Business Source Complete. A variety of fields were considered in the searches, including management, finance, entrepreneurship, international development, and sociology. Keyword searches included "Impact Investing," "impact investment," "social entrepreneurship," "social enterprise investment," "social finance," and "social impact investment." Using the keyword "Impact Investing," for example, yielded over 1.5 million results in Google, and 6,390 results in Google Scholar. Narrowing the keyword search in Google Scholar to titles of articles yielded 558 results. The term "Impact investment" yielded similar results (see Table 1.1). Practitioner contributions included various reports and case studies from government agencies, investment firms, foundations, and consulting firms. Furthermore, numerous reports appeared from organizations that provide services and resources to the social sector, such as the Global Impact Investing Network (GIIN), the Rockefeller Foundation, United Nations Development Program (UNDP), and JP Morgan.

This comprehensive review of existing literature addresses areas of similarities and inconsistencies in the diverse understandings of scholars and practitioners engaged in a critical analysis of the discourse, tracing noteworthy debates and prominent voices. It attempts to map the range of practices embraced under the Impact Investing umbrella, including the micro and macro levels; public, private, and public-private joint initiatives; and the use of asset classes. A total of 58 scholarly and practitioner references

TABLE 1.1 Keyword Search Results.

Key Word Source	"Impact Investing"	"Impact investment"
Google	1,540,000	615,000
Google Scholar	6,390 (anywhere in article) 558 (titles only)	8,180 (anywhere in article) 308 (titles only)

Source: Author. Haifa Ben Abid

were analyzed and a references analysis table constructed that highlights key statements and text extracts for each reference in order to assess the scope of literature, key themes, and foci.

IMPACT INVESTING: CLARIFYING THE CONCEPT

The History of Impact Investing: The Birth of a New Term

The term *Impact Investing* was reported to be first coined in 2007 at a meeting hosted by the Rockefeller Foundation (Bugg-Levine and Emerson 2011; Hummels 2016), which consisted of a gathering of like-minded people with different backgrounds, including philanthropy, the private sector, private-public partnerships, venture capital, financial markets, among others. Thus, since its inception, this investment strategy has been predominantly driven by practitioners (Freireich and Fulton 2009; Höchstädter and Scheck 2015; O'Donohoe et al. 2010). However, according to Hummels (2016) the practice itself has existed for much longer: "Investors, intending to create positive social or environmental outcomes while generating a financial return, had been around for decades. They simply operated in the margins of the financial system and remained more or less unnoticed." Similarly, Bugg-Levine and Goldstein (2009, p. 32) noted that Impact Investing has its underpinning in SRI:

> The seeds for Impact Investing were sown in the last quarter of the twentieth century with the socially responsible investment and corporate responsibility movement . . . what we see now is simply its latest iteration that links economics with the social and environmental aspects of the human experience. (p. 32)

The increasing popularity that Impact Investing is enjoying (Vecchi et al. 2016) stems from the massive efforts by the pioneers of this industry, which have been deployed to promote and streamline the concept over the last decade (Freireich and Fulton 2009; O'Donohoe et al. 2010). These pioneers have worked unrelentingly to put theory into practice by establishing a framework, a formal network, and a dedicated market for this nascent industry that has historically been characterized as "a small, disorganized, under-leveraged niche for years or even decades" (Freireich and Fulton 2009, p. 5).Despite claims that Impact Investing finds its underpinning mainly in praxis with bare theorization, scholars have expressed interest in the subject for years (Arosio 2011; Emerson and Cabaj 2000). Scholarly interest in investment geared toward social and environmental impacts is not a recent development (Arosio 2011). For instance, more than a decade ago, Emerson (2000) challenged the prevailing wisdom that financial returns and social returns were mutually exclusive (Clarkin and Cangioni 2016). Emerson and Cabaj (2000) proposed the possibility of investing in ways that combine financial returns and social and environmental impact, using the concepts of *socioeconomic value* and *social return on investment* (SROI). More recently, several renowned universities have included Impact Investing in their curricula (Höchstädter and Scheck 2015), and others have created dedicated platforms to generate knowledge, share experiences, and support impact investors, such as the Impact Investing Lab at the SDA Bocconi School of Management in Italy.

Challenging a Bifurcated System: Positive Impacts and Returns

Historically, the worlds of finance and philanthropy were bifurcated, separating profit-making from social and environmental problem-solving, respectively (Bugg-Levine and Emerson 2011). We have long relied on governments and community organizations to meet evolving social needs, while leaving markets, private capital, and the business sector to seek and deliver financial returns (Moore et al. 2012). However, this binary system is breaking down as Impact Investing has begun to bring funds from the financial world to address social problems (Harji and Jackson 2012; O'Donohoe et al. 2010). This move brings the potential to offer substantially larger amounts of funds to addressing social problems in the future (Freireich and Fulton 2009; Ormiston et al. 2015), signaling a booming industry (Bugg-Levine and Emerson 2011).

The innovation of Impact Investing lies partly in how, as a new investment concept, it has carved out a funding niche situated between philanthropy and mainstream financial investments (Nicholls 2010; Ormiston et al. 2015). As such, it offers a source of funding that can complement, rather than supplant, the efforts of governments and philanthropic organizations (Freireich and Fulton 2009; Harji and Jackson 2012; O'Donohoe et al. 2010). Complex global problems require multifaceted solutions and new alliances. Impact Investing is seen as an emerging instrument of financing development that offers novel means to harness financial capital to address social and environmental crises, with investors, governments, and philanthropists working cooperatively in unprecedented ways (Bugg-Levine and Emerson 2011). These new cooperative partnerships reflect how Impact Investing has "resonated as well with a new set of investors who have sensed a desire to integrate their investment and philanthropy but previously lacked the language to articulate it" (Bugg-Levine and Emerson 2011, pp. 8–9).

Types of Impact Investing: Financial-First versus Impact-First

Impact Investing has numerous variations, resulting in two broad categories: "financial-first" and "impact-first" (Ormiston et al. 2015). Financial-first impact investors, typically institutional investors, make investments with the aim of obtaining financial returns that are market-competitive and also have a social/environmental benefit. Conversely, impact-first impact investors, typically including foundations and family offices, pursue investments with high social/environmental impact, accepting below-market financial returns (Freireich and Fulton 2009; Harji and Jackson 2012; Ormiston et al. 2015). The defining feature of Impact Investing is this double objective: financial returns and positive social and environmental impacts. It could then be said that Impact Investing is a way of diversifying the value of an investment; thus, diversity represents a core characteristic of Impact Investing (O'Donohoe et al. 2010; Ormiston et al. 2015; Payne and Cook 2014). In various ways, diversity is the source of strength and competitive advantage for Impact Investing and may well be the driver of its success in the future.

Philanthropic organizations often engage in *mission-related investments* (MRI) or *program-related investments* (PRI), which tend to consistently prioritize social impacts over financial returns. Conversely, Impact Investing emphasizes "blended value" by aiming to achieve both substantial financial returns and measurable social impacts (Bugg-Levine and Emerson 2011; Ormiston et al. 2015). Yet Impact Investing is a flexible investment strategy that allows for prioritizing one over the other through impact-first or finance-first strategies. The chosen strategy will depend on the type of entity—whether an institutional investment firm or charity—its fiduciary and legal constraints and responsibilities and intended impact goals (O'Donohoe et al. 2010; Ormiston et al. 2015). As Ormiston et al. (2015, p. 356) explained, "investors' expectations regarding risk, return, and impact vary according to their intentions."

Although a broad array of configurations of financial-first and impact-first Impact Investing strategies exist, thus far, a much greater emphasis has been placed on financial-first investments, often with expectations of market-rate returns. While financial-first investments are clearly more appropriate for certain entities, given their needs and constraints, an emphasis on market-rate returns increases the risk of mission drift because institutional investors are wooed by the Impact Investing industry in ways that could undermine the integrity of Impact Investing and its core tenants. As a result, Impact Investing at times seems to fall prey to rebranding as commercial funds are repackaged in order to capitalize on its increasing popularity even if they do not technically qualify as such (Bolis et al. 2017). A continued expectation of near- or at-market returns will certainly incentivize rebranding efforts and undermine the distinguishing features of Impact Investing that set it apart from most institutional investment strategies.

Impact Investing and Similar Practices: Where Do the Differences Lie?

Impact Investing is closely related to a variety of investment strategies that seek to generate both financial and social value via investments, referred to as "positive" investment classes (Harji and Jackson 2012; Hebb 2013a and 2013b; Höchstädter and Scheck 2015; Scarlata and Alemany 2012). In this rapidly changing field, a proliferation of such positive investment classes and strategies has taken place in recent years, including SRI (Richardson 2013; Richardson and Peihani 2015; Robb and Sattell 2016), ethical investment (Richardson 2009), microfinance (Agbeko et al. 2017; Agbola et al. 2017; Banerjee et al. 2015; Fenton et al. 2017; Ngoasong and Kimbu 2016), corporate philanthropy (Gautier and Pache 2015), corporate social responsibility (Cochran 2007; Ramasastry 2015; Sharma 2015), business and human rights (Ramasastry 2015), innovative finance (Keohane 2016), Village Savings and Loan Associations (VSLAs) (Brunie et al. 2014; Ksoll et al. 2016), Pay for Success (PFS) financing (Godeke 2013), among other forms of private sector participation in social impact projects (Wentworth and Makokera 2015).

The distinctions between Impact Investing and these other forms of positive investment can be blurred, a point of debate among practitioners and scholars (Harji and Jackson 2012; Höchstädter and Scheck 2015). Ethical investment and SRI are essentially synonymous approaches; in fact, what we now call SRI was originally called ethical investment and refers to integrating social values in financial investments (Revelli 2016). According to Ormiston et al. (2015, p. 353), while Impact Investing shares similarities to SRI and ethical investment in particular, it sets itself apart from these classes by seeking "to achieve clearly defined and measurable social impact as opposed to simply avoiding negative externalities and focusing on high level environmental, social and governance (ESG) factors." Given this, Impact Investing "can thus be viewed as an evolution from socially responsible investment, though there is some overlap between the two fields" (Ormiston et al. 2015, p. 353). Other scholars consider Impact Investing as one form of SRI, such as Robb and Sattell (2016, p. 3), who use the term SRI to "describe sustainable investing, program-related investing, Impact Investing, and similar strategies that favor projects or shares of companies based on perceived social good."

The line dividing Impact Investing and microfinance is similarly blurred. In fact, given Impact Investing's emphasis on both intent and measurement of social impacts, as well as its preference for deploying capital in the form of debt rather than equity, it often prioritizes investments in financial services, particularly microfinance (Jafri 2018). Modern microfinance institutions (MFIs) first emerged in the 1970s in Bangladesh as a solution to the problem of credit constraint among poor people by providing financial services for those without access to traditional formal banking, mostly in the form of loans to individuals, groups, and small businesses (van Rooyen et al. 2012). Globally, more than 800 million people live in extreme poverty, defined as living on less than USD \$1.25 a day (United Nations Development Program 2016). Such people, including farmers and would-be entrepreneurs, are credit constrained due to collateral and other reasons. Without collateral, such as property that can be pledged as security for repayment of a loan, banks are generally unwilling to offer loans.

Theoretically, microfinance promises to eradicate poverty by allowing market forces to operate, which, in turn, enables the poor to invest in their future and bring themselves out of poverty (Donou-Adonsou and Sylwester 2016; Miled and Rejeb 2015). By reducing credit constraints, microfinance aims to enable clients to increase their incomes, repay their loans, and accumulate financial wealth. By providing microloans to entrepreneurs to start social enterprises or other small businesses, impact investors promote financial development and poverty reduction among the world's poor, while earning financial returns on the interest of the loans.

Measuring the actual impact of microfinance initiatives on poverty reduction has proved challenging (Banerjee et al. 2015; Miled and Rejeb 2015; Samer et al. 2015), a problem that Impact Investing has also faced (Jackson 2013b; Reisman et al. 2018; Wieland 2016). A large part of the challenge stems from the fact that the Impact Investing industry lacks comparable financial and impact data and a harmonized set of methodological procedures to collect and analyze data. According to Bolis et al. (2017), very few organizations "have datasets that include detailed information on both financial performance and impact performance, sufficient, for example, to compare financial performance against impact approach, enterprise type, etc. This is partly due to the difficulty of standardizing impact metrics and the cost of collecting data" (p. 15).

Evaluations of microfinance initiatives have revealed mixed results in terms of impacts on beneficiaries (Agbola et al. 2017; Banerjee et al. 2015; Miled and Rejeb 2015; van Rooyen et al. 2012). Likewise, assessments of Impact Investing–funded projects have found that the fiscal requirements, including rate of return and time horizons, are often not totally well matched to the needs of social enterprises and other social programs, negatively affecting outcomes (Bolis et al. 2015).

Impact Reporting and Investment Standards (IRIS),[1] a comprehensive system for impact measurement and management developed by GIIN, has made significant progress in providing consistent measuring and management of the impacts of investments, enabling investors to minimize negative effects and optimize positive effects (GIIN 2020).

IMPACT INVESTING: A RESPONSE TO A CHANGING INVESTMENT ENVIRONMENT

Twenty-First Century Investing: Features of the New Investment Environment

Given that Impact Investing aims to achieve both financial returns and social/environmental impacts rather than achieving one at the expense of the other, it has thus far proven capable of attracting substantial funding from the private sector (Carragher 2013; Freireich and Fulton 2009; Harji and Jackson 2012; Jackson 2013a; Runde and Rice 2016; UNDP 2016). Bugg-Levine and Emerson (2011) noted that the conditions that enabled the Impact Investing movement to emerge are the same conditions that continue to foster its growth, stating that "the forces that set off the first ripples of the impact investing movement continue to grow" (p. 11).

Changing Demographics: Investment Practices Among Millennials

The changing demographics are an integral feature of this new investment environment. Specifically, the entrance of Millennials—the cohort of individuals reaching young adulthood in the early 21st century—into the workforce are fueling the Impact Investing movement given that the priorities of many

---

[1] Available online through https://iris.thegiin.org/

Millennials seem to fit the ethos of Impact Investing well. According to a survey of 5,000 Millennials spanning 17 countries, 71 percent of respondents expressed interest in making impacts for the benefit of society or in working for organizations and companies that care about the environment and society (Rodin and Brandenburg 2014, p. 669). Evidence suggests that among the young and wealthy, there exists a great willingness to invest in society (Harji and Jackson 2012). As Harji and Jackson (2012, p. 771) explained, "this era has been the generation of unprecedented wealth, and the next cohort of wealthy individuals wants to approach things differently, combining their business activities with their commitment to society." The authors continued:

> In 2011, some USD $212 trillion existed in the world's financial stock (comprising equity market capitalization and outstanding bonds and loans) and in the next 40 years, some estimate Generation X and the Millennials could inherit up to USD $41 trillion from baby boomers... Unlocking even a small percentage of this capital would expand dramatically the resources available to address the world's biggest social and environmental problems. (parag. 771)

Runde and Rice (2016) have made similar observations:

> One of the trends driving interest in Impact Investing is generational—30 percent of Millennials believe that the number one priority of business should be to improve society. Traditionally, thinking around profit versus social good has been bifurcated, but this generation has a different view on social and corporate interests. (parag. 7)

Pointing to a 2015 study conducted by Morgan Stanley, Runde and Rice (2016) noted that the study "found Millennials to be twice as likely to both invest in companies or funds that target specific social/environmental outcomes." Relatedly, the numbers of millionaires and billionaires have increased dramatically in the decade, up 50 percent and 200 percent, respectively, between 2008 and 2014 (Runde and Rice 2016). The significance of these dual trends for the future of Impact Investing is clear. As Runde and Rice (2016) put it:

> This latest generation of high net worth individuals includes entrepreneurs like Mark Zuckerberg, Pierre Omidyar, and Jean and Steve Case... who are intent on transforming the world. For these

individuals, impact investment represents a new way to leverage their massive wealth and innovative thinking to deliver social good. (para. 8)

A Nascent Industry: Upward Trends and Institutionalization

A Global, Multibillion-Dollar Market

Private institutional investors are taking notice of these trends among Millennials. The largest of such investors have begun to integrate Impact Investing into their operations by assigning teams exclusively dedicated to the investment strategy (Runde and Rice 2016). For example, in 2015, "Goldman Sachs purchased the impact investment firm Imprint Capital. Morgan Stanley, BlackRock, and UBS have also recently established impact investment units" (Runde and Rice 2016).

Hence, it is no surprise that Impact Investing is now a booming, multibillion-dollar industry (Bugg-Levine and Emerson 2011; O'Donohoe et al. 2010; Saltuk et al. 2015; Vecchi et al. 2016). Yet, according to Ormiston et al. (2015, p. 355), "it is difficult to get an accurate indication of the size of the global market for impact investment, as little information on transactions is made publicly available, and there are various views as to what is or is not impact investment." Thus, figures vary markedly. The GIIN aimed to address these gaps in knowledge by conducting the first rigorous analysis and estimate of the size of the Impact Investing market (Mudaliar and Dithrich 2019). Based on the study's findings, GIIN estimates that over 1,340 organizations currently manage USD $540 billion in Impact Investing assets worldwide (Mudaliar and Dithrich 2019). The study also highlights the market's diversity with regard to types of investors, which include family offices, foundations, banks, and pension funds "who are based in every region of the world and investing worldwide" (Mudaliar and Dithrich 2019, p. 3). The authors of the study describe the market's key characteristics and players as follows:

> Over 800 asset managers account for about 50% of industry assets under management, while 31 development finance institutions (DFIs) manage just over a quarter of total industry assets. Most Impact Investing organizations are relatively small, with about half managing less than USD 29 million each, yet there are also many large players managing over USD 1 billion each. (Mudaliar and Dithrich 2019, p. 3)

The market potential is even larger. Over USD $13 trillion in professionally managed assets (one in four dollars) now consider sustainability principles (US SIF Foundation 2018).

Mechanisms for Institutionalization

Despite the fact that Impact Investing strategies have been around for decades, Impact Investing is still considered a nascent industry (Bugg-Levine and Emerson 2011; Nicholls 2010; Ormiston et al. 2015). This demonstrates that, for emerging investment strategies, the process of becoming institutionalized and mainstream can be long and slow. Developing the support infrastructure needed to facilitate Impact Investing activities and improve the legitimacy of the industry takes years of coordinated efforts by a wide range of actors.

However, significant progress to establish such infrastructure for the Impact Investing industry has been made in the last decade. In 2009, the GIIN was launched with the objective of increasing the scale and effectiveness of Impact Investing around the world through a large portal of activities to define and develop the relevant infrastructure for industry growth (O'Donohoe et al. 2010). Launched in cooperation by J.P. Morgan, the Rockefeller Foundation, and the United States Agency for International Development (USAID), the GIIN is "tasked to develop the critical infrastructure, activities, education, and research that would increase the scale and effectiveness of Impact Investing" (O'Donohoe et al. 2010). Now, GIIN arguably represents the core, constitutive element of this new infrastructure.

Beyond the GIIN, other key components of Impact Investing's support infrastructure have emerged in recent years (Ormiston et al. 2015). They include metrics such as IRIS and Global Impact Investing Rating System (GIIRS), both of which aim to "establish common standards for impact measurement and benchmarking" (Ormiston et al. 2015, p. 354). Additionally, new databases, such as ImpactBase and Impact Assets 50, have emerged in order to ease "the task of unraveling the landscape of impact investment funds and products" (Ormiston et al. 2015, p. 354).

Instruments such as social impact bonds[2] (SIB) have also been set up as a part of the emerging Impact Investing industry (Jackson 2013b). An increasingly popular Impact Investing instrument, SIBs are commonly used to fund social enterprises and development projects (Arena et al. 2015, 2016; Burand 2012; Demel 2012; Leventhal 2012; Park 2018). According to Park (2018, p. 1),

---

[2]See Chapter 14, "Social Impact Bonds: Promises and Results," by Maria Basílio.

social bonds are "debt securities sold to investors whose proceeds are used to finance projects with a defined social benefit such as affordable housing, education, food security, and access to healthcare."

Such instruments, which together form Impact Investing's support infrastructure, ease the entry for new impact investors by reducing risk and uncertainty. They do so largely by providing a track record and common standards. Yet much more work is needed in order to further institutionalize and streamline Impact Investing. Institutionalization remains one of the central challenges facing the industry (Harji and Jackson 2012; UNDP 2016).

KEY FEATURES OF IMPACT INVESTING

A Sense of Community: The Impact Investing Culture

One striking feature of Impact Investing, which brings together a broad base of stakeholders, is its distinctive investment culture marked by a sense of community among investors (Bugg-Levine and Emerson 2011; Ormiston et al. 2015). This feature is seemingly due both to its nascent status as "market building" and to its social/environmental impact component. Ormiston et al. (2015) found that relying on established networks and reaching out to create new ones was one of the four main strategies that early adopters of Impact Investing have employed to address its formidable challenges. In that study, such early adopters spoke of hosting events, bringing industry leaders together, reaching out, hiring consultants, asking for advice, and passing on investments that were not a good fit for them that might be a good fit for another organization. Together, these activities demonstrate a clear sense of community among Impact Investing investors and a culture of learning and cooperation.

Because Impact Investing is still a new investment strategy and thus still building a solid support infrastructure, interested parties recognize the need to take it upon themselves to actively help establish this infrastructure. That is, this community, created by impact investors and their networks, is constitutive of the support infrastructure. This strategy reduces risks by ensuring that impact investors are better informed, are making educated decisions, and are sharing risks with other investors through pooling their money together. Such risk reduction contributes to the ease of entry, a key factor to engage in Impact Investing as a new investor (Ormiston et al. 2015).

Compatibility with Existing Models and Practices: Portfolios, Industry Standards, and Investment Priorities

Another key feature of Impact Investing is its high degree of compatibility with existing investment models. At least, this is the view of one of the two schools of thought regarding Impact Investing's location in investment portfolios. This school purports that Impact Investing can be situated across the range of asset classes rather than representing its own distinctive asset class (Harji and Jackson 2012; Höchstädter and Scheck 2015; O'Donohoe et al. 2010; Ormiston et al. 2015). This means that Impact Investing can simply constitute a certain proportion of an existing portfolio, one way of mitigating risk with this new investment strategy. It also means that Impact Investing can be held to the same expectations and standards for returns, as discussed earlier, and for due diligence requirements (Ormiston et al. 2015). Such compatibility with existing investment models eases entry for new Impact Investing investors who do not need to deviate radically from their current investment practices. Rather, they are "adding value"—or "blending value" to use Bugg-Levine and Emerson's (2011) term—to their investments by simply considering social and environmental impact *in addition to* financial returns, applying the same methods used by existing investment models for developing portfolios and decision-making.

Flexible Investing for Broad Investor Interests and Needs

Given that Impact Investing holds two objectives simultaneously—financial returns and social/environmental impacts—a diversity of investors can find value in Impact Investing. Different investors have different needs, requirements, and priorities, and Impact Investing is flexible enough to match such diversity (O'Donohoe et al. 2010; Ormiston et al. 2015). For instance, institutional investors generally have more constraints regarding fiduciary responsibilities, required by law, and thus need to prioritize "financial-first" investments. Conversely, philanthropic organizations generally have more leeway to prioritize "impact-first" investments, although they, too, face legal constraints regarding the source of the investment, namely, whether endowment-based or not (Ormiston et al. 2015). Regardless of the priorities and constraints, both types of entities can find value in Impact Investing, since, again, Impact Investing does not pit financial returns against social/environmental impacts. It simply becomes a matter of priority: whether financial-first, impact-first, or an even distribution of both. Greater institutionalization and wider acceptance of Impact Investing will hinge in part on its ability to recognize that different entities face differing constraints and to identify ways for Impact Investing to respond to those constraints effectively and meet these entities' unique needs.

Refining the "Good" Return: Financial and Social Considerations

Given these distinctive features, Impact Investing is arguably a paradigm-shifting investment strategy with the potential to influence the entire field of investment. In particular, Impact Investing redefines the meaning of a "good return" and investment value (Bugg-Levine and Emerson, 2011). For Impact Investing, the value of investment is not limited to the financial realm but extends to social and environmental realms as well. Yet such an extension does not suggest that financial objectives should be compromised. In fact, a study by Ormiston et al. (2015) based on interviews with leaders of companies engaged in Impact Investing practices as early adopters found that one of the key strategies that these leaders and their companies used to navigate the unique challenges posed by this new form of investment was to maintain a "financial-first" approach, holding to the same standards and expectations for returns as institutional investments. With such a strategy, the social and environmental impacts become an "added value" (Ormiston et al. 2015).

Impact Investing shows that investment does not need to be a zero-sum game, where financial returns are compromised for the sake of social and environmental impact, or vice versa. Rather, a single investment can have double returns in two forms: financial and social/environmental (O'Donohoe et al. 2010). Financial returns and positive social/environmental impact can co-exist, and together enhance the overall value of the investment (Bugg-Levine and Emerson 2011). This occurs partly though supporting the mission and values of an organization, which, especially in cases of philanthropic organizations, cannot be captured solely by financial investment. The inclusion of social/environmental impact can also provide competitive advantage to investment portfolios, distinguishing them from the rest of the field (Ormiston et al. 2015).

Helping Investors "Walk the Walk": Aligning Mission, Values, and Investments

Impact Investing also offers a way to meet changing market demand. Increasingly, individuals and organizations seek positive social/environmental impact with their investments above and beyond financial returns (Freireich and Fulton 2009; Jackson 2013a; Ormiston et al. 2015; UNDP, 2015).

This trend demonstrates that one way that companies and organizations maintain their credibility, integrity, and loyalty of their clients and customers is to go beyond financial returns; they must "walk the walk," so to speak. If their missions and values claim a commitment to making social/environmental impacts, they must demonstrate it with their actions. That is, the positive social/environmental impact becomes a source of capital that is *distinctive* from financial capital, one that could be called "impact capital." A certain class of investors has shown clear interest in generating such impact capital, beyond financial capital. By demonstrating that the two objectives can be met within the same investment strategy, there is huge potential to win over institutional investors, who have historically been risk averse and have tended toward the *status quo* of focusing solely on financial returns (Ormiston et al. 2015).

A Prudent Entrepreneurial Spirit: Experimentation and Mitigating Risks

While impact investors are drawn to Impact Investing because of their desire to align mission and values, many of the early adopters maintain an entrepreneurial spirit that is reined in by caution and legal and other institutional constraints (Ormiston et al. 2015). Yet the observation that such early adopters, who have been quite successful in their Impact Investing endeavors, are not necessarily cavalier should be well received by the investment community as an encouraging sign that Impact Investing does not necessarily mean high risk or low returns on investment. Rather, by holding firmly to an entrepreneurial spirit, impact investors are able to recognize new opportunities, enter into novel ways of doing business, and experiment, while maintaining their responsibilities and keeping focused on their core business. In this sense, Impact Investing is, paradoxically, shifting paradigms without radicalism.

IMPACT INVESTING: LEVERAGE FOR DEVELOPMENT?

According to the United Nations (UN), achieving its sustainable development goals (SDGs) may require infusions of USD $1.5 trillion to USD $3 trillion annually (United Nations Conference on Trade and Development, 2014). While the funding available through governments and philanthropists may amount to billions in grants, loans, aid, and other sources of funding, it still falls far short of the needed resources to fulfil the SDGs (Rodin and

Brandenberg 2014). Through its seemingly simple dual commitment to social impacts and financial returns, Impact Investing represents a new and distinctive set of investment strategies and practices, one that is particularly effective at gathering support for economic development issues, even as Impact Investing's application goes well beyond development and developing countries.

The potential to leverage Impact Investing for development is massive. A growing body of research documents and analyzes the nexus between Impact Investing and development as Impact Investing has been used to fund an array of development projects in recent years (Bolis et al. 2017; Farley and Bush 2016; Jafri 2018; Jones and Turner 2014; Lindenberg and Pöll 2015; Ngoasong, et al. 2015). According to Jafri (2018, p. 2), impact investors can play a critical role in realizing development initiatives because they "fill the void in enterprise finance created by regulatory constraints on banks" and "accommodate the demand for yield by facilitating the entry of global capital into poor countries."

Within the set of strategies and practices that characterize Impact Investing lies an incredible range of configurations, some of which are much better suited to development projects than others. These configurations reflect investors' priorities and enterprises' needs regarding impacts and returns. Many such configurations are theoretical as of yet, demonstrating the broad potential for combining social impact with financial returns. This range of possibilities has been represented as a spectrum, with impact-first at one end and financial-first at the other (Bolis et al. 2017). This spectrum allows for Impact Investing to, at times, bear closer resemblance to philanthropy, such as when an investor agrees to less than a 100 percent return on his or her investment. At the other end of the spectrum, Impact Investing reflects typical institutional investments, prioritizing market-rate returns over the degree of social/environmental impact.

While financial-first strategies have been popular with impact investors, often because they more closely mimic institutional investments in terms of expectations for near-market returns and are considered lower risk than impact-first investments, many financial-first strategies are not a good fit for development projects. This is especially the case when financial-first strategies have expectations of near-market or at-market returns, which often are not appropriate goals for many social enterprises aimed at development and poverty reduction, in the short term, long term, or both. However, near-market return goals are appropriate for certain types of social enterprises, based on a variety of important factors, namely product or service and the enterprise's level of maturity. More research is needed in order to identify when near-market returns are possible for development projects and which impact-first configurations and configurations that balance financial-first and impact-first—those that would be located in the middle of this spectrum between financial-first and impact-first—would be better suited for many development projects (Bolis et al. 2017).

In their Oxfam report, Bolis et al. (2017) argued that as the potential for Impact Investing for economic development has garnered attention in the media and in academic literature, the promise of achieving market-rate returns has been overemphasized and even exaggerated. The expected rate of return for many social enterprises focused on economic development is often well below market-rate returns. Many development ventures could greatly benefit from Impact Investing but under different terms, such as lower financial returns or longer time horizons.

Social enterprises represent the organizational form that is arguably best suited for using Impact Investing for economic development projects, given the natural affinity between social enterprises and Impact Investing. Social enterprises, by definition, aim to address social/environmental problems using a for-profit business model that lends itself well to Impact Investing. Given the important role that social enterprises can play in economic development initiatives, there is need for greater clarification of the unique features and requirements of social enterprises and to adopt and adapt investment strategies and practices that are best suited to this type of enterprise. Rather than asking how social enterprises can achieve market-rate returns, we ought to ask how investors can best invest in social enterprises[3] so that they can achieve maximum impact and financial sustainability.

Because social enterprises include social impacts as part of their missions, they cannot compromise their commitment to the specified social impacts even if doing so would increase the rate of return; this is precisely what distinguishes them from other enterprises. As such, they are best served by investors who equally share their commitment to achieving social impacts, even at the expense of financial returns. Otherwise, a "mismatch," as Bolis et al. (2017) called it, can emerge between expectations, priorities, and outcomes.

Thus, the best way forward to leverage Impact Investing for development is to go beyond the emphasis on financial-first Impact Investing strategies that expect near- or at-market returns to further investigate other Impact Investing configurations—namely, impact-first strategies and especially

---

[3]See Chapter 26, "The Importance of Scale in Social Enterprises: The Indian Case," by Vikram Raman.

those that balance financial-first and impact-first—that may be more suited to the needs of economic development projects. More research is needed,[4] both to theorize as well as to document new experiments at the intersection of social impacts and financial returns in order to provide more empirical evidence regarding the extent to which Impact Investing can and does generate meaningful and measurable economic development outcomes, such as poverty reduction.

CONCLUSION

Is Impact Investing an innovation or a rebranding? In recent years, at both national and international levels, individuals and organizations concerned about creating sustainable solutions for pressing global and daunting local challenges paid increasing attention to Impact Investing as a fitting investment philosophy and a set of practices. It is clear from this review of the literature that Impact Investing shares some features of SRI, microfinance, and other "positive" forms of investment, with its "blended value," offering both financial returns *and* positive social and environmental impacts. However, such similarities do not mean that Impact Investing is merely a rebranded version of these other positive investment classes. Rather, Impact Investing does offer an innovative approach to investment that is resonating with new and established investors alike. Part of its innovation is its flexibility and compatibility with existing investment models and instruments, offering the world of investment a bridge between old and new paradigms. Impact investing thus reflects a new era of investment in the twenty-first century, further encouraged by the fact that it resonates with the ethos of high-net-worth youth entrepreneurs seeking to do good beyond doing well.

Nevertheless, Impact Investing faces serious challenges, such as measuring social and environmental impacts accurately and transparently and developing a robust infrastructure that can support this nascent industry and its growth. These considerations suggest future directions for research in this area. There is also a need for greater interrogation into Impact Investing's potential as a driving force for economic development. These and other considerations regarding the potential and future directions of Impact Investing will be valuable to scholars and practitioners alike, as we work collectively to clarify and shape this phenomenon to the greatest benefit for our global society.

---

[4]See Chapter 6, "Gender Lens Investing: Co-Creating Critical Knowledge to Build a Credible, Durable Field," by Edward T. Jackson and Elsa de Morais Sarmento.

ACKNOWLEDGMENTS

First and foremost, I would like to dedicate this study to my father's soul, who believed deeply in women's empowerment and who pushed me ahead with unfailing love and wisdom before he passed away; to my mother, for her endless love and backing; to my husband, for his support and patience; and to my children, Adam and Iyad; and to each of us, who deserve a greener, fairer, and safer world.

My fond thanks and sincere gratitude are due to each of my professors at the ULB-UMons-ULiège Doctoral School during my PhD Training Program, as well to each of my professors at the Academy of Louvain, FUSL Brussels, who all contributed to develop my research skills and build up my academic background, especially Dr. Anouk Claes for the encouragements and her inquisitive mind. My deep gratitude and thanks also go to Professors Virginie Xhauflair, Marc Labie, Hugues Pirotte, Valerie Swaen, and Camille Meyer, whose critiques and recommendations were key to improving this work.

I finally offer my special thanks to our editors, Elsa de Morais Sarmento and R. Paul Herman, for their enthusiastic encouragement to get me on the right path during the writing process, for their reviews to better frame this work, for giving me the opportunity to contribute to this book, and for their pioneering efforts to make this happen.

REFERENCES

Agbeko, D., Blok, V., Omta, S.W.F., et al. (2017). The Impact of Training and Monitoring on Loan Repayment of Microfinance Debtors in Ghana. *Journal of Behavioral and Experimental Finance* 14: 23–29.

Agbola, F. W., Acupan, A., and Mahmood, A. (2017). Does Microfinance Reduce Poverty? New Evidence from Northeastern Mindanao, The Philippines. *Journal of Rural Studies* 50: 159–171.

Arena, M., Bengo, I., Calderini, M., et al. (2015). Social Impact Bonds: New Finance or New Procurement? *ACRN Oxford Journal of Finance and Risk Perspectives* 4 (4): 168–189.

Arena, M., Bengo, I., Calderini, M., et al. (2016). Social Impact Bonds: Block-buster or Flash in a Pan? *International Journal of Public Administration* 39 (12): 927–939.

Arosio, M. (2011). *Impact Investing in Emerging Markets*. Singapore: Responsible Research.

Banerjee, A., Duflo, E., Glennerster, R., et al. (2015). The Miracle of Microfinance? Evidence from a Randomized Evaluation. *American Economic Journal: Applied Economics* 7 (1): 22–53.

Bolis, M., West, C., Sahan, E., et al. (2017). Impact Investing: Who Are We Serving? A Case of Mismatch Between Supply and Demand. Oxfam Discussion Paper. April. Oxford: Oxfam International and Sumerian Partners.https://policy-practice.oxfam.org.uk/publications/impact-investing-who-are-we-serving-a-case-of-mismatch-between-supply-and-demand-620240 (accessed 3 May 2020).

Brunie, A., Fumagalli, L., Martin, T., et al. (2014). Can Village Savings and Loan Groups Be a Potential Tool in the Malnutrition Fight? Mixed Method Findings from Mozambique. *Children and Youth Services Review* 47: 113–120.

Bugg-Levine, A., and Emerson, J. (2011). *Impact Investing: Transforming How We Make Money While Making a Difference.* Hoboken, NJ: Wiley.

Bugg-Levine, A., and Goldstein, J. (2009). Impact Investing: Harnessing Capital Markets to Solve Problems at Scale. *Community Development Investment Review* 2: 30–41.

Burand, D. (2012). Globalizing Social Finance: How Social Impact Bonds and Social Impact Performance Guarantees Can Scale Development. *NYU Journal of Law and Business* 9: 447–502.

Carragher, A. (2013). Impact Investing: A viable alternative to development aid? *SAIS Europe Journal of Global Affairs.*

Clarkin, J. E., and Cangioni, C. L. (2016). Impact Investing: A Primer and Review of the Literature. *Entrepreneurship Research Journal* 6 (2): 135–173.

Cochran, P. L. (2007). The Evolution of Corporate Social Responsibility. *Business Horizons* 50 (6): 449–454.

Cooper, H. M. (1988). Organizing Knowledge Syntheses: A Taxonomy of Literature Reviews. *Knowledge in Society* 1 (1): 104–26.

Cooper, H. (1998). *Synthesizing Research: A Guide for Literature Reviews,* 3rd ed. Thousand Oaks, CA: Sage Publications.

Cooper, H., and Hedges, L. V. (1994). Research Synthesis as a Scientific Enterprise. In *The Handbook of Research Synthesis* (eds. H. Cooper and L.V. Hedge), 3–15. New York: Russell Sage Foundation.

Demel, A. (2012). Second Thoughts on Social Impact Bonds. *NYU Journal of Law and Business* 9: 503–509.

Donou-Adonsou, F., and Sylwester, K. (2016). Financial Development and Poverty Reduction in Developing Countries: New Evidence from Banks and Microfinance Institutions. *Review of Development Finance* 6 (1): 82–90.

Emerson J. (2000). The Nature of Returns: A Social Capital Markets Inquiry into Elements of Investment and the Blended Value Proposition. Social Enterprise Series No. 17. https://www.fi-compass.eu/sites/default/files/publications/the-nature-of-returns-a-social-capitla-market-inquiry-into-elements-of-investment-and-the-blended-value-proposition.pdf (accessed 3 July 2020).

Emerson, J., and Cabaj, M. (2000). Social Return on Investment. *Making Waves* 11 (2): 10–14.

Emerson, J., and Spitzer, J. (2007). From Fragmentation to Function: Critical Concepts and Writings on Social Capital Markets' Structure, Operation, and Innovation. Working Paper. Oxford: Skoll Centre for Social Entrepreneurship. https://www.sbs.ox.ac.uk/sites/default/files/2019-10/FragmentationtoFunctionality2410Afinal.pdf (accessed 3 May 2020).

Farley, K. W., and Bush, C. B. (2016). Using Relationships as Resources in Social Impact Investing: Examining a Local Food Movement in Appalachia. *Journal of Appalachian Studies* 22 (2): 224–244.

Fenton, A., Paavola, J., and Tallontire, A. (2017). The Role of Microfinance in Household Livelihood Adaptation in Satkhira District, Southwest Bangladesh. *World Development* 92: 192–202.

Freireich, J., and Fulton, K. (2009). *Investing for Social and Environmental Impact: A Design for Catalyzing an Emerging Industry*. Cambridge, MA: Monitor Institute.

Gautier, A., and Pache, A. C. (2015). Research on Corporate Philanthropy: A Review and Assessment. *Journal of Business Ethics* 126 (3): 343–369.

Godeke, S. (2013). Community Reinvestment Act Banks as Pioneer Investors in Pay for Success Financing. *Community Development Investment Review* 9: 69–74.

Global Impact Investing Network (GIIN). (2020). How Are Investors Using IRIS+ to Measure and Manage Impact? https://iris.thegiin.org/introduction/#b3 (accessed 3 May 2020).

Harji, K., and Jackson, E. T. (2012). *Accelerating Impact: Achievements, Challenges and What's Next in Building the Impact Investing Industry*. New York: Rockefeller Foundation.

Hebb, T. ed. (2013). Special Issue: Impact Investing. *Journal of Sustainable Finance and Investment* 3: 71–175.

Hebb, T. (2013). Impact Investing and Responsible Investing: What Does It Mean? *Journal of Sustainable Finance and Investment* 3: 71–73.

Hedges, L.V., and Cooper, H. M. eds. (1994). *The Handbook of Research Synthesis*. New York: Russell Sage Foundation.

Höchstädter, A. K., and Scheck, B. (2015). What's in a Name: An Analysis of Impact Investing Understandings by Academics and Practitioners. *Journal of Business Ethics* 132 (2): 449–475.

Hummels, H. (2016). Impact Investments: The Emergence of a New Beacon in Investing? In *Principles and Practice of Impact Investing: A Catalytic Revolution* (eds. V. Vecchi, L. Balbo, M. Brusoni, et al.), 1–25. London: Routledge.

Jackson, E. T. (2013a). Interrogating the Theory of Change: Evaluating Impact Investing Where It Matters Most. *Journal of Sustainable Finance and Investment* 3 (2): 95–110.

Jackson, E. T. (2013b). Evaluating Social Impact Bonds: Questions, Challenges, Innovations, and Possibilities in Measuring Outcomes in Impact Investing. *Community Development* 44 (5): 608–616.

Jafri, J. (2018). Investing for Impact, Financing for Development: Private Debt and Shadow Banking in Pakistan. Financial Geography Working Paper #14. July. London: City, University of London. http://www.fingeo.net/wordpress/wp-content/uploads/2018/07/WP14_FINGEO_JAFRI_final_30-JUNE_sd.pdf (accessed 3 May 2020).

Jones, L., and Turner, K. (2014). At the Nexus of Investment and Development: Lessons from a 60-Year Experiment in SME Impact Investing. *Enterprise Development and Microfinance* 25 (4): 299–310.

Keohane, G. L. (2016). *Capital and the Common Good: How Innovative Finance Is Tackling the World's Most Urgent Problems*. New York: Columbia University Press.

Ksoll, C., Lilleør, H. B., Lønborg, J. H., et al. (2016). Impact of Village Savings and Loan Associations: Evidence from a cluster randomized trial. *Journal of Development Economics* 120: 70–85.

Leventhal, R. (2012). Effecting Progress: Using Social Impact Bonds to Finance Social Services. *NYU Journal of Law and Business* 9: 511–534.

Lindenberg, N., and Pöll, C. (2015). Financing Global Development: Is Impact Investing An Investment Model with Potential or Just Blowing Smoke?

German Development Institute/Deutsches Institut für Entwicklungspolitik (DIE) Briefing Paper 20/2015.https://papers.ssrn.com/sol3/papers.cfm?abstract_id=2781951 (accessed 3 May 2020).

Miled, K.B.H., and Rejeb, J.E.B. (2015). Microfinance and Poverty Reduction: A Review and Synthesis of Empirical Evidence. *Procedia-Social and Behavioral Sciences* 195 (31): 705–712.

Moore, M. L., Westley, F. R., and Nicholls, A. (2012). The Social Finance and Social Innovation Nexus. *Journal of Social Entrepreneurship* 3 (2): 115–132.

Mudaliar, A., and Dithrich, H. (2019). Sizing the Impact Investing Market. 1 April. Global Impact Investing Network (GIIN). https://thegiin.org/research/publication/impinv-market-size (accessed 3 May 2020).

Ngoasong, M. Z., and Kimbu, A. N. (2016). Informal Microfinance Institutions and Development-Led Tourism Entrepreneurship. *Tourism Management* 52: 430–439.

Ngoasong, M. Z., Paton, R., and Korda, A. (2015). Impact Investing and Inclusive Business Development in Africa: A Research Agenda. Innovation, Knowledge and Development Research Centre (IKD) Working Paper No. 76. January. Milton Keynes, UK: Open University. http://oro.open.ac.uk/42157/1/ikd-working-paper-76.pdf (accessed 3 May 2020).

Nicholls, A. (2010). The Institutionalization of Social Investment: The Interplay of Investment Logics and Investor Rationalities. *Journal of Social Entrepreneurship* 1 (1), 70–100.

O'Donohoe, N., Leijonhufvud, C., Saltuk, Y., et al. (2010). Impact Investments: An Emerging Asset Class. *Global Impact Investing Network (GIIN)*. 29 November. https://thegiin.org/research/publication/impact-investments-an-emerging-asset-class (accessed 3 May 2020).

Ormiston, J., Charlton, K., Donald, M. S., et al. (2015). Overcoming the Challenges of Impact Investing: Insights from Leading Investors. *Journal of Social Entrepreneurship* 6 (3): 352–378.

Park, S. K. (2018). Social Bonds for Sustainable Development: A Human Rights Perspective on Impact Investing. *Business and Human Rights Journal* 3 (2), 233–255.

Payne, G., and Cook, J. (2014). Redefining Impact Investing. *Corporate Knights*. 27 February.https://www.corporateknights.com/channels/natural-capital/redefining-impact-investing-13935048/ (accessed 3 May 2020).

Ramasastry, A. (2015). Corporate Social Responsibility Versus Business and Human Rights: Bridging the Gap Between Responsibility and Accountability. *Journal of Human Rights* 14 (2), 237–259.

Reisman, J., Olazabal, V., and Hoffman, S. (2018). Putting the "Impact" in Impact Investing: The Rising Demand for Data and Evidence of Social Outcomes. *American Journal of Evaluation* 9 (3): 1–7.

Revelli, C. (2016). Re-Embedding Financial Stakes Within Ethical and Social Values in Socially Responsible Investing (SRI). *Research in International Business and Finance* 38: 1–5.

Richardson, B. J. (2009). Keeping Ethical Investment Ethical: Regulatory Issues for Investing for Sustainability. *Journal of Business Ethics* 87 (4): 555–572.

Richardson, B. J. (2013). Socially Responsible Investing for Sustainability: Overcoming Its Incomplete and Conflicting Rationales. *Transnational Environmental Law* 2 (2): 311–338.

Richardson, B. J., and Peihani, M. (2015). Universal Investors and Socially Responsible Finance: A Critique of a Premature Theory. *Banking and Finance Law Review* 30: 405–455.

Robb, R., and Sattell, M. (2016). Socially Responsible/Impact Investing: Theoretical and Empirical Issues. Capitalism and Society 11 (2): Article 2. https://papers.ssrn.com/sol3/papers.cfm?abstract_id=2886082# (accessed 3 May 2020).

Rodin, J., and Brandenberg, M. (2014). *The Power of Impact Investing: Putting Markets to Work for Profit and Global Good*. Philadelphia: Wharton Digital Press.

Runde, D.F., and Rice, C. (2016). Leveraging Impact Investment for Global Development? Center for Strategic International Studies. https://www.csis .org/analysis/leveraging-impact-investment-global-development (accessed 3 May 2020).

Saltuk, Y., El Idrissi, A., Bouri, A., et al. (2015). Eyes on the Horizon: The Impact Investor Survey. Global Social Finance. 4 May. JPMorgan Chase & Co. and the Global Impact Investing Network (GIIN).https://thegiin.org/assets/ documents/pub/2015.04%20Eyes%20on%20the%20Horizon.pdf (accessed 3 May 2020).

Samer, S., Majid, I., Rizal, S., et al. (2015). The Impact of Microfinance on Poverty Reduction: Empirical Evidence from Malaysian Perspective. *Procedia-Social and Behavioral Sciences* 195: 721–728.

Scarlata, M., and Alemany, L. (2012). Deal Structuring in Philanthropic Venture Capital Investments: Financing Instrument, Valuation and Covenants. In *Entrepreneurship, Governance and Ethics* (eds. R. Cressy, D. Cumming, and C. Mallin), 121–145. New York: Springer.

Sharma, A. (2015). Who Leads in A G-Zero World? Multi-Nationals, Sustainable Development, and Corporate Social Responsibility in a Changing Global Order. *Washington International Law Journal,* 24 (3): 589–612.

United Nations Conference on Trade and Development (UNCTAD). (2014). *Trade and Development Report,* 2014. http://unctad.org/en/Publications Library/tdr2014overview_en.pdf (accessed 3 May 2020).

United Nations Development Program (UNDP). (2016). Human Development Report: Human Development for Everyone. New York: United Nations Development Program. http://hdr.undp.org/sites/default/files/2016_human _development_report.pdf (accessed 3 May 2020).

US SIF Foundation. (2018). Report on US Sustainable, Responsible and Impact Investing Trends. Washington, D.C.: US SIF Foundation.ussif.org/files/ Trends/Trends%202018%20executive%20summary%20FINAL.pdf (accessed 3 May 2020).

van Rooyen, C., Stewart, R., and de Wet, T. (2012). The Impact of Microfinance in Sub-Saharan Africa: A Systematic Review of the Evidence. *World Development* 40 (11): 2249–2262.

Vecchi, V., Balbo, L., Brusoni, M., et al., eds. (2016). *Principles and Practice of Impact Investing: A Catalytic Revolution.* London: Routledge.

Wentworth, L., and Makokera, C. G. (2015). Private Sector Participation in Infrastructure for Development. *South African Journal of International Affairs* 22 (3): 325–341.

Wieland, O. (2016). Development Financial Institutions: Impact Investing Practices in Scandinavian Context. *Advances in Economics and Business* 4 (8): 424–435.

CHAPTER 2

Investing for Impact: Socially Motivated Investors and Externalities

Raghavan Narayanan, MBA and Stoyan V. Tenev, PhD

Abstract

Externalities and the gaps they create between projects' social and private returns are prerequisite for the existence of socially motivated investors. This chapter defines socially motivated investors as private investors who, in addition to private returns, take social returns into consideration when making investment decisions. It develops a new taxonomy yielding three types of socially motivated investors: (i) value alignment investors, (ii) value commitment investors, and (iii) impact investors. *Value alignment investors* internalize all or most project externalities by design or social positioning. The *value commitment* investor narrows the gap between social and private returns by his or her willingness to sacrifice some private returns in order not to violate ethical norms to which he or she is committed; and finally, the *impact investor* makes his or her financial return contingent on the achievement of social impact, which in the absence of Impact Investing would be an externality. This chapter discusses the three cases in turn. For each, this chapter looks at: (i) the mechanisms for aligning with social interests, (ii) the mechanisms for aligning with investee's interests, and (iii) the viability of this behavior in market competition with traditional investors. Impact Investing builds on innovations that economize on transaction costs and make it possible to internalize externalities by linking them directly to investor returns, thus making investors' private returns contingent on the social impact achieved. This approach aligns incentives in support of social value creation while also aligning social and private returns. Social impact bonds are used as an example of such impact-based (pay-for-success) models where private investors put capital at risk to fund projects with social goals.

Keywords

Impact Investing; Socially Motivated Investing; Externalities; Social Impact Bonds; Socially Responsible Investing; Value Alignment; Value Commitment

INTRODUCTION

There was once a worldview where public sector investors pursued social goals and private investors financial returns. These assumptions do not hold anymore. Increasingly, investors combine, if not totally in practice, at least in rhetoric, the pursuit of social and commercial objectives. This comes about either through changes in investment behavior by existing types of players, such as government-owned enterprises seeking social value under the constraint of financial sustainability, or private enterprises seeking social value alongside financial returns; or through the emergence of new types of investors, such as non-government organizations, social enterprises, or new types of private investors seeking some combination of social impact and financial returns.

The process reflects a growing interdependence between business and society. With it, the social contract between business and society has been evolving. The social concerns and expectations regarding corporate behavior have been expanding to include environmental sustainability, employment discrimination, consumer abuses, employee health and safety, quality of work life, deterioration of urban life, and questionable practices of multinational corporations, among others (Agudelo et al. 2019).

As a result, there has been a convergence of investment behavior, sprouting surprisingly from an expansion of the spectrum of ownership and organizational forms these investors assume. Various terminologies abound to label this class of socially motivated investors: corporate social responsibility investors, socially responsible investors, and Impact Investing actors, to name a few. Within this convergence of investment behavior there are variety of ways in which investors can combine social and commercial objectives. Indeed, heterogeneity in investment styles and behaviors is an essential prerequisite for the very notion of socially motivated investing. Heterogeneity in investment behavior is based on the opportunities of investors making different choices regarding the pursuit of social and private/commercial objectives. The possibility of a choice between the pursuit of social and private/commercial interests in turn suggests divergence between the two. The gap between social and private interests is referred to as externalities. They are essential in understanding socially motivated investing.

In this chapter, we seek to develop a new typology for socially motivated investors and within that identify the characteristics that may differentiate impact investors, as being a distinct type within the class of socially motivated investors. The discussion builds on the notion of externalities and on heterogeneity of investors operating in the same market for investments where traditional investors motivated by commercial interests provide a sort of a benchmark.

The next section provides a conceptual framework for socially motivated investing, and the following section builds on the conceptual framework to develop a typology for socially motivated investing and defines Impact Investing in this context, as the last section concludes.

A CONCEPTUAL FRAMEWORK FOR SOCIALLY MOTIVATED INVESTMENT BEHAVIOR

Investors allocate capital to projects with the expectation of a financial return. They are distinct from the companies that receive the capital and execute the projects (i.e. the investees). Investors choose projects by their expected returns. A project's total net effects on society are captured by social returns. Private returns are those parts of the social returns that accrue to the investor.[1] Any gap between the two is due to externalities, positive

---

[1]See Pigou for the original definitions (Pigou 1932).

or negative. Externalities are a form of market failure, where market's functioning is impeded or completely blocked due to transaction costs (Arrow 1970). Gaps between social and private returns cause inefficiencies in the form of misallocation of private investments. Economic inefficiency creates pressure in the system to overcome it by some sort of collective action: laws and regulations or moral and ethical norms, each of which involves transaction costs of its own (Arrow 1970). Market structures and incentives interact with these non-market mechanisms and form the institutional structure of markets (Arrow 1970). At any given point, externalities are conditioned on the institutional structure (i.e. they reflect the technologies, market structure, laws and regulations, and prevailing social norms).

Externalities are a key driver of growth and development. They are the reason why the whole seems to be greater than the sum of its parts at all levels of the economy. At the level of the firm, Alchian and Demsetz (1972) stressed the importance of synergies and agency costs associated with team production. Jane Jacobs has drawn attention to the role of externalities in the growth of cities (Jacobs 1969). Porter (1990) has elaborated on the role of externalities in sectoral and local development. Endogenous growth models place the main emphasis on knowledge externalities (Barro and Sala-i-Martin 1999), while others (Antoci and Bartolinie 1999) have stressed the role of negative externalities in generating a self-perpetuating push for development. Externalities are the most likely explanation of the global productivity surplus that has been difficult to attribute to labor, capital, or technical progress (i.e. variations of the Solow residual), and that has accounted for the lion's share of growth (Moulier-Boutang 2011).

Given their importance for growth and development, externalities have been the focus of social and development programs. In fact, the very notion of impact employed in social and development programs closely resembles the concept of externalities, although it has been a challenge for these programs to internalize such "impacts" in their incentive structure. Indeed, some influential interpretations of the notion of impact define the concept as being the effects of activities (projects) that fall outside the sphere of direct control and influence of a particular development program, making impact very similar in nature to externalities even in the case of investors that are socially motivated in nature (Hearn and Buffardi 2016). The push by stakeholders to make the various development agencies more "impact oriented" reflects this perennial challenge.

Figure 2.1 presents the project space in the two dimensions of expected social and private returns. The 45-degree line shows projects where private and social returns are equivalent, with no externalities. Below the line are

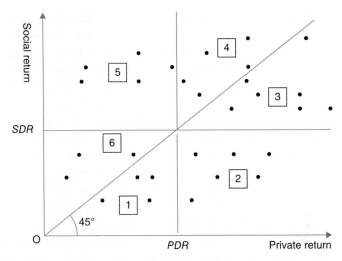

FIGURE 2.1   The Project Return Space. *Source:* Authors.

Notes: SDR = social discount rate; PDR = private discount rate.

projects with net negative externalities, and above the line, projects with net positive externalities. Investors make investment decisions based on a hurdle rate. Associated with social and private returns are social and private discount rates that are used as hurdle rates. Here it is assumed that the two are the same.[2] The two hurdle rates and the 45-degree line together divide the project space into six regions, fundamental for the subsequent discussion of investment behavior.

Projects in region 1 have net negative and those in region 6 net positive externalities, but expected returns in both regions fall below the social and private discount rates. These projects do not therefore meet investment thresholds, either from a private or social perspective. Projects in region 2 have an interesting return profile. They offer attractive private returns but social returns below the social discount rate, due to net negative externalities. They therefore present a dilemma: they lure private investors into socially undesirable undertakings. Projects in region 3 (net negative externalities) and region 4 (net positive externalities) exceed both private and social investment thresholds and should therefore be implemented. They may differ though in their distributional effects, with projects in region 3 more likely to have

---

[2]This assumption can be viewed as an equilibrium outcome in a model where public investment decisions are based on the social opportunity cost of the return to foregone private capital investment (see Moore et al. 2013).

losers among their stakeholders that may not necessarily be compensated by redistribution from within projects' total returns. Finally, projects in region 5 offer attractive social returns but private returns below the private discount rate. They therefore present the domain for traditional public investors.

The project return space reflects the following assumptions: (i) projects' returns are private equilibria whereby all gains from trade between various stakeholders that exceed the associated transaction costs (i.e. Coasian bargains) have been realized and remaining externalities are not Pareto-relevant, meaning the externally affected party cannot be made better off without the acting party (the project company and potential investee) be made worse off, given the transaction costs (Buchanan and Stubblebine 1962); (ii) as alluded to earlier, the transaction costs reflect the mode of economic organization (Arrow 1970) understood broadly to refer to the prevailing laws, regulations, taxes, and social norms; this implies that the projects' return profile reflects the same parameters; (iii) all opportunities for mergers and acquisitions between projects (investees) have been realized, so the resulting project space is atomized and individual projects' returns reflect remaining inter-project externalities (i.e. externalities that projects impose on one another).

Externalities may exist not only between the investees (through their projects) and the rest of society but also in the relationships between investors and the rest of society and between investors and investees. Investor-investee relationships, in particular, are fraught with externalities driven by different interests and asymmetric information. Investors face a principal-agent problem in their interactions with investees and use various financial tools and contractual mechanisms to manage risks and align interests. In fact, the principal-agent problem provides a useful framework for a unified treatment of externalities across the investment chain from investor to investee and from investee to the rest of society.[3] Useful, because it allows us to simplify the treatment of the problem by reducing it to asking first, under what conditions and how can the investor's and society's interests be aligned; and second, under what conditions and how can the investor then align the investee's interest with its own? This approach automatically takes care of the externalities at the project level (see Figure 2.2). Alignment between the investor and society is understood as investors taking social, in addition to private, returns into account in their investment decisions.

---

[3]To our knowledge, Arrow (1985) was the first to allude to the equivalence between the principal-agent problem and the externality problem. He gave the example of pollution control where "society may be regarded as the principal, and the polluter, whose actions cannot be fully monitored, as the agent" (Arrow 1985, p. 39).

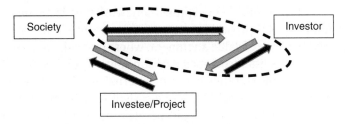

FIGURE 2.2   Externalities in a Principal-Agent Framework. *Source:* Authors.

Note: Gray arrows point from principal to agent, black lines point in the direction of externality effects. The oval encloses the causal sequence of aligning social and private interests: first by aligning the interests of society with those of investors, and second, by aligning the interests of investors with those of the investees. This indirect way of aligning social and investee's interests is the focus of the chapter, and the direct links between project and society are largely left out of the discussion.

Investment behavior is concerned with choosing projects for investment that satisfy a whole set of requisites and constraints. The hurdle rate is one such constraint, but the set incudes laws, regulations, and prevailing social norms including self-interested behavior as a behavioral norm in market transactions. It is this set, and not any one of the constraints, that should be viewed as the investor's goal (Simon 1964). A particular constraint can be singled out and treated like a goal if it is believed to be motivating the investor (Simon 1964). In this way, heterogeneity of investment behavior can also be explained in the same market (i.e. investors being motivated by different constraints within the same set of market constraints).

Given all this, what venues are open for investment behavior to internalize remining externalities and align with the social interests (i.e. to take social returns into account when making investment decisions)?

TYPOLOGY OF SOCIALLY MOTIVATED INVESTORS

For the purpose of this chapter, public investors are defined as investors who base their investment decisions solely on projects' social returns and the social discount rate; traditional private investors as investors who base their investment decisions solely on projects' private returns and the private discount rate; and socially motivated investors as private investors who, in addition to private returns and the private discount rate, take social returns and social discount rates into consideration when making investment decisions. The focus of this chapter is on socially motivated investors who, it is assumed, share the market space with the traditional private investors (i.e. there is no competition between public and private investors).

It would follow from the conceptual framework that there are only three scenarios under which private investors' interests can be aligned with the social interest: (i) a case of value alignment, where by design or by social positioning the investor's interest coincide or substantially overlap with those of society at large; the investor thus naturally internalizes all or most of projects' externalities in his or her decisions; (ii) a case of value commitment, where the investor is willing to sacrifice some private returns in order not to violate or to be able to follow ethical norms to which he or she is committed; commitment to ethical norms acts like a constraint on investor's behavior in a way that can internalize externalities beyond the Coasian bargains that were assumed to have already taken place in Figure 2.1; and (iii) a case of Impact Investing, where financial and contractual innovation helps reduce transaction costs and enables trade (a Coasian bargain) in positive externalities that are considered the project's main impact.

The three cases are discussed in turn. For each case, three issues are considered: (i) the mechanisms for aligning with social interests, (ii) the mechanisms for aligning with investee's interests, and (iii) the viability of this behavior in market competition with traditional investors.

Value Alignment

In value alignment, the investor, because of its investment style or position in society, has significant overlap between his or her private interests and the social interests. Examples are portfolio diversification and portfolio management techniques, where the investor has stakes in a large number of companies (and projects) with the high likelihood that he or she internalizes at least all interfirm externalities and possibly more; and, at the other extreme, local embedding, where the investor is so deeply embedded in the local community that he or she easily associates with all stakeholders affected by the project.

Let's take diversification first. It has been shown that if shareholders own diversified portfolios, and if companies impose externalities on one another, shareholders will internalize between-firm externalities and their objective will no longer be value maximization of individual projects and companies, but maximization of total portfolio value (Hansen and Lott 1996). The intuition is that if the investor owns shares in several companies in the right proportion, he or she will naturally internalize all the externalities these companies impose on each other. This is illustrated in Figure 2.3 with two projects (companies), A and B, imposing externalities on each other. A perfectly diversified owner who can influence companies'

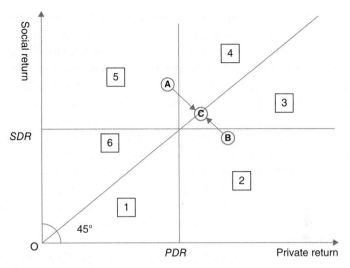

FIGURE 2.3   Internalization of Externalities Through Investment Diversification.
Source: Authors.

Notes: SDR = social discount rate; PDR = private discount rate.

behavior can under the right conditions achieve a combined project C where all the externalities are internalized. Such ownership structure can avoid many of the transaction costs associated with Coasian bargaining between separate owners and thus can take internalization of externalities further than what is assumed to have been achieved in Figure 2.1. Since diversification helps internalize externalities, it offers potential benefits over and beyond the reduction of risk. The results hold also with less than perfect diversification.

In fact, the most diversified investor of all is the government, if taxation is taken as the government acting as a "silent partner" with stakes in every firm and household (see Domar and Musgrave 1944). This is one if not the main reason for the expectation that the government acts in the public interest and as the perfect internalizing "machine." Internalization opportunities also exist when investors are also consumers or employees (Gordon 1990). They are especially powerful when combined with diversification as in the case of some pension funds such as CALPERS.[4]

The extent of shareholder diversification has been increased greatly by two well-known factors: the increase in institutional ownership of shares

---

[4]California Public Employees' Retirement System.

and the increase in indexing (or passive investing) as a portfolio strategy. The two factors show that diversification is a necessary but not a sufficient condition for internalization of externalities. For the latter to happen, institutional investors need also to be active investors and use existing mechanisms to change corporate behavior. Index investors are well diversified, but typically passive and spend little if any resources on influencing the behavior of their investee companies. Some of the institutional investors, however, take a more proactive stance and use available corporate governance mechanisms, including shareholder activism to change corporate behavior in line with broader social interests. Some pension funds, which combine diversification with the long-term interests of labor and consumers, have been particularly active in pursuing broader social objectives (for examples, see Hanse and Lott 1996). CALPERS, in particular, has become well known for shareholder activism and influencing corporate behavior.

Other institutional investors have also shown proclivity to act in the social interest. Venture capitalists are less diversified than some institutional investors but can be well diversified in particular industries. They are active investors and thus can influence corporate behavior significantly in line with social interests related to externalities within specific industries and possibly more broadly, beyond their industry focus, when the industry interests are aligned with the broader social interests, as, for instance, new technologies in renewable energy.

Active diversified investors do face limitations in the market in competition with traditional investors. If diversified active shareholders are successful in influencing corporate behavior, this may increase the value of their portfolio but reduce the (private) value of some individual firms (as is the case of company B in Figure 2.3). This creates a free rider problem whereby traditional investors may see an opportunity to take over individual firms, impose value maximization behavior, and derive significant private benefits (Hansen and Lott 1996). This imposes limitations on the prevalence and importance of this socially motivated investment behavior.

Local embedding is in some respects the opposite of diversification. It can be viewed as a case of vertical diversification because it involves exposure to stakeholders along the supply chain centered around a particular project. Local embedding occurs when the investor (say, a cooperative bank, credit unions, or a community development fund) invests in local projects that may have local externalities in terms of effects on consumers, employees, and other businesses in the locality. The local investor, because of its deep ties with the community, is exposed to these local interests. It may be in a position to internalize the projects' externalities and use available tools to influence the investee to take these effects into account. This is the idea behind the growing "invest locally" movement.[5]

Projects where the negative externalities are locally felt but project benefits are "globalized" or "nationalized," as in some large oil, gas, and mining (OGM) projects, illustrate the limitations of this approach. Local investors may be too small to take meaningful stakes and exert influence in projects of this nature that tend to be of bigger size. Even in such cases, there can be benefits of local investing and the, albeit limited, alignment of interests that it can bring. Some countries, such as South Africa,[6] have been encouraging the creation of community investing vehicles and a mandated minimum investment share in every mining project as part of the black empowerment movement in this country[7] (World Bank 2010; Wall and Pelon 2011). But the overall effect depends on how such policies are implemented. In many developing countries they have been implemented in ways that reduce the attractiveness of such projects for traditional investors and therefore may have hurt industry prospects overall.

The example illustrates two general points: (i) government action may enable socially motivated behavior; and the interactions between the two can expand internalization opportunities; (ii) heterogeneity of investment behavior, and in particular the importance of traditional investors in the marketplace, imposes limitations on the viability or socially motivated behavior and the nature and implementation of government policies in this regard.

Value Commitment

In value commitment, investor's behavior is driven by values and principles that act like ethical constraint on investment decisions. Ethics is the "rational pursuit of the long-run interest of society as a whole" (Harsanyi 1966) and therefore can align investors' behavior with social interests. This behavior is consistent with the non-consequentialist approach to moral judgment (Shaw and Barry 2001), although it can be made fully consistent with a consequentialist approach (Sen 1977), as, for instance, through a commitment to full responsibility for all the consequences of one's choice and action. It may involve making investment choices for their inherent worth rather than

---

[5]See, for example, https://www.locavesting.com/how-to-invest-local/.
[6]See, for example, https://www.reuters.com/article/us-safrica-mining/south-africa-proposes-30-%-black-ownership-for-mining-firms-within-5-years-idUSKBN1JB2HD.
[7]For some of the weaknesses in implementation and unintended effects of this approach see https://pmg.org.za/committee-meeting/2342/.

for some separable consequence (Besley and Ghatak 2014) (i.e. be a form of intrinsic motivation). Intrinsic motivation has been viewed as a solution to agency problems, including cases of externalities.

Commitment to moral values and ethical principles most clearly manifests itself in the capacity to choose an act that the investor believes will yield a lower level of personal welfare than an alternative that is also available to him or her (Sen 1977). Thus, it involves some trade-off between private and social returns and as such can take the internalization of externalities further than what has been achieved in private equilibria and Coasian bargaining as assumed in Figure 2.1.

This can lead to different choices in situations where private returns are higher than social returns, as in region 2 in Figure 2.4. Value commitment investors may avoid investing in projects in region 2 on the premise that these projects impose significant negative externalities and do harm to society despite their high private returns. CALPERS, for example, was one the first investors to shun investments in tobacco companies at a time where these investments were even more lucrative than now.[8] Goldman Sachs has recently made a public commitment not to take companies public without diversity on their boards.[9]

These examples are illustrative of value commitment investing of the passive type, where investors simply shy away from certain types of projects. Value commitment investing can also be of the active type when investors expend own resources or require the investee company to expend resources to reduce or eliminate some of the project's negative externalities, thus increasing their costs and lowering their private returns while keeping social returns intact. This would translate in horizontal movement of projects in regions 2 or 3 toward the 45-degree line, as, for example, from B to B' in Figure 2.4.

As an illustration, take the case of a project with significant negative externalities, say, pollution or environmental degradation, but offering attractive private returns. This project will be either in region 2 or in region 3. If the socially motivated investor wants to address the negative externalities, they will need to require significant investment in cleaner technologies that reduce emissions. Many socially motivated investors (i.e. the banks incorporating the Equator Principles) have environmental and social standards that they seek to enforce with their investee companies in order to mitigate

---

[8]See the debate on the merits of this approach at https://www.latimes.com/opinion/readersreact/la-ol-le-calpers-big-tobacco-20161222-story.html.
[9]For more information see https://www.cbsnews.com/news/goldman-sachs-diversity-ipo-women-minorities-david-solomon-davos/.

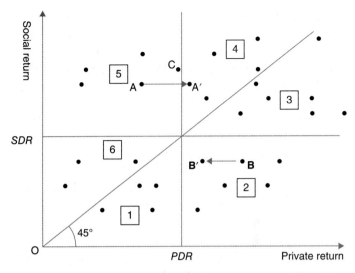

FIGURE 2.4   Internalization of Externalities Through Value Commitment Investing.
Source: Authors.

Notes: SDR = social discount rate; PDR = private discount rate.

or eliminate significant negative externalities. These standards typically go beyond national requirements in developing countries and thus impose additional costs to private companies operating in those environments. This lowers private returns and aligns them with the social returns. An estimate of such costs in the case of the performance standards of the International Finance Corporation (IFC) of the World Bank Group (WBG) indicates a magnitude of about 3.7% of nonrecurrent (i.e. initial) project costs, and about 0.3% of recurrent costs in the case of a typical manufacturing project in a developing country (Independent Evaluation Group 2009).[10] In a highly competitive environment, additional costs of such magnitude would be prohibitive.

---

[10]The assumptions about the project are as follows: project involving general manufacturing and services (GMS) in North Africa. The completed project would employ 1,500 people on a greenfield site. The capital cost of the project is USD $100 million. It was estimated that the manufacturing plant would need to invest about USD $11.2 million to meet both national and IFC Environment Health and Safety (EHS) requirements, with the IFC requirements contributing about USD $3.7 million (about 3.7% to total capital cost). Annual EHS operating costs to meet both national and IFC requirements were estimated at USD $1.3 million, with the IFC contribution estimated at USD $360,000 (about 27% of annual operating costs).

Value commitment investing of the active type does not increase a project's social returns (i.e. does not increase total social value); it simply redistributes it between various stakeholders. This may still be beneficial from a social point of view as it brings private and social values closer together. Nevertheless, there is significant difference between projects in region 2 and those in region 3. Although both types of projects may have significant negative externalities, projects in region 2 should not be implemented from a social point of view even if all the negative externalities were to be internalized. Projects in region 3, on the other hand, are both socially and privately attractive investments with all externalities internalized.

This is an important distinction to make because often value-commitment-type investors would justify investing in projects with significant negative externalities with the argument that their presence makes such projects better compared to the counterfactual (i.e. without them in the project). The argument is that these projects will be implemented anyway given the attractive private returns they offer, so it is better that they at least follow some good ESG standards (as, for instance, improvement from B to B' in Figure 2.3). This may be so, but if these projects are in region 2, it does not change the fact that from a social perspective these projects should not be implemented. Conducting a cost-benefit analysis to determine the exact location of such projects in the project return space is therefore of critical importance.

Projects in region 5 have the opposite profile from those in region 2. They are very appealing socially but do not offer sufficient private returns to motivate traditional investors to invest. Value commitment investors may invest in projects in region 5 where they have to accept returns lower than the discount rate in order to facilitate the implementation of projects with significant positive externalities (i.e. project C in Figure 2.4). Some renewable energy projects (i.e. solar in the early days of technological innovation when unit costs were much higher than today) may fall in this category. The difference between value commitment investors who confine their activities to projects in regions 3 and 4 (for example, of the passive type who shun projects in region, 2 as discussed earlier) and those who also invest in region 5 projects is that projects in region 5 will not happen without value commitment investors (or public investors for that matter) willing to sacrifice private returns (or public investors stepping in); projects in regions 3 and 4 will take place with or without value commitment investors.

Region 5 is the domain of public investors, however. If value commitment investors operate in this space, they are de facto becoming public investors as there is nothing to differentiate their behavior from that of public investors.

A hybrid practice has emerged recently—the practice of blended finance. Blended finance involves the combination of grants and commercial financing to support projects of the region 5 type. Graphically, as per Figure 2.4, the use of blended finance would imply a horizontal shift in the project space from where the projects are located in the direction of the 45-degree line (for example, from A to A' in Figure 2.4). This is because the financial subsidy element embedded in these instruments has limited ability to address non-financial risk. It tends to redistribute risks among investors, while inherent project risks, such as sponsor and management quality, market risk, macroeconomic conditions, and exchange rate risk remain untouched (Independent Evaluation Group 2019).

Value commitment investing implies a sacrifice of private returns compared to traditional investment behavior. Some asset managers and financiers promise their investors the holy grail of investing: value commitment without sacrificing financial return. Similarly, some foundations imply that they can create value through non-concessionary investments of their endowments and urge their peers to follow suit. The preceding discussion and lack of evidence in support of such claims should make one skeptical of these assertions.

Given these trade-offs between social and private returns, how can value commitment investment behavior be viable in competition with traditional investing? There are several possible answers to this question. One is given by Harsanyi's postulate of "low-cost" impartiality and public spirit, which says that people (and institutions, for that matter) tend to be public-spirited when it costs little to be public-spirited (Harsanyi 1966). Project C in Figure 2.4 offers an example of such low-cost public spirit as the project's private returns are very close to the hurdle rate. If this is the case, value commitment investing would be expected to be a marginal phenomenon, but it still could be quite effective especially if applied to projects on the margins of regions 5 and 2. Another possible explanation is that what appears as an altruistic act by the value commitment investor is in fact the purchase of some intangible benefits such as enhanced reputation, or indulgences for sins committed elsewhere. A third possibility is that only investors that operate in highly imperfect markets (i.e. enjoy some monopoly powers) are able to afford such acts, which are being financed by rents generated in such monopolistic practices. If this is the case, value commitment investment behavior should be observed by large, powerful financial institutions often in combination with equally large and powerful investee companies. A related final explanation is that large, powerful institutions can take a long-term enlightened perspective and realize that their long-term interests coincide with the public interest.

These multiple explanations suggest an intrinsic difficulty with observing and assessing acts on the basis of commitment: they may coincide with acts that maximize the private benefits of the investor but are not the motivating force for the particular behavior (Sen 1977). Elaborate tests and analysis are often necessary to be able to ascertain the real motives behind what appears or is presented as value commitment behavior.

In general, the overall market impact of value commitment investors interacting with traditional investors will depend on whether there are congestion or synergistic effects in the market for investments (Haltiwanger and Waldman 1985). Congestion effects exist when the more investors behave similarly, the worse off everyone is. And the opposite for synergistic effects. In the case of congestion effects, the impact of value commitment investors will be nullified by the behavior of traditional investors. This is more likely in the case of passive value commitments investors that simply avoid projects in region 2 and choose projects in regions 3 and 4. By avoiding region 2 projects, value commitment investors will tend to increase private returns there and make those projects even more attractive to traditional investors luring more capital into that region. At the same time, their concentration on projects in regions 3 and 4 will tend to depress returns there, making these projects less attractive for traditional investors. As a result, the macroeconomic and longer-term consequences of passive value commitment investing will tend to be negligible. What they will most likely achieve is to substitute for some traditional private investors and displace them from regions 4 and 3 into region 2. On the other hand, there is good likelihood that there will be synergistic effects between the choices of value commitment investors of the active type and those of traditional investors, especially in the case of projects in region 5 that can be moved into region 4. In this scenario, value commitment investors can have a disproportionately large impact on the market, especially when there are knowledge and learning spillovers from such investments.

IMPACT INVESTING

A potentially powerful new approach to investing internalizes externalities by linking impacts (i.e. positive externalities) to investor returns, thus making investors' private return contingent on the social impact achieved. This typically involves institutional innovation through which transaction (agency) costs are lowered, markets are created, and interests aligned between investor and investee. This is the only approach where impact in the form of externality is directly linked to investors' return and thus becomes the main goal of investment behavior. For this reason, the term Impact Investing is most appropriately reserved for this type of investment behavior.

The Global Impact Investing Network (GIIN) defines Impact Investing as making investments "with the intention to generate a measurable, beneficial social or environmental impact alongside a financial return."[11] Key word in the definition is "alongside"—social impact alongside financial return. The term suggests that returns to investors and social impact are not necessarily linked and contingent on each other. Without this link, impacts will not be fully embedded into the project's organizational arrangements and associated incentive structures and may not fully become the motivation and the intention of investment behavior.

Increasingly, investors and organizations, no matter whether businesses, nonprofits, or development agencies, define their goals at a higher level of the results chain, in terms of ultimate effects (i.e. social impacts). Proclaimed "intention to generate a measurable, beneficial social or environmental impact" might no longer be such a substantial differentiating characteristic of investors and organizations as in the past. What really differentiates impact investors are their underlying incentives (i.e. how their private financial returns relate to social impacts).

Real Impact Investing is investing under arrangements whereby returns to the investors are conditioned on the impacts achieved. The fundamental premise here is that incentives influence behavior and that behavior in turn influences performance (Dushnitsky and Shapira 2010). The key differences and defining characteristics are that in Impact Investing, investors have a stake and their investment is at stake in achieving the intended impact.

Thus defined, Impact Investing has the potential to have transformational effects on systems of social interactions. Ashby (1957, p. 53) differentiates between relationships of dominance, where one part of the system has an effect on another part but is not in turn affected by it, and relationships of feedback, where both are affected. The internalization through Impact Investing introduces a feedback mechanism and transform the system from one of domination to one of feedback.

Impact Investing is about expanding the pie and not simply redistributing it, as with some of the other approaches. It creates social value by aligning incentives around expanding positive externalities, which are internalized through Coasean-like bargaining between investor and investee.

---

[11]For more information, see GIIN at https://thegiin.org/impact-investing/need-to-know/#what-is-impact-investing.

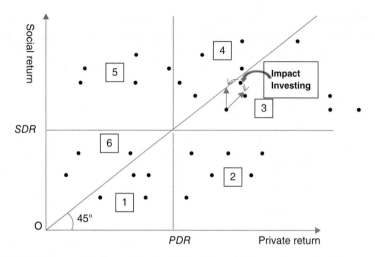

FIGURE 2.5   Internalization of Externalities Through Impact Investing. *Source:* Authors.

Notes: SDR = social discount rate; PDR = private discount rate;

Graphically, it involves shifts in the project space outward as presented in Figure 2.5.[12] The most valuable social contributions are from Impact Investing, which shifts projects into regions 3 and 4 from other regions in the project space.

Social impact bonds[13] (SIBs)[14] are a good example of an Impact Investing instrument. They are an impact-based (pay-for-success) model, where private investors put capital at risk to fund projects with clear social goals. If projects achieve their targeted social impact, the investment capital, plus an interest-based return, is repaid by an impact funder—usually a government department or private grant provider. If the impact goals are not met, investors can lose their interest return or lose some or all their capital investment. Impact funders can therefore only pay for the set of predetermined results.

---

[12]More precisely, the slope of the lines will be between the limiting cases of vertical to 45 degrees, which is the case where none of the social value created by the investor is appropriated in her private returns, and the parallel to the 45-degree line, which is the case where all of the social value created is appropriated.

[13]"Bonds" is really a misnomer because these instruments do not promise fixed income. Social impact bonds are more akin to pay-for-performance contracts, or outcome-based contracts, with possible equity-like risk.

[14]See Chapter 14, "Social Impact Bonds: Promises and Results," by Maria Basílio.

Some of the SIBs that have been implemented illustrate the logic of these arrangements. The state of New York in 2012 launched an SIB contract aimed at reducing juvenile recidivism. The investor Goldman Sachs paid USD \$6.9 million to implement the project. If the rate of recidivism is reduced by 10%, the principal will be repaid in full, with an additional USD \$2.1 million to be paid if rates are reduced by more than 10%. As per the contract, the maximum Goldman Sachs can lose has been limited to USD \$2.4 million. In July 2015, the program's independent evaluator concluded that the intervention had failed to reduce recidivism. Following the release of the findings, the program ended in August 2015 (Berlin 2016).

As the case illustrates, the design of an SIB demands an evidence-based results approach to addressing social problems. The independent monitoring and evaluation of SIBs' impacts and outcomes then become critical, promoting accountability and helping to keep projects on track. Well-defined, relevant, and measurable metrics of impact are key to the success of the SIB.[15] Measurement and evaluation are at the center of the organizational, financial, and incentive structure of these instruments, which is also unique from the perspective of the role of evaluation in organizational settings. Both accurate measurement of the social impact and its credible attribution to the intervention are critically important for the feasibility of SIBs.[16]

Similar to the SIB are the so-called income share agreements (ISA), whereby a financial institution funds a recipient who, in exchange, agrees to pay back a percentage of his or her income for a fixed number of years. ISAs have become popular in the United States as an alternative to the traditional student loans, and a number of private companies now offer ISAs for a variety of purposes, including as a funding source for college tuition. Under some arrangements, for example, if the student becomes a star in her field with corresponding increase in salaries, her payments to the financial institution increase; if she loses her job, the financial institution incurs a loss. So, there is genuine income and risk sharing (Boston 2019).

Given the equity-like features of Impact Investing, impact investors have the propensity to be active investors, although the way in which this is exercised depends on the particular circumstances. Specific to

---

[15]See, for instance, Deloitte's "Paying for outcomes: Solving complex societal issues through Social Impact Bonds" at https://www2.deloitte.com/content/dam/Deloitte/au/Documents/public-sector/deloitte-au-ps-paying-outcomes-social-impact-bonds-180914.pdf.

[16]The ideal would be to combine traditional cost-benefit analysis (CBA) and impact evaluation (based on control groups) to establish causality.

Impact Investing is the use and reliance on independent measurement and evaluation of impact, as in the case of SIBs.

Impact Investing has good chances of competing well with traditional investing because it does not involve trade-offs between social and private returns. These are new investment approaches, and as with anything new they generate hopes but also concerns and their market success is still uncertain. But they bring unique ways of aligning incentives around achieving social impacts, and as such we believe that the term "impact investor," as its name implies, should be reserved for them.

CONCLUSION

Socially motivated and impact investors exist because of projects' externalities. Externalities are prerequisite for the existence of socially motivated investors. There will be no distinct class of socially motivated investors without project externalities and the associated gaps between social and private returns. The socially useful role that socially motivated investors can play is related to correcting some of the inefficiencies arising from investment's externalities.

Socially motivated investors are defined as private investors who, in addition to private returns, take social returns into consideration when making investment decisions. Based on the ways they take social returns into account, three types of socially motivated investors are distinguished: (i) value alignment investors, (ii) value commitment investors, and (iii) impact investors.

Value alignment investors internalize all or most project externalities by design or social positioning. The value commitment investor narrows the gap between social and private returns by his or her willingness to sacrifice some private returns in order not to violate ethical norms to which he or she is committed. Finally, the impact investor makes his or her financial return contingent on the achievement of social impact, which in the absence of Impact Investing would be an externality.

Impact Investing builds on capacity and innovations that are able to link impacts, in the form of externalities (converted to positive impacts), to investor returns, thus making investor's private returns contingent on the social impact achieved. This approach aligns incentives in support of social value creation while also matching social and private returns. SIBs exemplify such impact-based (pay-for-success) models where private investors put capital at risk to fund projects with social goals.

No deliberate approach to Impact Investing can be followed without some attempt at measuring and assessing those externalities. This is, however, inherently difficult. Inherently because the same reasons for which externalities exist make it difficult to invest in better measuring such third-party effects. Measurement and evaluation are at the center of the organizational, financial, and incentive structure of these investment approaches. Both accurate measurement of the social value and credible attribution of results to the intervention are critically important.

Moreover, proper measurement of externalities and social impacts is critical for Impact Investing instruments such as SIBs. The design of SIBs demands an evidence-based results approach to addressing social problems. The independent monitoring and evaluation of SIB outcomes and impacts are at the center of the incentives structure of these instruments, because their feasibility depends on the extent to which social effects are accurately measured and attribution to the intervention is credibly established. A combination of CBA and post-experimental or experimental methods (e.g. randomized control trials [RCT]) are best suited for the purpose. But these are complex and costly tools that, combined with the institutional and structuring complexity of these Impact Investing instruments, suggest that investments need to be above certain critical size to justify the higher transaction costs. More recently, the GIIN has advocated for several simpler tools (e.g. qualitative analysis, mixed methods, beneficiary surveys) which look promising, but further research is needed to understand if these tools can credibly attribute impacts for instruments like the SIBs.

We believe that the term "impact investor," as its name implies, should be reserved for investors who seek actual value creation, by making their private returns dependent on the achievement of social impacts. The social investing field can grow responsibly only if individual investors, Impact Investing trade associations, and asset managers are transparent about the accuracy of their claims, demonstrated through credible evaluation methods.

ACKNOWLEDGMENTS

Elsa de Morais Sarmento and R. Paul Herman provided comments, guidance, and encouragement throughout the work on the chapter, for which the authors are grateful. The authors wish to thank Andrew Warner for useful discussions and suggestions on the formulation and interpretation of the project space.

DISCLAIMER

The findings, interpretations, and conclusions expressed in this paper are entirely those of the authors. They do not necessarily represent the views of the World Bank Group or its affiliated organizations, or those of the executive directors of the World Bank Group or the governments they represent.

REFERENCES

Agudelo, L., Jóhannsdóttir, L., and Davídsdóttir, B. A. (2019). A literature review of the history and evolution of corporate social responsibility. *International Journal Corporate Social Responsibility* 4(1). https://doi.org/10.1186/s40991-018-0039-y

Alchian, A., and Demsetz, H. (1972). Production, Information Costs, and Economic Organization. *American Economic Review*, 62(5): 777–795 (December 1972).

Antoci, A., and Bartolini, S. (1999). Negative externalities as the engine of growth in an evolutionary context. MPRA Paper No. 13908. https://mpra.ub.uni-muenchen.de/13908/ (accessed 22 March 2020).

Arrow, K. (1970). Political and Economic Evaluation of Social Effects and Externalities. In *The Analysis of Public Output* (Julius Margolis ed.). NBER. http://www.nber.org/books/marg70-1 (accessed 20 April 2020).

Ashby, R. W. (1957). *Introduction to Cybernetics,* 2nd ed. London: Chapman & Hall.

Barro, R., and Sala-i-Martin, X. (1999). *Economic Growth*. Cambridge, MA: MIT Press.

Berlin, G. (2016). Learning from Experience: A Guide to Social Impact Bond Investing. *MDRC (March)*.

Besley, T., and Ghatak, M. (2014). Solving Agency Problems: Intrinsic Motivation, Incentives, and Productivity. London School of Economics, Background paper for the 2014 World Development Report. Washington, DC: World Bank.

Boston, C. (2019). College Graduates Sell Stakes of Themselves to Wallstreet. Bloomberg Business Week (April 9) https://www.bloomberg.com/news/articles/2019-04-09/college-grads-sell-stakes-in-themselves-to-wall-street (accessed 22 April 2020).

Buchanan, J., and Stubblebine, W. (1962). Externality. *Economica* 29(116): 371–384 (November).

Deloitte (n.d.). Paying for outcomes Solving complex societal issues through Social Impact Bonds. https://www2.deloitte.com/content/dam/Deloitte/au/Documents/public-sector/deloitte-au-ps-paying-outcomes-social-impact-bonds-180914.pdf (accessed 1 February 2020).

Domar, E. D., and Musgrave, R. A. (1994). Proportional Income Taxation and Risk-Taking. *Quarterly Journal of Economics* 58(3): 388–422.

Dushnitsky, G., and Shapira, Z. (2010). Entrepreneurial Finance Meets Organizational Reality: Comparing Investments Practices and Performance of Corporate and Independent Venture Capitalists. *Strategic Management Journal* 31: 990–1017.

Foroogh, C. N., Jenkins, G. P., and Hashemi, M. (2019). Social Impact Bonds: Implementation, Evaluation, and Monitoring. *International Journal of Public Administration* 42(4):289–297. https://doi.org/10.1080/01900692.2018.1433206

Gordon, R. H. (1990). Do Publicly Traded Corporations Act in the Public Interest? NBER Working Paper Series, 3303.

Haltiwanger, J., and Waldman, M. (1985). Rational Expectations and the Limits of Rationality: An Analysis of Heterogeneity. *American Economic Review* 75(3): 326–340.

Hansen, R. G., and Lott, J. R. (1996). Externalities and Corporate Objectives in a World of Diversified Shareholder/Consumers. *Journal of Financial and Quantitative Analysis* 31(1):43–68 (March 1996).

Harsanyi, J. C. (1966). A General Theory of Rational Behavior in Game Situations. *Econometrica* 34 (3): 613–634 (July).

Hearn, S., and Buffardi, A. L. (2016). What Is Impact? London: Methods Lab, Overseas Development Institute. https://www.odi.org/sites/odi.org.uk/files/resource-documents/10352.pdf (accessed 22 April 2020).

Independent Evaluation Group (2019). IFC's Blended Finance Operations. Washington, DC: World Bank Group,. https://ieg.worldbankgroup.org/evaluations/ifcs-blended-finance-operations (accessed 22 April 2020).

Independent Evaluation Group (2009). Are IFC's Performance Standards Adding Value? And if Yes to Whom? Washington, DC: World Bank Group.

Jacobs, J. (1969). *The Economy of Cities*. New York: Random House.

Moore, M., Boardman, A., and Vining, A. (2013). The choice of the social discount rate and the opportunity cost of public funds. *Journal of Benefit-Cost Analysis* 4(3): 401–409. https://doi.org/10.1515/jbca-2012-0008

Moulier-Boutang, Y. (2011). What Defines Externalities Today? *Paris Innovation Review*, p. 10 (11 March). http://parisinnovationreview.com/articles-en/

what-defines-externality-today-yann-moulier-boutang (accessed 12 April 2020).

Pigou, A. C. (1932). *The Economics of Welfare,* 4th ed. London: Macmillan and Co.

Porter, M. E. (1990). *The Competitive Advantage of Nations.* New York: Free Press.

Sen, A. K. (1977). Rational Fools: A Critique of the Behavioral Foundations of Economic Theory. *Philosophy & Public Affairs* 6(4): 317–344 (Summer).

Sen, A. K. (2000). Consequential Evaluation and Practical Reason. *Journal of Philosophy* 97(9): 477–502.

Shaw, W., and Barry, V. (2001). *Moral Issues in Business,* 8th ed. Belmont, CA: Wadsworth.

Simon, H. A. (1964). On the Concept of Organizational Goal., *Administrative Science Quarterly* 9(1):1–22 (June).

Wall, E., and Pelon, R. (2011). Sharing Mining Benefits in Developing Countries: The Experience with Foundations, Trusts, and Funds. Washington, DC: World Bank. https://static1.squarespace.com/static/5bb24 d3c9b8fe8421e87bbb6/t/5c2930674d7a9c2ebbf43267/1546203244645/WB-Sharing-Mining-Benefits-in-Developing-Countries.pdf (accessed 22 April 2020).

World Bank (2010). *Mining Foundations,* Trusts and Funds*: A Sourcebook.* World Bank. http://siteresources.worldbank.org/EXTOGMC/Resources/Sourcebook_Full_Report.pdf (accessed 22 April 2020).

CHAPTER 3

Place-Based Impact Investing: Local and Regional Assets for Local and Regional Impact in Globally Diversified Portfolios

Lauryn Agnew, MBA

Abstract

Institutional investors have historically been averse to allocating investment assets in a way that aligns with their place-based missions or beneficiaries. These investors fear that any level of geographic focus could pose new or additional risks to a global portfolio and its expected rate of return. Place-based impact investing (PBII) can connect local communities and can create mutual shared value financially, socially, and environmentally for the citizens and community, as well as investors of all types. PBII is an investment strategy that focuses on investing in a specific location with the intention of addressing the needs of marginalized communities and improving their lives. This

61

chapter explores how globally diversified portfolios can invest in and better benefit local communities through PBII. It models how the six major asset classes — public equities, public fixed income, real estate, private equity, infrastructure, and cash — allocated by most institutional portfolios can produce local as well as global impact, generate competitive returns, and provide positive social and environmental outcomes. This chapter also discusses how communities can better engage investors across different asset class investments to finance sustainable areas and prosperous regions. Three distinctive communities — in the city of Curitiba, Brazil; the state of Telangana, India; and the city of North Richmond, California, United States — provide real-life examples of how to integrate community engagement, environmental planning, and long-term land use planning through PBII to better deliver sustainability and resilience to local and regional landscapes.

Keywords

Place-based Impact Investing; ESG Investing; ESG; Local Investing; Socially Responsible Investing; Sustainable Investing; Responsible Investing; Community Investing; Transit-Oriented Development; Sustainable Real Estate; Sustainability; Brazil; India; United States

INTRODUCTION

Place-based impact investing (PBII) helps to connect local communities and can create mutual shared value financially, socially, and environmentally for the citizens and community, as well as investors of all types. The Urban Institute — a think tank based in Washington D.C. that focuses on social and economic policy — defines PBII as the "deployment of impact capital to address the needs of marginalized communities" (Urban Institute 2020). Furthermore, the Urban Institute describes impact capital as investments that target both financial and social or environmental returns (Urban Institute 2020).

The Healthcare Anchor Network — a national collaborative network of 45 leading health care systems based in the United States — describes PBII as creating healthy and thriving communities through the increased availability of capital for social, economic, or environmental impact across various areas. These include, but are not limited to, affordable and supportive housing; minority, women, and employee-owned business creation, growth and retention; community and childcare facilities; stable, well-paying jobs; healthy food production and access; transit-oriented development;

economic development around arts and culture; renewable energy and energy efficiency; and Federally Qualified Health Centers (Zuckerman and Parker 2017).

This chapter pursues the research question of how globally diversified portfolios can invest into and better benefit local communities through a PBII approach. This chapter provides a framework for how institutional investors can prudently invest in a particular *place*, within their portfolios, while simultaneously benefiting the mission and beneficiaries of the organization, such as foundations, endowments, public pensions, and sovereign wealth funds. Furthermore, by leveraging the power of community engagement, as well as investor engagement, this framework aims to better connect local assets to local community-based solutions within investment portfolios.

To illustrate how this can be done, three examples of PBII are included: (i) a farming community in the southern Indian state of Telangana, which engages its marginalized farmers through education and collaborative networks to improve social, financial, and environmental conditions through pesticide-free farming practices, cooperatives, and micro-loans to farmers; (ii) the city of Curitiba, Brazil, which began its journey decades ago in response to urban sprawl, flooding risks, and environmental degradation, and which has realized positive outcomes by redirecting public funds to green infrastructure and through sustainable land use planning; (iii) and the marginalized low-income community of North Richmond, California, which managed to address the interrelated challenges of housing, job growth, air quality, and sea level rise through a broad collaboration among the local governments, regional housing and transit authorities, and environmental landscape conservancies.

These communities and their leaders across all disciplines demonstrate how intentional community design, combined with various asset pools, can be used to catalyze and fund local, impactful projects. These examples can be used as learning points and adapted to address the needs of any locality, region, or mission.

This chapter is based on a desk review of the literature and the professional experience of the author. Multiple impact investing articles and white papers covering environmental, social, and governance (ESG), impact themes, socially responsible investing (SRI, now updated to sustainable responsible Impact Investing), global diversification, and fiduciary duty were reviewed, and evidence integrated. The public equity research is based on tracking a model portfolio of local publicly traded companies identified by their geographic headquarters, following financial and fiduciary standards for institutional investors, and using financial optimization programs and ESG integration.

Current State of Place-Based Impact Investing Collaboratives

Most of the collaborative PBII efforts across the United States have been reviewed in a report by the Urban Institute (Ashley and Ovalle May 2018). The report identified a variety of alliances developing across the United States. Many alliances were based on information sharing and a loose network of community players, but not yet implemented nor pursuing financial co-investment vehicles. Other PBII collaboratives are backed by place-based foundations that partner with local community banks. They target lending to small businesses in underserved neighborhoods or to nonprofit organizations that deliver social services. Some regional efforts focus on private equity opportunities in new local businesses. Most alliances rely on relationships with community banks that can deliver steady returns, with low risk, and a large amount of local impact. Community Development Financial Institutions (CDFIs) work closely with their borrowers and generally have a very low risk of default due to their technical and financial assistance. They usually cannot, however, take on significant assets and deploy them quickly. The report also found a few state-identified bond funds that will assign the impact for regional bonds to regional investors within broader portfolios, but these do not originate the impact.

So far, no region has developed a "Collaborative PBII Initiative" that also includes strategies for the asset classes that institutional portfolios typically use. All investment portfolios have an impact, whether tracked or not, whether intentional in seeking that impact or not, or whether designed to be intentional about location, degree, and type of impact. Local impact can be more effective if investors collaborate with each other.

Several investors' misconceptions about PBII have contributed to a lack of intentional local investing. These misconceptions are related to: (i) the limited evidence that impact and profits can be achieved simultaneously; (ii) concerns that investors will not be making market returns with a focus on or alignment toward a specific place or mission; (iii) fears that geographic concentration raises investment risks; (iv) lack of local deal flows or proven strategies to diversify locally, while meeting minimum size requirements; (v) lack or insufficient resources and staff time to explore due diligence for these types of portfolios.

The concept of *place* is new to global institutional investors constructing a portfolio. However, many asset owners originate and manage their assets derived from place-focused institutions — such as local, state, or regional pension plans; universities and colleges; community foundations; corporate foundations; or focus their missions on location-identified landscapes, communities, or beneficiaries. For the purposes of this chapter, PBII is the act of investing in instruments designed to serve that geographic focus. Designing investment strategies to impact a *place* according to best practices and fiduciary standards can provide investors with reliable execution, diversification, and financial returns alongside local positive impact. Collaborating with other place-based investors for efficiencies of management and costs can provide the scale of capital for compounding impact.

PBII requires two formerly and seemingly unrelated specializations to come together: financial markets investing and community development. Investors that seek to provide capital locally for positive social and environmental impact need financial instruments, strategies, and portfolios that can qualify for strict fiduciary and financial standards, like due diligence, performance monitoring, and diversification of risks. Places like local or regional communities need to solve their internal challenges, which are unique to them, to build a sustainable and resilient future, and they will need capital to do this. Global financial markets have not evolved yet to pursue these place-based portfolios and strategies due to a perceived lack of demand for such. Place-aligned asset owners generally have limited broad-based strategic options to invest locally. This chapter connects both sides of this equation for the supply and demand for capital with a framework for centralized asset class portfolios that can be both geographically focused and financially suitable for those investors' and asset owners' portfolios, and provide an intentional positive impact for their *place*.

Institutional investors manage globally diversified portfolios that can include all asset classes. These portfolios can generate impact at a local, regional, and global level, depending on which projects, institutions, or individuals get funded through their respective investments. Investors seeking impact must understand that every investment, across all asset classes, has not only its own risk and return profile but also an impact profile (Agnew and Malta 2017). Each asset class has unique goals, also noted in Figure 3.1.

Financial instruments differ in their impact capacity. Securities like publicly traded equities and bonds have a more indirect impact. Equity portfolio owners individually and collectively can vote their proxies and engage with company management to influence corporate behavior regarding how the company addresses employee relations, diversity, environmental actions, and disclosures, among other management responsibilities. Bondholders provide liquidity and scale for long-term investments and markets. Real estate investments can identify and focus on particular sectors that provide specific impact for housing, commercial and industrial jobs, and community services like education and health care. Long-term infrastructure

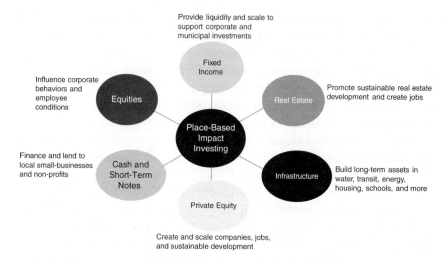

FIGURE 3.1   Sample Portfolio Impact Goals by Asset Class. *Source:* Author.

investments fund necessities like energy, water, sanitation, and transit. Private equity investments fund innovation and job growth through new business development. Short-term liquid assets like cash can be impacting local communities through lending to small businesses for job growth.

Most institutional investors optimize risk and return when making asset allocation decisions, based on the objectives stated in the investment policy statement (IPS). Since the typical main purpose is achieving a targeted financial return, investors historically have not measured their social and environmental impacts, unless specified by their organizational mandates. However, many of these portfolios are likely already generating some kind of positive impact, especially with portfolios that include municipal bonds, investments in infrastructure projects, money market instruments issued by financial organizations that follow socially responsible investing (SRI) principles, and even real estate investment trusts (REITs) that contribute to affordable or green housing. Investors can use the developing impact investing metrics like those from the United Nations Sustainable Development Goals (SDGs), discussed later in the chapter, so investors and beneficiaries could better track the impacts achieved by their portfolios.

TARGETING IMPACT THROUGH PLACE-BASED IMPACT INVESTING

The application of modern portfolio theory (MPT) includes multiple, diversified asset classes and sub-asset classes, where each asset class represents a particular set of risk and return expectations as well as correlations to other asset classes. This chapter explains how PBII strategies can be integrated into asset classes, ranging across public equities, bonds, real estate, infrastructure, private equity, and cash. (Asset classes not included here include hedge funds, Treasury-inflation protected securities [TIPS], and commodities.) This chapter describes investor portfolios using an equal-weighted asset allocation for visual simplicity of the figures in the development of a place-based, asset class-based impact investing model. Each investor can overlay their unique asset allocation for their optimal combination of risk and return — and impact — as targeted in their investment policy statement.

Intentionally seeking and measuring impact through the lens of PBII can be illustrated with the analogy of a target, where the target as a whole represents the globally diversified portfolio and the impact that it can achieve. As can be seen in Figure 3.2, achieving impact at a local level is at the center of the target (the bull's-eye). Investors seeking to achieve impact at this level would look for investments in local projects that enhance the quality of life of a particular locality and community. Projects at this level can include, for instance, the creation of more jobs and affordable housing near transit and can be achieved through investments in local financial institutions or bonds that specifically target these projects. The specific amount that gets allocated to these projects would be up to the investor and would depend on their overall investment policy statement, including their appetite for risk and general objectives. Building affordable housing near transit can help address economic displacement of low-income communities that have historically been pushed to the outskirts of big cities due to unaffordable rents, yet they still have to commute to urban centers where they are employed. Often, public transit is either unavailable or not available enough for them to reach their jobs, and they face additional challenges in their daily commute.

Larger infrastructure investments, such as water and sanitation, would fall under the scope of regional impact. These investments are also usually financed through fixed income instruments, and can also generate jobs, thus

Inside Circle:	Local	X%
Middle Circle:	Regional	Y%
Outer Circle:	Global	Z%

FIGURE 3.2   A Targeted Approach to Place-Based Impact Investing. *Source:* Author.

having a positive impact on the community. They are also more long-term in nature, requiring the monitoring and involvement of institutions not only at a local, but also at a regional level, which implies meeting the needs and demands of additional stakeholders.

The largest, all-encompassing circle of the target in Figure 3.2 represents the global portfolio and its global impact. Investments at this level entail impacts with a global scope, such as investing across multiple countries, and choosing investments that support a cleaner global economy and work toward slowing climate change. Achieving global impact encompasses achieving regional and local impact, and this targeted approach allows for more specific and measurable PBII strategies.

As can be seen in Figure 3.2, at the center of the target is its local focus, which may begin with a small portion, named "X%," of the entire portfolio, depending on the size of the *place* and the investors' investment criteria and mission. An investor seeking local impact could seek an investment in a local project, use local financial institutions or public bonds, and monitor the impact on the location, whether city or county or metro area.

Large, regional infrastructure investments could represent "Y%" of the portfolio (e.g. like water and sanitation, such as sewer and water treatment) and could impact a larger region. The remainder of the portfolio, "Z%," represents globally impactful investments, which could have both a local and a regional impact, but its intention could be to impact the entire planet (e.g. with clean air technologies or water and ocean measures through investment).

Tracking impact on each investment in the total portfolio would result in a 100% intentionally impactful portfolio, though only a portion may focus on a particular *place* in order to achieve additional focused impact. And therein lies the PBII challenge — how to build strong, diversified portfolios across as many asset classes as possible, while simultaneously providing a positive social and environmental impact to the designated *place*.

The following two figures can be used to better illustrate what the investment and asset allocation process could look like for a place-based investor (PBI). Figure 3.3 shows a simplified, equal-weighted portfolio across six commonly used asset classes. As shown in Figure 3.4, institutional investors can use the earlier mentioned bull's-eye analogy to target their desired impact across all six asset classes. Every asset class has the potential to achieve impact at a local, regional, and global level, and portfolio managers can adjust the percentage of funds allocated to each asset class according to the portfolio's objectives, risk and return characteristics, and desired impact.

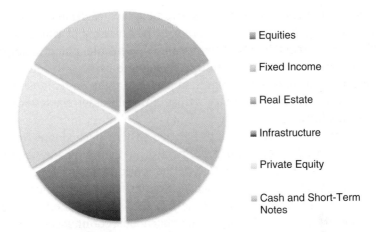

FIGURE 3.3 Simplified Asset Allocation. *Source:* Author.

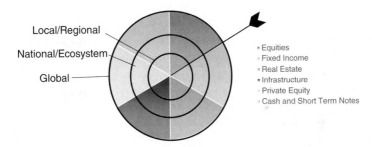

FIGURE 3.4 Asset Allocation and Impact Target. *Source:* Author.

Aligning Place-Based Impact Investing with the United Nations Sustainable Development Goals

The bull's-eye and geographical lens approach to PBII can also work in alignment with the 17 United Nations Sustainable Development Goals (UN SDGs). These goals aim to promote and advance sustainability and equity globally; however, their implementation can include a focus on a local or regional level, and their outcomes can be achieved through PBII.

The structure of the SDGs provides metrics to measure progress toward reaching these overall goals (Sustainable Development Knowledge Platform 2015). Institutional portfolio managers would be responsible for determining the best financial instrument or combination of investment tools for achieving a desired impact in alignment with a specific SDG or group of SDGs, and they would need to provide evidence of that impact.

To facilitate the alignment of UN SDGs to place-based and other impact investing strategies, SDGs can be grouped in a variety of ways, including according to the triple bottom line categories of people, planet, and profits. Each SDG can also be viewed through a geographical lens in connection to the specific geographical area where impact is sought. In its most complex form, investments can take place across multiple asset classes in several different locations.

As shown in Figures 3.5 and 3.6, two SDGs, SDG 11 for Affordable Housing and SDG 7 for Clean Energy, are pursued by investors. In this case, the example refers to the TONIIC network of impact investors, with investments made across cash, fixed income, private equity, public equity, and real assets (TONIIC 2019). These UN SDGs and related investments occur in specific places — locally in neighborhoods, communities, and cities. Many investors and beneficiaries of institutional investor portfolios might not be aware of the impact of their portfolios locally, at a higher level of

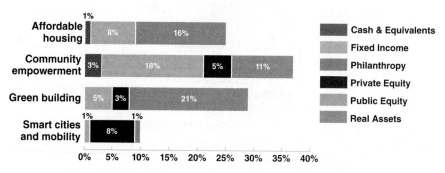

FIGURE 3.5   SDG 11: How SDGs Can Be Mapped to Investments Across Asset Classes and Possible Places: T100 SDG11 Investments. *Source:* TONIIC (2019).

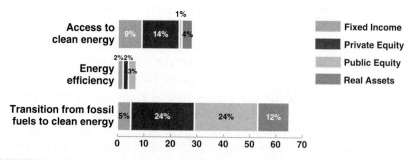

FIGURE 3.6   SDG 7: How SDGs Can Be Mapped to Investments: T100 SDG7 Investments by Asset Class. *Source:* TONIIC (2019).

geographical disaggregation. Providing them with this sort of impact metrics and linkages to global goals such as SDGs is one more step toward their engagement and evidence-based practice of Impact Investing.

CONSTRUCTING INSTITUTIONAL PLACE-BASED IMPACT INVESTING PORTFOLIOS

This section describes how institutional investors can incorporate intentional place-based impact goals within their globally diversified portfolios by choosing local or regional investment tools and intermediaries. It starts with describing the common challenges that institutional investors encounter when applying a PBII strategy, and it addresses how these challenges can be overcome through asset allocation and diversification of risks, combined with a consideration of ESG factors and a focus on achieving impact through a geographical lens.

The Institutional Investor Portfolio

A commitment to fiduciary duty and the requirement for proper due diligence and analysis in building portfolios have prevented the development of many local investment pools that can scale to include large allocations of institutional assets. Large investment pools typically hire fund managers who build global portfolios. The local portfolios that some investors (like community foundations) may develop are limited in size and scope and are generally not open to other investors, such as those who may also have a place-based alignment like local pension plans, endowments, or foundations. Community foundations that have initiated new and exploratory impact funds suggest they avoid outside investors because of a desire to gain experience before scaling, a fear that additional funds would not be effectively deployed, or that they could risk loss of control, or mission drift.

Asset allocation is the common starting point for constructing institutional quality investment portfolios. Diversification across asset classes, including geographic diversification, is considered a primary way to reduce portfolio risk, according to MPT. Investors now understand that multiple systemic risks to financial markets include climate change, social imbalances, and environmental degradation (Grippa et al. 2019). Consequently, investors can integrate ESG factors into portfolio investment choices when seeking long-term sustainability criteria to address such systemic risks, which is examined in the model below.

Aligning Investments with Place: Identifying the Geographic Area for Intentional Impact

Making capital available to a community creates a wide range of positive impacts and benefits, such as more affordable housing, supportive housing opportunities, childcare centers, and senior facilities. Institutional investors may have a geographic focus, either for their beneficiaries or their grants. Examples include the San Mateo County Employees Retirement Association in California, whose employees and retirees live in and around the San Francisco Bay Area,[1] and the Silicon Valley Community Foundation, the largest community foundation in the world by asset size, serving the communities and nonprofits of the Silicon Valley in the San Francisco Bay Area, funded by the philanthropy and donations of local investors, including those who have grown and sold high-growth technology ventures. However, it is quite uncommon for mission-driven, philanthropic, or public funds to invest their assets with an intentional preference to any single particular *place*, even including the locality in which it is based, despite the fact that the sources of the fund's assets could be coming from local citizens like teachers, firefighters, police, and local workers in a particular city, state, or region. One of the ways to make PBII more palpable to investors and fiduciaries entails engaging them with the idea that the assets in their portfolios can increase their community's or region's overall prosperity and well-being through the investment in local communities. For example, a pension plan's investments in local housing and transit development could provide ancillary benefits to its beneficiaries alongside their retirement checks, and a local community foundation could offer its donors local, investable strategies that support the local grant-making of community philanthropists.

Identifying the geographic area for intentional impact can be customized to the missions of the collaborating investors, the type of investments, and their intended reach. Some local leaders in the United States are innovating and sharing their insights on how to do so. For example, the Healthcare Anchor Network published a toolkit for health care institutions to act as anchor institutions via PBII (Zuckerman and Parker 2017). Along with this "How-to toolkit," the report included a summary of several programs across the United States, where a hospital system became an anchor — the dominant presence in the community and the catalyst for positive impacts from investing in local communities. For example, Trinity Health in the Detroit,

---

[1] For the purpose of this chapter, the author uses the terms San Francisco Bay Area and Bay Area interchangeably.

Michigan, area, and Bon Secours Health System in the Baltimore, Maryland, area, both offered low-interest-rate loans to nonprofit organizations in their regions through community investment intermediaries.

Longer-term assets in a portfolio can also engage in collaborative Impact Investing through real estate, infrastructure, and private equity investments in the community. This same report found that ethnic- and female-owned businesses increased their access to small business loans and that new, well-paying jobs were developed within new and existing businesses. Communities with access to additional capital saw improved access to transit, new cultural or artistic growth, new economic development, and renewable energy efficiency through collaborative PBII (Zuckerman and Parker 2017).

Many communities across the United Sates have developed some form of long-term plans. In the case of the San Francisco Bay Area, there are several plans to address improving transit, building housing, developing jobs, and adapting to sea level rise. These plans all require large amounts of funding, but unfortunately, they are neither analyzed nor packaged in forms that place-based investors can easily and confidently utilize within an investment portfolio. Identifying and gathering the various types of capital for each individual project separately has been the norm. As this chapter suggests through the following examples, financial collaboration across asset classes and among several projects within a *place* can result in more efficient and sizable investments across projects, but there is rarely local collaboration of this kind.

A San Francisco Bay Area Example: The Bay Area Model Equity Strategy

In 2012, the Bay Area Impact Investing Initiative (BAIII)[2] was launched to develop a blueprint for a collaborative effort to focus on positive social and environmental impact in the Bay Area while achieving competitive financial returns. The mission of the BAIII is to increase the quantity and effectiveness of impact investing in the Bay Area.

To understand the purpose of local impact investing, research was the driving force to build model portfolios that could have both a positive impact in the Bay Area and conform to the fiduciary standard for institutional assets to prioritize returns under prudent investment practices. It was clear that US-based institutional investors, including those in the Bay Area, were

---

[2]More details, including place-based investing examples and reports, at http://www.baiii .org.

unwilling to believe, without research and proof of concept, that having place-based impact goals does not compromise returns. By applying all asset classes to build model portfolios, the BAIII adopted broadly defined impact goals of long-term sustainability, shared prosperity, and resilience across the Bay Area.

The Bay Area Model Equity Strategy

The Bay Area Model Equity Strategy (BAMES) was developed for the United Way of the Bay Area[3] — a San Francisco Bay Area nonprofit — in order to align its endowment assets with a mission of reducing poverty in the Bay Area. Because having a good job is one of the best ways to escape poverty, the strategy developed a universe of the largest publicly held employers in the region. This strategy was designed to be overweighted in Bay Area headquartered companies, potentially providing an oversized voice for indirect impact through corporate engagement and proxy voting, as well as for engagement on employment issues, environmental practices and disclosures, and governance criteria.

BAMES was built to match the market's risk and return profile while overweighting Bay Area publicly traded companies. It is screened for ESG criteria so that higher ESG rated local companies are overweighted in the portfolio and lower ESG rated companies are underweighted. The portfolio is optimized to the market benchmark (Russell 3000, see Tables 3.1 and 3.2) so that all the industry sector weightings match the market, thereby minimizing tracking error (Agnew 2012).

The Bay Area has a robust and diversified economy, where about 19% of the S&P 500 companies are headquartered. This Bay Area–centric portfolio is nearly four times overweighted in companies headquartered in this Northern California region, at 75%. This portfolio keeps the industry sector weights neutral to the market through a portfolio optimization program. The overall portfolio's ESG score improves by over 30% from a rating of 45 upwards to 60 on a scale of 100. For the time period of January 1, 2011, to December 31, 2019, the total annualized out-performance of financial return is an annualized 206 basis points (or a full 2.06%) ahead of the broad market with only a 20 basis point (0.20%) increase in standard deviation (risk), since the portfolio's inception in 2011, and a tracking error of about 2%, which is within a range of tracking error that can be acceptable for institutional investors (up to 5%).

---

[3]More details at http://www.baiii.org.

TABLE 3.1 Bay Area Model Equity Strategy Performance Results, 2011 to 2019.

Year	Russell 3000	BAMES
2011	1.01%	1.56%
2012	16.37%	20.95%
2013	33.46%	33.38%
2014	12.54%	16.29%
2015	0.47%	0.82%
2016	12.64%	13.99%
2017	21.07%	27.43%
2018	−5.20%	−3.67%
2019	31.00%	31.45%
Cumulative Return	200.40%	253.34%
Annualized Return	13.00%	15.05%
Standard Deviation	12.63%	12.82%
% Bay Area Location HQ	19%	75%
Custom ESG Score	45 of 100	60 of 100

Source: Aperio Group (2020).

TABLE 3.2 Bay Area Model Equity Strategy Performance Results, including Q1-2020.

Year	Russell 3000	BAMES
2020 YTD 3/31	−20.88%	−17.66%
Cumulative Return	137.66%	190.93%
Annualized Return	9.81%	12.24%
Standard Deviation	13.50%	13.45%

Source: Aperio Group (2020).

The sharp downturn in the markets in the first quarter of 2020 due to the COVID-19 pandemic was reflected in the BAMES, but to a lesser degree than the broad market. While this one quarter of dramatic decline due to the pandemic reduced the long-term performance results, the ESG focused Bay Area portfolio continued to outperform its benchmark by an annualized 243 basis points (2.43% per year), and with less risk (standard deviation of 5 basis points lower) during that quarter's dramatic down market — essentially a more resilient portfolio.

To understand which factors contributed to BAMES outperforming the market, MPT and quantitative financial tools can provide an analysis of a portfolio's performance record to determine which characteristics (attributes) contributed to the relative performance differences from the broad market benchmark against which it is measured. Active strategies are expected to show differences in certain factors and styles, for example, by emphasizing factors like style (growth or value) or size (small-cap versus large-cap). Other factors like industry sector weightings, asset allocation, market timing, or trading and transaction cost differences can be explained by this analysis. These "tilts" can add or subtract from performance and

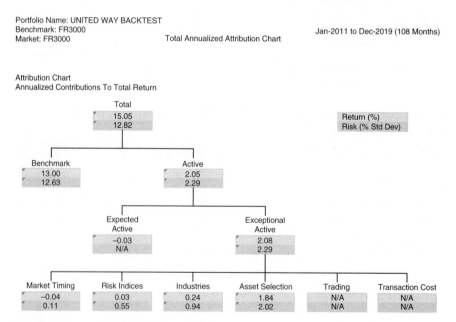

Portfolio Name: UNITED WAY BACKTEST
Benchmark: FR3000
Market: FR3000   Total Annualized Attribution Chart   Jan-2011 to Dec-2019 (108 Months)

Attribution Chart
Annualized Contributions To Total Return

Total
15.05
12.82

Return (%)
Risk (% Std Dev)

Benchmark	Active
13.00	2.05
12.63	2.29

Expected Active	Exceptional Active
−0.03	2.08
N/A	2.29

Market Timing	Risk Indices	Industries	Asset Selection	Trading	Transaction Cost
−0.04	0.03	0.24	1.84	N/A	N/A
0.11	0.55	0.94	2.02	N/A	N/A

FIGURE 3.7   Bay Area Model Equity Strategy, Performance Attribution. *Source:* Aperio Group (2020).

can be calculated by regression analysis against the benchmark. Security selection, also called Asset Selection, is one factor that remains if all the other factors are optimized or designed to match the market's exposure to those factors. The attribution report in Figure 3.7 indicates that this overweighting to the Bay Area geographically and amplifying high ESG-rated firms while reducing weights of low ESG-rated firms produced outperformance based on the attribute of stock selection. This approach can add portfolio value over time in both up and down markets. In financial terms, the "information ratio" is positive from this strategy. Figure 3.7 provides a performance attribution report for the period January 1, 2011, to December 31, 2019 (108 months), showing the attribution to stock selection as the major driver of out-performance.[4]

THE US COMMUNITY INVESTING INDEX, BY THE F. B. HERON FOUNDATION

The F. B. Heron Foundation has pioneered many elements of Impact Investing for several decades. Heron Foundation was one of the first to set its investment policy of the corpus to focus on pursuing impact across all asset classes. Heron has also been an early institutional investor focusing on PBII.

To encourage more attention toward the public equity asset class, and how it connects to the Heron mission of people and communities addressing and eliminating poverty, the Heron team created a US equity index of publicly traded stocks, working with index providers.

Heron tracks and measures four types of capital categories: human capital,[5] financial capital, civic capital, and natural capital. The US Community Investing Index, which has a Bloomberg ticker of CMTYIDX, overweights allocations to companies that advance communities and reduce poverty. Health care and technology companies are two of the larger sectors in this unique index.

As seen in Figure 3.8, this community index shows again how public equities can systematically be part of a PBII portfolio. The chart shows the financial returns outperformance of the index, relative to the S&P 500 benchmark, in multiple time periods, including the COVID-19 crisis in Q1-2020, as well as one-year, three-year, and five-year periods ending March 31, 2020. The index was initiated in October 31, 2005.

---

[4]Past performance is not a predictor of future results.
[5]For more on how to measure, value, and invest in human capital, see Chapter 4, "How to Invest in Human Capital," by R. Paul Herman and Kirstin Dougall.

FIGURE 3.8 The US Community Investing Index, F. B. Heron Foundation. Bloomberg price returns (not adjusted for dividends). Returns greater than one year are annualized.

Building Place-Based Impact Investing Portfolios

By combining the aspects of asset allocation, diversification, impact, and *place*, investors can compare traditional investing objectives and tools with those that align with a PBII objective, as shown in Table 3.3. PBII strategies include the same investing goals and objectives that traditional investment strategies have but with an intentional focus on *place* for impact. Table 3.3 summarizes the concepts by asset class as discussed in this chapter.

Investors can build their own custom portfolios by allocating to any combination of the six asset classes. As discussed above, these could be structured as multi-manager funds using qualified institutional investment managers as specialists in their various strategies and monitored by those investment teams, saving investors' time and resources needed to build these complex impact place-based portfolios. Investors with retirement savings accounts could also be offered these opportunities and choose some of these place-focused funds for their retirement assets. Pension plans, endowments and foundations, and donor-advised funds (DAFs) at community foundations could choose to invest some of their portfolios for local impact, aligning with their grants and missions.

Alternatively, a PBII team could develop a few standard blended portfolios, similar to some existing choices for DAFs: conservative, moderate, or aggressive in their risk and return profiles. Another alternative could create a mix of all the categories offering a simple, stable total return of 5% to 7% annually. Other enhancements to a security like this could include a guaranteed return upon delivery of impact, such as a social impact bond backed by a governmental authority. Terms like perpetual life (which could be attractive to DAFs), opportunity zone tax benefits for taxable investors, or some inheritance tax forgiveness could be included as incentives as well, for example.

TABLE 3.3 Comparing Traditional and Place-Based Portfolios.

	Investment Objectives		Asset Class	Sample Allocation	Financial Instruments/Projects	
	Traditional	Place-Based			Traditional	Place-Based
Growth	Influence corporate behaviors and employee conditions		Equities	50%	Public stocks, domestic and global	Overweight local companies
Income	Provide liquidity and scale to support corporate and municipal investments		Fixed Income	15%	Treasuries, global corporate, domestic corporate, muni bonds	Muni bonds, Green bonds, Social impact bonds
Real Returns	Promote sustainable real estate development and create jobs		Real Estate	10%	REITs, real estate development projects not specifically targeted toward well-being of all members of a community	Sustainable REITs, affordable housing projects, local and regional housing bonds and projects

TABLE 3.3 (*continued*)

| Investment Objectives | | Asset Class | Sample Allocation | Financial Instruments/Projects | |
Traditional	Place-Based			Traditional	Place-Based
Real Returns	Build long-term assets in water, transit, energy, housing, schools, and more	Infrastructure: including Forestry, Farmland, Water, Energy, Transit	5%	Bonds tied to specific projects, no specific focus on development of local communities	Bonds tied to specific projects, or public-private partnerships (PPP) for longer-term regional transit, housing, and community development solutions
Growth	Create and scale companies, jobs, and sustainable development	Private Equity, including Venture Capital	15%	Traditional venture capital funds	Innovation hubs, incubators, crowd-funding, and other alliances for investors, funding opportunities for social entrepreneurs
Liquidity	Provide financing and lending for local small-businesses and nonprofits	Cash and Short-Term Notes	5%	Money market instruments, funds, short-term notes	Community banking and loans, program-related investments (PRIs), community development financial institutions (CDFIs)

Source: Author.

80

Creating funds and securities is an expensive operation, legally speaking. Consequently, to develop a family of funds, and expect to break even, mutual funds need to have about USD $25 million in assets. Gathering commitments that total over USD $100 million to invest in the different categories of assets could achieve critical mass. Over time, as assets grow, fees and expenses could decline as a percentage of assets, and impact can grow. There may be a time when these PBII portfolios could be catalytic in the financing structures of community and regional projects.

CREATING INVESTABLE OPPORTUNITIES FOR SUSTAINABLE AND RESILIENT COMMUNITIES THROUGH INCLUSIVE COMMUNITY ENGAGEMENT

Local or regional PBII funds generally do not exist yet. However, they can indeed be built to attract and scale with just a small portion of each of the region's asset pools. Collaboration amongst various investors can compound impact through size and focus. One important form of collaboration is community engagement. Community involvement in identifying the unique set of solutions each community requires will result in a more effective and impactful portfolio, described below.

Community urban redevelopment does not happen overnight. It requires a commitment to the long-term nature of community change. Fixing one building in a crumbling urban neighborhood will do little to improve the conditions of those who live there unless there is a concerted effort to address the foundational issues of the community as well. In sectors like these, positive outcomes, like improved job creation, reduced crime, or increased graduation rates, can take 10 to 15 years to manifest.

By developing a strategy and sticking to it and by tracking a variety of metrics alongside financials, these redevelopments can tell a story of success. The first and most important step toward successful urban redevelopment begins with gathering input both from residents and from experts through holding community meetings for strategy development. Just changing one piece of the urban puzzle without considering the interrelatedness of it with the other issues in that community is inefficient and shortsighted. Housing, education, transit, employment, sustainability, and inclusive policies should be strategically considered together and be cohesively integrated into one long-term, strategic urban development plan.

Designing a Resilient Community in North Richmond, California

A good example of community engagement and successful plan development comes from North Richmond, California. For this community on the north-central area of the San Francisco Bay, the major focus was to address and mitigate the community's risks and consequences of sea level rise. The goal was to develop a proposal to reinvent the North Richmond community, allowing it to be a model for a vulnerable community becoming more resilient, inclusive, and sustainable for the future.

Their plan is called "ouR HOME"[6] (the capitalized R is to show the significance of the common letter in the five major resilience strategies: "thRive, filteR, gRow, Relate, gReen"), which focuses on adding sustainable and affordable transit-oriented housing, bike lanes and transportation access, and new business development. The plan also includes an extensive redesign of the shoreline parks, walkways, and drainages, with new floating pathways, flood management options, and water treatment facilities. Designing the long-term plan for Richmond is the first, critical step in the long process of redeveloping their community.

The chosen strategy for community engagement was the gathering of a broad representation of constituents and experts to assess the needs, risks, and potential solutions to reimagining North Richmond. Some of these individuals were from the North Richmond Community Advisory Board, consisting of mayor's office representatives, North Richmond residents, local commissions, regional committees, project or program facilitators, and general council members. These public sector stakeholders were offered a seat at the discussion table because their work impacted the North Richmond community in some key, unique way. Local corporations and large employers were at the table as well. Chevron, headquartered in Richmond, played a key part, along with the Richmond Community Foundation and a local community bank, in the development of the social impact bond for their housing restoration model, where funds were provided to repair blighted homes and resale them to first-time homebuyers in Richmond.

After many community engagement meetings and a process to capture input from the entire community, a grand plan was developed that included affordable and market rate housing, new businesses, industrial and green spaces, as well as a new waterfront park designed to mitigate the flooding

---

[6]More details at www.resilientbayarea.org. The plan is available at https://drive.google.com/file/d/1AkDL6T3rzts-GkYHsL42tQ5EbG2NWG05/view.

risks of sea level rise. The plan was very detailed with many working, suggested components, which provided the simplified examples below. Housing developments included new multi-family, affordable housing options along with various residential layouts. A myriad of small businesses are outlined in the plan, from technology stores, to storage yards, to bakeries. As North Richmond is an industrial-focused area, a great deal of planning was allocated to the construction of warehouses, commercial sites, production facilities, and water-treatment plants. And lastly, with a focus on mitigating the risks of climate change and harm upon the environment, several urban farms, agricultural sites, greenhouses, and recycling facilities were planned. A key element in this grand plan is restoration projects for the wetlands, native species, and wildlife of the area. Innovative sea level adaptation infrastructure was included in the plan as well, such as floating walkways and wetlands, to bird nesting islands and observation platforms.

Various community and environmental design tools can be used to achieve related benefits, as seen in this North Richmond example. Air quality parks, tree nodes, trail connections, and greenbelts can be established to improve natural areas and allow for environmental protection of open spaces. In terms of mitigating sea level rise, horizontal levees, muted marshes, and water conservation or collection systems can be constructed to preserve the coasts and areas affected by tides. Additionally, as many at-risk communities such as North Richmond face difficulties with housing availability and affordability, building small lot housing and community choice housing can increase ownership and options for citizens. New businesses and jobs, expected to arise from increased community spaces and resilience hubs, can enable communities to prosper economically as well.

In redeveloping complex projects like the North Richmond ouR-HOME design, each individual project would traditionally have its own financial funding sources to create an efficient "stack" of capital from multiple asset classes. Housing developers could seek funds from impact investors and public agency funding. Green space infrastructure funders could be funded by public entities or philanthropic organizations. Private and public sources of grant monies, risk capital, and long-term lending could all combine to create the complex capital stacks needed for each of these community projects. The financial planning process must also assess the timing of various investment flows and projects, since some infrastructure and predevelopment costs must be covered before revenue-generating assets can be completed.

Developing Investable Opportunities in a Community

The following examples of potential community projects and their unique capital stacks emulate the ideas from the North Richmond plan, but are simplified to illustrate how community design can be turned into investable opportunities for investors who choose to allocate their assets to *place*. Each piece of the community plan represents a different investment structure that has its traditional funding mechanisms well documented and understood. Each of the figures below represents a different capital stack for each piece (housing, new business development, urban farming, green infrastructure) of the community redevelopment project puzzle.

Affordable housing is generally funded through the US Department of Housing and Urban Development (HUD) bonds with the "equity gap" coming from philanthropy, public grants, and risk-taking equity. The tall building in Figure 3.9 represents mixed and affordable housing, with retail space on the bottom floor. On the right hand-side one can identify the capital stacks that could be used, which could include grants, bonds, business loans from community banks, and private equity.

The rooftop of Figure 3.10 represents a solar infrastructure on a school, financed using long-term bonds and public-private partnerships (PPP). Energy improvements at schools could be financed by PPPs and infrastructure bonds from public entities, ultimately paid for by members of the community through their taxes and fees. Grants and community bank loans can assist in the financing structure as well.

Urban farming (Figure 3.11) can be funded through grants, as well as risk capital and loans, and could be counted as a real estate asset in

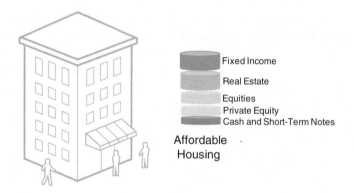

FIGURE 3.9   Affordable Housing Project Capital Stack. *Source:* Author.

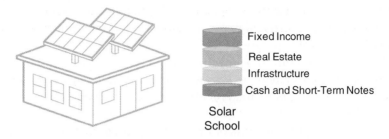

Fixed Income
Real Estate
Infrastructure
Cash and Short-Term Notes

Solar
School

FIGURE 3.10   School Remodeling Project Capital Stack. *Source:* Author.

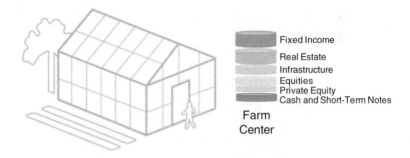

Fixed Income
Real Estate
Infrastructure
Equities
Private Equity
Cash and Short-Term Notes

Farm
Center

FIGURE 3.11   Urban Farming Project Capital Stack. *Source:* Author.

the portfolio. This greenhouse-looking building could serve as a community center and garden, as well as an indoor farm, using community capital, grants, and opportunity zone funds. New businesses can be financed by small business loans from community banks, as well as venture capital and angel investors, providing new jobs to the community.

The building in Figure 3.12 could be a "Center for Impact and Innovation," home to new businesses, venture capital incubators, and nonprofit

Real Estate
Infrastructure
Private Equity
Cash and Short-Term Notes
Equities

New Business
Hub

FIGURE 3.12   New Business Hub Capital Stack. *Source:* Author.

organizations. This Center's capital stack may include venture capital, opportunity zone funds, real estate investors, community funds, and public grants for job-training programs.

Green infrastructure and other large projects (e.g. transit hubs, watershed or eco-system management, or sea level rise environmental adaptation) may be funded through public infrastructure and resilience bonds, and landscape stewardship grants.

By combining various sorts of investable funds, each project will have a unique, complex capital stack, as shown in Figure 3.13, including risk capital or grants for early stage catalytic investments to the long-term funding through infrastructure or housing bonds. Investors can access different risk and return profiles within a capital stack and participate in the funding of local investments with impact.

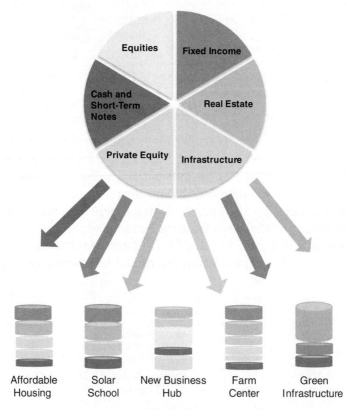

FIGURE 3.13   Portfolio-to-Projects Flow Chart. *Source:* Author.

Connecting Investment Portfolios to the Investable Projects: A Center for Place-Based Impact Investing

Connecting a local and regional asset allocation strategy to the capital stacks of various sustainable, local, and regional investment opportunities can be accomplished via a collaborative "Center for Place-Based Impact Investing." Facilitating the flow of funds into actionable, local impact investments could be the Center's purpose, along with the investors, in potential place-based funds managed by the Center or its appointees. The PBII facilitators at the Center could assess the various strategies used in each asset class, as well as track the impact for each manager, portfolio, and project. A Center for Place-Based Impact Investing could also perform the due diligence and monitoring processes. Therein, institutional funds of fiduciary assets can choose to invest in broad-based asset class portfolios that are designed to meet the highest-quality standards and seek a local impact (Figure 3.13).

A Regional Center for PBII can invest a small portion from any single regional investment pool into asset class-based collective funds, designed like mutual funds in some cases, and manage those funds for local impact and market-rate returns. Each fund is diversified in the asset class by including a variety of strategies and addressing different parts of each market. These various funds would be managed in accordance with fiduciary duty standards and can be invested with retirement (like super-annuation or 401(k)s)[7] and pension assets (Agnew 2016).

Impact can then be measured and tracked, while returns can be market-like for each asset class. Risk is not necessarily increased when held to the same standards as all other investments in a portfolio. Professional investment managers and/or independent expert evaluations (for external independent assessments) can be tasked with seeking local impact and making market-like returns.[8]

Additionally, in order to scale the number of assets that can be invested in a locality *(place)*, investors require confidence that fiduciary standards are met without sacrificing expected returns or accepting more risks. This framework is described below, with descriptions of each asset class strategy

---

[7]See Chapter 11, "Investing for Impact in Retirement Plans," by Megan Morrice.

[8]See Chapter 16, "Measuring and Evaluating Social Impact in Impact Investing: An Overview of the Available Standards and Methods," by Ana Pimenta and Elsa de Morais Sarmento, and Chapter 17, "Impact Measurement and Management Techniques to Achieve Powerful Results," by Jane Reisman and Veronica Olazabal.

for place-based impact. The sample portfolios provide examples across the San Francisco Bay Area, in the major asset classes used by investors. Similar examples can be developed for other locales.

Capital Stacks: Financing Local and Regional Projects

As explained above, every local or regional project can be financed by various financial instruments, each belonging to a particular asset class. An overview of how each asset class can be used, either alone or as part of a capital stack mix of asset classes, is given below.

Equities

In building a comprehensive public equity strategy for impact in the Bay Area, investments in public equity could be modeled following the example of the previously described BAMES. This portfolio expects strong attention to ESG criteria, long-term wealth creation for shareholders, and a positive impact on the Bay Area through shareholder activism and engagement on local issues.

- The equities allocation could be structured as a multi-manager portfolio to include both active and passive ESG integrated equity strategies; the BAMES approach could fit an "enhanced index" strategy to achieve market levels of expected return and risk.
- The equities can be very liquid and can be very volatile, but over the long term, public equities are an important contributor to growth of an overall portfolio.
- The fiduciaries of retirement funds could ensure that high standards for return per unit of risk, as well as impact on the local region, are pursued.
- Engaging the locally based corporations in an equity portfolio can realize both local, regional, and global impact.
- Impact criteria and metrics can include ESG performance, processes, and policies that benefit the locality.
- This asset class can relate to many SDGs, including:
  - SDG 8: Decent Work and Economic Growth, via metrics on pay level and equal pay for women
  - SDG 12: Responsible Consumption and Production, including "farm to table" food systems
  - SDG 13: Climate Action, with increased resilience of natural ecosystems

Fixed Income

Fixed income allocations can create positive impact through bonds funding the community. Providing liquidity to investable projects is a proven strategy for pursuing higher impact, and there are many types: small business loans, corporate bonds, municipal and government bonds, green bonds, and infrastructure bonds. Additional categories that focus on place-based financing opportunities could include direct lending, deposits at community banks and loan funds, local bond issuances, and middle market corporate loans. A portfolio implemented through vetted investment professional firms to provide both an overall market rate of return like its benchmark, the Barclays Aggregate Index (also known as the AGG), and evidence of the impact, output, and outcomes from that financing. Fixed income investments focused on place could have the following components:

- Highly rated on ESG and impact, such as school districts, community colleges, affordable housing, health and wellness centers, hospitals, and public transit
- Regional bonds to connect cities, counties, and provinces together
- Local community banks and credit unions, to spur more direct lending and community investing
- This asset class of fixed income can support impact related to these SDGs:
  - SDG 4: Quality Education, for building science and technology skills
  - SDG 6: Clean Water and Sanitation, including remediating pollution
  - SDG 9: Industry, Innovation, and Infrastructure, for longer-term research and development
  - SDG 11: Sustainable Cities and Communities, funding local governments
  - SDG 17: Partnerships for the Goals, as places are home to organizations across multiple sectors who need to work together

Real Estate

A place-based diversified real estate allocation could include some liquid options, like publicly traded sustainable real estate investment trusts (REITs), as well as property investments across the spectrum of residential homeownership, multi-family rental, commercial, industrial, retail, and affordable housing categories. The portfolio can include local and regional properties like medical, public, data center, renewable energy, and educational properties, and seek to invest in sustainable, regional solutions to housing disparity, affordability, and natural-resource shortages across the region. Examples of investment characteristics and criteria could include:

- Local and regional bonds, projects, and partnerships for affordable housing
- Attractive dividend yields from cash flows
- Impact metrics that promote net-zero energy and emissions for all building types, leasing of renewable energy infrastructure, and housing affordable for low- and middle-income families
- While real estate can be less liquid than public equities and fixed income, it offers long-term protection against inflation and helps diversify portfolios, especially those with a longer holding period.
- This real estate asset class can link to the following SDGs:
  - SDG 11: Sustainable Cities and Communities, linking the natural ecosystem with housing, schools, commercial, and industrial buildings
  - SDG 15: Life on Land, with sustainable buildings and homes
  - SDG 17: Partnerships for the Goals, to pursue environmental and social impacts

Infrastructure

Infrastructure allocations and investments could be bonds or private equity supporting specific longer-term projects, or public-private partnerships for longer-term regional transit, housing, and community development solutions. Green infrastructure projects to protect and maintain our public lands, including rivers and seashores, can be found in this asset class. Additional infrastructure opportunities include investments in clean and green energy sources and energy efficiency, Internet access, reducing congestion on the roads and highways, and reducing carbon footprints. Infrastructure investments can provide cash flow and an inflation hedge to investors and portfolios as well as move the regional economy forward in big ways toward the financing of sustainable cities, as a comprehensive report from the Urban Sustainability Directors Network, HIP Investor, and the City of Palo Alto summarized in 2016 (USDN 2016). This asset class of infrastructure could prioritize:

- Investments in renewable power, public transit, accessibility to families of all income levels, and greening projects

- Impact metrics can track the shift from fossil to renewable energy, the commutability and transit times and methods
- While highly illiquid due to multi-year projects, infrastructure can result in high local impact through job creation, funding for communities, and economic development for the long term
- Infrastructure opportunities could include cleaner energy for our homes, businesses, and cars; better transit options; affordable housing near transit; education and job training tied to job creation and job development in the region
- Adjusting to the risks of climate change and sea level rise can include cleaner water solutions and landscape resilience
- This infrastructure asset class clearly links to SDGs:
  - SDG 6: Clean Water and Sanitation, ensuring wastewater does not flow into natural lakes, rivers, and bays
  - SDG 7: Affordable and Clean Energy, supporting solar, wind, geothermal, and other renewable energies
  - SDG 9: Industry, Innovation, and Infrastructure, enhancing the modes of mobility to include electrified vehicles and group commuting
  - SDG 11: Sustainable Cities and Communities, prioritizing citizen benefits
  - SDG 17: Partnerships for the Goals, creating multi-sector financial vehicles

Private Equity, Including Venture Capital

The investment spectrum in private equity and venture capital allocations can include high-risk, high-reward investing, combined with innovation hubs, incubators, crowd-funding, and other alliances for investors. This can result in more funding opportunities for social entrepreneurs, launching a locally focused stock exchange, and networking among capital providers and capital seekers. This private equity and venture capital asset class can:

- Focus on triple-bottom-line (i.e. people, planet, profit) jobs in low-to-moderate income areas as well as green technologies in energy and water management
- Fund impact-oriented startups focused on their missions

- Can include limited liability partnerships and accommodate a multi-manager approach
- Create "runway" to support longer-term investment timeframe of 10 years
- Metrics to track impacts that include patents created and licensed, "green jobs" with "green-job-related incomes," and environmental improvements
- This asset class can link to SDGs:
  - SDG 8: Decent Work and Economic Growth, showing up in higher-paying jobs with more career potential
  - SDG 9: Industry Innovation and Infrastructure, encompassing more skilled talent and more resilient ecosystems

Cash and Short-Term Notes

Cash allocations and liquid short-term notes in a place-based impact portfolio could be invested in a diversified pool of notes with community development financial institutions (CDFIs), community banks, and credit unions. Members of the Global Alliance for Banking on Values (www.GABV.org) could be a fit. This asset class's risk-return profile resembles that of a "really good savings account for impact and risk-return" while providing an asset base to grow their impact. CDFIs create community impact by lending investors' deposits to small businesses and nonprofit organizations in the community — which they have been doing successfully for decades. This asset class can be an accessible impact choice for place-based impact investors:

- In combination with community banks, program-related investments (PRIs) from foundations can be supportive of impact.
- Can accelerate investments in qualified opportunity zones (QOZs) or similar tax-advantaged locations
- Metrics that track impact could be loans for nonprofits and small and medium enterprises.[9]
- This low-risk asset class can advance the following SDGSs:
  - SDG 1: No Poverty, with loans to ventures employing low-income families

---

[9]To invest in a mix of projects with varying risk, return, and impact profiles, see Chapter 2, "Investing for Impact: Socially Motivated Investors and Externalities," by Raghavan Narayanan and Stoyan Tenev.

- SDG 3: Good Health and Well-Being, to fund revenue-generating or expense saving health care practices
- SDG 10: Reduced Inequalities, can be directed to a diverse mix of communities locally

Table 3.4 could serve as a mapping tool on how different asset classes can be adapted to address certain themes in a particular impact area, such as climate change or building water and transit infrastructure, and it also suggests which strategy, as well as specific financial instruments (such as municipal bonds, infrastructure bonds, green bonds, green bank deposits) that investors can use to achieve outcomes aligned with PBII. Any region or locality can develop a similar table and choose the appropriate asset classes and financial instruments to achieve a desired impact.

Table 3.4 shows elements that could be part of a place-based locally focused portfolio. In the grid, the vertical columns represent each of the six major asset classes. Each asset class can provide impact related to social and environmental themes while being consistent to its asset class's risk and return profile.

Each column shows the variety of instruments and purposes the asset class provides. This factor plays a part in delivering a diversified portfolio within an asset class with a geographic focus and positive impact intentionality. Qualified investment managers with specific strategies could share in delivering both positive impact to the region and financial returns to the investors. Long-term strategic partnerships could result among these managers, community members, and investors.

GLOBAL EXAMPLES OF PLACE-BASED IMPACT INVESTING SUCCESS

Example 1: The State of Telangana, India

A recent case study approach by Ashok Kumbamu (Kumbamu 2017) documented the Center for Sustainable Agriculture (CSA) in Telangana in southern India, and described how a farming community built a strategy to provide stronger financial, social, and environmental conditions for farmers through collaborative education and investment of time and resources. This project improved the financial conditions of marginalized farmers in southern India.

TABLE 3.4 Examples of Impact Themes and Investable Opportunities for Bay Area Impact Investing Initiative.

Sustainability, Shared Prosperity, and Resilience	EQUITIES: Tilting Toward Local and Regional Companies	FIXED INCOME: Bonds and Lending	REAL ESTATE: Residential, Commercial, Industrial	INFRASTRUCTURE: Including Forestry, Farmland, Water, Energy, Transit	PRIVATE EQUITY: Including Venture Capital	CASH: including Short-Term Notes
Climate Change	Screens on portfolios; active corporate engagement	Local and regional green bonds	Sustainable buildings and communities	California Infrastructure Bank	DBL; PCV; Bay Area Council Equity Fund	Green Bank deposits
Transit	Tesla electric vehicles		Bay Meadows transit and housing	BART bonds, electrified vehicles		
Energy	Chevron, and renewable energy firms	Screened corporate. Muni bonds	Community Clean Energy; solar	Bay Area TOD	Clean energy ventures; Battery ventures	
Water		Santa Clara Water District bonds and projects		SF green water bonds	Water technology ventures	

Category						Bay Area Super CD; SME Lending
Community Development		Local CDFIs	NCCLF; PPP for Hunter's Point ReDev, Bay Meadows, and Stockbridge	California I-Bank; PPPs for Presidio SF, Treasure Island, Alameda	Verbhouse; HubSV	Bay Area Super CD; SME Lending
Health and Wellness	HIP Investor's Sustainable REITs ESG	Local housing bonds				
Sustainable Development		AFL-CIO Housing Investment Trust	Gerding Edlin	DBFOM		
Jobs, Education, and Job Training		White Oak direct lending	American Realty		Education tech ventures	

Source: Bay Area Impact Investing Initiative (2019) author.
Notes: Abbreviations in the table are explained as: SF (San Francisco), BA TOD (Bay Area Transit Oriented Development fund, including affordable housing), BART (Bay Area Rapid Transit system), HIP Investor (Human Impact + Profit) ESG (Sustainable Real Estate REITs strategy, www .HIPInvestor.com), AFL-CIO HIT (AFL-CIO Housing Investment Trust), DBFOM (Develop, Build, Finance, Operate, Maintain), NCCLF (Northern California Community Loan Fund, available at www.ncclf.org, CDFIs (Community Development Financial Institutions), CD (Certificate of Deposit), iforniaCommunity Loan Fund, available at www.ncclf.org, CDFIs (Community Development Financial Institutions), CD (Certificate of Deposit), PCV (Pacific Community Ventures), PPP (Public-Private Partnerships), DBL (DBL Partners), PCV (Pacific Community Ventures), PPP (Public-Private Partnerships). SME Lending (Small and Medium Enterprises), DBL (DBL Partners), PCV (Pacific Community Ventures), PPP (Public-Private Partnerships).

CSA, based in Hyderabad in the State of Telangana, was formerly a part of the Center for World Solidarity (CWS), a not-for-profit organization established in 1998 by multidisciplinary academics and community practitioners with an objective of enhancing livelihood opportunities for marginalized sections of Indian society. CSA separated from CWS, evolved as an independent professional resource organization, and registered as a Trust in 2004. CSA is a prominent alternative community development organization that has been working in south India for nearly two decades (starting with CWS in 1998) to build Sustainable Social and Solidarity Economies[10] (SSEs).

In 2010, CSA started organizing farmers in South India into agricultural producer groups to establish a community-based learning and sharing system. In addition to sharing best practices and developing networks for markets and other supply chain considerations, CSA created a community financial system to provide loans to small farmers through cooperatives for adopting organic farming methods, eventually helping farmers get access to traditional credit opportunities.

Over the first 10 years, CSA initiated an intensive community engagement initiative around its agro-ecological model for sustainable and pesticide-free farming. It was adopted by farmers in 11,000 villages and implemented over 3.6 million hectares in the states of Telangana, Andhra Pradesh, Maharashtra, and Punjab in South India. With the scaling-up of non-pesticide-management practices and community collaboration and education, pesticide use in project villages has decreased by over 50% over five years (from 2005–2006 to 2010–2011), reducing the cost of cultivation for many crops. Moreover, it not only made farming and food safer but also resulted in net savings of about INR 5000 (USD $78) to INR 13,000 (USD $204) per acre. In the project area, the number of cases of hospitalization because of pesticide poisoning also decreased. Farmer suicides, once too common, declined dramatically and in some villages to zero (Kumbamu 2017).

This project resulted in significant social, financial, and environmental benefits to the community (Kumbamu 2017). Like global microfinance, engaging to understand the dynamics of the people and community, and investing in the poorest of communities, can have demonstrated financial results and highly impactful community benefits over time.

---

[10]The organizing principles of the social economy are reciprocity and redistribution, rather than the profit and accumulation principles of a market-based economy.

Example 2: The City of Curitiba, Brazil

Curitiba has become known as one of the greenest cities in the world (Sustainable Development Knowledge Platform 2011). Curitiba's journey began in the 1960s when strong leadership and a team of urban planning architects addressed the interrelated problems of urban growth: sprawl, environmental degradation, and economic inequalities. Their solutions focused on comprehensive land use planning regarding transportation, infrastructure, and environmental sustainability (Gustafsson and Kelly 2012; Gray and Talberth 2011).

Financial incentives were tied to the programs for transportation by contracting private bus companies and compensating them for the services, distances, and upkeep of capital stock. The bus system is a financially self-sustaining program for the city, with very high usage by citizens throughout the community.

Collaborative and land use planning also created tremendous parks and green spaces. Using federal monies for parks, instead of dams, the city is able to control flooding, protect biodiversity and water quality, and limit carbon emissions. Creative zoning policies adopted by city planners protected approximately 20% of the city as parks, versus a US urban average of 8.1%.

The recycling and waste management systems are built on incentive programs and tied to social outreach. Eco-citizens are paid tokens for the trash they collect that are redeemable for food, transportation, and services in any of the city's 16 district servicing centers. The city then sells the salvage to recover costs.

These creative zoning policies enabled the density that created the demand for public transportation in the less environmentally sensitive areas. The policies that designated parkland for mitigating flooding improved the quality of life. The comprehensive recycling programs are tied to community services like job training, small business development, technical assistance, and new business launches through the district centers. Additional positive consequences of long-term sustainability planning include the financial impacts of 200,000 direct and indirect new jobs, lower fuel usage compared to other Brazilian cities, improved outdoor air quality and its associated health benefits, high participation rates for recycling, and rising property values and tax revenues. Developing parklands to control flooding risks has proven to be 5% less expensive in Curitiba than building concrete canals for water runoff (Adler 2016).

FINAL REMARKS AND KEY CONCLUSIONS

Communities face big challenges to building a better world. Big ideas and big investments will be required to tackle them. Issues such as housing, transit, or access to opportunity cannot be solved in isolation of one another. In any *place*, these challenges must be addressed together, through the big picture of community collaboration. Moving toward genuine collaboration in long-term planning, permitting, and production of impact will produce more broadly applied and compatible solutions, prioritized by the community's unique needs and risks, and ultimately funded and financed by many members of that regional community.

Investors have yet to allocate sufficient resources or to allocate enough focused staff effort to source, develop, and monitor enough local investment opportunities to build strong, diversified portfolios that meet the institutional standards of investment. Collaboration of place-based investors could solve this dilemma and build such portfolios. All of the stakeholders in a *place* can be a part of the collaboration to plan, design, and finance the transformations in their communities.

This chapter prescribes a framework by which assets can be pooled, investments and investment managers can be chosen by asset classes for intentional impact, and financial returns as well as a variety of local impacts can be delivered to the investors and the community. Collaborative PBII strategies can indeed create collective impact. Only through collaboration can the most beneficial design plans for the most intentional impact on our environmental and social goals be developed. Like the miracle of compound interest over time, community-based investments can compound the impact by collaborating, crossing cultural or disciplinary divides, working together, and rebuilding our communities, regions, and environment.

This chapter demonstrated that each asset class has a unique combination of risk, return, and impact. Second, evidence suggested that ESG integration can potentially improve returns and lower future risk. Third, risk of geographic concentration can be mitigated. Fourth, members of the community and region can collaborate on common goals, solutions, and funding priorities for more intentional, collective impact.

A centralized team can help communities understand their financing challenges in redevelopment and adaptation projects. Those challenges can be met with funds pooled by local investors, who seek strong returns alongside a local impact. Over time, the additional intention and channeling of funds for a community's benefit can produce more success stories to scale up PBII in localities and regions around the world, including via institutional investor portfolios.

ACKNOWLEDGMENTS

The author would like to acknowledge the following colleagues who contributed their insights in impact investing to evolve this place-based model strategy: Ian Galloway of the Federal Reserve Bank of San Francisco; Ben Thornley, formerly of Pacific Community Ventures, now at Tideline; Chad Spitler, then at BlackRock, now leading Third Economy LLC; Michael Dorsey from the Westly Group; Paul Solli of Aperio Group, Barbara VanScoy, formerly Community Capital Management, now at the F.B. Heron Foundation; Mark Sutton, former policy analyst at the Northern California Community Loan Fund; Vince Siciliano, retired president of New Resource Bank, now Amalgamated Bank; Tim Coffin of Breckenridge Capital; Steve Toben of the Flora (Hewlett) Family Foundation; R. Paul Herman of HIP (Human Impact + Profit) Investor; Marianna Grossman, formerly with Sustainable Silicon Valley, now Minerva Ventures; and Sarah Cleveland, advisor to institutional investors. Several volunteer interns have contributed to the development of the Bay Area Impact Investing Initiative (BAIII), and appreciation goes to Jatin Chadha, Stephen Malta, Rani Croager, James Stoner Holk, and Taarika Gopinath.

REFERENCES

Adler, D. (2016). Story of cities #37: How radical ideas turned Curitiba into Brazil's green capital. The Guardian (6 May 2016). https://www.theguardian .com/cities/2016/may/06/story-of-cities-37-mayor-jaime-lerner-curitiba-brazil-green-capital-global-icon (accessed 20 March 2020).

Agnew, L. (2012). Impact Investing for Small, Place-Based Fiduciaries: The Research Study Initiated by the United Way of the Bay Area. Working Paper 2012-5. Federal Reserve Bank of San Francisco (December 2012). http://www.frbsf.org/community-development/files/wp2012-05.pdf (accessed 20 March 2020).

Agnew, L. (2016). Regional Impact Investing for Institutional Investors: The Bay Area Impact Investing Initiative. In: *Routledge Handbook of Social and Sustainable Finance*. (O. Lehner, ed.). Routledge, pp. 710–727.

Agnew, L. and Malta, S. (2017). What is Place-Based Impact Investing? Bay Area Impact Investing Initiative (5 April 2017). http://baiii.org/what-is-place-based-impact-investing (accessed 5 March 2020).

Aperio Group LLC (2020). United Way Bay Area Client Report for Bay Area Impact Investing Initiative (BAIII).

Ashley, S., and Ovalle, J. (2018). Emerging Approaches in Collaborative Place-Based Impact Investing. Center on Non-Profit Philanthropy, *Research Report* (May 2018). https://www.urban.org/sites/default/files/publication/98452/investing_together_emerging_approaches_in_collaborative_place-based_impact_investing_7.pdf (accessed 20 March 2020).

Gray, E. and Talberth, J. (2011). A Compilation of Green Economy Policies, Programs, and Initiatives from Around the World. *World Resources Institute,* pp. 1–16. http://pdf.wri.org/green_economy_compilation_2011-02.pdf (accessed 20 March 2020).

Grippa, P., Schmittmann, J., and Suntheim, F. (2019). Climate Change, Central Banks, and Financial Risk. International Monetary Fund (December 2019). https://www.imf.org/external/pubs/ft/fandd/2019/12/climate-change-central-banks-and-financial-risk-grippa.htm (accessed 20 March 2020).

Gustafsson, H., and Kelly, E. (2012). Urban innovations in Curitiba: A case study. Eugene & Carol Ludwig Center for Community and Economic Development. Yale Law School (June 2012). https://www.alnap.org/system/files/content/resource/files/main/ludwiggustafssonkellycuritibareport.pdf (accessed 20 March 2020).

Kumbamu, A. (2017). Building sustainable social and solidarity economies: Place-based and network-based strategies of alternative development organizations in India. *Community Development*, pp. 1–16. DOI: 10.1080/15575330.2017.1384744.

Resilient by Design, Bay Area Challenge (2018). ouR-HOME (Contra Costa County) – Bay Area: Resilient by Design Challenge. http://www.resilientbayarea.org/our-home (accessed 20 March 2020). http://www.resilientbayarea.org/our-home (accessed 20 March 2020). http://www.resilientbayarea.org/projects (accessed 20 March 2020).

Sustainable Development Knowledge Platform (2011). Sustainable Urban Planning (Curitiba City). https://sustainabledevelopment.un.org/index.php?page=view&type=99&nr=57&menu=1449 (accessed 20 March 2020).

Sustainable Development Knowledge Platform (2015). Sustainable Development Goals. https://sustainabledevelopment.un.org/?menu=1300 (accessed 20 March 2020).

Toniic (2019). T100 Focus Report 2019: The Frontier of SDG Investing. https://toniic.com/t100-focus-the-frontier-of-sdg-investing/(accessed 20 May 2020).

Urban Institute (2020). Place-Based Impact Investing. https://www.urban.org/policy-centers/research-action-lab/projects/place-based-impact-investing (accessed May 23, 2020).

USDN (2016). USDN Innovation Products: Financing Sustainable Cities Scan and Toolkit. https://www.usdn.org/products-government.html#Financing Toolkit (accessed 20 March 2020).

Zuckerman, D., and Parker, K. (2017). Hospitals Aligned for Healthy Communities: Place-Based Investing. Hospitals Aligned for Healthy Communities: A toolkit to help hospitals and health systems build community wealth through inclusive hiring, investment, and purchasing. 2017 Hospital Toolkits. https://hospitaltoolkits.org/investment/ (accessed 20 March 2020).

How to Invest in Human Capital: Measuring and Integrating Human Capital Valuation to Realize Higher-Impact Portfolios

R. Paul Herman, BSci and Kirstin Dougall, MFA

Abstract

Impact investors can use human capital valuation (HCV) to identify promising investment targets. This investment strategy is based on the premise that a company's focus on human capital improves employee engagement, productivity, and well-being, which then generates stronger financial and social returns for investors. Companies that prioritize and invest in people, as well as measure and disclose human-capital metrics, frequently out-perform financial benchmarks. HCV has been historically underappreciated because there were limited common standards for measuring and reporting workforce assets as anything other than a "labor cost" to be minimized, versus an asset with a return on investment (ROI). However, with new standards from the International Standards Organization (ISO), Sustainability

Accounting Standards Board (SASB), and other coalitions focused on capturing intangible assets, the value of human capital is increasingly clear to investors who seek to include it as an essential metric. This chapter reviews key monetary and non-monetary human-capital valuation methods that investors can use to assess companies; describes emerging global standards for reporting human capital metrics; and offers valuable examples that illuminate how investors can use HCV information to make smarter investment decisions. Finally, this chapter describes three approaches investors can use to put HCV to work in a portfolio: (i) investing in HCV-focused funds or indexes; (ii) applying HCV ratings to evaluate holdings; and (iii) integrating HCV methods to create custom impact investing criteria. Readers will learn how HCV strategies can enhance portfolio resilience and pursue stronger returns while supporting sustainable workforces that value people as an asset.

Keywords

Human Capital; Human Resource Accounting; Human Resource Management; People as an Asset; Talent Management; Employee Engagement; ESG; Impact Investing; Human Capital Value; Intangible Capital; Socially Responsible Investing

WHY IMPACT INVESTORS SHOULD CARE ABOUT HUMAN CAPITAL VALUATION

While it is common for impact investors to seek investments with appealing environmental or sustainability characteristics, the value of people and the workforce as a whole—human capital—is often overlooked. Chief executive officers (CEO) frequently highlight that "people are our greatest asset," yet these people are accounted for as labor costs on income statements, rather than assets on the balance sheet (Herman 2011). Typically, more than 50% of cost structures (e.g. payroll, benefits, training, recruiting) are attributed to human capital. While generally accepted accounting principles (GAAP) mandate employees as labor costs, every dollar paid to employees is essentially an investment in building skills, experience, and expertise. Employees invent products, serve customers, and operate teams, and thus directly contribute to top-line revenue, just as manufacturing plants pump out products to be sold.

Thinking about labor as an investment is especially relevant in industries like technology, health care, and professional services, where people serve customers and create platforms. Whereas traditional manufacturing companies need property, factories, and equipment to scale their businesses, the critical building blocks in today's service-driven economy are people and human capital. Employees—and all the wisdom, expertise, and skills that need to be replaced if they leave a firm—are missing on companies' balance sheets. Workers can no longer be treated as replaceable cogs in a machine. There is substantiated evidence demonstrating that enterprises investing in the workforce or "human capital" can yield higher returns (Herman 2010; Hoque 2018). Leading companies of the twenty-first century invest in human capital, and leading investors seek out firms that do so.

Investors can choose to build human capital valuation (HCV) into portfolio strategies in a variety of ways. At the simplest, an investor can buy a mutual fund, Exchange-Traded Fund (ETF), index fund, or separately managed account (SMA) that focuses on human capital (see Table 4.2 of human capital–focused funds). A second approach would be to incorporate human capital valuation analyses performed by ratings providers into portfolio strategies (see Appendix 4.3 for HCV ratings methodologies). A third, and more intensive, sophisticated approach, is to integrate independently selected HCV metrics into a custom rating system, and then research or secure data in order to develop a unique investment strategy. The two main concepts of HCV that investors should take into account are: (i) "monetary" human capital valuation, a measure that calculates the intangible value of the workforce, and (ii) "non-monetary" human capital valuation, which measures variables that nevertheless affect profitability.

In this chapter, we will address the following questions: How should an impact investor look at a company and its workers? How should human capital value be measured in this relationship? What kind of data and metrics are meaningful in judging a mutually beneficial outcome? What kind of scorecard and rating systems can demonstrate how a company values the capital represented by the workers? How are ratings developed, and how can they help guide investor decision-making?

METHODOLOGY

A comprehensive literature review was performed to identify best practices in human capital valuation. The review covered books, articles, reports, and examples (including those based on case studies) that reference human capital valuation, human capital accounting, and human capital management, published from the 1960s through 2020. Original interviews were conducted with experts who are pioneers in the field of HCV, including economists, institutional investors, financial analysts, chief financial officers, human resource experts, standards bodies across for-profit companies, non-profit organizations, and investment firms (see Appendix 4.1).

MEASURING THE CONTRIBUTION OF HUMAN CAPITAL TO RETURNS

Investors face a major obstacle when it comes to measuring HCV and its contribution to financial performance. Workforce data is diverse and varies widely between different industry sectors. "The absence of a unifying language for human capital valuation is a challenge" (L. Bassi, personal communication, April 30, 2019). While there is an abundance of very useful sources of information and tools for describing human capital valuation among public companies, other organizations, and even countries, the variety of options and lack of standardization across firms and sectors often prevents clear comparisons that would allow for easy, accurate benchmarking.

In the absence of government mandates for human capital valuation reporting, over the past decade HCV ratings providers like those listed in Appendix 4.3 have bridged the gap while this language was being developed and codified through standards. Without legal standards, the onus was placed on corporations to voluntarily offer relevant data. Voluntary corporate disclosure standards emerged to address the material relevance of environmental, social, and governance (ESG) factors on business performance. "It's not about reporting; it is about valuing and measuring impact," said Mike Wallace from the Social and Human Capital Coalition, now called the Capitals Coalition (M. Wallace, personal communication, April 11, 2019). For some investors seeking indicators for positive outcomes, companies' self-reported data may be adequate.

Only recently has a shared vocabulary emerged for HCV. In a major policy shift, the United States (US) Securities and Exchange Commission recently updated disclosure requirements to include human capital resources that are material to managing the business (Securities and Exchange Commission 2019). Other nations such as South Africa have begun to mandate integrated reporting of material sustainability factors in order to be registered on the stock exchange (Institute of Directors Southern Africa 2016). This modernization of reporting rules enables companies to formally calculate their workforce investments, as well as uniformly analyze how these investments correlate with returns. As companies around the world are increasingly required to report their human capital investments as assets in financial filings, investors will gain access to better, more standardized data for benchmarking social and financial performance.

HUMAN CAPITAL VALUATION METHODS

The two major categories of human capital valuation methods are monetary and non-monetary.

Non-monetary methods assess human capital value by translating non-financial variables such as external expert ratings, internal human resource data, or employee self-assessments into economic value. While there have been numerous robust non-monetary methods developed by economists, it is challenging to achieve consistency across sectors or firms that each have unique circumstances. Despite inherent variability, non-monetary HCV data has rich potential for informing investors. Variables may include quantitative and qualitative measures, a mixture of self-reported data and data captured about companies from public sources (e.g. press releases, patent filings, or legal notices). Metrics can be reported in proportions or scorecards, either by companies or external analysts. To evaluate a company's HCV, investors can use standardized measures—such as employee retention or employee turnover, sick leave, injuries and deaths on the job, and legal actions filed by employees—as well as proprietary measures such as internal employee engagement surveys. For example, the Human Capital Management Institute found that turnover rates of high-performing employees negatively correlated with productivity levels and was one of the top five metrics that impact a company's performance (Higgins et al. 2019). Even though these non-monetary HCV metrics may not have an explicitly calculated monetary value, these metrics are quantifiable and link to financial metrics and outcomes that can be used to guide internal management strategy and/or drive productivity and shareholder value (Higgins et al. 2012; Fulmer and Ployhart 2013).

Monetary human capital data can be found in annual corporate disclosures, or in supplemental reporting, corporate responsibility reports, and corporate sustainability websites. Depending on the company and its reporting methods, HCV data can be scarce. Some forward-thinking companies like Infosys and JetBlue present workforce-focused supplemental material with their annual reports, illustrating the value of labor to their operations (Infosys 2011; J. Higgins, personal communication, April 15, 2019). This supplement alone is an indicator that the company is savvy to the importance of human capital and how it impacts company performance.

In accounting terms, labor was historically represented on financial statements as a cost on the income statement, or a liability on the balance sheet (G. Becker 1964; Lev and Schwartz 1971). This convention arises from the industrial revolution when most companies' assets were largely tangible and featured items like factories (plant, property, and equipment), cash, and securities. Historically, "most organizations treat talent like disposable products that are expensed as used, you hire somebody, use them up, and cast them aside and get a new one; and GAAP accounting supports that" (J. Higgins, personal communication, April 15, 2019). The generally accepted accounting principles (GAAP) still treat employees as a cost of doing business, which frames people and labor costs as an input to be minimized in order to improve profitability (FASB 2019b). These norms are changing, however, as companies begin characterizing their workforce as an asset on the balance sheet. This choice reflects employees' full contribution to value creation—through inventing products, discovering new solutions, and exceeding expectations with customers—and enables more accurate measurement of the "return on workforce investment."

At times in the past, voluntary corporate disclosure of human resource information was considered a risk because any problems with workforces or labor-management disputes could reflect badly on brand image, and ultimately hurt the firm's stock price. But this attitude of reluctant disclosure has been evolving as the perception of corporate value shifts more toward intangibles. "Human assets are so immense and important for a company that they have to find a solution to overcome discrepancies between only seeing employees as a cost factor and as an asset that creates value" (S. Becker, personal communication, May 22, 2019). Calls for expanded reporting requirements demonstrate investors' growing caution regarding under-reported human capital and workforce problems and their financial and reputational risks and indicate that investors are seeking transparency in how companies treat, invest in, and value their workforce.

According to Bryan Esterly of the SASB, "Our paradigm for how the capital markets view human capital really needs to shift from the historic legacy perspective as simply a cost center on an income statement to an intangible asset that the company manages and can measure and is directly associated with long term value creation and thus appropriate for more useful investor disclosures" (B. Esterly, personal communication, May 3, 2019). Putting aside the official balance sheet, what investors need is to develop a modern understanding of human capital valuation methods as well as a strategy to put these ideas into the due diligence process to create profitable portfolio positions.

INVESTOR METHODS FOR CAPTURING MONETARY HCV

The Heritage of Monetary Human Capital Valuation Methods

In the 1960s and 1970s, scholars around the globe generated Ph.D. theses and numerous frameworks exploring financial models for quantifying the value of human capital. The intention behind this research was to change how human capital was reflected on balance sheets in quarterly and annual reporting. Even the *Harvard Business Review* published a 1967 feature, called "Put People on Your Balance Sheet," that showcased examples of income statements and balance sheets from one of the first approaches ever piloted (Hekimian and Jones 1967).

"Human Resource Accounting" arose as a method of quantifying people as assets using objective and subjective criteria (Brummet et al. 1968; Flamholtz 1971; Flamholtz et al. 2002). Some models followed accounting principles typically used for tangible assets, which measure the "historical costs" or "replacement costs" that would be incurred to replace a worker, while also taking into account the associated costs of wages and training (Hekimian and Jones 1967; Brummet et al. 1968; Likert and Pyle 1971; Flamholtz 1974). This static cost approach evolved into more complex models that were centered around the future value of labor, including employee acquisition, wages, training and professional development, and benefits (Lev and Schwartz 1971).

Following this decade-long surge in scholarship was a 20-year lull that started when it became clear reporting standards were not changing to include HCV metrics (Flamholtz 2009; Fulmer and Ployhart 2013). Corporations around the world largely ignored HCV as a key component in annual reporting because of a lack of regulation or consistent guidelines. Some scholars and investors, however, reintroduced the idea of monetary HCV in the 1990s. Over the past three decades, renewed academic and professional interest reflects how intangible value in our 21st-century economy is closely linked with workforce capability. "Progressive leaders really understand that people are the most valuable asset; they say it, they mean it, but they didn't have any good way to measure it," said Jeff Higgins (personal communication, April 15, 2019) from the Human Capital Management Institute.

From a managerial accounting perspective, the costs and values of workers can be assessed relative to a company's revenue or profit. Basic approaches assess revenue or profit relative to the costs of the average full-time employee. Economists since the 1960s have put forward a variety of formulas for calculating this monetary cost of employees, including approaches developed by Hekimian and Jones (1967), Brummet et al. (1968), Likert and Pyle (1971), Jaggi and Lau (1974), and Lev and Schwartz (1971).

Investors interested in quantitative measures of human capital valuation can incorporate metrics and formulas developed by the Human Capital Management Institute (HCMI 2012). These models include the "Total Cost of Workforce" (TWC) and "Human Capital Return on Investment" (HC ROI) that push toward a comprehensive and straightforward method of calculating the impact and profit potential of workforce investments (see Appendix 4.2 for definitions). HCMI created these models to forecast business performance and to demonstrate how share prices and company workforce investments are positively correlated across industries (see this chapter's example using HCMI metrics for a publicly traded Asian telecom firm, anonymized as "BroadTek" below).

Investment Strategies Using Monetary HCV

Investors can evaluate companies by incorporating monetary formulas like HCMI's for calculating HCV. For example, an impact investor could use data from corporate annual reports to calculate a company's Total Cost of Workforce and a Return on Human Capital Investment (see Appendix 4.2). They could use this to build a model calculating the financial returns attributed to investments in human capital for the current year and for a historical period to view trends over time. To compare companies, investors could rank companies by their Return on Human Capital Investments from highest to lowest, giving more weight to the best monetary HCV performers. An alternative method would be to assess the percentage of total intangible assets attributed to human capital, which could then be used to calculate a return on assets (ROA) or also be added to a company's "Calculated Intangible Value" (Kenton 2019). This second approach would more systematically add human capital to the intangibles recognized by GAAP, including assets like brand recognition, goodwill, patents, trademarks, copyrights, proprietary technology, and customer lists (FASB 2019a).

NON-MONETARY HUMAN CAPITAL VALUATION FOR IMPACT INVESTORS

When it comes to non-monetary valuation, a broader and more complex array of variables present themselves. These include diverse sociological markers, corporate culture, geographical location, and the myriad complexities of human behavior. Non-monetary HCV ratings systems can be based on company survey data; expert review; qualitative information from interviews, earnings calls, or presentations; and quantitative sources from annual reports and quarterly filings, corporate responsibility reports, public legal and compliance databases, and internet analytics that identify trends (see Appendix 4.4 for a comprehensive list of material human capital metrics). Visibility and access to firm-level data are critical to investment managers. Hernando Cortina, then of Just Capital, which developed an index licensed to an asset manager to underlie an ETF that includes human capital metrics, observed that such metrics have "been a good differentiator of performance; when you have a company that is treating workers and customers well and has quality products, they tend to be less accident prone: not just environmental, but fewer product recalls, fines, bad media, controversies; they are more resilient and robust businesses" (H. Cortina, personal communication, April 11, 2019).

Exemplary Ratings Systems That Feature Human Capital Valuation

There are many organizations offering guidance and creating ratings systems that investors can use to develop custom datasets regarding companies of interest. These include Great Place to Work®, HIP (Human Impact + Profit) Investor, Human Capital Management (HCM), ISS, JUST Capital, MSCI, Refinitiv, RobecoSAM, Sustainalytics, and Fitz-Enz's Balanced Scorecards (Fitz-Enz 2000; Fitz-Enz 2019) (see Appendix 4.3 for full descriptions).

As an example, HIP (Human Impact + Profit) investor ratings track employee impacts through quantitative metrics from job safety to fair pay, board diversity, and employee lawsuits—all of which correlate to future risk and return potential for investors. HIP Investor's ratings of over 9,000 corporations globally incorporate four key human capital concerns: health, wealth, equality, and trust (Herman 2010).

JUST Capital's rankings are based in part on focus group research, where the opinion of "the American public is our materiality map" (H. Cortina, personal communication, April 11, 2019). Similar to HIP ratings, four of five JUST Capital core investment criteria are human-centered: workers, customers, communities, and shareholders. "How you treat your workers" is a primary concern of respondents, and so workforce management is the highest-weighted category with the greatest significance (A. Omens, personal communication, April 11, 2019; JUST Capital 2019b). Therefore, if a company scores poorly in the workers' category, it is very unlikely to be highly ranked by JUST.

Laurie Bassi of McBassi & Company, which surveys key performance indicators for investment strategy firms, uses the litmus test of whether executives view investments in human capital as a sustainability imperative. Moreover, as a measure of executive commitment McBassi takes note of whether human capital information is reported to the board of directors. "Our analysis shows clearly that leaders who choose the path of sustainable human capital investment are rewarded in the long run, but they must do so in spite of the pressures of the market; it takes courage to do that" (L. Bassi, personal communication, April 30, 2019; Bassi and McMurrer 2007).

Non-Monetary Human Capital Metrics That Impact Investors Can Use in Custom Analyses

The major challenge faced by investors seeking to use non-monetary HCV evaluations to guide investment decisions is identifying the appropriate metrics and gleaning the key HCV data that is relevant to each sector, industry, or company they seek to evaluate. Impact investors can develop their own profitability analysis by leveraging non-monetary HCV metrics in developing a custom dataset. For example, impact investors interested in evaluating the role of non-monetary human capital valuation within the airline industry could build a strategy incorporating HCV-relevant data as diverse as safety reporting, absenteeism, employee satisfaction, and customer experience surveys.

Some of the meaningful areas for expressing non-monetary human capital valuation include:

- Employee experience and engagement
- Workforce development
- Human resource metrics
- Workforce governance

Often, non-monetary human capital metrics are uncovered in a human resource setting, when companies are seeking to evaluate how much employees cost a business with absenteeism, turnover, or other factors. Metrics used for evaluating human capital flip this idea; rather than looking at labor simply as a cost, non-monetary HCV analysis treats labor as a value-add.

Employee experience data measures how employees feel about the company and the environment in which they work. Employee engagement and satisfaction ratings are a useful source of information and often have demonstrated correlations with productivity and business performance. Professor Alex Edmans of the London Business School (LBS) was among the first to show the distinct financial advantages experienced by companies listed in best-place-to-work rankings produced by Great Place to Work® and published annually in *Fortune* magazine (Edmans 2011). Edmans then expanded his analysis from US-based companies to firms located in two dozen countries across the globe. "In 'flexible' labor markets worldwide, employee satisfaction [is] correlated with better financial outcomes." Being certified as a "Great Place to Work®" or achieving similar recognition correlates with higher financial returns, compared to benchmarks (see Great Place to Work® example below). Interestingly, great workplaces did not reward investors in two strong-labor countries, Denmark and Germany, which likely shared the profit gains with employees more instead of shareholders (Edmans et al. 2017).

Increasingly significant to employees feeling good about their workplaces are the two themes of "trust" and "purpose," which connote meaningful work by employees (M. Bush, personal communication, April 30, 2019). Trust and purpose indicators may be also captured in internal surveys, third-party rankings, or evident in crowd-sourced employee-driven databases.

> Employees around the world all want the same thing in a workplace: trust. They define a great workplace as one where leaders demonstrate credibility, respect, and fairness.
>
> (Frauenheim 2019)

Another aspect of experience data is workers feeling they have the opportunity to contribute creatively and make a difference. "Innovation velocity ratio" is an emerging metric where "companies that had the highest percentage of people feeling the opportunity and the invitation to come up with new ideas and innovate had 5.5 times revenue growth of those least inclusive in their innovation activities" (M. Bush, personal communication, April 30, 2019). Internationally, other important workplace variables shape employee experiences.

For example, workers in the United States and Canada place a high value on a sense of "community," whereas work/life "sustainability" was found to be more important in Asia, "fairness" in Europe, and "psychological safety" in Latin American countries (Great Place to Work® 2019a). Leadership has also historically been an important driver, increasing productivity up to 25% while decreasing turnover, disengagement, and other employee relations issues. Discipline, managing for results, and communications skills (i.e. managing employee expectations) were key characteristics of top revenue-generating leaders (HCMI 2019; HCMI 2012). "Once you figure that out, then it's really just figuring out where can we get the data in any given company or industry to try to replicate as many of these value creation algorithms as possible" (J. Higgins, personal communication, April 15, 2019).

Many operational human resource metrics can be found in public documents in corporate, government, or crowd-sourced publications. Increasingly, company management and boards of directors prioritize human capital indicators and voluntarily publish related disclosures in proxy statements, supplemental annual report information, and corporate responsibility reports (Smith and Klemash 2019). However, many companies may retain human resource data for internal use, and so expert analysis and ratings can be a way to indirectly access proprietary HCV information. This may apply to more qualitative metrics, such as employee perceptions of trust in management, freedom to innovate, and purpose in their work, which have become important in retention, productivity, and corporate resilience (M. Bush, personal communication, April 30, 2019; Erb et al. 2019; Mayer et al. 2017).

> [C]orporate policies that promote more pro-diversity cultures, specifically treatment of women and minorities, enhance future innovative efficiency. This positive effect is stronger during economic downturns, and in firms that are more innovative, value intangibles and human capital more highly, have greater growth options, have higher cash flow, and have stronger governance.
>
> (Mayer et al. 2017)

Employee Participation

Employee participation in the governance of organizations has the potential to increase resilience and revenue growth for investors and other stakeholders. The financial multiplier effect of employee ownership can preserve jobs, increase longevity, and/or recirculate created value throughout local communities (Lingane 2015). As part of a risk mitigation strategy, investors can consider companies with employee stock ownership plans (ESOPs) and employee representation on boards or companies with a cooperative governance structure.

Incorporating Data from Human Resources Management Systems

Impact investors may be able to glean further non-monetary intelligence about a company by looking at the Human Resource Management Systems (HRMS) in place and asking how data generated informs financial reporting. HRMS have been developed to allow companies to assess human capital investments and human resource metrics and to enable optimization of resources as well as strategic planning. HRMS use largely commercial technology platforms that collect company workforce, compliance, and other metrics at routine reporting intervals and in real-time. Standardized variables and customized data are captured at the company and industry level. According to Dr. Stefanie Becker (personal communication, May 22, 2019), head of the working group Human Capital Reporting from the International Organization for Standardization (ISO), "most key performance indicators are already a standard part of bigger human resource systems, but some items like employee engagement are collected separately." Companies that are not using some level of human resource management may offer more limited visibility into the human capital metrics that are of interest to investors. According to Nancy Mancilla (personal communication, April 19, 2019), who leads a consulting firm specializing in sustainability metrics and reporting, "the granularity of investor requests are really helping fuel the need to produce that [human capital] information.... We generally need to automate a lot." While companies in the European Union (EU) have more human resource transparency, in the United States people analytics technology platforms (HRMS) are more prevalent (J. Higgins, personal communication, April 15, 2019) and could be increasingly harnessed for standardizing HCV reporting.

STANDARDS FOR HUMAN CAPITAL VALUATION

It may seem daunting to mine uncorrelated human capital valuation data across industries and sectors. Fortunately, impact rating companies and other third parties already offer methodologies, protocols, and aggregated and ranked data to make HCV valuations accessible to investors at all levels of skill and interest. Still, given the absence of government mandated reporting standards, the onus for reporting HCV data remains on corporations who voluntarily choose to make the information public, and who elect to follow one of the protocols for reporting created by a standards organization. Some of the players offering protocols for standards reporting include the following:

- **The Sustainability Accounting Standards Board (SASB)** (SASB 2019). A nonprofit organization that sets financial reporting standards, SASB was founded in 2011 to develop and disseminate sustainability accounting standards and incorporate non-monetary HCV into many datasets. SASB's mission is to establish industry-specific disclosure standards across environmental, social, and governance topics that inform investors about financial material information (**see SASB example**).

- **The Human Capital Management Institute (HCMI)** (Human Capital Management Institute n.d.). Founded on the belief that organizations must find better ways of measuring human capital investments, HCMI's goal is to fundamentally change the way organizations make decisions about their workforce, and to strive toward a future in which human capital measurement and information are as integral to business decision-making as financial information is today (**see HCMI example**).

- **The Social and Human Capital Coalition, now The Capitals Coalition** (Social and Human Capital Coalition 2019). The coalition is a collaboration of over 350 of the world's leading organizations from business, accounting, science and academia, membership organizations, standard setting groups, finance, policy, and civil society. The Capitals Coalition offers a protocol to measure and value the social and human capital impacts and dependencies of an entire business or an individual project, product, or operation. The Protocol seeks to determine how (and by how much) your business activities increase, decrease, and/or transform human capital, and the extent to which you depend on human capital resources. A long-term aspiration of the coalition is that every business using the protocol will scale and integrate this approach across their organization (**see Social and Human Capital Coalition example**).

- **The International Organization for Standardization (ISO)** (ISO 2018). ISO 30414 was created to focus on human resource management and provide guidelines for internal and external human capital reporting. Their objective is to consider and to make transparent the contribution of human capital to the organization in order to support the sustainability of the workforce. The ISO 30414 standards document is applicable to all organizations, regardless of the type, size, nature, or complexity of the business, whether in the public, private, or voluntary sector, or a not-for-profit organization. ISO 30414 provides guidelines for evaluating the following HCR areas: compliance and ethics, costs, diversity, leadership, organizational culture, organizational health, safety and well-being, productivity, recruitment, mobility and turnover, skills and capabilities, succession planning, and workforce availability.

- **The International Integrated Reporting Framework (IIRF)** (IIRC 2013). IIRF is a principles-based approach that "identifies information to be included in an integrated report for use in assessing an organization's ability to create value" (IIRC 2013). The IIRF is based on a framework that breaks down capital into six categories. Human capital is the fourth pillar on which IIRF evaluates and reports value creation for the company and its stakeholders (**see Groupe PSA example**).

- **The Global Reporting Initiative (GRI)** (GRI 2020). The Global Reporting Initiative (GRI) is an international independent standards organization that helps businesses, governments, and other organizations understand and communicate the impact of issues such as climate change and human rights on business outcomes. According to Mike Wallace of the Social and Human Capital Coalition, there is evidence that 75% of the S&P 500 are reporting formally or informally using the GRI framework (M. Wallace, personal communication, April 11, 2019). This broad coverage makes GRI a useful tool to compare companies and allows impact investors to access high-level human capital metrics they consider to be material (**see CBUS example**).

Impact investors interested in how a company, fund, or organization values human capital should begin by investigating whether any corporate reports exist that use one of these standards-based protocols to evaluate a given company. Within a sector, a group of standards-based HCV reports could guide an impact investor in developing a custom ratings scale that would, based on the available evidence, correlate to performance and ultimately profitability.

INTEGRATING HUMAN CAPITAL INTO THE INVESTMENT PROCESS

Investors including a human capital strategy can and should employ an overarching HCV framework that includes the following actions:

- **Investment Policy Statement:** Clearly state incorporating human capital valuation as a strategy. Identify monetary and non-monetary human capital metrics most applicable for the strategy's target asset classes. Specify conditions and timing for re-balancing.
- **Investment Decision-Making:** Prioritize allocations to investments, indexes, and funds that include human capital valuation based on financial reporting that can be found in supplemental balance sheets or corporate responsibility reports, standards-based reporting such as SASB or ISO, or non-monetary HCV such as safety or satisfaction reports.
- **Asset Allocation and Security Selection:** Consider including human capital themed indexes, mutual funds, ETFs, or separately managed accounts (SMAs) in portfolios.
- **Impact Reporting:** Mandate that portfolio funds or other holdings provide a baseline of human capital monetary metrics such as "Return on Workforce" or "Human Capital ROI" and non-monetary metrics such as attrition rates.
- **Engagement and Advocacy:** Engage with corporate investees and fund managers to clearly communicate your expectations about which human capital metrics are important, and what reporting formats and frequencies are desired.

EXAMPLES OF HUMAN CAPITAL VALUATION APPLIED IN IMPACT INVESTING

The examples highlighted in this section provide a range of examples of how companies are measuring and reporting human capital to the marketplace. Impact investors can see how these types of disclosures can inform their portfolio decisions. Companies that make an effort to manage human capital and track it as an investment should have characteristics that are better aligned with the types of risks, returns, and social values impact investors are seeking. Examples include companies calculating monetary HCV;

companies focusing on non-monetary human capital metrics to create value, and companies using standards to communicate social as well as financial value to potential investors.

Examples: Monetary Human Capital Valuation in Action

Monetary HCV Example: Asian Company "BroadTek" Uses Human Capital Financial Statements to Calculate Returns on Workforce Investments

"BroadTek," a pseudonym for a leading Asian telecommunications company, uses Human Capital Financial Statements (HCF$) developed by the Human Capital Management Institute to calculate returns on human capital investments. HCMI's model evaluates the value of human capital expressed as a quantitative ROI. The ROI of human capital is calculated by dividing the company's total profits by its total investment in human capital (HC ROI) (see Appendix 4.2 for further definitions and formulas). "How much cost you have and the output per dollar you invest turned out to be the most productive and most powerful productivity metric to measure the ROI contribution or value creation of the workforce and people," says Jeff Higgins, founder of HCMI (J. Higgins, personal communication, April 15, 2019). By conducting this analysis, BroadTek was then able to optimize future workforce investments to pursue and achieve higher returns (Higgins and Cooperstein 2019).

Takeaway for Impact Investors

The "Productivity and ROI of Human Capital" section of the financial statement shown in Figure 4.1 demonstrates how much of the company's returns are attributed to workforce investments (expressed as Total Cost of Workforce; see Appendix 4.2). The presence of and content in HCF$ statements can be used as a barometer of how much attention companies are paying to their workforce and human capital. Investors can screen or weight companies based on their HCF$ statements. Investors can also use these statements to benchmark performance against other companies using similar methods.

Monetary HCV Example: Global Technology Company Infosys Uses Present Value of Compensation Method to Calculate Returns on Workforce Investments

This example is an example of how a public company used the present value HCV method to publish a supplemental balance sheet listing the value

BroadTek Human Capital Impact Statement (Workforce Productivity Impact Section)

Revenue	Prior Year	Current Year	Variance	% Chg
Net Operating Revenue	$4,114,540,000	$4,444,560,000	$330,020,000	8.0%
Total Workforce Headcount (FTE)	4,645	4,750	105	2.3%
Revenue per FTE	$885,800	$935,697	$49,897	5.6%
Costs				
Total Expenses	$2,788,752,921	$2,809,406,376	$20,653,455	0.7%
Total Operating Expense	$2,262,997,000	$2,377,839,600	$114,842,600	5.1%
Total Cost of Workforce (TCOW)	$447,661,952	$467,567,712	$19,905,760	4.4%
TCOW Percent of Revenue	10.9%	10.5%	−0.4%	−3.3%
TCOW Percent of Expenses	16.1%	16.6%	0.6%	3.7%
TCOW Percent of Operating Expenses	19.8%	19.7%	−0.1%	−0.6%
Profit				
EBITDA[(1)]	$1,316,652,800	$1,511,150,400	$194,497,600	14.8%
Net Operating Profit	$573,155,422	$680,017,680	$106,862,258	18.6%
Profit per FTE	$123,392	$143,162	$19,770	16.0%
Productivity and ROI of Human Capital				
Total Market Capitalization [(2)]	$6,304,709,642	$6,800,176,800	$495,467,158	7.9%
Average Market Capitalization Value per FTE	$1,357,311	$1,431,616	$74,305	5.5%
Human Capital ROI Ratio	3.96	4.50	0.54	13.5%
Return on Human Capital Investment	128.0%	145.4%	17.4%	13.6%
TOTAL WORKFORCE PRODUCTIVITY IMPACT:	**$355,630,545**	**$700,578,523**	**$344,947,978**	**97.0%**

[(1)] *EBITDA = Earnings before interest, taxes, depreciation and amortization*
[(2)] *Total Market Capitalization for publicly traded organizations or independent bank/financial market valuation for private entities*

FIGURE 4.1   Human Capital Impact Statement Links to Financials. *Source:* Human Capital Management Institute (2019). Reprinted with permission from HCMI.

of their workforce as an intangible asset in their annual reports. Infosys, a software company based in India, included human capital assets in its annual reports starting when it went public in 1998, and continuing into the mid-2010s. "Balance Sheets Including Intangible Assets" were supplemental to formal financial reporting (Infosys 2011). The asset value of their workers was calculated using the Lev and Schwartz Present Value of Compensation method, which proposed an economic valuation of employees based on the present value of future earnings, adjusted for the probability of employees' death/separation/retirement (Lev and Schwartz 1971):

- Employee compensation includes all direct and indirect benefits earned both in India and overseas.
- The incremental earnings based on managerial level and age group have been considered.
- The future earnings have been discounted at the cost of capital of 11.21% (previous year 10.60%).

The total cost of Infosys' "human resources" is listed among intangible assets, potentially increasing the book value of the company. When the "value of human resources" for staffing types (software professionals and support) appear as assets, the return on investment attributable to those human resources is 5.1%, which is more similar to the ratios seen for a physical-asset business. People are viewed as assets in this framework.

Takeaway for Impact Investors

The Infosys supplemental financial statement shown in Figure 4.2 demonstrates that Infosys's human capital return on assets equaled more than 5%. This is a much lower return on assets ratio compared to the traditional manner of evaluating most software and service firms, but it is more accurate, as Infosys' means of production are people, not traditional property, plants, or equipment. Investors can screen for companies providing supplemental financial information, but in many countries, there are few. For example, in India, only a half dozen firms are readily providing this level of detail. Investors can also use these statements to benchmark performance against other companies that use similar methods of calculating workforce value.

	in ₹ crore, unless stated otherwise	
	2011	2010
Employees (no.)		
Software professionals	1,23,811	1,06,864
Support	7,009	6,932
Total	1,30,820	1,13,796
Value of human resources		
Software professionals	1,22,539	1,06,173
Support	12,566	7,114
Total	1,35,105	1,13,287
Total income [1]	27,501	22,742
Total employee cost [1]	14,856	12,093
Value-added	25,031	20,935
Net profit [1]	6,823	6,219
Ratios		
Value of human resources per employee	1.03	1.00
Total income/human resources value (ratio)	0.20	0.20
Employee cost/human resources value (%)	11.0	10.7
Value-added/human resources value (ratio)	0.19	0.18
Return on human resources value (%)	5.1	5.5

[1] *As per IFRS (audited) financial statements*

FIGURE 4.2 Infosys Supplemental Financial Statement Showing Calculated Returns on Human Resources. *Source:* Infosys Annual Report (Infosys 2011).

Examples: Using Non-Monetary Human Capital Metrics to Guide Investment

Example: Being a Global "Great Place to Work®" Creates Higher Growth

Organizations rated among the "best companies to work for" typically have a history of outperforming the market. A variety of funds and financial instruments around the world have packaged this "best-to-work" approach for investor convenience, with demonstrable effectiveness (see Figure 4.3). The *Fortune* 100 Best Companies to Work For, Parnassus Endeavor Fund, and the HIP Great Place to Work ESG Portfolio all demonstrated 30% to 100% higher return multiples beyond the benchmarks in Russell, S&P, and NYSE indexes for the same periods (Morningstar 2017; HIP Investor 2019; M. Bush, personal communication, October 22, 2019). These rankings and investment strategies are based on information collected through employee surveys, combined with quantitative salary and attrition data that measure employee experience. If investors are considering companies that do not appear on "best-to-work" lists, metrics such as employee satisfaction can be similarly measured through internal surveys that are often published for the public

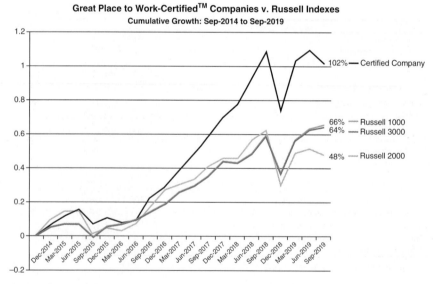

FIGURE 4.3   "Certified Great Workplaces" Outperform the Market. *Source:* FTSE Russell 2019.

in annual financial or corporate responsibility reports, but non-standardized company-reported data may not translate across companies or sectors.

Non-Monetary HCV Example: Indian Company HCL Technologies' "Employees First, Customers Second" Initiative Leads to Higher Growth and Economic Resilience

This example (based on a case study from Forrester) demonstrates how employee-centered management efforts led a company to remain competitive in a crowded market by encouraging transparency and employee innovation (Hammond et al. 2011). In 2005, multinational information technology company HCL Technologies, headquartered in India, launched a management initiative called "Employees First, Customers Second" (EFCS). The first part of this experiment was "inverting the management pyramid" where, instead of traditional top-down evaluations, "HCL opened the 360-degree performance review process to all employees where everyone could access the results." This innovative approach allowed employees to evaluate management's ideas openly and critically. The second part of the EFCS initiative invited employees to innovate solutions through a value portal, and to have more direct contact with customers (Nayar 2010; Frauenheim 2014). Within three years, HCL's compound annual growth rate was 24% despite the great recession. Their market capitalization nearly tripled, and they reported 35% revenue growth per employee (Nayar 2010; Hammond et al. 2011).

Takeaway for Impact Investors

The lesson for impact investors is to look for companies demonstrating engagement with employees in management processes, which can lead to higher commitment and translate into higher returns. Connecting workers more directly with customers increased product innovation, which led to increased growth and performance.

Examples: Using Standards to Assess Whether Companies Value Human Capital

HCV Standards Example: SASB Standard Used by PIMCO to Invest in Commercial Banks

This example of how PIMCO, a global investment management firm, uses human capital data generated through SASB reporting to make routine investment decisions (PIMCO 2017; SASB 2019). PIMCO portfolio managers incorporate "material non-financial information" generated from SASB reporting in daily investment analysis. Using SASB data, PIMCO generates ESG scores for potential investments. Their scoring system puts additional weight on the Governance and Social Pillars "given that the material non-financial risks facing bank investors have been historically related to Governance and Social exposures" (PIMCO 2017).

> Human capital is quite simply our assessment of the quality of the non-executive employee base. Does the company attract top candidates and provide them excellent training and advancement opportunities? We often do this using a simple thought experiment: Where would the bank rank for a top-tier graduate applying for a job, assuming that the candidate had received comparable offers from every bank? First-choice employers receive higher human capital scores; banks that attract employees with less sterling qualifications or reputations receive lower scores.
>
> (PIMCO 2017)

The geographical region heatmap in Figure 4.4 shows how human capital is assessed as one of five Governance criteria and is embedded within the Social criteria.

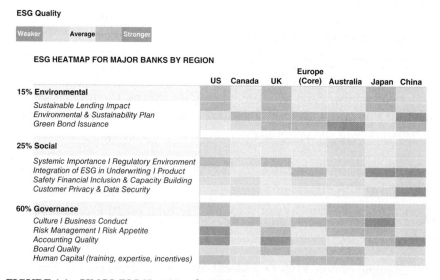

FIGURE 4.4   PIMCO ESG Heat Map for Major Banks by Region. *Source:* PIMCO 2017. Reprinted with permission from PIMCO and SASB.

Takeaway for Investors

This example shows how investors can use SASB materiality maps to identify sectors, regions, or individual companies that are performing well with regard to HCV. Investors can give greater weight to companies with higher Social and Governance performance according to SASB maps.

HCV Standards Example: How Novartis Used the "Social and Human Capital Protocol" to Calculate the Economic Value of Improving Health Across Africa

For some companies, human capital may also include customers as part of the value chain. Novartis International AG, a multinational pharmaceutical company, began considering consumer health as human capital in some of their markets. Looking specifically at the use of its products in Africa, Novartis estimated that customer health improvements resulting from their pharma products would also bolster end-users' ability to work and contribute to local economies. Figure 4.4 shows how improving "quality of life years" for customers (QALYs) translated into improving the workforces of South Africa and Kenya and increasing social and economic value, based on a case study conducted by WifOR, the Germany-based research institute (Seddik et al. 2018).

Takeaway for Impact Investors

This example based on that case study shows how Novartis used the Social and Human Capital Coalition Protocol to calculate how their products would not only benefit shareholders but also benefit customers by improving the quality of life for workers at large. Improved wellness ripples through society and creates a positive financial feedback loop for investors. Through reporting standards such as this, investors can more clearly quantify positive social impacts of their holdings alongside the financial upside.

(Note: Health gains on the left Y-axis and Social Impact on the right Y-axis by medicine)

HCV Standards Example: French Automaker Groupe PSA Demonstrates How Human Capital Contributes to Their Value Chain Using the International Integrated Reporting Framework

French automotive Groupe PSA uses the International Integrated Reporting Framework (IIRF) in its annual integrated reports to highlight the six types of capital that contribute to performance. Figure 4.5 is an example of how the inputs of human capital (and others) flow through their operational processes into value creation for stakeholders, including employees. Groupe

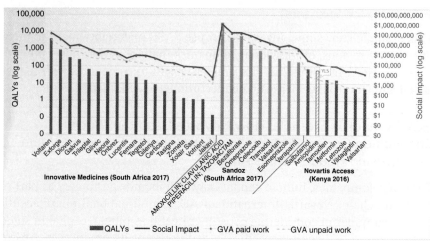

Health gains (left Y-axis) and Social Impact (right Y-axis), broken down by medicine

FIGURE 4.5 Novartis Regional Social and Human Capital Impact of Products. *Source:* Seddik et al. 2018. Reprinted with permission of Social and Human Capital Coalition and WifOR.

PSA captures human capital metrics they consider material to their business, including employee motivation, employee innovation, risk management related to safety, and ethical values (Groupe PSA 2017).

Takeaway for Impact Investors

Companies using frameworks such as the IIRF in their corporate reporting acknowledge the importance of human capital metrics as performance indicators. As a result of creating conditions for innovation and engagement, such companies may achieve higher growth than competitors. Investors can anticipate that companies using the IIRF model may exceed benchmarks. They can also assess how the stated corporate values of companies align with their chosen impact strategies.

HCV Standards Example: Managers of Australian Retirement Fund Assess and Adjust Holdings Using GRI Human Capital Guidelines

Construction and Building Unions Superannuation (CBUS), the largest Australian retirement fund, considers human capital metrics found in GRI's Social Standards as fundamental to selecting companies that generate "strong risk adjusted returns" (CBUS 2019; Global Reporting Initiative 2016). As active owners, CBUS managers highly value GRI reporting and work with their portfolio companies to strengthen transparency and increase disclosures. Three of CBUS's five key responsible investment principles incorporate human capital GRI metrics: cognitive diversity; health and safety; and labor and human rights in direct operations and supply chains (CBUS 2019). Leading by example, CBUS reports extensive human capital metrics in their integrated annual reports that cover all core and related workforce, including management, board members, full-time employees, and contractors within the organization and in their ancillary properties. Figure 4.6 shows a sample report from CBUS using GRI data to break down gender equity targets they consider relevant to company performance.

Takeaway for Impact Investors

CBUS is an example of an institutional impact investor. They use GRI Social Standards to screen companies to meet their responsible investment principles as well as their targets for risk-adjusted returns. Investors can follow CBUS's model by using GRI standards to create initial inclusion and exclusion criteria for their holdings, rate companies, and make adjustments over time.

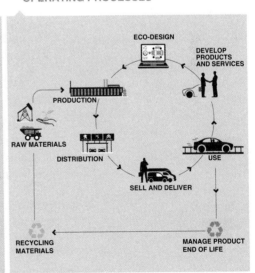

FIGURE 4.6   Human Capital in Groupe PSA Value Chain. *Source:* Groupe PSA Integrated Report 2017.

	2017		2018		2019	
	Males	Females	Males	Females	Males	Females
Permanent	135	127	173	163	226	200
Contract	12	6	9	20	24	38
Total employees	147	133	182	183	250	238
Full-time	142	99	165	120	220	155
Part-time	5	33	8	43	6	45
Contractors	0	1	9	20	24	38
Total employees	147	133	182	183	250	238

FIGURE 4.7   CBUS Superannuation Gender Parity 2019. *Source:* CBUS 2019 Annual Integrated Report, People, Culture and Remuneration Data Section (CBUS 2019).

STOCK INDEXES AND FUNDS BUILT ON HUMAN CAPITAL METRICS

If developing a customized approach to impact investing in HCV seems too laborious, there are numerous stock indexes that select companies based on human capital and human resource performance. Examples of indexes and funds that use HCV as a primary filter are listed in Box 4.1. Investors can select one or more of these to include in their portfolios. Alternately, investors can review the philosophies and holdings of each to inform or create their own HCV-inspired asset management strategies.

Box 4.1 Selected Investment Vehicles with Human Capital Value (HCV) Inclusion Criteria

Dow Jones Sustainability Indices (DJSI) Family of Indexes (DJSI 2019)

Every year, the largest public companies globally and in emerging markets are invited to take the RobecoSAM Corporate Sustainability Assessment (CSA). Questions address material economic, environmental, and social dimensions. Responses are weighted by industry relevance. Respondents are ranked and 10% are included in relevant DJSI indexes. Event-based factors may be subjectively evaluated on a case-by-case basis if they are deemed material (e.g. a major safety incident).

HCV Utility: *Useful for portfolio inclusion and exclusion. Select for indices highlighting CSA "Human" scoring such as the DJSI Europe Low Volatility index.*

S&P ESG Index Family (Core ESG Indices: ESG, S&P Dow Jones Indices, n.d.)

The S&P ESG index draws from the universe of S&P 500 companies. It uses DJSI SAM ESG scores but weights them across an average of 21 industries. A second set of SAM ESG criteria is applied to each environmental, social, and governance dimension, then a composite score is generated. Exclusions are made for low ESG performance and controversial industries (e.g. tobacco).

HCV Utility: *The social dimension of the CSA includes the majority of HCV factors, which can be targeted for investment or further research. The S&P ESG Index spans mid- to large asset classes and multiple geographies.*

HIP Great Place to Work® ESG Index and Portfolio (HIP Investor 2020)

HIP Investor's Great Place to Work® Index and Portfolio draws from publicly traded firms that appear on *Fortune*'s 100 Best Companies to Work For ranking produced each year by Great Place to Work®. The index is primarily weighted by companies' HIP Ratings score and rebalanced quarterly to exclude low performers. The index is benchmarked against the S&P 1500.

HCV Utility: *The HCV criteria assessed in HIP Investor's Great Place to Work® ESG Index and Portfolio includes employee satisfaction, a uniquely predictive HCV metric. Companies are weighted by their performance across the composite HIP pillars of "Health, Wealth, Earth, Equality, and Trust."*

JUST Index and ETF (JUST Capital 2019a)

The JUST index comprises Russell 1000 companies that are weighted by industry according to market capitalization and ranked in the top 50% by JUST Rankings. The index and ETF are rebalanced quarterly.

HCV Utility: *JUST Rankings are based on polling from a representative sample of Americans. Their data and rankings are concerned with public priorities and are grounded in qualitative evidence related to the human dimension of Human Capital. Their rankings are grounded in workforce-related metrics specific to the United States.*

(continued)

(continued)

Parnassus Endeavour Fund (Parnassus 2019)

The Parnassus Endeavor Fund selects US companies with outstanding workplaces and quality management teams. It emphasizes long-term value and is benchmarked against S&P 500 and rebalanced monthly.

HCV Utility: *The Parnassus Endeavor Fund is a specific targeted investment vehicle focused on HCV.*

Japan JPX/S&P CAPEX and Human Capital Index (S&P Dow Jones Indices 2019)

The JPZ/S&P specifically targets Japanese companies making investments in human capital that include variables from RobecoSAM scoring such as Human Capital Development and Talent Attraction and Retention.

HCV Utility: *JPZ/S&P is a specific targeted country investment vehicle that uses HCV data as core criteria.*

Source: Authors, based on desk review.

LOOKING FORWARD: NEW HUMAN CAPITAL VALUATION REPORTING WILL MAKE IMPACT INVESTING EASIER

Artificial intelligence (AI) and automated human resource management systems (HRMS) using big data are the next frontier. HCV data is collected by companies and funneled to impact investors for real-time management.

> There is naturally occurring data in the world through places like LinkedIn where the flow of people can be observed if you are clever enough at scraping; it's an imperfect measure ... but we live in a data desert where some data would be helpful.
>
> (Laurie Bassi, personal communication, April 30, 2019)

We are going to companies with the message that if you don't provide data, we will find other ways of finding it, including crowdsourcing. So, I think companies who are forward looking would want to be ahead of the curve and put the best foot forward by disclosing the data.

(Hernando Cortina, JUST Capital, personal communication, April 11, 2019).

Such efforts to scrape public data sources are under way to identify corporate HCV trends for investors. For example, there are some funds that scrape data, tracking the number of employees updating their profiles within a company without changing jobs; they end up shorting those companies because they expect layoffs. Professional raters and all investors can use LinkedIn, Glassdoor, Monster, and other public sources as proxies for gauging job flows and employee satisfaction.

AN INVESTOR'S ACTION PLAN FOR HUMAN CAPITAL VALUATION

HCV is vital to help the corporate and investment marketplaces identify risks and opportunities associated with workforce management. What can investors do to encourage companies to measure and report on their human capital? Below is a checklist to guide the conversation.

> **Ask companies for metrics and information:** All investors, whether individual or large asset managers, can ask companies for data directly through their management or investor relations teams (L. Bassi, personal communication, April 30, 2019; J. Higgins, personal communication, April 15, 2019; M. Wallace, personal communication, April 11, 2019). Investors can request that companies adopt any of the reporting standards described in the chapter and utilize their social and human capital guidelines.
>
> **Submit shareholder resolutions:** Investors owning a minimum threshold of shares can submit shareholder resolutions requesting routine disclosures of metrics, including those relating to human capital valuation.
>
> **Join forces:** Form or join a coalition and petition for disclosure requirements. For example, the Human Capital Management Coalition, comprised of pension fund managers with USD $3 trillion in assets under management, petitioned the SEC to mandate the following disclosures from publicly traded companies (Human Capital Management Coalition 2017). Within two years, the SEC subsequently recommended a rules change to allow accounting for the types of assets listed below (SEC 2019):

- Workforce demographics
- Workforce stability
- Workforce composition
- Workforce skills and capabilities
- Workforce culture and empowerment
- Workforce health and safety
- Workforce productivity
- Human rights
- Workforce compensation and incentives

Use the available tools: Use the tools that are available today. The reporting standards and frameworks are evolving to include more industry-specific, material human capital variables, such as SASB for investor disclosures, and GRI for multi-stakeholder reporting (S. Becker, personal communication, May 22, 2019; B. Esterly, personal communication, May 3, 2019). The simplest step an investor can initiate is to track and invest in indexes with HCV approaches (DJSI 2019; HIP Investor 2020; JUST Capital 2019a; Parnassus 2019). If a more personalized approach is desired, ratings systems are available to provide aggregated data vetted by analysts. HCV ratings are well suited for investors who are seeking expert input on portfolio inclusion and exclusion (McBassi & Company 2020; HIP Investor 2020; JUST Capital 2019b). Asset managers and active individual investors can also perform their own research using metrics suggested in this chapter that are aligned with their individual investing philosophies.

Reward HCV reporting: Any company or organization that is taking initiative to calculate monetary HCV as supplemental to consolidated reporting is paying attention; such reporting is in and of itself a positive signal of institutional awareness. Firms electing to report on workforce variables using third-party standards are committing time and resources to provide the market useful data for comparative analysis (M. Wallace, personal communication, April 11, 2019). The data and ideas presented in this chapter strongly suggest that investors can benefit from holdings that provide HCV data, regardless of the company's performance on HCV measures, compared to those that have no transparency.

Elevate the human capital conversation: Elevate discussion of your experiences by sharing them with other investors to create a generative space for discussions, modeling, and to understand and set expectations for best practices.

CONCLUSION

The evidence and examples (including those based on case studies) presented in this chapter demonstrate the clear benefits of integrating human capital value (HCV) into impact investment strategies. Until recently, HCV was an underutilized approach to appraising companies and their future financial prospects for growth and competitive success. Variability in measurement and reporting tools made benchmarking a challenge. Recent disclosure standards, such as the SASB and others, give companies the tools to provide the marketplace crucial non-monetary information about how they manage workforce assets. Such data allow all investors to assess human capital-related risks to businesses (such as safety issues, sufficient supply chains, and legal actions). Companies that measure human capital as an asset using monetary methods have a more accurate picture of how much their workforce investments contribute to returns. For investors seeking positive social as well as financial outcomes, companies that regard people as an asset and not a liability send a signal that their management practices may yield better outcomes for their workforce and even their customers.

Proactive impact investors can combine monetary and non-monetary human capital metrics described here to create custom models for building HCV-themed portfolios. Alternately, investors can take advantage of HCV ratings platforms to guide decision-making and strategy. Such ratings platforms provide a quick way to access information by offering company and fund-level scores or rankings and benchmarking based on their detailed analyses of human capital metrics. Those seeking a simpler approach can invest in HCV-oriented indexes, ETFs, or funds. Any of these HCV approaches augment portfolio building and can give investors a better, deeper understanding of a given company's prospective performance and profitability. This is a terrific win-win for investors, who can pursue better returns on investment while supporting companies that recognize and maximize the social and financial value created by their human capital.

ACKNOWLEDGMENTS

Many thanks to the expert interviewees for their generous contributions to this book and for their pioneering work to integrate human capital valuation into investing. Thanks also to Walt Morton and Lucia Pohlman for their thoughtful edits and insightful improvements. Finally, gratitude for the editors who worked tirelessly to bring this collection of ideas together to equip investors to use resources to achieve a more sustainable and humane world.

FURTHER READING FOR IMPACT INVESTORS

Disclosure and Standards

Global Reporting Initiative (GRI) Standards: www.globalreporting.org/standards/gri-standards-download-center/

Global Reporting Initiative (GRI) Examples: www.globalreporting.org/information/news-and-press-center/Pages/Corporate-case-studies.aspx

Human Capital Management Institute Financial Statements (HCF$): www.hcmi.co/solutions

International Integrated Reporting Framework (IIRF): integratedreporting.org/resource/international-ir-framework/

International Organization for Standardization (ISO): www.iso.org/standard/69338.html

Social and Human Capital Coalition Protocol: social-human-capital.org/#process

Sustainability Accounting Standards Board (SASB) Materiality Standards: www.sasb.org/standards-overview/materiality-map/

Sustainability Accounting Standards Board (SASB) Examples: www.sasb.org/knowledge-hub/

Human Capital Valuation Ratings

BCorporation Certification and Analytics: b-analytics.net/content/standards-navigator

Great Place to Work® Trust Index Employee Survey©: www.greatplacetowork.com/

HIP Investor Ratings: hipinvestor.com/how-clients-use-hip/ratings/

Human Capital Management Drivers, McBassi & Company, Analytics: mcbassi.com/analytics/

ISS Environmental and Social Disclosure: www.issgovernance.com/esg/ratings/environmental-social-qualityscore/

Sustainalytics: www.sustainalytics.com/esg-ratings/#1530569132662-3e9e89 29-5bee

JUST Capital Rankings: justcapital.com/rankings/

Refinitiv Diversity and Inclusion Index: www.refinitiv.com/en/financial-data/indices/diversity-and-inclusion-index

RobecoSAM Corporate Sustainability Assessment (CAS): www.robecosam.com/csa/

Health and Safety

Center for Safety and Health Sustainability: www.centershs.org/human-capital.php

Social Accountability International Standard: www.sa-intl.org/index.cfm?fuseaction=Page.ViewPage&pageId=1689

REFERENCES

Bassi, L., and McMurrer, D. (2007). Maximizing Your Return on People. *Harvard Business Review* 85 (3): 115–123, 144.

Becker, G. S. (1964). *Human Capital: A Theoretical and Empirical Analysis, with Special Reference to Education. New York: National Bureau of Economic Research.* https://doi.org/10.1177/000271626536000153.

Brummet, R. L., Flamholtz, E. G., and Pyle, W. C. (1968). Human Resource Measurement: A Challenge for Accountants. *Accounting Review* 43: 217–224.

Bush, M. C., and the Great Place to Work Research Team (2018). *A Great Place to Work for All.* Oakland, CA: Berrett-Koehler.

CBUS (Construction and Building Unions Superannuation) (2019). CBUS Annual Report 2019: Built on Trust. https://www.cbussuper.com.au/content/dam/cbus/files/governance/reporting/Annual-Integrated-Report-2019.pdf (accessed 3 May 2020).

Core ESG Indices: ESG, S&P Dow Jones Indices. (n.d.). https://us.spindices.com/index-family/esg/core-esg (accessed 4 May 2020).

DJSI (2019). Dow Jones Sustainability Index: DJSI Index Family. https://www .robecosam.com/csa/indices/djsi-index-family.html (accessed 30 December 2019).

Edmans, A. (2011). Does the Stock Market Fully Value Intangibles? Employee Satisfaction and Equity Prices. *Journal of Financial Economics* 101 (3): 621–640.https://doi.org/10.1016/j.jfineco.2011.03.021.

Edmans, A., Li, L., and Zhang, C. (2017). Employee Satisfaction, Labor Market Flexibility, and Stock Returns Around the World. European Corporate Governance Institute (ECGI), Finance Working Paper No. 433/2014.

Erb, M., Rohman, J., Frauenheim, E., et al. (2018). Innovation by All (Part 1 of 5: Innovation Insights Series). Great Place to Work®. https:// www.greatplacetowork.com/resources/reports/innovation-by-all (accessed 4 May 2020).

FASB (Financial Accounting Standards Board) (2019a). Accounting Standards Codification (ASC) 350 - Intangibles, Goodwill and Other. https://asc.fasb .org/imageRoot/76/120327576.pdf (accessed 3 May 2020).

FASB (Financial Accounting Standards Board) (2019b). 105 Generally Accepted Accounting Principles. https://asc.fasb.org/topic&trid=6532098 (accessed 18 November 2019).

Fitz-Enz, J. (2000). *The ROI of Human Capital: Measuring the Economic Value of Employee Performance*. New York: AMACOM.

Fitz-Enz, J. (2019). The Human Capital Scorecard. *American Management Association.* https://www.amanet.org//articles/the-human-capital-scorecard/ (accessed 14 December 2019).

Flamholtz, E. (1971). A Model for Human Resource Valuation: A Stochastic Process with Service Rewards. *Accounting Review* 46 (2): 253–267.

Flamholtz, E. (1974). Human Resource Accounting: A Review of Theory and Research. *Journal of Management Studies* 11 (1): 44–61.

Flamholtz, E. (2009). Towards Using Organizational Measurements to Assess Corporate Performance. *Journal of Human Resource Costing and Accounting* 13 (2): 105–117.https://doi.org/10.1108/14013380910968629

Flamholtz, E., Bullen, M.L., and Hua, W. (2002). Human Resource Accounting: A Historical Perspective and Future Implications. *Management Decision* 40 (10): 947–954. https://doi.org/10.1108/00251740210452818

Frauenheim, E. (2014). Vineet Nayar's Happy Feet. Workforce.com. https://www .workforce.com/2014/03/14/vineet-nayars-happy-feet/ (accessed 26 December 2019).

Frauenheim, E., (2019). How the World's Best Workplaces Create a Great Global Culture. Fortune.com. https://fortune.com/2019/10/02/worlds-best-workplaces-global-culture (accessed 15 August 2020).

Fulmer, I. S., and Ployhart, R. E. (2013). "Our Most Important Asset": A Multidisciplinary/Multilevel Review of Human Capital Valuation for Research and Practice. *Journal of Management* 40 (1): 161–192. https://doi.org/10.1177/0149206313511271

Great Place to Work® (2019a). Defining the World's Best Workplaces. https://www.greatplacetowork.com/resources/reports/defining-the-worlds-best-workplaces (accessed 3 May 2020).

Great Place to Work® (2019b). *World's Best Workplaces* 2019. https://www.greatplacetowork.com/best-workplaces-international/world-s-best-workplaces/2019 (accessed 23 December 2019).

GRI (Global Reporting Initiative) (2016). GRI 405: Diversity and Equal Opportunity. https://www.globalreporting.org/standards/gri-standards-download-center/gri-405-diversity-and-equal-opportunity-2016/ (accessed 4 May 2020).

GRI (Global Reporting Initiative) (2020). GRI Standards. https://www.globalreporting.org/standards (accessed 5 April 2020).

Groupe PSA (2017). Integrated Report: Creation of Values for Stakeholders – Automotive Division. https://www.groupe-psa.com/content/uploads/2018/03/2017-Integrated-Report--Creation-of-Value-for-Stakeholders.pdf (accessed 4 May 2020).

Hammond, J. S., Rymer, J. R., Gilpin, M., et al. (2011). Case Study: HCL Technologies Puts Employees First, Customers Second. Forrester. https://www.forrester.com/report/Case+Study+HCL+Technologies+Puts+Employees+First+Customers+Second/-/E-RES60172# (accessed 27 December 2019).

Hekimian, J. S., and Jones, C. H. (1967). Put People on Your Balance Sheet. *Harvard Business Review* 45 (1): 105–113.

Herman, R. P. (2010). *The HIP Investor: Make Bigger Profits by Building a Better World*. Hoboken, NJ: John Wiley & Sons.

Herman, R. P. (2011). Let's Value People as an Asset and Bring Financial Statements into the 21st Century. Huffington Post (28 October). https://www.huffpost.com/entry/lets-value-people-as-an-a_b_1063698 (accessed 24 March 2020).

Higgins, J., and Cooperstein, G. (2019). Human Capital Financial Statements. *Human Capital Management Institute (HCMI)*. https://www.hcmi.co/Docs/Case-Studies/Human-Capital-Financial-Statements (accessed 4 May 2020).

Higgins, J., Cooperstein, G., Peterson, M., et al. (2019). Top Five Metrics for Workforce Analytics. Human Capital Management Institute (HCMI) and Human Concepts. https://www.hcmi.co/Docs/White-Papers/Top-5-Metrics-for-Workforce-Analytics (accessed 4 May 2020).

Higgins, J., Sidda, H. R., Gilmyers, J., et al. (2012). Linking Human Capital to Business Performance. *Human Capital Management Institute (HCMI)*. https://www.hcmi.co/Docs/White-Papers/Linking-Human-Capital-to-Business-Performance-White-Paper (accessed 4 May 2020).

HIP Investor (2020). How Clients Use HIP. https://hipinvestor.com/how-clients-use-hip/ (accessed 30 December 2019).

Hoque, F. (2018). Incorporating Sustainable, Responsible and Impact Investing into Your Practice: A Roadmap for Financial Advisors. US SIF Foundation. https://www.ussif.org/store_product.asp?prodid=35 (accessed 4 May 2020).

Human Capital Management Coalition (2017). *Petition letter to the Security Exchange Commission regarding Rule* 192(1). http://uawtrust.org/Admin Center/Library.Files/Media/501/About%20Us/HCMCoalition/hcmcpetition july2017.pdf (accessed 10 December 2019).

HCMI (Human Capital Management Institute) (2012). Case Study: UPS – How Leadership Affects Workforce Productivity. https://www.hcmi.co/Docs/Case-Studies/How-Leadership-Affects-Workforce-Productivity (accessed 4 May 2020).

HCMI (Human Capital Management Institute) (2019). ROI of Internal Hires. https://www.hcmi.co/Docs/Case-Studies/ROI-of-Internal-Hires (accessed 4 May 2020).

IIRC (International Integrated Reporting Council) (2013). International <IR> Framework. https://integratedreporting.org/resource/international-ir-framework/ (accessed 4 May 2020).

Infosys (2011). Annual Report: 30 years of Infosys – Additional Information 2010-11. https://www.infosys.com/content/dam/infosys-web/en/investors/reports-filings/annual-report/annual/documents/ar-2011/download.html (accessed 4 May 2020).

Institute of Directors Southern Africa (2016). *King IV Report on Corporate Governance for South Africa* 2016. https://cdn.ymaws.com/www.iodsa.co.za/resource/collection/684B68A7-B768-465C-8214-E3A007F15A5A/IoDSA_King_IV_Report_-_WebVersion.pdf (accessed 4 May 2020).

ISO 30414:2018 (2018). Human resource management—Guidelines for internal and external human capital reporting. ISO (International Organization for

Standards). http://www.iso.org/cms/render/live/en/sites/isoorg/contents/data/standard/06/93/69338.html (accessed 12 December 2019).

ISS (Institutional Shareholder Services) (2019). E&S Disclosure QualityScore. https://www.issgovernance.com/esg/ratings/environmental-social-quality score/ (accessed 12.23.19).

Jaggi, B., and Lau, H. S. (1974). Toward a Model for Human Resource Valuation. *Accounting Review* 49 (2): 321–329. www.jstor.org/stable/245105.

JUST Capital (2019a). 2020 Overall Rankings.https://justcapital.com/rankings/ (accessed 15 December 2019).

JUST Capital (2019b). Just Capital Ranking Methodology. https://com-just capital-web-v2.s3.amazonaws.com/pdf/JUSTCapital2020RankingsMethodo logy.pdf (accessed 4 May 2020).

Kenton, W. (2019). Calculated Intangible Value (CIV). Investopedia. https://www .investopedia.com/terms/c/civ.asp (accessed 15 December 2019).

Lev, B., and Schwartz, A. (1971). On the Use of the Economic Concept of Human Capital in Financial Statements. *Accounting Review* 46 (1): 103–112. http:// www.jstor.org/stable/243891.

Likert, R., and Pyle, W. C. (1971). Human Resource Accounting: A Human Organizational Measurement Approach. *Financial Analysts Journal* 27 (1): 75–84. http://www.jstor.org/stable/4470773.

Lingane, A. (2015). Bay Area Blueprint: Worker Cooperatives as a Community Economic Development Strategy. *Carolina Planning* 40: 19-28. https://www.project-equity.org/wp-content/uploads/2017/02/Bay-Area-Blueprint_Worker-Coops-as-a-Community-Economic-Development-Strategy_CPJ2015_Lingane.pdf.

Mayer, R. C., Warr, R. S., and Zhao, J. (2017). Do Pro-Diversity Policies Improve Corporate Innovation? *Financial Management* 47 (3): 617–650. https://doi.org/10.1111/fima.12205

McBassi & Company (2020). Benchmarking, surveys, and research for associations. https://mcbassi.com/benchmarking-industry-associations/ (accessed 4 May 2020).

Morningstar (2017). Morningstar Ratings 101: What You Need to Know. http:// www.morningstar.com/content/marketing/global/company/morningstar-ratings-faq.html (accessed 30 December 2019).

Nayar, V. (2010). *Employees First, Customers Second: Turning Conventional Management Upside Down*. Boston: Harvard Business School Publishing.

Parnassus (2019) Parnassus Endeavor Fund Investor Shares. https://www
.parnassus.com/parnassus-mutual-funds/endeavor/investor-shares
(accessed 30 December 2019).

PIMCO (2017). ESG for Commercial Banks: Think like a treasurer, engage like
a partner, hold to account as a lender. *Sustainability Accounting Standards
Board (SASB)*. https://www.sasb.org/knowledge-hub/case-study-pimco/
(accessed 4 May 2020).

Refinitiv (2019). Diversity and Inclusion Index. https://www.refinitiv.com/en/
financial-data/indices/diversity-and-inclusion-index (accessed 12.11.19).

RobecoSAM (2019). Corporate Sustainability Assessment. https://www
.robecosam.com/csa/ (accessed 13 December 2019).

Rohman, J., (2016). The Business Case for a High-Trust Culture. Great Place to
Work®.

SASB (Sustainability Accounting Standards Board) (2019). Standards. https://
www.sasb.org/standards-overview/download-current-standards-2/
(accessed 11 December 2019).

Seddik, A. H., Branner, J., Helmy, R., et al. (2018). The Social Impact of
Novartis medicines: Two Case Studies from South Africa and Kenya.
WifOR Institute. https://www.wifor.com/uploads/2019/02/2018_Novartis_
Social-Impact-ZA-and-Kenya_Case-Study_WifOR-4.pdf (accessed 4 May
2020).

SEC (Securities and Exchange Commission) (2019). Modernization of Regulation
S-K Items 101, 103, and 105. *Human Capital Disclosure*: 44–54. https://www
.sec.gov/rules/proposed/2019/33-10668.pdf (accessed 4 May 2020).

Smith, J., and Klemash, S. (2019). How and why human capital disclosures
are evolving. *Ernst and Young (EY)*. https://www.ey.com/en_us/board-
matters/how-and-why-human-capital-disclosures-are-evolving (accessed 4
May 2020).

S&P Dow Jones Indices (2019). JPX/S&P CAPEX and Human Capital
Index. https://eu.spindices.com/indices/strategy/jpx-sp-capex-human-
capital-index (accessed 30 December 2019).

Social and Human Capital Coalition (2019). Social and Human Capital Protocol.
https://social-human-capital.org/protocol/ (accessed 4 May 2020).

Sustainalytics (2019). Sustainalytics. https://www.sustainalytics.com/ (accessed
11 December 2019).

APPENDIX 4.1: EXPERTS INTERVIEWED

TABLE A4.1   Experts Who Participated in Original Interviews for This Chapter in 2019 and 2020.

Interviewee	Position	Description
Laurie Bassi, PhD	CEO at McBassi & Company; People Analytics Advocate	Human Resources Analytics and Consulting Firm
Stefanie Becker, PhD	HR Expert People Insights, SAP; Convenor of Working Group Human Capital Reporting	Human Resources Management Technology Firm
Michael Bush, MBA	CEO, Great Place to Work®	Employee Experience Research and Recognition Firm
Hernando Cortina, MA Finance	Executive Director, Head of Index Strategy at ISS ESG; Formerly Research Director, Just Capital	Financial Services Firm
Bryan Esterly, CFA	Director of Research – Standards at SASB	Accounting Standards Developer
Jeff Higgins, MBA	Founder and CEO HCMI; ISO Human Capital Reporting Standard ISO30414 Expert	Workforce Analytics and Development Firm
Nancy Mancilla, MPS	Founder and CEO, ISOS Group	Management Consulting Firm
Alison Omens, MPA	Chief Strategy Officer at JUST Capital	Financial Research Firm
Mike Wallace	Executive Director, Social and Human Capital Coalition; Partner, Environmental Resources Management	Environmental Services Firm

APPENDIX 4.2: HUMAN CAPITAL MANAGEMENT INSTITUTE MONETARY HUMAN CAPITAL VALUATION FORMULAS

TABLE A4.2   Human Capital Financial Statements Metrics Defined.

Human Capital Return on Investment Ratio (HC ROI Ratio)
Definition:

(Total Operating Revenue – (Total Expenses – Total Cost of Workforce)) / Total Cost of Workforce

Measures the impact of financial investments in the workforce on operating profit. For example, a ratio of 1.1 means each dollar invested in the workforce would yield a 10% return.

Pros: Predictive, simple to calculate and understand; Emphasizes returns from labor without other expenses

Cons: Snapshot; Does not take into account present value

Return on Human Capital Investment (HC ROI)
Definition:

Total Operating Profit / Total Cost of Workforce

Percentage of operating profit relative to investment in workforce (Total Cost of Workforce)

Pros: Simple to calculate and understand contributions of HC to profit

Cons: Snapshot; Does not take into account present value; Focus on operating profit may obscure inefficiencies in non-revenue sectors of a company or overvalue workforce by factoring in revenue from non-operating activities

Total Cost of Workforce
Definition:

(Total Compensation Costs + Benefits Costs + Other Workforce Costs)

Total Cost of Workforce includes full and part-time employees, contractors, and temporary workers

Pros: Comprehensive cost capture

Cons: Time investment needed to collect all relevant workforce costs including training, benefits, settlements, and outsourced work can be extensive

Source: Higgins et al. 2012.

APPENDIX 4.3: HUMAN CAPITAL VALUATION RATINGS SYSTEMS

TABLE A4.3 Ratings Systems.

Balanced Scorecards (Fitz-Enz 2019)**:** These contain assessments of management activities for acquiring, maintaining, developing, and retaining human capital. They provide a way to measure the cost, time, and quality of key human factors that impact production of products and services.

Pros: Visual and easy to understand; Produced internally or externally for benchmarking over time.

Cons: Scorecards are subjective and therefore difficult to compare across firms.

Utility for Impact Investors: Companies that publish balanced scorecards are paying attention to internal human capital metrics and providing transparency for investors. Scorecards produced by external raters may provide a window into human capital practices that cannot be found elsewhere.

BCorp or Benefit Corporation Certification (BCorporation 2019)**:** These are certifications that score human capital and other ESG factors. Participating firms are scored according to standardized key indicators.

Pros: Scoring is global and consistent across companies. Companies are vetted by the certifier. Social factors have a dedicated sub-score. Scores are free to the public.

Cons: Data is largely self-reported. Certification is voluntary and paid for by the firms, which limits participation.

Utility for Impact Investors: Certification is rigorous and demonstrates a commitment to ESG. Scoring is standardized and allows benchmarking with other certified companies across social and governance factors as well as environmental.

Great Place to Work® (Great Place to Work® 2019b)**:** Employees and employers are surveyed about work environments and experiences in roughly 10,000 companies worldwide. Ratings predict productivity and operational efficiencies related to turnover, engagement, operating margin, and other variables (Rohman 2016).

Pros: There are demonstrated correlations between employee satisfaction and company performance on this employee survey and stock price. Scores are free to the public.

Cons: Survey data are self-reported, participation by companies is voluntary and requires payment from companies.

Utility for Impact Investors: Higher scores reflect workforce satisfaction and also correlate with higher growth compared to benchmarks, and therefore provide investors with indicators for both social impact and returns.

TABLE A4.3 *(continued)*

HIP (Human Impact + Profit) Investor Ratings (HIP Investor 2020): Uses standardized quantifiable metrics of people, planet, and trust to score companies. Provides weighted rankings in five top-level categories: Health, Wealth, Earth, Equality, Trust. Three of the five focus directly on human capital.
Pros: These ratings are conducted by expert analysts and enable consistent comparisons across companies and sectors, and over time.
Cons: Not all publicly traded companies are ranked. Scores are available by paid subscription.
Utility for Impact Investors: Higher scores in the Health, Wealth, and Equality categories indicate better performance on human capital indicators, which can be cross-referenced with financial performance to make investment decisions.

Human Capital Management (HCM) Drivers (McBassi & Company 2020): Surveys identify key performance indicators for human capital such as leadership practices, employee engagement, knowledge accessibility, workforce optimization, and organizational learning capacity.
Pros: Surveys are rigorous, performed by expert analysts, and standardized results lend themselves to benchmarking companies over time.
Cons: Survey input data is not available for public scrutiny and outside assessment. Scores are available by paid subscription.
Utility for Impact Investors: Companies with higher ratings on surveys are expected to have better performance on human capital indicators, which can be cross-referenced with financial performance to make investment decisions.

ISS E&S Disclosure Quality Score (ISS 2019): This scoring system measures risk in social and environmental areas by analyzing corporate disclosures. The more complete the disclosures, the greater potential for a higher score.
Pros: These scores are based on multiple established ESG reporting standards and can be used for benchmarking companies against peers by assessing published data. The ISS system identifies gaps in disclosure practices.
Cons: This is a proprietary measurement system. Scores are available by paid subscription.
Utility for Impact Investors: Higher ratings on surveys indicate better performance on social indicators. Higher scores can then be cross-referenced with financial performance to select or weight investments.

JUST Capital (JUST Capital 2019a): In-depth research is conducted on Russell 1000 Companies based on proprietary national survey results. Qualitative and quantitative surveys and focus groups are performed, followed by expert data review and evaluation of human capital practices. Firms are then ranked and weighted.
Pros: Original expert research informs individual company rankings. Companies are also rated by their industry sector for peer comparison.
Cons: Analysis is limited to companies in the Russell 1000 index.
Utility for Impact Investors: Higher ratings on surveys anticipate better performance on human capital indicators, which can be cross-referenced with financial performance to make investment decisions.

TABLE A4.3   *(continued)*

Refinitiv Diversity and Inclusion Index (formerly Thomson Reuters) (Refinitiv 2019): Ranks workforce diversity, which is a key indicator for innovation and financial performance. Lists the top 100 public companies.

Pros: Includes qualitative and quantitative data across thousands of global companies.

Cons: Diversity and inclusion are the only human capital measures.

Utility for Impact Investors: Higher ratings anticipate better performance on diversity indicators, which can be cross-referenced with financial performance to make investment decisions.

RobecoSAM (RobecoSAM 2019): SAM Corporate Sustainability Assessment (CSA). Corporate surveys are performed of ESG activities.

Pros: Surveys are designed to inform investment decisions with ESG data. Companies are scored based on their transparency as well as performance. ESG categories are scored independently. Questions map to the GRI reporting standard for comparability. Data is free to the public.

Cons: Only invited companies can participate. Those that choose to participate may indicate a self-selection bias and skew results.

Utility for Impact Investors: Higher ratings on surveys anticipate better performance on social indicators, which can be cross-referenced with financial performance to make investment decisions. Several HCV themed funds and indexes are based on this ratings system.

Sustainalytics (Sustainalytics 2019): Company-level ESG ratings based on assessments of materiality and risk.

Pros: Based on comprehensive expert analysis. Ratings are comparable across companies through a large database.

Cons: Human capital ratings are embedded in overall ESG score. Scores available by paid subscription.

Utility for Impact Investors: Higher scores anticipate better performance on social indicators, which can be cross-referenced with financial performance to make investment decisions.

APPENDIX 4.4: HUMAN RESOURCE METRICS AND WHERE TO FIND THEM

TABLE A4.4   Sources of Human Resource Metrics.

Human Resource Metric	Source of information
Employee turnover and retention rates	Company filings Corporate Social Responsibility reports
Internal promotion rates	Company filings Corporate Social Responsibility reports
Absenteeism	Company filings Corporate Social Responsibility reports
Illness and medical leave taken	Company filings Corporate Social Responsibility reports
Wellness support and programs such as allowances for fitness or health screening	Company filings Corporate Social Responsibility reports Employee-based company review outlets
Safety and Accident data, which may be required in certain industries	Company reporting Government filings Safety database such as Occupational Health and Safety Administration (OSHA)
Compensation including wages and benefits	Company filings and published documents Employee-based company review outlets
Pay ratios (a) between management and entry-level employees; (b) between management and median employee pay; and (c) gender-based ratios	Company filings and published documents Corporate Social Responsibility reports Bureau of Labor Statistics
Diversity and inclusion measures for (a) age; (b) gender; (c) ethnicity; and (d) disability	Company filings and published documents Corporate Social Responsibility reports Employee-based company review outlets Expert ratings platforms
Innovation factors such as patents or copyrights	Company filings Government filings
Legal actions either internal or from external sources	Government filings Legal publications
Workforce training, engagement, and development programs	Company filings and published documents Corporate Social Responsibility reports Employee-based company review outlets
Rates of volunteerism by employees	Company filings and published documents Corporate Social Responsibility reports Employee-based company review outlets
Community engagement programs	Company filings and published documents Corporate Social Responsibility reports Employee-based company review outlets

CHAPTER 5

Leadership by Results for Impact Investors and Investees

Rajen Makhijani, MBA

Abstract

A chief executive officer's (CEO) leadership contributions alone may be responsible for 10% to 14% of the firm's overall performance. Supporting quality leadership is critical for achieving superior impact and financial returns. But does the impact sector invest enough to provide such support to portfolio companies? Mission-driven organizations may be investing 75% less on leadership development than for-profit organizations, on a per employee basis. This is concerning, since 60% or more of leaders themselves self-identify as "not strong" on the very leadership capabilities they see as important to driving impact and financial returns. This suggests that impact investors recognize the criticality of leadership but are uncertain about the effectiveness of leadership development programs. Citing research and real-life examples, this chapter demonstrates how investing in leadership can accelerate impact by 10% to 30% per annum, along with increasing sales of impactful products and services sales worth—in the United States alone—USD $18 billion to USD $31 billion. The "Leadership by Results" framework can result in impact and profit six to eight times greater than the initial investment in leadership programs, a multitude of lives can be improved, and far greater innovation and efficiencies can be achieved. For such results, the leadership development programs must enable mindset shifts, not just skill and competency development. Impact investors must institutionalize such programs for their portfolio firms on an ongoing basis. The "Talent Accelerator" by LeapFrog Investments is one such example of institutionalized support, and a source of rich insights for impact investors.

Keywords

Leadership; Leadership by results; Leadership Mindsets; Leadership Development; Performance; Talent; Impact Investing; Results; Due Diligence; Top Team Effectiveness; Culture; CEO Development; Founders Syndrome; Private Equity; Venture Capital; IPO Self-Awareness Impact Washing; Ontology; Phenomenology; Hurdle Rate

INTRODUCTION

The Global Impact Investing Network (GIIN) estimates that the global impact investing market grew to USD $502 billion in 2019, measured by assets under management (AUM) (Mudaliar and Dithrich 2019). Sustainable investing assets in Europe, the United States (US), Canada, Japan, Australia, and New Zealand reached USD $30.7 trillion, a 34% increase in two years (Global Sustainable Investment Alliance 2018). This growth is tremendous, but is the impact investing sector allocating sufficient resources and attention to building leadership skills, capabilities, and mindsets of investees?

This chapter draws on a literature review, qualitative data, examples from companies, and the author's personal experience applying leadership frameworks, process, applications, and systems with a multitude of clients in the global south, particularly in Asia and Africa, including impact investors across investor types (private equity, venture philanthropy, and grant makers), such as LeapFrog, for profit educational businesses, social enterprises in skilling and employment, and human rights organizations.

This chapter focuses on the current state of leadership development efforts in the impact sector, pointing out key gaps and opportunities. It then establishes the criticality of leadership in delivering impact and financial results and highlights social enterprises' significant underinvestment in leadership development. This underinvestment is not because impact sector leaders are unaware of their leadership capability gaps. In fact, sector leaders from across the spectrum, from mission-focused, social-sector chief executive officer (CEO) and other top managers to leading impact investors, foundations, families, as well as nonprofit organizations, and social enterprises all acknowledge gaps in the very leadership capabilities that they see as important.

Next, details are provided about the typical reasons for such underinvestment. One underlying cause is that impact investors are uncertain about the effectiveness of leadership development programs, and the extent to which they actually help leaders to produce better financial and impact results. This mistaken assumption is driven by the use of inappropriate metrics (i.e. participant feedback-based metrics) to assess the success of leadership development programs.

This chapter advocates for the use of the "Leadership by Results" approach. Within this approach, impact investors are urged to initiate leadership development programs that are geared toward achieving an organization's Big Hairy Audacious Goals (BHAGs), in terms of both impact and profit. In the process of delivering such goals, leaders will be stretched and will develop personally and professionally to speed and scale the organization to even more impact and profit. The "Leadership by Results" approach fundamentally transforms all aspects of leadership programs—the trigger, conception, design, execution, and measurement—to ensure they are focused on both impact and financials.

This chapter also identifies specific trigger points within the deal life cycle where "Leadership by Results" programs can be initiated and provides examples of BHAGs for impact and financial goals. A strong recommendation is made that impact investors support leadership programs that enable mindset shifts, not just impart knowledge and skills. Cited research findings and a real-life example show how mindset shifts effectively change behaviors and create sustained results.

Three practical frameworks and a detailed example are also provided. Approaches like results-based finance, shared value, information communications technology (ICT) for development, human-centered design, among others, can enable impact investors, boards, and decision-makers in the impact sector to better analyze impact and financial outcomes, derive deeper insights into the underlying drivers of performance, and devise effective innovations for future improvement. The goal of delineating these practical frameworks is to provide impact investors with a starting point from which to review their own portfolio's impact, profitability, and organizational health, with a "leadership lens," by helping an impact investor answer the questions such as: (i) is there anything about an investee's leadership mindset that might be driving these outcomes, and (ii) what can an investor do to support the leaders of her portfolio company, and drive different results, financially and in terms of impact?

The first framework described, entitled "Leadership Archetypes," helps the impact investor to diagnose the underlying limiting mindset of the leaders in their portfolio companies. These limiting mindsets are impediments to the performance and delivery of results, both impact and financial. It provides practical tips for impact investors, to provide the most targeted and effective support to portfolio company leaders to shift the underlying mindset and produce superior results—in impact and financial terms.

The second framework, known as the "Ineffective Bus," helps impact investors identify which elements are missing at the leadership team level and address those gaps from a collective team perspective. Specific triggers in the deal life cycle are identified for such collective leadership support interventions. The third framework, "Leadership by Results," directly addresses the question of metrics. It helps translate the achievement of BHAGs, which are established in executive leadership programs, into clear and measurable objectives for impact and profit that are applicable to the organization as a whole. Impact investors can answer one or both of the following questions using the third framework: (i) for a given amount of investment into a leadership program, what should the minimum magnitude of the BHAG be; or, alternately, (ii) for a given BHAG (in impact and financial terms), what is the acceptable investment into the leadership program that would address and accomplish these breakthroughs? In this discussion, the attribution problem is also highlighted; in other words, a multitude of factors may contribute to the achievement (or nonachievement) of a BHAG, and attributing it to only a single factor (such as a leadership development program) may require the use of more complex quantitative methods, such as experimental or post-experimental evaluation methods.[1] Accordingly, limitations of this approach are acknowledged, and practical mitigation tactics are proposed.

Finally, an example is provided that moves the discussion from the level of an individual company's program to how an impact investor might

---

[1]See Chapter 16, "Measuring and Evaluating Social Impact in Impact Investing: An overview of the Available Standards and Methods," by Ana Pimenta and Elsa de Morais Sarmento.

institutionalize such programs across their portfolio. This example details how a reputed impact investor, LeapFrog Investments, explored, conceptualized, and established the LeapFrog Talent Accelerator to provide such leadership development support to its portfolio companies on an ongoing basis.

Thus, this chapter is organized in three sections. The first section establishes the criticality of leadership and underinvestment in leadership development by the impact sector. The second section recommends the "Leadership by Results" approach. This approach is characterized by a focus on achievement of BHAGs—impact and financial goals—through leadership development support. It also includes several other guiding principles to close the gaps in current leadership development approaches. The most important of these is to enable shifting of underlying mindsets, not just developing leadership skills, competencies, and capabilities, and to carry out holistic collective leadership journeys over time for the entire top team. The third and final section comprises three practical frameworks and a case. The frameworks are "Leadership Archetypes"; the "Ineffective Bus" or leadership team effectiveness framework; and finally, a framework to translate goal achievement into impact and financial return. The real-life example describes and distills insights from the feasibility assessment stage of LeapFrog Investment's Talent Accelerator as an example of institutionalized leadership development support for portfolio companies.

THE IMPACT SECTOR UNDERINVESTS IN LEADERS

The impact sector recognizes the criticality of leadership in producing impact and financial results. Sector leaders themselves acknowledge key gaps on the very capabilities that they regard as important. However, the sector still underinvests in leadership development overall.

Leadership Is a Critical Lever to Deliver Results

A study from Harvard Business School estimates that 30% to 40% of the performance of a company is attributable to industry effects, 10% to 20% to cyclical economic changes, and 10% to the CEO (Khurana 2002). Another study from Harvard puts this at 14% (Champy and Nohria 2001). Yet another study that surveyed 1,155 business leaders in the United States found that nearly 50% of a company's reputation is linked to the CEO's reputation (Kelly 2008). The significance of executive leadership carries over to nonprofits. In a study of nonprofits in India, a full 97% of the 203 nonprofit respondents said that leadership development is vital to their organizations' success. It is also a belief echoed by funders (Venkatachalam and Berfond 2017). Clearly, leadership matters.

A study on the criticality of social enterprise leaders in the impact sector is likely to yield similar results. In fact, leadership may be even more critical in the impact sector, since the sector demands more of its leaders, requiring them to realize both impact and profit. Most impact sector leaders emphasize the importance of leadership in their speeches at conferences and company town halls. But unlike the for-profit sector, this focus is underpursued and underinvested.

Impact Sector Chronically Underinvests in Leadership Development

Data available for nonprofits indicate that investment into talent and leadership remains very low (Stahl 2014):

- Only 1.24% of total grant dollars were allocated toward investments in nonprofit talent by the US 1,000 largest foundations on an average annual basis from 1992 to 2011.
- Out of the nearly USD $287 billion granted over those 20 years, only USD $3.5 billion was spent on supporting leadership in grantees or the community.
- Of the 2.4 million grants made during that period, only 24,000 included some form of talent-investment.
- In 2011, funders distributed 147,872 grants totaling USD $24.5 billion. Of these, only 1,111 grants went to talent development, for a total of USD $179 million or 0.7% of total grant dollars that year.

McKinsey arrived at the same conclusion after it surveyed nearly 200 social-sector CEOs and top managers at the helm of nonprofit organizations, foundations, social enterprises, and impact-investing funds in the United States. McKinsey's 2015 report, "What social sector leaders need to succeed," found that the social sector spent only ~1% on talent development, a value of approximately USD $400 million (Callanan et al. 2014a). By comparison, a 2014 study from the Center for Nonprofit and Public Leadership at the Haas School of Business at the University of California, Berkeley, found that the private sector spent about USD $12 billion on leadership development for established and emerging leaders in 2011 (Callanan et al. 2014b). When compared on a per employee basis, this translates to USD $120 per employee

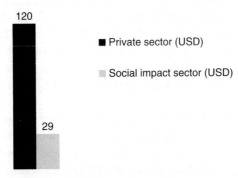

FIGURE 5.1 Annual Leadership Development Budget Per Employee in the Private and Social Impact Sector. *Source:* Callanan et al. (2014b).

annually in the private sector, versus USD $29 per employee in the social sector, as depicted in Figure 5.1.

Sector Leaders Themselves Acknowledge Gaps

In the same study, McKinsey found that social sector leaders agree on core capabilities that are essential for them to succeed in their missions (Callanan et al. 2014a). As Figure 5.2 illustrates, in spite of widespread agreement about

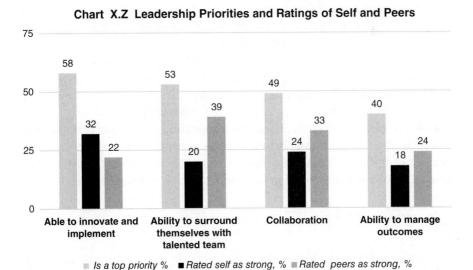

FIGURE 5.2 Leadership Priorities and Ratings of Self and Peers. *Source:* McKinsey (2014).

which leadership capabilities are essential, however, less than 30% of social sector leaders rate themselves as strong on these factors. Even when rating their peers, the results are somewhat better but distinctly low.

The Wrong Metrics Lead to Underinvestment

Impact investors typically understand the importance of leaders in generating results. But continued underinvestment in leadership development suggests that investors are uncertain about the effectiveness of leadership development programs in accelerating financial and impact results.

This is unsurprising because most leadership development programs measure success based on participant feedback. This tends to be true of programs run by experts, service providers, universities, and others with funding from investors and/or investees. More sophisticated providers may measure success of leadership programs via "Net Promoter Scores" (NPS) or other such methods, which are more appropriate for customers and referrals but not for leadership skills.

Surprisingly, few programs measure "learning" or assess whether participants learned a new concept. A "learning" metric consists of baselining the knowledge and awareness of the participant at the preprogram stage and measuring the same post program. However, these metrics are useful only where the goal is to improve the leaders' knowledge or some skills. Creating results requires the application of such knowledge and skills in the business, toward sharply defined stretch goals of impact and financial returns creation. Further, learning from experience is the number one way that leaders develop (McCauley et al. 2013). However, in many cases, the translation of the learning into organizational context, and its application in actual business, organizational, and people problems, is largely left to the individual.

Some programs do take a step forward and include feedback from stakeholders on competencies and measure the differential. Some also include Action Learning Projects (ALPs) so that leaders find an arena to practice their learning. These are certainly better than mere feedback. However, the effectiveness of these can be significantly enhanced by following "Leadership by Results" principles, described in further detail later in this chapter.

THE "LEADERSHIP BY RESULTS" APPROACH

A summary of the key ideas of the "Leadership by Results" approach is provided in Box 5.1. The rest of the chapter expands on these core ideas.

Box 5.1 The Key Ideas of the "Leadership by Results" Approach

The "Leadership by Results" approach advocates that the pursuit of BHAGs develops leadership. Hence, leadership development programs under this approach must provide customized support to leaders, that help them with the most critical elements that accelerate their achievement of both impact and financial goals, and their sustained development as leaders.

Since the goal is "sustained" development as a leader, it must result in an expansion of their capabilities over a considerable period time (sustainability), but also across contexts. It needs to be relevant for the achievement of BHAGs but also applicable across contexts, beyond the current BHAG at hand. This has three implications:

- Since achievement of organizational BHAGs requires top team members to work together, it is ideal that the leadership program be a custom program and a journey together over time, for the entire top team.
- The shift in leadership must be at the level of mindsets, not just skills and capabilities, since mindsets pervade across contexts. A corollary of this is that the support to the leader needs to be holistic; in other words, the mindset-shift may have to be focused on areas of life that are outside the BHAG but are being influenced by the same underlying mindset that is also in the way of the achievement of the BHAG.
- There needs to be agreement upfront on a "hurdle rate of return" and how it will be measured. This needs an agreement on how BHAG achievement will be measured, and how it will be translated into financial and impact returns. The "Leadership by Results" approach advocates a rule of thumb as the hurdle rate of return for leadership programs: the incremental EBITDA potential over three to five years must be about six to eight times the total financial cost of the leadership program, in addition to 50% to 100% acceleration in the achievement of select impact metrics over a three- to five-year period.

Source: Author.

Impact Investors Must Focus on Big Hairy Audacious Goals

Impact investors must change the trigger that catalyzes an investment in leadership development, from routine or exploratory, to doing it to deliver BHAGs. Several times, "routine" learning and development programs tend to be calendared by the learning and development department within the human resources function of larger organizations. These are characterized by low ownership by actual leaders in line functions and often result in very little impact (Ryan 2009).

"Exploratory" triggers for enrolling into leadership development programs refers to the times when senior leaders in portfolio companies are sent to university-run or other open enrollment programs. The motive of going to such programs is to network, take some time off the day-to-day, and expose the leader to new ideas. Similarly, leadership teams and the entire organization, too, "indulge" themselves in leadership development alongside all staff conferences, leadership retreats, and the like. These are all legitimate motives and triggers for leadership development. However, under the "Leadership by Results," the motive and the trigger to launch a leadership development intervention must change. The motive must be to create breakthrough results in impact and financial terms.

As Gandhi said, "Find the purpose, and the means will follow." The means refer not just to resources outside but also the inner resources of a leader.

The leadership development intervention must be designed to support leaders in their pursuit of specific BHAGs so they can enhance their effectiveness in leading themselves, leading others, leading the business, leading impact, and leading transformation to achieve the BHAGs. In this process, leaders deliver big results and develop leadership.

Triggers for Leadership Development Across the Investment Life Cycle

Throughout the investment life cycle, impact investors have several pivotal opportunities to push their investees to grow their leadership capacities by further committing to BHAGs, moments of significant threat, possible expansion, strategic change, and transition. The academic literature, business examples, and the author's personal experience in the field all support the recommendation to initiate results-based leadership development interventions at such turning points in order to enable CEOs and the entire leadership team to achieve BHAGs.

These moments include, but are not limited to, the following stages:

- **Pre-deal due diligence.** At this stage investors can carry out "leadership due diligence" with two objectives:
  - Explicitly test the "fit" of the founder, CEO, and top team to deliver on the investment thesis with regard to the impact and financial goals.
  - Ascertain and design the leadership development support that will be needed post-investment.
- **Immediately post-investment**, alongside the initial 100-day plan
- **First six months** (180 days) of the deal execution
- **At the two-year mark** (730 days)
  - A large number of the investors ask for advice at this point in time, typically because the investment thesis has not played out in practice, and it is now recognized that the leadership needs support.
- **Six quarters prior to a targeted exit** (e.g. if an initial public offering [IPO] is planned)

Apart from this, a CEO change, founder succession, enterprise technology implementations, and external shocks and opportunities like significant regulatory changes, new technologies, shifts in customer preferences, or supply chain changes, and significant partnership opportunities are also relevant to trigger change.

A real-life example of a BHAG from the author's own experience is described in Box 5.2. The example refers to a comprehensive performance acceleration program for a mission-driven for-profit educational group owned by a family and several impact investors, referred to as EduCo Group.

Box 5.2 EduCo Group's Comprehensive Performance Acceleration Program

EduCo Group aimed to fundamentally drive social mobility by making quality higher education available to those who lacked access due to affordability, opportunity cost, and geographic remoteness through a hybrid-distance education model. Higher education has been identified as a particularly important impact outcome because the gross enrollment

(continued)

(continued)

ratio (GER) in the country of EduCo Group's headquarters stood at 18%, as compared with 26% in Brazil and 30% in China. The government had set an aggressive target of increasing the GER to 30%. The emergence of the knowledge economy opened up demand for graduates from the industry, but supply from conventional providers of higher education had been growing at an abysmal 5.6% p.a. in the preceding 35-year period. Against this backdrop, EduCo Group had pioneered an innovative learning model that created cost savings of 37% to 75% for the provider, as compared to traditional models, while improving learning outcomes for the student by as much as 90%. EduCo Group's board, consisting of committed family owners and impact investors, had set aggressive reach and revenue goals that were being missed. They recognized they needed to support EduCo Group's leadership team through a dedicated program. They mutually agreed that the meta-indicator of success for the leadership program would be whether EduCo Group successfully raised capital through an initial public offering (IPO) at a valuation of USD $1 billion (50% increase in valuation in six quarters). If raised, this capital would be ammunition to further accelerate EduCo Group toward their mission and goal of being the single largest contributor to the national goal of GER of 30%. Moreover, such an IPO would be a strong message to the world that "doing good and doing well can indeed go hand in hand." This overall organizational BHAG was then translated to individual BHAGs for the top team. Examples of these translated goals included plans and regulatory approvals for five new campuses for higher education, and a pipeline of 100,000 learners for vocational education. Notably, in striving for this goal, EduCo Group substantively contributed to the country's achievement of GER of 26.3%.
Source: Author.

Additional real-life examples of pivotal moments where organizations and individual leaders strengthened their commitments to BHAGs by launching custom leadership development programs include:

- Starting off a new organizational unit within an organization (in this case, a fellowship) to accelerate outcomes of the departments that they are assigned to. Fellows work on crucial new transformation projects ranging from

- Service expansion: Increasing the number of civic services available via doorstep delivery from 40 to 100 within a year
- Process quality and responsiveness: Bringing a civic grievance redressal system to six-sigma standards, meaning 3.4 defects per million, or 99.99966% free of defects
- Accelerating consumer behavior shifts through a comprehensive approach: Changing consumer and industry behavior in the transport sector such that 25% of all new vehicles registered in the city are electrical vehicles, and other such goals
- Massive scale-up and Organization Transformation: Several times growth in revenue in five years, and increased incomes for learners, equivalent to certain percentage points of the gross domestic product (GDP) of the country, achieved by capturing life cycle value of a learner, digital transformation of the operating model, and market and ecosystem linkages for a vocational skills and employment player
- Leadership succession and culture preservation: Founder succession for a human rights nonprofit (without loss of donors, maintaining continuity, and bringing fresh strategy that builds on past successes)
- Capital Raising: Pivoting the funder base of an organization from concentrated and risky to diverse (from two to five funders) in six months

Custom and Collective Journeys for the Top Team

Having chosen a compelling organizational BHAG, impact investors must ensure all the design and execution elements of the leadership program are geared toward successful and sustainable delivery on the BHAGs. There are a number of principles that may be collectively referred to as the "Leadership by Results" approach, which can help impact investors and program designers to align their efforts toward sustainable results on BHAGs. Following is a list of two key principles:

- **Insist on a custom program, deeply anchored in the context of the organization, for the entire c-suite and/or top leadership team,** rather than sending one or a few individuals to an open enrollment leadership program. Start off with a Top Team Effectiveness Diagnostic. One of the tools that can be used is "The Ineffective Bus" (details in Figure 5.3). When carried out skillfully in a safe environment, this exercise fosters trust and collaboration. Top team members become stakeholders in one another's sustained leadership

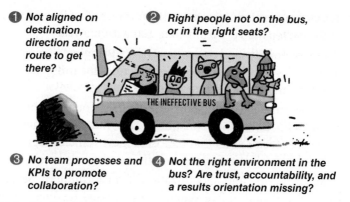

FIGURE 5.3   The Ineffective Bus. *Source:* Art © 2020 by C. Grisham; Content by Author.

development. Additionally, it lays the foundation for a broader culture shift in the organization.

- **Ensure that the leadership development program is a "journey," not an event.** Leadership development must consist of multiple touch points, which may include several classroom sessions, as well as coaching and mentoring support. The journey can be as long as is needed for the achievement of the BHAG, but it usually ranges between 6 and 18 months. If the BHAG needs more time to be accomplished, which is often the case, then stretch goals should be set based on key milestones on the journey to the ultimate BHAG. Several research papers and books agree. For instance, Satia et al. (2014) in their book, *Visionary Leadership in Health: Delivering Superior Value*, state, "where traditionally a one off, one-time leadership course was the norm, there is now a general consensus that this is not adequate." In the author's experience, the impact sector in particular tends to have "brown bag talks" over lunch and chooses shorter training formats but still counts them as leadership development. While lack of resources and paucity of time are often cited as constraints, one-time events usually remain at surface level and do not reach the critical level of changing mindsets.

Mindsets, Not Just Skills

Mindsets are mental lenses that dictate what information leaders take in and use, which make sense of and navigate the situations they encounter. Simply put, mindsets drive what leaders do and why. In order to support leaders in a way that is deep, powerful, and sustained over time, "Leadership by Results" approach advocates that leadership programs must enable awareness and shifting of mindsets and not just focus on providing knowledge, skills, and networks. The latter do help them to navigate the challenges from the world outside. But mindset shifts will ensure they identify the barrier within them. This would require enhancing their self-awareness in a deep and powerful way. Mindset shifts should not be generic and must be clearly linked to the specific impediments that inhibit a leader's individual and organizational BHAG achievement. Having identified these unique barriers, the duration of the program must be long enough, and with sufficient support, to enable guided application over time. This will enable the leader to deliver sustainable results of impact and profit. The behavior shifts will be cemented and sustained too. Box 5.3 provides an example of shifting mindsets of CEOs of investee companies.

Box 5.3 LeapFrog: An Example of Shifting Mindsets in a Group Setting

"Intense," "Transformative," and "Life changing moment."

The CEOs

"I don't think any of us could have envisaged just how far the program could have gone!"

The Impact Investor

LeapFrog CEO Indaba: An example of a powerful intervention can be found in the CEO Indaba initiative (LeapFrog Investments 2015) launched by LeapFrog Investments and supported by the European Investment Bank, KFW, and the European Union. The CEO Indaba initiative brought together the 12 CEOs of LeapFrog's investee companies from Asia and Africa in 2015 for the first time and reconvened them in 2016 in London. The 2016 edition focused on leadership development with a focus on self-awareness. This was not a "death-by-PowerPoint" experience where the participants were taught *about* leadership theories, nor was it a "case study" approach where the leaders learned about other leaders in facing similar situations, nor was it a set of psychometrics

(continued)

(*continued*)

where a rule engine and a database are used as a benchmark to tell the leader where they stand, vis-à-vis a general population of survey takers.

Instead, CEO Indaba was a longer-term "journey." It consisted of a "discovery phase" of one-on-one interviews with each of the participating CEOs to understand their needs and prepare them to make the best use of the leadership development program. Next, there was an experiential workshop in London. It comprised a set of conversations, exercises, and real-life situations (no role plays or simulations) where the leaders were asked to take immediate action, and which generated real-time results for them with real stakeholders.

For example, in exploring "Trust" and "Honesty," they did not explore these concepts using the famous trust equation (Maister et al. 2001). They also did not explore how Steve Jobs or Gandhi demonstrated trust and honesty, or their views about it. They also did not get into a simulation where they would be asked to put themselves in the shoes of the protagonist and make decisions, or indeed a simulation concerning their own organization. Instead, they were invited to interact with each other, "live-in-the-moment," in a way that would allow for trust and honesty to be demonstrated (or not). It was not a game, or any other made-up situation. The conversation, the people, the roles they play, and the stakes were all real. A safe platform was created to enable these authentic conversations to take place. The CEOs then took a hard and honest but nonjudgmental look at the results they had generated with their real peers, in real time, in a real conversation. They received feedback from peers and acknowledged the results and experience they were generating for their peers. They looked into the mirror—and noticed their behaviors, the unconscious choices that drove these results, and were able to identify the underlying mindset or "lens" that drove their choices. They identified the shifts they needed to make in these mindsets. But mere intellectual identification does not change mindsets. They identified opportunities and began acting from the new mindset, in real time, creating new results. It was of course quite uncomfortable.

Could "uncomfortable" be used as a complimentary description for a process? In this case, it was, with a very special meaning. After the workshop, CEOs shared their experience, and the impact it had, in a candid video (LeapFrog 2016). Quotes from the CEOs include "intense," "transformative," and a "life-changing moment." LeapFrog Investments, represented by Associate Directors Akua Owusu-Akonor and Claus Eckbo, shared their reflections and stated, "I do not think any of us could have envisaged just how far the program could have gone."

A coaching phase was envisaged post-workshop to support continued practice of new behaviors in real situations, to create new results. Many of these leaders went on to sustain these shifts and produce results in impact and financial terms, many of which cannot be detailed due to confidentiality reasons. Collectively, the portfolio companies of LeapFrog have gone on to reach over 188.6 million people across more than 35 emerging markets. Of this customer base, 154.5 million are low-income consumers often accessing insurance, savings, pensions, credit, and health care for the first time. In the process, LeapFrog has created and supported 128,048 jobs and livelihoods.

Source: Author and LeapFrog CEO Indaba (2016) video testimonials by CEOs and LeapFrog.

Holistic Support

Since mindsets pervade across contexts, the support to the leader needs to be holistic, meaning that the mindset shift may have to be focused on areas of life that are outside the BHAG but are being influenced by the same underlying mindset that is also in the way of the achievement of the BHAG. Hence, the program must have a clear "what's-in-it-for-me" at an individual level for every top team member, that may even extend to areas outside the BHAG, or even outside work.

Practically speaking, every member of the top team must have at least two goals. One should directly flow from the organizational BHAG, based on the leader's role and responsibility area. The other should be completely autonomously chosen by the leader, based on what is personally and/or professionally important to her. This will ensure ownership and internal motivation throughout the exercise. An example is provided in Box 5.4. For illustrative purposes, let's continue with the example of EduCo Group, the mission-driven, for-profit education company from Box 5.1 with an innovative distance education model[2] (Box 5.4). This example is not a fable; it is indeed a true story, though the client context has been changed.

Box 5.4 The Surprising Key to Restoring the Faith of a Leader in EduCo Group's Vision

The head of EduCo Group's student enrollments team was what is colloquially referred to as "the typical alpha aggressive salesperson." This worked well for the requirements of the job and for the organization's BHAG of aggressive growth of students. However, two challenges were creating friction for him and those around him.

The first challenge was that he occasionally demonstrated streaks of "impact-washing" (particularly prominent during month and quarter endings, when chasing aggressive targets). Tangibly, this would include overlooking on-ground reports from operations teams about students having been sold courses without due counseling. To put it mildly, this resulted in students whose expectations, fit, and purpose were misaligned with what was on offer, and the overall mission of EduCo Group. Enrollment numbers looked better, but they were not necessarily in line with the mission. This led to strains between the CEO and him. The CEO insisted on both mission and profit to sustain the pursuit of the mission, whereas the sales director saw some trade-offs being inevitable.

The second challenge was the sales director's lack of collaboration with his peers. This also had an adverse impact on EduCo Group's BHAG in both impact and financial terms. EduCo Group sought to spawn and grow adjacent businesses, including related services in student placements, and corporate assessment engines that would create a match between students and jobs, among others. The purpose of these businesses was to serve learners holistically, and they furthered EduCo Group's overall mission of supporting income and social mobility for students, not just providing them with a degree or qualification. Creating and growing these businesses required significant collaboration amongst the heads of businesses, and most crucially with the head of learner enrollments.

---

[2]The actual leader in this example belonged to another company in another country, with a different organization BHAG. This preserves confidentiality while still illustrating the point using a real leader's example.

Discussions, workshops, and trainings on collaboration, and concepts like "Shared Value," did not yield desired results. Eventually, a leadership program with "Leadership by Results" principles was launched. It commenced by creating the foundation of leadership self-awareness at the level of mindsets. Through a guided process, the leader had the opportunity to look at his mindset and "lens for life," holistically. What eventually became clear to him was that a failed personal relationship had made him angry and cynical about "high-sounding ideals." He had channeled that anger constructively, by immersing himself at work, and driving his team to chase targets. However, it had also made him less collaborative. And the disillusionment about ideals of love and trust had seeped into other areas of life. Mindsets are all encompassing and all pervading (Olley 2012). This mindset of cynicism due to perceived betrayal in a personal relationship was driving the behaviors of impact washing and lack of collaboration. This was a self-arrived, self-owned realization, aided of course by some questions from the facilitators, but was not a super-imposition.

Realizations are not enough. Mindset shifts must be evident in actions and results. The leadership program must explicitly facilitate and accelerate the application of mindset shifts. In the EduCo Group program, goal setting and coaching over nine months was designed toward this end.

EduCo Group's BHAG had been cascaded down to him, and informed his personal BHAGs:

- A leap in enrollment numbers of tightly defined target learners in line with EduCo Group's mission; supported by a behavior and mindset shift from "Impact-Washing driven by Cynicism" to "Impact-Driven, propelled by Genuine Mission Belief."
- BHAGs in the adjacent business development team were identified that demanded a collaborative and trusting mindset.
- A BHAG in the area of personal life, finding a partner and demonstrating trust in the relationship.
- Over the next nine months, the coach provided support on all the goals, including the relationship goal. This put some personal stakes for him in the program, and it also assisted in shifting the underlying mindset he had about his unit and EduCo Group's BHAGs. When one of the later modules of the program commenced in a classroom environment, the enrollments director revealed

(continued)

(continued)

in the check-in that he had transformed his relationship with someone he had hitherto been seeing, but not trusting. A spontaneous applause ensued from all participants. But the bigger surprise was yet to be revealed. He had planned for that very day to be his "ring ceremony" with his partner. In it, he would have announced to all invited friends and family about their intention to get married. Instead, he was sitting there in the leadership program, hundreds of kilometers away. He had chosen to postpone his engagement in order to participate in the leadership module. The enrollments director saw the leadership development program as instrumental in unlocking his impact, business success, and personal satisfaction. From the impact investor's perspective, the key to accelerating impact outcomes in line with the vision lay in an unexpected place—the mindset of the head of enrollments, specifically the degree of trust in his relationship with his partner.

Source: Author.

Mindsets Can Tangibly Be Shifted Using Ontological and Phenomenological Models

The importance of shifting mindsets is intuitively understood by many impact investors, leaders of portfolio companies, and leadership service providers. However, claims of shifting mindsets and personal transformation are often greeted with suspicion. This is not without reason. If mindsets are "lenses" that determine the worldview of leaders, it implies that they are deep-rooted and closely tied to the beliefs that shape how a leader views the world. Hence, claims that closely held beliefs collected over a lifetime can be shifted in a workshop or even a journey of 6 to 12 months may seem questionable. Further, if the "mindset-shifting" processes are recommended to be carried out together as a collective top team, there is even greater level of skepticism, since these beliefs are not just long-standing, but also deeply personal.

So, can mindsets be shifted at all? While many approaches attempt to do so, in the author's own experience, the ones that have been most powerful and successful are built on the foundations of disciplines within philosophy, ontology (the branch of metaphysics dealing with the nature of being), phenomenology (the science of phenomena as distinct from that of the nature of being), and epistemology (the theory of knowledge, and the distinction between justified belief and opinion). Some researchers and practitioners of leadership development have translated the insights from these "abstruse" branches of philosophy into practical insights, models, and methods for the purposes of leadership development.

The ontological model of leader and leadership opens up and reveals the actual nature of being when one is being a leader and opens up and reveals the source of one's actions when exercising leadership (Jensen, Erhard, and Granger 2012). Since it is not the purview of this chapter and book to delve too deeply into what causes mindset shifts, it may suffice to state that creating sustained shifts in mindsets is possible, including in collective settings.[3]

Use a Hurdle Rate for Impact and Financial Returns

There needs to be agreement upfront on how BHAG achievement will be measured, and how it will be translated into financial and impact returns. The "Leadership by Results" approach advocates a rule of thumb as the hurdle rate of return for leadership programs—the incremental Earnings Before Interest, Taxes, Depreciation and Amortization (EBITDA) potential over three to five years must be about six to eight times the total financial cost of the leadership program, in addition to 50% to 100% acceleration in the achievement of select impact metrics over a three- to five-year period.

The details of how this is deployed in actual practice are given later in the chapter (Box 5.9). The problem of attribution of results to the leadership program is also discussed in that section.

Other Practical Suggestions to Implement the "Leadership by Results" Approach

Apart from the BHAGs as the trigger, holistic mindset-shift support, collective journey over time for top teams, and measurement of impact and financial returns, here are a few practical tips and suggestions for impact investors and boards:

- **Once designed, impact investors must step back to** create a safe and empowered space for leaders of their portfolio companies. Furthermore, while impact investors must hold expert service providers

---

[3]Those interested in exploring more may refer to Jensen et al. (2012).

and participating leaders accountable to results, they must allow for confidentiality between the leadership experts and the leaders.

- **Encourage leaders to give the biggest co-investment of all, the investment of their time.** The popular saying "Put your money where your mouth is" is outdated. It can be rephrased as "Put your time where your mouth is." Again, the LeapFrog CEO Indaba (2016) offers a best practice. There was enormous (and understandable) pressure from investment partners to make the CEOs available for impact and business discussions, now that they had flown in from afar for three days in London. But LeapFrog as an institution understood the importance of going deeper, and that the transformation they were seeking required more time. As such, LeapFrog's CEO Indaba devoted two and a half days of the three-day retreat to the CEO's leadership self-awareness workshop.

- **Institutionalize the support.** Impact investors have a significant role to play in institutionalizing results-based leadership development efforts. LeapFrog Impact Investments took the lead in their ecosystem by creating the LeapFrog Talent Accelerator. The author had the opportunity to conceive, design, and build a business plan for the Talent Accelerator, building on two years of leadership development work with the CEOs of LeapFrog's investee companies. Eventually, this led to the creation of the Talent Accelerator with support from Prudential of a USD $1.5 million capstone investment (Prudential 2017). The chapter covers key learning and highlights from this experience in the example provided toward the end of the chapter.

THREE PRACTICAL FRAMEWORKS AND AN EXAMPLE

Thus far, the chapter has established the importance of leadership, the gaps, and the underinvestment in leadership development in the social sector. A case has been made to use the achievement of BHAGs as a means for leadership development. Critical points in the investment life cycle have been identified for impact investors to trigger "Leadership by Results" programs.

In this section, three practical frameworks and one example are provided, all of which enable and demonstrate a "Leadership by Results" approach. These frameworks are: (i) Common Leadership Archetypes in the impact sector, classified by the limiting mindsets; (ii) Leadership Team Effectiveness Framework; and (iii) illustration for translating BHAGs into financial and impact returns.

These three frameworks are connected to the key recommendations of this chapter, which are:

- Enable mindset shifts at a whole person level.
- Take entire top team on a collective leadership journey over time.
- Measure success of leadership development through financial and impact returns.
- Impact investors must institutionalize the "Leadership by Results" approach (brought to life through a real-life example).

Framework 1: Common Leadership Archetypes in the Impact Sector

In board of directors' reviews and other assessments of portfolio companies, impact investors and senior executive team members examine financial and impact outcomes. Investors tend to be well trained and adept to dig deeper and understand the impact, business, financial, and other drivers of success. Impact investors have already come a long way in uncovering insights and supporting their investees through other frameworks from a variety of disciplines. Examples include Theory of Change, Systems Thinking, Human-Centered Design, and Results-Based Finance. Often, they also identify the underlying leadership challenge. However, the diagnosis and remedy tend to be at the level of knowledge or skill. The Common Leadership Archetypes tool can help impact investors quickly dig in a level deeper. Investors and decision makers can construct a few hypotheses of what the underlying limiting mindset might be, and what the impact investor can do. After all, investee's leadership is a key lever of performance of the organization, potentially accounting for 10% to 14% of the performance, or more.

For this, the first step is to define the term "mindsets."

Mindsets and Attitudes

As stated earlier, mindsets are mental lenses that dictate what information leaders take in and use, which make sense of and navigate the situations they encounter. Simply put, mindsets drive what leaders do and why.

Mindsets can either be enabling or limiting. Four such pairs of mindsets have been identified: (i) Growth and Fixed Mindsets; (ii) Learning and Performance Mindsets; (iii) Deliberative and Implemental Mindsets; and (iv) Promotion and Prevention Mindsets (Gottfredson and Reina 2020).

Some of the archetypes that are commonly seen in the impact sector are described in the following sections, along with the impact they tend to have on their results and relationships. An anecdotal sectoral spread of these archetypes is also provided. How an impact investor can support such a leader is also described. For three such archetypes, real-life examples with anonymized backgrounds or sectors are also provided.

Fixed Mindset Archetypes in the Impact Sector

As against displaying a growth mindset, the fixed mindset leader archetype displays a limited and inflexible worldview. This archetype encompasses the *Charismatic Visionary* and the *Idealist*, described below.

- **The Charismatic Visionary**

The *Visionary and Charismatic, but Disempowering Founder* is arguably more widespread in the impact sector than in commercial investing. For instance, what distinguishes leaders in the health sector from those in the for-profit corporate world, or government sector, is a combination of peculiar situational and institutional parameters. Health leaders, particularly in developing countries, work long hours, have limited resources, face uncertain funding flows, deal with hostile traditional groups, and face volatile policy and economic situations (Satia et al. 2014). Unsurprisingly, personal charisma and visionary qualities act as a countervailing force to the generally depressing conditions and motivate employees to do more despite constraints. However, many visionary leaders also tend to hire helpers instead of developing talent (Zwilling 2015). The "Charismatic but Disempowering" leadership mindset, coupled with low funding into developing second line of leaders, creates a thin leadership pipeline. This increases both impact and business risk for investors. This can be seen in India, where only 47% of 203 surveyed Indian non-government organizations felt confident that anyone internally could effectively lead their organizations in the absence of their senior-most leaders (Venkatachalam and Berfond 2017). A survey of impact investees is likely to yield similar results.

The archetype can be easily detected by impact investors, including their strengths and the challenge they face (Table 5.1). To support such leaders, impact investors often send them to leadership courses on organization building, succession planning, and others. The leader themself acknowledges the need for such strengthening of the organizational systems and bench strength, even putting it as a top three priority. But they often

TABLE 5.1 The Charismatic Visionary.

Archetype	Visionary and charismatic but disempowering founder
Description	Surrounded by "Yes men" loyalists; often loses talent in top team
Mindset	Fixed mindset about own identity as irreplaceable, poor assessment of others' ability, talents, and intelligence
Outcomes	Path breakers but cannot scale beyond a point due to weak organizational systems and overreliance on leader
Where	Can be anywhere; particularly found in sectors that need high courage, grit, and sacrifice (e.g. Human Rights), innovation (ICT for Development, Fintech, Professional Services for Development), or "Techno-Managerial sectors" like Health and Education

Source: Author.

complain about not being able to find such talent. Frequently, they are able to narrate specific examples of having tried to groom others and give responsibility, but how none of it worked. This is also referred to as the "Founder's Syndrome" (Block 2004).

One such Asian founder and CEO was operating in a vital services sector. They aimed to expand access of the unserved in the country, which stood at the country's 36%, as compared to 81% for its neighboring countries. This despite the fact that the neighboring countries were middle-income countries, not the "developed global north." The founder was a passionate and driven individual, out to change this about her country, and do it decisively. In the nine years since inception, her organization had already reached over 4.4 million people via almost 900,000 customers across her country, with deep reach into rural areas that she focused on, having created a trusted brand name.

She "intellectually" saw that she could not do it all alone, especially if her company was to contribute to grow the national reach from 36%, to where it should be. She needed a professional CEO and recruited as many as three consecutive hires for top roles, where she paid top dollar to bring in talent. But all of them failed to either deliver, or to fit into the organization, or the developing country context. In describing the reasons, she would enumerate factors, such as whether the incoming CEO was foreign versus local, from within the sector versus outside the sector, too young or too old, and similar analyses that focused on superficial judgments of CEOs or of others.

When speaking about what she learnt about herself, she would say, "I have learned I am not a great judge of people. I need to get better at that." Supportive impact investors sponsored her for courses on talent assessment and provided consultancy assistance for her recruitment process. But it did not change the result.

The investor sensed, but could not give direct feedback to, the founder, that her own mindset, behavior, and approach could be the key driver in creating failure. Professionals who work at impact investing organizations find delivering negative feedback particularly tough. Founders may respect the impact investment organization, and its employees, but some professional managers may hesitate about their personal credibility to give mindset and attitude-related feedback to a charismatic and visionary founder. Even if they gave feedback, how would she take it? Will her mindset shift at all? Worse, could the impact investor end up doing more harm than good?

These hesitations notwithstanding, impact investors need to get such leaders to self-reflect. They need to bring in an experienced coach, or another visionary leader who the investee founder or CEO respects. In this case, the author carried out a self-awareness journey for the leader. She came to see for herself that her strong self-identity and the belief that "no one can match the passion of an entrepreneur' was the key impediment. Her pride in coming from zero to touching 4.4 million lives was her strength, but also her stumbling block to doubling that number. She saw how she herself may be unconsciously sabotaging professional managers; even while consciously, she wanted to hire the best, and see them succeed. Over the next two years, she shifted her mindset, cultivated new habits and behaviors, and handed over reins to a successor and became a chairperson instead. The organization continued a growth trajectory, and in some years reached annual growth rates as high as 70% in both net income and lives reached. She founded a new organization herself. The world gained two leaders.

- **The Idealist**

Extreme idealists are likely to self-select themselves out of Impact Investing. They may demonstrate a greater need for autonomy and "ideological purity." They may see the monitoring and reporting that comes with having investors on board as being an "administrative burden." For instance, in the context of idealists in nonprofits, it has been said that "even under the most favorable conditions, nonprofit leaders are often discouraged by how much of their energy is drawn away from "program work " into bureaucracy and tasks like administration, and perpetual fundraising that are necessary for running a nonprofit and dealing with external pressures and demands" (Joiner 2010). Thus, those idealists who decide to get impact investors on board may already be demonstrating a degree of pragmatism. Yet the underlying mindset of idealism may manifest from time to time and result in conflict between the founder and the impact investor. To support idealists, impact investors tend to send them to leadership courses on topics like "Shared Value" that teach frameworks and share examples of "profit with purpose." Investors may even support top teams, or all-staff retreats to a nice location, where the organization brainstorms about ways to create both profit and impact. The underlying assumption is that the problem is "*out there*"; i.e. exposing leaders to more examples and frameworks of "how" will lead to the solution. These courses and retreats are not without their utility. But it leaves out the "looking in" aspects, the critical questions of self-identity, and how the leader's own "meaning-making machine" or "lens" may be contributing to the challenge (Table 5.2).[4]

Beyond founders, professionals can also be idealists. An important sub-archetype with a professional background is the "New Convert," the corporate executive who joins the impact sector with idealistic zeal, crossing over from the "dark side," the name that they sometimes use for the for-profit corporate sector. A real example of a "New Convert" is described in Box 5.5.[5]

TABLE 5.2   The Idealist.

Archetype	The Idealist
Description	Well-intentioned but fixated about how the world should operate
Mindset	Fixed mindset about self-identity as idealist, and a narrow definition of what it means to operate as an idealist
Outcomes	Sub-scale operations: lower business model fit-to-market, false starts, and disillusionment
Where	Endemic across impact sector, particularly in nonprofits

Source: Author.

---

[4]Those interested in a deeper exploration of "lenses that make meaning" can refer to the disciplines of phenomenology and ontology. A quote provides a useful summary: "Whenever I think, believe, and act as though something were really true, it is more a reflection of my own spirit and passion than it is a reflection of true nature" (Snowden 2010). The "results-based leadership" approach advocates for these profound insights to be converted from philosophy into highly personalized "look-in-the-mirror" experiential formats, which help shift mindsets.

[5]The country, product, and sector have been changed to protect confidentiality.

Box 5.5 A "New Convert" Idealist Sees the Light

A Southeast Asian executive with decades of prior experience in multi-national corporations transitioned into serving as CEO of an innovative insurance company that was an investee of a global impact investor. The insurance company operated one of the most innovative business models to provide access to an important service to a demographic group that is specifically excluded by most other insurance product offerings: diabetics. While people with diabetes represent a genuine human need and a significant market, traditional business models had neglected them because they were harder to serve and involved riskier profiles. In recent years, the incidence of diabetes has been on the rise in Southeast Asia. In 2010, there were 58.6 million people with diabetes, which translates to an age-adjusted comparative prevalence of diabetes of 7.6% of the population. By 2019, this increased to 87.6 million, and the age-adjusted comparative prevalence swelled to 11.3%. These numbers are projected to further go up to 115 million and 12.2%, respectively. Total diabetes-related expenditure for 2010, 2019, and 2030 (projected) was USD $3.1billion, USD $8.06 billion, and USD $10.1 billion, respectively. Adult lives lost due to diabetes were 1.14 million and 1.15 million, respectively, for 2010 and 2019. Excluding a significant proportion of the population from insurance coverage clearly had a huge human cost. It drove up out-of-pocket expenditure on health, put pressure on public health systems and the economy as a whole, degraded quality of life, deprived many of treatment, and cost lives. Besides, if an appropriate business model was to be created, then there can be a way to generate profits and cash flows to sustain the operation.

Unsurprisingly, the "New Convert" leader was attracted to the company. However, two years later, the pressure from her board for financial returns made her disillusioned. She was about to resign. Through deep self-awareness work, the CEO was able to get aware of her own "lenses." She saw how she had been construing the board's emphasis on profitable expansion as "betrayal of what she had come to the sector for." She realized that she had developed a fixed mindset on what it meant to be an idealist, and saw its consequences on their decisions, behaviors, and results. The CEO saw that this lens was taking away the opportunity to serve her own ideals and make an impact. A self-owned shift to growth mindset made her broaden her time horizon. The CEO saw that by earning credibility with the board through adequate financial returns, she can actually achieve idealistic ambitions more effectively. With newfound energy, the

CEO created superior impact, and even led a second round of funding in the next nine months. This took the company's total funds raised to USD $9 million, and added to their funder list two marquee names in global impact investing. Thus, the pragmatic focus on financial returns made treatment accessible to those that would have been deprived.

Source: Author.
Note: For more information refer to https://diabetesatlas.org/data/en/region/7/sea .html.

For impact investors, the other tricky sub-archetype to identify is the idealist who self-identifies as a "realist." This sub-archetype is dogmatically bound to the idealism of market principles. Box 5.6 provides an example of the idealist who self-identifies as a "realist."

Box 5.6 A Real-Life Example of the Idealist Who Self-Identifies as a "Realist"

Consider a leader in a global skilling and employment nonprofit. He pushed for a model where employers had to pay recruitment fees for hiring students trained by them. In most developing country markets, employers are not used to paying. But his idealist mindset was fixated on the idea that markets must solve problems, that the superiority of the organization's skilling must be valued and compensated by getting employers to pay. This fixed mindset ended up reducing the actual impact delivered. It led to a significantly lowered field of play, as well as reduced impact and financial returns. While the leader had set the organization a target of five times their current growth, their fixed mindset may have been one of the factors that led to an actual contraction in the number of trainees, as well as significant attrition and friction within the organization.

Source: Author.

Extreme Deliberative or Extreme Implemental Mindset

Deliberating between potential action goals activates cognitive procedures (deliberative mindset), which facilitates the task of the pre-decision phase,

TABLE 5.3   The 30,000 Feet Leader.

Archetype	The 30,000 Feet Leader
Description	Grand ideas, complex "holistic" plans, and often an inability to communicate them simply
Mindset	When at its best, enables optimal thinking and acting through a deliberative mindset (i.e. heightened receptiveness to multiple types of information); but with an overplay of strengths, the 30,000 feet archetype ends up complicating matters
Outcomes	Complex business models with multiple inter-linkages, assumptions, and hence potential failure points, significant organizational energy lost in trying to second guess what the leader means and wants
Where	Found across the impact sector but especially where there is a need to change user behavior, and to create linkages in a broken value chain or ecosystem; examples include smallholder agriculture, reaching out-of-school children, and vocational skilling and employment

Source: Author.

which is to set preferences. Because undecided individuals do not know which direction their decisions will finally take them, a heightened receptiveness to all kinds of information (open-mindedness) seems appropriate and functional to task solution.

Similarly, planning out the implementation of the chosen goal should activate cognitive procedures (the implemental mindset) that facilitate the task of the pre-reaction phase (i.e. getting started on the chosen goal). As this requires more selective and focused orientation to processing information, close-mindedness, rather than open-mindedness with respect to available information, seems called for (Gollwitzer 2012).

- **The 30,000 Feet Leader**

Table 5.3 presents one of the archetypes that are seen in mission-driven organizations, the 30,000 Feet Leader, whose overplay of the deliberative mindset leads to overcomplexity and delays.

The 30,000 Feet Leader is the one where "soft skill" interventions fail, rather ironically. Typically, the impact investor and stakeholders describe the leader as "brilliant, but struggling to communicate her vision." Consequently, the focus of the coaching and leadership support tends to be on clarity of communication, rather than the fundamental and more complex question of why the complexity exists in the first place. Box 5.7 provides an example of one such real-life case.

> ### Box 5.7 The Need to Keep a Sharp Eye, When Supporting a 30,000 Feet Leader
>
> The organization was already a market leader. The Asian Managing Director, a mix between the Visionary and the 30,000 Feet Leader archetype, had a fascinating vision to transform the way the sector worked—to pursue an innovative and complex ecosystem approach. There was a clear BHAG: several times growth in the outcomes they delivered, expressed audaciously as a certain percentage point contribution to the achievement of an SDG in their country. The targeted business growth amounted to several times the current level in five years. The challenge was to take the top team and the organization along in the transformation journey. The coaching was initiated, contracted, and paid for by the managing director himself. The focus was communication and relationship skills. However, the external context and market realities changed adversely, whereas the focus of the coaching did not. The lesson for impact investors from this example is that the focus or the goals of the leadership intervention need to be thoughtfully designed. A conscious moment must be built into the journey to step back and ask if the BHAG and the focus of the leadership intervention are still relevant.
>
> *Source:* Author.

Impact investors and board members in particular have an important role to play in this since they are one step removed from the process than the coach and the coachee. This lesson is relevant across archetypes, but it is especially true for the 30,000 Feet Leader archetype. This is because such a leader's business model has multiple moving parts and assumptions. The impact investor can play the role of the risk monitor, which they often play anyway through their participation on investees' boards of directors.

Other Impact Sector Leader Archetypes

There are several other leader archetypes in the impact sector, two of which are described briefly below, the leader in the weeds and the insular expert.

- **The Leader in the Weeds**

The inverse of "The 30,000 Feet Leader," the "Leader in the Weeds" has an overplay of a strength, leading to a limitation. In this case, the leader considers only information related to goal attainment and shields against non-goal-related considerations. This closes the organization off to new and different ideas and information. Impact investors may find that some investees with a background in grassroots work may exhibit some behavior of this kind. Of course, that is not universally true, because some grassroot leaders with a learning and growth mindset are able to leverage the grassroots experience to innovate, be strategic, and devise dynamic scale solutions.

Impact investors may be tempted to send the "Leader in the Weeds" to leadership development programs aimed at building strategic skills. However, this may not work, if the leader happens also to be an idealist. The sponsoring impact investor needs to also recognize and shift the underlying mindset, and strong self-identity as an action-oriented grassroots' leader. Without facilitating a mindset shift, the investment in trainings that focus on the "how" may not yield many results.

- **An insular expert who struggles to be innovative**

Typically, a technocrat who misses the trees for the woods and compromises impact financial returns, or both. This archetype demonstrates a fetish for either a particular product, technology, or a certain approach or methodology to solving a problem. They "stick to the knitting" and emphasize performance on narrower, more technical metrics of success, rather than holistic outcomes. The underlying performance mindset involves being motivated toward gaining favorable judgments (or avoiding negative judgments) about one's competence (Gottfredson and Reina 2020). Such leaders are inclined to generate business models that become outdated.

Impact investors that invest in access to energy, environment technology, and related sectors are likely to find the "Insular Expert" archetype. Impact investors who try to support such leaders with skill and perspective building programs like human-centered design may continue to face challenges. They must help to shift the underlying mindset, from seeking favorable judgments about their competence, to being motivated toward increasing their competence and mastering something new.

Framework 1, "Common Leadership Archetypes," may be considered as a starting point for impact investors to dig for deeper insights at the level of drivers, not just symptoms, and craft their solutions such that leaders and leadership teams can deliver bigger and better results, both financial and impact results. Framework 2 builds on this and provides a practical framework for impact investors to quickly diagnose gaps in leadership teams and provide targeted support.

Framework 2: Leadership Team Effectiveness Framework

Sometimes the Impact Investor and/or founders ensure that there is an All-Star team in the management of the investee company. However, despite the impressive background of each of the top team members, they collectively fail.

Impact investors may think of the top team as being on a bus that is headed to a destination. This may be an interesting and useful analogy to analyze, diagnose, and address key gaps. Figure 5.3, "The Ineffective Bus," builds on this analogy and describes how one or more of the elements present in high-performance teams could be missing, leading to sub-optimal results in impact and financial returns.

Each of the four elements highlighted in Figure 5.3 can hinder high-performance teams. These are described below, with a particular emphasis on how these gaps manifest for mission-driven organizations:

- **"Not aligned on the destination, direction, and route"**

This is one of the most common gaps in top teams of impact organizations. In the author's experience, the top team typically tends to be divided into two camps, one that emphasizes financial return and another that emphasizes impact. This is particularly relevant to detect and address for investees in the scaling phase, where old-time loyalists and new professionals are both united by the overall vision and mission but diverge on the direction and strategy.

Most impact investors have robust discussions with the founder or CEO, but they must also offer support to the founder or CEO in facilitating team alignment, including the involvement of experts, particularly when team alignment is the key missing ingredient in achieving the organizational BHAG. Mapping this to the triggers described earlier, a team-alignment intervention can be timed immediately after the investment, as a part of the 100-day plan.[6]

Impact investors may consider various tools to drive alignment. One such tool is the Five HIP Management Practices (Herman 2010). The

---

[6]For more information on how to create a 100-day plan, see Bradt et al. (2009).

framework provides five practices: integrating impact into the vision and mission; tracking impact and profit in a balanced scorecard; understanding how impact drives financials; ensuring the highest levels of the organization are accountable; and integrating impact into every decision so as to align top teams toward delivering top performance in human impact and profit. The diagnostic generates a rating score that enables not just benchmarking, but action as well.

- **"Right People Not on the Bus, in the Right Seats"**

This is also often present in scale-up stage investee companies. The "all-hands-on-deck" approach works in the early stage. But as the business scales and matures, team composition, structure, and roles need to be systematically redesigned to match where the bus is headed.

Impact investors have a crucial role to play in supporting the founder or CEO to both bring in the new talent (which most investors do), but in also helping the CEOs and founders through a necessary mindset shift, to bite the bullet. Adding new staff to social enterprises often involves hard decisions, particularly if the origins of the organization were from nonprofit. As the founder brings in professionally skilled deputies, moments of self-doubt (or allegations from the outside) may arise that "the soul of the organization is being sold."

Expert help may be needed here to help the leader and top team on the dimensions of "Lead Self" and "Lead Others." But equally, help may be needed to determine how to design the leadership team structure and roles to give the organization the blended capabilities generating impact *and* financial returns. Impact investors can help investees by having a roster of such experts, and co-funding such efforts.

With regards to timing, it is ideal if due diligence on leadership risk has already been carried out at the pre-investment stage, as it typically establishes the key gaps in the team composition, role, and structure upfront and early. The post-deal initial six-month period can consist of carrying out the aforesaid changes. Alternately, the pre-exit preparation stage is also a useful time to redesign the structure, composition, and roles—especially if the goal is to sell to strategic investors or carry out an IPO.

- **"Team Processes, Key Performance Indicators (KPIs), and Meeting Rhythms enable collaboration on the bus"**

This factor is akin to ergonomics within the bus, and includes physical space layout, time-zones (or adjustment to work practices based on these), frequency of meetings, and other team processes. Some impact investors may hesitate to provide support on this dimension, since it seems very granular. But this is also the most easily identified and actionable area of support that can generate quick wins for the investee. In terms of timing, the investor should have a keen eye for such quick wins at all times in the deal life cycle.

- **"The atmosphere on the bus—Team Culture not enabling"**

This refers to how it "feels to be on this bus." It can be codified by the six-key enabling behaviors: (i) Trust, Straight talking, (ii) Ownership and Accountability, (iii) Courage to Challenge, (iv) Collaboration, (v) Interdependence, and (vi) Results Focus (Lencioni 2002). This goes to the heart of the team's collective practice of leadership.

Significant and sustainable results can be achieved by the investees if the impact investor sponsors custom programs and interventions aimed at creating self-awareness and collectively shifting of mindsets of the top team. In the author's experience, this is a no-regret, high-impact intervention at any time during the deal life cycle. When done well, the top team takes ownership to address all other gaps. The only time when some caution may be needed is in the first six months, if significant change in team composition is imminent and under way.

In summary, collective and collaborative exercise of leadership is the powerful ingredient that unblocks the engine. If the investor's money is the fuel, great leadership ensures the fuel is used to generate top performance, rather than being used up in friction. But how should such impact and financial performance be translated into returns? And how can such returns be attributed to the leadership development intervention? The next framework addresses that question.

Framework 3: Translation of Leaders' Goals into Return on Investment and Attribution

Translation of Goal Achievements into Returns on Investment

As stated earlier, the "Leadership by Results" approach advocates that the pursuit of BHAGs must be used as a trigger to launch leadership programs with a clear hurdle rate of return in mind, in impact and financial terms. With regard to this, Framework 3 helps impact investors to answer the following questions:

- At what rate of financial and impact return is it worth investing into a leadership development program? In other words, what hurdle rate of return should be used when evaluating a leadership development proposal? Consequently, what should be the "size of the BHAG," such that the returns are significant enough and greater than the hurdle rate?

- How will BHAG achievement be measured?
- How it will be translated into financial and impact returns?

Following is some guidance on how BHAGs can be measured and connected to returns.

Hurdle Rate and Size of BHAG. The "Leadership by Results" approach advocates a rule of thumb that the hurdle rate of return for leadership programs should be as follows: the incremental EBITDA potential over three to five years must be about six to eight times the total financial cost of the leadership program, Simultaneously, there should be a 50% to 100% increase in a critical impact metric over a three- to five-year period (or acceleration of 50% to 100% in a three- to five-year period in the rate of achievement of select impact metrics). As may be expected, the definition of the incremental achievement of impact is highly contextual to the organization, sector, and several other factors. Accordingly, the above should only be taken as broad directional guidance.

Measurement of the achievement of BHAGs. The gold standard is to make BHAGs as quantifiable as possible and translated into revenue, cost, valuation terms, and intended impacts; and for impact metrics to be specific to the organization. The impact and financial metrics should be closely aligned to the Theory of Change framework of the organization.

Translation of the BHAG into financial and impact returns. Typically, BHAGs are expressed in impact or business metrics (e.g. opening of a certain number of new student learning centers). These need to be translated further into incremental EBITDA generated due to the increase in the business metric, in order to calculate the financial return on the investment made into the leadership program. Similarly, the incremental impact (e.g. new learners reached) needs to be arrived at and divided by the investment made into the leadership program to arrive at the impact rate of return. In doing so, existing rules of thumb should be leveraged (e.g. how many new learners are typically reached, and how much incremental EBITDA is generated by adding a new learning center in the areas that the leader has chosen to expand their reach). Box 5.8 illustrates this with an example from the skilling and employment sector.

Box 5.8 An Example of How Much Investing in a Leadership Program That Motivates Leaders Can Increase Quality of Service

The BHAG of a skilling and employment social enterprise was to improve the quality of a nursing assistant program so that it became markedly superior to any other in the market. The program redesign involved making students more proficient. The key impact metric was the increase in income generation for the nursing assistant (15% in this case), as compared to market standard. The corresponding impact metric can include service metrics like increased on-call availability and higher quality of care for patients as the nursing assistant is now able to do more, with the same (or even reduced) nurse-to-patient ratio. The financial return metric for the hospital was the time of the senior nurse saved per shift, due to increased proficiency of the nursing assistant (in this case 25 minutes per shift). The impact thus delivered to the customer was converted into the financial value of impact delivered. This involved costing the senior nurse's time and calculating the capacity created for the hospital or elder care institution.

To calculate the financial returns for the investee, the customer sales teams must indicate the increase in nursing assistants' placement fees. The next step is to convert the increased revenue into increased Earnings Before Interest, Taxes, Depreciation, and Amortization (EBITDA). In the example provided, the innovation increases revenue by 50%. The current EBITDA is 15%. Assuming that the new method involves additional expenses (e.g. more consumables or instructor time needed), then the standard EBITDA is lowered by an agreed percentage. In this case, let us say that the EBITDA of the new way is 12.5%. If the fees per placement is USD $500, and the current volume of placements is 1,000, then the base line revenue is USD $500,000. The current EBITDA is USD $75,000. If the BHAG were to be achieved, the revenue increases to USD $750,000 and the new EBITDA is approximately USD $94,000. Thus, the additional EBITDA of achieving the leadership goal per annum is USD $19,000.

The next step is to translate this into return on investment (ROI) from the Leadership Program. A rule of thumb is suggested here: the incremental EBITDA potential over three to five years must be about six to eight

(continued)

(*continued*)

times the total financial cost of the leadership program. Thus, the incremental EBITDA over three to five years would be USD $57,000 to USD $95,000. Using the mid-point of the spectrum (USD $86,000) and the rule of thumb that the leadership program cost must be recovered six to eight times, the total investment that should be made in the leadership program would be between USD $10,750 and USD $14,285 (approximated close to the midpoint $\sim$ USD $12,500).

This can also further be "risk adjusted." For instance, in a collective top team leadership development journey, a certain success rate can be agreed upon between the impact investor and the service provider. Based on the author's experience, a well-designed and executed multi-touchpoint leadership journey (with potentially ongoing coaching for select top team members) over 6 to 9 months should enable one-third of the cohort to achieve 90% or more of their BHAGs; another one-third of the cohort must achieve 60% to 89% of their BHAGs, and the final one-third of the cohort may achieve less than 60% of their BHAGs. At an overall cohort level, this translates to approximately 65% to 80% of BHAG achievement.

Thus, building upon the skilling and employment example above, if it was a collective top team program for 8 leaders, then the acceptable range of investment into the leadership program would be 65% to 80% of USD $100,000 (i.e. USD $65,000 to USD $80,000).

The sponsor of the leadership program must upfront agree upon the broad principles and assumptions that are used in making such calculations. Assuming that the cost of the program is indeed within this range, then the other principles of "Leadership by Results" mentioned earlier need to be ensured by the leadership development program's sponsor or funder. Questions to be asked include: is the structure, design, and support envisaged by the leadership program going to help our Head of Program Design achieve this BHAG, and do so sustainably? Does it identify the mindsets that inhibit their innovation, collaboration, delegation, or other behaviors needed to deliver on the BHAG? Further, is this goal strategically in line with the organization's BHAG? Is this goal also exciting for the leader?

This is one of the key hallmarks of the "Leadership by Results" approach.

Source: Author.

Following a similar logic, as illustrated in Box 5.8, it is estimated that if across the impact sector, leaders and top teams could similarly be supported on the most critical individual and organizational BHAGs, the whole sector could accelerate impact by 10% to 30% per annum.

The basis for this is that typically the impact goals that a participant is asked to take up (BHAG) must involve 50% to 100% improvement in outcomes (reach, quality, sustainability, etc.) in a period of three to five years. If all participants in "Leadership by Results" programs were to achieve this, the acceleration of outcomes would be to the tune of 20% to 33% per annum. If the number of participants of such programs who could actually achieve the BHAG reached somewhere between 50% to 90%, then acceleration of impact could be to the tune of 10% to 30% per annum.

Attribution of Impact

As is evident in the above example of the nursing program, there are problems of attribution that need to be discussed, of both success or failure in achieving BHAGs. There can be many reasons as to why outcomes and impacts[7] may not be as envisioned, due to extraneous factors. Conversely, even when a target for a given goal is achieved (e.g. increasing the nursing assistant's income by 15% and saving 25 minutes of the senior nurse's time), can it be said that the achievement of that result could be attributed *only* to the leadership development program of the leader in charge of program design? It is possible that achieved results are compounded by other factors that also contributed to make it happen and that the leadership development program might only represent a given proportion of that end result.

Is it also possible that even if the goal of designing and running such a program is achieved, it might not translate into EBITDA numbers (due to a variety of factors, like market conditions, internal structure issues, and others)? Admittedly, rigorous academic standards of attribution and causality may be complex (and expensive) to apply, requiring knowledge of the methodologies.[8]

In this instance the recommendation is that "let not great become the enemy of good." This chapter recommends that the principles of "Leadership by Results" be used. These principles are likely to make everyone involved

---

[7] In a theory of change, outcomes are usually depicted as medium to long-term effects, while impacts are the ultimate long-term effects of an intervention.

[8] See Chapter 17, "Impact Measurement and Management Techniques to Achieve Powerful Results," by Jane Reisman and Veronica Olazabal.

more accountable and results focused. It is important that through the period of the leadership program (not a one-time event), there is close collaboration and review between the leadership expert, the investee leader, and the investor. This ongoing relationship will ensure that changes in the uncontrollable factors become evident to all in real time (or in advance) and are more easily factored in. Accordingly, the goals and the methods to quantify benefits can be promptly changed. In summary, a step toward "good" will ultimately lead us to finding our way to "great."

One such great step toward good was initiated by LeapFrog Investments, a reputed impact investor. Having seen the value of leadership development support for its investee companies, LeapFrog decided to explore the feasibility of institutionalizing such support through the "LeapFrog Talent Academy." This went on ultimately to be launched as "LeapFrog Talent Accelerator." Next, insights are shared from this experience of leading the feasibility study. The purpose of this is to advocate similar institutionalized support by other impact investors for their portfolio companies, as well as to distill lessons on key considerations when doing so.

Institutionalized Leadership Development Support: The Case of LeapFrog Investments Talent Accelerator

LeapFrog Investments decided to institutionalize leadership development support for its portfolio companies by establishing the LeapFrog Talent Accelerator. Next, this chapter sheds lights on its conception and feasibility assessment, courtesy of LeapFrog Investments and Dalberg Advisors. Box 5.9 starts by providing an example of the LeapFrog Talent Academy.

Box 5.9 Exploring and Planning for a LeapFrog Talent Academy

LeapFrog Investments is a successful high-impact investor with several awards and accolades to its name. LeapFrog invests capital, people, and knowledge in purpose-driven businesses, helping them to grow, be profitable, and have real social impact. A survey of the CEOs of LeapFrog's firms found that talent development is the single greatest challenge they face (Institutional Asset Manager 2017). This was the focus of the first CEO Indaba facilitated by the author in 2015. The author was also invited to facilitate the 2016 CEO Indaba focused on leadership self-awareness for the CEOs of its 12 companies. Given the success of the support provided by LeapFrog on matters of talent and leadership, LeapFrog took a pioneering step. They commissioned a feasibility study led by the author, in his capacity as global head and founder of Dalberg Advisors' Leadership and Talent practice, to explore how LeapFrog could institutionalize leadership development support, beyond just workshops, to its investee companies. *Source:* Author.

Considering the example of LeapFrog, their starting point was to explore the "why." As seen in Figure 5.4, the first and foremost reason to institutionalize leadership development support was to help portfolio company leaders deliver superior results in financial and impact terms, thereby accelerating value creation, building resilience, and managing risk for their portfolio companies. Another important advantage is the access to quality deals, via differentiation and edge over other investors. This differentiation can help investment companies sign deals, and thus deploy capital to the full-extent they desire; "dry powder," or uninvested capital estimates of traditional private equity in the United States, is USD $900 billion as of April 8, 2020 (Segerstrom 2020).

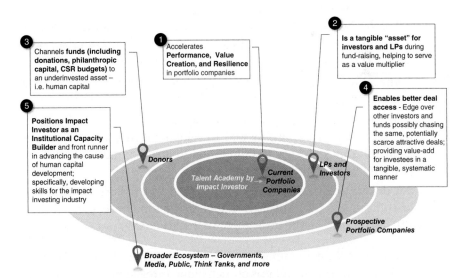

FIGURE 5.4 Benefits of Institutionalizing Leadership Development Support in Investee Companies for Impact Investors. *Source:* Dalberg Advisors, "Feasibility Assessment and Business Plan for LeapFrog Talent Academy," report commissioned by LeapFrog Investments.

The edge over other investors created by in-house leadership development programs can address one of the top challenges cited by impact investors: the lack of "high quality investment opportunities with track record," which was cited as a moderate to significant challenge by 74% of investor respondents to a recent GIIN survey (Mudaliar et al. 2019). Portfolio companies will likely prefer an investor that offers institutionalized support for one of their top concerns: talent. Finally, leadership development programs also have significant positive signaling effects on other stakeholders, such as investors, Limited Partners (LP), government, media, think tanks, and the general public.

As described earlier, LeapFrog Investments realized and acknowledged the value of investing into leadership development of their portfolio companies. Based on the strong demand from CEOs of portfolio companies, LeapFrog wanted to formally deepen and institutionalize these programs.

In order to achieve consistency, add value, and continue the focus on results, some design principles emerged:

- **Ensure impact is integrated into business goals:** Develop C-level, mid-level, and sales leaders with business-focused content that serves both short- and long-term goals.
- **Be inclusive of all cultures and geographies:** Ensure relevance to the global South context, with "profit with purpose" at the center.
- **Adapt by growth stage:** Tailor the offering to differing stages of growth, scale, and maturity of portfolio companies.
- **Understand it is a marathon, not a sprint:** Focus on building capabilities, not just one-off events.
- **Make leadership programs distinctive:** Do not substitute or overlap with what the Learning and Development functions of investee companies may already be doing. Add to it in the most relevant and powerful way.
- **Set dramatic goals:** Define stretch targets that enable application of learning and deliver business results, to the tune of six to eight times EBITDA return on the investment in the leadership programs.

Different execution and funding models were debated by LeapFrog and the most fit-for-purpose model was chosen along three dimensions: partnerships for execution, funding model, and scale-up plan:

- **Partnerships for execution: Weave the journeys, not white label with universities.**

Clearly, LeapFrog would not conceive, design, and run the programs themselves, since impact investors may not necessarily bring this expertise. LeapFrog chose to leverage partnerships to implement. LeapFrog needed to decide the type of partners, and the execution model. Several options were evaluated. Ultimately, most of the "off-the-shelf" leadership development programs from different service providers and universities were not a good fit, based on the key design principles listed above. Besides, many were also quite expensive. It was agreed that a "weaver" model would be used (i.e. a lean internal team would create, collate, and curate content and co-ordinate with multiple specialized agencies to stay focused on goals, and anchored in the key principles).

- **Funding model: Raise cornerstone investment from limited partners for initial period.**

  As Gandhi espoused, "Find the purpose and the means will follow." The LeapFrog experience demonstrated that impact investors can also leverage the support of donors and governments in building a leadership development institution. For instance, LeapFrog secured the support of their partner Prudential Financial Inc. via a cornerstone investment of USD $1.5 million in the Talent Academy, which ultimately became the Talent Accelerator. The LeapFrog Talent Accelerator is now in its third year of existence having accelerated the development of multiple dozens of leaders across Asia and Africa. Long-term sustainability options for the Talent Accelerator include co-payment by portfolio companies, and the investor's own contribution.

- **Scale-up plan: Pilot plans were drawn out to test the hypotheses.**

  The first program was kicked off with participants from four of LeapFrog's financial service partner firms, which employ 12,000 people and reach 42.5 million in Africa and Asia. This program included Resolution Insurance, one of the largest health insurers in Kenya; IFMR Capital (now Northern Arc Capital), a financial services company in India that provides credit and finance to 7.5 million consumers; and UT Life (now MiLife), which provides life insurance in Ghana and has an 80% annual growth rate (Prudential 2017). LeapFrog Talent Accelerator would eventually become a paid service provider to several companies, not just within its portfolio but also to portfolio companies of other investors. To guide this journey, financial and impact-based milestones were also defined.

CONCLUSION

Supporting quality leadership is critical for superior impact and financial returns. People are the "most important asset" according to many CEOs. Yet in mission-driven organizations, investment in leadership is 75% lower than for-profit corporations (in the US, USD $29 per employee versus USD $120 per employee, respectively).

If impact investors can increase leadership development spending to match that of for-profit corporations (on a per employee basis), and if such investment is carried out using "Leadership by Results" principles, then a multitude of lives can be improved, and far greater innovation and efficiencies can be achieved by the impact sector. These principles are likely to make everyone involved more accountable and results focused. The US social sector alone could add USD $19 to USD $33 billion worth of goods and services annually and could drive incremental annual growth of 2.4% to 4% for the sector. Investing in leadership can accelerate impact by 10% to 30% per annum. It would also accelerate job creation. A 2019 report by the Center for Civil Society Studies at Johns Hopkins University shows that nonprofits account for roughly 1 in 10 jobs in the US private workforce, with total employees numbering 12.3 million in 2016. Over the decade since 2007, the number of nonprofit jobs grew almost four times faster than the for-profit ones. For the first time, nonprofit employment now equals manufacturing. Retail trade, accommodation, and food services are the only US industries that employ more people than nonprofits (John Hopkins University 2019). Furthermore, the nonprofit organizations grew almost four times faster than for-profit companies in the last 10 years (John Hopkins University 2019). All these numbers can go up significantly, especially if social enterprises, B Corporations, and other commercial organizations looking to do good to society can add to these numbers and represent an expanding segment of the overall social sector. Given the sector's size and fast-paced growth, McKinsey projects that "improving performance even a little could mean a lot with respect to social outcomes" (McKinsey 2014). Decision-makers in the impact investment ecosystem must stand up, take note, and address the specter of such a large workforce being led by underinvested leaders.

Finally, and perhaps more importantly, the question is this: If an entire generation of impact sector leaders were to go through structured and supported "stretch" experiences, to what extent could we simultaneously unlock financial and impact returns and unleash the sheer human potential of mission-driven change makers?

ACKNOWLEDGMENTS

The author would like to acknowledge Scott Hensarling, Gareth McIlroy, and Graham Poston for their contribution to shaping his "inside-out" approach toward leadership development, with deep mindset shifts and big results; and those that enriched it further: Kanishka Sinha and Girish Manimaran (Stillwater); Sunil Savara (Lead Like Gandhi); Santhosh Babu (ODA); Peter Reding (Coach For Life); Aneace Haddad; and Wendy Chua and team. Thanks to mentors at ECS, Debu and Sukumar, who laid the foundation of the results-based approach, by putting people and change management at the heart of "bottom-up" operations transformation; and those at McKinsey Center for Asian Leadership that enabled a "top-down" view of using "leadership as a starting point of strategy"—Tsun-yan Hsieh, Sara Yik, Huijin Kong, Alper Tenguz, Florian Pollner, Faridun Dotiwala, and others. The author is deeply grateful for the trust placed by innumerable clients, including Vaughan Lindsay and Andy Kuper (LeapFrog Investments); Joel Nielsen (UNHCR); Ankur Bansal and Gaurav Goel (Samagra); Ruchira Gupta (Apne Aap); Danladi Verheijen and Eric Idiahi (Verod); Rajesh A.R. (Labournet); K. Martin, M. Smallwood, and S. Pradubsuk (USAID); Dr. Armin Bauer (Asian Development Bank); Markus Dietrich (GIZ); Elleke Maliepaard and Julian Frede (DEG); N. Welikala, E. Wickramaratne, and I. Bandara (National Development Bank); Richard Saldanha (Blackstone); Dr. Ranjan Pai (Manipal); Anu Prasad (ILSS); Neera Nundy and Megha Jain (Dasra); Maya Ziswiler (UBS-OF); Deepali Khanna (Rockefeller Foundation); Sanjay Singh (Indian School of Business); Micheal Olosky and Joyce Guo (Henkel); Yvonne Villinger (DB Schenker); Eduardo Perez Cejuela (SABIC); Sang-Hoon Lee and Nammin Lee (Doosan); Simon Duncombe and Carla Bonev (BHP); Giuseppe Pedretti (PLI); Santosh Katti (Graphene AI), and Dr. Nachiket Mor and Madhabi Buch (ICICI).

Leadership practices incubated in organizations need supportive colleagues from the mothership. The author is grateful to those who stepped forward: Charles Moore, Steve Stine, Daren Kemp, Stafford Bagot, and Euan Kenworthy (Heidrick); Paul Callan, Henrik Skovby, James Mwangi, Madji Sock, Naoko Koyama, Carlijn Nouwen, Wijnand De Wit, Joe Dougherty, Niall Saville, Nupur Kapoor, Krisha Mathur, Vibhor Goyal, and Samira Khan (Dalberg); and Pushp Gupta (Korn Ferry); Akua Doreen Akonor (LIKAD); and Manas Mainrai (BTS) who stepped across organization boundaries to form consortiums to take leadership services to the development sector. Sincere gratitude to friend-philosopher-guides that encouraged me on the path lesstrodden: Shalini Sarin, Ujwal Thakar, Manoj Kumar, Prabhat

Pani, Amit Chandra, Pritha Venkatachalam, Sanjiv Aiyar; Murali Rajamani, Neha Sharma, Keyur Shah, Zubin Mulla, Dhritiman Hui, Sujata Deshmukh, Chandrashekhar, Arun Nair, Professor Leena Chatterjee, and Samba Natarajan; and selfless contributors to purpose-driven clients: Aditya Minocha and Vidushi Shrikant; and to those that made this article possible, R. Paul Herman and Elsa de Morais Sarmento, the editors of this handbook; Rajneesh Chowdhury, for his tips on academic writing styles; and Cathy Grisham, for her effective illustration of "The Ineffective Bus." Last but not least, my gratitude to never-failing guides for life: my wife, Sonali Ahuja Makhijani, and my parents, Bharti Makhijani and the late Pritamdas Makhijani.

REFERENCES

Block, S., (2004) *Why Nonprofits Fail: Overcoming Founder's Syndrome, Fundphobia and Other Obstacles to Success.* Hoboken, NJ: John Wiley & Sons, pp. 135–155

Bradt, G. B., Check, J., and Pedraza, J. E. (2009). *The New Leader's 100-Day Action Plan: How to Take Charge, Build Your Team, and Get Immediate Results*, 2nd ed. Hoboken, NJ: John Wiley & Sons.

Callanan, L., Gardner, N., Mendonca L., et al. (2014a). What Social Sector Leaders Need to Succeed. McKinsey Insights (November 2014). https://www.mckinsey.com/industries/social-sector/our-insights/what-social-sector-leaders-need-to-succeed (accessed 12 May 2020).

Callanan, L, Silver, N., and Jansen, P. (2014b) *Leveraging Social Sector Leadership.* Grantmakers for Effective Organizations (GEO). Berkeley: Haas School of Business, University of California, p. 10.

Champy, J., and Nohria, N. (2001). *The Arc of Ambition: Defining the Leadership Journey.* New York: Perseus Books.

Mudaliar A., Bass, R., Dithrich, H., et al. (2019). Annual Impact Investor Survey, 9th ed. (June 2019). Global Impact Investing Network.

Mudaliar, D., and Dithrich, A. (2019). Sizing the Impact Investing Market. Global Impact Investing Network (April 2019). https://thegiin.org/research/publication/impinv-market-size (accessed 12 May 2020).

Global Sustainable Investment Alliance (2019). *Global Sustainable Investment Review* 2018.

Gollwitzer, P. (2012). Mindset Theory of Action Phases. In *Handbook of Theories of Social Psychology*, Edited by Lange, P., Kruglanski, A., and Higgins, E. London: Sage Publications. p. 528.

Gottfredson, R., and Reina, C. (2020). To Be a Great Leader, You Need the Right Mindset. *Harvard Business Review* (17 January).

Herman, P. (2010). *The HIP Investor: Make Bigger Profits by Building a Better World*. Hoboken, NJ: John Wiley & Sons.

Institutional Asset Manager (2017). LeapFrog launches Investments Talent Accelerator (12 December 2017). https://www.institutionalassetmanager.co.uk/2017/12/07/259075/leapfrog-launches-investments-talent-accelerator (accessed 12 May 2020).

Jensen, M. C., Erhard, W., and Granger, K. L. (2012). Creating Leaders: An Ontological/Phenomenological Model. In *The Handbook for Teaching Leadership: Knowing, Doing, and Being* (ed. Scott Snook, Nitin Nohria, and Rakesh Khurana). Thousand Oaks, CA: Sage Publications, Chapter 16.

John Hopkins University (2019). The 2019 Nonprofit Employment Report. Center for Civil Society Studies.

Joiner, S. (2010). *The Idealist Guide to Nonprofit Careers for Sector Switchers*. Idealist.org, p. 218.

Kelly, K. (2008). *CEO: Lowdown on the Top Job*. London: FT Prentice Hall.

Khurana, R. (2002). The Curse of the Super Star CEO. *Harvard Business Review* (September 2002).

LeapFrog Investments (2015). LeapFrog CEO Indaba. https://leapfroginvest.com/casestudy/case-study-ceo-indaba/ (accessed 12 May 2020).

LeapFrog CEO Indaba (2016). CEO candid testimonial. https://www.youtube.com/watch?v=rrJCZPrGcuU (accessed 12 May 2020).

Lencioni, P. (2002). *The Five Dysfunctions of a Team: A Leadership Fable*. Hoboken, NJ: John Wiley & Sons.

Maister, D., Green, C., and Galford, R. (2001). *The Trusted Advisor*. New York: Free Press.

McCauley, C., DeRue, D., Yost, P. et al. (2013). *Experience Driven Leader Development: Models, Tools, Best Practices, and Advice for On-the-Job Development*. Hoboken, NJ: John Wiley & Sons. Doi: 10.1002/9781118918838.

Olley, P. (2012). *Result: Think Decisively, Take Action and Get Results*. London: Pearson.

Prudential (2017). Prudential invests in LeapFrog Talent Accelerator to develop leadership skills for emerging-markets companies. Press Release (20 December).

Ryan, R. (2009). *Leadership Development: A Guide for HR and Training Professionals*. Oxford: Routledge, p. 173

Satia, J., Kumar, A., and Liow, M. (2014). *Visionary Leadership in Health: Delivering Superior Value*. New Delhi: SAGE India.

Segerstrom (2020). A decade of growth for U.S. private equity. FactSet (8 April). https://insight.factset.com/a-decade-of-growth-for-u.s.-private-equity (accessed 12 May 2020).

Snowden, D. (2010). Cognitive Edge. Phenomenology – Epistemology – Ontology. Cognitive Edge (August 2010). https://cognitive-edge.com/blog/phenomenology-epistemology-ontology/ (accessed 12 May 2020).

Stahl, R. (2014). Talent Philanthropy Project and the Foundation Center. Foundations That Invest in Non-profit Leadership: Count Them on Your Hands! Fund the People (16 July). http://fundthepeople.org/count/#_edn1 (accessed 12 May 2020).

Venkatachalam, P., and Berfond D. (2017). Building the Bench at Indian NGOs: Investing to Fill the Leadership Development Gap. Bridgespan (September 2017). https://www.bridgespan.org/leadership-development-at-indian-ngos (accessed 12 May 2020).

Zwilling, M. (2015). Five Shortcomings of a Visionary and How to Compensate. Forbes (June 16). https://www.forbes.com/sites/martinzwilling/2015/06/16/5-shortcomings-of-a-visionary-and-how-to-compensate/#6e931d224348 (accessed 12 May 2020).

Gender Lens Investing: Co-Creating Critical Knowledge to Build a Credible, Durable Field

Edward T. Jackson, OMC, EdD and Elsa de Morais Sarmento MA

Abstract

The long-term success of the gender lens investing (GLI) movement is dependent on a robust and continuous co-creation of *critical* knowledge that can independently interrogate the actors and factors in GLI, facilitate collective and organizational learning, and build new theory to accompany and inform the field-building process. This chapter explores the possible content and process in the co-creation of this critical knowledge; traces the definitional journey of GLI, highlights GLI's manifestations in practice, and examines five scaling strategies to build a bigger and more robust field. The chapter then considers how the empirical GLI knowledge base can be deepened in four specific areas: documenting private capital mobilization with the necessary rigor, examining failure, refining appropriate impact measurement methods, and responding to the financing needs of vulnerable populations. It concludes by outlining five key elements of a research agenda through

2030: (1) aligning research agendas' timeline with that of the SDGs; (2) establishing a community of practice; (3) applying theory-building as a core element; (4) deepening empirical knowledge; (5) encoding, disseminating, and sustaining knowledge through formal education, which will be capable of holding GLI champions and products to account while, with equal energy and verve, enabling the building of a scaled, high-impact, and lasting field of GLI practice in Impact Investing globally.

Keywords

Gender Lens Investing; Gender; Impact Investing; Impact Investments; Knowledge; Research; Field-Building; Community Campus Partnerships; Multi-Stakeholder Partnerships; Sustainable Development Goals; Agenda 2030

INTRODUCTION

Patriarchy is notorious for its ability to recover from losses to its power, to regroup, and then to act, often in novel ways, to restore its dominance. With increasing visibility and momentum, gender lens investing (GLI) is a vibrant and promising field of practice. GLI has demonstrated its capacity to redirect substantial flows of capital to women-led and women-friendly businesses in both the publicly traded and private markets. Gender participation in the labor market and gender equality is a known driver of economic growth. Research over the last decade confirmed the higher financial performance of public companies with strong female representation at the board level and in senior management.[1] Furthermore, more recent research shows that it goes beyond this, that there are clear connections between more women in leadership roles with improved environmental,

---

[1] Several studies point to a positive correlation between gender diversity in senior management and reported earnings (e.g. Kyaw, Olugbode, and Petracci, 2015; Catalyst 2011; Krishnan and Parsons 2008). Fortune 500 companies with three or more corporate female directors outperformed those with no women directors by 84% on return on sales (ROS) and 60% on return on invested capital (ROIC) (e.g. Krishnan and Parsons 2007). Microfinance institutions (MFIs) with more women clients have lower write-offs and lower credit-loss provisions, confirming that female creditors in general are a better credit risk for MFIs (D'Espallier et al. 2011).

social, and governance (ESG) performance (Banaham and Hasson, 2018). With full gender parity (i.e. women and men participating equally in the labor market), an additional USD $28 trillion could be added to global gross domestic product (GDP) by 2025 (McKinsey Global Institute 2015).

However, if GLI is to have any chance of becoming a durable, resilient field capable of reaching optimum scale and impact, its leaders must not make the mistake of relying solely on the proprietary knowledge of its practitioners, as committed and remarkable as they are. The long-term success of the GLI movement is, in fact, dependent on a robust and continuous co-creation of *critical* knowledge that can independently interrogate the actors and factors in GLI, facilitate collective and organizational learning, and build new theory to accompany and inform the field-building process.

The purpose of this chapter is to explore the possible content and process in the co-creation of this critical knowledge. It traces the definitional journey of GLI, highlights its manifestations in practice, and examines five scaling strategies to build a bigger and more robust field. The chapter then considers how the empirical knowledge base can be deepened in three specific areas: incentivizing private capital mobilization, responding to the financing needs of both vulnerable women and men, and refining appropriate impact measurement methods. The chapter then goes on to outline the elements of a research agenda that will be capable of holding GLI champions and products to account while, with equal energy and verve, enabling the building of a scaled, high-impact, and lasting field of practice.

Why Critical Knowledge Matters to Professional Fields

Practice almost always leads theory in the development of professional fields. Leaders and advocates among practitioners are in general particularly skilled and dedicated, very articulate about their vision about what is and what ought to be, and justifiably so. However, particularly in emerging fields whose material bases are still developing, piecemeal, or unpredictable (e.g. where revenue streams are still fragmented and business models not fully refined or stable), the first responsibility of champions is to activate their networks and mobilize resources for their own causes and organizations. Their primary concern, in this sense, is to market their products and services under often crowded, unpredictable, and very competitive circumstances.

In the case of financing and investment professionals, this promotional effort can be fragmented, noisy, sometimes aggressive, and often characterized by overly optimistic claims and rhetoric, intended to attract attention and raise substantial funds for proprietary products and services. The discourse and knowledge creation of such a field tends to be uncritical and short-term in scope, and characterized by self-serving, overstated prophecies of changing the world. Practitioners often not only come to believe their own slogans, but will mount high barricades to defend them, while remaining too often delinked from independent, longer-term, and more critical perspectives on their work and the global needs.

The results of practitioners submitting their field and abiding their practices to a culture of hyped, proprietary interests can be tragic in human terms. A decade ago, at the height of its size and influence, the micro-finance industry was completely unprepared for a series of suicides by some 200 borrowers in the state of Andhra Pradesh in India.[2] In despair from overindebtedness caused by egregiously aggressive and sometimes fraudulent sales techniques by microfinance agents, these borrowers saw no other way out of the impossible pressure they came under. In response to this crisis, the state government passed a law placing severe restrictions on the activities of microfinance firms,[3] including not allowing agents near the doorsteps of borrowers (Business Insider 2012).

At the level of the microfinance industry, champions were shocked, some immobilized by the tragedy in India. To be sure, there had been critiques of the excesses of scaling and commercialization by independent scholars, often documenting specific cases on the ground. However, most leaders of the field did not take these warnings seriously enough to alter or even moderate the behavior of industry actors.

Consequently, beyond the loss of human life, the microfinance sector at large suffered substantial reputational damage at every level, from the local to the global. And, while the field's willful inattention to critical knowledge was not the only factor in this case, it was probably the most significant one. GLI ignores this experience at its peril.

GENDER LENS INVESTING: EVOLVING DEFINITIONS

It is useful to track this process through the efforts of an early leader in this work, the Criterion Institute, an American nonprofit think tank. Initially, in 2014–2015, the definitional focus of the Institute and GLI as a whole was on

---

[2]The actions of field personnel of one company, SKS Microfinance Ltd., a rising star in the market in India, were found to have been associated with the suicides of 17 of the company's borrowers (Sanjai and Nair 2015).
[3]SKS's share price dropped, executives were replaced, and eventually the company developed a new, more moderate sales approach—though no one went to jail.

ways and means of channeling more capital to women-owned or -led small and medium-sized enterprises (WSMEs), to companies where workplaces are safe and fair for women employees at all levels, and to firms that sell products or services that enhance the lives of women and girls (Anderson and Miles 2015; Kaplan and VanderBrug 2014). This framing of GLI has been widely adopted by both publicly traded investment funds and products (e.g. UBS 2018; Pax World Ellevate Global Women's Leadership Fund 2019) and development finance institutions (e.g. Gaffuri and Willis 2019; FinDev Canada)[4], together with grant-funded programs (notably, Investing in Women 2019).

Beginning in 2017, the members of the GLI Working Group of the Global Impact Investing Network (GIIN), including, for example, the leading non-profit impact fund Root Capital, as well as SEAF and AlphaMundi, advised by Criterion and supported by Investing in Women, broadened the definition of GLI as also encompassing "a process that focuses on gender, from pre-investment activities (e.g. sourcing and due diligence) to post-deal monitoring (e.g. strategic advisory and exiting); or a strategy that examines, with respect to the investee enterprises, their vision or mission to address gender issues, their organizational culture, internal policies and workplace environment; their use of data and metrics for the gender-equitable management of performance and to incentivize behavioral change and accountability; and how their financial and human resources signify overall commitment to gender equality" (GIIN 2019).

A complementary method for integrating gender into the analysis of the ESG performance on investee companies was published in 2018 by Mennonite Economic Development Associates and USAID (2018)[5] in its Gender Equality Mainstreaming Framework, with the intent to support investors and capacity builders to implement better gender equitable practices while continuing to support companies' growth and impact generation.

Also in 2018, and again with the support of Investing in Women, the Criterion Institute went a step further and developed a way of applying a gender analysis to the full organizational structure, strategy, policies, and incentives to investment funds engaged in raising and placing GLI capital. At this level, GLI came to be defined as a set of pro-women policies and practices within an investment institution or fund that infuses gender mainstreaming at every level, from the recruitment of the executive management

---

[4]FinDev Canada website: https://www.findevcanada.ca/en.
[5]Available at https://www.meda.org/gem.

team to compensation and promotion incentives, to portfolio strategy, and investment monitoring (Criterion Institute 2018). Others, like the consulting firm DAI, conceptualized GLI to include not only women's access to capital, women-focused products and services and workplace equity, but also women in supply chains, women in leadership, and women as investors (DAI 2019).

At the same time, the Criterion Institute shifted its own internal strategy to an even more macro level, to help build the capacity of a wider range of actors—including asset managers and other investment professionals, business associations, governments, grant-makers, and grassroots organizations—to reimagine and transform *financial systems* as a whole in the interest of gender equality and social change. As part of this shift, the Criterion Institute made a long-term commitment to use this approach to reduce the effects, worldwide, of gender-based violence (GBV). This systems-level work required extensive and sustained advisory, design, training, and capacity building work in all parts of the world.

By early 2019, with its latest signpost along this definitional journey, the Criterion Institute (2019, p. 3) reformulated its definition of GLI to a more all-encompassing one, as "the incorporation of gender analysis into the practice of investments and the systems of finance. This includes how value is assigned, how relationships are structured, and how processes work." This definition provides a workable overall frame for both stakeholders focused on mobilizing and deploying capital at the levels of individual deals and investment institutions, as well as advocates for, and participants in, systems change.

To date, definitions of GLI have largely been shaped by practitioners based in the Global North. This has been an important starting point. Now, however, it is time for practitioners from the Global South to share the leadership of this effort. Moreover, engaged *scholars* from both the Global North and the Global South can, and should, play a key role in this ongoing definitional work. Recent efforts, such as the publication of "Mapping Gender Lens Investing in the Global South, Ghana, Kenya, Sri Lanka, and Vietnam," represent key stepping-stones in this direction (MacLeod 2019). Perhaps the most comprehensive Southern perspective on the GLI field was prepared by an Indian-African team for the International Development Research Centre (Maheshwari et al. 2019). However, until a broader cohort of new, Southern players fully takes up this task in their own hands, the definition of GLI will not achieve full maturation.

A PROFESSIONAL FIELD WITH VISIBILITY, FORCE, AND MOMENTUM

GLI is clearly a professional field with growing visibility, force, and momentum. While it is still not dominant nor fully in place within Impact Investing[6] or blended finance (along with other professional fields and investment areas), GLI has a recognizable, committed and creative set of champions (e.g. development finance institutions [DFIs][7], donor agencies, foundations) and a relatively broad constituency of actors (e.g. private asset managers, academics, etc.). Funded projects, fund launches, blogs, books, and technical reports on GLI are increasingly frequent (e.g. Johnston 2019; Gaffuri and Willis 2019; Value for Women 2019; Equileap 2018; Quinlan and VanderBrug 2017; Calvert 2016; Carlile et al. 2015). GLI is gaining traction and being an increasingly prominent theme in influential events on Impact Investing like the Social Capital Markets (SoCap) annual conference series in San Francisco or in multilateral gatherings related to development finance and the Sustainable Development Goals (SDGs), especially SDG-5 on gender equality. GLI asset growth accelerated from USD $2.4 billion in 2018 to USD $3.4 billion in June 30, 2019 (Veris Wealth Partners 2020).

The driver of this field-building effort is a coalition of US-based thought leaders, investment professionals, and philanthropists in alliance with UK-based and European DFIs, donor agencies, multilateral development banks, and investment banks. The most concrete and far-reaching achievement of this coalition has been in the Gender-Smart Investing Summit series in the UK in 2018 and 2020. Bringing together 350 GLI leaders from around the world, these events provide a forum "to drive collaborative dialogue and leverage our collective capacity to unlock barriers to deploying capital in a gender-smart way" (Gender Smart Investment Summit).[8] At the 2018 summit, the Western DFIs involved in the 2X Challenge to mobilize USD $3 billion for women's economic empowerment announced that they had formed a Gender and Finance Collaborative to advance knowledge and practice on increasing financing for women's businesses (2x Challenge:

---

[6] For instance, reference books such as those by Wendt (2018), Mungai (2018), and Allman and de Nogales (2015) take a light approach to GLI or the gender role in Impact Investing.
[7] For instance, European Bank of Reconstruction and Development (EBRD 2016).
[8] GenderSmart Investing Summit available at https://www.gendersmartinvesting.com/. Leading sponsors of the conferences have included UBS, the CDC Group, Investing in women, Morgan Stanley, the DFIs of Canada and the Netherlands, and others.

Financing for Women Initiative, 2019). The Canadian government launched in 2018 their Feminist International Assistance Policy, putting gender at the core of their foreign and development policy efforts. In parallel, the U.S. government launched various programs, including the Overseas Private Investment Corporation's (OPIC) 2X Women's Initiative.[9] In one, OPIC surpassed its goal of catalyzing investments of USD$ 1 billion and now targeting over USD $3 billion, globally.

One of the important limitations of these conferences to date, however, is that voices of GLI champions from the Global South have not been so frequently heard, either because they are muted, marginalized, or their representatives are simply not considered for these events. The 2018 Summit featured a few keynotes and workshop facilitators from Africa, the Americas, and Asia, but perhaps as many as 80% of delegates were based in the Global North. However, in the medium and longer term, emerging markets offer much more potential for growth in investment through a gender lens than do the older Northern economies (e.g. Value for Women 2019). For the GLI movement to grow significantly in the years ahead, therefore, much more North-South balance is required in terms of both speakers and participants, but also in the lead up to these events.[10]

A second point of vulnerability in the GLI field-building to date, and one shared with Impact Investing and blended finance, relates to the contradictions of capitalism itself. Economic inequality has deepened and broadened. There is widespread skepticism and anger, understandably directed at the richest 1% for their hoarding of the benefits of wealth creation and their commitment to the avoidance of paying taxes (see, for example, Rose 2020). GLI champions must find the right advocacy tools to deliver on its promise. This requires the engagement of the private sector and mainstream investors to move the needle toward impact and gender equality, with GLI products and services being more than additional financial instruments: they must demonstrably show they can effectively be used to *reduce* inequality.

BUILDING A LARGER, MORE ROBUST FIELD: FIVE SCALING STRATEGIES

Champions of GLI seek to build a larger, more robust field. In the realm of practice, there is a cluster of field-building strategies that could help shift GLI

---

[9]More information on https://www.dfc.gov/our-impact-priorities/2x-womens-initiative.
[10]As a practical matter, sponsors and leaders in the field must ensure attendance by more Southern delegates and put in place support for visitors to obtain travel visas in a timely manner.

from its current modest size toward a sector of finance that is much larger and more influential. Five such scaling strategies are worth highlighting.

1. *Less rhetoric, more evidence for higher and more effective financial commitment:* As with many emerging fields, including the early stages of both microfinance and Impact Investing, rhetoric and aspiration outpace delivery in GLI. But as the validity that gender matters in financial decision-making is demonstrated to established players in finance, boundaries are pushed forward as to what either investors or women's organizations can actually achieve and the role of GLI as an effective tool for social change. While an already impressive array of funds, vehicles, and instruments for GLI have come to market over the past five years, they are still collectively very small compared with the trillions of dollars in the broader capital markets and also the financing requirements for the full scale of SDG implementation. Larger and more gender-smart investment funds must be designed and launched, rapidly. Moreover, mobilization of capital does not signify deployment of that capital. GLI champions must, therefore, accelerate delivery—that is, actual *placement* of capital in businesses—while ratcheting down the volume of their discourse and the hubris of their claims.

   There is another dimension to be addressed. Some GLI advocates are focusing on changing the macro-environment—values, markets, policies—in order to redirect capital in favor of women and women's rights. A good (and impressive) example here is the Criterion Institute's campaign to secure USD $10 billion in commitments by financial institutions and governments to fight gender-based violence. By its very nature, much of this work involves dialogue among various stakeholders that must be supported by multi-year grants. While this work is important, indeed essential, it can also crowd out time, space, and money for actual investments *per se* in gender-smart businesses. Designed and targeted appropriately, such placement of capital at the micro-level confers immediate benefits on entrepreneurs, employees, customers, and communities. At the very least, there needs to be improved coordination among the various organizations working at the macro and micro levels of GLI.

   The NEPAD Spanish Fund (NSF)[11] for African Women's Empowerment was supported with Spanish Funds and managed by the African Union (AU). It intended to promote gender equality and

---

[11] https://www.nepad.org/nepad-spanish-fund-african-womens-empowerment.

increase the capacities and autonomy of women throughout the African Continent and to contribute to the acceleration of the achievement of the Millennium Development Goals (MDG), in particular MDG-3. Since its inception in 2007, it supported 79 projects reaching an estimated 1.2 million African women. At the institutional level, it strengthened the capacities of government institutions, Regional Economic Communities (RECs), and civil society structures, including grassroots women's organizations in several countries (LeBlanc et al. 2019). Working in close collaboration with the AU Member States, RECs, and development partners, the NSF support was also provided through networking among women's groups and scaling up economic and business opportunities. The focus of the NSF was on the following priority sectors: i) women economic empowerment, ii) institutional strengthening, and iii) the strengthening of civil society organizations, within the principles of democratic governance.

2. *More South at the steering wheel:* Like Impact Investing and blended finance, GLI has been mostly driven by champions and organizations based in the Global North (including donor agencies, DFIs, investment banks, foundations, think tanks and non-government organizations). The gender lens market continues to be mainly a North American phenomenon with a global investment focus. There are now eight funds open in Asia-Pacific, two funds in South America and one in Africa. Since the term appeared 10 years ago, there are now more than 50 publicly available GLI products, a 300% increase since 2015[12] (Veris Wealth Partners 2020).

However, this is still not enough. Southern leaders have also not been visible or audible enough in GLI gatherings. This must change. The potential for serious growth of GLI lies in developing markets, big and small, in all parts of the world. Africa (e.g. Mungai 2018) and Latin America (e.g. Value for Women 2019) are particularly fertile grounds. There are examples of decentralization to the South and ownership (e.g. the example of the NSF highlighted above). One of the loudest successes of the NSF happened in the African archipelago of Cabo Verde, where NSF's support[13] was a turning point

---

[12]Available at https://www.veriswp.com/gender-lens-investing-assets-grow-to-more-than-3-4-billion/.
[13]More information here: https://www.nepad.org/nepadspanishfund/countries/cape-verde.

for gender empowerment and mainstreaming in Cabo Verde's public policy (Morais Sarmento 2019). Country authorities realized that without a favorable legal framework, any gender initiatives could only have a minor impact. The GBV Law, passed in 2011, was the first gender law in Cabo Verde and became completely transformational, with society gaining an important mechanism to combat discrimination and inequality. By supporting the approval and wide implementation of the GBV Law, the NSF allowed the creation of a strong legal framework that had a multiplier effect in several sectors, triggering a wide range of activities, most of which are still unfolding and growing today.[14]

Indeed, if Northern actors really seek field building leverage, they should provide support that is adapted to the setting of the country/region of the Global South and the capacity of its implementing institutions. This can be done through multi-year grants, as well as longer-term investment capital to local gender-smart investors, intermediaries, investees, and ecosystem service providers, under close monitoring and scrutiny. And such commitments should be long-lasting as transformational change and impact takes time to occur. But patriarchy and misogyny are deeply established in many countries and economies of the South. Thus, the South needs not only to be empowered but be well prepared to the tasks at hand, which are often hardened by the country's framework conditions, such as good governance, lack of technical knowledge, staff turnover, and more.

3. *Replicating models that work:* In the interest of growing GLI, there is an interest and opportunity to look at models that worked well (at the local or regional level) and replicate them by adapting these to the specific local features, putting in place the elements proven to work within specific contexts and scales. This traditionally entails establishing the right networks, inciting the sharing of best practices, and creating communities of practice to integrate gender knowledge with the best investment practices. This scaling "sideways" can drive real growth. One example is that of Component 2 of Investing in Women: infrastructure exits in its second three-year phase, supported its impact funds to move from an initial concentration of WSMEs in

---

[14] By working on three different fronts, legislation, capacity-building, and the re-creation of networks and synergies with a wide range of institutions, the project brought about innovative aspects, by working with masculinity issues, introducing educational and training modules in the school curricula, and in the training of policy forces and health staff.

capital cities to gender engagement with investees in regional cities and focus "up-country." Another replication vector is to apply tested models to other countries altogether. Finding new geographic settings with reasonably hospitable conditions to support GLI programming is key to successful replication, together with skilled local allies and staff, and to share budget with them in meaningful ways. However, it can be challenging to raise funds to effectively implement even proven successful GLI methodologies to other geographies or sectors, especially in the Global South.

4. *Integrating into infrastructure:* Another strategy for increasing the scale of GLI is for its proponents to engage with infrastructure, that is, applying GLI principles and tools to large-scale infrastructure projects (e.g. dams, wind and solar farms, roads, bridges, airports, ports, etc.). One useful starting point in this regard is the recently published Gender Ambition Framework of the Private Infrastructure Development Group[15] (PIDG 2019). An initiative supported by Australian Aid, the framework provides investors with a rubric and metrics to classify infrastructure projects on their gender equality dimensions. Using this tool, investors can determine the extent to which an infrastructure investment opportunity will either "do the minimum" by addressing the basic needs and vulnerabilities of women; promote "empowerment" by building the assets and capabilities of women; or advance "transformation" by addressing unequal gender power relations and seeking institutional, policy, and societal changes (PIDG 2019). By applying this framework to large-scale infrastructure projects, GLI practitioners can increase the scale and influence of their field exponentially. This may open the door to renewed infrastructure-investment partnerships between public and private investors from different geographies, including those that prioritize gender.

5. *Demonstrating more* successful *exits:* Another important way of mobilizing significantly more capital for WSMEs and gender-smart enterprises more broadly is for funds to demonstrate successful exits by their investors—and, ideally, have those investors themselves testify to their satisfaction with the terms of their exits. Investors seek specific rates of return and social impact over specified time horizons. However, private investors are diverse, ranging from private equity

---

[15] Available at https://www.pidg.org/wp-content/uploads/2019/03/PIDG-Gender-Ambition-Framework-070219-FINAL.pdf.

funds to banks, insurance companies, and pension funds, for example. Each of these entities seeks investments aligned with their regulatory and market requirements for risk, return, tenor, and liquidity. Venture capital funds, therefore, will be interested in the accounts of exit by other venture capitalists rather than by a bank or foundation, both of which are regulated much differently from a venture fund. GLI advocates aiming to grow the field, therefore, must devote greater attention to facilitating and publicizing successful but also responsible exits (GIIN 2018) from their funds and vehicles and use those examples to mobilize much more private capital.

DEEPENING THE EMPIRICAL KNOWLEDGE BASE: FOUR THEMES

An important task in building critical knowledge for a growing field is to deepen its empirical knowledge base. To date, in GLI, practice has led the generation of empirical experience and data. This has been a useful but limited process. It is time for engaged scholars to collaborate with practitioners to not only expand the body of GLI knowledge but to also test, replicate, interpret, interrogate, and share it in the open, peer-reviewed literature. Three themes provide promising initial opportunities for doing so.

1. *Documenting private capital mobilization with the necessary rigor:* To date, the richest and most granular source of experience and data on how to mobilize private capital for WSMEs in the Global South is that of the Investing in Women (IW) initiative in Southeast Asia, an Australian government program, operating in Indonesia, Philippines, and Vietnam. IW's Component 2 (C2) has created and refined a unique model aimed at raising more private capital to invest in WSMEs in the three programming countries. As illustrated in Figure 6.1, C2 provides 10-year, accountable performance grants to carefully selected impact investment funds, which in turn utilize these funds to expand their local operations in these markets and deepen their pipeline development, due diligence, and monitoring. Grantees also use IW funding to set up or expand sub-funds or other vehicles and products to raise and deploy private funds for WSMEs (Jackson and Alvarez 2018).

   Further, in order to carry out their plans, each of the impact funds partnering with IW must also develop and implement a comprehensive GLI action plan, for whose execution they are also

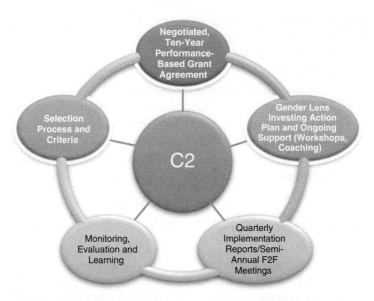

FIGURE 6.1   Investing in Women's Impact Investment Component. *Source:* Jackson and Alvarez (2018).

held accountable. The plans have been supported by training and coaching services provided by the Criterion Institute. These plans embed a gender-based analysis and gender mainstreaming measures in each fund's investment thesis and investment process, key performance indicators, human resources policies, organizational structure (including investment committees), and post-investment engagement with investees (Jackson and Alvarez 2018).

In its first phase, C2 provided grants to four proven, Western-based impact investment funds. Each negotiated proposal with IW on which the grant agreements are based. SEAF, a founding GIIN member, has used the grant to set up its Women's Opportunity Fund, which aims to raise USD $300 million in investment capital for WSMEs in the region (Lowe et al. 2019a). For its part, Root Capital, also an original GIIN member and already a leader in integrating gender into its portfolio management, has applied its C2 grant to expanding its lending in the agriculture sector to women-owned or -led cooperatives in Indonesia (Lowe et al. 2019b). A third fund partnering with IW, Patamar, used a portion of its grant to set up and run, with Kinara Investments, an annual theme-focused (e.g. food, fashion, etc.) incubator for WSMEs in Indonesia as a way to developing its pipeline of investees and to build a special-purpose fund for growth-stage WSMEs in the three programming countries (Lowe et al. 2019c). The fourth impact fund, C4D Partners, is levering its IW grant to deploy 30% of its USD $40 million Asia Fund into growth-stage WSMEs (Lowe et al. 2019d).

Time, of course, will tell how successful Investing in Women's partners will be in achieving their goals for private-capital mobilization, but progress so far is encouraging. By October 2019, the combined efforts of all four funds had resulted in deployment of AU $6.8 million into 24 deals with WSMEs across the three countries, one-third of which involved graduated companies from the Patamar/Kinara incubator. At the same time, these investments had collectively levered another AU $18.8 Million in private sector capital and co-investments, or 2.8 times IW's own investment in these companies (Lowe et al. 2019a).

Investing in Women's Component 2 has thus begun to build an empirical database that can and should be examined systematically by engaged scholars working with reflective practitioners.[16] To expand this empirical knowledge base, it will be essential to gather and analyze data on applications of the IW/C2 model to regional towns within the same three countries, in different Asian countries, and indeed in different regions of the world altogether.[17]

2. *Undismayed documentation of failure:* It is far too common for impact investors to showcase their investments' positive outcomes only. Notwithstanding the best efforts of all parties, some investee companies may underperform or fail altogether, the consequence of internal factors (e.g. management capacity, marketing decisions) or external factors (e.g. political instability, commodity-price shifts). There is a bias toward not reporting failure (disregarding or even

---

[16]Some questions that could drive deeper data collection and analysis might include, for example, what key factors, such as industry sector and use of technology, influence the growth and profitability prospects of investee WSMEs? How is WSME performance influenced by different management practices in, for example, governance, strategy, human resources, and technology? What investee cases have the most comprehensive gender-equality policies and practices, and to what extent do they affect business performance?

[17]Moreover, independent research should be undertaken, marshalling both qualitative and quantitative methods, to compare the IW/C2 model data with those of other incentive models, both grant-based and otherwise. How do the results in private-capital mobilization achieved by the IW/C2 model compare with program using repayable grants, with or without the requirement of gender action plans for the investment institutions involved?

hiding), and this double standard needs to be corrected (Bendell 2019). But documenting "positive net impact" or its absence must be accompanied by clear definitions and measurements. For instance, the framework offered by the International Finance Corporation's (IFC) Impact Management Principles[18] (IFC 2019) calls for more granular analysis and reporting, not only of every positive effect but also of the negative results a company may have.

Scholars and practitioners ought to use their research collaborations to fully document and understand the roots failure with a fair degree of honesty, to facilitate stakeholder learning and future improvements. The task of independent, critical research is to unflinchingly investigate what went wrong, who if anyone was responsible, and how such failure can be limited or avoided altogether in the future. The concept of reporting a rigorous "net impact" should also encompass the measurement of any eventual negative impacts (unintended, or unexpected) of the investment. This should be an integral part of the overall (social/environmental) contribution of the investment. If Impact Investing is about good intentions, then it must ensure its role is to fairly document its full net impact (positive and negative) with the necessary rigor and integrity. Positive net impact takes responsibility for the inevitable negative impacts of every investment and measures the overall contribution.

Impact Investing starts with good intentions, but it cannot end there. As the influx of funds continues, we have a collective role to ensure money is deployed with rigor and integrity to achieve both positive impact and financial performance. Researchers must make practitioners aware not to ignore or look away from the deals that lose money or enterprises that must be closed. Durable fields learn from what works and what does not; thus, documenting lessons learned is a key aspect of this work.

3. *Refining appropriate impact measurement methods:* As more capital is mobilized and deployed in GLI, stakeholders in the GLI ecosystem will turn their attention to investment implementation and monitoring and, in the medium- to longer term, to Impact Measurement and Management (IMM).[19] While the broader Impact Investing

---

[18]These principles tend to focus on the private sector of developing countries.
[19]See Chapter 17, "Impact Measurement and Management Techniques to Achieve Powerful Results," by Jane Reisman and Veronica Olazabal.

industry has made gains in recent years in making the case for investors integrating IMM systems and tools into the daily activities of the investment cycle, in practice, IMM in Impact Investing is still a mix of proprietary metrics and tools blended with some common standards and metrics (e.g. Bass et al. 2020; So and Staskevicius 2015; European Commission 2014). There are several debates about the most adequate toolset, and how to best combine qualitative methods (e.g. theory-based impact evaluation methods) with more advanced quantitative ones (e.g. experimental and post-experimental methods) to effectively determine long-term results of capital deployed, for the sake of triangulation, reliability, and generalization of results (e.g. Jimenez et al. 2018; So and Capanyola 2016; White 2010). The discipline of mixed methods should also be given more consideration (e.g. USAID 2013; Bamberger 2012).

But the "growth of metrics, ratings and certification-based approaches has sought to address this gap but this only goes so far, and there is a need for a more evaluative approach to assessing impact" (O'Flynn and Barnett 2017, p. 3). The prioritization of social impact cannot be done at the expense of prioritizing evidence-based impact. Evidence-based data can help depoliticize paradigms discussions, along with professional and political debates. The potential for evidence to help achieve social goals is huge (Parkhurst 2017). In this matter, Impact Investing needs to catch up and learn from other fields of knowledge such as evaluation, where impact assessment is practiced for decades (e.g. Masset et al. 2019; Gertler et al. 2016; Stockmann and Meyer 2016; Asian Development Bank and Australian Aid 2013; Lopez-Acevedo et al. 2012; Morra Imas and Rist 2009; UNDP 2002).

Given the diversity of gendered experience indifferent sectors and settings, there is not a single standard for measuring investing with a gender lens. General impact standards, principles,[20] and guidelines for good impact practice (e.g. GIIN 2014) emerged and exist, also more specifically for GLI, from workplace equity to access to appropriate capital. Nonetheless, there is already a considerable

---

[20]See, for instance, World Bank Group Evaluation Principles (World Bank et al. 2019), the Women's Empowerment Principles (WEPs) tool, available at https://weps-gapanalysis.org/, the EDGE (Economic Dividend for Gender Equality) used in Latin America, supported by the Inter-American Development Bank (IDB) Invest supports gender equality certification processes and adherence to national gender standards.

level of agreement in the industry on a basic set of IMM issues.[21] First, most impact investors accept the concept and application of the theory of change (see Jackson 2013). Investors know it as the investment thesis of a fund or institution. Second, there is wide acknowledgment that stakeholder engagement is necessary for accurate and credible monitoring and evaluation of investments (O'Flynn and Higdon 2019).

Moreover, the experience of the Investing in Women initiative underscores the importance of identifying and interrogating the various roles, contributions, costs, and benefits of diverse actors along the stakeholder network in a GLI investment (Figure 6.2). In this network, capital moves from the impact investment partner to the investee WSME and then on to its owners, employees, suppliers, and (through savings and quality) customers. It is at the level of the households of these stakeholders where families and individuals make decisions about resource allocation and spending that additional income from the enterprise is converted into, for example, school or clinic fees that improve children's education or health, more nutritious food for all household members, or investment in addition to the residential structure or in the new business of a family member. In turn, these decisions translate into SDG results (see Jackson and Alvarez 2018).

Third, there is also growing recognition across the Impact Investing industry that IMM metrics should be closely aligned with the

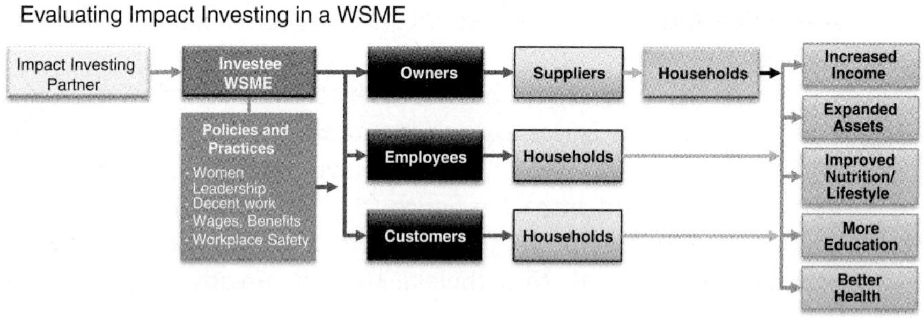

Evaluating Impact Investing in a WSME

FIGURE 6.2   Evaluating Impact Investing in a WSME. *Source:* Jackson and Alvarez (2019).

---

[21] IRIS+, a generally accepted system for measuring, managing, and optimizing impact also emphasizes the use of IMM for decision-making. Available at https://iris.thegiin.org/.

United Nations' Sustainable Development Goals (Ogunfowora 2020; Data2X and Open Data Watch 2016). Finally, it is understood by most practitioners that deploying tools, especially mobile, web-enabled platforms, can do much to achieve cost-effective impact assessment through lead data collection and analysis (Dichter et al. 2016).

GLI can and should learn from these efforts and build upon them, but also chart its own path. The work that remains to be done is to deepen these measurements through practice and applied research, by incorporate them into existing measurement systems, but also by creating new systems of accountability. The integration of gender-based analysis into IMM systems and tools is an important element in mainstreaming gender in GLI. Feminist theory and gender studies more broadly can sharpen the critical framing of evaluation methods and tools. It is critical that the field put in place safeguards to ensure that GLI scales and that it does not just become an example of "pink-washing." Indeed, through critical analysis and field-based research, gender scholars and evaluation scholars in both the North and the South can enrich and strengthen the field of GLI.

4. *Responding to the financing needs of all the vulnerable, in particular men:* Most GLI projects around the world would claim that they are engaging both men and women and that gender equality can only be achieved with the involvement of both male and female stakeholders.[22] However, the reality on the ground is that patriarchy and misogyny perpetrate such egregious injustices on women and girls that advancing women's power and resources, strategically and practically, must by necessity be the priority. But that approach is not suitable for every context. In many advanced economies, like Canada, and some developing economies, such as those in the Caribbean, men have fallen behind women in educational attainment, especially in post-secondary institutions, and, consequently, in the formal labor market. Thus, continuing discrimination against women in terms of wages and sexual harassment in the workplace can and does coexist with high unemployment or underemployment among young, uneducated men.

One source of relevant empirical data in this regard is found in the Caribbean. In 2019–2020, with the support of the Caribbean

---

[22] Often in gender empowerment initiatives the key involvement of men is undervalued or even despised, while, in fact, they are key actors in ending discrimination and GBV.

Development Bank, three local DFIs in the region—the Development Bank of Jamaica, the Development Finance Corporation of Belize, and the Saint Lucia Development Bank—undertook a gender analysis of their loan portfolios, as they each developed a customized gender equality policy and action plan to mainstream gender throughout their organizational strategy, operations, policies, and practices.

For example, the Saint Lucia Development Bank found that, overall, individual male borrowers account for 53% of all loans compared with 39% for individual female borrowers (the remaining 8% of loans are taken by companies and associations). This bias toward men is most striking in the productive sectors, such as agriculture, where male borrowers account for 63% of loans and females for only 17%.[23] However, in another part of the portfolio, female borrowers account for 69% of all education loans, while males receive 31% (Jackson et al. 2019).

The Development Finance Corporation (DFC) of Belize also carried out an analysis of sex-disaggregated data for its loan portfolio, with similar results. For the portfolio as a whole for the last three years, individual male borrowers received 61% of the loans representing 55% of the value of all loans, while individual women borrowers received 38% of the loans representing 23% of the value of all loans. In tourism, the dominance of male borrowers was striking; they received 83% of the loans in this sector while female borrowers received just 17%. In contrast, though, in the education sector, male borrowers accounted for 40% of all loans while women accounted for 60%. DFC also found that, for its portfolio as a whole, 11% of its loans to male borrowers are nonperforming and 20% are in delinquency, while only 3% of loans to women borrowers are nonperforming and 7% are in delinquency (Jackson et al. 2019).

Thus, in these countries and likely in most others, GLI must really be about gender balance as a whole, and that includes considerations around both men's and women's needs. That is, in Saint Lucia and Belize, there are very specific areas in which women face obstacles to accessing finance, especially in the productive sectors. But men are also underrepresented in education sector loans. DFIs must first assess vulnerabilities by tracing inequalities in access to finance and opportunities, tracking these different groups performance, to later address gaps in order to continue to learn and adapt through outreach,

---

[23]See, for instance, International Labor Organization (2018).

marketing, education, and also potentially through incentivized loan terms.

The extent to which these specific needs are met is an important subject for scholar-practitioner research collaboration. Some borrowers' businesses and projects will not take off; some student borrowers will drop out of their educational programs. While exacting a human price, these realities must be studied carefully and understood in detail. The appropriateness and effectiveness of the widest range of financial products should also be subject of deeper analysis. The gender mainstreaming work in Belize produced a capital continuum that identifies various types of grants and loans, some of which are within the core business of local development finance institutions and others which are the prime responsibility of other players. Researchers should seek to understand the financing needs and potential of the stakeholders involved at each point on the continuum.

What measures work (and what do not) and why, across sectors, regions of the country, borrowers' education levels, their ethnic and religious affiliation, are some of the questions tackled by researchers or evaluators, or blended teams of the former, often through evaluative research (Powell 2006). These questions can be examined through a whole array of methodologies, from qualitative and quantitative to mixed methods. The particular mix of methods needs to be pondered and adapted to address each particular context and evaluation question, to obtain evidence that is factual and triangulated, so that its reliability is ensured.

Confidentiality of data is often a considerable impairment to these judgments and needs to be overcome by technology, regulation, and confidentiality statements. The inclusion of best practices and lessons learned[24] in these types of assessments (or evaluations) reflects the analysis of areas of underperformance and failure, which must be uncovered, understood, and addressed. Similarly, unintended or unexpected effects of investments (positive or negative) need to be documented and acted upon with the necessary caution due to reputational issues. Moreover, comparative studies of similar continua for other countries should also be undertaken. Cross-national research lends itself to broader research consortia or networks with shared governance and resources, and technology provides huge opportunities for partnerships to come alive.

---

[24]See, for instance, International Labor Organization (2014).

CONSTRUCTING A GLI RESEARCH AGENDA THROUGH 2030

There is a much larger array of themes, issues, and questions on which scholars, evaluators, and practitioners can and should collaborate with investors
and policymakers. But how should a research agenda for GLI be constructed,
timed, and overlapped with key timelines, such as the monitoring for the
SDGs? Below are key elements that should be present as much as possible
in defining a research agenda for GLI up to 2030. First, it ought to be done
around a consensual purpose and a vision for change, and there is no better
consensus than the SDGs. For its implementation it needs to rely on a wide
set of stakeholders and relevant communities of practice to allow the field
to advance and impose itself as a credible research area. Next are methods
and application of knowledge. Finally, these efforts would not be complete
without a strategy to sustain and disseminate the knowledge that has been
created, especially through formal education. Five key stepping-stones are
important:

- *SDG timeline-aligned:* First, it makes sense to align research agendas'
  timeline with that of the SDGs,[25] whose final implementation year
  is 2030. That suggests that the research agenda for GLI should be 10
  years in length and target its completion in 2030, as well. This 10-year
  time horizon, in turn, could be developed into a series of shorter,
  more manageable phases each of, say, 3 to 5 years in duration. In
  parallel, research should be aligned with the relevant policy of the
  agenda. Some countries went far in this respect. The Government of
  Belize has decided to take full ownership of the SDGs. Its strategy
  is to attract foreign investments that are consistent with the goals
  of sustainable development.[26] Belize offered itself as a pilot country for the SDGs, fully integrating the SDGs into its "Growth and
  Sustainable Development Strategy" (GSDS),[27] the country's main

---

[25]With 54 gender-specific indicators, the SDGs indicator framework is more comprehensive and far-reaching than that of the MDGs.

[26]This is evidenced by the Ministry of Finance embarking on an initiative to move toward
program budgeting in all line ministries to enable the monitoring of individual ministry's performance in achieving GSDS and SDG targets. According to the "Belize's Voluntary National Review for the Sustainable Development Goals – 2017," a key challenge
in achievement of the GSDS and SDG targets is the collection and management of data
(Government of Belize 2017).

[27]"In late 2013, Belize volunteered to act as a "pilot country" within the UN system, to help
demonstrate how national development planning could work in harmony with the emerging 'Post-2015 Development Agenda' of the global community of nations. The GSDS, while

planning document for the planning period (2016–2019). Moreover, several countries embarked on developing Development Finance Assessments (DFA)[28] and Integrated National Financing Frameworks (INFF) to support cohesive nationally owned sustainable development strategies.[29] This is line with the Addis Ababa Action Agenda (AAAA), which sets forward strategic recommendations for leveraging private finance to make the achievement of SDGs a reality. Governments are now due to work with diverse sectors of society to ensure that within INFFs, domestic system of policies and institutional structures work toward an efficient management of resources and an adequate channeling of financial flows toward relevant goals (see, for instance, United Nations 2019).

The full implementation of the AAAA requires collective action, but a collective approach to financing seems a challenge, as financing actors, driven by their own assessment of priorities, tend to act independently (OECD 2019). In this respect, a research agenda can help study the nature of interlinkages between the SDGs, and

---

focused principally on the development vision for Belize as articulated in Horizon 2030, is also intended to be in line with this emerging United Nations framework" (Government of Belize 2016, p. 2). "The framework is applicable to the full range of growth and sustainable development issues elaborated in this GSDS: from medium-term, growth-oriented policies to stimulate industry and jobs; to long-term, investment-oriented programs to build human capital and ensure the future health of critical ecosystems" (Government of Belize 2016, p. 13). Available at http://med.gov.bz/wp-content/uploads/2016/10/FINALGSDS-April72016.pdf.

[28] See, for instance, "Development Finance Assessment and Integrated Financing Solutions Achieving the Sustainable Development Goals in the Era of the Addis Ababa Action Agenda" available at: https://www.undp.org/content/dam/rbap/docs/meetTheSDGs/Achieving%20the%20Sustainable%20Development%20Goals%20in%20the%20Era%20of%20the%20AAAA%20-%20DFAs%20as%20a%20tool%20for%20Linking%20Finance%20with%20Results.pdf.

[29] "The DFAs and integrated financing solutions support governments to use the concept of the INFF to help strengthen policies and actions for mobilizing different types of finance for economic, environmental and social results into a single, Development Finance Assessment Integrated Financing Solutions coherent framework" (Asia Pacific Effectiveness Development Facility and UNDP, p. 3). According to United Nations Development Program's (UNDP) "Development Finance Assessment Guidebook" (UNDP n.d.), a DFA is a diagnosis exercise, aiming at providing a comprehensive view of revenues and flows to finance the SDG. The DFA methodology currently focuses on five dimensions that encompass a wide spectrum of policy and institutional factors in financing sustainable development: integrated planning and financing processes, public-private collaboration, monitoring and review frameworks, and transparency and accountability.

between these and regional, national, and subnational policies, and inform on how these can be reinforced. The International Council for Science document (2017) entitled "A guide to SDG interactions: from science to implementation"[30] supports this idea, based on the premise that a "science-informed analysis of interactions across SDG domains—which is currently lacking—can support more coherent and effective decision-making, and better facilitate follow-up and monitoring of progress" (International Council for Science 2017, p. 7).

- *Establishing a wider community of (research) practice*: After defining the goals around which to work in, it makes sense to think about stakeholders and partnerships. In October 2017, the GIIN launched the *Gender Lens Investing Initiative* to explore the opportunities and challenges in dealing and scaling GLI. A *GLI Working Group* was also created (as a subset of the GIIN membership) with over 130 individuals from over 70 organizations as a platform to share learnings and explore the opportunities and challenges in catalyzing and scaling GLI. This initiative already offers GLI case studies, resources to help investors select GLI impact strategies and adopt metrics, and an online GLI resource repository.[31] There is a growing list of resources leaders[32] and initiatives that touch upon GLI. The ongoing DFA initiative, as mentioned above, is a United Nations and European Union (EU) working agenda that is running in parallel, and which should not be kept disjoint from GLI efforts. But all this can be expanded even further to involve groups of donor agencies, foundations, research bodies, and granting councils, ideally with North-South membership balance, that convenes high-level leaders and scholars to take the first year to collectively draft, debate, and finalize what a GLI research agenda should look like. This process could involve a global conference to launch the new research agenda, then intermediate regional gatherings, along with regular webinar engagements, publications, and the availability of more global resources.

- *Theory-building a core element:* All emerging (and mature) professional fields need to be informed, engaged, challenged, and, ultimately, strengthened through theory-building. For GLI, feminist and gender

---

[30]This report provides a particularly useful blueprint for countries to implement and achieve the SDGs, by examining the interactions between its 17 SDGs and its 169 targets, determining to what extent they reinforce or conflict with each other.

[31]Available at https://thegiin.org/gender-lens-investing-initiative.

[32]See more information at https://missioninvestors.org/gender-lens-investing.

studies should play a central role in this effort, but so should other disciplines, including finance and investment, management, economics, political science, public policy, and more. Space should be created for GLI to be more inclusive, culturally sensitive, and informed by indigenous epistemologies[33] and participatory frameworks. In parallel, GLI should also be more open to consider relationships with other cross-cutting issues beyond gender, and on how these elements mix and influence each other, such as gender and race, gender and violence, gender and extremism, for instance, developing more than a two-dimensional view. It is here that complexity lies when creating a theory of change (ToC), developing a theory, or even more simplistically a theoretical approach on how intended impacts can be derived from an intervention.

- *A deepened empirical knowledge base from practice*: According to UNWOMEN (2018), the challenges for gender-responsive monitoring are formidable, with only 10 out of 54 SDG gender-related indicators being reliably monitored at the global level. To strengthen this empirical knowledge base, progress on more SDG indicators must be tracked, gaps identified, and challenges in implementation highlighted. Beyond more funding for gender statistics, the gender data revolution needs to look beyond national averages, to tackle the deep-seated biases in definitions, classifications, and methodologies to ensure that data actually captures the diversity of the world we live in. A common misconception is that GLI works in silos or that even precludes men, while it actually is another set of analytical tools to uncover how to better drive returns. GLI funds and other vehicles, and products, programs, and projects all generate valuable data through practice. Investors need reliable data, not only to determine whether GLI investments are making the intended impact for women and vulnerable groups but also to measure and improve gender inclusiveness and women's empowerment in its multidimensional fronts. Data and gender impact assessments[34] are key to advocating for GLI since some investors still do not accept that investing in gender can lead to better results, even if there is increasingly more information that gender-diverse teams correlate with better returns.

  However, analytical frameworks for data collection and analysis need to expand beyond women-led small and medium enterprises,

---

[33]See, for instance, Gilbert (2019), Smith (2005), and Mbava (2019).
[34]See, for instance, European Institute for Gender Equality (2017).

so that GLI can also be perceived and connected to what happens at the workplace and to gender equity policies and practices, but also linked to other types of decisions, such as those for instance linked to climate financing. This is also why the 2030 Agenda calls for dramatic advances in statistics, financing, and policies for gender equality. Scholars and practitioners in the Global South and North should collaborate from a critical stance to deepen the field's understanding of what works and what does not, under which conditions, and where. In interrogating practice-generated knowledge, scholars can help the field learn from failure as well as success.

• *Encoding, enlivening, disseminating, and sustaining knowledge through formal education:* One of the most effective ways of encoding and enlivening and sustaining knowledge generated through research or applied practice is to develop formal university degree programs, graduate courses in GLI, or even blended or online courses.[35] But these need to go beyond creating specialized programs for female entrepreneurs and female-focused companies only. The teaching of the application of GLI needs to be available to all and included in the curricula as a framework and a set of tools that potentiates businesses' effectiveness, performance, and impact. Funding agencies should call for proposals and support efforts by universities in Africa, Asia, and the Americas to lead this process, perhaps routing some funds for Northern institutions to work as subcontractors and advisors to the lead Southern universities.

IMPACT INVESTING COMMUNITY-UNIVERSITY RESEARCH PARTNERSHIPS

Collaborative dialogue structures between community partners and universities on critical and complex issues are now part of the way business is done, as brokering support and action research engagement are part of the knowledge architecture of most research-oriented institutions. The GLI ecosystem is a dynamic community of practice, and certainly also a community of interest, populated and driven by practitioners—asset managers, DFI officers, bankers, philanthropists, consultants, but also governments and

---

[35] See, for instance, the Coursera course "Social Entrepreneurship and Gender Lens Investing," https://www.coursera.org/lecture/world-change/social-entrepreneurship-and-gender-lens-investing-3uEHu.

beneficiaries themselves—in all parts of the world. Collective action has the power to accelerate the advancement of GLI partnerships. In engaging with scholars to co-create critical knowledge to both energize and challenge the field-building process, this community can intentionally and systematically develop partnerships with universities and institutes at the global, national, and individual levels (Table 6.1). In turn, these partnerships can serve as the prime vehicles for the co-creation of knowledge by reflective practitioners and engaged scholars.

Much is already known about how to design and implement effective community-campus research partnerships (Hall et al. 2013). Reciprocity, mutual benefit, shared power, financial resources, and transparent operations are important principles adopted by the most productive and sustainable partnerships (Jackson 2014). Such principles could be applied

TABLE 6.1   Partnership Development Drivers.

External

- Access to wider networks (national/regional), new business opportunities (new markets for products and services), and partners
- Reputation enhancement
- Higher influence and business status (local/national/regional)
- New funding sources or access to other resources

Organizational

- Enhanced operational efficiency and effectiveness in meeting business objectives to meet targets and achieve mission
- Leveraging of internal capacity to attain business goals
- New opportunities for learning and enhancement
- Acquisition of different working modes
- More effective resource allocation and use of time

Individual

- Personal status and reputation
- New channels to exert influence and making the personal opinion heard
- Development of new contacts and relationships
- New opportunities for learning
- Acquisition of new skills
- More effective use of time and resources

Source: Authors, based on Caplan et al. (2007).

equally to a global research consortium, a national knowledge network, or an evaluation partnership between individual funds and local universities. However, there is another principle that is essential as well, a shared commitment to co-create, confront, learn from, share, and act upon *critical* knowledge. All these principles should be encoded in a written agreement between the parties that govern the collaboration.

There is a field of practice running parallel to that of GLI, broadly known as community-university engagement, a concept that encompasses community-service learning courses, community-based research projects, and student volunteering in communities. There are academic associations, conferences, and journals that highlight and disseminate the knowledge produced by these scholars and their community partners. Moreover, the engagement field is also a site of theory-building, drawing on feminist, indigenous, ecological, and constructionist epistemological traditions, among others. While some of these frames may inspire fierce challenges to GLI's culture and methods, they also may shine a light on certain practices in the field that permit and sustain elite capture and severe income inequality and, in response, amplify calls for positive social and environmental impacts among employees, suppliers, and customers in urban neighborhoods, small towns, and villages.

In the last two decades multi-stakeholder initiatives (MSIs)[36] are also increasingly put forward as a promising way to address complex challenges relating to sustainability and international development (Adviesraad Internationale Vraagstukken 2013). When one actor alone cannot address complex issues, but joint efforts are necessary, MSIs bring a variety of actors together to co-create solutions or address economic, social, and environmental challenges. MSIs have converted into key instruments for policy decision-making and action on global development topics. These transnational arrangements often fill a governance vacuum for safeguarding global public goods when no system of transnational legally enforceable law exists (Biekart and Fowler 2018). In general, approaches to engaging with MSIs have been "learning by doing" experiences, often pioneering interventions, done with a spirit of exploration, which have resulted in mixed results of success.

MSIs vary greatly in terms of their vision, mission for addressing intended economic, social or environmental issues, and usually portray

---

[36]The term MSI is adopted because the concept of "partnership" can be potentially misleading regarding the involved inherent power asymmetries (Stern, Kingston, and Ke 2015). A relationship between "partners" suggests a relationship between equals, which is not always the case.

unique engagements in terms of their nature, objectives, constitution, duration, governance, decision-making, resource intensity, and/or operational structure and roles played by actors. But the evidence indicates that MSI which are grown endogenously and are truly participative work the best. Donor-driven agendas frequently lead to the formation of parallel structures which can lead to fragmentation, and therefore yield a weak level of local/country ownership. MSIs often poorly address in a significant way the needs of Southern countries either because they are ad hoc, set up to look for short-term gains, or are too focused on one specific issue. "A first conclusion is to avoid searching for a specific and ideal MSI template, for example for each SDG or target" (Biekart and Fowler 2018). National and sub-national contexts differ. The cliché that "context matters" demands a more fine-grained understanding of what makes an MSI work. An understanding of these dynamics requires unpacking the incentives for collaboration and assessing how internal stakeholder balance eventually determines positive results over time.

FINAL REMARKS

No field of practice can flourish without independent, critical knowledge production challenging and guiding its development. This is as true for GLI as for any other professional endeavor. While the champions of GLI may not always appreciate a critical frame being applied to their work, ultimately, their efforts will be strengthened rather than undermined. It is time for scholars to work with practitioners and all relevant stakeholders in the ecosystem to design an appropriate GLI research agenda (which can have different tiers, at the global regional, national, and company level, as long as it is integrated and cascades from the SDGs) that will generate relevant, independent, and systematic knowledge about the full kaleidoscope of issues, products, factors, and actors at play in the emerging global ecosystem of GLI.

A "roadmap" to portray what the field encompasses and where it is going is urgently needed given the levels of investment available, the need to fulfill the SDGs, and the diverse contexts, goals, and participants involved in GLI. In clear-eyed, mutually accountable partnership with GLI practitioners, engaged scholars from both the Global North and Global South aiming to grow the field need to interact and work together as they both have an important role to play. But the levels of conversation, which have initially happened as investments take off and become successful, need to take place also around challenges and not so successful endeavors. GLI advocates must devote greater attention to publicizing not only successes but also responsible exits from their funds and vehicles and use those cases to mobilize more capital.

There is much to be done. The scope for growth of GLI is huge; public markets could grow to USD $30 billion in the next five years, with the potential to expand to more than 10 times that amount according to Veris Wealth Partners (Avery 2018). Most financial institutions already incorporating gender in their decision-making want to expand the breadth and depth of this work, viewing GLI as a useful frame and set of analytical tools for business expansion. Those who have not yet intentionally incorporated gender into financial analyses tend to recognize the importance of owing gender data and gender policies for better decision-making. Larger and more gender-smart investment funds must be designed and launched rapidly, along with more collaborative networks and accelerator programs focusing on women entrepreneurs. With data and technological advances, methods and gender scorecard methodologies have evolved significantly; existing tools need to be better used and new ones developed and tailored.

The five key elements of a research agenda— (1) aligning research agendas' timeline with that of the SDGs; (2) establishing a community of practice; (3) applying theory-building as a core element; (4) deepening empirical knowledge; and (5) encoding, disseminating, and sustaining knowledge through formal education—will be capable of holding GLI champions and products to account while, with equal energy and verve, enabling the building of a scaled, high-impact, and lasting field of GLI practice in Impact Investing globally.

ACKNOWLEDGMENTS

Although they are not responsible for any errors or omissions in this chapter, the following colleagues have influenced the analysis herein: Kaylene Alvarez, Denise Beaulieu, Elizabeth Burges-Sims, Cathy Clark, Nicole Etchart, Natalie Ewing-Goff, Anthony George, Kristy Graham, Karim Harji, Katharine Im-Jenkins, Hamdiya Ismaila, Jennifer Jones-Morales, Dorn Lafeuilee-Simon, Joan Larrea, Nancy MacPherson, Alima Mahama, Elizabeth McAllister, Nicole Meier, Anna Rose Miller, Refilwe Moekoena, Julia Newton-Howes, Lilly Nicholls, Catherine Potvin, Jane Reisman, Brian Rowe, Ariane Ryan, Kizzann Lee Sam, Magda Seydegart, James Soukamneuth, Sue Szabo, Beth Woroniuk, and Maria Ziegler. Special thanks are also due to R. Paul Herman, co-editor of this volume, for his contributions and advice.

REFERENCES

2X Challenge: Financing for Women Initiative (2019). Two new investors join the 2X Challenge initiative. https://www.2Xchallenge.org/press-news/2019/10/22/two-investors-join-the-2X-challenge-initiative (accessed January 29, 2020).

Allman, K., and de Nogales, X. E. (2015). *Impact Investment. A Practical Guide to Investment Process and Social Impact Analysis.* Hoboken, NJ: Wiley & Sons.

Anderson, J., and Miles, K. (2015). The State of the Field of Gender Lens Investing: A Review and a Road Map. Criterion Institute. http://criterioninstitute.org/wp-content/uploads/2012/06/State-of-the-Field-of-Gender-Lens-Investing-11-24-2015.pdf (accessed on 29 January 2020).

Asia Pacific Effectiveness Development Facility and UNDP (n.d.). Development Finance Assessment and Integrated Financing Solutions, Achieving the Sustainable Development Goals in the Era of the Addis Ababa Action Agenda.

Asian Development Bank and Australian Aid (2013). Tool Kit on Gender Equality Results and Indicators.

Avery, H. (2018). Gender-lens investing doubles in a year. Veris Wealth Partners (November 14). https://www.euromoney.com/article/b1btkm4lqly7sl/gender-lens-investing-doubles-in-a-year (accessed on 29 March 2020).

Adviesraad Internationale Vraagstukken (2013). Wisselwerking tussen actoren in internationale samenwerking naar flexibiliteit en vertrouwen. *Advies* 82, Den Haag: AIV.

Bamberger, M. (2012). Introduction to mixed methods in Impact Evaluation. Interaction and the Rockefeller Foundation Impact Evaluation Notes No. 3 (August 2012).

Banaham, C., and Hasson, G. (2018). Across the Board Improvements: Gender Diversity and ESG Performance. Harvard Law School Forum on Corporate Governance and Financial Regulation (6 September).

Bass, R., Dithrich, H., Sunderji, S., and Nova, N. (2020). *The State of Impact Measurement and Management Practice,* 2nd ed. New York: Global Impact Investing Network. https://thegiin.org/research/publication/imm-survey-second-edition (accessed January 29, 2020).

Bendell, A. (2019). Impact investors fail to measure negative outcomes. *Financial Times* (13 May 2019). https://www.ft.com/content/8ffb4e56-546d-11e9-8b71-f5b0066105fe (accessed 22 April 2020).

Biekart, K., and Fowler, A. (2018), "Ownership dynamics in local multi-stakeholder initiatives," *Third World Quarterly, April 2018.* DOI: 10.1080/01436597.2018.1450139.

Business Insider (2012). Hundreds of Suicides Linked to Microfinance Organizations (February 24, 2012). https://www.businessinsider.com/hundreds-of-suicides-in-india-linked-to-microfinance-organizations-2012-2 (accessed on 2 February 2020).

Calvert (2016). Calvert Women's Principles. https://www.calvert.com/includes/loadDocument.php?fn=28364.pdf&dt=fundpdfs%27.

Catalyst (2011). The Bottom Line: Corporate Performance and Women's Representation on Boards 2004–2008. https://www.catalyst.org/wp-content/uploads/2019/01/the_bottom_line_corporate_performance_and_womens_representation_on_boards_2004-2008.pdf (accessed 10 March 2020).

Carlile, L. R., Choi, L., Farrar-Rivas, P., and Pyott, A. (2015). Women, Wealth and Impact: Investing with a Gender Lens 2.0. VERIS.

Criterion Institute (2019). Key Concepts in Gender: A Primer for Investors. https://criterioninstitute.org/resources/key-concepts-in-gender-a-primer-for-investors (accessed on 29 January 2020).

Criterion Institute (2018). Designing a Gender Lens Investing Action Plan. Prepared for the Investing in Women Initiative. Manila. https://criterioninstitute.org/resources/gender-lens-investing-tool-designing-an-action-plan (accessed on 29 January 2020).

Criterion Venture (2012). The Landscape of Gender Metrics: Measuring the Impact of Our Investments on Women. http://criterioninstitute.org/resources/files/2012/08/The-Landscape-of-Gender-Metrics.pdf.

Criterion Institute (n.d.) Framing Gender Lens Investing. Prepared for the Investing in Women Initiative. Manila. https://indd.adobe.com/view/9b2f9581-74e2-45c9-891b-56a94684365c (accessed on 29 January 2020).

DAI (2019). Six Practical Ways to Tackle Gender Lens Investing. Washington, DC. https://www.dai.com/uploads/gender-lens-investing.pdf (accessed January 29, 2020). Data2X and Open.

Data Watch (2016). Ready to measure: Twenty Indicators for Monitoring SDG Gender Targets. https://opendatawatch.com/blog/ready-to-measure-twenty-indicators-for-monitoring-sdg-gender-targets/ (accessed 21 April 2020).

Dichter, S., Adams, T., and Ebrahim, A. (2016). The Power of Lean Data. *Stanford Social Innovation Review*, Winter. https://ssir.org/articles/entry/the_power_of_lean_data (accessed January 29, 2020).

D'Espallier, B., Guérin, I., and Mersland, R. (2011). Women and Repayment in Microfinance: A Global Analysis. *World Development* 39 (5): 758–772 (May 2011).

Equileap (2018). Gender Equality Global Report & Ranking, 2018 Edition.

European Bank of Reconstruction and Development (2016). Strategy for the Promotion of Gender Equality 2016–2020. Making Business Transformative: Creating Opportunities for All.

European Commission (2014). Proposed Approaches to Social Impact Measurement. GECES Sub-group on Impact. Measurement 2014. Directorate-General for Employment, Social Affairs and Inclusion Unit C2.

European Institute for Gender Equality (2017). Gender Impact Assessment, Gender Mainstreaming Toolkit. https://eige.europa.eu/publications/gender-impact-assessment-gender-mainstreaming-toolkit.

Gaffuri, A., and Willis, R. (2019). SheInvest: New initiative to mobilize EUR 1 billion for women across Africa. European Investment Bank (November 12, 2019). https://www.eib.org/en/press/all/2019-306-sheinvest-new-initiative-to-mobilise-eur-1-billion-for-women-across-africa (accessed on 29 January 2020).

Gertler, P., Martinez, S., Rawlings, L. B., et al. (2016). Impact Evaluation in Practice. World Bank and Inter-American Development Bank, 2nd ed.

GIIN (2019). Lasting Impact: The need for responsible exits, GIIN Issue Brief.

GIIN (2014). Guidelines for good impact practice. https://thegiin.org/assets/documents/Webinar%20Slides/guidelines-for-good-impact-practice.pdf (accessed 21 April 2020).

Gilbert S. (2019). Embedding Indigenous Epistemologies and Ontologies Whilst Interacting with Academic Norms. *Australian Journal of Indigenous Education* 1–7. https://doi.org/10.1017/jie.2019.18.

Government of Belize (2016). Growth and Sustainable Development Strategy for Belize 2016–2019.

Government of Belize (2017). Belize's Voluntary National Review for the Sustainable Development Goals. https://sustainabledevelopment.un.org/content/documents/16389Belize.pdf (accessed 21 April 2020).

Hall, B. L., Jackson, E. T., Tandon, R. et al. (2013). *Knowledge, democracy and action: Community university research partnerships in international perspectives*. Manchester, UK: Manchester University Press. https://www.manchesteropenhive.com/view/9781526137081/9781526137081.xml (accessed on 29 January 2020).

International Council for Science document (2017). A guide to SDG interactions: from science to implementation.

International Finance Corporation (IFC) (2019). Investing for Impact: Operating Principles for Impact Management.

International Labor Organization (2014). Evaluation Lessons Learned and Emerging Good Practices. Guidance Note 3. ILO Evaluation Unit (April 25, 2014).

International Labor Organization (2018). Gender at Work in the Caribbean: Country Report for Saint Lucia.

Jackson, E. T. (2014). Community University Research Partnerships. In *The Sage Encyclopedia of Action Research*. (eds. D. Coghlan and M. Brydon-Miller, 163–66). Sage Publications.

Jackson, E. T. (2013). Interrogating the Theory of Change: Evaluating Impact Investing Where It Matters Most. *Journal of Sustainable Finance and Investment* 3(2): 95–110. https://www.tandfonline.com/doi/full/10.1080/20430795.2013.776257 (accessed on 29 January 2020).

Jackson, E. T., and Alvarez, K. (2018). Catalytic Capital for Women's Economic Empowerment: Report of the C2 External Review of the C2 Component of the Investing in Women Initiative. A Report prepared for the Investing in Women Initiative, Manila and the Department of Foreign Affairs and Trade, Canberra. https://investinginwomen.asia/wp-content/uploads/2019/03/190206-C2-Review-Report_Catalytic-Capital-for-WEE_final_online-version.pdf (accessed on 29 January 2020).

Jackson, E. T., Beaulieu, D., Ewing-Goff, N., and Palacio, A. (2019). Mainstreaming Gender in Development Finance in Belize. NESsT Blog (December 10, 2019). https://www.nesst.org/nesst/guest-feature-mainstreaming-gender (accessed on 29 January 2020).

Jimenez, E., Waddington H., Goel, N., et al. (2018). Mixing and matching: Using qualitative methods to improve quantitative impact evaluations (IES) and systematic reviews (SRS) of development outcomes. CEDIL Inception Paper 5.

Johnston, J. (2019). Blending for Gender Balance. Blog (March 7, 2019). Convergence. https://www.convergence.finance/news-and-events/news/5lqarXZRuQEMKeyeI9cI8e/view (accessed on 29 January 2020).

Kaplan, S., and VanderBrug, J. (2014). The Rise of Gender Capitalism. *Stanford Social Innovation Review*, Fall 2014. https://ssir.org/issue/fall_2014 (accessed on 29 January 2020).

Kyaw, K., Olugbode, M., and Petracci, B. (2015). Does Gender Diverse Board Mean Less Earnings Management? *Finance Research Letters* 14: 135–141.

Krishnan, G. V., and Parsons, L. M. (2007). Getting to the Bottom Line: An Exploration of Gender and Earnings Equality. *Journal of Business Ethics* 78(1–2).

LeBlanc, R., Moore, D., and Sarmento, E. de Morais (2019). The Joint Evaluation of the NEPAD Spanish Fund for African Women's Empowerment 2007–2016. Final Evaluation Report. AUDA-NEPAD. Spanish Ministry of Foreign Affairs, European Union.

Lopez-Acevedo, G., Krause, P., and Mackay, K. (eds.) (2012). Building Better Policies, The Nuts and Bolts of Monitoring and Evaluation Systems. International Bank for Reconstruction and Development/International Development Association and World Bank.

Lowe, J., Habtemarian, S., and Wildman, H. (2019a). Case Study Series: SEAF Women's Opportunity Fund. Investing in Women Southeast Asia and Ernst and Young, Manila. https://investinginwomen.asia/wp-content/uploads/2019/10/IW-Case-Study_SEAF_OCT-2019_Final.pdf (accessed on 3 February 2020).

Lowe, J., Habtemarian, S., and Wildman, H. (2019b). Case Study Series: Root Capital. Investing in Women Southeast Asia and Ernst and Young, Manila. https://investinginwomen.asia/wp-content/uploads/2019/10/IW-Case-Study_Root-Capital_OCT-2019_Final.pdf (accessed on 3 February 2020).

Lowe, J., Habtemarian, S., and Wildman, H. (2019c). Case Study Series: Patamar Capital. Investing in Women Southeast Asia and Ernst and Young, Manila. https://investinginwomen.asia/wp-content/uploads/2019/10/IW-Case-Study_Patamar-Capital_OCT-2019_Final-002.pdf (accessed on 3 February 2020).

Lowe, J., Habtemarian, S, and Wildman, H. (2019d). Case Study Series: Capital 4 Development Partners ("C4D Partners"). Investing in Women Southeast Asia and Ernst and Young, Manila. https://investinginwomen.asia/wp-content/uploads/2019/10/IW-Case-Study_C4D-Partners_OCT-2019_Final.pdf (accessed on 3 February 2020).

MacLeod, E. (2019). *Mapping Gender Lens Investing in the Global South, Ghana, Kenya, Sri Lanka, and Vietnam*. Michael Snow, Jim Delaney, and Ariane Ryan (eds.). WUSC and Global Affairs Canada.

Maheshwari, P., Gokhale, A., Agarwal, N., et al. (2019). The Global Landscape of Gender Lens Investing. Intellecap and International Development Research Centre, Nairobi and Ottawa. file:///C:/Users/edwar/Downloads/

The-Global-Landscape-of-Gender-Lens-Investing.pdf (accessed March 3, 2020).

Masset, E., Rathinam, F., Nath, M., et al. (2019). Successful impact evaluations: Lessons from Dfid and 3IE. CEDIL Inception Paper 6.

Mbava, N. P. (2019). Shifting the Status Quo: Africa Influencing Global Evaluation Practice. *Evaluation Matters* Independent Development Evaluation (IDEV). African Development Bank.

McKinsey Global Institute. (2015). The Power of Parity: How Advancing Women's Equality Can Add $12 Trillion to Global Growth. https://www.mckinsey.com/featured-insights/employment-and-growth/the-power-of-parity-advancing-womens-equality-in-the-united-states#.

Mennonite Economic Development Associates and USAID (2018). The Gender Equality Mainstreaming (GEM) Framework. United States Agency for International Development. https://www.meda.org/gem (accessed on 29 January 2020).

Mungai, E. (2018). *Impact Investing in Africa. A Guide to Sustainability for Investors, Institutions, and Entrepreneurs.* Palgrave.

Morais Sarmento, E. (2019). Country Case study Cabo Verde/Cape Vert, The Joint Evaluation of the NEPAD Spanish Fund for African Women's Empowerment 2007–2016, NEPAD and AECID, Cooperacion Española, Ministerio de Assuntos Exteriores e Cooperación (Spanish Cooperation).

Morra Imas, L. G., and Rist, R. C. (2009). The Road to Results: Designing and Conducting Effective Development Evaluations. World Bank.

OECD (2019). Global Outlook on Financing for Sustainable Development 2019. Paris.

O'Flynn, P., and Barnett, C. (2017). Evaluation and Impact Investing: A Review of Methodologies to Assess Social Impact. IDS Evidence Report 222, Brighton: IDS.

O'Flynn, P., and Higdon, G. L. (2019). Is participation the antidote to "impact washing?" Institute of Development Studies. IDS Blog (September 19, 2019). https://www.ids.ac.uk/opinions/is-participatory-impact-investing-the-antidote-to-impact-washing/ (accessed January 29, 2020).

Ogunfowora, O. A. (2020). Social Impact Measurement and Impact Investing for Social Enterprises. PhD Thesis. Alliance Manchester Business School, Manchester University, Manchester.

Pax World Ellevate Global Women's Leadership Fund (2019). Pax World Funds. https://paxworld.com/funds/pax-ellevate-global-womens-leadership-fund/ (accessed 29 January 2020).

Parkhurst, J. (2017). The politics of evidence: From evidence-based policy to good governance of evidence. In: *Routledge Studies in Governance and Public Policy*. Routledge. Abingdon, Oxon, UK.

Powell, R. R. (2006). Evaluation Research: An Overview. *Library Trends* 55(1): 102–120. doi:10.1353/lib.2006.0050.

Private Infrastructure Development Group (2019). PDIG Gender Ambition Framework https://www.pidg.org/wp-content/uploads/2019/03/PIDG-Gender-Ambition-Framework-070219-FINAL.pdf (accessed 29 January 2020).

Quinlan, J., and VanderBrug, J. (2017). *Gender Lens Investing. Uncovering Opportunities for Growth, Returns and Impact*. Hoboken, NJ: Wiley & Sons.

Rose, G. (ed.) (2020). The Future of Capitalism (Special issue). Foreign Affairs, January/February 2020. https://www.foreignaffairs.com/articles/2019-12-10/future-capitalism (accessed 29 January 2020).

Sanjai, P. R., and Niar, V. (2012). Management Case-SKS Microfinance: Back from the Brink. LiveMint (March 24, 2012). https://www.livemint.com/Companies/RBD90ZgNGoQdojz6Dah8BM/Management-Case--SKS-Microfinance-Back-from-the-brink.html (accessed on 2 February 2020.

Smith. L. (2005). Building a Research Agenda for Indigenous Epistemologies and Education. *Anthropology & Education Quarterly* 36.

So, I., and Capanyola, A. (2016). How Impact Investors actually measure impact. *Stanford Social Innovation Review* (May 16). https://ssir.org/articles/entry/how_impact_investors_actually_measure_impact# (accessed 21 April 2020).

So, I., and Staskevicius, A. (2015). Measuring the "Impact" in Impact Investing. *Harvard Business School, MBA* 2015.

Stern, A., Kingston, D., and Ke, J. (2015). More than the Sum of Its Parts: Making Multi-Stakeholder Initiatives Work. Global Development Indicator. Washington, DC.

Stockmann, R., and Meyer, W. (eds.) (2016). *The Future of Evaluation: Global Trends, New Challenges, Shared Perspectives*. Palgrave Macmillan.

UBS (2018). UBS announces launch of new Global Gender Equality UCITS ETF (January 8). 2018 Media Release. https://www.ubs.com/global/en/ubs-news/r-news-display.html/en/2018/01/08/global-gender-equality-ucits-etf (accessed 29 January 2020).

United Nations (2019). Financing for sustainable development report 2019. Report of the Inter-agency Task Force on Financing for Development. New York.

United Nations Development Program (2002). *Handbook on Monitoring and Evaluating for Results UNDP Evaluation Office* (January 2002).

United Nations Development Program (n.d.). *Development Finance Assessment Guidebook, A tool for countries to enhance the Sustainable Development Goals.*

UNWOMEN (2018). Turning promises into action: Gender equality in the 2030 agenda for sustainable development.

USAID (2013). Conducting Mixed-Method Evaluations, Technical Note. Monitoring and Evaluation Series (June 2013).

Value for Women (2019). A Landscape Report: Impact Investing with a Gender Lens in Latin America. May 2019.

Veris Wealth Partners (2020). Gender Lens Investing: Assets Grow to More Than $3.4 Billion (4 March).https://www.veriswp.com/gender-lens-investing-assets-grow-to-more-than-3-4-billion/ (accessed 21 April 2020).

Wendt, K. (ed.) (2018). *Positive Impact Investing: A Sustainable Bridge Between Strategy, Innovation, Change and Learning.* New York: Springer.

White, H. (2010). A Contribution to Current Debates in Impact Evaluation. *Evaluation* 16(2): 153–16. Sage. DOI: 10.1177/1356389010361562

World Bank, International Finance Corporation, Multilateral Investment Guarantee Agency, Independent Evaluation Group (2019). *World Bank Group Evaluation Principles* (April 2019).

CHAPTER 7

Investing with a Gender Lens: Uncovering Alpha Previously Overlooked

Kristin Hull, PhD

Abstract

Women are an unparalleled force in the global economy. Across the world, women are successful entrepreneurs, business owners, employees, and thoughtful consumers. And yet when it comes to investing, considering women as a critical variable and input is a recent phenomenon. Incorporating a gender lens is a growing trend within environmental, social, and governance (ESG) and Impact Investing. Practitioners are bringing a gender lens into focus as a strategy to drive future growth, reduce risk, and produce positive impact. This chapter explores the decade-long history of this rapidly growing movement and illustrates approaches to incorporating a gender lens into an investment portfolio. A gender lens mandate can be woven into investment policy statements, investment criteria, and integrated into decision-making across all asset classes. Strategically evaluating all investments for leadership composition, products and services, operating metrics, and company policies can ensure a portfolio and an economy that is more gender balanced. The result is higher alpha potential, with higher upside possibilities, lower future risks, and more inclusion. Strategies range from investing in companies that include women in executive leadership and on the board of directors, to selecting women-owned businesses, and companies with products and services beneficial to women. Selecting female fund managers, financial advisors, and women-run wealth management firms are additional strategic ways to invest with a gender lens. Investors integrating gender in a systematic fashion are able to pursue higher-impact portfolios that are stronger and more resilient financially, while addressing Sustainable Development Goal 5 for gender equality.

Keywords

Gender Lens; Gender Alpha; Gender; Impact Investing; ESG; Diversity; Inclusion; Women in Leadership; Governance; Females in Finance; Sustainable Development Goals; SDG 5

INTRODUCTION

Women today are an unparalleled force in the global economy. Across the world, women are successful entrepreneurs and business owners, as well as employees and thoughtful consumers. Yet the absence of women's legal and property rights in many parts of the world, the persistent wage gaps at nearly every level of the corporate ladder, and the bias (both implicit and overt) against women in business, in leadership, and in society at large remains. This paradox creates an unprecedented and underexplored opportunity for investors (Quinlan and VanderBrug 2016). As Christine Lagarde, managing director of the International Monetary Fund (IMF) and the first woman to head up the European Central Bank (ECB), stated, "All economies [would] have savings and productivity gains if all women have access to the job market. It is not just a moral, philosophical, or equal-opportunity matter. It is also an economic cause. It just makes economic sense" (Quinlan and VanderBrug 2016). In fact, estimates show that overcoming gender inequality would greatly increase macroeconomic gains, national global gross domestic product (GDP), and ultimately global wealth (Elborgh-Woytek et al. 2013; Marone 2016). Research from the McKinsey Global Institute suggests that closing the gender gap in the workforce could add at least USD $12 trillion and up to USD $28 trillion to the global GDP by 2025 (Hunt et al. 2015).

Furthermore, it is estimated that up to 27% of GDP per capita in certain regions is lost due to gender gaps in the labor market (Cuberes and Teignier 2012), and evidence suggests that matching the female labor force participation rate (FLFPR) to that of males would lead to a GDP growth of 5% in the United States (US), 9% in Japan, 12% in the United Arab Emirates, and 34% in Egypt (Aguirre et al. 2012). Clearly, there is an investment case to be made for including women.

Gender lens investing (GLI), also known as "gender-smart" investing, is simply the consideration of women and girls when making investment decisions. GLI includes: (i) investing in companies with products and services that benefit women and girls; (ii) measuring positive and negative impacts across all asset classes and beneficiary types; and (iii) seeking investees and fund managers who are women-led or gender-balanced. In many contexts, "gender" is considered a neutral term referring to male or female identities. Yet when used in the largely male-driven financial and Impact Investing arenas, the term "gender" has come to refer solely to women, and often in reference to women in leadership positions.

The concept of GLI is gaining recognition and continues to grow in popularity as investors of all genders discover that adding a simple gender-based lens or filter can enhance the due diligence process. This chapter will explore compelling reasons for incorporating a gender lens, including the quest for stronger financial returns, as well as some investors' desire to signal market demand for greater diversity and inclusion by investing in companies that include women in leadership positions, or that provide employee benefits that help create gender-smart workplaces. Also to be discussed are various ways to incorporate a gender lens throughout the investment process, the investment policy statement (IPS), and across asset classes within a portfolio.

This chapter explains how all investors can include, embed, and develop a portfolio that achieves gender balance, positive impact, and financial benefits. This chapter serves as a "how-to guide" to GLI, answering questions on how to embed a gender focus into an IPS, and into the investment process, including security and fund selection, as well as manager selection. Engagement as a gender lens strategy is also discussed.

This chapter's methodology includes desk review of a combination of research studies from the field, direct conversations with fellow thought leaders in the space, and findings from the author's personal investing experience, as both a pioneering impact investor with early-stage companies and a portfolio manager of one of the first US-based gender-lens portfolios.

The next section dives into the background and history of GLI and provides context for this growing movement.

GENDER LENS INVESTING: DEFINITIONS, HISTORY, AND POTENTIAL FOR A GROWING MOVEMENT

Definitions: What Is Gender Lens Investing?

GLI is simply any investment made with women or gender equity as part of the investment criteria. Examples include investments made into a portfolio, fund, or individual enterprise run by a woman or a female-led team.

The Global Impact Investing Institute (GIIN) describes GLI as investing within the following two broad categories: (i) investing with the intent to address gender issues or promote gender equity and/or (ii) investing with specific approaches when forming investment decisions (GIIN 2017). The GIIN further elaborates that the first category includes investing in women-owned or -led businesses, investing in businesses that promote workplace equity, or investing in businesses that offer goods and services that significantly improve the lives of women and girls. The second category encompasses focusing on gender when sourcing and monitoring potential investments, as well as evaluating the investee's vision and mission in addressing gender issues; a company's organizational structure, culture, policies, and work environment; their use of data and metrics to manage gender-equitable performance and incentivize behavioral change toward increased equality; and their commitment to gender equality as evidenced in their financial and human resource decisions (GIIN 2017).

Given the extremely low percentages of funding currently invested in women-led businesses, ventures (Kapin 2019), funds (Sommer 2018), and wealth management firms (Segal 2019), specifically targeting and working with women in finance is a key way to invest with a gender lens. Given that the status quo has often excluded women, investments that include products or services beneficial to women, made with the intention to benefit women, or for women's financial enrichment are also strong examples. Joy Anderson, founder of the Criterion Institute—a US-based activist think tank devoted to gender equity—and an instrumental leader in helping launch, nurture, and grow the gender lens movement, says, "It's about incorporating a gender analysis into a financial analysis to get to better decisions" (Joy Anderson, personal communication).

Origins and History of Gender Lens Investing

While there is currently a surge in growth of requests for GLI vehicles, as well as an increasing number of examples of new approaches and products, up until recently this type of investing was rare. Catholic nuns are credited with being among the first women to use their investor voices to engage in shareholder activism, starting in the 1970s. These groups of religious women were also some of the first values-aligned investors, directing advisors and asset managers to remove what are now referred to as "sin stocks" from their investment portfolios. This type of investing, often referred to as socially responsible investing (SRI), focuses on the removal of "bad" companies (such as those producing alcohol, tobacco, pornography, etc.) from a standard index of publicly traded companies. While pioneering female investment managers engaged in SRI, building their own SRI investment firms as early as the 1980s, none of these early screening efforts actually took women into account in a direct way.

The first example of investments targeted specifically for women came with the invention of microcredit lending, which is the practice of making small loans to the previously unbanked, often to those without credit histories or collateral. Microfinance provides basic credit and deposit-taking on a very small scale to historically marginalized populations that generally do not meet the standard criteria to bank or receive credit from conventional banking institutions.

GLI has its roots in microfinance. Muhammed Yunus, economics professor and Nobel Peace Prize Laureate, is credited for pioneering the first micro-loans. Frustrated by the cycle of poverty he saw in his native Bangladesh, Yunus launched the Grameen Bank Project in 1976 to offer banking services to poor entrepreneurs being exploited by money lenders. Designed to support entrepreneurship and alleviate poverty, these first micro-loans were made to women stool makers. Grameen Bank began exclusively lending to women in the 1980s when it found that women repay their loans at more consistent rates and were willing to accept smaller loans than their male counterparts. Women continue to make up 75% of all microcredit recipients worldwide.

Over the past four decades, banks and investors have used microfinance to lend money to marginalized rural women in developing nations. Microfinance boosted the incomes and quality of life for many thousands of women and their families, simultaneously achieving positive financial and social impacts in countries such as Asia, Africa,[1] and Latin America.[2] When wealth

---

[1]See Chapter 8, "Gender Lens Investing in the African Context," by Michael Ngoasong and Richmond O. Lamptey.
[2]See Chapter 6, "Gender Lens Investing: Co-Creating Critical Knowledge to Build a Credible, Durable Field," by Edward Jackson and Elsa de Morais Sarmento.

management firms recognized this trend, the microfinance asset class was born, and over time microfinance was integrated into the fixed income asset class because of its high impact, low risk, and reliable financial returns.

Pro Mujer,[3] founded in 1990 in El Alto, Bolivia, by visionary leaders Lynne Patterson and Carmen Velasco, implemented an expanded micro-lending strategy combining microcredits with health-care services to groups of Bolivian women. Patterson and Velasco determined the health of their clients to be crucial to the success of microcredits and female empowerment in general. They thus took on a more systemic approach to poverty alleviation through access to capital. Pro Mujer has since become one of Latin America's leading women's development organizations, anchored in the belief that given the right opportunities, women can become powerful agents of change.

The first gender-focused public markets portfolio was launched in 1993 by Linda Pei and Leslie Christian. Their Women's Equity Mutual Fund was the first and only US opportunity to invest in companies with positive track records of hiring and promoting women. Upon Linda's death in 2006, Pax World took over managing the fund. In 2010, Morgan Stanley launched a strategy with a screen for women in leadership, at which time the GLI movement was yet to gain significant traction. Nia Global Solutions (a product of California, US-based Nia Impact Capital), a concentrated portfolio of public equities, was a pioneering strategy that launched in 2013. This gender lens product was the first to take an intersectional approach, combining both sustainability and gender equality as core investment criteria.

The Valeurs Feminines Fund, created in 2005 by the French money-management firm Conseil Plus Gestion, represents one of the earliest funds designed to invest in women-owned and women-led European businesses. Another early example is the Women in Agriculture Initiative at Root Capital. In 2008, while serving as president and chair of the board at the Hull Family Foundation, based in Oakland, California, our investment team looked into making an agricultural loan investment through Root Capital. In the due diligence process this question was asked: What percentage of the loans would go to women-run businesses? By raising this question, we used our investor voice and alerted the organization to the possibility of adding a gender lens to the way they engaged in their work. During the time the staff at Root Capital took to calculate the number of women-led

---

[3]See Chapter 9, "The Evolution from Gender-Focused Microfinance to Gender Lens Investing in Latin America: The Case of Pro Mujer," by Angélica Rotondaro, Maria Cavalcanti, and Carmen Correa.

business ventures in their portfolio, our investment team decided to direct all of our investment dollars toward women-run agriculture ventures. In collaboration with Root Capital, the Foundation seeded a new investment product which was then made available for other investors as well. In a similar vein, the Women's Foundation of California used their investor voice to work with their financial advisors in creating a screened public equities product incorporating their gender equity criteria (Judy Patrick, personal communication). These efforts underscore the importance of the investor voice in the creation of new gender lens products.

This last decade has seen a huge increase in innovative GLI vehicles. Many products are springing up globally across all asset classes, in both public and private markets, with demand growing each year. Veris Wealth Partners, a US-based wealth management firm has tracked gender lens funds, identifying only eight investing vehicles in 2014. Five years later, in 2019, the number had more than sextupled to more than 50. Assets invested in public market products designed with a gender lens grew from USD $100 million to USD $3.4 billion over the same time period (Veris Wealth Partners 2020). In 2018, several of the large institutions, including Royal Bank of Canada, UBS, and the Bank of Montreal, all launched their own gender-based public market strategies. Institutional and public interest continues to grow as foundations, pension funds, governments, not-for-profit organizations, research organizations, and individual investors see the many opportunities and the values alignment in adopting a women-focused approach.

Despite the growing interest in some areas of GLI, very little money has historically been invested in female entrepreneurs or women-led funds. Venture capital investment in all-female founding teams reached an all-time high of USD $3.3 billion in 2019, but dollars invested in female founders still only represent a minuscule fraction (2%) of the capital invested across the entire US startup ecosystem (PitchBook 2019). With such low numbers of venture capital dollars flowing into women-led businesses to date, researchers are seeking to understand the investor bias at play. Daryn Dodson—founder and managing director of Oakland, California–based Illumen Capital and member of the Dean's Management Board at Stanford University—states, "Our research has found that beyond disparities in the pipeline, there are additional systemic racial and gender disparities in how asset allocators evaluate and allocate money to women and people of color who are in the private investing space. Investors therefore leave money on the table" (Daryn Dodson, personal communication). With 98% of venture capital money directed toward male-led enterprises, and male-led teams, savvy investors may uncover significant opportunities by shifting their capital and specifically choosing to invest in women who continually are overlooked in early and venture-stage investing.

Part of the issue in moving more investment money with a gender lens is a dearth of information for investors. In response to this lack of knowledge, Project Sage of the Wharton Business School, Criterion Institute, Veris Wealth Partners, as well as the Tara Health Foundation and Nia Impact Capital are working to promote the expansion of this field of investing (Wharton Social Impact Initiative 2019). As an example, Rachel Robasciotti of San Francisco–based asset management firm Robasciotti & Philipson is working with activist investors such as Oakland-based Nia Impact Capital both to engage with US companies on changing policies associated with sexual harassment within the workplace culture and to incorporate such information into investment decisions. Robasciotti's organization Force the Issue[4] is providing gender lens investors and portfolio managers with critical information on company policies to inform their investment research (Rachel Robasciotti, personal communication).

Gender Lens Investing: A Growing Movement

The term "gender lens investing" is still quite new to the financial industry lexicon, having been introduced in 2009 and formalized during a 2013 conference in Connecticut, led by Joy Anderson, Suzanne Biegel, Sarah Kaplan, and Jackie VanderBrug, among others, and attended by 50 women and 100 men. While still in its infancy as a sector, this burgeoning subset of the impact investment movement is sure to expand rapidly in the coming years. As Joy Anderson attests, "Gender lens investing is gaining incredible momentum with an unprecedented amount of capital flowing into the space, [with] new products and services being developed across asset classes" (Joy Anderson, personal communication).

In fact, GLI is one of the most rapidly growing segments of the sustainable, ESG, and Impact Investing movements. Assets in strategies specifically including women grew from USD $100 million in year-end 2014 to USD $2.4 billion in year-end 2018 and to USD $3.4 billion as of June 30, 2019 (Figure 7.1), with more than 50 investable GLI vehicles globally, including 10 GLI products over $100 million in AUM, and six GLI products with more than $250 million AUM (Veris Wealth Partners 2020). As of September 30, 2018, Veris Wealth Partners counted 14 separately managed accounts, nine exchange traded funds, seven mutual funds, three gender equality bond issues, an exchange traded note, and a certificate of deposit, each focused

---

[4]More information at www.forcetheissue.org.

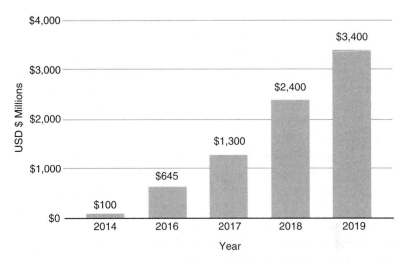

FIGURE 7.1   Gender Lens Investing, Global Assets Under Management in Public Equities. *Source:* Author adaptation from Veris Wealth Partners (2018 and 2020).

Note: AUM is mid-year as of June 30.

on gender. Geographically, these strategies across asset classes are produced and managed in the United States, Canada, Europe, Australia, Nigeria, and Singapore (Veris Wealth Partners 2018).

Adding fuel to this trend, the world is in the beginning stages of a massive global wealth transfer. Between the years 2020 and 2030, the world's most wealthy (net worth over USD $5 million) will pass down an estimated USD $15.4 trillion to the next generation (Wealth-X 2019). This global intergenerational wealth transfer is significant because the next generation of high-net-worth investors (HNWI) is younger, more willing to take risks, and more interested in the social impacts of their investments. Investing in socially responsible companies is important to the next generation. This group of HNWIs is also more likely to be women. As of 2020, women control 32% of wealth across the globe, and that is expected to rise to USD $93 trillion by 2023 (Zakrzewski et al. 2020)

As the wealth transfer progresses, these figures are likely to increase, and there will be more female wealth holders than ever before. As both wealth earners and inheriting kin, women around the globe will play a key role in investing these assets. This wealth transfer is another reason why the GLI sector is poised to grow exponentially over the coming decades.

From wealth advisors and fund managers, to start-up entrepreneurs and company leadership at the board and executive level, the need for greater diversity within the financial industry is significant. A compelling body of academic research points to the varied benefits of embracing inclusivity for companies and their investors. For example, gender diversity has been found to have a positive effect on group performance (Bear and Woolley 2011), and inclusion of women in groups has been related to improved group collaboration, as measured by collective intelligence (Woolley et al. 2010). Collective intelligence stems from the connections of units within a group and their patterns of behavior (Losada and Heaphy 2004), and collectively intelligent behavior is receptive to the accomplishments of desired outcomes, as opposed to merely following a prescribed process or routine (Bear and Woolley 2011). The increase of collective intelligence of a group due to the presence of women can be explained in part by women exhibiting higher social sensitivity, which is based on their greater ability to interpret nonverbal cues as well as the ability to accurately infer what others are feeling or thinking (Woolley et al. 2010).

Research by Díaz-García et al. (2013) suggests that gender diversity within a working team has a positive influence on radical innovation, particularly in uncertain situations. A study by McKinsey & Company has shown a statistically significant correlation between increased diversity among leadership teams and financial outperformance (Hunt et al. 2018). The same study also reports that greater gender diversity in executive teams enhances the likelihood of outperforming both in terms of profitability and value creation. Furthermore, companies with more ethnic and cultural diversity had a 33% higher chance of achieving industry-leading profitability. The McKinsey study also demonstrated that companies in the bottom quartile for both gender and ethnic and cultural diversity had a 29% lower likelihood of achieving above-average profitability (Hunt et al. 2018). This study indicates that there may actually be a performance penalty for companies that lag behind on gender and other types of diversity.

With findings that diverse teams are more innovative (leading to increased revenue generation) and that companies with women in leadership perform better during times of financial uncertainty, there is a strong financial case for inclusion. During the 2008 financial downturn, for example, hedge funds run by female managers returned −9.6% compared to a deeper drop of −19% for male fund managers (Denmark 2009). While the research is not yet in for the 2020 COVID-19 crisis, researchers will be looking for differences in ways male- and female-led teams manage portfolios during volatile market periods.

Another aspect of GLI can include taking into consideration corporate disclosures on gender pay gaps. Many large firms are recognizing the significant gender pay gap and are acknowledging that providing equal pay may be in their best interest due to the gains achieved in talent retention. Gap Inc., for example, was the first Fortune 500 company to announce in 2014 that it would be paying female and male employees equally for equal work (McElhaney and Smith 2017). Despite much work by Catalyst—a New York–based, leading nonprofit organization accelerating progress for women—and others, the gender pay gap remains a significant issue. Activist investors such as Natasha Lamb of Massachusetts-based Arjuna Capital and corporate engagement experts such as Meredith Benton of US-based Whistlestop Capital argue there is an economic case for talent retention. And in the time of #MeToo and #TimesUp, reducing corporate pay gaps is a significant way to reduce negative branding issues that can affect shareholder pricing (Natasha Lamb and Meredith Benton, personal communication).

FACTORS DRIVING INVESTORS TO ADOPT A GENDER LENS

GLI Intended Goals

Reasons for integrating gender-based factors into investment decisions vary. Goals range from enhancing risk-adjusted returns to empowering women and working toward gender equality. Some investors are looking to alleviate poverty and view increasing women's access to capital as a key strategy toward this end. Other investors are looking to achieve gender parity and choose to invest in women-owned businesses or in companies that commit to hiring, training, and promoting women as a strategy to achieve this goal. Others are looking to shift the financial industry by empowering more women in leadership and thus choose to invest with female investment advisors and female fund managers. Still other investors seek financial gains and see women in leadership as a method to achieve lower risk and increased returns.

Enhancing the investment process is the primary reason US-based Nia Impact Capital weaves a gender lean throughout all decision making. By incorporating a gender lens as a step or criteria during the investment process, investors stand to both reduce risk and possibly uncover alpha by potentially strengthening executive teams and company culture and by reducing groupthink that can occur in homogeneous, nondiverse teams.

For Aron Cramer, president and chief executive officer of Business for Social Responsibility (BSR), considering women and their needs within businesses has multiple benefits for women, for the businesses themselves, and for investors: "Business holds significant, untapped potential to contribute to women's advancement and stands to benefit tremendously by ensuring women are empowered" (Rhia Ventures 2020).

Many investors behind this growing movement strongly believe there is a pressing moral imperative for asset holders to promote gender equality, and that there is an economic imperative to include women in greater numbers at decision-making tables and across the economy. These factors together make a compelling case for inventors to adopt a gender lens. According to Suzanne Biegel, a prominent gender lens advocate and co-founder of the United Kingdom GenderSmart Summit, "Backing women is not just the right thing to do—it's the smart thing to do" (Suzanne Biegel, personal communication).

Benefits of Incorporating a Gender Lens in Investing: The Evidence

A large and growing body of research is demonstrating that gender diversity within companies of all sizes results in positive benefits ranging from increased productivity (MSCI 2016) to greater innovation (Díaz-García et al. 2013), better decision-making (Phillips et al. 2009), and higher employee retention (Nielsen and Madsen 2017) and satisfaction (Hunt et al. 2015). Many consider having more women in executive roles to be the right approach to achieving gender parity, and increasingly, research is finding that including women in leadership is also good for business and employees (Castrillon 2019).

Female Asset Managers Outperforming

Several studies have compared the performance of female asset managers to their male peers, and their findings suggest that women outperform men when it comes to investment returns. The Warwick Business School in the United Kingdom observed 2,800 men and women investing with Barclays' Smart Investor, tracking their performance over three years. Not only did the women outperform the FTSE 100 over the three-year time period, they also earned higher returns than their male counterparts (Stewart 2018). The women managers outperformed the benchmark by 1.94%, beating the male managers by 1.8 percentage points (p.p.). Similarly, Hargreaves Lansdown found that women investors returned on average 0.81% more than men over a three-year period. If these findings persisted over a 30-year period, the female-led portfolios would be worth 25% more than the average male portfolio after three decades of investing (Hargreaves Lansdown 2018).

In addition to earning greater returns, research suggests that women are more risk conscious than men (Byrnes et al. 1999). A study by Niessen-Ruenzi found that US female fund managers adopted more risk-averse strategies compared to their male counterparts (Niessen-Ruenzi 2015). Furthermore, research has found that women take fewer risks under stressful circumstances, while men are prone to more risk taking during uncertain times (Lighthall and Mather 2012).

Female investors appear to choose stocks that are less risky with lower volatility and maintain a longer-term perspective. This view is backed by the Warwick Business School study, which found that women were more likely to hold diverse portfolios, and typically experienced fewer losses (Stewart 2018). Female investors also trade less frequently; the Hargreaves Lansdown study found that women traded shares of individual stocks 49% less frequently than men, and traded funds 67% less often (Hargreaves Lansdown 2018).

In a similar vein, female investors with diverse experiences bring a distinct and valuable perspective to the due diligence process. As Kesha Cash, founder and General Partner of the Impact America Fund, stated, "You can either spend a lot of time trying to train [traditional investors] outside of their worldview, or you can use the time to empower the people who already get it and are ready to go" (Kesha Cash, personal communication). Having women and women of color making investment decisions can uncover new and different solutions, as well as bring to light a greater number and quality of female-centered products and services.

With several studies showing women to be superior investors that systematically outperform men, particularly when looking at hedge fund management (Mooney 2017), there is substantial alpha to be had by diversifying managers (Foster 2015). Yet despite this empirical evidence, there are dismally low numbers of women in every part of the financial system, largely due to historical and culture-based reasons that keep women out of financial services careers.

The Knight Foundation commissioned Harvard University to study diversity in asset management and uncovered startling results. The Knight Foundation/Harvard University study analyzed US-based funds across four different asset classes: (i) mutual funds, which include mutual funds, separately managed accounts, marketable securities, and exchange traded funds, (ii) hedge funds, (iii) private equity, and (iv) real estate. Funds and strategies managed by firms owned by women and people of color ("minority-owned") are still a small share of the overall fund universe. The study also found that bias exists when it comes to allocating funds led by women and people of color. While the 638 funds that included women in

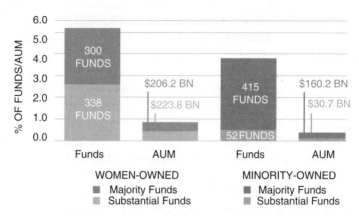

FIGURE 7.2   Number of Funds and Assets Under Management (AUM) of Women-Owned and Minority-Owned Investment Strategies.   *Source:* Knight Foundation (2019). Data from years 2011–2017 for US managers.

Note: For purposes of this study, "substantial" ownership is 25% to 49%, and "majority" is 50% and higher.

ownership totaled USD $430 billion, these funds made up approximately 1 in 20, or 5%, of total US fund vehicles. The assets allocated to these same funds made up under 1% of allocations (Figure 7.2). When looking at fund financial performance, women-owned firms were overrepresented in the top quartile. Despite this compelling research finding outperformance, and all of the studies cited above demonstrating various ways women have been shown to be strong money managers, some form of bias is at play resulting in female managers receiving far fewer asset allocations from investors (Knight Foundation 2019). Similar underrepresentation is prevalent in minority-owned investment funds as well, totaling 467 funds and nearly $191 billion AUM.[5] For the purpose of this study, "substantial ownership" is defined as 25% to 49.9% of a firm's owners and "majority ownership" is defined as 50% and higher. As shown in Figure 7.2, investment funds owned by women and minorities manage just 1.3% of assets in the USD $69 trillion asset management industry.

Women at the Top

Research focusing on the presence of women in corporate decision-making roles offers compelling reasons to invest in companies with women at the

---

[5]For an in-depth review, see Chapter 10, "Inclusive Investing: Impact Meets Diversity, Equity, and Inclusion (DEI)," by Julianne Zimmerman, Edward Dugger III, and Shijiro Ochirbat.

top, and thus to adopt a gender lens when selecting in which companies to invest. Women-led teams have been found to be more collaborative (Woolley et al. 2010), more communicative, and more open to learning, even when managed across remote locations (Post 2015). These findings suggest that women-led companies foster a more effective corporate culture leading to business success.

When it comes to tracking financial returns, greater diversity on boards and in executive management is empirically associated with higher returns on equity, higher price to book valuations, and superior stock price performance (Credit Suisse 2014). FP Analytics (FPA) found that the companies with the highest percentage of women in management were on average 47% more profitable than those with the lowest (FP Analytics 2020). Women interviewed for the FPA study explained ways in which they were leading their companies toward new revenue-generating possibilities, advancing innovation in stagnant industries, advocating for products and practices that safeguard against human exposure to harm, and increasing transparency in ways that translate to increased stakeholder trust.

The majority of companies that track their management's gender diversity report profit increases between 5% and 20%, with the majority seeing increases of 10% and 15% when gender diversity increased (Bureau for Employers' Activities 2019). Additionally, research looking at data from firms listed in the S&P 1500 found that female representation in top management improves company performance in terms of innovation and boosts revenues derived from innovative products (Dezso and Ross 2011).

In a 2019 study, the Bureau for Employers' Activities—a specialized unit within the International Labor Organization (ILO) in Geneva—found that gender diversity within corporations improves business outcomes and makes it easier to attract top talent (Bureau for Employers' Activities 2019). In the study's survey data of nearly 13,000 enterprises in 70 countries, more than 57% of respondents agreed that gender diversity initiatives improved business outcomes, translating to financial returns (Bureau for Employers' Activities 2019).

Board Representation

Research suggests that diverse teams make better decisions, and adding women to corporate boards is no different. The Credit Suisse Research Institute found that companies with one or more women on the board delivered lower net debt-to-equity ratios and better average growth (Curtis 2012). In fact, companies with higher female participation at board level or in top management were shown to produce higher dividend payout ratios as well.

In every country of the world, most companies still have work to do to achieve gender parity and to maximize the business benefits that gender diversity can offer. That said, Europe leads the way when it comes to board diversity. Norway passed the first quota mandate for women's representation on corporate boards in 2003. Since then, governments across the globe have looked to gender quotas as a tool to accelerate gender equality, with Europe leading in this regard. In 2006, the Norwegian government set a goal requiring both public and state-owned companies to reach 40% female board representation by 2008. Full compliance was achieved in 2009. France passed a bill in 2011 requiring the boards of privately held companies and publicly traded firms to include 40% female directors by 2016. Interestingly, Finland and Sweden—the two countries with the highest number of women on boards—are leading the world without having set any targets or legal requirements for gender diversity. The United States, however, has been slower to move when it comes to legislating board diversity. California was the first US state to pass a board diversity bill, SB-826, in 2019. Several other US states are currently in the initial stages of following suit in some form, bringing the issue top of mind for entrepreneurs and investors alike.

Women Founders and Women-Led Startups

There are a growing number of studies that build the case for investing in women-led startups and female entrepreneurs. A summary of alpha generating research findings and some interesting US-based examples, as cited in Forbes, are provided below (Kapin 2019):

- Women-led private technology companies use capital more efficiently and can achieve a 35% higher return in investment (ROI). When backed by venture funds, providing capital infusion can achieve 12% higher revenues than their male-run counterparts (Kauffman Fellows 2016).
- Women-founded companies outperformed those founded by men by 63% (San Francisco–based First Round Capital).[6]
- US-based startup accelerator Mass Challenge[7] and Boston Consulting Group (BCG) found that women-founded businesses achieved more than double the amount of revenue per dollar invested compared to

---

[6]More information at www.firstround.com.
[7]More information at www.masschallenge.org.

men-founded startups; thus women-owned companies prove to be better investments than their male-owned counterparts. The authors of the study that encompassed 350 startups also calculated that venture capitalists could have earned an additional $85 million over five years had they equally invested in both women- and men-founded startups (Abouzahr et al. 2018).

- Startups founded and co-founded by women performed better over time and generated 10% more in cumulative revenue over a five-year period, despite the severe funding gap (Abouzahr et al. 2018).
- Companies in the MSCI World Index with strong women leadership measured an annual return on equity (ROE) of 10.1%, whereas companies without strong women leadership reported annual ROE of 7.4% (Lee et al. 2015).
- From 2007 to 2018, the number of US women-owned businesses grew by 58% and their revenues increased by 46%. These rates are higher than those for all businesses. Furthermore, these numbers are driven by women of color who started businesses at a much faster rate during this period. The number of firms owned by African American women grew by 164% in the reported period (Geri Stengel of American Express).
- Boston Consulting Group (BCG) reports a strong and statistically significant relationship between the diversity of management teams and overall company innovation (Lorenzo et al. 2018). Companies with above-average diversity on their management teams had higher innovation revenue than companies with below-average leadership diversity (45% of total revenue for more diverse teams versus 26% of total revenue for less diverse teams) (Lorenzo et al. 2018).
- Gallup reported that companies embracing diversity have 22% lower turnover rates (Anita Borg Institute 2014).
- According to Project Diane,[8] a demographic study authored by digital undivided,[9] LatinX women-owned businesses grew by more than 87% between 2007 and 2012.
- At the beginning of 2018, women were estimated to be the sole or majority owners of 12.3 million businesses in the United States, and the rate at which women were starting additional businesses amounted to 1,800 per day (American Express 2018).

---

[8] More information at www.projectdiane.digitalundivided.com.
[9] More information at www.digitalundivided.com.

- According to Golden Seeds[10]—a US-based early-stage investment firm investing in women-led startups—many women-led startups reap the benefits of being led by serial entrepreneurs, including having a wealth of experience needed to scale quickly. In 2017, one-third of companies in which Golden Seeds invested were led by serial entrepreneurs (Nethero 2018).

HOW IMPACT INVESTORS CAN PURSUE GENDER INVESTING

The United Nations Women's Empowerment Principles

In 2010, the United Nations Women collaborated with the UN Global Compact to develop the Women's Empowerment Principles (WEPs). The seven WEPs (Table 7.1), adapted from Calvert Investments' Women's Principles, are grounded in the understanding that businesses have a stake in, and a responsibility for, gender equality and women's empowerment. The WEPs were designed to advance gender equality and shift markets by recognizing both the power and responsibility of companies to seek gender parity, as well as the potential benefits women bring to business and the economy.

The WEPs offer specific guidance for investors, as well as for the businesses in which they choose to invest. Nia Impact Capital is part of a growing movement of investors encouraging companies to sign on to the WEPs, and using shareholder advocacy encourages companies to adjust their corporate practices to align with gender equality goals. Companies that follow the UN WEPs may in fact be more attractive to investors and may offer more upside in terms of returns on investment (ROI), and less downside when it comes to risk of brand from poor governance decisions.

Key Ways to Leverage and Align Investment Portfolios with a Gender Lens

How can impact investors begin investing with a gender lens? A gender lens can be incorporated in all stages of the investment process, in all sizes of companies and across asset classes. Just as consumers are using a gender lens when making purchases, choosing restaurants and suppliers, and seeking to support women-owned businesses, investors can use a gender lens and an

---

[10]More information at www.goldenseeds.com.

TABLE 7.1 Women's Empowerment Principles.

	Principle	Description
1	**Establish high-level corporate leadership for gender equality**	Establish company-wide goals and targets for gender equality and women's empowerment and measure progress through clear performance indicators.
2	**Treat all women and men fairly at work without discrimination**	Respect and support human rights, including eliminating any pay gaps. Foster an inclusive workplace culture and remove gender-based discrimination from all policies and practices.
3	**Ensure the health, safety, and well-being of all female and male workers**	Ensure all employees' equal access to health insurance, including part-time workers, and to support services for survivors of violence and harassment.
4	**Promote education for gender equality**	Promote education, training, and professional development for women such that they have access to tools for career advancement.
5	**Implement enterprise development, supply chain, and marketing practices that empower women**	Establish supplier diversity programs that actively seek to expand business relationships with women-owned enterprises and support them in access.
6	**Promote equality through community initiatives and advocacy**	Work with community stakeholders and officials to eliminate discrimination and exploitation and to open opportunities for women and girls.
7	**Measure and publicly report on progress to achieve gender equality**	Develop incentives and accountability mechanisms to accelerate WEPs implementation. Collect, analyze, and use gender statistics and gender-disaggregated data and benchmarks to measure and report results at all levels.

Source: Author adaptation from United Nations (2010).[11]

eye for diversity and equality when making investment decisions. The multiple ways to integrate a gender lens when selecting investments and making portfolio allocations can be seen in Table 7.2. And for additional resources, see Appendix.

---

[11]For more detail see https://www2.unwomen.org/-/media/field%20office%20eseasia/docs/publications/2016/05/wep-booklet-en.pdf?la=en&vs=5928.

TABLE 7.2   Examples of GLI Criteria and Actions for Investors.

Criterion 1: Measure and Quantify Women in Leadership

Look to ensure that every company in your portfolio includes women in leadership. There is a need for greater diversity at the board level and in executive leadership regardless of company size. Until recently, the onus has been on women to prove that inclusive workplaces represent a solid business proposition. With accumulating research illustrating the benefits of inclusive practices to both companies and their shareholders, the tide is turning toward viewing diversity and a culture of inclusion as competitive advantages.

Possible action: Select companies that include women in executive management and on the board of directors.

Criterion 2: Use Your Investor Voice: Activism and Engagement with a Gender Lens

Moving forward in this age of inclusion, and at a time when innovation is paramount, all-male boards will be questioned and the burden will shift toward men to justify nondiverse leadership teams. In the meantime, investors can send a strong message by voting with their dollars. At Nia Impact Capital,[12] the firm invests only in companies that include women in leadership. Nia uses its platform and investor voice to share the accumulating research on the benefits of women in corporate leadership, encouraging many portfolio companies to increase their gender diversity numbers.

Possible action: Use your platform and investor voice to inform companies of the benefits of women in leadership, and encourage companies to increase their gender diversity practices, including hiring and promotion practices.

Criterion 3: Engage Formally and Proactively as an Asset Owner to Achieve Gender Parity

Investors can incorporate a gender lens when voting proxies and by using their investor voice to advocate for gender-balanced policies and practices in companies they own. Writing letters to companies and filing shareholder resolutions are effective ways to begin dialog toward greater equality. Nia Impact Capital views the voting of proxy statements as both a shareholder's right and a responsibility. From women in board leadership, to CEO pay, and workplace equity, Nia uses its investor voice by voting proxy statements in alignment with fair and equitable corporate policies and procedures. If your portfolio managers or financial advisors do not already offer this service, As You Sow, a nonprofit shareholder advocacy group based in Berkeley, California, can assist investors with these goals.

Possible action: Vote proxy statements in alignment with fair and equitable corporate practices.

Criterion 4: Invest in Women-Led Investments and Funds Across All Asset Classes

Financial inclusion is a significant part of how society can achieve gender equity. Currently, women receive less than 4% of venture capital funding. Impact investors should check for any biases—including implicit bias—to ensure capital can be to women and not miss out on higher-alpha opportunities by inadvertently excluding half of startup businesses. Investors who do not engage in private equity can

---

[12]More information at www.niaimpactcapital.com.

TABLE 7.2 *(continued)*

check with their banks to ensure cash deposits are being used to provide loans to female entrepreneurs. Additionally, investors can check with any lending companies in their portfolios to ensure they lend to women and women-owned businesses.

Possible action: Choose funds or investment products managed by female portfolio managers; when selecting municipal bonds, choose projects that positively impact women or improve the lives of women and girls (for example, retrofitting of public housing for single mothers).

Criterion 5: Invest in Businesses That Produce Products and Services That Solve Everyday Problems for Women and Girls

Companies with women in charge hire more women, with benefits to business. Providing leadership opportunities to diverse candidates is essential for both a company's financial bottom line as well as broader societal inclusion goals, and as investors and advisors, it is important to select companies that have women in mind. In order to transition to a just, sustainable, and inclusive economy, those companies that are actively innovating on behalf of women and girls need our investment. From avoiding harmful companies (such as oil, gas, and extraction, to companies that do not include women in leadership) to investing in solutions-focused companies such as those focused on renewable energy, affordable housing and health care solutions, impact investors can allocate their investment portfolios to invest in a world that works for everyone.

Possible action: Choose companies that produce goods and/or services beneficial to women; purposefully invest in women-owned businesses, either by making loans or by investing in privately held companies.

Criterion 6: Evaluate Company Employment Policies and Practices

Companies with generous family leave make it easier for women to excel in their careers while also raising a family. Hiring and board recruitment policies as well as sexual harassment protocols can have a large impact on company culture. By choosing to invest in companies that embrace diversity goals, as well as gender-inclusive policies and practices, investors can align their dollars with their values while supporting companies that are likely to outperform their competition.

Possible action: Select companies based on their internal policies and practices; this could include hiring practices, Board recruitment policies, sexual harassment policies, diversity and inclusion trainings, maternity and paternity leave policies, childcare, and more.

Criterion 7: Allocate to Women-Led Funds and Advisors

When selecting wealth management services and investment funds, choose female investment advisors and portfolio managers. To change the face of finance moving forward, many of us will need to bring a gender lens to all levels of investment decisions. The good news: female managers have been shown to outperform their male counterparts, so diversifying a portfolio along gender lines may serve all parties.

Possible action: Choose to work with investment management firms owned by women.

Source: Author.

Gender Lens Investing Examples Across Asset Classes

Impact investors can allocate among an increasing number of GLI strategies across multiple asset classes. The following section provides examples in cash equivalents and short-term notes, fixed income, public equities, private equity, and individual companies with a gender focus.[13]

Gender Lens Cash Equivalents and Short-Term Notes

CNote, founded by Cat Berman and Yulia Tarasava, is an Oakland, California–based firm offering savings products, some of which pay up to 40 times the interest of a traditional savings account. CNote invests in community-focused projects that help grow small businesses, build affordable housing, and help underserved communities thrive. With several specialty products focused on community development financial institutions (CDFIs) that lend specifically to businesses led by women of color, CNote provides a dependable way to earn more interest while investing in women.[14]

CNote marries the return of a longer-term investment, like a bond, with the liquidity and accessibility of a more traditional bank deposit. CNote was founded on two core principles: financial products should not just serve a wealthy few, and financial prosperity does not have to be a zero-sum game; one can make money and do good at the same time.

During a crisis such as COVID-19, CDFIs are on the frontlines working to support and save small businesses and *retain employment* in the United States. CDFIs have both historically outperformed other asset classes post–natural disasters and recessions and are also the first responders to rebuild small businesses and local economies when such events occur.

Gender Lens Public Fixed Income

Publicly listed bonds are an emerging vehicle for companies committed to reducing gender inequality. The proceeds fit into one of the three tiers of GLI: women-led companies, companies that promote gender equality in the workplace, or companies selling products and services beneficial to women.

---

[13]Nia Community Investments invests exclusively with a gender lens. Some of the company examples listed here are included in the Nia Community Investments portfolio. For a full list of investments, see www.niacommunity.org.

[14]More information at www.myCnote.com.

In 2017, the National Bank of Australia issued and sold AUD $500 million gender equity bonds. The bonds were invested in a portfolio of businesses which have received a gender citation from Australian government body the Workplace Gender Equality Agency (Pendal Group 2019).

Gender Lens Fixed Income

Capital Sisters International is a female-founded bond instrument that was created as a platform to advance economic justice and financial inclusion for marginalized women entrepreneurs in the informal business sector. Capital Sisters International's mission is to connect impoverished women in developing countries who need micro and small business loans with willing investors. Capital Sisters delivers its mission through an Investment Program and an Advocacy Program. The Investment Program provides capital to microfinance institutions in developing countries. The Advocacy Program works to raise awareness about the need for new and reformed public policies to enable greater financial inclusion.[15]

Root Capital Women in Agriculture Fund is a nonprofit social investment fund that grows rural prosperity in poor, environmentally vulnerable places in Africa and Latin America by lending capital, delivering financial training, and strengthening market connections for small and growing agricultural businesses.[16]

Gender Lens Private Debt

Bay Area Medical Academy (BAMA) is a female-founded San Francisco–based medical training facility that provides job-focused training in high-growth, high-demand areas of the health care field, fulfilling the workforce needs of medical facilities in the Bay Area. BAMA prepares individuals (predominantly women) from different socio-economic, cultural, and educational backgrounds for successful, long-term careers in the medical field. Simonida Cvejic is a Macedonian immigrant to the United Sates. As a female founder, she has unique insights into the issues at play both in the medical field and for female immigrants when it comes to job training and placement.[17]

Kubé Nice Cream, founded by Kai Nortey, is an artisan food producer of raw, plant-based, hand-crafted coconut cream "nice cream" based in

---

[15]More information at www.capitalsisters.org.
[16]More information at www.rootcapital.org.
[17]More information at www.bamasf.com.

Oakland, California. The standard international pasteurization process of coconut cream and milk uses a toxic preservative and bleaching chemical called sodium metabisulfite. Kubé is the emerging leader in harnessing the power of raw, unpasteurized coconut cream. Kubé believes that real, fresh, and healthy foods, without chemicals, support healthier outcomes for all people and for the earth. Kai Nortey, coming from a lactose-intolerant community, uniquely understands their needs. As a woman of color, she is perfectly suited to carry out her business model with sales to a largely lactose-intolerant audience. Kubé is also committed to hiring and training previously incarcerated women in the San Francisco Bay Area. Her plan is for Kubé to scale globally.[18]

LaborX is a US-based female founded marketplace for hiring talent from nontraditional backgrounds. They are currently focused on six US cities, including San Francisco, Los Angeles, and New York. LaborX matches employers with an untapped, skilled, and loyal talent selection. LaborX is the LinkedIn for the previously "LinkedOut," meaning they work to connect women and people of color with employment opportunities. Yscaira Jimenez is a woman of color of Dominican heritage who uniquely understands the gap in employment opportunities as well as bias in hiring.[19]

Weal Life is a female-founded, San Francisco Bay Area Public Benefit Corporation that developed and markets an application (app) to facilitate and make it easier to care for one another, particularly during a health crisis, or for those who are aging or suffering from chronic illness. Knowing that caring for family disproportionally relies on women, Weal Life crowdsources care from people within known personal networks so that individuals can heal and thrive. This helpful service leverages mobile technology to capture value from underutilized capacities of family, friends, neighbors, and others who can help streamline life logistics such as transportation, meals, errands, or shopping for medical supplies. Founder Keely Stevenson is well positioned to bridge the needs of care for women and their families.[20]

Gender Lens Public Equities

In public equities, there are several different factors to consider: is the firm offering the strategy female-owned? Are the portfolio managers women?

---

[18]More information at www.kubenicecream.com.
[19]More information at www.laborx.co.
[20]More information at www.theweallife.com.

How is the portfolio designed? Often, managers start with a screen to see that a company includes women in leadership, at the executive level, on the board of directors, or both. Some managers choose to include corporations that have signed on to the WEPs (as featured above, a joint initiative of the UN Global Compact and UN Women). Others exclude "sin stocks" or products such as weapons, gambling, or alcohol.

Gender Lens Global Equities

Mackenzie Global Leadership Impact Exchange Traded Fund (ETF)[21] (Global All-Cap, 411 holdings, Canadian ticker: MWMN), launched in December 2017 as an exchange-traded fund in Canada. This ETF invests in companies that have female representation on the board of directors and in senior management, a female CEO or chief financial officer (CFO), and are signatories to the United Nations WEPs.

Nia Global Solutions (Global All-Cap, 50 holdings), was launched in 2013. Nia Impact Capital is a separately managed account, accessible by investors on eight platforms. Nia Global Solutions invests in solutions-focused companies along Nia's solutions themes including sustainable planet, health care, natural and organic foods, sustainable and affordable transportation, financial inclusion, education, and communication. The Nia investment process emphasizes products and services beneficial to women, like Hologic's breast cancer detection and Etsy's empowerment of women in small business. All companies include women in senior management or board positions.[22]

Pax Ellevate Global Women's Leadership Fund (World Large Stock, 412 holdings, USA tickers PXWEX and PXWIX), launched in October 1993 for all investors and August 2006 for institutional investors. The Pax fund invests in developed markets, tracking the Impax Global Women's Leadership Index, a custom index based on the MSCI World Universe, and screens for criteria that measure women in leadership, and only includes signatories to the Women's Empowerment Principles.[23]

Valeurs Feminines (European Large-Cap, France ticker = FOX) launched in late 2019. This fund uses two criteria for European large caps:

---

[21] More information at www.mackenzieinvestments.com.

[22] www.niaimpactcapital.com.

[23] More information at https://impaxam.com/products/gender-lens-investing/impax-ellevate-global-womens-leadership-strategy.

strong women in leadership and a focus on women consumers. Additional ESG screens are applied.

Gender Lens Private Equity

Many gender lens–focused opportunities are currently found in private equity. From early stage startups, to larger companies seeking their Series A or B, to established private equity funds, female-led companies have been historically overlooked. The current numbers of women-owned companies and funds receiving investment dollars in the United States are still shockingly low (as cited in the Women Founders section above) and present a major opportunity for increased capital deployment.

Startup Ventures with a Gender Lens

Investors may invest in individual companies with a gender lens. While often not suitable for large institutional investors, investing in smaller, earlier-stage companies started by women can be an important way to diversify a portfolio, and move capital toward women, as female founders have been statistically overlooked by many investors.

Emerging Women is a US-based company that supports and inspires women to express themselves authentically through the work that they do. Chantal Pierat and her women-run team provide the tools, knowledge, and network to help women lead. Emerging Women helps women start and grow their businesses in a way that integrates core feminine values like connection, collaboration, intimacy, beauty, and heart. Emerging Women also provides a platform and specific training for leaders and entrepreneurs, with the aim of empowering women to have a strong voice in shaping the world's future.[24]

Southeastern Roastery is a minority and women-owned coffee company based in the Washington, DC, area, and a member of the Specialty Coffee Association. The founder, Candy Schibli, a former chemical engineer, has worked in international relations for over a decade and is passionate about social justice for women across the globe.[25]

Private Equity and Venture Capital Funds

Chloe Capital is a US-based "touring" venture capital firm investing in seed-stage women-led innovation companies across North America. Chloe's

---

[24]More information at www.emergingwomen.com.
[25]More information at www.southeasternroastery.com.

#InvestInWomen nationwide tour exposes the firm's all-female investment committee to a unique deal flow of "over-prepared, yet under-valued founders," as Chloe Capital says. Chloe Capital works to amplify their entrepreneurs' visibility, networks, and resources through programming and seeks to accelerate its investment exit to pursue superior returns.[26]

Alante Capital is a US-based, women-led venture capital fund investing in innovative companies that enables a resilient, sustainable future for apparel production and retail. Alante is investing across the apparel industry into innovations in production, distribution, and waste recovery, seeking scalable solutions that leave lasting, positive impacts on people and the planet. Alante focuses on bridging the gap between emerging technologies and apparel brands and retailers, helping to improve efficiency and resiliency across the USD $3.1 trillion textile and apparel industry.[27]

Rethink Impact is the largest US-based venture capital firm investing in female leaders who are using technology to solve the world's biggest problems. Rethink Impact believes that the next generation of extraordinary companies (in health, environmental sustainability, education, and economic empowerment) will find success through their relentless pursuit of mission, for the benefit of all communities.[28]

Impact America Fund (IAF) has a mission to generate financial returns while enhancing the quality of life for underserved communities in the United States. IAF, led by Kesha Cash, invests in high-growth companies that are scaling solutions in the health and wellness, education, essential services, and financial inclusion sectors. IAF is making impact investments in sectors and in communities that need it most. IAF addresses gender, racial, and social equity issues by directing capital to the businesses championing progressive and inclusive business practices.[29]

Portfolia is a US-based, low-entry (USD $10,000 minimum investment) participatory venture fund, led by women with the intention to help women discover, interact with, and invest in new companies and entrepreneurs. Portfolia provides women with opportunities to invest in innovative and growing companies as individuals or with community with their colleagues, friends, and mentors. Both women-led and designed with the specific purpose of growing the field of women investors in private equity.[30]

---

[26]More information at www.chloecapital.com.
[27]More information at www.alantecapital.com.
[28]More information at www.rethinkimpact.com.
[29]More information at www.impactamericafund.com.
[30]More information at www.portfolia.co.

Force for Good Fund is a fund created by US-based B Corporation through its initiative called LIFT Economy. The Force for Good Fund nurtures, supports, and invests in women and people of color-owned "Best for the World" B Corporations (i.e, companies that score in the top 10% of B Corps worldwide). The fund provides capital that can be incredibly difficult to access for early-stage, socially, and environmentally responsible businesses run by women and people of color. The Force for Good Accelerator and Fund provides an innovative opportunity to support these early-stage entrepreneurs with the guidance, access to capital, and connections needed for success.[31]

Rhia Ventures is a US-based, women-led social impact investment firm focused on connecting capital with entrepreneurs to accelerate innovative solutions in reproductive and maternal health. Specific investments seek to support innovations in contraception.[32]

Fund of Funds

Illumen Capital is a San Francisco Bay Area–based, private equity impact fund of funds, dedicated to working with active fund managers to reduce their investment biases. Managing Director Daryn Dodson founded Illumen to provide a pathway for investors, foundations, and family offices to access the world's top impact funds and actively reduce bias throughout global financial markets. By partnering with Stanford University, Illumen Capital creates and applies bias-reducing interventions to help venture capital and private equity fund managers unlock latent financial return and impact, and to create a more equitable, empathetic, and prosperous world.[33]

THE IMPORTANCE OF AN INVESTMENT POLICY STATEMENT FOR GENDER LENS INVESTING

The purpose of an investment policy statement (IPS) is to spell out the goals and stated objectives of any given portfolio, providing direction and parameters for the investment managers. The IPS can serve as a central document, grounding all stakeholders on both the goals and expectations as well as strategies to be used. Often, strategies such as asset class allocations, as well as time horizons or any constraints, are articulated within the IPS. For institutions and pensions, as well as endowments and family offices, the investment

---

[31] More information at www.lifteconomy.com.
[32] More information at www.rhiaventures.org.
[33] More information at www.illumencapital.com

policy statement can be used as a market signal, as well as a document sharing expectations with fund providers on just what types of products and assets will be needed.

Increasingly, institutions are seeking to articulate their values in addition to asset allocation goals within their IPS. When adopting new strategies or shifting objectives, the IPS is the place to communicate parameters for investment decisions.

Current examples include US-based Nia Community Investments,[34] for which all new investments and managers must be led by women and/or people of color. The Rockefeller Brothers Fund recently announced a commitment for 25% of their endowment to be managed by women and diverse managers (Valerie Rockefeller, personal communication). These trend setting entities are models that other capital allocators can follow. Consider including the following goals and criteria in an IPS, as in Figure 7.3.

"We seek to invest in companies with diverse boards."

- Can include criteria for how many women are present on boards, such as: boards must be half women, a third women, have at least 3 women, at least 1 woman, etc.

"We invest exclusively in companies founded by women."

- Only include companies with women founders.

"We invest in companies that include women in leadership."

- Depending on the level of conviction, can be stated as primarily or exclusively or a specified percentage.

"A percentage of all investment managers we engage will be women led teams"

- Depending on level of conviction, this could vary from 25% to 100% for example.

"We invest in companies that produce products and services beneficial to women."

- Examples include: women's health care, sustainable fashion, automobiles designed with female drivers in mind.

"We invest in companies that include strong diversity and inclusion processes and procedures to ensure more women are promoted to leadership."

- Examples include: transparent hiring practices, always including more than two women in all applicant pools, generous family leave policies where men are also encouraged to take time off.

FIGURE 7.3   Sample Gender Driven Language to Include in an Investment Policy Statement. *Source:* Author.

---

[34]More information at www.niacommunity.org.

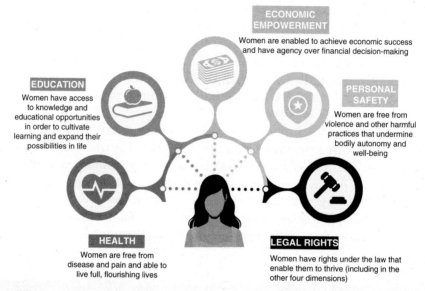

FIGURE 7.4   Tara Health Foundation Five Dimensions of Women's Lives Framework. *Source:* Barrett et al. (2017).

GLI Example 1: Tara Health Foundation

US-based Tara Health Foundation was founded by Doctor Ruth Shaber with the primary focus of improving women's health. Tara Health Foundation has developed an investment strategy that spans public equities and private markets, all targeting women's health in various ways (see Figures 7.4 and 7.5). In each asset class, Tara Health seeks to address missing products in the market and also uses foundation grants to support field-building research on women's health investing opportunities. Tara Health Foundation invests along five dimensions they deem essential for women's health and gender parity. The foundation also uses their investor voice for company activism, including encouraging companies to offer paid family leave in the United States, the only developed country that does not offer this benefit at the federal level.[35]

GLI Example 2: Nia Global Solutions

Nia Global Solutions, launched in 2013 as a separately managed account product and managed by Nia Impact Capital, is an example of a public equities product including a gender lens. In addition to selecting only

[35]More information at www.tarahealthfoundation.org.

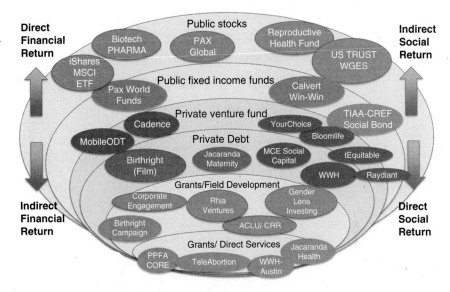

FIGURE 7.5 Example Investments Across All Asset Classes, including Grants.
Source: Tara Health Foundation.[36]

Tara Health Foundation 100% Mission Driven Balanced Portfolio

companies that include women in leadership (on the executive management team and/or on the board of directors), this concentrated portfolio of solutions-focused companies includes products and services beneficial to and important to women. Nia Impact Capital also uses its investor voice to vote proxy statements in favor of diverse boards of directors and to engage with companies to raise issues of gender equity and share best practices. Figure 7.6 illustrates sample portfolio company selections of publicly traded companies and how they fit the various Nia gender lens criteria, spanning leadership positions, products, and services with women in mind, and women's health care policies and practices.

CONCLUSION

The past several years have seen record numbers of women—and men—gathering to march in the streets to protest government policies, gun violence, and the use of fossil fuels, as well as to advocate for the fair treatment of women around the globe. As these global movements

---

[36]More information at www.tarahealthfoundation.org.

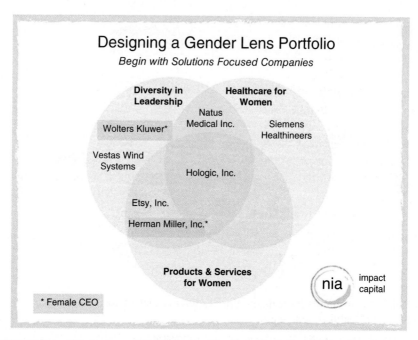

Designing a Gender Lens Portfolio
Begin with Solutions Focused Companies

FIGURE 7.6   Gender Lens Criteria for the Nia Global Solutions Equity Portfolio.
Source: Nia Impact Capital (2020).

gather steam, many investors are looking to use finance as a lever for social change in support of their feminist values. At the same time, large banks and wire houses are also increasing their women-centered offerings as a strategy to keep and grow their female clients.

The field of GLI is still a relatively new practice yet becoming a quickly growing field within the financial sector, and an area of great interest for investors, researchers, and portfolio managers alike. With international demonstrations of support including the Women's March, and myriad celebrations of Women's History Month, as well as a growing body of research highlighting the business case for diverse leadership, impact investors looking to "change the face of finance" have strong winds in their sails.

Every investment has an impact in the world, from banking decisions, to fixed income selections, to public equity holdings. Layering a gender lens into financial decisions and portfolio construction strategies can leverage an entire portfolio of assets to make a positive impact on gender parity issues around the world while also potentially protecting investment portfolios from unnecessary risk and increasing exposure to overlooked alpha previously left on the table. Impact investors can work toward women's equality while also reaping the potential benefits of financial returns associated with gender inclusion.

Investing with a gender lens is also a compelling way to bring more women into the financial fold. By including a gender lens in the investment process, both male and female impact investors can leverage their assets to achieve more balance in the workplace and at decision-making tables. Strategically evaluating all investments for leadership composition, products and services, operating metrics, and company policies can ensure a portfolio and as an extension, an economy that is gender balanced. The result can be higher alpha potential, with higher upside possibilities, lower future risks, and more inclusion. Investors integrating a gender lens in a systematic way can pursue higher impact portfolios that are stronger and more resilient financially, while addressing Sustainable Development Goal 5 for gender equality.

ACKNOWLEDGMENTS

I would like to thank the editors for their guidance and for advancing the field of Impact Investing. I extend my gratitude to R. Paul Herman for his tremendous industry leadership and his encouragement of my efforts to change the face of finance. Enormous thanks to Srdana Pokrajac and Lucia Pohlman for their careful edits and support for this chapter. Thank you also to each of the Nia team and my colleagues in the Impact Investing space for working alongside me to empower investors to invest for a sustainable and inclusive world.

REFERENCES

Abouzahr, K., et al. (2018). *Why Women-Owned Startups Are a Better Bet*. Boston Consulting Group. https://www.bcg.com/en-us/publications/2018/why-women-owned-startups-are-better-bet.aspx (accessed May 17, 2020).

Aguirre, D., Hoteit, L., and Rupp, C., et al. (2012). Empowering the Third Billion: Women and the World of Work in 2012. Booz and Company (15 October).

American Express (2018). Number of Women-Owned Businesses Increased Nearly 3,000% since 1972, According to New Research. American Express (August 21). https://about.americanexpress.com/press-release/research-insights/number-women-owned-businesses-increased-nearly-3000-1972-according (accessed May 17, 2020).

Anita Borg Institute for Women and Technology (2014). Innovation by Design: The Case for Investing in Women. https://anitab.org/wp-content/uploads/ 2014/03/The-Case-for-Investing-in-Women-314.pdf (accessed May 17, 2020).

Barrett, K., Hobble, R., and Rosqueta, K. (2017). *The XX Factor: A Comprehensive Framework for Improving the Lives of Women & Girls*. The Center for High Impact Philanthropy at the University of Pennsylvania. http://www.impact .upenn.edu/the-xx-factor   https://tarahealthfoundation.org/wp-content/ uploads/2018/01/CHIP_XXFactor_2017.pdf (accessed May 21, 2020).

Bear, J. B., and Woolley, A. W. (2011). The Role of Gender in Team Collaboration and Performance. *Interdisciplinary Science Reviews* 36:2: 146–153. DOI: 10.1179/030801811X13013181961473 (accessed May 16, 2020).

Brennan, B. (2018). Top 10 things everyone should know about women consumers. Bloomberg (January 11). https://www.bloomberg.com/company/ stories/top-10-things-everyone-know-women-consumers   (accessed   20 April 2020).

Bureau for Employers' Activities (2019). *Women in Business and Management: The business case for change*. Global Report. International Labor Organization (ILO). https://www.ilo.org/global/publications/books/WCMS_700953/ lang--en/index.htm (accessed 20 April 2020).

Byrnes, J. P., Miller, D. C., and Schafer, W. D. (1999). Gender Differences in Risk Taking: A Meta-*Analysis. Psychological Bulletin*, 125(3): 367–383. DOI: 10.1037/0033-2909.125.3.367.

Castrillon, C. (2019). Why Women-Led Companies Are Better for Employees. Forbes   (March   24).   https://www.forbes.com/sites/carolinecastrillon/ 2019/03/24/why-women-led-companies-are-better-for-employees/# 2a9d0b013264 (accessed May 16, 2020).

Credit Suisse (2014). The CS Gender 3000: Women in Senior Management. https://www.credit-suisse.com/about-us-news/en/articles/news-and- expertise/cs-gender-3000-report-2019-201910.html (accessed   20   April 2020).

Curtis, M. (2012). *Gender Diversity and Corporate Performance*. Credit Suisse Research Institute. https://publications.credit-suisse.com/tasks/render/file/ index.cfm?fileid=88EC32A9-83E8-EB92-9D5A40FF69E66808 (accessed 12 May 2020).

Cuberes, D., and Teignier, M. (2012). Gender Gaps in the Labor Market and Aggregate Productivity. *Working Papers 2012017*, University of Sheffield, Department of Economics.

Denmark, F. (2009). Female Hedge Fund Managers Outperform Male Counterparts. Institutional Investor (November 9). https://www.institutionalinvestor.com/article/b150q908ltv3b3/female-hedge-fund-managers-outperform-male-counterparts (accessed May 17, 2020).

Dezso, C. L., and Ross, D. G. (2011). Does Female Representation in Top Management Improve Firm Performance? A Panel Data Investigation. Robert H. Smith School Research Paper No. RHS 06-104. SSRN: https://ssrn.com/abstract=1088182.

Díaz-García, C., González-Moreno, A., and Sáez-Martínez, F. J. (2013). Gender Diversity Within R&D Teams: Its Impact on Radicalness of Innovation. *Innovation* 15(2): 149–160. DOI: 10.5172/impp.2013.15.2.149.

Elborgh-Woytek, K., Newiak, M., Kochhar, L., et al. (2013). Women, Work, and the Economy: Macroeconomic Gains from Gender Equity. https://www.imf.org/external/pubs/ft/sdn/2013/sdn1310.pdf (accessed May 16, 2020).

Foster, L. (2015). Women and Alpha: "Money Is on Everybody's Mind." CFA Institute (June 16). https://blogs.cfainstitute.org/investor/2015/06/16/women-and-alpha-money-is-on-everybodys-mind/ (accessed May 16, 2020).

FP Analytics Report (2020). Women as Levers of Change. FP News (26 March). https://foreignpolicy.com/events/women-as-levers-of-change-virtual (accessed 12 May 2020).

Global Impact Investing Network (2017). Gender Lens Investing Initiative. https://thegiin.org/gender-lens-investing-initiative (accessed 16 May 2020).

Hargreaves Lansdown (2018). Women Who Invest Tend to Outperform Men. Press release (6 February). https://www.hl.co.uk/about-us/press/press-releases/women-who-invest-tend-to-outperform-men (accessed 12 May 2020).

Hunt, V., Layton, D., and Prince, S. (2015). Why Diversity Matters. *McKinsey & Company (January).* https://www.mckinsey.com/~/media/McKinsey/Business%20Functions/Organization/Our%20Insights/Why%20diversity%20matters/Why%20diversity%20matters.ashx (accessed May 16, 2020).

Hunt, V., Prince, S., Dixon-Fyle, S., et al. (2018). Delivering Through Diversity. *McKinsey & Company (January).* https://www.mckinsey.com/~/media/mckinsey/business%20functions/organization/our%20insights/delivering%20through%20diversity/delivering-through-diversity_full-report.ashx (accessed May 16, 2020).

Kapin, A. (2019). 10 Stats That Build the Case for Investing in Women-Led Startups (January 28). https://www.forbes.com/sites/allysonkapin/2019/

01/28/10-stats-that-build-the-case-for-investing-in-women-led-startups/#7ff18ea859d5.

Kaufmann Fellows (2016). The Rising Tide: A "Learning-By-Investing" Initiative to Bridge the Gender Gap. https://www.kauffmanfellows.org/journal_posts/the-rising-tide-a-learning-by-investing-initiative-to-bridge-the-gender-gap (accessed May 17, 2020).

Knight Foundation (2019). Diversifying Investments: A Study of Ownership Diversity and Performance in the Asset Management Industry. https://knightfoundation.org/reports/diversifying-investments-a-study-of-ownership-diversity-and-performance-in-the-asset-management-industry (accessed 12 May 2020).

Lee, L. E., Marshall, R., Rallis, D., et al. (2015). Women on Boards: Global Trends in Gender Diversity on Corporate Boards. MSCI ESG Research Inc. (November 2015). https://www.msci.com/documents/10199/04b6f646-d638-4878-9c61-4eb91748a82b (accessed May 17, 2020).

Lehmann Nielsen, V., and Madsen, M. B. (2017). Does Gender Diversity in the Workplace Affect Job Satisfaction and Turnover Intentions? *International Public Management Review* 18 (1). https://journals.sfu.ca/ipmr/index.php/ipmr/article/view/318 (accessed May 16, 2020).

Lighthall, N., and Mather, M. (2012). Risk and Reward Are Processed Differently in Decisions Made Under Stress. *Current Directions in Psychological Science* 21(2): 36-41. DOI: 10.1177/0963721411429452.

Lorenzo, R., Voigt, N., Tsusaka, M., et al. (2018). How Diverse Leadership Teams Boost Innovation. Boston Consulting Group (23 January). https://www.bcg.com/en-us/publications/2018/how-diverse-leadership-teams-boost-innovation.aspx (accessed May 17, 2020).

Losada, M., and Heaphy, E. (2004). The Role of Positivity and Connectivity in the Performance of Business Teams. *American Behavioral Scientist* 47(6): 74065. DOI: 10.1177/0002764203260208.

Marone, H. (2016). Demographic Dividends, Gender Equality, and Economic Growth: The Case of Cabo Verde. IMF Working Paper (9 August). https://www.imf.org/en/Publications/WP/Issues/2016/12/31/Demographic-Dividends-Gender-Equality-and-Economic-Growth-The-Case-of-Cabo-Verde-44178 (accessed May 16, 2020).

McElhaney, K., and Smith, G. (2017). *Eliminating the Pay Gap: An Exploration of Gender Equality, Equal Pay, and a Company That Is Leading the Way.* University of California, Berkeley. https://www.icrw.org/wp-content/uploads/2017/11/Eliminating-the-Pay-Gap-Kellie-McElhaney-and-Genevieve-Smith.pdf (accessed May 17, 2020).

McKinsey Global Institute (2015). How advancing women's equality can add $12 trillion to global growth. *Report.* https://www.mckinsey.com/featured-insights/employment-and-growth/how-advancing-womens-equality-can-add-12-trillion-to-global-growth (accessed 12 May 2020).

Mooney, A. (2017). Female hedge funds outperform those run by men. Financial Times (September 16, 2017). https://www.ft.com/content/8bffa2c4-99f3-11e7-a652-cde3f882dd7b (accessed May 26, 2020).

MSCI (2016). The Tipping Point: Women on Boards and Financial Performance. https://www.msci.com/documents/10199/fd1f8228-cc07-4789-acee-3f9ed97ee8bb (accessed May 16, 2020).

Nethero, D. (2018). Why Investing in Women-Led Startups Is the Smart Move. Entrepreneur (March 8). https://www.entrepreneur.com/article/309555 (accessed May 17, 2020).

Niessen-Ruenzi, A. (2015). Sex matters: Gender differences in the financial industry. In: K. *Responsible Investment Banking.* (Ed. Wendt, pp. 439–443). Switzerland: Springer Publishing.

Pendal Group (2019). IWD 2019: The growing role of gender equality bonds. *Report.* https://www.pendalgroup.com/wp-content/uploads/2019/03/IWD-2019-Special-gender-equality-bonds.pdf (accessed 12 May 2020).

Phillips, K. W., Liljenquist, K. A., and Neale, M. A. (2009). Is the Pain Worth the Gain? The Advantages and Liabilities of Agreeing with Socially Distinct Newcomers. Personality and Social Psychology Bulletin. Research Paper (29 December). DOI: 10.1177/0146167208328062 (accessed 16 May 2020).

PitchBook (2019). PitchBook-All Raise Report on Venture Financing in Female-Founded Startups Shows Progress, Yet Continued Gender Inequity. Press Release (12 November). https://pitchbook.com/media/press-releases/pitchbook-all-raise-report-on-venture-financing-in-female-founded-startups-shows-progress-yet-continued-gender-inequity (accessed 12 May 2020).

Post, C. (2015). When Is Female Leadership an Advantage? Coordination Requirements, Team Cohesion, and Team Interaction Norms. *Journal of Organizational Behavior*, 36(8): 1153–1175 (November 2015). https://doi.org/10.1002/job.2031.

Quinlan, J. P., and VanderBrug, J. (2016). *Gender Lens Investing: Uncovering Opportunities for Growth, Returns, and Impact.* Hoboken, NJ: John Wiley & Sons.

Rhia Ventures (2020). Hidden Value: The Business Case for Reproductive Health. https://rhiaventures.org/wp-content/uploads/2020/01/Hidden-Value_The-Business-Case-for-Reproductive-Health.pdf.

Segal, J. (2019). Asset Managers Owned by Women and Minorities Have to Work 10X as Hard for Assets. Institutional Investor (January 28). https://www .institutionalinvestor.com/article/b1cwvq3mc37xwk/Asset-Managers-Owned-by-Women-and-Minorities-Have-to-Work-10X-as-Hard-for-Assets (accessed May 16, 2020).

Sommer, J. (2018). Who Runs Mutual Funds? Very Few Women. New York Times (May 4). https://www.nytimes.com/2018/05/04/your-money/who-runs-mutual-funds-very-few-women.html (accessed May 16, 2020).

Stewart, N. (2018). Are Women Better Investors Than Men? Warwick Business School (28 June 2018) https://www.wbs.ac.uk/news/are-women-better-investors-than-men (accessed 12 May 2020).

Tara Health Foundation (2020). www.tarahealthfoundation.org (accessed May 21, 2020).

United Nations (2010). The Women's Empowerment Principles, Equality Means Business Initiative. https://www.unwomen.org/-/media/ headquarters/attachments/sections/library/publications/2011/10/women-s-empowerment-principles_en%20pdf.pdf?la=en&vs=1504.

Veris Wealth Partners (2018). Gender Lens Investing: Bending the Arc of Finance for Women and Girls. *Report.* https://www.veriswp.com/wp-content/uploads/2018/10/GLI_Bending_the_Arc2018-web.pdf (accessed 12 May 2020).

Veris Wealth Partners. (2020, March 05). Gender Lens Investing: Assets Grow to More Than $3.4 Billion. https://www.veriswp.com/gender-lens-investing-assets-grow-to-more-than-3-4-billion/ (accessed 24 May 2020).

Wealth-X (2019). *A Generational Shift: Family Wealth Transfer Report* 2019. https://www.wealthx.com/wp-content/uploads/2019/07/Wealth-X_Family-Wealth-Transfer-Report_2019.pdf (accessed May 2020).

Wharton Social Impact Initiative (2019). Project Sage 2.0 Tracking Venture Capital with a Gender Lens. University of Pennsylvania. https://socialimpact .wharton.upenn.edu/research-reports/reports-2/project-sage-2 (accessed 12 May 2020).

Woolley, A., Chabris, C., Pentland, A., et al. (2010). Evidence of a Collective Intelligence Factor in the Performance of Human Groups. *Science 330*: 686–688. New York. 10.1126/science.1193147.

Zakrzewski, A., Newson, K., Kahlich, M., et al. (2020). Managing the Next Decade of Women's Wealth: BCG. https://www.bcg.com/publications/2020/ managing-next-decade-women-wealth.aspx (accessed 28 May 2020).

APPENDIX 7.1:   RESOURCES

Gender Equity Now https://thinkgen.org/	The Gender Equity Now (GEN) Certification is the gold standard for gender equity in the US workplace. Businesses that are GEN Certified meet standards of excellence across five tenets of workplace culture. A composite assessment of employee experience and employer policies provides a data-driven standard of equity-centered work environments. The GEN Certification rewards business leaders who go beyond talk to meaningful action. Nia Impact Capital was the first US GEN certified company.
Emerging Women https:// emergingwomen .com/	Emerging Women is a global network of brilliant women creating new leadership paradigms and supporting the rise of leaders across all sectors of society. With an ethos of authenticity, consciousness, and connection, the Emerging Women mission is to catalyze the power of feminine leadership in order to fill the pipeline of women leaders and create a more sustainable future, where life and humanity are at the center of all business activity. Emerging Women supports and inspires women to express themselves authentically by providing the tools, knowledge, and network for women to lead in a way that integrates core feminine values like connection, collaboration, intuition, empathy, and heart. Emerging Women is a global platform for leaders and entrepreneurs to catalyze their vision, create powerful connections, and explore the many issues that women in business face today. Based in Colorado, Emerging Women offers international events, networking circles, and online content that build community and know-how for women leaders.

Crowdfund Mainstreet[37]	Crowdfund Main Street is a women-led registered Crowdfunding portal that seeks to bring together small business innovation and the financing that makes it possible to start or grow these ventures. Crowdfund Main Street makes it possible for individuals to find and invest in small businesses doing the kind of work they believe in and want to support —and champions women-led startup ventures.
Investibule https://investibule.co/	Investibule is a crowdfunding impact investment vehicle that brings together a wide range of community-based investment opportunities into one easy-to-use platform. Investibule allows investors to discover investments tailored to their interests and investment profile. Investors can easily sort and filter for women-led entities in which to invest.

---

[37] https://crowdfundmainstreet.com/campaigns?category=WOMAN_FOUNDERS.

CHAPTER 8

Gender Lens Investing in the African Context

Michael Z. Ngoasong, PhD and Richmond O. Lamptey, PhD

Abstract

African women face serious constraints in obtaining credit, cultivating business networks, when dealing with cultural norms that favor men, and with gender-neutral policies. This has led to calls for breaking stereotypes of women as survivalist entrepreneurs through gender lens investing (GLI) initiatives. This chapter investigates the practice of GLI by analyzing how fund managers draw on the gender lens narrative to break down gender stereotypes through the provision of microcredit, to develop women entrepreneurs' agency, and attract investments. Through the analysis of the gender lens narrative of Impact Investing Funds in Africa and two in-depth case studies of microfinance organizations in Ghana and Cameroon, this chapter reveals explicit and implicit GLI strategies for investing in women-owned businesses in resource-scarce contexts and adds to the sustainable finance research by analyzing the application of GLI in Africa. The cases highlight important policy and practice implications facing gender lens investors seeking to address the persistent gender inequalities in access to entrepreneurial finance.

Keywords

Gender Lens Investing; Impact Investing; Gender; Women-Owned Businesses; Microfinance; Africa; Cameroon; Ghana

INTRODUCTION

Gender lens investing (GLI) is a global trend. Existing studies estimate total publicly available equity and fixed income within GLI to have grown to over USD $2.4 billion in assets under management (Smucker 2019) and the total capital with a gender lens having reached USD $4.8 billion in 2020, more than doubling the USD $2.2 billion in 2018 (Biegel and Hunt 2020, p. 6). The Global Impact Investing Network (GIIN) estimates USD$6.8 billion in impact investments to West Africa and USD $7.8 billion to East Africa in 2014 (GIIN 2015a, p. 2; GIIN 2015b, p. 8) and at least USD $12 billion to Sub-Saharan Africa (GIIN, 2019).

GLI has led to a growing number of women-focused investment opportunities in Western economies (Reilly and Miller 2014), Asia and Middle East (USAID 2018), Latin America (Goddard and Miles 2016), and Africa (AgDevCo 2018). These prioritize women in efforts to build successful businesses through long-term investments and support the delivery of positive impacts at scale to redress power imbalances, to give women more autonomy in the management of their lives. GLI can counteract the persistent 9% gender gap regarding bank account ownership globally, which leaves 41% of women unbanked (Developing World Markets 2019).

Current evidence reveals increasing market opportunities for gender lens impact investors (AgDevCo 2018; GIIN 2018) and argues for it to be framed in terms of gender equality, access to entrepreneurial finance, as well as bringing these forward in the strategies, operations, and reporting of both fund managers and investees (Quinlan and VanderBrug 2017). However, GLI is not only about pursuing gender equality as a social good. GLI is also a strategy for financial outperformance, where women are both clients and input (talent) for producing stronger institutions, higher financial returns, and a more equitable world (Women's World Banking 2018). Stronger women-in-leadership metrics are now known to be correlated with superior company performance (Smucker 2019).

GLI can be defined as a set of "investment strategies applied to an allocation or to the entirety of an investment portfolio, which (i) seeks to intentionally and measurably address gender disparities, or (ii) examine gender dynamics to better inform investment decisions," or both (GIIN 2018, p. 2). From this perspective, GLI is seen as both an effective means for channeling funds toward interventions that advance gender equality and empower women and girls and a strategic tool for investors to identify investment opportunities with unrealized value (like undercapitalized women entrepreneurs with good growth prospects), to uncover potential risks (like sexual harassment, low staff retention, value chain abuses), and improve the transparency of gender equality practices (Quinlan and VanderBrug 2017; W20 Japan 2019).

Resource-scarce contexts expose why women entrepreneurs engage in untapped markets, facing constraints that challenge their business to avoid a survivalist, subsistence, or necessity mode, despite displaying similar growth potential of male entrepreneurs (Ford Foundation-Dalberg 2019; Ngoasong and Kimbu 2019). Constraints women face include difficulties in obtaining credit, cultivating business networks, dealing with gender policies, and cultural norms that typically favor men. This has led to calls for breaking stereotypes of women as survivalist entrepreneurs through GLI initiatives that increase women's economic contribution to the economy (AgDevCo 2018). More than 50% of investors consider contributing to the United Nation's Sustainable Development Goals (SDGs) of Gender Equality (SDG-5), poverty eradication (SDG-1), and inequality reduction (SDG-10) as a very important motivator for making impact investments (GIIN 2019).

The GLI focus on Africa is related to the recognized role of women as entrepreneurs or owner-managers of businesses in the formal and informal sectors (Ngoasong and Kimbu 2019), seen as crucial for developing women's self-independence, income generating potential, and contributing to the transformation of the economy (Ngoasong and Kimbu 2016; Financial Sector Deepening Trust 2017; Ford Foundation-Dalberg 2019). Apart from debt, equity, quasi-equity, and patient capital investments (Ngoasong et al. 2015), African countries have experienced some of the highest gender imbalances in the entrepreneurial sector worldwide (Kimbu et al. 2019). For women entrepreneurs in Africa, a typical stereotype is that without adequate financing, many are restricted to informal (unregulated) survivalist businesses, despite displaying similar growth aspirations to male entrepreneurs (Ngoasong and Kimbu 2019). This chapter responds to these calls by analyzing the practice of GLI in the resource-scarce context of Africa, seeking to enhance the understanding of how GLI is practiced.

Many studies focus on the perspectives of investors and development agencies. For example, Lang et al. (2015) examine three varieties of GLI, namely: (i) investments that focus on increasing access to capital for women; (ii) investing in workplace equity (e.g. increasing women's representation on boards and in senior leadership positions as a way to alter the gender landscape at the top, as well as policies that benefit women more broadly, such as wage equity and paid maternity leave); and (iii) investment in businesses that offer products and services that target women (e.g. female hygiene products, maternal health care, clean cook stoves in the developing world). Our aim is to move beyond the investor perspective, to focus on fund managers at the country level in Africa. A review of the literature and some of the funds operating in Africa uncovered narratives describing what GLI investing means for different types of funds. In analyzing two empirical cases in Africa, this chapter adds to the sustainable finance research by increasing the analysis of the results of the application of GLI in Africa.

By considering Impact Investing within a gender lens, this chapter addresses a key research question: how do fund managers of microfinance institutions (MFIs) break down gender stereotypes, by extending microcredit and support services to women entrepreneurs in resource-scarce context in Africa? To address this question, this chapter combines desk research on impact investments in Africa and in-depth qualitative analysis of two case studies of MFIs in Ghana and Cameroon.

The remainder of this chapter is organized as follows. First, the challenging opportunities for GLI in Africa are presented. Second, the methodology used to carry out the study is described. Third, the practice of GLI in Africa and the findings from two MFIs are offered. Finally, emergent theoretical frameworks, followed by recommendations and future research opportunities, are discussed.

METHODOLOGY

This research was inspired by a qualitative research approach to understanding women's entrepreneurship in Africa. The analysis is based on desk research, focus groups, and interviews and underpinned by existing studies linking gender and entrepreneurial finance (Palmer 1995; Marlow and Patton 2005; Chant and Sweetman 2012) and women entrepreneurs' motivations within the resource-scarce context of Africa (Kimbu and Ngoasong 2016; Tillmar 2016). The desk research consisted of reviewing GLI initiatives taking place in Africa, retrieved from policy documents, technical reports, magazine articles, and independent evaluations.

Inspired by these studies, this chapter analyzes current narratives framed by a gender lens perspective used by impact investment funds, focusing on those targeting women entrepreneurs in Ghana and Cameroon. This chapter relies on a wider set of data collection, done as part of two projects on Impact Investing set in Africa, during July 2014 to April 2015 and January 2017 to April 2018.[1] For the wider study, data was gathered through more than 60 semi-structured interviews with key informants drawn from impact investors, fund managers, owner-managers of small and medium-sized enterprises (SMEs), and government authorities discussing Impact Investing in Africa from the perspective of the informants' organization and roles.

From the above data, two MFIs were studied in depth, I-Microfinance Ltd in Ghana and C-Credit Ltd in Cameroon (Table 8.1). Both raised funds from gender lens investors and in turn extended micro-credit to women entrepreneurs. The two case studies typify the perspectives of country-level fund managers seeking to break down gender stereotypes, by extending microcredit and support services to women entrepreneurs in the resource-scarce context in Africa. These two empirical cases were examined in-depth to illustrate GLI in Ghana and Cameroon, leading to the development of a model to better understand GLI application in resource-scarce contexts.

In the case of I-Microfinance Ltd, two semi-structured interviews were conducted with the general manager and a relationship officer, as a first point of contact for women entrepreneurs at the branch level, who often went to the field to undertake capacity building and advocacy. A CEO of one of the three gender lens investors for I-Microfinance Ltd was also interviewed. In the second case of C-Credit Ltd Cameroon, two interviews were conducted with the CEO and the general manager. The general manager also attended a focus group discussion. The GLI perspectives of fund managers matter because of their role in deploying a gender lens narrative in soliciting, screening, and selecting investments in women-owned businesses, but also in developing the agency for women owner-managers to effectively operate such businesses and create the desired financial return and social impacts locally.

The focus group discussion was informed by GLI principles and involved the analysis of factors considered by fund managers when screening and approving or rejecting applications for capital, capacity building initiatives, women's leadership and management, advocacy, and policy initiatives to

---

[1] Both authors conducted fieldwork in Ghana while Richmond O. Lamptey was a graduate research assistant at Ghana's Centre for Impact Investing. Sections of the first project are reported in Ngoasong et al. (2015).

TABLE 8.1　Microfinance Institution Characteristics and Data Collection.

	I-Microfinance Ltd Ghana	C-Credit Ltd Cameroon
Microfinance institution	Microfinance Bank	Non-Banking Financial Institution
Location	Ghana	Cameroon
Founding Year	2009	1999
Key informant interviews	2	2
Position of Interviewees	1. General Manager 2. Relationship Officer	1. CEO 2. General Manager, North West Region
Gender Lens Investors interviewed	CEO	Board Member
Focus Group	No focus group	10 participants, all women: 2 from C-Credit Ltd (general manager for Northwest region and women) entrepreneur client 8 other women entrepreneurs
Documents analyzed	Company documents, observations (fieldnotes), online documents	Company reports, observation during meetings between credit managers and entrepreneurs (fieldnotes), online documents

Source: Authors' field work.

promote inclusiveness for women and girls (Quinlan and VanderBrug 2017; Carlile et al. 2015).[2]

　Both cases also rely on field observations, particularly of loan officers holding one-to-one loan application meetings with women entrepreneurs in branch offices, explaining how support would be provided (interactions

---

[2]A regional manager of C-Credit, Ltd and one woman entrepreneur client attended the focus group; participants' experiences were discussed with MFIs (such as C-Credit Ltd).

between loan officers and clients at the branch) and on the revision of sample loan applications.

Semi-structured interviews and focus group discussions were tape-recorded and transcribed, while dialogues and informal discussions were captured as field notes. The content analysis technique was used to analyze the data (Jaiyeoba and Haron 2016), and a narrative analysis was applied for discussing the emergent GLI themes from MFIs (Kimbu et al. 2019).

Qualitative work of this sort presents limitations as regards extrapolating results from a small set of interviews to the general population (Jaiyeoba and Haron 2016; Ngoasong and Kimbu 2019). To address this limitation, this chapter also draws from a wider set of primary data collection. Interviews with academics and practitioners at the Ghana Centre for Impact Investing in Accra, part of a larger project on Impact Investing in Africa, served to discuss the findings of these two case studies and facilitated triangulation of the information, thereby enhancing the reliability of results.

WHY GENDER LENS INVESTING IN AFRICA MATTERS

GLI in Africa matters due to the financing challenges underpinning gender inequality, namely the debates linking gender and entrepreneurial finance (where businesses owned by men are more likely to be funded by investors), the biases facing women compared to men, and the societal transformation occurring in African countries, where gender biases are still key considerations in investment decisions. This chapter investigates how GLI is attempting to address these biases in African countries, offering new paths to solve specific and global problems in this domain.

Persistent gender inequality is long lived in the entrepreneurial finance landscape of most African countries, producing severe financing bias against women. Women still need to rely on their husbands or other family members to provide collateral security for loans from banks (Kimbu and Ngoasong 2016). Another bias is in the way women's voices and choices are relatively less recognized as compared to men, who are in control of income opportunities. This can be addressed by developing agency for women to pursue income-generating opportunities through GLI initiatives (DAI 2019). This includes behavior and orientation guidance, not only concerning formal and informal practices within their businesses but also toward their wealth creation potential, as expected from any entrepreneur (Marlow and Patton 2005).

Unless gender balance is prioritized, there is a risk that male entrepreneurs will continue to be prioritized by investors (Marlow and

Patton 2005). The entrepreneurship literature addresses the link between gender and entrepreneurial finance. Marlow and Patton (2005) question why men access finance disproportionately more than women. In the African context, a number of reasons have been identified for this disproportionate access: women-led business tend to be smaller in size and underrepresented in loan applications; women's roles are perceived to be connected to household duties, while men are traditionally interpreted as primary financial breadwinners; the vast majority of investors are men, leading to likelihood of implicit bias; succession planning and ethnic and traditional practices restrict women's access to land titles and collateral needed to access finance (MacLeod 2019; Ngoasong and Kimbu 2019). These biases illustrate how GLI overlaps with the debate linking gender and entrepreneurial finance and justify gender-aware interpretations increasingly being deployed by impact investors (MacLeod 2019; AgDevCo 2018).

Three interlinked areas have also been suggested as justification for a gender lens focus in understanding the role of women entrepreneurs in development, namely the social transformation goals, commercial goals, and community needs that women-owned businesses serve (Kimbu and Ngoasong 2016). First, GLI can help women pursue social transformation goals, such as advancing their perceived "status" to female entrepreneurs and using their businesses as platforms for alleviating poverty. Second, commercial goals enable women entrepreneurs to pursue financial independence (economic status), supplement their household income, and support the survival or sustainability of their business. Third, operating a business enables women entrepreneurs to contribute to development through the sales of goods or services and providing employment opportunities.

GLI matters for all African countries, given the entrepreneurial opportunities that women entrepreneurs cannot realize as a result of the major resource constraints they face, including "(i) poor SME support, (ii) lack of opportunities for business leadership roles compared to men, (iii) less access to financial services and products compared to men, and (iv) lower level of knowledge assets compared to men" (Mastercard 2017, p. 27).

There are also country-specific challenges for Cameroon and Ghana. In Ghana, micro enterprises are dominated by women-owned businesses, representing 79.8% of the SME sector (Lamptey 2017). Concerning Cameroon, it has the highest rate of total early-stage entrepreneurial activity (TEA) in Africa, with a female/male TEA ratio of 0.92 compared to an average of 0.70 across Africa and 0.67 globally (Ngoasong and Kimbu 2019). The legal and commercial infrastructure and government support programs relating to entrepreneurial activities around agriculture are more developed compared to those of Ghana. However, Cameroon has one of the highest business discontinuation rates and the lowest rates of opportunity-oriented early-stage entrepreneurial activity in Africa (Ngoasong and Kimbu 2019).

Despite the promise and potential of GLI, it is important to recognize existing critical voices about gender-focused narratives pursued by international development agencies and private investors. In a detailed review of the development finance literature, Chant and Sweetman (2012) report the findings of international development programs' evaluations and argue that even if the provision of access to finance for women can facilitate the attainment of gender equality, an enabling environment—that promotes gender equality and women's empowerment—is crucial to the success of GLI.

ADOPTING GENDER LENS INVESTING

Though GLI is relatively nascent, several frameworks have been advanced for analyzing the practice of GLI by fund managers. This chapter focuses on those at the investor-fund manager and fund manager-investee levels, respectively.

With respect to the investor-fund manager level, since 2013, Veris Wealth Partners has produced an annual guide for investors, with the aim to apply a gender lens to assess the multiple facets of an investment opportunity (Carlile et al. 2015). The guide suggests that adopting GLI involves looking into women-owned and managed investment firms and advisors, as per the percentage of women in management at all levels, including those in search of new advisors and investment managers. When women are found to be underrepresented, the guide advises investors on how to proceed with actions toward greater gender equality. The Forum for Sustainable and Responsible Investment's practical guidebooks go further to include gender alongside social and environmental problems, advising investors on how to adopt explicit strategies to address those and demonstrate impacts (USSIF 2014).

Fund manager-investee level, the Aspen Network of Development Entrepreneurs incorporated a gender lens component in their impact manager training and launched a Metrics and Research Working Group, where fund managers share progress. The group trains fund managers to actively pursue gender inclusive practices by disaggregating performance metrics by gender wherever feasible when considering how to invest (Edens and Lall

2014). Disaggregation by gender is also an important theme in the GLI guide produced by the Global Fund for Women, in collaboration with Root Capital, Thirty Percent Coalition, and Trillium Asset Management (Global Fund for Women 2015). The Calvert Foundation's Women's Principles adapted by the United Nations to the seven UN's Women's Empowerment Principles (UN Women 2011) is another important GLI strategy focused on key elements of GLI (Calvert 2019). Taken together, these frameworks guide fund managers' dealings with investees as well as their reporting back to investors to demonstrate as evidence of impacts and to raise additional capital.

Moving from principles to practice, Quinlan and VanderBrug (2017) also provide a useful framework that depicts key areas for analyzing the adoption of a combination of GLI goals, namely through the promotion of women's leadership, increasing women's access to capital, investing in products and services beneficial to women and girls, promoting workplace equity, and related shareholder engagement and policy work. For fund managers wanting to use their portfolios to support the advancement of women and girls, Carlile et al. (2015) propose two main investment options. First, investing in dedicated gender lens solutions and explicitly adopting one or more gender lens goals, which reflects the goals discussed in Quinlan and VanderBrug (2017). Second, integrate significant gender criteria into the security selection[3] and engage in shareholder advocacy to advance gender inclusiveness (Carlile et al. 2015). Fund managers can engage in shareholder advocacy by using their rights as partners to advocate for gender in evaluation metrics.

With respect to microfinance, the above frameworks provide suggestions on how evidence can be collected to demonstrate GLI. For example, how to focus on the improved socio-economic status of women recipients of capital (which was provided to enable them to start their own businesses and reduce their economic dependence on behaviors that put them at risk of contracting HIV [USSIF 2014]), through explicit GLI strategies that actively seek to understand and produce these opportunities and impacts for women (Global Fund for Women 2015).

There is also a debate as to whether the very small investments that are provided by microfinance institutions are enough to demonstrate an explicit GLI strategy, or whether MFIs are better off pursuing a more implicit strategy where gender is one of many other resource-scarce challenges that need to be

---

[3]Security selection is the allocation to specific financial securities in a fund's portfolio; for GLI, this is vital for financial advisors seeking to maintain or grow their gender lens investor base.

addressed in African countries. The Calvert Foundation's GLI guide demonstrates how even investments starting as low as USD $20 can catalyze gender inclusive change. At the end of 2013, 800 investors had adopted Calvert's approach, leading to more than USD $20 million in loans for community development for women, including through microfinance (Calvert 2019).

THE PRACTICE OF GENDER LENS INVESTING IN AFRICA

GLI Narratives of Regional Fund Managers in Africa

Similarly to GLIs in Asia (USAID 2017) and in Latin America (Goddard and Miles 2016), GLI in Africa takes mostly the form of partnerships between development finance institutions (DFIs) and private venture funds, to create funds that undertake GLI into women-owned businesses (AgDevCo 2018), improve the employability and retention of female staff, and foster equitable hiring practices (DAI 2019; PNUD 2019).

Tables 8.2 and 8.3 provide a summary of multi-country funds operating in Africa and their GLI narratives. To uncover how these funds took part in GLI, we focused on the narratives used by fund managers, sustainability reports, their use of environmental, social, and governance (ESG) standards, interview data, and field notes. Though narratives are not evaluative evidence on their impact, this information is useful for the analysis of the context in which GLI is practiced, producing intended financial and social impact outcomes for women. The last column provides information on some of its reported impact on gender and business.

The analysis reveals some heterogeneity in the application of GLI strategies. Table 8.2 features "explicit gender strategies" (gender-first and gender-sensitive), and Table 8.3 highlights "implicit gender lens narratives" (gender-aware) (MacLeod 2019). An explicit GLI strategy is implemented when the fund manager has a clearly defined investment strategy for GLI. Grofin Africa, Investisseurs and Partennaires, and Acumen Fund applied explicit GLI strategies, in which they recognized gender lens as part of their sectoral focus. Developing World Markets and JCS/Goodwell Investments focused on financial inclusion through investments in MFIs that prioritized women-owned micro businesses. The conversations held with impact funds in-country, revealed that commercial banks implementing small business finance initiatives started to pursue this approach of supporting businesses which had developed a strategy related to women's empowerment issues.

TABLE 8.2 Gender Narratives Underpinning Explicit GLI Strategies in Africa.

Fund	Description	African Countries	GLI narratives	GLI Impact
Explicit GLI strategies				
Developing World Markets	A fund that has invested or arranged USD $1.5 billion in financing for more than 200 socially or environmentally positive companies in developing and emerging countries.	Egypt, Zambia, South Africa, Kenya, and Rwanda	Objective 4 of impact framework aims to "Improve Gender Equality" through (1) Women Clients, (2) Women-Tailored, Services and (3) Women Senior Leadership Representation, via portfolio MFIs (Developing World Markets 2019).	In 2017, 79% of clients in DWM portfolio of 54 MFIs are women, and 33% of the MFIs provide various women-tailored services; 22% of female representation in senior leadership (compared with the global average of 15%) and 28% for portfolio management team members (Developing World Markets 2019).
Grofin	A USD $500 million fund specialized in USD $100,000 to USD $1.5 million investments.	Egypt, Ghana, Ivory Coast, Nigeria, Senegal, Kenya, Rwanda, Tanzania, Uganda, Zambia, and South Africa	GroWoman gender lens investment strategy to substantially increase the percentage of women-owned/led businesses in its portfolio; implements a GLI metrics (Grofin 2018).	Between 2014 to 2018, the cumulative number of investee businesses owned/managed by women increased from 79 to 188 and direct women jobs sustained from 3,362 to 9,526; USD $66.8 million cumulative investments overall.

AGRA	An agricultural fund that provides start-up capital of up to USD $150,000 over a period of 2 years to farmer-centered, gender and youth inclusive SMEs.	Kenya, Ghana, Burkina Faso, Ethiopia, Malawi, Mali, Mozambique, Nigeria, Rwanda, Tanzania, Sudan, Sierra Leone, and Liberia	Empowering women and strengthening families through strategic investment funds.	400 projects grant-funded; 247 grants worth USD $130 million in 11 countries through 24 consortia impacting the livelihood of 8 million farmers majority of whom are females due the gender-integrated approach in agricultural transformation in Africa (Alliance for a Green Revolution in Africa 2018).
MASSIF	A EUR 387 million fund that invests in small businesses and micro-entrepreneurs, women and youth entrepreneurs.	South Africa, Kenya, Ethiopia, Zimbabwe, Ghana, Ivory Coast, Nigeria, and Sierra Leone	The gender narratives of the fund evidenced in the fund policies are manifested at the portfolio level through investments in financial intermediaries (e.g. MFI) that support women-owned ventures, agriculture, and micro, small, and medium-size enterprises.	One portfolio MFI evaluated had a minimum of 60,000 jobs created, of which 50% are for women and income improvement for the other 30,000 (Netherlands Ministry of Foreign Affairs 2015).

(continued)

TABLE 8.2 (*continued*)

Fund	Description	African Countries	GLI narratives	GLI Impact
Investisseurs and Partenaires (I&P)	A group investing to maximize economic, environmental, social, and governance impacts. The size of its most recent fund, IPDEV 2, is USD $102 million.	Benin, Burkina Faso, Ivory Coast, Mali, Senegal, Cameroon, Gabon, Uganda, and Madagascar	A broad objective to promote gender equality in the formal SME sector in Sub-Saharan Africa and a specific purpose to integrate a gender perspective into I&P partner companies' main impact areas: (1) SME leaders, (2) employees, (3) clients, (4) suppliers and distributors, (5) funds (Investisseurs and Partenaires 2018a, 2018b).	40% or more of new investments (seed or equity) are women-impact SME; gender equity in I&P Développement 2 (IPDEV 2) teams and national funds (between 40% and 60% women) (Investisseurs and Partenaires 2018b).
Acumen	A global community that provides patient capital in the range of USD $250,000 to USD $3 million to businesses.	Kenya, Uganda, Tanzania, Rwanda, Ethiopia, Burundi, South Sudan, Ghana, and Nigeria	Invests in women as a way to achieve business and social goals (e.g. ventures that provide products to improve maternal health, affordable early childhood education, and water and sanitation) (Acumen 2015, 2018).	Provides fellowships for young female students. Lean Data Gender Tool with Unilever to empower 5 million women across the value chain. (Acumen 2015, 2018).

JCS Capital / Goodwell Investments	Raised over five funds with over USD $150 million in capital and invests in financial inclusion, early stage fintech businesses, and inclusive growth sectors.	Ghana, Nigeria, Kenya, and South Africa	Gender embedded at the portfolio level; uses internal working groups for understanding and deploying gender-lens analysis to adapt standard tools to local contexts; invests in MFIs that specifically target women-led businesses and businesses that provide services to women (Goodwell 2019).	Between 2016 and 2019, the customer base of these MFI portfolio had increased from 10,000 to 20,000 customers, of which 86% are female; 39% of 883 employees in the portfolio companies were women at the end of 2017 (Goodwell 2019).
Injaro	A USD $49 million fund that invests in SMEs along the agricultural value chain in West Africa.	Ghana, Burkina Faso, and Ivory Coast	Uses gender-based screening tools to ensure investment readiness of women-owned and/or women-focused businesses.[4]	At the fund manager level, 50% of the employees are women; at portfolio level 50% of the 658 jobs created by investee SMEs in 2017 went to women. A woman entrepreneur who benefited from Injaro's grower scheme noted, "Before, I supported 70 smallholder farmers, with the supply of farm inputs. I now support over 150 farmers with seeds, fertilizer, and money."[5]

Sources: Authors' elaboration based on the literature review and field work (interviews).

[4]Interview data.
[5]Interview data.

TABLE 8.3 Gender Narratives Underpinning Implicit GLI Strategies in Africa.

			Implicit GLI strategies	
Novastar	A fund that invests USD $250,000 in early-stage and up to USD $6 million in growth-stage businesses.	Mauritius, Kenya, Nigeria, and Ethiopia	Tracks the number of employees by gender in investee businesses primarily due to select investors interest (GIIN 2017).	Examples are Bridges International Academies, which operate in six countries in Africa, providing educational solutions at the basic level expanding access and enrolment for girls.
Inspired Evolution II	A USD $216 million specialized investment fund offering development, energy, and resource efficiency growth investments.	South Africa, Mauritius, and Kenya	Strives to include women and reduce gender inequalities optimizing opportunities for women as partners, employees, management, board members, and community beneficiaries; gender split in carbon footprint classified under "other metrics" rather than core matrix (Inspired 2017).	Metrics from 2018 show women make up 30% of 739 employees, 3 of 25 board members, and 8 of 21 board members (Inspired 2018).
Oasis Capital Ghana	A private equity fund that invests in USD $500,000 to USD $5 million in small and medium-sized businesses.	Ghana and Côte D'Ivoire	Considers gender analysis when required by funds, e.g. founders with vision and passion for women's education via pioneering business for and by women.[6]	Investment in Legacy Girls' College, which offers high-quality education. To be expanded from 13 students to over 400 schoolgirls in Ghana (Proparco 2020).
Vital Capital Fund	A USD $350 million private equity fund investing in food, water, health care, and housing.	Ghana and Angola	Invest in sectors that improve vocational education, researching women's resilience to food insecurity, capacity-building program for social workers (Vital Capital 2015).	Invested USD $10 million in WaterHealth International, which enabled 5.8 million rural individuals, where the majority of these population are women, secured access to water in Ghana.

[6]Interview data.

288

Sources: Authors' elaboration based on the literature review and field work (interviews).

In the cases depicted in Table 8.3, GLI is more implicit. For instance, technical assistance facilities and grants are used to create schemes targeting women as key beneficiaries, such as training programs, support for the adoption of new governance frameworks to realize financial return, and metrics that include gender. Oasis Ghana Ltd provided targeted investments to women entrepreneurs in education and other essential services. In such cases, gender is included among one of many variables of the preliminary impact assessment of the fund, rather than being the main variable.

Case Study: Case Studies of Impact Investing with a Gender Lens

This section examines how Impact Investing within a gender lens perspective can be deployed by MFI's fund managers to break down gender stereotypes (i.e. by extending microcredit and support services to women entrepreneurs in resource-scarce context in Ghana and Cameroon). Two case studies are illustrated before proceeding to the discussion of the emergent themes, as a framework for a better understanding of GLI.

I-Microfinance Ltd, Ghana

I-Microfinance Ltd is a growing fund, established in 2009. Currently, it has 97 staff members and has directly invested in more than 2,000 women entrepreneurs and women-owned businesses through nine branches nationwide. The fund's headquarters are based in Accra for ease of access to investors. However, they also extended their microcredit activity to rural Accra, where women dominate micro-businesses along the coast, in fish mongering, smoked fish for bulk selling, tabletop sales of cooked food, and small provision shops. Second, the northern regions of Ghana have communities with relatively high incidence of poverty, considering the nature of economic activities, such as farming, basket weaving, livestock farming and sales, shea butter farming and processing. These are resource-scarce contexts with limited resource base for women entrepreneurs, in addition to a high proportion of people having very low purchasing power (Ngoasong and Kimbu, 2019). To address this, I-Microfinance works with women groups or associations, such that each woman can have the opportunity to access microcredit, as an associated member of group lending schemes.

As a microfinance institution, I-Microfinance Ltd is still seeking to secure a savings and loan banking license, which is a second-tier banking segment within the banking sector in Ghana. In addition to an anonymous high-net-worth investor and grant funding from a DFI (USAID), I-Microfinance raised capital from two international corporate investment vehicles that support its gender lens narrative. These two vehicles are the African Tiger Holding Ltd. (formerly known as African Tiger Mutual Fund, Ltd.) and Goodwell Investments BV, in partnership with JCS Investments Ltd, the local fund manager that operates the Goodwell West Africa Microfinance Fund.

The investments from the latter two sources were estimated at USD $2 million and confirmed in an internal report that was shown to us during the fieldwork. The report included statements about how the objective of promoting financial inclusion for women in rural and semi-urban communities was crucial in securing GLI. The motivation for GLI comes from Goodwell Investments BV. This was confirmed locally through an interview with a Ghana-based partner at JCS Investments Ltd. When asked what the nature of GLI looks like in the context of Ghana, the following narrative was provided:

> We were the first foreign company to invest in rural banking targeting women. We believe rural banking sector must become an asset class, which can support the rural economy. Some funders were convinced and have supported us by giving grants for trainings. Also, when we started, there was virtually no financial inclusive fund domiciled in Ghana. Since then, we have seen the microfinance sector grown a lot, there are now over 600 MFIs.
>
> *(General Manager, I-Microfinance)*

The interviews helped explain how African Tiger Holding Ltd. had been investing in the northern region of Ghana for over 20 years and why they were keen to incorporate GLI into their existing investments targeting rural women in the region. To achieve this, the fund actively sorted local opportunities for investing in women. When asked to describe how they aligned their investment strategies to secure buy-in from African Tiger Holding Ltd., the following statement was provided:

> We present what our company has achieved for women and what is in it for impact investors. They [investors] bought into the vision to support the low-income women group who are into small businesses. They have brought in funding to support the company to grow

and achieve its objective. They sit on the Board. Our CEO crafts the strategy with the management team and presents it to the Board for approval. They review all actions on a quarterly basis. Monthly management reports are produced and sent to Board members.

(General Manager, I-Microfinance)

The above quotation elicits an explicit GLI strategy as the fund deliberately prioritized access to capital for women (Quinlan and VanderBrug 2017). I-Microfinance fund managers managed multiple objectives due to different sources of funds, which were not equally gender lens focused. GLI for I-Microfinance Ltd meant prioritizing women entrepreneurs in rural and semi-rural regions in Ghana.

I-Microfinance worked with women groups to promote collective mobilization, which is an important approach to supporting micro-entrepreneurship in African countries (Ngoasong and Kimbu 2016; Tillmar 2016). The group lending schemes it runs were core to their GLI strategy. An example is the group of women producing shea butter in the northern region of Ghana. This group-based capacity building enabled I-Microfinance to provide education and training for women (UN Women 2011). At the time of the fieldwork for this research, in 2017, there were 60 women in one group, trained and funded to weave baskets that were then sold across the region. The proceeds were shared among the women according to agreed group norms. Other group-based funded projects included a project to sell rice palm boilers and another supporting the women who produced and sold shea butter.

In terms of management and governance, underpinning a GLI strategy (Calvert 2019), though gender lens investors sat on the I-Microfinance's Board, a separate contractual arrangement existed for each investor, within which transactional arrangements related to financing and profitability were monitored. Concerning GLI practice (fund manager to women entrepreneur), targeting specific categories of women customers (Goddard and Miles 2016), 70% of I-Microfinance loans were borrowed by women, especially those who run their businesses in rural villages.

Another major challenge for Ghanaian women entrepreneurs is that there is hardly any entrepreneurial finance scheme that does not require collateral for the granting of loans:

Whilst the interest on our loans to individual businesses is 6% to 7% per annum, rural women are charged 4% interest rate on microloans. Whilst we ask for collaterals for loans to individuals and middle-income businesses, we don't ask for collateral to rural women entrepreneurs. We partnered with [an international NGO], we manage the funding and they provide a caretaker for street children. We give the funds to women and monitor them, educate and provide financial management training.

(General Manager, I-Microfinance)

The GLI strategy of I-Microfinance Ltd Ghana consisted of aligning their policies with the gender lens mission of global impact investors, which enabled them to access gender lens investment financing. This funding was then deployed locally, through extending microcredit and capacity building for women entrepreneurs and enforcing agreed governance mechanisms.

C-Credit Ltd Cameroon

C-Credit Ltd was founded in 2000 as a savings and loan cooperative in the north west region of Cameroon. C-Credit Ltd's primary goals are to provide services to improve economic and social well-being of women, through a fair rate of interest on savings and loans; and to provide quality financial services that will enable the cooperative to be competitive. As a member-driven cooperative, its membership rose from 633 in 2011 to 1,200 in 2015, all of whom are women. Members are rural and semi-urban women entrepreneurs, who are owners and managers of micro and small businesses in a range of sectors.

C-Credit Ltd displays a GLI strategy around women's leadership (Quinlan and VanderBrug 2017). They prioritize women, as seen through their women-focused membership, women-elected board of directors, and equity funding from women-focused investors.[7] This is related to women's representation in the governance and management of their GLI strategy (Calvert 2019). An internal report provided by C-Credit Ltd outlines the alignment of their strategies to an impact investor in five principles: (i) created for women only, (ii) incorporation of savings and loans to promote women's activities, (iii) training female small-scale business projects and record keeping, (iv) facilitation of training for women through community development initiatives, (v) prevention of HIV/AIDS through family planning advocacy. Another evidence of explicit GLI is the focus on offering products and services to women, for example, through access to capital for

---

[7] About 10% of their total assets in 2015.

women-owned businesses. This evidence was consistent with the views of participants at the focus group discussion, many of whom stated how they are required to demonstrate how their business reflects the gender lens principles of C-Credit when applying for loans and training opportunities.

The experiences of C-Credit Ltd female borrowers points to the importance of overcoming biases associated with male-dominated patriarchal cultures and ethnic traditions. Examples of biases that were uncovered in the focus group discussion included "families actively seeking early marriages for girls," "limited rights for some women in polygamous marriages," "succession processes that favor girls." These unique gender-related challenges are related to respect and support for human rights and nondiscrimination (UN Women 2011) that GLI aims to address. These are factors typical of a resource-scarce context in that they constrain women's ability to demonstrate the collateral required to own property or secure loans from banks (Ngoasong and Kimbu 2019). To address this, C-Credit categorizes women who do not have collateral and provides an initial amount as small as 10,000 Francs CFA (USD $16.50), progressing to loan amounts over 200,000 Francs CFA (USD $329.40), where collateral is required in the form of business asset or other property.

Apart from effects on access to finance, cultural barriers also affect the performance of women-owned businesses:

> The cultural backgrounds and barriers that we have in our society today hinder many women from getting involved in businesses, no matter how they struggle. I have had a group of women whose businesses were doing well but they were still scared of declaring their savings to family members. They tell me to "keep it quiet, never allow X to know." Many barriers are really hindering these women.
>
> *(Interview, General Manager, C-Credit)*

The quotation above also relates to what Kimbu and Ngoasong (2016) call self-independence in the sense that creating and operating a business can enable women to develop newly found confidence necessary to give visibility and recognition to their voice. The following quotation highlights the need for independence in the form of income to supplement household income and reduce dependency on their husbands (Kimbu and Ngoasong 2016).

> Women want to generate income. Some are single mothers who need to rent houses, pay school fees and feed their family. Without income generation they may turn to prostitution or other dirty businesses.

Economically, if they don't get involved in a business activity, the economy will not improve. We also see that women are a vulnerable group when it comes to contracting HIV and a target for thieves.

(CEO, C-Credit)

Serving the needs of both full-time and part-time women entrepreneurs is also part of the ethos of C-Credit Ltd. However, not all women entrepreneurs aspire to full financial independence. During the focus group discussions in Cameroon, some women entrepreneurs described their preferences as part-time owner-mangers, which allowed them to combine family responsibilities (Marlow and Patton 2005). This includes, for instance, running part-time catering businesses from their homes, combined with the management of their households, as a complement to the full-time income generated by their husbands.

In the focus group discussion, participants also identified business and management skills as a major challenge facing women entrepreneurs. A resource-scarce context can impact entrepreneurs as they need certain skills to be able to deal with cultural barriers and low purchasing power of buyers. This is where the capacity building programs implemented by C-Credit became valuable. In the focus group discussion, a women entrepreneur who had benefited from the training offered by C-Credit Ltd mentioned this:

I received a text message about a workshop for clients interested in business skills and financial information for growing their business. We were told by the local Field Officer that if our businesses are growing and we are selling more services this can result in us depositing larger sums with C-Credit Ltd and in turn increase how much we were later able to borrow to expand my business further.

(Microfinance Borrower of C-Credit Ltd, Focus Group)

From a GLI perspective, workplace equity at the level of investees was more implicit in the practices of C-Credit, because women entrepreneurs were not required to demonstrate workplace equity in their loan applications (Quinlan and VanderBrug 2017). However, by carrying out capacity building programs related to education and professional development promotion for women, the CEO explained that "there is some expectation" that women entrepreneurs will not only employ young girls, but also that they will transfer the skills taught to improve their performance in the business as employees.

DISCUSSION

The aim of this chapter is to explore the understanding of how GLI is practiced, by analyzing how MFI Fund managers break down gender stereotypes when extending credit, microcredit, and other support services to women entrepreneurs in resource-scarce contexts in Africa. Its conceptual underpinnings are entrepreneurial motivations (Kimbu and Ngoasong 2016) and GLI strategies (Quinlan and VanderBrug 2017) used by fund managers of MFIs to identify and invest in women-owned businesses.

Both cases seen in the previous section, Credit Ltd Cameroon and I-Microfinance Ltd Ghana, illustrate the challenges and opportunities faced by the GLI community in breaking down stereotypes in communities where ethnic traditions continue to favor men (Ngoasong and Kimbu 2016). To uphold their commitment to diversity, inclusive of gender and ethnicity, MFIs rely on group-based approaches to maintain close interactions through regional branches and fieldworkers.

For both MFI study cases analyzed, GLI strategies take the form of prioritizing women in the choice of investees, women-focused membership, women ownership or management of businesses. GLI is also combined with attracting equity from either women-focused investors or investors that target businesses in sectors where women operate. Fund managers applied a gender lens to their investments' strategy and due diligence processes to select women entrepreneurs in order to ensure the intended gender impact (Carlile et al. 2015). Through GLI approaches, these MFI Fund managers break down gender-related barriers by understanding and acting upon women's motivations, and by providing both financial and non-financial support to their endeavors.

From a comparative perspective, C-Credit Ltd Cameroon can be said to pursue a more explicit GLI strategy due to its exclusive focus on women as owners and clients. This is because it operates as a woman-led and women-only cooperative with democratic principles in terms of elected leaders and primarily serves women clients. Though I-Microfinance Ltd Ghana primarily targets women, the ownership and management structures are not exclusively female.

The two MFIs compare to Calvert's (2019) women-centered approach to responsible investing in the area of community relations (support for women-owned businesses, ensuring women have equal access to credit), environment (women as agents of change), Indigenous people's rights (access to education/training), and human rights (treatment of women).

They are, however, lagging in workplace and product-safety, given their focus on access to capital.

However, a gender-lens perspective does not necessarily translate into an exclusive focus on women, as both cases of I-Microfinance and C-Credit appear to suggest. The UN Women's Principle 2, to treat all women and men fairly at work, and Principle 3, to ensure the health, safety, and well-being of all women and men workers (UN Women 2011), suggest that equal treatment must be applied. Though the persistent biases that women entrepreneurs have in African countries, namely in Cameroon and Ghana, can justify the appropriateness of strategies that exclusively focus on women's entrepreneurial needs, more research is needed to also understand how workplace equity in the businesses created and operated by women entrepreneurs works for both men and women, in favor of full gender equality.

CONCLUSION

This chapter enhances the understanding of GLI's practices in an African context, focusing on how MFI Fund managers break down gender stereotypes in Ghana and Cameroon, by extending microcredit and support services to women entrepreneurs in a resource-scarce context. This chapter further elicits explicit and implicit gender lens narratives (MacLeod 2019).

Persistent gender inequality has long existed in entrepreneurial finance (Kimbu and Ngoasong 2016). GLI attempts to break down persistent biases in the African entrepreneurial sector by identifying and acting upon women's entrepreneurial motivations and by developing women enterprises' agency for business execution. MFI Fund managers who can identify gender lens investors and develop strategies for incorporating women's entrepreneurial motivation and investment preferences into their country level fund strategies are actively contributing to address this imbalance. GLI also provides opportunities for women entrepreneurs and for addressing women's specific needs (Goddard and Miles 2016). Some of these include access to capital and management skills, maternity and reproductive health challenges, and overcoming patriarchal cultures that favor men in property ownership.

The in-depth analysis of two case studies of MFIs in Ghana and Cameroon revealed important insights as to how fund managers have deployed a gender lens perspective to local support of women-owned businesses. These MFIs achieved it by focusing on explicit GLI strategies related to access to capital for women entrepreneurs and by investing in services beneficial to women entrepreneurs (e.g. capacity building and training). Fund managers also deliberately engaged in discussions about gender equality and took gender considerations on board in the choice of their investment portfolio.

Some of the visible results include a growing number of women entrepreneurs that have secured access to finance who would not probably obtain it otherwise, the training and professional development they obtained, their group-based community projects, and the products and services for local communities produced consequently. However, adopting a GLI strategy still goes further, toward pursuing goals such as workplace equity (Quinlan and VanderBrug 2017) and engaging in shareholder advocacy to advance gender inclusiveness (Carlile et al. 2015). The evidence from the case studies suggests that these remained either implicit or had not yet been achieved by MFIs.

GLI also represents an opportunity for developing the agency of women entrepreneurs and their staff for successful business execution. This relates to the capacity building programs and group-based lending projects described in the two case studies, which exposed women to behaviors, orientation, and actions necessary to navigate formal and informal practices within their businesses. Recognizing the relevance of agency helps gender lens impact fund managers distinguish "need-based" versus "opportunity-based" women-owned businesses in their screening and due diligence processes, to better deploy the resources necessary to develop the capabilities of women entrepreneurs. The grants and technical assistance facilities from DFIs enabled country fund managers to develop the entrepreneurial agency of women entrepreneurs through training (human resources) and formal (regulated) management practices necessary for business exploration and execution (Lang et al. 2015).

RECOMMENDATIONS

The gender bias in African countries is long-standing and known to be persistent. It may not be eradicated solely by GLI without public policy support. Most national governments already provide ad hoc support to women entrepreneurs and women-owned businesses through scattered initiatives, but most public policies on entrepreneurship in Africa can be considered largely gender neutral (Kimbu et al. 2019; Tillmar 2016).

More active public policies could incentivize greater access to finance and reduce the number of bottlenecks facing women entrepreneurs in

Africa. A starting point is the creation of an enabling environment that offers the right framework conditions for female entrepreneurship. This includes investing in public infrastructure relevant to women (e.g. funded nursery schools and sanitary facilities), easing market access through safe public transportation and Internet, reproductive health policy initiatives, targeted tax incentives, and property legislation that give women access to collateral security for accessing capital. An enabling environment is necessary for maximizing impacts generated by funds and businesses already adopting GLI strategies.

Moreover, increased awareness about the role fund managers can play in breaking down stereotypes through GLI strategies is needed. Fund managers can encourage the institutionalization of commitments toward greater diversity, concerning gender but also ethnicity, for instance during the selection of board of directors candidates. Rather than assuming stereotypical views that ascribe business opportunities in certain sectors of the economy as more suitable for women, a GLI narrative opens more opportunities to women and empowers them with the confidence needed to pursue their true aspirations and realize their full potential.

Furthermore, MFI Fund managers should adopt factsheets for GLI indicators (GIIN 2018) as an integral part of their impact assessments. These are central for assessing impact and reporting it back to investors and beneficiaries, including increasing the chances of raising more capital from investors. They should adopt already existing tools more widely to demonstrate impact, such as the Calvert Foundation tool that tracks how to start from investing minimal amounts in women-owned businesses and progressing to larger amounts as the business grows and addresses gender lens metrics (Calvert 2019), while incorporating the UN Women's (2011) empowerment principles. By adopting suitable frameworks and tools for impact measurement, GLI can go beyond access to finance, to include other initiatives (e.g. capacity building activities and raising awareness of the many biases related to gender-specific roles) to help all Africans to strive for excellence, irrespective of their gender.

Though women in African countries display a similar growth-orientation as those in western countries, the pace of growth of their businesses is much slower due to existing biases (Ngoasong and Kimbu 2019). GLI in Africa requires an in-depth understanding of what motivates women to aspire to be entrepreneurs and match their aspirations to the gender lens strategies of investors. This scrutiny needs to be done to ensure appropriate GLI strategies, in support of women entrepreneurs who develop growth aspirations, thus requiring larger investments to pursue market opportunities that target larger segments of society, with greater societal impacts.

ACKNOWLEDGMENTS

This research benefited from grants from the Open University (UK) for a scoping project by the first author and PhD Studentship on impact investments in Ghana awarded to the second author.

We thank participants at the Diana International Conference on Women's Entrepreneurship, Babson College, Wellesley, Massachusetts (2–4 June 2019) and Africa Academy of Management Conference in Lagos, Nigeria (8–11 January 2020) for comments suggestions.

We are grateful to the editors of this book for their critical comments and guidance.

REFERENCES

Acumen (2015). Women and Social Enterprises: How Gender Integration Can Boost Entrepreneurial Solutions to Poverty. *A Report by Acumen and International Centre for Research on Women*.

Acumen (2018). A Lean Data How-To Guide: Understanding Gender Impact Phase 1. *A Guide by Acumen Fund* (November).

AgDevCo (2018). Gender Lens Investing: The Case for Empowering Women. Practical findings for the Investment Community. *A Joint Report by AgDevCo and UKAID* (March).

Alliance for a Green Revolution in Africa (2018). Investing in agriculture to reduce poverty and hunger. https://www.gatesfoundation.org/how-we-work/resources/grantee-profiles/grantee-profile-alliance-for-a-green-revolution-in-africa-agra (accessed 12 March 2020).

Biegel, S., and Hunt, S. M. (2020). Project Sage 3.0: Tracking Venture Capital, Private Equity, and Private Debt with a Gender Lens. https://socialimpact.wharton.upenn.edu/research-reports/reports-2/project-sage-3/ (accessed 5 August 2020).

Calvert (2019). The Calvert Women's Principles. Calvert Research and Management. https://www.calvert.com/includes/loadDocument.php?fn=28364.pdf&dt=fundpdfs%27 (accessed 21 March 2020).

Carlile, L. R., Choi, L., Farrar-Rivas, P., and Pyott, A. (2015). Women, Wealth & Impact: *Investing with a Gender Lens 2.0. A Report by Veris Wealth Partners Report* (March).

Chant, S., and Sweetman, C. (2012). Fixing Women or Fixing the World? "Smart Economics," Efficiency Approaches, and Gender Equality in Development. *Gender and Development* 20(3): 517–529.

DAI (2019). Six Practical Ways to Tackle Gender Lens Investing. A Practical Guide by Development Alternatives, Inc. (DAI).

Developing World Market (2019). Developing World Markets 2018 Impact Report.

Edens, G., and Lall, S. (2014). The State of Measurement Practice in the SGB Sector. *A Report Prepared for Aspen Network of Development Entrepreneurs* (June).

Financial Sector Deepening Trust (2017). Summary Paper: Retrospective Impact Assessment 2005-2015, Financial Sector Deepening Trust Tanzania During 2016. https://www.itad.com/knowledge-product/summary-paper-retrospective-impact-assessment-2005-2015-financial-sector-deepening-trust-tanzania/ (accessed 24 February 2020).

Ford Foundation-Dalberg (2019). Impact Investors Foundation. Impact Investors' Foundation: Nigeria and Ghana Impact Investing and Policy Landscape. *A Joint Report by Ford Foundation and Dalberg* (September-December).

Global Fund for Women (2015). Investing for Positive Impact on Women: Integrating Gender into Total Portfolio Activation. https://www.globalfund forwomen.org/wp-content/uploads/2015/11/Investing-for-Positive-Impact-on-Women.pdf (accessed 3 March 2020).

Global Impact Investing Network (2015a). The Landscape for Impact Investing in West Africa: Understanding the Current Status, Trends, Opportunities, and Challenges. *A West Africa Regional Chapter Report by the GIIN (December).*

Global Impact Investing Network (2015b). The Landscape for Impact Investing in East Africa. *East Africa Full Report by the GIIN in partnership with Open Capital Advisors* (August).

Global Impact Investing Network (2017). Novastar Ventures' Use of Impact Data. https://thegiin.org/research/publication/impact-measurement-and-management-cases (accessed 3 March 2020).

Global Impact Investing Network (2018). Gender Lens Impact Investing Factsheet 2018 (March). https://missioninvestors.org/resources/gender-lens-impact-investing-factsheet (accessed 15 September 2018).

Global Impact Investing Network (2019). Annual Impact Investor Survey. https://thegiin.org/assets/GIIN_2019%20Annual%20Impact%20Investor%20Survey_webfile.pdf (accessed 4 March 2020).

Goddard, C., and Miles, K. (2016). The Sky's the Limit: Increasing Social Investment Impact with a Gender Lens. The Young Foundation. *A Report by Gender Futures for Young Foundation* (March).

Goodwell (2019). Connecting the Dots: Impact Report 2019. Goodwell Investments.

Grofin (2018). GroFin Integrated Report 2018.

Inspired (2017). Inspired Evolution Impact Report 2018.

Investisseurs and Partenaires (2018a). Opportunities to address the gender gap in African SMEs. *I&P Gender Policy Report* (March).

Investisseurs and Partenaires (2018b). I&P Développement II. *Annual ESG and Impact Report March* 2018.

Jaiyeoba, H. B., and Haron, R. (2016). A Qualitative Inquiry into the Investment Decision Behavior of the Malaysian Stock Market Investors. *Qualitative Research in Financial Markets* 8(3): 246–267.

Kimbu, A. N., and Ngoasong, M. Z. (2016). Women as Vectors of Social Entrepreneurship. *Annals of Tourism Research* 60: 63–79.

Kimbu, A. N., Ngoasong, M. Z., Adeola, O., and Afenyo-Agbe, E. (2019). Collaborative Networks for Sustainable Human Capital Management in Women's Tourism Entrepreneurship: The role of Tourism Policy. *Tourism Planning and Development* 16(2): 161–178.

Lamptey, R. O. (2017). Curbing SME Financing Challenges in Ghana: The Role of Impact Investing. *Proceedings from the International Conference on Entrepreneurship Business and Technology,* Accra, Ghana (27–28 March 2017).

Lang, K., Humphreys, J., and Electris, C. (2015). Investing for Positive Impact on Women: Integrating Gender into Total Portfolio Activation. A Trillium Asset Management White Paper (November).

MacLeod, E. (2019). Mapping Gender Lens Investing in the Global South: Ghana, Kenya, Sri Lanka, and Vietnam. http://assets.wusc.ca/GLI-mapping-in-Global-South-v3.pdf.

Mastercard (2017). Mastercard Index of Women Entrepreneurs 2017. *A Mastercard Report* (March).

Marlow, S., and Patton, D. (2005). All Credit to Men? Entrepreneurship, Finance, and Gender. *Entrepreneurship Theory and Practice* 29(6): 717–735.

Netherlands Ministry of Foreign Affairs (2015). MASSIF Evaluation: Financial inclusion in developing countries, 2006-2014. MASSIF Final Report 2014 (November).

Ngoasong, M. Z., and Kimbu, A. N. (2016). Informal Microfinance Institutions and Development-Led Tourism Entrepreneurship. *Tourism Management* 52: 430–439.

Ngoasong, M. Z., and Kimbu, A. N. (2019). Why Hurry? The Slow Process of Growth in Women-Owned Businesses in Resource-Scarce Contexts? *Journal of Small Business Management* 57(1): 40–58.

Ngoasong, M., Paton, R., and Korda, A. (2015). Impact Investing and Inclusive Business Development in Africa: A Research Agenda. IKD Working Paper No. 76, Open University, Milton Keynes, UK.

Palmer, I. (1995). Public finance from a gender perspective. *World Development* 23(11): 1981–1986.

Proparco (2020). A new generation of women in Ghana in Ghana with Legacy Girls College. https://www.proparco.fr/en/actualites/grand-angle/legacy-girls-college-new-generation-women-ghana (accessed 15 September 2018).

Quinlan, J. P., and VanderBrug, J. (2017). *Gender Lens Investing: Uncovering Opportunities for Growth, Returns, and Impact*. Hoboken, NJ: John Wiley & Sons.

Reilly, J., and Miller, A. (2014). Gender-Wise Philanthropy: Strengthening Society by Investing in Women and Girls. *A Report by the Australian Women Donors Network*.

Roberts, A. (2016). The Limitations of Transnational Business Feminism: The Case of Gender Lens Investing. *Soundings* 62: 68–83.

Smucker, M. (2019). How Are Gender Lens Funds Performing? *CFA Institute*. https://blogs.cfainstitute.org/investor/2019/06/24/how-are-gender-lens-funds-performing/ (accessed 18 March 2020).

Tillmar, M. (2016). The gendered contextualization of SME cooperation in urban East Africa. In *Women's Entrepreneurship in Global and Local Contexts* (eds. C. Diaz-Garcia, C. Brush, E. Gatewood, F. Welter), 105–123, Northampton, MA: Edward Elgar.

UN Women (2011). Women Empowerment Principles. https://www2.unwomen.org/-/media/field%20office%20eseasia/docs/publications/2016/05/wep-booklet-en.pdf?la=en&vs=5928 (accessed 18 March 2020).

USAID (2017). Championing economic growth best practices in Asia and the Middle East. *Final Report of the Asia and Middle East Economic Growth Best Practices Project, USAID Task Order AID-OAA-M-12-00008*.

USSIF (2014). Investing to Advance Women: A Guide for Individual and Institutional Investors. Investing. https://www.ussif.org/Files/Publications/SRI_Women_F.pdf (accessed 18 March 2020).

Vital Capital (2015). Crafting Impact: Presenting Vital Capital's Approach to Impact Investing. https://www.vital-capital.com/images/upload/texts/48465097050528.pdf (accessed: 20 March 2020).

W20 Japan (2019). Gender Lens Investing: Emerging Global Trends. Concept Note. https://www.mofa.go.jp/files/000455165.pdf (accessed: 17 February 2020).

Women's World Banking (2018). "About Us." https://www.womensworldbanking.org/about-us/ (accessed 24 February 2018).

The Evolution from Gender-Focused Microfinance to Gender Lens Investing in Latin America: The Case of Pro Mujer

Angélica Rotondaro, PhD Maria Cavalcanti, MBA, MS and Carmen Correa, BS

Abstract

As an economic power, women are the world's largest emerging market. Globally, women investor groups saw their private wealth grow from USD $34 trillion to USD $51 trillion between 2010 and 2015. Estimates point to women holding about a third of the world's wealth—USD $72 trillion by 2020—and by 2028, female consumers will control around USD $15 trillion of global consumer spending. This chapter addresses the broadening of microfinance operations in Latin America, from a gender focus to employing a gender lens investing (GLI) methodology.

Building on the 30 years' experience of Pro Mujer—a Latin American organization empowering women and girls through a holistic approach, including access to financial services, education, and health care—this chapter describes the organic development and implementation of a GLI strategy as a response to the demands and needs of women entrepreneurs in Latin America. Pro Mujer's financial services portfolio transitioned from being a purely microfinance organization to include increased diversification with more tailored investment instruments designed with a gender perspective. This chapter describes the implementation of a GLI strategy based on an organizational self-assessment, through an institutional cultural change, which extended to changes in portfolio management, digital transformation and education. This transformation process allowed Pro Mujer to become a reference organization in the GLI space in Latin America.

Keywords

Gender Lens Investing; Gender; Microcredit; Impact Investing; Gender Gap; Gender Equality; Gender Equity; Poverty Reduction; Women Entrepreneurs; Small and Medium-sized Enterprises; Inclusion; Latin America; Mexico

INTRODUCTION: BUILDING THE BUSINESS CASE FOR GENDER LENS INVESTING IN LATIN AMERICA

As an economic power, women are the world's largest emerging target group. By 2028, female consumers will control around USD $15 trillion of global consumer spending. When women earn a competitive income, they tend to allocate 90% of those funds to their households, including food, health care, and education (Quinlan and VanderBrug 2017). Yet investing in women pays dividends in other areas as well.

One common finding is that the main reason women-led businesses fail in the Latin American region is lack of access to capital (IFC 2017). In Latin America, the finance gap for women-led small and medium-sized enterprises (WSMEs) stands at USD $93 billion (IFC 2017, p. 37), indicating that an opportunity exists for gender lens financing in the region. Furthermore, this need extends beyond formal markets. While the credit gap in Latin America and the Caribbean is significant, at USD $5 billion for women's micro businesses and USD \$93 billion for WSMEs, McKinsey forecasts an opportunity for a gross domestic product (GDP) annual growth of USD \$2.6 trillion for Latin America in 2025, if women participated as entrepreneurs and economic leaders to an identical extent as men in the economy.

The gender gap can be assessed through many different lenses, from uneven labor market participation to unequal salary scale, from lack of women professionals in science, technology, engineering, and math[1] (STEM) fields to low deal flows led by female entrepreneurs, from low political representation[2] to gender insensitive public policies. In the financial industry, women account for only 18% of the jobs. The CFA Institute,[3] with more than 150,000 members in 165 countries, found that women represent less than one in five CFA Institute country members, well below the percentage of female workers around the world (Adams et al. 2016).

Similarly, the gender investing gap can also be considered through many lenses. Looking at venture capital (VC) and private equity (PE), for example, only 9.65% of partners in the top 280 United States venture firms are women in decision-making positions (Wilhelm 2019). According to a Boston Consulting Group (BCG) report, when women business owners pitch their ideas to investors for early-stage capital, they receive significantly lower financial investment, on average more than USD \$1 million less than men (Abouzahr et al. 2018). On the other hand, it is clear there is a market opportunity for closing the gender gap and to add USD \$28 trillion, or 26%, to the annual global GDP in 2025 (Woetzel et al. 2015).

This chapter is based on the case study of Pro Mujer, a forerunner in providing microcredit, technical assistance, education, and health care to women and girls in Latin America, and addresses the processes it went through to develop and apply a broader approach to gender lens investing (GLI) in the region. It applies qualitative research methods to

---

[1] Another commonly mentioned gender gap relates to STEM, although the figures seem to be stable with an overall 24 percent of women in STEM worldwide (UNESCO Institute of Statistics 2019). However, it should be noted that, of the female doctorate graduates in the fields of science and engineering, 86% are white or Asian. Less than 4% are Latinos, and less than 3% are black. A similar situation can be observed in the job market as well. Only one out of 20 employed scientists and engineers are black or Latino women (Silva 2019).

[2] According to the World Economic Forum (WEF) report, in 2019, women with political representation accounted for only 25.2% of parliamentary seats and 21.2% of ministerial positions worldwide (WEF 2019).

[3] More information on https://www.cfainstitute.org/.

the analysis of Pro Mujer's 30 years' experience in providing financing, education, and health care services for women in Latin America, through five semi-structured interviews with Pro Mujer's top management, as well as with key partners in the region.[4] It also includes a literature review of GLI internationally and in Latin America, and documentation from Pro Mujer and its partner organizations.

The next section offers an overview of the transformation of GLI in Latin America in order to set the background for Pro Mujer's case study, from gender inclusion to gender investing in the region. The following section explores the definition for GLI and the need to develop a clear scorecard to avoid misappropriation of some GLI core goals. Then the next section describes the importance of catalytic capital and alliances for leveraging GLI. The following section consolidates key learnings and recommendations from Pro Mujer. Finally, the chapter concludes with reflections about the way ahead for scaling up GLI in Latin America.

GENDER LENS INVESTING IN LATIN AMERICA AND BEYOND: BACKSTAGE HIGHLIGHTS

One of the tipping points for the transformation of how financial funding and credit lines evolved in Latin America was the "upgrading" of many countries in the region from low to middle-income countries (MIC). This phenomenon led to scarcer and costlier microfinancing capital for microfinance borrowers and prompted a geographic reallocation of philanthropic resources to Africa and Southeast Asia, resulting in a reduction of worldwide donations to Latin America. Between 2014 and 2015 approximately 6.3% of the overall amount of USD $16.2 billion donated by the US foundation for international causes were directed to Latin America (Foundation Center 2018). Along this process, women became disproportionately affected by limited access to finance and quickly became the main constituency for microfinance institutions (MFIs), contributing to their proliferation around the globe and to the common belief that women are generally better credit risks in microfinance than men (D'Espallier et al. 2011). Nevertheless, today in Latin America, the credit gap for women-led micro businesses is approximately USD $5 billion, and in the case of women-led SMEs it sums up to USD $93 billion (IFC 2017).

---

[4] The interviews with key partners include Deetken Impact from Canada and VIWALA in Mexico.

These new microfinance market dynamics in the region brought forth a binary strategy: (i) a bottom-up strategy, in which the microcredit organization plays the role of an aggregator of services to be provided to the target group of women; and (ii) a top-down strategy by investing in companies that provide products and services to women and girls, while at the same time promoting more equitable workplaces and supply chains.

In Latin America, GLI has been gaining traction with several VC funds, incubators, and accelerators beginning to focus on women-led start-ups. This is the case of the Ilu[5] Women's Empowerment Fund, a joint venture between Pro Mujer and Deetken Impact, a Canadian Impact Investment Fund Manager, which is focused on the Latin American market, and VIWALA, a company set up in partnership between Pro Mujer and New Ventures Mexico, which provides revenue-based loans to women-led SMEs across Mexico.

Another relevant initiative was the creation of the Equality Fund, launched in 2018. It aims at mobilizing USD $1 billion for gender equality, through a financial tool which combines traditional philanthropy with GLI and public sector funding. This fund operates worldwide and already counts on committed capital from the Global Affairs Canada summing up CAD[6] $300 million in investments, and another CAD $100 million from donations. The Equality Fund's primary focus is to support grassroots organizations and movements that advance women's rights through grants worldwide. One example of the movements these grants support is the Women's Voice and Leadership (WVL) in the Caribbean, which aims to strengthen women's and lesbian, gay, bisexual, transgender, and queer (LGBTQ) rights organizations and movements in the region. The Equality Fund was idealized and incubated by the Match International Women's Fund, which recently merged both organizations into one. Together, they amassed a coalition of supporting organizations, including Calvert Impact Capital, the African Women's Development Fund (AWD), the Canadian Women's Foundation, and the Community Foundation of Canada, all in partnership with the Government of Canada. The private debt strategy is being structured and will be led by Calvert Impact Capital.

Calvert Foundation and their Impact Capital are also one of the predecessors in GLI. In 2012, it launched the Women Investing in Women

---

[5]*Ilu* is a word in Aymara language that means "to plant" and has been selected to name the fund because it represents the investors' intention to cultivate a world where women and girls in Latin America and the Caribbean can take leadership over their lives in the most productive ways.

[6]Canadian dollars.

(WIN-WIN) initiative, which focused on both empowering women as investors and empowering women and girls through their investments, with gender cutting across more traditional impact sectors. The initiative was translated in two debt funds, each raising USD $20 million, applying ticket sizes between USD $1 million to USD $5 million with an open geographical criterion. The Win-Win 1.0 was launched in 2012 and was sector agnostic, while Win-Win 2.0, launched in 2014, focused on clean energy technology firms.

The Criterion Institute[7] is a central opinion leader for the creation, consolidation, and piloting of gender empowerment projects, while at the same time addressing gender-based violence. Together with investors, philanthropists, and social change experts, the Criterion Institute has tested strategies where finance could address gender-based violence. Examples include the structuring of investments addressing the root causes of gender-based violence with terms and processes that align the uses of capital with the outcome sought or the proposition to channel capital to companies intentionally making a difference to reduce gender-based violence and away from companies who are not reducing it. The intention is to move USD $10 billion in investment capital into these strategies benefiting women and families.

The Small Enterprise Assistance Funds (SEAF),[8] an investment fund founded in 1989 as a private equity investment subsidiary of the international development organization CARE, has also been applying gender lenses to their investing. SEAF aims to provide growth capital to SMEs in emerging and transition markets where there is a lack of available financing sources. It has developed its own GLI scorecard[9] to support both assessing new investees in terms of gender inclusion and empowerment perspective, but also to align current portfolio companies and to track-record their GLI strategy along their investment horizon.

Politics have played a role in the genesis of GLI in Latin America. From a political representation perspective, Latin America is a region with a larger number of women occupying presidential positions. Argentina has had two women elected presidents, Isabel Perón and Cristina Kirchner. In Bolivia,

---

[7]The Criterion Institute (https://criterioninstitute.org/) is an activist think tank that aims at proving how finance can work for social change. It is committed to investing one-third of its own resources toward reimagining possibilities for using finance as a tool to effectively address gender-based violence.

[8]For more information, see http://www.seaf.com.

[9]SEAF's Gender Equality Scorecard is available at https://www.seaf.com/womens-economic-empowerment-and-gender-equality/gender-equality-scorecard/.

Jeanine Áñez led after the resignation of Evo Morales. In Chile, after several years under a military system, Michelle Bachelet was elected in 2006, and once again in 2014 for another four-year term. Beatriz Merino was the first female Prime Minister of Peru, followed by Rosario Fernández and Ana Jara. In Brazil, Dilma Rousseff was elected in 2011. In Central America, women presidents or acting presidents have included Violeta Chamorro in Nicaragua, Rosalía Arteaga Serrano in Ecuador, Mireya Moscoso in Panama, and Laura Chinchilla in Costa Rica (Da Paz and Moura 2019).

Gender empowerment via legislation has become a greater focus with women as presidents of these countries. In Brazil, examples of this include the increase in the number of women in ministerial positions; several programs and new legislation for equal opportunities, such as the implementation of labor rights for domestic employees; and a comprehensive communication campaign against gender-based violence. In Argentina, under female presidents, a program for Gender Equality and Equal Opportunities at Work was established, as well as the Gender Policy Council and Observatory on the Integration of Women in the Armed Forces (Da Paz and Moura 2019).

From a civil society perspective, movements have united women throughout Latin America, using social media to organize large-scale nationwide protests against gender-based violence. Examples include the social movement founded in Argentina in 2015 in response to brutal gender-based violence, and now spreading via the social-media hashtag #NiUnaMenos ("not one woman less"), dedicated to fighting gender inequality, abuse, and murder of women. In March 2020, Mexico experienced one of the biggest ever feminist mobilizations, the national women's strike to fight the continuing epidemic of femicides in the country. This act of protest showcases that Latinas are aware of both the need to push for stronger regulations against gender-based violence and the need to call for a change in the region's *machismo* culture.

Fortunately, Latin America's historical cycle of withholding capital from women-led businesses, commonly underpinned by pervading gender biases, is transforming into a virtuous cycle to close the financing gap for women entrepreneurs. This is a crucial change in response to new cultural, social, and economic norms, and the increasing demands and requirements of ESG metrics (like women's pay ratios relative to men) to support women's better positioning in the workplace, as investors and investees, and in the development of value chains that deal with the economic market potential to develop products and services for women. A leading force in this transformation is Pro Mujer and its focused gender lens Investing process.

PRO MUJER'S GENDER LENS INVESTING PROCESS

Pro Mujer's Background

"One of our underlying principles is never to take our clients for granted and to ensure that we continuously deliver relevant products and services to underserved women in Latin America" (Pro Mujer).

Since its inception in 1990, Pro Mujer has touched millions of lives in Latin America, and now operates in countries such as Argentina, Bolivia, Peru, Mexico, Nicaragua, and Guatemala, in three primary business sectors: financial services, health and well-being, and education. The Pro Mujer group is a holding of for-profit and nonprofit entities housed under a non-governmental organization (NGO) umbrella. Pro Mujer currently employs approximately 1,600 people, over 65% of whom are women employed at all levels of the organization, including field workers, middle management, senior leadership, and boards of directors.

Pro Mujer's financial services operations have loaned over USD $3.6 billion in microcredit operations to over 2 million women, alongside the delivery of financial inclusion literacy programs that enabled clients to better manage their personal finances and strengthen their businesses. Pro Mujer has also provided over 9 million health care interventions to its patients, including primary beneficiaries and their families. Its education-related activities have focused on digital literacy programs and entrepreneurship training. All Pro Mujer's business sectors have both profit and nonprofit operations. For example, in the health and well-being sector, in addition to offering consultations and medical services through its revenue-generating enterprises, Pro Mujer also offers free health care campaigns and wellness workshops to educate women on how to look after their own health needs and those of their families.

While most platforms' business models focus primarily on the use of technology, Pro Mujer's main demographic target is underserved women in Latin America, a group sometimes not yet fully conversant in technology and lacking in broad digital access. As part of its five-year strategic plan, Pro Mujer adopted a three-prong platform business model. The platform comprises in-house and external partner resources. Products and services can be delivered via a hybrid three-prong service model—offering high-touch support from its field agent network and brick-and-mortar facilities, and digitally via different interfaces. Assisted women continue to value the relationship of trust built over 30 years through a true interpersonal network. But while the personal and brick-and-mortar networks allow for

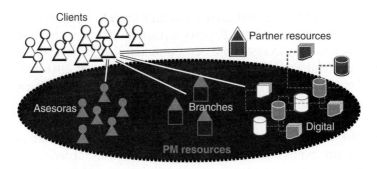

FIGURE 9.1   The Pro Mujer System Map. *Source:* Courtesy Pro Mujer.

trust building, the digital component enables scale, disintermediation, data collection, immediate feedback loop, continuous process efficiency, and lower transaction costs (Figure 9.1).

Based on a learning process, where listening to customers and loan officers is valued, Pro Mujer has been actively diversifying its portfolio during the last three years. It included new products, such as micro-insurance, savings accounts, housing lending, and mobile banking. The organization's average repayment rate varies according to the countries where it operates, but averages 95%, or 19 of 20 clients repaying loans successfully. This high repayment rate results from the front-line experience with communal banking methodology and the thorough work of loan officers. See Figure 9.1 for a visual of this system's approach.

The Transitioning Process

Although the transition from being primarily a gender-focused microfinance organization to a comprehensive platform offering different financial instruments for supporting women entrepreneurs with different needs at various stages of their life was perceived by Pro Mujer's management as a natural process, there is considerable change management involved behind this diversification, which had been ongoing for the previous three years. The central elements of this change management involved creating a vision, organizational review, team building, portfolio management, digital transformation, and a series of trainings for the internal and external publics. It started with two main interrelated elements, human and financial capital, aligned with a shared vision.

In order to create a vision, two complementary perspectives were taken into consideration. The first from "outside-in," by identifying new market needs and trends, and the second "inside-out," based on the internal knowledge and learnings from 30 years on the ground providing microcredit, access to health care services, and education. For the inside-out perspective, top management team members implemented between 2016 and 2017 a series of visits, interviews, and meetings throughout Latin America, involving beneficiaries in different countries, cultures, languages, and generations, along with team members and credit representatives.

For the outside-in perspective, market studies were reviewed, aiming at understanding trends and changing needs of women entrepreneurs, and new market studies were commissioned. For instance, Pro Mujer commissioned a study from the Failure Institute to identify the causes and consequences of business failure of low-income women-led startups in Latin America.[10] One of its insightful findings identified that 75% of women entrepreneurs in Mexico fail due to low or no access to startup credit. This led to the creation VIWALA, a financial instrument in Mexico in in 2018, further described in this chapter.

This two-way perspective resulted in a roadmap based on four pillars:

1. Leveraging financial resources in order to keep up with the micro-entrepreneurs' loans and the inclusion of catalytic capital to leverage financial resources to be invested in SMEs
2. The establishment of new financial products
3. The organizational set-up needed for the desired transformation of Pro Mujer
4. The implementation of a series of educational programs for both the beneficiaries, along with Pro Mujer's employees

The human capital was the first step in this process, which started with the appointment of a new chief executive officer (CEO) for Pro Mujer, with years of relevant experience in Impact Investing in the region, and who brought along an extended network. With that, followed a review of roles, responsibilities, and positions in the organization, resulting in decentralizing top management responsibilities from the headquarters in New York to different countries in Latin America, putting Pro Mujer leadership on the front line and allowing field offices to deliver a faster response to client needs. For instance, the chief financial officer (CFO) is based in Argentina, most finance back offices are in Nicaragua, the chief operations officer

---

[10]The low-income female entrepreneurs: failure and empowerment assessment were developed by the Failure Institute in Mexico in 2017.

(COO) is in Uruguay, the legal counsel is in Bolivia, the human resources director is in Peru.

Another relevant part of the reorganization involved the creation of different business units for each of the complementary services provided by Pro Mujer. An example is the case of Bolivia, where three business units—health care, financial services, and education—run in parallel. For health care, in 2019, Pro Mujer launched the health social enterprise InnovaSalud, a joint venture with Solydes, a nonprofit organization with a long-standing commitment to eradicating poverty. Today, Pro Mujer's health services in Bolivia have been successfully transferred to InnovaSalud as part of its innovative primary care and health insurance program. Through this initiative, Pro Mujer is expanding its health care services to reach a greater number of underserved communities, aiming to reach 1 million beneficiaries in five years. InnovaSalud operates 42 medical offices and 11 pharmacies across Bolivia and provides medical care to 60,000 patients. Besides the changes in its organizational structure, there was an ongoing process of awareness building related to the need to develop new financial services and to define new structures, beyond the last 30 years: cash flow, for the microloan services.

From a portfolio management perspective, Pro Mujer diversified and developed two new financial instruments aiming at providing capital to women entrepreneurs in different phases of their venture's business life cycle. In 2019, Pro Mujer partnered with Canadian impact investment management firm Deetken Impact to launch the Ilu Women's Empowerment Fund, a GLI fund financed by a broad set of private sector investors and the U.S. International Development Finance Corporation (DFC, formerly OPIC) (see Box 9.2).

In Mexico, targeting the missing middle credit for SMEs, Pro Mujer, together with New Ventures Mexico, launched VIWALA,[11] a financial instrument for revenue-based lending (see Box 9.3).

In education, a series of trainings were delivered to bring about more knowledge and awareness to both employees and beneficiaries, aiming at developing soft and hard skills required for a better entrepreneurial behavior. One program is VIVE (Ven, Inspírate y Vende/Come, Get Inspired and Sell)[12] in Mexico, a collaboration between Pro Mujer and Trust for the Americas, a nonprofit organization affiliated with the Organization of American States (OAS). The program focus is developing commercial and personal skills

---

[11] https://www.viwala.com/home.
[12] Pro Mujer, 2019.

among entrepreneurs, in addition to increasing awareness of gender-based violence prevention and detection. The program ended January 31, 2020, reaching a total of 2,075 women and 486 men in low-income communities of Hidalgo and Puebla, where Pro Mujer operates.

As part of its digital transformation, Pro Mujer launched a digital wallet system (*Billetera Movil*) in Nicaragua and implemented a new core banking system and an enterprise resource planning (ERP) for its managerial processes, to better track its financial and operational activities.

PRO MUJER'S GENDER LENS INVESTING AND SCORECARD

GLI can have different definitions to different audiences, along with many scorecards and sets of indicators. This leads to three main problems. The first is that investors are confused about how to apply a gender lens in their investing selection process. The second is the risk of applying a simplistic approach where the easiest Environmental, Social, and Governance (ESG)[13] compliance boxes are ticked, in the belief that having one woman on the company's board is enough to tackle this issue. This leads to the third problem, which is the risk of "pinkwashing."[14] There is, consequently, the need to consolidate definitions and delimit the taxonomy.

GLI definitions abound and differ in their comprehensiveness. For the International Development Bank (IDB Invest), GLI "includes investment strategies in private markets (private debt, private equity, seed, angel, and venture capital) as well as within public markets (public equities, fixed income). GLI is a pro-active, intentional investment strategy that crosses

---

[13]ESG is a new term in capital markets used by investors to measure and evaluate corporate policy, process, and performance related to environmental, social, and governance issues that can lead to stronger, resilient financial performance. Like intangible capital, ESG factors are a subset of performance indicators, which include sustainable, ethical, and corporate governance issues, such as measuring and managing the company's carbon footprint, water, waste, energy, as well as employee turnover, satisfaction, and pay ratios, and ensuring there are systems in place to ensure accountability (Financial Times 2020). While some ESG assessments primarily focus on the policies or processes of a company, other ESG assessments measure the results and performance, including products and services (Herman 2010), such as the HIP (Human Impact + Profit) Investor Ratings (www .HIPinvestor.com).

[14]"Pinkwashing" refers to the exploitation of marginalized sexual identities to promote insidious agendas. In recognizing and countering its premises, individuals may reclaim appropriated movements, reorienting them toward meaningful, collective social change (Farag 2019).

asset classes and strategies" (Buckland et al. 2019, p. 20). In 2017, the Global Impact Investing Network (GIIN) launched the Gender Lens Investing Initiative[15] with the objective of collecting information and serving as a knowledge hub for Impact Investing discussions related to GLI. The GIIN developed a comprehensive definition for GLI that has been widely adopted and is further described in Box 9.1.

Box 9.1 Gender Lens Investing Categories, as Defined by the Global Impact Investing Initiative

GLI comprises two broad categories:

1. Investing with the intent to address gender issues or promote gender equity, including:
   - Investing in women-owned or women-led enterprises
   - Investing in enterprises that promote workplace equity
   - Investing in enterprises that offer products or services that substantially improve the lives of women and girls
2. Investing with the following approaches to inform investment decisions:
   - A process that focuses on gender, from pre-investment activities (e.g., sourcing and due diligence) to post-deal monitoring (e.g., strategic advisory, IPO, M&A, exiting)
   - A strategy that examines, with respect to the investees' enterprises:
   - The vision or mission to address gender issues
   - The organizational structure, culture, internal policies, and workplace environment
   - The use of data and metrics for the gender-equitable management of performance and to incentivize behavioral change and accountability
   - How financial and human resources signify overall commitment to gender equality

Source: GIIN (2017).

---

[15]More information at https://thegiin.org/gender-lens-investing-initiative.

ILU WOMEN'S EMPOWERMENT FUND GLI SCORECARD

Pro Mujer defines GLI as "an investment that generates financial returns while at the same time advancing gender equality." The Ilu Women's Empowerment Scorecard, developed collaboratively by Pro Mujer and Deetken Impact, aims to be a core tool for monitoring, evaluation, decision-making, and reporting. This GLI scorecard, while still a work in progress, enables the Ilu Women's Empowerment Fund to assess a company's eligibility for gender-focused investing and supports the identification of gaps, planning, follow-up improvements, target setting, and results planning.

The scorecard is multidimensional and includes four pillars based on different gender lenses, which are given an equal weight: (i) Leadership and Governance, (ii) Women Served, (iii) Value Chain Equity and Advocacy, (iv) Workplace Equity (see Figure 9.2).

What differs in the case of this scorecard is the purpose it serves and the methodology behind it. It is important to mention that the scorecard should not be a mere self-assessment, but rather one element in a process that does justice to the complexity of addressing issues like gender bias and inclusion. Its main objectives are three-fold. First, it is a tool to scan a company's potential for gender equality through its governance structure and the way the venture does (or does not) develop products and services for women and girls. Second, after companies have been selected, the picture provided by the scorecard informs the firm's development plans and is attached to the investing schedule. And third, it provides a series of data and metrics tracking leading to a historical database to provide evidence of progress over time.

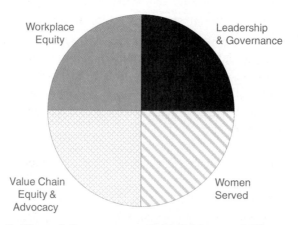

FIGURE 9.2 Ilu Women's Empowerment Fund GLI Scorecard Pillars. *Source:* Interviews with Pro Mujer and Deetken Impact (2020).

Each of these pillars comprises different criteria and guiding questions to better exemplify their meaning and support the assessment of organizations applying them. Table 9.1 shows a simplified version of the scorecard.

Besides evaluating the level of alignment and commitment to gender inclusion and empowerment, the scorecard aims to measure companies' *status quo* at the beginning of the investment process. The scorecard then serves as a tool in the development of a plan to overcome weaker scores and to measure progress.

In a "practice what you preach" mode, Pro Mujer performed its own assessment using this GLI scorecard. For Pillar 1: Leadership and Governance, Pro Mujer scored high, with 71% of women in C-Suite and 56% in middle management positions. Also, from a Governance perspective, there is a formal commitment to gender equality and women's empowerment, as these issues are central to the organization's existence.

For Pillar 2: Women Served, Pro Mujer provides an ongoing self-analysis about how women are considered as a relevant target group. As women are the primary group of clients that aligns with the mission, there is additional focus on identifying and serving the changing financing demands of low-income women. This would also involve complementary needs like access to health care and education and include how to provide even more customized products and services, like the newly developed digital wallet, or engaging with impact investing partners to develop mezzanine investing options.

Pillar 3: Value Chain Equity and Advocacy intends to create a domino effect in the opening of spaces for women entrepreneurs that leads to the provision of business opportunities in support of economic growth. Pro Mujer undertook initiatives to support gender-sensitive enterprises, like Ilu Women's Empowerment Fund with Deetken Impact. A key milestone includes valuing the businesses that integrate women entrepreneurs in their value chain.

For gender equity advocacy, at Pro Mujer this is delivered through financial and nonfinancial support to civil society organizations working to empower women and girls, or partnerships with local or global organizations, or teaming up with other companies working on gender equality and women's empowerment.

For Pillar 4: Workplace Equity, Pro Mujer assessed its working environment and employment structures and found a lack of women professionals in information technology, which was a male-dominant area. Pro Mujer devoted resources to developing a strategy to hire and train more women in technology, as well as to create a mid-management level to allow professionals to grow in this career path.

TABLE 9.1   Ilu Women's Empowerment GLI Scorecard Lens and Criteria.

Criteria	Guiding Questions
PILLAR 1. Leadership and Governance	
A. Leadership	Is the business women led?
B. Ownership and Control	Is the business women-owned? What % of board are women?
C. Governance	Does the governance environment support gender equality and women's empowerment?
PILLAR 2. Women Served	
A. Client Diversity	Are the business's clients primarily women?
B. Production & Marketing	Has the business developed a strategy that centers the differentiated needs of women clients, either stand-alone or clearly included in a broader strategy?
C. Access to Finance	Does the business include gender considerations and gender barriers in its financial inclusion activities?
	Does the business offer nonfinancial services that are specific to women and girls?
PILLAR 3. Value Chain Equity and Advocacy	
A. Value Chain Equity	Does the business take proactive steps in procurement to expand relationships with women or women-led businesses in the value chain and when contracting vendors?
B. Advocacy	Does the business pursue specific activities or have specific objectives to generate social impact by redressing gender inequalities in the broader community or value chain in which it works?
PILLAR 4. Workplace Equity	
A. Equal Pay	Does the business have a visible and actionable nondiscrimination and equal opportunity policy in writing, either stand-alone or clearly included in a broader corporate policy?
B. Workforce Participation	Does the business take proactive steps to recruit, promote, and/or retain women?
C. Workplace Environment	Does the business promote an inclusive work environment that supports gender equality in the workplace?

Source: Authors, and interviews with Deetken Impact.

Although most findings proved positive, challenges were identified by this exercise, which the organization acknowledged.

By applying the scorecard, Pro Mujer not only confirmed that there is more work to be done but also learned specifically which gaps to address. With three decades working to address the needs of women in Latin America, Pro Mujer is aware that gender equality is a continuous effort to be undertaken. As a reference organization, Pro Mujer is constantly checking market requirements and adapting its products and services to them.

UNITE TO CONQUER: THE CRUCIAL ROLE OF PARTNERSHIPS FOR LEVERAGING CATALYTIC CAPITAL FOR GENDER LENS INVESTING IN LATIN AMERICA

Catalytic[16] financial and social capital have an important role to play in bridging the sustainable development goals (SDGs) gaps. Programs were created by governments and development finance institutions (DFIs) to incentivize and enable organizations to allocate resources effectively to bridge the gender gap. Examples include the 2X Challenge Financing for Women, which relies on the commitment of the G7 and other 12 DFIs to collectively mobilize USD $2.5 billion in committed capital to provide women in developing-country markets including South Asia, East Asia and Pacific, Africa, Middle East and North Africa, Eastern Europe, and Latin America and the Caribbean with improved access to leadership opportunities, quality employment, finance, enterprise support, and products and services that enhance economic participation and access.[17] To be eligible for the 2X investment, organizations and funds need to fulfill at least one of their four direct criteria (Figure 9.3). For each criterion, a minimum target threshold has been predefined, varying according to different business sectors. The 2X Challenge foresees both direct and indirect investment. For indirect investments to qualify (meaning those done through financial intermediaries), they need to meet one of the direct 2X criteria. "For instance,

[16] According to the MacArthur Foundation, catalytic capital serves the purpose of unlocking conventional investment in several ways: (i) help in the development of new and innovative products and business models; (ii) help demonstrate that hard-to-reach geographies and populations most in need are, in fact, investable; (iii) help establish a track record for new and diverse managers; and (iv) can aid companies to scale to a level appropriate for conventional investment.

[17] More information about the 2X Challenge is available at https://www.2xchallenge.org/.

Sector-Specific Thresholds

2.A Women in Senior Management*

Grp.	Sector	%
Low	Infrastructure, Power, Telecoms	20%
Mid	Financial Services, Manufacturing	25%
	Agribusiness & Food, Professional Services, Consumer Services	
High	Healthcare, Eduction	30%

3.A Women in the Workforce*

Grp.	Sector	%
Low	Infrastructure, Power, Telecoms	30%
Mid	Financial Services, Manufacturing – Heavy, Agribusiness & Food, Professional Services	40%
High	Healthcare, Eduction, Consumer Services, Manufacturing – Light[3]	50%

*Room for judgement: Investees in unique sectors or geographies may require case-by-case consideration.

		Criteria	Threshold
Direct Criteria	**1** Entrepreneurship	1A. Share of woman ownership	51%
		OR	
		1B. Business founded by a woman	Yes/No
		OR	
	2 Leadership	2A. Share of woman in senior management[1]	20–30%[2]
		OR	
		2B. Share of woman on the Board or IO	30%
		OR	
	3 Employment	3A. Share of woman in the workfore[1]	30–50%[2]
		AND	
		3B. One "quality" indicator beyond compliance	Yes/No
		OR	
	4 Consumption	4. Product or service specifically or disproportionately benefit woman	Yes/No
		OR	
Indirect	**5** Investments through Financial Intermediaries[3]	*On-Lending facilities: Percent of the DFI loan proceeds supporting businesses that meet direct criteria[1]*	30%
		Funds: Percent of portfolio companies that meet the direct criteria.[1]	30%

FIGURE 9.3 2X Challenge Financing for Women Criteria. *Source:* Courtesy OECD (2019).

the financial intermediary would qualify if 51% women-owned, if 30% of the investment committee is women, if banks prioritize women in their portfolio (e.g., a fund focuses on investing in women-owned businesses, or a bank offers financing product tailored for female clients)" (2X Challenge Criteria 2018, p. 3).

Ilu Women's Empowerment Fund (IWEF) was selected by DFC as one of its 2X Women's Initiative investments, due to its focus on gender-smart investment management and emphasis on supporting companies that advance women's economic empowerment.

IWEF was established in 2019 by Pro Mujer and Deetken Impact. IWEF makes debt investments of USD $1 million to USD $3 million in businesses that are aligned with the criteria of the 2X Women's Initiative. As part of its gender-smart investment management strategy, IWEF has implemented a gender-smart scorecard to assess and monitor portfolio companies "Over time, the fund's goal is to seek ways to encourage portfolio companies to advance gender-smart business practices through structured feedback, CEO-level commitments or tailored engagement programs" (Alexa Blain, Deetken Impact). Investors in the Ilu Women's Empowerment Fund include the US International Development Finance Corporation (DFC, formerly OPIC), Vancity Credit Union, Cooperativa ABACO, Canadian foundations, family offices, and individuals. DFC has committed USD $10 million of senior debt financing to the fund. DFC's investment will advance its 2X Women's Initiative, which has catalyzed more than USD $1 billion in capital to empower women in developing countries around the world (see Box 9.2).

Box 9.2 Ilu Women's Empowerment Fund

The Ilu Women's Empowerment Fund is a joint venture between Pro Mujer and Deetken Impact established in 2019. It makes senior and subordinated debt investments in Latin America and the Caribbean of USD $1 million to USD $3 million. The target fund size is USD $35 million, with USD $25 million committed and USD $15 million deployed. After successfully closing the first fundraising round from catalytic investors, Deetken Impact and Pro Mujer plan to raise a second round of another USD $10 million. The fund focuses on high-impact businesses that promote women's economic empowerment and entrepreneurship in Latin America and the Caribbean. It typically invests with a term of three to five years for senior debt and five to seven years for subordinated

(continued)

(continued)

debt. Portfolio investments include financial institutions that provide integrated and thoughtfully designed services for low-income women including access to health care, educational loans, financial services, and technical assistance, as well as gender-smart investments in renewable energy, affordable housing, and social enterprise. The fund's current portfolio includes 13 companies across Latin America and the Caribbean. The gender-smart investment management process begins with a screening questionnaire for potential investees, which considers the business through four gender lenses in Table 9.1. Results are reviewed by the fund's Gender Smart Subcommittee, which advises the Investment Committee. Opportunities that pass this screening phase proceed to due diligence, during which a comprehensive gender-smart scorecard is used to evaluate the portfolio of selected companies based on 33 gender factors, and to measure performance over time. Scorecard factors are also aligned with the SDGs and the IRIS+ Core Metrics for GLI. In addition to its use during selection and due diligence, the scorecard is used to identify leading practices and opportunities within the portfolio.

Source: Interviews with Ilu Women's Empowerment Fund, Deetken Impact, and Pro Mujer.

One of the companies the Ilu Women's Empowerment Fund invested in is PISCIS, a sustainable trout farming and processing industry founded in Peru in 1978 with processing facilities in Quichuay (Huancayo) and in Characas (Puno). PISCIS began exporting trout from Lake Titicaca in 1981, initially to Sweden and today to a variety of countries. The PISCIS sustainable trout farming business provides workplace equity to over 70% of women employees at their fish processing plant in southern Peru. Ilu Fund invested CAD $1 million as senior debt.

Another GLI aligned initiative is VIWALA, a debt instrument whose uniqueness lies in the fact that the loan payback is tied to a startup's monthly revenue along a time frame of 36 months, with the interest rate defined according to the business sector and the startups' financial health. VIWALA was established by New Ventures Group (NVG), with the support from USAID and in a partnership with Pro Mujer. The overarching goal of VIWALA is to finance early-stage SMEs with significant social and/or environmental impact in Mexico, offering them a new flexible easy-to-access financing mechanism. VIWALA will channel a significant portion of their investments to high-impact businesses that are women-led and/or focus on gender impact. Through the VIWALA's example, the group aspires to pave the way for further GLI throughout Latin America. In 2019, of the 130 social entrepreneurs who were identified and accelerated, 30 entrepreneurs were trained on financials, of which eight women-led entrepreneurs were funded through VIWALA.

Box 9.3 VIWALA's Seed Capital

VIWALA is a non-banking financial institution with an innovative loan instrument where the payback is attached to a start-up's revenues. VIWALA is a partnership between Pro Mujer and New Ventures Mexico and has attracted investment of USD $1.2 million with USAID and a Mexican family office. The target group are women entrepreneurs with startups with an annual income from USD $100,000 to USD $1 million. Investments range from USD $30,000 and USD $250,000 with the initial geographic focus being Mexico.

The selected startups go through a process of defining interest rates according to their business segment potential risk. The repayment terms are defined according to the companies' capacity to pay and based on their monthly revenues along a time span of 36 months.

According to VIWALA's Managing Director, Karla Gallardo: "Most of the companies knocking at the door are men-led. If we want to invest in women, we must search for them." For this reason, it is starting a series of Readiness Workshops, covering topics like the relevance of gender empowerment for business, as well as managerial training about smart money and financial statements.

Source: Interview with VIWALA.

KEY LEARNINGS AND RECOMMENDATIONS

This chapter provides an overview of the front-line experience of Pro Mujer and its key partners in Latin America, looking at how Pro Mujer envisioned change and put it into practice with the introduction of new financial services solutions to convey its mission, while at the same time being aware of the changing needs of women entrepreneurs in a large region.

Key insights were amassed based on Pro Mujer's 30-year journey in financial inclusion and GLI. Table 9.2 brings together these key learnings,

TABLE 9.2 Pro Mujer's Key Learnings and Recommendations.

Dimensions	Learnings	Recommendations
Detailed Knowledge of the Context	A deep understanding of the regional context and the target group is required. In Latin America, for example, there is high level of business informality, ranging between 30% and 60%, depending on the country and city. This requires creative financing guarantees. In addition, it is necessary to follow up the capital needs of women entrepreneurs closely.	Analyze the gender regional context through contextual analysis tools. Get to know your target group in-depth; otherwise, look for a partner with deep understanding of the region and target group. Rank your target groups by importance according to key characteristics. Assess the types of financing instruments you are offering and its suitability to each target group, if needed, by contracting formal evaluations or impact assessments.
Leadership and Organizational Culture	The organizational structure and corporate culture should be assessed for feasibility and capacity, along with the ability for including GLI in a portfolio that is primarily of microloans.	Identify who are the stakeholders possibly backing the new GLI strategy and those against.[18] Mitigate risks and potential internal opposition to GLI. Maintain a culture of permanent dialogue and regular meetings.

[18] A reference for context analysis is the IFC Stakeholder Identification and Analysis available at https://www.ifc.org/wps/wcm/connect/e7705f54-6cd2-44b8-87fb-609a87a3f4a9/PartOne_StakeholderIdentification.pdf?MOD=AJPERES&CVID=jqetJIm.

Planning/ Self-assessment	One important part of the planning was the design of the five-year action plan, which looked at the customer needs (for microloans), SMEs requirements for growth, digital trends, as well as required financial capital and partnerships to leverage GLI inside out. The development of a GLI scorecard and its use for Pro Mujer's own self-assessment proved to be a valid tool to spot the non-obvious gaps that needed to be improved to strengthen its positioning in GLI.	Do your homework first: assess your company/fund gender positioning and previous performance as to gender before committing to or choosing a GLI approach. Ask: Have you assessed what is the gender and ethnicity ratio of your investment committee? Who are your limited partners (LP)? Are there women in decision-making positions? Choose and apply a suitable GLI tool to design an action plan.[19] Work on your overall theory of change or your specific gender theory of change.[20,21] After developing an action plan, develop your own or apply an existing GLI scorecard to guide you through the main action plan issues of your organization.

(continued)

---

[19]The Criterion Institute has an open-source planning tool available at https://criterioninstitute.org/resources/gender-lens-investing-tool-designing-an-action-plan.
[20]For more information about how to develop a theory of change, please refer to https://www.triodos-im.com/knowledge-centre/theory-of-change.
[21]For examples of how women-led investment advisors are "changing the face of finance" to include more women, see Chapter 7, "Investing with a Gender Lens: Uncovering Alpha Previously Overlooked," by Kristin Hull.

TABLE 9.2 *(continued)*

Dimensions	Learnings	Recommendations
Required Initial investment	Identify and carefully weigh the benefits versus the cost to your organization or fund for focusing on gender empowerment. Be aware that there are investments associated with the required change management for an organization or fund to become aligned with GLI. This includes, for example, an upfront investment for aligning the portfolio with a GLI strategy. Assess the tangible and intangible costs (resources and time) while developing the GLI strategy. In the long run, the investments toward a GLI strategy and portfolio will pay for themselves.	Compute tangible and the intangible costs (resources and time) of the GLI strategy and financially assess these. Respond to "so what" types of questions. Set clear objectives and intentions from the GLI strategy.
Gender Architecture and Capacities	It is extremely important to make sure that a gender inclusive strategy does not turn out to be gender exclusive. The strategy is not just about women and girls. Men and boys must also be engaged; otherwise, the richness of diversity will be lost, and the ability to work together across genders, or, worse, the same mistakes of a male-dominant economy and society will be repeated.	Work on new ideas of gender and masculinity in the sense of integrating men and boys in all that relates to gender empowerment and investing. Be inclusive, not exclusive. Train and engage your front-line team to understand the GLI products and how they co-relate with the microloan experience and portfolio. Develop a career plan with a gender lens in the organization.[22] Increase the number of women in leading positions.

---

[22]The UN Global Compact, UN Women, IDB Invest, and IDB Lab developed a tool to support companies in the process to include more women in the workforce as well as in leading positions—the Women's Empowerment Principles Gap Analysis Tool—from Principles to Practice, available at https://weps-gapanalysis.org/about-the-tool/.

Information Technology tools in the digital era	With the rise of fintech,[23] and based on Latin America's expected mobile penetration rate of 73% in 2025, the search for digital solutions is a must, whether for accessing credit or for health care and educational purposes. Pro Mujer has been working on solutions for digital wallet, a chatbot for health care services, as well as intensifying the use of social media channels. Pro Mujer has also been partnering with organizations like CISCO to build a training course for digital capacity building of its customers and internal teams.	Do not neglect the ongoing and foreseen changes for a more digital economy and society, which has been accelerated by the COVID-19 lockdowns and as means to reduce costs and reach out to excluded target groups. Partner with organizations that can offer the digital tools that fit the needs of your target group and that are designed for your organization's information technology state and structures.
Scorecard	The process of defining a GLI scorecard was intense in the sense of devising a set of indicators based on existing references, while at the same time considering the specific needs for the Ilu Fund's GLI investing strategy. Its implementation involved a preliminary (testing) phase in which Pro Mujer and Deetken Impact used the scorecard for its own assessment only before rolling it out to prospective investable SMEs.	To provide an alignment and comparability among GLI initiatives, funds, companies, and entrepreneurs could start by considering some of the already available gender scorecards[24] and adapt it according to the type of businesses.

(continued)

---

[23]See Chapter 30, "Fintech for Impact: How Can Financial Innovation Advance Inclusion?," by Frederic de Mariz.

[24]An example of GLI scorecards includes the SEAF Gender Equality Scorecard, which is based on six gender vectors, available at https://www.seaf.com/inclusive-sustainable-development-through-gender-equality/.

TABLE 9.2 *(continued)*

Dimensions	Learnings	Recommendations
Results measurement over time	Ongoing self-assessment tools are key for monitoring performance and self-checks (for raising red flags). Intended results must be compared with achieved results regularly. Regular benchmarks with other companies in the same segment are especially useful. There are several advantages of reporting impact publicly.	Set GLI metrics from the start (baseline) and measure how they evolve over time. Apply a close monitoring of performance indicators over time, of immediate, intermediate results, and impacts. Constantly ask the question and act upon it: Are we creating the right conditions to allow our investee companies to become gender equality organizations and leaders? Develop a culture of reporting impact, both as part of the follow-up meetings between investors and investees, as well as a sort of open-source information that will allow comparison between different GLI investors (benchmark), so as to provide a knowledge base to support this sector's growth.
Partnering	Partnering is a key element in providing the right structures to leverage catalytic capital	Partner with organizations that are highly experienced in the area of gender lens financial services. These partners should be chosen if they know the language, the final customer needs, and how to approach them. There is a substantial learning when working with the right organizations, which can save time and get the company ahead of the market and competitors faster. The general rule for setting good partnerships includes complementary experiences and capabilities to avoid duplicating efforts; values' alignment; transparency; predefined agreements to allow exiting the partnership comfortably.

Source: Authors (2020).

which are combined with recommendations specifically related to the process of including GLI in Pro Mujer's financial services portfolio. These can be particularly useful not only for financing organizations aiming to apply GLI, but also for entrepreneurs who are developing products and services for women and girls, as well as women entrepreneurs requiring business credit or investment.

THE WAY AHEAD

Will VC funds or startups always need a white-haired man on their boards to be taken seriously? When men do the pitching, they can frequently access millions more than women. Is this just the case of a *männlich* language? Or is it more to do with stereotyping women in business?

Impact Investing and GLI cannot expand if the old framework that has been ruling investing systems continues to be applied in the same manner. However, the transformation toward a more gender-inclusive society can happen more naturally. For that, in-depth intrinsic change is required. This goes from involving more women in leadership positions in private equity funds, to better preparing women-oriented startups and the links of their value chains. In addition, it is necessary to better educate all, including men and boys, to be more gender aware.

Top women executives with decision-making power are necessary to balance power and promote new work environments in their own organizations. Changes in companies might include, for instance, having two co-CEOs (to allow for a female CEO), and the development of programs and strategies for mentoring women and creating middle-management positions specifically for women in professional areas where female employees are more uncommon, looking more closely into the gender equality policies in place, among others.

Fostering GLI is not a simple matter, and a single tool will not provide the solution. Many tools are required to refurbish an old building or to build a new architecture or style. In recent years, there has been a growing amount of capital flowing fast, moving GLI from an investment niche to a multi-billion-dollar financing area. But scaling needs to be done responsibly.

Incentives, regulations, and the rule of law play a key role in the way business is done by enforcing practices that can directly and positively impact women. Governments need to be engaged to provide the right incentives and tax exemptions to facilitate and accelerate the change in old business practices, in addition to implementing more stringent regulations, enacting more gender-equal rule of law, and penalizing gender violence and femicide. Furthermore, GLI methodologies must also be used to generate valuable data to display less obvious inequalities. Exposing biases and educating through a gender perspective can generate a different mindset and propel structural change for future generations.

Pro Mujer's case shows these achievements are possible and at hand. By promoting gender equality for decades, Pro Mujer has enabled opportunities for women seeking to thrive. The organization is leveraging its community and online spaces to share information and build upon its learnings through data and analysis, to provide guidance to others to follow on its path. Those interested in embarking in GLI do not need to be experts in this field, but rather what they need to possess is the intentionality and commitment to want to do it. Any impact investor can purposefully accomplish gender-sensitive results and incorporate gender-balanced programs and criteria by keeping an open mind and by partnering with organizations that can give the necessary inspiration, support, and tools to make gender equality a reality.

REFERENCES

Abouzahr, K., Taplett, F., Krentz, M., et al. (2018). Why Women-Owned Startups Are a Better Bet. *Boston Consulting Group*. Boston Consulting Group (6 June). https://www.bcg.com/en-pt/publications/2018/why-women-owned-startups-are-better-bet.aspx (accessed 20 March 2020).

Adams, R., Barber, B., and Odean, T. (2016). Family, Values, and Women in Finance (1 September) https://ssrn.com/abstract=2827952 (accessed 12 February 2020).

Biegel, S., Hunt., S., and Kuhlman, S. (2019). Project Sage: Tracking Venture Capital with Gender Lens. https://socialimpact.wharton.upenn.edu/research-reports/reports-2/project-sage-2/https://socialimpact.wharton.upenn.edu/research-reports/reports-2/project-sage-2/ (accessed 10 March 2020).

Buckland, L., Cordobés, M., Oueda, C., et al. (2019). Gender Lens Investing: How Finance Can Accelerate Gender Equality in Latin America and the Caribbean. IDB Invest (March).

Da Paz, M., and Moura, N. (2019). Mulheres na América Latina: o perfil das presidentes Latino-Americanas. Revista eletrônica da Estácio Recife. https://reer .emnuvens.com.br/reer/article/view/341/150 (accessed 29 January 2020).

Deetken (2019). *Deetken Annual Report* 2019. https://deetkenimpact.com (accessed 2 March 2020).

D'Espallier, B., Guérin, I., and Mersland, R. (2011). Women and Repayment in Microfinance: A Global Analysis. *World Development* 39(5): 758-772 (May 2011). https://doi.org/10.1016/j.worlddev.2010.10.008.

Farag, E. (2019). Feminism 101: What Is Pinkwashing? *FEM News* (2 March). https://femmagazine.com/feminism-101-what-is-pinkwashing/ (accessed 10 March 2020).

Economist (2020). The violet tide: Mexico's new feminist wave. *Economist* (5 March 2020). https://www.economist.com/the-americas/2020/03/05/mexicos-new-feminist-wave.

Foundation Center (2018). U.S. Foundation Funding for Latin America, 2014–2015, with additional analysis on Central America. https://www.issuelab.org/resources/31177/31177.pdf (accessed 10 March 2020).

GIIN (2017). Gender Lens Investing Initiative. Global Impact Investing Network. https://thegiin.org/gender-lens-investing-initiative (accessed 4 March 2020).

Herman, R. Paul (2010). *The HIP Investor: Make Bigger Profits by Building a Better World*. Hoboken, NJ: John Wiley & Sons.

IFC (2017). MSME Finance Gap: Assessment of the shortfalls and opportunities in financing micro, small and medium enterprises in emerging markets. International Finance Corporation. World Bank Group. https://www.ifc.org/wps/wcm/connect/03522e90-a13d-4a02-87cd-9ee9a297b311/121264-WP-PUBLIC-MSMEReportFINAL.pdf?MOD=AJPERES&CVID=m5SwAQA (accessed 26 March 2020).

IFC (2019). Moving Toward Gender Balance in Private Equity and Venture Capital. International Finance Corporation, World Bank Group. https://www.ifc.org/wps/wcm/connect/79e641c9-824f-4bd8-9f1c-00579862fed3/Moving+Toward+Gender+Balance+Final_3_22.pdf?MOD=AJPERES&CVID=mCBJFra (accessed 20 April 2020).

Lavca Association for Private Capital Investment in Latin America (2019). Women Investing in Latin America. https://lavca.org/vc/women-investing-latin-american-vc-decision-makers (accessed 12 March 2020).

McKinsey Global Institute (2015). How advancing women's equality can add $12 trillion to global growth. https://www.mckinsey.com/featured-insights/employment-and-growth/how-advancing-womens-equality-can-add-12-trillion-to-global-growth (accessed 6 March 2020).

OECD (2019). *Strengthening the gender dimension of aid for trade*. Paris. http://www.oecd.org/dac/Aid-for-trade-Strengthening-Gender-DImension.pdf (accessed 29 April 2020).

Pro Mujer (2017). *Pro Mujer Annual Report* 2017. https://promujer.org/get-know-us/financial-reports (accessed 29 January 2020).

Pro Mujer (2018). *Pro Mujer Annual Report* 2018. https://promujer.org/get-know-us/financial-reports (accessed 29 January 2020).

Pro Mujer (2019). *Pro Mujer Annual Report,* 2019. https://promujer.org/get-know-us/financial-reports (accessed 29 January 2020).

Quinlan, J., and VanderBrug, J. (2017). *Gender Lens Investing: Uncovering Opportunities for Growth, Returns and Impact.* Hoboken, NJ: John Wiley & Sons.

Silva, V. (2019). 8 Statistics and Facts about Women in STEM. Built by Me, STEM Learning News (20 April). https://www.builtbyme.com/statistics-facts-women-in-stem/ (accessed 6 April 2020).

UNESCO (2017). Gender Lens Investing: How Finance Can Accelerate Gender Equality in Latin America and the Caribbean. United Nations Educational, Scientific and Cultural Organization. https://unesdoc.unesco.org/ark:/48223/pf0000253479 (accessed 12 March 2020).

Value for Women (2019). A Landscape Report: Impact Investing with a Gender Lens in Latin America. https://v4w.org/ (accessed 28 March 2020).

Wigglesworth, R. (2020). The ESG revolution is widening gaps between winners and losers. *Financial Times* (3 February 2020).

Wilhelm, A. (2019). The Slow Progress of Women in Venture. Crunchbase News (14 February) https://news.crunchbase.com/news/the-slow-progress-of-women-in-venture/ (accessed 12 March 2020).

Woetzel, J., Madgavkar, A., Ellingrud, K., et al. (2015). How advancing women's equality can add $12 trillion to global growth. McKinsey Global Initiative. https://www.mckinsey.com/featured-insights/employment-and-growth/how-advancing-womens-equality-can-add-12-trillion-to-global-growth (accessed 3 March 2020).

World Economic Forum (2019). *Gender Gap Annual Report* 2020. https://www.weforum.org/reports/gender-gap-2020-report-100-years-pay-equality (accessed 10 March 2020).

CHAPTER 10

Inclusive Investing: Impact Meets Diversity, Equity, and Inclusion

Julianne Zimmerman, MSci, Edward Dugger III, MPA-UP, and Shijiro Ochirbat, MBA, MPA

Abstract

During the 2010s decade, as gender lens investing (GLI) took root and the sustainable development goals (SDGs) became a standard frame of reference for Impact Investing, various entities pointed to the moral and economic hazards—and associated financial opportunity—posed by extreme hyper-concentration of finance in an overwhelmingly white, cisgendered, male minority. Yet just as Impact Investing writ large is still often misperceived as an asset class or concessionary return category, investing with a racial, social, or economic justice, or diversity, equity, and inclusion (DEI) lens ("Inclusive Investing" or "DEI investing") is frequently misconstrued as a concessionary or philanthropic asset class, or worse, a goodwill gesture. In actuality, Inclusive Investing is an asset-class-agnostic approach to capturing financial benefits and impacts of diversity, equity, and inclusion in a portfolio, via manager selection, investment strategy, portfolio construction, or intentional and unintentional operational outcomes. Inclusion lenses thus provide investors insight into otherwise obscured risks and illuminate otherwise unseen opportunities. Capital allocators can define race, ethnicity, gender, or other Inclusive Investing strategies as specific or as broad as they wish, across return objectives, impact goals, and geographies. Inclusive Investing is not even new: religious and community investing roots long predate both the emergence of Impact Investing and the formulation of DEI standards. This chapter posits one possible framework that can be utilized by new Inclusive Investors to formulate and embark upon an Inclusive Investing discipline. The historical example of Inclusive Investing pioneer UNC Ventures (UNCV) illustrates some kinds of financial and impact outcomes inclusive investors can target and achieve.

Keywords

DEI; Diversity; Equity; Equality; Inclusion; Inclusive Investing; Impact Investing; Racial Equity; Gender Lens Investing; Social Equity; Gender Equity; Sustainable Development Goals; LGBTQ

INTRODUCTION: "DEI" IS NOT AN ASSET CLASS

In the most pragmatic terms, investing for racial, social, gender, or other equity objectives ("DEI investing" or "Inclusive Investing") may be defined simply as: *systematically applying material investment considerations that are causally connected to the intentional and unintentional ways in which specific populations of people are included in, excluded from, or impacted by a given investment practice.* Such considerations include, but are not limited to, capital hyper-concentration, investment risk, and market opportunity, as well as economic, environmental, or other impacts.

Financial return objectives for Inclusive Investing range from wholly concessionary to market-leading, and may span asset classes, markets, geographies, and jurisdictions. Inclusive Investing impact objectives may likewise be defined with respect to immediate or multi-year time horizons, local or global reach, single or multiple populations, or other scopes, and may be readily quantifiable or challenging to render in concrete terms. Like other Impact Investing disciplines, Inclusive Investing is not any one kind of investment instrument but rather a way of approaching investing across categories.

Although the parlance of Impact Investing has emerged in the twenty-first century, Impact Investing and Inclusive Investing have ancient antecedents. For as long as investing has been practiced in one form or another, investors have applied a wide range of perspectives to determine which propositions were acceptable financially as well as legally, morally, socially, and/or ethically. Jewish and Muslim traditions include specific rules for acceptable financial practices that have been in continuous interpretation and application for millennia.[1] In the eighteenth century, religious leaders in the United States and Great Britain began to articulate concrete criteria for rejecting investments that harmed or enslaved other persons, formally declaring such practices to be fundamentally at odds with adherents' belief in human dignity.[2]

In the middle of the twentieth century, the prevailing wisdom and practice in capital markets moved increasingly in the opposite direction, widely solidifying around an extreme of the pendulum swing codified by Milton Friedman (Friedman 1970). In the late twentieth and early twenty-first century, momentum has begun to swing toward a more balanced viewpoint, nudged in that direction by a variety of friendly and not-so-friendly dissenters to the Friedman position.[3] Globally, state pension funds such as the Norwegian Pension Fund[4] have explicitly linked sustainability, ESG, and alignment with the sustainable development goals (SDGs) to their fiduciary duty and return generation strategies. In 2019, the US-based Business Roundtable issued a public statement committing the 181 signatories to "lead their companies for the benefit of all stakeholders—customers, employees, suppliers, communities and shareholders."[5]

All the while, a variety of faith-based investors including the Religious Society of Friends (Quakers),[6] several orders of Catholic nuns (Walsh 2018), the Aga Khan Network (Aga Khan Development Network 2020), and others have persisted in investing intentionally for both financial return and social integrity objectives. In recent years, ecumenical associations, such as Interfaith Center on Corporate Responsibility (ICCR 2020), have convened

---

[1] See. for example, Troster (2014), Chitillapaly (2016), and Lumberg (2017).

[2] See, for example, http://nationalhumanitiescenter.org/tserve/nineteen/nkeyinfo/ama brel.htm.

[3] See, for example, Denning (2013), Kenzie (2017), and Posner (2019).

[4] See, for example, https://www.nbim.no/en/the-fund/responsible-investment/.

[5] For more information, see https://www.businessroundtable.org/business-roundtable-redefines-the-purpose-of-a-corporation-to-promote-an-economy-that-serves-all-americans.

[6] See, for example, Friends Fiduciary (2018) and Quakers in Britain (2020).

faith-based and secular capital allocators to exchange intelligence, share practices, and collaborate on investments seeking both financial return and positive social change.

As various Impact Investing schema have emerged over the past few decades—including socially responsible investing (SRI); environmental, social, and governance (ESG) practices; gender lens investing (GLI); and others—so too have social enterprises, social impact and green bonds, hybrid and blended capital, negative and positive screen mutual funds and exchange traded funds (ETFs), donor advised funds (DAFs), opportunity zone (OZ) funds, and a host of other means to deploy capital in service of those schema. These various approaches, methods, and instruments enable impact-minded investors to affect a full spectrum of financial return and impact objectives. Moreover, in response to rising investor demand and competition for those investors' assets, several of the world's largest asset managers—including Blackstone, Goldman Sachs, and others—have launched new Impact Investing initiatives and/or reclassified existing assets under Impact Investing headings.

Thus, contrary to the frequently voiced complaint that there are no products available to meet impact investors' demands, the reality is that the growing profusion of available products poses practical challenges for advisors, consultants, and other professionals. The proliferation of methodologies and vehicles makes it difficult for finance professionals to keep apace and properly informed (Leijonhufvud et al. 2019). For individual investors, the number and variety of options can feel just as overwhelming (Leung 2019). This should not be surprising, because Inclusive Investing cuts across financial disciplines that are themselves large, multifaceted, and complex. However, it does not have to be paralyzing. After all, the universe of conventional investment propositions is no less complex, merely more familiar.

This chapter opens with a desk review and provides a suggested framework for first-time inclusive investors to categorize and analyze inclusion scopes in their investment holdings. It includes a brief illustrative review of the Inclusive Investing practice pioneered by UNC Ventures (UNCV) under Edward Dugger III, UNCV president. It concludes with actionable guidelines for first-time inclusive investors to manage, overwhelm, and take prudent steps to formulate and execute a new Inclusive Investing discipline.

ALIGNING PURPOSE WITH EVIDENCE AND PRACTICE

Contrary to persistent misconceptions that Inclusive Investing implies increased risk and/or decreased returns, Figures 10.1–10.3, and 10.4 present

PUBLIC EQUITY	**DIVERSE HEDGE FUNDS SHOW HIGH PROMISE** **Cumulative Return*** **82.4%** vs. **51.0%** WOMEN, MINORITY NON-DIVERSE OWNED FUNDS FUNDS *Single manager weighted index (2006-2011) **Barclays Capital (2011)**	**GENDER DIVERSITY CORRELATES WITH PROFITABILITY** *"Companies in the top quartile for racial diversity are **35%** more likely to have financial returns above their respective national industry medians. And the respective rate for gender diversity is **15%**."* **McKinsey & Co (2007)**
PRIVATE EQUITY	**VC FEMALE PARTNER HIRES BOOST RETURNS** **1.5% & 9.7%** HIGHER MORE RETURNS PROFITABLE EXITS **yield from 10% increase in female partners** **Harvard Business Review (2018)**	**DIVERSE ASSET MANAGERS DO NOT UNDERPERFORM** **"We found little support for the claim that diverse-owned asset managers** *(hedge funds, mutual funds, PE funds, real estate funds)* **underperform their non-diverse peers"** **Knight Foundation (2019)**
FIXED INCOME	**WOMEN ON BOARDS OF DIRECTORS** *"Share of women on bank boards is associated with higher profitability."* *"The presence of women on boards may be a distinguishing feature of bank stability."* **International Monetary Fund (2017)**	**BETTER RISK PROFILE** **Compared with men:** - female loan officers command a **4.7% lower probability of default** - female borrowers have **4.2% lower default rate** **Credit Suisse (2016)**

FIGURE 10.1 Benefits of Inclusive Management, by Asset Class. *Source:* Authors, based on desk review of the sources mentioned herein.

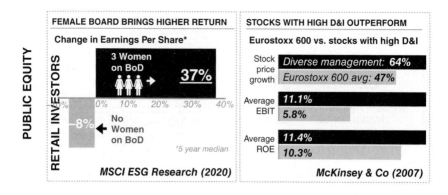

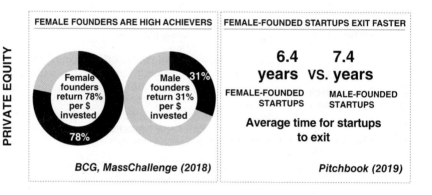

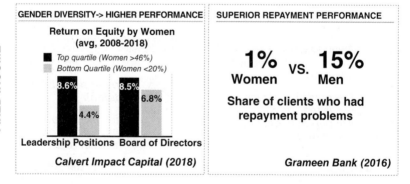

FIGURE 10.2   Benefits of Inclusive Portfolio Construction, by Asset Class. *Source:* Authors, based on desk review of the sources mentioned herein.

RETAIL INVESTORS

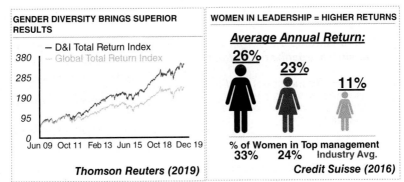

INSTITUTIONAL INVESTORS

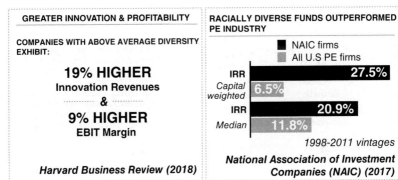

PHILANTHROPIES

IMPROVED FUNDRAISING	IMPROVED PROBLEM-SOLVING
"Greater diversity generates increased board engagement leading to higher participation in fundraising."	*"Diverse groups of problem solvers outperform the groups of the best individuals at solving problems. Diverse nonprofit organizations, and the diversity of perspectives within them, will lead to better solutions to social problems."*
RMH Foundation (2018)	*Independent Sector (2016)*

FIGURE 10.3   Financial Benefits of Inclusive Investing, by Investor Category. *Source:* Authors, based on desk review of the sources mentioned herein.

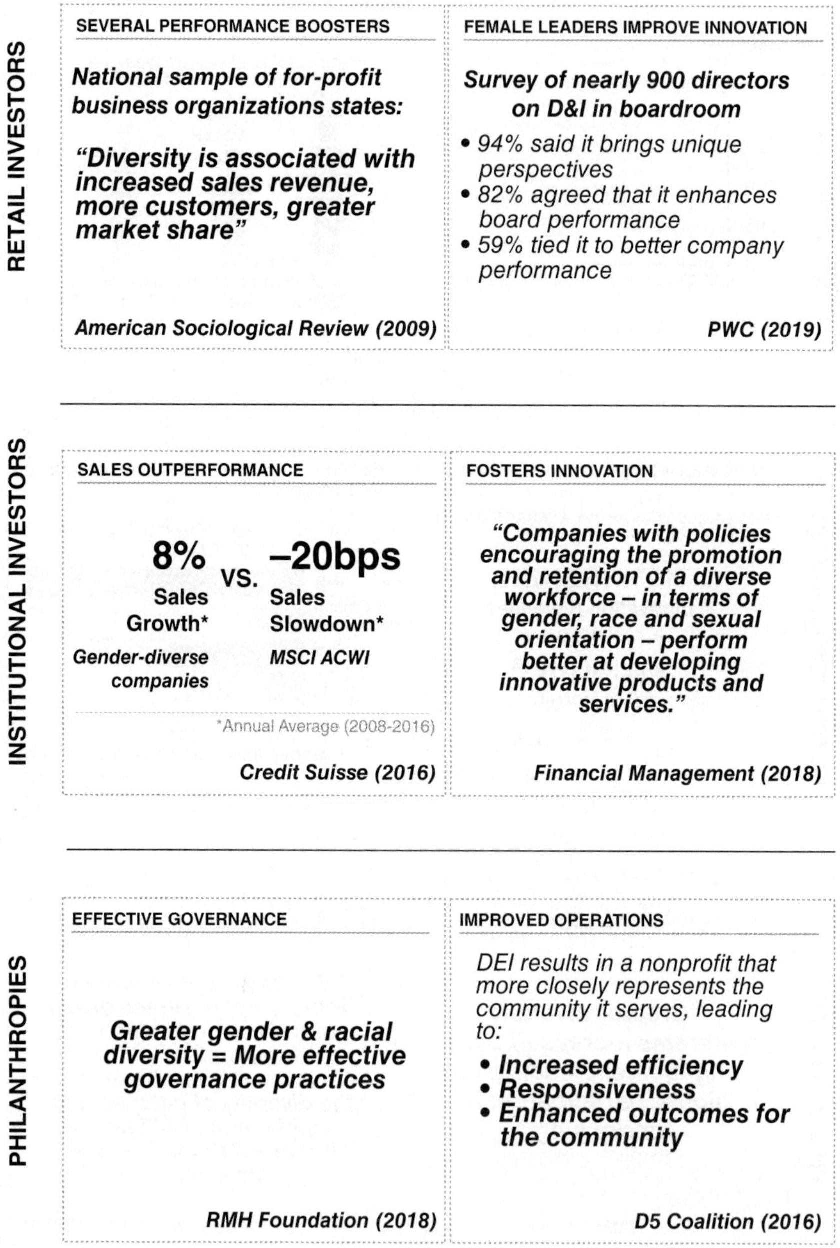

RETAIL INVESTORS

SEVERAL PERFORMANCE BOOSTERS

National sample of for-profit business organizations states:

"Diversity is associated with increased sales revenue, more customers, greater market share"

American Sociological Review (2009)

FEMALE LEADERS IMPROVE INNOVATION

Survey of nearly 900 directors on D&I in boardroom

- *94% said it brings unique perspectives*
- *82% agreed that it enhances board performance*
- *59% tied it to better company performance*

PWC (2019)

INSTITUTIONAL INVESTORS

SALES OUTPERFORMANCE

8% VS. **–20bps**

Sales Growth*   Sales Slowdown*

Gender-diverse companies   *MSCI ACWI*

*Annual Average (2008-2016)

Credit Suisse (2016)

FOSTERS INNOVATION

"Companies with policies encouraging the promotion and retention of a diverse workforce – in terms of gender, race and sexual orientation – perform better at developing innovative products and services."

Financial Management (2018)

PHILANTHROPIES

EFFECTIVE GOVERNANCE

Greater gender & racial diversity = More effective governance practices

RMH Foundation (2018)

IMPROVED OPERATIONS

DEI results in a nonprofit that more closely represents the community it serves, leading to:

- *Increased efficiency*
- *Responsiveness*
- *Enhanced outcomes for the community*

D5 Coalition (2016)

FIGURE 10.4   Business Performance Benefits of Inclusive Investing, by Investor Category. *Source:* Authors, based on desk review of the sources mentioned herein.

a sampling of findings from sources from around the world that demonstrate how applying inclusive practices for capital allocation—as well as for hiring, promotion, and compensation—at the very minimum presents no downside in terms of risk or return, and instead has been consistently correlated with advantageous financial and business outcomes.

The disconnect between evidence and investing practice is perhaps most pointedly evident in the venture capital sector, where in 2017, across Seed to Series D investments in the United States, "the typical founding team was a two-person, all-male, all-white, US university–educated team residing in Silicon Valley" (Shieber 2019). The same pattern is replicated in the UK and elsewhere as well.[7] Yet Morgan Stanley (2018) reported that nearly 80% of surveyed investors said female and multicultural entrepreneurs receive the right amount of capital—or more—than their business models deserve. This sentiment prevails in spite of numerous findings, such as the examples highlighted in Figures 10.1 through 10.4, that women and people of color consistently outperform their white male peers at growing stable businesses and generating returns to investors, and also that on average companies with diverse leadership go public or get acquired faster than their homogeneously white male counterparts. In addition, women and people of color also represent a growing economic power, as both valuable customers and determiners of culture, who are not well served by their white male peers. The market is thus failing to use readily available public information to appropriately price risk and opportunity.

This is the textbook definition of a market dislocation.

Moreover, given the existence of this long-standing market dislocation, capital allocators who believe their public and private equity holdings are appropriately diversified in an investment sense are likely sitting on substantially greater embedded risk than they have consciously accepted, as well as suboptimal return (Summers 2018). Therefore, there is a greater and more pervasive exposure to higher risk and lower return than is widely recognized, which is undesirable by any standard.

Furthermore, this pattern self-perpetuates, as flows of venture and other forms of capital concentrate wealth and opportunity in an ever-narrower demographic segment based on homophily, rather than merit. This hyper-concentration of capital is not benign and is also not an exclusively American phenomenon. For several years running, the World Economic Forum (2017) has listed financial inequity among the top threats to global economic security. Hyper-concentration of capital by race, social class, and gender—or factors other than merit—doesn't harm only institutional and private investors; it harms everyone.

---

[7] See https://pitchbook.com/news/articles/vc-firms-have-a-diversity-problem-do-they-care.

There are, however, institutional and private practitioners of Inclusive Investing strategies. Across asset classes, the majority of purpose-built Inclusive Investing instruments are offered by small or emerging managers. Conventionally viewed as presenting higher risk than larger, long-established entities, small and first-fund impact vehicles often financially outperform conventional funds (Matthews 2015), particularly within the Impact Investing sphere, and deliver advantageous impact performance (Price 2020).

White (2014) concluded, "Regardless of the mix of asset classes, foundations should allocate more assets to diverse managers just as they would with any other investment strategy—because it performs, complements other strategies, and/or provides needed asset or sub-asset class exposure to the overall portfolio" (p. 8). More narrowly, Zimmerman (2019) asserted that inclusive venture capital investing serves to reduce societal damage and portfolio risk associated with hyper-concentration of capital, while offering advantageous financial returns.

Accordingly, Inclusive Investing practices are appropriate for investors and capital allocators seeking to optimize portfolio performance, even if they have no stated impact mandate or investment policy statement (IPS) specification.

For those capital allocators and investors who do have defined impact objectives, inclusion lenses may satisfy a variety of personal or organizational motivations. For example, DEI lenses can enable investors to:

- Comprehensively address wider social and environmental justice objectives, by recognizing that not only SDGs 5 and 10, but all 17 SDGs[8] are interconnected with diversity, equity, and inclusion, as by the Return on Investment and Social Equity (RISE) Community.[9]
- Redress societal inequities and promote economic vitality, as in the diversity initiatives of the Pensions and Lifetime Savings Association,[10] GLI fund of the Equality Fund,[11] African Women Leadership Fund,[12] Raven Indigenous Capital Partners Fund,[13] and Indigenous Infrastructure Investment Fund.[14]

---

[8] See https://www.un.org/sustainabledevelopment/sustainable-development-goals/.
[9] See https://robasciotti.com/social-justice-investing/.
[10] See https://www.plsa.co.uk/About-us/Diversity.
[11] See https://www.equalityfund.ca.
[12] See https://competitions.potential.com/awlf/.
[13] See https://ravencapitalpartners.ca.
[14] See https://www.impactip.com.au.

- Bring portfolio holdings into alignment with an individual oi institutional investor's values of environmental, social, or economic justice, as in Ford Foundation committing USD $1 billion of its USD $12 billion endowment to mission-aligned investments (Ford Foundation 2017).
- Better serve an institutional entity's constituencies, as in pension funds seeking greater transparency on DEI-related matters (Walker 2019), increasing DEI-related shareholder activity (Kramer 2018), reorienting their portfolios (Shank 2016; Seddon-Daines and Chinwala 2017) or boards (Gan, 2017; Preesman 2016) to better resemble their members, or similarly, university officials participating in Intentional Endowments Network (IEN) working groups,[15] Equity Summit,[16] or other convenings to make their endowment investment practices more congruent with their student, faculty, staff, and alumni bodies.
- Gain access to new networks and deal flow (Businesswire 2019), as declared by private equity firm TPG[17] announcing their investment in Harlem Capital.[18]

INCLUSIVE INVESTING METHODOLOGY: ADAPTING THE SCOPE 1, 2, 3 APPROACH TO ASSESS *WHO ARE THE PEOPLE IN YOUR PORTFOLIO?*

Contemplating such a broad universe of options can be so overwhelming that individual investors and advisors often find it difficult to figure out where to begin practicing Inclusive Investing. Ironically, the challenge may be most acute for highly sophisticated professionals with long successful tenure in conventional finance. Accordingly, practitioners of all types who are starting to contemplate diversity lenses may find it useful to employ an organizing framework.

One possible option is to adapt the Scope 1, 2, 3 operational envelopes framework for greenhouse gas (GHG) emissions used by many ESG, climate impact, and sustainability practitioners.[19] For many impact investors, this structure is already familiar; for others it may be novel. In either case,

---

[15]See https://www.intentionalendowments.org/working_groups.
[16]See www.equitysummit.com.
[17]See company website, https://www.tpg.com.
[18]See company website, https://harlem.capital/.
[19]See, for example, information on WRI and WBCSD on the Greenhouse Gas Protocol, available at https://ghgprotocol.org/sites/default/files/standards_supporting/FAQ.pdf.

an Inclusive Investing variation on the Scope 1, 2, 3 framework may provide a straightforward, intuitive way for investors to organize complex materiality considerations.[20] In much the same way as complex GHG emissions are attributable to direct and indirect operational mechanisms, multilayered diversity and inclusion impacts may similarly be categorized as direct and indirect.

As illustrated, the three scopes represent different categories of GHG emissions, organized by operational sources. Scope 1 emissions are attributable directly to the company's primary operations. Scope 2 emissions are attributable to resources, materials, supplies, and services purchased or utilized by the organization in support of its primary operations; this generally encompasses goods and services that the company uses in its production cycle, for example. Scope 3 emissions are attributable to the organization's upstream supply chain, secondary operations, and downstream use of its products or services, encompassing the organization's wider network and including customers, clients, and suppliers. Figure 10.5 provides a simplified visualization of Scope 1, 2, 3 GHG emissions.

For Inclusive Investing, impact investors would focus on measures of inclusion that are materially relevant to their investment endeavors, rather

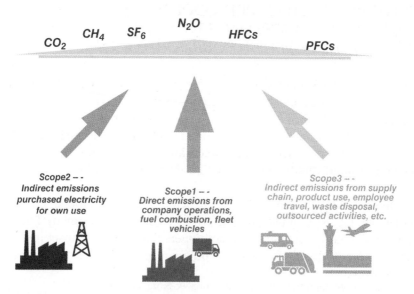

FIGURE 10.5   Scope 1, 2, 3 Greenhouse Gas Emissions. *Source:* Authors.

---

[20]Scope 1, 2, 3 is detailed Chapter 12, "Fossil-Fuel-Free Investing: Weaving a New Investment Paradigm," by Chander Balakumar.

than on measures of GHG emissions. Depending on materiality, capital allocators might selectively prioritize inclusion factors specific to gender (whether simple male-female binary, or full-spectrum encompassing LGBTQ/NB),[21] race, ethnicity, disability, age, class, immigrant or refugee, Indigenous/First Nations, or other inclusion lenses.[22]

Thus, adapting the GHG methodology to serve the purposes of Inclusive Investing, Inclusion Scope 1, 2, 3 mechanisms[23] might thus be defined as follows, and as illustrated in Figure 10.6:

- **Scope 1** inclusion is attributable to the managers represented in the impact investor's portfolio or capital allocator's platform.
- **Scope 2** inclusion is attributable to the managers' practices, the strategies they employ, and the public or private companies or other assets in which they invest.

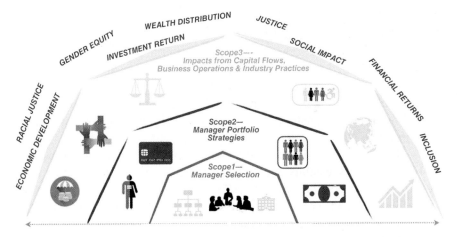

FIGURE 10.6 Inclusion Scope 1, 2, 3. *Source:* Authors.

---

[21] LGBTQ/NB stands for lesbian, gay, bisexual, transgender, queer/nonbinary.

[22] Note that there are arguably some situational or contextual cases where intentional homogeneity may be necessary or locally optimal to accommodate exogenous constraints or to achieve other social/economic equity impact objectives (e.g. all-female financial institutions serving female customers in gender-segregated societies, or all-Indigenous/First Nations providing health care services on sovereign lands).

[23] Note that for institutional investors or capital allocators, there may be the equivalent of Inclusion Scope 0 work to be done on the institution's own internal hiring, promotion, compensation, and sourcing performance. Although this is of vital importance, it is a separate endeavor in its own right and is not addressed here.

- **Scope 3** inclusion is attributable to the intentional and unintentional effects created by the portfolio holdings, including the sectors in which they operate (upstream and downstream and laterally in their value chain) and their networks of industrial, commercial, and financial partners.

Thus, capital allocators contemplating material Inclusion Investing matters could map Inclusion Scope 1, 2, and 3 as:

Scope 1: How inclusive is the manager pool, and how inclusive are the managers in the pool?

Begin by assessing the inclusivity of the investor's existing holdings: How diverse is the manager pool, and how inclusive is each manager? How are existing selection criteria and practices serving to either increase or limit inclusivity, whether by design or otherwise? How does this current status fall short of capturing financial and other benefits of full inclusivity?

Based on this internal assessment, revise manager selection criteria and evaluation practices, or define new criteria, practices, and/or mandates, as needed to increase equity and inclusion in the manager pool. Require managers, consultants, and advisors to report on managers' internal DEI composition and standards, at minimum starting with self-reported composition of each firm's partners/owners, investment committee, team, and staff.

Note that this is the scope where *emerging manager* programs typically focus, establishing set-asides or allocations for selecting fund managers or general partners (GPs) that satisfy certain racial, social, gender inclusion criteria, or fit a prescribed DEI profile. For example, capital allocators may set mandates requiring that a minimum specified portion of their allocations are made to managers with a minimum percentage ownership by people of color, Indigenous people, women, LGBTQ/NB persons, people with disabilities, etc. These initiatives are designed to increase the number or accelerate the growth of under-represented managers able to wield significant financial assets, as compared to status quo capital allocations. Properly designed, executed, and improved over time, they can serve as effective on-ramps both for underrepresented managers to gain entry into an investor's holdings, and also for the investor to transition from a noninclusive investing approach (0% of portfolio subject to intentional inclusion requirements) to a fully inclusive investing approach (100% of portfolio subject to intentional inclusion requirements).

Scope 2: What are the inclusion strategies and outcomes in each manager's portfolio?

Again, begin by assessing current holdings. What are the intended and actual racial, social, and gender performance of managers' strategies, whether in publicly traded or privately held entities or properties? Are they self-consistent, do the strategies produce the intended outcomes? Are the strategies and outcomes congruent with currently available data relevant to the asset class and approach? Do those strategies serve (intentionally or unintentionally) to increase or limit inclusion and equity?

Based on this assessment, revise portfolio strategy, standards, allocation, evaluation, or other criteria and practices, and/or define new mandates and criteria for consultants, advisors, or investment committee members, as appropriate to increase inclusion and equity across portfolio holdings.

Note that this is the scope where many *gender lens*, *equity lens*, or other readily quantifiable investment strategy methodologies typically focus.[24] For example, capital allocators may set mandates requiring managers to measure and report on inclusion by race, gender, disability, or other specified DEI factors in their public or private market holdings. These requirements are designed to increase systemic racial, gender, or other social equity as a direct and measurable upgrade over *status quo* portfolio construction.

Scope 3: Who is impacted by inclusion or exclusion, and how do portfolio holdings increase or decrease equity through their operations?

Once again, begin by assessing existing portfolio holdings. What are the direct and indirect racial, social, and gender effects of the industrial, commercial, and financial activities represented in the investor's own portfolio holdings and their managers' portfolio holdings? How do the activities of the portfolio holdings (intentionally or unintentionally) serve to increase or limit inclusion? As with GHG Scope 3 analyses, Inclusion Scope 3 analyses are by far the most complex of the three scopes. Investors and capital allocators embarking on this scope for the first time may find it less daunting to hire experts in the field,[25] as simply determining which considerations are

---

[24]See also Chapter 18, "Transformative Evaluation and Impact Investing: A Fruitful Marriage," by Courtney Bolinson and Donna Mertens.

[25]Impact assessments can be made internally through monitoring and evaluation (internal self-assessments). For greater accuracy and credibility, impact assessments ideally should

most material, urgent, or actionable can be challenging, and measuring and analyzing expected and unexpected equity effects can be even more so.

Based on this assessment, revise or define sectoral, geographic, or other elements of the IPS, consider shareholder action, divestment, direct investment, hybrid capital structures, performance or impact bonds, revenue-based financing, and other means as appropriate to exercise the full capacity of the portfolio to increase inclusion and equity or reduce effects of exclusion and inequity through the activities of portfolio holdings.

Note that this is where many financial inclusion, environmental justice, gender-based violence, human trafficking, and other systems-change-oriented approaches typically focus. These initiatives are designed to reduce negative impacts or deliver positive impacts to one or more racial, social, gender, or other designated populations persistently excluded from or negatively impacted by status quo business, government or policy, nonprofit, or other practices. For example, on the basis of a strategically defined Scope 3 objective to reduce specific disproportionate systemic harms, a capital allocator might preferentially select managers who invest in affordable clean energy, water, or other infrastructure in underserved jurisdictions, or exclude investments in companies that participate in the for-profit prison industry, or sign onto shareholder initiatives to eliminate forced arbitration, all of which disproportionately impact people of color and women and deepen systemic inequities, particularly in poorer communities.

Fully realized inclusion is of course multidimensional, and therefore extremely challenging to undertake comprehensively from a standing start, so it is advisable to begin by establishing a small set of clear, specific, and measurable objectives. Moreover, given the complexity inherent to bringing any new lens to an investment portfolio, it is generally advisable to resist any impulse to remake an entire portfolio at one go, and rather take an intentionally iterative approach to measuring and evaluating, correcting and improving, and learning with practice. Such an approach is consistent with the GHG reduction analogy, for which the Intergovernmental Panel on Climate Change (IPCC) and other knowledgeable bodies recommend

---

be done by independent teams of expert evaluators who apply consistent research standards and impact evaluation methodologies to identify, catalogue, and analyze differential direct and indirect effects on populations. See Chapter 17, "Impact Measurement and Management Techniques to Achieve Powerful Results," by Jane Reisman and Veronica Olazabal, and Chapter 16, Measuring and Evaluating Social Impact in Impact Investing: An Overview of the Main Available Standards and Methods," by Ana Pimenta and Elsa de Morais Sarmento.

an iterative approach, as articulated in "Informing an Effective Response to Climate Change" (National Research Council 2010, p. 5):

> Many climate-related decisions must address and incorporate uncertainty, the expectation of surprises, and factors that underlie the need to improve long-term decision making and crisis responses. Decision makers will differ in their assessment of the degree of risk that is unacceptable. These are not issues that are unique to climate choices. Decision makers in government and the private sector, as well as individuals, frequently make decisions with only partial or uncertain information and update these decisions as conditions change or more information becomes available. These include decisions with long-term implications such as saving for retirement, buying insurance, investing in infrastructure, or launching new products. The range of possibilities depends on future conditions and shifts such as a recession or technology breakthrough and the availability of information. Most people recognize the need to act despite uncertainty and that it is impossible to eliminate all risk. Effective management can benefit from a systematic and iterative framework for decision making.... Decision makers in both public and private sectors should implement an iterative risk management strategy to manage climate decisions and to identify potential climate damages, co-benefits, considerations of equity, societal attitudes to climate risk, and the availability of potential response options. Decisions and policies should be revised in light of new information, experience, and stakeholder input, and use the best available information and assessment base to underpin the risk management framework.

Many, if not all, of these considerations apply for investing in general, and Impact or Inclusive Investing in particular.

Perhaps the most opportune moment for advisors and consultants to begin identifying material considerations for Inclusive Investing is when reviewing an existing IPS or drafting a new IPS. In light of the evolving US Securities and Exchange Commission (SEC) guidance on ESG disclosure and specifically determination of materiality,[26] and similarly evolving guidance

---

[26]See, for example, https://www.sec.gov/news/public-statement/clayton-mda-2020-01-30, https://www.sec.gov/news/public-statement/peirce-mda-2020-01-30, https://www.sec.gov/news/public-statement/lee-mda-2020-01-30.

by other national counterparts, investment managers and advisors may find that obligations to prudence, loyalty, and/or care dictate exploring considerations for which the definition of materiality is fluid or even subjective. It may be that the absence of clear and certain a priori standards underscores the fiduciary necessity of iteratively making reasoned determinations of whether and how Inclusion Scope 1, 2, 3 considerations map to client interests.

As noted elsewhere in this chapter, this is not a trivial exercise, but it is also far from insurmountable. Whereas prevailing wisdom holds that inclusion is constrained by available talent ("we have a pipeline problem") and/or deal flow ("there aren't enough investable companies"), these and other closely related, deeply rooted misconceptions are demonstrably false (Zimmerman 2019). A historical example provides helpful illustration, as described next.

INCLUSIVE INVESTING IN PRACTICE: UNC VENTURES

This section is based on a first-person narrative from Edward Dugger III. During the reported 10-year performance period, Dugger served as president of US-based UNCV and was directly responsible for its portfolio.

In the last years of Reverend Dr. Martin Luther King Jr.'s truncated life, he turned his attention from advancing civil rights more broadly to directly addressing the debilitating economic injustices suffered by people of color. He explicitly called out the immorality of institutionalized poverty and stifled economic mobility and linked them to the systemic barriers people of color face to securing high-quality jobs and wealth-building capital. Many structural financial barriers have continued to contribute to persistent economic injustice after Rev. Dr. King's death. In the 1980s, a small alliance of rising executives and venerable Wall Street luminaries began to recognize the inequitable allocation of equity capital as both a symptom and significant driver of economic injustice and made it a target for their active intervention.

Drawing on their expertise in finance to fix a flaw in finance, they formed a private venture capital firm originally known as UNC Ventures, later simply UNCV, with an investment objective to counter racially based economic injustice by proving the concomitant opportunity represented by chronically capital-deprived founders of color. UNCV thus pioneered a new approach to venture investing that included diversity as both a primary criterion and an intentional outcome, an early precursor to today's Impact Investing in general and Inclusive Investing specifically.

The UNCV founders included a recent PhD graduate of Harvard Business School and a recent graduate of Harvard Law School, backed by the chief executive officer (CEO) of Morgan Stanley, the chairman of the Executive Committee of JP Morgan, and the CEO of North Carolina Insurance Company. Drawing on their disparate professional and generational perspectives, the founders formulated the UNCV investment approach and articulated a corresponding operating thesis that the lack of access to capital by people of color was not a failure of human ingenuity or capacity by a historically subjugated set of people, but rather a failure of the market to appropriately recognize opportunity and assess entrepreneurial risk.

In essence, the UNCV strategy was designed to expose residual classist and white supremacist tendencies in the venture capital sphere, by intentionally seeking out founder teams who did not fit already well-established venture capital selection patterns,[27] thereby tapping into a reservoir of "undiscovered" investment opportunity. The inclusion strategy was thus expressly designed to eliminate selection biases associated with educational background, economic status, and employment history, in addition to the primary focus on race.

The UNCV theory of change postulated that by investing in overlooked founders of color: (i) the fund could both disprove the prevailing wisdom that people of color were not "investable"[28] and generate compelling financial returns by taking advantage of the market failure; (ii) the success of the fund would then entice more investors to channel capital to black and brown entrepreneurs; and (iii) the resulting increase in capital flows to black and brown entrepreneurs would catalyze long-term structural change.

Acting on this thesis and theory of change, UNCV developed and pursued an Inclusive Investing strategy with the goal of generating returns comparable to traditional venture funds.

UNCV's institutional limited-partner (LP) investors—for the most part, large insurance companies, foundations, and pension funds—had already come to the realization that conventional investment practices were exclusionary and recognized that UNCV offered a fundamentally different approach that had never been implemented before. Rather than a venture practice with an inclusion perspective tacked on, UNCV was an inclusion practice using the tools of venture capital to achieve both impact and financial objectives.

---

[27] See Shieber (2019).

[28] This myth persists today. See, for example, Germano (2018). Gender-related myths are likewise persistent and continue to play out. See, for example, Alba (2015) and Noguchi (2020).

Viewing UNCV's inclusion venture practice through the Inclusion Scope 1, 2, 3 framework provides important insights into the way UNCV successfully transformed a conventionally return-only financial vehicle—a venture capital fund—into a dual-purpose vehicle that could deliver both financial return and inclusionary impact. Central to the UNCV theory of change was the understanding that UNCV would be an intermediator for the flow of capital: both the recipient of Limited Partner capital allocations (Scope 1) and the allocator of venture capital investments into portfolio companies (Scope 2), as well as the architect of broader systemic impacts (Scope 3), as summarized in Table 10.1.

The UNCV strategy proved a viable alternative to the conventional venture capital approach. UNCV's financial performance over its last 10 years (1988 to 1997) exceeded most venture funds of its vintage, as measured using industry standard indicators: 32% internal rate of return (IRR) on portfolio investments, registering in the upper quartile for all venture funds, compared to 22% industry-wide (Cambridge Associates 2011), and corresponding to 2.1 times paid in capital.

True to its design, UNCV accomplished intentional impact outcomes, including:

- Moved founders of color into over 10 growth sectors of the economy, including software, medical instruments, computer peripherals, radio and TV broadcasting, office development, and environmental services
- Provided the catalytic capital for the growth of 2 of the top 10 largest African American controlled companies, both of which had successful IPOs
- Provided the capital footings for portfolio companies to raise over USD $2 billion from conventional capital sources
- Achieved 30% employees and managers of color across the portfolio
- Generated over 7,000 family supporting jobs
- Grew businesses that created over USD $1 billion of shared wealth
- Seeded the financial and business worlds with 40 professionals of color who subsequently became prominent sector leaders

Notably, although there was no gender component to the UNCV strategy, one of the top-performing UNCV portfolio companies was co-founded by an African American woman.

TABLE 10.1 Viewing the UNCV Practice Through the Inclusion Scope 1, 2, 3 Framework.

Scope 1	**Inclusion in manager selection.**
	LPs chose to invest in UNCV (LPs selected UNCV as a manager) because the UNCV practice was designed from its inception to generate competitive returns by advancing inclusion, starting with its own internal team composition.
	Beyond its investment strategy, UNCV made binding agreements with its LPs to advance professionals of color into senior leadership and investment positions. To support such efforts, UNCV instituted an apprenticeship program structured both to provide employment opportunities for business professionals of color within the firm itself, and also to seed other firms in venture and other financial sectors with skilled financial practitioners of color.
Scope 2	**Inclusion in manager's portfolio.**
	As a manager, UNCV set mandates for assessing and reporting on its own inclusion performance across its portfolio. For example, UNCV's investment strategy mandated that 100% of its investment capital to be used to finance scalable businesses controlled by people of color, with "control" defined as authority over day-to-day operations and at least 30% ownership.
	UNCV required portfolio companies to be at least 30% staffed by both managers and employees of color.
	Further, UNCV's strategy called for using its investments to move founders of color into high growth sectors of the US economy, where often UNCV investees were the only non-white leaders.
Scope 3	**Effects of inclusion or exclusion and equity or inequity resulting from the portfolio.**
	The UNCV inclusion investing strategy explicitly aimed to generate societal impact through and alongside venture capital performance, via an intentional process of creating more shared business opportunities, privilege and wealth for founders of color and their diverse teams, customers, and suppliers, as well as for LPs.
	UNCV actively worked with its portfolio companies to ensure that they maintained inclusive business practices. UNCV required each portfolio company to report quarterly or annually on the racial composition of its workforce, the diversity of its supply chain, and the participation of shareholders and stakeholders in wealth-building asset appreciation and profits. UNCV utilized this information to produce annual reports highlighting the successes of its portfolio companies in creating quantifiable financial and inclusion success within and beyond each portfolio company's core business operations.
	UNCV also preferentially sourced from diverse-owned suppliers for its own operations and intentionally established syndicate relationships with diverse capital partners.

Source: Authors.

In short, UNCV explicitly challenged the conventional wisdom that venture capital investments in companies led by people of color would underperform sectoral standards, and moreover that DEI investment necessarily had to grow incrementally over a long period of time.

UNCV also validated its operating thesis that success was a function of opportunity. However, disappointingly, despite being widely hailed at the time in *Black Enterprise, Esquire, Pensions & Investments,* the *Boston Globe,* the *Wall Street Journal,* and other prominent media outlets, and becoming legendary among the Black community, the UNCV success story did not serve to inspire imitators and emulators, and was not immediately effective in attracting significant numbers of LPs to Inclusive Investing.

Thus, although UNCV provided a high-profile validation of the "investability" of founders of color and thereby successfully executed on theory of change hypothesis (i), UNCV was not immediately successful in fulfilling its other two system change objectives.

Nearly 20 years after the UNCV fund was harvested, although the UNCV example has been largely forgotten by the wider venture capital and LP communities, Inclusive Investing is at last starting to attract wider LP attention.

HOW TO BEGIN: DETERMINE WHAT IS MATERIAL AND RELEVANT

An Inclusive Investing strategy may be single-asset or multi-asset, retail or institutional, philanthropic, or competitive return, active or passive, local or global. As defined above, an Inclusive Investing strategy *systematically applies material investment considerations that are causally connected to the intentional and unintentional ways in which specific populations of people are included in, excluded from, or impacted by a given investment practice.*

For institutional, individual, or philanthropic entities seeking financial returns anywhere along the spectrum from wholly philanthropic to market-leading, along with and/or resulting from DEI impacts, a crucial first step is to simply identify core impact objectives and associated parameters (Trelstad 2016). This is a question-driven process. Table 10.2 provides some indicative (not comprehensive) questions as general starting points for exploring and defining material and appropriate Inclusive Investing considerations. Any IPS will necessarily be adapted to the specific needs, objectives, and aspirations of the investor or client.

TABLE 10.2 Sample Questions to Shape a New Inclusive Investing Process.

Objectives	What specific DEI-related (racial/social/gender/other) impacts, outcomes, or changes are intended?
Intensity and immediacy of impact	What scope and time frame are appropriate to those DEI-related (racial/social/gender/other) objectives? What measurable outcomes are aligned with investor time horizons?
Impact risk	How sensitive is the investor to combined financial and impact outcomes? What kind of risk (reputational, legal, opportunity, operational, etc.) is associated with either achieving or faltering on the intended impacts, outcomes, or changes?
Inventory	What does the current portfolio actually contain? Who is included, excluded, positively and negatively impacted by that current portfolio? What risks are embedded as a result? What impact opportunities or financial return potentials are suboptimal?
Gaps, conflicts, and obstacles	How do the intended objectives and current portfolio/practices differ or conflict? What obstacles are in the way of fulfilling the intended DEI-related impacts, outcomes, or changes?
Execution	What new steps can be taken? What existing practices can be altered?
Evaluation	How will both impact and financial results be measured, tracked, evaluated, and reported?
Steady state	How will impact and financial results inform future criteria, processes, and allocations?

Source: Authors.

As outlined above, the answers to these questions can then be mapped to Inclusion Scopes 1, 2, 3 and used to shape an investment strategy encompassing one or more asset classes as appropriate. As with any new strategy, investors and capital allocators may want to start with a small portion of their portfolio and revise or expand their Inclusive Investing allocation as they gain experience and confidence.

Inclusive Investing Methodology: Applying Inclusion Scope 1, 2, 3

Even the best frameworks serve as general guides or outlines, rather than detailed maps or fully completed scripts, and so it inevitably falls to the practitioner to define an actionable plan and achievable first steps. Applying Inclusion Scope 1, 2, 3 or any other systemic approach is not a one-time exercise, but an ongoing discipline of mapping investment objectives, constraints, capacity, practices, and outcomes through one or more inclusion lenses. This requires the practitioner—whether investor, capital allocator, advisor, or consultant—to persistently interrogate existing investments, sourcing and selection practices, and outcomes against the intended objectives, and to revise IPS, mandates, practices, criteria, and other implementation elements as needed to achieve those objectives.

There are many ways to get started. For example, depending on the individual or organizational persona, capacity, time sensitivity, and motivation for undertaking Inclusive Investing, capital allocators and investors may choose to inaugurate a new inclusive investment strategy simply by adopting another entity's preexisting investment thesis. Alternatively, they may define a particular intentional impact objective and undertake an in-depth inventory of the alignment or misalignment between their existing investments and the identified objective, mission, and/or constituencies. Or they could begin by experimenting with a small amount of capital in an inclusive investment vehicle which is ready at hand and discern an Inclusive Investing perspective experientially.

A novice inclusion investor might thus prefer to take either an analytical or exploratory approach. Both approaches are iterative, but in practice they are quite different, as outlined in Table 10.3. Each of the steps outlined here comprises several sub-steps, neither the analytical nor exploratory sequence is definitive or immutable, and these two outlines are neither prescriptive nor the only options; rather, these two approaches simply represent two possible ways of undertaking a new Inclusive Investing initiative.[29]

---

[29]It is worth noting that for some colleges and universities, the analytical approach may recall prior institutional experiences of undertaking gender and other diversity initiatives in admissions, sports, and student life, or faculty tenure cases. In much the same way as the Inclusion Scope 1, 2, 3 framework adapts an existing structure to serve a new investing perspective, where a prior diversity approach has proven effective and delivered celebrated results, its familiarity and the experience of success may serve to reduce anxiety associated with introducing Inclusive Investing into the endowment. A formerly traveled DEI

TABLE 10.3   Analytical and Exploratory Approaches to Beginning Inclusive Investing.

	Analytical Approach to Beginning Inclusive Investing	Exploratory Approach to Beginning Inclusive Investing
Step 1	Specify one or more financial and impact objectives for Inclusive Investing.	Set aside a small pool of capital for experimentation, and define the timescale.
Step 2	Map objectives to appropriate Scope(s) 1, 2, 3.	Identify and select one or more readily accessible Inclusive Investing vehicles corresponding to capital pool and timescale.
Step 3	Assess materially relevant concerns for each objective and scope, including timescale.	Deploy capital in selected vehicle(s).
Step 4	Inventory existing portfolio against materially relevant concerns, and identify gaps or misalignment.	Track and evaluate reported financial and inclusion impact performance.
Step 5	Identify and select appropriate asset class(es), and vehicle(s) for Inclusive Investment.	Map to corresponding Scope(s) 1, 2, 3.
Step 6	Deploy capital in selected vehicle(s).	Assess how well (or poorly) outcomes fulfill personal or organizational values and needs.
Step 7	Track and evaluate financial and inclusion impact performance against objectives, by scope.	Identify objectives and boundaries for further experimentation (or switch to analytical approach).
Step 8	(Repeat)	(Repeat)

Source: Authors.

As mentioned in the opening of this chapter, for institutions and high-net-worth and ultra-high-net-worth (HNW/UHNW) individuals and families, there exists a rapidly multiplying assortment of Inclusive Investing instruments spanning all asset classes.

---

roadmap may thus serve as an excellent foundation or template for continuing to instill inclusion and equity into every aspect of institutional life, including the financial sphere. Even in the absence of individual continuity, institutional memory of success with other DEI-related initiatives provides an excellent starting point for establishing measurable Inclusive Investing standards, strategies, and norms for the endowment.

For accredited and qualified investors of any identity, there are now hundreds of public and private market funds, not to mention novel hybrid and philanthropic vehicles, pursuing Inclusion Scope 1, 2, and/or 3 investment strategies under a variety of descriptions. Moreover, DAFs offer a shallow entry, by enabling donors to utilize tax-deductible charitable capital to fund impact investments (Macpherson et al. 2018).

For individuals at the retail scale, there are similarly numerous inclusion investment options, ranging from community capital and crowd-funding platforms to ETFs and managed funds. Many retirement and pension administrators now offer at least some inclusion-focused products. For those whose plan administrator does not yet offer any inclusion-focused products, it is certainly appropriate to ask for suitable products to be added. Alumnae/i of schools, colleges, and universities can also inquire of their alma maters how the endowment is invested to reflect and serve all of its student, faculty, staff, and alumni constituencies.

Regardless of investor identity, a strategy is only as good as its execution. For many experienced investors and capital allocators with extensive conventional investment experience, and likewise for many experienced philanthropists with extensive charitable endeavor experience, successfully executing Inclusive Investing strategies will also necessitate substantive revisions and upgrades to internal sourcing, selection, and assessment processes. These may include:

- Identifying and removing systemic biases baked into long-established "best practices" that preclude, discount, or disqualify inclusive and diverse managers (Lyons-Padilla et al. 2019), and especially those leading new funds or strategies (Niño 2019);
- Establishing new processes and requirements akin to the Rooney Rule (Sports Illustrated 2017), Inclusion Rider (Judkis and Merry 2018), or blind auditions (Rice 2013), among others, to ensure that underrepresented managers are both actively sought and given either impartial or preferential evaluation, as necessary to fulfill inclusion objectives;
- Defining new sourcing and selection criteria to support allocating capital to diverse managers (White 2014), and specifically seeking small and/or new funds and strategies;
- Other changes to accustomed practice as necessary to meet Inclusive Investing financial and impact objectives and capture corresponding benefits, across one or more Inclusion scopes.

No one need learn on their own. Communities of expertise and practice exist for all capital allocator and investor identities, and new networks, associations, and conferences are springing into existence. In addition to those cited above, there are numerous other digital, virtual, and in-person communities of practice, as well as platforms for field building and knowledge sharing. Some indicative examples of these communities and platforms are provided in Appendix 10.1, and some further resources are offered in Appendix 10.2.

CONCLUSION

Contrary to persistent misconceptions that Inclusive Investing or DEI implies increased risk and/or decreased returns, this chapter presents evidence that Inclusive Investing presents little or no downside in terms of risk or return, but rather has been consistently correlated with advantageous financial and business outcomes.

Inclusive Investing practices are therefore appropriate for investors and capital allocators seeking to optimize portfolio performance, even if they have no explicit or implicit impact objective.

Evidence notwithstanding, and despite historical antecedents stretching back millennia and continuing through more recent examples such as the UNCV case described here, deeply rooted misperceptions and biases persist in sustaining investment "best practices" that systematically steeply favor white male managers and entrepreneurs alike. These counterfactual beliefs and practices have been found to incur precisely the increased risk and sub-optimized return hazards that they purport to avoid.

In 2020, in conjunction with related approaches including ESG, SRI, GLI, and SDG investing strategies, Inclusive Investing is finally starting to attract investor (including LPs) attention.

For investors of all categories, there is a rapidly expanding universe of Inclusive Investing products and instruments, spanning the full spectrum from wholly concessionary to market-leading financial returns, and a wide range of capital requirements and liquidity.

Just as with any new investment strategy, and regardless of the mix of asset classes, institutional and private investors alike should persistently revise investing criteria, practices, methodologies, and policies in light of the best available information and peer learnings. By adopting an iterative, evidence-based Inclusive Investing discipline, investors stand to benefit themselves and create meaningful social impact as well.

REFERENCES

Abouzahr, K., Taplett, F., Krentz, M., et al. (2018). Why Women-Owned Startups Are a Better Bet, BCG Mass challenge (6 June). https://www.bcg.com/publications/2018/why-women-owned-startups-are-better-bet.aspx (accessed 1 March 2020).

Abramson, J. (2019). All In, Women in the VC Ecosystem. Pitchbook. https://files.pitchbook.com/website/files/pdf/PitchBook_All_Raise_2019_All_In_Women_in_the_VC_Ecosystem.pdf (accessed 1 March 2020).

Abramson, J., Cohen, S., Feldman, J., et al. (2019). All In: Women in the VC Ecosystem. PitchBook, All Raise, Goldman Sachs' Launch, Microsoft for Startups. https://files.pitchbook.com/website/files/pdf/PitchBook_All_Raise_2019_All_In_Women_in_the_VC_Ecosystem.pdf (accessed 1 March 2020).

Aga Khan Development Network (2020). AKFED Companies. Aga Khan Fund for Economic Development. https://www.akdn.org/our-agencies/aga-khan-fund-economic-development/akfed-companies (accessed 27 February 2020).

Alba, D. (2015). It'd be crazy if venture capital firms didn't fix their gender problem. *Wired* (21 May). https://www.wired.com/2015/05/ellen-pao-trial/ (accessed 12 March 2020).

Barclays Capital (2011). Hedge Fund Pulse: Affirmative Investing: Women and Minority Owned Hedge Funds. (June). http://www.managedfunds.org/wp-content/uploads/2011/08/HF-Pulse-Affirmative-Investing-June-2011-Letter.pdf (accessed 1 March 2020).

Bradford, H. (2019). Impact Investing finds its way on lists of more major players. *Pensions & Investments* (08 July). https://www.pionline.com/print/impact-investing-finds-its-way-lists-more-major-players (accessed 27 February 2020).

Businesswire (2019). TPG Announces Investment in Harlem Capital. Businesswire (24 June). https://www.businesswire.com/news/home/20190624005397/en/TPG-Announces-Investment-Harlem-Capital (accessed 27 February 2020).

Calvert Impact Capital (2018). Just Good Investing. https://www.calvertimpactcapital.org/storage/documents/calvert-impact-capital-gender-report.pdf (accessed 1 March 2020).

Cambridge Associates (2011). US Venture Capital Index and Selected Benchmark Statistics, Private Investments. Cambridge Associates LLC (31 December).

Chitillapaly, J. (2016). Sharia investment, the positive social impact of Islamic finance. *Lifegate* (21 November). https://www.lifegate.com/people/news/what-is-sharia-investment-characteristics (accessed 27 February 2020).

D5 Coalition (2016). State of the Work: Stories from the Movement to Advance Diversity, Equity, and Inclusion. http://www.d5coalition.org/wp-content/uploads/2016/04/D5-SOTW-2016-Final-web-pages.pdf (accessed 1 March 2020).

Dawson, J., Kersley, R., and Natella, S. (2016). The CS Gender 3000. The Reward for Change. Credit Suisse (September). http://www.insurance.ca.gov/diversity/41-ISDGBD/GBDExternal/upload/CSRI-CSGender3000-2016.pdf (accessed 1 March 2020).

Denning, S. (2013). The Origin of "The World's Dumbest Idea": Milton Friedman. *Forbes* (26 June). https://www.forbes.com/sites/stevedenning/2013/06/26/the-origin-of-the-worlds-dumbest-idea-milton-friedman/#49f4aa89870e (accessed 27 February 2020).

Desvaux, G., Deillard-Hoellinger, S., Baumgarten, P., et al (2007). Women Matter: Gender Diversity, a Corporate Performance Driver. McKinsey & Company. https://www.raeng.org.uk/publications/other/women-matter-oct-2007 (accessed 1 March 2020).

Eastman, M., Rallis, D., and Mazuchelli, G. (2016). The Tipping Point: Women on Boards and Financial Performance. MSCI ESG Research (December). https://www.msci.com/documents/10199/fd1f8228-cc07-4789-acee-3f9ed97ee8bb (accessed 1 March 2020).

Ford Foundation (2017). Ford Foundation commits $1 billion from endowment to mission-related investments. Latest News (5 April). Ford Foundation. https://www.fordfoundation.org/the-latest/news/ford-foundation-commits-1-billion-from-endowment-to-mission-related-investments/ (accessed 27 February 2020).

Friedman, M. (1970). The Social Responsibility of Business is to Increase Its Profits. *New York* (13 September).

Friends Fiduciary (2018). The Quaker Difference. https://friendsfiduciary.org/about-us/the-quaker-difference/ (accessed 27 February 2020).

Gane, D. (2017). Focus Group: Diversity more than a "trend." *IPE* (July/August Edition). https://www.ipe.com/pensions/investors/focus-group/focus-group-diversity-more-than-a-trend/10019660.article (accessed 27 February 2020).

Germano, M. (2018). The real reason minority-owned businesses aren't getting funded. *Forbes* (11 December). https://www.forbes.com/sites/

maggiegermano/2018/12/11/investors-think-they-are-fair-but-minority-owned-businesses-are-left-out/#115f50db67d5 (accessed 12 March 2020).

Gompers, K. (2018). The Other Diversity Dividend. *Harvard Business Review* (July–August 2018 Issue). https://hbr.org/2018/07/the-other-diversity-dividend (accessed 1 March 2020).

Herring (2009). Does Diversity Pay?: Race, Gender, and the Business Case for Diversity. *American Sociological Review*, 74(3): 208–224 (1 April).

Hunt, V., Layton, D. and Prince, S. (2015). Why Diversity Matters. McKinsey & Company (1 January). https://www.mckinsey.com/business-functions/organization/our-insights/why-diversity-matters (accessed 1 March 2020)

ICCR (2020). The Nexus of Faith and Finance. https://www.iccr.org/our-approach/connection-between-faith-investing (accessed 27 February 2020).

IMF (2017). Women in Finance: A Case for Closing Gaps. International Monetary Fund Discussion Notes. https://www.imf.org/en/Publications/Staff-Discussion-Notes/Issues/2018/09/17/women-in-finance-a-case-for-closing-gaps-45136 (accessed 1 March 2020).

Judkis, M., and Merry, S. (2018). What is an inclusion rider? Michael B. Jordan is taking on Frances McDormand's Oscars proposal. Washington Post (8 March). https://www.washingtonpost.com/news/arts-and-entertainment/wp/2018/03/05/what-is-an-inclusion-rider-explaining-frances-mcdormands-call-to-action-at-the-oscars/ (accessed 26 May 2020).

Kapila, M., Hines, E., and Searby, M. (2016). Why Diversity, Equity, and Inclusion Matter. Independent Sector (6 October). https://independentsector.org/resource/why-diversity-equity-and-inclusion-matter/ (accessed 1 March 2020).

Kenzie, J. (2017). It's time to think Milton Friedman's shareholders value argument. *Chicago Booth Review* (7 December). https://review.chicagobooth.edu/economics/2017/article/it-s-time-rethink-milton-friedman-s-shareholder-value-argument.

Knight Foundation (2019). Diversifying Investment: A Study of Ownership Diversity and Performance in the Asset Management Industry. https://knightfoundation.org/reports/diversifying-investments-a-study-of-ownership-diversity-and-performance-in-the-asset-management-industry/ (accessed 1 March 2020).

Kramer, L. (2018). NYC Pension Funds, Push for Board Diversity Yields Impressive Results. Institutional Allocator (21 August). http://institutional-allocator.com/nyc-pension-funds-push-for-board-diversity-yields-impressive-results/ (accessed 27 February 2020).

Leijonhufvud, C., Connaker, A., Levin, J., et al. (2019). Democratizing Impact Investing, One Financial Advisor at a Time: Full Session Transcript. SOCAP-19 (19 February). https://www.totalimpactconference.com/blog/2020/2/19/financial-advisors-are-on-the-front-lines-of-democratizing-access-to-impact-investing-experts-weigh-in-on-the-future-of-the-industry? mc_cid=fae6fba769&mc_eid=80c9cc1c53 (accessed 27 February 2020).

Leung, M. (2019). More the investing options, more the chances of bad choices. How to deal with it? *Economic Times* (27 November). https://economictimes.indiatimes.com/markets/stocks/news/why-more-investing-options-mean-bad-decisions-how-to-deal-with-it/articleshow/72221661.cms (accessed 27 February 2020).

Lorenzo, L. (2018). How and Where Diversity Drives Financial Performance. *Harvard Business Review* (30 January). https://hbr.org/2018/01/how-and-where-diversity-drives-financial-performance (accessed 1 March 2020).

Lumberg, J. (2017). A History of Impact Investing. Investopedia (22 June). https://www.investopedia.com/news/history-impact-investing/ (accessed 27 February 2020).

Lyons-Padilla, S., Markus, H., Monk, A., et al. (2019). Race Influences Professional Investors' Financial Judgements. *Proceedings of the National Academy of Sciences* 116 (35): 17225–17230 (27 August). https://www.pnas.org/content/116/35/17225 (accessed 02 March 2020).

Macpherson, R., Kearney, S., and Kulow, E. (2018). How to Use Donor-Advised Funds to Make Impact Investments. *Stanford Social Innovation Review* (25 October). https://ssir.org/articles/entry/how_to_use_donor_advised_funds_to_make_impact_investments (accessed 2 March 2020).

Mathews, J. Sternlicht, D., Bouri, A., et al. (2015). Introducing the Impact Investing Benchmark. Cambridge Associates and the Global Impact Investing Network. https://thegiin.org/assets/documents/pub/Introducing_the_Impact_Investing_Benchmark.pdf (accessed 27 February 2020).

Mayer, R., Warr, R., and Zhao, J. (2018). Do Pro-Diversity Policies Improve Corporate Innovation? *Financial Management*, 47(3): 617–650 (Fall 2018). Wiley. https://onlinelibrary.wiley.com/doi/full/10.1111/fima.12205 (accessed 1 March 2020).

Morgan Stanley (2018). The Growing Market Investors Are Missing. https://www.morganstanley.com/pub/content/dam/msdotcom/mcil/growing-market-investors-are-missing.pdf (accessed 12 March 2020).

NAIC (2017). Examining the Results: The Financial Returns of Diverse Private Equity Firms. National Association of Investment Companies

(8 April). https://2rp8zq2kdoxy38kvwx23zbuc-wpengine.netdna-ssl.com/wp-content/uploads/2020/04/2017-performance-report.pdf (accessed 17 May 2020).

National Research Council (2010). Informing an Effective Response to Climate Change. National Academies Press. https://www.nap.edu/read/12784/chapter/1 (accessed 27 February 2020).

Niño, N. (2019). Why is #FinanceSoWhite? *Fast Company* (19 September). https://www.fastcompany.com/90405621/why-is-financesowhite (accessed 2 March 2020).

Noguchi, Y. (2020). Investor's Naked Selfies Ignite #MeToo Moment: Female Founder Fights Back. NPR (6 January). https://www.npr.org/2020/01/06/793134459/investors-naked-selfie-ignites-metoo-moment-female-founder-fights-back (accessed 12 March 2020).

Posner, C. (2019). So Long to Shareholder Primacy. Harvard Law School Forum on Corporate Governance (22 August). https://corpgov.law.harvard.edu/2019/08/22/so-long-to-shareholder-primacy/ (accessed 1 March 2020)

Posner, E. (2019). Milton Friedman Was Wrong. *Atlantic* (22 August). https://www.theatlantic.com/ideas/archive/2019/08/milton-friedman-shareholder-wrong/596545/ (accessed 27 February 2020)

Preesman, L. (2016). Dutch funds slow on diversity. *IPE* (July/August Edition). https://www.ipe.com/dutch-funds-slow-on-diversity/10014056.article (accessed 27 February 2020).

Price, D. (2020). Emerging impact fund managers represent an emerging source of impact alpha. Impact Alpha (25 February). https://impactalpha.com/emerging-impact-fund-managers-represent-an-emerging-source-of-impact-alpha/ (accessed 27 February 2020).

PwC (2019). PwC's 2019 Annual Corporate Directors Survey. PwC. https://www.pwc.com/us/en/services/governance-insights-center/assets/pwc-2019-annual-corporate-directors-survey-full-report-v2.pdf.pdf (accessed 1 March 2020).

Quakers in Britain (2020). Quakers welcome Supreme Court appeal ruling on ethical investments. (29 April). https://www.quaker.org.uk/news-and-events/news/quakers-welcome-supreme-court-appeal-ruling (accessed 17 May 2020).

Rice, C. (2013). How blind auditions help orchestras to eliminate gender bias. *Guardian* (14 October). https://www.theguardian.com/women-in-leadership/2013/oct/14/blind-auditions-orchestras-gender-bias (accessed 2 March 2020).

Schecter, A. (2017). It's time to rethink Milton Friedman's "shareholder value" argument. (7 December). https://review.chicagobooth.edu/economics/2017/article/it-s-time-rethink-milton-friedman-s-shareholder-value-argument (accessed 27 February 2020).

Seddon-Daines, O., and Chinwala, Y. (2017). Diversity from an Investor's Perspective: Why and how the most forward-looking asset owners are addressing diversity and inclusion. New Financial (November). https://www.plsa.co.uk/Portals/0/Documents/Policy-Documents/2017/Diversity_from_investor_perspective_FINAL_30_10_2017.pdf?ver=2017-10-31-163101-643 (accessed 12 March 2020).

Shank, T. (2016). Increasing opportunities for minority and women owned asset managers in institutional investments. The Roosevelt Institute. https://rooseveltinstitute.org/wp-content/uploads/2016/10/castingAWiderNet.pdf (accessed 27 February 2020).

Shieber, J. (2019). Investors Are Still Failing to Back Founders from Diverse Backgrounds. TechCrunch (12 February). https://techcrunch.com/2019/02/12/investors-are-still-failing-to-back-founders-from-diverse-backgrounds/ (accessed 12 March 2020).

Sports Illustrated (2017). Rooney Rule leaves a legacy and impact far beyond NFL. *Sports Illustrated* (14 April). https://www.si.com/nfl/2017/04/14/ap-fbn-rooney-rule (accessed 26 May 2020).

Stutts, K. (2018). Diversity, Equity, and Inclusion in Nonprofits and Philanthropy: Promising Practices for Advancing RMHF Health Fellows' Recommendations'. Richmond Memorial Health (RMH) Foundation. https://www.rmhfoundation.org/wp-content/uploads/2018/10/RMHF-DEI.pdf (accessed 1 March 2020).

Summers, K. (2018). Lost opportunities and unseen risks loom when investing without intention. https://www.igfoa.org/content/documents/final_igfoa_dispatch_dec_2018.pdf (accessed 15 May 2020).

Thomson Reuters (2019). Factsheet: Diversity and Inclusion Total Return Index. https://www.refinitiv.com/content/dam/marketing/en_us/documents/fact-sheets/diversity-and-inclusion-index-fact-sheet.pdf (accessed 1 March 2020).

Trelstad, B. (2016). Making Sense of the Many Kinds of Impact Investing. *Harvard Business Review* (28 January). https://hbr.org/2016/01/making-sense-of-the-many-kinds-of-impact-investing (accessed 27 February 2020).

Troster, R. (2014). Beyond the Letter of The Law: The Jewish Perspective on Ethical Investing and Fossil Fuel Divestment. *Soujourners* (3 December). https://sojo.net/articles/disinvest-reinvest/beyond-letter-law-jewish-perspective-ethical-investing-and-fossil-fuel (accessed 27 February 2020).

Walker, D. (2019). Pension funds probing deeper on pay, discrimination claims. *Pensions & Investments* (1 April). https://www.pionline.com/article/20190401/PRINT/190409986/pension-funds-probing-deeper-on-pay-discrimination-claims (accessed 27 February 2020).

Walsh, D. (2018). Nun Funds: The Original Impact Investors. *Shelterforce* (24 January). https://shelterforce.org/2018/01/24/nun-funds-original-impact-investors/ (accessed 27 February 2020).

White, T. (2014). Who Manages the Money? How foundations should help "democratize capital": A case study of the W.K. Kellogg. In cooperation with ABFE: A Philanthropic Partnership for Black Communities. Progress Investment Management Company. https://www.abfe.org/wp-content/uploads/2014/10/White+Paper+-+Who+Manages+the+Money+14.pdf (accessed 02 March 2020).

World Economic Forum (2017). The Global Risks Report 2017. 12th ed. ISBN: 978-1-944835-07-1. http://wef.ch/risks2017 (accessed 12 March 2020).

Zimmerman, J. (2019). Field Note: Recognizing Social Impact Investment Opportunity, 2019. Reinventure Capital (8 October). https://reinventurecapital.com/field-note-recognizing-social-impact-investment-opportunity-2019/ (accessed 27 February 2020).

APPENDIX 10.1: STARTING EXAMPLES OF COMMUNITIES OF PRACTICE AND KNOWLEDGE-SHARING PLATFORMS

Around the world, numerous communities of practice exist where Inclusive Investors share intelligence, experience, and questions. More are forming all the time. As the communities of practitioners grow, knowledge-sharing platforms also proliferate. This appendix provides just a small set of examples (sites listed were accessed 27 February 2020).

Communities of Practice

Astia	LBAN
https://astia.org	https://lban.us
Beyond the Billion	Mission Investors Exchange
https://beyondthebillion.com	https://missioninvestors.org
Black and Brown Founders	MosaicGenius
https://blackandbrownfounders.com	https://www.mosaicgenius.com
Confluence Philanthropy	Native Women Lead
https://www.confluencephilanthropy.org	http://nativewomenlead.org

Communities of Practice

Confluence Philanthropy
https://www.confluencephilan
thropy.org
ConnectUP
https://connectupmn.com
Disability
https://disabilityin.org
Financial Alliance for Women
https://financialallianceforwomen
.org
Gender-Smart Investing Summit
https://www.gendersmartinvesting
.com
Global InvestHer
https://www.globalinvesther.com
GoldenSeeds
https://goldenseeds.com
INTENT Manifesto
https://www.intentmanifesto.com
Intentional Endowments Network
https://www.intentionalendow
ments.org

Nexus global
https://nexusglobal.org
Oxfam
https://www.oxfam.org/en/take-
action/join-global-movement-change
Pipeline Angels
https://pipelineangels.com
Portfolia
http://portfolia.co
Refugee Investment Network
https://refugeeinvestments.org
Social Venture Circle
https://svcimpact.org
Total Impact
https://www.totalimpactconference
.com
TBLI
https://www.tbligroup.com
Women Moving Millions
https://womenmovingmillions.org

Knowledge Sharing Platforms

Project Diane
https://www.projectdiane.com
Project Sage
https://socialimpact.wharton
.upenn.edu/news/five-things-
know-project-sage/
Rotman Institute for Gender and
the Economy
https://www.gendereconomy.org

Stanford SPARQ
https://sparq.stanford.edu/products/
publications
UNPRI Principles for Investors in
Inclusive Finance
https://sptf.info/images/PRI-
Principles-for-Investors-in-Inclusive-
Finanace-PIIF-Overview.pdf

APPENDIX 10.2: ADDITIONAL RESOURCES FOR FURTHER EXPLORATION

For those readers who wish to learn more, this appendix provides a small sampling of resources. These are offered as starting points for further discovery and are far from a comprehensive set. All sites listed here were accessed 27 February 2020.

Bonds/Fixed Income

Breckinridge Capital Advisors: https://www.breckinridge.com/insights/details/betting-on-social-progress/ https://www.breckinridge.com/insights/details/why-gender-lens-investing-matters/

SSIR/Social Impact Bonds library

https://ssir.org/tags/Social+Impact+Bonds#

Private and Public Markets

Accenture: https://www.accenture.com/us-en/about/inclusion-diversity/persons-with-disabilities

Cornerstone Capital

https://cornerstonecapinc.com/advancing-the-gender-lens-framework/
https://cornerstonecapinc.com/two-lenses-one-vision-investing-for-lgbtqi-and-gender-equity/
https://cornerstonecapinc.com/investing-to-advance-racial-equity/
https://cornerstonecapinc.com/the-art-of-the-possible-investing-to-address-inequality/
https://cornerstonecapinc.com/structural-complicity-sexual-and-gender-based-violence-as-an-emerging-investment-risk/

Criterion Institute

https://criterioninstitute.org/our-work

Cultural Survival

https://www.ohchr.org/Documents/Issues/IPeoples/EMRIP/StudyGood
Practices/CulturalSurvival.pdf

edx

https://www.edx.org/course/financial-development-and-financial-
inclusion

NextWave Impact Investor Landscape

http://app.impactinvestorlandscape.org/index.html

Triple Pundit

https://www.triplepundit.com/search/inclusion

World Bank

https://www.worldbank.org/en/topic/financialinclusion

World Economic Forum

https://www.weforum.org/agenda/2019/04/what-companies-gain-including
-persons-disabilities-inclusion/

Public Markets

Boston Common Asset Management: http://news.bostoncommonasset.com/
racial-justice-investing/

Robasciotti & Philipson/RISE

https://robasciotti.com/2019/12/19/investing-at-the-intersection-of-racial-
justice-climate-change/https://www.youtube.com/watch?v=K0Zl6iPTL2w
&feature=youtu.be

Retail and Community Capital

AllRaise: https://www.allraise.org
Boston Impact Initiative: https://bostonimpact.org
Boston Ujima Project: https://www.ujimaboston.com
CNote: https://www.mycnote.com
Cooperative Capital: http://www.cooperativecap.com/company
Funders' Network: https://www.fundersnetwork.org/inclusive-economies-investment-displacement-engagement/
Republic: https://republic.co

Faith-based

IASJ: https://iasj.org/about-us/
ICCR: https://www.iccr.org/investing-rights-way-guide-investors-business-and-human-rights
UNDP: Islamic Finance and Impact Investing: https://www.undp.org/content/dam/istanbul/docs/Islamic_Finance_Impact.pdf

Government sources

ASEAN: https://www.unescap.org/sites/default/files/Inclusive%20Business%20in%20ASEAN%20-%20Progress%20Report_ESCAP_iBAN_ASEAN.pdf
Canada / Equality Fund: https://www.equalityfund.ca
European Commission: https://ec.europa.eu/social/main.jsp?catId=737&langId=en
OECD: https://play.google.com/store/books/details?id=VfPCDwAAQBAJ&rdid=book-VfPCDwAAQBAJ&rdot=1&source=gbs_vpt_read&pcampaignid=books_booksearch_viewport
UK Government Inclusive Economy: https://www.gov.uk/government/collections/social-investment
UN Dept of Economic and Social Affairs: https://www.un.org/development/desa/socialperspectiveondevelopment/issues/financial-inclusion.html

Angel/Seed Stage

Angel Capital Association: https://www.angelcapitalassociation.org/data/Documents/diversity-and-inclusion-handout-summit-2.pdf?rev=3DAB
HBAN: https://www.hban.org/learning-centre/news/inclusiveness-an-interesting-way-to-improve-angel-results
WCAF/WBAF: https://books.google.com/books?id=VfPCDwAAQBAJ&pg=PA239&lpg=PA239&dq=inclusive+angel+investing&source=bl&ots=TJxC5Y13vK&sig=ACfU3U1DgF7gfdEVJO4o6W9TFXakcXReUw&hl=en&sa=X&ved=2ahUKEwja55nisM_nAhWolnIEHRpIBvkQ6AEwEXoECAwQAQ#v=onepage&q=inclusive%20angel%20investing&f=false

CHAPTER 11

Investing for Impact in Employee Retirement Plans

Megan E. Morrice, MBA

Abstract

Although once only available to institutional and ultra-high-net-worth investors, the perimeter of the Impact Investing ecosystem is expanding. Everyday investors are realizing they have the power to align their dollars with their desire for a more sustainable world. Simultaneously, changes are emerging in how most individual's largest investment portfolio, retirement funds, are invested. This includes a global shift from defined benefit (DB) plans, where investment risk and portfolio management are entirely controlled by the company or country in charge, to defined contribution (DC) plans, where employees bear the investment risk and portfolio choices. This trend from DB to DC primarily started in the United States and Australia, but many countries have followed. Historically, DC plans faced barriers integrating more impactful portfolios, such as regulation, low contribution rates, and participants' endeavors to choose the most appropriate investments. Evidence is growing that participation rates and contributions to retirement plans, along with employee engagement at work, increase when employees are offered sustainable investing options. Additionally, smart retirement plan design uses modern features like investments that match employee's environmental, social, and governance (ESG) interests. Automatic enrollment with appropriate default investments is critical to help employees save sustainably. The tools are ready to implement sustainable investing in retirement plan assets that currently do not have it, as long as plan fiduciaries are ready to be leaders and not laggards. This chapter shows how investment managers, plan fiduciaries, and plan participants can take action to invest more sustainably via retirement plans.

Keywords

Retirement Plans; 401(k); 403(b); Pensions; ESG; Socially Responsible Investing; Impact Investing; Defined Contribution; Defined Benefit; Sustainable Investing; Fiduciary Duty; Behavioral Finance

INTRODUCTION

Although once only accessible by institutional and ultra-high-net-worth investors, the perimeter of the Impact Investing ecosystem is expanding. According to the Global Impact Investing Network (GIIN), at the end of 2018, USD $503 billion in impact investments were allocated to bring about positive change. This number only includes impact investments as "investments made with the intention to generate positive, measurable social and environmental impact alongside a financial return" (Abhilash et al. 2019, p. 52). However, trillions of dollars must be mobilized to address the annual funding gap of USD $2.5 trillion that is needed to fulfill the United Nations Sustainable Development Goals (SDGs) (UNCTAD 2014).

In recent years, an increase of available products and increased technology has broadened access to investments with not only a financial return, but also a social and environmental impact. At an opportune time, everyday investors are realizing they have the power to demand their dollars to be aligned with their desire for a more sustainable world. When assets that employ additional sustainable investing strategies, like negative screening[1] or environmental, social, and governance (ESG) integration[2] are

---

[1] The process of excluding companies based on certain criteria.
[2] That is, the inclusion of ESG data in investment decision and analysis.

included under the umbrella of impactful investing, the total assets under management are much higher. The Global Sustainable Investment Alliance (GSIA) estimates that at the start of 2018, USD $30.7 trillion was allocated in sustainable investing assets across Europe, the United States, Canada, Japan, and Australia and New Zealand (Global Sustainable Investment Alliance 2018).

For most nonaccredited investors, the largest asset after a house is retirement funds (Desjardins 2018). Nonetheless, making choices for a portfolio that is more impactful can utilize the USD $46 trillion of capital that is currently invested in legacy finance in the retirement investment market (Willis Towers Watson 2020). Retirement arrangements vary by country. Historically, many companies funded public or private pensions that were managed centrally by investment professionals and paid annuity-life income to workers in retirement. Today, it is more common to have the investments in retirement plans self-managed by the individual worker. This shift has been most dramatic in the United States and the United Kingdom, but this trend also applies in Asia, Europe, and Latin America (Merton 2014). To optimize future risk and return, and eventually provide for retirement needs, these funds need to be invested looking decades forward into which investments are more likely to succeed. Yet many everyday investors (and even some investment professionals) choose funds in retirement portfolios by looking backward at historical performance, rather than proactively evaluating future risks and upside for the funds they select. The long-term investment risks of climate change or industry transformation are frequently overlooked or underestimated, as well as limited by the fund choices offered by the plan and its fiduciaries.

This chapter reviews the growing demand for sustainable portfolios in retirement plans, discusses the different types of retirement plans in the world, the current regulatory environment and global fiduciary standard, plus presents case studies of retirement funds that are creating more impactful portfolio choices in Australia (where retirement schemes are called superannuation). It consolidates much of the research available on sustainable defined contribution (DC) plans through a desk review, presents original evidence taken from 14 semi-structured interviews between April 2019 and January 2020 with leaders in the retirement and sustainable investing fields in the United States and Australia (see the Appendix of this chapter for further details), and draws on deep dive examples globally. A case study on impact portfolios discusses the setting up of a default ESG option at the United World College (UWC) in the United States. This chapter also highlights the gaps between the desire for sustainable investments and the supply of solutions with a focus on the psychology behind investing.

The following section describes the demand for sustainable portfolios in retirement plans and different types of retirement plans. Then the chapter reviews regulation in the United States, UK, and European Union (EU), including specifically fiduciary duty and guidance by the US Department of Labor. Next, the chapter reviews case studies in Australia, a world leader in sustainable retirement plans, and in the United States, a country very new to sustainable investing in DC plans. The following section highlights three key features of successful sustainable retirement savings plans, as well as a few benefits of creating the plans. The final section provides four guidelines for both companies and individuals to help catalyze the flow of assets into impactful retirement funds. Companies can take steps to offer impactful retirement plans to their employees by: (i) getting educated on sustainable investing, (ii) engaging employees through their retirement plans, (iii) preparing for inspired incremental change, and (iv) educating participants with managerial buy-in. Individuals can make their retirement savings more impactful by: (i) researching and preparing, (ii) talking to their colleagues and building consensus, (iii) identifying who to approach, and (iv) approaching companies with other potential solutions.

RETIREMENT PLANS DEMAND AND TYPES

Demand for Sustainable Portfolios in Retirement Plans

The global demand for sustainable, responsible, and impact investments continues to rise. Of the GSIA's estimate of USD $30.7 trillion in sustainable investing assets, Europe accounts for the largest share, at USD $14.1 trillion in Assets Under Management (AUM), followed by the US with USD $12 trillion USD in AUM (Global Sustainable Investment Alliance 2018). In Australia, the results of the recent Responsible Investment Association Australasia research show that 9 in 10 respondents expect their money to be invested responsibly and ethically. If their current fund engaged in activities not consistent with their values, 4 in 5 would consider moving their investments to another provider (Responsible Investment Association Australasia 2017). In the United States, research from the Natixis "2017 Global Survey of Individual Investors" found that 84% of respondents "consider it important to invest in companies that are ethically run" (Natixis 2017).

Meanwhile, the appetite for ESG retirement plan investments also continues to grow. The Natixis 2016 DC Plan Participant Survey revealed that 74% of US respondents would like to "see more socially responsible investments in their retirement plan offering," and 62% said they would "increase their contributions if they knew their investments were doing social good." Overall, 82% of survey respondents say they want investments in their retirement plan that reflect their personal values (Natixis 2016). In a field experiment where participants were given a real vote on their pension fund's sustainable investment policy, 67.9% of participants voted for more sustainable investments (Bauer et al. 2020). A 2017 survey by Strooga Consulting reported that two-thirds of DC plan investors said they would like to know more about the sustainability risks in their investment accounts, and over 80% agreed or strongly agreed that "a company's good performance on select sustainability issues could result in outperformance over the long-term" (Strooga 2017).

Although there is strong support across all ages and genders for sustainable investing, women and Millennials have consistently shown the highest interest. Five in six (84%) of women are interested in sustainable investing (Morgan Stanley Institute for Sustainable Investing 2017). A Natixis survey found that the interest among women in ESG investments was consistently above men, although in aggregate not by much. Nearly four in five (79%) women would like to see more socially responsible investments in their retirement plans, as opposed to 69% of males. Women were also more likely to be concerned about the environmental, social, and ethical records of the companies they invest in (68% of females, compared to 59% of males) (Natixis 2016). Millennials are also a key driver in sustainable investing in retirement plans. A full 85% of high-net-worth Millennials say they consider their investment decisions a way "to express their social, political, and environmental values," and 93% indicate that a company's action and results in these areas are important considerations when they invest (Ehrenfeld 2016). Nine in 10 (90%) of all Millennials want sustainable investing options as part of their 401(k)[3] plans, as shown in Figure 11.1 (Morgan Stanley Institute for Sustainable Investing 2017).

Retirement Income Architecture: Defined Benefit and Defined Contribution

The architecture of national options (or the lack thereof) for retirement investing are diverse. The Organization for Economic Co-operation Development (OECD) encapsulates the retirement income work globally in three main tiers, as shown in Figure 11.2. This chapter will focus on the second tier and the third tier.

---

[3] The most popular American DC retirement plans today are 401(k)s.

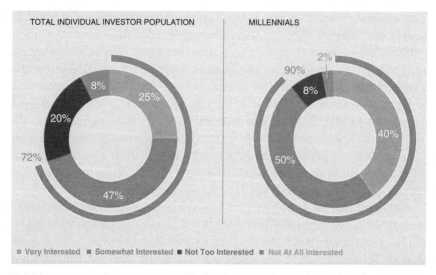

FIGURE 11.1 Level of Interest in Pursuing Sustainable Investments If They Were an Option for 401(k) Plans. *Source:* Morgan Stanley Institute for Sustainable Investing (2017), p. 6.
Reproduced with permission of Morgan Stanley.

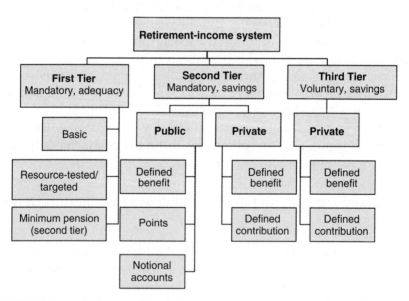

FIGURE 11.2 Architecture of Tiers of Retirement Income Plans in the World.
Source: OECD (2013).

The second tier is "designed to provide some targeted standard of living in retirement related to the working years, and generally considered to be a mandatory system, and may be offered through the public or private sectors. These benefits may be provided through a DB or DC arrangement. The benefit provided is normally related to the level of contributions, income levels and years in the workforce. These benefits may be fully funded, partially funded or operate on a pay-as-you-go basis as part of a social security arrangement" (CFA Institute/Mercer 2015, p. 7). The third tier is "voluntary and provided by the private sector; may be offered through occupational schemes and/or private savings accounts. This tier is fully funded and often operates in conjunction with the second tier"[4] (CFA Institute/Mercer 2015, p. 7).

Many countries provide for their employees' retirement through national or corporate pension plans, which guarantee participants receive an income benefit at a specific future date, typically when they retire from service. Under DB plans, most often known as pensions, the benefit in the future that participants receive is "defined" with the manager of the plan, assuming the investment risk and responsibility for allocating and investing for their citizen's or employee's retirement. The public sector provides DB plans in 18 OECD countries. Private, occupational plans are mandatory or quasi-mandatory in Iceland, the Netherlands, and Switzerland (OECD 2017). However, pension systems around the world all face strain because of increases in life expectancy beyond originally planned expectations. The UN projects global population will exceed 2 billion people over age 60 worldwide by 2050 (UN 2015, p. 25). Currently, about one in seven (14%) people in major developed economies is over 65, ranging from 5% in Mexico to 12% in Australia and the United States to 20% in Japan and Italy. The global proportion is expected to nearly double to 26% by the mid-twenty-first century (OECD 2018). The aging in demographics over 100 years in Europe and North America has occurred in just a single generation for some Asian countries. Asia-Pacific countries, outside the OECD, are much younger, with an average of 6% of the populations over 65 years of age today, though expected to nearly triple to 17% by mid-century (OECD 2018).

Largely due to the strain of aging demographics, DB plans have become expensive to manage. There has been a decline of traditional DB plans

---

[4]According to the OECD (2013), the first tier is a redistributive tier that "comprises programs designed to ensure pensioners achieve some absolute, minimum standard of living" designed to prevent poverty. It is normally provided by the public sector and may provide a basic universal pension or be subject to resource testing at the individual level, or a combination of both approaches.

by governments and employers due to the expense and complexity. More emphasis has been placed on accruing assets in individual retirement savings accounts, shifting the onus of saving and investing for retirement on workers, and DC plans have become the main vehicles for these savings (Gandhi 2019). With a DC plan, the contribution, rather than the benefit, is "defined" and any benefits are not guaranteed. In DC plans, the employee, employer, or both contribute on a regular basis to fund the retirement arrangement. In a DC plan, the risks (investment risk, longevity risk, interest rate risk, inflation risk) and the investment rewards fall solely on the individual to invest smartly for their goals. DC plans offer no guarantees on the future benefits that workers can expect from the plan in retirement. These are summarized in Table 11.1.

Stacy Scapino, previously Global Leader Investments Multinational Client Segment at Mercer, classifies international DC systems as:

- **The open-architecture, broad investment choice** system in largely Anglo-Saxon countries (United States, UK, Ireland, Australia), where the administrative provider offers a large range of funds from which employers and employees can select.
- **The government-mandated or collectively bargained guaranteed return** system, prevalent in Germany and Belgium, in which insurance contracts provide set returns on participant savings.

TABLE 11.1   Differences Between Defined Contribution and Defined Benefit Plans.

Defined Contribution Plans	Defined Benefit Plans
"Defines" the contribution amount into the plan.	"Defines" the benefit amount that participants can expect to receive.
Individual accounts.	Pooled accounts.
Investment risk on individual participants in plan.	Investment risk on the company or government who runs the plan.
Benefits are not guaranteed.	Fixed benefit related to pay and or length of serves, or fixed dollar amount.
Fixed or variable contribution.	Contributions can vary based on needs.
Examples include 401(k) plans 403(b) plans in the United States, Superannuations in Australia, or workplace retirement plans.	Examples include pensions.

Source: Author.

- **The government- or state-approved provider** system is used in countries like Chile and New Zealand, where employees may have a degree of investment choice. In countries like Thailand, Hong Kong, and Mexico, employers select a provider from several licensed entities, and the provider determines participants' investment choices, much like the US 403(b) system.
- **Personal pension brokered markets**, in which participants use DC savings to purchase individual pensions through brokers, as in the Czech Republic and Israel.
- **The state insurance model**, common in emerging markets such as Morocco and Pakistan, in which participants make payments into the state's insured funds (Aston 2018, p. 11).

This shift from DB to DC plans, although led by companies in the United States and Australia, has been global (Aston 2018). Even Japan and Canada, which historically have only been DB, are starting to show an increase in the allocation toward DC. In South Africa, the majority of private sector employees belong to DC arrangements, while public sector funds are largely invested in DB systems. In 2019, the total assets of the aggregate of DC plans in the six largest pension markets in the world exceed DB assets for the first time. DC assets are growing at a faster rate than DB assets (8.4% per year for DC compared to 4.8% per year for DB) and are fast becoming the dominant global model (Willis Towers Watson 2020).

In the 1990s, a series of regulations were introduced throughout Latin America to address the long-term financial sustainability of an aging population, some countries moved from relying on defined-benefit pay-as-you-go public pension systems to privately managed individual accounts.

DB plans are provided by the public sector in 21 Latin American and Caribbean (LAC) countries, and privately managed DC plans are required in six LAC countries (Chile, Costa Rica, Dominican Republic, El Salvador, Mexico, Uruguay). In addition, although workers in Columbia and Peru have the option to choose a public, DB arrangement, a significant number opt into contributing to the privately managed DC plans that are also available (OECD, IDB,[5] and World Bank 2014).

The differences among these models, as well as the nomenclature, regulation, and fiduciary responsibilities, and prevalence of sustainable options, vary greatly across the world.

The next sections address the challenges to implementing responsible investing in retirement plans. To ensure clarity to the reader, we follow the local nomenclature, which differs by region and country. In the United States,

---

[5] Inter-American Development Bank.

the most popular type of DC plan is named after its section in the congressional act that established DC plans, the 401(k). In Australia, the superannuation retirement system is known as "super." In other parts of the world, "workplace plans" or "employer plans" might suffice.

REGULATION IN THE UNITED STATES, UNITED KINGDOM, AND EUROPEAN UNION

Fiduciary Duty

Retirement plans around the world are highly regulated. It is critical to understand the responsibilities of fiduciaries who are responsible for managing someone else's money. A common concern among plan sponsors, or the designated parties that set up retirement plans, is ensuring they honor and do not violate their fiduciary duty.[6] Fear of fiduciary liability for investment decisions is a critical driver of behavior. However, what is considered to be prudent investing is not static and has evolved over time. This section will now examine current guidance in the United States, UK, and EU.

In the UK, the Law Commission defines the fiduciary relationship as "status-based," where the relationship falls under a previously recognized category like agent and principal or trustee and beneficiary, or as "fact-based," where the particular facts of the relationship such as acting on behalf of the other person, cause a fiduciary nature. The Law Commission states that the "irreducible core fiduciary duty is the duty of loyalty, which indicates that a fiduciary must not profit from the relationship, have a conflict, divide their loyalties between different relationships or use information obtained in confidence" (Walker et al. 2018, p. 11). The EU follows the prudent person rule, which is an ethical obligation to act in the best interest of the plan beneficiary.

In the United States, private sector retirement plans are governed by the Employee Retirement Income Security Act of 1974 (ERISA). Under ERISA, as seen in Figure 11.3, fiduciary duty spans the duty of loyalty, the duty of prudence, and the duty to diversify.

To improve the financial system, asset owners have worked to modernize the interpretation of fiduciary duty to include material financial risks related to sustainability (Willis Towers Watson 2020). There are an

---

[6]The term "fiduciary" derives from the Latin "fides," meaning "trust" or "faith," and the phrase embodies the core values and duties of care, loyalty, and prudence.

FIDUCIARY DUTY (ERISA)		
Duty of Loyalty:	**Duty of prudence:**	**Duty to diversify:**
A fiduciary must "run the plan solely in the interest of participants and beneficiaries and for the exclusive purpose of providing benefits and paying plan expenses"	A fiduciary must "discharge his duties with respect to a plan with the care, skill, prudence and diligence under the circumstances then prevailing that a prudent man acting in a like capacity and familiar with such matters would use in the conduct of an enterprise of a like character and with like aims"	A fiduciary must "diversify plan investments so as to minimize the risk of large losses"

FIGURE 11.3   Fiduciary Duty in the United States (ERISA).   *Source:* Walker et al. (2018).
Reproduced with permission of the World Business Council for Sustainable Development.

increasing number of people that believe that not considering long-term investment value drivers (including ESG issues) in investment decisions is a failure of fiduciary duty. In "Fiduciary Duty in the 21st Century," the Principles for Responsible Investing (PRI) state that "integrating ESG issues into investment research and processes will enable investors to make better investment decisions and improve investment performance consistent with their fiduciary duties. This will result in capital being allocated towards well-governed companies, putting investors in a better position to contribute to the goals of a greener economy and a more sustainable society" (PRI 2015).

Department of Labor Guidance in the United States

In the United States, the Department of Labor (US DOL) provides periodic guidance to ensure that fiduciaries follow principles that do not render them personally liable, including guidance on the regulatory landscape specific to ESG. The Interpretive Bulletins (IBs) they published have lacked a consistent message from different administrations.

However, in October 2015 the US DOL clarified a 2008 bulletin that many interpreted as discouraging private sector retirement plans from considering social and environmental factors in their investments. The 2015 bulletin, IB 2015-01, states that "fiduciaries should appropriately consider factors that potentially influence risk and return," and "environmental, social, and governance issues may have a direct relationship to the economic value of a plan's investment." It further states that fiduciaries may not accept lower expected returns in pursuit of these factors, but that material ESG "issues may have a direct relationship to the economic value of a plan's investment" (Lessne et al. 2019). In cases like these, ESG factors are part of the core due diligence and analysis of the investment and should not have extra scrutiny. The US DOL has consistently recognized that fiduciaries may consider noneconomic goals as "tiebreakers" when choosing between investments that are otherwise equal in their risk-return profile.

The 2016 bulletin, IB 2016-01, states that ESG topics may be incorporated into proxy voting policies and engagement with corporations (US Department of Labor 2016). In summary, the US DOL's 2015 and 2016 bulletins state ESG factors can be appropriately used in investment analysis for retirement plans, but they put forth restrictions.

In 2018, the US DOL issued Field Assistance Bulletin (FAB) No. 2018-01, in an attempt to further clarify how investment professionals should interpret the US DOL's prior IBs (Tang 2018). Although the FAB did not overturn the prior IBs, it reaffirmed the use of material ESG factors. The current 2016–2020 US administration has had a more careful tone about sustainable investing. The report says that fiduciaries "must not too readily treat ESG factors as economically relevant to the particular investment choices at issue when making a decision. It does not ineluctably follow from the fact that an investment promotes ESG factors, or that it arguably promotes positive general market trends or industry growth, that the investment is a prudent choice for retirement or other investors. Rather, ERISA fiduciaries must always put first the economic interests of the plan in providing retirement benefits" (US Department of Labor 2018).

The FAB does specify potentially using an ESG-themed fund as a qualified default investment alternative (QDIA), when new participants join or add funds, as an area for fiduciaries for particular attention. One of the provisions of the Pension Provision Act of 2006 (PPA) was "automatic enrollment," which permitted employees to opt out of a retirement plan instead of having to opt in. Plans with automatic enrollment always require a QDIA, or a default investment to use when the employee has not yet made their investment selections and receive "safe harbor" protection from potential litigation by employees who could claim the QDIA selection was against their best interests.

In 2007, the US DOL outlined the conditions for a plan fiduciary to not be liable for investment losses incurred by them investing the funds of plan participants. Those investment options include target-date funds, balanced funds, and managed accounts (Invesco 2015). Many advisors have interpreted the US DOL guidelines as permitting the use of ESG factors in a default option's investment strategy; however, some fiduciaries have been hesitant to proceed without specific guidance for QDIAs as opposed to the plan investments in general. It is still unclear whether ESG factors are permissible to consider as part of a QDIA, especially with the line into 2018-01 FAB "nothing in the QDIA regulation suggests that fiduciaries should choose QDIAs based on collateral policy goals" (Groom Law Group 2018 p. 2), although many would argue that ESG factors are completely separate from policy goals. The US DOL has "not considered whether the use of ESG factors in a default option's investment strategy impacts its ability to comply with existing QDIA regulations" (Jeszeck 2018, p. 40).

In conclusion, the US DOL has not provided much clarity around how retirement plans can incorporate ESG factors. In particular, US DOL has not addressed whether a DC plan may incorporate sustainability factors in the plan's default option and if there would be protection from potential litigation. However, ERISA is a process statute, which only describes what a good or bad process is, according to Judy Mares,[7] former Deputy Assistant Secretary and Advisor of US DOL. Additionally, FAB 2018-01 is a supplement and not a replacement of previous DOL publications (Lessne et al. 2019). A FAB usually cannot substantially change preexisting regulations without public notice and comment, of which 2018-01 was not subject (Mercer 2018). There is currently regulatory ambiguity, but making changes to established processes is time-consuming. Further clarification from the US DOL is needed, but for now advisors need to make sure they do not sacrifice the economic interest of their clients to incorporate sustainability into DC plans.

Guidance in the United Kingdom and the European Union

Regulators have provided much more clarity in the UK and the EU. In September 2018, the UK Department of Work and Pensions published a response to the Pension Protection Fund and Occupational Pension Schemes Regulations 2018, making it clear that it is the duty of pension trustees to consider all financially material risks and opportunities, and those include, but are not limited to, ESG topics like climate change (Sacker 2018). A core element of the regulations is that certain retirement plans will be required to update their Statement of Investment Principles (known as Investment Policy Statements in other countries) to reflect how they

---

[7] Judy Mares, interview data (see Appendix).

take social and environmental impact into account, as well as stewardship policies. These increased ESG disclosure requirements in Statement of Investment Principles are set to shift the landscape of how ESG considerations are incorporated into UK pension investment decision making (Walker et al. 2018).

A sweeping reform of the pensions industry in the EU came about in January 2019, two years after the EU adopted a revised Institution for Occupational Retirement Provision Directive. It requires retirement plan providers with over 100 members to evaluate potential ESG risk and disclose that data to members. EU member states were given two years to integrate the directive into national law. The Directive (European Union 2016) required occupation retirement plans to:

- Invest according to the Prudent Person Principle, potentially including the long-term social and environmental impact of their investments (Article 19).
- Have a transparent system of governance that includes the consideration of ESG factors (Article 21).
- Establish a risk management function that includes ESG risks (Article 25).
- Complete and document a risk assessment at least every three years. When ESG factors are included, the risk assessment should include emerging risks like climate change, social risks, resource use, and stranded assets (Article 28).
- Produce a Statement of Investment Policy Principles every three years or when there are significant changes, whichever comes first. These should be available to the public and include how the policy includes ESG factors (Article 30).
- Inform prospective members if and how ESG factors are used in the investment approach (Article 41).

Generally, the new laws reinforce that retirement plans must invest according to prudent person principles, improve internal risk management, and make more information and data available to its participants (PRI 2016).

Globally, sustainable investing choices in retirement plans have become more prevalent in Australia and its superannuation systems, offering wider choice to everyday investors. Meanwhile, the US retirement plan options have been slow to incorporate sustainability for the challenges described above in interpretations of regulation and fiduciary duty. The next section details the Australia system as a leading best practice and the US system as a lagging practice.

Case Study: Australia, a World Leader in Sustainable Retirement Plans

---

Australia's "superannuation" retirement system is one of the most highly rated systems in the world (Jones 2019), and includes: i) the Age Pension, a means-tested, government funded tax-financed pension, ii) a Superannuation Guarantee, a mandatory retirement savings program that employers are required to contribute a percentage of worker's earnings, and iii) Voluntary Savings, or the ability for the individual to contribute to their "Super" or retirement savings account (Eisenberg 2013). The employer's contribution is currently mandated at 9.5% of a worker's gross earnings, which totaled AUD $2.3 trillion (USD $1.8 trillion) at the end of 2017, and this rate will rise to 12% of employee gross pay by 2020 (Eisenberg 2013). In the 1980s, a little less than half the workforce was covered by pension plans. However, in the last four decades, plans have shifted from a DB, which guaranteed the participants receive an income benefit at a specific future date, to the above three-tiered approach. According to a survey by the Global Retirement Reality Report, "the sense that superannuation is 'deferred pay' has doubtless helped this conviction, particularly compared to some European countries in our survey, where expectations of the state were much higher" (State Street Global Advisors 2018).

Besides being touted for their retirement savings, Australians have also shown a strong commitment to sustainable investing. The majority of all assets in Australia and New Zealand are invested in sustainable strategies (Whyte 2017). Specific to retirement investing, four in five (81%) of the largest super funds now have embedded a formal commitment to Responsible Investing (RI). Nearly half of super funds offer a total of 75 responsible-investing options (Responsible Investment Association Australasia 2017). A KPMG analysis of 49 super funds with greater than AUD $5 billion in AUM found that over half of the funds are signatories of the UN's PRI (Howes 2018). A few of the leading RI super funds include Australian Ethical, First State Super, Christian Super, and HESTA (Responsible Investment Association Australasia 2017).

Australian Ethical, the fastest-growing super fund by member growth from 2012 to 2017, has more than 41,500 participants. It invests in companies that are working to build a clean energy future and promote human rights, as well as wholly avoid harmful practices from higher-emission industries

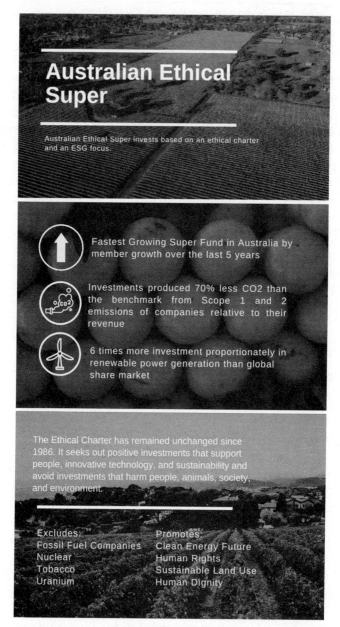

FIGURE 11.4   Highlights of Australian Ethical's Leadership in Sustainable Retirement Plans. *Source*: Author constructed image based on data from Australian Ethical 2018 Sustainability Report (Australian Ethical 2019).

like coal, and oil, as well as weapons and tobacco, as summarized in Figure 11.4. As of December 31, 2017, Australian Ethical's sum of equity investments produced 66% less CO_2 emissions than their benchmark and have proportionately six times more investment in renewable power generation compared to the global equity market (Australian Ethical Investment Ltd 2019).

Australian Ethical also discusses climate risk at every board meeting as a standing item on the board agenda, has set a portfolio decarbonization target of zero portfolio emissions by 2050, and measures the extent of alignment of its investments to reduce exposure to the energy sector in line with the +2° Celsius limit of a global warming pathway. Additionally, Australian Ethical pursues corporate engagement and advocacy, uses various sustainability metrics, including revenue from activities contributing toward certain UN SDGs (provided by ESG data provider MSCI), and information about the impact of certain investments (Responsible Investment Association Australasia 2017).

Another super fund with an ESG and ethical mandate is HESTA, a super fund focused on its members in the hospitality industry. HESTA has more than 870,000 members, mostly women, with AUD $50 billion (USD $30.8 billion) in assets. HESTA is committed to creating better futures for its members both through retirement outcomes and by supporting a healthy economy, environment, and society.[8] HESTA has strong governance and accountability processes developed with a proactive understanding of its member's interests from surveys to monitoring issues raised at its call centers. These member interests are then incorporated into their investment strategies.

HESTA invested AUD $30 million into its Social Impact Investment Trust and committed AUD $35 million to the LeapFrog Fund, an alternative investment fund that invests private equity and private debt in high-growth Asian and African companies that provide affordable health care. HESTA's target focus for impact investment is in the health and community services sector, which has values-alignment with HESTA's membership of health care workers. LeapFrog companies reach 188 million people, of which 154 million are low-income consumers buying financial and health products and services, across 35 emerging markets[9]. In addition to their membership, the management has evolved to be primarily women. HESTA surveys 100% of its fund managers on the gender diversity of their underlying investments, with a target of at least 30% of the

---

[8]More information available online at https://www.hesta.com.au/members.html.
[9]More information available online at www.leapfroginvest.com.

board of directors being women. The membership organization also engages managers on how they identify and manage other gender diversity risks and opportunities in their investment holdings (Responsible Investment Association Australasia 2017).

HESTA has also worked with the Criterion Institute, a nonprofit think tank that works with social change organizations and investors on how to engage and shift financial systems. One of Criterion's programs works to leverage investment capital, including funds managing workplace retirement plans, to address gender-based violence. HESTA, along with 10 other investment firms, sponsored Criterion's Gender Lens Investing and Market Risk (GLIMR) analysis tool. Within GLIMR, Criterion has analyzed OECD gender data and data from the Georgetown University Women, Peace, and Security Index, drawing out correlations between gender patterns and market risk. For instance, there is a correlation between countries with a high level of violence against women and current and future instability in terms of country or political risk (Hudson et al. 2008/09). Two-thirds of women in the Pacific Islands experience gender-based violence, according to the World Health Organization (WHO), and one in three women worldwide. The global cost of violence against women is estimated at USD $1.5 trillion or 2% of global gross domestic product (GDP) (Puri 2016). The Criterion Institute has been working with impact investors and family offices, as well as banks, insurance companies, private advisors, and other super funds, on how to pursue Impact Investing and gender lens investing. It identifies major trends leading to overlooked and undervalued patterns and then educates investors on how to implement gender equality and social change strategies that help to uncover risks to be avoided and opportunities to be pursued.[10]

While Australian firms and systems encourage this leadership, the world's largest economy is lagging. The next section explains the gaps and where innovative retirement plans are breaking through to implement higher impact portfolio choices.

United States, Emerging Innovations in Sustainable Retirement Plans

Many retirement plans in Europe have adopted ESG investment strategies, but in the United States, there is less adoption and more regulatory

---

[10]Tanya Black, interview data (see Appendix).

ambiguity. Very little of the USD $8.4 trillion in US ERISA[11]-governed private DC plans have shifted to match the overwhelmingly expressed demand for ESG funds. Few plans offer their employees the option to include ESG funds in their 401(k) or 403(b), even in plans established by mission-driven business and nonprofits. The Vanguard Group reported that only 8% of its 1,900 employee plans included a socially responsible investment offering, most of which offered only a single fund rather than a suite of offerings. Out of the 18% of participants who were offered one, only 3% actually invested; almost 1 in 5 firms (19%) larger than 5,000 employees offered a socially responsible fund choice, while only 1 in 12 firms (8%) with fewer than 5,000 employees offered one to participants (Utkus and Young 2018). According to the Plan Sponsor Council of America annual survey of US DC plans in 2016, only 2.4% of the 590 respondents had an ESG investment option as one of the funds participants could choose from (Jeszeck 2018).

Similar to the larger divestment movement in foundation endowments, it can be hard for larger organizations to change the *status quo* even when there seems to be a clear alignment with the organization's programmatic mission and grantmaking. Although almost 200 foundations worldwide have committed to divest, there are thousands, including the largest American foundations with explicit missions to combat climate change, who have not. Since 2014, 200 foundations with assets totaling USD $24 billion, signed on to Divest-Invest Philanthropy.[12] Most of the signatories are mostly small and medium-sized foundations. For example, according to its government filing Form 990-PF in 2017, the MacArthur Foundation continues to finance the fossil-fuel industry. As of 2019, other large funders like the Ford Foundation, the William and Flora Hewlett Foundation, and the David and Lucile Packard Foundation have yet to divest (Williams 2019). Additionally, according to both the 2018 government filings Form 5500 for the Sierra Club

---

[11]In 1974, the federal Employee Retirement Income Security Act (ERISA) was enacted to prescribe minimum standards for most voluntarily established retirement and health plans in private industry in the United States. Under ERISA, "plan sponsors and fiduciaries must (1) act solely in the interest of the plan participants and beneficiaries; and (2) invest with the care, skill, and diligence of a prudent person with knowledge of such matters and (3) diversify plan investments to minimize the risk of large losses. Plan fiduciaries that breach any of these fiduciary duties can be held personally liable to repay any losses resulting from the breach, and restore any profits that have been made through use of plan assets (Jeszeck 2018)." ERISA has a primary focus on protecting individuals in these plans.
[12]Divest-Invest Philanthropy is an international platform for institutions interested in divesting from fossil fuels and investing in climate change solutions (www.divestinvest .org/).

and the Natural Resources Defense Council, even these large environmental nonprofits have not divested from fossil fuels or offered employees fossil-fuel free retirement plans.

However, there are innovative organizations, financial advisors, firms, and membership organizations that are listening to people who care for and want to improve nature and the environment, as well as the well-being of the community.

For some organizations, all it takes is awareness of where their money is currently allocated. Although Katelyn Kriesel, a financial advisor at Hansen's Advisory Services in Fayetteville, New York, has known Marsha Tait, the executive director of LiteracyCNY, for most of her life, they only recently started working together. Hansen's Advisory is a socially responsible investment firm that focuses on ESG inside their client's portfolios, and on creating higher-impact portfolios that meet client values. When Marsha discovered that the investments in LiteracyCNY's investment portfolio could undermine the mission of the nonprofit, she wanted to invest in a more sustainable way. "We are an adult education organization and we serve people who read, write or speak English below a sixth-grade level. About 65% of our students are refugees and immigrants because this is a refugee resettlement city. So, the notion of inadvertently investing in, for example, for-profit prisons where some of our own students' relatives or others may get caught in this wave of immigration reform, was a clear line to interfering with our mission," says Tait.[13]

Timothy Yee, president and founder of Green Retirement Inc.,[14] is a leading financial advisor in the retirement industry that works with organizations that understand the importance of a more sustainable world, such as 350.org, Hog Island Oyster Company, and Healthcare Without Harm. The nonprofit 350.org[15] is one of those organizations, advocating for a world fueled by community-led renewable energy, and ultimately working to end the era of polluting fossil fuels. Green Retirement currently offers fossil-fuel free (of producers and pipelines) retirement portfolios for 350.org's employees. Hog Island Oyster Company, a restaurant and retail outlet, also changed to fossil-fuel free and socially responsible in its 401(k) fund choices. "Red tide" blooms of toxins directly impact the farming of its oysters, so Hog Island understands the material risk that environmental changes could have on their business model. Nonetheless, even at organizations working for

---

[13]Marsha Tait, interview data (see Appendix).
[14]More information at http://www.greenretirement.com/.
[15]More information at http://350.org/.

environmental health and justice, it still takes a concerted effort to transition the retirement plan from traditional investments to sustainable ones. At Healthcare Without Harm, a nonprofit with a mission to transform health care worldwide, change required a year-long campaign launched by an internal champion in human resources to get its 401(k) changed. Financial advisors like Yee play a critical role in working with clients to incorporate ESG into investments, even if the change is incremental.

Social(k)[16] is a pioneering firm in bringing these sustainable investments to retirement plans. Social(k) has invested over USD $150 million on behalf of 7,500 participants working at more than 300 organizations. Social(k)'s clients include many sustainability-focused member organizations, of which the firm is also a member (e.g. B Corp, US SIF, Green America, 1% For The Planet, and RSF Social Finance), as well as other organizations working toward an inclusive and sustainable world (e.g. As You Sow, BALLE, Social Venture Network, and Wallace Global Fund). Rob Thomas,[17] president and founder of Social(k), believes impactful, sustainable, responsible investing and ESG are deeper forms of due diligence. Thomas firmly believes that integrating ESG issues into investment research is the obligation of those working with other people's money, and he reported the biggest challenge in the industry is getting plan sponsors to realize they have an obligation to do more than they currently are with the 401(k)s of their participants.

The World Business Council for Sustainable Development (WBCSD) is an organization of more than 200 businesses pursuing a sustainable future. Although the organization is working on aspirational goals on some of the biggest sustainability challenges, even WBCSD members have yet to make the transition to a sustainable retirement plan. In 2018, the WBCSD announced an aspirational goal to move 1% of USD $1 trillion, equaling USD $10 billion, in retirement assets under management of its member companies to ESG retirement benefit accounts in the next two years (Khalamayzer 2018). Tony Calandro,[18] Strategic Partner at Povaddo, found in his research that almost three-quarters of Fortune 1000 company employees considered offering socially responsible investment options in their retirement plans as relevant (Povaddo 2017). As Calandro points out, few firms "look at the 401(k) as a social impact vehicle, which gives everyday employees the ability to invest with their values."

---

[16]More information at https://socialk.com/.
[17]Rob Thomas, interview data (see Appendix).
[18]Tony Calandro, interview data (see Appendix).

CREATING SUCCESSFUL RETIREMENT SAVINGS PLANS

Planning for successful retirement outcomes has seen the risk shifting from employers and governments to individuals. Many critics have said that much of the financial industry has been designed to profit more from fees than to encourage employees to save for retirement. Issues with DC plans, such as contribution levels being too low and people struggling to choose appropriate investments, can be overcome by implementing behavioral science insights on what makes a successful DC plan. Features can also be implemented to make it easier to optimize a DC plan for not only employee financial health but also the sustainability of the planet. This section will discuss some of the behavioral science insights, as well as highlight three key features of successful sustainable retirement savings plans: auto-enrollment into an impact default, sustainable target-date funds (typically designed and named for the year of retirement, like 2030, 2040, 2050, and balanced across different asset classes), and technology- enabled plans.

Although more choices are thought of as better in many decision-making situations, research shows that too many choices can inhibit making a timely decision.[19] Similarly, this paralysis is also encountered when employees are offered an overabundance of choice in their retirement plans. As the number of funds in a retirement plan increases, the retirement plan participation decreases. In laboratory experiments, for every additional 10 investment choices, participation rates are predicted to be reduced by 2%. For example, an employee that only has five funds in their retirement plan has expected participation of 72%, while in a plan with 35 funds, the predicted participation rate is 67.5% (Iyengar and Kamenica 2010). According to research by the Investment Company Institute and BrightScope, between 2006 and 2015, the average large 401(k) added an average of seven investment options, going from 20 investment options on average in their plan lineup in 2006 to 27 in 2015 (BrightScope 2018). Luckily, more plan sponsors are becoming aware of the best practices and limiting the total number of funds offered to 15 or less. While that can lead to more participation and contributions, this

---

[19] In 2000, psychologists conducted an experiment with fruit jam at an upscale supermarket. One day, consumers had to choose from a display with an "extensive choice" of 24 different types of jam. On another day, they had to choose from a "limited choice" of 6 jams. Even though more people stopped by the booth for the larger display, they were one-tenth as likely to buy (only 3% purchased) than people who saw the small display (30% purchased, or 10 times higher). Additionally, when surveyed later, those consumers that selected their jam from the smaller display were more satisfied with their purchase (Iyengar and Lepper 2000).

smaller lineup of funds inhibits an approach to add sustainable ESG funds to a plan to cover those who want it and non-ESG funds for those who do not.

Most people spend more time planning their annual vacation than their retirement (Hicken 2014). In fact, a survey of faculty and staff at the University of Southern California found that the majority (58%) spent less than one hour determining their contribution rate and electing the investments in their retirement plan. Besides the amount of time spent, there is also the skill involved in selecting appropriate funds. The average employee is not financially savvy enough to know how to design an investment portfolio appropriate for their goals and risk profile from investment options presented to them across asset classes. Many people use shortcuts, rules of thumb, or "saving heuristics." Hewitt Associates finds that the distribution of contribution rates spikes at multiples of 5%, such as 60%, 65%, 70% in equities, not 62% or 67%. Another popular heuristic that Benartzi and Thaler have dubbed the 1/n rule is the strategy of diversifying across funds by spreading money equally. For example, five funds equally split at 20% each, or 10 funds equally allocated at 10% each, even if those funds have different risk and return profiles. Although popular, this can be quite an ineffective method of diversification due to the lack of regard for the underlying asset classes (Benartzi and Thaler 2007). Thus, employees need guidance and suggestions to better invest for their own future.

Feature: Auto-Enrollment into an Impact Default

Adding a default option that is a sustainable fund is a great way to increase flows into better investments for the workers' financial health, and also for a positive social and environmental impact. The UK's National Employment Saving Trust (NEST), a defined contribution plan established by the UK's government, fully integrates ESG factors into the plan's default investment option, which covers 99.8% of participants. Representatives from NEST consider ESG factors material for understanding investment risk (Jeszeck 2018). HSBC invested £1.85 billion (USD $2.3 billion) of its UK employees' savings by selecting a sustainable fund as the default equity option for its defined contribution pension arrangement (Flood 2016). The Future World Fund, managed by Britain's largest fund house Legal & General Investment Management, applies a climate "tilt," which excludes coal companies and reduces exposure to companies with higher than average carbon emissions and fossil fuel reserves, and increases exposure to companies with revenue from lower-carbon solutions (Walker et al. 2018).

In the United States, until recently, the default option in most defined contribution plans was not to participate at all. Most employees had to "opt-in" to the plan and then elect how much they were willing to contribute and then decide on the investment allocation. As previously mentioned, one of the provisions of the Pension Provision Act of 2006 (PPA) was "automatic enrollment," which permitted employees to opt out of a retirement plan instead of having to opt in. Today, 71% of DC plans use auto-enrollment (Callan 2018). Vanguard, which manages more than 3.4 million 401(k)s, found that companies with auto-enrollment had 86% participation, compared to 59% participation in plans with voluntary enrollment. That increase is also conservative, as it includes all the workers at companies even though most employers only offer it to their new employees (Rosenberg 2010). Plans with automatic enrollment always require a default investment, or QDIA, and offer large potential to continue to increase flows into sustainable DC retirement plans as long as the country's current regulation guidelines are properly followed. See Box 10.1 for a case study of an environmental, social, and governance (ESG) default option in a retirement plan.

Box 11.1 Case Study in the United States, an Environmental, Social, and Governance Default Option in a 403(b) Retirement Plan

Some advisors have found ways to work within the current system of regulation. As a former US Marine and former Benedictine monk, now turned financial advisor, Doug Lynam of LongView Asset Management set up one of the first ESG-themed custom target-date solution as a QDIA for a 403(b)[20] for the United World College (UWC) in the United States that adheres to the traditional fiduciary standards. Lynam, who entered a Benedictine monastery when he was 22, eventually took over the monastery's finances and was not pleased with what he discovered. Even with all the monks working full time, including Lynam as a math and science teacher at a seventh- through twelfth-grade school for 18 years, the organizations could not achieve financial stability. The monastery went bankrupt in the 1990s, and Lynam learned about finance through the "school of hard knocks."[21] Budgeting and money management learnings

---

[20] A 403(b) is similar to 401(k)s, but they serve employees of educational institutions and nonprofits organizations rather than private-sector workers.
[21] Doug Lynam, interview data (see Appendix).

led Lynam to becoming a de facto financial advisor for monastery guests as well as teaching personal finance and investing at the school.

One of his colleagues from the school, in her 60s, asked for retirement planning assistance, and he was shocked to discover she had only saved USD $16,000. She had assumed the school was taking care of her account, but the recordkeeping service was not a fiduciary. Lyman found the retirement plan had poorly performing funds and no behavioral economics features built into it. After 20 years as a teacher and a monk, he became a financial advisor in 2015 and formed his own registered investment advisory firm (RIA) in 2016. He then merged his firm with LongView Asset Management in 2017, where he is now a partner. In 2019, LongView was the first financial services firm in New Mexico to become a certified B-Corp for sustainability.

When Lynam began working with UWC-USA, it made sense to match the 403(b) investments with their mission of building a more sustainable, inclusive global community. UWC-USA, based in New Mexico, is the North American campus of UWC International, which has 18 schools and colleges in 18 countries on four continents (United World College 2017–2020). UWC-USA is a values-driven organization that cares about global thinking as well as the financial wellness of their employees. Lynam worked with the president of UWC, Victoria Mora, PhD, who was 100% committed to building an impactful, sustainable, ESG-friendly default or QDIA. However, it took some time to convince her business office, faculty, staff, and ultimately, her executive committee and board, since they were one of the first retirement plans to implement an ESG QDIA. Lynam credits Dr. Mora with the vision to see the opportunity that ESG investing presents and be willing to try something new. They started with the basics of the plan, including behavioral economics features, lower fees, and higher performance funds, and then progressed to discussing and implementing sustainable investment choices.

The core issues that Lynam focuses on when designing a plan are lowering greenhouse gas emissions, reducing potential emissions from fossil fuel reserves, improving land use and biodiversity, eliminating toxic spills and releases, operational waste, water management, factory farming, cluster munitions, and child labor.

Using the teacher-focused company TIAA's platform as a recordkeeper, Lynam was able to build model portfolios using ESG funds that

(*continued*)

(*continued*)

change allocations with the plan participants' age, like a target-date fund. He mentioned that "by using our own choice of mutual funds, we were able to bring the cost down to 27 basis points (0.27% of assets managed), so it is a big savings from some of the ESG target date funds out there, especially for a smaller USD $1.8 million plan."[22] According to Lynam, "we naturally had a lot of discussions about the DOL's fiduciary duty requirements under ERISA and what the law says and doesn't say about the use of ESG investing programs" (Manganaro 2019).

Source: Author based on desk review and interview data.

Feature: Sustainable Target Date Funds

Target-date funds help employees "set it and forget it" by outsourcing the portfolio asset allocation to a professional fund manager. Target date funds are portfolios that mix securities across equities, fixed income, and cash and automatically become more conservative as retirement approaches. Instead of plan participants being responsible for routinely updating their funds, the manager of the target date fund is determining the ideal asset allocation for the target retirement date. Today, 7 out of 10 new dollars invested into 401(k)s in the United States are going into target-date funds.[23]

The Northeast Clean Energy Council, based in Boston, has a mission to help mitigate climate change by developing the clean energy industry in the northeastern United States. The company recently revised its 401(k) plan investment offerings to include a target date fund series, Natixis Sustainable Future funds,[24] which includes impact-positive, ESG-focused equity and bond funds, as the default option for participants. President Peter Rothstein says, "we have the expertise to understand that these new business models have the potential to be climate solutions and to grow the economy at the same time. With that perspective, it makes sense for us to incorporate ESG investing for our retirement plan" (Miller 2019).

---

[22] Doug Lynam, interview data (see Appendix).
[23] Jim Roach, interview data (see Appendix).
[24] Available online at https://www.im.natixis.com/us/natixis-sustainable-future-funds.

Feature: Technology as an Enabler

Technology is rapidly transforming many practices around money, and investing in retirement plans is no exception. Technology can assist in lowering investment minimums to participate, auto-enrollment and fund selection, and even is beginning to change the underlying holdings inside workplace retirement plans. As technology platforms are inherently global, the ability to scale technology advances from one country to another is large.

Financial advisors, in addition to using existing ESG-focused target-date funds like Natixis, can also create their own glide-path portfolios using technology. In the United States, platforms like Matrix enable a custom mix of mutual funds and ETFs into a "push-button" portfolio, provided the underlying funds meet strong financial and sustainability criteria. QBOX Fiduciary Solutions is an RIA specializing in providing fiduciary related services to retirement plans by embracing a truly open architecture strategy. QBOX has partnered with some of the leading impact-focused advisory firms, creating ESG-based "push-button" models for 401(k) plan participants that pursue higher impact and sustainability. QBOX's models for plans and participants include the HIP Investor Fossil Fuel Free portfolios.[25]

Beyond being able to customize based on a packaged product, like a mutual fund or ETF or other basket of many securities, it is now possible in some plans to customize based on the individual security. OpenInvest, a Registered Investment Adviser and Public Benefit Corporation based in California (US), has applied technology and finance solutions used in sophisticated hedge funds to provide sustainable investing solutions to individual investors, financial advisors, and institutional investors. OpenInvest has partnered as an investment manager with Good Super, a superannuation fund in Australia, to provide participants with ESG thematic indexes, which are currently pooled across participants. Traditionally, an issue with ESG investing in retirement plans has been the inability to individualize based on each participant's values or their particular investment desires, versus setting up ESG options that are the same for all of the participants at a plan level. "Our technology is capable of handling individual participant engagement where each participant has a 'virtual slice,'" explains Josh Levin, Chief Strategy Officer at OpenInvest, "but there are still major record-keeping and accounting steps necessary to implementing this fully."[26] Changes in technology will continue to enable advisors to offer tailored separately managed accounts to their retirement plan clients efficiently and more cost-effective than ever before.

---

[25] Greg Moerchin, interview data (see Appendix).
[26] Josh Levin, interview data (see Appendix).

BENEFITS OF SUCCESSFUL SUSTAINABLE RETIREMENT SAVINGS PLAN

This section highlights the benefits of a successful sustainable retirement savings plan by providing specific examples on how talent is influencing choices at companies toward higher impact portfolio choices, which can lead to higher contributions and participation rates in workplace plans and, importantly, spur higher employee engagement.

Benefit: Higher Contribution and Participation Rates

Despite the fact that very little of the USD $8.4 trillion dollar DC marketplace is invested in ESG funds, there is developing evidence that offering employees the investment selection that they are demanding can increase contribution and participation rates. San Francisco–based company stok, a sustainable real estate services firm serving clients like Subaru of America and LinkedIn, has a majority Millennial workforce that is deeply mission-driven. The workforce was not engaged with a 401(k) that was investing in guns, fossil fuel, and palm oil, and this was reflected in their low participation rate of 14% and an average contribution rate of 1.6%. "Employees were saying, 'I work all day long to mitigate the impacts of climate change.... I'm not going to turn around and invest in fossil fuels and toxic products and bad labor practices," says Burke Pemberton, principal at stok (Peters 2016). To understand how fund choices rated on ESG and impact, stok partnered with HIP Investor and Communitas Financial Planning, and later Money Intelligence, to show employees how their portfolio rated. The results of the effort were that plan participation increased to 95%, and the average contribution rate rose to 7.1% after only two years (As You Sow 2020).

BW Research, an applied research firm whose clients include the Solar Foundation, added a Natixis ESG Target Date Fund in July 2018. The executives of the company, headquartered in both Wrentham, Massachusetts, and Carlsbad, California, spent time in front of their employees emphasizing the importance of saving for retirement. BW's participation rate jumped from 57% to 100% in the first six months, and it was not an automatic reenrollment. Monthly contributions also increased by 230%.[27] The synergistic effect of offering employees sustainable investment options that they prefer and effectively communicating the new choices and related benefits to employees is essential. Although there is not yet enough evidence to draw conclusions about causation, there is evidence that offering ESG retirement choices increases employee interest in retirement plan communications and meetings, thereby ultimately increasing their participation and contribution rates to the plan.

---

[27] Jim Roach, interview data (see Appendix).

Benefit: Attracting Talent and Increased Employee Engagement

In addition to helping retirement plan participation and contribution rates, offering ESG funds inside of a company's retirement plan is a great way to engage employees and attract and retain top talent. At the California firm stok, 20% of employees feel that having the world's first "push-button" fossil-free, gun-free, palm-oil free 401(k) portfolio was a "significant differentiating factor in their compensation package" (As You Sow 2020). BW Research considers the offering of an ESG fund in their 401(k) one of their top five benefits.[28] Philip Jordan, vice president and principal researcher of BW Research, says it added the ESG funds "equally because sustainability is important to the firm's work and for the competitive advantage for hiring talent. We see including ESG options in the plan as a strategic advantage for recruitment and retention, as well as an option that feels good to do emotionally regardless of the impact on the bottom line."[29]

Companies that foster employee engagement and innovation increase human and intellectual capital, which is great for their bottom line. *The Sustainability Advantage,* by Bob Willard, has quantified +12% higher profitability due to highly engaged employees being +18% more productive and customer satisfaction +12% higher (Willard 2012). In fact, Boston Research Group conducted a national study to see how engagement with a company 401(k) would be related to employee engagement. They found that the participants with a more positive perception of the quality of their retirement plan appreciated their employer for providing it and had higher levels of employee engagement (McKinnon 2018).

HOW A RETIREMENT PLAN CAN BECOME MORE SUSTAINABLE

Companies, who play a larger role than ever before in individuals' retirement plans, can be a huge driving force in increasing the impactfulness of the plans they offer. Four key steps are described in the following sections: getting educated on sustainable investing, engaging employees through their retirement plans, preparing for incremental change, and educating participants with strong support from management. These lessons, while primarily from the United States, can be applied across the world.

---

[28] Jim Roach, interview data (see Appendix).
[29] Philip Jordan, interview data (see Appendix).

Guidelines for Companies to Offer Impactful Retirement Plans

Get Educated on Sustainable Investing

Open-source information on sustainable, responsible Impact Investing exists at the Global Impact Investing Network with educational materials for decision-makers and plan participants.[30] Also, the Global Sustainable Investment Alliance (GSIA)[31] is a collaboration of sustainable investment organizations from around the world, including EuroSIF, Responsible Investment Association Australasia, Responsible Investment Association of Canada, UK Sustainable Investment and Finance Association (UK SIF), US Forum for Sustainable and Responsible Investment (US SIF), and Association of Investors for Sustainable Development (VBDO) (GSIA 2018).

In the United States, it is critical for plan sponsors to document their processes. The US DOL bulletins make it clear that workplace plans should be putting "economic interests" first, so the documentation should show that sustainable options are economically viable. Most advisors who work on setting up these accounts do not have to change their fund selection process since it already includes an evaluation of financial performance, but this research can be an important first step in this documentation.

Engage Employees Through Their Retirement Plans

All too often, the retirement plan is thought of as a cost center, when it can be thought of as an employee engagement tool. Retirement savings and planning are one of the top benefits that attract quality employees, and having an innovative offering is a great differentiator. When making the case internally, remind the decision-makers that a sustainable retirement plan can be a key part of achieving the company's goals and objectives. It shows employees that that company is invested in their future and truly interested in listening to and incorporating their desires and requests. For a mission-driven company, having a retirement plan that is aligned with the mission indicates true authenticity, which today's employees are demanding. In fact, the most significant driver of adding an impact, sustainable, or ESG option is values alignment with the company (USSIF 2011).

Another leading driver of adding an ESG option are requests from plan stakeholders, like employees. If the firm is considering starting a new ESG-friendly retirement plan or updating the investments in the current plan, it is important to review the information currently held on employees' interests. Is an annual survey of employees conducted where questions that could be relevant are asked? In Australia, HESTA reviews its members'

---

[30] Available online at https://thegiin.org/.
[31] Available online at http://gsi-alliance.org/.

requests to the call center. A stand-alone poll of employees could be conducted to gauge interest in ESG, as well as overall satisfaction with the plan. There are multiple other ways to find what issues areas and ESG themes are most important to employees, as well as help them feel emotionally invested in the design of the plan, which can help for contributions.

Prepare for Inspired Incremental Change

As Timothy Yee of Green Retirement[32] stated, "there is no perfect solution, but that does not mean intransigence. It does not mean you can sit on your hands and do nothing. You have got to do something because currently, the *status quo* is not working." Changing the existing fund options can be a long process over months or years. Larger companies typically have an investment committee that might only meet a few times a year. It can be hard to push for radical change within a heavily regulated industry, like financial services. Alex Bernhardt, former Head of Responsible Investment, US, of Mercer Investments, has worked with many Fortune 500 companies and warns "it can take a long time." For one of his plan sponsors, Bernhardt included ESG education in every meeting for almost two years before action toward impact was achieved in the plan. It can be easier to start by simply adding one ESG fund to the existing lineup before a complete revamping of the plan and attempting to make it a completely sustainable offering. However, Bernhardt thinks this is a great way to "test the waters" for both the organization and the participants without overwhelming them.

For example, Bloomberg's Investment Committee worked with Mercer (its DC retirement plan consultants) to complete due diligence on ESG funds for inclusion in their USD $2.5 billion 401(k) plan. The committee selected US-based Parnassus Investments' Core Equity Fund to add to their plan line-up in 2015 (Pensions and Investments 2018). Even though it started with simply adding one fund, Bloomberg has become a signatory of the PRI as a plan sponsor in 2017 (Bloomberg signed as a service provider in 2009) (Walker et al. 2019). Bloomberg's retirement plan also created an ESG specific section in its Investment Policy Statement (IPS), which describes how ESG considerations are integrated and managed in the plan, as well as making an attempt in every fund search to identify at least one investment fund that considers ESG factors. After adding the fund, Bloomberg also began to review the plan's carbon emissions footprint (Pensions and Investments 2018).

---

[32]Timothy Yee, interview data (see Appendix).

Educate Participants with Managerial Support

A common thread with many of the successful DC retirement plan roll-outs is strong employee education efforts with managerial support. Plan participants' desire for ESG options in combination with traditional ways of increasing participation and contribution rates, such as increased communication about the plan, can produce stronger participation. Employees who otherwise have not been excited about retirement planning can be motivated by their commitment to sustainability. As mentioned earlier in the chapter, stok increased plan participation from 14% to 95%, as well as contribution rate from 1.6% to 7.1%. "Most companies have to provide a 401(k) education meeting, and usually these are around financial lessons, and they're generally not that well attended, or it's not that exciting," says R. Paul Herman, CEO of HIP Investor, the ESG advisor to stok. "In companies that have created 401(k)s that have gone fossil free, that's created an excitement among employees" (Peters 2016).

BW Research had the executives of the company spending time in front of their employees discussing the importance of strong retirement savings, and their participation rate went from 57% to 100% in the first six months, and monthly contributions increased by 230%.

Guidelines for Individuals to Make Their Retirement Saving More Impactful

An individual investing via an employer-sponsored plan has much less control over investment choices than an account outside of work completely in their control, despite that a larger percent of their investable assets are in the workplace retirement plan. However, employees can improve the sustainability of investment options by engaging their leaders and managers internally. Four key steps are described in the following sections: how to research and prepare, how to talk to colleagues and build consensus, how to identify who to approach, and how to approach with potential solutions.

Research and Prepare

In order to make a good case, it is important to spend time researching the current plan and options. Request all documents related to the plan, from the accounts statement to the documents provided about the overall investment choices and general administration. In the United States, sites like BrightScope[33] show how plans compare against other companies' for design,

---

[33] Accessible online via www.brightscope.com, owned by Institutional Shareholder Services.

performance, and investments. Also, As You Sow[34] shows how the funds in plans rank on core impact themes of climate impact, gender equality, exposure to guns and weapons of war, forest deconstruction, and tobacco.

Talk to Colleagues and Build Consensus

Multiple voices are stronger than one. Building a coalition of coworkers who share the same investment desire for action can move an employer faster toward a sustainable plan. Demand from 10 or 50 or 100 people can be more of a driver than from just one person. Some companies have "green teams" or other affinity groups that can help build coalitions interested in investing sustainably. A "Lunch and Learn" could be arranged to ask questions to the plan's administrator or to engage participants in researching fund choices to include. Communicating with colleagues on the company's intranet, corporate chats, Slack channels, company newsletter, or social media can help build a coalition and develop a plan for action.

Identify Who to Approach

Human resources departments are typically responsible as the retirement plan administrator, and specific roles are frequently listed on BrightScope[35] when there is public disclosure, like the US Form 5500. Current fiduciaries of the plan are typically public information for larger firms. Many companies have departments that focus on sustainability or initiatives that focus on employee engagement, so they could be willing allies. If resources for collaborations within the company are lacking, LinkedIn can help identify colleagues that might want to align their investing with their values based on volunteer work that indicates they care about climate change or social justice or have other connections to extracurricular mission-driven organizations. At smaller companies, it might be possible to approach the founder or C-Suite directly to discuss your concerns, especially in firms less than 200 employees, where leaders know their staff.

Approach with Potential Solutions

A prudent strategy when approaching a company is not to be confrontational and instead to express concern over employee financial health and the financial risk of the current fund choices. If the company is working toward a clean energy future, the risk of potential future investments in fossil fuels could be

---

[34] Accessible online via www.asyousow.org/invest-your-values.
[35] Available online via www.brightscope.com.

of interest. If the company that claims diversity is a core part of their mission, cite data on the financial risk of having a portfolio that does not support racial and gender diversity, such as the North Carolina State study showing that diverse firms innovate more and earn more patents than less-diverse firms (Mayer et al. 2017). Even with a smaller company, the current investment advisor to the plan might not be educated in sustainable investing and could resist any changes unless presented with compelling evidence.

Including research, as well as suggestions of sustainable ESG funds with three or more years track records that the plan could be invested in, can be helpful to engaging the plan leaders or advisors. Relevant examples from companies in this chapter, like Bloomberg, that added just one additional ESG fund, to companies like stok, that give the option for employees to have a 100% sustainable plan, can be cited to show it can be accomplished.

CONCLUSION

Integrating impactful investing and ESG considerations in retirement plans is a growing area of interest for workplaces and employees around the world. As the risk for planning successful retirement outcomes has been shifting from employers and governments to individuals by shifting more money from DB plans into DC plans, there are increased opportunities for plan providers, plan advisors, and fiduciaries in the overlapping areas of sustainability and long-horizon investing. Investors need the ability to incorporate wider sustainability motives in their strategies to deal with climate change and help work toward achieving the UN SDGs.

Sustainable investing interest for retirement plans is fostering a growing body of research on the long-term financial, social, and environmental outcomes of these plans. Issues with DC plans, such as people struggling to choose appropriate investments, can be overcome by implementing behavioral science insights on what makes a successful DC plan. Behavioral research shows that as the number of funds in a retirement plan increases, the retirement plan participation decreases. Further research is still needed to determine whether adding ESG funds follows previous research's findings that more choice inhibits decisions due to the total number of funds, or if participants feel like they have a clearer choice by knowing they have a preference for the ESG funds over the nonsustainable ones.

Companies offering impactful portfolio choices in their retirement savings plans have seen higher contributions and participation rates in workplace plans, like stok and BW Research, and increased employee engagement. Stok saw their participation rate increase from 14% to 95%, and the average contribution rate increase from 1.6% to 7.1% (As You Sow 2020). BW Research saw their participation rate jump from 57% to 100% in the first six months, and monthly contributions increased by 230%. Sustainable retirement plans are a strategic advantage for attracting and retaining talent, as well as an option that feels good emotionally to those who participate. Strong communication on the plan offerings and managerial support are key.

The tools are ready to implement sustainable investing into the retirement plan assets that currently do not have it, as long as plan leaders incorporate smart design. This includes auto-enrollment with appropriate ESG default investments and easy-to- select sustainable target-date funds balanced across different asset classes. Improvements in technology have already made it easier for participants to save and for companies to inform, educate, and engage their participants about the full value of impactful investing via their retirement plans.

Regulation can be slow moving, but many countries have recognized the importance of taking a holistic approach to employee financial health. The future of DC plans is likely to further embrace technology-enabled plans, deeper customization, and an increased focus on the specific desires and needs of individual participants. Everyday investors are realizing they have the power to align their retirement plan dollars with their desire for a more sustainable world.

REFERENCES

Abhilash, M., Bass, R., and Dithrich, H. et al. (2019). Annual Impact Survey. The Global Impact Investing Network. https://thegiin.org/assets/GIIN_2019%20 Annual%20Impact%20Investor%20Survey_webfile.pdf (accessed 19 May 2020).

Anderson, J. (2017). Using tools of finance to address domestic violence against women in the Pacific. *Impact Alpha*. https://impactalpha.com/using-tools-of-finance-to-address-domestic-violence-against-women-in-the-pacific-21196816a487/ (accessed 22 March 2020).

As You Sow (2020). Fossil free action toolkit: How to make a change and invest your money fossil free. https://fossilfreefunds.org/fossil-free-action-toolkit (accessed 10 July 2019).

Aston, Nigel (2018). 10 Best Practices for Global DC Plans: DC Goes Global. State Street Global Advisors. https://www.ssga.com/dc/2018/10-best-practices-for-global-dc-plans%20-%20DC%20Goes%20Global.pdf (accessed 10 July 2019).

Australian Ethical Investment Ltd (2019). Ethical investments: The tide is rising. https://www.australianethical.com.au/super/ (accessed 10 December 2019).

Bauer, R., Ruof, T., and Smeets, P. (2019). Get Real! Individuals Prefer More Sustainable Investments (21 February). http://dx.doi.org/10.2139/ssrn.3287430.

Benartzi, S., and Thaler, R. H. (2007). Heuristics and biases in retirement savings behavior. *Journal of Economic Perspectives* 21 (3): 81–104 (Summer 2007). https://doi.org/10.1257/jep.21.3.81.

Bradford, H. (2019). Global sustainable assets hit $30.7 trillion in 2018 – report. *Pensions & Investments.* https://www.pionline.com/article/20190401/ ONLINE/190409960/global-sustainable-assets-hit-30-7-trillion-in-2018-report (accessed 9 January 2020).

BrightScope (2018). The BrightScope/ICI Defined Contribution Plan Profile: A Close Look at 401(k) Plans, 2015. BrightScope and Investment Company Institute. https://www.ici.org/pdf/ppr_18_dcplan_profile_401k.pdf (accessed 10 October 2019).

Callan Institute (2018). 2018 Defined Contribution Trends. https://www.callan .com/wp-content/uploads/2018/01/Callan-2018-DC-Survey.pdf (accessed 10 October 2019).

CFA Institute/Mercer (2015). An Ideal Retirement System. https://www.cfa institute.org/-/media/documents/support/future-finance/an-ideal-retire ment-system.ashx (accessed 9 January 2020).

Desjardins, J. (2018). Chart: What Assets Make Up Wealth? *Visual Capitalist* (18 January). https://www.visualcapitalist.com/chart-assets-make-wealth/ (accessed 11 January 2020).

European Union (2016). Directive (EU) 2016/2341 of the European Parliament and of the Council of 14 December 2016 on the activities and supervision of institutions for occupational retirement provision (IORPs). https://eur-lex .europa.eu/legal-content/EN/TXT/?uri=CELEX:32016L2341 (accessed 15 April 2020).

Flood, C. (2016). HSBC's UK pension scheme to invest £1.85bn in eco-friendly fund. *Financial Times* (7 November). https://www.ft.com/content/a5af8328-a4ef-11e6-8898-79a99e2a4de6 (accessed 19 December 2019).

Ehrenfeld, J. (2016). U.S. Trust Study Finds 10 Common Success Traits for Building and Sustaining Wealth. U.S. Trust Insights on Wealth and Worth. https:// www.privatebank.bankofamerica.com/publish/content/application/pdf/ GWMOL/2016_USTrust_Insights-WealthWorth-PressRelease.pdf (accessed 5 August 2019).

Eisenberg, R. (2013). To Solve the U.S. Retirement Crisis, Look to Australia. *Forbes* (19 August). https://www.forbes.com/sites/nextavenue/2013/08/19/to-solve-the-u-s-retirement-crisis-look-to-australia/#58cbf8e547b5.

Gandhi, A. (2019). Investing in (and for) Our Future. World Economic Forum. http://www3.weforum.org/docs/WEF_Investing_in_our_Future_report_2019.pdf (accessed 20 May 2020).

Global Sustainable Investment Alliance. (2018). 2018 Global Sustainable Investment Review. https://www.invesco.com/pdf/QDIA-BRO-1.pdf (accessed 22 March 2020).

Groom Law Group (2018). DOL and ESG Investing: Evolving Guidance. Groom Law Group, Chartered. https://www.groom.com/wp-content/uploads/2018/04/DOL_and_ESG_Investing_Evolving_Guidance.pdf.

GSIA (2018). Global Sustainable Investment Review 2018. Global Sustainable Investment Alliance. http://www.gsi-alliance.org/trends-report-2018/ (accessed 10 July 2019).

Hudson, V., Caprioli, M., Ballif-Spanvill, B., et al. (2009). The Heart of the Matter: The Security of Women and the Security of States. *International Security*, 33(3): 7–45 (Winter 2008–09). https://www.mitpressjournals.org/doi/pdf/10.1162/isec.2009.33.3.7 (accessed 23 March 2020).

Hicken, M. (2014). Workers spend more time planning vacation than retirement. CNN Money (19 August). https://money.cnn.com/2014/08/19/retirement/401k-investments/index.html (accessed 8 February 2020).

Howes, P. (2018). Super Insights Report 2018. KPMG International. https://assets.kpmg/content/dam/kpmg/au/pdf/2018/super-insights-report-2018.pdf (accessed 10 December 2019).

Invesco (2015). QDIA Q&A A Resource for plan sponsors. *Invesco*. https://www.invesco.com/pdf/QDIA-BRO-1.pdf (accessed 18 October 2019).

Iyengar, S. S., and Kamenica, E. (2010). Choice Proliferation, Simplicity Seeking, and Asset Allocation. *Journal of Public Economics* 94(7–8): 530–539. http://dx.doi.org/10.1016/j.jpubeco.2010.03.006 (accessed 10 July 2019).

Iyengar, S. S., and Lepper, M. R. (2000). When Choice Is Demotivating: Can One Desire Too Much of a Good Thing? *Journal of Personality and Social Psychology*, 79(6): 995–1006. (accessed 11 July 2019). http://dx.doi.org/10.1037/0022-3514.79.6.995/.

Jeszeck, C. A. (2018). Retirement Plan Investing: Clearer Information on Consideration of Environmental, Social, and Governance Factors Would Be Helpful. United States Government Accountability Office. https://www.gao.gov/assets/700/691930.pdf (accessed 28 November 2019).

Jones, S. (2019). Australia ranks third in world's best pension systems. *Investment* (21 October). https://www.investmentmagazine.com.au/2019/10/australia-ranks-third-in-worlds-best-pension-systems/ (accessed 10 February 2020).

Khalamayzer, A. (2018). Why it's time to align retirement funds with sustainability goals. *GreenBiz Group Inc.* (1 February). https://www.greenbiz.com/article/why-its-time-align-retirement-funds-sustainability-goals (accessed 15 December 2019).

Lessne, A., Tovrov, S., West, A., et al. (2019). Sustainable Investing in Defined Contribution Plans: A Guide for Plan Sponsors. Defined Contribution Institutional Investment Association (DCIIA), May 2019. https://cdn.ymaws.com/dciia.org/resource/resmgr/docs/DCIIA_Sustainable_Investing_.pdf (accessed 29 March 2020).

Manganaro, J. (2019). Mission-Based Employer Embraces ESG TDFs, In-Plan Income. Plan Sponsor. https://www.plansponsor.com/in-depth/mission-based-employer-embraces-esg-tdfs-plan-income/ (accessed 15 March 2020).

Mayer, R., Warr, S., and Zhao, J. (2017). Do Pro-Diversity Policies Improve Corporate Innovation? *Financial Management.* 47 (3): 617–650 (Fall 2018). https://doi.org/10.1111/fima.12205 (accessed 28 March 2020).

McKinnon, L. (2018). *Known: How to Create a Great 401(k).* LMC17, LLC.

Mercer (2018). Department of Labor's Field Assistance Bulletin on ESG Investing. Mercer LLC. https://www.mercer.com/our-thinking/wealth/department-of-labors-field-assistance-bulletin-on-esg-investing.html (accessed 29 March 2020).

Merton, R. (2014). The Crisis in Retirement Planning. *Harvard Business Review.* (July-August). https://hbr.org/2014/07/the-crisis-in-retirement-planning (accessed 14 March 2020).

Miller, M. (2019). Bit by Bit, Socially Conscious Investors Are Influencing 401(k)'s. *The New York Times* (27 September). https://www.nytimes.com/2019/09/27/business/esg-401k-investing-retirement.html (accessed 29 September 2019).

Morgan Stanley Institute for Sustainable Investing (2017). Sustainable Signals: New Data from the Individual Investor. Morgan Stanley & Co LLC and Morgan Stanley Smith Barney LLC (7 August). https://www.morganstanley.com/pub/content/dam/msdotcom/ideas/sustainable-signals/pdf/Sustainable_Signals_Whitepaper.pdf (accessed 25 August 2019).

Natixis (2017). ESG may entice investors to save more. Natixis Global Asset Management. Press Release (15 June). https://www.natixis.com/natixis/upload/docs/application/pdf/2017-06/pr_esg_report_-_ngam_-_15-6-2017.pdf (accessed 29 March 2020).

Natixis Investment Managers. (2016). Running on Empty. https://www.im .natixis.com/us/resources/2016-survey-of-defined-contribution-plan-participants (accessed 29 March 2020).

OECD (2017). Architecture of national pension systems. In *Pensions at a Glance 2017: OECD and G20 Indicators*. Paris: OECD Publishing. https://doi.org/10 .1787/pension_glance-2017-6-en (accessed 29 March 2020).

OECD (2018). *Pensions at a Glance Asia/Pacific 2018. Paris: OECD Publishing.* https://doi.org/10.1787/pension_asia-2018-en (accessed 29 March 2020).

OECD, IDB, and World Bank (2014). *Pensions at a Glance: Latin America and the Caribbean*. Paris: OECD Publishing. http://dx.doi.org/10.1787/pension_ glance-2014-en (accessed 27 March 2020).

Pensions and Investments (2018). Millennials embrace ESG option in Bloomberg's 401(k) plan. *Pensions & Investments* (17 February). https:// www.pionline.com/article/20180207/ONLINE/180209884/millennials-embrace-esg-option-in-bloomberg-s-401-k-plan (accessed 29 March 2020).

Peters, Adele (2016). How to Convince Your Employer to Divest Your 401(k) from Fossil Fuels. *Fast Company.* (19 May). https://www.fastcompany.com/ 3059618/how-to-convince-your-employer-to-divest-your-401k-from-fossil-fuels (accessed 22 July 2019).

Povaddo (2017). Corporate America's POV: A Povaddo Survey Examining Corporate Activism and Employee Engagement Inside Fortune 1000 Companies. http://www.povaddo.com/downloads/Povaddo_Corporate_America©s_ POV_May_2017.pdf (accessed 14 May 2019).

PRI (2015). Failing to consider long-term investment value drivers—which include environmental, social and governance issues—in investment practice is a failure of fiduciary duty. Principles for Responsible Investment. https://www.unpri.org/fiduciary-duty/fiduciary-duty-in-the-21st-century/ 244.article (accessed 19 October 2019).

Puri, L. (2016). The economic costs of violence against women. Speech presented a high-level discussion at UN Women (21 September 2016). https:// www.unwomen.org/en/news/stories/2016/9/speech-by-lakshmi-puri-on-economic-costs-of-violence-against-women (accessed 23 March 2020).

Responsible Investment Association Australasia (2017). Responsible Investment Benchmark Report 2017 Australia. https://responsibleinvestment.org/wp-content/uploads/2017/07/Responsible-Investment-Benchmark-Report-Australia-2017.pdf (accessed 29 January 2020).

Rosenberg, T. (2010). The Opt-Out Solution. *Opinionator* (11 January). https:// opinionator.blogs.nytimes.com/2010/11/01/the-opt-out-solution/ (accessed 12 February 2020).

Sacker & Partners LLP. (2018). Government response: Clarifying and strengthening trustees' investment duties (9 December). https://www.sackers.com/publication/government-response-clarifying-and-strengthening-trustees-investment-duties/ (accessed 29 March 2020).

State Street Global Advisors (2018). Global Retirement Reality Report 2018 Australia Snapshot. State Street Global Advisors.

Strooga Consulting (2017). The ESG Product Quarterly. Strooga Consulting's ESG Series. (https://static1.squarespace.com/static/57503f96f850825fdde650fc/t/5bc4d0fa7817f70a2395c0e2/1539625211110/ESG+Product+Quarterly+-+Marketing+Edition+2Q2017.pdf (accessed 29 March 2020).

Tang, K. (2018). The Department of Labor and ESG Guidance: Is the Pendulum Shifting? *Seeking Alpha* (20 June). https://seekingalpha.com/article/4182928-department-of-labor-and-esg-guidance-is-pendulum-shifting (accessed 29 March 2020).

UNCTAD (2014). *World investment report 2014: Investing in the SDGs – an action plan. UNCTAD. Geneva.* https://doi.org/10.18356/3e74cde5-en.

United Nations (2015). *World Population Aging.* Department of Economic and Social Affairs Population Division. https://www.un.org/en/development/desa/population/publications/pdf/ageing/WPA2015_Report.pdf (accessed 29 March 2020).

US Department of Labor (2016). US Labor Department Provides Updated Guidance on Proxy Voting by Employee Benefits Plans. Press Release (28 December). https://www.dol.gov/newsroom/releases/ebsa/ebsa20161228.

US Department of Labor (2018). *Field Assistance Bulletin No.* 2018-01. https://www.dol.gov/agencies/ebsa/employers-and-advisers/guidance/field-assistance-bulletins/2018-01.

USSIF (2011). Opportunities for Sustainable and Responsible Investing in US Defined Contribution Plans. US SIF: The Forum for Sustainable and Responsible Investment. https://www.ussif.org/store_product.asp?prodid=8 (accessed 20 June 2019).

Utkus, S., and Young, J. (2018). How America Saves 2018: Vanguard 2017 Defined Contribution Plan Data. Vanguard Group, Inc. https://pressroom.vanguard.com/nonindexed/HAS18_062018.pdf (accessed 29 March 2020).

United World Colleges (2017–2020). Schools like no other. https://www.uwc.org/schools (accessed 19 December 2019).

Walker, C., Messervy, M., and Bernhardt, A. (2018). Aligning Retirement Assets Toolkit #1: The responsible retirement plan opportunity. World Business Council for Sustainable Development. https://docs.wbcsd.org/2018/12/ARA-The_responsible_retirement_plan_opportunity.pdf (accessed 19 June 2019).

Walker, C., Messervy, M., and Bernhardt, A. (2019). Aligning Retirement Assets Toolkit #2: The responsible retirement plan opportunity. World Business Council for Sustainable Development. https://docs.wbcsd.org/2019/06/WBCSD_ARA_toolkit_Global_version.pdf (accessed 19 June 2019).

Whyte, A. (2017). McKinsey: ESG No Longer Niche as Assets Soar Globally. *Institutional Investor.* (27 October). https://www.institutionalinvestor.com/article/b15cc1dxds8k97/mckinsey-esg-no-longer-niche-as-assets-soar-globally.

Willard, B. (2012). The New Sustainability Advantage: Seven Business Case Benefits of a Triple Bottom Line. *Sustainability Advantage.* Gabriola Island, BC: New Society Publishers.

Williams, T. (2019). Major Climate Funders Are Still Invested in Fossil Fuels. Why Is That? Inside Philanthropy (December 19). https://www.insidephilanthropy.com/home/2019/12/19/major-climate-funders-are-still-invested-in-fossil-fuels-why-is-that (accessed 10 February 2020).

Willis Towers Watson. (2020). Global Pension Assets Study. Thinking Ahead Institute. https://www.thinkingaheadinstitute.org/en/Library/Public/Research-and-Ideas/2020/01/Global-Pension-Asset-Study-2020 (accessed 29 March 2020).

APPENDIX 11.1:   EXPERTS INTERVIEWED

Interviewee	Current or Former Title	Current of Former Company	Interview Date	Interview Topic
1. Timothy Yee, CPFA, C(k)P, CHSA, NQPA, CSRIC	President	Green Retirement	4 April 2019	Sustainable 401(k)s
2. Tania Black	Regional Manager and Senior Counsel	Criterion Institute	10 April 2019	Gender lens investing in Australia
3. Rob Thomas	President	Social (k)	12 April 2019	Sustainable 401(k)s
4. Josh Levin	Chief Strategy Officer	OpenInvest	18 April 2019	Sustainable Superannuation in Australia

Interviewee	Current or Former Title	Current of Former Company	Interview Date	Interview Topic
5. Tony Calandro	President	Purposeful Strategies	26 April 2019	World Business Council for Sustainable Development project
6. Greg Moerchen, AIF	Partner	QBOX	6 May 2019	401(k)s
7. Katelyn Kriesel	Socially Responsible Financial Advisor	Hansen's Advisory Services	14 May 2019	Sustainable 401(k)s
8. Judy Mares	Former Deputy Assistant Secretary and Advisor	United States Department of Labor	17 May 2019	401(k)s
9. Marsha Tait	Executive Director	Literacy CNY	23 May 2019	Setting up a sustainable workplace retirement plan
10. Alex Bernhardt	Principal, Head of Responsible Investment	Mercer	17 June 2019	Sustainable Retirement Plans
11. Laraine McKinnon	Founder	LMC17	13 September 2019	401(k)s
12. Jim Roach, AIF	Senior Vice President, Retirement Strategies	Natixis	11 November 2019	Sustainable 401(k)s
13. Doug Lyman	Principal	Longview Asset Management	17 December 2019	Sustainable 403(b)s
14. Philip Jordan	Vice-President & Principal Researcher	BW Research	9 January 2020	Workplace retirement plan enrollment process

CHAPTER 12

Fossil-Fuel-Free Investing: Weaving a New Investment Paradigm

Umachander Balakumar, MSci

Abstract

The climate crisis is upon us, and investors need to think beyond pure financial returns, as some of those gains are based on extractive behavior and hence unsustainable. As the impacts of climate change transform our planet's ecologies and threaten its ability to sustain life as we know it, the financial sector needs to seriously consider its role in the crisis, as well as the financial risks posed by climate change. If investors switch to using a fossil-fuel-free strategy, they can mitigate both financial and environmental risks associated with fossil fuels and climate change and build stronger, more resilient portfolios. Some investors incorrectly equate a fossil-fuel-free approach to an emissions-free portfolio and halt their adoption efforts in fears of lackluster returns and poor asset class diversification. Instead, investors should work to limit their portfolio's overall fossil fuel exposure, while seeking high environmental efficiency. To build a fossil-fuel-free portfolio, investors can also bolster their due diligence processes to utilize scope-based emissions and environmental, social, and governance (ESG) metrics. This chapter will review the various financial, environmental, and health motivations that drive investors to adopt fossil-fuel-free strategies, beginning with an examination of China as a case study, and then explore which metrics are relevant for fossil-fuel-free portfolios, and lastly present a novel framework to assess investments—including private equity, hedge funds, commodities, real estate, public debt, green bonds, and cryptocurrency—toward a fossil-fuel-free paradigm

Keywords

Energy; Fossil Fuels; Fossil Fuel Free; Green Energy; Renewable Energy; Climate Change; Global Warming; Climate Action; Science Based Targets; ESG; Sustainable Investing; Impact Investing; SDG; China; Metrics; Emissions; GHGs; Subsidy; Sustainable Development Goals; Green Bonds; Cryptocurrency; Plastic

INTRODUCTION

Given the increasingly tangible consequences of climate change, and the political and geological risks associated with fossil fuel production and exploration, the future profitability of the fossil fuel industry is at risk, and potentially dubious. Recent reports, including the International Panel on Climate Change's (IPCC) Global Warming of 1.5°C report on global warming, are shaking long-held beliefs about the inexhaustibility of fossil fuel reserves and ongoing supplies and the appropriate business, investor, taxation, and policy responses to resulting environmental consequences.

Investors who lead the charge on climate-action investing can force companies and industries to consider their operational efficiency in the context of future sustainability, which can generate superior financial returns *and* environmental benefits. While seeking risk-adjusted return, or alpha,[1] is essential to investing—even in the fossil-fuel-free paradigm—the investor's challenge is leaving behind financial profit maximization being acceptable at any cost, especially when the world is on the cusp of irreversible climate change.

---

[1] Alpha is used in financial markets to describe the active return of an investment relative to a suitable market index.

In early March 2019, the world's largest sovereign wealth fund announced it was divesting from fossil fuels. Norway's sovereign wealth fund, which is valued at USD $1.1 trillion, expunged assets dedicated to oil and gas production and exploration. As Europe's second-largest producer of fossil fuels, Norway divested primarily to limit their exposure to price depreciation and dividend uncertainty related to the future demand for oil, the volatility of future prices, and the threats associated with climate change. Though Norway's divestment was not in itself purely altruistic, it did have far-reaching implications for the fossil fuel sector in the form of investor activism.

Dan Adler, vice president of the Energy Foundation, whose mission it is to "promote the transition to a sustainable energy future by advancing energy efficiency and renewable energy," commented on two paths on climate change action: policy and market driven.[2] Policy-driven thinkers believe greater policy changes need to be enacted and that markets cannot be trusted fundamentally to address climate change, while market-driven activists believe that markets are the only things that move fast enough to quickly transition away from fossil fuels. Institutional investors, regardless of which side of the debate they are on, play a crucial role in pushing the market and policy makers to adopt new markers beneficial to a clean energy future that others can follow. In this chapter, we will focus on investor-led climate change actions, but we will also consider the improved efficacy when these actions are grounded in policy; but before we do so, we need to first define fossil fossils.

In everyday terms, fossil fuels are dead animal and plant remains accumulated over tens of millions of years that have decomposed or fossilized underground. These fossilized remains contain high levels of carbon, which makes them a quality fuel and an energy source, and their use has been instrumental in the development of efficient energy solutions, and powering the growth of economies with oil and coal central to its DNA. The main types of fossil fuels that are in use today are crude oil, coal, and natural gas. From early cave tribes lighting coal to stay warm, to Alexander the Great igniting petroleum fires to fend off charging war elephants, to China and India's aggressive construction of power plants fueled by coal extracted from Australian mines and global sources, like OPEC nations, the use of fossil fuels is ubiquitous throughout human history. While lives may have been at risk from inhaling smoke in a cave or a cabin, the risks have never been greater to the entire Earth's ecosystems we all need to live and breathe, literally.

---

[2]Interview data. See Appendix 12.1.

In the past century, however, the amount of fossil fuels burned for human purposes has skyrocketed. Using history as precedent, many investors falsely believe that fossil fuels can continue to be extracted without devastating environmental consequences, and that fossil fuel investments can continue to generate financial dividends. The global economy now finds itself at a crossroads. Continue down the path of extractive, polluting, and oppressive fossil fuel exploitation—or accept scientifically established findings and create a new approach to energy, commerce, and investment that is adapted to the twenty-first century.

The science is clear: unadulterated use of fossil fuels cannot continue. Investors have a pivotal role to play in this transition. Garvin Jabusch, the chief investment officer of Green Alpha Advisors,[3] describes how investors would be "insane to hold fossil fuels for the long run" because the best-case economic scenario for fossil fuels might only extend for the next five or so years. To understand what is ahead, investors need to look no further than China—the world's biggest producer of fossil fuels and home of the world's biggest clean energy market. China presents a national case study that illuminates the benefits of contributing toward a fossil-fuel-free world, as well as the implications of not doing so.

This chapter draws on a comprehensive literature review to describe the global historical and current use of fossil fuels. Material from reports, industry studies, articles, and interviews were drawn from to paint a complete picture of the world's growing energy needs and the subsequent growth of the fossil fuel industry. An analysis comparing energy and consumer discretionary sector stock movements from 2016 to 2018 by companies' Scope 1 and 2 emissions was also analyzed to provide insight into the metrics and process behind selecting appropriate fossil-fuel-free portfolio investments. Original semi-structured interviews were conducted with non-governmental organizations (NGO), asset managers, and industry experts leading the charge in investor-backed climate change initiatives to document current real-world action being taken (see Appendix 12.1).

This chapter is organized as follows. The next section uses China as a stand-in for the global markets to comment on fossil fuel usage, transitions toward clean energy, and the implications of government intervention. Further sections describe the metrics and tools investors have available in evaluating potential fossil-fuel-free investments. Taking those tools and metrics, the last section describes the building of a fossil fuel portfolio and provides examples of investment opportunities across a myriad of different asset classes.

---

[3]Interview data. See Appendix 12.1.

CHINA: LESSONS FROM THE BIGGEST POLLUTER AND BIGGEST GREEN ENERGY MARKET MAKER

Shanghai's smog alert system is met with shuffling silence as its population of more than 24 million don face masks and head indoors, as a gray haze envelops one of Asia's largest financial hubs. The smog is ripe with PM2.5 (fine particulate matter with a diameter equal to or smaller than 2.5 microns), which when inhaled regularly can result in respiratory illnesses, lung cancer, and even heart disease. Scenes of citizens donning face masks, purchasing air purifiers, and telling their children not to play outside paint a pedestrian picture of life in the city. Smog is now synonymous with winter in many parts of China. With pollutant densities reaching more than 20 times the recommended levels established by the World Health Organization (WHO), China has increasingly come under scrutiny from its own citizens.

With 18% of the world's population—the largest percentage of any country on Earth—China is home to 1.4 billion residents. In 2017, China was responsible for 31% of the world's fossil fuel consumption. Data from the United Nations Environment Program (UNEP) reveals that China consumed close to 4.7 billion metric tons of fossil fuels in 2017, which equates to roughly 3.4 metric tons per resident per year (Cassidy 2019). As a point of comparison, an average adult is recommended to limit consumption to 64 ounces a day, which over a year equates to 0.66 metric tons of water. Chinese residents consume almost five times more fossil fuels than their daily recommended water intake. The United States, comparatively, consumes less fossil fuel overall with a population one-quarter the size, but still uses twice as much per resident.

China is the largest consumer and producer of coal in the world. Its coal industry is a monolith, providing the majority of energy in the country. In the early to mid-2000s, coal met 80% of the country's energy needs. In recent years that number has dropped down closer to 62%, yet China still finds itself relying heavily on coal as a primary fuel source (Taplin 2019). Though China's voracious appetite for fossil fuels exceeds that of any other country, it is simultaneously host to the world's largest green energy market, an endeavor set in motion by the consequences of heavy fossil fuel use and industry. This pattern is mirrored globally, where local renewable energy markets grow in response to the environmental and health consequences of fossil fuels.

China's wanton reliance on coal and its subsequent economic success is forcing its residents to pay a heavy toll. Ahead of the 2015 Paris Climate Accord, China pledged to make 20% of its energy portfolio non–fossil fuels (Duggan 2015). The Chinese government took action by enforcing strict emission mandates and offering generous clean energy subsidies. Two years later, China was generating 26.4% of its power from non–fossil fuel sources, exceeding its goal (Dong and Ye 2018).

To transform an economy built extensively on coal, China introduced subsidies to encourage and spread the development of clean energy technologies. Funded by tax surcharges on end-users, these subsidies are allocated toward funding new renewable energy ventures and projects. In 2020 alone, China is set to dispense CNY ¥2.63 billion (USD $376 million) to solar projects, CNY ¥2.97 billion (USD $425 million) to wind farms, and CNY ¥73.79 million (USD $10.58 million) toward biomass generators (Cassidy 2019).

The success of these subsidies is showcased by the parity of green energy patents filed in China compared to other countries. In 2016, Forbes reported that China held over 150,000 or 29% of the total number of renewable energy patents in the world, with the United States coming in second, totaling 100,000 patents (Dudley 2019). China's significant early investments in wind and solar energy have been so successful that they are now reducing funding for said projects, as the economics are favorable without subsidies. In 2019, China announced that solar technology had reached "grid parity"—meaning that the cost of producing solar energy was now cheaper or equal to the cost of producing coal energy—and it would begin to cut the number of solar projects funded by subsidies.

China might have managed to curtail its appetite for fossil fuels with government intervention, but it did not come without pitfalls. While China's efforts to subsidize clean energy were incredibly effective, the country's easeful path to reaching grid parity for solar energy was equally enabled by stagnant energy needs. This all changed in early 2019, when the country's energy needs started to grow. Chinese fossil fuel emissions, which were on the decline since 2012, rose 4% in the early half of 2019. Without subsidies, fewer solar energy projects were being added to the grid, and the country turned to coal to meet its energy supply deficit. Consequently, China's demand for coal, oil, and gas increased by 3%, 6%, and 12%, respectively (Myllyvirta 2019).

The bad news does not end there. The ever-increasing number of clean energy projects in China has reached such a scale that government subsidies cannot keep up. Having once had a subsidy surplus of CNY ¥15 billion in 2012, China found itself with a deficit of over CNY ¥100 billion (USD $14.5 billion) at the beginning of 2019 (Boqiang 2018). As a result, the country has been forced to cut funding every year. These deficits and decreasing subsidies have been felt in the global energy market as well. With

Chinese clean energy investments dropping by 39% in early 2019 compared to 2018, global investments experienced a similar 14% decrease during the same period.

Overall, China is a compelling case study because it shows both the power and limits of public-sector approaches to clean energy development. Due to the sheer size of its energy market and demand for energy, China is a powerful exemplar of how timely and strategic renewable energy subsidies can reduce and replace fossil fuels with clean energy technology. Through the use of subsidies, China ultimately saw the development and proliferation of clean energy within its overall energy mix.

What China was not anticipating was the speed at which its renewable energy market would grow and respond to government subsidies. With staggering increases in the development of clean energy projects, China found itself fiscally unable to subsidize all the viable clean energy projects it had committed to supporting. Coupled with funding deficiencies and growing energy demands, which both intensified in 2019, the country's success story broke down. Today, continued fossil fuel use is essential in China because of growing demand and because clean energy projects lack the necessary capital to become viable alternatives.

China's story epitomizes the current global situation. China's overreliance on fossil fuels highlights the deleterious effects on the environment and health that will be experienced around the globe with continued fossil fuel use. As in China, many other countries' energy demand has surpassed the public sector's ability to subsidize clean energy, threatening the ability for renewable energy technologies to become mainstream.

Investors have a pivotal role to play. Private investment can and must supplement these funding shortages by allocating more assets to the clean energy sector. If continued development and procurement of green energy ventures are to become mainstream, then investors need to collaborate with governments to lead the charge in supplementing and promoting these projects. Investors need to build robust fossil-fuel-free portfolios.

METRICS

The Intergovernmental Panel on Climate Change (IPCC) published a special report in October 2018, detailing the effects of climate change if temperature increases are not kept within a 1.5° Celsius (or 2.7° Fahrenheit) increase of pre-industrial levels (IPCC 2018). This and other IPCC reports can be considered the absolute benchmarks of the changes required globally to reduce emission levels fast enough to avoid the most catastrophic of climate change. The 1.5°C IPCC special report details the number of viable scenarios that could achieve various temperature goal reductions. As Table 12.1 shows from the IPCC special report, the number of scenarios that overshoot emission targets prematurely but return to levels in accordance with a 1.5°C or less change in temperature. Out of a possible 90 scenarios in which we can keep temperature change below 1.5°C, 81 of those, or 90% of the scenarios, involve us overshooting our emissions beyond an acceptable level before bringing it back down (IPCC 2018). This should worry investors.

However, there are more far scenarios included in the IPCC report that show us overshooting our emissions and then settling at a 2°C (3.6°F)[4] change in temperature. While keeping warming to 2°C might be easier, the difference of another +0.5°C above 1.5°C triggers a world of difference. A comprehensive study by Carbon Brief found that if our emission levels are kept in line with a 1.5°C change in temperature, there is a 3% likelihood of having an ice-free Arctic summer in a given year (Pearce 2020). That number jumps to 16% when considering a 2°C change. Likewise, there is an 80% chance that we will experience an ice-free Arctic summer in this century if we follow a 2°C temperature goal, compared to a 10% chance if we align with the 1.5°C target (Pearce 2020). An ice-free arctic signals rising sea levels and the displacement of coastal communities to a degree that our current infrastructure is not prepared to handle, especially in light of what were inadequate past global responses to other problems, such as conflict-affected refugees.

Building an Investment Policy Statement (IPS) for the mandate of keeping temperature change within a 1.5°C threshold in a fossil-fuel-free portfolio allows investors to take greater responsibility, but other factors relating to the types of emissions are to be considered as well. Investments within a fossil-free portfolio construction should be considered with the 1.5°C target in mind, but investors can choose alternative targets if desired. While mission levels in the IPCC report are primarily described in the context of carbon dioxide (CO_2) and methane (CH_4), the methodologies described throughout will focus on CO_2 and CO_2 equivalent emissions (CO_2e) given that metric's prevalence across industry reports.

---

[4]If you consider the Earth's temperature like your body, then a 2°C rise, equivalent to or 3.6°F higher, to your body temperature of 37°C or 98.6°F, would result in a temperature of 39°C or 102.2°F, which would not only give you a fever, it could send you to the hospital consistent with the conditions of measles or mumps.

TABLE 12.1 Pathway Classifications.

Pathway group	Pathway class	Pathway selection criteria and description	Number of scenarios	Number of scenarios
1.5°C or 1.5°C consistent	Below 1.5°C	Pathways limiting peak warming to below 1.5°C during the entire 21st century with 50–66% likelihood	9	90
	1.5°C low-overshoot	Pathways limiting median warming to below 1.5°C in 2100 and with a 50% to 67% probability of temporarily overshooting that level earlier, generally implying less than 0.1°C higher peak warming than below 1.5°C pathways	44	
	1.5°C high-overshoot	Pathways limiting median warming to below 1.5°C in 2100 and with a greater than 67% probability of temporarily overshooting that level earlier, generally implying 0.1 to 0.4°C higher peak warming than below 1.5°C pathways	37	
2°C or 2°C consistent	Lower 2°C	Pathways limiting peak warming to below 2°C during the entire 21st century with greater than 66% likelihood	74	132
	Higher 2°C	Pathways assessed to keep peak warming to below 2°C during the entire 21st century with 50 to 66% likelihood	58	

Source: Rogelj et al. (2018).

Science-Based Targets: Scope 1, 2, and 3 Emissions

In order to build fossil-fuel-free portfolios, investors need to become familiar with the variety of meaningful metrics that can be used to vet and compare the future risks of companies. While it is relatively straightforward to compare a solar-energy developer to an oil and gas company, the analysis will focus on the harder process of quantifying fossil fuel usage in non-energy sectors. Gauging a company's use and dependence of fossil fuels requires a deep understanding of emissions along their supply chain.

While most investors know what they want to measure, accurately gauging a company's supply chain emission profile is easier said than done. Investors today find themselves at a crossroads, asking:

- How should I define "ideal" corporate practices?
- What methodologies and key metrics are "correct" to measure emissions?
- Where can I find reliable data?
- How can I compare data across asset classes and industries?
- What limitations are set by the investment board and IPS, and is there any flexibility?

As some investment managers attempt to create their own definitions, and others follow their peers, there is not yet unanimous consensus amongst investors about how to proceed, especially with regards to what levels of fossil fuel usage is acceptable for companies. The primary difficulty, and opportunity for industry growth, is establishing acceptable norms and identifying goalposts for ideal corporate behavior. The Greenhouse Gas (GHG) Protocol, established in 1998, first laid the groundwork for what could be considered internationally accepted accounting and reporting standards in line with a global low-emission economy. Going forward, more third-party assessment frameworks and other forms of quantifiable intervention are needed, much like the United Nations (UN) Sustainable Development Goals (SDGs), in order to protect and align the interests of investors, investees, and the environment.

Consider the Science-Based Targets Initiative, a joint collaboration between the World Wildlife Fund, World Resource Institute, the UN Global Compact, and the Carbon Disclosure Project (CDP) to encourage companies to set emission targets based on scientifically established findings, not anecdotes. One of its most impactful achievements is its ability to coalesce corporate support for a consistent agreed-upon set of definitions and metrics for measuring companies' carbon footprints. This is of immense value to investors. By using science-based targets (SBT), investors can rely on a vetting process driven by verifiable quantitative analysis, which often complements their existing due diligence framework. This quantitative approach enables comparisons across companies, industries, and asset classes—an essential step forward for the investment industry.

To provide the most transparency to investors and actionable intelligence to companies, the initiative has broken down the total universe of corporate GHG emissions into three distinct categories: Scope 1, Scope 2, and Scope 3 emissions.[5] These three different scopes cover the various different emissions possible across a supply chain and are further detailed in Figure 12.1. The Science Based Targets Initiative identifies and publishes specific emissions targets for nearly[6] 900 companies at each of the scope levels. These targets are science-based and are derived from a quantitative analysis of what each company's emissions need to be in order for global emissions to be in line with the IPCC's 1.5°C benchmark.

In committing to a science-based target, typically GHG emissions reductions by a certain year, like 100% by 2030, corporations are first encouraged to reduce their Scope 1 and 2 emissions. Scope 1 encompasses all *direct* emissions, from the company's boiler room to the fuel used by its business vehicles. Scope 1 emissions therefore evaluate emissions from properties, business units, and other aspects owned or controlled by the company, as illustrated in Figure 12.1. Scope 2 emissions are considered to be *indirect* emissions related to energy purchased from utilities and independent power producers, or produced from on-site power. Scope 2 emissions capture the GHG emissions of electricity that is used by a business, but is frequently produced by an outside party and delivered through the grid. Scope 3 emissions are also *indirect* emissions and consist of emissions that result from upstream (suppliers) and downstream (customers) actions in the supply chain. Upstream activities are defined as steps in the supply chain process that gather and bring in all the raw materials necessary to create a product. Downstream activities include the life cycle of a product from its sale, use, and ultimate disposal. Consumer use of products are the biggest contributors of Scope 3 emissions, with increased consumer demand and use of products driving emissions (Science Based Targets 2019b).

[5]See also Chapter 10, "Inclusive Investing: Impact Meets Diversity, Equity, and Inclusion (DEI)," by Julianne Zimmerman, Edward Dugger III, and Shijiro Ochirbat.
[6]As of May 2020, see the companies and their goals at https://sciencebasedtargets.org/.

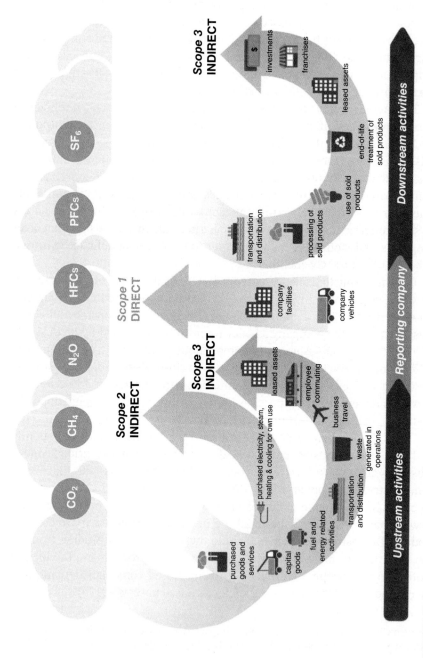

FIGURE 12.1 Scope 1, 2, and 3 Greenhouse Gas Emissions Explained. *Source:* World Resources Institute and WBSCD (2014).

424

These downstream emissions often make up the largest part of an enterprise's GHG emissions, and through its Scope 3 category, SBTs are the first major attempt to systematically measure the emissions of products using an entire life cycle approach. As such, SBT will hopefully be a catalyst for companies to consider the complete life cycle of their products and their related effects on the environment. That being said, the majority of companies that have accepted SBTs have only committed to reducing Scope 1 and 2 emissions, with Scope 3 being optional. Current hurdles facing broad Scope 3 emission targets is the sheer scale and variability of supply chains across different industries, companies, and regions, which requires a multi-stakeholder process to avoid conflicts of interest.

Consider Coca-Cola as a case study. With a business model contingent on outsourcing its manufacturing process, the majority of Coca-Cola's emissions fall into Scope 3 emissions. Given that it has factories and distribution centers located around the world, Coca-Cola's Scope 3 emissions are directly correlated to the market and region in which it operates. A can of coke in Africa does not have the same emissions as that in Chile, or Sweden, or the United States. Depending on the region, the transportation method of delivering the can (or in some cases bottle), the type of energy required to refrigerate it before consumption, and the energy demands of recycling the can once the Coke is consumed all change drastically. These distinctions require differing amounts of fossil fuel and produce different amounts of emissions. Measuring these complex product delivery, consumption, and waste systems is incredibly difficult.

By the end of May 2020, the SBT initiative collected formal goal-setting participation of 375 companies. SBT commits to:

- Showcase companies that set SBT through case studies, events, and media. Highlight the increased innovation, reduced regulatory uncertainty, strengthened investor confidence, and improved profitability and competitiveness generated by companies that have committed to setting SBT.
- Define and promote best practices in setting SBT, with the support of a technical advisory group.
- Reduce barriers to adoption by offering resources, workshops, and regular guidance.
- Independently assess and approve company targets.

Big brands and corporations, such as Coca-Cola and Swiss packaging giant Tetra Pak, have set SBTs. With a growing number of companies choosing to pursue SBTs, investors are able to apply specific information from all parts of a company's global supply chain, downstream and upstream. One example is the HIP Investor Science Based Targets for Climate Action strategy, focusing on the 50-plus US-listed securities, including holdings like toolmaker Stanley Black and Decker, which has committed to a 100% GHG reduction by 2030 goal.

The Science Based Targets initiative eases the process for investors significantly with readily available calculation tools. SBT's tools are designed to interpret the emission standards of various sectors, calculate sector-specific emission outputs, and even recommend relevant performance metrics.[7] Given the SBT initiative's emphasis on measurement and reporting, SBTs are laying the foundation of what will hopefully be a core addition to the standard reporting practices required for all companies worldwide.

If required, companies' commitment to and performance against SBT would become an ideal framework for investors to assess all potential investments in a fossil-fuel-free paradigm. Even as a voluntary program, SBTs are increasingly quintessential to investors worldwide that are seeking to invest in lower carbon footprint companies. Furthermore, these new reporting standards should not be confused with lesser shareholder return. By reducing emissions, companies can reduce the cost of energy, improve their operational efficiency, improve shareholder relations, and also differentiate their presence in an increasingly environmentally conscious global market.

It is important to note, however, that SBT do not consider factors pertaining to the social impact and governance policies of a business. SBTs should not be confused with providing the full answer in terms of environmental sustainability. Coca-Cola HBC (or Hellenic Bottling Company), the third largest bottler of Coca-Cola, announced that by 2020 it would commit to reducing Scope 1 and 2 emissions by 50% per liter of beverage, and would additionally reduce total value chain (meaning Scope 1, 2, and 3) emissions by 25% from a base year of 2010. This is an ambitious goal, considering Coca-Cola HBC operates in over 28 countries and is responsible for more than 2 billion-unit sales globally, equivalent to 5.7 trillion two-liter bottles (Science Based Targets 2019a). HBC's products could fill over 4.5 million Olympic-sized swimming pools every year.

Other Key Metrics: Pursuing Fossil Fuel Free in Tandem with ESG

In the context of creating a fossil-fuel-free portfolio, it is essential that investors also take additional environmental, social, and governance (ESG)

---

[7]For more information please see https://sciencebasedtargets.org/methods-2/.

factors into consideration in order to prevent the rise of new or tangential externalities beyond climate change.

For example, even if HBC meets its SBT goals, maintaining those levels of production with containers made of plastic does not come without a cost, especially in countries without robust recycling systems. Other environmental factors beyond GHG emissions need to be considered to achieve holistic sustainability.

Consider the 2015 eye-opening study from the University of California at Santa Barbara on the state of ocean plastics (Jambeck et al. 2015). The study estimates that 12.7 million metric tons of plastic enter the oceans annually.[8] Coca-Cola, unsurprisingly, was found to be the most polluting brand by the Break Free from Plastic movement, which organizes beach cleanups and conducts global audits of the plastics it finds. Corporations that use plastic packaging or encourage single-use plastics products need to take responsibility. Also, take a look at the isolated mountain village of San Cristóbal de las Casas in Mexico. The town's residents reportedly have access to running and drinking water as little as once every two days. Instead of water, residents consume on average more than two liters of soda per day. At the edge of town, however, the Coca-Cola factory is permitted to extract approximately 300,000 gallons of water every day. The result? With an indigenous population already genetically predisposed to diabetes, the mortality rate from diabetes has increased 30% from 2013 to 2016 (Lopez and Jacobs 2018).

In order to address the lingering secondary and tertiary effects of fossil fuel use, investors adopting a fossil-fuel-free portfolio should incorporate a range of ESG metrics. Tracking emissions should come first, but to build a well-rounded fossil-fuel-free portfolio investors need to acknowledge the extractive industries, environmental degradation, human rights violations, and human health issues that have arisen from our use of fossil fuels, and take steps to minimize them. These steps can either take the form of shareholder resolutions or new ESG benchmarks built directly into investor policy statements.

But given the vast universe of ESG metrics, how do investors choose the correct metrics that have tangible effects?

One of the leaders in adapting an ESG and impact methodology is the F.B. Heron Foundation[9] based in New York City, which adapted a pure impact portfolio. By aligning their value of "empowering people and institutions" to every investment within their portfolio, Heron seeks not only

---

[8] The blue whale is the world's largest animal. Estimated to weigh around 181 metric tons or 400,000 pounds fully grown, the blue whale now numbers between 10,000 to 25,000 mammals in the wild. Annual plastic waste pollution accounts to the equivalent of 70,000 adult blue whales in weight, almost triple the estimated population.

[9] For more information see https://www.heron.org/ .

to pursue financial returns but to realize impact through their investments. By not limiting themselves to generating impact through grantmaking, Heron is at the forefront. Heron strategically invests their endowment to work hand in hand with their grantmaking in order to further the foundation's mission and values. Since 1997, Heron's impact assets have grown considerably, and the foundation continues down its trail-blazing path by having a 100% values-aligned investment portfolio.

Building on the concept of "net contribution" by asking whether the world is better off with the existence of a corporation or potential investment vehicle, Heron actively invests in companies and municipal issuers that have a net positive effect on their immediate communities and the world at large (Heron Foundation 2019).

As an institutional investor, Heron also addresses the common misconception that adopting an impact or fossil-fuel-free portfolio means sacrificing asset diversity. Heron did not sacrifice portfolio diversity in its pursuit of impact, and has in fact increased its mix and distribution among asset classes on its path to a 100% impact portfolio.

The next section will specifically address how the broad use of these different metrics can build a multi-asset class portfolio without sacrificing market-level returns.

BUILDING A FOSSIL-FUEL-FREE PORTFOLIO

Building a fossil-fuel-free portfolio requires utilizing a variety of knowledge and techniques, such as setting scope-based emissions caps, utilizing ESG metrics, and taking into account asset-class specific metrics addressing fossil fuel use. A fossil-fuel-free or carbon-free portfolio does not equate to unilaterally eliminating every source of emissions from a portfolio; it means taking active steps to control and limit your portfolio's exposure to fossil fuels while maximizing its current use.

This section describes these issues in detail and is divided into two subsections. The first will focus on the importance of metric selection and utilization; the second will detail several potential investments to consider within private equity (PE), hedge funds, commodities, real estate, public debt including green bonds, and cryptocurrency.

The methodology described below should be applied after an investor has decided on their strategic asset allocation (SAA). The methodology should be applied to the total universe of investments that meet an investor's desired risk-return profile. Controversial investments into geoengineering (the act of using technology to manipulate the environment) will be excluded in this example, given their often-precarious claims and dubious outcomes. Carbon offset investments, which allow an investor to pay to mitigate their carbon footprint, will be considered, but only when they are made in the correct geopolitical context, such as an investment into clean energy in a resource-constrained nation.

To begin, consider a fossil-fuel-free portfolio in the context of publicly available securities that are available to both retail and institutional investors. Proper fossil-fuel-free due diligence for public equities begins with setting appropriate emission caps at the sector level. While a simple carbon footprint target is a great place to start, by taking into consideration Scope 1, 2, and 3 emissions, investors can set more granular and informed goals. As such, to the extent possible emissions caps should be based on a combination of Scope 1, 2, and 3 emissions, as laid out by the Science Based Targets Initiative, as seen in the previous section. Scope 1 emissions deal with all direct emissions, Scope 2 addresses indirect emissions from energy providers, and Scope 3 encompasses all indirect emissions from the entire supply chain. By segmenting emissions into these various categories, investors can better understand what specific points in a potential investment's supply chain have the greatest exposure to fossil fuels.

When first building a fossil-fuel-free portfolio of public equities, it is often practical to only consider Scope 1 or 2 emissions. Unfortunately, given the complexity and size of many large company supply chains, Scope 3 emission data will often be too difficult or cost-prohibitive to research. When and wherever possible, however, investors should utilize Scope 3 data were available, but that is not to say that any validity is lost when only looking at Scope 1 and 2 data. If industries change due to investor demand of emissions data, then those same companies will encourage their supply chain providers to disclose, and emissions information becomes more readily available for all to use. Data from Scope 1 and 2 emissions are sometimes reported by companies themselves, or available through NGOs such as the CDP. Scope 1 emissions, which are a company's direct emissions, are being reported by more and more companies worldwide. This allows investors, given two comparable investments, to compare their fossil fuel use and choose the appropriate lower emissions one.

But how would an investor go about doing so if both investments belonged to different sectors? By conducting increased due diligence into the fossil fuel use within a sector, investors will be able to select appropriate emission-based targets rather than be forced to compare apples and oranges when comparing cross-sector investments.

It is crucial that emission caps are not applied uniformly to each sector. For example, if the methodology is being applied to an international shipping company, the investor should recognize that Scope 1 emissions will be fairly high given the amount of fuel needed to transport goods. Conversely, investments into sectors like technology will have investments with low exposures to Scope 1 and 3 emissions and some exposure to Scope 2 emissions.

It would be easy to set an all-encompassing emission cap across the portfolio, but a blanket emissions cap would potentially result in an unbalanced or overweight portfolio in one or several sectors. All sectors are not created equally in their exposure to fossil fuels. Blanket caps fail to take into account sector differences in fossil fuel use, and also rarely recognize companies in carbon intensive sectors that are taking big steps to reduce their fossil fuel use. A proper SBT emissions cap requires investors to calculate the fossil fuel use within the sector, to ensure the appropriate scopes caps are being considered in the correct context.

For example, emissions from the energy sector are going to be drastically different from the technology sector. Let's compare Microsoft, a technology sector stock, and Equinor, an energy sector stock. Microsoft produced 90,723 metric tons and Equinor produced 13.51 million metric tons of carbon-dioxide-equivalents ($mtCO_2e$[10]) of Scope 1 greenhouse gases in 2018. If an investor had decided to adopt a uniform Scope 1 emissions cap of 100,000 $mtCO_2e$ regardless of the sector, such a cap would have excluded a leading energy company like Equinor that is taking active steps to reduce its emissions. As a multinational Norwegian energy- and petroleum-producing company, one would not readily consider Equinor as an addition to a fossil-fuel-free portfolio.

However, while some fossil-fuel-free investors seek to screen any energy producer of coal, oil, or natural gas, some investors are opting for the goal of minimizing or optimizing fossil fuel intensity. From 2014 to 2018, Equinor has reduced its total Scope 1 emissions by 8.56%, while also increasing its renewable clean energy production from 536 GWH to 1,251 GWH through increased investments into solar, wind, and hydropower (Equinor 2018). To put that into perspective, the entire European Union (EU) produced close to 3.1 million GWH in 2017 to meet its growing energy needs (Eurostat 2020). Furthermore, while Equinor's carbon footprint might be gigantic compared to Microsoft, it still constitutes less than 0.25% of the world's GHG emissions

---

[10]Carbon-dioxide equivalents seek to unify under one metric the effects of carbon (1x), methane (about 25x), nitrous oxide (about 300x), and other super-pollutants (as high as 10,000x or more).

while being the eleventh-largest oil producer in the world (Equinor 2018). Equinor showcases how companies that are fossil fuel producing or reliant can still be considered to be included in a fossil-fuel-free portfolio that seeks to reduce GHG intensity but remain diversified across sectors.

Fossil-Fuel-Free Portfolios: Risk and Returns

Figure 12.2 compares the standard MSCI ACWI Index[11] (in British pounds, GBP) to a subset of the index that removed all companies that own oil, gas, and coal reserves. The fossil-fuel-free subset had greater annual returns between 2017 and 2019, and possessed a higher annualized return since its inception on November 30, 2010. The MSCI ACWI ex–Fossil Fuels Index, which seeks to exclude firms with fossil fuel businesses and reserves, did produce higher returns more often than not, and by 100 to 300 basis points (1% to 3%). Similarly, the energy sector weights differed greatly between the two, with the parent MSCI ACWI index holding 4.5% and its ex–fossil fuel counterpart holding less than a percent or 0.98%. This translated to small discrepancies in the risk or standard deviation of both benchmarks. Though exclusion of all fossil fuel companies is the easiest method in adopting a fossil-fuel-free portfolio, institutional investors are choosing to remain diversified across sectors, including energy. If this is the case, could these portfolios benefit from the application of fossil-fuel-free methods? It is often not the best choice.

CUMULATIVE INDEX PERFORMANCE – GROSS RETURNS (GBR) (NOV 2010 – APR 2020)

ANNUAL PERFORMANCE (%)

Year	MSCI ACWI ex Fossil Fuels	MSCI ACWI
2019	23.24	22.38
2018	–3.26	–3.27
2017	14.59	13.84
2016	27.84	29.40
2015	5.82	3.84
2014	13.23	11.22
2013	22.68	21.15
2012	13.47	11.67
2011	–6.32	–6.17

FIGURE 12.2 Comparative Cumulative Index Performance of MSCI ACWI and MSCI ACWI excluding Fossil Fuels. *Source:* MSCI (2020).

---

[11]The MSCI ACWI Index is the Morgan Stanley Capital International All Country World Index that contains large and mid-cap stocks across 23 developed and 26 emerging markets.

A blanket ban on fossil fuel investments, especially in equity markets, does not translate to significantly higher returns. It is important to examine the historical and current fossil fuel use within each sector to precisely evaluate and benchmark investments from a risk, return, and emissions standpoint.

Developing a fossil-fuel-free portfolio requires investors to wed standard risk-return methodologies with projections of the future of the fossil fuel industry. Consider Figure 12.3, which details a precursory look at a subset of investments taken from the S&P 500 Energy benchmark in 2019 when the energy sector performed particularly poorly compared to the broader economy (Egan 2019). Note how the chart is plotted similarly to a risk-return profile, but with the additional dimension of total Scope 1 and 2 emissions, and the percent change of emissions from 2016 to 2018. Returns are showcased according to total Scope 1 and 2 emissions. The risk, or standard deviation of returns, is used as a scaling measure so that the bigger the plot,

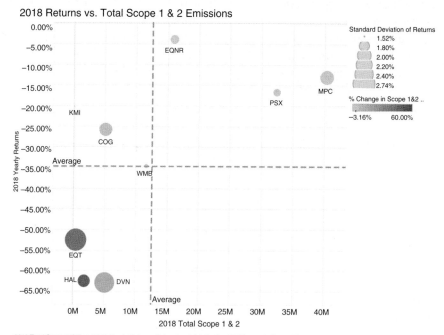

2018 Total Scope 1 & 2 vs. 2018 Yearly Returns. Color shows details about % Change in Scope 1&2 emissions from 2016 to 2018. Size shows details about 2018 Standard Deviation. The marks are labeled by Stock Ticker1.

FIGURE 12.3   Custom Analysis of Energy Equities on Risk-Return Ratios and GHG Emissions, 2016 to 2018. *Source:* Author's analysis of annual sustainability and returns data from 2016 to 2018.

the greater the company's standard deviation or risk. Reference lines are also included in the Figure 12.3 to showcase the different averages within this investment universe and segment the graph into different quadrants. The reference line, which measures the average emissions within the sector, can also be utilized differently by investors. Investors could choose to not hold any securities above the sector-wide average for emissions, or they could only consider the bottom 25% or lower quartile of investments that have the least emissions. See Table 12.2 for exact figures.

Focusing solely on minimizing fossil fuel exposure, investments into Kinder Morgan (KMI) and Cabot Oil & Gas Corporation (COG) in the second quadrant (upper left) would be considered acceptable for the portfolio because they offer the lowest fossil fuel exposure while having higher historical yearly returns; and investments in the first quadrant (Equinor, Philips 66, Marathon Petroleum Corp.) would not be considered given their above-average fossil fuel exposure. Meanwhile, investments in the third quadrant (EQT, Haliburton, Devon Energy, and Cimarex) could be potential investments, but they offer lower than average returns and would need further due diligence investigation of their fundamentals.

Taking a different view of the same energy stocks, this time juxtaposed with consumer discretionary stocks, reinforces the importance of sector-based considerations from a different perspective. Graphed along the

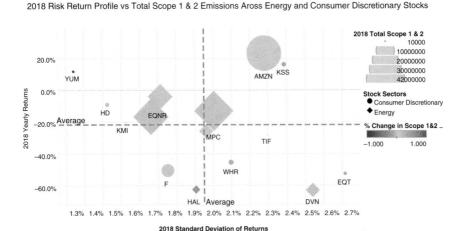

FIGURE 12.4   Custom Analysis of Energy and Consumer Discretionary Equities on Risk-Return Ratios and GHG Emissions, 2016 to 2018. *Source:* Author's analysis of annual sustainability and returns data from 2016 to 2018.

TABLE 12.2 Custom Analysis of Energy Stock Returns and Emissions ($mtCO_2$).

Stock	Stock Ticker	2018 Yearly Returns	2018 Standard Deviation of Returns	2016 Total Scope 1 and 2 GHG Emissions	2018 Total Scope 1 and 2 GHG Emissions	Change in Emissions from 2016 to 2018 (%)
Marathon Petroleum Corp.	MPC	−12.97%	2.00%	41,016,333.94	40,290,381.13	−1.77%
Kinder Morgan Inc.	KMI	−20.08%	1.52%	78,767.00	84,234.00	6.94%
Phillips 66	PSX	−16.64%	1.66%	32,123,411.98	32,395,644.28	0.85%
Halliburton Company	HAL	−62.40%	1.90%	1,187,939.20	1,793,077.13	50.94%
Cabot Oil & Gas Corporation	COG	−25.70%	1.96%	4,840,000.00	5,090,000.00	5.17%
EQT Corp.	EQT	−52.43%	2.71%	301,503.00	428,988.00	42.28%
Devon Energy Corp.	DVN	−62.78%	2.54%	4,441,424.00	5,070,315.24	14.16%
Equinor ASA	EQNR	−3.85%	1.71%	16,061,705.99	15,970,961.89	−0.56%

Source: Author's analysis of annual sustainability and returns data from 2016 to 2018.

434

TABLE 12.3 Custom Analysis of Consumer Discretionary Stock Returns and Emissions ($mtCO_2$).

Consumer Discretionary Stocks	Stock Ticker	2018 Yearly Returns	2018 Standard Deviation of Returns	2016 Total Scope 1 & 2	2018 Total Scope 1 & 2	Change in Emissions from 2016 to 2013 (%)
Amazon.com, Inc.	AMZN	23.37%	2.28%	N/A	35,250,000.00	N/A
Ford Motor Company	F	−50.37%	1.75%	4,600,000.00	4,792,771.00	4.19%
Hasbro, Inc.	HAS	−12.51%	1.72%	13,762.00	13,077.00	−4.98%
The Home Depot, Inc.	HD	−9.02%	1.42%	439,906.00	516,645.00	17.44%
Kohl's Corporation	KSS	16.32%	2.39%	663,995.00	553,923.00	−16.58%
Whirlpool Corporation	WHR	−45.23%	2.10%	833,000.00	753,000.00	−9.60%
Yum! Brands, Inc.	YUM	11.91%	1.24%	2,173,315.00	203,485.72	−90.45%
Tiffany & Co.	TIF	−27.91%	2.30%	42,757.00	44,571.00	4.24%

Source: Author's analysis of annual sustainability and returns data from 2016 to 2018.

435

standard risk-return profile, Figure 12.4 displays emissions as a factor of size. The graph highlights the glaring emission discrepancies that exist in securities; sector classifications of emissions showcase how skewed emission caps can become. This is especially true in this comparison, as the consumer discretionary sector produces significantly less emissions than the energy sector. The most glaring firm on the graph is Amazon, which only started reporting emissions from 2018, but produces not only more emissions than others in its own sector but also more compared to energy sector stocks. Even though Amazon is an attractive investment, fossil fuel investors need to consider the risks related to that massive carbon footprint.

Though quadrant-based analysis is a helpful start when considering sector-level investments, other factors related to emissions should also be taken into consideration. Companies that are actively taking steps to mitigate their emissions should likely be considered for inclusion in a fossil fuel portfolio. Why? Because when investing in companies that are reforming dirty industries, investors incentivize those companies and their peers to further reduce their emissions. It is a form of positive reinforcement that signals to companies that investors are looking to future risks to bottom-line profits and the environment.

Energy Productivity

Depicted in Table 12.2, Equinor is one of the few energy companies that was able to reduce its total emissions from 2016 to 2018. Why does this matter? From an investor's point of view, Equinor is essentially a first mover in the energy sector because it is investing heavily in renewables and adapting into a clean energy provider. Coupled with EQNR's returns in 2018, the company is well positioned to respond to increasing supply and demand risk in the future.

Ophir Bruck, the US Network Manager for the Principles of Responsible Investing (PRI), speaks to how inclusion of some leading fossil fuel companies that allocate a certain threshold or directionality of their capital expenditures toward renewables could be considered for inclusion in a fossil-fuel-free portfolio. Furthermore, by lessening its reliance on fossil fuels, EQNR will be better able to weather the geopolitical risks that often plague energy producers and fossil fuel extraction.

Compared to EQT, the US largest producer of natural gas, and other firms that increased their emissions, Equinor is significantly less risky, as seen by its comparatively lesser price volatility. EQT increased its total Scope 1 and 2 emissions by 42.28% and fell 52.43% in value between 2016 and 2018, as seen in Table 12.2. From the lens of overall fossil fuel exposure, EQT possesses below-average total emissions, but its overall increase in emissions is concerning. Adding it to a fossil fuel portfolio is risky and would not be recommended.

Bringing about a new investment paradigm centered around minimizing fossil fuel use and maximizing returns would not include a company that has not taken any steps to reduce climate change risk. In fact, when assessing companies, it is not only important to consider their total emissions and changes to emissions, but also how efficiently they use energy, as well as their broader performance on ESG criteria. Why is energy productivity important to consider? Investors are still seeking revenue in a fossil-fuel-free portfolio, and investments in energy productive companies mean a portfolio dedicated to lowering energy use while maximizing economic output and total shareholder value.

Assessing investments with respect to energy productivity means measuring the production output per unit of energy consumed. This ratio highlights the carbon efficiency of companies, enabling investors to identify which companies get the most out of their energy supply. As a metric, energy productivity is gaining ground among investors because it enables them to directly calculate the efficiency of companies based on the amount of energy they consume. At the company level, this calculation is done by dividing total revenue or production units by the total amount of energy used, which can be in the form of kilowatt hours of energy expended or barrels of cure oil consumed. The same metric can also be applied to the energy sector, where it is commonly labeled carbon intensity.

Carbon intensity through a fossil fuel lens can be thought of as the amount of greenhouse gases released per unit of energy consumed or the total amount of greenhouse gases produced divided by gross domestic product or GDP. Equinor, for example, has a carbon intensity of 9kg CO2 per barrel of oil equivalent (BOE) for their upstream production activities, compared to the industry average of 18kg CO_2/boe (Equinor 2019). Weighing different investments with respect to carbon intensity opens up more of an individual company's fossil fuel profile and importantly helps investors see individual and also industry trends. In that spotlight, Equinor has further pledged to reduce their carbon intensity by 50% by 2050, a goal in line with securing their place within a future low-carbon economy (Equinor 2020).

Metrics as Building Blocks

Andrew Montes, Director of Digital Strategies at As You Sow,[12] evaluates thousands of mutual funds and exchange-traded funds to assess if they are

---

[12]Interview data. See Appendix 12.1.

fossil-fuel-free, and if not, to what degree those funds may be fossil-intensive. This initiative and free, global online website started at As You Sow when the nonprofit's team asked what their organization's 401(k) retirement plan fund choices were invested in, since the nonprofit's mission is to make the world better for people and the planet.[13]

Specifically, investors should investigate a fund's prospectus[14] because even if a fund is billed as fossil-fuel-free, that does not necessarily mean it will stay that way in the future. A fund's prospectus will hold the asset manager accountable if there are clearly stated sustainability goals and prevent any detrimental style drift. With an average of 1,000 users logging into FossilFreeFunds.org each week, the demand for selecting prudent fossil-fuel-free funds is growing fast.

Other key factors or metrics to consider when selecting investments for a fossil-fuel-free portfolio include ESG metrics. While Scope 1 and 2 emissions comprise the majority of an individual company's exposure to fossil fuels, if the governance or social practices of a company are not aligned with reducing fossil fuel use and maximizing efficiency, then fossil fuel's long-term risks will still persist for that company. ESG metrics can and need to be utilized to further the investment decision-making process in building a fossil-fuel-free portfolio. Not only do ESG metrics and their aggregate ESG scores allow investors to rate investments across their environmental, social, and governance, this also enables investors to create a more well-rounded portfolio.

This chapter took a brief look at how investors consider individual securities within a sector, but what about mutual funds and exchange-traded funds (ETFs)? How can investors begin assessing these funds, and specifically these asset managers? As You Sow, a non-government organization dedicated to shareholder advocacy and increasing corporate transparency addresses this issue straight on using a combination of five investment screens. As You Sow assesses funds and ETFs applying five fossil fuel criteria to grade each fund quantitatively to show the percentage of fossil fuel firms in the fund and a representative grade of "A, B, C, D, and F." The five criteria are:

1. **Carbon Underground 200**

    The Carbon Underground 200, compiled and maintained by the firm Fossil Free Indexes™ LLC,[15] identifies the top publicly traded

---

[13]To learn about how your retirement plan could be more sustainable, see Chapter 11, "Investing for Impact in Employee Retirement Plans," by Megan Morrice.

[14]A document detailing investment information including strategy, past performance, fee structure, and others.

[15]See more at https://fossilfreeindexes.com/.

firms with fossil fuel reserves—100 in coal, plus 100 in oil and gas —globally, ranked by the potential carbon emissions content of their reported reserves.

2. **Coal Industry**

The coal criterion consists of companies engaged in mining coal as designated by Morningstar, as well as the top 100 coal reserve holders from the Carbon Underground 200.

3. **Oil and Gas Industry**

The oil and gas criterion consists of companies from six Morningstar subcategories: drilling, extraction and production, integrated, midstream, refining and marketing, and equipment and services. It also includes the top 100 oil and gas reserve holders from the Carbon Underground 200.

4. **Macroclimate 30**

The Macroclimate 30[16] is an exclusion list of the 30 largest public-company owners of coal-fired power plants in developed markets plus China and India. Macroclimate compiled the list of 30 companies using open-source data on coal-fired power plants worldwide.

5. **Fossil-Fired Utilities**

The fossil-fired utilities criterion consists of companies from four Morningstar subcategories: independent power producers (IPPs), diversified utilities, regulated electric utilities, and regulated gas utilities. Companies that are engaged in 100% renewable operations, pure transmission utilities, or otherwise don't burn fossil fuels to generate power are removed from this list.

These five exclusionary screens filter out investments against the criteria above to provide transparency to investors and, more importantly, allow them to make more informed investment decisions when evaluating funds and ETFs.

An example of a scorecard is provided in Figure 12.5 of the SPDR S&P 500 ETF Trust (SPY), which breaks down assets within the ETF that fall within each of the screens detailed to the holdings level. This level of granularity can be hard-pressed to find, and this scorecard by As You Sow energizes investors to not heavily rely on asset managers for fossil fuel exposure details, and discern by themselves greater amounts of detail from publicly available information.[17] Investors can use this scorecard to compare investments, choosing higher-rated investments over lower-rated ones.

---

[16]More details at https://macroclimate.com/coal#.
[17]More information at https://fossilfreefunds.org.

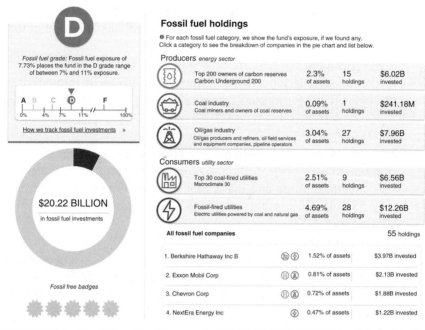

FIGURE 12.5   Fossil-Free-Fuel Scorecard of SPDR S&P 500 ETF Trust. *Source:* Fossil Free Funds.[19]

As You Sow decided on their five screens based on metrics that they believed were important to evaluating fossil-fuel-free investments. The number and quality or metrics of the screens can all be decided by the investor, and therefore investors have a certain degree of freedom in choosing which metrics they want to include and in how many screens they use. Even if investors are not savvy enough in their metrics and screen selection, then potentially fossil-fuel-heavy investments can find themselves in the portfolio. In addition to the FossilFreeFunds.org tool, another online tool called CleanPortfolios.com[18] brings together the financial, fossil-free ratios, and other fund information to simulate how close to a fossil-fuel-free portfolio is possible.

Beyond ESG environmental factors, social and governance metrics also pay a key role in building a fossil-fuel-free portfolio. Scope 1 and 2 emissions paint a portion of the bigger picture of an individual company's exposure to

---

[18] More details at http://www.CleanPortfolios.com, built and operated by CleanMoney.US.
[19] Available at https://fossilfreefunds.org/fund/spdr-sp-500-etf-trust/SPY/fossil-fuel-investments/FSUSA00B4A/FEUSA00001.

fossil fuels, but if the governance or social practices of a company are not aligned to reducing or maximizing fossil fuel use, then associated long-term risks will still persist. The use of ESG variables allows investors to plug the gap in data when GHG Scope-based information is scarce, especially in private equity (PE) and other alternative investments that have less strict reporting standards. Therefore, the careful selection and alignment of ESG metrics become necessary in contemplating alternate assets.

Consider the aligned ESG practices of PE investment "Formula E." Formula E is the environmentally conscious version of "Formula 1," the branded adrenaline-fueled racing series consisting of cars reaching max speeds of 300 kilometers per hour (186 miles per hour) over street and road courses. The electric cars that race in Formula E reach speeds of 280 km per hour (174 mph) and do so while limiting their environmental impact on an individual car and racing series basis. Having been awarded the ISO 20121 certification for "sustainable event management," Formula E set a high bar when it recycled and saved 200,000 plastic bottles, used 10 kilometers worth of non-PVC recyclable trackside branding, and even established an advanced battery recycling program (Formula E 2020). This is a clear example of a company's ESG practices aligning to reduce and maximize fossil fuel use. The methodology discussed thus far deals with gleaning available emission and ESG information from public and private companies, but the same can be applied to other alternative assets as well.

Potential Investments

After detailing the various metrics and tools investors have at their disposal to evaluate investments, the next section examines different investment opportunities present in the major asset classes. These fossil-fuel-free investment choices will further be detailed by their relevant financial instruments and strategies.

Private Equity (PE)

An asset class marred by limited mandatory reporting regulations and oversight is a highly sought-after asset class by institutional and accredited investors worldwide, due to the potential of very high returns, despite typical liquidity restrictions of 7 to 12 years. PE collectively was one of the few asset classes that weathered the financial crisis of 2008 with positive returns. Such upside performance during a recession made this asset class much more sought after in ensuing years. Today's PE market is saturated.

The role of investment manager is a general partner (GP) competing for asset allocation by asset owners—pensions, sovereign wealth funds, foundations, and high-net-worth investors. Investors in PE are typically limited partners (LP), and too many LPs have now crowded the market to such a degree that PE funds are able to raise more capital, resulting in more and more "dry powder" to invest capital in more investee deals (Feliz 2019). Dry powder is the available capital that GPs have on hand to deploy to their investments. Though having large amounts of dry powder can be beneficial in periods of economic downturn or meeting unforeseen financial obligations, a trend of increased dry powder could also means lost opportunities to have those funds invested in growth markets; though it is of high value going into stressed markets, which may offer more attractive valuations.

When considering fossil-fuel-free investments within PE, consider the strengths and weaknesses of the asset class. As previously stated, reporting regulations are not as stringent as in public markets and available data sets around environmental sustainability are either incomplete or nonexistent. The strengths may outweigh the weaknesses. Since sustainable-minded LPs may be a large portion of a fund, especially larger pensions that tend to be more activist, LPs can encourage or mandate the GP collect ESG and other sustainability information related to the investments. This privilege allows LPs at times to push GPs to enact better business practices within their investments to meet an LP's overall IPS. These scenarios are frequently seen in Europe,[20] which has implemented various styles of PE ESG disclosure frameworks that LPs and GPs can adapt or modify to meet their individual investment needs (Guarascio 2019). Some LPs have demanded their GPs link their "carried interest"[21] to meeting ESG metrics and results—including possible SDGs. Private markets also face their own share of hurdles and challenges. Similar to "greenwashing," GPs have started to treat ESG and other environmental factors as check boxes on an investment, rather than a sustained effort toward bettering business practices. With the addition of lack of transparent quantitative data in private markets, the problem is compounded and LPs have a greater need to get the GP to properly collect, verify, and report the correct metrics. Successful PE investments are possible and have already been made with respect to a fossil-fuel-free portfolio.

---

[20]See Chapter 29, "Impact Investing and European Wealth Managers: Why Impact Investing Will Go Mainstream and Evolve to Suit Every European Investor," by Trang Fernandez-Leenknecht.

[21]"Carried interest" refers to a type of performance fee paid out to GPs usually as a percentage of the investment's total performance after meeting or exceeding pre-determined criteria, which can be financial returns and also be ESG, sustainability, and fossil-fuel-free metrics

Tesla Motors, once a private company, was valued at USD $17.00 a share during its initial public offering (IPO) in 2010. During the time of the offering, investors and the public alike showed great skepticism in an electric automotive company. Yet on close of day May 18, 2020, Tesla's share price of USD $813.63 represented more than 47 times its original price from 2010. Given its leadership in influencing other car manufacturers to increase their electric car capacities, thereby reducing overall emissions across all models, it is easy to see why Tesla would find a home in every fossil-fuel-free portfolio. But not all PE investments are as obvious for inclusion in a fossil-fuel-free portfolio. Besides being a maverick electric car manufacturer, Elon Musk, the CEO of Tesla Motors, has been strategic in promoting clean energy transitions, including the PowerWall in South Australia, which was sparked by a Twitter request, and ultimately resulted in a lower-cost, more-resilient energy source.

In late 2018, Tesla deployed the world's largest lithium ion battery in South Australia. The Hornsdale Power Reserve is essentially a 100 megawatt (MW) battery that stores energy from the Hornsdale wind farm and primarily supplements any energy deficiencies in the grid as a local "frequency control ancillary service" (FCAS). This service allows the grid to shore up energy deficiencies while also facilitating the trading of electricity within the system from various sources such as home-battery units. The need for the massive battery farm arose from growing complaints of frequent blackouts further exacerbated during South Australia's sweltering summer months. With storms known to frequent the region, South Australia has always been privy to its share of minor blackouts. Yet in December 2016, a series of storms would unleash the largest and longest blackout. A cataclysmic chain of failures beginning with the severance of several high-voltage power lines resulted in regions in the developed country being left without power for days. Storms are not the only concern. In early January 2018, temperatures soared to as high as 47.4°C (or 117°F) in the town of Wudinna and demand for power peaked. Air conditioners become the region's saving grace and Achilles heel as power needs neared the 3,000 MW capacity for South Australia (ABC News 2018). To combat these frequent power outages, South Australia opened a USD $150 million Renewable Technology Fund, targeted toward energy storage infrastructure. Tesla's battery storage farm, though expensive, AUD $90.6 million, provided returns of AUD $13 million in its first six months of operation, equating to a 14.3% financial return on investment (ROI). The addition of the 100 MW, though small relative to the total grid capacity, offered a glimpse of how marginal capacity can be used to avoid rolling blackouts.

Tesla's battery farm project exemplifies how the company is actively seeking opportunities to reduce society's reliance on coal and other fossil fuels. Potential PE investments like Tesla can be considered dubious by some, especially in their earlier years, especially if they challenge long-held market sentiments, like toward fossil fuels. PE investments especially in their early stages can be shaped by the GPs managing them, either through direct intervention via management team changes or indirectly via guidance targets. Though GPs regularly engage their individual portfolio companies, LPs can play a key role as well. Active engagement via a Limited Partner Advisory Committee (LPAC) gives LPs who have invested into a fund insight and the opportunity to guide current and future investment decisions. For example, LPs within an LPAC can set forth criteria in the beginning for tracking individual investments according to their fossil fuel usage and suggest guidance on reducing emissions over a period of years. Additionally, when expanding the opportunity set to cover new investments, the LPAC can lay out guidelines in selecting appropriate fossil-fuel-free investments that have the capacity to meet certain fossil fuel emission thresholds. This is why PE can be considered a special asset class, because investors can exercise a greater amount of influence in the management of the assets or portfolio companies. Therefore, investors will not only need to consider the type of investments within PE but also the importance of the relationship being cultivated with GPs to ensure proper adhesion to fossil-fuel-free and other investment guidelines.

Hedge Funds

Hedge fund investments have grown significantly in the last two decades, aided by advances in high-frequency trading, new financially engineered products, and a multitude of investment strategies. Much like PE, hedge funds do not face the same stringent reporting requirements as found in the public markets. With Assets Under Management (AUM) of USD $3.24 trillion as of early 2020, the hedge fund sector has grown significantly since 2000 (Williamson 2020). But growth has not been without controversy. Many still blame some renegade hedge funds as contributing to the subprime mortgage bubble that rippled into the 2007–2008 global financial crisis.

Within a fossil-fuel-free portfolio, hedge funds are a viable asset class, offering a smorgasbord of managers and strategies to choose from. One such strategy that fits within a fossil-fuel-free portfolio is the use of weather derivatives. Derivatives are financial instruments or agreements between a buyer and seller, where the buyer agrees to pay the seller a predetermined amount at a certain time for an underlying commodity. As financial products, derivatives are useful because they allow both buyers and sellers to hedge risks associated with uncertain market conditions. Hedge funds utilize weather derivatives to minimize the risks associated with climate change inherent in their portfolios that do not normally account for any fossil fuel exposure.

Unlike weather insurance, which is purchased to cover high-risk, low-probability events, weather derivatives are marketed toward hedging low-risk, high-probability events. For example, consider an agricultural business whose revenue will be greatly affected if temperatures are 5 degrees lower than expected. By purchasing a weather derivative, the business hedges against the 5-degree fall in temperature, while also purchasing weather insurance in the case of the temperature drop being part of a greater natural disaster. Though weather derivatives can be based on temperature changes, they can also be derived from precipitation levels (i.e. rainfall and snowfall), or the likelihood of regularly occurring natural events in a region, such as monsoons.

The most commonly used application of weather derivatives is by utility companies to hedge weather risk associated with increased power consumption during particularly high or low temperatures. Weather derivatives come in the form of heating degree day (HDD) or cooling degree day (CDD) contracts. HDD contracts speculate on the amount of energy required to warm a building when temperatures drop below the accepted standard of 18°C (or 64°F). CDD contracts meanwhile consider how much energy is required to cool a building when temperatures exceed the same temperature standard (Clements 2012). When looking at temperature forecasts, assuming our current rate of greenhouse gas emissions, temperatures are expected to increase by up to 4.8°C (8.6°F) by 2100. Such a drastic increase in temperature not only threatens our coasts but also our global food production, which is climate and weather dependent. Weather derivatives therefore can be incorporated into a fossil-fuel-free portfolio through specific hedge fund strategies or be added on their own.

The addition of weather derivatives within a fossil-fuel-free portfolio allows investors to capitalize on rising temperatures, though that does come with the quandary of betting alongside the immediate effects of climate change. Though the contracts do offer protection against the losses associated with increasing temperatures and their ever-increasing effects, it does little to curtail the problem of fossil fuel consumption.

Multi-strategy hedge funds that utilize ESG metrics and fossil fuel exclusionary screens based on emission targets could offer greater diversification benefits than a single instrument. Unfortunately, the burden of research on the underlying holdings of these hedge funds and their strategies is left to the investor. But if an increasing number of large LPs begin to demand more disclosure around ESG and fossil fuel metrics, then this burden can be lessened.

Meanwhile, the clever use of other instruments and structured products will have to be utilized in building a fossil-fuel-free portfolio. There are a growing number of structured products encouraging the reduction of fossil fuel risk that can be considered good additions to a fossil-fuel-free portfolio such as Power Purchase Agreements (PPAs).

In 2019, Nephila Weather, the ESG-arm of the hedge fund Nephila Climate, introduced the world to the use of Proxy Generation Power Purchase Agreements (pgPPAs). Fossil fuel exposure reduction is a goal for a fossil-fuel-free portfolio, but that can only be accomplished by also increasing clean energy investments. These agreements are risk-mitigating tools that can not only act to reduce fossil fuel exposure, but rather make clean energy investments more attractive to investors who are concerned with the risks inherent in a transitioning energy market. These risks are centered around how unpredictable demand is in the energy markets and the expected outputs of clean energy investments. Similar to PPAs, which allows buyers to lock in to a predetermined rate of cost per unit of energy, pgPPAs instead use a proxy index of expected output to define the associated risk when the clean energy project fails to meet the expected output (Nephila 2019). This allows investors to view their clean energy investments holistically and take steps to reduce any shortfall production risks.

Commodities

Many institutional investors have been ambivalent about including commodities in their portfolio, given their track record of cyclical returns and risky trading strategies that primarily utilize the swaps and futures markets. Consider the Bloomberg Commodity Index (BCOM), which was created in 1998 and is now one of the most widely used commodity benchmarks. Weights within the benchmark are categorized within broad categories, consisting of energy, grains, industrial metals, precious metals, and livestock.

Historically, energy has always been the largest group within the index, accounting for more than 30%, yet 2020 marked the first time since the index's inception that the group dropped below 30% (Bloomberg 2019). Traditionally consisting of physical commodity exchange contracts involving crude oil, diesel, and natural gas exchange contracts, the energy group's allocation was lowered in line with market trends and the activities of the Organization of the Petroleum Exporting Countries (OPEC). Commodity as an asset class would appear best served within a fossil-fuel-free portfolio by simply excluding any fossil fuel commodities, but there are other opportunities in an increasingly stressed energy market dominated by OPEC decisions.

As discussed previously, renewable energy is entering the global energy mix with low-cost clean energy projects such as solar. With price points becoming more competitive for clean energy projects in addition to their low environmental impact, many countries have begun a wider adoption of renewable energy to fuel their next generation of energy needs. As clean energy begins to take a noticeable foothold globally, market share is slowly being lost by fossil fuels, and as a result, many have called on OPEC to cut prices to remain competitive.

OPEC's 15 member nations, whose main exports are fossil fuels, include countries such as Saudi Arabia and Venezuela, are responsible for close to 44% of the world's oil production, and are home to 81.4% of the world's oil reserves (OPEC 2020). Broken down, OPEC[22] exists to control the supply of oil within the market so no one member nation is flooding the market and downwardly impacting prices. This is easier said than done. In essence, this amounts to setting oil production limits or a cap on how much oil revenue a member nation can generate. The process is similar to how the diamond industry artificially controls the supply and demand of diamonds to ensure prices stay competitive over an indefinite time horizon. The issue? Much like how the diamond industry faces competition from diamond substitutes like moissanite or lab grown diamonds, market share is further divided within OPEC with the presence of non-member OPEC countries and renewable energy alternatives. Therefore, in keeping with supply and demand principles, OPEC's decisions greatly influence the crude oil market, creating market inefficiencies that can be exploited by potential investors.

"Backwardation" occurs in the futures market when the current commodity or spot price is higher than the price in the futures market. This occurs mainly because current demand has propped up the current spot price, and with dwindling demand or excessive supply expected, futures prices are much lower. The inherent risk of the futures market then becomes apparent. Investing in the commodity futures markets requires nuanced knowledge of the sector to predict and take advantage of supply-demand inefficiencies and macroeconomic trends. This holds especially true for

---

[22]Having significant control over almost a majority of the current oil production, OPEC's mission is to "coordinate and unify the petroleum policies of its Member Countries and ensure the stabilization of oil markets in order to secure an efficient, economic and regular supply of petroleum to consumers, a steady income to producers and a fair return on capital for those investing in the petroleum industry" (OPEC 2020).

commodities such as crude oil where the OPEC dictates a large portion of production amounts.

One such way to take advantage of such supply-demand inefficiencies is to short sell the commodity at the current spot price and buy futures contracts at a lower price. This strategy does possess unlimited downside loss risk, but if the spread or difference in the spot and future prices is expected to increase, profits can be earned. Taking advantage of backwardation with fossil fuel commodities within a fossil fuel portfolio implies investors anticipate demand and prices of fossil fuels to fall due to a variety of factors, including the wide adoption of clean energy alternatives or an unexpected global pandemic. The latter of these factors saw oil futures reach negative price values for the first time on April 20, 2020, due to the impact of the COVID-19 crisis on oil demand (Gilbertie 2020).

Real Estate

The growing availability of various qualitative and quantitative metrics means investors still have many untapped opportunities in their fossil-fuel-free portfolio, especially when considering investments into real estate. Real estate investments, particularly in urban environments, have come under increasing scrutiny for their environmental sustainability with respect to their design, materials, and power consumption. Dense urban areas are hamstrung by their need to reduce waste and maximize energy savings, and new guidelines, green certification programs, and legal mandates are issued every year in cities around the globe. LEED (Leadership in Energy and Environment Design) is one of these designations.

For a building to be certified as LEED, it needs to meet a range of criteria across five categories: sustainable sites, water efficiency, energy and atmosphere, materials and resources, and indoor environmental quality. Though there are four different levels of LEED certification ranging from Certified to Silver to Gold to Platinum, LEED-certified buildings on average utilize between 25% to 30% less energy than their noncertified counterparts.

LEED is not the only sustainable real estate building certification that is popular. Originating in Germany in the 1990s, Passive House buildings on average reduce their energy consumption by 60% to 70%, a feat accomplished by lowering energy consumption while focusing on the comfort and health of its inhabitants. Furthermore, the World Green Building Trends 2016 (World Green Building Council 2016) report found demand for green buildings doubling each year, and building owners reported greater asset values numbers compared to non-green buildings, a median increase of 7%.

These new green building designations present attractive opportunities to institutional investors because they promote savings in operations costs, which then translates into higher ROI upon sales of the buildings.

A study by the World Green Building Council found that green buildings, on average, possess higher rental and lease rates, lower operating expenses, and higher occupancy rates (World Green Building Council 2013). Because consumers and investors are increasingly sustainability-oriented, the leasing and occupancy rates are higher for green buildings. Real estate investments, in particular, showcase how fossil fuel use cannot always be avoided altogether, but instead needs to be maximized through efficient design, quality construction, regular retrofits, and routine maintenance.

Public Debt

A well-diversified portfolio includes debt instruments. Public debt instruments, with relatively lower risk and correspondingly smaller returns, are a cornerstone in any portfolio seeking to preserve principal, earn a yield, and hedge risk. From a fossil-fuel-free perspective, fixed income investments are valuable to the extent that they steer projects away from fossil fuels and their associated risks. Take, for example, a corporate infrastructure project surrounding oil pipeline creation. Bonds for the project would predominantly fund construction costs, with a share of the future revenue from the project translating to dividends to bond holders. If recent history is any indication, such projects face harsh public scrutiny for their negative environmental impact, as well as the risk of abandonment. Such was the case in the now cancelled USD $1 billion Constitution Pipeline project in the United States, which sought to connect Pennsylvania's shale gas fields to New England. The project began with a proposed budget of less than USD $700 million, but costs quickly ballooned as the pipeline encountered increasing legal complications due to its proposed route across 251 bodies of water. With environmental agencies refusing to grant permits, the project was ultimately abandoned in early 2020 with an expected loss of USD $354 million to investors (Esch 2020). Fossil fuel infrastructure endeavors such as the failed Constitution Pipeline project highlight the innate risks investors often do not calculate when investing in the lower-risk asset class.

Green Bonds

Enter green bonds. Green bonds help dedicated fixed income portfolios to turn a new leaf. While municipal bonds typically serve the public good for citizens and society, and often include projects that benefit the environment, the green bond label helps investors identify and invest in issuances with an outsized environmental benefit. Green bonds can include a range of environmental projects, including those that directly transition public infrastructure away from fossil fuels, such as renewable energy generation projects, municipal fleet electrification, expanded public transportation systems, and energy efficiency retrofits, but also those that support sustainability more broadly, like recycling centers and green infrastructure. In the first half of 2019, however, 40% of total USD $170 billion green bond issuances worldwide went toward funding green energy projects.

Figure 12.6 details the explosive growth of green bonds from less than USD $5 billion in 2014 to over USD $175 billion in 2018. But why are green bonds exploding? An analysis by Moody's showed that green bonds defaulted at a lower rate compared to traditional bonds when comparing 10-year cumulative default rates. Furthermore, green bonds can be an attractive investment product to institutional investors, like pension funds, who are seeking impact linked to their mission and beneficiaries and stability in primarily fixed-income portfolios. Adoption of green bonds globally will not only support developed countries in meeting funding deficiencies for clean energy and other climate action projects but also allow resource-constrained countries to secure funding toward renewable energy and climate-smart infrastructure instead of fossil fuels.

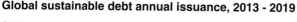

Global sustainable debt annual issuance, 2013 - 2019

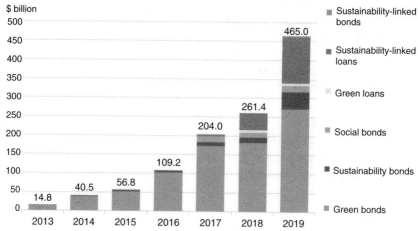

FIGURE 12.6 Growth of Sustainable Debt Annual Issuance, 2013 to 2019.
Source: Bloomberg NEF (2020).

Cryptocurrency

Fossil fuels can be completely avoided in new asset classes, such as cryptocurrency. The introduction of cryptocurrency has many in arms over the jurisprudence of digital currencies. Based solely on the sentiment of its holders, cryptocurrency is highly volatile, its production is energy intensive, and its regulation decentralized. With prices peaking at over USD $19,000 in December 2017 for a single coin, many investors are starting to warm up to cryptocurrency, but Bitcoin and its peers are not appropriate for fossil-fuel-free portfolios.

Cryptocurrencies are surprisingly energy intensive. Rows and rows of machines are needed to mine cryptocurrency efficiently on a 24-hour and 7-days-a-week basis. One of the largest costs of a crypto mining operation is energy; it takes vast amounts of energy required to run the machines, but also to cool them. With such active usage, computers and servers tend to overheat, and crypto-miners have to find ways to cool their machines and maintain an optimal temperature.

A recent study published by researchers from Hunan University looked into the global energy usage of mining the Monero cryptocurrency (Li et al. 2019). Delving into production outputs, energy usages, and equivalent greenhouse emissions, researchers were shocked to find that it took 645.62 GWh of electricity to mine a crypto-currency named Monero worldwide in 2018, and 30.34 GWh in mainland China. The average American household consumes close to 7,200 KWh of electricity every year, meaning the energy required to mine Monero is equivalent to powering close to 19,000 American households annually, and that's only one cryptocurrency.

A similar finding in 2020 was reported regarding Bitcoin transactions. Each Bitcoin transaction reportedly used as much energy as an average British household uses over two months. The annual figure for energy consumption for all cryptocurrency is stated to be around 77.78 terawatt hours, which is equivalent to the annual energy consumption of countries like Chile (Knapton 2020). The disproportionate energy consumption of cryptocurrency does not bode well given our current dependence on fossil fuels.

There are, however, a few clever workarounds. Iceland is now considered to be a "cryptocurrency capital," given its relatively cool temperatures and renewable energy grid fueled by abundant geothermal heat escaping from the Earth's crusts that merge the Americas and European tectonic plates, as well as prolific hydroelectric power from melting snow and frequent rainfall. By capitalizing on the colder climate and relatively low cost of renewable energy, crypto-miners are able to reduce their energy costs while still consuming large amounts of electricity (Hern 2018).

Even with miners moving to renewable energy grids, it is an arduous task to track where and which conditions individual coins were mined from. If a cryptocurrency became available that regulated its crypto-mining process with respect to the energy sources used, then it could be an asset class worth considering for a fossil-free goal. Until then, cryptocurrency is too energy hungry relative to today's energy sources to be considered for a fossil-fuel-free portfolio.

FINAL REMARKS

Is adopting a framework of divestment from all fossil fuel companies and projects the only answer to meeting IPCC's temperature goal? Many organizations, including 350.org, a nonprofit dedicated toward halving our fossil fuel use by 2030 to meet IPCC's 1.5°C goal, are proposing and taking active steps toward 100% divestment from all proposed fossil fuel projects (350.org 2020). A full divestment of all future fossil fuel projects means the broader adoption of only renewable energy projects, a worthwhile goal if we are to mitigate the irreversible damage of climate change and a definite consideration for impact investors. Such organizations and investors consider the inclusion of fossil-fuel-based companies in a fossil fuel portfolio heresy.

Yet 100% divestment is not always a suitable goal for all investors. Ophir Bruck,[23] US network manager from PRI on the topic, highlighted that from his viewpoint as an impact investor, it would not make sense to include oil and gas companies in his portfolio, but for investors who care more about their investment's risk-return profile, the mentality could be different. Building a portfolio solely based on reducing total fossil fuel exposure abandons companies and investments that are taking measured steps in reducing and maximizing their current fossil fuel use. Furthermore, existing energy companies are necessary actors in the larger ecosystem that will transition our world to clean energy.

The type of fossil-fuel-free framework investors choose to adopt has more to do with the risk tolerance and their definition of impact. Investment guidelines and fossil fuel considerations need to begin with the investment-policy statement, with board buy-in to ensure consistency and longevity of the strategy, especially when taking into account energy sector investments. The energy sector is particularly vulnerable if a majority of assets are suddenly divested. These vulnerable factors include the industry-trained workforce,

---

[23] Interview data (see Appendix).

which will need to transition to clean energy or other industries, and the assets key to the drilling, exploring, and storage of fossil fuels.

Stranded assets can be thought of as the leftover pieces of what will happen if we fully change into a global clean energy market. What happens to the oil companies' rights on oil reserves that are still undrilled? If we are to even meet the IPCC's goal of 2°C, then 80% of our current oil reserves need to remain in the ground and undrilled until 2050 (McGlade and Ekins 2015). Rather than simple divestment from fossil fuel companies, a broader framework that incentivizes companies to be more energy productive while lowering their fossil fuel use needs to be considered. But there are pitfalls.

Investments into companies that simply increase their clean energy investments as a way to reduce their overall increasing fossil fuel production will need to be weeded out, as well as those who offload their fossil fuel production to subsidiaries or offshoots to appear more fossil-fuel-friendly on their balance sheets. The methodology discussed so far deals with emission reductions in line with the IPCC's target of 1.5°C but does not consider those emissions within a timeline. A broader mandate in an investment policy statement can include companies that have emission targets in line with meeting the global goal of halving emissions by 2030, but in reality, few are reporting such metrics.

Building a fossil-fuel-free portfolio relies on the use of scope-based emissions and ESG data, which are often not reported, and even if reported, are usually not comprehensive. According to the Science Based Targets Initiative, as of May 2020, nearly 900 companies have pledged to take science-based climate action, and 374 companies have pledged to concrete science-based targets to reduce their emissions, including some pledging to cut by 100% in 2030, like Unilever, Novo Nordisk, and Stanley Black and Decker. The number of companies subscribing is growing monthly, and active investors can further motivate those who have not.

Shareholder engagement is the biggest weapon investors have in the fight for full disclosure, and Green Century Funds understands that disclosure and advocacy are needed in order to bring about greater systemic change. As a leader in environmental and socially responsible investing, Green Century Funds provides institutional investors with socially responsible mutual fund investments. Erin Gray[24] of Green Century Investments stated, "Shareholder engagement is a tool that is most effective [at] working to make incremental change on a specific issue."

---

[24]Interview data (see Appendix).

Institutional investors that wield large swathes of capital and influence by their allocations need to lead the charge in increasing disclosure practices so investors have more available information to make better-informed investment decisions toward emission-reducing portfolios. More and more investors are leading the charge in pushing for more environmental and social best practices, forcing companies to disclose material information related to their carbon footprints and greater ESG impact.

Another possible solution is increased regulation, especially in public markets. Companies worldwide are required by law to submit audited financials, and those legal requirements can be amended to include emissions and other nonfinancial metrics. One way to tackle this lack of data would be for investors to work closely with regulatory bodies—including securities and exchange commissions, and stock exchange overseers—to create mandated reporting guidelines on ESG practices. Such guidelines would not only create more transparency, but they would allow investors to directly view the impact of their investments, especially when it comes to individual dollar contribution toward fossil fuels.

Finally, fossil-fuel-free portfolios require increased due diligence to assess an investment's carbon emissions. Those increased efforts should not prevent investors from adopting the paradigm. Reducing current fossil fuel use and maximizing efficiency is necessary for the world to recover from generations of wanton fossil fuel reliance. Investors are in a unique position to use their capital to directly influence companies and persuade them to adopt practices in line with the IPCC's report. Emissions need to be lowered to prevent irreversible damage to the environment and health of those around us.

These actions do not mean that returns need to be sacrificed. By adopting a long-term view and investing in companies that are actively reducing emissions, investors can be first-movers in a global trend. As first adopters, investors are poised to reap the benefits when the global energy supply switches to renewable sources. First movers like Dean Takahashi of Yale, who transitioned the university's endowment into a major allocation to private equity funds, reaped the rewards of being one of the first to make that bet.

Getting policymakers, investors, and global leaders to the table may be difficult, and as executive director of a Detroit-based family foundation, and my mentor, Doug Stewart, would say, "Let's hope these conversations lead us to a more mature form of capitalism that rewards creating value in an investment via financial performance and measurable social or environmental impact" (Stewart 2019). With a long investment horizon and unavoidable consequences of the climate crisis, investors who do not adopt a fossil-fuel-free paradigm will need to take action, join the discussion, or risk being left behind.

ACKNOWLEDGMENTS

My sincere thanks to Paul R. Herman, Elsa de Morais Sarmento, and Lucia Pohlman for reviewing, editing, and filtering through all the eclectic topics I wanted to include. I am immensely grateful to my mentor, Doug Stewart, for introducing and feeding my passion for impact investing. My deepest gratitude to my father, Balakumar Damodaran, for tolerating my presence the last 27 years and believing in me.

Finally, to my loving, caring, and supportive fiancée, Prapitha, my sincerest appreciation. Your patience and pep talks during the writing process provided much inspiration, especially during moments of mind-numbing quarantine. It was a great boon to have someone to bounce ideas off of and push me outside my comfort zone. My most heartfelt thanks.

I also thank John Ferris and his Jeep, whose emissions have led me to begin my own emission-offset garden during the COVID-19 quarantine of spring 2020.

REFERENCES

ABC News (2018). Southern states swelter as power supply struggles. ABC News (19 January). https://www.abc.net.au/news/2018-01-19/parts-of-australia-to-pass-40c-as-another-hot-weekend-looms/9342274 (accessed 1 March 2020).

Bitcoin (2020). How does Bitcoin work? Bitcoin (1 January). https://bitcoin.org/en/how-it-works (accessed 3 March 2020).

Bloomberg NEF (2020). Sustainable Debt Sees Record Issuance At $465Bn in 2019, Up 78% from 2018. BloombergNEF (8 January). https://about.bnef.com/blog/sustainable-debt-sees-record-issuance-at-465bn-in-2019-up-78-from-2018/ (accessed 7 February 2020).

Boqiang, L. (2018). How renewable energy subsidies are taking the wind out of China's sails. World Economic Forum (22 May). https://www.weforum.org/agenda/2018/05/china-is-a-renewable-energy-champion-but-its-time-for-a-new-approach/ (accessed 29 Feb. 2020).

Cassidy, E. (2019). Which Countries Use the Most Fossil Fuels? Resource Watch Blog (2 May). https://blog.resourcewatch.org/2019/05/02/which-countries-use-the-most-fossil-fuels/ (accessed 27 February 2020).

Clements, A. (2012). Weather Derivatives: Hedging on Mother Nature. Open-Markets (19 April). https://openmarkets.cmegroup.com/2927/hedging-a-bet-on-mother-nature (accessed 3 March 2020).

Dong, W., and Ye, Q. (2018). Utility of renewable energy in China's low-carbon transition. Brookings Institution (18 May). https://www.brookings.edu/2018/05/18/utility-of-renewable-energy-in-chinas-low-carbon-transition/ (accessed 27 February 2020).

Dudley, D. (2019). China Is Set to Become the World's Renewable Energy Superpower. *Forbes* (11 January). https://www.forbes.com/sites/dominicdudley/2019/01/11/china-renewable-energy-superpower/#7d614391745a (accessed 29 February 2020).

Duggan, J. (2015). China makes carbon pledge ahead of Paris climate change summit. *Guardian* (30 June). https://www.theguardian.com/environment/2015/jun/30/china-carbon-emissions-2030-premier-li-keqiang-un-paris-climate-change-summit (accessed 27 February 2020).

Egan, M. (2019). Energy Stocks Are the Biggest Losers of 2019 – And the Decade. CNN (19 December). https://www.cnn.com/2019/12/18/investing/worst-stocks-oil-energy/index.html (accessed 19 May 2020).

Equinor (2019). 2018 Sustainability Report. https://www.equinor.com/en/how-and-why/sustainability/sustainability-reports.html.

Equinor (2020). Our New Climate Roadmap. https://www.equinor.com/en/how-and-why/climate.html (accessed 21 February 2020).

Esch, M. (2020). Costs, delays scuttle $1B U.S. pipeline venture. Global News (24 February). https://globalnews.ca/news/6590708/constitution-pipeline-natural-gas-usa-abandoned/ (accessed 2 March 2020).

Eurostat (2019). Electricity production, consumption and market overview. Electricity production, consumption and market overview. Statistics Explained. https://ec.europa.eu/eurostat/statistics-explained/index.php/Electricity_production,_consumption_and_market_overview (accessed February 20, 2020).

Feliz, N. (2019). Alternatives in 2019: Private Capital Dry Powder Reaches $2Tn. Preqin (29 January). https://www.preqin.com/insights/blogs/alternatives-in-2019-private-capital-dry-powder-reaches-2tn/25289 (accessed 9 January 2020).

Formula E. (2020). Formula E Recognitions. Reports and recognitions | FIA Formula E. https://www.fiaformulae.com/en/discover/sustainability/reports-recognitions (accessed March 26, 2020).

Gilbertie, S. (2020). Will Oil Prices Go Negative Again? *Forbes* (23 April). https://www.forbes.com/sites/salgilbertie/2020/04/23/will-oil-prices-go-negative-again/#5b516fab7e9c (accessed 23 April 2020).

Guarascio, F. (2019). EU Rules on Responsible Investments to Kick in from 2021: Document. Reuters (19 November). https://www.reuters.com/article/us-eu-regulations-sustainablefinance/eu-rules-on-responsible-investments-to-kick-in-from-2021-document-idUSKBN1XE1U3 (accessed 8 January 2020).

Hern, A. (2018). How Iceland Became the Bitcoin Miners' Paradise. *Guardian* (13 February). https://www.theguardian.com/world/2018/feb/13/how-iceland-became-the-bitcoin-miners-paradise (accessed 3 March 2020).

Heron Foundation (2019). Introduction to Net Contribution. https://www.heron.org/intro-net-contribution (accessed February 20, 2020).

IPCC (2018). Global Warming of 1.5 °C. Intergovernmental Panel on Climate Change. https://www.ipcc.ch/sr15/ (accessed 24 March 2020).

Jambeck, J., Geyer, R., Wilcox, C., et al (2015). Plastic Waste Inputs from Land into the Ocean. *Science* 347(6223): 768–771.

Knapton, S. (2020). Bitcoin using more electricity per transaction than a British household in two months. *Telegraph* (1 March). https://www.telegraph.co.uk/science/2020/03/01/bitcoin-using-electricity-per-transaction-british-household/ (accessed 3 March 2020).

Li, J., Li, N., Peng, J., et al. (2019). Energy Consumption of Cryptocurrency Mining: A Study of Electricity Consumption in Mining Cryptocurrencies. *Energy* 168: 160–168.

Lopez, O. and Jacobs, A. (2018). In town with little water, Coca-Cola is everywhere, so is diabetes. *New York Times* (14 July). https://www.nytimes.com/2018/07/14/world/americas/mexico-coca-cola-diabetes.html (accessed 1 March 2020).

McGlade, C. and Ekins, P. (2015). The Geographical Distribution of Fossil Fuels Unused When Limiting Global Warming to 2°C. *Nature* 517(7533): 187–190.

MSCI (2020). MSCI ACWI Ex Fossil Fuels Index (GBP). MSCI. https://www.msci.com/documents/10199/d6f6d375-cadc-472f-9066-131321681404 (accessed 20 April 2020).

Myllyvirta, L. (2019). Guest post: Why China's CO2 emissions grew 4% during first half of 2019. Carbon Brief (5 September). https://www.carbonbrief.org/guest-post-why-chinas-co2-emissions-grew-4-during-first-half-of-2019 (accessed 1 March 2020).

Nephila (2019). Using Risk Transfer to Achieve Climate Change Resilience. https://mklstatic01.azureedge.net/~/media/nephila/climate/risk-transfer-for-climate-resilience.pdf?rev=73370dcb8b94446fae44196d1d1c0398 (accessed 18 April 2020).

OPEC (2020). OPEC: Our Mission. https://www.opec.org/opec_web/en/about_us/23.htm (accessed 8 April 2020).

Pearce, R. (2020). Interactive: The Impacts of Climate Change at 1.5C, 2C and Beyond. Carbon Brief. https://interactive.carbonbrief.org/impacts-climate-change-one-point-five-degrees-two-degrees/?utm_source=web&utm_campaign=Redirect (accessed 23 March 2020).

Rogelj, J., D. Shindell, K. Jiang, S., et al. (2018). Mitigation Pathways Compatible with 1.5°C in the Context of Sustainable Development. In: *Global Warming of 1.5°C. An IPCC Special Report on the impacts of global warming of 1.5°C above pre-industrial levels and related global greenhouse gas emission pathways, in the context of strengthening the global response to the threat of climate change, sustainable development, and efforts to eradicate poverty* (V. Masson-Delmotte, P. Zhai, H. O. Pörtner, D. Roberts, J. Skea, P.R. Shukla, A. Pirani, W. Moufouma-Okia, C. Péan, R. Pidcock, S. Connors, J. B. R. Matthews, Y. Chen, X. Zhou, M. I. Gomis, E. Lonnoy, T. Maycock, M. Tignor, T. Waterfield, eds.).

Science Based Targets (2019a). Science Based Targets Case Study: Coca-Cola HBC. https://sciencebasedtargets.org/wp-content/uploads/2016/05/Science-Based-Targets-Case-study-Coca-Cola-HBC.pdf (accessed 1 March 2020).

Science Based Targets (2019b). Science-Based Target Setting Manual. https://sciencebasedtargets.org/wp-content/uploads/2017/04/SBTi-manual.pdf (accessed 1 March 2020).

Stewart, D. (2019). Rebutting the Case Against Impact Investing. Mission Investors Exchange (12 March). https://missioninvestors.org/resources/rebutting-case-against-impact-investing (accessed 20 April 2020).

Taplin, N. (2019). China's Banks Are Choking on Coal Dust. *Wall Street Journal* (9 April). https://www.wsj.com/articles/chinas-banks-are-choking-on-coal-dust-11554833294 (accessed 27 February 2020).

Williamson, C. (2020). Hedge Fund Industry AUM Slips Below $3 Trillion. Pensions & Investments (22 April). https://www.pionline.com/hedge-funds/hedge-fund-industry-aum-slips-below-3-trillion (accessed 30 April 2020).

World Green Building Council (2013). The Business Case for Green Building. https://www.worldgbc.org/news-media/business-case-green-building-review-costs-and-benefits-developers-investors-and-occupants.

World Green Building Council (2016). World Green Building Trends 2016. https://www.worldgbc.org/news-media/world-green-building-trends-2016.

World Resources Institute and WBSCD (2014). Corporate Value Chain (Scope 3) Accounting and Reporting Standard Supplement to the GHG Protocol Corporate Accounting and Reporting Standard. GreenHouse Gas Protocol. https://www.ghgprotocol.org/sites/default/files/ghgp/standards/Corporate-Value-Chain-Accounting-Reporing-Standard_041613_2.pdf (accessed 27 February 2020).

APPENDIX 12.1: EXPERTS INTERVIEWED

Interviewees	Entity	Position
Dan Adler	Energy Foundation	Vice President, Policy
Ophir Bruck	Principles for Responsible Investment (PRI)	US Network Manager
Erin Gray	Green Century Funds	Institutional and Client Relations Manager
Garvin Jabusch	Green Alpha Advisors	Chief Executive Officer
Andrew Montes	As You Sow	Director of Digital Strategy

APPENDIX 12.2: FOSSIL-FUEL-FREE TOPICS AND INFORMATION

Fossil-Fuel-Free Topics	Source of Information
Science Based Targets (Scope-based emissions)	Company annual filings Corporate Sustainability reports https://sciencebasedtargets.org/
Greenhouse Gas Protocol Standards	https://ghgprotocol.org/standards
Fossil-Free Funds	https://fossilfreefunds.org/
Carbon Disclosure Project (CDP)	https://www.cdp.net/en/scores
UN Sustainable Development Goals	https://sustainabledevelopment.un.org/sdgs
401(k)s and Fossil-Fuel-Free Portfolios	https://HIPinvestor.com/401k/
Clean Portfolios in 401(k)s and IRAs	https://www.cleanportfolios.com/

CHAPTER 13

The Role of Transition Finance Instruments in Bridging the Climate Finance Gap

Pauline Deschryver, MSci, MPA and Frederic de Mariz, PhD

Abstract

With the growth of green bonds and other viable impact-oriented investment vehicles, impact investing outcomes are on the rise. The monumental challenge of financing the energy transition and the United Nations Sustainable Development Goals (SDG), together with the limits of the existing finance instruments, have primed the markets for and sparked innovation in new financial policies, products, and services. This chapter is the first study dedicated to "transition finance instruments," defined as investment vehicles specifically aimed at "greening" (improving, cleaning) the "brown" (dirty, polluting) industries and transforming the practices of the least sustainable sectors and companies, bridging the gap of reliable information on the potential and credibility of the transition instruments, and offering the most comprehensive analysis of barriers and possible solutions to date. It focuses on the role of transition finance in the low-carbon climate resilient pathway by analyzing the determinants of growth of the green bond market, assessing the green bond market's rigidity, and identifying constraints on its scalability. The observation of the green bond market illuminates the rich landscape of new innovative instruments being developed to the evolving demands of investors, the profiles of investees, and the readiness of market participants to the challenges of climate change. This chapter then explores pathways for transition bonds to attract more funding while also credibly and consistently attaining sustainable outcomes. The findings confirm that issuers and investors are eager to develop flexible instruments that extend beyond pure green to include transitions from brown, but only if credible and commonly shared guidelines and frameworks are established.

Keywords

Green Finance; Transition Finance; Green Bonds; Sustainable Development Goals; SDGs; Climate Change; Sustainable Investing; ESG; Environmental; Social; and Governance; Impact Measurement; Socially Responsible Banking

INTRODUCTION

Transitioning to low-carbon, climate-resilient (LCCR) and sustainable development pathways requires a holistic approach to finance and investment. The relatively new term of "transition" for financial market participants is increasingly critical for responsible investing. New transition finance instruments have the potential to massively increase capital allocations in and diversification of assets in the LCCR-aligned investment universe (Robinson-Tillett 2019).

This approach entails shifting public and private finance from "brown" (dirty, polluting) to "green" (cleaner) investments and integrating environmental considerations into all relevant investments and government activities. Brown investments refer to polluting industries and companies, and green investments refer to businesses, projects, and sectors that generate beneficial environmental outcomes. While green finance focuses on environmental issues, it belongs to the broader field of so-called "sustainable" finance, which also encompasses socioeconomic and governance issues (Aglietta and Rigot 2012). Green finance offers a way to implement the transition from brown to green at scale, through a wide spectrum of financial initiatives, processes, products, and services—all designed to protect the natural environment and mitigate climate-related impact on markets, investments, and the economy (Aglietta et al. 2015).

This transition-oriented approach benefits from the momentum of green finance. Both movements, however, face similar challenges in expanding. There is slow global consensus on what defines climate finance, and even less on transition finance for now—and there is a lack of credible and commonly accepted guidelines for transition bonds. Green finance embraces a large diversity of policies and instruments dedicated to advance the global climate and sustainable development agenda. It also includes the recognition of, and advocacy for, the policies and infrastructure necessary for development as a green-finance sector. But focusing exclusively on green assets is likely to miss the largest thrust of the transition, requiring even those firms with larger gaps to finance the path to climate solutions (Study Group on Environmental Innovation Finance in Japan 2020). The bulk of the economy lies in non-green assets, for which green finance is not suitable. Yet the whole system must be part of the transition equation.

Players in the green finance industry have been actively developing new instruments and channels to fund green initiatives—including green and sustainable bonds, carbon market instruments, "green" monetary policies, new blended combinations of financial technologies, green investment funds, community green funds, and more. Green bonds in particular gained international salience as critical climate and sustainability finance instruments. Green bonds offer several attractive characteristics to both investors and issuers. Assets invested in green bonds increased from USD $1.5 billion in 2007 to USD $389 billion in 2018 (CBI 2018a). Despite this rapid growth, green bonds represent less than 2% of the global bond market today (Refinitiv 2019). In the meantime, fossil fuels and other "brown" activities still benefit from ample funding in fixed-income and equity markets, especially from financial institutions and asset managers.

Accordingly, this chapter's central research question assesses the extent to which transition instruments propose a distinctive and valuable investment strategy compared to green finance for potential issuers, in terms of levels of origination, performance metrics, and reporting. We emphasize that green and transition bonds, along with new innovative green instruments and policies, can play distinctive roles in the ecosystem of green and sustainable finance. While the legitimacy and the contribution of green bonds in financing the United Nations (UN) Sustainable Development

Goals (SDGs) has been proven (Tolliver et al. 2020), that of transition bonds as a credible investment vehicle for sustainable outcomes remains to be clarified.

While green bonds are one of the first tools developed for financing the LCCR pathway, the market is continuing to evolve with the emergence and development of new sustainable instruments. These expansions and innovations are critical, given the size of the challenge: by 2050, an investment of USD $27 trillion will be needed to finance a global energy transition (IRENA 2019). In developing countries alone, the financing gap to achieve the SDGs is estimated at USD $2.5 trillion per year, mainly for basic infrastructure (roads, rail, ports, power stations, water, and sanitation); food security (agriculture and rural development); climate change mitigation and adaptation; health; and education (UNCTAD 2014).

Another way to approach the green agenda is to finance the transformation of brown activities to align with LCCR demands. In this regard, regulators have advanced ideas such as "weighting factors," a mechanism that allocates capital with a tilting preference away from carbon intensive assets and toward LCCR-aligned companies and assets. Other stakeholders have developed alternative instruments, such as transition bonds and sustainability-linked instruments, which have broadened the investable universe and present interesting benefits to investors in terms of financial return. According to research by Standard & Poor's, there is a positive correlation between environmental, social, and governance (ESG) performance and companies' financial performance (Burks and London 2019). At the same time, this development expands the range of instruments that issuers and intermediaries, such as banks, can originate and market to clients.

Increasing volumes of capital are critical to advance the global climate and sustainable development investment agenda. This capital can be mobilized through a large spectrum of financial instruments, tailored to various investment strategies and profiles, and flowing into climate, sustainability, and cleaner production investments. Green and transition financing can contribute to infrastructure projects for positive environmental and social outcomes. Embedding sustainability considerations into infrastructure development is instrumental to address adaptation and mitigation issues and enhance resource efficiency (Déséglise and Lopez Freijido 2020). Understanding the fundamental factors that promote their growth is of prime importance. In this analysis, a major question is the evaluation of the real and perceived greenwashing risks linked to transition finance. Which risks need to be mitigated? Which opportunities optimize impact and risk-adjusted returns? What pathways need to emerge for faster scaling to climate solutions?

The methodological approach combines an analysis of market prices for green and transition bonds, along with a thorough revision of the latest literature, combined with interviews with investors, issuers, and intermediaries, such as banks and consulting firms. As of 2020, the existing literature was limited on financing the sustainability transition (Fabian 2015; Campiglio 2016; Louche et al. 2016; Polzin 2017). This chapter bridges the gap of reliable information on the potential and credibility of the transition instruments, offering the most comprehensive analysis of those barriers and possible solutions to date.

While this chapter focuses mainly on transition bonds, it also tackles other alternative transition finance mechanisms. It answers several questions: What are the major barriers that each category of market participant faces with a transition bond issuance? Is there a standardized process to issue a transition bond? To what extent would a transition bond issuance differ from a green bond issuance? Which risks are associated with a transition bond issuance for each category of stakeholders? Are transition bonds a trustworthy instrument, financially and technically, to fund sustainable companies and assets? How can policy-makers attract asset managers and investors to transition investments?

This chapter answers these questions by examining the roles transition instruments can play for issuers and investors in their broader portfolios and investment strategies, and by identifying and explaining the various financial instruments that can capitalize the transition of brown assets toward a low-carbon economy. The chapter then delineates key recommendations for investors and the industry at large to overcome credibility and growth barriers, which if enacted would enable the recycling of private investment from fossil fuels into LCCR segments of the economy.

AN OVERVIEW OF GREEN FINANCE

Objectives and Limits of Green Finance

Green finance is blossoming at the crossroads of financial, socioeconomic, and environmental issues, and transition finance is raising hard-to-answer questions. Green finance is characterized by a desire to sustainably manage and improve the relationship between humans and the natural world, and to responsibly mitigate the risks of climate change and other systemic environmental threats that the financial sector and the economy are facing. Green finance is primarily concerned with environmental aspects such as pollution, greenhouse gas emissions, biodiversity, and water and air quality, but the sector also includes aspects related to climate change, including energy efficiency, renewable energies, and prevention and mitigation of the impacts of climate change.

As such, green finance serves a clear and distinct objective: to allocate capital for sustainable purposes and for the benefit of the low-carbon transition. In practice, according to the Organization for Economic Co-operation and Development (OECD), its purpose is to "achieve economic growth while reducing pollution and greenhouse gas emissions, minimizing waste and improving efficiency in the use of natural resources" (OECD 2020).

However, if green finance is fully realized as a sector and reaches mass-market adoption along with widespread fossil-fuel divestment, it raises troubling questions: by choosing to only finance "green" companies and industries, what are the socioeconomic risks and other immediate impacts on highly emitting "brown" sectors, such as job losses? Additionally, are green technologies and the companies stewarding green innovations developed enough to utilize such an influx of cash? Or would it be impractical and overblown to direct such capital to the relatively small and nascent industry? Yet, by choosing a sequenced approach (i.e. investing in cleaner, but still fossil-fuel-based, sources of energy like natural gas), it is possible that the energy sector will become further invested in hard-to-abate activities. This could result in a long-term "lock-in" effect and thus prevent the world from adhering to scientific guidance from the International Panel on Climate Change (IPCC) and international treaties like the Paris Climate Agreement.

Transition finance would fall under the definition of green finance, which the Green Finance Study Group of the G20 defines as finance that provides any environmental benefit (G20 2016). Transition finance would also stand in opposition to brown finance, which is defined as domestic and international finance flows that support carbon-intensive projects and pathways that do not sufficiently consider future climate risks. Specifically, transition finance supports the effective management of physical and transition risks linked to climate action and economic transformation for a low-carbon and climate-resilient future.

Transition finance attempts to balance the two risks explored above. Financing the transition from "brown" to "green" means moving away from fossil fuels—and other industries that do not consider the negative externalities of economic production and consumption on the environment—toward a far cleaner energy system that uses energy and other carbon-intensive resources more efficiently. This translates to better natural resource management, especially on agricultural lands and in forests (Deichmann and Zhang 2020).

Green finance offers the financial sector the tools to effectively redirect capital toward an LCCR future while reducing the asymmetry of information regarding the risks linked to climate change. Public and private actors, spanning institutional investors, banks, regulators, central banks, insurers, rating agencies, governments, and multilateral organizations, are mobilizing in order to better understand the risks posed by climate change and to seize the opportunities of this expanding area. The structuring and distribution of "green" products is an important vector of growth for all players.

One way to classify green tools and products is by their environmental impact as perceived by investors. Investors can decide between: (i) encouraging and accelerating sectors that are already green; (ii) supporting activities and assets that will not be able to green quickly, largely because of economic and technological barriers faced by firms, or (iii) sanctioning "brown" companies and industries by divesting.

For the first option, the main recipient sectors are the production, distribution, and storage of renewable energies; energy efficiency in domestic and industrial buildings; green transport, recycling, pollution prevention, conservation of energy, and reforestation. Within these activities, a whole range of green options exists, from light to dark green, with dark green being the most orthodox. Green bonds are one of the most common instruments used to finance decidedly green eligible sectors and assets.

For the second option, the targeted activities are segments of the fossil fuel and mining industries, in particular minerals essential to the low-carbon economy, such as lithium and cobalt, and heavy industries such as cement, aluminum, and iron. For many considering investing in these industries, a debate remains: is it really green finance or, rather, transition finance? This is the part of the spectrum going from "light green" to "light brown," which today divides investors as well as the regulatory and supervisory authorities. As the objective of transition finance is to support the effective management of physical and transition risks, however, most of the industries above squarely fit as transition investment opportunities.

Green Bonds, Increasingly the Primary Instrument of Green Finance

Green bonds are bonds that are specially designed to finance climate and environmental projects. They present attractive characteristics to both issuers and investors. They ensure access to the increasingly important financial flows, particularly among institutional investors—dedicated to finance the energy transition and climate change adaptation. Issuers see in green bonds an interesting way to take a position for marketing as well as strategic reasons. For investors, green bonds give access to a more diversified range of assets, including sovereign bonds, allowing them to balance their portfolio. These bonds are generally linked to assets and backed by the issuer's balance sheet. Green bond issuers are usually public entities (e.g. communities, state, international agency) but can also be private companies. The process of issuing a green bond usually begins with adopting the framework established by the Green Bond Principles. These principles and guidelines, developed by the International Capital Market Association (ICMA), promote transparency in the green bond market and call for standardized disclosures of project details. In accordance with these principles, a green bond annual report must include the list and description of the allocated projects (use of proceeds) and their expected impact (ICMA 2018).

In 2007, the first green bond came from the European Investment Bank (EIB), which allocated bond proceeds to eco-friendly projects with a EUR €600 million Climate Awareness Bond focused on renewable energy and energy efficiency. Since this original issuance, the green bond market steadily increased from USD $1.5 billion in 2007 to USD $389 billion outstanding in 2018 (CBI 2018a). The first corporate green bond was issued in 2013 by the largest Swedish real estate company, Vasakronan, in association with the Scandinavian Individual Bank (SEB) for a Swedish krona SEK 2.35 billion bond (approx. EUR €250 million).

The appetite for green bonds continues to grow, with total issuance reaching USD $167.3 billion in 2018—marking a 3% year-on-year increase (CBI 2018a). In 2019, green bond issuance surpassed USD $100 billion in the first half of the year for the first time. Dealogic and Bloomberg registered USD $228.2 billion for 2019 (Figure 13.1). Europe is the most important market, with 48% of issuances in 2019. Asia is the most dynamic market, with a compound average growth rate over 2015–2019 of 74% in emerging countries of the region (versus 63% in its developed market, and 43% in Europe). North America comes second in volume of issuances (19%), and USD-labeled issuances over the period represent 29%, against 49% in EUR. The green bond market continues to expand with an increasing number of issuances, larger bond sizes, a broader group of issuers, and a growing investor base.

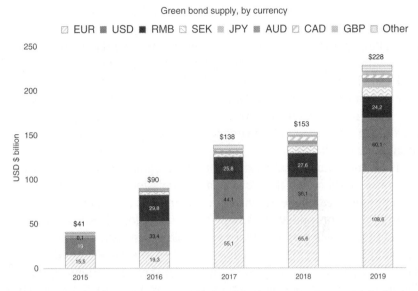

FIGURE 13.1   Overview of the Green Bond Supply Since 2015. *Source*: Dealogic, Bloomberg (as of 20 January 2020).

Green Bond Certification: Growing Diversity Toward Transparency and Integrity

Several nonbinding frameworks define green bonds. The most established framework comes from the ICMA. The ICMA developed the Green Bonds Principles (GBP), which are voluntary guidelines. The grand majority of green bond issuances are GBP compliant. If green bonds are not GBP labeled but meet or almost meet the criteria, they are usually referred to as "climate-aligned bonds." The climate-aligned bond market is estimated to have twice the amount of issuances as the labeled green bond market (CBI 2018b; Migliorelli and Dessertine 2019).

The Climate Bond Initiative (CBI) is another certification standard that focuses on green bonds that fund climate solutions and related projects. The criteria to be included in the CBI database are to be labeled as green bonds by issuers, have at least 95% of the proceeds aligned with the Climate Bonds Taxonomy, and offer sufficient information about the projects financed (CBI 2017).

In addition to GBP and CBI certifications, many countries and regional jurisdictions have developed their own national green instrument guidelines.

Several regional organizations (e.g. EU, ASEAN countries) and countries (e.g. UK, China, Mexico, and Morocco) have adopted green bond frameworks. Regional and international working groups have also been established (for example, the Green Finance Expert Group, the Network for Greening the Financial System led by the Central Bank). The Climate Finance Disclosure Working Group (TCFD), the UN, the World Bank (WB) Roadmap for a Sustainable Financial System, and the High-Level Panel of Experts on Sustainable Finance are all programs that help standardize and consolidate the green bond market.

To address the critical lack of globally recognized definition of what is considered sustainable, the European Commission (EC) has put in place an ambitious Sustainable Finance Agenda and has mandated the European Union (EU) Technical Expert Group (TEG) to develop guidelines, standards, and methodologies pertaining to sustainable investment classification and corporate disclosure. The TEG has published the Green Bond Standard (TEG, 2019), which defines green bonds under three conditions: (i) the strict alignment of the issuer's green bond framework with the European Green Bond standards; (ii) the allocation of bond proceeds to green projects; and (iii) the verification of the alignment to the EU-Green Bond standard by an accredited External Verifier.

Despite Strong Growth, Green Bonds Face Several Barriers

Several limits constrain the expansion of the green bond market. The market is challenged by a consistent shortage of sufficiently large bonds, the complex process of bringing green bonds to market and reporting on them, and the reputational risks faced by issuers and investors if accused of greenwashing (Deschryver and De Mariz 2020).

Green Bond Issuances Are Not Large Enough for Most Investors

Government and corporate green bonds are rarely big enough in size for traditional investors. To be bankable and to ensure liquidity and inclusion in bond indexes, the primary vehicle for fixed income purchases, a green bond can hardly be less than USD $300 to $500 million. Governments at the national, regional, and local levels do not have sufficiently large and environmentally friendly project portfolios to reach that threshold (Cochu et al. 2016). Similarly, corporate bond issuers do not have eligible capital expenditures portfolios of this size on their balance sheets.

The shortage of financeable projects is also due to a narrow sectoral scope. As mentioned by an investor in Euromoney (Bowman 2019), "The early growth was from renewable energy assets but that is done now.... Many companies have a limited amount of renewable and energy efficient assets on their balance sheets." The president of the European Central Bank (ECB), Christine Lagarde, highlighted this problem when discussing the possibility of orienting the ECB's bond purchase policy toward corporate green and nonpolluting bonds. Lagarde pointed out the current deficit of green assets, along with the nascent development of a green taxonomy (Lagarde 2019). Consequently, investors of all types are now looking for green bonds in sectors other than utilities, such as green transportation and green buildings. Such an expansion of scope might increase the amount of USD $300 million dollar or greater in size green bond issuances that meet investor needs. Among investors, pension funds in particular experience a lack of variety and liquidity of green bond issuers, and the shortage of scalable investment vehicles (Reichelt and Keenan 2017). This is unfortunate because pension funds are the largest asset owners of all investors, and their support is critical for the green bond market to become institutionalized. The absence of a large potential of eligible projects for corporate green bonds hampers further growth.

Lack of Standardization in the Green Bond Market Threatens Integrity of Label

The absence of a mutually agreed upon definition as well as a standard framework for certifying, issuing, and reporting on green bonds presents major obstacles to the development of the green bond market.

The variation and sheer number of green bond frameworks has yet to stabilize and standardize. Various organizations have defined different guidelines and best practices for green bonds, as described earlier. Additionally, several green bond issuers have developed and published their own green bond frameworks. Development banks, for example, the Asian Development Bank (ADB) and the International Finance Corporation (IFC) as well as other actors such as the Nordic Investment Bank have done so.

This variety works against and stands in opposition to the adoption of a consistent certification system that is equivalent to standardized credit ratings for the "vanilla" bond market. This lack of a common standard results in "no unique definition among investors of what green investing entails"

(Della Croce et al. 2011, p. 11) and has become a major barrier. Furthermore, the fungibility of green bonds exposes them to the whole company's business risks. Thus, a green label is not a hedge against environmentally related financial risks, especially when these instruments are more likely in sectors exposed to such risks (Ehlers and Packer 2017).

Reputational Risks Scare off Issuers and Investors Alike

This lack of standardization also presents potential reputational risks and drawbacks. The risk of greenwashing can be strong enough to prevent issuers from issuing a green bond. The term "greenwash," coined by environmentalist Jay Westerveld in 1986 (Becker-Olsen and Potucek 2013), is an unsupported or misleading statement about the environmental benefits of a product, service, technology, or business practice. It also extends to a growing trend where companies spend more time and money on the branding and marketing of green products than on implementing sustainable business practices themselves.

Another risk in the green bond market is the lack of traceability into how bond proceeds are used, because no existing framework requires issuers to allocate directly into green projects, nor do they limit allocation to only green projects. The risk of misallocation exists because the proceeds of green bonds are fungible: the funds raised via a green bond can finance any other business activity of the issuer, including non-green projects. In other words, the money raised from a green issuance is potentially interchangeable with the issuer's other source of capital, thereby carrying the risk to be allocated differently to what it was supposed to (i.e. to green projects). In China for example, which accounted for 39% of global CO_2 emissions in 2016, issuers are allowed to use up to half of the proceeds to pay off bank loans and invest in working capital (Morgan Stanley Research 2017).

Another common criticism is that green bonds, when used to refinance projects, are a simple means of "repackaging" conventional bonds without a substantial addition of benefits (Shishlov and Morel 2016). The 2017 revision of the US tax code reduced issuers' ability to refinance their existing debt by eliminating prepaid transactions. The revision helps explain the slowdown in new green issuances from municipalities but also points to the percentage of green bond issuances that were simply repackaged conventional bonds (De La Gorce 2019). In 2018, municipalities completed 20% fewer green issuances compared to 2017, with a total volume halved (Boeke Burke and Bredeson 2019).

THE SUSTAINABLE FINANCE MARKET STANDS TO BENEFIT FROM THE DEVELOPMENT OF TRANSITION FINANCE

In addition to green bonds, there are alternative green instruments that offer attractive benefits to investors and issuers in the LCCR pathway, including transition bonds, sustainability-linked instruments, and portfolio construction weighting factors. Next, clarification will be provided about whether transition bonds pertain to green finance.

Transition Bonds: Characteristics and Specificities

A preliminary definition of a transition bond is a fixed income instrument, whose proceeds are earmarked to fund the decarbonization of an organization via projects that are not considered green yet and, therefore, not certifiable or eligible to access green financing instruments. Transition bonds would still have to comply with the four core components of the principles specified by the ICMA (i.e. use of proceeds, process for project evaluation and selection, management of proceeds and reporting). Moreover, when choosing transition bonds, both issuers and investors face reputational risks and could fall prey to greenwashing. Transition bonds could also threaten to cannibalize green bonds given the current ambiguity on the former instrument.

The concept of supporting the transition to an LCCR future, in contrast to only focusing on pure LCCR outcomes, is aligned with governmental efforts in several different jurisdictions. The importance of transition is exemplified by Spain's creation of the ministry for the ecological transition, France's national strategy for the ecological transition to sustainable development, and the UN's SDGs. The imperative to shift away from fossil fuels and transition toward a low-carbon future sparked the emergence of transition bonds: a source of financing for carbon-intensive companies that aspire to green their business model and operations.

Transition bonds emerged in 2018 as a new category of labeled bonds. These bonds, which attempt to close the gap between conventional bonds and green bonds, aim to raise capital for issuers in hard-to-abate "brown" industries—such as oil production and coal mines—and raise capital to finance their transition and shift toward cleaner modus operandi and business models. Transition bonds are a form of green bonds that finance decarbonization activities within high-carbon sectors that would otherwise be bypassed by conventional green bond issuers. Transition bonds mark a shift away from the purist frameworks of green bonds, which take a black-and-white approach by supporting only "green industries" that have low levels of greenhouse gas (GHG) emissions, such as renewable energies.

Transition bonds stem from a shared willingness among investors to support issuers that are shepherding the transition toward a more sustainable economy, even if these issuers are not yet green or sustainable. Building on the methodology of CICERO (Norway's Center for International Climate Research) that defines "shades of green" (and later on, adopted and modified by several market participants), transition finance expands this spectrum by including "brown" shades. Transition bonds serve issuers in light green or light brown industries, but only if said companies or government entities have a significant and credible strategy to align their operations and business model with a low-carbon climate resilient future (Figure 13.2). For "brown" issuers, such as companies in steel and cement, investing in low-carbon technologies is very expensive to implement, and access to financing can be the difference in making the switch (Rootzén and Johnsson 2017, 2016). It is important to note that some brown issuers are excluded from both the green bond and the transition bond markets by most guidelines and investors (e.g. coal-mining companies). In this regard, the draft guidelines on transition

Shades of green	Dark green	Medium green	Light green/brown	Dark brown
Definitions	Alignment with the implementation of a LCCR pathway today	Steps towards the LCCR vision but not quite there yet	Climate-friendly short-term gains that do not contribute to the long-term LCCR solution	Fossil-fueled technologies that lock in long-term emissions
Examples of projects	• Wind energy projects • Solar plants	• Plug-in hybrid buses • Sustainable buildings	• Energy efficiency improvement in a fossil-fuel based activity	• New infrastructure in coal
Profile of industry by LCCR strategy & efforts	Industries that do not emit GHG emissions	Industries which unequivocally reduce GHG emissions	Industries which reduce GHG emissions but still have emission-intensive parts in their lifecycle	Industries with large GHG emissions that have made little or no effort to mitigate them
Profile of transitional risk exposure	High to medium opportunity to benefit through the growth of low-carbon products and services	Limited exposure to climate transition risks	Exposure to climate transition risk but with mitigation and adaptation strategies	High potential of "stranding" assets and high exposure to transition risks

Green bonds can fall in these three shades*

Proceeds of Transition bonds could fall in these two shades*

*Conditioned to the categorization of the issuer, as assessed by key ESG rating agencies and data providers, Second-Party Opinion institutions, and Climate Bond Initiative.

FIGURE 13.2   Shades of Green and Spectrum of Industries on the LCCR Pathway. *Source*: Authors, based on Harald and Clapp (2015) and MSCI (2019).

*Conditioned to the categorization of the issues, as assessed by key ESG rating agencies and data providers, second-part opinion institutions and the Climate Bond Initiative.

finance published in April 2020 by a group of Japanese researchers gathered under the Transition Finance Study Group (TFSG), and at the request of a nonprofit organization pertaining to environmental finance, point out that the current lack of standardization of ESG evaluation methods prevents from offering a reliable assessment of the goals and achievements of companies in the transition journey, and recommend focusing on projects, assets, and activities. The TSFG differentiates green finance from transition finance, assigning specific and distinct objectives to each category. The TSFG also argues that further requirements are necessary in the case of transition finance to guarantee the credibility of the transition journey. Building on ICMA's core principles for green bonds, the TSFG adds ex-ante and ex-post issuance evaluations on the length of the transition period and CO_2 emission targets. Each evaluation should be performed by different bodies according to the TSFG, which is not an obligation under the Green Bond Principles (Transition Finance Study Group 2020).

Transition bonds depart from green bonds in three main ways (more details in Table 1):

- Transition bonds' use of proceeds target climate transition-related activities, rather than strictly eligible green projects.
- Transition bonds focus on the issuer's commitment to be greener, whereas green bonds focus primarily on the direct use of the proceeds for green projects or on the issuer's profile.
- There is an explicit requirement that issuers articulate their transition philosophy "in the context of their current business model and their future strategic direction" and lay out a sound strategy, governance, metrics, and targets that define how they intend to achieve their transition journey.

Existing Frameworks for Transition Bonds

To date, there is neither formal framework nor universally established taxonomy for transition bonds. AXA Investment Managers have presented their own pioneering system, titled "Transition Bond Guidelines," which lays out a classification system that identifies companies that are brown today but have the ambition to go green in the future.

Under AXA's framework, transition bonds possess many of the same fundamental principles as green bonds, such as earmarked funding and a commitment to regularly report on the use of proceeds. Issuers must assign proceeds to "activities linked to climate transition." A non-exhaustive list

TABLE 13.1   Differences and Similarities Between Transition Bonds and Green Bonds.

	Green bonds	Transition bonds
Similarities	Proceeds are earmarked	
	Financing, or partial to full refinancing, of projects supporting a green transition	
	Requirement of robust disclosure addressing:	
	• Use of proceeds	
	• Selection of projects	
	• Management of proceeds	
	• Reporting and the monitoring process	
Differences	• Eligibility of light to dark green issuers and projects (only)	• Eligibility of brown issuers
	• Some credentials and market adoption:	• Shorter maturities in general
	• Existence since 2007	• Primarily tied to decarbonization targets
	• Growth of the market	• No commonly shared framework
	• Strong reputation of many issuers	• Allocation of proceeds to climate transition-related activities
	• An enabling ecosystem	• Focus on the whole transition story of the issuer (in AXA's Transition Bond Guidelines)
	• Allocation of proceeds to eligible green projects	
Eligible categories	Per the *Green Bond Principles*, eligible green projects:	Per *AXA's Transition Bond Guidelines*, eligible climate transition-related activities:
	• Renewable energy	
	• Energy efficiency	• Energy
	• Pollution prevention and control	• Co-generation plants: gas-powered combined heat and power
	• Environmentally sustainable management of living natural resources and land use	• Carbon capture and storage
	• Terrestrial and aquatic biodiversity conservation	• Gas transport infrastructure that can be switched to lower carbon intensity fuels
	• Clean transportation	• Coal-to-gas fuel switch in defined geographical areas, with defined carbon avoidance performance
	• Sustainable water and wastewater management	• Waste-to-energy
	• Climate change adaptation	• Transportation
	• Eco-efficient and/or circular economy adapted products	• Gas-powered ships
	• Production technologies and processes	• Aircraft alternative fuels
	• Green buildings	• Industry
		• Cement, metals, or glass energy efficiency investments

Source: Authors, based on Takatsuki and Foll (2019) for AXA and ICMA (2018) for Green Bond Principles.

of project categories includes carbon co-generation, carbon capture, and carbon storage plants. So-called "brown" issuers are also asked to tell an articulated story about their transition, backed by short-term targets.

At the institutional level, the EU Taxonomy Report on Sustainable Finance ("EU Taxonomy") provides the most comprehensive definition for which areas are sustainable and ruling out which are not. Activities that can "make a substantial contribution to climate change mitigation" are subdivided in three broad categories in the June 2019 TEG Report (TEG 2019, p. 30; see Table 13.2 for greater detail):

- *Low-carbon activities:* Activities with low GHG "in an absolute sense" (e.g. production of electricity from wind power, forest restoration and rehabilitation, electric cars or trains). This category is the simplest to define.
- *Enabling activities:* Activities that enable reductions of GHG "in another sector," also benefitting from a strong level of political acceptability and technical clarity (e.g. installation of energy efficient boilers in buildings, as it enables carbon emissions reductions even though the manufacturing process itself does emit some GHG).
- *Transition activities:* Activities that "are not currently close to a net-zero carbon emissions level" (p. 30) but "contribute to a transition to a net-zero emissions economy in 2050." Transition activities must also "avoid lock-in to carbon-intensive assets or processes" (p. 30).

The last category is the most complex and controversial. The EU TEG defines transition activities by a set of metrics and thresholds that delimitate the scope of these activities. For example, building renovation and advanced cement manufacturing are on the list, if they do not emit more than 50g of CO_2 per kilometer, and 0.498 tons of CO_2 equivalent emissions (CO_2e) per ton of cement, respectively. By setting a specific threshold of 100g of CO_2 per kWh of electricity produced, under which activities make "a substantial contribution to climate change mitigation" (p. 57), the EU Taxonomy excludes projects like gas-fired power plants from "transition activities," which emit more than this ceiling.

Transition activities are further defined in the final TEG report (TEG 2020), providing additional guidance to evaluate such activities: (i) best performance in terms of greenhouse gas emission levels in the sector or industry; (ii) compatibility with the development and deployment of low-carbon alternatives; and (iii) no lock-in effect in carbon-intensive assets. Moreover, a key change since the TEG June report is the exclusion

TABLE 13.2 Three Kinds of Green Activities in the EU Taxonomy.

Types of activity	Definition	Technical screening criteria	Example
Low-carbon activities ("green activities")*	Activities associated with sequestration or very low and zero emission. These activities require caption to increase their development and wider deployment.	Likely to be stable and long term	• Zero-emission transport (e.g. electric cars or trains) • Near to zero carbon electricity production (e.g. solar power) • Restoration of forest
Enabling activities ("greening by")	Activities that enable low-carbon performance or enable substantial emissions reductions	• Likely to be stable and long term, if the activities are already low-carbon • Subject to regular revision tending to zero, if the activities are not yet operating at this level	• Manufacture of wind turbines • Manufacture of household appliances rated in the highest energy label class • Installation of efficient boilers in building
Transition activities ("greening of")	Critical activities to the economy that contribute to a transition to a net-zero emissions economy in 2050 but are not currently close to this level yet	• Subject to regular revision, approaching zero over time • $<100\,g$ CO_2e/kWh reducing in five-year increments to $0\,g$ CO_2e/kWh by 2050	• Building renovation • Buses for interurban transport $<50g$ CO_2/km • Cement manufacture $<0.498tCO_2e/t$ of cement

Source: Authors, based on the TEG's Report on the EU's Taxonomy (TEG 2020).
Note: * The mention of greening of/by is from the June 2019 TEG's Report on the EU Taxonomy; these labels have changed in the final version in March 2020.

of solid fossil-fuels (including activities related to dedicated storage and/or transportation of any fossil fuels, including gaseous or liquid fossil fuels) as eligible transition activities, considering that they would "ultimately undermine climate change mitigation objectives" (p. 21).

Nevertheless, while ruling out these "brown" activities, the final TEG report acknowledges the need to "assist companies and other issuers in explaining incremental improvements in their activities and receiving some positive recognition in the market" (p. 51). Thus, it does not exclude the possibility of including "brown" activities in transition bonds, as TEG's ambition is that the Taxonomy would ultimately include three levels of performance: "substantial contribution" [green], "significant harm" [brown], and a category for activities that do neither (TEG 2020).

It is interesting to note that the draft guidelines by the TSFG distinguish green finance from transition finance, contrary to the EU Taxonomy, which includes both categories under different thresholds. The TSFG proposes eligible project categories that include natural gas–powered and biofuels projects, either through conversion from oil or maintenance that increases carbon efficiency. Thus, transition finance enables the financing or the refinancing of the transformation of high-emitting assets and activities through a process with intermediate goals and eventually leading to net-zero emissions. Conversely, according to the TSFG, green finance implies to finance or refinance new or existing green assets or activities. The TSFG takes the example of dismantling a coal-fired plant and successively constructing a solar plant; such a project would be eligible to green finance. These guidelines reflect the increasing interest of sustainable finance in Japan; in a process similar to that of the EU Taxonomy, consultations are open until May 2020, before the publication of a final report at the end of this year.

In addition to TEG and TSFG, two Canadian initiatives have notable approaches to transition finance: Corporate Knights and the Council for Clean Capitalism. These organizations similarly propose clean transition bond guidelines, which include a taxonomy of the different projects and issuers that would align with a green transition. As with green bonds, the sectors covered by transition bonds differ from one framework to another, emphasizing the lack of commonly agreed guidelines.

In terms of eligible sectors, AXA's framework allows for a large and flexible spectrum of sectors. It comprises:

- Greenhouse gases emitting sectors (e.g. materials, extractive industry, chemicals, and transport), or

- Sectors that do not currently have—and may not have in the future —enough green assets to finance but have financing needs to reduce the carbon footprint of their business activities, their products, and their services

In practice, transition bonds are allocated to projects contributing to the environmental transition of carbon-intensive sectors (e.g. ships powered by liquefied natural gas, energy efficiency projects in industry), as well as gas assets in countries where energy production currently depends on coal. The use of transition bonds for transition projects can assist the oil and gas sector in diversifying beyond fossil fuels. Other carbon-intensive sectors such as steel and cement, which can be produced in cleaner and more carbon-efficient ways, are also be eligible.

Among its three categories of green bonds, the European Bank of Reconstruction and Development (EBRD) published a framework for its own "green transition bond," which presents a more restrictive approach. The bank identifies the following sectors as applicable for transition bond investments:

- Decarbonization and resource efficiency, including circular economy products in manufacturing
  - For example, chemical production, cement production, steel production
- Food production
  - For example, improving resource efficiency in agribusiness, promoting sustainable land use
- Activities to enable a green transition
  - For example, electricity grids, supply chains, low-carbon transport, green logistics, ICT solutions
  - Construction and renovation of buildings

Building on its framework, EBRD launched a EUR €500 million global green transition bond in October 2019 dedicated to financing and refinancing projects that enable significant improvements toward decarbonization, a reduction in environmental footprint, or improved resource efficiency in key sectors of the economy. A minimum of 50% of the capital being designated to a given project must be specifically designated to the green transition of the asset or project.

However, some sectors have gray areas that require special attention and expert guidance. One such area is natural gas, described in detail in Box 13.1.

Box 13.1 Focus: Financing Natural Gas, a Key Question for Investors

Natural Gas Is at the Core of the Debate of Transition Investments

On the one hand, natural gas is a fossil fuel that emits CO_2 on combustion, and the extraction of the fuel releases 40% more methane than initially estimated; methane is 28 times more virulent than CO_2 (Hmiel et al. 2020).

On the other hand, natural-gas emissions are 30% less than oil and half as much as coal. Natural gas represents a quarter of global energy consumption (IEA 2019b). Compared to coal and oil, natural gas appears to be a good candidate to lead a fast and economically feasible path to an LCCR future with cleaner air. On the other hand, gas extraction released 40% more methane than initially estimated; methane is 28 times more intensive than CO_2 alone (Hmiel et al. 2020). In addition, methane leaks are invisible to the naked eye and require infrared cameras to observe.

In Europe, natural gas is not eligible for sustainable financing under the EU Taxonomy. The EC-mandated TEG considered that it does not meet the required CO_2 reduction threshold. If unabated natural-gas fired power generation is ruled out at this stage, gas-fired power with carbon capture and sequestration may qualify, and blended gas-fired power is subject to the emissions intensity threshold. Nevertheless, the Platform for Sustainable Finance—replacing the TEG—can determine the role for natural gas (and/or nuclear power), if any, in the taxonomy through the use of delegated acts and a review clause that enables the Commission to include performance criteria for "brown" activities.

Moreover, the EIB pledged in July 2019 that it would no longer invest in projects linked to fossil fuels, including gas, by 2022. However, in November 2019, the EC included natural gas infrastructure projects on its list of Projects of Common Interest (PCI) eligible for EIB funding. Beyond the EU, it is also interesting to note that MSCI Global Climate Index includes a "future fuels" category comprising companies engaged in the production and use of natural gas. In MSCI's index, natural gas is considered to be a "transitional" fuel—with an expected role of reducing GHGs in the transition to a post-petroleum economy (MSCI 2017).

These divergences between EIB, MSCI, and TEG exemplify that it is extremely complex to provide sufficient energy for a rapidly growing global economy, while also phasing out fossil energy for environmental reasons.

(continued)

(*continued*)

Additionally, any investment in new infrastructure could lock the economy in fossil gas for decades, with gas-powered long-term infrastructures becoming "stranded assets." The persistence in prolonging dependence on natural gas could put territories at risk of reaching a structural deadlock in 2030 (Foresight Climate & Energy 2018).

Additionally, according to some authors, the imperative of "energy transition" might also serve as a "tool for maintaining the existing order" (Aykut and Evrard 2017). Far from being the spearhead of a profound transformation of the energy sector, the energy transition could be a means for the fossil fuel industry and other corporate and political actors to ensure and maintain control over the scope and content of these transformations.

Therefore, in the long term it is necessary to anticipate a certain decline of natural gas, in addition to or instead of capture and storage of CO_2, or gas greening techniques—namely a deployment of biogas or hydrogen—which is for now actively in the research and development phase.

Source: Author, based on the literature review.

Issuance of Transition Bonds

To date, few transition bonds have been issued. Those that have made it to market were either denominated as "transition" bonds or as "green" (or "sustainable") bonds with a brown issuer.

In May 2018, the Spanish oil company Repsol issued a EUR €500 million green bond. Its use of proceeds was dedicated to financing and refinancing 312 projects and targeted a reduction of 1.2 million tons of CO_2 equivalent emissions, which amounts to a reduction of 25% or greater in CO_2 emissions by 2020 relative to 2005 levels. Climate Bonds Initiative (CBI), the company that reviewed the bond for green certification, argued that the 312 projects only represented an incremental change in the oil company's business model, and that any investment in refineries, even if focused on efficiency and reduced emissions, is likely to extend plant operating lifetimes and therefore indirectly increase emissions over time. As a green bond certifier, CBI requires fundamental "wholesale business-model shifts" that lead to "deep, rapid, and sustained reduction in emissions" (Whiley 2017). Following CBI's decision, Bloomberg, Barclays, MSCI, S&P, DJI, and Solactive indices did not include the bond. Nevertheless, the second-party opinion provider Vigeo Eiris validated the bond as green and considered it aligned with the GBP (Vigeo Eiris 2017).

Another example comes from Marfrig, the Brazilian company that is the world's second-largest producer of beef. In August 2019, Marfrig issued a USD \$500 million sustainable bond to fund the purchase of beef from Brazilian cattle producers who would respect strict environmental rules. Originally, the company wanted to issue a green bond, which would have had to comply with the green label requirements. The difficulty to meet the minimum standards of many green investors and the reputational risks tied to this audacious issuance led to a rebranding. A "sustainable transition bond" label aimed at reflecting Marfrig's efforts to green its supply chain and fight deforestation. The bond was validated by the second-party opinion of Vigeo Eiris, which acknowledged the compliance with the Green and Social Bond Principles voluntary guidelines and the contribution to "the preservation of biodiversity, the avoidance of land deforestation, the protection of indigenous rights and the avoidance of the use of forced labor within the supply chain" (Vigeo Eiris 2019). Vigeo Eiris also stressed its concerns about the issuer's ability "to effectively manage and mitigate the environmental and social risks associated" with the bond, challenges that Marfrig also endorsed "given the characteristics of (their) industry," justifying the "transition" label. The issuance provoked strong reactions in the green bond community given the core activity of the issuer and of the project itself (Petheram 2019). Opponents to the bond claim that it does not finance new sustainable activities nor invest in climate solutions; supporters argue that it fosters a transparent and critical debate about sustainable practices and deforestation. Despite the controversy, the issuance was three times oversubscribed, and Marfrig got its lowest coupon ever at 6.625%.

In November 2019, the French financial institution Crédit Agricole issued a 10-year EUR €100 million transition bond with a coupon of 0.55%. The proceeds are dedicated to a selection of loans contributing to the environmental transition of carbon-intensive sectors. Examples provided by the bank include LNG-powered ships, investments in energy efficient industries as well as gas power assets in countries where power generation currently relies on coal. According to Credit Agricole's estimates, the underlying projects should reduce the volume of carbon emissions by 26,500 tons of CO_2.

The limits of transition finance appear in the example of Teekay, a Bermuda-headquartered company specialized in oil tankers. Teekay, one of the world's largest shipowners, failed to achieve its goal by raising only USD$ 125 million out of the USD $150–200 million expected. The fund aimed at acquiring energy efficient tankers. Investors considered that it was not admissible to qualify as green the financing of polluting ships used to transport oil or coal, even if they would be less polluting than their predecessors (Nauman 2019). A set of industry guidelines could help dispel these concerns for future transactions. The market would need a strict framework around the use of these terminologies, and to differentiate clearly green bonds from transition bonds, by considering them as two different categories.

The Development of Alternative Instruments: Cannibalization or Consolidation of the Green Bond Market?

Transition bonds enable firms that would not qualify to issue green bonds to access capital to transition their business models toward an LCCR future. Under certain conditions, green bonds and transition bonds can avoid cannibalizing each other, and in fact they can coexist in ways that benefit the whole market. "Light green" projects remain eligible for green bond financing on a case-by-case basis (see CICERO's shades of green for details), while "brown" issuers can only have access to transition bonds when they have thoroughly documented transformation strategies—then creating a new bond label for issuers and projects in the light green and light brown categories represents an opportunity to protect the green bond market from greenwashing and still fund critical efficiency and carbon emissions reduction projects.

Transition bonds can also bridge the investment gap between the lack of supply for green bonds and the increasing demand for sustainable investment opportunities. In addition to meeting investor demand, transition bonds can address the critical and massive need for capital and financing for energy infrastructure systems around the world, investments that are necessary to limit global warming to 1.5 degrees Celsius (Figure 13.3). According to the Intergovernmental Panel on Climate Change (IPPC), the amount of capital needed for energy infrastructure globally is estimated to be USD $2.38 trillion per year between 2016 and 2050 (de Coninck et al. 2018). Yet today, the green bond market represents only a fraction of this amount, with a cumulative issuance between 2007 and 2018 reaching only USD $521 billion (CBI 2018a).

The opportunity of transition bonds must be perceived in a context where fossil-fuel industries continue to benefit from massive energy subsidies (Climate Transparency 2017). As emphasized by Christian de Perthuis,

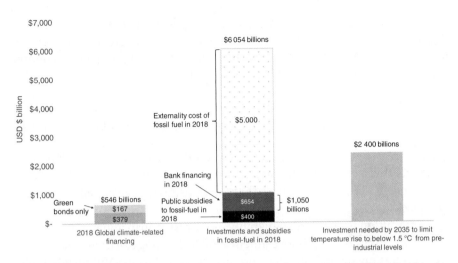

FIGURE 13.3   The Climate Finance Gap. *Source*: Authors, using data from Coady et al. (2015), CBI (2018b), IEA (2019a), Rainforest Action Network (2019), Climate Policy Initiative (2019).

head of the Climate Economic chair at Paris Dauphine, reducing CO_2 emissions means divesting from fossil fuels (de Perthuis 2019). In 2018, direct price subsidies for fossil fuels reached over USD $300 billion in 2018 globally[1] (IEA 2019a), and bank financing for over 1,800 companies active across the fossil fuel lifecycle amounted to USD $654.123 billion (RAN 2019). Through taxes, citizens have to shoulder the cost of directly subsidizing the fossil fuel industry, while also absorbing the hidden costs of burning fossil fuels on society, which were estimated to be USD $5.2 trillion in 2017 alone by the International Monetary Fund (Yeo 2019). All this capital, which supports fossil fuel energy production, could be reallocated to the transition towards cleaner outcomes. The elimination of energy subsidies could reduce deaths related to fossil-fuel emissions by over 50 percent and fossil-fuel-related carbon emissions by over 20 percent, and create substantial revenue gains estimated at 3.6 percent of global GDP in 2015 (Coady et al. 2015). An application is going to happen in South Korea. Following the victory of the Democratic Party in April 2020, South Korea is going to implement a Green New Deal. It pledges to end domestic and overseas coal financing by 2029, create a Regional Energy Transition Centre to support

---

[1] Oil is the most heavily subsidized energy carrier, expanding its share in the total to more than 40% according to IEA 2018 data.

workers transition to green jobs, and massively invest in in renewable energy infrastructures. The country is the world's seventh-largest carbon emitter, with coal supplying 40% of its energy. South Korea will be the first country in East Asia committing to achieve net-zero by 2050.

Alternative Instruments to Bridge the Transition Finance Gap

In addition to transition bonds, there are other transition-linked financial products that help bridge the gap between sustainability-oriented investors and firms in "brown" industries that are transitioning sustainable business practices.

One option is to link sustainability indicators to loan and bond financing (or related indexes). In this investment vehicle, funding can be allocated without earmarking definite projects, but pricing is tied to specific sustainability goals with time-sensitive targets. As such, if the conditions for sustainable development are not met by the issuer, interest rates would increase. Unlike transition bonds, financing linked to sustainability indicators can support companies without substantial portfolios of green projects and provide capital for general business purposes if sustainability goals are met. By linking companies' ESG performance to pricing, investors create an incentive for the issuer to be greener. The instrument also motivates companies and municipalities to measure any sustainability improvements, as well as their broader social and environmental impact. This approach has recently gained significant momentum in the loan market.

A frequent green bond issuer, the Italian electricity producer Ente Nazionale per l'Energia Elettrica (ENEL) issued the first bond linked to the UN's SDGs in June 2019 for USD $1,500 million dollars. ENEL's bond focuses on specific objectives within four SDGs: energy, industry, sustainable cities, and climate action. Regarding SDG 7 "Clean and Affordable Energy," ENEL committed to having more than 11.6 GW of additional renewable generation capacity by December 2021, an increase from 46% to 55% of its total capacity. The SDG-linked bond provides ENEL with euro banknotes that have annual interest payments tied to environmental goals. While ENEL earmarked the bond's use of proceeds for ordinary needs – including more than half of its "brown" electricity generation activities – ENEL will incur penalties on the cost of the loan if it fails to meet its renewable energy targets. More specifically, its coupon would increase by 25 basis points through a step-up mechanism if the company fails to achieve the above key performance indicators (KPI). There was strong investor appetite for ENEL's issuance, with demand reaching USD \$4 billion. ENEL said the deal saved them 20 basis points compared to a conventional bond (ENEL 2019).

The system of ENEL's bond echoes the proposition by the Japanese TSFG to add a variable coupon system in the case of bonds, or interest rate increase clause in the case of loans, that would sanction the nonachievement by the issuer of its transition commitments in terms of transition period and/or CO_2 emission target reduction (Transition Finance Study Group 2020).

Another transition-related financial instrument is regulation. Some proposals favor adapting financial regulation in order to encourage greater demand for green assets, and to disincentivize investment in brown assets (Thomä and Hilke 2018). For example, the EU High-Level Expert Group on Sustainable Finance (2018) raised the prospect of introducing a "green supporting factor" and a "brown penalizing factor" in prudential rules, and the Central Banks and Supervisors Network for Greening the Financial System (NGFS) also discussed the introduction of penalties for holding carbon intensive assets. A "green supporting factor" means lowering the amount of capital held in reserve as collateral for green assets, considering they are not subject to a variety of climate-related risks. Conversely, the "brown penalty factor" means increasing the capital requirement for "brown" assets (e.g. fossil fuel investments), as they represent a climate-related threat to financial instability.

Such regulatory changes would increase banks' demand for green investments and reduce their demand for carbon-intensive investments. Moreover, the penalty would account for the transition risks resulting from a haphazard adjustment to a low-carbon economy. In the European banking system, the brown factor could be implemented through a dedicated systemic risk buffer, or it could be integrated into the requirements of Pillar 2 of the Basel II framework concerning banks' internal capital assessment and regulatory supervision. Hence, at this institutional level, regulation would encourage banks to develop climate-related risk management capacities (Awazu Pereira da Silva 2019).

Another possible instrument, a "green supporting factor" in the form of lowered capital requirements on climate-friendly credits or green bonds, has failed to garner industry support since its first proposition by the EC's Vice-President for the Euro and Social Dialogue Valdis Dombrovskis. Academia, financial supervisors, and think tanks have opposed the limited impact in terms of cost and availability of capital of this measure (Thomä and Gibhardt 2020) and the threat to European financial stability by encouraging risky lending practices. Such an incentive would need to be justified by empirical or theoretical evidence that green assets are less risky, but these claims are still debatable (Cooper 2018; Ehlers and Packer 2017).

It is also possible to raise the capital requirements on brown companies and industries. A brown penalty is likely to act as a relative noticeable deterrent on lending to high-carbon industries. The impact on capital reserves would be more important for the brown factor compared to the green because the applicable universe of assets is larger the former (Thomä and Hilke 2018). However, if the NGO community largely supports this option, it would need to overcome a fierce opposition from carbon-intensive industries and some financial institutions to be implemented.

In this debate, and following the suggestions of market observers during the consultation period, the final Taxonomy document of the TEG of the EC (March 2020) does not preclude the possibility of introducing a brown taxonomy (i.e. a taxonomy of activities that cause significant harm to the environment). Such a taxonomy could be used as the basis for raising capital requirements on assets with high-sustainability risks – a so-called brown penalizing factor. Additionally, the brown category could be combined with incentives to reduce environmental damage. The TEG laid out that such a taxonomy would motivate companies and other issuers to disclose their strategy and financing plans, and gradually seek to be more sustainable and contribute to the EU's energy transition, consequently changing their activities from "brown" to "green."

An additional strategy, green weighting factors, comes from the private sector. The global financial institution and asset manager Natixis developed its own internal green weighting factor, which has the potential to be replicated across the industry. This internal analytical tool introduces a green and brown adjustment coefficient that can be applied to the bank's risk-weighted assets (RWA) analysis, which quantifies the amount overall capital needed to be put aside by the bank in order to cover defaults and other risks. It is based on a seven-color scale ranking from dark green to dark brown for each client or project funded. The metrics are climate-focused and comprise environmental externalities such as waste, water, biodiversity, and pollution. In Natixis's tool, all green holdings are adjusted to a lower risk scale, and are allocated a reduction of up to 50% in risk-weighted assets, while holdings with negative environmental impacts are adjusted upward, and require up to an additional 24% in risk-weighted assets (Paris Action Climat 2020). To date, this "additional decision thermometer" does not impact or interfere with the regulatory RWA, but rather aims at influencing (or "greening") internal capital allocation decisions, and provides an additional tool for monitoring the climate and environmental transition of the bank and its clients.

Which Roles Can Market Participants Play to Foster Green and Transition-Oriented Finance?

To reach the trillions of dollars needed to annually to transition to a LCCR future, banks and investors are pushing to expand the sustainable finance market beyond the usual issuers of green bonds: states, local authorities, development banks, financial institutions, companies, and energy companies. To bridge this gap, the "sustainable" finance market seeks to mobilize all market participants in the climate transition by pushing its boundaries and utilizing alternative instruments, under the watchful eye of stakeholders, civil society and demanding investors.

While many challenges remain, these alternative instruments (transition bonds, ESG-linked financing, regulation, weighting factors, etc.) also present specific advantages to investors and issuers: they address the limited supply of green bonds, while offering more flexibility and fewer constraints. Transition bonds are available to firms that do not qualify for green bonds issuance or do not have significant green expenditures, yet still are willing to commit to sustainable transitions and targets. Transition bonds offer a viable pathway for investors to exert pressure on the world's largest emitters, and for companies in dirty industries to secure the necessary capital to bring their business models into alignment with the Paris Agreement and a zero-carbon economy.

To date, however, transition bonds are highly controversial in the market and the asset class is yet to be firmly established. As there is no consensus on what defines climate finance, delineating climate transition finance instruments is even more difficult. Investors fear that companies could obtain funds for projects with no real environmental benefits. As evidenced by the transition bonds showcased in this paper, including the USD $500 million sustainable transition bond from Brazilian beef giant Marfrig, the EUR €500 million bond by the Italian gas company SNAM, and the SDG-linked bond from ENEL, there is often investor controversy, but the fear of greenwashing doesn't diminish investor appetite as most issuances are oversubscribing with lower yields and spreads.

To gain credible legitimacy, transition bonds should be referenced by dedicated, commonly accepted, and trustworthy guidelines, ideally one framework that becomes the international standard. A distinct framework, based on a consistent and differentiated language and labels, would also protect the green bond market from being diluted and reputationally degraded. These guidelines would have to include "coherence checks" (Shishlov and Morel 2016) in order to certify that so-called green and transition bonds are truly aligned with a LCCR pathway. An alternative framework would follow a 2°C trajectory, given that each activity sees its carbon intensity gradually decreasing, at a level and a rate depending on the specificities and technological breakthroughs experienced by the sector.

Several bodies are working to develop these required guidelines. The executive committee of the Green Bond Principles, developed under the aegis of the ICMA, has just created a working group on "transition bonds," coordinated by several financial institutions (AXA IM, HSBC, and JP Morgan). The objective is to understand why companies in the carbon-intensive sectors have been largely absent from the green bond market so far and to give guidelines for future emissions. The group, consisting of fifty financial and environmental institutions, launched in 2019, and will meet throughout 2020 to establish a common framework to make transition bonds a credible instrument for the future (Working Group Climate Transition Finance 2020).

CONCLUSION

Achieving the objectives and commitment of the Paris Agreement in a 2° C scenario (Peake and Ekins 2017) – and any further progress towards scenarios like 1.5°C pathways – requires a major mobilization of capital toward LCCR infrastructure. Furthermore, achieving the SDGs necessitates a tremendous acceleration and massification of investments at the country level and international level (UNCTAD 2014). In response, the diversity and quantity of green financing instruments are increasing rapidly to meet investor demand for climate and sustainability investments. From this perspective, broadening the green finance landscape with new instruments oriented towards the climate transition offers market participants opportunities to expand their green and sustainable investment capacity. Specifically, transition instruments have the potential to attract both institutional and socially responsible investor funding to sustainable projects.

While the green bond market has experienced strong growth, it is also facing challenges to consolidating its legitimacy and scale. Green bonds only represent the tip of the iceberg, with less than 2% of the global bond markets. There is an opportunity to develop and reinforce alternative instruments – investment vehicles that are better-suited for the moderate bulk of the economy – by setting up a transparent framework for the credible development of transition finance instruments.

If legitimized through the enforcement of credible and commonly agreed upon principles and frameworks, transition bonds can open up a new promising market for financing the low-carbon climate resilient transition. They can also help to raise public awareness of the challenges of sustainable finance. While transition bonds are tainted by accusations of greenwashing, partly explained by their lack of standardization, in practice transition bonds protect the green bond market from greenwashing by delimitating specific bond types within the total range of sustainable activities.

Innovation has always been one of the key assets of the financial sector. As industries and companies that are heavily reliant on fossil-fuels have a critical economic and societal weight globally, if said organizations and sectors are making change and taking significant efforts to adapt their business model and strategy to a long-term low-carbon pathway, they should be a part of the 2050 climate solution. There is a critical opportunity to develop and scale-up adapted instruments in order to avoid the massive economic consequences of stranded assets while supporting the implementation of a robust LCCR pathway.

REFERENCES

Aglietta, M., and Rigot, S. (2012). Investisseurs à long terme, régulation financière et croissance soutenable. *Revue d'économie financière*, 108(4): 189.

Aglietta, M., Hourcade, J.-C., Jaeger, C., et al. (2015). Financing transition in an adverse context: climate finance beyond carbon finance. *International Environmental Agreements* 15: 403–420.

Awazu Pereira da Silva, L. (2019). Research on climate-related risks and financial stability: An "epistemological break"? Conference of the Central Banks and Supervisors Network for Greening the Financial System (NGFS), Paris, 17 April 2019. https://www.bis.org/speeches/sp190523.htm (accessed 16 March 2020).

Aykut, S. C., and Evrard, A. (2017). Une transition pour que rien ne change ? Changement institutionnel et dépendance au sentier dans les «transitions énergétiques» en Allemagne et en France. *Revue Internationale de Politique Comparee* 24(1–2): 17–49.

Becker-Olsen, K., and Potucek, S. (2013). Greenwashing. In *Encyclopedia of Corporate Social Responsibility* (pp. 1318–1323). Springer Berlin Heidelberg.

Boeke Burke, E., and Bredeson, A. (2019). 2019 U.S. Municipal Green Bond & Resiliency Outlook: Will the Self-Labeled Market Rebound? www.spglobal.com/ratingsdirect (accessed 20 April 2020).

Bowman, L. (2019). ESG: Green bonds have a chicken and egg problem. Euromoney. https://www.euromoney.com/article/b1fxdsf5kpjxlg/esg-green-bonds-have-a-chicken-and-egg-problem (accessed 15 February 2020).

Burks, B., and London, M. W. (2019). The ESG Advantage: Exploring Links to Corporate Financial Performance. https://www.spglobal.com/_assets/documents/ratings/the-esg-advantage-exploring-links-to-corporate-financial-performance-april-8-2019.pdf (accessed 21 April 2020).

Campiglio, E. (2016). Beyond carbon pricing: The role of banking and monetary policy in financing the transition to a low-carbon economy. *Ecological Economics*, 121: 220–230.

CBI (2017) Green Bond pricing in the primary market. https://www.climate bonds.net/files/files/Greenium Q3-Final-20180219.pdf (accessed 15 February 2020).

CBI (2018a). *Green Bonds. The State of the Market*. London. https://www.climate bonds.net/files/reports/cbi_gbm_final_032019_web.pdf (accessed 26 March 2020).

CBI (2018b). *Bonds and climate change. State of the Market* 2018. https://www .climatebonds.net/files/reports/cbi_sotm_2018_final_01k-web.pdf (accessed 18 February 2020).

Climate Policy Initiative (2019). *Global Landscape of Climate Finance 2019*. London. https://climatepolicyinitiative.org/wp-content/uploads/2019/11/2019-Global-Landscape-of-Climate-Finance.pdf (accessed 27 March 2020).

Climate Transparency (2017). Financing the transition from brown to green: How to track country performance towards low carbon, climate-resilient economies. (ODI and HVGP). Berlin, Germany. www.climate-transparency .org. http://www.climate-transparency.org/wp-content/uploads/2017/12/Financing_the_transition.pdf (accessed 26 March 2020).

Coady, D., Parry, I., Sears, L., et al. (2015). IMF Working Paper. How large are global energy subsidies? Washington D.C. https://www.imf.org/external/pubs/ft/wp/2015/wp15105.pdf (accessed 26 March 2020).

Cochu, A., Glenting, C., Hogg, D., et al. (2016). Study on the potential of green bond finance for resource-efficient investments. European Commission, 1–174.

Cooper, G. (2018). *Banque de France calls for "brown penalising factor."* *Environmental Finance*. https://www.environmental-finance.com/content/news/banque-de-france-calls-for-brown-penalising-factor.html (accessed 16 March 2020).

De Coninck, H., Revi, A., Babiker, M., et al. (2018) An IPCC Special Report on the impacts of global warming of 1.5°C above pre-industrial levels and related global greenhouse gas emission pathways, in the context of strengthening the global response to the threat of climate change. https://www.ipcc.ch/site/

assets/uploads/sites/2/2019/02/SR15_Chapter4_Low_Res.pdf (accessed 26 March 2020).

Deichmann, U., and Zhang, F. (n.d.). *Growing Green. The Economic Benefits of Climate Action.* Washington D.C. http://documents.worldbank.org/curated/en/501061468283462662/pdf/Growing-green-the-economic-benefits-of-climate-action.pdf (accessed 26 March 2020).

De La Gorce, N. (2019). Green Finance: Modest 2018 Growth Masks Strong Market Fundamentals for 2019. https://www.icmagroup.org/assets/documents/Regulatory/Green-Bonds/Public-research-resources/SP-Global2019-01-29Green-Finance-Modest-2018-Growth-Masks-Strong-Market-Fundamentals-For-2019-130219.pdf (accessed 15 February 2020).

Della Croce, R., Kaminker, C., and Stewart, F. (2011). *The Role of Pension Funds in Financing Green Growth Initiatives.* http://www.oecd.org/finance/private-pensions/49016671.pdf (accessed 16 February 2020).

De Perthuis, C. (2019). *Le Tic-tac de l'horloge climatique,* 1st ed. *De Boeck Sup.*

Deschryver, P., and De Mariz, F. (2020). What Future for the Green Bond Market? How Can Policymakers, Companies, and Investors Unlock the Potential of the Green Bond Market? *Journal of Risk and Financial Management* 13(61).

Déséglise, C., and Lopez Freijido, D. (2020). Financing sustainable infrastructure at scale. *Journal of International Affairs* 73(1): 33–48.

Ehlers, T., and Packer, F (2017). Green bond finance and certification. BIS Quarterly Review (September 2017). https://www.bis.org/publ/qtrpdf/r_qt1709h.pdf (accessed 15 February 2020).

ENEL (2019). Enel signs first credit line linked to United Nations sustainable development goals. https://www.enel.com/media/press/d/2019/10/enel-signs-first-credit-line-linked-to-united-nations-sustainable-development-goals (accessed 15 February 2020).

Fabian, N. (2015). Support low-carbon investment. *Nature* 519(7541): 27–29.

Foresight Climate & Energy (2018). New gas infrastructure risks fossil fuel lock in. https://foresightdk.com/new-gas-infrastructure-risks-fossil-fuel-lock/ (accessed 12 March 2020).

G20 (2016). *G20 Green Finance Synthesis Report.* http://unepinquiry.org/wp-content/uploads/2016/09/Synthesis_Report_Full_EN.pdf (18 February 2020).

Harald, F. L., and Clapp, C. (2015). *CICERO Shades of Green. CICERO.* https://www.cicero.oslo.no/en/posts/single/cicero-shades-of-green (accessed 25 March 2020).

Hmiel, B., Petrenko, V. V., Dyonisius, M. N., et al. (2020) Preindustrial 14CH4 indicates greater anthropogenic fossil CH4 emissions. *Nature* 578;10–14 (May 2019).

ICMA (2018). *The Green Bonds Principles: Voluntary Process Guidelines for Issuing Green Bonds. International Capital Market Association.* https://www.icmagroup.org/assets/documents/Regulatory/Green-Bonds/June-2018/Green-Bond-Principles---June-2018-140618-WEB.pdf (accessed 26 October 2019).

IEA (2019a). Energy subsidies: tracking the impact of fossil-fuel subsidies. International Energy Agency. https://www.iea.org/topics/energy-subsidies (accessed 26 March 2020).

IEA (2019b). *The Role of Gas in Today's Energy Transitions.* https://webstore.iea.org/download/direct/2819?fileName=TheRoleofGas.pdf (accessed 2 March 2020).

IRENA (2019) *Global energy transformation: A roadmap to 2050* (2019 edition). https://www.irena.org/publications/2019/Apr/Global-energy-transformation-A-roadmap-to-2050-2019Edition (accessed 29 March 2020).

Lagarde, C. (2019). Letter from the ECB President to Mr Ernest Urtasun. https://www.ecb.europa.eu/pub/pdf/other/ecb.mepletter191122_Urtasun~2dc928d018.en.pdf (accessed 17 February 2020).

Louche, C., Busch, T., Crifo, P., and Marcus, A. (2016). Call for Papers. *Organization & Environment* 29(4): 529–532.

Migliorelli, M., and Dessertine, P. (2019). *The Rise of Green Finance in Europe: Opportunities and Challenges for Issuers, Investors and Marketplaces,* 1st ed. Edited by Palgrave Studies. Cham, Switzerland: Palgrave Macmillan.

Morgan Stanley Research (2017). Behind the Green Bond Boom. Morgan Stanley. https://www.morganstanley.com/ideas/green-bond-boom (accessed 15 February 2020).

MSCI (2017). MSCI Global Climate Index Methodology. https://www.msci.com/eqb/methodology/meth_docs/MSCI_Global_Climate_Index_Methodology_June2017.pdf (accessed 26 March 2020).

MSCI (2019). Bloomberg Barclays MSCI Green Bond Index Consultation. https://www.msci.com/documents/1296102/12275477/Bloomberg+Barclays+MSCI+Green+Bond+Index+Consultation.pdf/e887b067-1513-c94d-4441-e18b39f6170d?t=1561734332189 (accessed 15 February 2020).

Nauman, B. (2019). Investors balk at green bond from group specialising in oil tankers. Financial Times (18 October). https://www.ft.com/content/b1d4201c-f142-11e9-bfa4-b25f11f42901 (accessed 22 March 2020).

OECD (n.i.). *Green Finance and Investment*. Paris. https://www.oecd-ilibrary .org/environment/green-finance-and-investment_24090344 (accessed 17 February 2020).

Paris Action Climat (2020). Natixis met en œuvre son Green Weighting Factor. Paris Action Climat. https://parisactionclimat.paris.fr/fr/natixis-met-en-oeuvre-son-green-weighting-factor (accessed 23 March 2020).

Peake, S., and Ekins, P. (2017). Exploring the financial and investment implications of the Paris Agreement. *Climate Policy* 17(7): 832–852.

Petheram, R. (2019). Beef giant issues controversial Sustainable Transition Bond Framework: Environmental Finance. Environmental Finance. https://www.environmental-finance.com/content/news/beef-giant-issues-controversial-sustainable-transition-bond-framework.html (accessed 15 February 2020).

Polzin, F. (2017). Mobilizing private finance for low-carbon innovation: A systematic review of barriers and solutions. *Renewable and Sustainable Energy Reviews* 77: 525–535.

Rainforest Action Network (2019). Banking on Climate Finance. Fossil fuel Finance Report Card 2019. https://www.banktrack.org/download/banking_on_climate_change_2019_fossil_fuel_finance_report_card/banking_on_climate_change_2019.pdf (accessed 27 March 2020).

Refinitiv (2019). Green Bonds H1 Review. https://www.refinitiv.com/ perspectives/market-insights/tracking-the-growth-of-green-bonds/ (accessed 15 February 2020).

Reichelt, H., and Keenan, C. (2017) Pension Fund Service. http://pubdocs .worldbank.org/en/554231525378003380/publicationpensionfundservice greenbonds201712-rev.pdf (accessed 15 February 2020).

Robinson-Tillett, S. (2019). *Analysis: IPCC warning on meat consumption adds to scrutiny of beef producer Marfrig's $500m "transition bond." Responsible Investor*. https://www.responsible-investor.com/articles/marfrig (accessed 26 March 2020).

Rootzén, J., and Johnsson, F. (2016). Paying the full price of steel: Perspectives on the cost of reducing carbon dioxide emissions from the steel industry. *Energy Policy* 98: 459–469.

Rootzén, J., and Johnsson, F. (2017). Managing the costs of CO_2 abatement in the cement industry. *Climate Policy* 17(6): 781–800.

Shishlov, I., and Morel, R. (2016) Beyond transparency: unlocking the full potential of green bonds. https://www.cbd.int/financial/greenbonds/i4ce-greenbond2016.pdf (accessed 15 February 2020).

Study Group on Environmental Innovation Finance in Japan (2020). Concept Paper on Climate Transition Finance Principles. https://www.meti.go.jp/press/2019/03/20200331002/20200331002-2.pdf (accessed 25 April 2020).

Takatsuki, Y., and Foll, J. (2019). Financing brown to green: Guidelines for Transition Bonds: AXA IM – Real Assets. AXA IM. https://realassets.axa-im.com/content/-/asset_publisher/x7LvZDsY05WX/content/financing-brown-to-green-guidelines-for-transition-bonds/23818 (accessed 15 February 2020).

TEG (2020). Taxonomy: Final report of the Technical Expert Group on Sustainable Finance. https://ec.europa.eu/info/sites/info/files/business_economy_euro/banking_and_finance/documents/200309-sustainable-finance-teg-final-report-taxonomy_en.pdf (accessed 12 March 2020).

TEG (2019). EU taxonomy technical report. https://ec.europa.eu/info/sites/info/files/business_economy_euro/banking_and_finance/documents/190618-sustainable-finance-teg-report-taxonomy_en.pdf (accessed 15 February 2020).

Thomä, J., and Gibhardt, K. (2019). Quantifying the potential impact of a green supporting factor or brown penalty on European banks and lending. *Journal of Financial Regulation and Compliance* 7(3): 380–394.

Thomä, J., and Hilke, A. (2018). The green supporting factor: Quantifying the impact on European banks and green finance. 2 Degrees Investing Initiative. 2018/1. https://2degrees-investing.org/wp-content/uploads/2018/04/The-Green-Supporting-Factor.pdf (accessed 22 April 2020).

Tolliver, C., Keeley, A. R., and Managi, S. (2020). Drivers of green bond market growth: The importance of Nationally Determined Contributions to the Paris Agreement and implications for sustainability. *Journal of Cleaner Production*, 244.

Transition Finance Study Group (2020). Transition Finance Guidance: Interim Report. Tokyo. http://rief-jp.org/wp-content/uploads/Transition-Finance-Interim-Report2.pdf (accessed 25 April 2020).

UNCTAD (2014). *World Investment Report 2014*. New York. https://unctad.org/en/PublicationsLibrary/wir2014_en.pdf (accessed 24 March 2020).

VigeoEiris (2017). Second Party Opinion on the Sustainability of Repsol's Green Bond. https://www.repsol.com/imagenes/global/en/Repsol_GreenBond_Second_Party_Opinion_tcm14-71044.pdf (accessed 15 February 2020).

VigeoEiris (2019). Second party Opinion on the sustainability of Marfig Global Fod's sustainable transition Bond. VigeoEiris. http://www.marfrig.com.br/Arquivos/Second_Party_Opinion__Sustainable_Transition_Bond_Marfrig.pdf (accessed 22 April 2020).

Whiley, A. (2017). An oil & gas bond we knew would come eventually: Repsol: Good on GBPs, not so sure on green credentials: | Climate Bonds Initiative. CBI. https://www.climatebonds.net/2017/05/oil-gas-bond-we-knew-would-come-eventually-repsol-good-gbps-not-so-sure-green-credentials (accessed 26 March 2020).

Working Group Climate Transition Finance (2020). Working Group Climate Transition Finance. *GBP, ICMA and SBP.* https://www.icmagroup.org/assets/documents/Regulatory/Green-Bonds/Climate-Transition-Finance-WG-ToR-FINAL221119.pdf (accessed 12 March 2020).

Yeo, S. (2019). Where climate cash is flowing and why it's not enough. *Nature* 573(7774): 328–331.

Social Impact Bonds: Promises and Results

Maria Basílio, PhD

Abstract

Social impact bonds (SIBs) appeared in the aftermath of the financial crisis as a promising financial instrument to deliver more and better social services. They are the result of public-private partnerships and represent the involvement of the private sector in domains that were once exclusive to governments and third-sector organizations.

Despite SIBs expansion, there is no agreement in the literature about their merits and drawbacks. The empirical evidence regarding their results is limited, which contributes to additional difficulties in reaching conclusions and furthering the debate between advocates and critics of SIBs.

This chapter presents an overview of this new financial instrument, discusses its promises and results, and the role of similar and more recent instruments, such as development impact bonds and environmental impact bonds. Further, the difficulties in implementation are presented and their potential to contribute to the attainment of the Sustainable Development Goals (SDG) is explored.

Keywords

Social Impact Bonds; Public-Private Partnerships; Impact Investing; Pay-for-Success; Sustainable Development Goals; Social Finance

INTRODUCTION

Among the different instruments used for impact investment, social impact bonds (SIBs) are becoming more popular. Impact Investing consists of investments made on a market-structure approach in order to generate a measurable social or environmental impact and simultaneous financial return.

According to OECD (2015), there is a modification in the way social services are being delivered, through several innovative financing mechanisms. Moreover, investments with the specific focus of promoting development have been increasing with social Impact Investing spanning a broad range of sectors, from moderate-income housing, to health care, water and sanitation, and rural development (Simon and Barmeier 2010).

Under the umbrella of Impact Investing, diverse instruments and investment approaches can be considered, including microfinance, cash-on-delivery aid, green bonds, social venture capital, and developmental impact bonds. Nevertheless, SIBs appear to be the most attractive in the Impact Investing industry (Carè and Wendt 2018).

SIBs were introduced in the United Kingdom (UK) in 2010 and have since expanded, mostly in developed countries, from the United States to Europe. They were developed to address systemic and complex issues that led to poor and ineffective services for the most vulnerable and marginalized groups (Dear et al. 2016). SIBs offer a mechanism to channel more funding (i.e. private funds) to solve or at least improve interventions in domains like unemployment, foster care, education, health, and recidivism. Even though they are not seen as the primary source of funding for the delivery of social services, SIBs can offer an important complementary mechanism to public sector and third-sector interventions.

However, the expected benefits obtained from SIBs are far from consensual, and the results are mixed. As argued by Dey and Gibbon (2018, p. 378), "while SIBs can deliver benefits to both public and private sectors in certain circumstances, initial studies suggest that the claims being made about impact bonds in overcoming societal problems may be exaggerated."

The goal of this chapter is to present and demystify SIBs as a relevant financial instrument, not only for Impact Investing but beyond, by describing key concepts, exploring its recent expansion, and considering pros and cons of this innovative financial mechanism, along with two related and more recent extensions—Development Impact Bonds (DIBs) and Environmental Impact Bonds (EIBs)—which may have the potential to become more relevant to attain the Sustainable Development Goals (SDG) given their focus on developing and emerging countries, alongside their social and environmental scope.

SOCIAL IMPACT BONDS: KEY CONCEPTS

Governments' budgets are clearly insufficient to address social issues such as poverty, inequality, unemployment, and other multidimensional problems. This fact provides the rationale to allow for the participation of other types of investors.

Among the different instruments used for impact investment, SIBs were considered very promising. SIBs appeared in 2010 in the United Kingdom in the aftermath of the 2008 financial crisis. This innovative financing instrument became popular as governments were very enthusiastic with the opportunity to deliver better social services to the public without compromising public accounts and, through this solution, overcoming overstretched budgets.

Typical areas for introducing SIBs are education, foster care, unemployment, criminal justice, health, and homelessness, where emphasis is placed on prevention and main benefits accrue to savings to public budgets, compared to using corrective solutions. For instance, in the field of criminal justice, the prevention of recidivism will generate savings in police, courts, and prisons.

A SIB is a result of a public-private partnership (PPP), that is, public entities (at local or state level) contract on a pay-for-success basis with a private-sector intermediary. A relevant group of investors provides upfront funding for the project. After raising the funds from private investors, a service provider contracts with the operator and is provided with the required capital and technical assistance in return. The service provider works closely with the targeted population in order to deliver the required social outcome (Lindenberg and Pöll 2015). The interesting feature is the shift of responsibility from the government to a service provider and the risk of failure to private investors; that is, the government will pay for the outcome only if the intervention has been successful. If the project fails to meet agreed outcomes, investors will take the loss.

The term "bond" used for SIBs could be misleading because this is not a fixed-income security. A SIB is, in essence, a payment by results (PbR) or payment for success contract, and the return is contingent on the performance of the service providers in achieving specified social outcomes. The emphasis is on outcomes rather than outputs,[1] which is very important because it replaces "payment for an activity" with "payment for the achievement of policy objectives" (OECD 2016).

There are four main stakeholders involved in an SIB: the investor, the service provider, the outcome sponsor, and the evaluator. The investor (typically, foundations, high-net-worth individuals, banks, institutional investors, or asset managers) pre-finances the activities of a service provider, meaning that it covers (all or some of) the upfront costs of service provision. The outcome sponsor (normally central or local government bodies) agrees to pay the investor once the agreed outcomes have been achieved. The service provider works with the targeted population, and an independent verifier (evaluator) assesses whether the outcomes are met according to the contractual arrangements of intended outcomes and impacts. There is traditionally a fifth stakeholder, the specialist intermediary, who is responsible for the design of the SIBs project, securing the contract with the sponsors, facilitating investment, and managing the project's delivery (Belt et al. 2017, Fraser et al. 2018b). Figure 14.1 highlights these stakeholders' relationships.

The interest in this new financial instrument is not equally spread among different countries and regions. SIBs appeared mostly in developed countries, with 47 active contracts in the United Kingdom, 26 in the United States, followed by 11 in The Netherlands and 10 in Australia, according to the database from Social Finance. Currently there are 138 active contracts (Table 14.1).[2]

Under the same label of impact bonds and applying the same model, DIBs and EIBs have emerged more recently. DIBs emerged as a way to invest in developing countries and mainly differ from SIBs in that typically private investors are rewarded by donors instead of host country governments. The first DIB was launched in 2015 implemented in India (Rajasthan), with

---

[1] An output is a direct result of an activity, considered the first level of results (more connected to the short run). An outcome is the following level of results, after outputs (mid-term results), while impacts correspond to the last level of results, considered in the long run. Outcomes are harder to attain and measure than outputs.

[2] More details available at https://sibdatabase.socialfinance.org.uk/ (accessed 12 February 2020).

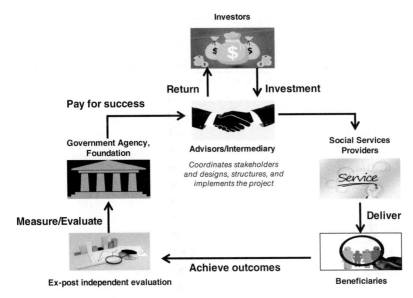

FIGURE 14.1   Social Impact Bonds Model. *Source:* Author, adapted from OECD 2015.[3]

a focus on girls' education, namely, to increase the enrollment retention and learning outcomes for 15,000 marginalized girls in 166 public schools in Rajasthan (Loraque 2018; OECD 2016). EIBs have the goal to finance environmentally sustainable initiatives, namely in water provision, clean energy, parks management, and sustainable agricultural practices. Their development is at a much more nascent stage than SIBS and DIBs (Balboa 2016; Dey and Gibbon 2018). Two of the few EIBs currently under implementation are on urban water management in Washington, DC, and Atlanta. Table 14.1 summarizes current active impact bonds contracts.

The majority of initiatives were developed in Europe and North America. The UK alone accounts for more than one-third of the SIBs that exist worldwide, and the four countries detailed next (UK, the United States, The Netherlands, and Australia), account together for nearly 70%. Under the label of "Other" are remaining countries, such as France, with five projects; Canada and Portugal, with four; and Germany, Israel, Japan, and India with three. The remaining 27 countries in the database have just one or two SIBs projects.

In the UK, projects implementation was policy driven, through a *top-down* approach, with the government leveraging funds from the Big Lottery Fund to create seven investment funds of a total of £191 million from which commissioning authorities could apply for to cover SIBs payments.

---

[3] Images from https://pixabay.com/pt/.

TABLE 14.1   Active Impact Bonds Contracts.[4]

Field of implementation	United Kingdom	United States	The Netherlands	Australia	Other	Total	
Child and family welfare	6	6	0	4	4	20	14.5%
Workforce development	15	2	8	1	18	44	31.9%
Housing/ Homelessness	16	4	0	3	0	23	16.7%
Health	8	3	1	1	9	22	15.9%
Education and early years	1	2	0	0	11	14	10.1%
Criminal justice	1	8	1	1	1	12	8.7%
Poverty and Environment	0	1	1	0	1	3	2.2%
Total	**47**	**26**	**11**	**10**	**44**	**138**	100%
	34.1%	18.8%	8.0%	7.2%	31.9%	100%	

Source: Adapted from sibdatabase.socialfinance.org.uk (accessed on 12 February 2020).

In other countries, such as the United States, Australia, and Canada, the approach developed was *bottom-up,* with projects being promoted by private partners, mainly foundations, charities, and other philanthropic investors (Vecchi and Casalini 2019).

Family and childcare, education, and employment for vulnerable social groups, homelessness among Not in Education, Employment, or Training (NEETs) and recidivism are among the main thematic areas for SIBs implementation (OECD 2015 and 2016). According to Table 14.1, SIBs have been particularly used to tackle social problems in workforce development (31.9%), followed by housing problems (16.7%) and health issues (15.9%).

To date, implemented SIBs average length is 4.4 years and average financial value is €3.2 million. Typically, SIBs are low capital-intensive, because of their focus on services, rather than hard infrastructure. They have been mainly implemented on small-scale initiatives (Vecchi and Casalini 2019).

SIBs do not seem to be appropriate for every project or policy area. Some preconditions for its application include cashable savings outweighing the

---

[4]The other database on SIBS contracts is Instiglio, available on www.instiglio.org/en/projects/.

higher cost of capital and transaction costs occurred in a SIB contract; the availability of clear and measurable outcomes; the possibility of achieving a successful outcome in order to motivate investors to pre-finance and bear the risk; and the existence of contracts that fully specify the responsibilities of each stakeholder (investors, public entities, and service providers), requiring the appropriate legal and political conditions (Belt et al. 2017; Chamaki et al. 2018).

EXPECTED BENEFITS AND REASONS FOR CONCERN

SIBs' main advantages, as pointed out in the literature, are to a certain extent the same as those for PPPs. To private investors, they represent new investment opportunities to market access, which were once exclusive to the public sector and third-sector organizations, thus allowing greater diversification and profitability. In addition, there are increased opportunities to engage in more socially responsible investments and a better prospect to engage with more green/social business practices, with a better alignment with today's social and environment concerns and investors' public image in this regard.

For the public sector side, the advantages are even clearer. First is the leveraging of public funds, allowing projects to proceed even when public funding is unavailable for the whole implementation costs, or when previous interventions have failed or achieved mixed results at best. Second is risk transfer to social/private investors. There is an explicit identification, quantification, and allocation of risks, which is translated into more efficiency in risk management.[5] Third, the use of a performance-based mechanism for payments induces increased monitoring, quality improvements, and potentially more innovative approaches. The focus on outcomes rather than processes also allows for a greater focus on intended impacts and results in efficacy enhancements. Fourth, it brings about more efficiency in the procurement process; that is, the need to prepare outcome-based specifications makes the commissioning authorities focus exactly on what is essential. Lastly, a stronger emphasis on prevention rather than corrective solutions increases performance and reduces costs to public entities.

Summing up, SIBs are seen as a key instrument by which to increase efficiency and effectiveness of public services delivery, increasing value for money and accountability for all intervening parts.

---

[5] By contrast, in traditional procurement, risks tend to be ignored.

SIBs are known to offer a win-win-win mechanism. Private investors win a return on investment, public entities win savings, and society wins a public good (a social service), although this is a questionable statement because several concerns may be pointed (Balboa 2016; Dey and Gibbon 2018). First, financial risks are distributed unevenly. The commissioner must pay the investor only when the project meets predefined performance targets. If targets are missed, investors lose their investment. Service providers, which receive financing upfront, do not have any immediate financial risk (Berndt and Wirth 2018).

In addition, the SIB model can also present disadvantages, some of them related to the general PPP model, namely, the high cost of the procurement process, the length and complexity of negotiations, difficulties in clearly specifying the outcomes to be delivered and its measurement, and potential conflicts of interests among the different stakeholders.

Moreover, there might be other implementation concerns involved, such as client picking, creaming, and parking (OECD 2015), such as using payment by results schemes. Providers may be incentivized to respond to financial pressures and incentives by choosing selected elements to the target groups (picking), and selecting individuals who are more likely to trigger an outcome payment (creaming), while, on the other hand, deprioritizing those individuals unlikely to generate an outcome payment (parking) (Rees et al. 2013). Another challenge is the ability to effectively measure performance, ensuring that project targets are really met, and budget savings are effectively generated (Dermine 2014). In the evaluation phase, attributing results to the intervention (the SIB itself) can become a challenge if measurement practices were not introduced, data was not collected, and the right methodologies were not applied correctly. Without an independent evaluation process, namely, using experimental or post-experimental methods for clear assessment of this instrument's attribution (i.e. allowing comparisons with a control group), evaluation results might be not reliable and/or valid (Fox and Morris 2019; Fraser et al. 2018a).

THE THEORY BEHIND

Fraser et al. (2018b) conducted a systematic review of the literature on SIBs in high-income countries, covering 101 references in academic (38 references) and gray[6] literature (63 references) from 2009 until 2015. The majority of

---

[6]Gray literature: information, or research results produced by organizations, outside the commercial or academic publication and distribution channels, such as technical reports, evaluation reports, projects, working documents, or government documents.

papers analyzed were theoretical, with only one quantitative study found reporting on SIBs outcomes. The authors identified three theoretically distinct narratives about SIBs, *a public sector reform narrative* (associated within the broader scope of New Public Management theories), a *private financial sector narrative* (located within social entrepreneurship theories), and a *cautionary narrative*. The first two narratives dominate the *gray* literature, with a win-win rhetoric; and the cautionary narrative, more sceptical, is more associated with the academic literature.

Additionally, three major themes are explored in Fraser et al. (2018b): values, outcomes, and risk transfer. The first theme analyzes the question of public versus private values; that is, the PPP nature of SIBs influences the traditional values of the public and the private sectors, both in theoretical and ideological terms. Questions were raised on the extent to which public entities should be moved by profitability, or otherwise, if private sector agents should pursue different interests than traditional profit maximization, thus seeking more socially minded returns. The second focuses on outcome measurement in public services, being a more consensual topic for both the proponents and the critics of SIBs. In general, the shift from processes to outcomes measurement is seen as a positive aspect, although technical problems subsist in pricing the outcomes (Joy and Shields 2013). The third theme regards risk transfer, and the practical and ideological consequences that this may have for specific services and policy in general terms (Fraser et al. 2018b). Table 14.2 presents a summary of the SIBs literature veins.

The empirical evidence is still too limited to support any of the narratives, although the cautionary narrative seems to be more plausible. Since the Fraser et al. (2018b) literature review, the scientific debate has continued along the same lines, with arguments being presented *for* and *against* SIBs (Maier et al. 2018). More recently, Broccardo et al. (2019) developed a systematic review of the literature on SIBs, with an exclusive focus on academic contributions. Ninety papers were analyzed, published from January 2010 to June 2019. The authors concluded that the research on SIBs is a new field of interest and the literature is growing at a very high rate, with 21 papers published in 2018 and 17 in just the first semester of 2019. These authors reinforced the idea that the debate on SIBs reveals political and ideological considerations. A large body of the literature is concerned with the financialization of the welfare state, and SIBs represents a boundary shift in terms of the nature of public services, concerns also supported by the cautionary narrative.

TABLE 14.2 Theoretical Lines of SIBs Literature.

Themes/ Narratives	Public sector reform narrative	Private financial sector narrative	Cautionary narrative (miscellaneous)
Competing public and private values	Public sector entities have important shortcomings in terms of service design, delivery, and accountability. Using private sector management techniques and values (financial incentives, market discipline) allow remedying these issues (Liebman 2011; Mulgan et al. 2011).	Blending public and private values will offer private sector investors an opportunity to effect socially worthwhile change through social entrepreneurship whilst simultaneously pursuing commercial interests (Cohen 2011; Liebman 2011; Nicholls and Murdock 2012).	SIBs are one more example of *financialization*. This is a process whereby both macroeconomic and public policymaking is subordinated to financial sector interests. Concerns also arise related to competition and the adoption of performance management schemes, in nonprofit and voluntary sector provider organizations, because this may lead to a diminution or distortion of their social mission (Lake 2015; Warner 2013; Tse and Warner 2018).
Outcome measure-ment	SIBs are an extension of outcomes-based contracting. They introduce greater accountability and transparency between commissioners and service providers.	The expertise of external entities, such as the specialist intermediaries, is crucial to the implementation of SIBs. Such entities bring enhanced data monitoring techniques and skills to allow an independent evaluation, to ensure that outcome payments are earned in a valid and fair way.	The shift from process to outcome measures aligns SIBs to an evidence-based approach. However, outcome measures need to be very carefully defined and calibrated by commissioners, providers, and investors.
Risk transfer	The financial risk is transferred to private/social investors. Public entities do not need to release any public funds unless projects achieve success.	Two distinct views: for some, SIBs are a niche for pro-social investors who will take higher risks and smaller returns; for others, investors desire guaranteed returns or higher yields to compensate for the higher risk.	Risk calculations are likely to be highly context-specific, making it difficult to benefit from the accumulation of past experience in SIBs investing. Some SIBs projects have benefited from government support, suggesting that private sector investors may be more risk-averse, requiring government or philanthropic funds to guarantee or underwrite their investment.

Source: Adapted from Fraser et al. (2018b) and Tan et al. (2019).

SUCCESSES AND FAILURES OF SIBS

Despite their expansion, the expected benefits obtained from SIBs are far from consensual and the few results obtained so far seemed to be mixed. In addition, the majority of SIBs are in the early phase of implementation, so there is still lack of empirical data on its effectiveness (Pandey et al. 2018). The main problems to date are data paucity, due to the small numbers of SIBs completed, and the scarcity of information publicly disclosed on ongoing projects (Broccardo et al. 2019).

Due to the tailored nature of each SIB, specific evaluations need to be conducted for each. As such, it is not yet possible to draw definitive conclusions about the perils and merits of SIBs in general terms (Maier et al. 2018). The existing findings and conclusions are case-specific. Some examples are presented next.

The world's first SIB project—the Peterborough One Service—was launched in 2010, with the aim to reduce recidivism at Peterborough Prison over a five-year term, involving three cohorts of prisoners (OECD 2016). The Peterborough SIB pilot was originally intended to operate until 2017. Support from the One Service[7] was available to cohort members for a period of up to 12 months post-release, and engagement was on a voluntary basis. For the first two cohorts of released prisoners, the program operated in a payment by results basis under the SIB model, but the intervention was modified during the process and the third cohort received support under a fee-for-service arrangement (Disley et al. 2015). There is still a lack of information about the cost-effectiveness of this SIB, but independent evaluations in the Final Process Evaluation Report of this project, performed by Disley et al. (2015), show that stakeholders did not report any major costs or disadvantages. However, transaction costs were high, with 300 hours of legal advice spent by the intermediary alone (Maier et al. 2018).

In addition, mentioned positive effects include, first, the individualized support given to service users. Housing, finance, and employment were the predominant needs identified, and prior research suggests that this kind of support was central to the process of preventing recidivism. Second was the

---

[7]Social Finance (a not-for-profit organization in the UK that partners with the government, the social sector, and the financial community) raised £5 million from trusts and foundations to launch the first-ever SIB to reduce re-offending among short-sentenced offenders leaving Peterborough prison. It funded the One Service, an umbrella organization designed to respond to the complex needs of offenders and to prevent recidivism. Source: https://www.socialfinance.org.uk/peterborough-social-impact-bond.

strong and constructive partnership among all stakeholders, and third, a number of innovations in the program—for instance, flexibility of funding and the resultant adaptations of the service in response to local conditions and service user needs, although these were stated as not necessarily being a result of SIB funding mechanisms (Disley et al. 2015).

In their analysis of the first six years of SIBs implementation, Dear et al. (2016) considered 60 projects launched in 15 countries. Overall, 22/60 projects reported performance data, and from those, 21 had delivered measurable improvements for participants on at least some of their target outcomes. In addition, 12 projects made outcome payments, either to investors or to be recycled into service delivery, depending on the project's financial structure

However, it is necessary to go beyond success stories and also examine failures or unfeasible SIBs, to prevent future poor performance. Chamaki et al. (2018) presented two examples of unsuccessful SIBs. The first was the "Be Active Program," launched in 2009 in Birmingham, UK, with the aim of providing free access to local sports centers during off-peak hours. Although some positive results were achieved (more people were encouraged to participate in physical activity, with improvements in health, decreased rates of smoking, and an increase in subjective well-being), the benefits matched costs and did not materialize in the savings required by project investors. The second SIB project was the US-based Wyman Center's Teen Outreach Program (TOP), a program designed to prevent teenage pregnancy. The program involved 8,000 female students during four years and successfully reduced the incidence of pregnancy during participants' school years. However, the savings generated were not sufficient to cover project costs (Chamaki et al. 2018; Dao 2012).

Further, Edmiston and Nicholls (2018) presented additional critical reflections related to SIBs' adequacy as a funding mechanism to welfare provision. The authors explored four social impact bonds in the UK context: the Essex Multi-Systemic Therapy (MST) SIB, the Merseyside New Horizons SIB, and two London Homelessness SIBs. Through an in-depth study, involving stakeholder documentation analysis, process and impact evaluations, as well as qualitative fieldwork with cross-sectoral stakeholders,[8] they concluded there was very little definitive evidence to suggest that services funded through SIBs led to any relative improvement in social outcomes compared

---

[8] Forty-one qualitative interviews were undertaken with policymakers, public sector commissioners from local and central government, third-sector service providers, social finance intermediaries and entities, social investors, and service users (Edmiston and Nicholls 2018).

to more conventional performance by results commissioning models. In addition, the benefits of service innovation appeared to originate more from the novelty, size, and experimental nature of the contract. However, they concluded that SIBs helped overcome some of the existing limitations of PbR contracting by redistributing the financial risks of nondelivery.

THE ROLE OF IMPACT BONDS IN SUSTAINABLE DEVELOPMENT GOALS

The Sustainable Development Goals (SDGs) were established to achieve a better and more sustainable future and to address problems related to poverty, inequality, climate, environmental degradation, prosperity, and peace and justice.[9] Given that the majority of the challenges are still concentrated in developing countries, DIBs and EIBs are particularly appropriate to deal with these challenges.

But the complexity surrounding the design and implementation of impact bonds may prevent them from fulfilling their potential, particularly in emerging economies. Munoz and Kimmitt (2019) identify four main challenges that are emphasized in these economies. The first is the challenge of ill-defined social issue and target groups. Consequently, it is key to ensure the adequacy between social problems under consideration and the type of social intervention designed to tackle it. The failure to identify, prioritize, and evaluate key social problems and target groups will most likely be translated into higher transaction costs or the unfeasibility of the project. The second problem concerns the political and regulatory framework. As a form of PPP, SIBs rely strongly on contracts between the stakeholders involved. Moreover, the alignment with broader government agendas or areas of national interest may foster or block the SIBs development. Therefore, as a prerequisite, agents should examine the development and adequacy of the regulatory environment and the alignment with political interests. Third is stakeholder involvement; with numerous participants pursuing sometimes opposing objectives, it is critical to develop efforts to bring actors together during design stages enabling contractual agreements, taking into account the degree of commitment and fostering alignment across stakeholders. Last is the suitability of social economy service providers; service providers should have enough accountability capacity: the ability to deliver the defined social outcomes but also to measure the performance and report the results.

---

[9]More details available at https://www.un.org/sustainabledevelopment/sustainable-development-goals/.

Policy agents should consider "the extent to which local social economy can adequately respond to the delivery and measurement of outcomes, ensuring quality and effectiveness" (Munoz and Kimmitt 2019, p. 5).

Despite the difficulties in implementation in emerging economies, SIBs and their variants (EIBs and DIBs) are at the forefront of stimulating social entrepreneurship and solving complex social issues. The next sections present some examples of DIBs and EIBs in different stages of implementation.

DEVELOPMENT IMPACT BONDS

DIBs can be used to increase rigour and transparency in global health interventions (Welburn et al. 2016). For instance, DIBs are being considered in Mozambique (to prevent malaria), South Africa (to prevent and treat HIV), Uganda (to control sleeping sickness), and Brazil (to withdraw chronically sick patients from hospital and offer a better solution).[10] In the case of sleeping sickness, or human African trypanosomiasis (HAT), both its chronic and acute forms are exclusively confined to sub-Saharan Africa, where they affect the poorest of the rural population. Both forms of the disease are fatal if not treated. As such, a DIB is being developed to control this disease. The cash flow profile of the DIB reflects the high upfront financial effort needed, followed by long-term lower cash needs to interrupt transmission and to maintain disease control. Usually, traditional donor grant funding does not advance large amounts of cash, and the DIB allows circumventing this difficulty with private investors providing the capital needed upfront. The risk transfer from donors to social investors improves the probability of DIB financing over direct funding. If the intervention fails, the investors lose their investment. But if it succeeds, international donors repay the social investors with interest (Welburn et al. 2016).

As emphasized above, one important area of DIBs intervention is related to the control of tropical diseases. If a DIB for sleeping sickness can be successfully developed and used to underpin disease control in Uganda, the financing approach could be extended to other geographical areas and to different tropical diseases, where adequate disease control tools already exist but are insufficiently applied (Welburn et al. 2016).

Different DIBs were already developed to tackle a variety of social issues, namely, in education, poverty alleviation, or to increase productivity in the

---

[10]According to the Instiglio database.

agricultural sector, just to cite some examples. Educate Girls, the first DIB, was launched in 2015 to run until June 2018 and was established with the goal of improving the enrollment, retention, and learning outcomes for 15,000 neglected girls in Rajasthan, India. The three-year impact evaluation of the "Educate Girls" program reported that the project surpassed the DIB targets for both learning gains and enrollment (IDinsight 2018).[11] The project was considered a success. It scaled-up its operations, reaching new districts, such as the Khandwa district of Madhya Pradesh with more 1100 villages. It also expanded its partnerships and created new programs through a new Educate Girls' Adolescent Girls Program, with a focus on marginalized adolescent girls in rural India.

More recently, in November 2017, the Village Enterprise DIB was launched, targeting approximately 12,000 households in Western Kenya and Northern Uganda, with the goal of poverty alleviation, through the empowerment of families providing training and skills to develop sustainable microenterprises and simultaneously seed capital (Loraque 2018). In order to accurately measure the DIB results, Innovations for Poverty Action (IPA), an independent, third-party evaluator, completed a large-scale, three-year randomized controlled trial to evaluate the DIB effectiveness. Among the results, in general terms, the evaluator concluded that the microenterprise graduation program led to increased consumption, assets, and income, as well as improvements in nutrition and subjective well-being. Its cost-effectiveness appears high; researchers estimated a full cost recovery within three to four years.[12]

Another DIB project, developed in Peru, was explored by Belt et al. (2017). The goal was to increase productivity and market sales of cocoa and coffee produced by the Asháninka people.[13] This project has shown the opportunities for DIBs development in emerging economies within the agricultural sector. Results highlighted a successful completion of the project, with most targets largely achieved and important lessons for future

---

[11] More specifically, in Outcome 1: Learning Gains, students in treatment villages gained an additional 8,940 ASER learning levels relative to students in control villages, representing 160% of the final target. In Outcome 2: Enrollment, by the end of Year 3, Educate Girls enrolled 92% of all 837 eligible out-of-school girls in treatment villages, representing 116% of the final target for enrollments (IDinsight 2018).

[12] More details available at https://villageenterprise.org/our-impact/rct/.

[13] An indigenous community living in the Peruvian Amazon. The goal was to assist their cooperative—the Kemito Ene *Association*—in establishing a system of coffee and cocoa production that is environmentally sound, and to increase market sales (Belt et al. 2017).

TABLE 14.3 Targets Descriptions and Levels of Achievement.

Outcome indicator	Description	Level of achievement
1	60% of the members of the association increase their supply to the association by at least 20%, thereby improving their income.	75%
2	At least 60% of the members of the association improve their cocoa yield to 600kg/ha or more.	Not achieved
3	The association buys and sells at least 35 tons of cocoa in the last year of the DIB project.	100%
4	At the end of the project, 40 producers have 0.5 ha of newly established coffee plots with leaf rust–resistant varieties.	100%

Source: Adapted from Belt et al. (2017).

contracts. Four outcome indicators were established for the project, with the verification report presenting different levels of achievement (Table 14.3).

Among the lessons gathered from this experience, some have to do with the long preparation time and transaction costs required for designing the impact bond, the need for a clearly defined and easily measurable outcome matrix, the need for timely collection and monitoring of data by project staff, and the overall advantages of this model over conventional development projects and grants.[14]

ENVIRONMENTAL IMPACT BONDS

Concerning EIBs, fewer cases exist to date. EIBs present similar aspects to green bonds: they are used to fund environmentally sustainable projects. But unlike green bonds, EIBs have their financial return of the investment tied directly to the success of the project. Next, we detailed two innovative projects in water management in the United States, DC Water and the Atlanta EIB.

DC Water[15] was the first EIB of the country, implemented in Washington, DC, to fund the construction of a green infrastructure project in the Rock Creek sewerage system, to manage stormwater runoff and improve water quality.

---

[14]More details available on Belt et al. 2017.
[15]Based on information retrieved from https://www.quantifiedventures.com/dc-water and https://www.epa.gov/sites/production/files/2017-04/documents/dc_waters_environ mental_impact_bond_a_first_of_its_kind_final2.pdf.

Box 14.1 Project Summary

Background: Initially intended to solve the problems of many outdated pipes within their combined sewer system, dumping an average of 2.5 million gallons of combined sewer overflow[16] annually into three rivers (including the Rock Creek tributary that ultimately flows into the Chesapeake Bay), DC Water planned a solution using a series of massive underground tunnels. Two main problems were detected: first, the tunnels were underground, "invisible to the customer," which complicates public acceptance of the price of the city's water service. Second, it was very expensive, amounting to USD $2 billion. The opportunity appeared with the design of an EIB that enabled risk to be transferred from government agencies like DC Water to outside investors, minimizing the impact on taxpayer funds. The DC Water EIB was the first use of the Pay for Success model in the water sector and the first to be issued as a tax-exempt municipal bond.

Beneficiaries: Local residents and community organizations

Outcomes: To reduce combined sewer overflows

Indirectly: new green spaces and workforce development

Government Agency: District of Columbia Water and Sewer Authority (DC Water)

Measurement: Volume

Investors: Institutional investors: Goldman Sachs Urban Investment Group and Calvert Foundation

Capital raised: 25 million USD

Issue date: September 2016

Length: 30-year tax-exempt municipal bond with a mandatory tender in year five

Financial Structure: The bonds were issued at a US$25 million face value and an initial 3.43% interest coupon, payable semi-annually, for the first five years. The stated maturity date is October 1, 2046. The mandatory tender date is April 1, 2021.

Payments: At the five-year mandatory tender, there is provision for a USD $3.3 million payment, payable to investors by DC Water or to DC Water by investors, contingent on the relative success or failure of the

(*continued*)

---

[16]This overflow brought bacteria, trash, and heavy metals along with it, contaminating watershed and disturbing the ecosystem.

(continued)

project. Failure to achieve the predefined targets will result in no return on investment, including a total loss of principal (i.e. performance risk to the investor of up to 100%). However, DC Water designed its EIB to share performance risk between itself and investors by reducing DC Water's cost of capital (the interest paid to investors) in the event of flow reduction underperformance and increasing DC Water's cost of capital (the return to investors) in the event of overperforming flow reduction.
    Intermediary: Quantified Ventures

Atlanta's EIB was the first publicly offered EIB, making this financial product accessible to public municipal bond markets. The goal was to finance six green infrastructure projects in the Proctor Creek Watershed to manage stormwater, reduce local flooding, alleviate water quality impacts, increase access to green space, and create local green jobs.

Box 14.2 Project Summary[17]

Background: The neighborhoods around Proctor Creek in Atlanta have been adversely affected by frequent flooding and poor creek water quality. Urbanization pressures combined with increasing rainfall and extreme storm events worsened the existing problems, resulting in a polluted Proctor Creek threatening the health and well-being of nearly 60,000 people.
    In order to finance six green infrastructure projects in Proctor Creek neighbourhoods, namely, combination of bio retention cells in public parks, stormwater bump-outs in the right-of-way, and larger floodplain, wetland, and stream restoration projects, an EIB was developed.
    Beneficiaries: Low-income communities around Proctor Creek
    Outcomes: Flood reduction and improvement of water quality
    Indirectly: local job creation (workforce development) and access to green spaces
    Government Agency: The City of Atlanta's Department of Watershed Management (DWM)

---

[17]Based on information https://www.quantifiedventures.com/atlanta-eib and https://conservationfinancenetwork.org/2019/06/24/atlanta-environmental-impact-bond-breaks-into-public-market.

Measurement: Volume of stormwater captured or detained by green infrastructure, as measured by hydrologic surveys, as the metric for determining payments to bondholders

Investors: Municipal bond investors. The municipal bond was highly rated by S&P (A+) and Moody's (Aa3).

Capital raised: USD $14 million

Issue date: January 2019

Length: 10-year term

Financial Structure: The bonds were backed by Atlanta DWM's Water and Wastewater Enterprise Revenues. To attract investors, a two-tier performance structure was developed. The estimated base interest rate is 3.55%. If the project achieves a "high" performance (probability of 27.7%), investors will receive a performance payment totaling US$1 million resulting, in an estimated 4.67% effective interest rate (above market net interest rate).

Payments: Two scenarios were assumed: a "base" and a "high" performance scenario. If the project captures more stormwater in aggregate than expected ("high performance"), investors will receive a pro rata share of an additional US$1 million payment. This is compensated, however, by a lower "base" rate that is paid on the bond. The rate was designed to be set at a below-market rate, so that when taking into account the respective probabilities of "base" or "high" performance, the overall expected value of the EIB's yield would be similar to that for an otherwise traditional bond, without the performance payment mechanism. This structure allowed DWM to hedge some of the uncertainty around how effective the green infrastructure projects will be at capturing stormwater while offering investors a known floor for their return with potential for upside.[18]

Intermediary: Quantified Ventures

Comparing Atlanta's project to the DC Water, two particular aspects are of note. First, Atlanta's EIB used a simpler two-tier structure (just base rate and upside), while the DC Water EIB used a three-tier structure, allowing the city to recoup some of the EIB's proceeds from investors in case the project underperformed. Second, Atlanta's issued public bonds, offered on an open market (the Atlanta EIB was sold on Neighborly's online platform). By contrast, DC Water EIB used private bonds and sold to specific prearranged investors. This difference highlights the potential to expand EIBs as a tool

---

[18]https://www.quantifiedventures.com/atlanta-eib.

available to finance a wide variety of municipalities' projects (the Atlanta bond was fully subscribed, mostly by mainstream institutional investors).

The next phase was to make EIBs bonds available for retail sales. This idea emerged with the Atlanta's EIB, "allowing any Atlanta resident to invest in their city's green infrastructure if they wished," but it was considered "too challenging."[19]

The cases presented in the last two sections are examples of successful projects that contribute to the SDGs in several dimensions, where the more obvious are Educate Girls (India)—*reduced inequalities* and *quality education*; Village Enterprise (Kenya and Uganda)—*no poverty* and *reduced inequalities*; Asháninka cocoa and coffee case (Peru)—*responsible consumption and production*. EIB projects are linked to the Goals of *clean water and sanitation* and *sustainable cities and communities*. In addition, in the *health* domain, several promising experiences are under way.

There is still a long path ahead, but the rising number of projects launched recently and the several successful stories which are already known encourage the view of impact bonds assuming a more active role to catalyze private resources to much-needed social and environmental interventions in order to attain the SDGs.

CONCLUSION

Official aid flows and philanthropic contributions will not be sufficient to achieve the SDGs. As such, the entire spectrum of Impact Investing and blended finance[20] has an important role in closing the SDG funding gap, with annual needs amounting to USD $2 trillion. Impact investment strategies could bridge the gap between patient capital and venture capital scaling up sustainable development projects (Business and Sustainable Development Commission and Convergence 2017; Carè and Wendt 2018).

Moreover, the recent financial crisis brought additional challenges to public sector budgets. With the escalation of social problems, several governments and third-sector organizations are facing financial problems due to a scarcity of resources. As Dermine (2014) argues, many nonprofit

---

[19]https://conservationfinancenetwork.org/2019/06/24/atlanta-environmental-impact-bond-breaks-into-public-market.

[20]The strategic use of public and/or philanthropic funding to catalyze private sector investment in SDG-related investments in developing countries (Business and Sustainable Development Commission and Convergence 2017).

organizations are struggling to keep their public financing and are currently facing severe problems when trying to launch new programs.

This new context may represent an opportunity for SIBs as an alternative financing mechanism to contribute to the fulfilment of the SDGs. Although seen as controversial instruments, SIBs are still in their infancy, and as such there remains a lot to be seen.

As already mentioned, conclusions are case-specific and linked to the tailored nature of each contract, making it difficult to put together a SIBs database of broad lessons learned. Despite these limitations, further analysis of SIBs projects is needed in order to assess their potential in an informed way. The analysis of their value as a win-win-win instrument, mostly defended by the gray literature, has evolved to a more sceptical and cautious analysis of their merits and drawbacks, mostly due to more recent academic research.

Despite the availability of less complex and less costly options to finance social services, SIBs have particular advantages over traditional approaches, such as their focus on monitoring and measuring social outcomes, their transparency and accountability prospects, combined with the alignment of different interests and objectives of multiple stakeholders involved in the partnership.

At the same time, several challenges persist. The idea of using private resources is appealing, but the need to make outcomes attainable and the accountability pressures may create perverse incentives. Designing contracts to offer segmented or incremental returns could generate the necessary balance between financial revenues and environmental and social processes. In addition, to fully justify the option for impact bonds, SIBs need to be compared more thoroughly to traditional social policy tools that deliver the same sort of services. This can be done by developing a public sector comparator, assessing, for instance, the results against a control group through experimental evaluation methods.

Some of these challenges are common to the entire Impact Investing industry. The market potential of these instruments is limited by different kinds of barriers (Chiappini 2018). First, it is necessary to develop regulation to protect investors, providing transparency and stability, preventing problems of asymmetric information, and avoiding the development of a shadow market. Second, the availability of independent information about social and financial performance of each project is of critical importance. And this is not an easy task given the proliferation of impact metrics covering diverse social areas and the lack of data to support studies about financial performance. Third, the market should evolve and develop to embrace the younger generations that are more willing to invest in projects/products aimed at social impact and sustainability.

For development policy, critical questions are raised (Simon and Barmeier 2010): Are impact bonds an effective new tool for long-term development, and how likely are they to reach the scale necessary to be part of an overall development strategy? Promising results show that SIBs and their variants should be particularly incentivized in developing countries, despite greater challenges in its implementation, as they have the potential to mobilize much-needed private funds to deal with very complex social problems. Impact bonds represent a step, although small, toward the attainment of the SDGs, namely, to end poverty, fight inequality, and stop climate change.

REFERENCES

Balboa, C. M. (2016). Accountability of Environmental Impact Bonds. *Global Environmental Politics* 16:2, 33–41.

Belt, J., Kuleshov, A., and Minneboo, E. (2017). Development Impact Bonds: Learning from the Ash ́aninka Cocoa and Coffee Case in Peru. *Enterprise Development and Microfinance* 28:1–2, 130–144.

Berndt, C., and Wirth, M. (2018). Market, Metrics, Morals: The Social Impact Bond as an Emerging Social Policy Instrument. *Geoforum* 90, 27–35.

Broccardo, E., Mazzuca, M., and Frigotto M. L. (2019). Social Impact Bonds: The Evolution of Research and a Review of the Academic Literature. *Corporate Social Responsibility and Environmental Management.* DOI: 10.1002/csr .1886.

Business and Sustainable Development Commission, and Convergence (2017). The state of blended finance. http://s3.amazonaws.com/aws-bsdc/ BSDC_and_Convergence__The_State_of_Blended_Finance__July_2017.pdf

Carè, R., and Wendt, K. (2018). Investing with impact: An integrated analysis between academics and practitioners. In M. La Torre and M. Calderini (eds.), *Social Impact Investing Beyond the SIB: Evidence from the Market.* London: Palgrave Macmillan.

Chamaki, F. N., Jenkins, G. P., and Hashemi, M. (2018). Social Impact Bonds: Implementation, Evaluation, and Monitoring. *International Journal of Public Administration,* DOI: 10.1080/01900692.2018 .1433206.

Chiappini, H. (2018). Social impact investments beyond social impact bonds: A research and policy agenda. In M. La Torre and M. Calderini (Eds.), *Social*

Impact Investing Beyond the SIB: Evidence from the Market. London: Palgrave Macmillan.

Cohen, R. (2011). Harnessing Social Entrepreneurship and Investment to Bridge the Social Divide. London: EU Conference on the Social Economy.

Dao, V. (2012). Social Impact Bond: Feasibility Analysis of the Wyman Teen Outreach Program (Unpublished doctoral dissertation). University of Chicago.

Dear, A., Helbitz, A., Khare, R., Lotan, R., Newman, J., Gretchen, C. S., and Zaroulis, A. (2016). *Social Impact Bonds: The Early Years.* London: Social Finance.

Dermine, T. (2014). Establishing social impact bonds in Continental Europe. M-RCBG Associate Working Paper Series no. 26, Harvard Kennedy School.

Dey, C., and Gibbon, J. (2018). New Development: Private Finance over Public Good? Questioning the Value of Impact Bonds. *Public Money & Management* 38:5, 375–378. DOI: 10.1080/09540962.2018.1477676.

Disley, E., Giacomantonio, C., Kruithof, K., and Sim, M. (2015). The payment by results Social Impact Bond pilot at HMP Peterborough: Final process evaluation report. Crown copyright. https://www.rand.org/pubs/research_reports/RR1212.html.

Edmiston, D., and Nicholls, A. (2018). Social Impact Bonds: The Role of Private Capital in Outcome-Based Commissioning. *Journal of Social Policy*, 47(1), 57–76. DOI: 10.1017/S0047279417000125.

Fox, C., and Morris, S. (2019). Evaluating Outcome-based Payment Programmes: Challenges for Evidence-based Policy. *Journal of Economic Policy Reform.* DOI: 10.1080/17487870.2019.1575217.

Fraser, A., Tan, S., Kruithof, K., Sim, M., Disley, E., Giacomantonio, C., Lagarde, M., and Mays, N. (2018). *An Evaluation of Social Impact Bonds in Health and Social Care: Final Report.* London: Policy Innovation Research Unit (PIRU).

Fraser, A., Tan, S., Lagarde, M., and Mays, N. (2018). Narratives of Promise, Narratives of Caution: A Review of the Literature on Social Impact Bonds. *Social Policy and Administration* 52 (1): 4–28. DOI: 10.1111/spol.12260.

Gustafsson-Wright, E., and Gardiner, S. (2015). *Policy Recommendations for the Applications of Impact Bonds: A Summary of Lessons Learned from the First Five Years of Experience Worldwide.* Washington, DC: Brookings Institution.

IDinsight (2018). Educate Girls Development Impact Bond Final Evaluation Report 10 June 2018. https://www.educategirls.ngo/pdf/Educate-Girls-DIB-Final-Evaluation-Report_2018-06-10.pdf.

Joy, M., and Shields, J. (2013). Social Impact Bonds: The Next Phase of Third Sector Marketization? *Canadian Journal of Non-profit and Social Economy Research* 4, 39–55.

Lake, R. W. (2015). The Financialization of Urban Policy in the Age of Obama. *Journal of Urban Affairs* 37 (1): 75–78. DOI: 10.1111/juaf.12167.

Liebman, J. B. (2011). *Social Impact Bonds: A Promising New Financing Model to Accelerate Social Innovation and Improve Government Performance.* Boston: Center for American Progress 9.

Lindenberg, N., and Pöll, C. (2015). Financing Global Development: Is Impact Investing an Investment Model with Potential or Just Blowing Smoke? German Development Institute/Deutsches Institut für Entwicklungspolitik (DIE) Briefing Paper 20/2015. https://ssrn.com/abstract=2781951.

Loraque, J. (2018). Development Impact Bonds: Bringing Innovation to Education Development Financing and Delivery. *Childhood Education* 94:4, 64-68, DOI: 10.1080/00094056.2018.1494454.

Maier, F., Barbetta, G. P., and Godina, F. (2018). Paradoxes of Social Impact Bonds. *Social Policy & Administration* 52 (7), 1332–1353. https://doi.org/10.1111/spol.12343.

Mulgan, G., Reeder, N., Aylott, M., and Bo'sher, L. (2011). Social Impact Investment: The Challenge and Opportunity of Social Impact Bonds. Young Foundation. http://www.youngfoundation.org/files/images/11-04-11_Social_Impact_Investment_Paper_2.pdf. *See also* http//www.socialfinance.org.uk.

Munoz, P., and Kimmitt, J. (2019). A Diagnostic Framework for Social Impact Bonds in Emerging Economies. *Journal of Business Venturing Insights* 12. DOI: 10.1016/j.jbvi.2019.e00141.

Nicholls, A., and Murdock, A. (2012). The nature of social innovation. In *Social Innovation*, A. Nicholls and A. Murdock (eds), 1–30. London: Palgrave Macmillan.

OECD (2015). Social Impact Bonds-Promises and Pitfalls, Summary Report of the OECD Experts Seminar, Paris, 15 April 2015, France, http://www.oecd.org/cfe/leed/SIBsExpertSeminar-SummaryReport-FINAL.pdf.

OECD (2016). Social impact bonds: State of play & lessons learnt. Retrieved from https://www.oecd.org/cfe/leed/SIBs-State-Play-Lessons-Final.pdf (accessed 20 November 2017).

Pandey, S., Cordes, J., Pandey, S. K., and Winfrey, W. (2018). Use of Social Impact Bonds to Address Social Problems: Understanding Contractual Risks and Transaction Costs. *Non-profit Management and Leadership* 28. 511–528. DOI: 10.1002/nml.21307.

Rees, J., Whitworth, A., and Carter, E. (2013). Support for all in the UK Work Programme? Differential payments, same old problem. Working Paper 115. Third Sector Research Centre (December).

Simon, J., and Barmeier, J. (2010). More Than Money: Impact Investing for Development. Report. Center for Global Development. https://www.cgdev.org/sites/default/files/1424593_file_More_than_Money_FINAL_web.pdf.

Tan, S., Fraser, A., McHugh, N., and Warner, M. (2019). Widening Perspectives on Social Impact Bonds. *Journal of Economic Policy Reform.* DOI:10.1080/17487870.2019.1568249.

Tse, A. E., and Warner, M. E. (2018). The Razor's Edge: Social Impact Bonds and the Financialization of Early Childhood Services. *Journal of Urban Affairs* 1–17. DOI: 10.1080/07352166.2018.1465347.

Vecchi, V., and Casalini, F. (2019). Is a Social Empowerment of PPP for Infrastructure Delivery Possible? Lessons from Social Impact Bonds. *Annals of Public and Cooperative Economics* 90: 353–369. DOI: 10.1111/apce.12230.

Warner, M. E. (2013). Private Finance for Public Goods: Social Impact Bonds. *Journal of Economic Policy Reform* 16(4): 303–319. DOI: 10.1080/17487870.2013.835727.

Welburn, S. C., Bardosh, K. L., and Coleman, P. G. (2016). Novel Financing Model for Neglected Tropical Diseases: Development Impact Bonds Applied to Sleeping Sickness and Rabies Control. *PLoS* Neglected Tropical Diseases. DOI: 10.1371/journal.pntd.0005000.

Climate and Money: Dealing with "Impact Washing" and a Case for Climate Impact Bonds

Jyotsna Puri, PhD, Aemal Khan, MA, and Solomon Asfaw, PhD

Abstract

Techniques for robustly measuring impact have remained rudimentary and are not employed frequently or systematically enough in the Impact Investing sector, including in impact bonds. The first challenge is the wide chasm of language, concepts, and the different worlds of investors and practitioners, who apply and develop impact instruments on the one hand, and evaluators or impact assessment professionals who design and implement measurement and reporting systems on the other. A second challenge is to identify a balance between the convergence of approaches and standards in evaluation, and continued innovation in the financial sector. This tension is felt intensely in impact measurement. Robust and credible impact measurement requires coordination, co-building, and co-ownership between the Impact Investing sector and the measurement and evaluation communities. Addressing these challenges can help mitigate the underlying risks of "impact washing" and close the transparency and accountability gaps. The illustrative case of climate impact bonds (CIBs) demonstrates a potentially innovative way in which organizations can structure contracts to leverage finance while also providing incentives for rigorous measurement and climate-related outcomes. CIB's advantages relate to the shift of accountability from "outputs" toward "impacts" (in both private and public sectors), the redistribution of risk away from impact funders, and the fostering of further innovation. However, CIB's risks and limitations also need to be carefully considered, such as the transaction costs involved in establishing CIBs, logistical difficulties of coordinating multiple stakeholders, search costs, contract negotiation costs, and those concerning monitoring and evaluating impacts.

Keywords

Impact Investing; Climate Change; Climate Action; Climate Impact Bonds; Impact Measurement; Sustainable Development Goals; Impact Washing

INTRODUCTION

Climate change is now affecting every country on every continent. It is disrupting national economies and affecting lives, negatively impacting people, communities, and countries, and this will increase in the coming years, decades, and centuries. People are experiencing significant impacts of climate change, which include changing weather patterns, rising sea level, and more extreme weather events. Greenhouse gas emissions from human activities are driving climate change and will continue to rise. Without action, the world's average surface temperature is projected to rise over the twenty-first century and is likely to surpass 3 degrees Celsius ($+3°C$, or $5.4°F$) this century (IPCC 2018). The poorest and most vulnerable people are being affected the most. To address climate change, countries adopted the Paris Agreement at the COP21 in Paris in 2015. In the agreement, all countries agreed to work to limit global temperature rise to well below 2 degrees Celsius ($+2°C$, or $3.6°F$), and given the grave risks, to strive for 1.5 degrees Celsius ($+1.5°C$, or $2.7°F$). Implementation of the Paris Agreement is essential for the achievement of the Sustainable Development Goals (SDGs) and provides a roadmap for climate actions that will reduce emissions and build climate resilience.

Responding to climate change, however, requires collective action from public and private sector actors. Public finance, including municipal bonds and multilateral climate funds, can meet only a fraction of the total needs for climate finance, and the trillions needed to pursue mitigation and adaptation. If climate finance is to reach the scale required to mitigate and adapt to climate change adequately, then public funding must be used in catalytic ways to mobilize investors across all asset classes.

About USD $440 billion of climate-oriented capital is still required each year until 2030 to meet the climate adaptation and mitigation needs of developing countries (UNEP 2018).[1] In 2018, the total global long-term bond market issuances summed to USD $17 trillion,[2] while global equity issuances totaled USD $560 billion. Green-bond issuances in 2018 totaled USD $167 billion globally,[3] not yet at the scale of the USD $5 trillion needed annually. Clearly, climate change will require significant additional resources from the private sector in the form of business-as-usual investments into myriad subsectors that include not just clean energy but also adaptation and resilience initiatives across all sectors.

One route for galvanizing additional resources from the private sector is Impact Investing. According to the Asian Development Bank's (ADB) estimate, there is approximately USD $23 trillion currently available that needs to be leveraged and deployed in Impact Investing (ADB 2019). Arguably, Impact Investments can provide not just financial resources, but also the necessary frameworks to address and achieve the objectives of the SDGs and the Paris Agreement (GIIN 2016).

As one of the largest global climate funds and as the operating financial entity of the United Nations Framework Convention on Climate Change (UNFCCC), the Green Climate Fund (GCF) has an explicit private sector focus related to climate finance. The Private Sector Facility (PSF) of the GCF is mandated according to the Governing Instrument[4] to "directly and indirectly finance private sector climate change activities at the national, regional, and international levels" (UNFCCC 2010). Within this mandate, the PSF has the ability to support investment through a flexible suite

---

[1]For more information, see https://unepdtu.org/wp-content/uploads/2019/04/agr-final-version-2018.pdf.

[2]For more information, see https://www.sifma.org/resources/research/fact-book/.

[3]For more information, see https://www.climatebonds.net/resources/reports/2018-green-bond-market-highlights.

[4]UNFCCC COP Decision 1/CP.16/Add.1, creating the GCF.

of financial instruments, including grants, debt, equity, guarantees, and (reimbursable) grants.[5]

Within the GCF and beyond, there is a growing recognition that public institutions face several challenges when leveraging resources for Impact Investing. Specifically, there is a lack of rigor in the measurement of impact in Impact Investing. This can lead to an accountability and transparency gap, and potential instances of "impact washing." Impact washing is defined as the tendency of impact investments to claim direct social and environmental impacts when, in reality, these outcomes are not occurring as a direct *consequence of the investment*.

There are many reasons why measurement methods in the Impact Investing industry have not yet dealt with this problem. One possible reason is that frequently the verifiers of impact are the bond issuers themselves, creating an obvious but frequently ignored conflict of interest. These have led Impact Investing intermediaries to draw up "performance contracts" or "output contracts" that measure activities rather than true social or development outcomes and impacts. All of this, unfortunately, increases the likelihood of impact washing.

One way to mitigate the "impact washing" concern is to use theory-based impact evaluation approaches[6] that allow establishment of credible logical impact pathways and consider end results (impacts). Using theory-based impact evaluation methods requires (constructing) counterfactual frameworks, identifying measurable metrics, and need an overall evidence-based communication of impact. This approach can help to measure the causal attributable impact of an investment. It could gear Impact Investing toward gathering more momentum, by *credibly* measuring and reporting evidence-based impact and avoiding occurrences of "impact washing" (e.g. Verrinder et al. 2018).

This chapter is divided into four main sections. The next section presents an overview of challenges in Impact Investing–related measurement. The following section describes the architecture of a hypothetical climate impact bond (CIB) that illustrates how contracts may be constructed to become incentive-compatible with achieving impact and credible measurement. The last section discusses possible next steps and concludes with recommendations for further work and opportunities to improve the Impact Investing ecosystem and industry.

---

[5]The PSF has 17 multi-instrument projects with a grant component (the largest grant component equaling USD $34 million), and one is a reimbursable grant-only project.
[6]See, for instance, Mayne (2015) and Riché (2012).

IMPACT INVESTING: DEFINITION AND MEASUREMENT CHALLENGES

Investments that also deliver a positive net impact on people or planet have existed for decades, and continue to scale up globally. Investments in microfinance, low-income housing, and green technology have become widespread. More than a decade ago, these practices began to be summarized under a common term called "Impact Investment" (Bugg-Levine and Emerson 2011).[7],[8]

In 2009, the Monitor Institute articulated the first definition of Impact Investing as those that "actively place capital in businesses and funds that generate social or environmental goods and at least return the nominal principal to the investor" (Monitor Institute 2009, p. 5). In this definition, Impact Investing went past the relatively modest goalpost of avoiding negative outcomes or negative investment screens, and instead spotlighted investments that created positive impacts (Brest et al. 2013). In subsequent years, numerous organizations, such as Credit Suisse, the World Economic Forum (WEF), the Boston Consulting Group (BCG), J. P. Morgan, and networks such as the Global Impact Investing Network (GIIN) used this definition (Vecchi et al. 2017). Appendix 15.1 offers a benchmark of the most relevant definitions.

At the center of the goal of making an impact investment lies the investor's intention to seek environmental, social, and governance returns. However, simultaneously, impact investment is *expected to deliver a financial return,* ranging from a minimum that repays the capital provided, to a more traditional market-rate return on capital (GIIN 2016). Consequently, an essential feature for an impact investor is his or her ability to *measure impact,* that is, to calculate empirically, and demonstrate beyond doubt, that the investment achieved the intended objectives with respect to its social and environmental gains (which in most cases cannot be easily monetized) (GIIN 2016).[9] Therefore, impact *measurement* takes on a salient role in the

---

[7]According to the Rockefeller Foundation, the term was first used at a conference held by the organization in 2007. See https://www:rockefellerfoundation.org/our-work/initiatives/innovative-finance.

[8]HIP (Human Impact + Profit) Investor Inc. was incorporated on December 6, 2006, and the first "HIP Scorecard" was published in *Fast Company* in April 2007.

[9]Note, however, that qualitative performance indicators are widely used in Impact Investing and are more common than quantitative metrics. Although these are useful, it is widely acknowledged that qualitative indicators are much harder to compare and aggregate across industries, therefore not providing the sort of metrics needed for benchmarking investments (Climate Bonds Initiative 2019).

Impact Investing industry precisely because, unlike financial returns, in the absence of rigorous measurement, there is no objective *numeraire*[10] to measure social and environmental (and climate) returns.[11]

Over time, Impact Investing has also become widely recognized as an instrument capable of bringing together a government or a multilateral organization's overarching interest in realizing social goals or public goods and its capacity to bear risks (see, for example, Mazzucato 2018), into coordinated cooperation with the private sector's ability to leverage resources, construct incentive-compatible contracts, and its interest in returns on investment. Within this broad group of investments exist a range of different terminologies and investment types, such as "sustainable investing," "ethical investing," "community development finance," and others. A large part of the rise of these strategies is due to public pressure and a concomitant rise of "citizen governance" (Box 1998).

Persistent Challenges to Impact Measurement and "Impact Washing"

As the volume of capital and activity in the Impact Investing sector has grown over the years, discussions about the significance of social and environmental impact measurement have accelerated (Rockefeller Foundation 2012). There is extensive consensus that one of the key challenges in Impact Investing is the unclear and varied impact measurement standards across the industry (GIIN 2016 and 2017; Godsall and Sanghvi 2016) and that current methodologies for measuring impact in Impact Investing can be improved.[12] Karim and Jackson (2012) argue that "while the Impact Investing industry is still very nascent and is more than ten years old, measurement methodologies are not well developed and remain fraught with various methodological and implementation difficulties" (p. 5).

One of the critical challenges that have been underscored in this sector is the unclear impact measurement standards of the industry (GIIN 2016

---

[10]Numeraire is a basic standard by which value is computed. It is an economic term of French origin, which acts as a benchmark in comparing the value of similar products or financial instruments.

[11]For more on Impact Investing industry terms and definitions, see Chapter 1, "Impact Investing: Innovation or Rebranding?" by Haifa Ben Abid.

[12]Throughout 2016, the Rockefeller Foundation facilitated various discussions and meetings to exchange and cross-pollinate ideas among evaluation practitioners and investors. These discussions affirmed the need for robust evidence of social impact.

and 2017). Godsall and Sanghvi (2016) highlight that most impact investment funds select and borrow metrics and key performance indicators (KPIs) from different frameworks. This makes it difficult for asset managers because there is no single source from where they can draw indicators and measurement guidance that covers all aspects of impact. Godsall and Sanghvi (2016) also argue for the need to build up a uniform approach to impact measurement to empower investment funds.

There has been an effort made by the GIIN to formalize the quantitative metrics of the IRIS[13]+ for measuring, managing, and optimizing impact (GIIN 2019). However, there is an agreement that there is room for improving the current impact measurement methodologies in Impact Investing. Still, challenges remain as to the ability to measure impact credibly in the Impact Investing industry and the conceptual understanding of impact measurement training. An insufficient collaboration between impact investors and the evaluation community—knowledgeable about impact measurement—has persisted for decades.

According to Clifford et al. (2013, p. 35), impact measurement corresponds to "changes (outcomes) intentionally achieved in the lives of beneficiaries as a result of services and products, delivered by an organization, for which the beneficiary does not give full economic value." While there is no fundamental understanding until now on social impact measurement (European Union and OECD 2015), impact measurement is referred to as the quantified environmental, economic, and social changes that have been caused and can be attributed to impact investments. In this definition, two things are underscored. First, that any measurement method must focus on a *change* caused by the investment where the change is the long-term "impact" or nearer-term "outcomes," or in some cases it may just be the "output" in special cases. Second, the change must be *caused* by the investment; in other words, the change should be attributable to the investment (Gertler et al. 2016). It should be a change that would *not have occurred otherwise* (in the absence of the investment), and it should be a positive change that is social, environmental, or governance-related. This means that the investment should make it very clear at the beginning what change it is aiming to bring about.

So far, the Impact Investing industry has shown a glaring gap in standardization of social impact measurement methods or definitions (European Union and OECD 2015). This gap is widened by the fact that the definition of "impact" in Impact Investing is still a fuzzy concept and has not been

---

[13] IRIS stands for Impact Reporting and Investment Standards.

standardized. Indeed, theoretical and conceptual definitions of impact vary greatly among different stakeholder groups (Maas and Liket 2011). Some stakeholders treat impact as the direct change that has occurred due to activities (traditionally called "outputs," the first line of effects stemming from activities in a typical intervention logical framework).

For example, an impact investor may target investments in solar energy lamps to enable students to study for extended periods of time. Typically, traditional investors will set targets (and report) on the number of solar lights sold (outputs). Reporting will typically also include a few anecdotal stories of how children perform during the exam because of clean air. But what impact investors should care about is how many children study for longer hours at night and improved learning outcomes, compared to *not* having the solar lighting investment. Final outcomes from the investment will be reflected in better school grades, and long-term impacts include employment and higher salaries due to better-educated students. This difference, between what is typically measured and what impact investors should actually measure, is the difference between outputs and *attributable* outcomes/impacts (ultimate effects that occur solely due to the implementation of the investment). Unfortunately, in the Impact Investing sector, there are currently large incentives to assess only activities or outputs of investments, rather than the more useful (and impactful) change at the outcome or impact level.

A large number of existing definitions, along with lack of harmonized and evidence-based methods for impact measurement, have led to accountability and transparency gaps, and potentially to "impact washing." Impact washing occurs for several reasons. First, there is a lack of communication between the Impact Investing industry and the evaluation and measurement communities, which is compounded by the absence of a common language. Second, robust impact measurement is undermined by perverse incentives in the Impact Investing industry, which reward investors that "dumb down" or otherwise diminish what impact means, what impacts must be tracked, and how impact should be measured. In many instances, it is also a failure on the side of measurement professionals to recognize these sorts of incentives. So in many cases, measured "impact" is usually quantifying activities undertaken by the firm (e.g. number of meetings) or, at the most, outputs delivered by those activities. These are much easier and cheaper to understand, measure, and report.

Overall, this absence of credible and useful measurement is related to the lack of a clear understanding of what "impact" truly means, the implementation costs of sophisticated measurement methods (such as those establishing causality)—which are perceived to be high or even prohibitive for smaller companies—and the commonly found investor's desire not to overload their teams by having to account for more difficult-to-measure nonfinancial impacts. However, measurement ideally should not only be about measuring at baseline and end line; rather, it should be about understanding what would have happened without the investment (the so-called counterfactual). This requires applying counterfactual methods, which include experimental and quasi-experimental methodologies. Perceptions of high costs in impact measurement occur because sophisticated methods are usually required for measuring causal change that is otherwise often confounded by many biases (such as selection, endogeneity, and omitted variable bias). However, today there are a variety of tools and data to mitigate these costs (including geographic information systems and big, high-frequency data) that may be used for rigorous impact measurement while keeping costs low. The higher cost of these sorts of impact measurements (where impact is defined as a longer-term effect) puts additional financial pressure on investors to keep measurement "simple" and is one of the underlying reasons why Impact Investing has been slow to scale up. All of these reasons have contributed to methodologies and processes not being adequately adapted to the realities and unique constraints of the Impact Investing industry.

SOCIAL IMPACT BONDS

Social impact bonds (SIBs) have been getting a great deal of attention. SIBs are innovative in that they bring together a variety of actors to leverage additional resources for social/development causes. SIBs are briefly discussed here since the idea of a climate impact bond (discussed in the next section) borrows extensively from the SIB framework.

A SIB[14] is a financing tool in which governments or commissioners agree with social service providers (e.g. social enterprises or nonprofit organizations) and investors to pay for delivering predefined social outcomes (Social Finance 2011, OECD 2015). Governments or commissioners then collaborate with investors (as the investment firms are also the entities issuing the bonds). Typically, investors belong to the private sector, but they can also be from philanthropic foundations.

Funds raised through bonds are used to cover the operating costs of service providers. In turn, service providers agree to implement the investment project and deliver a set of pre-agreed measurable outcomes. Essentially, SIBs

---

[14]See Chapter 14, "Social Impact Bonds: Promises and Results," by Maria Basilio.

act as performance-based contracts on future social outcomes. If intended outcomes are achieved, the commissioner or government pays the bond's issuer or investors. SIBs are also referred to as Payments-for-Success (P4S) bonds in the United States and Pay-for-Benefits (P4B) bonds in Australia (OECD 2015; Gustafsson-Wright et al. 2015).

SIBs are useful because, whereas governments are typically resource-constrained to support public and social services, governments are more likely to have a smaller amount of capital necessary to leverage private investment to finance such services. Investors are rewarded if suppliers meet agreed-upon outcomes. However, they lose all or part of their investment if the expected results are not achieved. On the face of it, SIBs may appear to be a win-win for everyone involved if outcomes are achieved (Michael et al. 2018). Since SIBs are still nascent in terms of coverage and scale, it is too soon to discuss the overall performance of SIBs and their success rates.

Clearly, SIBs—and a similar iteration of them, development impact bonds (DIBs)—have the advantage of leveraging the private sector and other resources into otherwise constrained areas. Additionally, they are outcome-oriented, and they create concrete financial incentives for achieving social or development outcomes. Nonetheless, their use has remained nascent for a few reasons, chiefly that most impact investors expect market rates of return, while most commissioners or governments do not expect to pay high financial returns, even if a risk would imply that financial rate of return. On the other hand, these financial returns are usually guaranteed (if outcomes are achieved), and typically the risk of project failure is low. Another reason is that SIBs or DIBs have not been used at scale is that they typically involve multi-actor contracts and require at least three to four separate contracts to be signed and executed. This leads to high transaction costs for each SIB or DIB, which are often not commensurate with the small scale of most of the SIBs that have been issued thus far. Additionally, SIBs tend to originate and be planned outside of developing countries. So far, the trend has been that the Global North supports these bonds that are being used in the Global South. Any profits and returns, therefore, go to agencies and investors in the Global North.

THE CASE FOR CLIMATE IMPACT BONDS: A HYPOTHETICAL EXAMPLE

In this section, an example of a climate-resilient investment is developed to illustrate the possibilities and the steps involved in setting up a CIB. The case of the structuring of a CIB is illustrated using hypothetical investment.

Climate Impact Bonds: A Brief Introduction

A CIB is a form of financing that aims to achieve climate-related outcomes or results in which the investor pays for climate-related outcomes. The investor provides upfront funding to a service provider or implementer, who implements the project.

CIBs use some of the same structural constructs of SIBs, but they differ in significant ways. CIBs focus more manifestly on climate-related outcomes and use rigorous measurement systems. They also deal with the challenges of scaling up witnessed in SIBs. Further, a CIB addresses the key accountability gap present in most impact bonds because it includes incentives and clauses for implementing rigorous and transparent measurement systems.

CIBs are better suited to achieve scale because they guarantee the return of principal to investors, while also including an incentive clause for service providers to ensure a higher probability of success in achieving impact outcomes, and as such, they facilitate greater expected gains (or savings).

Background of the Hypothetical CIB

The hypothetical CIB shown below for the purpose of this exercise borrows some of its structural constructs from SIBs.

This hypothetical project is implemented in country Z with the objective of developing a CIB. Consider the name of this illustrative project as "Strengthening Climate Resilience of Agricultural Livelihoods in Agro-Ecological Regions of Country Z." This project provides support to the government of country Z to strengthen and increase resilience to climate change, particularly related to climate risks faced by vulnerable smallholder farmers living in two different regions of the country.

Country Z Agro-Ecological Regions I and II are expected to encounter increased rainfall-related uncertainty and consequent drought incidence, which is expected to slow development and put the lives of those in agriculture-dependent households at risk. To mitigate these climate change–induced challenges and to increase the adaptability of its smallholder farmers, the hypothetical investment project aims to promote viable climate-resilient value chains that will benefit vulnerable smallholder farmers, with a focus on building the resilience and adaptive capacity of women.

Table 15.1 displays the summary of the major components of the climate resilience project, which includes the intervention description, project structure, key actors, and planned outcome metrics of the CIB.

TABLE 15.1   Summary of "Climate Resilience of Agricultural Livelihoods in Agro-Ecological Regions of Country Z."

Country: Z	Duration: 7 years

Intervention description: Capitalize on opportunities to strengthen and promote viable climate-resilient value chains relating to smallholder agriculture in the target regions, specifically targeting value chains that are gender-sensitive and provide viable economic opportunities for women.

Contract signed	1 March 2018
Project completion	12 October 2025
Overall bond principal	USD $60 million
Investor	Private sector
Downside risk taker	GCF, Green Climate Fund
Service provider	Hypothetical International Organization (HIO
Implementors/Executors	Ministry of Agriculture (MOA), Water Management Authority (WAMA), Z Meteorological Department (ZMD), the Food and Agricultural Organization (FAO), and the World Food Program (WFP)
Beneficiaries	Rural smallholder farmers in Argo-Ecological Regions I and II

Planned outcomes and metrics

1. Increase the capacity of smallholder farmers to plan for climate risks. **Metric**: By the end of year 7 is for 75% of farmers to have at least a 25% increase in their income.
2. More resilient agricultural production and lifestyle diversification. **Metric**: By the end of year 7, 80% of farmers have agricultural productivity that shows a reduction in the variability by 1 standard deviation (SD), or 68%, from the baseline.

Source: Authors.

In this hypothetical example, there are various stakeholders involved: the government of country Z, the GCF, the private sector, and a third-party verifier (independent evaluator). The service provider is a hypothetical international organization (HIO), and implementers are hypothetically the Ministry of Agriculture (MOA), Water Management Authority (WAMA), Z Meteorological Department (ZMD), the Food and Agricultural Organization (FAO), and the World Food Program (WFP).

TABLE 15.2 Stakeholders Involved in the Creating of a CIB for the Hypothetical Project.

Role	Stakeholders
Outcome funder	Ministry of Planning and National Development
Investor	Private sector
Downside risk taker	GCF: Global Climate Fund
Service provider	HIO
Implementor/Executor	Ministry of Agriculture
Third-party verifier	Third-Party Independent Evaluator
Beneficiaries	Rural smallholder farmers

Source: Authors.

Fundamentally, this structure is about shifting risk onto the seller, rather than the buyer, of outcomes. The purpose of this redistribution of risk is to reorganize stakeholder incentives in such a way that intervention becomes an attractive proposition, prompting stakeholders to fund an intervention that would otherwise not be funded. A CIB has the potential to bring together experts in the agricultural, rural livelihood, and climate sectors, while also leveraging private sector resources. Table 15.2 shows the six primary actors or agents involved in developing the CIB and their roles.

The structure of this hypothetical CIB is dependent on four contracts:

The **first contract** is between the private sector investor (payer) and HIO (the service provider). This is a grant agreement that outlines payment schedules predicated on verifiable outcomes.

The **second contract** is between the GCF and the private sector investor. This is a contract that indicates that GCF will provide downside risk protection (unfunded) for the private sector investor.

The **third contract** is between the service provider (HIO) and the implementor (MOA). In this contract, HIO covers its engagement with the MOA with a contribution agreement conditioned on the delivery of all the activities.

The **fourth contract** is between the payer (private sector) and the independent evaluator.

The following steps comprise setting up the key components of a CIB structuring.

In the **first step**, a private sector investor or payer draws up a contract with a service provider (in this example, HIO) to pay USD $60 million if HIO verifiably achieves key resilience-related results. As the risk-taker, the private sector may decide to provide a particular share of the overall contracted amount (say 15%) to HIO as an upfront payment to cover for transaction and preparation costs. This is upfront working capital. In the contract, the private sector and HIO would agree upon a set of achievable outcomes over the seven years, which, in turn, would be measured and verified by an independent verifier (e.g. an impact evaluator). The private sector investor would engage the service provider to come up with a framework and oversee the implementation (ideally, they might do this themselves or ask a trusted entity to provide the service).

The payment schedule agreed upon by a private sector and HIO would recognize the additional risk that HIO is taking, and would compensate HIO for this risk while recognizing that HIO would also be compensated for the cost of capital. A possible payment mechanism for the project is depicted in Table 15.3.

The **financing structure** of the CIB includes the resources required from the private sector, to pay the upfront working capital to the HIO (a service provider in this CIB), and the resources from the service provider to the executor (MOA) on the achievement of the outcomes. If the MOA achieves all of the outcomes, at or beyond the agreed quantitative targets, the revenue generated as a result of project interventions will also be used to contribute to farmer and water user organizations for operations and maintenance (O&M).

Risk-adjusted payments (column C of Table 15.3) are made on the principal from payer to service provider if annual targeted outcomes are verifiably achieved.[15] If verifiable impacts (column B) are not met, then the payment (column five) is done according to what is stated, 25% during the first year, 10% in the second year, 5% in the third year, and so on. According to this schedule, the service provider bears the risk: if outcomes are not met, 70% of the principal is guaranteed[16] (see column E of Table 15.3). If the program achieves or goes beyond the minimum target, interest rates vary (see column D). There is an in-built incentive for the service provider (HIO) to deliver on the intended outcomes of the investment because returns will be higher

---

[15]The figures in Table 15.3 are all hypothetical.

[16]This corresponds to the payment schedule in case conditions are not met for any of the seven years; then as stated in column E: 25% in year 1, plus 10% in year 2, plus 5% each of years 3 through 6, plus 15% in year 7, equaling 70% overall for failing to meet the targets.

TABLE 15.3 Proposed CIB Payment Schedule.

Timeline	Verifiable impact: Share of the farmers whose income growth is at least 25%	Risk-adjusted payments (%)[17]	Principal payment per year (in %) conditional on the achievement of the outcomes (indicated in column B)	Additional conditions if minimal project outcomes not achieved
Column A	Column B	Column C	Column D	Column E
Year 1	No target yet	No payment	25%	25%
Year 2	No target yet	No payment	10%	10%
Year 3	40% or more	10%	10%	If less than 40%,[18] then 5% of the principal
Year 4	50% or more	12%	10%	If less than 50%, then 5% of the overall principal
Year 5	60% or more	16%	10%	If less than 60%, then 5% of the overall principal
Year 6	65% or more	18%	10%	If less than 65%, then 5% of the overall principal
Year 7	75% or more	20%	25%	If less than 75%, then 15% of the overall principal
Total Payout		Up to 76% if successful in all years	100%	

Source: Authors.

[17] Please note that the risk-adjusted payments are additional to the principal payment, and do not have to add up to 100%, unlike column D.

[18] Verifiable impact for year three, column B of Table 15.3.

compared to not achieving any. In particular, the investor or payer will pay a 10% return on investment if the service provider can prove that it was able to improve the income of at least 40% of the smallholder farmers by 25% by year 3, as a consequence of the investment (see Table 15.3). If the service provider can prove that 75% of the targeted population enjoyed a 25% increase in income in the seventh year because of the investment, then the investor will pay additional 20% return over the full principal (i.e. in addition to the remaining payment of the principal in the seventh year).

In the **second step**, GCF could provide downside risk protection (unfunded) for the private sector investor. In return for GCF providing downside risk protection, the private sector investor can pay a premium (perhaps a share of the interest that they would receive on the bond). Also, the private sector investor can equally share the upside with GCF (excess proceeds shared with the investor). In the instance where the outcomes are not achieved, GCF would make the private sector investor whole for the principal amount.

In the **third step**, HIO as the service provider would work with the implementor/executor (in this case, the MOA or the Ministry of Finance [MOF] in country Z) to build the mechanisms to achieve measurable climate resilience outcomes of the beneficiaries, a group of smallholder farmers in the two agro-ecological zones of country Z. By so doing, it would refer to the contract that the private sector and HIO have signed and recognize that there are primary and secondary climate-resilience related outcomes that will need to be achieved during the duration of the investment.

In the **fourth step**, HIO and the MOA of country Z would then bring in local and international experts to develop and design the investment. Implementation would be left to the government of country Z who would be free to bring in local implementors, as well as course-correct depending on changes in contexts.

In the **fifth step**, the external third-party verifier would set up the results framework and act as the independent verifier. At the beginning of the investment development process, an independent third-party evaluator sets up the measurement systems required for verifying the overall effects caused by the investment, so that they can provide credible and verifiable proof of whether the investment caused the changes expected by the investor or payer. In so doing, the evaluator builds a predefined protocol for measuring causal changes.

In the **sixth step**, the private sector would make subsequent payments to HIO based on the risk-adjusted schedule that they would have agreed upon (Table 15.3). The upfront capital will support innovative investments needed to assist the most vulnerable and disadvantaged populations most affected by climate change. Besides, failure risk from the service provider (HIO) and executor (MOA) will be transferred to the private sector investor, which in turn will be transferred to GCF. This project ensures that climate risks across all the stakeholders and beneficiaries are addressed, while also putting in place the necessary technical, financial, and institutional foundations to promote and accelerate resilient agricultural value chains that can be viable in the face of climate change.

How would the smallholder farmers gain? Assume there are 0.500 million smallholder farmers, and the expected income increase is 25% in local currency for at least 75% of the farmers (consider, for example, current farmer income as USD $100, and income increase is USD $25). The government of country Z could establish an escrow account and capture the excess in farmer incomes during the seven years, after a threshold of USD $15 (where 15% is the trigger for the outcome payment). This means the government of country Z could capture 10% incremental income beyond the benchmark of 15% times the 0.500 million smallholder farmers 25% minus 15% = 10%; which is for 500,000 farmers equivalent to USD $10 times 0.500 million, which adds up to USD $5 million per year starting from year three. Over the last five years, the escrow account would grow up to USD $25 million in local currency. The government of country Z will subsequently use these proceeds to pay the bond interest first, then the bond principal, then whatever is left is shared among the government, service provider, and private sector investor. After the seventh year, the farmer keeps the entire additional income.

Measuring Attributable Change Using Theory-Based Impact Evaluation

As an integral part of the process, the private investor would bring in an independent evaluator to discuss the verification of outcomes. Ideally, there should be three different moments for evaluations to take place at different stages of the project life cycle: baseline (start of the project), midline (midway the implementation), and end line (at the end or after the project ends). Impacts should be tracked during the duration of the investment, that is over the seven years, with the end line evaluation occurring when the investment finishes or at a suitable time after impacts have consolidated enough to be measured. This process would be independent of HIO and the government of country Z.

The independent evaluator would work closely (but independently) with the implementers on the ground to discuss and regularly communicate the intermediate outcomes that the evaluator would be able to verify. The evaluator could use measurement systems that she or he designed from the start of the project implementation or use existing verified baseline data, working collaboratively with the implementing or executing agency during the monitoring process. Beyond using secondary data, the evaluator could also collect primary data, using surveys, interviews, and a variety of other methodologies[19] by applying mixed-methods.

The independent third-party evaluator can also be hired to set up measurement systems required for verifying the overall effects caused by the investment. These systems can also be implemented so that they are able to provide credible and verifiable proof of whether the investment caused the changes expected by the investor or payer (or to what extent these can be attributable to it). This is related to attributing the impacts directly to the project, the so-called attribution.[20] In so doing, the evaluator uses a predefined research protocol and theory-based counterfactual frameworks for measuring causal changes, which specifies how *causal* measurement will occur. This will establish the processes for data collection so that impacts are objectively verified through strong internally valid research methods, and causes of achievement/nonachievement are better understood.

A theory-based framework to impact evaluation demonstrates the causal links from activities to changes that can be assigned or attributed to the intervention while examining fundamental assumptions. Evaluations based on these methods are called theory-based impact evaluations. These can measure and explain changes in outcomes, outputs, or long-term impacts caused by a given intervention (investment project, program, or policy). This method helps uncover why, what, and how these changes occurred, together with any unintended consequences of programs. Additionally, theory-based impact evaluations can inform the way forward through lessons learned.

These are the five key elements of a successful theory-based impact evaluations:

---

[19]See Chapter 16, "Measuring and Evaluating Impact in Impact Investing: Key Characteristics for a Generally Accepted Solution and a Diagnosis of the Main Available Methods," by Ana Pimenta and Elsa de Morais Sarmento, and Chapter 18, "Transformative Evaluation and Impact Investing: A Fruitful Marriage," by Courtney Bolinson and Donna Mertens.

[20]On attribution and contribution, see Forss et al. (2011), for instance.

Theory of Change (ToC):[21] The elaboration of a ToC is crucial. It will link inputs to outputs, outcomes and impacts. It explains how the intervention is expected to deliver its intended impact (i.e. how activities materialize in outputs, outputs in outcomes, and outcomes in impacts).

Understanding the context: The economic, social, and political setting in which the intervention takes place can influence how the causal links play out. It is thus important when designing an evaluation to understand the context and how different factors (internal and external) can play out in the future. Establishing assumptions and risks for a ToC is a common practice.

Establishing credible counterfactuals to evaluate impact rigorously: Suitable counterfactuals[22] need to be identified to avoid selection bias and to measure assignable impact.

Factual analysis: Causal links within a theory-based framework to impact evaluation should be established on the basis of factual analysis. Targeting analysis (i.e. examining effects on beneficiaries of the intervention) is the most type of factual analysis.

Mixed methods: A combination of quantitative and qualitative methods is usually required to undertake most theory-based counterfactual approaches.

Figure 15.1 depicts a hypothetical ToC, which outlines how the CIB-related investment may have improved the adaptive capacity of targeted populations. In the hypothetical country Z, the CIB is expected to increase the capacity of smallholder farmers affected by climate change and provide better economic opportunities to farmers.

---

[21] ToC is essentially a comprehensive description and illustration of how and why a desired change is expected to happen in a particular context. It is focused in particular on mapping out what has been described as the "missing middle" between what a program or change initiative does (its activities or interventions) and how these lead to desired goals being achieved. It does this by first identifying the desired long-term goals and then works back from these to identify all the conditions (outcomes) that must be in place (and how these related to one another causally) for the goals to occur.

[22] The counterfactual is based on a treatment (the group that receives the intervention/investment) and control group. According to Spiess-Knaf and Scheck (2017), a counterfactual "measures what would have happened to beneficiaries in the absence of the intervention, often by means of a control group" (p. 142). The base case (known as the control group) reveals what would have happened without the intervention and serves as a starting point for determining the impact of an intervention.

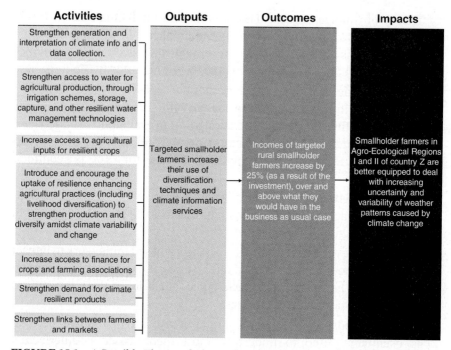

FIGURE 15.1 A Possible Theory of Change for a Hypothetical Climate Impact Bond.
Source: Authors.

The ToC above explains how the capacity of smallholder farmers will be improved against climate risks. Inputs to the project are funds provided by the private sector, for the installation of equipment and the workforce to deliver the intervention. Activities include the dissemination and use of tailored weather or climate-based forecasts, for which smallholder farmers will be trained. Agreements with cell phone service providers will be established to transmit messages to the farmers. Another critical activity includes increasing access to water for agricultural production through irrigation schemes and storage. These activities are expected to result in timely, precise, and dense weather forecasts that will be available to smallholder farmers. These smallholder farmers are also trained on the use of sustainable agriculture practices and the use of improved seeds. It assumes that smallholder farmers are aware of the services of weather forecasting and accept these services. In the long term, these smallholder farmers use these services and can plan for and manage climate risk. It is thus expected that this will result in higher income and stable agricultural productivity, which in turn will translate into increased smallholder farmers' climate resilience.

For establishing credible counterfactuals to evaluate impact rigorously, experimental methods, such as randomized control trials (RCT) and quasi-experimental methods can be used for the hypothetical CIB. However, experimental designs that use counterfactuals are often harder to implement for a variety of reasons, which include intensive micro-data collection and measurement over the lifetime of the project, institutional systems, and the context in which the intervention takes place, in which unexpected external factors can have an effect on the intervention. We argue that this is mostly true for development programs, where the incentives to report credibly are not as strong and where there is instead a more significant focus on the realization of other goals other than financial returns. The CIB space, however, presents a singularly salient opportunity to deal with several of these challenges.

If evaluation designs that use RCTs cannot be used for some reason (e.g. not integrating it in the implementation design before the start of the project, issues with sample size and thus sufficient statistical power, lack of resources), it is often possible to use quasi-experimental designs.[23] A wide variety of quasi-experimental approaches exist in the literature. The most common quasi-experimental approaches are Propensity Score Matching methods. The quasi-experimental studies employ a variety of methods including Inverse Probability Weighting to simulate the conditions of an experiment in which treatment and nontreatment groups are randomly assigned, allowing for the identification of a causal link between treatment and outcome variables. Other methods include regression discontinuity design (RDD) and instrumental variable (IV) approaches.[24] Some of the indicators used by the IRIS+[25] propose (implicit) comparators (even if they are not called as such). These implicit comparators include regional and country averages. However, these can be coarse comparators and are likely to be biased.

---

[23] In nonexperimental studies one must invoke some identifying assumptions to solve the selection problem. The same is also true when differences between treatment and control groups at baseline emerge despite randomization. More systematic differences at baseline between treatment and control groups require econometric techniques to create a better counterfactual by removing preexisting significant differences in key variables.

[24] Instrumental variable regression are alternative approaches for nonexperimental approaches. In a nonexperimental setting, program eligibility rules can sometimes be used as instruments for exogenously identifying participants and nonparticipants. Discontinuities and delays generated by program eligibility criteria can help identify impacts in a neighborhood of the cut-off points for eligibility.

[25] See https://iris.thegiin.org/.

Box 15.1 highlights the institutional dynamics and challenges encountered when institutionalizing a multi-year Learning-Oriented Real-Time Impact Assessment (LORTA) program, and specifically its impact measurement in GCF investments. It also discusses opportunities for learning going forward. The GCF Independent Evaluation Unit initiated the LORTA program in 2018 to understand *what works in climate interventions, for whom, how much, and why*. LORTA supports quality baseline data, generates real-time learning on the likelihood of impacts, and measures the causal impact of GCF using theory-based counterfactual frameworks.

Box 15.1 Learning from the Use of Theory-Based Impact Evaluations for Climate Investments in a Multilateral Setting.

Overall, the structures and processes within the GCF present major challenges for credibly measuring attributable change caused by its investments.

- The complexity of GCF investments poses challenges for effective evaluation and attributable impact measurement. GCF investments include a diversity of actors and interactions, networks and feedback loops, the openness of systems, nonlinearity and emergence.
- All GCF investments are required to demonstrate country ownership and be country-led. Since any effort to rigorously and credibly measure impacts/change requires all key actors to agree on the production, use, ownership, analysis, and release of data and findings, there needs to be multi-partner communications and agreements.
- A previous study by Fiala et al. (2019) showed that there is a lack of planning and provision for credible measurement systems, reporting, and quality theories of change in the GCF, and that these are not fully incorporated nor developed in the design of proposed GCF investments. This makes the assessments of impact challenging, reinforcing the need of the GCF to rely solely on ex-post and mostly descriptive data.

Lessons learned from this process:

- The success of theory-based impact evaluation requires partnerships and mutual trust between implementers and evaluators.

Implementers must understand and trust that these evaluations will assist them in improving the program, and that better real-time measurement will enhance program quality and results.

- There is a need to adopt a flexible approach that can help minimize the burden of theory-based impact evaluations on program implementation staff. Open discussions on trade-offs between design options on one hand, and threats to internal validity on the other, can help all actors agree on a suitably flexible approach.

- Cooperative relationships between evidence creators, advocates, and policy targets are important for use, uptake, and learning. How evidence is generated and how findings are communicated are key and use multiple channels over time, increasing the chance of positive outcomes. The effective integration of research findings and even the research process itself into the policy process is important to ensure that evaluative research can help inform the evidence needs of the GCF and, most importantly, the climate needs of developing countries.

Source: Authors.

CONCLUSIONS AND IMPLICATIONS

This chapter discusses critical challenges that are important while discussing leveraging the Impact Investing industry to realize the climate-related effects. The first is the wide chasm of language, concepts, and worlds between investors and practitioners who apply and develop impact instruments on the one hand, and evaluators or impact assessment professionals who design and implement measurement and reporting systems on the other. Although there are frameworks such as principles of responsible investing (PRI) and other standards that have urged organizations, including large hedge funds, to adopt these principles in their investments (see, for example, BlackRock 2020), there is still a considerable "accountability gap" in the measurement and reporting of impact investments, including a "transparency gap."

The second challenge is to identify a balance between the convergence of approaches and standards and continued innovation. This tension is felt intensely in impact measurement (Cohen 2018). Asset owners are asking for standard indicator sets, reporting frameworks, and impact measurement systems, to make it simpler for them to look across investment opportunities and develop an aggregate perspective of the impact performance of different investments. Making an impact also depends on how rigorously it can be demonstrated. Robust and credible impact measurement requires greater coordination, co-building, and co-ownership between the Impact Investing sector and the Measurement and Evaluation communities. Unfortunately, these two worlds have so far seldom intersected. Methods development and tailoring can be supported by the evaluation community who can leverage the power of their expertise, supported by big data, data software, and increased processing capacity to keep on improving the quality and rigor of impact measurement. Increased collaboration and dialogue between the Impact Investing and the evaluation communities will help both industries cross the language chasm between investing with impact and rigorously evaluating the intended impact. This can then help mitigate the underlying causes of "impact washing" and close the accountability gap.

The third challenge is that it is still unclear whether these organizations are genuinely pursuing robust impact measurement approaches to credibly inform social, environmental, or climate objectives alongside financial returns. Unless there is a push to measure impacts that matter, the Impact Investing industry will remain nascent. One possible way to encourage and ensure better impact measurement is to work closely with multilateral agencies that have the ability and power to apply greater pressure to demand more responsible investing.

The illustrative case of CIBs demonstrates a potentially innovative way in which organizations can structure contracts to both leverage finance while also providing incentives for rigorous measurement and climate related outcomes. But CIB's risks and limitations need to be considered to minimize surprises and increase the opportunity for participants to benefit from it and for the overall continuation of designing solutions that provide for the market. Despite being attractive, impact bonds have risks and limitations, some that can be mitigated (namely through good design), others tolerated, while still some need to be considered at a more strategic level. Moreover, CIB might not result in long-term solutions because payment is trigged by short-term outcomes that might not always be long-lasting.

Some of these risks have to do with transaction costs involved in establishing these instruments, logistical difficulties of developing complex contracts between multiple stakeholders that involve large sums of money and effort (which increase with the number of stakeholders involved—which creates a trade-off to enlist more funders), time, and expenses associated with uncovering the right contracting parties, negotiating contracts, and monitoring and evaluating impacts. These difficulties are likely to be greater than for most output-based contracts, where government pays for services outright, although perhaps no greater than for existing pay-for-performance arrangements, such as the purchasing of ex-post carbon credits.

Some of the advantages have to do with the shift of accountability from outputs to impacts (a long-term criticism for the private sector but also of the public), the redistribution of risk away from impact funders, and the fostering of innovation. There can also be substantial long-run savings in case the CIB is successfully implemented, standardized, and scaled.

The potential for change and for building trust is high. The IFC (2018) estimates that impact investments from households and private institutions could be scaled up to USD $5.1 trillion for assets managed in private markets, and this can be scaled up to USD $25 trillion if investments in public equities and green and social bonds are included. This could make a vital contribution to meeting the financing needs of SDGs and the nationally determined contributions within the Paris Agreement. Indeed, if the Impact Investing industry can continue to be mission-driven and respond to these investor demands, using its wealth of inspiration, innovation capital, proactivity, creativity, and diversity, while co-developing methods and measurement with evaluation communities, it is likely that the future will be far more sustainable.

ACKNOWLEDGMENTS

The authors would like to thank Elsa de Morais Sarmento, R. Paul Herman, Martin Prowse, and Iben Hjorth, who commented deeply on this draft. We also benefited greatly from early conversations with Karim Harji, Rene Kim, Matthijs de Bruijn, Edward Jackson, and Peter O' Flynn. We also thank participants at the LORTA workshop held in Mannheim, Germany, and workshop participants at the Impact Investing workshop held in Prague, Czech Republic, in 2019, as well as conversations with the private sector group at the Independent Evaluation Group of the Asian Development Bank (ADB). Many special thanks to Mr. Nathan Subramaniam at the ADB for providing the payment schedule illustration.

DISCLAIMER

REFERENCES

Abt, W. (2018). Almost Everything You Know About Impact Investing Is Wrong. Stanford Social Innovation Review (18 December). https://ssir.org/articles/entry/almost_everything_you_know_about_impact_investing_is_wrong# (accessed 27 May 2020).

Bamberger, M., Rugh, J., and Mabry, L. (2011). *RealWorld Evaluation: Working Under Budget, Time, Data, and Political Constraints*. Los Angeles: SAGE Publications.

BlackRock (2020). A Fundamental Reshaping of Finance. https://www.blackrock.com/corporate/investor-relations/larry-fink-ceo-letter (accessed 27 March 2020).

Box, R. (1998). Citizen governance: Leading American communities into the 21st Century. https://us.sagepub.com/en-us/nam/citizen-governance/book7005 (accessed 17 May 2020).

Brest, P., and Born, K. (2013). Unpacking the Impact in Impact Investing. *Stanford Social Innovation Review* (14 August). https://ssir.org/articles/entry/unpacking_the_impact_in_impact_investing (accessed 15 February 2020).

Bugg-Levine, A., and Emerson, J. (2011). *Impact Investing: Transforming How We Make Money While Making a Difference*. San Francisco: Jossey-Bass.

Clifford, J., Markey, K., and Malpani, N. (2013). *Measuring Social Impact in Social Enterprise: The State of Thought and Practice in the UK*. London: E3M.

Climate Bonds Initiative (2019). *Climate Bonds Standard version* 3.0. https://www.climatebonds.net/files/files/climate-bonds-standard-v3-20191210.pdf (accessed 17 May 2020).

Cohen, R. (2018). *On Impact: A Guide to the Impact Revolution*. London: Ronald Cohen.

European Union and OECD (2015). Policy brief on social impact measurement for social enterprises. https://www.oecd.org/social/PB-SIM-Web_FINAL.pdf (accessed 27 September 2019).

Fiala, N., Puri, J., and Mwandri, P. (2019). Becoming bigger, better, smarter: A summary of the evaluability of the Green Climate Fund Proposals. IEU Working Paper No. 1.

Forss, K., Marra, M., and Schwartz, R. (2011). *Evaluating the Complex: Attribution, Contribution and Beyond*. New Brunswick, NJ: Transaction Publishers.

Gertler, P. J., Martinez, S., Premand, P., et al. (2016). *Impact Evaluation in Practice*. Inter-American Development Bank and World Bank. https://openknowledge.worldbank.org/handle/10986/25030 (accessed 28 May 2020).

GIIN (2016). *Annual Impact Investor Survey*. Global Impact Investing Network. https://thegiin.org/assets/2016%20GIIN%20Annual%20Impact%20Investor%20Survey_Web.pdf (accessed 1 March 2019).

GIIN (2017). *B Impact Assessment (and GIIRS Rating)*. Global Impact Investing Network. https://iris.thegiin.org/b-impact-assessment-metrics (accessed 28 Feb 2019).

GIIN (2019). *About IRIS+*. Global Impact Investing Network. https://iris.thegiin.org/about/ (accessed 28 May 2020).

Godsall, J., and Sanghvi, A. (2016). How impact investing can reach the mainstream. McKinsey (22 November). https://www.mckinsey.com/business-functions/sustainability/our-insights/how-impact-investing-can-reach-the-mainstream (accessed 5 March 2019).

Gustafsson-Wright, E., Gardiner, S., and Putcha, V. (2015). *Potential and Limitations of Impact Bonds: Lessons from the First Five Years of Experience Worldwide,* Global Economy and Development Program, Brookings Institution. http://www.brookings.edu/~/media/Research/Files/Reports/2015/07/social-impact-bonds-potentiallimitations/Impact-Bondsweb.pdf?la=en (accessed 5 March 2019).

IPCC (2018). Global Warming of 1.5°C. An Intergovernmental Panel on Climate Change Special Report. (eds. Masson-Delmotte, V., Zhai, P., Pörtner, H. O. D., et al.) https://www.ipcc.ch/sr15/.

Jackson, E. T. (2013). Evaluating Social Impact Bonds: Questions, Challenges, Innovations, and Possibilities in Measuring Outcomes in Impact Investing. *Community Development* 44(5): 608–616.

Karim, H., and Jackson, E. (2012). Accelerating Impact Achievements, Challenges and What's Next in Building the Impact Investing Industry. Technical Report. DOI: 10.13140/RG.2.2.26485.78565.

Maas, K., and Liket, K. (2011). Social impact measurement: Classification of methods. Environmental Management Accounting and Supply Chain Management Eco-Efficiency in Industry and Science, pp. 171–202. DOI: 10.1007/978-94-007-1390-1_8.

Mayne, J. (2015). Useful Theory of Change Models. *Canadian Journal of Program Evaluation* (2 January). DOI: 30.10.3138/cjpe.30.2.142.

Mazzucato, M. (2018). *The Entrepreneurial State: Debunking Public vs. Private Sector Myths*. London: Penguin Books.

Monitor Institute. (2009). Investing for Social and Environmental Impact. https://www2.deloitte.com/content/dam/Deloitte/global/Documents/Financial-Services/gx-fsi-monitor-Investing-for-Social-and-Environmental-Impact-2009.pdf (accessed 1 March 2019).

OECD (2015). *Social impact investment: Building the evidence base*. OECD: Paris.

Puri, J., Rastogi, A., Prowse, M., et al. (2020). *Good will hunting: Challenges of theory-based impact evaluations for climate investments in a multilateral setting*. World Development Review. https://www.sciencedirect.com/science/article/abs/pii/S0305750X19304334?via%3Dihub (accessed 17 May 2020).

Riché, M. (2012). *Theory Based Evaluation: A wealth of approaches and an untapped potential*. European Commission. https://pdfs.semanticscholar.org/4bfc/0fbea08e814da8e4b6c4efe240832002ce61.pdf?_ga=2.36631456.1896053265.1590701932-181275455.1588688611 (accessed 17 May 2020).

Rockefeller Foundation (2012). Unlocking Capital, Activating a Movement: Final Report of the Strategic Assessment of the Rockefeller Foundation's Impact Investing Initiative. https://assets.rockefellerfoundation.org/app/uploads/20150904105231/Impact-Investing-Evaluation-Report-20121.pdf (accessed 1 March 2019).

Social Finance (2011), A Technical Guide to Developing Social Impact Bonds. https://www.socialfinance.org.uk/resources/publications/technical-guide-commissioning-social-impact-bonds (accessed 1 March 2019).

Spiess-Knaf, W., and Scheck, B. (2017). *Impact Investing: Instruments, Mechanisms and Actors* (ed. Mario La Torre). Palgrave Studies in Impact Finance.

Vecchi, V., Brusoni, M., and Cusumano, N. (2017). Position Paper: Public Private Collaborations for Social Impact Creation, pp. 2–4. https://www.sdabocconi.it/upl/entities/attachment/Public_Private_Collaborations_for_Social_Impact_Creation_v1.pdf.

Verrinder, N. B., Zwane, K., Nixon, D., et al. (2018). Evaluative Tools in Impact Investing: Three Case Studies on the Use of Theories of Change. *African Evaluation Journal* 6(2). doi.org/10.4102/aej.v6i2.340.

APPENDIX 15.1 DEFINITIONS OF TERMS USED IN THE IMPACT INVESTING INDUSTRY

Name of Organization	Impact Investing Definition
Global Impact Investing Network (GIIN)	"Impact investment has the intention to generate measurable positive social and environmental impact" Source: https://thegiin.org/impact-investing/need-to-know/
The Rockefeller Foundation	Impact investment has the intention of generating social or environmental impact Source: https://www.rockpa.org/wp-content/uploads/2017/10/RPA_PRM_Impact_Investing_Intro_WEB.pdf
Monitor Institute	Impact investment is actively placing capital in businesses that generate social or environmental good. Source: https://www2.deloitte.com/content/dam/Deloitte/global/Documents/Financial-Services/gx-fsi-monitor-Investing-for-Social-and-Environmental-Impact-2009.pdf
World Economic Forum (WEF)	Impact investment that intentionally seeks to create that is actively measured the positive social or environmental impact. Source: http://reports.weforum.org/impact-investing-from-ideas-to-practice-pilots-to-strategy/introduction-to-the-mainstreaming-impact-investing-initiative/
Omidyar Network	Impact investment that seeks to generate social change. Source: https://www.omidyar.com/about/impact-investing

Name of Organization	Impact Investing Definition
Social Impact Investment Taskforce	Impact investment intentionally targets and measures the achievement of specific social objectives. Source: https://www.pmc.gov.au/sites/default/files/publications/social-impact-investing-taskforce-interim-report.pdf
Organization for Economic Co-operation and Development (OECD)	Impact investment that expects a measurable social return. Source: https://www.oecd.org/newsroom/impact-investment-needs-global-standards-and-better-measurement.htm
HIP (Human Impact + Profit) Investor Inc.	All investments have a measurable impact, whether positive or negative; and all investments have a measurable financial return. Thus, all investments have the potential to generate a strong financial return and a high net-positive impact at the same time. Source: https://www.HIPinvestor.com

Sources: Authors, based on the literature review.

Measuring and Evaluating Social Impact in Impact Investing: An Overview of the Main Available Standards and Methods

Ana Pimenta, MEcon and Elsa de Morais Sarmento, MA

Abstract

One of the main benefits of impact measurement is that it can support investors and advisors in their decision-making processes to identify, monitor, report, and compare alternatives, thus enabling investors to better allocate their resources to high-value holdings and create more impact from the same amount of capital. This chapter reviews how the main existing standards, methods, and tools measure social impact in Impact Investing. The financial sector's impact measurement practices have emerged in a somewhat uncoordinated fashion, and only recently have they received increased attention and begun to coalesce around generalized practices. As the Impact Investing industry scales, it is bringing a significant number of new players into a market traditionally dominated by the public and social sectors. These new players, predominantly from the private sector, are entering the field from a diversity of industries and geographies. Their entry has resulted in a proliferation of different approaches, standards, and methods being used to measure and evaluate impact. Research and evaluation methodologies that are widely applied in the scientific field of evaluation are not yet well known in the Impact Investing field and are equally not widespread throughout the investment community. This chapter offers a concise description of the most widely used toolbox of standards and methods for measuring impact for each stage of the investment and measurement cycles.

Keywords

Impact Measurement; Impact Investing; Impact Evaluation; Social Impact; Evaluation; Theory of Change; Standards; Social Value; Expected Return Methods; Sustainable Development Goals; IRIS; SROI

INTRODUCTION

There is a world in between intending to create impact and actually proving impact. Entrepreneurs wanting to attract capital from more demanding impact investors and demonstrating impact can get easily lost in an intimidating web of measurement standards, methods, tools, and acronyms.

Impact investors can be quite diverse in their approach to attaining impact. They may use their capital to focus on specific asset classes, sectors, themes, geographies, desired impact, or even combined financial and social returns. Investors may incorporate social or environmental aspects into traditional investing to complement a portfolio that already incorporates some elements of socially responsible investments. Investors' financial return expectations can range from patient capital to market-beating profits.

The need for an effective way to communicate social and environmental performance requires a credible, consistent, and rigorous set of metrics that includes social, environmental, and financial performance indicators.[1]

According to the Global Impact Investing Network (GIIN), impact investment has the intention to generate measurable positive social and environmental impact. Impact Investing sets itself apart from other forms of investing by actively focusing on generating both financial returns and impact. For the International Financial Corporation (IFC), Impact Investing concerns "investments made in companies or organizations with the intent to contribute measurable positive social or environmental impact, alongside a financial return" (IFC 2019c, p. 1). There are four key compulsory elements according to this most commonly adopted definition: (i) intent, (ii) positive impact contribution, (iii) impact measurement, and (iv) financial return. Thus, the imperative to measure impact and generate reliable evidence about investments' contribution towards social and environmental goals are part of Impact Investing's core definition.

Impact has been used widely in this field to describe the positive change generated by activities, which most of the time corresponds only to the first level of most immediate results—outputs. The evaluation field and international development often use impact to identify significant or lasting changes in people's lives, brought about by a given intervention. Impact has also been associated with effects that target the root causes of a social problem. Others use the term more narrowly to refer to an organization's specific and measurable role in affecting a given social or environmental result—attribution—which requires a counterfactual assessment. Within

---

[1] "Indicators are measurable variables that can be used to represent the change that has been achieved in terms of outputs, outcomes, or impacts. They are usually linked to the overall objectives of the intervention and aim to illustrate to what extent these have been reached. There are qualitative and quantitative indicators: qualitative indicators are best suited to understand changes in attitudes, motivation or behaviors and explain the underlying reasons for this (Muir and Bennett 2014). They often provide a high explanatory value but are relative and subjective. Quantitative indicators aim at explaining an observed phenomenon in a numerical way; for instance, how many, how much or how often. The advantage of quantitative indicators is their objectivity and comparability. However, they are often only able to capture some aspects of social impact and it is difficult to depict, for instance, attitudes or feelings, without losing much explanatory value" (Spiess-Knaf and Scheck 2017, p. 167).

the impact evaluation profession, stating that an intervention has "impact" usually requires proving attribution, based on the existence of a relevant control group against which to judge a counterfactual (i.e. what would have happened anyway without the intervention).

By having the clear intention of bringing about positive social or environmental outcomes, Impact Investing necessarily calls for social and environmental returns measurement, combined with financial returns measurement. This has given rise to a large number of tools and approaches for impact measurement across the sector (O'Flynn and Barnett 2017). In fact, an analysis of the existing literature on Impact Investing and social entrepreneurship reveals a wealth of studies. Besides well-accepted industry standards, literature abounds about multiple research themes (e.g. Gupta et al. 2020; de Bruin and Teasdale 2019), namely, independently developed approaches to social impact assessment. Adding to the methods-focused literature, a significant body of knowledge has pursued a debate to advance impact measurement from a theoretical perspective, derived from the view that standardized metrics can often prove inadequate to measure outcomes. This has called for the adoption of multiple methods for the evaluation of the impact of an investment (Brest and Born 2013).

There is already evidence of positive correlation between financial returns and social impact. Reports from the Omidyar Network show that its for-profit portfolio has a slight positive correlation between financial returns and social impact[2] (Bardhan et al. 2018). Despite Impact Investing's financial benefits, it will only be credibly accepted by financial markets if impacts are effectively measured, evaluated, and ideally valued within decision-making processes. That is, when there is clear evidence of creation of social and environmental impact through consistent harmonized methods that are widely understood and recognized.

The aim of this chapter is to map and describe the main standards and methodologies that exist to measure and evaluate impact, thus bringing more awareness and coherence to the field of Impact Investing. Thus far, there is a wide range of available literature focused on impact measurement and evaluation methodologies, but little guidance on its application to Impact Investing. The financial sector's impact measurement practices have emerged

---

[2]"[Omidyar Network's] analysis showed that our for-profit Impact 'Stars' outperformed our 'Impact Laggards' in financial returns (and, by definition, in impact). [Omidyar Network] also found that those investments that generated the least financial return—including write-offs—also tended to have the lowest levels of social impact" (Bardhan et al. 2018, p. 19).

in a somewhat uncoordinated fashion, and only recently have they received increased attention and begun to coalesce around generalized practices (e.g. GIIN 2018; IMP 2018a).

The next section describes the importance of measuring and evaluating impact for impact investors. The section after that reviews the evolution and current status of impact measurement practice in impact investing. The following two sections describe the standards and methods most used by private impact investors. The next section describes an integrated model for impact measurement. Finally, the last section offers concluding remarks.

THE IMPORTANCE OF MEASUREMENT IN IMPACT INVESTING

Impact Measurement Matters

Impact measurement is key to demonstrate whether investments achieve their intended purposes (Barr et al. 2016). Measurement is also critical to understanding how money invested in a specific organization or project contributes to solving the problem that motivated the investment in the first place (Brest et al. 2009), and to ensure that funds are being invested in companies that are aligned with an investor's mission and strategy (Ormiston and Seymour 2011). In this sense, impact measurement pertains to the activities performed by investors and investees to evaluate and report on the change beyond financial returns they have generated.

Impact measurement can increase the engagement and motivation of all stakeholders, as well as contribute to better marketing and increased legitimacy of Impact Investing (Ormiston 2019). Besides providing credibility, impact measurement can help the industry differentiate itself and contribute to its growth (O'Flynn and Barnett 2017; Hoffman and Olazabal 2018).

One of the main benefits of impact measurement is that it can support investors and advisors in their decision-making processes to either increase, decrease, or maintain their investment in a specific project (Barr et al. 2016). In addition, it helps investors identify, monitor, report, and compare alternatives, thus enabling investors to better allocate their resources to high-value holdings and creating more impact from the same amount of capital. Moreover, some investors remunerate fund managers according to their impact performance, besides financial results. If the process of measuring impact is not granted the same importance as measuring financial value, however, the whole concept of Impact Investing can be misinterpreted, distorted, or even crippled.

Impact Investing has the potential to help developing countries and regions, particularly in Africa, Asia, and Latin America, complementing public sector investments, particularly in sectors such as health care, education, and finance. This requires more consistent impact measurement practices to build confidence and transparency, to attract more and better investments. Beyond the usual challenges of measuring impact, Africa and other emerging economies also face other limitations, like the lack of reliable data on social and environmental performance (UNDP 2015).

Furthermore, impact measurement resonates with the mandates of stakeholders beyond investors, such as (i) beneficiaries: participatory and inclusive approaches allow them to help improve the effectiveness and spread of social gains; (ii) investees: which can use impact metrics to substantiate their performance and improve their impact track record; (iii) portfolio managers: impact measurements can be used to select investments and benchmark their effectiveness; and (iv) evaluators or impact management organizations: which can learn and help support the adoption of more tailored and complex methodologies, bringing an added layer of credibility to the measurements.

Measuring impact can also serve a bigger purpose, sharing good unbiased data can mobilize additional capital and support for high-impact interventions. This can build out a robust set of best practices and lessons learned, which can enable the creation of impact benchmarks and result in even more capital flowing into solutions that effectively address today's pressing issues (Case 2017). Impact Investing objectives should increasingly connect with the planet's main social and environmental problems. The Sustainable Development Goals (SDGs) framed these problems into 17 wide-ranging aspirations, with the ambition to "end poverty" and "protect the planet." The 17 SDGs provide an incredible opportunity to connect investors to entrepreneurs and investees who are solving the world's most critical problems. Measuring how impact investments are contributing toward each of the SDGs is key not only for impact reporting but also for the achievement of this global agenda (Pineiro et al. 2018).

Scope of Impact Measurement

Impact happens at different levels within communities, countries, society, people, and planet. Thus, the scope of an impact assessment should be considered from the outset. There are three basic possible levels:

- **Micro level:** changes on an individual or a project or program level
- **Meso level:** wider community changes or at an organizational level
- **Macro level:** changes at a societal level, within an entire industry, sector, or population

These levels should not be confused with impacts or outcomes that define the primary beneficiaries that could be situated on a meso or macro level, along with other changes that might surpass the primary target group that happen on a micro level (Spiess-Knaf and Scheck 2017).

Dimensions of Impact Measurement

The Impact Management Project (2018) defines five key dimensions of impact performance: (i) What?, (ii) Who?, (iii) How much?, (iv) What was the contribution?[3], and (v) Risk. These types of questions cover most relevant inquiry areas for an impact assessment. They constitute the pillars of any measurement analysis and can be translated into different types of evaluation questions that underly formal impact measurements such as independent evaluations. These questions are:

- **What**: What types of effects (outputs, outcomes, and impacts) are the investment achieving and how important are they to the people (or planet) experiencing it?
- **Who**: Who are the stakeholders experiencing these effects and how underserved are they in relation to those effects?
- **How Much**: How much of the intended effects occurred? What is the degree of change experienced by beneficiaries and relevant stakeholders and by how many? Does it happen at scale and drive effects deeply? Does it last for a long time?
- **Contribution**: What is the investment/intervention contribution to what would likely happen anyway?
- **Risk**: The likelihood that effects will be different than intended. The risk to people and planet that the impact does not occur as expected.

---

[3]This example is focused on "contribution" and not on "attribution" of impacts. For attribution to be established, ideally a comparison needs to be made between factual (the treatment group) and counterfactual changes over time (the control group or those who have not received the intervention). Constructing or reconstructing an adequate counterfactual may prove to be a challenge, particularly if done ex-post, and if a portfolio is being assessed with a considerable number of investments.

These five dimensions indicate the types of data that investors need to collect to assess impact, but they do not prescribe specific indicators or how impact management should be operationalized. Applying these dimensions into an investor's portfolio management system depends on what kind of performance assessment is intended across each category. A company's impact is the combination of its activities' effects on people and the planet. Once data has been collected against each of the impact categories for an effect, an assessment can be made on the impact of that effect. The impact can be classified according to the IMP guidelines shown in Table 16.1 and can serve as a departing point to make decisions about investments, proceed to more due diligence, or make changes to an impact thesis or Theory of Change (ToC).

In order to do this, the impact of the underlying investment or asset should be determined. Simply put, five possible classifications should be considered: (i) may cause harm, (ii) does cause harm, (iii) acts to avoid harm—the enterprise company reduces significant effects on important negative outcomes for people and planet, (iv) benefits stakeholders—the company not only acts to avoid harm, but also generates various effects on positive outcomes for people and the planet; v) contribute to solutions, the company not only acts to avoid harm, but also generates one or more significant effect(s) on positive outcomes for otherwise underserved people and the planet (IMP 2018b). Table 16.1 provides a template for assessing a company's impact across the five dimensions and interesting examples on how to use this framework to classify investments and assets.

Stages of Impact Measurement

Impact can be measured at different stages during the investment cycle, from the pre-investment planning phase to post-exit. By measuring key metrics at baseline and during project implementation, impact measurement can demonstrate the value of investments (Barr et al. 2016). There are four main stages for impact measurement, which accompanies the traditional project cycle:

1. **Estimating impact**: Performed during pre-investment or as a part of the due diligence process. Impact investors are interested in estimating the impact that a potential investment may create. This understanding helps investors prioritize goals and decide where to invest resources to create maximum impact. Social and environmental metrics can be incorporated into due diligence checklists

TABLE 16.1 Classifying the Impact of an Investment.

	Effect #1	Effect #2	Effect #3	Effect #4	Effect #5
What	Unclear	Important negative outcomes	Some positive outcomes but a negative outcome: CO_2 carbon emissions	Important positive outcome: Access to healthcare services	Specific important positive outcomes: Decent living wage
Who	Not identified	Various	The Planet Underserved	Patients urban area, not underserved	Employees, the underserved
How much	Unclear	Various	Some degrees of positive change	Marginal change	High degree of positive change
Depth	Unknown	Various	Marginal	Hundreds	Thousands
Scale	Unknown	Various	Various	At scale	At scale
Duration	Medium/Long-term	Medium/Long-term	Medium/Long-term	Medium term	Long-term
Contribution	Minimal	Low	Likely the same without investment	Likely better than without investment	Likely better than without investment
Risk	Unknown	Various	Low risk	Medium risk	Low risk
Classification of Impact	May cause harm	Does cause harm	Act to avoid harm	Benefits stakeholders	Contributes to solutions
	NO	NO	NO	NO	YES

Is the company/investment acting to avoid harm to its stakeholders?

Is the company/investment delivering any positive outcomes?

Are any of the company/investment's effects contributing to solutions to social or environmental challenges?

Source: Adapted from IMP (2018b).

and help understand choices and tradeoffs with regards to impact, screen out unwanted sectors or companies, and determine a potential investment's fit with the investor's focus, expertise, and values.

2. **Planning impact**: During deal negotiation and early in post-investment, impact investors decide what should be measured and how. Next, they devise a plan to measure impact and pick tools and methodologies most adequate for their business and resources. For example, an investor could develop a data collection plan to monitor and evaluate impact at specific junctures (e.g. midterm, end-term) throughout the entire life cycle of the investment through a combination of internal and external resources (e.g. independent evaluators). Traditional financial return models are limited in their ability to capture long-term value creation, and social metrics help to ensure that this is captured and considered in decision-making. Metrics can also support in the identification of assumptions of the impact thesis and risk mitigation. Frameworks such as the Global Impact Investing Rating System (GIIRS) and the Impact Reporting and Investment Standards (IRIS) can be used as a component of risk assessment process.

3. **Monitoring impact**: Once an investment has been made, progress and performance can be monitored on an ongoing basis. Metrics can identify progress made toward intended results and be used to track investments to ensure that financial and social goals are being met. Metrics can serve as a management tool to ensure that a project/company/organization is on track to achieve its intended impact. Any data created from monitoring tools supplements financial data to inform, for instance, whether an investee's performance is on track (investors can compare agreed targets versus actuals on specified impact metrics). Impact monitoring should be performed on a continuous cycle for the duration of the investment, helping an organization to pivot and improve their model if they see that a financial or social dimension of their business is not being left behind. Depending on the impact measurement plan agreed, there can be midterm evaluations (internal or external) to assess impact midway toward the completion of the project and to provide corrective measures and recommendations for the way forward.

4. **Evaluating impact**: Once an investment is complete, at the end of an investment cycle, the impact generated by the investment is evaluated (internally or ideally through independent external evaluations)

in order to prove and demonstrate social value. Metrics can help grasp and capture the value achieved—especially for social impact goals—and report on the share of the impact investors have helped create, and also prove impact and attribution. Overall, metrics allow being accountable to stakeholders and report on social/environmental value creation. This is particularly crucial for fund managers—who manage other people's funds on the basis of a likelihood to achieve social outcomes—and for ventures that must demonstrate impact to investors.

There are several ways to view the Impact Measurement and Management (IMM) cycle and its alignment with the investment cycle. In Figure 16.1, yet another layer is connected to the former two, developed based on the UN Results Based Management (RBM) cycle.[4] The Better Evaluation group's Rainbow Framework is now mapped to the investment and IMM cycles. The Rainbow Framework organizes the processes often undertaken in Monitoring and Evaluation (M&E) into seven (rainbow) color-coded clusters according to M&E logical stages: Manage, Define, Frame, Describe, Understand Causes, Synthesize, and Report Use.

Typologies of Impact Investors from an Impact Measurement Perspective

Different mindsets and perceptions of impact and value have steered impact investors to adopt different approaches to measure the social and environmental effects of their investments. Table 16.2 attempts to characterize impact measurement practices, this type from the perspective of the adoption of impact practices by investors themselves. This draws on the applied work of Reeder et al. (2015), who interviewed a set of impact investors and grouped them according to their incentives, practices, and forms of human relationships. This taxonomy portrays three types of impact investors according to their practices: "system builders," "case by case," and "intermediate outcome." System builders and case-by-case investor types are able to build their own impact evidence from their evaluative work and from impact experiences and studies done before by others. System builders take the ToC frameworks as a departing point to establish impact pathways, but then move forward by applying rigorous evaluation and research methods and by drawing from past studies on what works to

---

[4]This is more commonly used in donor and government-funded programs.

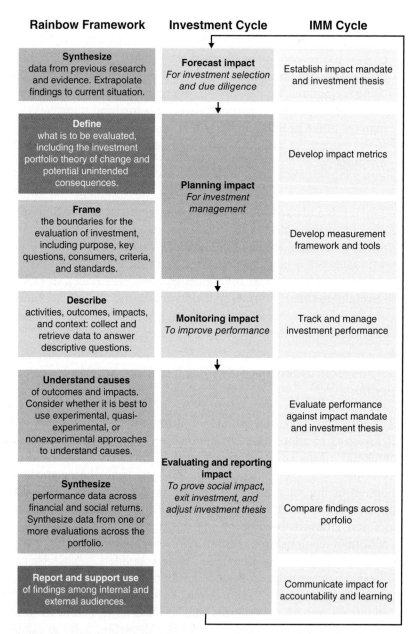

FIGURE 16.1   Mapping Impact Measurement and Management and the Investment Cycle to the Rainbow Framework.   *Source*: Better Evaluation website.

Note: Reproduced with permission.

---

[5] Available at https://www.betterevaluation.org/en/themes/monitoring-and-evaluation-impact-investing.

TABLE 16.2 Emerging Typology for Distinguishing Impact Investors and Their Measurement Practice Culture.

Central Task	Forms of Human Relationships	Other Considerations	Drawbacks
		System builders	
Produce a system that is as objective, robust, and quantified as possible. Tend to use more sophisticated analysis to understand how an intervention works.	Expert-to-expert interactions designed to build up a body of knowledge. Expert to audience communications designed to disseminate knowledge.	Tend to highlight, test, and compare individual components of an assessment (parameters of value, assessments of attributable changes in outcomes), to develop a transparent database drawing on a large array of data. ToC perspectives are seen as a starting point, to be complemented by other analyses. Such investors tend to either be highly socially minded or have alternative sources of funding.	Run the risk of imposing preconceived ideas of value and ignoring what the stakeholders feel has truly been the main benefit of a given intervention. Dialogue and more participatory approaches could yield valuable insights.

(continued)

TABLE 16.2 *(continued)*

Central Task	Forms of Human Relationships	Other Considerations	Drawbacks
		Case by Case	
Focus on understanding the particular context around a given intervention ("case"). The aim is to produce an assessment that informs about the investment's full social value.	Focus is on the "here and now," on a particular "case" and not on what others have done in the past or on generalizations of existing evidence. Facilitator role played to draw out stakeholder views on key outcomes.	ToC perspectives are important. Metrics tend to be chosen on a case-by-case basis and are interpreted within the context of expert judgment, informed about the specificities of the intervention. Investors are likely to adopt a pragmatic approach to monitoring impact and caution the need for processes to be proportionate to the benefits they achieve.	Run the risk of not considering and building upon what has been done in the past (existing research evidence and evaluation findings of other cases) before making overstated claims.
		Intermediate outcomes	
Focus more on short-term tangible results and the assessment of the scale of intermediate outcomes achieved.	Practitioner to expert interactions designed to draw out main sources for calculations	These investors are more interested in measures of operational stability and execution than in studies that take a longer and wider perspective.	Ultimate effects on society or the environment are often not considered or assessed less clearly.

Source: Adapted from Reeder et al. (2015).

deliver robust evidence. They can also forge partnerships with those savvy in impact studies (see, for instance, Petrick 2013, where the Social Venture Fund partnered with Omidyar Network). Those investors committed to an "Intermediate Outcome" perspective focus more on short-term tangible results with the use of less robust methods where ultimate effects on society or the environment are overlooked.

A BRIEF OVERVIEW OF THE EVOLUTION AND CURRENT STATUS OF IMPACT MEASUREMENT IN IMPACT INVESTING

Measuring and evaluating impact is far from being a new or emergent field. As far back as the 1950s, it was relatively common to evaluate the impact of health care, housing, and educational programs. Actors from the public, philanthropic, and non-governmental organization (NGO) sectors have been incorporating impact measurement and evaluation processes into their projects for decades (see, for instance, Reisman and Olazabal 2016; World Bank Operations Evaluation Department 2003). Long before impact measurement became a buzzword in the Impact Investing world, program evaluation as an applied and research field had established itself in the 1960s. It has since been widely used in areas such as public policy and international development (see, for instance, Madaus and Stufflebeam 2002; Peter et al. 1998). Guba and Lincoln documented these developments and provided a valuable critique of the state evaluation, which have meant different things in different historical contexts. They argue that there is no "right" way to define evaluation; rather, they describe it as a construction (Guba and Lincoln 1989, p. 21).

For the purpose of this chapter, evaluation is concerned with the effectiveness, efficiency, impact, and sustainability of social interventions. Probably the most frequently given definition for evaluation is "the systematic assessment of the worth or merit of some object" (e.g. Trochim 2020; Stufflebeam and Shinkfield 2007; DePoy and Gilson 2007; OECD 2005). But this definition is partial as there are many types of evaluations that do not necessarily focus on an assessment of worth or merit (e.g. formative evaluations). Evaluation is without any doubt a systematic endeavor and a "methodological area that is closely related to, but distinguishable from more traditional social research. Evaluation utilizes many of the same methodologies used in traditional social research, but because evaluation takes place within a political and organizational context, it requires group skills, management ability, political dexterity, sensitivity to multiple stakeholders and other skills that social research in general does not rely on as much" (Trochim 2020).

Scientific-experimental models have been some of the most dominant among employed evaluation strategies. These include experimental and quasi-experimental designs; econometrically oriented perspectives (e.g. cost-effectiveness and cost-benefit analysis), and its recent articulation of theory-driven evaluation (Trochim 2020). Drawing their methods and research principles from sciences—especially social sciences—these methodologies require accuracy, objectivity, and impartiality to general internal and external validity of the information generated. A second class of evaluation strategies comprises management-oriented systems models (e.g. the program evaluation and review technique [PERT] and the critical path method [CPM]). In the third class are qualitative or anthropological models, which stress the importance of observation and the analysis of the evaluation context. These methods value the subjective human interpretation in the evaluation process. Examples are the various existing qualitative schools, the grounded theory approach of Glaser and Strauss, or the naturalistic or Fourth Generation of Evaluation (FGE) methods.[6] Finally, a fourth class of evaluation strategies is named participant-oriented models, where evaluation participants are at the core of the evaluation process, especially those for whom the evaluation findings are destined (e.g. end users, clients, beneficiaries). Examples of participant-oriented models are client-centered and stakeholder approaches.

These are enduring heated debates even within the evaluation profession. The world's leading evaluators and economists have been engaged for decades in a passionate argument over the worth of observational studies versus randomized controlled trials (RCTs), widely considered the golden standard in impact evaluation.[7] The tendency for a bipolar debate (e.g. quantitative versus qualitative) led the previous IEG director, Caroline Heider, to write an article with the title "Embrace All Evaluation Methods—Can We End the Debate?" (Heider 2013). As a matter of fact, professional evaluators should master all four categories of evaluation strategies and should take from each what they need depending on the type of evaluation being conducted, especially due to the emphasis of mixed methods for triangulation of findings. There is no inherent incompatibility between these strategies and

---

[6]According to Guba and Lincoln (1989), FGE is based on a divergent paradigm known as the "constructivist, naturalistic, hermeneutic, or interpretative paradigm" (p. 83). For more information see, for example, Patton (2003) and Lay and Papadopoulos (2007).

[7]For a taste of the debate, see ILO (2015) and Jones (2009).

the methods featured within them. Each brings its value added to the evaluation study and debate.

In fact, in recent years attention has increasingly turned to how one might integrate results from evaluations that use different strategies, carried out from different perspectives, and using different methods. Clearly, there are no simple answers here. The problems are complex, and the methodologies needed will and should be varied.

Nonetheless, as Impact Investing grows, reliable data collection on performance outcomes still remains the exception rather than the norm. "While nearly all impact investors—95%—say that they measure and report on impact, current practice is, on the whole, limited to output measures of scale: number of people reached, number of jobs created" (Acumen and Root Capital 2015, p. 5). The impact focus, following on the heels of accountability, has been driven mainly by funders who want to know whether their investments are making a difference and by an increasing professionalization of the sector, which has led to the emergence of more standard norms and tools, including the use of credentialed experts such as auditors and evaluators. "While this is disappointing, it is also understandable. The prevailing wisdom within the sector is that collecting data about social performance is burdensome and expensive, and some impact investors and social entrepreneurs would assert that it is a distraction from the 'core' work of building a financially sustainable social enterprise. Practitioners believe this because we've allowed ourselves to be convinced, incorrectly, that the tools we inherited from traditional M&E methodologies are the only way to gather social performance data. This is no longer the case" (Acumen and Root Capital 2015, p. 5).

Social Impact Assessment

In the development field, discussions about social impact assessment emerged during the 1970s as a response to new environmental legislation whose promoter was (and still is) the International Association for Impact Assessment. But unlike environmental-impact assessment, social impact assessment is not constrained by international guidelines and regulations, allowing for a greater diversity of approaches.

In the United Kingdom, for instance, the government has been fostering the implementation of impact measurement for over 20 years. After the translation of the Social Value Act into law in 2013, social impact measurement became a requirement in public procurement for all public services.

Despite these measures, social impact measurement is still far from becoming an exact science, as recognized by the British government (Young 2014).

The current objective of social impact assessment is to guarantee that planned interventions maximize benefits for people and the planet, while minimizing interventions' costs for communities and the environment. These external effects—namely, when externalities are involved—are often not taken adequately into consideration by decision makers. One of the reasons is that they are hard to identify and quantify.

But social value is more than a set of accounting practices. Social value measurement needs to account for a complex web of interactions resulting from the compound of benefits generated by the different stakeholders involved, time lags, unanticipated events. This can make social impact assessment extremely challenging, especially when referring to monetization and causal attribution. In reality, this is highly context-specific to the sector, geography, types of beneficiaries, and more.

Social impact assessment features two main schools of thought. The first focuses on social impact assessment to make estimates about social change. The main method involved is ex-post assessment of planned interventions, coupled with demographic and socioeconomic trends and a relevant set of other statistical data to look at wider effects and extrapolate what might occur in other locations where similar interventions are proposed (Lockie et al. 2008).

The second school of thought uses social impact assessments to assist public entities in decision-making, through, for instance, the identification of affected parties, inclusion of community viewpoints, and participatory opportunities to share and debate plans and results. Community involvement is a very popular tool and one of the most dominant themes in the literature on impact assessment (O'Faircheallaigh, 2009).

The overall evidence in the social sector as to whether outcome measurement has led to improved performance is mixed (Ebrahim and Rangan 2014). Hall (2005) holds that in three decades since the early 1970s, impact assessments and evaluations done by the social sector (mostly nonprofits and foundations) lacked rigor. Besides, it did not serve to influence policy because key decision makers did not pay sufficient attention to the findings and recommendations. Foundations had also a mixed record of using evidence from evaluations and impact assessments in their decision-making process (Ebrahim and Rangan 2014), because philanthropy is often spurred by the interests of donors, instead of relying on observed evidence of what works. However, the situation has changed significantly in recent years, namely, with the emerge of Impact Investing.

Impact Investing

More recently, particularly following the formalization of the term "Impact Investing" in 2007, impact-focused interventions have been spreading from the public and nonprofit sectors into the investment sector, and many stakeholders are making a significant effort toward effectively measuring impact. Interest in the subject has increased tremendously, and governments, academics, and practitioners have been dedicating time and resources to develop tools and frameworks that capture the essence of social value creation, not only at the project or firm level but also at the global level[8] (Brest and Born 2013; Ormiston et al. 2015). In fact, one of the prime directives of the GIIN, established in 2009, was to increase the size and the effectiveness of Impact Investing through the creation of common and tailored tools and resources to better measure and manage impact (Reisman and Olazabal 2016). Further, the adoption of the SDGs by the United Nations in 2015 has been a call to action to both the public and private sectors to measure and evaluate their strategies and contributions to this global agenda.

This rise in interest about measuring the impact of projects, programs, and public policies has resulted in the proliferation of new customized standards and methods (Hoffman and Olazabal 2018; Mulgan 2010). The resulting heterogeneity is a fraught and controversial topic in the sector. Several believe that the use of common metrics would compromise and devalue the social value being created—a unified taxonomy would inherently zoom out from more nuanced impacts, as well as reduce complexity—and the possibility of reducing impact to a single value or performance metric is simply inappropriate and imprecise (Emerson 2003; Ruff and Olsen 2016). On the other hand, the overwhelming majority of stakeholders involved in the social sector face challenges in the measurement and quantification of impact due to low levels of familiarization and knowledge in quantitative approaches (Emerson 2003), but also in the utilization of mixed methods.[9]

According to Mudaliar et al. (2019), impact measurement is now central to most impact investors, with only 2% reporting they are not measuring. Around 63% use proprietary metrics that are not aligned with any existing

---

[8]Different organizations measure impact in different ways. For instance, Calvert Impact Capital measures impact in three dimensions: Investor Impact, Portfolio Impact, and Enterprise Impact.

[9]With an effort to be as inclusive as possible, Tashakkori and Creswell (2007) have broadly defined mixed methods as "research in which the investigator collects and analyzes data, integrates the findings, and draws inferences using both qualitative and quantitative approaches or methods in a single study or a program of inquiry" (p. 4).

frameworks, and 66% solely use qualitative information. These measurement practices suggest that there is a clear divergence between methods recommended by academic literature and experts and those in fact used by practitioners. Due to a lack of awareness of the range of tools available, as well as the best way to apply each tool to particular situations and projects, companies and institutions often find a framework they like and attempt to reshape it to suit their unique purposes and goals. Yet given practitioners' lack of knowledge and experience tackling impact's methodological complexities, in addition to the time and cost requirements necessary to learn frameworks, choose metrics, collect data, and analyze impact, practitioners often don't have the necessary capacity to reinvent the measurement wheel.

The experience of development finance institutions (DFI), multilateral development banks (MDBs), as well as some governments—which have been working at this far longer than private impact investors—shows that the necessary number of impact measurement and evaluation studies have not yet been produced to prove what works, where, and when. This is also related to the adoption of rigorous methods, which has resulted in a "costly evaluation gap" (Savedoff et al. 2006). This still points to a long road ahead.

As such, the practitioner experience demonstrates the need for clear, widely adopted, and institutionalized measurement frameworks.[10] A good example of this is the social return on investment (SROI) method, which has been the basis for a multitude of measurement approaches led by institutions such as Pacific Community Ventures (PCV), the Calvert Social Investment Foundation, the REDF, and the Social Venture Technology Group (SVT). Additional initiatives like IRIS[11] and the Impact Management Project (IMP)[12] seek to establish common metrics and standards, respectively. When it comes to finding a common approach for measuring outcomes, however, challenges increase—particularly when measuring across different sectors and geographies (Ormiston et al. 2015).

To move this field forward, the development of an integrated model of impact measurement is needed, one that can be used across the full investment life cycle to build a stronger evidence base. It is also fundamental that impact investors and the social sector work together to share and establish best practices (Reisman and Olazabal 2016).

---

[10]This does not rule out the use of specific tailored metrics and the design of specific methodologies to fit the impact assessment needs of different stakeholders during the investment cycle.

[11]See https://iris.thegiin.org/metrics/.

[12]See https://impactmanagementproject.com/.

FRAMEWORKS FOR MEASURING AND REPORTING ON IMPACT

Impact measurement tools are critical to enable impact investors to do their job more efficiently and gather data that is reliable to show impact around its dual value proposition. The need for some degree of measurement standardization is real and can provide investors and investees with a common starting point and foundation to come together to adopt key metrics and evaluation methods that can be harmonized and contrasted amongst the industry. Standardization serves a number of purposes, including:

- **Aligning definitions.** Investor and investee share common definitions, agree on the specifics of each indicator, and are on the same page when reporting on impacts.
- **Harmonizing reporting** across project, portfolio, company, and/or fund, avoiding reinventing the wheel, serving to answer questions such as what is the impact investor's theory of change? Investors and funders can better assess systemic impact.
- **Reducing the reporting burden.** Investees often have multiple sources of funding and multiple funders to report to. If all investors use and require a common set of metrics, it can reduce the reporting burden on social entrepreneurs.
- **Adopting more specific tailored metrics** for their investments and provide ideas on the alignment with other frameworks, namely the SDGs.
- **Reducing costs** concerning devising new indicators and consequently new methodologies for data collection and analysis, and the lowering of the reporting burden by avoiding reinventing the wheel.
- **Increasing knowledge sharing** among organizations[13] and communities of practice. Standardized metrics allow learning about how impact is measured by other comparable organizations, and what best practices look like.

Bridging this gap between existing methods and unproven vanguard ideas, several institutions have been working to develop frameworks that satisfy the needs for both standardization and customization (GIIN 2018;

---

[13] Progress Out of Poverty Index (PPI), used to measure poverty-related outcomes, is a free tool available here: https://www.povertyindex.org/.

IMP 2018). Several standardized metrics to measure social impact in Impact Investing have already been in place for several years, such as IRIS and the GIIRS. Many of these work around the higher-end results level of the logic model framework (outcomes and impacts) and are already providing solutions to the dual need of standardization and customization but also of alignment toward higher end goals such as the SDGs.

Social Impact Measurement Frameworks

Social impact measurement frameworks have been applied since the early 1990s to make intangible results more tangible and measurable for a series of different organizations from social companies, nonprofits, and public entities (e.g. SROI, OASIS, etc.), so that they can be used for decision-making and strategy development.

Several frameworks for measuring social performance employ a "results chain" or the so-called "logic model," which has its roots in the evaluation of programs and projects. These were quickly disseminated across the public sector, and international development cooperation and logic models emerged as a primary means through which organizations identified impacts and established performance metrics.

Conventional wisdom in this field indicates that results should be measured as far down the logic chain as possible, to outcomes and wider societal impacts. This expectation has its roots on a normative view that socially focused organizations, especially if they seek public financing, should be able to provide evidence of their ability in solving societal problems.

Impact measurement requires asking complex causal questions, including: Are the activities and outputs leading to sustained improvements in the lives of beneficiaries? These approaches are thus less frequent and harder to implement, as organizations have the most control over their activities and immediate outputs, whereas outcomes take longer to materialize, span several stakeholders, and are often moderated by outside events beyond their control.

Maas (2014) and Maas and Liket (2011) have provided a comprehensive list of 30 quantitative frameworks for social impact measurement available in the market at the time.[14] Many of these are adaptable and can meet the needs of different types of organizations. From the assessment of these 30 different

---

[14]Not all of those 30 are currently being widely applied. Aside from those mentioned by Maas (2014), there is quite an extensive list of qualitative guidelines, principles, and standards available in the market, some of which are listed in Appendix 16.2.

TABLE 16.3 Selected Quantitative Social Impact Measurement Frameworks.

Framework name, Owner, and Year	Description	Frameworks Characteristics
Measuring Impact Framework[15] World Business Council for Sustainable Development Year of inception: 2008	Designed to help corporations understand their contribution to society. Based on a four-step methodology that attempts to merge business perspectives of its contribution to development with the societal perspectives of what is important where that business operates. Companies are encouraged to make the assessment as participative as possible. It thus requires consultation among internal and external stakeholders.	**Purpose:** All (Screening, Monitoring, Reporting, Evaluation) **Time perspective:** All (Prospective, Ongoing, Retrospective) **Orientation:** Input **Time Frame:** Short and Long Term **Beneficiaries:** Meso (company) and Macro (society) **Approach:** Process and Impact
Bottom of the Pyramid Impact Assessment Framework[16] Ted London, William Davidson Institute Year of inception: 2007	Helps organizations focus on three areas of well-being (economic, capability, and relationship) and provides a thorough understanding of their intervention's poverty alleviation impacts. The aim is to understand the relationship between profits and poverty alleviation, and who at the base of the pyramid is impacted, who benefits, and how they are affected. The framework evaluates and articulates impacts, guides strategy, and enables better investment decisions, building upon the different well-being constructs developed by 1998 Nobel Prize winner Amartya Sen.	**Purpose:** All (Screening, Monitoring, Reporting, Evaluation) **Time perspective**: All (Prospective, Ongoing, Retrospective) **Orientation:** Input **Time Frame:** Short Term **Beneficiaries:** All (Micro, Meso and Macro) **Approach:** Process and Impact

(continued)

[15]More information at https://www.wbcsd.org/Programs/People/Social-Impact/Resources/Understanding-the-business-contribution-to-society.

[16]More information at https://wdi.umich.edu/wp-content/uploads/BoP-Roadmap.pdf.

TABLE 16.3 (*continued*)

Framework name, Owner, and Year	Description	Frameworks Characteristics
Poverty Social Impact Assessment (PSIA)[17] World Bank Year of inception: 2000	A systematic analytical approach to the analysis of the distributional impact of policy reforms on the well-being of different stakeholder groups, with a particular focus on the poor and vulnerable. Not a tool for impact assessment itself, but rather a process for developing a systematic impact assessment. Emphasizes the importance of setting up the analysis by identifying the assumptions on which the program is based, the transmission channels through which program effects will occur, and the relevant stakeholders and institutional structures. Next, impacts are estimated, and social risks are assessed, using analytical techniques that are adapted to the investment under scrutiny.	**Purpose:** Screening, Reporting, Evaluation **Time perspective:** Retrospective Orientation: Input **Time Frame:** Short and Long Term **Beneficiaries:** Micro (individual) and Macro (society) **Approach:** Process and Impact
Social Impact Assessment (SIA) Interorganizational Committee on Guidelines and Principles for Social Impact Assessment Year of inception: 1994	Includes adaptive management of impacts, projects, and policies (as well as prediction, mitigation, and monitoring) and needs to be involved (at least considered) in the planning of the project or policy from inception. Can be applied to a wide range of interventions and undertaken wide a range of actors.	**Purpose:** All (Screening, Monitoring, Reporting, Evaluation) **Time perspective:** All (Prospective, Ongoing, Retrospective) **Orientation:** Input **Time Frame:** Short Term **Beneficiaries:** Macro (society) **Approach:** Process and Impact

---

[17]More information at https://www.worldbank.org/en/topic/poverty/brief/poverty-and-social-impact-analysis-psia.

Robin Hood Foundation Benefit-Cost Ratio[18]

Robin Hood Foundation

Year of inception: 2004

Uses a common measure of success for interventions of all types: how much an intervention boosts future earnings (or, more generally, living standards) of poor families above that which they would have earned in the absence of Robin Hood's help. Second, a benefit-to-cost ratio is calculated for the intervention, dividing the estimated total earnings boost by the size of Robin Hood's grant. The ratio for each grant measures the value it delivers to poor people per dollar of cost to Robin Hood, comparable to the commercial world's rate of return.

Purpose: Screening, Reporting, Evaluation
Time perspective: All
Orientation: Output
Time Frame: Short and Long Term
Beneficiaries: Macro (society)
Approach: All (Process, Impact, Monetization)

Social Cost-Benefit Analysis (SCBA)

Analyzes the costs and social impacts of an investment that are expressed in monetary terms and then assessed according to one or more of three measures: (1) net present value (the aggregate value of all costs, revenues, and social impacts, discounted to reflect the same accounting period); (2) benefit-to-cost ratio (the discounted value of revenues and positive impacts divided by discounted value of costs and negative impacts); and (3) internal rate of return (the net value of revenues plus impacts expressed as an annual percentage return on the total costs of the investment).

Purpose: Screening, Reporting, Evaluation
Time perspective: All (Prospective, Ongoing, Retrospective)
Orientation: Input
Time Frame: Short and Long Term
Beneficiaries: Macro (society)
Approach: All (Process, Impact, Monetization)

(continued)

---

[18]It is based on the Cost-Benefit Analysis Method. More information at https://www.issuelab.org/resource/measuring-success-how-the-robin-hood-foundation-estimates-the-impact-of-grants.html.

TABLE 16.3 *(continued)*

Framework name, Owner, and Year	Description	Frameworks Characteristics
Participatory Impact Assessment[19] Feinstein International Center Year of inception: early 1990s	Seeks to answer the question "What difference are we making?" through a participatory approach to measuring impact on livelihoods Offers not only a useful tool for discovering what change has occurred, but also a way of understanding why it has occurred. The framework does not aim to provide a rigid or detailed step-by-step formula or set of tools to carry out project impact assessments, but describes an eight-stage approach and presents examples of tools that may be adapted to different contexts.	**Purpose:** All (Screening, Monitoring, Reporting, Evaluation) **Time perspective:** All (Prospective, Ongoing, Retrospective) **Orientation:** Input **Time Frame:** Short and Long Term **Beneficiaries:** Micro (individual) and Macro (society) **Approach:** Process and Impact

Source: Adapted from Maas (2014).

---

[19]More information at https://fic.tufts.edu/publication-item/participatory-impact-assessment-a-design-guide/.

impact measurement frameworks, the findings of Maas (2014) highlighted that most frameworks found tended to be input oriented rather than output or impact oriented, and that all could claim short-term effects, while only 12 were able to include long-term effects. Moreover, her assessment reveals that most frameworks are based on a process approach, where only 11 frameworks were able to convert all effects into monetary units. She also revealed that while most frameworks could be used for reporting, only a few were conceived with reporting in mind.

From those listed, only eight frameworks were specifically conceived to measure social impact quantitatively and complied with the requirement of having some sort of impact assessment based on "what would have happened" had the intervention or investment not taken place (i.e. as assessment of the contribution of the investment). Seven of these frameworks currently in use for social assessment are described in Table 16.3.

Within the current Impact Investing market, three main dominant framework archetypes have been adopted (IFC 2019a). The first type of framework described in this section is called "Impact Target Framework" and is more commonly used by private institutional investors. The second and predominant framework is called "Impact Ratings" and is used by MDBs and DFIs. This is a variation of an impact rating framework, but with a higher level of refinement in methods. This archetype was developed from a sort of a modified framework from the original Balanced Scorecard[20] performance management tool, originally developed by Robert Kaplan and David Norton (1997). In 2000, its co-developer, Robert Kaplan, adapted it for social purpose organizations by including a fifth perspective social impact. The third type of framework, called "Impact Monetization Framework," has been traditionally used by the public sector to help governments make decisions about major public projects through comparing project costs and benefits, discounted to the value of today's currency. A known example is IFC's Anticipated Impact Measurement and Monitoring (AIMM)

---

[20]The Balanced Scorecard collects and integrates a range of metrics along the impact value chain and seeks to measure holistically a company's operational performance of all involved parts and interlinkages in four outcome domains: financial, customer, business process, and learning and growth. It helps coordinate evaluation, internal operations metrics, and external benchmarks, but does not substitute them. More at www.balancedscorecard.org.

system,[21] which is a combination of the impact ratings and impact targets frameworks.[22]

All the three measurement frameworks can be used as part of a robust impact management system and can be developed in such a way that they are embedded throughout and integrated impact management processes aligned with the investment cycle, which includes ideally some form of: (i) an impact thesis, supported by evidence; (ii) an evidence-based, ex-ante assessment; (iii) continuous monitoring of impact-creating evidence (IFC 2019a).

Each of these frameworks can be implemented in a simple or more complex way. The target framework, which sets basic goals, is a useful starting approach, one to which the other two could be added. All three archetypes can be embedded throughout an impact measurement system, and should be built on an impact thesis, anchored in evidence, and used to assess and monitor impact (Table 16.4). As investors consider the archetype(s) that are most fit for purpose, following are some general considerations to support decision-making.

Assessing the Most Appropriate Framework: Three Applications

Ebrahim and Rangan (2014) delved into three organizations widely regarded by their peers as thoughtful leaders and innovators in performance measurement: Acumen Fund, Robin Hood Foundation, and Millennium Challenge Corporation (MCC). The three provide capital to operating nonprofits, social enterprises, or government agencies, either as investors or grant makers. These three organizations' intentions are different regarding assessment.

Acumen Fund's primary social metric is the number of lives reached in base-of-pyramid markets (an output measure). When it invests in a company that manufactures anti-malarial bed nets, Acumen will count the number of mosquito nets made and distributed. But beyond these output metrics, how

---

[21] Also see IFC (2019b). More information about the AIMM at https://www.ifc.org/wps/wcm/connect/Topics_Ext_Content/IFC_External_Corporate_Site/Development+Impact/Areas+of+Work/sa_AIMM/#:~:text=The%20Anticipated%20Impact%20Measurement%20and,financial%20sustainability%20and%20development%20impact.

[22] IFC has developed a comprehensive system to guide operations to achieve strong development impact consisting of five interlinked parts based on IFC's Development Goals: AIMM, Monitoring, Diagnostics, Evaluations, and Modelling. https://www.ifc.org/wps/wcm/connect/Topics_Ext_Content/IFC_External_Corporate_Site/Development+Impact/Areas+of+Work/.

TABLE 16.4 Compatibility Within Impact Measurement Framework Archetypes.

Archetype	Suitability	Impact Thesis	Impact Assessment and Monitoring	Impact Evidence
Impact Target	Because of the challenge of cross-industry comparability, this approach is often best-suited for more specialized investors that operate in a specific or a limited number of sectors (such as financial services). Due to the clarity and simplicity of this approach, it is often the impact measurement framework requiring the least upfront investment, operational costs, and skills, making it attractive to many new and/or smaller impact investors. Target impact frameworks may also be more attractive for investors focusing on sectors with established ToC, supported by strong evidence of causality between output (reach) and outcomes.	For investments seeking impact within a specific or limited number of sectors.	Relatively straightforward and cost-effective approach. Specific impact assessment and monitoring skills may be needed, but to a high degree, possible to embed.	The stronger the evidence of causality, the stronger the impact's credibility. Evidence can be relatively simple and built on a sector's ToC.

(continued)

TABLE 16.4 (*continued*)

Archetype	Suitability	Impact thesis	Impact Assessment and Monitoring	Impact Evidence
Impact Rating	Because so many quantitative and qualitative dimensions can be incorporated into an overall rating, this approach is often best-suited for investors that prioritize and seek to manage against multiple aspects of impact (e.g. direct project impact and systemic impact, impact aspects beyond "reach" including breadth, depth, duration, and so forth). Rating impact measurement frameworks are often suitable for impact investors wanting to cover multiple sectors and geographies, as it allows for comparability within a portfolio.	For investments seeking to deliver on multiple aspects of impact (e.g. direct impact and systemic impact across multiple dimensions).	Build extra dimension onto the target framework. The complexity of approach may be scalable but will include an additional level of sector economic competences and some additional monitoring resources.	The stronger the evidence of causality, the stronger the impact's credibility. The multidimensional approach and benchmarking requires use of investment and context-specific evidence.

| Impact Monetization | Because of its complexity, expertise, data needs, and economic rigor, this approach is often better suited for larger investors or investments (where sufficient budget can be allocated to early implementation of more rigorous methods). This requires a careful selection of the investments, choice of industries, and geographies, to ensure data collection and availability over the investment life cycle, to provide strong evidence of causality and comparability. As it relies on financial metrics to define both social and financial dimensions, this framework is interesting for investors seeking to bridge the communication between social measurement and the more mainstream investment industry. | Investments seeking impact within certain industries and geographies, with rich data available. | Builds extra dimension onto the target framework. Complexity will be high and require significant ex-ante economic competence and analysis, as well as some increased monitoring resources. | The stronger the evidence of causality, the stronger the impact's credibility. Placing a monetized value on externality required a very high level of evidence, preferably with a clear, proven ToC. |

Source: Adapted from IFC (2019).

do they measure outcomes, such as reduction in malaria or improvements in health? Acumen's strategy is to use existing research to make credible claims about the link of their activities to community impact (Ebrahim and Rangan 2014). It thus reviews the literature and consult experts to establish a link between a specific output and impact (for instance, how bed net distribution leads to malaria reduction) and then to count the outputs.

Robin Hood Foundation has a mission to fight poverty in New York City, and requires each of the grants to nonprofits to undergo a cost-benefit analysis every year. It focuses on long-term impacts in the well-being of individuals (e.g. income growth). One of its most recognizable metrics is the expected increase in lifetime earnings of its clients (Ebrahim and Rangan 2014). For grants focused on education, for example, they identify results that can be immediately measured (e.g. school attendance, standardized test scores). Then they rely on studies that empirically establish a link between those activities and outputs and their ultimate goals (e.g. income growth). Some longitudinal studies have relationships in which they estimate how a 10% increase in test scores is correlated with high school graduation rates, which in turn is associated with a given rise in annual income growth. Robin Hood picks these relationships to estimate their benefits until better research comes along (Ebrahim and Rangan 2014). Initially, the foundation required the grantees to be responsible for these measurements, but it soon realized few grantees were able to do this type of work. Consequently, Robin Hood enhanced its own internal capacity for developing outcome metrics, employing a full-time researcher and contracting a research organization for further support (Ebrahim and Rangan 2014).

The MCC is an American government agency providing grants to emerging market countries to reduce poverty through economic growth. Its approach is more complex than the previous two, given it sets up five-year Compacts and it operates with a long-term time horizon. The MCC looks at both individual outcomes and broader impacts on society (e.g. poverty reduction and economic development). Unlike Acumen and Robin Hood, who have influence on the process as it pertains to outputs and in some instances to outcomes, MCC's big bet is on impacts on poverty, and that depends on how effective and efficient implementers—such as governments, public institutions, and other partners on the ground—are in building efforts to reduce inequality and poverty.

For example, MCC's Ghana Compact awarded USD $547 million to the government to build roads and ferry boats to get agricultural goods to markets. They start by estimating the number of farmers likely to benefit from these investments (beneficiaries), and what those benefits would look like (e.g. reduced cost and time to market, access to new markets, increased exports, and job creation). The main outcome metric would be increased farmer incomes, and as impact, a reduction in regional poverty rates. These data are used then to estimate an economic rate of return (ERR). Once the Compact contract enters into force, an M&E process (which is formalized by instruments such as indicator tracking tables) is introduced to allow for midcourse correction. Midterm evaluations are also conducted.

According to Ebrahim and Rangan (2014), among these three funding organizations, two features of their measurement approaches stand out. All three organizations created metrics in partnership with the implementing organizations, with the objective of managing the impact performance process in the best possible way and not to overburden implementers. MCC (which when operating in a given country becomes a Millennium Challenge Account) works closely with government agencies to strengthen their capacities for implementing projects and monitoring progress, often offering support from its own staff and external experts. Robin Hood worked with grantees to identify key outputs and metrics. Acumen focused on metrics helpful to the entrepreneur in setting up their business. These types of relationships in the form of partnerships are not as common as one might think. Funders demand accountability reporting but most frequently leave funded organizations to fend for themselves, without providing technical support or the funding required to do so.

These examples reflect more sophisticated stakeholders—funders and investors—with the required expertise and resources to assess long-term results. These three funding organizations rely on outcomes and impacts measurement, but only to the extent to which they are able to provide the right support to sort out funding shortages and operational challenges of the organizations they work with, withholding the capacity to monitor throughout, either by commissioning their own research or independent evaluations, or both.

The experiences of these funders also suggest this process is not a smooth one and that there are considerable challenges (see, for instance, Rose 2014). Assessing impact requires a minimal level of inquiry expertise, commitment to longitudinal research, and deployment of resources that are more often than not beyond the capacities of implementers and at times of their funders.

Theory of Change and the Logic Model

A theory-oriented approach has the capacity to identify the crucial elements of an intervention and their coherence. It allows an analysis of the achievement of results but also looks into how and why these were achieved or not. A theory-oriented approach is appropriate for dealing with the complexity of multilevel governance systems, found in evaluation work. In order to carry out a theory-based evaluation, three essential elements need to be interrelated: the intervention, the objectives, and the intervention process (Rogers et al. 2000). Accordingly, ToC needs to be developed on a case-by-case basis as a function of the focus of the assessment of particular interventions (or investments).

A ToC is a method to help the mapping of *what* is the desired/expected change and *how* it can happen. A ToC traditionally includes the underlying logic, assumptions, influences, causal linkages, and expected outcomes of an intervention. It explicitly shows the path from resources applied in the process (inputs) and actions taken (activities), to its main immediate results (outputs) and changes obtained (outcomes and impacts). It is a versatile tool used for multiple purposes, allowing investors and organizations to: (i) conduct due diligence, (ii) construct and validate an impact thesis, (iii) select investments, (iv) identify causal factors, leverage points, and barriers, (v) set goals, (vi) monitor and report, and (vii) align incentives.

Making a ToC explicit provides a common ground for understanding to all parties involved about the processes of change, to align ideas about what is to be achieved and how, and the level of resources needed to make that change (Jackson 2013).There is a wide consensus around the ToC being the most pertinent and immediately translatable evaluative tool for measurement in Impact Investing (e.g. Flynn et al. 2015; Jackson 2013; Jackson and Harji 2014). A ToC can be used widely, at different moments in time over an investment life cycle (Verrinder et al. 2018; So and Staskevicius 2015).

Two core key components of Impact Investing are intent and impact. In addition, a third should be added, the ToC (Jackson 2013), as depicted in Figure 16.2.

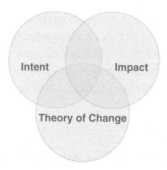

FIGURE 16.2   Core Components of the Definition of an Impact Investment. *Source:* Jackson (2013), p. 97.

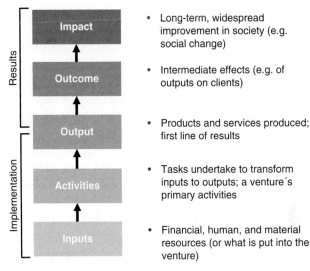

FIGURE 16.3 Results Chain Underlying a Theory of Change. *Source*: Authors' elaboration.

The ToC can be applied widely to the Impact Investing field, besides the traditional application to philanthropic, nonprofit, public policy, and international development cooperation (Verrinder et al. 2018; So and Staskevicius 2015; Jackson 2013). Investors can use the ToC to determine the level of results (impact) they are interested in achieving and measuring. Beyond determining what specific goals of the intervention are and what investors should be measuring, it can be used to set impact targets (e.g. for investors and investees) and to determine the key performance indicators (KPIs) that must be monitored as part of the IMM process. This can be used to create an incentive-based system orientated toward social impact (e.g. funding milestones or performance bonuses).

The ToC relies on a logical sequence of results called the results chain. It was originally developed for the United States Agency for International Development (USAID) in the late 1960s and has its roots in the evaluation of projects and programs. Its dissemination and quick adoption by evaluation specialists have made ToC (and its depiction as logic frameworks) emerge as a primary means through which social and public sector organizations identified impacts and performance metrics.

A results chain can be understood from a simple depiction, in Figure 16.3, which starts at the implementation stage of an activity (intervention/ investment/project/program/policy), where inputs are deployed through activities to be converted into the first line of short-term results, called outputs. These outputs are then translated into intermediate-term effects called outcomes, which in the long-term are converted into widespread improvements to society (impacts). Specific definitions of these terminologies are offered in Appendix 16.1.

These are thus the three main categorizations of results, depicted in three levels: outputs, outcomes, and impacts,[23] which are seen from the perspective of different moments in time (short-term, medium-term, and long-term). But there can be numerous other time partitions that might be relevant to look at, at which social impact can be achieved. Outputs, outcomes, and impacts can still be further decoupled into a more detailed chain of results over time, toward the higher-level systemic society changes, as shown in the results staircase of Figure 16.4.

Impacts report to what extent the life situation of target groups' living conditions have improved, whether this can be extended for other target groups more widely (e.g. other family members, scaling up to other regions),

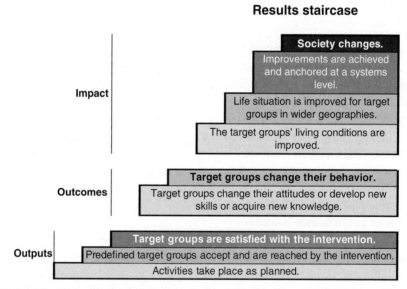

Results staircase

Impact
- **Society changes.**
- Improvements are achieved and anchored at a systems level.
- Life situation is improved for target groups in wider geographies.
- The target groups' living conditions are improved.

Outcomes
- **Target groups change their behavior.**
- Target groups change their attitudes or develop new skills or acquire new knowledge.

Outputs
- **Target groups are satisfied with the intervention.**
- Predefined target groups accept and are reached by the intervention.
- Activities take place as planned.

FIGURE 16.4   The Results Staircase. *Source*: Inspired by the "Results Staircase" by PHINEO (2016).

---

[23]For the purposes of this chapter, impact refers to change occurring in communities or systems.

to what extent these improvements are achieved and anchored at a systems level,[24] and finally to what extent society changes can take place (e.g. poverty reduction, economic development). Outcomes look at the effect of activities and outputs on target groups, whether there were changes in skills, capacity, or behavior. Lastly, below, the first steps refer to outputs that are derived from the activities of an intervention, and how many people were reached by it.

A clear distinction is thus needed between outcomes and impacts, with the former referring to lasting changes in the lives of individuals and the latter to lasting results achieved at a community or societal level. This is important, as the impact process is part of a longer evolution of moving from a focus of investments meeting certain investment criteria to thinking through what the investment is actually aiming to achieve, if the thought behind it is plausible and whether achieving intended impact is likely. Assumptions and risks need to be determined for each level of change with the ToC. One also needs to assume there might be other explanatory factors not perceived at the time (or unexpected) that might influence the achievement of those results. Within the depiction of a results chain or a logic model, they can be depicted as in Figure 16.5. Other aspects to bear into consideration are unintended (and unexpected) results that can be produced by the activities.

In formal program evaluation, the ToC is used to identify and test causal mechanisms of an intervention and pinpoint the assumptions in the path of the materialization of results, from activities to desired impacts. It can also be used to shape strategies and implementation plans and make adjustments throughout the life of an investment.

Similarly, impact investors can use a different ToC for each of their investments (and also integrate a different ToC at a higher level for a portfolio, by combining different investments' ToC into a single one for a portfolio) at various points in the investment cycle.

Logic Model

A ToC is usually depicted graphically and translated into a logic model, also known as a logical framework or "log-frame." The primary purpose behind a

---

[24]Systems are interconnected frameworks, with several relationship layers and connections between people, sectors, and organizations. The behaviour of complex systems is emergent and unpredictable. See, for instance, https://mcconnellfoundation.ca/systems-change/.

logic model is to depict and clarify the formation of impact. Its visual depiction resonates better with audiences that may not be familiar with impact measurement approaches or with the complexity of the causal links of the impact phenomena.

This framework is commonly used in the evaluation and measurement industry and started being a requisite in the Impact Investing sector. Impact investors use this approach to outline complex linkages and assumptions in the logical sequence of change. A logic model of a potential investment lends itself to the thorough analysis of an organization's assumptions and identification of areas where extensive due diligence may be necessary. This is especially valuable when an entrepreneur or impact investment fund is attempting to raise funds.

The logic model is frequently combined with other tools (such as IRIS) to demonstrate the relationship between planning and intended results, to choose the best metrics and align with standards, and to support the calculation of reliable outcomes and impact. Logic models can also be combined with scorecards,[25] which usually comprise different KPIs that allow a closer supervision of the performance of an investment. Table 16.5 wraps up a description of the logic model characteristics.

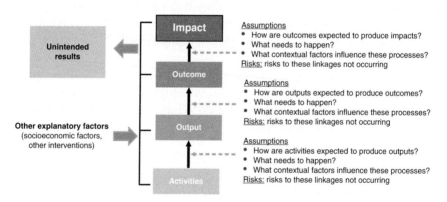

FIGURE 16.5   Formulation of Assumptions and Risks.   *Source*: Authors' elaboration.

---

[25]Scorecards can be used to estimate the performance of a single investment, or combine the results of multiple investments into an overall scorecard at a portfolio level.

TABLE 16.5   Review of Logic Model's Characteristics, Strengths, and Weaknesses.

Degree of Implementation: Widespread	
Key Characteristics	Project Cycle/ Measurement Cycle
Provides a sound framework for impact measurement	Estimating Impact (and Due Diligence)
Illustrates the logic of impact through a visual roadmap, helping to visualize and understand how investments can contribute to achieving intended impact	Planning (and investment selection)
	Monitoring
Establishes impact pathways to intended impact (also as part of due diligence processes) and can serve to uncover unintended impacts	Evaluation of impacts (in a formal evaluation process needs to be aligned with the evaluation matrix and evaluation questions)
Main Strengths	**Main Weaknesses and Challenges**
Versatile tool for multiple purposes, due diligence, investment selection but also when designing an intervention, monitoring, evaluating, and reporting	Reduces the process of change to a linear process[26]
Simplicity, easy to understand	Ideally requires the definition of assumptions and risks that should be carefully assessed, and this is often not done consistently
Allows investors to overlay dimensions that are important to mission and in their own analysis of investees logic models	
Identifies causation points to pressure test and potential barriers	
Investors can identify underlying impact assumptions that can be reviewed during implementation	
By mapping an investee's ToC on a logic model, investors can easily identify hypothesis of causation that may require further investigation	

---

[26] Although some investments may have a clear path to impact, social change, for instance, is often nonlinear and multidimensional, involving complex interactions.

TABLE 16.5 *(continued)*

Degree of Implementation: Widespread	
Main Strengths	Main Weaknesses and Challenges
Serves to align incentives among several stakeholders Wide adoption and familiar tool in the evaluation field, social and economic development sectors, as well as many social ventures Provides a logical framework for goal setting (outputs, outcomes, and impacts) Allows to overlay dimensions that are important to mission Identification of hypothesis of causation for further scrutiny and review	Contribution to big goals (e.g. poverty reduction, qualify of life, competitiveness), that is, the pathway from outcomes to impacts is often blurred and not specific enough, leading to measurement problems during ex-post evaluations of impact Ex-ante identification of indicators to assess outcomes and impacts

Source: Authors' elaboration, based on the literature review.

MCC Malawi Compact Example

On April 7, 2011, the Millennium Challenge Corporation (MCC) signed a USD $350.7 million Compact with the government of the East African country of Malawi (GoM) for a Power Sector Revitalization Program, a national program developed to electrify Malawi and reform the energy sector, with a five-year timeline completed by 2018.

Malawi has a remarkably low national electrification rate. By 2014, in a ranking of 215 countries and territories, Malawi ranked the fifth worst for electricity access (World Bank data). In 2014, electrification rates stood at 12% of the population. By then, more than 85% of the population in rural areas (still used fuel wood for cooking).

The overall goal for the Compact was to reduce poverty through sustainable and equitable economic growth, by increasing the competitiveness of the agricultural, commercial, and industrial sectors in Malawi. The specific objectives of the Compact were to:

- Increase investment and employment income by reducing the cost of doing business
- Expand access to electricity for the Malawian people and businesses
- Increase value-added production to support economic growth in Malawi

The underlying economic rationale for the Compact focused on reducing power outages and technical losses, enhancing the sustainability and efficiency of hydropower generation, and increasing the potential energy throughput; thus, the program would reduce energy costs to enterprises and households, thereby lowering the cost of doing business and improving productivity in agriculture, manufacturing, and service sectors.

In order to achieve these agreed key goals and objectives, this program comprised three projects (namely, the Infrastructure Development Project, the Power Sector Reform Project, and the Environment and Natural Resources Management Project) and several subcomponents, as described in Figure 16.6.

The program also included sustainability measures related to institutional reform, regulation, legislation (e.g. Electricity Law Amendment), policy (e.g. anti-sexual harassment policies at ESCOM), training and capacity building, institutional and funding arrangements (e.g. establishment of funds), support to new land and agricultural management practices, support to natural resource–based economic development activities by women and vulnerable groups, gender enhancement activities, studies, and purchase of equipment (e.g. dredgers).

This complex national program with several projects, layers of intervention, and effects benefited the entire population in Malawi. The ToC was reconstructed, and following discussions with MCC and MCA-Malawi, the intervention logic was finalized as a key instrument of the ex-post end-term evaluation of the Compact (Figure 16.6).

STANDARDS

This section introduces the current standards used in the Impact Investing industry. According to the funds database[27] developed by GIIN, about 40% of impact investors use the IRIS and the GIIRS. Impact investors can also use and mix several other standards such as environmental, social, and governance (ESG) metrics, the Global Reporting Initiative (GRI), the Principles for Responsible Investment (PRI), the Sustainability Accounting Standards Board (SASB) Standards, and the SDGs (Best & Harji 2013; Dufour 2015). The most prominent standards are reviewed and compared in Table 16.6.

---

[27]Impact Base (2018), information from a total of 237 impact-focused investment funds (only registered funds with the following status were considered: completed, closed, and open with post first close).

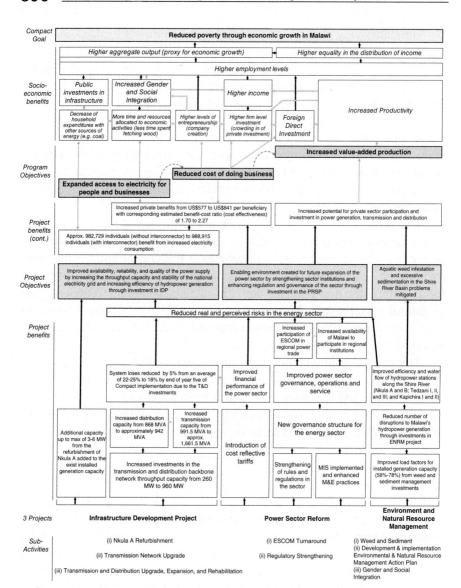

FIGURE 16.6   Reconstructed Logic Model for the Millennium Challenge Corporation's Malawi Compact. *Source*: Morais Sarmento et al. (2018).

TABLE 16.6 Overview of Impact Standards' Characteristics, Strengths, and Weaknesses.

	Key Characteristics	Main Strengths	Main Weaknesses
ESG metrics	Environmental, social, and governance indicators (inputs, outputs, outcomes) to track impacts on people, planet, and trust	Simplicity of the approach Transparency Can be directly matched to client values Can link to profit, cash flow, risk, and financial return	Does not easily allow the measurement of impacts
PRI	Set of six voluntary principles that offer a list of possible actions to put ESG matters into practice	Encourages and guides best practices	Does not measure or guide the calculation of outputs, outcomes, or impacts
GIIRS	Rating standard, as well as an analytics platform. Attributes points to four performance areas: workers, customers, communities, environment	Comparability[28] Builds track record Comprehensive Transparency	Does not allow the measurement of outcomes or impacts Can be time- and labor-intensive and thus costly
GRI	Reporting standard that helps organizations understand and communicate the impact of their operations on critical sustainability issues	Free resource Global standards Comparability Transparency Medium comparability: allows sector specific information but not exclusively in quantitative terms	Does not allow the measurement of outcomes or impacts Labor intensive: extensive data gathering and detailed reporting requirements Relevance: Social impact is one component amongst much other information Reliability: self-reported, not necessarily with external certification

(continued)

---

[28]GIIRS ratings can be compared to peers, and the standardized GIIRS approach limits the need to make additional judgments or adjustments when it is being assessed.

TABLE 16.6 *(continued)*

	Key Characteristics	Main Strengths	Main Weaknesses
IRIS	Accessible taxonomy of standard metrics, with a catalogue of quantitative and qualitative metrics, split into six performance areas: financial, operational, product, sector, social, environmental	Free resource Simplicity and practicality Can be used by numerous different industries Comparability Accessibility Common language for the Impact Investing market	Does not allow the measurement of impacts For some metrics it is difficult to judge if the results are "good" or "bad"
SASB Standards	Set of metrics to assist companies in disclosing relevant and highly material sustainability information for investors	Free resource Cost-effective Transparency Rigorous Validated by investors and investment analysts	Does not measure outcomes or impacts For some metrics it is difficult to judge if the results are "good" or "bad"
SDGs	17 universal goals (objectives) and 169 targets (metrics) focused on the three dimensions of sustainable development: economic, social, and environmental set by the UN to build a better world for all	Measures outputs, outcomes, impacts Greater attention to ecological and environmental issues than the Millennium Development Goals (MDGs) Harmonized global accounting Truly global, can be used by all kinds of organizations, sectors, and geographies and be customized or cascaded	Lack of data for reporting Trade-offs in choices Ensuring responsibility and accountability for progress toward meeting the SDGs

Source: Authors' elaboration, based on the review of the literature.

ESG Metrics

ESG metrics are a set of criteria used to quantitatively measure companies according to their ESG characteristics. They assess sustainability and relevant future risks and upside potential of an investment. ESG metrics are used widely by various financial industry stakeholders worldwide and across all industries[29] and are particularly useful for investors, banks, and other financial institutions when analyzing, investing, and advising on portfolios internally and externally (Figure 16.7).

ESG metrics are clear and transparent, and they enable fund managers to include extra-financial criteria in their investment strategy, portfolio construction, and decision-making processes. Due to their regular use, many firms now offer products that help to screen, track, and measure ESG investments, such as the Bloomberg Terminal,[30] which is used by more than 18,000 customers to analyze more than 11,500 companies in 83 countries; as well as the HIP (Human Impact + Profit) Investor Portal, rating 129,000 investments

E Environment	S Social	G Governance
CO2 carbon emissions Carbon footprint and carbon intensity Climate change policies, plans, and disclosures Biodiversity Food security Water-related issues (e.g. overfishing, waste disposal). Renewable energy (solar, wind) Recycling Waste production Green products Population growth	Human Rights Equality Child labor Ethical supply chain sourcing Public stance on social justice Labor conditions and standards Employee treatment, pay, benefits Employee engagement, training and development, safety policies including sexual harassment prevention Diversity and inclusion (gender, age, race, ethnicity) in hiring, salaries and in advancement opportunities	Quality and diversity of board directors and management team Board of director composition (independence and conflicts of interest) Corruption Shareholder rights Transparency in communicating with shareholders Executive compensation, bonuses, and perks. Compensation tied to metrics that drive long-term business value "Golden parachutes" and large bonuses for executives

FIGURE 16.7 Environmental Social Governance Pillars Explained. *Source*: Authors.

---

[29] ESG metrics are typically focused on performance, processes, and policies. ESG metrics can be used as positive filters (e.g. firms with more than 10% revenue exposure to green wind power) or negative filters (e.g. revenue exposure to fossil fuels, weapons, alcohol, slave labor). Using ESG metrics as filters or screens can be directly matched to customer preferences and specific values.

[30] https://www.bloomberg.com/impact/products/esg-data/.

globally across 85 countries.[31] These ESG metrics can also be audited by external parties, which adds an additional layer of credibility for investors.

Integrating ESG metrics with traditional investment analysis techniques is known as ESG integration. As ESG factors can be leading indicators of impact and profit, ESG metrics can be valuable to impact investors.

Clear evidence has emerged that ESG metrics and integration are associated with several economic benefits. ESG disclosures are connected to higher revenues, lower costs, and lower capital costs and constraints (Amel-Zadeh and Serafeim 2018).

Ortas et al. (2015) investigated companies' ESG metrics and linkages to financial implications of their commitment to the United Nations Global Compact (UNGC), a Corporate Social Responsibility (CSR) initiative; the research focused on three countries (Spain, France, and Japan). The results showed that ESG performance had a significant impact on the financial performance for companies adopting the principles of the UNGC, and that despite requiring a degree of organizational change, this compliance fostered stakeholder engagement, ultimately resulting in improvements in companies' ESG performance. Box 16.1 provides an example of an ESG application.

Box 16.1 An Example of ESG Metrics and Criteria

Althelia is an asset manager that aligns investments with ecology, linking sustainable production with protection. According to Althelia's ESG Principles and Policy, the projects they invest in must achieve results in three categories: performance, process, and policy:

- POLICY: Comply with national, environmental, social, and labor laws and legislation
- PROCESS: Conform with the International Labor Organization's (ILO) Core Conventions on child labor, forced labor, equality, rights of association
- PERFORMANCE: Provide employment that pays a living wage, which is quantifiable on a per-hour or salary basis

Source: Althelia Ecosphere (2016).

---

[31] The HIP Investor Ratings portal (https://www.HIPinvestor.com/portal/) rates the ESG of 9,000 global equities, 119,000 muni bonds, 200 sovereigns, 200 real estate investment trusts, and 1,000 mutual funds and exchange traded funds (ETFs).

Principles for Responsible Investment

The United Nations and a group of the world's largest institutional investors launched the Principles for Responsible Investment (PRI)[32] in 2006. PRI is composed of six voluntary principles that offer a list of possible actions related to ESG matters (Table 16.7). Due diligence questionnaires specific to each asset class or industry are used to evaluate how specific investment managers or companies treat ESG factors.

Investment managers, asset owners, and investment service providers can sign and commit to the PRI principles to be officially recognized as sustainable investors. PRI requires: (i) the payment of an annual membership fee; (ii) a public report of the organization's responsible investment activity through the Reporting Framework; (iii) an allocation of at least half of a firm's assets under management to responsible investments; (iv) a dedicated staff member or team responsible for implementing responsible investing policies;

TABLE 16.7 Principles for Responsible Investment and Possible Actions.

Principle
Principle 1: We will incorporate ESG issues into investment analysis and decision-making processes.
Principle 2: We will be active owners and incorporate ESG issues into our ownership policies and practices.
Principle 3: We will seek appropriate disclosure on ESG issues by the entities in which we invest.
Principle 4: We will promote acceptance and implementation of the principles within the investment industry.
Principle 5: We will work together to enhance our effectiveness in implementing the Principles.
Principle 6: We will each report on our activities and progress toward implementing the Principles.

Source: PRI webpage.[33]

[32]https://www.unpri.org/
[33]https://www.unpri.org/pri/an-introduction-to-responsible-investment/what-are-the-principles-for-responsible-investment.

and (v) a commitment from senior-level leadership along with accountability mechanisms to correct implementation. An example is provided in Box 16.2.

Box 16.2 Example of Principles for Responsible Investment

New Forests is an asset manager mainly focused in sustainable forests and land in the Asia-Pacific and US regions. Its Responsible Investing (RI) Transparency Report shares information about PRI principles, including progress toward implementing the principles:

- SG 02.1: Indicate which of your investments policy documents (if any) are publicly available
  - Formalized guidelines on environmental factors, social factors, governance factors
  - Asset class-specific and sector-specific RI guidelines
- SG 02.2: Indicate if any of your investment policy components are publicly available
  - Your investment objectives that take ESG factors/real economy influence into account
  - Governance structure of organizational ESG responsibilities
  - ESG incorporation approaches, and active ownership approaches

Source: New Forests Pty Limited (2019).

Global Impact Investment Rating System

GIIRS is a comprehensive and transparent approach used frequently by private equity and venture capital investors seeking impact. GIIRS[34] is a tool for rating impact, but it is also an online analytics platform intended to assess firms' and funds' social and environmental performance, which has the largest database of social and environmental performance data for private companies and funds. GIIRS Fund Ratings include three main dimensions: (i) an overall impact business model rating, (ii) an overall operations ratings,

---

[34]For more information along with information on resources and service providers, see www.giirs.org, https://b-analytics.net/giirs-funds and www.thesroinetwork.org.

TABLE 16.8 GIIRS Operational Ratings.

Category	Description of Metrics
Governance	Mission and engagement; governance; transparent reporting; and anticorruption
Community	Supply chain, local community, job creation, diversity, civic engagement, and charitable giving
Workers	Compensation, training, and benefits; worker ownership; and work environment
Environment	Company land, office, and plant; inputs; outputs; transportation and distribution; and supply chain
Socially and environmentally focused business models	Covers models of impact, including consumer-focused models, worker-focused models, supply chain–focused models, ownership-focused models, community-focused models, and environment-focused models

GIIRS Composite Score is based on predetermined relative weightings, which depend on a company's geography, sector, and size, and are made transparent within a ratings system.

Source: GIIRS and SROI Network (2016).

and (iii) a fund manager assessment.[35] The GIIRS Company Assessment Score is a combination of two categories: Impact Business Models Rating and the Operational Rating (Table 16.8).

One of GIIRS's strengths is that it allows the construction of a track record (time series data) and the comparison of an organization's performance against more than 13,000 other companies and 90 funds. Another major advantage is that it uses the IRIS metrics as a departing point (Gelfand 2012), but takes it a step further by aggregating and presenting results in a single number that can be used for comparisons across sectors (Kroeger and Weber 2016) and to industry benchmark reports. Its major weakness[36] is that it does not evaluate the actual impact of the interventions; instead, it

---

[35] Fund Manager Assessment contains approximately 60 questions covering three fund impact areas: Impact Targets, Investment Criteria, and Portfolio Management.

[36] The use of the B Impact Assessment requires the filling of a detailed form and a paid subscription, which may be time and cost consuming.

enables investors to track, report, and quantify inputs and outputs. Box 16.3 illustrates an example of GIIRS.

Box 16.3 An Application of the GIIRS

Vital Capital is a leading impact private equity fund focused on sub-Saharan Africa, which uses the GIIRS rating system to measure and evaluate their social and environmental performance.

Kora, one of Vital Capital's investees in the infrastructures and energy industries, earned an overall score of 116 (on a 200-point scale), which is a combination of:

- Operational Rating: 4 (out of 5) stars
- Impact Business Model: Platinum, due to socially oriented basic services (consumers), supply chain, and workforce development community practices (community)
- Vital Capital Fund Rating = (10% Fund Manager Assessment) + (90% Investment roll up)
- Fund Manager Assessment = 56.6 (Portfolio Management) + 48.4 (Investment Criteria) + 54.2 (Targeted for investment) = 159.3 (on a 200-point scale)
- Investment roll up = Weighting all five companies' scores: 116 (Kora), 109 (Aldeia Nova), 121 (Focal Energy), 122 (SGWK), 152 (Water Health International), will result in a score of 121.3 (of 200 possible)
- Overall fund rating = (10% × 159.3) + (90% × 121.3) = 125.1 (of 200 possible)

As the emerging markets funds' average rating is 114.6, Vital Capital is one of the 10 leading funds in emerging markets.

Source: Vital Capital Fund (2015).

Global Reporting Initiative

The GRI[37] was developed in the 1990s as a guideline for sustainability reporting. It is now a known global sustainability reporting standard and a

---

[37]https://www.globalreporting.org/ and database: https://database.globalreporting.org/.

process to help organizations understand and communicate the impact of their business on critical sustainability issues (GRI 2019).

The main reason to use GRI is to publicly report economic, environmental, and social impacts through globally accepted standards. Its main strength is providing organizations with a set of standards that can be applied and utilized across different countries to disclose and report economic, environmental, and social impacts, thus enabling more uniform and transparent sustainability reports. However, its main weakness is that it is more of a framework for reporting; it does not directly measure or evaluate the impact generated. Box 16.4 provides a simple example of reporting.

Box 16.4 An Example of GRI Reporting

U Ethical, established in 1985, is one of the largest and oldest ethical investment management companies in Australia. Their sustainability report follows the GRI standards and indicators. For example:

- GRI 102-16 (Values, principles, standards, and norms of behavior)

  Mission: To improve our world through the power of purposeful investing.

  Values: (i) Authenticity: we do the right thing, not the easy thing, (ii) Progress: we are open-minded, innovative and future-focused and (iii) Impact: we strive for better investments and a better world.

  Exclusion principles: cause unacceptable damage to the natural environment, infringe on human rights, have unacceptable occupational health and safety practices, support oppressive regimes, cause, or perpetuate injustice and suffering

  Excluding the bad: thermal coal, unconventional oil and gas extraction, uranium for nonmedical uses, armaments, adult entertainment, gambling, predatory lending, animal cruelty, alcohol production, tobacco manufacturing

- GRI 102-22 (Composition of the highest governance body and its committees): 50% male-to-female ratio of board members

Source: U Ethical (2019).

TABLE 16.9   GRI 306: Waste 2020.

GRI	Disclosure
306-1	Waste generation and significant waste-related impacts
306-2	Management of significant waste-related impacts
306-3	Waste generated
306-4	Waste diverted from disposal
306-5	Waste directed to disposal

Source: GRI 306: Waste 2020.[38]

Table 16.9 summarizes the disclosures and reporting requirements for one of the GRI Standards, the GRI 306 (Waste), which is a specific topic in the 300 series (environmental topics).

Impact Reporting and Investment Standards

The Impact Reporting and Investment Standards (IRIS) is a free resource developed in 2009 jointly by the Rockefeller Foundation, Acumen Fund, and B Lab, with support from Hitachi, Deloitte, and PricewaterhouseCoopers, and released by the GIIN. IRIS provides a taxonomy for defining standard metrics for measurement, and tools to make these metrics accessible, which are used within the Impact Investing community. "The IRIS initiative was formed to address the needs of the Impact Investing industry, including fragmented impact measurement approaches, lack of performance comparability among organizations and portfolios, and an absence of sector analyses, such as performance benchmarking" (Bouri 2011). The first IRIS report was released in September 2011, with data from more than 2,000 mission-driven organizations. Since then, IRIS has been adopted by funds and organizations that operate globally.[39]

IRIS also includes cross-sector performance indicators[40] that can be used by organizations operating in any sector. IRIS currently comprises a

---

[38] Available at https://www.globalreporting.org/standards/gri-standards-download-center/.

[39] IRIS partnered with several organizations such as Microfinance Information Exchange (MIE), Aspen Network for Development Entrepreneurs (ANDE), GIIRS, and Pulse (a data management platform for fund managers) to add several thousand companies whose performance data generate industry benchmarks and market analysis.

[40] An example is the metric "Target Beneficiary Demographic." It is defined as "demographic groups of beneficiaries targeted by the organization's operations." These could be children and adolescents, disabled groups, minorities, previously excluded populations, women, and others.

catalogue of 559 generally accepted performance quantitative and qualitative metrics[41] split into six performance areas: financial, operational, product, sector, social, and environmental.[42] These metrics are widely used by private impact investors, particularly in emerging markets (Mudaliar et al. 2019). The biggest strengths of IRIS are its simplicity and practicality, which contributed to establish a credibility and legitimacy that is far beyond its peers (Kroeger and Weber 2016). IRIS also has the capacity to be used by numerous different players, from small to big companies, for-profit to nonprofit organizations, private to public entities, and for different sectors and geographies. Its biggest limitation is that it does not measure outcomes or impacts (Best and Harji 2013; Brest and Born 2013), and that for some of its metrics it is difficult to judge whether a company's score or number is "good" or "bad" (Kroeger and Weber 2016). Box 16.5 provides an example of its use.

Box 16.5 An Example of the Use of the IRIS Framework

Sarona is an asset management firm focused in emerging markets. Sarona targets financial returns as well as positive ethical, social, and environmental values, including IRIS metrics:

- OI6213 (full-time employees: female): 62,000 women in 2018 (18% more than in 2017) representing 33% of the 187,000 full time jobs of all ventures in Sarona's portfolio
- OI3757 (occupational injuries): 241 in 2018 (reduction from 666 in 2017) of all firms invested in by Sarona
- OD4108 (environmental impact objectives): 113 billion liters of graywater recycled each year, 5 GW of clean energy capacity, 68% of companies actively pursue at least one environmental objective

Source: Sarona (2019).

Sustainability Accounting Standards Board

The SASB standards[43] are a set of material metrics developed to assist companies in disclosing relevant and meaningful sustainability information that

---

[41] IRIS Catalog of Metrics at https://iris.thegiin.org/metrics/.
[42] Impact categories are: Agriculture, Air, Biodiversity and Ecosystems, Climate, Diversity and Inclusion, Education, Employment, Energy, Financial Services, Health, Real Estate, Land, Oceans and Coastal Zones, Pollution, Waste, Water, and Cross Category.
[43] https://www.sasb.org/.

meets investor needs. SASB standards were developed by the SASB Foundation in 2011, an independent nonprofit based in the United States, with the guidance of 100-plus investment professionals and industry experts. SASB developed 77 industry-specific standards, each describing the predominant business model and industry segments.

The SASB's Materiality Map (Figure 16.8) is also an online, interactive tool that identifies sustainability issues and compares disclosure topics across different industries and sectors that can influence a company's financial condition or operating performance. In the left-hand column, SASB identifies 26 sustainability-related business issues.

The SASB standards are voluntary and can be used by companies in making disclosures in US Securities and Exchange Commission (SEC) filings. These standards are also recognized by the European Commission as a suitable framework for companies to use when providing information to investors. Baxter Healthcare, Gap Inc., and FedEx are all firms using SASB standards. An example of an application of the SASB Standards is provided in Box 16.6.

Box 16.6 An Example of an Application of the SASB Standards

Adobe is an American multinational computer software company focused in the creation of multimedia and creativity software products. Adobe has adopted the SASB Standards to report key performance indicators regarding their governance, society, community, sustainability, and policies activities. Adobe's 2018 corporate social responsibility report shows:

Reference Indices	KPI	2017	2018
SASB TC-SI-330a.3	% Female Employees	31%	32%
SASB TC-SI-330a.3	% White (Caucasian) Employees	63%	61%
SASB TC-SI-130a.1	Total Energy consumption (Gigajoules)	853,042	803,693

Source: Adobe (2018).

Next, Figure 16.8 depicts the SASB Materiality Map.

Sustainable Development Goals

The SDGs are a group of 17 universal goals and objectives set by the United Nations (UN) General Assembly in 2015 to build a better world for all.[44]

---

[44]See the SDGs in detail here: https://sustainabledevelopment.un.org/topics/sustainabledevelopmentgoals.

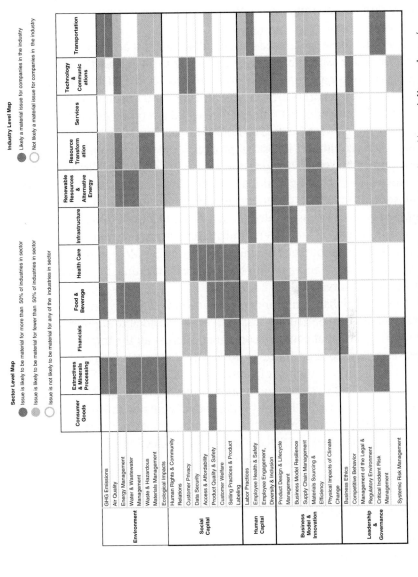

FIGURE 16.8 SASB Materiality Map. *Source:* Adapted from SASB website, available at http://materiality.sasb.org/.

The SDGs break silos across themes, sectors, countries, regions, networks, and professions. They are holistic and portray well-being as a complex and multifaceted phenomenon. The SDGs apply to both developed and developing countries, and address all sectors and needs, from ending poverty to improving education and health, to preserving the environment and creating sustainable cities.

The SDGs have galvanized a tremendous amount and a growing amount of private sector capital, but there is still much to do to close the funding gap. More than 60% of all impact investors surveyed by the GIIN in their annual industry survey report (GIIN 2019) stated they are tracking performance to the SDGs (Saldinger 2019). The GIIN released a report, "Achieving the Sustainable Development Goals: The Role of Impact Investing" (GIIN 2017), featuring a series of impact investors' profiles[45] and showcasing how they have been approaching the SDGs to tackle a variety of global problems (e.g. access to clean water, improving health and well-being, climate change mitigation). In these profiles, several experienced impact investors explain why and how aligning to the SDGs has enabled them to develop impact strategies and goals, communicate with stakeholders, and attract new capital, and why they think the SDGs can be a source of business opportunities. More information about impact investors' alignment with the SDGs can be found, for instance, at the GIIN's annual surveys (GIIN 2019).

Toniic, a "global community of asset owners seeking deeper positive net impact across the spectrum of capital,"[46] also decided to support the efforts of reporting data that could be comparable across all the impact investment ecosystem. So as to align Toniic's efforts with those prevailing in the industry, it mapped the impact themes of interest to its members to the SDGs Goals and Targets, and those to a selection of impact metrics from the IRIS Catalog 4.0. The report "Toniic SDG Themes Framework" contains this useful mapping, between the SDGs and Toniic Impact Themes Framework Version 1.1,[47] and the mapping between the SDGs Targets and a selection of the IRIS metrics, to support investors in identifying relevant outcomes and output indicators for impact management and measurement. Table 16.10 provides a depiction taken from this report that illustrates how they aligned the SDGs with the IRIS metrics, for SDG-1.

---

[45]See the report here: https://thegiin.org/assets/GIIN_Impact%20InvestingSDGs_Final profiles_webfile.pdf.
[46]Available at https://toniic.com/.
[47]See Chapter 17, "Driving Impact in Impact Investing Through Impact Measurement and Management," by Jane Reisman and Veronica Olazabal.

TABLE 16.10 Alignment Between SDG-1 Targets and Selected IRIS Metrics.

SDGs	SDGs Targets (Selected): Outcomes	IRIS Metric Catalog 4.0 GIIN (Selected): Output Metrics
SDG1: No poverty	**1.1** Reduce number of individuals living below USD $1.25 per day	**PI1748** Client Savings Premium
	1.2 Reduce number of individuals living below national poverty line	**PI2476** Communities Served
		PI2242 Supplier Individuals: Poor
		PI3193 Client Individuals: Poor
		PI7815 Payments to Supplier Individuals: Poor
	1.3 Increase number of individuals covered by social protection systems	**PI9991** Supplier Individuals: Smallholder
		PI6372 Client Individuals: Smallholder
	1.4 Increase number of individuals with access to basic services (banking, land, rights, technology)	**PI8381** Number of Loans Disbursed
		PI5160 Average Loan Size Disbursed
		PI5476 Value of Loans Disbursed
	1.5 Increase resilience of individuals to natural disasters	**FP2630** Loans Receivable Gross
		FP9954 Value of Loans Fully Repaid on Time
	1.A Increase resources allocated to poverty reduction programs	**PD5833** Percent Affordable Housing
		PI2998 Individuals Trained: Total
	1.B Promote policies to support accelerated investment in poverty eradication	**PI5691** Jobs Maintained at Directly Supported/Financed Enterprises: Total
	Impact Metrics Applicable to all SDG Targets	**PI3687** Jobs Created at Directly Supported/Financed Enterprises: Total
		PI4060 Client Individuals: Total
		PI8330 Client Individuals: Female
		OI5247 Full-time Wages: Female Management
		PI4237 Client Individuals: Minorities/Previously Excluded
		OI3862 Full-time Wages: Minorities/Previously Excluded Management
		PI3180 Revenue Generated at Directly Supported/Financed Enterprises
		PI9652 Client Organizations: Total

Source: Toniic (2018).

611

The Bertelsmann Stiftung and the Sustainable Development Solutions Network (SDSN) jointly prepared a development report scoring each of the 193 United Nations members on their performance across the SDGs (the "SDG Index") (Sachs et al. 2019; Lafortune et al. 2018). The SDG Index allows for easy comparison between different impact issues and geographies, because for each SDG, each indicator is normalized and rescaled from 0 (worst) to 100 (optimal). This standardization, and the SDGs' related capacity for comparison, is one of its greatest advantages. It is also a very complete standard since it incorporates most of the world's global problems, proposing specific targets and metrics, and measuring not only outputs but also outcomes and impacts. Box 16.7 contains an example of SDG reporting.

Box 16.7 Example of an Impact Investor Reporting on the SDGs

Impact Finance is an investment fund advisor specialized in investing in projects that generate positive economic, social, and environmental impacts for people in poverty and the Base of the Pyramid (BoP). Their impact report explains Impact Finance's 10 sub-strategies, which are directly linked to six SDGs: SDG-1 (no poverty), SDG-2 (zero hunger), SDG-8 (decent work and economic growth), SDG-12 (responsible consumption and production), SDG-13 (climate action), and SDG-15 (life on land). For each SDG they specify, monitor, and report metrics using a proprietary tool called Kharmax. Impact Finance's report presents key performance indicators for impact across the firm's entire investment portfolio, plus detailed metrics for some of their relevant investments.

Impact Finance portfolio impact data
- SDG1 (no poverty):
  - Number of beneficiaries at the BoP: 198,001 (2018) vs 180,193 (2017)
- SDG15 (life on land):
  - Number of hectares of organic agriculture: 108,547 (2018) vs 119,134 (2017)

Impact metrics regarding the companies invested
- Terrafertil Group – SDG 8: share of women among full-time employees: 52% (2019)
- Coopecan – SDG 12: hectares of improved pasture: 350 (2019)
- Hylea – SDG 13: hectares of forests preserved: 292,500 (2019)

Source: Impact Finance (2019).

The Corporate Citizenship (2018) report "The SDGs: Materially impacting the bottom line 2018, Annual Review of Progress on the Global Goals" assessed if the SDGs were delivering results for the bottom line: "We have seen a steady rise in the number of companies using the SDGs as a framework to report their societal contributions. We have also observed increasing interest for the investment community to channel investment flows towards opportunities seen to deliver against the Global Goals" (p. 4).

A SELECTION OF METHODS FOR IMPACT MEASUREMENT

Impact investors want to know and seek from investees the evidence about reliability, and comparability of results. The lack of rigor, transparency, and validity in measuring impact can lead to significant gaps in accountability, and possible impact washing.[48]

By **functional type and their overall purpose**, impact assessment methods can broadly be clustered into three main **functional categories** (Spiess-Knaf and Scheck 2017):

- **Rating systems:** Screenings, mostly done by independent third parties using a fixed set of metrics, often represented with a final score or symbol (e.g. stars, 100-point scale)
- **Assessment systems:** Mainly quantitative (sometimes translated to monetary terms) results of social interventions at a certain point in time, usually without explicitly analyzing operational data over time

---

[48]See Chapter 15, "Climate and Money: Dealing With 'Impact Washing' and a Case for Climate Impact Bonds," by Jyotsna Puri, Aemal Khan, and Solomon Asfaw.

- **Management systems:** Ongoing M&E methods that can measure and manage operational performance as drivers of impact.

The clear assignment of a given method to one of these three categories of methods and impact frameworks is often not possible, as many belong to multiple categories.

In evaluation theory and practice, the hierarchy of evidence or ranking evidence produced by measurement methods has been at the core of discussions about the validity of evaluation processes. Based on the reliability and validity of findings, methods for impact measurement are traditionally clustered into three broad categories, arranged lower to higher in order of credibility, robustness, and use of data and methods: "after-only" designs, "before-after" designs, "before-after with control group."

"After-only" designs measure impact (the independent variable) only after the participants have been exposed to the intervention. For instance, beneficiaries are interviewed after experiencing the impact of a given product or service so they can provide their feedback. Beneficiaries can be asked to recall the product or service and assess their satisfaction. The chief limitation is that this method does not afford any control over extraneous factors that could have influenced the ex-post measurements. Findings from these methods can thus be misleading, putting at risk the internal validity of the impact assessment. After-only designs are not true experiments since little or no control is exercised over any of the variables. This underlines the need for more complex designs.

"Before-after" designs involve measuring the dependent variable (the selected variable for measuring impact) both before and after the participants have been exposed to the intervention using historical comparisons of data. The effect of the intervention, if any, is established by observing differences before and after the intervention. However, before-after designs still have a number of weaknesses.

The "before-after with control group" design involves establishing two groups of participants (the whole population or a representative sample to ensure generalization and thus external validity): an experimental group that receives the intervention and a control group that would not be subjected to the intervention but that would be similar to the treatment group in all relevant characteristics for the study. The two groups would be matched to ensure the two would be identical in key variables, to ensure that any confounding factors would impact both groups in a similar way. This means that any differences in the independent variable drawn from the two groups

TABLE 16.11 Hierarchy of Evidence.

Level of Evidence	Description
Level I (Highest Rigor)	Evidence from systematic reviews, meta-analysis[49] or meta-evaluations of all relevant RCTs or evidence-based practice guidelines based on systematic reviews of RCTs or three or more RCTs of good quality that have similar results
Level II	Evidence obtained from at least one well-designed RCT
Level III	Evidence obtained from well-designed controlled trials without randomization (i.e. using quasi-experimental methods)
Level IV	Evidence from well-designed case-control[50] or cohort studies[51]
Level V	Evidence from systematic reviews of descriptive and qualitative studies (meta-synthesis)
Level VI	Evidence from a single descriptive or qualitative study
Level VII (Least Rigor)	Evidence from the opinion of authorities and/or reports of experts or expert committees or organizations

can be attributed to the intervention and that would be the amount of estimated impact from the intervention.

The hierarchy of evidence can be found in several streams of the academic literature where it is analyzed with a greater level of detail, from the health to the social sciences. The hierarchy presented in Table 16.11 is adapted from Evans (2003), which was based on a literature review, a research on existing hierarchies and an examination of the strengths

---

[49] A meta-analysis is a valid, objective, and scientific method of analysing and combining different results. Usually, to obtain more reliable results, a meta-analysis is mainly conducted based on RCTs, which have a high level of evidence (Ahn and Kang 2018, p. 103). A meta-analysis applies statistical procedures to summarize the results of available studies and provides a powerful tool to combine analysis for all extracted data and gives weighted values for each study's effect sizes. A meta-analysis also indicates whether publication bias is present in assessing positive and negative studies.

[50] Identifies stakeholders who have the outcome of interest (cases) and control stakeholders without the same outcome and looks for the reaction to the exposure of the intervention.

[51] Identifies two groups (cohorts) of stakeholders, one that did receive the intervention and one that did not, and follows these cohorts in time to assess the outcome of interest.

and limitations of different research methods. Levels of evidence are thus assigned to different types of studies, which provides the grade (or strength) of their findings, based on the methodological quality of their design, validity, and applicability.

The Center for Social Impact Bonds also uses a similar hierarchy of evidence based on five layers, which is depicted by a pyramid. The top tier includes meta-analysis of studies that rely on experimental methods. RCTs are considered the most rigorous and robust evaluation method. The methods at lower tiers, including "no comparison" and "historical baseline," are less rigorous and can be less effective at dismantling impact washing. Overall, impact measurement should move beyond "before" and "after" measurements to between "with" and "without" the intervention types of assessments.

The hierarchy of evidence can also be considered from three dimensions used in evaluation: effectiveness, appropriateness, and feasibility. In Table 16.12, four levels of evidence are proposed (excellent, good, fair, and poor) to classify the strengths of each research design according to these three dimensions. Research methods that contribute to generate valid evidence for each category are suggested.

Expected Return Methods

Expected returns are quantitative methodologies that highlight how meaningful the impact of investments is by analyzing its economic and financial impact on society and the environment. They are mainly characterized by its quantitative approach, which allows the translation to monetary terms, which can go from inputs to impacts, depending on the chosen method. They offer different but considerable degrees of comparability for estimating impact across portfolios and investments and allow organizations to remove biases and share the same language for decision-making.

Methods are constantly evolving and expected returns can take different forms and calculations methods. Each has its pros and cons and is as reliable as the data they use. Changing the data can yield different results within the same method (e.g. developing countries might have weaker results). For expected return methods, the literature mostly mentions the best alternative charitable option (BACO), cost-benefit analysis (CBA), cost-effectiveness analysis (CEA), the ERR, and SROI. This list is not exhaustive, and Appendix 16.2 offers more resources.

Table 16.13 summarizes the main characteristics of the expected return methods, which will be described in this section.

TABLE 16.12   Hierarchy of Evidence: Ranking of Research Evidence Evaluating Interventions.

	Effectiveness[52]	Appropriateness[53]	Feasibility[54]
Excellent	Systematic Review and Meta-Evaluations	Systematic Review and Meta-Evaluations	Systematic Review and Meta-Evaluations
Good	RCT Observational Studies	RCT Observational Studies Interpretative Studies	RCT Observational Studies Interpretative Studies
Fair	Uncontrolled trials with dramatic results Before and After Studies Non-Randomized Controlled Trials	Descriptive Studies Focus Groups	Descriptive Studies Action Research[55] Before and After Studies Focus Groups
Poor	Descriptive Studies Case Studies Studies of poor methodological quality	Expert Opinion Case Studies Studies of poor methodological quality	Expert Opinion Case Studies Studies of poor methodological quality

Source: Adapted from Ackley et al. (2008).

Beyond the expected return methods depicted in Table 16.13 and described next, there are a myriad of other methods, such as the social accounting and auditing (SAA), which is a useful method to assess the

---

[52] Effectiveness addresses the multidimensionality of effects concerning whether the intervention worked as intended and whether it was appropriate for its recipient.

[53] The evidence of appropriateness relates to the psychosocial dimensions of the intervention, addressing questions related to its impact on stakeholders, its acceptability, and whether it would be used by the beneficiaries.

[54] Feasibility refers to the broader environmental issues related to implementation, cost, and practice change.

[55] Action research is a collaborative approach to inquiry. It poses questions, analyses responses, validates new actions on the basis of responses, and then continues to ask further questions. As such, action research tests ideas as they come up and offers real-time feedback about what is working.

TABLE 16.13 Review of Expected Return Methods' Characteristics, Strengths, and Weaknesses.

	Key Characteristics	Degree of Implementation
BACO: Best Alternative Charitable Option	Compares potential social output of an investment against the best existing charitable option	Mostly used by Acumen and other nonprofit investment funds Not used often by investors
CBA: Cost-Benefit Analysis	Monetizing method, which aggregates all benefits and costs associated with a specific intervention	Mainly used by DFIs, public entities, big foundations Widely utilized in the infrastructure sector
CEA: Cost Effectiveness Analysis	Ratio of cost to a nonmonetary benefit (outcome)	Mainly used by public and health care sectors
ERR: Economic Rate of Return	Provides a single metric showing how an investment's economic benefits compare to its costs through an implicit interest rate at which the discounted benefits and costs of a project are equal	Used widely by the public sector and large non-governmental organizations
SROI: Social Return on Investment	Monetizing method that compares social or environmental costs of an activity with the benefits of achieving a specific goal or outcome. Also, a learning and planning framework to identify opportunities and strategies for increasing impact.	Mainly used by investors in public sector and in large nonprofit or social contexts

Source: Authors' elaboration.

performance of social, economic, and environmental objectives[56] (see, for instance, European Commission and OECD 2015).

Worth mentioning is also the Hewlett Foundation Expected Return,[57] which calculates the expected returns on investment "by assembling standardized, thorough, and explicit assumptions. Expected Return ultimately reduces potential biases in grant selection and makes grant-making more rigorous. The resulting documentation can be examined, challenged, and updated, and consequently leads to better decisions" (Hewlett Foundation 2008, p. 7). It allows very different results to be compared based on their shared ability to reduce poverty and increase well-being.

In addition to guiding investment decisions, expected return analysis can also inform an organization's strategy. For instance, the William and Flora Hewlett Foundation used expected return analyses to unfold a new program in global development, with the aim of improving the well-being of populations living on less than USD $2 per day in Nigeria[58] (Brest 2009). Using expected return analysis to guide choices among investments requires a common metric. To this end, the Hewlett Foundation developed an index that incorporated income, health, and education for this program. Next, it calculated the likelihood of success. To calculate the risks, it consulted experts at the Center for Global Development, the Brookings Institution, and Oxfam. The foundation also considered its experience with similar grant making in other countries. They needed to revise the ToC as they understood there were too many moving parts to work out well. Taking into account all the risks, they assigned the program a given percent probability of success. Next, the Hewlett Foundation calculated its contribution (an estimate of the share of the total effects it would be responsible for), considering the program also relied on donations by other organizations. Given this, the evaluation team estimated that the foundation's contribution would account for only a given percent of the total observed changes. The Hewlett Foundation then estimated the total benefit of its investment in transparency and accountability work in Nigeria. Finally, the foundation calculated the total cost of its investment, which also included the administrative costs for monitoring, and

---

[56]This technique can be as detailed as needed and can be combined with other metrics such as SROI. It is not easily comparable against other organizations because it is highly individualistic.

[57]See https://www.hewlett.org/wp-content/uploads/2016/08/Making_Every_Dollar_Count.pdf.

[58]More details on Brest (2009), pages 54 and 55.

evaluating grants. If the foundation had based its decision-making only on one outcome measure, it would not get the right perspective of the return and benefits on its activity in Nigeria.

More recently, and due to some of the limitations and weaknesses of existing methods, newer approaches have been developed to measure social impact. These are not yet commonly used, but they should be referenced as examples of how academic researchers and other organizations are tackling the issue of impact measurement. An example is the comparability method (Kroeger and Weber 2014), which uses the life satisfaction indicator as a unified measurement unit for social value created. The Viviani and Maurel benchmark review (Vivian and Maurel 2010) compares the financial and social outcomes of an organization with a benchmark(s) (e.g. organizations with similar activities). Eimicke and Buffett (2018) developed the impact rate of return (IRR), an approach that seeks to translate the benefits to the investment required, just as internal rate of return does. On the more practical side, there is HEC's Social Impact Assessment Strategy Report (HEC 2019). Given the newness of some of these methods, its practical applications to the Impact Investing sector are still limited.

Best Alternative Charitable Option

The global nonprofit Acumen Fund's model is to raise charitable funds from individuals, foundations, and corporations and invest it as equity or debt in organizations (for-profit businesses or not-for-profit organizations) serving BoP markets. The BACO method conveys the net cost per unit of social impact and helps portfolio managers and investors compare the potential social output of an investment against the best existing charitable option. Instead of providing an absolute number for social impact across a diverse portfolio, BACO aims to quantify an investment's social impact and compare it to the universe of existing charitable options for that explicit social issue. It measures quantitative results and involves monetization. This method belongs to the "assessment" category of the functional type of impact measurement systems.

The following formula indicates to what extent the investment is more cost-effective than the best alternative charitable option (Acumen Fund 2007):

$$BACO\ Ratio = \frac{NC_c/TSI_c}{NC_i/TSI_i}$$

with *NC* being the Net Cost[59] in monetary units, *TSI* the Total Social Impact in terms of outputs generated, *c* the best alternative charitable option, and *i* the fund investment. This ratio is a multiplier that compares the best alternative charitable option with the investment option and pursues the investment if the ratio is higher than one. Acumen's assessment of TSI focuses on the number of people affected in BoP markets, multiplied by a factor that estimates how they might be affected.

Box 16.8 provides an application of this method, whereby the net costs of each project are divided by the unit of social output (e.g. measured in people protected by mosquito nets, multiplied by years of durability).

Box 16.8 Acumen Fund Application of the BACO Method

Acumen Fund is analyzing the possibility of attributing part of a USD $325,000 loan to AZ Textile Mills Ltd, a manufacturer and exporter of insecticide-treated polyester bed nets based in Tanzania, Africa. This loan will finance long-lasting insecticide treated bed nets that would protect people against the mosquitoes that transmit malaria for 5 years. The other option would be to make a grant to an NGO that would use the money to distribute traditional bed nets (only effective for 2.5 years). The main steps to calculate the BACO Ratio are:

- Charitable option "net cost": USD $3.50 per bed net for 92,857 nets, plus an administrative fee of USD $32,500, totaling USD $357,500
- Charitable option "total social impact": 185,714 people (1 net for 2 people) protected per year (for 2.5 years) resulting in 464,285 people years of malaria protection
- Investment option "net cost": 20% of the total USD $325,000 which equals USD $65,000
- Investment option "total social impact": 2,000,000 people protected per year resulting in 10,000,000 people years of malaria protection. Since Acumen invests 20%, it will result in 2,000,000 people years of malaria protection.

(continued)

---

[59]The net cost of an investment is the total investment, plus administrative costs, subtracted from the expected benefits.

(*continued*)

- BACO Ratio = $\dfrac{357,500/464,285}{65,000/2,000,000} = \dfrac{0.77}{0.0325} = 23.7$

Thus, the Investment option saves more than four times the lives at one-sixth the net cost, equaling almost 24 times more net benefits than the charitable option.
Source: Brest et al. (2009).

BACO does not completely account for the long-term impact of Acumen's investments, "beyond the five- to seven-year investment period—nor the more qualitative 'system change' that may result (i.e., enabling local African production of life-saving anti-malarial bed nets and demonstrating that African manufacturing can be as efficient as production in Asia)" (Acumen 2007, p. 4). BACO is a process-oriented approach, there is a clear focus on outputs, and not on impact or monetization.

Additionally, the methodology is heavily reliant on the comparable charitable alternative. It is easier when organizations provide similar goods and services. If not (e.g. comparing an investment in bed nets with a grant to research a malaria vaccine), it often struggles with the difficulty of comparing "apples to oranges" when determining which option is more cost-effective at improving on a broader scale. Even intra-sector comparisons are difficult to make as the unit of social output needs to be the same for all the investment opportunities under consideration (Jäger 2010). Acumen is continually improving this methodology, and BACO serves as an extremely useful tool in understanding the larger context of Acumen's funds.

Cost-Benefit Analysis

CBA is a monetizing method that aggregates all the benefits and costs associated with a specific intervention. It calculates costs and benefits of a social venture and compares it to each other in order to evaluate whether the venture should be pursued or not.

The formula is generically defined as follows:

$$CBA = \sum_{t=0}^{T} \left[\frac{C_t}{(1+r)^t} - \frac{B_t}{(1+r)^t} \right]$$

C represents the costs in monetary units, *B* the benefits in monetary units, *r* the discount rate, and *t* the period of time. The strength of CBAs is that it allows the comparison of different investments across sectors and countries because all inputs and outcomes are converted into the same base, a monetary value (Cordes 2017). As it monetizes all the benefits and costs, investors can use CBAs to compare various investments in diverse areas and sectors, including in government and infrastructure. However, CBA is one of the most demanding and challenging methods due to its resource intensive nature (data, time, and cost). SROI is an example of a CBA. Box 16.9 depicts an example of CBA.

Box 16.9 Robin Hood's Example for the CBA

Robin Hood uses CBA to analyze the net benefits of learning English as a second language (Robin Hood 2014):

- Benefits: model assumes a 2% increase in earnings due to improved English literacy and USD $13,000 average earnings for a recent immigrant with low skills
- Costs: program costs of USD $50,000 for 1,000 participants to complete a year-long English as a Second Language program. About 30% of participants would not have access to language training if not for this program.
- Benefits: $B_1 = 1 \times 30\% \times \$13 \times 2\% = USD\$78$
- Costs: $C_1 = USD \$50,000$
- Cost Benefit Ratio $= \dfrac{78,000/(1+2\%)^1}{50,000/(1+2\%)^1} = \dfrac{76,741}{49,020} = 1.57$

Thus, for the incremental USD $1 invested by Robin Hood, the collective living standards rises by USD $1.57.

Source: Robin Hood 2014.

Cost-Effectiveness Analysis

The cost-effectiveness analysis (CEA) is mostly used when monetizing outcomes and impacts of an investment or project is not possible or very difficult, preventing a CBA analysis from being conducted instead.[60] CEA is commonly

---

[60]The choice between CBA or CEA depends on how easily benefits can be monetized.

used, for example, in health care, where it is difficult to put a value on outcomes, but where outcomes themselves can be counted and compared (e.g. number of patients recovered, or lives saved).

The CEA is calculated as a ratio of a monetary cost to an outcome measured in physical units (e.g. cost per life of saved AIDS patient). CEA is expressed through the following equation:

$$CEA = \frac{C}{E}$$

C represents the cost of the intervention in monetary units, and E the effect of the intervention in number of outcomes. The ratio represents the cost per unit of effectiveness (e.g. monetary units invested per life saved). Projects can be rank ordered by CEA ratio from lowest to highest. CEA is simple, feasible, and accurate, and is used frequently in the public and health care sectors, although it can be applied to all industries and geographies. It is most useful before the start of an intervention because it enables the comparison of two different courses of action, but it can also be used during the impact measurement stage. It allows ranking different programs within one program area, with the outputs to be ranked by cost-effectiveness often being social or environmental in nature. As with CBA, the level of detail will typically depend on the specific topic being addressed but can take a broad view of costs and benefits to reflect all stakeholders involved. CEA can also be used to build counterfactual scenarios comparing the effectiveness of the intervention to alternative scenarios or other similar interventions.

The main disadvantage of CEA is that results cannot be aggregated or cross-compared unless the analysis is done in exactly the same area of investment (O'Flynn and Barnett 2017). The CEA example is provided in Box 16.10.

Box 16.10 A Centers for Disease Control and Prevention CEA Example

The Centers for Disease Control and Prevention (CDCP) use the CEA to compare the relative costs and outcomes of two or more similar interventions in the United States. This example tackles measuring the "new HIV diagnoses detected" by two programs:

- Program A costs: USD $500,000
- Program A outcomes: 12 new HIV diagnoses detected by the program annually

- Program B costs: USD $37,000,000
- Program B outcomes: 5,000 new HIV diagnoses detected by the program annually
- $CEA_A = \frac{\$500,000}{12} = USD\ \$41,667$
- $CEA_B = \frac{\$37,000,000}{5,000} = USD\ \$7,400$

Thus, program B delivers a lower cost per HIV diagnosis detected.
Source: CDC (2019).

Economic Rate of Return

The Economic Rate of Return (ERR) provides a single metric showing how an investment's economic benefits compare to its costs. Since the value of a benefit accruing to people sooner is greater than the value of the same benefit accruing later, benefits and costs are discounted over time. The ERR is thus the implicit interest rate at which the discounted benefits and costs of a project are equal. The ERR uses the CBA method to compare the economic costs and benefits of an investment. It discounts all the costs and benefits over time, to calculate the interest rate that makes these net benefits equal to zero. The ERR is expressed in percentage terms and represents the rate at which benefits equal costs after discounting. This method is often used by the public sector and big private non-governmental organizations.

The ERR can be calculated through the IRR[61] formula:

$$ERR = IRR_{\sum_{t=0}^{T}(B_t - C_t)}$$

B represents the benefits in monetary units, *C* the costs in monetary units, and *t* the period of time of the duration of the investment.

The Millennium Challenge Corporation (MCC) uses ERR extensively in its work. MCC's objective is to contribute to poverty reduction through economic growth. MCC forms partnerships with developing countries committed to good governance and economic freedom, by offering grants designed to complement other US and international development support programs. There are three primary types of MCC grants: (i) Compacts (large, five-year

---

[61] The IRR is calculated by finding the discount rate at which the sum of the present value of future cash flow less the initial investment equals zero.

grants for selected countries that meet MCC's eligibility criteria); (ii) concurrent Compacts for regional investments (grants that promote cross-border economic integration, and increase regional trade and collaboration); and (iii) threshold programs, like smaller grants focused on policy and institutional reform.

MCC's evidence-based approach is rooted in its mission and its comprehensive results framework, which measures, collects, and reports on the outputs, outcomes, and impacts of MCC investments. MCC has a very strong commitment to making decisions based on data and evidence, and this permeates all stages of the agency's engagement in a country. MCC's results framework has been conceived to foster learning and accountability, and it has served as a model for global conversations about development results and aid effectiveness for more than a decade. Some of the main tools MCC uses to achieve, measure, learn, and report its results are country scorecards, constraints analyses, CBA, beneficiary analysis. And M&E plans are some. This evidence informs and shapes future project design and decisions. Box 16.11 explains how the ERR is used by MCC.

Box 16.11 Millennium Challenge Corporation Application of the Economic Rate of Return

In MCC's cost-benefit analyses, the costs of a project include all necessary economic costs, from financial expenses covered by MCC and other parties, as well as opportunity costs of nonfinancial resources expended. Benefits include the increased income of a country's population or the increased value-added generated by producers (firms and households) that can be attributed to the proposed project. Value-added is defined as the value of gross production (or sales) minus the cost of intermediate inputs produced (and purchased from) outside the firm.

MCC requires that its projects' ERRs exceed a 10% hurdle rate to be considered for investment (this is a common discount factor for development projects). MCC makes all ERR analyses available via interactive, downloadable spreadsheets. These spreadsheets are unique to a project or activity as defined within a Compact, or to a set of closely related interventions with the same benefit stream.

MCC's methodology for cost-benefit analysis, which produces an ERR metric, is best described as microeconomic growth analysis, which captures the expected increases in local incomes. This analysis includes income or value-added that is expected to be generated through environmental and social improvements, such as the effect of clean water on health outcomes for improved female educational attainment on incomes. However, it does not incorporate the non-income-related value of environmental and social improvements, given MCC's mission.

The ERR calculation considers two scenarios:

- Scenario 1: The expected outcome with the project
- Scenario 2: The expected outcome without the project (the counter-factual)

Scenario 2, called the "counterfactual," reflects an estimate of what is likely to happen in the future if the project does not take place. While this may be considered a "status quo" scenario, the estimation of future economic outcomes without the project also accounts for dynamic trends. For example, a growing economy would be expected to continue on its recent (or projected) growth trajectory without the project, and private investments would likely be made. In other cases, investments could be expected to decline in the counterfactual, for example, if electrical outages would be expected to increase without the project.

Next, through economic analysis the difference in incomes or value-added between the two scenarios are compared, factoring in the timing of accrued costs and benefits. Investments meeting MCC's hurdle ERR of 10% are those for which benefits are at least as high as costs after adjusting for the time value of money. Projects that are likely to generate larger increases in household incomes per dollar invested will have higher ERRs.

In addition to producing these ex-ante ERRs, MCC began computing revised ERRs upon Compact closeout in 2011, called "closeout ERRs." These ERRs provide an estimate of a project's cost-benefit relationship based upon the information available at the time of closeout, when MCC's costs and some indicators of benefits are known. Closeout ERRs are still forecasts, given that many projects' benefits do not start until after Compact closeout, and these benefits can continue for 20 years or more. Moreover, impact evaluation findings, which provide a measure of the degree of any project impact to date, are typically not available at the time of closeout ERR estimation. Closeout ERRs are thus distinct from an ERR based on measured benefits resulting from the MCC's projects.

(continued)

(continued)

All MCC projects are independently evaluated, and these independent evaluations often include evaluation-based ERRs. These ERRs still rely on forecasts for the later portion of MCC's CBA evaluation horizon, which spans 20 years. Nonetheless, independent evaluation-based ERRs complete the accountability loop in a way that is rare among investors.

Source: MCC Economic Rates of Return webpage.

Another example is in Box 16.12 of how the ERR can be calculated for the Mozambique Compact.

Box 16.12 An Example of the Calculation of an Economic Rate of Return for the Mozambique Compact

The Millennium Challenge Corporation (MCC) works in partnership with several developing countries to deliver sustainable economic growth and poverty reduction. The following project used ERR to evaluate a water and sanitation project in Mozambique.

- Project's benefits for one borehole in terms of time saved for households in wet and dry seasons:

$$= \#households \times \#trips \times (TimeWalking + TimeWaiting)$$

$$\times Opportunity\ cost$$

$$= B_{t=3}^{wet\ without\ project} = \frac{125 \times 3.8 \times (66 + 23)}{60} \times 4.8 = 3{,}368\ MT$$

$$= B_{t=3}^{wet,users\ with\ project} = 44 \times \left(\frac{2.2 \times (33 + 19)}{60} + \frac{1.6 \times (66 + 21)}{60} \right) \times 4.8$$

$$= 880\ MT$$

---

[62] Country spreadsheets with ERR calculations are available here: https://www.mcc.gov/our-impact/err. MCC also conducts cost-benefit and beneficiary analysis; this can be consulted here: https://www.mcc.gov/our-impact/beneficiary-analysis.

$$= B_{t=3}^{wet,non-users\ with\ project} = \frac{81 \times 3.8 \times (66+23)}{60} \times 4.8 = 2{,}190\ MT$$

$$= B_{t=3}^{wet} = B_{t=3}^{wet\ without\ project} - B_{t=3}^{wet,users\ with\ project} - B_{t=3}^{wet,non-users\ with\ project}$$

$$= B_{t=3}^{wet+dry} = (B_{t=3}^{wet} \times 67\%) + (B_{t=3}^{dry} \times 33\%) = \frac{542MT}{day} or\ 197{,}799MT/year$$

- Project's benefits for 160 boreholes:

$$= B_{t=3}^{wet+dry} = 197{,}799 \times 160 = 31{,}647{,}770MT$$

- Benefits considering the percentage of hand pumps in service:

$$= B_{t=3}^{wet+dry} = 31{,}647{,}770MT \times 85\% = 26{,}900{,}604MT$$

- Project's costs: Investment costs + Annual recurring costs

$$= C_{t=3} = 67{,}336{,}162 + 4{,}204{,}800 = 71{,}540{,}962MT$$

- Year 3 net benefits: Benefits $_{t=3}$ – Costs $_{t=3}$

$$= NB_{t=3} = 26{,}900{,}604 - 71{,}540{,}962 = -44{,}640{,}357MT$$

Please note that net benefits are negative until year 5 (inclusive), from year 6 net benefits are positive until the end of the project's life.

- Project's net benefits: Total benefits – Total costs

$$= NB = \sum_{t=1}^{t=20} NB_t$$

- Project's ERR = IRR(NB) = 46.7%.

Thus, the net benefit of this project over the full project life is 46.7%.
Source: MCC (2014).
Note: MT stands for Meticals, the currency of Mozambique (MZN).

Social Return on Investment

The social return on investment (SROI) is an international standard method to account for both monetizable and nonmonetizable impact, initially developed by the Roberts Enterprise Development Fund (REDF); Roberts is one of the named co-founders of KKR, the famed private equity fund.

SROI is an approach in which the economic value—both financial returns and the socioeconomic value of a given investment—are combined to result in blended value. SROI produces information on the social impact of an enterprise and monetizes outcomes. SROI is comprised of socioeconomic goals (e.g. increased welfare, jobs creation, etc.), impact indicators (e.g. income growth, job creation, private sector development), along with methods and tools to collect, manage, and share data (it can include both subjective, self-reported indicators and objective indicators, existing data and new data, desk research and interviews, surveys, and other types of analytical tools such as social media analysis).

Overall, it is a more holistic approach and provides an impact-oriented perspective of the return on investment (Brest et al. 2009; O'Flynn and Barnett 2017; So and Staskevicius 2015). It provides information for screening and due diligence and reporting. A review of the social impact sector points out SROI as the most developed method with a robust framework for implementation and facilitates the dissemination and usefulness of findings (Watsona and Whitley 2017).

In terms of reporting principles, it offers high comparability through quantitative measures. SROI[63] recognizes seven generally accepted principles, known as the social value principles: (i) involve stakeholders; (ii) understand what changes; (iii) value the things that matter; (iv) only include what is material; (v) do not over claim; (iv) be transparent; and (v) verify the result.

As a set of principles applied in a standard framework, SROI is both quantitative and qualitative. SROI can consider both the qualitative and quantitative relationship between inputs (activities performed) and impact (a given intended change in well-being). If applied quantitatively, the SROI Value Map[64] can be used, which is basically a type of financial modeling (i.e. impact modeling) of a change of well-being as experienced by stakeholders

---

[63]SROI is a framework seeking to establish Social Generally Accepted Accounting Principles (SGAAP), similar in structure to traditional financial accounting standards.

[64]An SROI Value Map is a discounted cash flow calculation that compares total value creation to total input costs, to obtain net value creation and an SROI ratio.

due to the program intervention (it can be regarded as a kind of a CBA, the difference being that it is guided by SROI principles, which borrows insights from financial accounting and sustainability reporting).

The SROI ratio is calculated by dividing the discounted value of benefits by the discounted value of investment required to achieve proposed benefits:[65]

$$SROI = \frac{\sum_{t=0}^{T} \frac{B_t}{(1+r)^t}}{\sum_{t=0}^{T} \frac{C_t}{(1+r)^t}}$$

B represents benefits in monetary units, C the costs or investment in monetary units, r the discount rate, and t the period of time.

The estimation of each outcome's benefits (B_t) should consider its unit value (financial proxy), the number of beneficiaries that experience change, the duration of change, what would have happened if this change had not occurred (deadweight), who else contributed to change (attribution), how this change affects outcomes that would have occurred elsewhere (displacement), and finally how the value varies in future years (drop-off). Box 16.13 provides an example of an application of the SROI.

Box 16.13 An Application of SROI in New Zealand

Since 1894, Te Whānau o Waipareira has offered advocacy services to the Whānau community in New Zealand. They used the SROI method to demonstrate the value of their Incredible Years Parenting (IYP) Program. IYP is designed to improve parental capabilities to prevent, reduce, and treat children's conduct problems:

- Total investment includes the cost of the program (NZD $412,500), volunteers (NZD $8,978), additional facilities (NZD $52,500), and the program supervisor (NZD $10,219), which totals to NZD $484,196.
- Total benefits include the sum of the 17 outcomes for the three stakeholders (parents or caregivers; children; and facilitators).

(continued)

---

[65]There are some variations in the calculation, but most methods tend to consider not only the economic value generated, but also the social value; this is the "Blended Value SROI" (So and Staskevicius, 2015).

(continued)

These are calculated considering the following: $Outcome_x = $ nr.beneficiaries $\times$ financial proxy $\times$ (1 − deadweight) $\times$ (1 − attribution) $\times$ (1 − displacement)

- To value the benefits of the outcome "Being a better parent":
  - 54 stakeholders experiencing the outcome
  - NZD $95 (estimated cost of a family coach per hour) $\times$ 2.5 hours $\times$ 14 sessions = NZD $3,325
  - 20% of deadweight based on the likeliness of the change to happen without being involved in this program
  - 25% attribution due to training on other programs and social services
  - 0% displacement because it does not affect other activities
  - 20% reduction in the influence that the service will have after the first year
- $Outcome_1^A = 54 \times$ NZD $3,325 \times (1 - 20\%) \times (1 - 25\%) \times (1 - 0\%) = $ NZD $107,730
- Considering the 20% reduction in the following years:

$$Outcome_2^A = \text{NZD } \$107{,}730 \times (1 - 20\%) = \text{NZD } \$86{,}184$$

$$Outcome_3^A = \text{NZD } \$86{,}184 \times (1 - 20\%) = \text{NZD } \$68{,}947$$

- Replicating these calculations for all outcomes:

$$Outcomes_1 = \sum_{1}^{i=17} (Outcome_1^i) = \text{NZD } \$771{,}889$$

$$Outcomes_2 = \sum_{2}^{i=17} (Outcome_2^i) = \text{NZD } \$601{,}025$$

$$Outcomes_3 = \sum_{3}^{i=17} (Outcome_3^i) = \text{NZD } \$469{,}282$$

- Adding up all benefits and costs, and considering a discount rate of 1.75%, the SROI ratio for the three years of the program is the following:

$$\text{SROI ratio} = \frac{\dfrac{771{,}889}{(1+1.75\%)^0} + \dfrac{601{,}025}{(1+1.75\%)^1} + \dfrac{469{,}282}{(1+1.75\%)^2}}{484{,}196} = \overset{.}{3}.75$$

Thus, for each NZD \$1 invested, a total of NZD \$3.75 of social value is created.

Source: Incredible Years Parenting Program (Lakhotia 2019).

SROI focuses on answering five key questions: (i) Who changes?, (ii) How do they change (positive and negative changes, intended and unintended)?, (iii) How do you know (gathers evidence beyond individual opinion)?, (iv) How much is you?[66], (v) How important are the changes?[67]

SROI requires a lot of information and time to be calculated properly, which makes its implementation across Impact Investing funds an expensive and complicated solution.

SROI analysis should only be conducted when it is possible to identify causal effects with reasonable confidence (Maier et al. 2014). A key limitation has to do with every SROI analysis in dealing with causality. Causality claims stemming from SROI analyses fall normally behind the gold standards of scientific research. Beyond statistical data about effects often not being available, it is not uncommon for SROI analyses to "neglect the qualitative illumination of impact value chains necessary to understand the mechanisms leading to desired outcomes, even though the cost of examining such mechanisms with qualitative methods is not prohibitive" (Maier et al. 2014, p. 12). Another related issue to featuring causality is about the setting of deadweights and attributions (as experimental designs in most cases are not feasible, evaluators need to work around it by accounting for deadweight as random effects and larger societal developments). For instance, SROI does not consider how the management team may perform and does not capture the catalytic effect of investments (So and Staskevicius 2015).

---

[66] Accounts of all the other influences that might have changed things for the better or worse.
[67] Refers to the relative value of the outcomes to all the people, organizations, and environments affected.

Another critical issue is the temporality of effects, in particular related to which discount rate to choose (the application of social time preference concept) and the linearity of social returns (e.g. the intervention might provide diminishing returns over time).

Given the many enterprise-specific factors considered in each application of the SROI method, and the weight it gives to context-specific stakeholders, SROI does not allow for comparison across different investments or projects. However, it does create a "common language" to estimate impact (So and Staskevicius 2015). Whether SROI analysis should be more standardized to increase the comparability of SROI reports and the availability of benchmark data is a much-debated issue. On one hand, standardization would streamline procedures, making SROI training simpler, and thus lowering the costs of its application. On the other hand, standardization inhibits customizing, thus making them potentially less legitimate and valuable for organizational learning.

AN INTEGRATED APPROACH FOR IMPACT MEASUREMENT

Different players in the Impact Investing ecosystem have distinct impact measurement and management needs. The approach to impact management may vary considerably depending on the theme, resources, and the expertise and sophistication of the stakeholders involved, which then establishes the degree of rigor of the methodological choices. Approaches and the level of rigor should be aligned along the impact stakeholder chain and the needs to demonstrate impact credibly (beneficiaries, asset, asset manager, founder).

It is useful to have an idealization of the concept of an integrated model for impact management, and what it entails along the different stages of pre-asset allocation (assessing potential impact and devising an impact strategy) and post-asset allocation (M&E and reporting) so to consider the different options and tools to apply.

Table 16.14 summarizes most standards and methods described in the previous sections according to the project and measurement cycle.

During the first stage—due diligence or impact risk assessment—assessing impact potential and its risks is crucial. A model for impact measurement is needed at this stage as funders are asked about historical impact data to demonstrate the kind of impact the asset is claiming to generate, how it materializes (what is its impact thesis), and how much impact is due to be generated for a given amount of capital. All impact investors should develop their own ToC to understand how their investments translate into

TABLE 16.14 Standards and Methods According to the Measurement Cycle.

	Estimating Impact	Planning Impact	Monitoring Impact	Evaluating Impact	Reporting Impact
	for due diligence	*through strategy*	*to improve project/program during implementation*	*to demonstrate social and environmental impact*	*to communicate impact*
Standards					
• ESG					
• GIIRS					
• GRI					
• IRIS					
• PRI					
• SASB Standards					
• SDGs					
Expected Return Methods					
• BACO					
• CBA					
• CEA					
• ERR					
• SROI					
Theory of Change					
• Logic Model					
Mission Alignment Methods					
• Social Value Criteria					
• Scorecards					
Quasi-Experimental & Experimental Methods					
• Historical baseline					
• Randomized Control Trials					
Mixed Methods					

Investment Process Alignment:	Due Diligence	Pre-Approval	Post-investment

Source: Adapted from Ivo, So, and Staskevicis (2015).

635

intended impacts and conduct the necessary research to explore and validate their assumptions and risks. This can be accompanied by a more graphic depiction of the results chain in the form of a logic model. Drawing upon existing literature, namely on experimental or quasi-experimental studies to test the hypothesis underlying the causal links, is key for establishing the validity and reliability of relationships across the results chain.

The pre-investment process involves a number of tools to screen candidates and conduct due diligence, which could include using, for instance, a social return on investment calculation to compare the impact of potential investments, then mapping out the potential investee's ToC to understand how the investment will convert theory to action and to identify causal links.

Developing a solid impact strategy is the next step at this stage before execution starts. This includes identifying risks and mitigation strategies, identifying hypothesis underlying the thesis, assessing information from similar interventions or impact metric databases available on the market in order to establish the relevant targets and metrics at all levels (impact investor or funder, investee, beneficiaries, etc.) along the results chain (outputs, outcomes, and impacts). Consequently, this implies identifying the sequence of beneficiaries and developing a set of indicators along the value chain and the right methods for data collection and analysis, besides systems, from very early on. Overall, this implies developing an impactful intervention that meets the needs of asset owners and managers aligning outcome expectations among all players in the ecosystem.

Additionality is also an important consideration when devising an impact strategy. "To have investment impact requires meeting the criterion of additionality—that an investment increases the quantity or quality of the enterprise's social output beyond what would otherwise have occurred" (Brest and Born 2013). It refers to whether the intended social outcomes would have occurred anyway without the investment, where the counterfactual is what ordinary, socially neutral investors would have provided in any event. "Investor-level additionality is the additional impact the investor is creating on the enterprise; enterprise level additionality is the additional impact that the enterprise has on society. As additionality is an important concept in understanding the actual difference that an impact investment is making, it should be an important consideration that cuts across many of the methods mentioned above" (Brest and Born 2013).

In the pre-approval stage, after due diligence, the investor and investee work collaboratively to fine-tune the impact measurement strategy for data collection, analysis, and reporting, starting by determining key performance indicators (KPIs) to track using agreed tools (monitoring scorecards, M&E systems, etc.). Screens can also be used but scorecards are considered a more robust form of performance measurement and tracking over time (So and Staskevicis 2015).

During the post-asset allocation, impact measurement might become more challenging. Resources and expertise need to be in place to start setting up the systems and collect baseline data. Beneficiaries need to be identified and interactions need to be set to ensure data is collected regularly, and that this is relevant to answer if the intervention had an impact. Data needs to be collected, analyzed, and managed efficiently across teams and between different types of players to monitor the social/environmental impact performance of the investee.

During impact reporting, telling an impact story should be done consistently using reliable data ideally collected at different points in time that pleases each different type of audience.

The challenge is that each player in the Impact Investing ecosystem might need their own unique performance indicators and might hold themselves accountable to different standards, thus several different impact management structures might need to be developed. Besides, these processes ought to be done collaboratively among all players. Collaboration along this cycle between investors and investees during due diligence, pre-approval (impact planning), and post-investment (M&E, or reporting) stages is not a quick win. An integrated approach and platform are needed.[68] For the most advanced and sophisticated type of actors, quasi-experimental or even experimental methods might be used. This is also used to validate the ToC.

Investors and investees have different combinations of resources, maturity, and sophistication for impact measurement. Figure 16.9 portrays the main methods used for the four types of combinations of early-stage investors and mature impact investors with more to less sophisticated investee organizations—distinctions between the quadrants are in bold text. The methods pointed out below are not exclusive to a single category; they only represent from the perspective of the authors the most commonly used by each type of actor(s).

---

[68] For instance, SoPACT has developed a platform called Impact Cloud, which allows funders, mission-driven organizations, and sustainable organizations to easily measure and manage their social and environmental impact. This is available at https://info.sopact .com/impact-cloud.

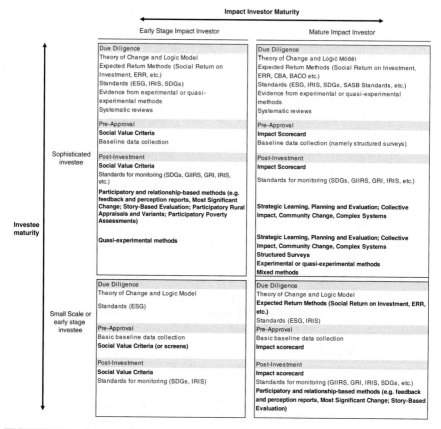

FIGURE 16.9   Integrated Approach for Impact Measurement.   *Source*: Authors, inspired by So and Staskevicis (2015).

Note: Systematic reviews sum up the best available research on a topic through synthesizing evidence of several studies, especially published research. Strategic learning, planning, and evaluation; collective impact; community change; and complex systems are methods to bring together organizations across sectors by building a common agenda around shared measure of success. They link performance measurement to strategy using methods such as formative and developmental evaluation, balanced scorecards, strategy maps, dashboards, and related tools.

There are some methods and tools that are most appropriate for a mature impact investor who is working with a sophisticated investee. A best practices integrated model ought to be developed for each intervention so that learning is embedded in whole process and lessons learned might be gathered for future implementation.

Guidelines for good impact practice can take different shapes depending on the internal context of an organization and can be applied differently according to the impact measurement objectives of an investor or investee. Fundamentally, investors need to align their vision and measurement with their guiding principles—fundamental norms, rules, or values that represent what their vision is of the future, what is a desirable system. The Social Impact Investment Taskforce (2014) produced a subject paper on impact measurement that outlines seven best-practice guidelines that impact investors should integrate in their investment practices: *Set Goals; Develop Framework and Select Metrics; Collect and Store Data; Validate Data; Analyze Data; Report Data;* and *Make Data-Driven Investment Management.*

For the construction of an impact framework that is relevant and effective for any organization, these are the most relevant steps:[69]

- Create a vision, a mission, and goals for your investment(s)/portfolio.
- Elaborate an intervention structure.
- Build a ToC (or several nested ToC).
- Decide what is worth measuring and which data is critical to validate your vision and mission, focusing on intended outcomes and impacts.
- Decide what is realistic to measure, looking at the instruments already in place and your resources. Some metrics are very difficult to collect and measure. Consider your resources at hand.
- Align with the mission with resources available for impact measurement.
- Look at your needs for reporting and communication and decide on the most appropriate impact measurement framework.
- Choose the right impact indicators to demonstrate impact.
- Balance standardization with harmonization. Align metrics to a relevant standard to allow compatibility (e.g. IRIS) and with the SDGs.
- Decide on the methods for impact measurement along your investment cycle.
- Craft your final "customized" impact management system.
- Decide on how to report and communicate your impact metrics.

---

[69] Inspired by Dodd (2017).

Lessons Learned for Impact Investors

Omidyar Network, the impact investment firm of eBay founder Pierre Omidyar, operates as a limited liability corporation for its for-profit investments and as a 501 (c)(3) private foundation for its grants to nonprofit organizations. From 2004 to 2014, its first 10 years of operation, it invested and donated a combined USD $750 million in 380 organizations (about half nonprofit and for-profit) in 40 countries, reaching about 150 million individuals and touching the lives of more than 1.2 billion people worldwide. Omidyar Network's lessons learned offer some valuable insights (Box 16.14).

Box 16.14 Lessons Learned by the Omidyar Network

- Impact analysis was done from the early start. From inception, Omidyar tried to achieve social impact at scale.
- Ensuring change occurs at a wider sector level. For example, instead of simply analyzing the impact of an investment in a given company and its clients, the firm looked at whether that investment had a broader impact on the sector. Building more competitive and inclusive sectors (e.g. financial sector) can serve a higher number of people and be more impactful.
- Assess depth as well as reach. The depth of reach is the most important assessment to analyze if grantees really understand the true impact of its activities. Some investees provided important yet relatively light improvements to the life of a typical user. Providing easy and free access to basic services is a positive thing, but it is a very different impact than causing a reduction in child mortality.
- Because most of Omidyar Network's contributions were in early-stage enterprises, it can take several years for the impact of their contributions to emerge (20% of its investees were "Impact Stars," young organizations that demonstrated "superior impact, both direct and on their sectors").

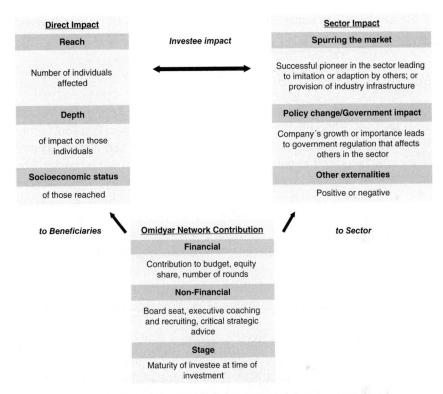

FIGURE 16.10   Omidyar Network's Measurement Model. *Source*: Adapted from Bardhan et al. (2018).

> • Expand the definition of risk to account for aspects such as mindsets and talents of the leadership team, but also the logical statements underpinning how the product or service can lead to impact.
>
> *Source*: Based on Bardhan et al. (2018).

Finally, Omidyar Network's impact measurement model integrates the direct impact of the investees, the impact on the sectors of the investees, and Omidyar Network's own contributions to both (Figure 16.10). It features three dimensions: (i) direct impact, (ii) sector impact, and (iii) network contribution. This highlights how devising an impact measurement plan can be complex, requiring effort and focus and allocating the right resources.

Nesta also offers some lessons from several years of Impact Investing (Box 16.15).

Box 16.15 Lessons Learned by Nesta

- Ensure that a collaborative and realistic impact plan is set out before every investment. Setting mutual expectations about the time and effort required to measure impact in an impact plan is crucial. The impact plan is an opportunity to ensure the venture is well resourced to deliver on impact measurement, and that timelines for data collection and analysis are sensitive to business milestones.
- Maintain a clear focus on impact. It is necessary to strike the right balance between maintaining a focus on impact and the flexibility to changing business demands. As a result of inflexibility, some ventures became increasingly detached from their impact plans to a point where measurement and engagement ceased to be relevant.
- Pursue a robust but flexible approach to impact plans and ongoing impact conversations so that wherever a portfolio company starts to deviate from its impact plan, there is mutual dialogue to develop a strategy for getting back on track or modifying the plan.
- Engage the investment committee. All committee members must be equipped to participate in substantive social impact conversations for the sake of maintaining proper oversight and accountability for impact.

Source: Based on Nesta (2017).

CONCLUSION

Although evaluation and impact measurement share a long history dating back from the 1950s, starting with DFIs, public institutions, and the social sector, private impact investors are relatively new to this field during the twenty-first century. Consequently, they have in general less experience in implementing impact measurement frameworks and techniques—especially the most advanced ones, or combining them appropriately along the investment cycle—due to the inherent complexity of measuring social and environmental change deriving from single or multiple contained interventions.

There are hundreds of standards and methods proposed by numerous actors, including academic researchers, social enterprises, consultancy firms, public institutions, philanthropic organizations, and traditional investors. Given the multitude of available options and lack of standardization in most areas, it becomes challenging for impact investors to select and apply the most appropriate standard(s) or method(s) for each stage of the investment cycle for the case of their specific investment(s) (Maas and Liket 2011). In the face of such high heterogeneity, investors sometimes opt for not measuring social impact or customize existing frameworks to their own needs (O'Flynn and Barnett 2017; GIIN 2018).

The consequence is frequently a measurement oversimplification, which can be experienced in a multitude of different measurement frameworks, which often end up tracking outputs (e.g. number of people with disabilities employed), instead of outcomes and impacts (e.g. change in the economic and social well-being of disabled people once employed) (Brest and Born 2013; White 2010; Dufour 2015). Numerous impact investors also fail to consider potential (unexpected or unintended) negative impact of their interventions or consider that all impact generated is due to their own action, thus failing to perform a proper analysis of attribution (White 2010). It is thus imperative to connect impact investors to the evaluation community and experienced impact organizations, who can share their knowledge, experiences, and best practices. Robust impact management practices and formal evaluations can address the two biggest concerns facing impact investors—the credibility of impact decisions and the attribution of impact to the investment(s)—while supporting better portfolio management for higher social, environmental, and financial returns.

Nevertheless, private impact investors have specific needs that might go beyond those addressed by these organizations. Thus, there is also an opportunity for the private sector, the public, and NGO sectors to share and learn from one another (Reisman and Olazabal 2016).

Impact measurement has been undertaken over time for multiple purposes, including evaluating effectiveness, meeting accountability requirements, and guiding organizations in improving the next cycle of decision-making. But similar to other areas where impact measurement is used, in Impact Investing, more evidence still needs to be collected to demonstrate that impact measurement practices are being implemented correctly, leading to concrete improvements in impact, reporting, and decision-making.

The state of impact measurement practices within the Impact Investing industry is moving forward fast, expanding, and diversifying across several sectors and geographies with a clear willingness to carefully explore and analyze the boundaries to impact measurement. Achieving a consensus on how to continue to move on forward sustainably seems to be a major challenge for the field and for all those pushing toward greater standardization in impact measurement (Reeder et al. 2015). The work led by the GIIN and IRIS, the OECD, and the IFC, among others, can no doubt encourage agreement around the use of a common set of frameworks, indicators, and techniques—which is nonetheless needed in certain instances for benchmarking across institutional performance, portfolios, and investments. But impact investors need to keep their hearts and minds open to a more formalized and regular practice of impact measurement, which has a crucial role to play in steering the field in the right direction, toward an agenda where it can prove itself to achieve social and environmental good through long-term systemic change.

ACKNOWLEDGMENTS

Our thanks to R. Paul Herman for applying the insights and knowledge of his 18 years of Impact Investing experience.

REFERENCES

Acumen and Root Capital (2015). Innovations in impact measurement: Lessons using mobile technology from Acumen's Lean Data Initiative and Root Capital's Client-Centric Mobile Measurement. https://acumen.org/wp-content/uploads/2015/11/Innovations-in-Impact-Measurement-Report.pdf (accessed 13 May 2019).

Acumen Fund (2007). Acumen Fund Concepts: The Best Available Charitable Option. https://acumen.org/wp-content/uploads/2013/03/BACO-Concept-Paper-final.pdf (accessed 13 April 2019).

Adobe (2018). 2018 Adobe Corporate Social Responsibility Report. https://www.adobe.com/content/dam/acom/en/corporate-responsibility/pdfs/Adobe-CSR-Report-FY2018.pdf#page=7https://www.adobe.com/content/dam/acom/en/corporate-responsibility/pdfs/Adobe-CSR-Report-FY2018.pdf#page=7 (accessed 13 March 2020).

Ahn, E., and Kang, H. (2018). Introduction to Systematic Review and Meta-Analysis. *Korean Journal of Anesthesiology*, 71(2): 103–112. DOI: 10.4097/kjae.2018.71.2.103.

Althelia Ecosphere (2016). ESG Principles and Policy. https://althelia.com/wp-content/uploads/2016/10/Althelia-Ecosphere-ESG-Policy.pdf (accessed 13 December 2019).

Amel-Zadeh, A., and Serafeim, G. (2018). Why and How Investors Use ESG Information: Evidence from a Global Survey. *Financial Analysts Journal 74(3)*. CFA Institute.

Bardhan, S., Kubzansky, M., and Bannick, M. (2018). *Omidyar Network's First 10 Years: An Impact Analysis*. Omidyar Network. https://www.omidyar.com/sites/default/files/Omidyar%20Network's%20First%2010%20Years%20An%20Impact%20Analysis.pdf (accessed 13 May 2019).

Barr, J., Rinnert, D., Lloyd, R., et al. (2016). The Value of Evaluation: Tools for Budgeting and Valuing Evaluations. Department for International Development, UKaid, and Iitad.

Best, H., and Harji, K. (2013). *Social impact measurement use among Canadian impact investors*. Venture Deli and Purpose Capital. https://karimharji.com/wp-content/uploads/Social-Impact-Measurement-Use.pdf (accessed 2 May 2020).

Bouri, A. (2011). How Standards Emerge: The Role of Investor Leadership in Realizing the Potential of IRIS. *Innovations: Technology, Governance, Globalization*, 6(3): 117–131.

Brest, P., and Born, K. (2013). Unpacking the impact in Impact Investing. *Stanford Social Innovation Review* (14 August). https://ssir.org/articles/entry/unpacking_the_impact_in_impact_investing (accessed 21 March 2019).

Brest, P., Harvey, H., and Low, K. (2009). Calculated impact. Stanford Social Innovation Review (Winter). https://ssir.org/articles/entry/calculated_impact https://ssir.org/articles/entry/calculated_impact (accessed 21 March 2019).

Eimicke, W. B., and Buffett, H. W. (2018). *Social Value Investing: A Management Framework for Effective Partnerships*. New York: Columbia University Press.

Case, J. (2017). Data: The next frontier for Impact Investing. *Stanford Social Innovation Review* (20 June). https://ssir.org/articles/entry/data_the_next_frontier_for_impact_investing (accessed 9 February 2020).

Centers for Disease Control and Prevention (CDC) (2019). HIV Cost-effectiveness. https://www.cdc.gov/hiv/programresources/guidance/costeffectiveness/ (accessed 30 November 2019).

Commonwealth (2018). Toolkits for Effective Implementation of the Sustainable Development Goals. Proceedings of the Toolkits for Effective Implementation of the Sustainable Development Goals Workshop Emperors Palace Resort, Johannesburg, South Africa. https://thecommonwealth.org/sites/default/files/inline/CommonwealthWorkshopToolkitsEffectiveSDG ImplementationFinal%20Report.pdf (accessed 13 May 2019).

Cordes, J. J. (2017). Using Cost-Benefit Analysis and Social Return on Investment to Evaluate the Impact of Social Enterprise: Promises, Implementation, and Limitations. *Evaluation and Program Planning*, 64: 98–104. https://doi.org/10.1016/j.evalprogplan.2016.11.008.

Corporate Citizenship (2018). The SDGs: Materially impacting the bottom line. 2018 Annual Review of Progress on the Global Goals. https://corporate-citizenship.com/wp-content/uploads/The-SDGs-Materially-Impacting-the-Bottom-Line-FINAL.pdf.

de Bruin, A., and Teasdale, S. (eds.). (2019). *A Research Agenda for Social Entrepreneurship.* https://www.e-elgar.com/shop/gbp/book-series/asian-studies/elgar-research-agendas.html Elgar Research Agendas. Cheltenham, UK: Edward Elgar Publishing.

DePoy, E., and Gilson, S. F. (2007). *Evaluation Practice: How to Do Good Evaluation Research in Work Settings.* Oxford, UK: Routledge.

Dodd, R. (2017). Best Practices for Social Impact Metrics Selection. SoPact, IMPACT METRICS10, Jul 2017. https://www.sopact.com/perspectives/best-practices-for-metrics-selection (accessed 24 February 2020).

Dufour, B. (2015). State of the art in social impact measurement: methods for work integration social enterprises measuring their impact in a public context. 5th EMES International Research Conference on Social Enterprise: "Building a scientific field to foster the social enterprise eco-system," EMES, Helsinki, Finland. https://hal.archives-ouvertes.fr/hal-01458730/document (accessed 24 February 2020).

Ebrahim, A., and Rangan, V. K. (2014). What Impact? A Framework for Measuring the Scale and Scope of Social Performance. *California Management Review*. DOI: 10.1525/cmr.2014.56.3.118.

Emerson, J. (2003). The Blended Value Proposition: Integrating Social and Financial Returns. *California Review Management*, 45: 4. http://www.blendedvalue.org/wp-content/uploads/2004/02/pdf-proposition.pdf (accessed 24 February 2020).

European Commission and OECD (2015). Policy Brief on social impact measurement for social enterprises: Policies for social entrepreneurship.

Evans, D (2003). Hierarchy of Evidence: A Framework for Ranking Evidence Evaluating Healthcare Interventions. *Journal of Clinical Nursing 12(1): 77–84.* Blackwell Publishing Ltd,

Flynn, J., Young, J., and Barnett, C. (2015). Impact investments: A literature review. CDI Practice Paper. Brighton: IDS.

GECES Sub-group on Impact Measurement (2014). Proposed Approaches to Social Impact Measurement in European Commission Legislation and in Practice Relating to EuSEFs and the EaSI. https://www.imfino.com/en/pages/industry-know-how/proposed-approaches-to-social-impact-measurement-in-european-commission-legislation-and-in-practice-relating-to-eusefs-and-the-easi/.

Gelfand, S. (2012). Why IRIS? *Stanford Social Innovation Review* (10 October). https://ssir.org/articles/entry/why_iris (accessed 19 March 2019).

GIIN (2017). Achieving the Sustainable Development Goals: The Role of Impact Investing. Global Impact Investing Network (8 September).

GIIN (2018). Roadmap for the future of Impact Investing: Reshaping financial markets. Global Impact Investing Network. Supported by the Rockefeller Foundation. https://thegiin.org/assets/GIIN_Roadmap%20for%20the%20Future%20of%20Impact%20Investing.pdf (accessed 2 May 2020).

GIIN (2019). 2019 Annual Impact Investor Survey. Global Impact Investing Network.

GRI (2019). GRI Standards. Global Reporting Initiative. https://www.globalreporting.org/standards (accessed 29 March 2019).

Guba, E. G., and Lincoln, Y. S. (1989). *Fourth Generation Evaluation.* Thousand Oaks: CA: SAGE.

Gupta, P., Chauhan, S., Paul, J., et al. (2020). Social Entrepreneurship Research: A Review and Future Research Agenda. *Journal of Business Research*, 113: 209–229. May 2020. DOI: doi.org/10.1016/j.jbusres.2020.03.032.

Hall, P. D. (2005). A Solution Is a Product in Search of a Problem: A History of Foundations and Evaluation Research. Hauser Center for Nonprofit Organizations. Kennedy School of Government, Harvard University. https://pdfs.semanticscholar.org/f7d8/1c3b098235c8ecc71b227c95b92d4fe0a51f.pdf?_ga=2.222042072.1355125893.1596389503-849321471.1596389503.

HEC (2019). Social Impact Assessment Strategy Report. HEC Paris Society and Organizations Center Movement for Social, Business Impact. https://contents.hec.edu/s3fs-public/2019-02/S%26O%20Social%20impact%20Assessment%20Strategy%20Report_%20page-page_web%20format_feb

%202019_HEC%20Paris.pdf?znXUzmBiNK9w1vlecjQPkDVFLI4I92Ia#_ga=2.186769256.1755744210.1596389682-1261784266.1596389682.

Heider, C. (2013). Embrace All Evaluation Methods: Can We End the Debate? (November 13). World Bank Blogs. https://ieg.worldbankgroup.org/blog/embrace-all-evaluation-methods-can-we-end-debate (accessed 20 May 2020).

Hewlett Foundation (2008). Making Every Dollar Count: How Expected Return Can Transform Philanthropy. https://www.hewlett.org/wp-content/uploads/2016/08/Making_Every_Dollar_Count.pdf (accessed 13 April 2019).

Hoffman, S. A., and Olazabal, V. M. (2018). The Next Frontier for Measurement and Evaluation: Social Impact Measurement for Impact Investing and Market Solutions. *African Evaluation Journal*, 6(2). https://doi.org/10.4102/aej.v6i2.342.

IFC (2019a). *Creating Impact. The Promise of Impact Investing*. International Finance Corporation, Washington, DC. https://www.ifc.org/wps/wcm/connect/publications_ext_content/ifc_external_publication_site/publications_listing_page/promise-of-impact-investing (accessed 2 May 2020).

IFC (2019b). IFC's Anticipated Impact Measurement and Monitoring (AIMM) System: Project Assessment and Scoring Guidance Note. March 2019. International Finance Corporation, Washington, DC. https://www.ifc.org/wps/wcm/connect/45565802-1b1c-4697-a4cf-45d675dd5640/AIMM-General-Guidance-Note-Consultation.pdf?MOD=AJPERES&CVID=mDqGyqA (accessed 20 April 2019).

IFC (2019c). Growing Impact: New Insights into the Practice of Impact Investing. https://www.ifc.org/wps/wcm/connect/8b8a0e92-6a8d-4df5-9db4-c888888b464e/2020-Growing-Impact.pdf?MOD=AJPERES&CVID=naZESt9 (accessed 20 April 2019).

ILO (2015). Fooled by randomization: Why RCTs might be the real "gold standard" for private sector development. http://www.ilo.org/wcmsp5/groups/public/---ed_emp/---emp_ent/---ifp_seed/documents/briefingnote/wcms:335698.pdf.

IMP (2018a). A Guide to Mapping the Impact of an Investment. Impact Management Project. https://29kjwb3armds2g3gi4lq2sx1-wpengine.netdna-ssl.com/wp-content/uploads/A-guide-to-mapping-the-impact-of-an-investment.pdf (accessed 15 March 2020).

IMP (2018b). A Guide to Classifying the Impact of an Investment. Impact Management Project. https://29kjwb3armds2g3gi4lq2sx1-wpengine.netdna-ssl.com/wp-content/uploads/A-Guide-to-Classifying-the-Impact-of-an-Investment-3.pdf.

Impact Base (2018). The global online directory of impact investment vehicles. https://www.impactbase.org/ (accessed 8 August 2018).

Impact Finance (2019). Impact Report 2019. http://www.impact-finance.com/index.php (accessed 13 December 2019).

Jackson, E. T. (2013). Interrogating the Theory of Change: Evaluating Impact iInvesting Where It Matters Most, *Journal of Sustainable Finance & Investment*, 3(2): 95–110, DOI: 10.1080/20430795.2013.776257.

Jackson, E. T., and Harji, K. (2014). *Assessing impact investing*, Five doorways for evaluators. Rockefeller Foundation.

Jäger, U. P. (2010). *Managing Social Businesses: Mission, Governance, Strategy and Accountability*. London: Palgrave Macmillan.

Jones, H. (2009). The "gold standard" is not a silver bullet for evaluation. Opinion, p. 127 (March). Overseas Development Institute (ODI). https://www.odi.org/sites/odi.org.uk/files/odi-assets/publications-opinion-files/3695.pdf.

Kaplan, R., and Norton, D. (1997). *Balanced Scorecard: Strategien erfolgreich umsetzen*. Stuttgart: Schäfer-Poeschel.

Kroeger, A., and Weber, C. (2016). Measuring and comparing social value creation: Advantages and disadvantages of a new comparability method, IRIS, GIIRS, and SROI. In *Routledge Handbook of Social and Sustainable Finance*, L. M. Othmar (ed.), Chapter 24. New York: Routledge.

Lafortune, G., Fuller, G., Moreno, J., et al. (2018). SDG Index and Dashboards Detailed Methodological paper. https://github.com/sdsna/2018GlobalIndex/raw/master/2018GlobalIndexMethodology.pdf (accessed 2 May 2020).

Lakhotia, S. (2019). Ngā Tau Mīharo ō Aotearoa: Incredible Years Parenting Program, Forecasting Social Return on Investment Analysis. http://www.socialvalueuk.org/app/uploads/2019/05/Assured-SROI-Report-Incredible-years.pdf (accessed 27 December 2019).

Lay, M., and Papadopoulos, I. (2007). An Exploration of Fourth Generation Evaluation in Practice. *Evaluation*, 13(4): 486–495. Thousand Oaks, CA: Sage Publications. DOI: 10.1177/1356389007082135.

Lockie, S., Franetovich, M., Sharma, S., et al. (2008). Democratization versus engagement? Social and economic impact assessment and community participation in the coal mining industry of the Bowen Basin, Australia. Impact Assessment and Project Appraisal, (26): 3, 177–187. DOI: 10.3152/146155108X357257.

Maas, K. (2014). Classifying Social Impact Measurement Frameworks. Giving thoughts. Conference Board. http://citeseerx.ist.psu.edu/viewdoc/download?doi=10.1.1.679.4208&rep=rep1&type=pdf (accessed 31 March 2019).

Maas K., and Liket K. (2011). Social Impact Measurement: Classification of Methods. In *Environmental Management Accounting and Supply Chain Management, Eco-Efficiency in Industry and Science,* Book 27, R. Burritt, S. Schaltegger, M. Bennett, T. Pohjola, M. Csutora (eds.). Dordrecht: Springer. DOI: doi.org/10.1007/978-94-007-1390-1_8.

Madaus, G., and Stufflebeam, D. (2002). Program Evaluation: A Historical Overview. *Evaluation Models*, p. 3–18. DOI: 10.1007/0-306-47559-6_1.

Maier, F., Schober, C., Simsa, R., et al. (2014). SROI as a Method for Evaluation Research: Understanding Merits and Limitations. *Voluntas: International Journal of Voluntary and Nonprofit Organizations* 26(5): 1805–1830. Welfare Mix and Hybridity (October 2015). *Springer.* DOI: 10.1007/s11266-014-9490-x.

Millennium Challenge Corporation (MCC) (2014). Mozambique's Water and Sanitation Project, Rural Water Points Activity. https://assets.mcc.gov/content/uploads/2017/05/mcc-err-mozambique-water-and-sanitation_ruralwater_closeout.xls (accessed 2 May 2020).

Morais Sarmento, E. de, et al. (2018). End-Term Evaluation Report for the Malawi Compact. Millennium Challenge Corporation.

Mudaliar, A., and Dithrich, H. (2019). Sizing the impact investing market. Global Impact Investing Network (GIIN). https://thegiin.org/research/publication/impinv-market-size (accessed 7 April 2019).

Muir, K., and Bennett, S. (2014). *The Compass: Your Guide to Social Impact Measurement*. Sydney: Centre for Social Impact.

Mulgan, G. (2010). Measuring social value. *Stanford Social Innovation Review (Summer).* https://ssir.org/articles/entry/measuring_social_value (accessed 31 March 2019).

Nesta (2017). Setting our sights: A strategy for maximizing social impact. September 2017. https://media.nesta.org.uk/documents/impact_strategy.pdf (accessed 13 May 2019).

New Forests Pty Limited (2019). RI Transparency Report 2019. PRI Association. https://ncwforests.com.au/wp-content/uploads/2019/07/2019-Public-Transparency-Report-for-New-Forests-Pty-Limited.pdf (accessed 13 December 2019).

O'Faircheallaigh, C. (2009). Effectiveness in Social Impact Assessment: Aboriginal Peoples and Resource Development in Australia. *Impact Assessment and Project Appraisal* 27(2): 95–110.

O'Flynn, P., and Barnett, C. (2017). Evaluation and Impact Investing: A Review of Methodologies to Assess Social Impact. *Institute of Development Studies. Evidence Report* 222. https://opendocs.ids.ac.uk/opendocs/handle/20.500.12413/12835 (accessed 2 May 2020).

OECD (2002). Glossary of Key Terms in Evaluation and Results Based Management. Paris: Organisation for Economic Co-operation and Development. https://www.oecd.org/dac/evaluation/2754804.pdf.

OECD (2005). *Evaluating Public Participation in Policy Making*. Paris: Organisation for Economic Co-operation and Development.

Ormiston, J. (2019). Blending Practice Worlds: Impact Assessment as a Transdisciplinary Practice. *Business Ethics: A European Review*, 28(4): 423–440. DOI: https://doi.org/10.1111/beer.12230

Ormiston, J., Charlton, K., Scott D., et. al. (2015). Overcoming the Challenges of Impact Investing: Insights from Leading Investors. *Journal of Social Entrepreneurship,* 6(3). DOI: http://dx.doi.org/10.1080/19420676.2015.1049285 (accessed 2 May 2020).

Ormiston, J., and Seymour, R. (2011). Understanding Value Creation in Social Entrepreneurship: The Importance of aligning mission, Strategy, and Impact Measurement. *Journal of Social Entrepreneurship,* 2(2): 125–150. DOI: https://doi.org/10.1080/19420676.2011.606331.

Ortas, E., Álvarez, I., and Garayar, A. (2015). The Environmental, Social, Governance, and Financial Performance Effects on Companies That Adopt the United Nations Global Compact. *Sustainability*, 7: 1932–1956. DOI: 10.3390/su7021932.

Patton, M. Q. (2003). *Qualitative Research & Evaluation Methods: Integrating Theory and Practice*. Thousand Oaks, CA: Sage Publications.

Peter, H., Rossi,Freeman, H. E., et al. (1998). *Evaluation: A Systematic Approach*. Thousand Oaks, CA: Sage Publications.

Petrick, S. (2013). Impact Investing in the area of long-term unemployment: Entrepreneurial approaches within selected European countries. Social Venture Fund.

PHINEO (2016). Social Impact Navigator: The practical guide for organizations targeting better results. Supported by the World Bank and Bertelsmann Stiftung. https://www.phineo.org/uploads/Downloads/PHINEO_Social_Impact_Navigator.pdf (accessed 20 April 2019).

Pineiro, A., Dithrich, H., and Dhar, A. (2018). Financing the Sustainable Development Goals: Impact Investing in Action. Global Impact Investing Network. https://thegiin.org/assets/Financing%20the%20SDGs_Impact%20Investing%20in%20Action_Final%20Webfile.pdf (accessed 14 February 2020).

Reeder, N., Colantonio, A., Loder, J., et al. (2015). Measuring Impact in Impact Investing: An Analysis of the Predominant Strength That Is Also Its Greatest Weakness. *Journal of Sustainable Finance & Investment,* 5: 1–19. DOI: 10.1080/20430795.2015.1063977.

Reisman, J., and Olazabal, V. (2016). *Situating the next generation of impact measurement and evaluation for impact investing.* Rockefeller Foundation. http://assets.rockefellerfoundation.org/app/uploads/20161207192251/Impact-Measurement-Landscape-Paper-Dec-2016.pdf (accessed 21 February 2020).

Robin Hood, R. (2014). Metrics Equations. https://robinhoodorg-production.s3.amazonaws.com/uploads/2017/04/Metrics-Equations-for-Website_Sept-2014.pdf (accessed 30 November 2019).

Rogers, P., Petrosino, A., Huebner, T., et al. (2000). Program Theory Evaluation: Practice, Promise, and Problems. *New Directions for Evaluation* 87: 5–13.

Rose, S. (2014). Regional and Sub-National Compact Considerations for the Millennium Challenge Corporation. MCC Monitor (September 2014). Center for Global Development.

Ruff, K., and Olsen, S. (2016). The next frontier in social impact measurement isn't measurement at all. *Stanford Social Innovation Review* (10 May). https://ssir.org/articles/entry/next_frontier_in_social_impact_measurement https://ssir.org/articles/entry/next_frontier_in_social_impact_measurement (accessed 21 March 2019).

Sachs, J., Schmidt-Traub, G., Kroll, C., Lafortune, G., et. al. (2019). Sustainable Development Report 2019. Bertelsmann Stiftung and Sustainable Development Solutions Network (SDSN). https://s3.amazonaws.com/sustainabledevelopment.report/2019/2019_sustainable_development_report.pdf (accessed May 2, 2020).

Saldinger, A. (2019). A deepening relationship between impact investing and the SDGs. Devex (21 November). https://www.devex.com/news/a-deepening-relationship-between-impact-investing-and-the-sdgs-96075 (accessed 2 May 2020).

Sarona (2019). Value-driven leadership for collaboration: Growth that matters. 2019 Annual Values Report. https://www.saronafund.com/user-files/uploads/2019/09/Sarona-Values-Report-2019-Final-Web.pdf (accessed 13 December 2019).

Savedoff, W., Levine, R., and Birdsall, N. (2006). When will we ever learn? Improving lives through impact evaluation. Report of the Evaluation Gap Working Group. Center for Global Development. https://www.cgdev.org/sites/default/files/7973_file_WillWeEverLearn.pdf (accessed 22 March 2019).

Sicoli, G., Bronzetti, G., and Baldini, M. (2019). The Importance of Sustainability in the Fashion *Sector*: ADIDAS Case Study. *International Business Research*. DOI: 10.5539/ibr.v12n6p41.

So, I., and Staskevicius, A. (2015). *Measuring the "impact" in impact investing*. Harvard Business School Social Enterprise Initiative with supervision of Alnoon Ebrahim. https://www.hbs.edu/socialenterprise/Documents/MeasuringImpact.pdf (accessed 13 March 2020).

Social Impact Investment Taskforce (2014). Measuring impact. Subject paper of the Impact Measurement Working Group. Social Impact Investment Taskforce. Established under the UK's Presidency of the G8. https://www.thinknpc.org/wp-content/uploads/2018/07/IMWG_Measuring-Impact1.pdf (accessed 13 March 2020).

Spiess-Knaf, W., and Scheck, B. (2017). *Impact Investing: Instruments, Mechanisms and Actors*. London: Palgrave Macmillan.

Stufflebeam, D. L., and Shinkfield, A. J. (2007). *Evaluation Theory, Models, & Applications*. San Francisco: Jossey-Bass.

Tashakkori, A., and Creswell, J. W. (2007). Editorial: The New Era of Mixed Methods. *Journal of Mixed Methods Research*, 1(3).

Toniic (2018). Toniic SDG Themes Framework. https://toniic.com/download/sustainable-development-goals-framework/.

Trochim, W. M. K. (2020). *Research Methods: The Essential Knowledge Base*. Conjoint.ly, Sydney, Australia. ABN 56 616 169 021.

U Ethical (2019). Annual Sustainability Report 2019. https://www.uethical.com/about-us/annual-reports (accessed 13 December 2019).

UNDP (2015). Impact Investment in Africa: Trends, Constraints and Opportunities. United Nations Development Program Regional Service Centre for Africa. https://www.undp.org/content/dam/undp/library/corporate/Partnerships/Private%20Sector/Impact%20Investment%20in%20Africa/

Impact%20Investment%20in%20Africa_Trends,%20Constraints%20and %20Opportunities.pdf (accessed 22 February 2020).

UN-OHRLLS (2018). Apia Outcome Inter-Regional Meeting for the Mid-Term Review of the SAMOA Pathway. Apia, Samoa 30 October–1 November 2018.

Verrinder, N. B., Zwane, K., Nixon, D., et al. (2018). Evaluative tools in impact investing: three case studies on the use of theories of change. *African Evaluation Journal*, 6(2). DOI: doi.org/10.4102/aej.v6i2.340.

Vital Capital Fund (2015). Crafting Impact: Presenting Vital Capital's approach to impact investing Impact Investing. https://www.vital-capital.com/ images/upload/texts/48465097050528.pdf (accessed 1 December 2019).

Viviani, J. L., and Maurel, C. (2019). Performance of Impact Investing: A Value Creation Approach. *Research in International Business and Finance, 47: 31–39 (CNRS 4).*

Watsona, K. J., and Whitley, T. (2017). Applying Social Return on Investment (SROI) to the Built Environment. *Building Research and Information* 45(8): 875–891 DOI: doi.org/10.1080/09613218.2016.1223486>.

White, H. (2010). A Contribution to Current Debates in Impact Evaluation. *Evaluation*, 16(2): 153–164. https://www.researchgate.net/publication/ 249744039_A_Contribution_to_Current_Debates_in_Impact_Evaluation (accessed 2 May 2020).

World Bank Operations Evaluation Department (2003). *The First Years* (P. G. Grasso, S. S. Wasty, and R. V. Weaving, eds.). Washington, DC: World Bank.

Young, L. (2014). Social value act review report to government. https://www.gov .uk/government/uploads/system/uploads/attachment_data/fle/403748/ Social_Value_Act_review_report_150212.pdf (accessed 20 April 2019).

APPENDIX 16.1: DEFINITIONS AND TERMINOLOGY

Term	Definition
Accountability	Obligation to demonstrate that work has been conducted in compliance with agreed rules and standards or to report fairly and accurately on performance results vis-à-vis mandated roles and/or plans. For evaluators, it connotes the responsibility to provide accurate, fair, and credible monitoring reports and performance assessments. For public sector managers and policymakers, accountability is to taxpayers/citizens.[70]
Activities	Actions, programs, or projects the organization carries out.
Additionality	The extent to which an investment has made a difference and has resulted in a change.
Attribution	Refers to that which is to be credited for the observed changes or results achieved. It represents the extent to which observed effects can be attributed to a specific intervention or to the performance of one or more partner taking account of other interventions, (anticipated or unanticipated) confounding factors, or external shocks.
Base case	Identifies what would have happened without the intervention and serves as a starting point for determining the additionality of an intervention
Base-line study	An analysis describing the situation prior to an intervention, against which progress can be assessed or comparisons made.
Benchmark	Reference point or standard against which performance or achievements can be assessed. A benchmark refers to the performance that has been achieved in the recent past by other comparable organizations, or what can be reasonably inferred to have been achieved in the circumstances.

[70]Note: Accountability in development may refer to the obligations of partners to act according to clearly defined responsibilities, roles, and performance expectations, often with respect to the prudent use of resources.

Term	Definition
Beneficiaries	The individuals, groups, or organizations, whether targeted or not, that benefit, directly or indirectly, from the intervention.
Counterfactual	The situation or condition that hypothetically may prevail for individuals, organizations, or groups where there is no intervention. Measures what would have happened to beneficiaries in the absence of the intervention, often by means of a control group.
Data Collection Tools	Methodologies used to identify and collect (store and organize) information sources and collect information (data) during an evaluation.
Effect	Intended or unintended change due directly or indirectly to an intervention.
Effectiveness	The extent to which the intervention's objectives were achieved, or are expected to be achieved, taking into account their relative importance.
Efficiency	A measure of how economically resources/inputs (funds, expertise, time, etc.) are converted to results.
Evaluability	Extent to which an activity or a program can be evaluated in a reliable and credible fashion. Evaluability assessment calls for the early review of a proposed activity in order to ascertain whether its objectives are adequately defined and its results verifiable.
Evaluation	The systematic and objective assessment of an ongoing or completed project, program, or policy, its design, implementation, and results. The aim is to determine the relevance and fulfillment of objectives, efficiency, effectiveness, impact, and sustainability. An evaluation should provide information that is credible and useful, enabling the incorporation of lessons learned into the decision-making process of both recipients and donors. Evaluation also refers to the process of determining the worth or significance of an activity, policy, or program. An assessment, as systematic and objective as possible, of a planned, on-going, or completed intervention.

Term	Definition
Ex-ante evaluation	An evaluation that is performed before implementation of an intervention.
Ex-post evaluation	Evaluation of an intervention after it has been completed. It may be undertaken directly after or long after completion. The intention is to identify the factors of success or failure, to assess the sustainability of results and impacts, and to draw conclusions that may inform other interventions.
External evaluation	The evaluation of an intervention conducted by entities and/or individuals outside the donor and implementing organizations.
Finding	A finding uses evidence from one or more evaluations to allow for a factual statement.
Formative evaluation	Evaluation intended to improve performance, most often conducted during the implementation phase of projects or programs.
Goal	The higher-order objective to which an intervention is intended to contribute.
Impact	Primary and secondary long-term effects of interventions (positive and negative) produced by an intervention, directly or indirectly, intended or unintended, that go beyond the primary beneficiaries and reach additional target groups such as communities and families or that lead to changes on an institutional level.
Impact value chain	Illustration and logical link between inputs, activities, outputs, outcomes, and impacts.
Independent evaluation	An evaluation carried out by entities and persons free of the control of those responsible for the design and implementation of the intervention. The credibility of an evaluation depends in part on how independently it has been carried out. Independence implies freedom from political influence and organizational pressure. It is characterized by full access to information and by full autonomy in carrying out investigations and reporting findings.

Term	Definition
Indicator	Quantitative or qualitative factor or variable that provides a simple and reliable means to measure achievement, to reflect the changes connected to an intervention, or to help assess the performance of a given stakeholder.
Input	Financial, human, and material resources are used in delivery of the intervention.
Internal evaluation	Evaluation of an intervention conducted by a unit and/or individual reporting to the management of the donor, partner, or implementing organization.
Lessons learned	Generalizations based on evaluation experiences with projects, programs, or policies that abstract from the specific circumstances to broader situations. Frequently, lessons highlight strengths or weaknesses in preparation, design, and implementation that affect performance, outcome, and impact.
Logical framework (Logframe)	Management tool used to improve the design of interventions, most often at the project level. It involves identifying strategic elements (inputs, outputs, outcomes, impact) and their causal relationships, indicators, and the assumptions or risks that may influence success and failure. It thus facilitates planning, execution, and evaluation.
Materiality	Data that is of such relevance and importance that it could substantively influence the assessments of providers of financial capital with regard to the organization's ability to create value over the short, medium, and long-term.
Midterm evaluation	Evaluation performed toward the middle of the period of implementation of the intervention.
Monitoring	A continuing function that uses systematic collection of data on specified indicators to provide management and the main stakeholders of an ongoing intervention with indications of the extent of progress and achievement of objectives and progress in the use of allocated funds.

Term	Definition
Outcome	The likely or achieved short-term and medium-term effects of an intervention's outputs. Social effect (short-term and medium-term change), achieved for the target beneficiaries as a result of the intervention undertaken.
Output	The products, capital goods, and services that result from an intervention; may also include changes resulting from the intervention that are relevant to the achievement of outcomes. Also referred to as tangible results from the intervention, effectively the points at which the services delivered enter the lives of those affected by them, expressed.
Participatory evaluation	Evaluation method in which representatives of agencies and stakeholders (including beneficiaries) work together in designing, carrying out, and interpreting an evaluation.
Performance	The degree to which an intervention operates according to specific criteria/standards/guidelines or achieves results in accordance with stated goals or plans.
Performance indicator	A variable that allows the verification of changes in the intervention or shows results relative to what was planned.
Performance measurement	A system for assessing performance of interventions against stated goals.
Project or program objective	The intended physical, financial, institutional, social, environmental, or other results to which a project or program is expected to contribute.
Relevance	The extent to which the objectives of an intervention are consistent with beneficiaries' requirements, country needs, global priorities, and partners' and donors' policies. Note: Retrospectively, the question of relevance often becomes a question as to whether the objectives of an intervention or its design are still appropriate given changed circumstances.
Results	The output, outcome, or impact (intended or unintended, positive, and/or negative) of an intervention.

Term	Definition
Results Chain	The causal sequence for an intervention that stipulates the necessary sequence to achieve desired objectives beginning with inputs, moving through activities and outputs, and culminating in outcomes, impacts, and feedback. In some agencies, reach is part of the results chain.
Results framework	The program logic that explains how the objective is to be achieved, including causal relationships and underlying assumptions.
Results-based management	A management strategy focusing on performance and achievement of outputs, outcomes, and impacts.
Stakeholders	Agencies, organizations, groups, or individuals who have a direct or indirect interest in the intervention or its evaluation.
Summative evaluation	A study conducted at the end of an intervention (or a phase of that intervention) to determine the extent to which anticipated outcomes were produced. Summative evaluation is intended to provide information about the worth of the program.
Sustainability	The continuation of benefits from an intervention after major assistance has been completed. The probability of continued long-term benefits. The resilience to risk of the net benefit flows over time
Target group	The specific individuals or organizations for whose benefit the intervention is undertaken.
Theory of change	The means (or causal chain) by which activities achieve outputs and outcomes, and use resources (inputs) in doing so.
Triangulation	The use of three or more theories, sources or types of information, or types of analysis to verify and substantiate an assessment. Note: By combining multiple data sources, methods, analyses, or theories, evaluators seek to overcome the bias that comes from single informants, single methods, single observer, or single theory studies.
Validity	The extent to which the data collection strategies and instruments measure what they purport to measure.

Source: Based on Spiess-Knaf and Scheck (2017), Social Impact Investment Task Force (2014), GECES Sub-group on Impact Measurement (2014) and OECD (2002).

APPENDIX 16.2: GLOBAL, NATIONAL, AND COMPANY LEVEL INITIATIVES, FRAMEWORKS, AND TOOLKITS

The widespread growth of frameworks, standards, and methods for the measurement of impact, and social and nonmonetary value have led to a spread of initiatives globally. Corporate Citizenship (2018) developed a "measurement map" designed to map the key initiatives offering measurement tools relevant to companies, helping them to navigate this space.

TABLE 16.15   Global and National Initiatives, Frameworks, Standards, and Indexes

Global and National		
Big Goals	**Well-being**	**Toolkits**
SDG Index[71]	OECD Better Life Index[72]	Commonwealth SDG Implementation Toolkit[73]
UN Global Compact[74]	Global Happiness and Well-Being Policy Report[75]	UNECA Toolkit to Support Alignment of Development Goals[76]
SIDS Accelerated Modalities of Action Pathway (Samoa Pathway)[77]	Indigo Well-Being Index[78]	Economic Commission for Africa (ECA) Integrated Planning & Reporting Toolkit (IPRT)[79]

---

[71] See, for instance, the dashboard for India: https://sdgindiaindex.niti.gov.in/#/.

[72] More information at http://www.oecdbetterlifeindex.org/#/11111111111.

[73] Commonwealth (2018). Conceived by the Commonwealth can be used to host national M&E systems in an integrated manner. It can facilitate to a great extent the implementation of the SDGs and the Samoa Pathway. http://sit.pmatglobal.com/.

[74] More information at https://www.unglobalcompact.org/.

[75] More information at http://www.happinesscouncil.org/.

[76] More information at https://www.uneca.org/content/uneca-toolkit-support-alignment-development-goals

[77] The Samoa Pathway was adopted in 2014, to address priority areas for Small Island Developing States (SIDS), calling for urgent actions to achieve sustainable development. (UN-OHRLLS, 2018, parag. 21). More at https://sustainabledevelopment.un.org/sids/samoareview.

[78] More information at http://global-perspectives.org.uk/volume-three/infographics/.

[79] More information at https://www.unescap.org/sites/default/files/Session_6_ECA_Ben%20McCarthy_IPRT_0.pdf.

TABLE 16.15 *(continued)*

Global and National		
Big Goals	**Well-being**	**Toolkits**
Ocean Stewardship 2030[80]	UK's Office for National Statistics National Well-Being Index[81]	Global Compact Self-Assessment Tool (UN Global Compact)
Sendai Framework[82]	Happy Planet Index[83]	Samoa Pathway Toolkit[84]
ILO Elimination Child Labor	World Happiness Report[85]	Human Rights Impact Assessment Toolkit (NomoGaia)
	Gallup Global Emotions Report[86]	
	Bloomberg Healthiest country Index[87]	
	UN Human Development Reports[88]	
	Base of the Pyramid Impact Assessment Framework (William Davidson Institute) Global Climate Risk Index[89]	
	PPI Progress out of Poverty Index (CGAP, Grameen Foundation, Ford Foundation)	
	Oxford Poverty & Human Development Initiative (OPHI)[90]	

Source: Authors.

---

[80]More information at https://www.unglobalcompact.org/.

[81]https://www.ons.gov.uk/peoplepopulationandcommunity/wellbeing.

[82]The Sendai Framework contains seven global targets and 38 global indicators to measure progress made by all countries on disaster risk reduction by the year 2030.

[83]More information at http://happyplanetindex.org/.

[84]This is currently under development by the United Nations.

[85]More information at https://worldhappiness.report/.

[86]More information at https://www.gallup.com/analytics/248906/gallup-global-emotions-report-2019.aspx.

[87]More information at https://www.bloomberg.com/news/articles/2019-02-24/spain-tops-italy-as-world-s-healthiest-nation-while-u-s-slips?srnd=premium-europe.

[88]More information at http://hdr.undp.org/en/global-reports.

[89]More information at https://germanwatch.org/en/17307.

[90]https://ophi.org.uk/.

TABLE 16.16 Company Measures, Frameworks, Investors, and Toolkits.

Companies			
Company Measures	Business Frameworks	Investors	Toolkits
Bespoke Key Performance Indicators (KPIs)[91]	GRI[92]	Socially Responsible Investing[93]	The Global Value Toolkit[94]
Impact studies and casestudies[95]	Sustainability Accounting Standards Board (SASB)[96]	Principles for Responsible Investment	
Strategy-linked plans[97]	LBG Framework[98]	The Equator Principles[99]	

---

[91] Most companies identify indicators and metrics relevant to their corporate responsibility and sustainability strategies. Consider, for instance, Coca-Cola's sustainability plan at https://www.cokecce.com/system/file_resources/1/Our_Sustainability_Plan_Overview_Booklet.pdf.

[92] Described in the section regarding standards.

[93] Also known as ethical, green, or sustainability investing. One of the first examples was the Dow Jones Sustainability Index, launched in 1999. Indices such as this act as benchmarks for investors who integrate sustainability considerations in their portfolios. https://www.spglobal.com/esg/csa/indices/.

[94] Provides knowledge, tools, and resources for companies and other societal actors wishing to tackle the SDGs together with business. https://www.global-value.eu/toolkit/.

[95] These can measure direct or indirect impacts from the micro level (e.g. local communities), sectors, or at a more macro level (country or region). and also include knock-on or ripple economic impacts. See, for instance, Dell's FY19 "Corporate Social Responsibility Report A Progress Report on our 2020 Plan" at https://corporate.delltechnologies.com/content/dam/delltechnologies/assets/corporate/pdf/progress-made-real-reports/dell-fy19-csr-report.pdf For case studies, see https://bimpactassessment.net/case-studies and corporate case studies at Global Reporting: https://www.globalreporting.org/information/news-and-press-center/Pages/Corporate-case-studies.aspx A series of impact stories are reported by Impact Reporting UK at https://impactreporting.co.uk/success-stories/ For academic papers see the Adidas case study on sustainability by Sicoli et al. (2019).

[96] Described in the section about Standards.

[97] A growing number of companies are implementing sustainability plans linked to global strategy to integrate business imperatives with social ones. See, for example, Unilever's Sustainable Living Plan at https://www.unilever.com/sustainable-living/.

[98] LBG is global standard in measuring and managing corporate community investment and a global network of more than 300 companies working together to address the challenges of measuring corporate community investment. More information at http://www.lbg-online.net/framework/.

[99] A risk management framework adopted by financial institutions.

TABLE 16.16 *(continued)*

Companies			
Company Measures	Business Frameworks	Investors	Toolkits
Environmental Profit & Loss[100]	World Business Council for Sustainable Development (WBCSD) Measuring Impact Framework and Measuring Socio-economic Impact[101]	International Finance Corp.'s Development Outcome Tracking System (DOTS)[102]	
Integrated reports[103]	Foundation Strategy Group's Shared Value Initiative[104]	ESG screens[105]	
	Business in the Community (BITC) CR Index and Responsible Business Tracker[106]		
	ISO26000 Social Responsibility[107]		

Source: Authors, inspired by Corporate Citizenship (2018).

---

[100]Dating from 2011 PUMA's Environmental Profit and Loss Account (EP&L) was ground-breaking in its assessment of long-term hidden environmental business costs. See the report here: http://danielsotelsek.com/wp-content/uploads/2013/10/Puma-EPL.pdf.

[101]The WBCSD developed two main tools to help business get started: (i) the "WBCSD Measuring Impact Framework," launched in 2008, designed to help companies understand their contribution to society and use this understanding to inform their operational and long-term investment decisions, and have better conversations with stakeholders; (ii) the "Measuring Socio-economic Impact," a guide for business to help companies navigate the complex landscape of socioeconomic impact measurement, and select the options that work best for them.

[102]More information at http://documents.worldbank.org/\discretionary-curated/ en/287171468326410253/Development-Outcome-Tracking-System-DOTS-indicator-framework.

[103]A new approach to reporting that shows how organizations deal with value creation, by bringing together strategy, governance, and performance and demonstrating the links between financial performance and the wider social, environmental, and economic context. Examples hosted by the International Integrated Reporting Council at http://examples.integratedreporting.org/home and award-winning reports at http://examples.integratedreporting.org/recognized_reports.

[104]Created and supported by FSG, it is a global community of leaders who find business opportunities in societal challenges. More information at https://www.fsg.org/shared-value-initiative.

[105]Described in the section on Standards.

[106]More information at https://www.bitc.org.uk/the-responsible-business-tracker/.

[107]More information at https://www.iso.org/iso-26000-social-responsibility.html.

TABLE 16.17   Social Impact Additional Information.

Social Impact		
Impact Investing	Social Impact Frameworks, Standards, and Methods	Social Impact Organizations[108]
Global Impact Investing Network (GIIN): IRIS[109]	Issue-based frameworks/standards[110]	Social Enterprises[111]
Root Capital – Social and Environmental Scorecard[112]	AA1000 Accountability Principles Standards 2008[113]	Cooperatives[114]
Bridges Ventures[115]	B Impact – GIIRS[116]	Inspiring Impact[117]
Acumen Fund: BAC[118]	B Impact – Assessment[119]	

---

[108]Those that prioritize doing work that consciously, systemically, and sustainably serves or attempts to address a local or global community need.

[109]Described in the section about Standards.

[110]See, for instance, the Ethical Trade Initiative at https://www.ethicaltrade.org/; Fair Trade at https://www.fairtradecertified.org/; and Forest Stewardship Council at https://fsc.org/en.

[111]See, for instance, the Ethical Trade Initiative at https://www.ethicaltrade.org/; Fair Trade at https://www.fairtradecertified.org/; and Forest Stewardship Council at https://fsc.org/en.

[112]Root Capital conducts social and environmental due diligence on all prospective borrowers to determine how they align with our mission to build sustainable livelihoods for rural communities in Africa and Latin America: https://rootcapital.org/wp-content/uploads/2018/01/Social_and_Environmental_Scorecards_ENG.pdf.

[113]Primarily intended for use by organizations developing an accountable and strategic approach to sustainability; free tool available at https://www.accountability.org/wp-content/uploads/2016/10/AA1000APS_english.pdf.

[114]See, for instance, Co-operatives UK at https://www.uk.coop/.

[115]A specialist fund manager that uses financial and social and environmental goals. More information at https://www.bridgesfundmanagement.com/.

[116]Described in the section about Standards.

[117]A group of third-sector organizations from impact measurement experts to membership bodies engaged towards high-quality impact measurement. The Inspiring Hub Impact features more than 200 resources and tools to support impact measurement; more information at https://www.inspiringimpact.org/.

[118]Nonprofit raising charitable donations to invest in companies, leaders, and ideas to change the way the world leads with poverty. More information at https://acumen.org/. Acumen developed the BACO method described in the section about methods.

[119]A credible free tool any company can use to measure its impact on its workers, community, environment, and customers, available at.https://bimpactassessment.net/.

TABLE 16.17 *(continued)*

Social Impact		
Impact Investing	**Social Impact Frameworks, Standards, and Methods**	**Social Impact Organizations**
Impact Investing Hubs[120]	Social Return on Investment (SROI)	
	Cost Benefit Analysis (CBA)	
	Cost Effectiveness Analysis (CEA)	
	Economic Rate of Return (ERR)	

Source: Authors, inspired by Corporate Citizenship (2018).

Beyond Impact Investing frameworks, certifications, tools, and methods there are organizations that work within the boundaries of profit and non-profit, such as social enterprises and cooperatives.

---

[120]See, for instance, the Impact Investing Hubs in Australia, https://www .impactinvestinghub.com.au/; Geneva, https://geneva.impacthub.net/; and the Social Impact Investing Hub at http://www.socialimpacthub.org/impact-investing-hub/.

Impact Measurement and Management Techniques to Achieve Powerful Results

Jane Reisman, PhD and Veronica Olazabal, MCRS

Abstract

Seen as a barrier to scaling Impact Investing, efforts to build field-level consensus about how to approach impact measurement have intensified. Impact Measurement and Management (IMM) must evolve if the industry is to grow and scale within the tenets of credible Impact Investing. Numerous standard bearers, professional associations, academics, investors, and intermediaries have made a purposeful effort to build consensus around terminology and practice. Commonly referred to as IMM, this coalition of the willing has been leading the charge to align standards for data collection and management. This global mobilization has allowed an alignment and socialization of consensus-based best practices around generally accepted metrics for different thematic areas of impact and the United Nations' Sustainable Development Goals (SDG). This chapter delves into the evolution of measurement practices for Impact Investing, focusing on three significant developments: the five dimensions of impact and its use in impact management, the IRIS+ system, and the alignment with SDG goals. Drawing from right-sized conventional methods, evaluative thinking, and innovative evaluation approaches, the burden for the Impact Investing industry can be lessened, avoiding the unnecessary burden of reinventing the wheel. This chapter pinpoints where there has been critical successes and spotlights examples of progress for establishing the credibility of IMM, but also highlights existing needs for a continued reduction of bespoke approaches and for the adoption of field-level practices for articulating, defining, measuring, and managing for impact.

Keywords

Impact Investing; Impact Measurement and Management; IMM; Impact Management; Social Impact Evaluation; Innovative Finance; Sustainable Development Goals; IRIS+; Five Dimensions of Impact; Impact Management Project

INTRODUCTION

Impact Measurement and Management: The Lever for Driving Impact in Impact Investing

Impact Investing, the term *du jour* for the next generation of innovative finance solutions to address global challenges, was formalized at a 2007 conference in Bellagio, Italy, hosted by The Rockefeller Foundation.[1] A key differentiator between Impact Investing and other forms of sustainability and socially responsible investing is the intentional effort to practice impact measurement and management in order to create a positive impact on people and planet. This differentiator is clearly pronounced in the set of fundamental tenets for credible Impact Investing put forward by the Global Impact Investing Network (GIIN). These tenets speak to intentionality, use of evidence and impact data in investment design, managing impact

---

[1] This formalization of an industry coalesced a number of related efforts that had been in place for one or more decades that focused on social return on investment alongside financial return, philanthropic program–related investments, microfinance lending, and more. The Bellagio meeting, supported by The Rockefeller Foundation, produced a roadmap for building out this growing Impact Investing arena into an industry.

performance, and contributing to the growth of the industry based on these shared conventions (GIIN 2019b).

The fundamental tenets of Impact Investing are a clear response to the threat of "impact washing," a term customarily used to cast doubt on the viability of an industry that makes claims for social and environmental benefits without normative evidence or data to support these claims. Even worse, the lack of evidence, data, or active impact management holds the possibility of creating more harm than good (Karnani 2007) or detracting capital that might otherwise have been deployed as charitable grants and donations (Kramer 2017).

Seen as a barrier to scaling Impact Investing, over the last few years efforts to build field-level consensus about how to approach impact measurement have intensified and become highly animated. A number of standard bearers, professional associations, academics, practitioners, investors, and intermediaries have made a purposeful effort to build consensus around terminology and practice, including definitions, protocols, metrics, transparency, methodologies, and stakeholder engagement related to data, evidence, and decision-making for measuring and managing impact performance. Commonly referred to as Impact Measurement and Management (IMM) or impact management for short,[2] a coalition of the willing has been leading the charge to collaborate and align existing standards for data collection and management (Olsen et al. 2019, p. 60). These field builders have mobilized thousands of stakeholders globally who are beginning to align around and socialize consensus-based best practices, particularly the five dimensions of impact, generally accepted metrics for different thematic areas of impact and alignment with the UN Sustainable Development Goals (SDG) (United Nations 2015).

Additionally, principles are also being promoted around conventions for quality of data collection and methods, such as ensuring data represent the voice of people most affected (World Economic Forum 2017), data transparency and comparability (OECD 2019), and that high-quality data are collected in a way that is verifiable (IFC 2019). Increasingly, more attention is being given to robust approaches to measuring and managing impact, often drawing from methods used in the allied fields of accounting and evaluation (Ruff and Olsen 2018), involving both conventional and innovative ones that make use of advances in technologies and an orientation toward embedding evaluative thinking into the design of programmatic strategies

---

[2]See the Impact Management Project here: impactmanagementproject.com (accessed 27 March 2020).

(Picciotto 2015). The game-changing aim of these consensus-driven and field building efforts is to shift the focus of measurement from being viewed as a commodity to one where measurement is the means toward "impact management" (i.e. reduce the negative and increase the positive social and environmental impacts resulting from investment decisions). "As the practice of impact measurement and management grows, its standards, principles, and frameworks are quickly moving from optional supplements to financial accounting to necessary anchors of it" (Olsen et al. 2019, p. 60).

This chapter brings these developments to life, focusing on three specific and significant developments for advancing Impact Investing through IMM: (i) the five dimensions of impact and their use in impact management; (ii) IRIS+ system[3] to measure, manage, and optimize impact; and (iii) SDG goal alignment. This chapter brings each of these developments to life with case examples of how they are practiced within the Impact Investing ecosystem. It is important to note that these practices are not mutually exclusive, that each case example illustrates a key development in IMM and can incorporate elements of other significant developments as well. For instance, the Toniic T100 Project (discussed as a case example) animates SDG alignment and leverages the five dimensions and the IRIS+ system.

The next section discusses the journey over the past 10 years, to illuminate how IMM has been evolving and advancing toward a consensus-based discipline among actors in the Impact Investing ecosystem. This is followed by focused attention on three developments and illustrative examples of each. The chapter wraps up with three concise recommendations about the types of efforts needed to advance the positive momentum for driving impact through IMM.

METHODOLOGY

This chapter is based on desk review of the literature, case examples, engagement with IMM, and evaluation work by the authors. The examples provided deliberately include Impact Investing organizations at different parts of the ecosystem and represent different levels of assets, ranging from billion-dollar asset managers to single million-dollar investors. The variation in these examples supports the case that resources are not a limiting factor for employing IMM to drive impact. Importantly, these examples are all focused at the asset manager (impact investor) level and should not necessarily be

---

[3] IRIS stands for Impact Reporting and Investment Standards.

conflated with IMM at the enterprise level, for which there would be other signs of significant progress (such as the proliferation of B Labs' certification process for B Corps).

An Evolving Landscape for Impact Measurement and Management

Early efforts to normalize measurement in Impact Investing were choppy. In 2009, as a global convener and field builder for growing the Impact Investing marketplace, the GIIN began to manage and regularly update a catalogue of standard metrics commonly referred to as IRIS: the Impact Reporting and Investment Standards.[4] This catalogue intentionally aligned with 40 standards and reporting frameworks associated with specific sectors and provided an on-ramp to the industry's effort to track impact currently in use at that time. The Impact Investing industry coalesced in support of IRIS as a recognized industry best practice for standardized metrics and indicators. Importantly, IRIS's focus on inputs and outputs as proxies for impact notably differed from the contemporary public and global development sectors' conventions and practices, which equated impact with changes in beneficiaries or end users.

Over time, asset managers developed bespoke measurement approaches that they promoted as part of their competitive market advantages. Often called integrated reporting, these bespoke methods typically integrate reporting on financial performance alongside social and environmental reporting. Like early versions of IRIS, these metrics typically resided and still do at either the output level or attempted to provide social return on investment (SROI) calculations based on available, but often limited, evidence or assumptions.

Only a decade later, a noticeable growth of measurement solutions in the marketplace occurred. For instance, the CDC Group (the United Kingdom's development finance institution) produced a handbook that is an overview of tools and methods (2019) and features both conventional evaluation methods and those that take advantage of advances in technology that have the potential for enabling quick, low-cost, and valuable impact measurement. Lean data methods, originally developed by Acumen and now spun off to 60 Decibels,[5] exemplifie a quick and low-cost measurement approach, with great uptake by impact investors across the globe and across

---

[4]See more information here: iris.thegiin.org/ (accessed 27 March 2020).
[5]See acumen.org/blog/acumen-launches-60-decibels/ for further detail (accessed 27 March 2020).

various industry sectors. This method uses both standard and customized survey questions to obtain customer (stakeholder) feedback, primarily using mobile-based data collection.

While scaling IMM may seem to value quick and low-cost methods over more intensive approaches, the choice of approach will also be related to the depth of change that aligns to intentions of investors and enterprises, scale of anticipated impact, complexity of externalities that may require measurement of system factors, and stage of growth of investee companies and models. Similar to the public and global development sectors, methodological measurement and evaluation choices are related to the relevant decisions needed to be made about a problem, as well as the overall life stage of the effort (e.g. innovation, emergent strategy, proven solution, etc.; Reisman and Olazabal, 2018). For instance, Upaya Social Ventures, discussed shortly below, offers a proven solution focused on transforming the lives of the very poor in India and has developed their IMM system to be longitudinal in order to track change over time and to better manage for impact.

Interestingly, it is also commonplace to combine multiple approaches. The GIIN's 2019 annual survey of impact investors (GIIN 2019a) revealed that the majority of the investors surveyed who measured impact use qualitative information (66%) or proprietary metrics not aligned to any external frameworks (63%). Yet, nearly half of these investors also use metrics aligned with IRIS (49%) and a third use standardized frameworks and assessments (37%). The GIIN's study, surprisingly, also revealed that the UN global goals, well known as the SDGs, have become widely adopted as part of impact measurement. The majority of survey respondents (71%) have mapped their investments to the SDG goals and half (51%) have incorporated the SDGs into their measurement systems.

The landscape for measuring impact is further muddled by some asset managers and owners interchanging screening and sustainability rating tools focused on internal environment, social, and governance (ESG) factors with impact measurement approaches. While ESGs are more commonly applied to analysis of public companies, impact measurement is focused on the growing industry of companies adopting intentional impact strategies. However, these approaches are nonetheless often conflated. Take, for instance, the United Nations Principles for Responsible Investment (UNPRI)[6] and the International Finance Corporation-led (IFC) Operating Principles for Impact Management (IFC 2019). Both are accountability frameworks; however, UNPRI is most appropriate for ESG-oriented public

---

[6]See United Nations Principles of Responsible Investment here: www.unpri.org/ (accessed 28 March 2020).

companies, while the IFC-led principles offer impact investors specifically a process for ensuring that impact considerations are integrated into their investment decisions throughout the investment life cycle.[7]

The authors have taken a broad view of the IMM field to situate this chapter within this wide aperture. Figure 17.1 is organized across four quadrants, illustrating the landscape of approaches currently at play. These range from high-level frameworks, conventions, and principles to concrete platforms and methods for data collection and analysis.

The horizontal x-axis is anchored on one end by proprietary/market-based methods and on the other by field-oriented/consensus-driven standards and methods. This line shows the shifts from a competitive market of IMM approaches (which continues to thrive) to one in which standard-setting organizations are striving to build shared norms for IMM.[8] The former offers innovation and testing of new approaches such as the approaches offered by Aeris and SoPact. The latter offers standardization in definitions, measures, and principles, and thereby the underlying foundation for creating comparisons within and across impact portfolios, such as those led by the GIIN and IMP. If successful, these publicly available field-oriented/consensus-driven approaches can guide future development of approaches and methods, as well as become incorporated into existing ones. In fact, a number of proprietary/market-based methods are already incorporating field-oriented/consensus-driven approaches.

The anchors for the vertical y-axis are screenings/ESG/sustainability focus at the top and thematic/impact investing focus on the bottom. This distinction is too-often glossed over in discussions about IMM. The screenings/ESG/sustainability approaches, such as those offered by Bloomberg, Morningstar, and UNPRI, focus on "how" public companies (primarily) conduct internal practices related to ESG. The thematic/Impact Investing focus, such as those by Social Value International (SVI) and Toniic (an impact investing network), addresses external impact on people and planet resulting from businesses' services and products. Over time, the IMM field has been moving closer to the practices and impact focus used by public and global development sectors' conventions for measurement and evaluation. For these, process matters, but so do the impacts (i.e. how are the impacts

---

[7]It should be made explicit here that a public company may have impact investments in their investment portfolios, but most impact investors are not necessarily formed as a publicly listed company, rather, typically as a family office or limited partnership.

[8]See Impact Management Project norms for further detail: impactmanagementproject .com/impact-management/impact-management-norms/ (accessed 27 March 2020).

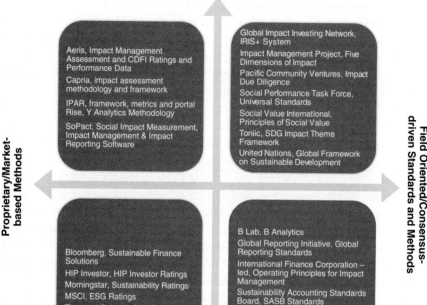

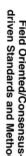

FIGURE 17.1 The Landscape of Impact Measurement and Management Approaches. *Source*: Authors' analysis.

of the intervention, services, or products, directly, indirectly, or both, connected to people and planet?).

It is thus no wonder that the abundance of measurement approaches overwhelms most people who are doing their best to make sense of measurement for Impact Investing. This proliferation of approaches can have a dizzying effect on most investors, let alone enterprises who are subject to multiple reporting protocols.[9] The GIIN's tenets for differentiating and growing the field of Impact Investing serve as a useful starting point for framing and

---

[9]This is not unlike government-led development finance and the relationship between donors and the international non-governmental organizations who receive, for instance,

providing additional structure to the future of impact in Impact Investing. As noted earlier, these tenets speak to intentionality, use of evidence, and impact data in investment design, managing impact performance, and contributing to the growth of the industry based on these shared conventions.

The way forward would see the Impact Investing IMM industry and the evaluation community come closer together (Harji and Jackson 2018), so that evaluation methods that have been developing for over 70 years can become more commonly incorporated into the Impact Investing IMM toolkit (Picciotto 2015). The evaluation community, which shares a commitment to driving impact through reliable measurement and management practices, developed a portfolio of approaches, rallying around shared principles and practices about the importance of utilizing data for driving impact and data's integrity. In addition, the evaluation field is adaptive and continues to grow new approaches that become socialized and adopted. Clearly, there is great opportunity here for the Impact Investing IMM industry and the evaluation community to be powerful allies in innovating and advancing positive momentum in IMM standards and practices. The future should see a continued evolution of evaluation methods that are rightsized and in tune with the needs and life cycle of Impact Investing (Hoffman and Olazabal 2018). This chapter now turns to highlighting significant developments through case examples.

Impact Management Project's Five Dimensions of Impact and Its Use

The first significant development to note is the traction that is building toward a global consensus around five dimensions of impact under the leadership of the Impact Management Project (IMP). Led by a structured network of standard-setting organizations and engaging a community of over 2,000 enterprises and investors, the IMP has been working since 2016 to build consensus and share best practices in IMM in order to provide complete standards for impact measurement, management, and reporting.

Obtaining a consensus around the five dimensions of impact for Impact Investing (Table 17.1) already represents a major breakthrough that provides the basis for establishing standard categories for identifying, tracking, and assessing impact performance, in line with the Impact Management Project. These are necessary preconditions for managing for impact and comparing

---

contracts and grants in US dollars through the aid system, and then are held accountable to reporting to multiple donors.

TABLE 17.1 Five Dimensions of Impact.

	Dimensions of Impact
What?	Outcomes the enterprise is contributing to, and how important the outcomes are to stakeholders
Who?	Types of stakeholders that are experiencing the outcome and how underserved they were prior to the enterprise's effect
How Much?	How many stakeholders experienced the outcome, what degree of change they experienced, and how long they experienced the outcome for
Contribution?	Whether an enterprise's and/or investor's efforts resulted in outcomes that were likely better than what would have occurred otherwise[10]
Risk?	Likelihood that the impact will be different than expected, and that the risk will be material from the perspective of people and planet who experience impact[11]

Source: Impact Management Project.[12]

impact performance. In reviewing the five dimensions of impact, it is important to keep in mind that the Impact Investing field uses the term "impact" liberally, which is in part why the dimensions of impact are so valuable to the field. During the short history of Impact Investing, this term has included both outputs and outcomes and has not accounted for the time dimensions commonly found in public and global development results chains, such as short, intermediate, and long-term changes (traditionally called outputs, outcomes, and impacts, respectively).

The IMP's five dimensions of impact lean in the direction of characterizing impact along the lines of outcomes, which it considers as changes in well-being, organizations, or systems.

---

[10]Contribution is intended to be a broad-based term that can be used to address practices adopted by diverse disciplines, such as the finance industry's interest in additionality and the evaluation industry's interest in attribution.

[11]The risk dimension anticipates that financial risk assessments may not capture impact risks and so must be considered separately from financial risks. Three data categories address impact risk: (i) types of risks that undermine delivery of the outcome; (ii) likelihood and severity of impact risk; (iii) mitigation strategy to reduce the level of impact risk. See the Impact Management Project for further detail: impactmanagementproject .com/impact-management/impact-management-norms/ (accessed 27 March 2020).

[12]See the Impact Management Project here: impactmanagementproject.com (accessed 27 March 2020).

While on the face of it, these five dimensions of impact address evaluative questions typically incorporated into public and global development sectors' monitoring and evaluation (M&E), they succeed in breaking the pattern for impact investors of excessive reliance on bespoke approaches around the selection of impact dimensions. They also may alter commonplace practices in the Impact Investing field that limit understanding of impact by using intention as a proxy for impact or restricting impact measurement solely to outputs (Reisman et al. 2018).

The level of detailed analysis that is necessary for adequately addressing the five dimensions of impact requires far more rigor and depth to put in place methodologies to measure impact than simply using a small set of key performance indicators (KPI) primarily focused on outputs.[13] Take the categories "how much" and "contribution." They can be further broken down into scale, depth, and duration. Asked early enough in the life cycle of an investment, this evaluative reflection can be the distinguishing feature between a regular investment and an investor managing an impact investment. However, the methods for collecting and analyzing data for these categories are not prescribed by the IMP.

Two illustrative examples follow about how the five dimensions are put into practice by impact investors. The first illustration involves a field leader in building out the Impact Investing industry and continues to be a catalytic, philanthropic investor, The Rockefeller Foundation. The second illustration features Upaya Social Ventures, a nonprofit organization committed to addressing the global problem of poverty through market solutions.

Case Study: Case Example: The Rockefeller Foundations' Zero Gap Portfolio

The Rockefeller Foundation is a pioneer in the Impact Investing space, which it formalized in 2007. Throughout the last decade, The Rockefeller Foundation has continued to strengthen the sector through the testing of new financing mechanisms, supporting the development of new industry agencies, and providing catalytic capital to increase private sector engagement in innovative and high-impact solutions for riskier investments.

The Rockefeller Foundation's understanding of how Impact Investing can achieve social change has become quite sophisticated. Today, they

---

[13] See www.oecd.org/dac/evaluation/2754804.pdf (accessed 27 March, 2020).

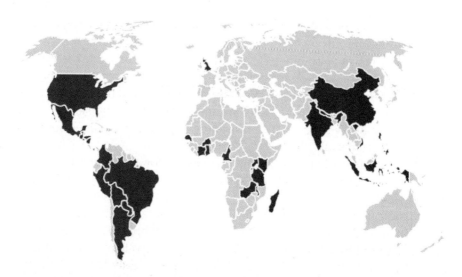

FIGURE 17.2   Reach of The Rockefeller Foundation's Zero Gap Portfolio, 2019.
Source: Courtesy of The Rockefeller Foundation.

understand that achieving impact is a complex endeavor, necessitating the best thinking in the measurement and evaluation fields, far more challenging than simply achieving financial returns, and requiring diligent attention throughout the investment life cycle. Its Innovative Finance portfolio has now a global reach (Figure 17.2), with the flexibility to deploy concessional capital across multiple regions, sectors, and asset classes.

Launched in 2015, the Zero Gap initiative seeks to close the SDG financing gap by mobilizing private capital. The Zero Gap portfolio is structured to support the next generation of financing mechanisms and products to mobilize institutional and retail capital at scale and in support of the SDGs. Among other requirements, all Zero Gap grants and investments must qualify through a set of impact principles, including: (i) impact, (ii) innovation, (iii) additionality,[14] and (iv) scale and replicability. The Zero Gap grant portfolio currently supports the development of 44 innovative financial instruments, of which 17 have been piloted in the capital markets and in 2018, extended to program-related investments (PRIs), with five active Zero Gap investments and a rapidly growing portfolio—with total capital deployed since 2008 of USD $95 million.

---

[14]"Additionality" is defined as the extent to which a new input (action or item) adds to the existing inputs (instead of replacing any of them) and results in a greater aggregate. See IMP's glossary in impactmanagementproject.com/impact-management/impact-management-norms/ (accessed 27 March 2020).

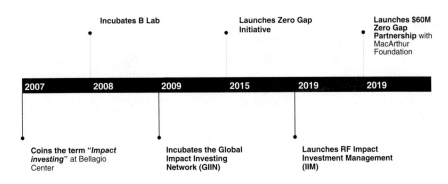

FIGURE 17.3   Evolution of The Rockefeller Foundation's Impact Investing Portfolio.
Source: Courtesy of The Rockefeller Foundation.

And in 2019, the Rockefeller Foundation launched Impact Investment Management (RFIIM), an asset management platform designed to aggregate capital from like-minded partners (Figure 17.3). RFIIM is managed by The Rockefeller Foundation's Innovative Finance team. The first entity on RFIIM's platform is the Zero Gap Fund,[15] with equal capital commitments from the MacArthur Foundation and Rockefeller Foundation, aimed to scale and accelerate The Rockefeller Foundation's maturing Zero Gap portfolio around the globe.

Impact measurement and management are a key part of this work and start in the pre-due-diligence stages of the investment life cycle and then carries into the lifecycle of The Rockefeller Foundation's impact investments (Figure 17.4). Using the various tools and conventions that have been developed over the last decade, The Rockefeller Foundation has designed an impact measurement and management approach that is clear at the portfolio level and that carries through at a deal-by-deal level.

The philosophy underpinning its IMM approach is that in order to manage social impact and generate returns, there must be clear lines of visibility and accountability at the deal and thus company level for both financial and social and/or environmental performance. As a result, The Rockefeller Foundation's Impact Investing team works to ensure the five dimensions of the IMP (who, what, how much, contribution, and risk) are explicit, understood, and documented across each of their investment partnerships. Given the goal of addressing the SDG finance gap, and like Toniic (discussed next), each

---

[15]The Zero Gap Fund is the first fund under RFIIM and for which a large portion of deals come from the maturing grant portfolio of the Zero Gap Initiative. It is inclusive of the C3 partnership with the MacArthur Foundation.

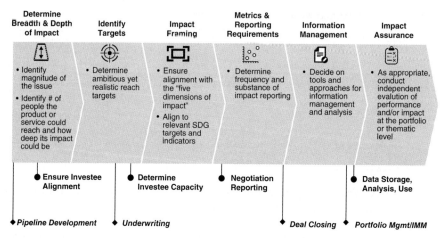

FIGURE 17.4 The Rockefeller Foundation's Impact Measurement and Management Across Its Impact Investment Process. *Source*: Courtesy of The Rockefeller Foundation.

investment is also mapped to the SDG goals. And these discussions result in the core social performance metrics that will serve as markers for impact success.

Prioritizing operational management is critical to delivering results, and so The Rockefeller Foundation has also codified their approach to align to the IFC-led Operational Principles for Impact Management and have committed to ensure the impact integrity of their work through regular impact verification and evaluation.

Case Study: Case Example: Upaya Social Ventures

Upaya Social Ventures portrays the case of a small effort that has gone far and takes very seriously the full range of the five dimensions of impact. Founded in 2011, Upaya operates as a nonprofit social venture organization that both operates an accelerator and makes equity investments in a selected group of entrepreneurs in under-resourced regions of India. A typical equity investment is USD $50,000. By the end of 2019, Upaya had invested USD $400,000 across 16 companies that had generated cumulative revenues of nearly USD $11 million. A focused fundraising campaign in 2019 resulted in doubling its pool of investable funds to USD $1 million and additional funding for Upaya's operations, including managing an accelerator, identifying investee companies, managing its portfolio, and evaluating impact. Upaya is using a philanthropic tool for its investments, referred to as a "recoverable grant fund" to form its investment pool that operates as patient capital (Cochrane 2020).

Committing 10% of its budget to impact measurement and management, Upaya developed a framework that is consistently applied throughout their investment cycle, similarly to The Rockefeller Foundation. With a mission to create dignified jobs for the extreme poor, Upaya invests as an equity investor in early stage entrepreneurs with businesses often considered too large for micro-loans, but often deemed too risky for investment by local banks or venture capitalists.

Upaya's focus on the extreme poor is a good demonstration of a clear "who" for impact investments (i.e. early stage entrepreneurs that don't fit neatly into the standard investment criteria, but who are committed to creating dignified jobs, or drastically improve incomes and livelihoods for people living in extreme poverty). Upaya's investment strategy also speaks to "contribution" to impact as Upaya fills a gap by investing in entrepreneurs who are often considered too risky, yet results in a financial payoff for investors seeking impact.

Initially defining success—the "what"—as short-term revenue growth for entrepreneurs and dignified jobs for jobholders, Upaya's dual approach of financial investments and consulting support represent their commitment to the scalable growth of enterprises and its effect on the well-being of the households of the people they employ. As Upaya's co-founder and chief impact officer explains, "My job is to analyze data to validate our thesis that these jobs help households emerge from extreme poverty" (Shenoy 2019b).

In keeping with the direction of impact that moves past outputs to outcomes, Shenoy elevates the "depth of impact" as their ultimate success measure. As she puts it, "In the decade plus I have been doing this work, I have often heard mission-driven organizations talk about the importance of scale...that their services ought to extend and 'touch' the greatest number of beneficiaries. While reporting large and wide outreach is a commendable goal, it should not preclude measuring the *depth* of impact" (Shenoy 2019a). An example of depth is the progression from job creation to jobholders' increased income (compared to old jobs), and quality of life indicators resulting from this increased income. This is a more refined version of Upaya's "what" as well as "how much" change is expected to occur.

Upaya's approach to measurement is based on rigorous outcome (evaluation) studies. They send third-party enumerators to visit a random sample of jobholders and administer a 10-minute survey. The survey data is used to ascertain program modifications (i.e. using data to inform impact management; Shenoy 2020). Over the years, Upaya has learned how good intentions do not necessarily translate into impact, something they learned from their steadfast attention to data.

For example, the jobholders at one investee company reported a 200% increase in their household incomes and were spending considerably more on food and consumer goods. But over the course of one year, despite jobholders' intentions, the more transformational outcome of improvements in housing condition did not occur. Upaya acted and engaged in further data collection to better understand why transformational change was not materializing. The data analysis revealed that jobholders faced difficulty in obtaining approval for bank accounts and unbanked money was prone to theft. As a result, the investee company was able to correct this by devising a savings scheme through payroll deductions that had shown promising effects in longer-term outcomes.

Upaya's 2019 impact report shows that keeping their eye (and IMM) on transformative change was a valuable strategy.[16] In their sample of 1,296 jobholders surveyed, access to jobs and more reliable income resulted in school attendance for over 90% of their children, three square meals for 61% of households, and access to a bank account for 52% of jobholders.

Shenoy's recent blogpost (Shenoy 2020c) compares their commitment to measuring the depth of change to the GIIN's recent survey on IMM practices. Less than half of GIIN's survey respondents (43%) measured depth or significance of impact in their IMM practice. In a call to action, Shenoy urges a greater commitment to rigorous and high-quality IMM, in other words, not only tracking changes in the "what" but also evaluatively exploring the "how" and the "why" change happens.

"Looking ahead with all this positive momentum, hopefully the 2021 GIIN industry survey will show us that the remaining roadblocks have fallen, allowing for more rigorous analysis and reporting. The next wave should show us that practitioners are incorporating and managing learnings from their impact data to improve their programs in order to deliver better results

---

[16]See www.upayasv.org/our-impact for more information (assessed 27 March 2020).

to investors. We all know that some programs are effective, and others not so much . . . let's openly acknowledge that and use our impact data to drive real change!" (Shenoy 2020c).

The IRIS+ System

Next, another significant contribution to ensuring impact at the center of Impact Investing is introduced. The earlier discussion of the IRIS catalogue of metrics with a primary focus on outputs took a major turn in 2019. Although the GIIN continuously updated IRIS since its original launch in 2009, its fifth version transformed IRIS from a catalogue of metrics to an end-to-end system for measuring, managing, and optimizing impact. Significant aspects of this system include: (i) treatment of IMM as an end-to-end system, (ii) identification of both investable strategies and core metric sets based on research evidence within thematic area verticals, and (iii) movement toward outcomes by including one or more outcome for each thematic area (e.g. affordable housing, financial inclusion, food security).

While these types of features are conventional practices in evaluation for the public and global development sectors, it is a great leap forward in the Impact Investing arena. Additionally, IRIS+ emphasizes the importance of stakeholder voice in developing and selecting impact measures, a participatory approach that has been an essential principle in the evaluation profession for decades, to ensure that measures of success also matter to people who are the end-customers and beneficiaries of services and products. Last, IRIS+ emphasizes the importance of developing a theory of change to guide IMM. This intentional focused approach to measurable social or environmental impact lays the groundwork for more thoughtful and systemic approaches to achieving impact (Verrinder et al. 2018). It also links measurement work more directly to producing data that can guide better decision-making for managing and optimizing impact.

Global asset manager Nuveen offers a strong illustration of an impact investor that has applied features of the IRIS+ system in its approach to impact measurement and management.

Case Study: Case Example: Nuveen

Nuveen, a long-time impact investor and fifteenth largest asset manager in the world, with USD $1.1 trillion in 2019, was identified by IRIS+ as an

(continued)

> (*continued*)
>
> exemplary use case for applying IRIS+ to deepen its IMM practice (GIIN 2020). Nuveen's pursuit of impact is a direct response to its client base of educators, health care professionals, researchers, and other workers in the nonprofit sector who looked to Nuveen to generate reasonable risk-adjusted returns for their retirement while also building investment portfolios aligned with their public-minded values. Over USD $1 billion of Nuveen's Assets Under Management (AUM) is invested globally in direct investments explicitly aimed at achieving important social and environmental outcomes for underserved people and the planet. These investments comprise private equity, private debt, and real estate in three impact verticals: (i) inclusive growth related to financial services, health care, and education, (ii) resource efficiency related to waste management, energy efficiency, and circular economy, and (iii) affordable housing.

This illustration focuses on Nuveen's affordable housing strategy, which represents USD $350 million AUM invested in real-estate equity in 2019. The specific impact objective of this portfolio is to preserve and provide safe, affordable, and sustainable housing for low-income and other underserved individuals and families in the United States. Nuveen used the IRIS+ system throughout each stage of portfolio construction and management.

One clear way that Nuveen incorporated IRIS+ was by validating its impact thesis (also known as theory of change) by using the research evidence base provided by IRIS+. For example, Nuveen's initial impact thesis included positive educational outcomes for children living in affordable housing. However, the research evidence base published in IRIS+ does not support educational outcomes as a direct result of affordable housing. Consequently, Nuveen eliminated this outcome area from its impact thesis. On the other hand, access to supportive services is supported in IRIS+'s research evidence base as an impactful strategy for affordable housing investments, and Nuveen maintained that in its impact thesis metric sets.

Beyond the impact thesis, the Nuveen team also matched the indicators that they identified for data collection with the core metric set established in IRIS+. To the extent possible, Nuveen made the effort to incorporate these research evidence-based metrics in its IMM system, due to the credibility of these metrics and Nuveen's recognition of the opportunity to establish comparability of measures across the Impact Investing industry. Doing so did not preclude Nuveen from adding measures or selecting from the additional measures in the extended catalogue of metrics that had evolved within IRIS for nearly a decade.

As is the case for the IMP, IRIS+ also emphasizes the use of impact measurement and management for decision-making. Nuveen provides a striking example of how it thoughtfully approached the use of data for decision-making in a critical decision about implementing its investment strategy. Nuveen further engaged in evaluative thinking by transparently addressing the tradeoffs in their impact results with their impact thesis and decisions for ongoing investments.

Several years ago, for example, Nuveen realized that it faced a decision about trade-offs in its US affordable housing portfolio, an equity-based Impact Investing portfolio representing USD $350 million. As noted earlier, this portfolio was developed based on evidence about strategies that effectively increase access to safe, affordable, and sustainable housing for cost-burdened households. Nuveen's impact thesis recognized that affordability was only one part of the equation and that the companies Nuveen invested in also needed to provide cost-burdened households with other benefits that save costs and support their well-being and stability of housing. For instance, increased availability of green units reduces a household's utility bill costs. Access to social services and proximity to transit services for residents in Nuveen's investment companies' housing units support residents' well-being. Each of these benefits contribute to the stability of housing for the households served by the investment companies that provide affordable housing.

Nuveen's initial investments focused on investments in companies providing housing in urban infill locations that already tended to have good access to public transportation. As its portfolio expanded over the years, Nuveen expanded to serving additional populations in new geographies, particularly rural populations. Along with this expanded geographic focus, the investment companies in rural geographies were less likely to have close proximity to transit services. Nuveen's impact data reflected this shift and showed that the access to transit score (availability of transportation) for their tenants had fallen (Figure 17.5) over time as it expanded its geographic diversification as reflected by the number of states. Clearly, Nuveen faced an impact tradeoff between optimizing its portfolio for access to public transit versus serving rural populations.

The result was Nuveen's prioritization of preserving affordability for low-income populations across America, even if it meant investing in properties that lacked good access to public transit. To manage this tradeoff,

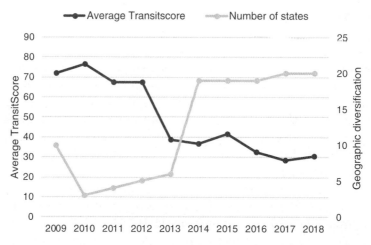

FIGURE 17.5 Access to Transit Scores and Geographic Diversification in Nuveen's Affordable Housing Portfolio in the United States (2009–2018). *Source*: Global Impact Investing Network (2020).

Nuveen made the decision to explore how the firm could add value as an investor in affordable housing serving low-income populations by encouraging or funding alternative transportation services for more rural locations, thus addressing the enabling conditions for achieving the results they were driving toward.

Nuveen considers similar impact tradeoffs throughout their investment life cycle, using data adopted from IRIS+ metrics to assess the extent to which potential investments meet their impact criteria (outputs and outcomes), along with their financial due diligence. Where possible, and like The Rockefeller Foundation, Nuveen considers whether it could add value by addressing impact shortcomings in their deal terms or through developing partnerships. This evaluative thinking is a core component of effective impact management.

Sustainable Development Goal Alignment

The application of the UN's SDGs has had a significant effect on creating a standardized way to clarify, communicate, and manage impact intentions. The SDGs offer a common language and framework for articulating and coordinating around the "what" dimension referred to in the "five dimensions of impact," which has appealed to impact investors, as noted earlier. In contrast to the UN's last set of major global goals, the UN Millennium Development

FIGURE 17.6 The 17 Sustainable Development Goals. *Source*: United Nations.

Goals (MDGs), which were seen primarily as a public sector effort, the UN engaged the private sector, civil society, and other global development actors in developing the SDGs in implementing strategies for achieving the world's most pressing goals (United Nations 2015).

There are 17 SDGs, each associated with targets and indicators (Figure 17.6). The goals themselves are broad (e.g. end hunger, zero poverty, and inclusive and resilient cities), and the global indicator framework includes 231 unique indicators. The utility that the SDG framework provides for the Impact Investing community specifically is that it: (i) serves as a place to start discussions around the "what," and (ii) provides a common taxonomy and language to connect with other investors. As an example, Toniic, a network of impact investors, developed a rigorous approach to applying the SDGs across its investor and investment portfolios, described next.

Case Study: Case Example: Toniic T100 Project

Among the leading groups actively pursuing a rigorous approach to measuring and evaluating impact and committed to contribute to and align with field-building conventions is Toniic, a global network of active impact investors who invest across all asset classes. In 2016, as a result of

(continued)

(continued)

the scarce evidence of the viability and scalability of Impact Investing and the risk of impact washing, Toniic launched the T100 project in pursuit of deepening the understanding of impact for all investors and intermediaries and to empower academic research. Further described in the case study, *Putting "Impact" at the Center of Impact Investing: A Case Study of Toniic's T100 Project* (Reisman and Millet 2017), this robust, longitudinal research study is aimed to demonstrate how both the finance community and cross-sector global partners can consider the role of private investment capital in achieving impact on global goals. Most T100 participants are part of the 100% Network, a subgroup of Toniic members that have committed to deploying 100% of one or more of their portfolios to deeper positive net impact across all asset classes, and to share their data with one another and in aggregate and anonymized reporting for the longitudinal T100 study.

Toniic developed an SDG framework that spans the full set of SDGs and associated targets that are adapted to the investor level rather than national level. Each target has corresponding IRIS metrics associated with it. Published as a public good and called the SDG Impact Theme Framework (2016), Toniic encourages each Toniic member to use this in their investments' portfolio analysis.

Toniic developed its SDG Impact Theme Framework initially for three primary purposes: (i) to help investors increase clarity in visualizing the impact of their portfolios, (ii) to help them identify co-investors, and (iii) to help them find relevant investment opportunities. The framework was co-developed by Toniic members in a workshop format, shaped by the Toniic team, and then improved by outside reviewers who are expert in specific impact areas. The current version of the framework contains 63 impact themes associated with the 17 SDGs and is being adopted as a common standard by several other organizations, which are contributing feedback.[17]

The following table (Table 17.2) illustrates how SDG themes and investor impact themes can be aligned with one another.[18]

---

[17]See Toniic's SDG framework for more detail: toniic.com/sdg-framework/ (accessed 27 March 2020).
[18]Ibid.

TABLE 17.2   Toniic Impact Theme Alignment to the SDGs

UN PRIMARY SDG	TONIIC IMPACT THEME	UN SDG GOALS
SDG-1: End poverty in all its forms everywhere	Access to basic goods and services	8
	Financial Inclusion	9, 17
	Affordable housing	11
	Smallholder farmers	2
SDG-2: End hunger, improve nutrition, and promote sustainable agriculture	Food security	3, 4
	Food waste	12
	Healthy food	3
	Smallholder farmers	1
	Sustainable agriculture	15
SDG-3: Ensure healthy lives and promote well-being for all at all ages	Access to healthcare	1
	Aging	10
	Maternal and reproductive health	5

Source: Toniic (2018).

By associating specific SDG impact themes to investments, investors can see how their portfolio aligns and contributes to the SDGs. It also provides a ready-made set of impact outcomes, in the form of the 169 SDG targets, such as SDG-1, which calls for ending poverty in all its forms, and its Target 1.1, which pertains to reducing the number of individuals living below USD $1.25 per day. Detailed financial and impact data may be collected for each investment.

Until 2019, investors/fund managers were expected to gather as much data as possible for each of their investee companies, by using existing reports or by engaging with their investees. In some cases, Toniic staff members supported this data collection effort. They also worked closely with T100 participants to guide their data reporting into the portfolio tool and, thus, increase the reliability of the data entries. One participating member, the KL Felicitas Foundation in the United States, combines data collection for the SDG Impact Theme Framework with other measurement approaches, such as data that addresses the five dimensions from the IMP and New Philanthropy Capital's proprietary risk assessment inventory to assess negative impact as well as positive impact.

In March 2020, Toniic launched Toniic Tracer, a new platform that enables investors, entrepreneurs, and funds (issuers) to share and compare data about their impact investments, along with corresponding goals, performance, and outcomes.[19] Toniic Tracer represents a leap forward in financial and impact reporting. It leverages technology and leading standards, like the IMP Impact Class Matrix and the IRIS+ catalogue, while continuing to use the SDGs Framework. Toniic Tracer builds on the body of data already included in the T100 Project to provide insights to issuers and investors, publicizes example investments in every asset class, while at the same time powering academic research. The platform structure should ease the reporting burden for participants and facilitate collaboration and communication with industry partners.

Toniic is making publicly available the results of their aggregated analyses in annual publications, comparing them with GIIN's research to support further insights on impact performance as well as sharing anonymized data with a global consortium of trusted academic researchers to develop a twenty-first-century portfolio theory that incorporates social and environmental impact in decision-making. The data is also important to each investor to better understand their own investment decisions and intended impacts. The T100 members have elevated the role of IMM in their Impact Investing practice and are engaged in concerted efforts to improve the quality of data and to work collaboratively with the investee companies to identify measures, create data collection systems, and set targets (Toniic 2018). The aggregated data are also valuable for understanding patterns of impact investment such as variation of asset class investments for each SDG, relationship between geographic location of investor and geographic focus of investors. For instance, Toniic's 2018 report called out an "investor home bias," which is a finding documented by others that investors are most likely to invest in their own region. The implication for this bias is that capital in the more affluent global north is more likely to remain in the north than to be invested in the relatively less resourced global south. European investors diverge from this pattern though and are more likely than any other region to be geographically diverse in their investments (Figure 17.7).

---

[19] See toniic.com/toniic-tracer/ (accessed 27 March 2020).

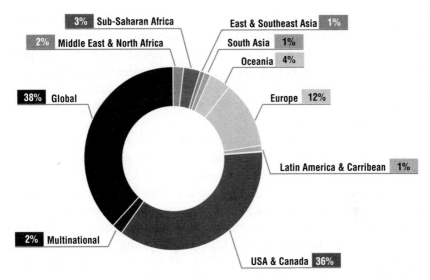

FIGURE 17.7 Toniic's 2018 Impact Geography of Investments. *Source*: Toniic (2018).

Over time, and with the third year of reporting completed in 2019, Toniic has explicitly shared the value of the framework as contributing to field building for Impact Investing. One specific aim is to "empower the research community to begin exploring systemic issues such as impact risk factors, the availability and accessibility of specific impact themes within each asset class, and how best to incorporate externality pricing into security valuation and analysis." The 76 portfolios and USD $2.8 billion in committed capital as of 2019 provides a robust data set contributing to this goal and longitudinal study (Toniic 2019).

This chapter concludes with a summary and three concrete recommendations aimed at ensuring that impact drives Impact Investing.

CONCLUSION

Achieving impact is a complex and sophisticated endeavor, a reality the public and global development sectors know quite well and that the Impact Investing community is just starting to learn. Yet, after only a decade, there is promising and visible traction in how IMM is evolving for Impact Investing. The four examples discussed in this chapter illustrate the evolution of IMM across a range of actors in the Impact Investing ecosystem, from early to more mature companies, and from investors with sizable AUM to networks of investors with far less capital to deploy. This variation of actors validates the GIIN's notable differentiator for Impact Investing as an intentional effort to practice IMM in order to create a positive impact on people and planet (GIIN 2019b). The type of investor or their assets under management do not predict how investors engage in adopting best practices in IMM. Rather, the driving force is the intentional decision to thoughtfully apply IMM and use the data to drive impact.

But what will it take to scale these efforts and continue to ensure that impact drives Impact Investing? First, in a world where blended finance is becoming the norm, the intersectionality of work at the nexus of public and private financing is critical. Both sectors offer quality ways to manage their impact with blended finance also promising to spur blended methods for measuring and managing impact. The Organization for Economic Co-operation and Development (OECD) (2019), the Donor Community for Enterprise Development (DCED),[20] the IFC of the World Bank Group, and others in the global development sphere have been blazing trails and working toward harmonized efforts and standards in this area.

Second, policies and standards will provide structural incentives to motivate more actors in the Impact Investing system to conform to principles and standards. The Business Roundtable's[21] 2019 statement about the principles of corporate governance publicly modernized their position from a viewpoint where corporations exist primarily to serve their shareholders toward a viewpoint commonly referred to as "stakeholder capitalism," which incorporates impact and sustainability as integral to the role of business in society. The 2019 Statement on the Purpose of a Corporation declares, "While each of our companies serves its own corporate purpose, we share a fundamental commitment to all of our stakeholders."[22] The specific stakeholders listed in addition to shareholders are customers, employees, suppliers, and communities (both people and environment).

This prominent business organization took a bold step toward a normative change that expands the role of corporate responsibility to include people

---

[20]See www.enterprise-development.org/measuring-results-the-dced-standard/ (accessed 28 March 2020).

[21]The Business Roundtable comprises chief executives of leading US companies, representing every sector of the economy, and exist to advocate for policy solutions that foster US economic growth and competitiveness.

[22]See Statement on Purpose of a Corporation: opportunity.businessroundtable.org/wp-content/uploads/2019/08/BRT-Statement-on-the-Purpose-of-a-Corporation-with-Signatures.pdf (accessed 27 March 2020).

and planet alongside financial returns.[23] The roundtable even encourages investors to support companies committed to building long-term value by supporting their employees and communities. Yet they fell short of structural change or advocating for government policies that require accountability to impact. Skeptics have also noted that some businesses who are signatories to the statement have continued to be active opponents to legislation that takes actions on climate and other environmental protections (Winston 2019). So the next step—beyond a voluntary call to action to drive for impact—would necessitate structural changes in how value is accounted for, verification of impact, and the like.

Third, with the evolution in technology and technological capabilities, the data and measurement space are changing quickly. Lower-cost methods for collecting data directly from stakeholders using SMS and other mediums, such as big data, blockchain, and artificial intelligence, are among these technological advances that will increase the availability of evidence, data, metrics, and benchmarks. Solutions to allow interoperability across data sets are not yet available but are on the horizon and will become more crystalized with the adoption of conventions around impact, standardized core metric sets, and adoption of core principles. These shifts will not only influence Impact Investing, innovative finance, and blended finance discussions, but even more importantly, the global sustainability discussions writ large.

The not too distant future is on the horizon, and with it an urgency to consider how financial vehicles, whether Impact Investing or other types of investments (e.g. the more conventional private and government sector financing institutions), will generate a more sustainable future for people and planet. IMM can help in this endeavor by equipping investors with the means to proactively drive toward the impact promise their investments hold, acting as a game changer in achieving the SDGs. The other side of the horizon will see the widespread practice of IMM among impact investors, aligned with the growing body of standards and methods, where learnings from impact measurement are endogenized to manage and optimize impact to drive real change.

---

[23] "Stakeholder capitalism" is actually not a new idea. It was an approach generally taken by business in the first half of the twentieth century until it was replaced by shareholder capitalism, also known as free-market capitalism, as the gospel of business popularized by Nobel Prize winner economist Milton Friedman.

DISCLAIMER

The findings, interpretations, and conclusions expressed in this paper are entirely those of the authors. They do not necessarily represent the views of The Rockefeller Foundation or its affiliated organizations, or those of the executive directors of The Rockefeller Foundation or the institutions they represent.

REFERENCES

Cochrane, K. (2020). Upaya Fundamentals: How Is Upaya Funded. Upaya Social Ventures blog post (10 July 2019). www.upayasv.org/blog/2019/7/10-how-is-upaya-funded (accessed 27 March 2020).

GIIN (2019a). *Annual Impact Investor Survey 2019,* 9th ed. Global Impact Investing Network.

GIIN (2019b). *Core Characteristics of Impact Investing.* Global Impact Investing Network.

GIIN (2020). *IRIS+ Use Case: Nuveen. Global Impact Investing Network (forthcoming).*

Harji, K., and Jackson, E. T. (2018). Facing Challenges, Building the Field: Improving the Measurement of the Social Impact of Market-Based Approaches. *American Journal of Evaluation* 39(3): 396–401. DOI: `10.1177/1098214018778817`.

Hoffman, S. A., and Olazabal, V. M. (2018). The Next Frontier for Measurement and Evaluation: Social Impact Measurement for Impact Investing and Market Solutions. *African Evaluation Journal* 6(2): 342.

IFC (2019). *Investing for Impact: Operating Principles for Impact Management.* International Finance Corporation.

Karnani, A. (2007). Micro-finance Misses Its Mark. *Stanford Social Innovation Review.* 2007.

Kramer, L. (2018). Down the Rabbit Hole? Impact Investing and Large Foundations. *Stanford Social Innovation Review* (12 June).

Olsen, S., Miller, C., Carpenter, B., et al. (2019). The Free Market Must Account for Environmental and Social Impact. *Stanford Social Innovation Review,* 17 (4): 59–60.

OECD (2019). Social Impact Investment 2019: The Impact Imperative for Sustainable Development. OECD Publishing. Paris. doi.org/10.1787/9789264311299-en.

Picciotto, R. (2015). *The Fifth Wave: Social Impact Evaluation*. The Rockefeller Foundation.

Reisman, J., Olazabal, V., and Hoffman, S. (2018). Putting the "Impact" in Impact Investing: The Rising Demand for Data and Evidence of Social Outcomes. *American Journal of Evaluation*, 39(3): 389–395. DOI: 10.1177/1098214018779141.

Reisman, J., and Olazabal, V. (2016). *Situating the Next Generation of Impact Measurement and Evaluation for Impact Investing*. The Rockefeller Foundation.

Reisman, J., and Millet, H. (2018). *Putting "Impact" at the Center: A Case Study of Toniic's T100 Project*. The Rockefeller Foundation.

Ruff, K., and Olsen, S. (2018). The Need for Analysts in Social Impact Measurement: How Evaluators Can Help. *American Journal of Evaluation*, 39(3): 402–407. DOI: 10.1177/1098214018778809.

Shenoy, S. (2019a). The Importance of Capturing Feedback from Your Target Audience. American Evaluation Association blog post (13 May 2019). aea365.org/blog/sim-tig-week-moving-beyond-scale-the-importance-of-capturing-feedback-from-your-target-audience-by-sachi-shenoy/ (accessed 27 March 2020).

Shenoy, S. (2019b). Panel presentation at SOCAP PNW 360. Seattle (March 2019).

Shenoy, S. (2020). Let's acknowledge the real value—and cost—of measuring impact. Upaya Social Venture blog post (5 February 2020). www.upayasv.org/blog/2020/2/5/the-valueand-costof-measuring-impact (access 27 March 2020).

Simler, C. (2019). *Impact Measurement: A Practical Guide to Data Collection*. CDC Group.

Toniic. (2018). *T100* Powered Ascent Report.

Toniic. (2019). T100 Focus: *The Frontier of SDG investing*.

United Nations (2015). *Transforming our World: The 2030 Agenda for Sustainable Development Goals*. United Nations Department of Economics and Social Affairs. *A/RES/70/1*.

Verrinder, N., Zwane, K., Nixon, D., et al. (2018). Evaluative tools in Impact Investing: Three Case Studies on the Use of Theories of Change. *African Evaluation Journal* 6(2). DOI: //doi.org/10.4102/aej.v6i2.340.

Winston, A. (2019). Is the Business Roundtable Statement Just Empty Rhetoric? (30 August 2019). www.hbr.org/2019/08/is-the-business-roundtable-statement-just-empty-rhetoric (access 20 March 2020).

World Economic Forum (2017). Engaging all Affected Stakeholders. Developed by Action Group 3 of the World Economic Forum's initiative to Accelerate Impact Measurement and Management.

CHAPTER 18

Transformative Evaluation and Impact Investing: A Fruitful Marriage

Courtney Bolinson, MS and Donna M. Mertens, PhD

Abstract

This chapter examines the "marriage" of Impact Investing with a transformative framework for evaluation. Currently, Impact Investing measurement usually consists of tracking key performance metrics or calculating the social return on an investment at the post-investment stage. However, because Impact Investing often targets wider social or environmental impact goals, such as the Sustainable Development Goals, this approach to measurement becomes insufficient. By applying measurement techniques ahead of the investment decision, and by using methods that incorporate data on the cultural context and complexities that influence the success of an investment—such as data collected directly from the vulnerable populations that an investment seeks to impact—investors get an upper hand. With this kind of measurement technique, known as transformative evaluation, investors can select the companies and projects that are most likely to perform economically, socially, and sustainably, as well as identify and acquire the tools that will assess impact with the necessary rigor. By combining

697

a literature review and expert advice with personal experience in the field conducting transformative evaluations for impact investments, this chapter makes the case for applying a transformative methodological framework to Impact Investing. The chapter describes transformative methodological frameworks and their origins in the field of program evaluation. A six-phase approach is introduced, including the activities and methods to be applied during each phase of the Impact Investing process. Three examples of Impact Investing evaluations are provided, serving to illustrate the transformative approach and explore how its application affects Impact Investing outcomes. The chapter concludes with an appeal for the wider adoption of transformative evaluation frameworks across the entire investment cycle.

Keywords

Transformative Evaluation; Impact Investing; Sustainable Development Goals; Social justice; Evaluation Methodology; Evaluation; Nonmonetary impact

INTRODUCTION

Social and Environmental Impact Investing. The words of this phrase are all action oriented. Investing is the action of using money to accomplish a goal. Impact describes the generation of certain nonfinancial outcomes, which the Impact Investing sector strives to measure quantitatively, typically as return on investment. The meanings of "social" and "environmental" inherently include interactions among people, and among people, natural resources, and the environments in which they live. When these four words are considered together, they point toward the intentional movement and utilization of financial capital to transform the ways people live.

Complexities arise, however, concerning imposition of certain outcomes from outside actors, and their powerful ability to shape the interactions between people and their environments. These complications include tradeoffs between short-term economic security and environmental goals, as well as the importance of self-determination for historically marginalized groups. These issues cannot be ignored, especially when the main goal of Impact Investing is to help meet the Sustainable Development Goals (SDGs), which embody the international community's commitment to social, economic, and environmental justice.

Impact investors can make better decisions when they have access to data that is grounded in the contextual complexities of the communities in which they work. Such data can be generated through a transformative approach to evaluation. As an accepted systematic approach, transformative evaluation enables engagement with communities in culturally respectful ways, in order to better understand what is needed for transformative change to occur (Mertens 2009, 2018; Mertens and Wilson 2019). The argument put forward in this chapter is that while the "marriage" between the investment community and the use of a transformative lens for evaluation is a novel approach, it has the potential to bear fruits in the form of increased social, economic, and environmental impact.

The international community endorses the need for transformational change in order to meet the SDGs (van den Berg, Magro, and Mulder 2019), and has set the goal of leaving no one behind in this endeavor. Assessment of progress toward meeting the Millennium Development Goals (MDGs) indicated that while progress was made on many fronts, significant parts of the population were left behind, specifically women, girls, and people with disabilities (UNICEF 2013). To avoid this problem going forward, sustainable development strategies need to better engage stakeholder groups, as well as aim toward triple-bottom-line outcomes rather than single-metric improvements. Impact Investing is primed to do just that, given its alignment with the SDGs and its ability to direct capital toward companies and projects aligned with transformational change. If economic and social needs are deprioritized to reach environmental goals, however, it is likely that the shortcomings of the MDGs will be repeated.

A transformative lens for evaluation is defined as an approach that consciously prioritizes the appropriate inclusion of vulnerable and marginalized groups in order to ensure these groups are not left behind. It is designed to support the development of interventions, including impact investments, that are culturally and contextually responsive to the needs of those living in poverty, and address the SDGs more effectively. It includes data collection on both monetary and nonmonetary impacts, allowing investors to better understand what kind of support is necessary to realize their intended impact goals. The adoption of a transformative lens requires an expansion of the impact investment community's perception of impact measurement and evaluation, beyond a narrow focus on metrics to one that promotes a broader purpose for data collection and analysis that reflects an ethical commitment to addressing the needs of those who are traditionally left behind (i.e. members of vulnerable and marginalized communities who experience discrimination and oppression).

In order to be environmentally, economically, and socially responsible, it is important for the Impact Investing community to have access to data that specifically focuses on the cultures and contexts that either support or inhibit the achievement of their goals. Reisman, Olazabal, and Hoffman (2018) noted that the inclusion of beneficiaries' voices is not currently given enough attention in Impact Investing. Take, for example, Impact Investing's focus on climate change mitigation. The sector's commitment to climate action is evident in its fierce advocacy of science-based targets for carbon emissions, which were recently adopted by over 300 firms (George 2019). While this achievement is laudable, reaching these targets requires investing in initiatives that are not only environmentally responsible but also economically viable and responsive to the needs of the vulnerable and marginalized. Impact investors can increase the probability of meeting their goals if they include the concerns and experiences of the vulnerable and marginalized, who are currently experiencing the most serious health problems from climate pollution (Agency for Healthcare Research and Quality 2018). Given that Impact Investing seeks to contribute to the SDGs, its associated measurement and management would benefit from the use of a transformative evaluation framework.

Impact Investing assessment methodologies traditionally prioritize performance metrics, such as returns on investment or other quantitative metrics that can be measured post-investment. For example, Novo Nordisk committed to a quantitative reduction of their emissions based on science-based emission reduction targets (Nielsen 2010). While this is a valuable commitment, its focus on quantitative metrics does not address the culture or the complexities that influence the success of Novo Nordisk's investments in reducing emissions. In contrast, a transformative approach tracks quantitative and qualitative measures at baseline before an intervention, during the midterm, and at the post-investment investment phase. The data collected informs feedback loops that guide future decisions, expanding the scope and role of evaluation from judging completed projects, to providing a means to influence decisions about who and what is funded. Accordingly, data from transformative evaluations can help investors guide funds in ways that are culturally responsive to marginalized and vulnerable populations. Investors can benefit from expanding the role of impact evaluation and measurement in order to identify the conditions needed for just impact *before* an investment is made, as well as before revising an investment's impact thesis[1] or strategy.

The title of this chapter refers to a "marriage" between Impact Investing and evaluation. Impact investors and evaluators share the goal of contributing to positive social change; however, collaborations across these two fields have been limited because of a "lack of a common language, inconsistent definitions and misperceptions of each other's interests and abilities" (Reisman, Olazabal, and Hoffman 2018, p. 392). The evaluation industry has a history of using systematic inquiry and developing tools and frameworks that comprise the evaluation arsenal (Grasso, Wasty, and Weaving 2003). The premise of evaluation is asking a variety of interrogative questions, such as: What worked; and for whom? Did the intervention achieve its desired goals; and how? To what extent can impacts be attributed to the intervention? Evaluative inquiries also often include so-called "why" and "so what" questions. Evaluations can focus on the measurement of different dimensions of performance (e.g. effectiveness, impact) retrospectively, but they can also adopt a prospective approach that integrates evaluation across the full life cycle of a project. The primary outputs of evaluation are learning and the provision of data to inform decision making.[2]

A transformative approach to evaluation and impact measurement in Impact Investing is based on the ethical assumption that Impact Investing must support progress toward social, economic, and environmental justice by design.

---

[1] An impact thesis is the articulation of the social mission of an investment fund. It is usually driven by the set of values operationalized by an individual or organization and can reference a theory of change. It often references specific impact objectives, such as access to clean water or affordable housing, and may also reference a target population, business model, or set of outcomes through which the investor intends to deliver impact. An impact thesis may also include geographies, target sectors, the growth stage and scalability of the potential investees, and the risk appetite of the investor (Saltuk and Idrissi 2012).

[2] Attention to accountability, more explicit in the development cooperation field, is an equally relevant output of evaluation.

Reisman and Olazabal (2016) described the current state of courtship between the Impact Investing and the evaluation fields as follows: "The impact investment community adopted the term 'measurement' to encompass what the traditional evaluation sector typically refers to as 'monitoring and evaluation" (p. 10). However, differences in terminologies should not prevent meaningful conversations across these two disciplines. The "marriage" described in this chapter is designed to support a broader role for evaluative activities, inclusive of measuring, monitoring, and evaluating impact as well as broader understandings of evaluation. Such activities can also contribute to the development of an Impact Investing social mission statement (sometimes referred to as an impact thesis) and related investment strategies.

This chapter applies the transformative methodological framework for evaluation to Impact Investing and demonstrates how its use can improve early investment decision-making and impact measurement, resulting in improved social, environmental, and financial returns. It demonstrates that the "marriage" of transformative evaluation and Impact Investing measurement can further support impact investors in accomplishing the SDGs. It also details best practices, such as developing close relationships between impact investors and evaluators. Healthy working relationships with frequent contact are well suited for delivering timely and reliable data, which can be used to inform decision making in a prompt and judicious manner throughout the whole life cycle of an impact investment.

METHODOLOGY

This chapter relies on a desk review of transformative evaluation and impact investment literature, as well as case studies and examples that illustrate the process and advantages of using a transformative lens in the Impact Investing sector pre-, mid-, and post-investment. In addition, the authors draw on direct field experience gained from piloting the first formal transformative evaluation in the Impact Investing sector, which was for Engineers Without Borders Canada in 2019. Throughout the course of that pilot study, experts in Impact Investing were interviewed about the advantages and challenges of using a transformative approach to evaluation in Impact Investing. This chapter combines the literature review, experience from the pilot study, and advice from experts about transformative evaluation.

THE TRANSFORMATIVE METHODOLOGICAL FRAMEWORK

Methodological frameworks are typically used to provide structure regarding how a given task is performed or to guide thinking about the strategies used (Mertens 2020). The transformative methodological framework originates from the field of program evaluation. The transformative framework was developed with the explicit goals of contributing to social, economic, and environmental justice (Mertens and Wilson 2019). These goals align with the SDGs and with impact investors' intentions of enhancing economic, social, and environmental returns through their investments.

The Transformative Framework Explained

"The transformative paradigm emerged in response to individuals who have been pushed to the societal margins throughout history and who are finding a means to bring their voices into the world of [evaluation]" (Mertens 2009, p. 3). The transformative framework for evaluation arose in response to the calls of members of vulnerable and marginalized communities and their advocates, who expressed dissatisfaction with outsiders coming into their communities to introduce interventions based on a misunderstanding of their needs, culture, and context—leaving them no better, or even worse off, than before the intervention (Mertens, Cram, and Chilisa 2013; Mertens 2009).

The evaluation field has a long history. Its birth as a professional field is usually tied to the 1960s and the introduction of social interventions during President Johnson's Great Society (Mertens and Wilson 2019). The transformative approach to evaluation emerged in the 1990s, and was developed as a framework to guide methodological choices in ways that are rooted in the experiences of members of vulnerable and marginalized communities, with the goal of supporting transformative changes valued by community members and their advocates. The application of the transformative evaluative approach is relevant for impact investors, especially those who have goals that align with the SDGs, because investors can utilize the framework to better inform their investment decisions through the inclusion of vulnerable and marginalized stakeholders.

Transformative evaluations are characterized as follows:

- An ethical stance that promotes social inclusion and challenges oppressive structures that sustain inequality and discrimination
- A participatory and reflective entry process into a community, designed to build trust, address power differences, and make goals and strategies more transparent
- The dissemination of findings in ways that encourage the use of results to enhance human rights and social, economic, and environmental justice
- A commitment to addressing the intersectionality of relevant dimensions of diversity—such as gender, disability, indigeneity, poverty status, and language—by incorporating culturally responsive, equity-focused, feminist, and indigenous approaches that are relevant in the evaluation context (Mertens and Wilson 2019; Mertens 2020)

The application of a transformative lens in Impact Investing invokes different types of questions than more traditional approaches. The following chart contrasts the types of evaluation questions that would emerge under a traditional approach to evaluation, with those associated with a transformative approach (Table 18.1). Additional examples of the application of these characteristics in Impact Investing are provided through case studies and examples later in the chapter. For a more detailed list of transformative evaluation principles and methodological implications, see *A Transformative Evaluation Toolkit for the Impact Investing Sector* (Bolinson and Mertens 2019).

Transformative Evaluation Design

Typically, a transformative design involves several phases that allow for the identification of a broad range of stakeholders, ensures that vulnerable and marginalized voices are included in respectful ways, develops relationships with stakeholders, and delineates strategies for working together (Mertens 2018; Mertens and Wilson 2019). These phases are meant to facilitate the application of the four characteristics of transformative evaluation described in the previous section: an ethical stance promoting social inclusion, a

TABLE 18.1 Sample Evaluation Questions and Transformative Evaluation Questions in Impact Investing.

OECD / DAC[3] evaluation criteria	Standard evaluation questions	Transformative evaluation questions
Relevance	**To what extent** were activities, outputs, and outcomes of the project/ investment/business model consistent with the overall goal and the attainment of its **objectives?**	**To what extent** were activities, outputs, and outcomes of the project/investment/business model consistent with the overall goal and the attainment of its objectives for vulnerable and marginalized populations?
		To what extent does the theory of change (impact thesis) demonstrate a clear commitment to diversity and inclusion?
		To what extent did the project/investment/business model fit in the social setting, including cultural norms and beliefs?
Relevance (Design)	**What elements** were considered in the stakeholder analysis during the design of the project/investment/ business model?	Was there a stakeholder analysis in design of the project/investment/business model that considered a 360° perspective on vulnerable, marginalized, or impacted populations (for possible unintended effects)?
		To what extent was the project/investment/business model designed in a participatory manner by all affected stakeholders (direct and indirect)?
		To what extent were vulnerable and marginalized stakeholders involved in the design and adaptations of the project/investment/business model?
		To what extent were power dynamics considered throughout the project/investment/business cycle?

(continued)

[3]OECD stands for the Organization for Economic Co-operation and Development, an international organization with 27 member nations headquartered in France. DAC stands for Development Assistance Committee, a committee of the OECD that discusses issues surrounding aid, development, and poverty reduction in developing countries.

705

TABLE 18.1 (continued)

OECD / DAC[3] evaluation criteria	Standard evaluation questions	Transformative evaluation questions
Efficiency	How was the project/investment/business model implemented and how did that compare to its implementation initial plan? Were activities cost-efficient? Were objectives achieved on time? Was the project/investment/business model implemented in the most efficient way compared to alternatives? Were there guidelines for conflict resolutions?	How was the project/investment/business model implemented and how did that compare to its implementation initial plan in particular for vulnerable and marginalized populations? Were activities equally cost-efficient for all stakeholder types? Were objectives achieved on time for all stakeholder types, in particular for vulnerable and marginalized populations? How was efficiency compromised by power dynamics? How was efficiency compromised by conflict? How was efficiency compromised by fair treatment (e.g. discrimination) or less acceptable practices (e.g. harassment, bullying)?

Effectiveness	To what extent were the project/investment/business model objectives achieved?	To what extent were the project/investment/business model objectives achieved for vulnerable and marginalized populations?
		How accessible was the project/investment/business model to vulnerable and marginalized members of the target population?
		To what extent were power dynamics addressed throughout the project/investment/business cycle?
		What barriers needed to be overcome to ensure equity in terms of participation and impact?
		How could those barriers be overcome?
	To what extent was the project/investment/business model serving intended participants?	To what extent was the project/investment/business model serving intended participants, in particular those who are marginalized and vulnerable (e.g. women, the young, indigenous populations)?

(continued)

TABLE 18.1 *(continued)*

OECD / DAC[3] evaluation criteria	Standard evaluation questions	Transformative evaluation questions
Impact	**To what extent** was impact (ultimate long-term goals) realized for intended beneficiaries?	**To what extent** did impact materialize for participants' own goals, in particular those who are marginalized and vulnerable (e.g. women, the young, indigenous populations)?
	What was the return on investment?	Were quantitative results disaggregated to reveal the return on investment for marginalized and vulnerable populations?
	Were there unexpected (+/−) impacts?	Were there unexpected (+/−) impacts for *those who are marginalized and vulnerable?*
	Were there unintended (+/−) impacts?	Were there unintended (+/−) impacts for *those who are marginalized and vulnerable?*
Impact (Counter-factual)	**What** would have occurred without the project/investment/business model? (**So what?**)	**What** would have occurred without the project/investment/business model for *marginalized and vulnerable populations?*

Source: Authors.

participatory and reflective entry process, the dissemination of findings to improve design and policy, and addressing intersectionality.

A typical transformative evaluation design is displayed in Table 18.1. The purpose of this design is to provide opportunities for better design, monitoring, collection, and use of data throughout the full course of a project or investment—and to do so in a way that respectfully engages the full range of stakeholders involved directly or touched upon indirectly by any of the intervention's effects, including those who are most vulnerable and marginalized. The purpose is to ensure that whichever project or investment is ultimately supported is culturally responsive and inclusive of those most in need, as well as to demonstrate the effectiveness and impact[4] of the project or investment once implemented. The example in Table 18.1 uses a six-phase approach that moves from relationship building to mixed methods data collection, through to the final use of impact data for transformative purposes. Mixed methods—which is the use of both quantitative and qualitative data collection—are recommended in order to capture the cultural and contextual complexities that affect the achievement of the desired goals, and because they aid data triangulation and enhanced reliability of the findings.

According to Table 18.1, most projects begin with the identification of a problem and a preliminary understanding of what the solution might be (Phase 0). The intent of applying a transformative lens is to challenge these preexisting assumptions, and to arrive at a more accurate understanding of what the problem is and what types of solutions directly respond to the culture and context of the impacted stakeholder groups and geographic areas. Phase 1, building relationships, is a critical first step that supports the identification of relevant stakeholders, especially from vulnerable and marginalized populations. Evaluators and investors need to engage in a critical self-reflection, to ensure they are aware of how their own perspectives and experiences might enhance or detract from the creation of relationships. These relationships should be fostered throughout the life cycle of the project or investment—to inform, advise, test program designs, develop program theory (i.e. impact thesis), and implement.

---

[4] In the evaluation field, effectiveness—according to a traditional results logical framework—comprises outputs (short-term effects) and outcomes (medium-term, intermediate effects). Impact is seen as the accomplishment of ultimate (long-term) goals.

TABLE 18.2 A Six-Phase Approach Toward a Transformative Evaluation.

Phases	Phase 0: Problem Identification	Phase 1: Build Relationships	Phase 2: Contextual Analysis	Phase 3: Pilot	Phase 4: Implement	Phase 5: Determine Effects and Impact	Phase 6: Use Findings for Transformative Purposes
	Identify the nature of the problem and appropriate solutions.	Identify relevant stakeholders, especially from vulnerable or marginalized groups, through an insightful and 360° stakeholder analysis.[5]	Consult beneficiaries and groups of interested stakeholders along with advisors (e.g. through focus groups, advisory committees, interviews, or other methods). In this process, systematically collect data and contextual information, ideally using mixed methods to capture complexity and triangulate information[6] for increased reliability.	Test or "pilot" the inclusive project or investment. Use adequate mix of methods to collect data from relevant vulnerable or marginalized stakeholders regarding the pilot version of the project or investment.[7]	Fully implement the project or investment. Utilize mixed methods data collection to document quality of experiences, as well as to provide baseline data and start the monitoring process on	Analyze monitoring and evaluative data collected previously to determine the impact of the project or investment for achieving intended outcomes.	Use the evidence and findings for refinements of subsequent stages or new projects or investments Use evidence and findings to improve and expand partnerships, relationships, anc coalitions.

[5]Common methods for stakeholder analysis can be found here: https://masterofproject.com/blog/7514-top-5-stakeholders-analysis-techniques-in-projects-stakeholder-analysis-in-project-management.

[6]For instance, through literature review, GIS mapping, statistical analysis, or other methods to gather cultural, historical, political, or other contextual information.

[7]This evaluation should focus on the relevance, efficiency, and effectiveness (performance) of the project or investment.

Develop partnerships, relationships, and coalitions—especially with those most affected or negatively affected by the project or investment. Develop active participatory approaches for working together throughout the entire project or investment cycle.	Revisit and update the understanding of the nature of the problem and appropriate solutions based on stakeholder consultations and contextual analysis. Design an inclusive project or investment.	Utilize mixed methods[8] to evaluate the pilot. Adapt the project or investment design based on the data analysis, stakeholder consultations, and evaluation results.[9]	key performance indicators (KPI).[10] Collect data on unexpected and unintended outcomes (monitor throughout the project cycle). Evaluate performance at midterm or at key points to document quality of implementation, challenges, and to implement corrective measures.	Examine relationship quality with vulnerable and marginalized stakeholders. Determine if there are any unintended or unexpected impacts, especially on vulnerable and marginalized populations. Use evidence and findings for improvements and policy change.

Source: Adapted from Mertens (2018).

---

[8] Mixed methods include interviews, focus groups, observation, financial data, photo voice, baseline surveys, and more.

[9] Ex ante evaluations, which are performed at the start of a project cycle, can be conducted.

[10] Key performance indicators include return on investment, jobs created (quantitative data), and qualitative data (e.g. perceptions, quality of experience as captured in interviews).

711

Phase 2 conveys the need for in-depth contextual analysis,[11] where stakeholders—especially those who are vulnerable or marginalized—can engage via focus groups, advisory committees, or other participatory approaches, in order to convey their experiences in relation to whatever problem a project seeks to address. Data from the contextual analysis should be fed back into the program theory (i.e. impact thesis); relevant information shared by stakeholders should be taken into consideration and incorporated into the design of the project or investment. In addition to stakeholder consultations, other data collection methods and sources include literature reviews, observations, and field experience—all of which can and should be used to deepen the understanding of cultural, political, historical, and other contexts, and additionally can provide more reliable information through information triangulation.[12] Additionally, a critical aspect of this transformative approach is to provide an accurate understanding of the nature of the problem. Contextual analysis helps surface more nuanced understandings. For example, if a bank wants to increase the number of women they employ, it is critical to identify and understand the reasons why women are not employed or do not stay in their jobs. Contextual analysis and participatory approaches can reveal that the problem might result from

---

[11]Examples of contextual analysis questions from an investment perspective:

What dimensions of diversity are used as a basis of discrimination and oppression in this context? (Mertens and Wilson 2019)

How does a potential investment respond to or address this?

What are the consequences associated with the current course of action in the community? (Reason and Bradbury 2006).

What principles or values underpin the investment strategy?

To what extent has an investment process been created that is truly worthy of human aspirations? (Reason and Bradbury 2006).

How do sexism, racism, able-bodyism, audism, and classism serve to create barriers for women, indigenous peoples, people of color, people with disabilities, or people who are deaf with regard to the investment process or social business model? (Mertens 2009).

What barriers confront vulnerable and marginalized individuals in their access to the product or program being evaluated, and how can those barriers be overcome?

What is the role of the local community, including those most vulnerable and marginalized, in the development or design of the potential investment product or service?

How can investment practices be localized to reflect the cultural complexity of the target beneficiary community?

What is the impact of the investment product or service on issues of cultural and community relevance?

[12]Information triangulation can be done through both stakeholder consultations and the other methods of analysis and sources of information.

the larger surrounding culture, the bank's internal culture, or possibly a hostile environment (e.g. sexual harassment). The impact thesis would differ depending on what the evaluation found—ranging from those that focus on changing attitudes toward women, to providing a safe work environment in specific offices.

Phase 3 comprises piloting the project and testing the impact thesis before full implementation commences. Mixed methods of evaluation should be employed as they better capture complexity and can respond to a multitude of stakeholders with different kinds of needs. During this pilot phase, an even broader group of stakeholders and vulnerable and marginalized individuals should be engaged and consulted, with a focus on evaluating the potential effectiveness and impact of the project design. Data should be applied toward understanding what works and does not work with the current design, paying particular attention to the needs, barriers, and constraints of the most vulnerable and marginalized members of the target population. Quantitative measures such as amount of investment, addition of jobs, or reduction of pollutants can be included in the pilot phase to test the cultural appropriateness of such measures. Based on the recommendations obtained from the consultations and data collected during the pilot phase, the project or investment design should be updated, and a new version should be fully implemented during Phase 4. In Phase 4, data can be collected about the quality of the implementation using both quantitative and qualitative methods.

In Phase 5, determining effects and impacts, experimental or quasi-experimental designs can be included with collection of both quantitative and qualitative data. The data should be analyzed to determine the effectiveness and impact of the project or investment. In Phase 6, findings are used to improve the project or investment for its next iteration. Data can also be used for other transformative purposes, like informing policy, depending on the scale of the project and the type of data collected.

Because a transformative design is highly contextualized, the specific methodologies, approaches, techniques, and activities in each phase will vary according to the context, as well as with the type of project or investment. The practical application of a transformative evaluation may include part, all, or more than what is demonstrated in this six-phase example. Not all phases will be relevant in all contexts, and additional phases might need to be added. For example, in a case described later in the "Examples" section, Burns, Tashima, and Matranga (2019) used five-phases in their evaluation, which was designed to determine whether their project achieved its goal of increasing the number of female entrepreneurs receiving funding. What makes a design *transformative* is adherence to the four elements described earlier: an ethical stance promoting social inclusion, a participatory and reflective entry process, the dissemination of findings to improve social, economic, and environmental justice, and addressing intersectionality.

APPLICATION TO IMPACT INVESTING

This section describes the role that a transformative framework can play for investors in each investment stage. For each stage of investment, all six transformative design phases can be applied. As a new investment stage begins, a new transformative evaluation process should begin as well.

The phases of a typical transformative design can be applied throughout an investment cycle, in a cyclical way, just as they are applied in other social project contexts. For the purposes of this chapter, an investment cycle involves the stages described in Table 18.2.

In an investment context, an "evaluator" can be a member of the investment team who is knowledgeable about evaluation methodologies and monitoring and is tasked with measuring the portfolio's impact. The evaluator could also be someone contracted externally (e.g. a consultant), which in some contexts better enables relationship building with marginalized groups and can also provide additional credibility as outside evaluators produce independent third-party evaluations. Ideally, impact investors would work with an expert evaluator to apply the transformative framework throughout the investment cycle, from the very beginning (impact thesis and investment strategy development). The use of a transformative lens from the earliest stages allows for the identification of the right stakeholders, inclusion of the right metrics and processes, and use of the right data collection methods—so that accurate information can be provided about not only impact, but also the most relevant externalities, and other unintended and unexpected effects. This allows for the development of investment projects that are culturally responsive and inclusive from the very beginning.[13]

In situations where the investment thesis or strategy has already been developed, a transformative framework can still generate benefits if applied in subsequent stages of the investment process, such as pre-investment, investment, and post-investment through to final exit. Using a transformative lens in later stages benefits investors by identifying areas in need of

---

[13]For additional information about how a transformative framework is aligned with Impact Investing, and which types of Impact Investing fit best with a transformative approach, see *A Transformative Evaluation Toolkit for the Impact Investing Sector* (Bolinson and Mertens 2019).

TABLE 18.3   Investment Cycle Stages.

Investment stage	Description/Key elements
Impact thesis and investment strategy development	Articulation of the impact thesis of the portfolio or fund
Pre-investment	Sourcing, screening, due diligence (pre-term sheet), term sheet, and due diligence (post-term sheet)
Investment	Investment decision, deal structuring (investment and terms), social impact metric selection, contract, disbursement of funds, and monitoring
Post-investment (ongoing investment management)	Impact measurement and management, portfolio management
Exit	Exit to ensure the company has access to the resources it needs to scale; selection of aligned buyers according to various criteria (Schiff and Dithrich 2018)

Source: Adapted from Bolinson and Mertens (2019).

revision, enabling course corrections toward more culturally responsive and inclusive interventions. The previous example of employing more women in the banking sector serves to illustrate this point. If an investment firm notes that two years into a five-year project several women were hired but left the bank shortly thereafter, they could identify the reasons that led them to leave. This could shift the focus to addressing the elements that contribute to a hostile environment and enable the project to nimbly achieve its goals.

Impact Thesis Application

Impact investors typically begin by developing their impact thesis, theory of change, or another explicit description of their portfolio's impact goals and relationship with the foreseen investments and activities (Saltuk and Idrissi 2012). An impact thesis provides a critical foundation for the Impact Investing process. It drives investment decisions, management choices, impact measurement approaches, and may articulate principles governing the relationships between the investor and their investees. By applying a transformative framework at an early stage—ideally before the thesis or

TABLE 18.4 The Six-Phase Transformative Framework for Impact Thesis Development.

Phase 1: Build Relationships	Phase 2: Contextual Analysis	Phase 3: Pilot	Phase 4: Implement	Phase 5: Determine Impact	Phase 6: Use Findings for Transformative Purposes
Build a diverse team of investment professionals. Build relationships[14] with the full range of stakeholders, including vulnerable and marginalized individuals intended to positively benefit from possible investments. Consult with vulnerable and marginalized stakeholders regarding their day-to-day experiences, needs, interests, and goals, relevant to possible investments.	Based on consultations with all stakeholders, including those who are vulnerable and marginalized, observations, and relevant literature, develop a draft impact thesis for the investment or portfolio. Clarify how the possible investment or portfolio will directly or indirectly benefit (or harm) different communities, especially those that are vulnerable and marginalized. Identify systems of oppression, and barriers to social justice. Build inclusive environmental, social, economic, or other impact considerations into the investment design model.	Share the draft thesis with the relevant stakeholders, including vulnerable and marginalized groups, and gauge their reactions. Revise and finalize the thesis based on feedback from the target beneficiary populations, including vulnerable and marginalized groups.	Use the impact thesis to guide the development of an investment strategy. Select KPIs and set up monitoring systems to assess the impact thesis over time.	Collect data, including on unexpected and unintended outcomes. Analyze data to determine the appropriateness of the impact thesis for addressing the desired social, economic, or environmental impacts.	Refine the impact thesis over time to better reflect the needs and desires of vulnerable and marginalized beneficiary populations. Use data to find ways to improve and expand relationships with stakeholders, especially those most vulnerable and marginalized. Use data to support needed policy changes

Example Activities

Source: Authors.

---

[14]Without the building of these relationships, there will be critical blind spots through the rest of the process.

716

theory of change is being developed—impact investors can better select, understand, and define the problem(s) they seek to address via their portfolio, particularly in respect to the needs and interests of vulnerable and marginalized populations that investors are seeking to benefit. Using a transformative framework at the design stage is critical for identifying and building relationships with the right stakeholders early enough for them to inform the selection of indicators and data collection methods. Without this participatory approach, investors may miss crucial information regarding unintended and unexpected effects of their investments, which might negatively impact their profits, social goals, and even image. Table 18.3 demonstrates what a transformative evaluation process could look like for the stage of impact thesis development.

Pre-Investment Application

Once the impact thesis is developed, the investor moves to the pre-investment stage. During this period, attention is paid to issues of sourcing, screening, due diligence (preterm sheet), term sheet, and due diligence (post-term sheet). The application of a transformative framework to the development of sourcing processes would examine possible barriers and facilitators to sourcing vulnerable and marginalized entrepreneurs and/or enterprises focusing on the most vulnerable and marginalized populations by hearing from those populations directly. An investor could then develop sourcing processes that address the identified barriers, as well as catalyze the facilitators to create a more equitable sourcing process. Developing an inclusive sourcing process using a transformative framework looks similar to the impact thesis example (Table 18.3), with a few key differences. During the relationship-building phase (Phase 1), investors should focus on building relationships with vulnerable and marginalized *entrepreneurs* (those they are seeking to source more inclusively), not just vulnerable and marginalized populations generally.

The contextual analysis phase (Phase 2) would focus on the sourcing context, including the current barriers and facilitators to sourcing in ways that are more inclusive of vulnerable and marginalized entrepreneurs, or entrepreneurs focusing on vulnerable and marginalized populations. Based on the contextual analysis and consultations with these stakeholders, investors should design an inclusive sourcing process that addresses the identified barriers and catalyzes the facilitators to create a more equitable sourcing process. Once this sourcing process is designed, it can be piloted and revised (Phase 3) by sharing a draft sourcing process with relevant stakeholders, including vulnerable and marginalized entrepreneurs, and revising the process based on their reactions and feedback. Investors can then implement (Phase 4) the piloted version of the inclusive sourcing process, and subsequently collect data on the effectiveness and impact of the implemented sourcing process (Phase 5). Finally, data on effectiveness and impact should be used (Phase 6) to refine the inclusive sourcing process, enabling impact investors to effectively source vulnerable and marginalized entrepreneurs or businesses focused on the most vulnerable and marginalized populations.

For screening, a transformative framework can be used to design a process that prioritizes investments based on their alignment with the four principles of transformative evaluation and/or based on the prioritized needs of the target beneficiary population. A transformative framework can also be useful for designing and conducting due diligence processes that involve vulnerable and marginalized populations to better determine the relevance, appropriateness, and potential impact of an impact investment. The same six phases would be applied in each of these cases.

Investment Application

It is at the investment stage that most investment decisions are made, deals are structured (instruments and terms), impact metrics are selected, contracts are issued, and funds are disbursed. Applying a transformative framework to the investment stage can guide impact investors to work with investees to select impact metrics that are inclusive and appropriate for vulnerable and marginalized beneficiary populations, and which also allow for the disaggregation of data by relevant subgroups and inclusive data categories. The process used to select stakeholders is crucial. Deliberate efforts need to be made to include women and members of vulnerable and marginalized communities in respectful ways. A transformative framework could also be used to address power relations by ensuring that the voices of the full range of stakeholders are included. An example of an investor applying a transformative framework to the investment stage is the UnLtd Big Venture Challenge—a program that supports social ventures to become growth and investment-ready. UnLtd structures their investments in order to create mission "locks" for their ventures via social purpose statements that are written into governing documents, as well as operational commitment in their venture's Articles of Association (Smith et al. 2017). Careful monitoring of progress and implementation is an important part of this stage of investment and can take the form of database systems, performance assessments, and implementing monitoring metrics such as IRIS+ metrics to monitor specific outputs and performance. Such monitoring can alert investors when midterm corrections are needed to ensure the project is being inclusive and is moving toward the accomplishment of its goals.

Post-Investment and Exit Application

The post-investment stage includes activities such as portfolio management, and impact measurement and management. At this time, an impact investor may want to commission an impact measurement and management process or provide resources to an investee enterprise to conduct data collection and impact measurement and management. This could take the form of implementing performance assessments to look into outcome and impact indicators, or the implementation of post-experimental or experimental evaluation methods (such as randomized control trials).[15] A transformative framework could be used to develop impact measurement and management processes that are more inclusive, culturally responsive, and participatory. The discussion of M-Shule in the "Examples" section illustrates how this might be done.

When it comes time to exit an investment, impact investors have an obligation to exit responsibly. This entails exiting at the right time to "ensure the company has access to the resources it needs to scale, maintain management in place, and select aligned buyers according to criteria such as their vision for scaling the company, track record and experience in the sector" (Schiff and Dithrich 2018, p. 18). The transformative framework can be used at this stage to review what has been learned from the perspective of the investor, entrepreneur, or investee, and target impact beneficiaries. The final phase of a transformative evaluation can go beyond impact, toward an assessment of the sustainability of an investment and provide guidance on how it can be made even more responsive to the vulnerable and marginalized in the future. Table 18.5 demonstrates this in four phases.

A transformative approach to learning identifies intended, unintended, and emergent outcomes of the investment. It instigates inclusive and participatory conversations between the investee and/or investor and the relevant vulnerable and marginalized populations, which are focused on what those impacts mean for them. The learnings gained from the evaluation process are to guide future strategy or portfolio construction decisions, and impact

---

[15]Randomized control trials (RCT) need to be prepared from the design stage. International Initiative for Impact Evaluation (3ie) provides a range of materials and a database where RCT studies can be consulted: https://developmentevidence.3ieimpact.org/.

TABLE 18.5 Four-Phase Transformative Framework for Post-Investment Learning.

	Phase 1: Build Relationships	Phase 2: Contextual Analysis	Phase 3: Determine Impact	Phase 4: Use Findings for Transformative Purposes
Example Activities	Maintain close contact and relationships with the full range of stakeholders, including relevant vulnerable and marginalized stakeholders.	Revisit contextual analysis results from earlier applications of a transformative framework (i.e. during earlier investment stages). If this is the first time a transformative framework is being used, consult individuals and groups of stakeholders through focus groups, advisory committees, interviews, or other methods on the local context. Also utilize surveys, extant data, literature reviews, GIS mapping, or other methods to gather cultural, historical, political, or other contextual information.	Analyze the impact measurement data to determine the nonmonetary impact of the investment(s)	Refine aspects of the investment thesis and strategy, pre-investment processes, and investment processes according to the results of the impact measurement process in order to make better investments in the future. Share learnings with the beneficiaries, stakeholders, and the broader Impact Investing community so other investors can refine their strategies to be more socially, economically, and environmentally effective.

Source: Authors.

thesis revisions. For this to happen it is also crucial to share lessons with the right stakeholders, and to communicate effectively and comprehensively with asset owners and prospective investors. A transformative framework can also be used to demonstrate evidence of impact or progress toward impact if an investor exits before scale.

Examples

This section presents three examples of evaluations conducted in Impact Investing. Two of the examples (Village Capital and M-Shule) illustrate a transformative approach to evaluation; the third example (Global Agri-development Company) provides insights into the failings that result from an impact investment that does not use such an approach.

Village Capital and Peer-Selected Investment

Village Capital is an impact investment firm that funds projects in the United States, India, Sub-Saharan Africa, and Latin America. Village Capital was founded by Ross Baird and Victoria Fram because they were concerned about the paucity of female-founded or co-founded ventures in Impact Investing, as well as the lack of Impact Investing funding being allocated to Black and Latinx entrepreneurs. In just over 10 years, they have supported over 100 seed-stage investors. Village Capital wanted to test the hypothesis that a collaborative due-diligence model such as their own, which took a bottom-up approach to investing, would increase the number of investments in female, Black, and Latinx entrepreneurs.

Because Village Capital did not regularly collect data to test their hypothesis, they conducted a study to assess the quality of their investment decision-making strategies, which somewhat aligns with a transformative approach (Burns, Tashima, and Matranga 2019). This case study highlights how Village Capital's adopted methods and process decisions mirrored a transformative framework and identifies additional steps that would have been taken if a full transformative evaluation had been undertaken.

Village Capital started by recognizing a problem characterized by oppressive structures that sustained inequality and discrimination, which is aligned with the first principle of the transformative framework. Village Capital's primary focus was on ameliorating gender and race biases in how funds are awarded to entrepreneurs. They hypothesized that using a peer-selected investment process for decision-making would mitigate bias based on race and gender. While Village Capital did not intentionally follow a transformative framework in the design and implementation of their study, multiple aspects of their process reflect a transformative design.

Village Capital succinctly described their methodology as follows: "Using quantitative and qualitative analysis, and pulling from both internal and external databases and surveys, we spent the past 10 months studying the processes and outcomes of 39 Village Capital programs from 2013 to 2017 in the US, India, Sub-Saharan Africa, and Latin America. The dataset comprised a group of more than 1,200 entrepreneurs in total, including alumni of Village Capital peer selection programs and control groups[16] of applicants who did not participate in the programs" (Burns, Tashima, and Matranga 2019, p. 7). Their primary data collection and analysis were focused on determining to what extent women, Black, and Latinx entrepreneurs were not adequately represented in the group of funded entrepreneurs.

Table 18.6 maps the study description to a transformative framework in five phases. In Phase 1, Village Capital formed partnerships with the MacArthur Foundation, the Aspen Network of Development Entrepreneurs, the Global Accelerator Learning Initiative, and Social Enterprise at Goizueta, a research center at Emory University. Had they applied fully a transformative evaluation framework, their relationship building would have been strengthened by including women, Black, and Latinx entrepreneurs.

In Phase 2 of the study, they collected baseline data that indicated that only 15% of venture capital went to female-founded or female co-founded ventures, and that less than 2% of the awards went to Black and Latinx entrepreneurs. In Phase 3, they used a mixed methods approach to data collection—obtaining data from a wide range of stakeholders, observing one project, and collecting quantitative data on the ratings of applications and the awarding of funds. They collected quantitative data on the number of awards made to ventures that were founded by people of color, as well as those founded or co-founded by women. They also collected quantitative data on the ratings given to the 1,200 proposals that were submitted, including the amount of capital the entrepreneurs were able to raise and the amount of revenue they generated. Next, the results were disaggregated by gender (Phase 4). Disaggregation by race was not possible as there was insufficient data to do so.

Analysis of seed-stage investments indicated that 44% of the ventures Village Capital funded were female-founded or co-founded, and 26% of ventures had founders of color. This supported their hypothesis that Village

---

[16]Control or comparison groups are commonly used in experimental and quasi-experimental designs in formal impact evaluations.

TABLE 18.6 Village Capital Peer-Selected Investment Study, Mapped onto a Transformative Framework.

Phase 1: Building Relationships	Phase 2: Contextual Analysis	Phase 3: Assessment of the Intervention	Phase 4: Analysis and Reporting	Phase 5: Use of Results
Performed desk review to determine the scope of the problem. Hired study teams. Established partnerships with other foundations and research center.	Collected baseline data from Village Capital, put into a database with indicators such as funding level by gender and race. Conducted interviews and focus groups with potential ventures who were actively seeking funding as they submitted proposals.	Conducted interviews with current and past Village Capital staff, board members, program mentors, and current and alumni ventures. Made field observations of one of Village Capital's projects. Collected quantitative performance data one and two years after the program (e.g. debt, equity capital raised, revenue, sex, and race).	Disaggregated (by gender and race) and analyzed data of ventures that were funded and not. Compared funded ventures with three other groups that did not apply for funding (control group). Disaggregated data by gender (insufficient data for race disaggregation).	Reexamined the review process to eliminate gender and racial bias. Examined new strategies to reduce racial bias.

Source: Authors.

Capital had considerably increased the percentage of ventures founded by women and people of color in their portfolio, as at baseline only 15% of ventures were female-founded, 2% were started by Black and Latinx entrepreneurs. The design did not permit a rigorous test of what would have happened without the peer selection process, but the results do indicate that their peer-selection process did mitigate the gender bias. For example, compared to baseline, more women were included in Village Capital's list of proposals, and more ultimately rose to the top of the review set and were awarded seed-stage grants. However, the results suggested further improvements to their investment process were needed: on average, male-founded companies were ranked higher than female-founded companies, even though companies founded by women had stronger revenue performance than the higher ranked male-founded companies. In addition, their analysis revealed that too few members of minority racial groups (e.g. Black and Latinx) were funded to do meaningful comparisons.

The Village Capital example (Burns, Tashima, and Matranga 2019) illustrates the potential for a transformative framework to address disparities in funding for female- and male-founded companies. The authors of Village Capital's study indicated that they intended to continue focusing on the issues that arose in the evaluation process to determine how to improve the program going forward.

Their nonintentional use of a sort of a transformative framework provided valuable insights into gender bias, but it did not do the work of developing strategies to actually promote bias reduction based on race and gender (Phase 5). A more comprehensive application of a transformative framework would have raised questions about the implicit bias operating in the review process, which might have led to the development of specific actions to change reviewers' beliefs about female-founders and entrepreneurs of color. In other words, while Village Capital's adoption of a peer-reviewed due diligence process was effective in many ways, it was not sufficient to address the underlying foundations of gender and racial bias throughout the decision-making process.

In addition to what Village Capital accomplished, a more comprehensive application of a transformative framework could have engendered additional activities, which could have more fully addressed the issues they encountered, such as providing training to reviewers to be more aware of their internal biases. Activities on how to use safeguards in the review process also could have played out well. Further, devising interventions to support women and members of racial minority groups in the development of their proposals and business models would have also warranted a stronger strategy to increase their representation in the funded projects.

Global Agri-Development Company and the Absence of a Transformative Framework

While the Village Capital example provides an opportunity to explore the application of a transformative lens to evaluating the effectiveness of investment strategies, the example presented next, from Ghana, reveals the high cost of not using a transformative lens. Kish and Fairbairn (2018) describe the evaluation of an impact investment farming project in southeast Ghana. This example demonstrates inconsistency between what impact investors claim they are doing and what their investments achieve on the ground.

The Global Agri-Development Company (GADCO) is a commercial rice business in southeast Ghana. The business aims to generate impact by addressing food insecurity in Ghana, increasing local employment, and boosting the productivity of local smallholder farmers. GADCO was an inaugural impact investment in West Africa made by Acumen, a nonprofit impact fund, along with other development agencies, impact investment funds, and grants (Kish and Fairbairn 2018).

Kish and Fairbairn (2018) explain that while stories of the investment's positive impact circulated, researchers found that instead, "employment has remained low since the company's 2010 founding because the farm is highly mechanized and mainly draws skilled labor from other parts of the country" (p. 582). In fact, no one from the village had been hired, even though local employment was part of the company's agreement. In addition, researchers found several other issues, such as no clear link to local entrepreneurship, that the operation's farming practices were not environmentally sustainable, and negative feedback from the local Fievie community that revealed a general feeling that the company had not helped their community. Local entrepreneurship could not have been fostered because no local entrepreneurs were included; the founding entrepreneurs were from Nigeria and Brazil. In addition, the company's managers were given rent-free access to the villagers' farmland in exchange for 2.5% revenue sharing. To make things worse, two years into the agreement no funds had been transferred to the villagers.

Kish and Fairbairn (2018) concluded that the GADCO project secured funding because the fund managers and entrepreneurs reiterated their value stories frequently enough and with such conviction that they beguiled "conscious" moneyed audiences. Their cajoling ultimately funded the project, despite GADCO's broken promises to reduce food insecurity, increase local employment, and increase the productivity of local smallholder famers. It is a great loss, both to the investor and society at large, when resources are deployed to ineffective or unsuccessful social businesses.

GADCO and/or its investors could have used a transformative framework at multiple stages of the investment to improve outcomes. First, if a transformative framework had been applied before the investment was made, the evaluation would have involved the local Fievie community to clarify whether food insecurity, employment, and farm productivity were the most pressing challenges to be addressed. If these were not the most pressing challenges, as defined by the local vulnerable and marginalized population, then investors whose impact theses were directed at that particular population, sector, or SDG may have decided not to invest. If local community members did feel that the goals of the social enterprise were aligned with their most pressing needs, then the investors could proceed with the investment feeling assured about GADCO's alignment with community needs and thus their own impact theses. Later, the transformative framework could have involved the local Fievie community in setting GADCO's impact goals and in selecting culturally relevant impact measurement methods. Expectations would have been set early on, along with initial impact measurements, and a clear impact measurement plan would have allowed Acumen and other investors to better hold GADCO accountable to the delivery of intended social and economic outcomes. Additionally, the results of the impact measurement process would have provided valuable data for GADCO to iterate upon and improve the social aspect of their business.

Engineers Without Borders, M-Shule, and a Transformative Evaluation Pilot

This example illustrates the use of a transformative framework during the post-investment phase of Impact Investing. Impact investors often work with their investees to set up impact measurement systems. In this example, Engineers Without Borders Canada (EWB) commissioned a transformative evaluation pilot with one of their seed-stage investees, M-Shule. EWB deploys investment capital, talent, and mentorship to founding-stage social enterprises in Sub-Saharan Africa. M-Shule is an adaptive, mobile education platform that uses a short message service to deliver personalized English and math lessons to students in upper primary school in Nairobi, Kenya, and beyond. M-Shule also provides data insights to schools and families regarding individual student performance.

TABLE 18.7 EWB Pilot Transformative Framework.

	Phase 1: Build Relationships	Phase 2: Problem Identification and Contextual Analysis	Phase 3: Design of the Evaluation	Phase 4: Data Collection	Phase 5: Data Analysis and Interpretation	Phase 6: Utilization of Results
Example Activities	Identified target population and gatekeepers.[17] Built relationships with gatekeepers and vulnerable and marginalized members of the target population, such as the local school association, school directors, and head teachers. Set up a Local Advisory Committee (LAC), inclusive of school staff, parents and students.	Conducted in-depth contextual analysis on M-Shule's social, political, and economic context, including a general profile of Kenya and Nairobi and an investigation in Kenyan education policy, primary school education data, and general trends in digital technology, and education sector stakeholder identification.	Consulted LAC for the design of the evaluation to ensure the needs of the LAC and the stakeholders they represented were met by the design. Adjusted evaluation methods based on LAC feedback, including participant recruitment strategies, planned timing of the focus groups, which subject teachers to interview, and how best to involve parents.	Conducted focus groups, key informant interviews, and demographic surveys with parents, teachers, and students from a marginalized school district to determine the effectiveness of the M-Shule product. Regularly interacted with evaluation participants before, during, and after data collection.	Coded and analyzed data for emergent themes and sub-themes.[18] Shared results with the LAC during a co-inter-pretation meeting where the evaluators asked the committee for their interpreta-tions of the meaning of the data.	Shared results with M-Shule via a report and a facilitated discussion focused on how M-Shule could incorporate the evaluation results into their business decisions. Shared results with evaluation participants, including a response from M-Shule on their planned use of the evaluation results. Participant reactions and responses were reported back to M-Shule for further learning.

Source: Authors.

---

[17] Evaluators worked with M-Shule to determine which of their target neighborhoods contained the most marginalized populations and pulled an evaluation sample from those neighborhoods. Gatekeepers were identified via observation and word-of-mouth by an evaluator who spent time in the sample neighborhoods and met with key individuals at the local school association.

[18] Detailed instructions for how to analyze qualitative data using coding and theming can be found in Miles, Huberman, and Saldaña (2014).

As a seed stage investor, EWB was motivated to demonstrate the social impact of their portfolio. EWB hypothesized that by using a transformative framework to assess the cultural responsiveness and business performance of seed stage social enterprises, they could enable those investees to effectively communicate their initial impact outcomes, as well as their potential for future impact. EWB also saw the opportunity for a transformative evaluation to support data-driven operational and strategic decision-making, which would improve investees' offerings to target clients and communities (Wakiaga and Bolinson 2019). With support from the 2018 Aspen Network of Development Entrepreneurs Catalyst Fund for Impact Measurement, EWB partnered with M-Shule to commission a pilot transformative evaluation of the social enterprise between June 2018 and June 2019. EWB used a six-phase transformative design in a slightly different order than the previously presented frameworks in this chapter. Table 18.7 lists the main activities in each phase of the EWB transformative evaluation pilot.

A meta-evaluation[19] conducted by EWB to evaluate the effectiveness of the transformative framework—applied in a seed stage context post-funding allocation—revealed unique elements and findings that EWB had not unearthed through their conventional impact measurement process. These new elements centered on the inclusion of vulnerable and marginalized constituencies and the involvement of a local advisory committee (LAC) during the evaluation design, implementation, interpretation of data, and reporting stages (Bolinson 2019). According to the meta-evaluation report (Bolinson 2019), the transformative framework produced valuable results for M-Shule. Ultimately, the transformative evaluation helped M-Shule decide to pivot from a business-to-consumer model to a business-to-business one (Bolinson 2019). "The transformative evaluation successfully validated data M-Shule had already collected, provided data that could help them refine their business strategy, prioritize product improvements, and refine the product, provided an alternative form of impact measurement that was more attainable than other methods, and improved M-Shule's relationship with its stakeholders" (Bolinson 2019, p. 8). For example, even though the data collected was similar to what M-Shule was collecting in regular

---

[19]Meta-evaluation is a type of meta-analysis of a set of relevant evaluations concerning a given topic, which evaluates the methodology; see Stufflebeam (1978). In this case, following the conclusion of the pilot, EWB evaluators conducted key informant interviews with evaluation stakeholders, including members of the implementing evaluation team, members of M-Shule who were involved in the evaluation, and members of the EWB Investment Team. The meta-evaluation data was analyzed to pull out key aspects of the transformative evaluation and its implementation process (Bolinson 2019).

customer engagements, the transformative process was more rigorous, and emphasized a greater diversity of stakeholders, including those most vulnerable and marginalized (Bolinson 2019). M-Shule used the evaluation results to improve their product and services for vulnerable and marginalized beneficiaries, advancing social justice for their clients.

Not only did M-Shule gain valuable data to inform their product development and broader decision-making, EWB also gained valuable data as an investor. As expected, the transformative framework provided high-quality outcome-level data that EWB could use to evidence the social impact of their investment and improve the venture's future implementation and design. Since it was a pilot project, EWB used lessons learned from the process to develop a more inclusive and culturally responsive portfolio-level impact measurement and management process. Future evaluations of M-Shule and other similar projects could be enhanced by the collection of quantitative baseline data on relevant indicators (e.g., educational achievement, rate of employment) with post-implementation comparisons. Integration of experimental or quasi-experimental designs into a transformative evaluation could provide further insight into ventures' effectiveness in achieving impact goals.

CONCLUSION

Good business sense tells of the importance of product-market fit. A transformative framework ensures product-market fit is defined from the perspective of vulnerable and marginalized communities, rather than only entrepreneurs or investors. If impact investors embed a transformative framework early on in their investment processes, using it to design the intervention, set impact goals for the portfolio, and to source, screen, and evaluate potential investments based on their alignment with community interest and need—investors will not only be selecting appropriate investments, but they will be selecting those more likely to outperform economically, socially, and sustainably.

At the start of this chapter, we described the complexities of social, economic, and environmental impact investments, especially those aimed at contributing to larger objectives, such as the SDGs. The SDGs seek to address massive global challenges that require transformative systemic changes to increase social, economic, and environmental justice. Because of the level of complexity involved, especially when vulnerable and marginalized communities are affected, sharp attention ought to be given to the appropriate inclusion and participation of members of vulnerable and marginalized communities, identification of relevant contextual factors, lessons learned, and unintended outcomes. These elements follow from the six-phase transformative framework presented in this chapter.

Impact measurement's "marriage" with the transformative evaluation approach introduces a new analytical lens and new methodologies. By enhancing decision-making through contextual analysis and participatory engagement with target beneficiary populations, transformative evaluation can help impact investors act justly and decisively in the face of entangled complexity. The framework enables this because it prioritizes the inclusion of vulnerable and marginalized populations, in order to expose and ame- liorate inequalities based on gender, disability, race, ethnicity, and other characteristics that are used as the basis for discrimination. The MDGs and experiences from international development and cooperation reveal that if vulnerable or marginalized groups are left out of the design phase, interventions are often unable to meet their intended results fully. To counter this, if impact investors are to fulfill their social goals they must meaningfully identify and include all stakeholders they intend to serve, along with those that might be negatively affected, and do so from the earliest stages of the investment cycle, starting with the development of an impact thesis.

An important consideration not explicitly addressed in this chapter is the financial cost of using a transformative framework throughout the investment cycle. Brest and Born (2013) argue that "evaluation costs must be justified in terms of their likely benefits in improving the investment decision." The use of standardized metrics and science-based targets are arguably less expensive than the more intensive work of transformative evaluation. However, what is not often present in the former is an explicit and conscious attempt to include vulnerable and marginalized groups early on in order to more fully understand the nature of the problem, contextual factors, and appropriateness of investment decisions.

Impact investors should begin their transformative evaluation process early, at the initial stages of portfolio design, in order to ensure alignment with the self-identified and prioritized needs and desires of target popula- tions through all investment phases. Without this approach and the data it generates, investments are at risk of being ineffective with regard to the SDGs and could even harm or negatively affect target beneficiaries. Avoiding these financial and nonfinancial risks should justify the added cost of transformative evaluations, especially for impact investors committed to the social impact of their work.

The transformative framework can be easily adapted and applied to Impact Investing contexts anywhere in the world, and should be duly considered by impact investors, philanthropists, and non-governmental organizations, but also by governments, and anyone else working under the Impact Investing umbrella. The case studies in this chapter demonstrate how transformative frameworks can be implemented at different stages in the investment process and highlight the gaps in performance and measurement that are felt by investees and investors in its absence. Because the nascent application of transformative frameworks to Impact Investing is only beginning, there is a general lack of good examples. One existing resource that new practitioners can turn to is the Transformative Evaluation Toolkit for the Impact Investing Sector by Bolinson and Mertens, which has a few additional case studies beyond those discussed in this chapter (2019).

This chapter demonstrates an opportunity for further piloting, experimenting, and documenting the implementation and lessons learned from applying a transformative framework to Impact Investing. Future applications of the transformative framework can incorporate quantitatively driven strategies, such as gap analysis, or experimental or quasi-experimental designs, in order to demonstrate effectiveness in a quantitative manner. If social impact is truly a goal, investors must commit to doing the work of engaging all the stakeholders they wish to serve, not leaving anyone behind, and investing resources toward inclusive, contextual, and participatory engagement methods such as those described in the transformative framework. A long-lasting partnership between transformative evaluation and Impact Investing will result in better outcomes for all and is crucial to effectively addressing intersectional challenges such as the SDGs.

ACKNOWLEDGMENTS

The authors would like to acknowledge Engineers Without Borders Canada, Claire Mongeau at M-Shule, and the Aspen Network of Development Entrepreneurs for courageously funding and participating in the first formal application of transformative evaluation in the impact investing sector. It is through the experience of that initial project that this chapter was born.

REFERENCES

Agency for Healthcare Research and Quality. (2018). *National Healthcare Quality and Disparities Report*. Rockville, MD: Agency for Healthcare Research and Quality.

Bolinson, C. (2019). *Using Transformative Evaluation in Impact Investing: A Case Study with Engineers Without Borders Canada and M-Shule*. Engineers Without Borders Canada.

Bolinson, C., and Mertens, D. (2019). *A Transformative Evaluation Toolkit for the Impact Investing Sector: How entrepreneurs and impact investors can deepen their data collection*. Engineers Without Borders Canada.

Brest, P., and Born, K. (2013). Unpacking the Impact in Impact Investing. https://ssir.org/articles/entry/unpacking_the_impact_in_impact_investing (accessed 6 March 2020).

Burns, A., Tashima, R., and Matranga, H. (2019). *Flipping the Power Dynamic*. Village Capital. https://newsandviews.vilcap.com/reports/flipping-the-power-dynamics-can-entrepreneurs-make-successful-investment-decisions.

George, S. (2019). 87 major firms commit to setting 1.5C science-based targets. *Edie Newsroom*. (22 September). www.edie.net/news/6/87-major-firms-commit-to-setting-1-5C-science-based-targets/.

Grasso, P., Wasty, S. S., and Weaving, R. V. (2003). *The first 30 Years*. Washington, DC: World Bank Operations Evaluation Department.

Kish, Z., and Fairbairn, M. (2018). Investing for Profit, Investing for Impact: Moral Performances in Agricultural Investment Projects. *Environment and Planning A: Economy and Space* 50(3). DOI: 10.1177/0308518X17738253.

Mertens, D. M. (2009). *Transformative Research and Evaluation*. New York: Guilford Press.

Mertens, D. M. (2018). *Mixed Methods Design in Evaluation*. Thousand Oaks, CA: Sage.

Mertens, D. M. (2020). *Research and Evaluation in Education and Psychology*. (5th ed.) Thousand Oaks, CA: Sage.

Mertens, D. M., Cram, F., and Chilisa, B. ed. (2013). *Indigenous Pathways into Social Research*. Walnut Creek, CA: Left Coast Press.

Mertens, D. M., and Wilson, A.T. (2019). *Program Evaluation Theory and Practice*. (2nd ed.). New York: Guilford Press.

Miles, M. B., Huberman, A. M., and Saldaña, J. (2014). *Qualitative Data Analysis A Methods Sourcebook*. (3rd ed.). Thousand Oaks, CA: Sage.

Nielsen, D. (2010). Case study: Novo Nordisk. *CDP Network*. http://www.cdp.net/en/articles/climate/case-study-novo-nordisk.

Reason, P., and Bradbury, H. (2006). Introduction: Inquiry and participation in search of a world worthy of human aspiration. In *Handbook of Action Research* (P. Reason and H. Bradbury, eds.), 1–14. London: Sage.

Reisman, J., and Olazabal, V. (2016). *Situating the next generation of impact measurement and evaluation for Impact Investing.* Rockefeller Foundation.

Reisman, J., Olazabal, V., and Hoffman, S. (2018). Putting the "Impact" in Impact Investing: The Rising Demand for Data and Evidence of Social Outcomes. *American Journal of Evaluation* 39(3): 389–395. DOI:10.1177/1098214018779141.

Saltuk, Y., and Idrissi, A. E. (2012). *A Portfolio Approach to Impact Investment.* J.P. Morgan.

Schiff, H., and Dithrich, H. (2018). *Lasting Impact: The need for responsible exits.* Global Impact Investing Network.

Smith, B., Fox, T, Bartram, D., et al. (2017). *Spotlight paper: Purpose, growth, impact mission locks insights from practice.* UnLtd.

Stufflebeam, D. L. (1978). Meta Evaluation: An Overview. *Evaluation and the Health Professions* 1(1): 17–43. DOI: 10.1177/016327877800100102.

UNICEF (2013). Global consultation on addressing inequalities in the post-2015 development agenda. http://www.unicef.org/media/media_67926.html (accessed 17 January 2020).

Van den Berg, R., Magro, C., and Mulder, S. S., eds. (2019). *Evaluation for Transformational Change.* Exeter, UK: International Development Evaluation Association.

Wakiaga, L., and Bolinson, C. (2019). *Using Transformative Evaluation in Impact Investing: A Case Study with Engineers Without Borders Canada and M-Shule.* Engineers Without Borders Canada.

Geospatial Analysis of Targeting of World Bank's Development Assistance in Mexico

Mario Negre, PhD, Dr. Hannes Öhler, PhD, and Željko Bogetić, PhD

Abstract

All development interventions with social objectives can arguably be considered "Impact Investing" in a broad sense. Evidence shows that spatial targeting of aid to the poor at the subnational level can improve efficiency and help maximize the poverty-reducing effects and impact of development programs on the poor, ultimately improving equity. Following the geographic targeting methodology in Öhler et al. (2019), this chapter examines the subnational allocation of World Bank development interventions in Mexico. The chapter focuses on spatial targeting of poverty, an analytical lens that may be necessary to affect transformative change in the context of spatial economic disparities, and it analyses the congruence of World Bank interventions with the spatial distribution of the bottom 40% of the population. Principal results are as follows. First, World Bank funding is positively correlated with the bottom 40% in Mexico in both absolute and relative (to population) terms, despite factors that may have constrained the extent to which the World Bank could lend at the subnational level. Second, the allocation of World Bank project funding is uncorrelated with the distribution of government's public expenditure. And third, government's public expenditure is only positively correlated with the bottom 40% when the overall state population is not controlled for. When accounting for population, however, results show that poorer Mexican states (i.e. states with larger proportions of bottom 40) receive less funds from the federal government than other states.

Keywords

Geographic Targeting Inequality; Poverty; Mexico; Aid Allocation; Shared Prosperity

INTRODUCTION

All development interventions with social objectives can be considered "Impact Investing" in a broad sense. In 2013, the World Bank adopted two ambitious goals: eliminating global extreme poverty and improving shared prosperity in every country in a sustainable way. This implies reducing the poverty headcount ratio from 10.7% globally in 2013 to 3.0% in 2030 and boosting the income growth of the poorest 40% in each country. These two goals are part of a wider international development agenda and are intimately linked to the United Nations' Sustainable Development Goals (SDGs) 1 and 10, respectively. These goals are not only aspirational; they are operationalized through countries' World Bank strategies and projects, which are now designed to advance the World Bank Group's twin goals and SDGs to the maximum extent possible across a variety of contexts.

In addition to the need to strengthen international development's focus on the poor, given that public resources for poverty reduction are always scarce, it is important to look for ways to increase the impact of what limited amount of development aid is available. Targeting poverty aid at the subnational level is one such way to increase funding efficiency of development programs—helping to maximize poverty-reduction effects and their impact on the poor (Elbers et al. 2007; Karlan and Thuysbaert 2016).

When combined, geo-referenced poverty and aid data enable researchers to evaluate the effectiveness of the geospatial distribution of development interventions (see, e.g. Briggs 2017; Öhler et al. 2019). This analysis can be performed by correlating the geographical allocation of World Bank projects at regional level with regional measures of the concentration of the poor.[1] Relatively high correlations between these two spatial distributions are consistent with effective geographic targeting, whereby resources are disproportionally directed toward regions with higher absolute count or proportion of the poor. However, low correlations between poverty and aid distribution may not necessarily point to poor targeting, because in some cases there are valid reasons not to allocate aid to areas where the bottom 40% are living (see Section 2 of this chapter). Therefore, a regression approach is necessary, controlling for these factors. A simple regression analysis does not account, however, for general equilibrium effects, because different aid allocation patterns within countries may have different effects on economic co-benefits, such as higher growth and market and energy access, which itself may also affect the poor.

This chapter examines the subnational allocation of World Bank development interventions in Mexico, a spatially large middle-income country with high levels of regional income disparity. It spotlights the bottom 40% of Mexican citizens in terms of poverty, a demographic group that is the focus of the World Bank's second development goal.[2] This chapter is novel in that it considers the whole universe of World Bank funding in Mexico—including project loans and investments from the International Bank for Reconstruction and Development (IBRD) and International Finance corporation (IFC), as well as budget support from the IBRD and advisory services from both IBRD and IFC. This comprehensive set of funding and support mechanisms is greater in scope than has been explored in the literature thus far, as existing research looks mainly at narrowly defined investment projects (e.g. Briggs 2017, 2018; Öhler and Nunnenkamp 2014; Öhler et al. 2018). Another unique contribution of this paper is its analysis of the correlation between the territorial distribution of the bottom 40% and the government's own territorial distribution of public expenditures. This additional lens allows this chapter to determine whether the territorial distribution of the

---

[1] In particular, it would be interesting to examine the geography of projects in the five poorest Mexican states (Chiapas, Guerrero, Oaxaca, Puebla, and Veracruz). Such an analysis, however, is currently limited by spatially insufficiently precise data on World Bank projects and income distribution in these states.

[2] This chapter thus follows the specific, albeit somewhat arbitrary choice made by the World Bank and the international community (in target 1 of SDG 10) that growth in the incomes of the bottom 40% is particularly relevant for overall economic growth and the welfare of societies.

government expenditure is more, or less, pro-poor than that of the World Bank, and whether World Bank interventions tend to "follow" the spatial distribution of public expenditures.

Following the methodology in Öhler et al. (2019), the chapter looks at whether aid and funding from the World Bank and from the Mexican government flow to states where the bottom 40% of Mexican citizens are concentrated. First, we create visual maps of where funding is distributed. To accomplish this, the unique geospatial datasets for the subnational distribution of World Bank and IFC aid, including funding as well as analytical and advisory work,[3] are merged into one dataset. The government's public expenditures are also aggregated and mapped. These geospatial data are then compared with the distribution of the bottom 40% of the Mexican population. Once these three layers are identified, this study analyzes any correlations between the layers and performs a regression analysis to take into account other confounding factors that affect in-country allocation.

There are three principal results. First, World Bank lending is positively correlated with the bottom 40% in both absolute and relative (to population) terms. Second, the allocation of World Bank project funding is uncorrelated with the distribution of government's public expenditures. And third, public expenditure is only positively correlated with the geospatial distribution of poverty when looking at the absolute number of citizens categorized as bottom 40% in each state. When accounting for population, however, the results show that poorer Mexican states (i.e. states with larger proportions of bottom 40) receive fewer funds from the federal government than other states.

The chapter proceeds as follows. The next section discusses conceptual issues and operational factors that must be taken into account when analyzing the subnational allocation of development aid within countries. The following section introduces the data and methodology, while the next section presents the results. The final section presents conclusions.

---

[3] Investment projects are the dominant type of assistance across development institutions, including at the World Bank. The other two types of financial assistance are (1) budget support loans, also referred to as development policy lending by the World Bank, which constitute 25% of the World Bank's annual lending portfolio on average, and (2) Program-for-Results financing, which is a new instrument with a limited but growing portfolio. In addition to financial assistance, the World Bank also provides extensive knowledge or "advisory services and analytics (ASA)" to partner countries. The term "interventions" in this analysis refers to all kinds of World Bank interventions (including ASA and budget support), and not to investment projects only.

BACKGROUND AND CONTEXT

Assessing the within-country allocation of aid requires the consideration of a number of conceptual criteria and operational factors that may play a role in the subnational allocation of aid. These criteria and factors discussed in depth in Öhler et al. (2017, 2019) are outlined in this section insofar as they are relevant for World Bank development assistance in Mexico. First, aid has been found to be at least partly fungible across sectors within countries (Feyzioglu, Swaroop, and Zhu 1998; Pack and Pack 1993).[4] Hence, it may not be possible to target specific income groups because governments may adjust their own spending according to the aid investments they receive. Furthermore, not all aid modalities are able to spatially target the poor within countries. This applies in particular to budget support operations.[5]

In general, within-country allocation of aid by the World Bank is derived from the Country Partnership Framework (CPF), which is the bank's operational strategy in each country. CPFs outline development objectives, as well as specific projects and analytical products that support those objectives, for a period of three to four years. Spatial targeting, depending on the country context, may be one among many, more or less specific criteria that defines these development interventions. But spatial targeting per se is not *a fortiori* a criterion for aid allocation. Still, given the high and increasing spatial concentration of poverty, it would appear necessary and desirable for the World Bank's interventions to be sensitive to the spatial configuration of poverty.

Alongside poverty targeting, efficiency concerns play a role in deciding on the allocation pattern of development assistance. In particular, physical access may influence the within-country allocation of aid. The costs of delivering aid to more remote areas are higher, and therefore aid allocated to remote communities is often less efficient. Political economy considerations among donors may also affect the allocation of projects to remote areas, which tend to be less visible than projects in a capital city or major metropolitan region. Furthermore, in countries or subnational regions and states (as in Mexico) where security risks are an issue, security considerations are likely to affect the allocation of aid. Donors are inclined to shy away from difficult environments with weak local institutions and entrenched forms of poverty where the likelihood of success is low (Nunnenkamp, Öhler, and Sosa Andrés 2017). In addition, general equilibrium considerations

---

[4]Van de Sijpe (2013), however, finds limited fungibility in the case of education and health care aid supplied through technical cooperation.
[5]See below on how to combat this issue in the empirical analysis.

may shape the allocation of aid within countries. For example, energy and infrastructure projects may be located in areas with a low share of the poor while still having high general equilibrium impacts on people experiencing poverty.

Political economy considerations of receiving governments may also influence the allocation of aid within countries (Nunnenkamp, Öhler, and Sosa Andrés 2017). For instance, Kirk (2005, p. 287) highlights that the allocation of World Bank aid within India "has been strongly conditioned by states' political clout with the central government, owing to their ruling parties' ties to the central coalition." However, Nunnenkamp, Öhler, and Sosa Andrés's (2017) empirical analysis does not support this claim. Also, Dreher et al. (2019) do not find evidence for favoritism of World Bank funding with respect to the birth areas of country leaders and the amount of funding these areas receive.

More generally, the allocation decisions of donors are supposed to be driven by the preferences and development challenges of the recipient countries. The World Bank relies on the country partnership framework (CPF) to operationalize this approach. The framework is designed to help identify the key objectives, instruments, and development results through which the World Bank intends to support a country in its efforts to reduce poverty and boost shared prosperity. In preparing a framework intervention, the World Bank starts from the recipient country's own vision, but aims to select programs that are aligned with its twin goals and the World Bank's comparative advantage vis-à-vis other donors (Öhler et al. 2017).[6] Related to this, coordination and division of labor among the World Bank and other donors within recipient countries may influence the pattern of subnational allocations (Öhler 2013).

With respect to the subnational allocation of World Bank lending in Mexico, certain factors constrain the extent to which the World Bank is able to lend at the subnational level. For example, the Mexican government's requirements on subnational external borrowing, imposed for reasons of fiscal discipline, cap the overall subnational debt and constrains borrowing to "productive investments" only. This requirement precludes the usual combination of lending, technical assistance, and capacity building provided by World Bank projects. Also, Mexico's budget cycle requires contracts to be budgeted, procured, completed, and paid for within a one-year time frame. This favors small-scale and less ambitious contracts. In addition, World

---

[6]See World Bank (2014) for a comprehensive description of the objectives and the country engagement model underpinning the country partnership framework.

Bank requirements for counterpart or "matching" funds from the recipient country's government are difficult to secure within a single year's budget cycle, and are near to impossible to secure on such short notice in poorer states, for whom the availability of any counterpart funding is extremely limited. Finally, foreign loans to subnational levels must pass through a specific government financial intermediary, which levies its own fees for service, adding to the costs and administrative requirements of the project. Moreover, the poorest states may be those with the most limited capacity for project administration.

DATA AND METHODOLOGY

All World Bank interventions active in one or more Mexican states in the period 2008–2017 were subject to the geospatial analysis.[7] The basic questions addressed are: (i) what is the correlation between the location of World Bank interventions in Mexico and the geographical distribution of the bottom 40%, and (ii) what other factors influence the allocation of World Bank funding? This analysis is novel because it considers IBRD investment projects, but also budget support operations and knowledge-based interventions—generally referred to as Advisory Services and Analytics (ASA)—and projects administered by World Bank's IFC, which have not been the subject of geospatial analyses to date.

The data required for the geospatial analysis was constructed in the three following steps.

First, geocoded aid data for Mexico is provided by the World Bank's Global Reach team and AidData—an open data initiative for international development. These flows mainly, but not exclusively, capture investment projects. With data from the World Bank's Global Reach team and the AidData initiative, a significant share of the World Bank investment projects in Mexico in 2008–2017 have been geocoded and successfully assigned to Mexican states (22 out of total of 43 projects). In addition, 23 World Bank knowledge products (ASA), 13 World Bank budget support operations, and 115 International Finance Corporation (IFC) projects were included through

---

[7]The empirical analysis has been carried out in a similar vein as in the Independent Evaluation Group (IEG)'s evaluation of the World Bank goal of shared prosperity (World Bank 2018a) and a resulting World Bank Policy Research Paper by Öhler, Negre, Smets, Massari, and Bogetić (2017). A later version has been published in *PLOS ONE* as Öhler et al. (2019).

an additional geocoding exercise.[8] However, the datasets did not provide a geographic breakdown of the overall amount of project commitments. Instead, this study utilized information on the locations (administrative areas) where (part of) a project takes place, which these databases typically contain, to split total project commitments equally across the subnational administrative areas (states) in which each project is active.

Budget support operations are by nature practically untraceable across the territory of the beneficiary country. This leads to two possible approaches. One is simply not to account for this funding modality. The other one consists of assuming that all contributions to the government's budget are fungible in the sense that the government can then, to a certain extent, adapt its budget allocations accordingly. In this case, one can consider that any World Bank budget support allocation implicitly follows the government's overall regional public budget allocation. Both approaches are considered in this chapter.

Second, to calculate the regional distribution of the poorest 40% of Mexico's population, this study used a harmonized survey[9] provided by the World Bank's Poverty and Equity Global Practice. The survey contains a welfare indicator (income), a geographic identifier, and a sample weight for each household. Together, these variables were used to estimate the number of individuals that belong to the bottom 40% in each of Mexico's 32 states.

Third, the study calculated the share of World Bank funding (measured as project commitments) that each Mexican state received (and the project commitments in per-capita terms), as well as the share of the bottom 40% of *all* Mexican citizens who live in each state (in absolute terms and relative to the state's population). Simple bivariate correlations are calculated between the two variables, to assess, at a basic level, the geographical allocation of World Bank project funding.

As a complementary approach, a distribution's indicator is also calculated. It measures *the share of World Bank funding going to the bottom 40%*. In this case, a value of 0.4 (or 40%) implies a spatially neutral distribution of World Bank funding with respect to the bottom 40%; a value higher than 0.4 implies that the bottom 40% receive a higher share of funding compared to the rest of the population; and a value lower than 0.4 means that the bottom 40% are disadvantaged with respect to the distribution of World Bank

---

[8]For the period of analysis, 2008–2017, there were 43 IBRD loans to Mexico plus some 20 ongoing projects. In addition, 164 ASA, 122 IFC loans/investments and 13 IFC advisory projects have been carried out.

[9]Encuesta Nacional de Ingresos y Gastos de los Hogares (ENIGH) of 2008.

interventions. The formula of this "distribution" indicator is:

$$DI = \sum_{i=1}^{N} Aid\ share_i * \frac{B40_i}{Population_i},$$

where *Aid share$_i$* is the share of World Bank funding allocated to state *i*, *B40$_i$* the number of bottom 40% in state *i*, and *Population$_i$* the population in state *i*.

In addition, a regression analysis is performed to account for other factors affecting the allocation of World Bank funding within states. The share of World Bank funding each state receives is considered as the dependent variable. Zero-inflated beta regressions are undertaken because beta distributions are well suited in the case of continuous variables bound between 0 and 1.[10]

The estimation equation is as follows:

$$y_i = \beta * B40_i + \theta'X + \varepsilon_i, \tag{19.1}$$

where y_i is the share of World Bank funding going to state *i*; $B40_i$ is the logarithm of the number of the bottom 40% living in state *i*; *X* is a set of control variables; and ε_i is an idiosyncratic error term.[11] Robust standard errors are estimated.

A control is applied for the total population of a state (in log) to identify the effect of the number of the bottom 40% living in a state, independent of the share of the population size of the state. In addition, conflict-related deaths per 100,000 inhabitants are used to gauge security and general risks in each state.[12] Government expenditures are included because the World Bank may have taken government budgetary allocations across states into account in determining its own subnational resource allocations.[13] Finally, as

---

[10]Beta distributions are characterized by high flexibility, thereby allowing varying degrees of skewness. Zero inflated beta regressions are particularly suited to proportion data and data with a large number of zero observations.

[11]Using the log of the number of the bottom 40% or the log scale of the share of the national bottom 40% living in a state is econometrically equivalent.

[12]The source for the conflict-related deaths data is: UCDP (Uppsala Conflict Data Program; https://ucdp.uu.se/). This statistic is especially relevant in Mexico, where the security situation in many areas of several states make development project off limits for the World Bank.

[13]The Mexican government may adapt its allocations in response to the aid it receives from the World Bank. In general, in the policy dialogue on World Bank funding, the government has considerable, even decisive say on the allocation of projects within the country.

a proxy for possible political influence, there is a dummy variable equal to one if the same party is in power at the state and federal level at any given year in the period of analysis between 2008 and 2017. This serves to investigate any potential political favoritism with respect to the location of development projects in Mexico, as there are analyses showing that political party affiliation may affect governments' development programs and, especially, their continuity[14] in times of political change at the state and local levels (World Bank, 2018b). However, to date there is no analysis on whether favoritism has affected the spatial distribution of World Bank interventions in Mexico.

EMPIRICAL RESULTS

Correlation results between funding and the bottom 40%

The analysis considers 22 World Bank investment projects, 23 analytical products, 13 budget support operations, and 115 IFC projects over the 2008 to 2017 period.[15]

Figure 19.1 displays the geographic distribution of the share of Mexico's bottom 40% living in each state (first map), as well as the shares of both IBRD investment projects funding (second map) and government's public expenditure (third map) allocated to that state.

At the outset, it is important to keep in mind that poverty in Mexico is highly concentrated in a small number of states in the southern half of the country. This can be seen in the dark areas on the map on the left, which shows where most of the bottom 40% live. A visual inspection comparing the allocation of funds with the distribution of the bottom 40% across states shows that states in the northeast are relatively underfunded, while states in

---

Indeed, this is so because of the country-based model of World Bank partnership with the government client where the bank needs the approval of the client to proceed with any project.

[14]This may be particularly so because elections at subnational and local levels are very frequent, usually every 1 to 3 years, resulting in a short-term horizon of state and local officials and a large turnover of staff, which tends to affect the continuity of many development projects.

[15]In an earlier analysis, a negative correlation for Mexico (−0.04) for World Bank projects was found (Öhler et al. 2019). In that analysis, Mexico's data included only 10 investment projects covering the 2005–2014 period. This lower correlation than in the present analysis could be caused by a lower number of projects being used in the earlier analysis, or to an improvement in the patterns of allocation in more recent times. Compared to nine other Latin American and Caribbean countries, the targeting correlations for Mexico were the lowest.

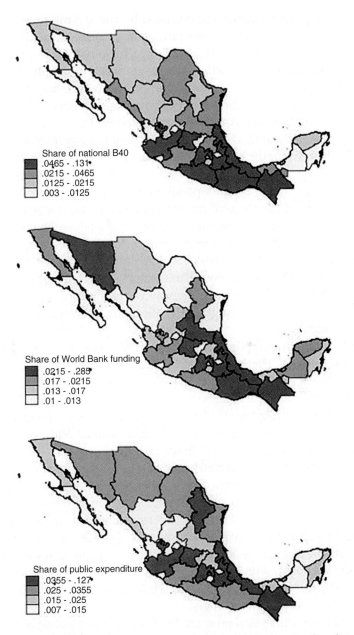

FIGURE 19.1 Share of National Bottom 40%, World Bank Project Funding (22 Projects), and Public Expenditure Per State. *Source*: The authors' calculations based on data from the World Bank's Global Monitoring Database, the bank's Global Reach team, AidData, and the World Bank's BOOST initiative.

the south are proportionately more funded by World Bank projects focused on the bottom 40%. This results in a rather low correlation coefficient of 0.18 (or 18%) for World Bank projects, as shown in Table 19.1. However, the distribution of the bottom 40% and the share of government's public expenditure appears to be highly correlated, with a correlation coefficient of 0.82 (or 82%). Whether this is due to the correlation with general population, or rather than specifically with the bottom 40%, is investigated below.

On average, World Bank project funding is marginally more likely to go to states where many of the bottom 40% live, as well as to comparatively poorer states when measured in per capita terms (0.15). Figure 19.2 displays the share of bottom 40% in a state's population (as an indicator of how poor a state is) instead of the share of the national bottom 40. It also maps World Bank funding and public expenditure in per-capita terms. The figure shows that relatively poor states (Chiapas, Guerrero, Puebla, Veracruz) do not seem to receive IBRD investment funds in corresponding fashion to the proportion of bottom 40% in their population. This results in a low correlation coefficient of 0.15 (Table 19.1). Importantly, security is a significant concern in many areas of these states, likely limiting the allocation of World Bank funds and projects to those areas.

The important exception is Oaxaca, which receives a fair amount of World Bank funds. The IEG Mexico country program evaluation and the associated field visit demonstrate that this is not an accident: Oaxaca has been targeted by the World Bank to receive substantial technical assistance on public sector management—due to close collaboration with and demands from Mexico's federal government—which continued and even increased over the period of analysis (World Bank, 2018b).

A high correlation is observed between the government's public expenditure and presence of the bottom 40%, which upon further scrutiny appears to be due to the fact that more populated states receive more funding (Table 19.1; see also regression results below). Considering public expenditure per capita, the calculations obtain a negative correlation (-0.42) with the proportion of bottom 40% in a state's population. In particular, the states in the north, which share a border with the United States, receive a disproportionally high amount of government's public funds while the poorer states in the south appear to be relatively underfunded.

World Bank's analytical products funding, both in absolute as well as per capita terms, are clearly allocated according to the distribution of the bottom 40% (Figure 19.3). The correlation is relatively high, with a correlation coefficient of 0.66 in the case of the former, and 0.41 in the case of the latter

TABLE 19.1 Simple Pairwise Correlations Between World Bank Funding and the Mexican Government's Public Expenditure (in Absolute and Per-Capita Terms), and Bottom 40% (in Absolute and Relative Terms).

	Share of total national B40 population living in each state	Share of B40 in a state's population
SHARE OF FUNDING		
Share of World Bank project funding (22 operations)	0.18	
Share of analytical product funding (23 products)	0.66	
Share of World Bank project and budget support funding (35 operations)	0.63	
Share of IFC project funding (115 operations)	0.69	
Share of IFC advisory funding (13 operations)	0.48	
Share of public expenditure	0.82	
PER CAPITA FUNDING		
World Bank project funding per capita		0.15
Analytical product funding per capita		0.41
World Bank project and budget support funding per capita		0.07
IFC project funding per capita		−0.24
IFC advisory funding per capita		−0.16
Public expenditure per capita		−0.42

Source: The authors' calculations based on data from the World Bank's Global Monitoring Database and the bank's Global Reach team.

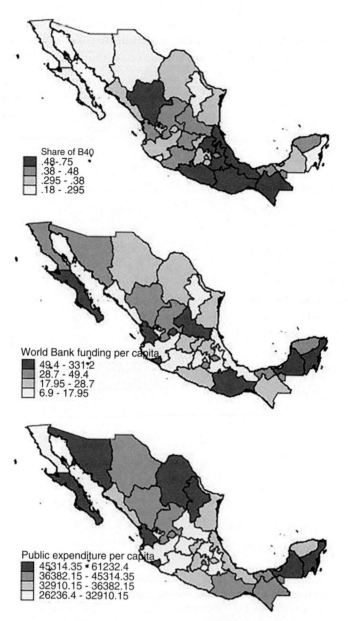

FIGURE 19.2　Share of Bottom 40% in a State's Population, World Bank Project Funding Per Capita (22 Projects) and Public Expenditure Per Capita Per State. *Source*: The authors' calculations are based on data from the World Bank's Global Monitoring Database, the bank's Global Reach team, AidData, and the World Bnk's BOOST initiative.

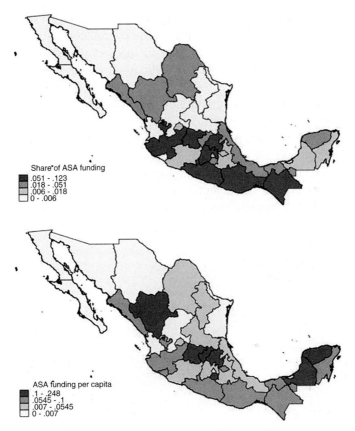

FIGURE 19.3 Share of World Bank's Analytical Products Funding, Total and per Capita (23 products). *Source*: The authors' calculations are based on data from the World Bank's Global Monitoring Database and the bank's Global Reach team.

(Table 19.1). Note, however, that analytical products are characterized by a far lower volume of funds compared to investment projects.[16]

Insofar as the World Bank's budget support to the government is perfectly fungible and congruent with the government's general budget, it can be assumed to follow governments' general geographic allocation. Since the Mexican government's public expenditure is very highly correlated (0.82)

---

[16] In a robustness test, the number of analytical products in each state is considered, disregarding the amount spent for each operation, as an alternative measure of where the World Bank focuses its analytical work. The correlations are, although still positive, considerably lower (0.46 and 0.14).

with the number of the bottom 40% in a state, including budget support in the World Bank's allocation figures increases the overall correlation coefficient to 0.63. This significant increase is due to the fact that this aid modality channels a large amount of funds. However, in our second set of correlation coefficients, the correlation decreases from 0.15 to 0.07 (Table 19.1), due to the negative correlation between public expenditure per capita and the share of bottom 40% in a state's population.

IFC projects' allocation is displayed in Figure 19.4. In contrast to the World Bank's analytical products funding (Figure 19.3), these projects are negatively correlated with the geographical distribution of the bottom 40%. Indeed, the correlation coefficient amounts to –0.24 (Table 19.1). This may not come as such a surprise since the IFC as the private finance arm of the

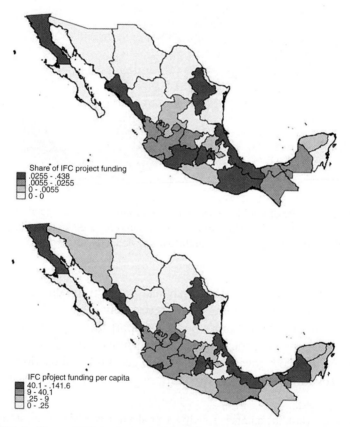

FIGURE 19.4 Share of IFC Project Funding and IFC Project Funding per Capita (115 Projects). *Source*: The authors' calculations are based on data from the World Bank's Global Monitoring Database and the bank's Global Reach team.

TABLE 19.2   Distribution Indicator: To What Extend Is World Bank and IFC Funding and Government Expenditure Pro-Bottom 40%, Neutral to the Bottom 40%, or Less Than Neutral to the Bottom 40%?

	0.40 = neutral distribution
World Bank project funding	0.45
Analytical product funding	0.46
World Bank project and budget support funding	0.41
IFC project funding	0.37
IFC advisory funding	0.47
Government's public expenditure	0.39

Source: The authors' calculations are based on data from the World Bank's Global Monitoring Database, the bank's Global Reach team, AidData, and the bank's BOOST initiative.

World Bank Group has profitability as the dominant business objective, with development as an accompanying objective ("double bottom line").

The distribution indicator[17] roughly resembles the above geographic targeting correlations of World Bank investment projects. Results are displayed in Table 19.2 and show a disproportionate targeting of the relatively poor (bottom 40%) in the case of World Bank projects, indicating that 45% of project funds are allocated to the bottom 40%. By contrast, the allocation of government's public expenditure with a value of 0.39 is marginally below a neutral distribution allocation (0.40). Adding budget support to the World Bank allocation brings down the indicator to 0.41, a nearly neutral allocation, similar to the Mexican government's allocation.

REGRESSION RESULTS

A regression analysis with a number of control variables allows deeper insights into allocation patterns. This is done for World Bank (IBRD)

---

[17]See methodology section for distribution indicator formula. A value of 0.4 (or 40%) implies a spatially neutral distribution of World Bank funding with respect to the bottom 40% (or the 40% poorest share of the population), a value higher than 0.4 implies that the bottom 40% receive a higher share of funding compared to the rest of the population, and a value lower than 0.4 means that the bottom 40% are disadvantaged with respect to the distribution of World Bank interventions.

TABLE 19.3 World Bank IBRD Project Funding (22 Projects) and Government's Public Expenditure

	(1)	(2)	(3)	(4)	(5)	(6)	(7)
	World Bank funding				Government expenditure		
B40	0.256***	0.423**	0.404**	0.470**	0.670***	−0.227**	−0.219**
	(0.045)	(0.182)	(0.182)	(0.212)	(0.096)	(0.099)	(0.087)
Population		−0.206	−0.143	−0.518		1.188***	1.175***
		(0.214)	(0.216)	(0.483)		(0.101)	(0.086)
Conflict-related deaths			−0.017	−0.022			0.004
			(0.030)	(0.033)			(0.013)
Same party			0.259	0.303			−0.151
			(0.393)	(0.360)			(0.094)
Public expenditure				0.356			
				(0.414)			
Observations	32	32	32	32	32	32	32

Source: The authors' estimations based on data from the World Bank's Global Monitoring Database, the bank's Global Reach team, AidData, and the bank's BOOST initiative.
Notes: The dependent variable in columns (1) through (4) is the share of World Bank IBRD project funding (23 operations). Robust standard errors in parentheses. *** $p < 0.01$, ** $p < 0.05$, * $p < 0.1$.

projects (Table 19.3) and for analytical product funding (Table 19.4). The data covers the 22 World Bank projects that were geocoded by the World Bank's Global Reach team and AidData.

The results for 22 World Bank (IBRD) projects and government public expenditure show that World Bank funding is positively correlated with the bottom 40% in both absolute and relative (to population) terms (columns 1 and 2 of Table 19.3, respectively). Interestingly, the allocation of World Bank project funding is not significantly correlated with the distribution of government's public expenditure (column 4 of Table 19.3). The other control

TABLE 19.4 World Bank's Analytical (ASA) Products Funding (23 products)

	(1)	(2)	(3)	(4)
B40	0.471***	0.849**	0.878***	0.943***
	(0.148)	(0.334)	(0.284)	(0.281)
Population		−0.468	−0.315	−0.635
		(0.429)	(0.380)	(1.064)
Conflict-related deaths			0.002	−0.004
			(0.060)	(0.067)
Same party			1.042**	1.079**
			(0.463)	(0.464)
Public expenditure				0.287
				(1.009)
Observations	32	32	32	32

Source: The authors' estimations are based on data from the World Bank's Global Monitoring Database.

Notes: The dependent variable in columns (1) through (4) is the share of World Bank analytical product funding (23 products). Robust standard errors in parentheses. *** $p<0.01$, ** $p<0.05$, * $p<0.1$.

variables—namely, population, conflict-related deaths, same party in power at the state and federal level—are statistically not significant either.[18]

The Mexican government's public expenditure is only positively correlated with the number of bottom 40% when the overall state population is not controlled for (column 5). When accounting for population, the coefficient becomes significant and negative (columns 6 and 7). This implies that poorer states (i.e. states with larger proportions of bottom 40% in their population) receive fewer funds from the federal government than other more economically prosperous states.

---

[18]The coefficient of the bottom 40% loses its significance in columns 2 through 4 when budget support operations in the dependent variable are considered (not shown). Not surprisingly, however, the coefficient on public expenditure turns out to be significant and positive. Recall that it is assumed that the bank's budget support distribution follows the government's distribution of the overall public budget across Mexican states.

With respect to the World Bank's analytical product funding toward 23 products, two results stand out (Table 19.4). First, the effect of the bottom 40% appears to be larger for products than in the case of investment projects. This suggests that analytical products tend to be better targeted to where the national bottom 40% live. World Bank product funding successfully targets states with large numbers of the national bottom 40, and states with high proportions of bottom 40% in the regions' population. Second, the dummy variable indicating whether the same party is in power at the federal and state level has a positive and significant effect on the allocation of analytical product funding. This may be due to different levels of government belonging to the same party coordinating with the bank more closely on analytical diagnostics, potentially resulting in more funding for analytical products. It may also be easier for the World Bank to agree with the government on various analytical products when there are less confrontational partisan relationships between different levels of government.

In the regression analysis of IFC project funding in Table 19.5, the bottom 40% appears to have no statistically significant effect on the allocation of IFC projects. In particular, poorer states (i.e. states with a larger proportion of bottom 40% citizens in their population) do not receive more project funds from IFC. Interestingly however, the allocation of IFC funds is positively and significantly correlated with the allocation of IBRD project commitments (at the 10% level).

CONCLUSION

This chapter examines the subnational allocation of the World Bank development interventions funding to Mexico, a spatially large middle-income country with significant regional income disparities. Compared to previous studies, this chapter uniquely considers the whole universe of different types of World Bank funding in a country—including investment projects, analytical products, budget support, IFC projects, and advisory services (although it does not consider all the interventions in Mexico which had not been geocoded). This is important because World Bank support goes beyond projects as their broader interventions are often "packaged" in combination with additional funding mechanisms and knowledge services.

Following the methodology in Öhler et al. (2019), the chapter looks at whether World Bank funding flows to states in Mexico where the bottom 40% are concentrated. The chapter accomplishes this by firstly merging unique geospatial datasets on the subnational distribution of World Bank funding

TABLE 19.5   IFC Project Funding (115 Projects)

	(1)	(2)	(3)	(4)
B40	0.360	−0.401	−0.254	−0.169
	(0.274)	(0.403)	(0.313)	(0.411)
Population		1.110**	0.922*	0.173
		(0.446)	(0.507)	(0.983)
Conflict-related deaths			0.105	0.088
			(0.084)	(0.100)
Same party			0.434	0.632
			(0.713)	(0.890)
Public expenditure				0.848
				(1.227)
IBRD project commitments				0.266*
				(0.137)
Observations	32	32	32	32

Source: The authors' calculations are based on data from the World Bank's Global Monitoring Database and the World Bank's Global Reach team.
Notes: The dependent variable is the share of IFC project funding (115 projects). Robust standard errors in parentheses. *** $p<0.01$, ** $p<0.05$, * $p<0.1$.

and the population identified as the bottom 40%; secondly, by correlating these two variables; thirdly, by calculating a distributional indicator of the World Bank's funding targeting; and fourthly, by carrying out a regression analysis to control for other potential determinants of within-country aid allocations.

The analysis shows three principal results. First, World Bank (IBRD) funding is positively correlated with bottom 40% in both absolute and relative (to state population) terms. This is good news; the World Bank allocates its projects where the bottom 40% live, which is broadly in line with the World Bank's stated goals of poverty reduction and shared prosperity.

Second, the allocation of World Bank funding is uncorrelated with the distribution of government's public expenditure across Mexican states. Intuitively, it means that the World Bank funding neither follows government's public expenditure, nor does it fill a gap where the government expenditures are limited. This may reflect the fact that the World Bank and Mexican government have different resource allocation processes, as well as multiplicity of objectives in different government programs.

And third, government's public expenditure is only positively correlated with the number of bottom 40% when not controlling for state population. When accounting for population, the coefficient becomes significant and negative. This implies that poorer states (i.e. states with larger proportions of bottom 40%) receive fewer funds from the federal government than other states.

While this analysis is devoted to funding flows and its congruence with the spatial distribution of poverty, an important question is: What is the impact of these allocations on the ground? Granular data to answer that question are not available, but a recent World Bank's Independent Evaluation Group's (IEG) evaluation of the World Bank Group's Mexico program during the same period—which covered all of the operations, analytical products, IFC projects, and advisory services (not just the geocoded subset analyzed in this chapter)—shows that World Bank Group has been broadly successful in its development interventions in Mexico, in terms of achievement of its objectives, especially those related to public finance and human development (Independent Evaluation Group 2018). This suggests that impact investments can achieve results in Mexico, despite the challenging economic and social environment. In fact, the "World Bank project funding approved for the poorest states—south and southeast states of Chiapas, Guerrero, Oaxaca, Puebla, and Veracruz—from FY2014 to FY2018 was on average 48.8% larger than the national state average" (World Bank Group 2020, p. 19). Further, in the ongoing country strategy for 2020–25, the World Bank Group has set a new target of allocating 75% more resources to these states relative to the national average.

This study offers broad conclusions that can be applied to Impact Investing, such as that it is possible for socially oriented and impact-oriented investors to more efficiently focus impact investments in areas where the level of development is low, poverty is high, and institutions are weak. Additionally, this chapter indicates that Impact Investing is a long-term process. Given that spatial disparities in Mexico remain large and will likely endure over the long-term, it is reasonable to assume that even with significant funding, it will take time for these flows to materialize into broader economic and social impacts.

This evokes the final question of this chapter: What are the implications of these findings for Impact Investing, the broad subject of this volume? The main implication is perhaps an elementary one. To reach the poorest, geographic targeting is essential. Investing can utilize geospatial analysis and targeting in countries and regions where poverty is highly concentrated, or more hidden but is known to exist in smaller pockets of even richer regions. Geospatial analysis can be included in the due-diligence process, as well as used to analyze entire portfolios. As this study demonstrates, the geospatial correlation between poverty and investment is often surprising. If equipped with this additional data, investors may be more likely to source and deploy their investments to geographies with higher levels of poverty or other risk factors.

ACKNOWLEDGMENTS

The authors would like to express gratitude to Jeff Chelsky (IEG, World Bank) and Anjali Kumar (formerly with Independent Evaluation Group, World Bank) for helpful comments and discussions on an earlier version of this paper. An early version of the paper was prepared as an input into the independent evaluation of World Bank Group's support to Mexico (Independent Evaluation Group 2018). It was presented at the World Bank country team discussions of the new World Bank country partnership strategy in Mexico City, December 6–7, 2018, and also at the first "gLocal" international event on geospatial analysis in evaluation, "Taking Evaluative Evidence (well) into the 21st Century," held in IEG, Washington, DC, on June 3, 2019 (Independent Evaluation Group 2019).

DISCLAIMER

The findings, interpretations, and conclusions expressed in this paper are entirely those of the authors. They do not necessarily represent the views of the World Bank Group or its affiliated organizations, or those of the executive directors of the World Bank Group or the governments they represent.

REFERENCES

Briggs, R. C. (2017). Does Foreign Aid Target the Poorest? *International Organization* 71 (1): 187–206.

Briggs, R. C. (2018). Poor Targeting: A Gridded Spatial Analysis of the Degree to Which Aid Reaches the Poor in Africa. *World Development* 103: 133–148.

Dreher, A., Fuchs, A., Hodler, R, Parks, B.C., Raschky, P. A., and Tierney, M. J. (2019). African Leaders and the Geography of China's Foreign Assistance, *Journal of Development Economics* 140: 44–71.

Elbers, C., Fujii, T., Lanjouw, P., Özler, B., and Yin, W. (2007). Poverty Alleviation Through Geographic Targeting: How Much Does Disaggregation Help? *Journal of Development Economics* 83 (1): 198–213.

Feyzioglu, T., Swaroop, V., and Zhu, M. (1998). A Panel Data Analysis of the Fungibility of Foreign Aid. *World Bank Economic Review* 12 (1): 29–58.

Independent Evaluation Group (IEG) (2019). Taking Evaluation (well) into the 21st Century. gLocal week, Washington DC (June 3–7). https://ieg .worldbankgroup.org/future-of-evaluation (accessed February 2020).

Independent Evaluation Group (2018). *An Independent Evaluation of the World Bank Group's Support to Mexico (2008-17)*. World Bank: Washington DC. https://ieg.worldbankgroup.org/evaluations/mexico-country-program (accessed February 2020).

Karlan, S. D., and Thuysbaert, B. (2016). Targeting Ultra-Poor Households in Honduras and Peru. World Bank Economic Review (August 19). https:// academic.oup.com/wber/article-abstract/doi/10.1093/wber/lhw036/ 2669742?redirectedFrom=fulltext (accessed February 2020).

Kirk, J. A. (2005). Banking on India's States: The Politics of World Bank Reform Programs in Andhra Pradesh and Karnataka. *India Review* 4 (3–4): 287–325.

Nunnenkamp, P., Öhler, H., and Sosa Andrés, M. (2017). Need, Merit, and Politics in Multilateral Aid Allocation: A District-Level Analysis of World Bank Projects in India. *Review of Development Economics* 21 (1): 126–156.

Öhler H. (2013). Do Aid Donors Coordinate Within Recipient Countries? AWI Discussion Paper 539. Heidelberg University.

Öhler, H., Negre, M., Smets, L., Massari, R., and Bogetić, Ž. (2017). Putting Your Money Where Your Mouth Is: Geographic Targeting of World Bank Projects to the Bottom 40 Percent. *World Bank Policy Research Paper No. 8247* (November).

Öhler, H., Negre, M., Smets, L., Massari, R., and Bogetić, Ž. (2019). Putting Your Money Where Your Mouth Is: Geographic Targeting of World Bank Projects to the Bottom 40 Percent. *PLOS ONE* 14(6): e0218671.

Öhler, H., and Nunnenkamp, P. (2014). Needs-Based Targeting or Favoritism? The Regional Allocation of Multilateral Aid within Recipient Countries. *Kyklos* 67 (3): 420–446.

Pack, H., and Rothenberg Pack J. (1993). Foreign Aid and the Question of Fungibility. *Review of Economics and Statistics* 75 (2): 258–265.

Van de Sijpe, N. (2013). Is Foreign Aid Fungible? Evidence from the Education and Health Sectors. *World Bank Economic Review* 27 (2): 320–356.

World Bank (2018a). *Growth for the Bottom 40 Percent: The World Bank Group's Support for Shared Prosperity. Independent Evaluation Group.* Washington, DC: World Bank.

World Bank (2018b). *An Independent Evaluation of the World Bank Group's Support to Mexico (2008–17). Independent Evaluation Group.* Washington, DC: World Bank.

World Bank Group (2014). World Bank Group: A New Approach to Country Engagement. Report 87846 (April 29). World Bank, Washington, DC. http://documents.worldbank.org/curated/en/940631468324888939/pdf/878460BR0R2014050Box385206B00OUO090.pdf (accessed February 2020).

World Bank Group (2020). *Country Partnership Framework for the United Mexican States for the Period 2020–25.* Washington, DC: World Bank.

Evaluating the Impact of Portfolio Allocations to Large Firms Along the Value Chain to Develop Small and Medium-Sized Enterprises

Maximilian Foedinger, MBA, MPA and Elsa de Morais Sarmento, MA

Abstract

The European Bank for Reconstruction and Development (EBRD) was one of the first multilateral development banks (MDBs) to have a clear specific commitment to small and medium enterprises (SMEs) in the form of a dedicated SME strategy. It has been a leading innovator in private equity, sponsoring a number of SME focused funds that were at the time the first of its kind geographically or by target market. Sustainability is one of EBRD's key principles, seeking long-lasting impacts and results in markets that thrive. EBRD looks beyond the lifespan of a single activity, like a loan and the design of projects, to produce changes that will last independently of its support. EBRD's goal is to contribute to the development of a robust private sector, with dynamic businesses that innovate, access know-how and financing, and continue to prosper and grow in the countries where it operates. This chapter is based on original work and a literature review to develop a new quantitative framework to measure impact and the magnitude of "spillovers"—or ripple effects—that EBRD financing of larger corporate clients has on SME suppliers along the supply chain. This novel methodology is designed to measure impact and spillovers directly and indirectly, namely, by: (i) identifying the impact of projects by investors, like EBRD, on SME suppliers and its channels; and (ii) capturing the overall magnitude of the impact of projects and investments in larger clients on SMEs, with a view to providing adequate business advice for SMEs.

Keywords

Impact investing; Small and Medium Enterprises; SME; Large Enterprises; Impact; Impact Assessment; EBRD; Multilateral Development Banks; Value Chains; Financial Performance; Spillovers; Ripple Effects

INTRODUCTION

The European Bank for Reconstruction and Development (EBRD) is an international financial institution founded in 1991. The documents establishing the EBRD stated the organization shall in member countries "promote, through private and other interested investors, the establishment, improvement and expansion of productive, competitive and private sector activity, in particular small and medium sized enterprises" (Bronstone 1999, p. 177).

As a multilateral developmental investment bank, the EBRD uses investment as a tool to build market economies. Initially focused on the countries of the former Eastern Bloc, it expanded to support development in more than 30 countries from Central Europe to Central Asia. In 2012, EBRD expanded operations in North Africa. Similar to other multilateral development banks (MDBs), the EBRD has board members from around the world (Europe, North America, Africa, Asia, and Australia, with the biggest shareholder being the United States. Headquartered in London, the EBRD is owned by 69 countries and two European Union (EU) institutions, the 69th being India, since July 2018. However, it only lends regionally in its countries of operations. Despite its public sector shareholders, it invests in private enterprises, together with commercial partners.

EBRD has had for several years a clear specific commitment to small and medium enterprises (SME) in the form of a dedicated SME strategy. At the end of 2013, EBRD adopted a radical new approach to SMEs in its Small Business Initiative Review (SBI), inter alia, a more strategic approach, a wider range of instruments, and more efficient, faster processes and procedures. The SBI was a milestone in SME support, providing a more coordinated strategy and approach to its SME activities, which encompassed country by country SME Action Plans. The SBI unit developed an enhanced "toolbox" of products and services across five pillars. Key innovations and developments included significant increases in targeted SME credit lines, the use of risk sharing and guarantee instruments, the Medium-size Co-financing Facility, and the use of local currency denominated instruments. In addition to financing, the EBRD enables SMEs access to business advice to support their growth. This is possible due to the support from donor organizations (most of its activities have been donor-funded since the very beginning). To date, more than 20 bilateral and institutional donors have supported EBRD with over EUR €230 million in funding. In what concerns policy and strategic orientations, the EBRD has been an innovator in private equity, sponsoring a number of SME focused funds that were the first-of-its-kind geographically or by target market.

EBRD embeds sustainability as one of its key principles. It seeks long-lasting results[1] to advance markets that thrive. EBRD looks beyond the lifespan of a single activity, like a loan and the design of projects, to produce changes that will last independently of the EBRD. The goal is to develop a robust private sector of dynamic businesses that innovate, access know-how and financing as needed, and continue to prosper and grow. The EBRD is working together with other institutions to identify issues that are preventing greater collaboration between investors and impact enterprises.

---

[1] The term "results" is used to include three elements of materialization of effects over time: outputs (short-run results stemming from activities), outcomes (medium-term results originated by outputs), and impacts (long-term results). Impacts are considered the ultimate effects (or results) defined by an intervention (investment/support provided). The term "intervention" is used in this chapter to describe specific activities undertaken to make a positive difference in outcomes and impacts of interest. It covers policies, programs, and investments, sometimes called projects.

Impact investing is becoming a mainstream investment strategy worldwide and is increasingly considered one of the instruments with potential to deliver on the 17 Sustainable Development Goals (SDG). Impact investing is an investment approach, where intentionality to create a social or environmental good matter. Intentionality is also a criterion by which investments are made across asset classes. Moreover, the outcomes of Impact investing, including both the financial return and the social and environmental impact, should be regularly measured. However, the challenge persists as how to embed impact and impact measurement strategies into investment decision-making, multicriteria decision analysis, and the application of systems approaches (Wendt 2018).

Value chains and global value chains (GVCs) are increasingly influencing programming and cooperation among investors and actors. Bilateral donors' experience with value chains tends to be particularly focused in the agriculture and food sectors, tourism, and textiles and apparel. Multilateral donors tend to have more experience in financial services, transportation, business, and professional services (Morais Sarmento 2018). However, there is still a lack of consensus concerning several aspects of how value chain projects should be designed, implemented, and evaluated. Donors and project implementing agencies still use a variety of terms, concepts, and graphical representations. Studies and literature reviews point to no single "silver bullet" for success (Morais Sarmento 2018). Development Impact is multidimensional and results from a combination of a well-structured and thorough value chain analysis, but several other elements need to be accounted for. A myriad of factors at play at different levels of an intervention can hinder or exacerbate success. Internal success factors can be influenced by project design, but also by factors related to its implementation capacity and scope of intervention (e.g. type of donor financing). In addition, external factors (e.g. political instability, conflicts, war, pandemics, or environmental catastrophes) may also affect project implementation and ultimately the success of the intervention.

EBRD loans to large companies are likely to have cascading ripple effects on SMEs, when SMEs are suppliers to larger companies. A loan to a large-sized company may trigger growth on the total supply chain (SC). To ensure the connection between loans to larger companies and the subsequent impacts on SMEs, EBRD decided to develop a methodology that allows the assessment of the impact of its commercial loans on the supply chains of their investees and borrowers. So far, EBRD's impact practice focused mostly on an assessment of loans provided to its borrowers, investees, and clients (typically a large firm), mainly in the form of financial indicators—such as return on investment (ROI), or sales "turnover"—but seldom connected to the supply chain and smaller companies participating in it ("upstream" or "downstream"). A systematic approach to assessing the impact on the supply chain had not yet been put in place. In order to launch and apply such a tool, EBRD hired expert advice to develop such a methodology and test its application in four pilot countries.

The key objective of this chapter is to present a pilot approach to measure the magnitude of impact and the spill-overs that EBRD corporate loans and projects have on SMEs as suppliers, through the identification of channels through which SME suppliers can be impacted. The chapter provides a definition of measures of impact (and other methodological considerations), combined with the selection and design of appropriate indicators to assess the impact that EBRD financing for larger clients has at the supplier or SME level, and how integration into supply chains can affect SMEs. This is done namely by: (i) identifying the impact of EBRD loans and projects on SME suppliers and related channels, and (ii) capturing the overall magnitude of the impact of projects with larger clients and borrowers on SMEs, with a view to EBRD providing appropriate business advice for SMEs. The testing of this methodology has not yet been finalized, so what is presented in this chapter is how a methodology was developed to address a large impact investor interested in SME development to methodically measure impact across the supply value chain of its borrowers and investees.

This chapter is based on original work and a literature review to develop a new quantitative framework to measure impact and the magnitude of spillovers that EBRD corporate loans and projects have on SME suppliers.

The following three sections provide a literature review on value chains and SMEs, donor engagements with the private sector, and best donor practices. The next three sections describe the approach and principles underlying the development of the EBRD methodology, the methodology itself, and the assessment of results. The final section concludes this chapter with views toward the future.

VALUE CHAINS AND SMALL AND MEDIUM ENTERPRISES

The value chain concept was popularized by Porter (1985) to describe a firm's value-adding activities for what it can influence or control—like suppliers and procurement criteria and quality standards. In his book *The Value Chain and Competitive Advantage,* Michael Porter (1985) defines value chains as the set of activities that an organization carries out to create value for its customers. Porter's division of the value chain into primary and support activities was largely based on the manufacturing model prevalent at the time (Chartered Global Management Accountants 2014). Porter also introduced the concept of a value system, which linked an entity's value chain to the value chains of upstream suppliers and downstream buyers, recognizing that the development of competitive advantage depends not only on the entity-specific value chain but also on the entire value system of which the entity is a part. However, this concept of a value system remained essentially linear; inputs that can be materials, products, or intellectual content are sourced and then converted by a series of entities each aiming to create additional value for the ultimate end customer.

Initial value chain analysis was largely focused on the manufacturing sector, but it expanded into a wider range of industries, including construction, mining, health care, financial services, banking, consulting, telecom, and others. Most products nowadays are rarely consumed "directly" at the place of its production. They are transformed, combined with other products and services, packaged, and transported until they reach the end consumer. The boundaries of value creation activities have become increasingly blurred. At the heart of the concept of the chain is the idea of connectedness, between goods and services produced by a complex set of activities and actors. But with globalization, the organization of global production and international trade have changed significantly within the last three decades. Market globalization has been facilitated by the decline in trade barriers and import tariffs. In addition to the import and export of materials and services, a significant component of globalization has been foreign direct investment (FDI) into production or other business activities in another country.

The GVC is a concept that captures the accelerating process of globalization and fragmentation of production.[2] Within this expanded scope, the traditional value chain is now more commonly understood as all the activities, functions, roles, and organizations involved in the production, delivery and consumption of products from raw materials to final consumption and back again through reverse flows. "The OECD defines a GVC as "all the activities that firms engage in, at home or abroad, to bring a product to the market, from

---

[2]Numerous other terms are used in the literature to reflect on this process, referring to firm-level strategies, such as "vertical specialization, outsourcing, offshoring, internationalization of production, international production sharing, disintegration of production, multistage production, intra-product specialization, production relocation, slicing up the value chain, and international segmentation of production" (Todeva and Rakhmatullin 2016).

conception to final use. . . . It is essential to understand how GVCs work, how they affect economic performance, and what policies help to derive greater benefits from them" (OECD 2013a). The academic research on GVC is also particularly well documented by the work of Hernández and Pedersen (2017) and Inomata (2017). This "systems view" promotes the idea that firms do not act as functional silos but rather as a linked chain. Indeed, the way competition is viewed has shifted from the concept of individual firms competing against each other to chains competing against chains. This paradigm shift facilitates coordination and collaboration among actors in the chain to deliver products that meet the needs of the consumer in an efficient and effective manner.

Increasingly, firms participating in global trade find themselves inserted into governed value chains and GVC. But how do SMEs fit and stand to benefit from value chains? And how do local manufacturers fit into these value chains? This occurs by offering new prospects to SMEs (and other firms), by accommodating specialization in narrow business functions and niche activities, and by helping surpass barriers to exporting, thus overcoming the common limitations of, for instance, developing countries (e.g. skill set constraints) and the path-dependence on the degree of industrial development.

The key issue thus is how producers of all sizes, geographies, and types should participate in value chains, rather than whether they should do so. Greater integration into value chains can help countries to sustain productivity growth, as a country's gross domestic product (GDP) per capita rises (EBRD 2018).

Enabling SMEs to scale via value chains requires addressing "informality" in the economy and creating the appropriate business environment. Moreover, the lack of a supporting, enabling environment can lead to higher production and trade costs. This in turn can result in lower productivity and growth for the economy as a whole, as firms with high-growth potential adopt suboptimal expansion strategies.

Emerging Economies, Value Chains, and Small and Medium Enterprises

Primary drivers in global production and trade are now emerging economies. Until recently, trade integration and growth for many in the developing world were fueled by the insertion of local producers in value chains led by firms from high-income economies, in particular in North America, Europe, and Japan. But low growth in the dominant northern economies, along with sustained growth in emerging countries, in particular China and

India, have spurred a shift in the primary trade and growth drivers, with crucial implications for the structures of production and global demand. The rise of South-South trade, the growing inclusiveness of innovation, and the emergence of new technologies will lead developing countries to innovate new products, seek growth markets, serve new consumers, and optimize production processes.

Value chains are particularly important for developing economies. Integration in GVCs is commonly associated with enhanced FDI and knowledge spillovers to the local economy. For several countries, GVCs have not yet totally materialized as a chain, encouraging further integration into international markets with improved capabilities in skills, learning, and innovation and upgraded products. Higher value-added investments in GVC in developing markets have so far mostly benefited attractive countries from both a platform and market perspective, those which feature a certain degree of local knowledge capacities and growing skills of an emerging middle class, and rising incomes of producers and consumers. Countries with large domestic markets became even more attractive (e.g. China and India) to amplify the benefits of growth.

The rising integration of some developing economies into GVCs has resulted from a concurrence of factors, including targeted policies to promote integration and internationalization of firms, new forms of business strategies in house and in partner countries, and new forms of public-private partnerships (OECD 2013a). Value chains are not uniform in their governance or incentive structure. The implications of participating in a value chain will depend on its type and structure.

SMEs in developing countries face particular challenges for integration into value chains due to the following constraints:

- Size too small, age too young, or structure not developed enough
- Access to finance may be more limited
- Lesser collateral to attract investors, or offset risks themselves
- Complexity of establishing connections with SMEs in often remote locations
- Scale: problems matching supply with demand due to smaller scale and capacity
- Degree of informality (diverse legal status of SMEs, lack of formal accounts, insecure resources)
- Specialization in inferior goods vis-à-vis superior goods[3]

---

[3] "Superior goods" increase in consumption with rising income; "inferior goods" decrease in consumption as income rises.

- Lack of managerial expertise, experience, and capacity to deal with bureaucracy and information
- Inadequate market information to secure adequate bargaining power
- Access to technologies and designer talent base
- Lack of capacity to offer suitable mitigation strategies to higher perceived risks
- Access to information about markets (prospects, price, quality, quantity, timeliness) innovation—making a product or service different (through cost efficiency, design, labeling and placement); and interaction—the capacity to work with clusters, associations, trade specialists, etc.

A major challenge, however, is that for several developing countries participation in GVC continues to be marginal. Industrialization, productivity, and diversification of many of these economies remain limited as they continue to be dependent on low-wage labor, commodity exports, and low-end primary production. The benefits of globalization have continued to be unevenly distributed, with gains going to countries with more education, skills, wealth, and power.

For developing economies, the quest to maximize benefits from value chain participation has to do with capturing a higher share of domestic value-added by essentially moving up the value chain. However, these countries face several challenges. First, they are located far away from industrial clusters, whereby most production networks are regionally oriented and concentrated around three main hubs of North America, Europe, and East Asia. Second, Preferential Trade Agreements (PTAs) play an important role in shaping GVC benefits. These can create cost and regulatory incentives to source among members, but also strict rules of origin, which can disincentivize the use of cheaper inputs from third countries.

Impact Measurement in Value Chains

In recent years, governments, donors, and non-governmental organization (NGOs) have increasingly embraced value chain development (VCD) for stimulating economic growth and combating poverty. VCD has been adopted by a broad range of entities, such as development agencies, for example, Deutsche Gesellschaft für Internationale Zusammenarbeit (GIZ), Netherlands Development Organisation (SNV), Swisscontact, United States Agency for International Development (USAID), government agencies, non-governmental organizations (NGOs); and international organizations, for example, International Labor Organization (ILO), Food and Agriculture

Organization of the United Nations (FAO), UN Industrial Development Organization (UNIDO)).

In line with the emergence of VCD programming and the rising interest in the subject, there has been a proliferation of VCD guides and a burst of activity to diagnostic tools to help practitioners conduct value chain analysis, usually as input for the design of interventions.[4] However, there are significant differences as to how chain-related concepts are interpreted, which have important repercussions for the design of interventions, and consequently for the attainment of development impacts. Guides also vary in terms of their conceptualization of value chain concepts, approaches to development (e.g. a focus on better market links versus business environment), objectives and overall complexity as to their developmental goals (e.g. poverty reduction, decent work, economic growth), targeted users (government, private sector, NGOs), and incorporation of local actors into strategy formulation, among other factors (Donovan et al. 2015).

In general, the quality of evidence for what has worked is weak for most types of studies (Morais Sarmento 2018). There are not many evaluation or impact studies on GVC, especially in sectors other than agriculture. There is some academic research, such as impact studies on trade policies in several parts of the world (e.g. Megersa 2019), but no studies where clear attribution is featured.[5] Most research in this area only develops pointers about key determinants of success. For bilateral programs, few have been evaluated, but those that have reported tangible results (OECD and WTO 2013). The UK's interim monitoring of its value chain activities and aid-for-trade projects found improved incomes, working conditions, and employment for partner country workers.

There have been some studies on certification and impact evaluations but mostly in agriculture;[6] not much is found for other sectors. Studies exist (such as systematic reviews) for corporate codes and sustainability standards, but these show mixed evidence. There are some Randomized Control Trials (RCT) in the agriculture and forestry sectors, featured for instance in the

---

[4]See, for instance, Schneemann and Vredeveld (2015); ValueLinks at www.valuelinks.org; GIZ and UNIDO's EQuIP GVC Tool: Tool 7 of the EQuIP Toolbox, at http://www.equip-project.org/wp-content/uploads/2015/08/EQuIP_Tool-7_V150821.pdf.
[5]That is, impact evaluations with post-experimental or experimental methods.
[6]For instance, "The African Development Bank's Support for Agricultural Value Chains Development: Lessons for the Feed Africa Strategy" (AfDB 2018) and "Mid-Term Evaluation (MTE) of the Trade in Global Value Chains Initiative (TGVCI)" by Nelson et al. (2016), are available here: https://www.gov.uk/government/publications/evaluation-trade-and-global-value-chains-initiative.

ISEAL[7] website. In agriculture, there has been a substantial focus on export VC and not so much on domestic markets. There has been a lack of evidence found for learning and leadership skills along with social dialogue in GVC as success factors.

Another challenge is the difficulty of getting access to data, which goes beyond time and resources. Access to data is often also very restricted. In order to establish impacts, there is need for more data on business performance to link outcomes from these initiatives (e.g. how improvements in worker's health impact on decreasing absenteeism and increased productivity); otherwise, what is mostly done are assessments based on opinions obtained from key informant interviews.

There are some emerging policy briefs for individual studies which mention success factors, but findings have not been totally scrutinized across (OECD 2014) and this remains a critical area for investigation. Detailed cases of value chains in specific industries provide valuable insights into actors and processes but offer little information on measures for optimization and efficient coordination of the resource flows within the value chain (Todeva and Rakhmatullin 2016). Development impacts of value chains are also dependent on the income distribution within the chains.

In one of the most recent evaluations on the topic of value chains, the "African Development Bank's Support for Agricultural Value Chains Development: Lessons for the Feed Africa Strategy" evaluation (AfDB 2018), the bank identified five critical factors and five key enablers that characterized successful implementation of value chain in Africa. The five critical factors for all AfDB's value chain interventions are: (i) the analysis of the full value chain; (ii) strategizing for inclusiveness; (iii) responsiveness to market changes; (iv) taking profitability with value additions; and (v) planning for sustained impact. Five other key elements termed "enablers" were also identified: (i) availability of appropriate infrastructure and Information Communication Technology (ICT); (ii) conducive policy and regulatory environment; (iii) availability of appropriate business support; (iv) access to finance; and (v) private sector participation and linkages between value chain actors.

Donor Engagements with the Private Sector

Multilateral and bilateral donor agencies have, for decades, sought ways of providing effective technical assistance to country producers. These engagements can be classified into the following four broad categories (Table 20.1).

---

[7]ISEAL represents the global movement of "credible sustainability standards," available at https://www.isealalliance.org/.

TABLE 20.1   Categories of Impact Investors'[8] Engagements with the Private Sector

Business Matchmaking	Direct facilitation or grant support mechanisms to help business linkages between developed and developing country firms
Incentivizing Investment	Financial support to remove risk for developed country firms to invest in developing countries, especially those tied to the investor's mission or investment policy
Technical or Business Advisory Services	Direct or grant-supported technical and business advisory services to firms
Leveraging Multisector Finance	Co-financing among sectors—combining private, bi-lateral, or multilateral funding vehicles—to develop SMEs and their communities

Source: Adapted from Donor Committee for Enterprise Development (2012).

Recently, these agencies have embarked on experiments of fostering private sector partnerships. The central idea is to combine technical assistance with connectivity. Typically, these programs and strategies related to engaging multisector partners have included interventions at the large "macro," middle," "meso," and small "micro" levels (Table 20.2).

Critical Success Factors for Donor Engagements in Value Chains

What creates success? The answers are not straightforward and to a considerable extent are context dependent. A preliminary answer is that a myriad of internal and external factors at different stages of the project life cycle exist. Internal project success and effectiveness can be influenced by design factors (e.g. implementation agencies' capacity, interest and knowledge of investors, or local champions necessary to make a project work, presence

---

[8] Any impact investor bringing tools more than just investing can apply this toolkit, and do so across all asset classes, ranging from loans and fixed income to private debt to private equity and other financing approaches; the goal is to amplify the impact with a range of interventions.

TABLE 20.2 Typology of Impact Investor Interventions for Engagement Across Sectors

Macro-level interventions	Focus on creating a business-enabling environment: building economic, legal, and regulatory foundations (property rights, financial regulations, governance frameworks, and public financial management policies) to ensure that the right conditions exist for the private sector to thrive.
Meso-level interventions[9]	Target market failures and imperfections to enhance competitiveness and integrate all actors into national, regional, and international markets. Such interventions include building value chains, "aid for trade," and transfer of technological innovations.
Micro-level interventions	Include investments in firms and people and entail building support services to enhance longer-term development and growth across multiple sectors (business and NGOs). Examples include technical and financial support for SMEs and investments in health, education, and vocational skills training to foster a thriving workforce.

Source: Adapted from, and based on, the reviewed literature and in particular on Gibb et al. (2008); Kurokawa and te Velde (2008); Kindornay and Reilly-King (2013).

of functional local markets and value chains). Success can also depend on factors related to project implementation (e.g. political problems, withdrawal of financing by funders, expropriation). In addition, external factors (e.g. political instability, conflicts and war, or environmental catastrophes) may also affect project implementation and ultimately the success of the intervention (Figure 20.1).

As such, the analysis of critical success factors for an impact investor's interventions is not simple and overlaps substantially across different stakeholders, and cannot be taken in isolation of intrinsic characteristics and success factors of value chain participants and stakeholders

---

[9] A "meso" level indicates a middle size that falls between the small "micro" and larger "macro" levels.

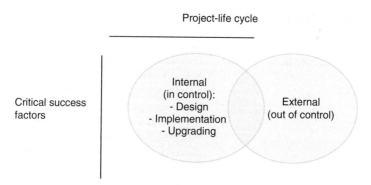

FIGURE 20.1   Generic Factors Affecting Success in Value Chains from an Impact Investor Perspective. *Source:* Adapted from Morais Sarmento (2018).

themselves—including financiers and impact investors, implementing agencies, firms, beneficiaries—and the value chain upgrading process itself.[10] The analysis needs to have a multidimensional approach, whereby critical success factors for an investor (such as a donor) are combined with critical success factors on the ground, within actors, and processes surrounding the value chain.

Another alternative is the grouping of general success factors into a three-level category: micro, macro, and meso. Micro-level includes intrinsic factors related to the firm (e.g. management quality, market orientation, product development and product process and product marketing capacity ties) and its relative competitiveness. Also, it entails building support services to enhance longer-term private sector development and growth (e.g. investments in education, and vocational skills training). In here, it is

---

[10]Upgrading describes the dynamic movement within the value chain by examining how producers shift between different stages of the chain. It allows achieving higher value-added production in the form of product, functional, and intersectoral upgrading via better skills and know-how, capital and technology, and processes, productivity increases, and eventually greater job creation. Upgrading, associated with "moving into higher value-added stages," is commonly followed by positive spillovers regarding technology and productivity (Marcato and Troncoso 2017). However, economic upgrading does not automatically lead to social upgrading. Benefits are not equally distributed among all production stages, and a position in higher-value added activities leads to larger economic benefits, including higher incomes, high-wage employment, and positive spillovers regarding technology (OECD 2013b).

important to distinguish in the analysis whether a "buyer-driven value chain" or a "producer-driven value chain" is being considered.

At the meso-level, it has to do with the targeting of market failures and imperfections to enhance competitiveness and integrate all actors into national, regional, and international markets. Such interventions include building value chains, "aid for trade," transfer of technological innovations, R&D, the existence of research institutes, and universities and the capacity to be able to find and to hire qualified staff. Based on the Danish International Development Agency's (DANIDA, 2016) evaluation, this can be translated into going beyond the value chain to the sector level, laying the foundation for achieving more systemic changes of benefit for the wider chain through a strategic approach to address sector-wide issues, and to have sector-wide impact.

At the macro-level, it refers to the framework conditions which enable a company to export and be integrated in international markets and chains, which allows the overall private sector to thrive (e.g. legal and regulatory frameworks, barriers to trade, legal systems, transport and logistics, governance frameworks, and public financial management policies and political stability; see Table 20.3).

One challenging aspect to the identification of critical success factors is the high dynamism and mobility of value chains, which make it very costly and intensive to analyze and map out fully, in particular for cross-border value chains (for instance tracking subcontractors from A to Z and to understand how value added is created by neighboring activities and conclude if in fact there is clear evidence of the value chain's contribution to employment and multiplier effects). It is also hard to track data at the enterprise level, especially for services.

There is no single "silver bullet" for success. Development impact is multidimensional; what is needed is a well-structured argumentation, and many elements in order, to come to the right judgments. Myriad factors are at play among different levels of intervention, which can hinder or exacerbate success. Many value chain actors (e.g. "small holders") are marginalized even from their own local economies and kept aside from the benefits of value chains. To include these groups in the mainstream economy, value chain projects must often be considered alongside broader programs for market systems and social protection.

From an impact investor perspective, overarching key success factors that can bring about development impacts in value chain projects were condensed

TABLE 20.3 Taxonomy of Critical Success Factors

Level	Examples
Micro	Market driven and behavioral change
	Stakeholder analysis for greater segmentation and tailored approaches (e.g. distinguish between incentives for commercial farmers and subsistence farmers)
	Ownership and participation
	Existence of a minimum criterion for value chain for intervention across countries
Meso	Availability of labor and human capital
	Innovation systems
	Partnering
	Going beyond the value chain to the sector level, laying the foundation for achieving more systemic changes of benefit for the wider chain through a strategic approach to address sector-wide issues to have sector-wide impact
Macro	Market analysis
	Trade environment
	Institutional quality
	Integration of policy components in projects to enhance a conducive environment
	Standards and certification systems
	Developmental analysis (poverty, income distribution, employment, etc.)

Source: Adapted from Morais Sarmento (2018).

in Table 20.4. Another aspect to consider are the tradeoffs between critical success factors.

Beyond what is described above, the particular ways in which the political economy and the relationships in a particular context articulate with the mechanisms is important. It is not enough to look at the mechanisms only, but it is also key to have an understanding as to how that mechanism works in that precise context (as it might work well in one context but not in another). Then, there are particular drivers for success to be attained in a particular country but not in another country. For instance, in South Africa, elements of black economic empowerment have been fundamental drivers to build

TABLE 20.4 Overarching Key Success Factors for Impact Investors

	Factors	Description
Design	**Analysis of the full value chain and reliance on good quality of information**	The analysis of the full value chain should rely on sound data and quality information sources. Key stakeholders should be identified and interviewed in the design stage. This involves good data collection at the statistical level but also "soft" information about the interests and motivations of key stakeholders. Reliance on a thorough needs assessment and feasibility studies can be determinant to better tailor the project, the needs of stakeholders, and constraints of the value chain.
	Selection of the right value chain	Requires a nuanced understanding of the value chain and value propositions in the context of each of the existing and upcoming priority sectors. Relies on the definition of strategic value chain and the methodology to identify these and the experts for the assessment of the relevant criteria and the sourcing approach. Includes the utilization of the appropriate value chain toolkits for analysis and selection.
	Thorough project design	Analysis of value addition across the value chain for each actor, an overall constraint analysis (which includes elements described in greater detail below), drawing on: (i) identification of weak links in the value chain constraining firm upgrading, hindering the materialization of impacts on poverty reduction and development; (ii) engagement with private sector trade experts and researchers, alongside internal experts, throughout the project cycle to ensure all the dimensions of sustainability are brought in; (iii) a holistic approach that takes into account the four dimensions of sustainability[11] into programs or

---

[11]Sustainability should be embedded in value chain selection and implementation through a holistic approach. Four dimensions of analysis – social, environmental, institutional, and economic – should be always present. But including these four dimensions in the value chain selection phase (and later phases) is made easier if they are already part of the program or project objectives and requirements.

TABLE 20.4 (*continued*)

Factors	Description
	projects, from the design stage through to implementation, making this sustainability holistic approach a requirement for the formulation of program/project and its objectives. Good knowledge and use of available tools which entail sustainability dimensions.[12]
Creating a coalition of champions	Setting up a critical mass of solid institutions that can collaborate and jointly spearhead the value chain agenda. The idea is to bring in a coalition of entities that can become "champions"[13] for the agenda or the needed reforms. It can also involve creating a training ground to have a new set of local/national champions trained (e.g. for different stages of the project and also for sustainability purposes).
Establishment of collaborative networks	Both at design, implementation and upgrading, throughout the relevant stakeholder range, which includes private sector, PPPs, collaboration with lead firms is of particular relevance. The selection of implementing potential partners should be based on comprehensive and strategic assessment of their capacities and incentives to perform this role. Issues to consider are public-private sector relationships, relationships between the national, regional, and local levels (including potentials for upscaling and linking to sector policy development). Private sector advisory boards have been used to gather participants and bring institutions to the table to agree on common value chain goals, to enable the elaboration of concrete action plans.

---

[12]Among the most important are GIZ's "Guidelines for Value Chain selection: Integrating economic, environmental, social and institutional criteria," GIZ's ValueLinks, ILO's "Value Chain Guide for Decent Work," "Making Markets Work for the Poor (M4P)," the UN's "The Corporate Responsibility to Respect Human Rights," "Conducting an Effective Human Rights Impact Assessment," and AgriProFocus's "Gender in Value Chains," and HSA qualitative tools for environmental measurement.

[13]Reform champions are powerful lead organizations that have pivotal roles in bringing about reform and policy or institutional change.

TABLE 20.4 (*continued*)

	Factors	Description
	Responsive-ness to market changes	Focusing on responsiveness to markets requires permanent adaptability, preparedness to identify market variations and a team that is able to steer across a changing environment.
	Team skills	Preparedness, identification, and availability of adequate training for the internal project team.
	Inclusive development focus	Strategize for inclusiveness, meaning the utilization of inclusive growth business models in the design (and implementation) of projects that ensure considerations for good working conditions, human rights, and gender. This pertains to the development of a capacity to identify a wide range of topics and embed it in an integrated fashion into project design (e.g. environment, gender, human rights,[14] and others related to human or environmental vulnerability), considering the different perspectives of the myriad of stakeholders involved in the value chain. Particular attention should be given to specific disadvantaged and/or excluded groups.
Implementation	**Effective and efficient project imple-mentation**	Having the implementation team well prepared to deliver a clear communication strategy concerning the importance of the chosen approach during project implementation and early negotiations between internal and external stakeholders is key to obtain a strong compromise and deliver on expected results.
	Embeddedness of a holistic perspective of sustainability	Embedding a holistic approach that takes into account the four dimensions of sustainability: social, environmental, institutional, and economic into program/project, from the design stage (value chain selection, development) through to implementation.

---

[14]For instance, considerations on whether there are grievance mechanisms in place, in case of human rights violations.

TABLE 20.4   *(continued)*

	Factors	Description
	Convener role of EU Delegations	To set up, maintain, and feed the dialogue channels and platforms established and motivate leading institutions to continue to perform.
	Implementation of monitoring and evaluation tools	Includes the clarification of the project's objectives and goals, Theory of Change (ToC), outcomes, and impact indicators, and the fostering of a shared understanding of the required intervention among donors and beneficiaries. In particular, it also involves monitoring of the weak links in the value chain constraining firm upgrading and hindering the materialization of impacts on poverty reduction and development. The incorporation of an evaluability assessment (EA)[15] can be also considered. In recent years, given the increase in the amount of evaluations of international development projects, EA has been incorporated as part of the project cycle.
Post-implementation	Credible evaluation of results	Without an independent and credible assessment of the achievement of the support provided there is no evidence of what worked for each value chain.

Source: Adapted from Morais Sarmento (2018).

the talent, skills, expertise, and infrastructure of the local communities and economies.[16]

---

[15]An evaluability assessment is "conducted to determine the ability of an intervention to demonstrate in measurable terms the results it intends to deliver" (MCC 2015). An evaluability assessment uses specific, transparent standards and best practices for assessing the following five dimensions of a project: (i) problem diagnostic, (ii) project objectives and program logic, (iii) risks and assumptions, (iv) project participants and beneficiaries, and (v) accountability and learning metrics.

[16]In South Africa, Black Economic Empowerment requirements were incorporated in the FairTrade standards of buyers from all types of institutions, to address power inequality in the commercial wine industry in South Africa (Melkeraaen 2009). In 2009, the Tourism Sector Codes of the 2003 Broad-Based Black Economic Empowerment Act were finalized. A scorecard for private businesses to fill out was created to determine if they were meeting the Broad-Based Black Economic Empowerment Act's goals (Staritz and Reis 2013).

A great deal of the success hinges on global processes, not only national ones and thus on relative competitiveness. Competition is global. The fact that one country improves labor conditions does not necessarily translate into an overall gain, as investors less conscious about impact could seek other countries with less stringent markets and regulations.

Critical Success Factors for SMEs' Participation in Value Chain

SMEs have the potential to contribute with significant positive impacts to development results due to their economic importance in developing countries. Targeting SMEs is an important means of enhancing private sector engagements' development impacts (Bella et al. 2013). Making more finance available to SMEs can enhance development impacts of projects and partnerships by alleviating access to finance constraints that these firms often face in developing countries.

According to the OECD's recent work, quantitative work on the determinants of SME participation in GVC is limited (OECD 2018), basically due to difficulties in measuring SME engagement in GVCs (given the need to access to firm level data) and the absence of a conceptual framework. As such, the literature traditionally relies on the determinants of firm engagement in export markets. On the basis of this literature, two main categories of determinants of SME participation in GVCs can be identified: those related to firm characteristics and those related to the policy environment. Internal firm characteristics are only partly responsible for SME participation in GVCs, the extent to which policies provide an enabling environment, addressing the core disadvantages that SMEs struggle with is also key.

Some of the critical success factors for a firm to get involved in a value chain are described in Table 20.5. But beyond those already mentioned, the governance of the value chain matters. Suppliers to global retailers are confronted by a much more demanding set of critical success factors than if they sell to small retailers and specialist buyers (Kaplinsky et al. 2003).

TABLE 20.5   Factors Affecting SME Participation in Value Chains.

Structural (related to firm characteristics)	Size of the firm
	Internal resources
	Demand for their products in the market
	Comparative advantage
	Lead times to get a product in the market (distance to the market)
Macro	Business climate: aspects of the environment: infrastructure, roads, courts procedures
	Institutional aspects: how fast government operates

Source: Adapted from Morais Sarmento (2018).

BEST PRACTICES FOR IMPACT INVESTORS

A common trend is that impact investors are making their strategies more demand-led or tailored to different types of business partners. Impact investors and MDBs as donors are planning to consult national industry bodies more systematically for future policy formulation in relevant thematic areas (Heinrich-Fernandes 2017).

Some impact investors (mission-based, commercial, multilateral, bilateral) embed in their interventions some dimension of policy dialogue, to create a more conducive environment to enforce change and support improvements in the value chain environment. This involves not only deepening the level and scope of policy dialogue with national authorities, but also calling upon other value chain stakeholders. Depending on the interventions, some can take a more holistic approach, encompassing a wide range of improvements in sectoral policies. Others can take a narrower approach, specific to a given sector or commodity (e.g. norms and standards, taxation), although these two approaches can be taken together and be combined.

Over time, impact investors have changed their policies, procedures, modes of work, and funding mechanisms to enable more strategic engagement with the private sector. They have created new internal roles or adapted their staff functions, as well as entire teams and units to the new requirements of wider partnerships across multiple sectors, including with the private sector (Donor Committee for Enterprise Development 2017). This entails larger central units and teams to lead on private sector engagement, but also the assigning of new leadership roles to senior staff, hiring of new outreach staff and focal points for closer interactions with the private sector, mandating technical staff to develop partnerships and allocating more of their time and resources to networking. This has also included teams, units, and departments being mandated to work cross-functionally for the sake of greater engagement with the private sector, and more formalized and systematic division of work and tasks that might involve knowledge sharing between headquarters and field offices and demand greater institutional coordination.

This organizational adaptation to a new reality seems to be key. In order to implement their new vision of private sector engagement, most of the organizations interviewed in the study by Heinrich-Fernandes (2017) changed the structure and roles of staff, teams, and units. While the specific arrangements differ, two complementary types of changes were common across organizations:

- The creation of new leadership positions and responsibilities at headquarters
- A decision to leverage the skills, creativity, and networks of staff at all levels and in different technical areas to enhance private sector engagement

Impact investors and their portfolios have also been exploring new funding procedures and vehicles to work with private businesses. A trend is the use of flexible, centrally managed funds, which can be accessed by all technical colleagues to support strategic collaborations with business, outside existing program frameworks. Several organizations now use special innovation funds to support early-stage and high-risk ventures. New funding mechanisms also tend to be open to a variety of stakeholders and sectors, and offer different types of financial support, including non-grant instruments.[17]

Picking up on the points mentioned above on relationships, best practices among impact investors also relate to bringing diverse groups together and working through multi-stakeholder, multisector partnerships, whereby governments, lead firms, global brands, factory owners, unions, and workers work together to improve working and living conditions.

Most major national donor agencies and international organizations have developed their own value chain approach, with varying degrees of full-fledged methodologies and tools. Interventions that are based on

---

[17]NGOs, for their part, have also set up mechanisms to diversify their funding income and invest it in more flexible ways—such as for capacity-building and preparatory discussions with businesses, which currently take place outside the scope of donor grant agreements.

these value chain approaches have increased considerably and have been labeled as "value chains for development" (Staritz 2012). Examples include those by the World Bank and the International Finance Corporation (IFC), the Organization for Economic Co-Operation and Development (OECD), the International Labor Organization (ILO), UNIDO, the Food and Agriculture Organization (FAO), and national donor agencies such as United States Agency for International Development (USAID), Swiss Agency for Development and Cooperation (SDC), Deutsche Gesellschaft für Internationale Zusammenarbeit (GIZ), Danish International Development Agency (DANIDA), Swedish International Development Agency (SIDA), and Australian Government's Overseas Aid Program (AUSAID). Others have not explicitly developed a value chain approach, but in broader private sector development (PSD) programs there is a role to be played by GVCs (e.g. DFID's "Making Market Systems Work Better for the Poor," or M4P).

But there is still a lack of consensus concerning how value chain projects should be designed, implemented, and evaluated. Donors and project implementing agencies use a variety of terms, concepts, and graphical representations. In contrast to the area of microfinance, VCD has not had a clearly articulated set of best practices (USAID 2010). The Donor Committee for Enterprise Development's (DCED 2001) "Blue Book" identified good practice in the delivery of business development services (BDS) for small enterprises but has not been updated since. During the past years, the BDS approach to enterprise development has been mainly enriched by alternative approaches and frameworks such as the value chain approach and "Making Markets Work for the Poor."

The Economic and Social Commission for Asia and the Pacific (2015) reflections emphasizes that when it comes to design policy options for national trade strategies and economic policies to enhance the competitiveness of firms and value-added content of production, "there are no simple 'one-size-fits-all' prescriptions available or desirable and that in fact some of the factors influencing developments in this area may not even be under the control of trade policymakers."[18]

Moreover, there is little systematic impact evaluation evidence across poverty impacts from value chain interventions, which brings added difficulty in relating good practices in this domain with poverty reduction objectives. This is problematic because not only does more need to be known about effectiveness of these initiatives, but also little is known

---

[18]Economic and Social Commission for Asia and the Pacific (2015), available at https://www.unescap.org/sites/default/files/E71_8E_0.pdf.

about which types of interventions are effective, on both the policy and the implementation sides. Most of the evidence is anecdotal for the positive outcomes and impact of value chain initiatives. These assessments are complex and expensive, which often deters donors and implementers from proceeding with them.

USAID's Marketlinks[19] suggests a common set of principles underlying best practices, which if applied sensibly can improve the design and implementation of value chain projects:

- Focus on a long-term industry vision and maintain a systemic perspective.
- Engage multiple stakeholders, but clearly define roles in upgrading the value chain.
- Increase breadth and depth of benefits to value chain participants.
- Leverage resources from the Impact investing ecosystem.
- Avoid redundancy with what is already being done by other private sector stakeholders.
- Sequence interventions appropriately.
- Strive for adequate incentives and win-win relationships to ensure sustainability and develop a clear exit strategy.
- Build flexibility into the program to respond to changing market conditions and project environments.
- Carefully assess resources and consider the scale of impact.

The OECD's High-Level Meeting of the Global Partnership for Effective Development Co-operation held in 2014 remarked that GVC offers a framework for thinking about how to wire together diverse policies (trade, infrastructure, taxation, development assistance, education) to help low-income countries create enabling conditions for development; however, further work on this topic is still needed. It also pinpointed that the principles agreed in Paris, Accra, and Busan[20] remain relevant in today's rapidly changing development landscape and that a wide range of partners are using these principles as the basis for their own accountability, including donors.

---

[19]Marketlinks is a knowledge sharing platform, hosted by USAID. It captures and disseminates good practices in inclusive market development around the world, available at https://www.marketlinks.org/.

[20]The Proceedings of the Busan High Level Forum on Aid Effectiveness are available at http://www.oecd.org/dac/effectiveness/HLF4%20proceedings%20entire%20doc%20for %20web.pdf.

APPROACH AND PRINCIPLES UNDERLYING THE DEVELOPMENT OF THE EBRD METHODOLOGY

The following sections of this chapter will concentrate on presenting how the methodology was developed and what instruments it makes use of. This is still being developed. The EBRD's pilot framework is to be implemented (and tested) in four pilot countries: Bulgaria, Croatia, Egypt, and Tunisia. Countries were selected based on the business cases available, as well as on the mix of industries in each and the potential to yield results for the piloting of this methodology.

A different selection criterion was devised with the EBRD for selecting pilot cases in each country, which ended up including a diversity of sectors and industry types with the aim of allowing the assessment of impact on diverse supply chains. The rational for this selection was to measure impact on different kinds of SMEs. As such, the following sectors were selected: aerospace (durable goods), food processing (consumer goods), food retail (trade), and tourism (services). The supply chain in the aerospace industry is mainly technology driven, and midsize companies qualify as a supplier. As for the food processing industry, its supply chain includes very small companies that supply ingredients (e.g. raw milk, fruits). Having as diverse number of suppliers as possible also influenced the selection of the industries for the piloting of this methodology. Figure 20.2 depicts the levels of analysis, at country, sector, and industry level.

The assessment of cross-border supply chains ended up not considered for now in the development of this impact assessment methodology, partly

FIGURE 20.2   Countries, Sectors, and Industries Selected for the Piloting of the Methodology. *Source:* Authors.

due to problems with data collection and harmonization, but also because the aim was to draw a picture of regional supply chains, thus allowing EBRD to design tailor-made interventions to support SMEs in specific countries.

Another limitation was the depth and the direction of supply chains. In order to have robust, reliable data, only the first link in supply chains—direct suppliers—is considered. The effort needed to dig deeper into a second or third tier of the supply chain would have exponentially expanded the data collection efforts, without necessarily providing more comprehensive insights at this point in time for the testing of the methodology. Furthermore, only upstream supply chains were considered, so as to have the same methodology for all industry types in each country. Besides, some of the selected industries will mainly have final customers (e.g. food retail, tourism), and therefore a downstream analysis would not add valuable additional information.

The impact assessment methodology adheres to the following principles:

- The methodology must provide insights in quantifiable indicators illustrating SME performance on financial indicators (e.g. sales, profits, and investments), socioeconomic indicators (e.g. employment, work environment), and quality aspects (e.g. product quality or standards, innovation, and more).
- Be applicable in the selected EBRD countries, given the data available in those countries.
- Be generalizable to other countries of EBRD operations (beyond those four already selected).
- Data limitations (namely in term of its availably) should be considered, as well as different accounting and record keeping practices in each country.

DEVELOPMENT OF THE METHODOLOGY

Purpose and Scope

The research question that led to the development of this methodology was: What are the impacts of EBRD support through large firms on the value chain and SMEs? In the initial stage of the setting up of the methodology, the scope of the impact study was determined, then research questions were developed, along with the identification of relevant stakeholders for the EBRD cases to be piloted. The scope of the study is an ex-post impact assessment, which intends to assess impact once the EBRD support is completed.

Defining a time horizon for impact assessment is crucial, as it takes time before immediate results (outputs), but especially intermediate results (outcomes) and long-term results (impacts) of EBRD support consolidate for any investment, loan, or project. Traditionally, in impact assessments the time horizon highly depends of the nature of the intervention and the economic lifetime of the activities and assets[21] involved. The time horizon in this context is defined by the measurement between two points: the first measurement point is the year just before EBRD intervention and second is the year just after EBRD intervention. Still some tangible assets are considered indirectly (e.g. of capacity of a supplier was increased).

Approach and Impact Pathways

To understand how and if an intervention, such as EBRD's support, works, activities related to the intervention need to be connected in a way that shows how they can lead to the intended results. This includes describing a causal impact pathway from two sides: (i) how activities concur to intended outputs, outputs to outcomes, and finally to impacts;[22] and (ii) specifying a set of causal assumptions showing under what conditions the various links in the causal pathway are expected to relate for the materialization of results.

A variety of terminologies to describe the causal pathways abound in the literature, including results chains, logic models, and impact pathways. In this case, the term impact pathway will be used. Impact pathways describe causal paths, clarifying the linkages between the sequence of steps from getting from activities to ultimate results (impact). An impact pathway is made up of different components. A Theory of Change[23] (ToC) complements

---

[21] For example, if the EBRD support was used to build certain facilities such as stores, then the time horizon would depend on the economic lifetime of the assets (i.e. for stores 10–15 years).

[22] Considering a three-tier partition of time, short run is for outputs, medium term for outcomes, and longer term for impact materialization.

[23] A Theory of Change depicts activities and results (outputs, outcomes, and impacts) in the following way: activities (actions undertaken by those involved in the intervention); goods and services produced (direct outputs resulting from the activities undertaken); reach (target groups, those intended to receive the intervention's goods and services and its first effects); capacity changes (e.g. in opportunities, attitudes, skills, knowledge, aspirations of those who have received or used the intervention's goods and services); behavioral changes; direct benefits (improvements in the condition of individual beneficiaries, e.g. increased clients, increased procurement of inputs, goods and services); well-being changes are the longer-term cumulative improvement in overall well-being of individual beneficiaries (e.g. food security, gender equality, poverty reduction).

an impact pathway by going more in-depth and describing the causal assumptions behind each link in the pathway, and what needs to be in place for those causal linkages to be realized. Beneficiaries are the target groups whose well-being the intervention intends to enhance.

EBRD's interventions may have created differentiated impact pathways on different supply chains. It is thus necessary to analyze the specifics of EBRD support (transactions) and its effects on large firms' operations (EBRD clients). This information was gathered through semi-structured interviews to know more about the purpose of the support and the nature of EBRD's financing support (e.g. loans and equity provision) at the preliminary stage of the piloting of this methodology.

Direct and indirect impact pathways on large firms, its supply chain, and SMEs needed to be studied and specified. For instance, in the case of an expansion of a (client) company, EBRD financing may have been used to open additional branches, increase production capacity, warehousing, or the purchasing of more updated production equipment. Indirect effects on suppliers (SMEs) need to be thus also established and can occur several times over an elapsed period of time, materializing in more than a single one-time effect. Indirect and spill-over effects on processes may also occur and trigger increased demand for products (e.g. the opening of a new branch for a retail chain may increase the number of goods procured).

Services are a possible additional impact channel. Services may be related to the hiring of a supervising engineer, but also related to the provision of advertising materials, and specific advisory work (e.g. human resources, tax, environmental protection). Impact channels and spillovers depend largely on the type of the intervention and its effects along the chain. The analysis of the intervention and its impact pathways determines which supply chains are to be scrutinized in the impact assessment.

Regarding indirect impacts of EBRD support through supplier relations (or second level effects), the focus is on data collection for the largest SME suppliers (which are intended to represent around 80% of the total procurement of large firms). Selected SMEs were contacted by the large firm and EBRD to increase the willingness to provide the required information. Figure 20.3 highlights the details of the methodological approach.

Sector indirect impacts, such as demonstration effects,[24] commercial replicability (e.g. state and subsidies), and more systemic impacts such as

---

[24]Examples of demonstration effects are innovations, adoption of new standards, implementation of human rights policies, and any other good practices involved in introducing new concepts, which are then disseminated in the sector or value chain, resulting in additional impacts on SMEs (financial and socioeconomic).

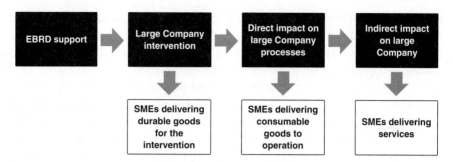

FIGURE 20.3 Methodological Approach: Direct and Indirect Effects of EBRD Support as an Impact Investor or Lender to Large Firms. *Source:* Authors.

investment climate effects and the role of regulations and institutions (e.g. tradable green certificates) are also likely to be produced by EBRD's support as an impact investor. EBRD financing support to large firms, via loans or equity, might also trigger effects such as enhanced market trust, which can spur additional finance from other financial institutions.

To demonstrate that there is impact, the country pilots will collect counterfactual data, mostly through secondary data, and harmonized across the four countries. The following aspects need to be considered: (i) standardization of indicators (secondary data), and (ii) data quality and reliability[25] (data source and methodology). However, it is not guaranteed that robust data sources for all countries and time periods are available. Due to the already identified lack of standardization for several indicators, which are industry and country specific, it was not yet possible at this point of the implementation of the methodology to get hold of all the intended counterfactual data. The selection of indicators for the counterfactual analysis will be attempted again during the country field visits. The availability of counterfactual data is most likely to occur for financial indicators, so these are expected to be more widely used across all

---

[25] In the counterfactual model, a causal factor is a "necessary factor without which the outcome (e.g. treatment success) would not have occurred" (Höfler 2005, p. 3). But that causal factor might not be required to be sufficient for the outcome, and multiple causal factors can be allowed. "For instance, physical diseases and almost all mental disorders are multicausal, resulting from a complex interplay between genetical and environmental factors. Furthermore, a causal effect does not have to be a direct effect. This is desirable because an intervention like drug prescription by a doctor (if the patient complies) often causes an outcome by triggering a whole cascade of consecutive events (of biological, biochemical, mental or social origin), which, in turn, affect the outcome (directly or indirectly)" (Höfler 2005, p. 3).

countries. Socioeconomic, work environment, and qualitative indicators, as described below, have so far not shown to be robust enough for this type of analysis.

Indicator System

Baseline information regarding key stakeholders and the relevant activities will be collected through surveys, namely on EBRD operations (operation leaders, local representatives), client firms (activities and key financials, contacts), and some key supplier SMEs (name and contacts, key financial, socioeconomic, and more qualitative data).

Indicators will be derived from the data collection methods (both primary and secondary data) and categorized along three dimensions, as depicted in Figure 20.4.

Financial performance indicators relate to companies' financial performance metrics, such as costs (e.g. sales per employee), efficiency (e.g. productivity), investments in assets, research and development (R&D), product prices, sales, and profits. These will be derived from companies' financial statements (secondary data, before and after EBRD support) and from the questionnaires deployed for large firm and SMEs (primary data). Financial indicators are calculated based on information retrieved from balance sheets, income statements, and cash flow statements. The intricacy of company performance systems in each country adds complexity to this work. Selected indicators cover dimensions of profitability, balance sheet structure, and liquidity. In order to ensure comparability, indicators will be calculated based on financial reports (balance sheet, profits and loss statements, and cash flow statements).

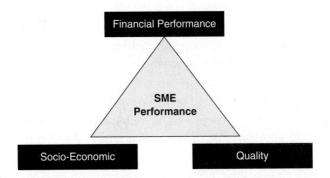

FIGURE 20.4   Categories of Indicators for SME Impact Assessment. *Source:* Authors.

Socioeconomic indicators measure effects on socioeconomic dimensions, such as economic performance, employment (gross and net job creation), working conditions, and salaries. They provide a picture of the investment in human capital and the work climate. The indicators also consider growth and quality of human resources. Data is collected from traditional company reporting instruments.

Quality indicators reflect effects on dimensions such as product standards, staff education, client, or workforce satisfaction. Quality indicators complement the analysis of a company's performance not covered from the financial reporting or the socioeconomic reporting side. Indicators were selected to describe innovation, sustainability, and environmental protection (considering production effects on the environment, such as reductions in pollution emissions, e.g. waste, CO_2), and natural resources depletion. Data collection for these indicators is challenging. Company records concerning the management of waste or identification of measures taken to protect the environment could not so far be found in the record keeping of most SMEs. Despite the fact that to some extent utility bills can provide some raw data, a different path was taken to collect additional data, using a scoring system, as described below.

A Scoring System to Collect Additional Data

A scoring system was introduced to generate additional data, through the quantification of more qualitative type of information. This allows, for instance, the mapping of changes in companies' practices that are not captured through companies' records. These indicators are derived using a set of four questions with dichotomous answers options.[26] An illustration of the concept is shown below, through four questions concerning a company's practices toward waste reduction:

- Question 1: Was waste reduction achieved? Answer options: Yes/No (4 points in case of Yes, 0 otherwise)
- Question 2: Was preparatory work for the waste reduction executed? Answer options: Yes/No (3 points in case of Yes, 0 otherwise)
- Question 3: Do plans for waste reduction exist? Answer options: Yes/No (2 points in case of Yes, 0 otherwise)

---

[26] In order to get a numeric value, the "yes" answer referred to a score of 1. "No" answers options were treated as zero.

- Question 4: Is there a waste reduction concept in place, but not yet implemented? Answer options: Yes/No (1 point in case of Yes, 0 otherwise)

The answer options gradually change from achieved changes (Question 1) to implementation (Question 4). In case a reduction of waste was actually achieved (Question 1), the highest number of points are given: four points. The number of rewarded points goes down by one in the case of a "yes," as questions below portray more actions instead of concrete achievement of results. Thus, a "yes" for Question 4 only yields one point as it refers only to the reduction concept being in place. Thus, the maximum score for all questions sums 10 points (4+3+2+1). If all questions were answered with a "no," the resulting score would be 0. This indicates that no waste reduction was achieved and that there is also no intention to introduce the necessary plans for it.

The information to calculate the indicators for the scoring system is obtained through interviews with SMEs, where these questions are asked. Its accuracy depends on the openness and reliability of the SME interlocutor's knowledge about the subject. The formulation of the questions is intentionally simple, so that answers can be provided quickly, without the need to consult a large number of people dealing with the subject in the company.

Oscillators

The members of a supply chain can belong to a variety of different sectors. In some instances, benchmarking company indicators against each other will not provide meaningful findings (e.g. for a service company the average return on sales differs from a retail chain). This challenge was resolved by introducing oscillators. Oscillators[27] are typically leading indicators[28] whose value indicates the strength of a trend (Naved and Srivastava 2015). In the

---

[27]"Oscillators are widely used as a tool of technical analysis, they are popular mainly because of their leading signal generating ability, being as leading indicators, they don't lag behind the price action. They are most profitable in a sideways market, in contrast to trend following indicator like moving average, which is more profitable in a trending market. Oscillators take the form of lines drawn below the price plot and usually moves in a predefined range" (Naved and Srivastava 2015, p. 925).

[28]Leading indicators anticipate peaks and troughs in the target variable, possibly with a rather constant lead time, have good forecasting properties not only at peaks and troughs, show statistical reliability of data collection (i.e. provide an accurate measure of the quantity of interest), and should be free of major high-frequency movements (Elliott et al. 2006).

case of the present methodology, oscillators are calculated by comparing indicators before and after the EBRD intervention. Using the example from the previous scoring section: the result R of a given company at the time t_1 (before) was three points and at the time t_2 (after) was four. The oscillator is calculated as follows: $Oscillator = \dfrac{Rt2}{Rt1}$.

In the example provided above, the ratio yields 1.333. Results above one show a positive trend, while indicators below one show a negative trend. The oscillators allow a clearer observation of the trend, which was an EBRD requirement for the methodology.

Proposed Indicators

The final set of indicators selected for the EBRD methodology is composed of a mix of quantitative and qualitative indicators. The indicator structure is made up of three sets of thematic indicators: financial, socioeconomic, and qualitative ones:

- Six financial indicators measure the overall financial performance of companies. The indicators are obtained from income statements, balance sheets, and liquidity ratios.
- Three socioeconomic indicators measure changes in the number of staff, salaries, and work environment through human development indexes.
- Six qualitative indicators provide information on quality certifications, rejection rate of goods, patent application field, new product development rate of local purchase, and environment protection.

Financial indicators are described next in Table 20.6.

Three socioeconomic indicators were selected to measure changes in the number of staff, salaries, and work environment through human development indexes, depicted in Table 20.7.

Six qualitative indicators provide information on quality certifications, rejection rate of goods, patent application field, new product development rate of local purchase, and environment protection (Tables 20.8 and 20.9).

TABLE 20.6   Financial Indicators

Sales ratio

Sales (or gross turnover) is an important indicator for the expansion of an SME over time. Moreover, sales are linked to gross production and can be linked to value added (production) in case there is a need to show more meso or macro impacts of EBRD interventions on value added or GDP. The ratio compares the situation of the SME before and after EBRD's intervention.

Earnings before taxes ratio

Earnings before taxes (EBT) is a measure of a company's ability to produce income in a given year. It is calculated as the company's revenue less its expenses (such as overhead), but not subtracting its tax liability. EBT represents profit available to the firm after the payment of interest and before deducting payment of taxes. Thus, it can be calculated by subtracting the interest from the more common measure earnings before interest and taxes (EBIT). The ratio compares the situation of the SME before and after EBRD's intervention.

Earnings before interest, taxes, depreciation, and amortization

Earnings before interest, taxes, depreciation, and amortization (EBITDA) is the net income retained by the firm before deducting taxes, interests, and depreciation. EBIDA shows the company's ability to pay interest and repay its investment. It is calculated by subtracting the interest and depreciation and amortization from EBIT. The ratio compares the situation of the SME before and after EBRD's intervention.

Personnel productivity

This ratio compares total sales to personnel costs and expenses, thus showing the amount of revenue generated per unit of currency spent on personnel. Over time, the ratio can be used as an indicator for changes in the productivity of a company. When the ratio increases, it may indicate a more efficient use of staff or increased automation. The ratio compares the situation of the SME before and after EBRD's intervention.

Free cash flow

The free cash flow (FCF) refers to the available cash for shareholders after all other obligations are accounted for. These net cash flows (when discounted over a number of years) describe the company's potential value for investors and creditors availability for reinvestment of profits, reserves (addition to the balance sheet), or payment of interest or credit redemption. The free cash flow indicator has to be complemented with a narrative section to provide background information about the specific situation of the company. The ratio compares the situation of the SME before and after EBRD's intervention.

Return on total capital

This indicator shows the return on total capital (ROTC), a return on investment ratio that quantifies how much return a company has generated through the use of its capital structure (both total equity and liabilities). In this ratio, taxes and interest expenses are added to net income in order to achieve a better comparability. ROTC gives a fairer assessment of a company's use of funds to finance its projects and functions better as an overall profitability metric. ROTC can be used to evaluate how well a company's management has used its capital structure to generate value for both equity and debt holders. The ratio compares the situation of the SME before and after EBRD's intervention.

Source: Authors.

TABLE 20.7 Social and Work Environment Indicators

Indicator: Total number of staff

This indicator needs to be compared with the "Personnel expenses to operating expenses" ratio. In case of a reduced productivity, clarifications are needed (e.g. if the new staff is in an R&D department a potential impact lag has to be envisaged). The ratio compares the situation of the SME before and after EBRD's intervention.

Indicator: Average salaries

This indicator compares salaries before and after the intervention. Higher salaries may indicate a higher qualification is needed and thus a premium for better qualified employees needs to be paid, but it may also be related to shortages in the labor market. The indicator has to be always interpreted in connection with other indicators, such as productivity and EBT. Generally, higher salaries are a good sign when coupled with higher productivity. Higher salaries have an impact on the local economy, especially in disadvantaged areas.[29] The ratio compares the situation of the SME before and after EBRD's intervention.

Source: Authors.

TABLE 20.8 Qualitative Indicators

Indicator: Quality certifications ratio

Certifications can be mandatory for a new product line or voluntary certifications like Investors in People,[30] and those by the European Foundation for Quality Management (EFQM). It is calculated by assigning a numeric value to a qualitative statement: certifications already obtained before EBRD intervention (one point), certification process intended after EBRD intervention (two points), certification processes started after EBRD intervention (three points) and certification processes finished after EBRD intervention (four points). The ratio compares the situation of the SME before and after EBRD's intervention.

Indicator: Rejection rate of goods

The rejection rate gives a good picture of how production capacity within a company evolves. A lower rejection rate (*ceteris paribus*, that is under the condition that the quality standards have not changed) indicates suppliers improved processes. The ratio compares the situation of the SME before and after EBRD's intervention.

Indicator: Patents applications filed

The amount of patents applications filed provides an indication of the innovation degree of the company. The ratio compares the situation of the SME before and after EBRD's intervention.

---

[29] Salary increases may need to be adjusted by the inflation rate.
[30] A standard for human resource management.

TABLE 20.8   *(continued)*

Indicator: New product development

Combined with patents, the development of new products represents a proxy for innovation. In some instances, new product development cannot be protected via a patent or companies do not want to use patents.[31] Together with the R&D ratio and patent applications, this indicator triangulates information and provides additional evidence as to the innovation abilities of a company. A new product or service as defined by this indicator is one that was not offered by the company previously. The ratio compares the situation of the SME before and after EBRD's intervention.

Indicator: Rate of local purchase

The share of domestic purchases to total purchases of supplies before and after the intervention indicates whether local sourcing increased or not. The downside of this indicator is to obtain an accurate calculation, the total supply chain of the supplier needs to be analyzed.[32] The ratio compares the situation of the SME before and after EBRD's intervention.

Source: Authors.

TABLE 20.9   Environmental Protection Scores.[33]

Indicator: Environmental protection score

Three indicators were developed referring to the reduction of waste, water, and energy consumption. Given the nature of the inquiry and the scarce data available, a set of qualitative answers will be used, and rated as described in the scoring system subsection. For each statement, a numeric value will be assigned and summed up, from 4 to 1. Sums will be calculated before and after EBRD intervention.

Source: Authors.

ASSESSMENT OF RESULTS

Quantification of Impacts

The quantification[34] of outcomes and impacts for large firm and the SMEs in their value chain implies data collection from two structured questionnaires

---

[31] In this case, the firm's motivation is the patent application form they need to file describing the innovation in detail, which may cause counterfeiting by entities that do not take patent protection seriously, or when enforcement measures for patent protection are weak.

[32] As example, if a purchase of 100 bought from a local company was imported by this supplier, the indicator may give an inaccurate picture. Still, despite its limitations, the indicator provides a good estimate of how local sourcing develops.

[33] Please refer to the subsection of the scoring system to understand how it works.

[34] Statistics and quantitative analysis cannot contribute to causal inference unless the factor of interest X and the outcome Y are measurable quantities.

for each firm profile, large and SME. Data will be collected at firm level (for large firms and SMEs) before and after EBRD's support to large companies.

For large firms, collected data will consider the nature of the intervention supported by the EBRD, key results (outputs, outcomes, and impacts of interventions), and key SME suppliers part of the interactions, those which benefited indirectly from the EBRD support in order to minimize the burden for large companies (see Appendix 20.2). Selected SMEs should represent a large proportion of the procurement of the large firm recipient of the EBRD intervention (about 80%).

For selected SMEs in the value chain, a different tailored structured questionnaire will be used.[35] Questions will focus on obtaining the information needed to calculate the financial, socioeconomic, and quality indicators described in the section above, as well as some additional data on the background of SMEs (see Appendix 20.3).

Data—before and after EBRD support—will be used to build a traffic light system to report results compared to the baseline. As regards the counterfactual, controls will be put in place, and questions will be posed to both large firms and SMEs regarding attributability of effects found during the validation stage described below.

The Traffic Light System Explained

In performance reporting, traffic light ratings function visually as an indicator of performance relatively to a goal. Traffic light indicators, also known as "RAG" (red, amber, and green), are commonly used in dashboards and other kinds of performance reporting. They serve to visualize status, report changes, and pinpoint areas where performance is on track and where attention is needed.

Traffic lights are adopted for three related reasons:

- They are easy to recognize. The traffic light symbology can be recognized by every automobile driver globally. Attaching a traffic light system to a performance report instantly indicates that a summary of status is being communicated.
- Traffic lights provide a consolidated view of complex attributes. The traffic light scale is a simple metaphor with three possible indications of overall performance. Even with simple variables such as profit,

---

[35]Surveys will be delivered by local consultants in each country.

client satisfaction, or risk, information is synthesized into a single status, which can be communicated to give a snapshot overview.

- Traffic lights are easy to explain. Once an organization reaches a consensus on the parameters that deem a traffic light indicator red, amber, or green, the rest becomes easy to understand at the naked eye.

Traffic light indicators are part of a family of indicators that can combine indices and scales. Indices are typically used when a single measure or metric does not tell the full story. An index can reflect a composite of measures.[36] Index metrics are averaged together or combined using quantitative methods. The index is then transposed onto a scale, so that it can be harmonized, interpreted, and used.[37]

When measuring the impact of interventions on the supply chain, a traffic light indicator typically reflects a synthesis of many attributes. In its user-friendly version, it uses a simple scale in which red means underperformance; yellow means no major changes, and green means a positive impact.

Traffic Light System Application Within the Methodology

Traffic light system colors are assigned to a Normal Distribution (bell-shaped curve) of a single oscillator. Green is assigned for positive results beyond standard deviation[38] (SD) of one and red for a SD below one (Table 20.10). When plotted against a Normal Distribution, it shows the variance of that particular variable compared to the average.[39] This will depict the different impacts on the whole supply chain.

---

[36]"A composite indicator is formed when individual indicators are compiled into a single index on the basis of an underlying model. "The composite indicator should ideally measure multidimensional concepts which cannot be captured by a single indicator, e.g. competitiveness, industrialization, sustainability, single market integration, knowledge-based society, etc." (OECD and JRC 2008, p. 13).

[37]For example, wind chill is an index that combines temperature and wind speed into a temperature perceived by the skin. Wind chill once calculated is shown on a temperature scale.

[38]The SD measures the difference of each observation from the mean. A sigma (σ) is used in statistics as a representation of an SD. One SD connotes 68% of the observations; two SDs connote 95%; and three SDs connote 99.7%, or nearly all except outliers.

[39]In the case of extreme values, for instance an overall negative impact (e.g. EBT dropped for the whole supply chain), counterfactual data needs to be analyzed in greater detail, to identify confounding effects and external shocks that have might influenced results negatively (e.g. economic crisis or a pandemic).

TABLE 20.10 Interpretation of the Traffic Light System.

Green	SD > 1, points to better developments than those occurring for the average member of the supply chain.
Amber	0 < SD < 1 indicates that some positive changes took place.
Red	Value < 0: indicates negative changes took place (e.g. sales or profitability went down). The cause of these changes will be further investigated to establish its relationship with the support intervention and what impact it may bring about on the company. As an example, a drop in sales turnover may have occurred during EBRD's intervention period but it could be a loss of a client unrelated to EBRD support. External effects need to be appraised and taken on board to circumscribe the judgment to factors related to the intervention.

Source: Authors.

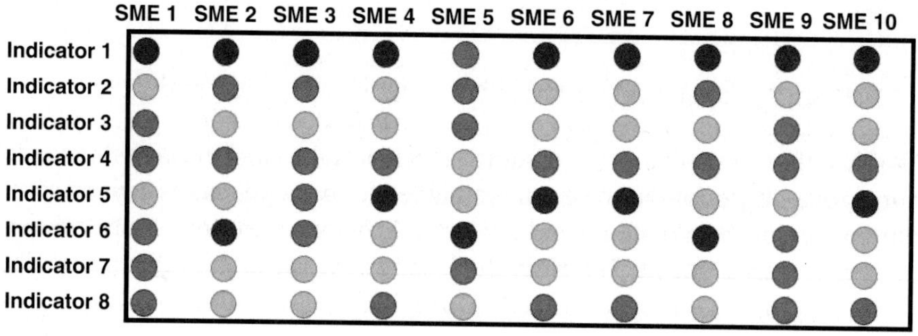

FIGURE 20.5 Traffic Light System. *Source:* Authors.

In addition to the color coding, several dashboards will be developed to report results. Further, for findings that need more in-depth considerations (e.g. cash flows) an accompanying narrative will be provided. A traffic light system table such as that of Figure 20.5 will compare indicators across all SMEs and display them graphically in a single chart.[40]

Validation of Findings with Key Stakeholders and Aggregation of Impacts for SMEs and National Level

A round of data validation is foreseen when presenting preliminary findings (measured impacts) to large firms (EBRD clients) and selected SMEs, to verify

[40]The figure shows the overall concept of how the data will be presented but will be subject to changes and improvements as the methodology is piloted.

whether they regard findings as plausible and make any necessary corrections or further investigate incoherence.

From the subset of SMEs analyzed and the knowledge of the share they represent in the total of large firms' procurement and their supply chain, an estimation of overall impacts for all SMEs, at the supply chain, industry and country level can be calculated. For some indicators (such as sales or employment), total impact for a country might be more easily estimated if data regarding sales, value added, and input-output matrixes are available (to account for backward linkages of the SMEs to their suppliers). The layout for such a macro-level impact assessment is still being refined and will also depend on the data-finding missions in each country.

Following the consultation rounds with firms and any methodological and data adjustments, key results will be shared with EBRD for feedback and comments.

FINAL REMARKS

Following the COVID-19 pandemic in 2019–2020, addressing change is now more than ever an integral part of a company's everyday life. The question to be resolved is how to deal with this volume of change and make transition as smooth as possible, while keeping up profitability. SMEs growth and survival can be threatened if their access to credit is barred. A quick response to evolving markets and SMEs needs is key, and impact investors, MDBs, and development finance institutions (DFIs) can play a key role in addressing market failures in credit and financial markets and responding to moments of crisis.

A recent EBRD report on "Regional Economic Prospects in the EBRD Regions: COVID-19: From Shock to Recovery" (EBRD 2020) reveals that efforts to respond to the pandemic have also created an opportunity to "tilt to green," applying additional pressure on the accelerator toward a low-carbon economy. The report also advises public authorities not to deploy measures hastily in favor of industries based on fossil fuels.[41] Countries where the EBRD traditionally works are not yet very climate change aware, and its firms are unlikely to switch spontaneously to green production habits. But if they face added customer or government pressure, and if careful

---

[41] See Chapter 12, "Fossil-Fuel-Free Investing: Weaving a New Investment Paradigm," by Umachander Balakumar.

policy action and green benefits are designed, firms can not only help speed the recovery of the economy—which will be largely depend on the types and duration of measures to contain the virus—but also convert it into a greener one.

The policy response to the pandemic made governments deploy unprecedented packages of measures to mitigate the economic impact of the containment measures, from liquidity injections to large fiscal packages, to blanket sovereign guarantees on borrowing by SMEs, aimed at preventing the collapse of businesses with viable long-term business models. However, in spite of the increasing importance of supporting SME development and growth, relatively little research exists on whether, why, and how banks, and in particular MDBs and DFIs financing SMEs around the world,[42] go about assessing the impact of their operations on these firms and their value chains.[43] Efforts to collect comprehensive data on SME financing were scaled up in the past within the G-20 framework (Consultative Group to Assist the Poor, 2010), but still remain incipient (e.g. Megersa 2019).

It has already become a good practice for DFIs and MDBs and many private sector lenders to integrate environmental, social, and governance (ESG) considerations into the lending process and to adopt ESG safeguard policies and standards to circumscribe the projects and activities they finance (Wendt 2018). This has been particularly applied to the financing of key infrastructure projects in economies in transition or developing countries (McIntyre 2015). "Lenders such as the EBRD that focus on private sector lending, the performance standards of ESG are imposed upon private corporate entities, against which most requirements of international law could never be formally applied" (Wendt 2018, p. 2).

On the other hand, projects and programs in support of value chains are becoming widespread among impact investors, international institutions, and donors because they offer a practical way of working directly with the private sector. For many development agencies, donors, and governments, supporting VCD has become a principal element of their poverty-reduction strategies. Improved chain relations and overall chain performance are

---

[42]Notable exceptions are Kwakkenbos and Romero (2013); Calice, Chando, and Sekioua (2012); Dalberg (2011); Perry (2011); and Beck, Demirguc-Kunt, and Peria (2008, 2010).
[43]In what concerns impact evaluations of SME programs, notable exceptions are Giorgi and Rahman (2013); López-Acevedo and Tan (2011); Bah, Brada, and Yigit (2011); López-Acevedo and Tinajero (2010); Castillo, Maffioli, Monsalvo, Rojo, and Stucchi (2010); Tan (2009); Tan and Lopez-Acevedo (2005); World Bank (2010); and Oldsman and Hallerg (2004).

expected to yield tangible benefits in terms of economic performance. The potential to include SMEs as active partners in VCD, by providing them with more tailored advice based on greater knowledge gathered by impact assessments along the value chain, offers impact investors, especially those at scale like MDBs and pensions, opportunities for achieving outcomes at greater scale, with increased impact and sustainability.

Impact assessments of SMEs and their supply chains pose several challenges, even for impact investors and MDBs, which stretches beyond time and resources, and often require the ability to access and collect firm-level data, which is often very restricted due to confidentiality issues, especially as most SMEs are private enterprises with no required transparency unless mandated by the leaders, or required by capital providers, or the regulating government and jurisdictions. The increase in ESG metrics across the whole supply chain—upstream and downstream—are gaining interest and momentum among impact investors. In order to establish impacts, more data on business performance is needed, to link different effects from these interventions, from outcomes to impacts, otherwise what is mostly seen are assessments of outputs, based solely on a few opinions obtained from key informant interviews.

A chain is only as strong as its weakest link. Building up data and information systems focused on the underinvested links of the chain and making the findings widely available can help reduce information asymmetries and market failures and support jobs, incomes, communities, and innovations from all parts of the global supply chain, thus contributing to the achievement of SDGs in multiple regions, financed across all asset classes.

DISCLAIMER

The views and findings expressed in this chapter are those of the authors and do not reflect the official position of the EBRD or any other organization. Any errors or omissions are the sole responsibility of the authors.

ACKNOWLEDGMENTS

We would like to thank the EBRD for the opportunity to develop and test this methodology.

REFERENCES

African Development Bank Group (2018). The African Development Bank's Support for Agricultural Value Chains Development: Lessons for the Feed Africa Strategy. Summary Report. December 2017.

Bah, E., Brada, J., and Yigit, T. (2011). With a Little Help from Our Friends: The Effect of USAID Assistance on SME Growth in a Transition Economy. *Journal of Comparative Economics* 39(2): 205–220 (June).

Beck, T., Demirguc-Kunt, A., and Peria, M. M. (2008). Bank Financing for SMEs Around the World: Drivers, Obstacles, Business Models, and Lending Practices. World Bank Policy Research Working Paper 4785. Washington DC: World Bank.

Bella, J. Di, Grant, A., Kindornay, S., et al. (2013). Mapping Private Sector Engagements in Development Cooperation September. Research Report, NSI, North South Institute.

Bronstone, A. (1999). *The European Bank for Reconstruction and Development: The Building of a Bank*. Manchester, UK: Manchester University Press.

Calice, P., Chando, V. M., and Sekioua, S. (2012). Bank Financing to Small and Medium Enterprises in East Africa: Findings of a Survey in Kenya, Tanzania, Uganda, and Zambia. African Development Group Working Paper Series 146 (March).

Castillo, V., Maffioli, A., Monsalvo, A. P., et al. (2010). Can SME Policies Improve Firm Performance? Evidence from an Impact Evaluation in Argentina. Office and Evaluation Oversight Working Paper, OVE/WP-07/10. Inter-American Development Bank.

Chartered Global Management Accountants (CGMA) (2014). Rethinking the value chain: The extended value chain. CGMA Briefing. https://www.cgma .org/content/dam/cgma/resources/reports/downloadabledocuments/the-extended-value-chain.pdf.

Dalberg (2011). Report on Support to SMEs in Developing countries through financial intermediaries. https://www.eib.org/attachments/dalberg_sme-briefing-paper.pdf.

DCED (2001). Business Development Services for Small Enterprises: Guiding Principles for donor intervention. Donor Committee for Enterprise Development (February).

DCED (2017). How donors can make the transition to strategic private sector engagement: Programming innovations and organizational change. DCED Briefing Note (March).

Donovan, J., Franzel, S., Cunha, M., et al. (2015). Guides for a Value Chain Development: A Comparative Review. *Journal of Agribusiness in Developing and Emerging Economies* 5(1): 2–23.

EBRD (1990). Agreement Establishing the European Bank for Reconstruction and Development. Basic Documents of the EBRD. https://www.ebrd.com/news/publications/institutional-documents/basic-documents-of-the-ebrd.html (accessed 20 March 2020).

EBRD (2018). Transition Report 2017–18: Sustaining Growth.

EBRD (2020). Regional Economic Prospects in the EBRD Regions: COVID-19: From shock to recovery. April 2020.

Elliott, G., Granger, C., Timmermann, A. ed. (2006) *Handbook of Economic Forecasting*, vol. 1. University of California, San Diego: Elsevier.

Gibb, H., Foster, J., and Weston, A. (2008). Human Rights and Private Sector Development: A Discussion Paper. Ottawa: North-South Institute.

Giorgi, G., and Rahman, A. (2013). SME Registration Evidence from a Randomized Controlled Trial in Bangladesh. World Bank Policy Research Working Paper 6382 (March).

Heinrich-Fernandes, M. (2017). How donors can make the transition to strategic private sector engagement: Programming innovations and organisational change. DCED Briefing Note (March).

Hernández, V., and Pedersen, T. (2017). Global Value Chain Configuration: A Review and Research Agenda. *BRQ Business Research Quarterly* 20(2): 137–150 (April–June).

Höfler, M. (2005). Causal Inference Based on Counterfactuals. *BMC Medical Research Methodology* 5(28). https://doi.org/10.1186/1471-2288-5-28.

Inomata, S. (2017). Analytical Frameworks for Global Value Chains: An Overview. Global Value Chain Development Report 2017.

Kaplinsky, R., and Morris, M. (2003). *A handbook for value chain research. Brighton. UK.* https://pdfs.semanticscholar.org/f76b/dee3c4c206a7ef5b6eb6b39baef10c1b136d.pdf?_ga=2.264772363.50380683.1596555065-849321471.1596389503.

Kindornay, S., and Reilly-King, F. (2013). Investing in the Business of Development: Bilateral Donor Approaches to Engaging the Private Sector. The North-South Institute and Canadian Council for International Co-operation.

Kurokawa, K., Tembo, F., and te Velde, D. (2008). Donor Support to Private Sector Development in Sub-Saharan Africa: Understanding the Japanese OVOP Program. JICA-ODI Working Paper 290. Overseas Development Institute. London.

Kwakkenbos, J., and Romero, M. J. (2013). Engaging the Private sector for Development: The Role of Development Finance Institutions? In: *ÖFSE (Hg.) Österreichische Entwicklungspolitik, Analysen, Informationen mit dem Schwerpunktthema, Private Sector Development – Ein neuer Businessplan für Entwicklung?* 25–30. Berichte, Wien.

López-Acevedo, G., and Tan, H. W. (2011). *Impact Evaluation of Small and Medium Enterprise Programs in Latin America and the Caribbean*. Washington, DC: World Bank.

López-Acevedo, G., and Tinajero, M. (2010). Mexico: Impact Evaluation of SME Programs Using Panel Firm Data. World Bank Policy Research Working Paper 5186 (January).

Marcato, M., and Baltar, C. T. (2017). Economic and social upgrading in global value chains: concepts and metrics. Texto para Discussão. Unicamp. IE, Campinas, n. 318 (November).

MCC (2015). Policy for Monitoring and Evaluation. Millennium Challenge Corporation. https://www.mcc.gov/resources/doc/policy-for-monitoring-and-evaluation.

McIntyre, O. (2015). Development banking, ESG policies and the normativisation of good governance standards. In K. Wendt (ed.), *Responsible Investment Banking, Risk Management Frameworks, Sustainable Financial Innovation and Softlaw Standards*, pp. 143–157. New York: Springer.

Megersa, K. (2019). Effectiveness of Aid for Trade programs providing market information and advice to businesses. Helpdesk Report. Institute of Development Studies.

Melkeraaen, S. (2009). *Black Economic Empowerment in the South African wine industry: Fair Trade, power relations and socio-economic rights*. Norwegian University of Life Sciences.

Morais Sarmento, E. (2018). Study on Sustainable Value Chains, European Commission.

Naved, M., and Srivastava, P. (2015). Profitability of Oscillators Used in Technical Analysis for Financial Market. *Advances in Economics and Business Management* (AEBM) 2(9): 925–931 (April–June).

Nelson, V., Martin, A., Ewert, A., et al. (2016). Mid-Term evaluation of the Trade in Global Value Chains Initiative (TGVCI). Evaluation Management Unit Natural Resources Institute, University of Greenwich.

OECD (2013a). Interconnected Economies: Benefiting from Global Value Chains – Synthesis Report. Paris. DOI: 10.1787/9789264189560-en.

OECD (2013b). Interconnected Economies: Benefiting from Global Value Chains – Synthesis Report. Paris. DOI: 10.1787/9789264189560-en.

OECD (2014). Policy Brief, Trade in Value Added. Paris. https://www.oecd.org/corporate/PB-Trade-In-Value-Added-Mar-2014.pdf.

OECD (2018). Participation and Benefits of SMEs in GVCs in Southeast Asia. Progress report. Working Party of the Trade Committee, Trade and Agriculture Directorate (18–19 June), OECD Conference Centre. Paris. TAD/TC/WP (2018)9.

OECD and WTO (2013). Aid for Trade at a glance 2013: Connecting to value chains. https://www.wto.org/english/res_e/booksp_e/aid4trade13_e.pdf.

OECD and JRC (2008). *Handbook on constructing composite indicators: Methodology and user guide*. JRC, European Commission. https://www.oecd.org/els/soc/handbookonconstructingcompositeindicatorsmethodologyanduserguide.htm (accessed 12 May 2020).

Oldsman, E., and Hallerg, K. (2004). Evaluating Business Assistance Programs. In *Evaluating Local Economic and Employment Development, How To Assess What Works Among Programs and Policies*, pp. 229–250. OECD, Paris.

Perry, G. (2011). Growing Business or Development Priority? Multilateral Development Banks' Direct Support to Private Firms. Center for Global Development (April).

Porter, M. (1985). *The Value Chain and Competitive Advantage*. Free Press, New York.

Satoshi, I. (2017). Analytical Frameworks for Global Value Chains: An Overview, Global Value Chain Development Report 2017.

Schneemann, J., and Vredeveld, T. (2015). Guidelines for Value Chain selection, Integrating economic, environmental, social, and institutional criteria. Deutsche Gesellschaft für Internationale Zusammenarbeit (GIZ) GmbH on behalf of the German Federal Ministry for Economic Cooperation and Development, International Labor Organization.

Staritz, C. (2012). Value Chains for Development? Potentials and limitations of Global Value Chain approaches in Donor interventions. Working Paper 31. Austrian Research Foundation for International Development.

Staritz, C., and Reis, Guilherme J. G. (eds.) (2013). *Global Value Chains, Economic Upgrading, and Gender, Case Studies of the Horticulture, Tourism, and Call Center Industries*. World Bank.

Tan, H. W. (2009). Evaluating SME Support Programs in Chile using Panel Firm Data. Policy Research Working Paper 5082, Impact Evaluation Series 39.

Tan, H. W., and López-Acevedo, G. (2005). Evaluating Training Programs for Small and Medium Enterprises: Lessons from Mexico. World Bank Policy Research Working Paper 3760 (November).

Todeva, E., and Rakhmatullin, R. (2016). Industry Global Value Chains, Connectivity and Regional Smart Specialization in Europe. An Overview of Theoretical Approaches and Mapping Methodologies. JRC Science for Policy Report, European Union.

United Nations Economic and Social Commission for Asia and the Pacific (2015). Global value chains, regional integration and sustainable development: linkages and policy implications. Seventy-first session Bangkok, 25–29 May.

USAID (2010). Implementation best practices for value-chain development projects. Washington, DC. https://www.marketlinks.org/sites/marketlinks .org/files/resource/files/Implementation_Best_Practices_VC_Projects.pdf.

Wendt, K., ed. (2018). *Positive Impact investing: A Sustainable Bridge Between Strategy, Innovation, Change and Learning.* Springer. https://doi.org/10 .1007/978-3-319-10118-7.

World Bank (2010). WBRD Financial Sector Strategy - Dealing with the Legacy of the Crisis and Supporting the Development of Sustainable Financing of the Real Economy in EBRD Countries of Operations (12 October).

APPENDIX 20.1:   DETAILS ON INDICATORS USED

Financial indicators

Indicator: Sales Ratio	
Formula	Description
Sales (or gross turnover) is an important indicator for the expansion of an SME over time. Moreover, sales are linked to gross production and can be linked to value added (production) in case there is a need to show more meso or macro impacts of EBRD interventions on value added or GDP. The ratio compares the situation of the SME before and after EBRD's intervention. Source: Income statement Input: Sales from income statements	$\dfrac{\text{Gross sales of SME after EBRD intervention}}{\text{Gross sales of SME before EBRD intervention}}$ Values: Absolute number in local currency Interpretation: Values >1 indicate a positive impact

Indicator: Earnings before taxes ratio

Earnings before taxes (EBT) is a measure of a company's ability to produce income in a given year. It is calculated as the company's revenue less its expenses (such as overhead), but not subtracting its tax liability. EBT represents profit available to the firm after the payment of interest and before deducting payment of taxes. Thus, it can be calculated by subtracting the interest from the more common measure of earnings before interest and taxes (EBIT). The ratio compares the situation of the SME before and after EBRD's intervention.

Source: Income statement

Input: EBT from income statements

$$\frac{\text{EBT after EBRD intervention}}{\text{EBT before EBRD intervention}}$$

Values: Absolute number in local currency

Interpretation: Values >1 indicate a positive impact

Indicator: Earnings before interest, taxes, depreciation, and amortization (EBITDA)

Earnings before interest, taxes, depreciation, and amortization (EBITDA) is the revenue retained by the firm before deducting taxes, interests, and depreciation. EBIDA shows the company's ability to pay interest and repay its investment. It is calculated by subtracting the interest and depreciation and amortization from EBIT. The ratio compares the situation of the SME before and after EBRD's intervention.

Source: Income statement

Input: EBT from income statements

$$\frac{\text{EBITDA after EBRD intervention}}{\text{EBITDA before EBRD intervention}}$$

Values: Absolute number in local currency

Interpretation: Values >1 indicate a positive impact

Indicator: Personnel productivity

This ratio compares total sales to personnel costs and expenses, thus showing the amount of revenue generated per unit of currency spent on personnel. Over time, the ratio can be used as an indicator for changes in the productivity of a company. When the ratio increases, it may indicate a more efficient use of staff or increased automation. The ratio compares the situation of the SME before and after EBRD's intervention.

Source: Balance sheets, profit and loss statements

Input: Personnel expense, total operating expenses

$$\frac{\text{Sales}}{\text{Personnel expenses}} \times 100 \text{ after EBRD intervention}$$

$$\frac{\text{Sales}}{\text{Personnel expenses}} \times 100 \text{ before EBRD intervention}$$

Value: Ratio

Interpretation: Values >1 indicate a positive impact

Indicator: Free cash flow

The free cash flow refers to the available cash for investors after accounting for all other expenses. These net cash flows (when discounted over a number of years) describe the company's potential value for investors and creditors availability for reinvestment of profits, reserves (addition to the balance sheet), or payment of interest or credit redemption. The free cash flow indicator has to be complemented with a narrative section to provide background information about the specific situation of the company. The ratio compares the situation of the SME before and after EBRD's intervention.

Source: Balance sheet, profit and loss statement

Input: Cash flow from operating activities, CAPEX net

Cashflow from Operating activities after EBRD intervention
−CapEx net after EBRD intervention
= Net cashflow after EBRD intervention

Cashflow from Operating activities before EBRD intervention
−Capex net before EBRD intervention
= Net cashflow before EBRD intervention

Value: Absolute number in local currency

Interpretation: Values >1 indicate a positive impact

Indicator: Return on total capital (ROTC)

This indicator shows the return on total capital (ROTC), a return on investment ratio that quantifies how much return a company has generated through the use of its capital structure (both total equity and liabilities). In this ratio, taxes and interest expenses are added to net income in order to achieve a better comparability. ROTC gives a fairer assessment of a company's use of funds to finance its projects, and functions better as an overall profitability metric. ROTC can be used to evaluate how well a company's management has used its capital structure to generate value for both equity and debt holders. The ratio compares the situation of the SME before and after EBRD's intervention.

Source: Balance sheet, profit and loss statement

Input: Cash flows from operating activities, net Capital Expenditures (CapEx)

$$\frac{\text{Net income+income tax+interest expenditure}}{\text{Total liabilities and shareholder equity}} \text{ x 100 after EBRD intervention}$$

$$\frac{\text{Net income+income tax+interest expenditure}}{\text{Total liabilities and shareholder equity}} \text{ x 100 before EBRD intervention}$$

Value: Absolute number in local currency

Interpretation: Values >1 indicate a positive impact

Source: Authors.

Social and work environment indicators

Indicator: Total number of staff

This indicator needs to be compared with the "personnel expenses to operating expenses" ratio. In case of a reduced productivity, clarifications are needed (e.g. if the new staff is in an R&D department a potential impact lag has to be envisaged). The ratio compares the situation of the SME before and after EBRD's intervention.

Source: Company records

Input: People employed

Stafff change ratio =

$$= \frac{N^o \text{.staff after intervention}}{N^o \text{ staff before intervention}}$$

Value: Ratio

Interpretation: Values >1 indicate that the number of staff increased

---

Indicator: Average salaries

This indicator compares salaries before and after the intervention. Higher salaries may indicate a higher qualification is needed and thus a premium for better qualified employees needs to be paid, but it may also be related to shortages in the labor market. The indicator has to be always interpreted in connection with other indicators, such as productivity and EBT. Generally, higher salaries are a good sign when coupled with higher productivity. Higher salaries have an impact on the local economy, especially in disadvantaged areas.[44] The ratio compares the situation of the SME before and after EBRD's intervention.
Source: Company records
Input: Salaries

$$\frac{\text{Median of Salaries after intervention}}{\text{Median of Salaries before intervention}}$$

Value: Ratio
Interpretation: Values >1 indicate that salaries increased

Source: Authors.

Qualitative indicators

Indicator: Quality certifications ratio

Certifications can be mandatory for a new product line or voluntary certifications like inter alia, Investors in People,[45] and those by the European Foundation for Quality Management (EFQM). It is calculated by assigning a numeric value to a qualitative statement: certifications

Number of certifications before EBRD intervention (one point) + number of certification process intended after EBRD intervention (two points) + number of certification process started after EBRD intervention (three points)

---

[44]Salary increase needs to be corrected by the inflation rate.
[45]A standard for human resource management.

already obtained before EBRD intervention (one point), certification process intended after EBRD intervention (two points), certification processes started after EBRD intervention (three points), and certification processes finished after EBRD intervention (four points). The ratio compares the situation of the SME before and after EBRD's intervention.

+ number of certification process finished after EBRD intervention (four points)

Number of certifications before EBRD intervention (one point)

+ number of certification process intended before EBRD intervention (two points)

+ number of certification process started before EBRD intervention (three points)

+ number of certification process finished before EBRD intervention (four points)

Value: Ratio

Interpretation: Values >1 indicate that quality improvement measures were adopted.

Source: Company records, Interviews
Input: Company documents, Questionnaires

Indicator: Rejection rate of goods

The rejections rate gives a good picture of how production capacity within a company evolves. A lower rejection rate (*ceteris paribus*, that is under the condition that the quality standards have not changed) indicates suppliers improved processes. The ratio compares the situation of the SME before and after EBRD's intervention.

Source: Company records, interviews
Input: Company documents, questionnaires

$$\frac{\%\text{of rejected supply after EBRD intervention}}{\%\text{of rejected supply before EBRD intervention}}$$

Value: Ratio

Interpretation: Values >1 indicate that the quality of delivery has improved

Indicator: Patents applications filed

The amount of patents applications filed provides an indication of the innovation degree of the company. The ratio compares the situation of the SME before and after EBRD's intervention.

$$\frac{N° \text{ of patents after EBRD intervention}}{N° \text{ of patents before EBRD intervention}}$$

Value: Ratio

Interpretation: Values >1 indicate more patents compared to situation before EBRD's intervention

Source: Company records

Input: Patents applications filed in

Indicator: New product development

Combined with patents, the development of new products represents a proxy for innovation. In some instances, new product development cannot be protected via a patent or companies do not want to use patents.[46] Together with the R&D ratio and patent applications, this indicator triangulates information and provides additional evidence as to the innovation abilities of a company. A new product or service as defined by this indicator is one that was not offered by the company previously. The ratio compares the situation of the SME before and after EBRD's intervention.

New products development ratio =

$$\frac{\text{New products developed after EBRD intervention}}{\text{New products developed before EBRD intervention}}$$

Value: Ratio

Interpretation: Values >1 product development increased compared to situation before EBRD intervention

Source: Company records

Input: Products developed

---

[46]In this case, a firm's motivation is that in the patent application form they need to describe the innovation quite in detail—it may cause counterfeiting by entities that do not take patent protection seriously or when enforcement measures for patent protection are weak.

Indicator: Rate of local purchase

The share of domestic purchases to total purchases of supplies before and after the intervention indicates whether local sourcing increased or not. The downside of this indicator is to obtain an accurate calculation, the total supply chain of the supplier needs to be analyzed.[47] The ratio compares the situation of the SME before and after EBRD's intervention. Source: Company records Input: Supplier data	$\dfrac{\%\text{domestic supplies to total supplies after EBRD intervention}}{\%\text{domestic supplies to total supplies before EBRD intervention}}$ Value: Ratio Interpretation: Values >1 indicate an increase of local sourcing

Source: Authors.

Environmental protection scores[48]

Indicator: Environmental protection score

These three indicators refer to the reduction of waste, water, and energy consumption. Given the nature of the inquiry and the scarce data available, a set of qualitative answers will be used, and rated as described in the scoring system sub-section. For each statement, a numeric value will be assigned and summed up, from 4 to 1. Sums will be calculated before and after EBRD intervention. Source: Company records, interview Input: Company documents, questionnaires	Value: Ratio based on scores Interpretation: Values >1 indicate increased efforts in environment protection

[47] As example, if a purchase of 100 bought from a local company was imported by this supplier, the indicator may give an inaccurate picture. Still, despite its limitations, the indicator provides a good estimate of how local sourcing develops.

[48] Please refer to the subsection of the scoring system to understand how it works.

Waste Reduction[49]

Reduction of waste executed after EBRD intervention (4 points) +

+ Preparation for waste reduction executed in the last reporting period (concrete measures like installations of waste separation, bought but not yet operational after EBRD intervention (3 points) +

+ Plans for waste reduction made after EBRD intervention (2 points) +

+ Waste, consumption reduction concepts in place, but no changes after EBRD intervention (1 point)

Water preservation[50]

Water preservation measures were executed after EBRD intervention (4 points)

+ Preparation of water preservation was executed in in the last reporting period (concrete measures like reduction of water usage, recycling systems bought but not yet operational) after EBRD intervention (3 points)

+ Plans of water preservation were made after EBRD intervention (2 points)

+ water preservation concept in place, but no changes after EBRD intervention (1 point)

Water preservation measures were executed before EBRD intervention (4 points)

+ Preparation for water preservation was executed in the last reporting period (concrete measures like reduction of water usage, recycling systems bought but not yet operational before EBRD intervention) (3 points)

+ Plans for water preservation were made before EBRD intervention (2 points)

+ water preservation concept in place, but no changes before EBRD intervention (1 point)

---

[49] Below a ratio is presented.
[50] Below a ratio is presented.

Energy conservation[51]

Energy conservation measures were executed after EBRD intervention (4 points)

+ Preparation for Energy conservation measures were started in the last reporting period but not yet operational after EBRD intervention (3 points)

+ Plans for Energy conservation measures were made after EBRD intervention (2 points)

+ Energy conservation measures concept in place, but no changes after EBRD intervention (1 point)

Energy conservation measures were executed after EBRD intervention (4 points)

+ Preparation for Energy conservation measures were started in the last reporting period but not yet operational after EBRD intervention (3 points)

+ Plans for Energy conservation measures were made after EBRD intervention (2 points)

+ Energy conservation measures concept in place, but no changes after EBRD intervention (1 point)

Source: Authors.

APPENDIX 20.2:   IMPACT ASSESSMENT DRAFT QUESTIONNAIRE FOR LARGE FIRMS

Company General information

---

1. Company name:

2. Sector:

□ Trade □ Production □ Service (NACE code: _____)

3. For how many years does the company exist?

□ Less the 5 years □ 5 to 10 years □ More than 10 years

4. Ownership

□ Local, with a foreign minority shareholder

□ Foreign owned □ Subsidiary of a multinational company

□ Privately owned (no shares held by state) □ Publicly owned, listed

□ State-owned

---

[51] Below a ratio is presented.

Information on EBRD Transaction

5. When was the transaction closed?

(date)

6. Has the CAPEX started before the EBRD loan commitment?

□ No

□ Yes, _____ month(s) before

7. How many tranches were foreseen and disbursed?

	Date of disbursement (past and future)	Amount in local currency
1st Tranche		
2nd Tranche		
3rd Tranche		

8. Was any other type of support provided by EBRD? *(please select one option only)*

□ No

□ Yes, attended EBRD-sponsored event/conference/study tour

□ Yes, received training sponsored by EBRD

□ Yes, received EBRD grant

□ Yes, received assistance by a consultant hired by or co-funded by EBRD

□ Yes, received technical assistance by EBRD in assessing performance and drafting an action plan

(e.g., corporate governance, energy efficiency, inclusion policies)

9. The purpose the loan is to: *(please select one option only)*

□ Restructure existing debt	
Invest in existing facility to:	□ increase capacity of existing production line
	□ introduce a new product line
Open a new branch/production facility to:	□ increase capacity of existing production line
	□ introduce a new product line

10. What is the share of EBRD in the total investment (%)?

%

11. Were there any other financial institutions involved? *(please list institutions and amount)*

Institution	Amount (in local currency)

12. Was the investment supported by Grants? *(please select one option only)*

□ Yes	*(indicate amount in local currency)*
□ No	

13. Are investment activities completed? *(please select one option only)*

□ Yes	
□ No	*(indicate expected completion date)*

Suppliers Information

14. Please provide a contact list of your local suppliers, if possible disaggregated by durable, supply and service, and amount of purchase

(name of suppliers)	*(contact)*
(name of suppliers)	*(contact)*

15. Share of domestically sourced inputs/raw materials (% of COGS divided by value of inputs)

1. _____ (… %)
2. _____ (… %)
3. _____ (… %)

16. Total number of local suppliers

17. Do you have a supplier development program?

☐ Yes ☐ No

18. In case the previous answer is yes, please describe the nature of the program.

19. What share of local suppliers participate in the program?

inputs

Value before EBRD loan Year 20xx[52]	Value after EBRD loan Year 20xx[53]
. . . .%	. . . .%

Company information

	Value before EBRD loan Year 20xx[54]	Value after EBRD loan Year 20xx[55]
20. Sales turnover *(in local currency)*		
21. Number of staff *(full time/part time)*		
22. EBITDA *(in local currency)*		
23. EBT *(in local currency)*		

---

[52]Local consultants will adapt questionnaires to each case study, specifying the year of EBRD intervention.

[53]Local consultants will adapt questionnaires to each case study, specifying the year of EBRD intervention.

[54]Local consultants will adapt questionnaires to each case study, specifying the year of EBRD intervention.

[55]Local consultants will adapt questionnaires to each case study, specifying the year of EBRD intervention.

<u>Estimation of economic conditions</u>

24. How would you rate the development of your company during the last 12 months? *(please select one option only)*

25. How would you rate the development of the domestic economic situation during the last 12 months? *(please select one option only)*

26. Do you plan to expand your business during the next two years?
(please select one option only)

☐ No
☐ Yes, by increasing production
☐ Yes, by opening new branch(es)
☐ Yes, by introducing a new service/product
☐ Yes, by starting to export to new markets
☐ Other: _____
☐ Don't know

27. How do you rate the outlook for the domestic economy for next year? *(please select one option only)*

Very bad   Bad   No changes   Good   Very good
(1) ———— (2) ———— (3) ———— (4) ———— (5)

28. Can your company get loans under acceptable financial conditions?

(please select one option only)

☐ No

☐ Yes

☐ Yes, but might be difficult.

APPENDIX 20.3:   IMPACT ASSESSMENT DRAFT QUESTIONNAIRE FOR SMES

General

---

1. Company name:

---

2. Sector:

☐ Trade ☐ Production ☐ Service (NACE code: _____)

---

3. For how many years does the company exist?

☐ Less the 5 years ☐ 5 to 10 years ☐ More than 10 years

---

4. Ownership

☐ Local ☐ Local, with a foreign minority shareholder

☐ Foreign owned ☐ Subsidiary of a multinational company

☐ Privately owned (no shares held by state) ☐ Publicly owned, listed

☐ State-owned

Estimation of economic conditions

5. How would you rate the development of your company during the last three months? *(please select one option only)*

Not satisfied	Little satisfied	Somewhat satisfied	Satisfied	Very Satisfied
①	②	③	④	⑤

6. How would you rate the development of the domestic economic situation during the last 12 months? *(please select one option only)*

Not satisfied	Little satisfied	Somewhat satisfied	Satisfied	Very Satisfied
①	②	③	④	⑤

7. Do you plan to expand your business during the next two years? *(please select one option only)*

 ☐ No
 ☐ Yes, by increasing production
 ☐ Yes, by opening new branch(es)
 ☐ Yes, by introducing a new service / product
 ☐ Yes, by starting to export
 ☐ Other: _____
 ☐ Don't know

8. If the answer to Question 7 is "Yes," do you need a loan to realize this expansion?

☐ Yes ☐ No

9. If the answer to Question 8 is "Yes," were you able to get a loan in the past 12 months?

☐ Yes ☐ No

10. If the answer to Question 9 is "No," what are the reasons? *(Multiple answers possible)*

☐ Interest rates were not suitable ☐ Insufficient collateral
☐ Financial ratios were not good enough ☐ Loan application process too complicated
☐ Equity was too low ☐ Other, please describe _____

11. How long have you been working with *(name of the client)*?

_____ years

12. What kind of goods/services are you providing to (*name of the client*)?

13. Have you ever worked with the EBRD before (e.g. loan/advisory/training/TC/ASB, etc.)?

□ Yes □ No

14. Financial information in domestic currency:

	One year before EBRD intervention	Year of EBRD intervention	One year after EBRD intervention
Gross sales turnover			
Net sales			
Net Sales to gross sales turnover (excluding VAT)			
Foreign sales (if known) as % of total sales			
Personnel expenditures			
Number of staff (full-time, and part-time)			
Training expenditures			
Number of people trained			
EBITDA			
EBT			
Interest expenditure			
Income tax paid			
Net income			
Total equity			
Total liabilities			
Shareholder equity			
Non-current provisions			
Interest-bearing debts			
Cash flow from operating expenditures			
Net CapEx			

---

[56]Local consultants will adapt questionnaires to each case study, specifying the year of EBRD intervention.

15. Specific business information

	One year before EBRD intervention	Year of EBRD intervention	One year after EBRD intervention
In case of an increased demand of goods/services from company (name of the client), has it caused cash flow problems?	☐ Yes ☐ No	☐ Yes ☐ No	☐ Yes ☐ No
What is the share of rejection of all goods due to defects or other quality reasons (%)?			
Production bought by company (name of the client) (in local currency/EUR) and share (%)			
Number of new products developed			
Number of patents filed			
Share of domestically sourced inputs / raw materials (% of name of the client)			
Share of export (% of sales turnover)			
Total number of certifications held			
Number of certifications your company intends to acquire			
Number of certifications the acquisition process for which has started			
Number of certifications acquired in the relevant year			

	One year before EBRD intervention	Year of EBRD intervention	One year after EBRD intervention
Waste reduction measures were executed			
Preparation of waste reduction measures done but not yet operational			
Plans for waste reduction were made			
Waste reduction concept already in place			
Water preservation measures were executed			
Preparation of water preservation measures done but not yet operational			
Plans for water preservation were made			
Water preservation concept already in place			
Energy conservation measures were executed			
Preparation of energy conservation measures done but not yet operational			
Plans for energy conservation were made			
Energy conservation concept already in place			

[57]Local consultants will adapt questionnaires to each case study, specifying the year of EBRD intervention.

CHAPTER 21

Two Decades of Front-Line Impact Investing

Jean-Philippe de Schrevel, MBA

Abstract

Impact investing pioneer Jean-Philippe de Schrevel, the founder and managing partner of Bamboo Capital Partners, recounts lessons from his two decades of investing in emerging and frontier markets. He provides insight into the five pillars of impact investing best practice, imparting wisdom from his years of experience in the field. Jean-Philippe outlines the importance of investing in leaders with a capacity and willingness to execute on their vision, and not those held hostage by their own ego and pride. He examines the necessity of grounding each investment in a theory of change, which must be measured rigorously to avoid green-washing. He then considers the use of different types of capital in certain markets and looks at how partnerships are crucial for scale and advancing an entrepreneur's vision at a faster rate. Finally, Jean-Philippe provides his insight into the role of technology as a critical success factor for Impact Investing and its potential in providing communities with access to affordable goods and services, leapfrogging years of development in the process.

Keywords

Impact Investing; Theory of Change; Blended Finance; Greenwashing; Partnerships; Technology

INTRODUCTION

I created BlueOrchard Finance in 2001 and Bamboo Capital Partners in 2007 with one intention: to demonstrate that you can invest profitably in companies delivering basic products and services to low-income populations in frontier and emerging markets.

Why? Firstly, because our world is confronted with major challenges, such as poverty and climate change. And secondly, it is now widely accepted that the traditional way of public aid and private charity will fall considerably short in addressing these issues. In short, there's a need for an alternative way of raising capital and investing in order to drive change.

As a result, organizations that have historically been involved in public aid and private charity are now starting to evolve their propositions. Large non-governmental organizations are beginning to embrace Impact Investing, whereas in the past, they typically devoted their resources to grants. Similarly, governments are starting to partner with private organizations, while institutions like the Red Cross, one of the largest humanitarian organizations in the world, are now looking at the prospect of social bonds (International Committee of the Red Cross 2017).

This is not a complete departure from traditional philanthropy, but an acknowledgment that it is not the only weapon in the arsenal that can confront major global challenges. Large foundations, non-governmental organizations, and governments would not have envisaged using private capital—both debt and equity—to solve problems previously addressed with philanthropic capital 10 years ago.

However, if we are to succeed in addressing these challenges at scale, massive amounts of private capital will have to be invested in sustainable, profitable, and scalable businesses offering solutions to specific problems. This is not to say that philanthropy is useless and that every problem can be tackled by the market and private enterprise. Charity should increase, but it should also become more efficient and targeted at what the market cannot by itself achieve.

The market cannot solve all the world's problems. Furthermore, there are some domains which are not entirely appropriate for private enterprises, such as early education, care services, public goods, and social services in communities. Often, these communities are living in extreme poverty and cannot be helped by market-based solutions. People within these communities live on less than US $1 per day and struggle to survive. They deserve to be fed and have access to health care, but it cannot be provided for them on a cost basis because they cannot afford it. This is the sweet spot for charity and philanthropy. It would almost be irresponsible if the market began to invest in these areas.

It is equally important to recognize that for demographics living outside of extreme poverty, where a market-based approach can be deployed, the populace can pay for its services. This allows charity and philanthropy to focus on the demographics that need it the most, while private sector solutions can be embedded in markets where they previously might not have existed.

The conclusion that should be drawn from this is that private sector capital must be geared up to take over where charity and philanthropy should not operate, or where it cannot be fast-tracked. Philanthropic capital can also be used as a fantastic catalyst for private investment intentionally seeking to generate social and environmental positive impact together with sound financial returns.

It is this philosophy and approach that has underpinned my work over the last two decades, where I have traveled throughout emerging markets and launched different impact investment products and funds.

Along the way, my experience in the sector has led me to devise five pillars of impact investing best practice:

1. Investment firms must first and foremost invest in leaders who have the capacity and willingness to execute on their vision.
2. Each investment must be grounded in a sound theory of change, which must be measured rigorously to avoid "greenwashing" or "social washing."
3. There is a place for each type of capital and there is a need to recognize that using inappropriate sources of capital can spoil a market and potentially kill a company, which is also known as absorptive capital.
4. Partnerships are crucial for scale and help an entrepreneur advance the impact they have on the ground at a much faster rate.

5. The use of technology is a critical success factor and provides communities with access to affordable goods and services, sometimes leapfrogging years of development.

Over the course of this chapter, I will explain each pillar of Impact Investing best practice and provide real-world examples to demonstrate how these principles work in practice.

FIVE PILLARS OF IMPACT INVESTING BEST PRACTICE

Invest in True Leaders

The first pillar of Impact Investing best practice and an extremely important consideration for all fund managers is the need to invest in portfolio companies that are led by true leaders.

Too often, enterprises created with a social purpose in mind are built around charismatic leaders who excel at inspiring people around them but who unfortunately turn out in many cases to be very poor managers. They are usually incapable of building a management team or delegating management to a team of experts. Pride often stands in their way; ego is their worst enemy.

Companies often fail because their founder was unable to realize that they should let other people execute their vision. Such founders will then justify their failure by stating that they did not want to compromise on their mission, and that, after all, they were pursuing social goals and were not primarily driven by profit. However, this is too often only a poor excuse for bad management practices, such as delaying tough cost adjustment measures, looking for scale and a larger footprint while disregarding unit profitability, or poor communication with company directors or shareholders.

Leaders often emerge from associations or not-for-profit organizations that they created and guided, sometimes over decades, toward more sustainable market-based approaches. This is their merit and they should be celebrated for their accomplishments. However, their downfall is their inability to let go when their mission is accomplished for fear of losing status in the industry. The consequence is that they then become the very obstacle to the growth of what they originally set out to develop.

To provide an example, in 2008, a chief executive and the senior managers of a non-governmental organization had founded a microfinance company but did not have enough capital to maintain control and scale it. Therefore, they decided to enter a joint venture (JV) with an impact investor. The JV would maintain control of the company, while the founders and social entrepreneurs would lead the company, but they now had the resources to take the company to the next level. However, the impact investor had the requirement to sell their stake in the portfolio company. As part of the joint venture, they agreed to sell their stake in the bank in 10 years' time.

However, 10 years later, the social entrepreneurs reneged on their promise. They no longer wanted to sell their stake because they wanted to maintain control over the company, which had become very profitable. This was in spite of the fact that by selling their stake in the bank branches, they would have allowed it to scale up and a new buyer would have taken it to the next level to achieve a greater impact than originally planned. This is one inherent risk with Impact Investing—if a social entrepreneur is overcome with pride or ego, the investor will be held hostage if it has a minority shareholding position with no viable exit, with the negative fallout from deteriorating relationships between investors and management.

There are ways that investors can overcome this issue. At the very start, they need to have a very honest and frank conversation with the entrepreneur. The attention should be on them, but they should be reminded that it will be a wider team that executes on their vision and generates the desired impact.

There are alternative options for the entrepreneur—they could move onto the board of directors or shift to an adviser capacity. They need to be convinced that greater impact will be achieved by a wider team—not just their efforts to execute on their vision. They need to feel loved, but underneath everything, there needs to be a transition plan that can be put in place if they begin to waver from their original mission.

The purpose of Impact Investing is to create solid companies that will generate lasting and growing social, environmental, and financial returns. A careful assessment of the capacity and willingness of the entrepreneurs to execute on their vision is probably the single most important condition for success.

A Theory of Change

When an entrepreneur launches a business to meet a need in the market and generate profits, they develop a product or service and write a business plan to achieve its objectives. An impact investor is no different.

A theory of change is essential, and it is driven by an impact investor's cause—the thing they are trying to change. Their investments in a company will benefit this cause, but also contribute a financial return to their portfolio.

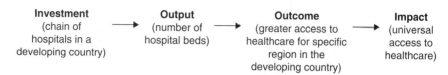

FIGURE 21.1   Impact Investing Theory of Change. *Source*: Author.

For example, the cause could be climate change. Therefore, investing in the distribution of solar energy solutions for off-grid markets will contribute to the cause by removing the need to cut trees or burn diesel.

To measure the impact of their investments against their cause, an impact investor needs to track the outputs. For example, an impact investor's cause might be universal access to health care. Therefore, to support their cause, they invest in a chain of hospitals in developing countries. The output they would measure would be the increased number of hospital beds in the specific region or country of investment.

Investment outputs are mapped against contributions to an impact investor's cause—known as outcomes, which underline the overall theory of change. For example, by increasing the number of hospital beds in a specific region, the outcome would be greater access to health care for communities in that region. This in turn supports the impact investor's original cause of universal access to health care. An impact investor's theory of change is represented visually by Figure 21.1.

An example of an impact investor's theory of change can be analyzed through one of Bamboo Capital Partners' portfolio companies, BBOXX. BBOXX is a next-generation utility that provides pay-as-you-go solar home systems to rural communities, predominantly in Sub-Saharan Africa. The solar home systems include solar panels supplied with batteries to store electricity, which is payable with mobile money. The systems enable households to power domestic appliances, such as TVs and radios (BBOXX 2020).

An investor whose primary causes are to reduce climate change and infant mortality might invest in BBOXX. In Sub-Saharan Africa, one of the primary causes of infant mortality and a significant contributor to CO_2 pollution is cooking inside huts and houses using polluting sources of energy such as kerosene. In 2016, household air pollution was responsible for 7.7% of global mortality (World Health Organization 2016). However, by using one of BBOXX's solar home systems, the polluting sources of energy are replaced with a clean source of energy. In this instance, the outputs measured would include number of households electrified and number of solar panels deployed. The outcome would be a reduction in pollutants and the impact a lower infant mortality rate, which support the investor's causes.

Cynics sometimes mock Impact Investing by arguing that every action in life is impactful in some shape or form. But it is the intentionality of investments and the anchoring of them in a well-established theory of change, where the flow of results is depicted logically, that sets true impact investors apart.

However, one of the biggest threats to true impact investors is "greenwashing," an industry term for investments that focus too heavily on financial returns and neglect the impact element while claiming that their investments contribute significantly to social or environmental change. At best, greenwashing is a deliberate skewing in favor of financial performance with very limited regard for the original lauded impact objectives. At worst, it is outright lying to investors. Greenwashing is predominantly a by-product of marketing activity. Investment firms will claim that their investments are socially responsible and generate significant impact on the ground, when upon closer examination, this is not necessarily the case.

To return to our health care example, impact firm "A" and impact firm "B" both want to revolutionize access to health care in emerging markets. Impact firm A invests in tertiary care hospitals with hundreds of beds in large, established cities within these markets. Impact firm B invests in a new chain of rural hospitals with a price point that enables the treatment of many poor people. Both the approaches taken by these firms are valid, but impact firm B will generate a greater impact by providing access to health care to people in rural areas for the first time. Impact firm A will probably yield higher financial returns because of its focus on an easier, and more profitable, established part of the market. This will generate a profit, but it will not reach the masses. The problem arises if impact firm A is not transparent about the level of impact it has generated through its investments. This would be a case of greenwashing or "social washing."

Greenwashing can have serious implications for the reputation of Impact Investing. To prevent it, the sector is focusing heavily on developing a standardized set of metrics to help capture, monitor, and report on impact outputs and outcomes. Regardless of the size of the investment firm, every company that claims to be an impact investor should report using the same benchmark. Third-party tools can ensure the standardization of impact measurement. GIIRS ratings and IRIS metrics (IRIS 2020) are the industry's two leading tools. GIIRS ratings collect relevant data to ascertain whether individual investments will fulfil their objectives, providing a rating for the asset manager of its ESG management and the impact performance of its portfolio (B

Analytics 2020). The IRIS metrics measure the social, environmental, and financial performance of an investment and are designed to be filtered based on investment priorities and focus areas. The move toward standardized metrics should be pursued—it will help impact investors' benchmark results and ensure the industry is singing from the same hymn sheet.

The arrival of large, multinational asset managers to Impact Investing is a great sign that Impact Investing is moving toward the mainstream. The movement has become more prominent in recent years, with the Global Impact Investing Network estimating the size of the market in April 2019 to be US $502 billion. But this also calls for strict adherence to Impact Investing principles and transparency. It is therefore the responsibility of the community to protect its reputation by reporting on the same benchmarks (Global Impact Investing Network 2019).

Adopting a sound theory of change will help impact investors protect the industry's reputation by measuring the outputs and mapping them to the outcomes that support an investor's cause and ultimately generate a significant impact in communities that need it the most.

Use Appropriate Sources of Capital

From angel investing to private equity commercial capital, there is a continuum of capital sources that should be targeted at companies at specific growth stages. Using inappropriate sources of capital can undermine the viability of a company or spoil a market. For example, using grants for commercial investment-ready companies is a waste of money and runs the risk of distorting a market, while using commercial private equity for early stage companies will usually put unnecessary pressure on the entrepreneur.

For example, in India, about 10 years ago, a development finance institution (DFI) started lending to small businesses at highly subsidized rates. In the same region of the country, microfinance institutions that I had invested in at BlueOrchard Finance were lending on commercial terms. The subsidies destroyed the lending market because the businesses went straight to the subsidized loans from the DFI over the loans offered by the microfinance institutions.

Several years later, the same DFI no longer offered subsidies, and the small businesses were left with nothing. At this point, the microfinance institutions were no longer lending on commercial terms and they had not been replaced. The DFI subsidies provided a short-term solution to cheap financing, without solving the long-term problem of access to finance within this specific region of India.

The DFI should have applied its subsidy to other sectors where the market-based solution was less mature, or they should have subsidized microfinance solutions in areas that were most underserved and difficult to access. In these instances, the microfinance institutions would have thrived and served their customer base more efficiently, ultimately scaling the market-based approach without killing the market.

In fact, the DFI subsidies completely ruined a long-term, scalable solution. The use of subsidies in the microfinance market for small businesses in India was devastating and completely spoiled the market. This type of market distortion is unfortunately still very prevalent in emerging economies.

Today, there are new forms of investing currently being tested that depart from traditional financial instruments. For example, the structuring of dividend pay-outs or interest rate payments from top line revenues to ease or accelerate financial returns without putting too much pressure on the company. Impact investors should not shy away from being creative in the way they provide financial resources to the businesses they support and the way they are rewarded.

A growing practice in the Impact Investing sector is the creation of funds using blended finance. The idea is simple. When structuring a fund, you create several layers of risks and returns. You create a "first loss layer" and then "senior layers" on top. All layers share the same investment portfolio. But if there is a loss in your portfolio, the first loss layer takes the hit, thereby protecting the senior layers of investors. The tiering of investment funds is not a new concept. In fact, layering funding in an investment vehicle has been a common practice for the last two decades. I created a layered fund at BlueOrchard Finance with the IFC over 15 years ago. It was a collateral debt obligation for microfinance companies with a senior piece, mezzanine, and equity, and worked well.

The difference with a first loss layer in an impact fund lies in the type of investor. The first loss layer appeals to traditional donors, charities, and philanthropic organizations. Instead of irrevocably donating a dollar to a cause they support, they can now invest in the first loss of an impact fund tackling the same cause, but their investment will have a major catalytic effect. Their investment is designed to trigger the investment of private companies who will benefit from their protection, and instead of seeing one dollar being invested into the cause, it now multiplies to four or five dollars. On top of this, if the investment manager has done a proper job, this philanthropic dollar may well come back and the donor gets to invest it again, or to eventually donate it. This is truly efficient philanthropy.

The private companies investing in the senior layer also benefit from a blended finance approach. They receive financial returns that they would not have expected because they are protected by the first loss layer, and the lower returns generated by the impact portfolio become market-based risk adjusted returns. This overcomes a major barrier to Impact Investing by institutional investors who have a fiduciary responsibility.

The idea is that in 5 to 10 years' time, a first loss piece is no longer needed because private companies will have tested these markets and become more comfortable investing in them. Blended finance does not have the longest track record, but it has already been embraced by an increasing number of governments, supranational organizations, and not-for-profit organizations. This new form of structuring capital is an incredible opportunity to partner with the private sector and contribute to causes they care about. Bamboo Capital Partners has developed a series of blended finance funds with a range of partners, including the International Fund for Agriculture Development, the United Nations Capital Development Fund (UNCDF), the International Trade Centre, SmartAfrica, and the international non-governmental organization (NGO) CARE USA.

These blended finance funds are in the early stages of their life cycle, but we have already overcome some challenges that are inherent with the nature and structure of these funds. One of the difficulties presented by blended finance applied to open-ended structured funds resides in the ongoing management of the size of its different tranches. A degree of liquidity needs to be offered to investors coming in the senior tranches of the fund, while some proportionality between tranche sizes must be maintained in order to keep the risk return profile of each tranche (Figure 21.2).

The other challenge is to educate investors coming into the senior tranches about the necessary level of protection given by the first loss

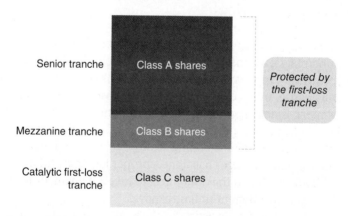

FIGURE 21.2   Blended Finance Structure. *Source*: Bamboo Capital Partners.

tranche as the Impact Investing space still lacks reliable aggregated performance data on similar past investment portfolios. In the future, reliable default statistics over a long period of time will enable us to provide senior tranches of blended finance funds with an investment rating that would greatly ease decision-making and portfolio construction for private investors.

The Value of Partnerships

The aim of any impact investor should be to grow a portfolio company and take it to the next stage of its development and one step closer to achieving the original vision of its founder. One of the most effective ways of achieving this is by encouraging partnerships with larger, established private sector companies. They can help fast-track smaller companies to scale quicker and increase the impact they have on the ground.

To demonstrate how this works, examine the recent partnership between BBOXX and French energy giant EDF. Before its partnership with EDF, BBOXX had made some progress in Togo. It had supplied electricity to 26,000 Togolese households and opened 20 shops, which employed around 100 people. However, in order to achieve scale, BBOXX partnered with EDF to create the joint venture BBOXX Togo. BBOXX Togo provides a reliable, affordable, and CO_2-free contribution to the government of Togo's electrification program known as CIZO, which aims to supply over 500,000 households with solar home systems by 2030 (ESI Africa 2019). As part of the partnership, EDF will provide investment to accelerate the deployment of the solar home systems and technological knowledge to improve battery performance. Therefore, the partnership has taken BBOXX one step closer toward its original vision—to provide people with access to a clean source of renewable energy—at an accelerated rate.

In many ways, the third and fourth pillars of Impact Investing best practice intertwine. Blended finance highlights how combining different sources of capital in one fund can generate a significant impact. There needs to be closer coordination or partnership between grant givers, early stage investors, and growth investors because it will allow for more efficient support of companies and avoid detrimental market disruption. Typically, different types of organization or investor go to the segment of the market that suits them best. However, in certain investment vehicles, these different sources of capital can partner efficiently with one another to generate impact by adopting a blended finance approach.

The Agri-Business Capital Fund (ABC Fund) launched by the International Fund for Agricultural Development (IFAD) in February 2019 is a good example of how this can work in practice (IFAD 2020). The ABC Fund provides small loans to rural small and medium-sized businesses (SMEs), farmers' organizations, and rural financial institutions. The fund was launched with a first loss layer of €50 million, with commitments from the European Union, the Government of Luxembourg, and the international NGO Alliance for a Green Revolution in Africa (AGRA). It is an example of how a supranational organization, a government, and an international NGO are partnering to address an area of the market, which would be much harder for them to address as individual entities. The advantage of blended finance is that each party keeps its place in the funding structure. Furthermore, the first loss layer in the ABC Fund is designed to attract private investors to the African rural SME market via senior layers of funding—a catalyst for further investment to deliver a greater impact on the ground.

Finally, newcomers to Impact Investing would be wise to approach asset managers who have been in the market for several years in order to avoid making the same mistakes and learn from their experience. There are economies of scale in asset management, and the current multiplication of small first-time impact funds are far from efficient. Bamboo Capital Partners and others in the sector will continue to offer new entrants to Impact Investing from other sectors or disciplines the opportunity to be housed under their platform. By taking advantage of this market experience, new players will benefit from advice, networks, and installed fund management capabilities. Therefore, they are more likely to generate a significant impact with their new product or fund at the first time of asking.

Technology as the Critical Success Factor

Whether an impact investor is investing in a company that installs solar home systems in Sub-Saharan Africa or provides microfinance loans to low-income populations in India, the common thread running through both investments is democratization. The democratization of essential services (i.e. making them available to everyone), such as energy, finance, and education, is fundamentally driven by technology. Technology is the catalyst that contributes to better outcomes from individual investments, which ultimately supports an impact investor's causes.

Technological progress provides people, especially those living in rural areas, with accessibility to essential services at an affordable price. At present, we are witnessing an extraordinary acceleration of development in ground-breaking technologies that are set to be at the heart of new business models. New technologies will enable entire continents to leapfrog the traditional linear economic development that developed economies have followed in the past.

For example, in the last decade, Africa has lived through the mobile phone revolution, leapfrogging the traditional infrastructure of landlines. According to GSMA, mobile adoption in Africa has grown rapidly with overall subscriber penetration reaching 44% in 2017, up from 25% at the start of the decade (GSMA 2019). The mobile phone in Africa is not purely a communications device, but it is the main gateway to the Internet for millions of Africans and enhances access to a multitude of services, including banking.

Mobile money is quickly transforming economies in several African countries and bypassing traditional bank branching. In 2017, GSMA notes that the value of mobile money transactions on the continent grew by 14.4% to US $19.9 billion. Mobile money has had a revolutionary impact on financial inclusion in Africa. It has become a vital tool in digitalizing transactions in the public and private sectors. Many providers collaborate with government to digitalize person-to-government payment streams, which is improving fund collection and allowing greater transparency (GSMA 2019).

Mobile money is also serving as the backbone of distributed energy generation in off-grid regions. There is a drive toward clean sources of energy in Africa to bypass polluting sources of energy, such as kerosene and burning wood. There are currently 1.1 billion people—14% of the global population—without access to energy (IEA 2017). By providing these additional 1.1 billion people with access to energy, they will in turn gain access to the internet, mobile money, and a whole host of other services.

Looking ahead, there is a new type of technology which is on the verge of revolutionizing society—blockchain. Like other technologies such as big data and artificial intelligence, blockchain, with its characteristics of security, transparency, and decentralization, will be used as the backbone of new business models. Blockchain will enable the direct delivery of decentralized services and increase "people-to-people" connectivity all over the globe. Furthermore, blockchain will be conducive to the creation of secure digital identities, something that a vast number of marginalized populations lack. Access to a digital identity will unleash many opportunities to serve those populations better—for example, digital payments (including aid to refugees paid by multilateral organizations), digital land ownership titles, and the creation and tracking of personal digital credit history. Finally, if applied to public finances, blockchain has the potential to force absolute transparency and accountability, thereby strengthening democracies around the world.

In conclusion, technology is at the heart of Impact Investing. It is the catalyst that can drive better outcomes to support an impact investor's cause. Technology has already had a big effect in democratizing services such as banking and energy access in rural areas, while new technologies such as blockchain have the potential to take this one step further and completely transform business models.

CONCLUSION

The five pillars of Impact Investing best practice are by no means the definitive guide to success. However, they are guidelines that all impact investors should follow closely if they truly wish to be viewed as impact investors.

The purpose of Impact Investing is to create solid companies that will generate lasting social, environmental, and financial returns. By investing in good leaders who are willing to execute on their vision, impact investors stand a good chance of success. Furthermore, if their investments are guided by a theory of change, they will generate outcomes that support their overarching cause.

When they structure their funds, impact investors need to be careful and use the right type of capital to avoid undermining a company or spoiling a market. Blended finance will allow them to combine multiple types of capital and encourage partnerships between different types of organizations looking to generate impact on the ground. Meanwhile, partnerships between smaller and larger private companies can accelerate business development and deliver on the founder's original vision. Finally, underpinning everything is technological change. Investing in companies that utilize new technologies to leapfrog traditional infrastructure and provide access to services such as banking to new demographics will support an impact investor's overall theory of change.

Impact Investing is opening a whole new world of opportunities for the further inclusion of low-income populations. Impact Investing will be key to achieving the vision of Nobel Peace Prize winner Dr Mohammad Yunus: "to put poverty in the museum" (YouTube 2013). Also, his Nobel Peace Prize (not the prize for Economics) was awarded for "creating the conditions under which peace can exist," the core of UN SDG 16, a rare goal for investing, but achievable.

REFERENCES

B Analytics (2020). Company Ratings. https://b-analytics.net/content/company-ratings (accessed 21 February 2020).

BBOXX (2020). Home – BBOXX. www.bboxx.co.uk/ (accessed 21 February 2020).

ESI Africa (2019). Togolese government approves innovative solar subsidy. https://numerique.gouv.tg/projet/cizo (accessed 21 February 2020).

Global Impact Investing Network (2019). Sizing the Impact Investing Market. https://thegiin.org/research/publication/impinv-market-size (accessed 21 February 2020).

GSMA (2019). The Mobile Economy Sub-Saharan Africa 2018. https://www.gsma.com/r/mobileeconomy/sub-saharan-africa/ (accessed 21 February 2020).

IEA (2017). Energy Access Outlook 2017. https://www.iea.org/access2017/ (accessed 21 February 2020).

International Committee of the Red Cross (2017). The world's first "Humanitarian Impact Bond" launched to transform financing of aid in conflict-hit countries. https://www.icrc.org/en/document/worlds-first-humanitarian-impact-bond-launched-transform-financing-aid-conflict-hit (accessed 21 February 2020).

International Fund for Agricultural Development (2020). Agri-Business Capital (ABC) Fund. https://www.ifad.org/en/abcfund (accessed 21 February 2020).

IRIS (2020). IRIS Metrics. https://iris.thegiin.org/metrics (accessed 21 February 2020).

World Health Organization (2016). Mortality from household air pollution. https://www.who.int/gho/phe/indoor_air_pollution/burden/en/ (accessed 21 February 2020).

YouTube (2013). Gold Medal Ceremony Honoring Professor Muhammad Yunus. https://www.youtube.com/watch?v=BrcCADu5xvQ (accessed 21 February 2020).

CHAPTER 22

China's Rapidly Evolving Practice of Impact Investing: A Critical Perspective

Zhao Jianbo, PhD

Abstract

Impact Investing has grown rapidly and is increasingly popular around the globe. Following this trend, China's Impact Investing market is similarly expanding and diversifying, but it has not yet matured, and still holds huge market opportunities. While today China's Impact Investing industry is in an embryonic stage of development, in the future the country is expected to become an international leader in impact-oriented finance. The seeds for future growth are already present; many entrepreneurs in China have not yet realized they are social entrepreneurs and potential impact investors. They simply do what they think is right, practicing their mission and generating innovative solutions to environmental and social problems. The impact-oriented culture of Chinese entrepreneurship is sure to fuel the growth of impact investing. Based on a literature review and several interviews, this chapter offers a fresh and critical perspective on

843

the growth and development of China's Impact Investing, and how the country has been using its unique value propositions. It will investigate Impact Investing frameworks deployed in China, as well as a spectrum of adjacent schema, including venture philanthropy organizations, and "base of the pyramid" strategies. In China, as in the rest of the world, the greatest challenge to the Impact Investing industry continues to be the identification of investable opportunities that simultaneously optimize financial and social outcomes.

Keywords

China; Impact Investing; Venture Philanthropy; Base of the Pyramid; Poverty Alleviation; Social Innovation; Emerging Markets; Public Policy

INTRODUCTION

While still in its infancy, China's Impact Investing market is increasingly diversified, with huge market opportunities ahead. The economic transformation that has taken place in China over the past half century, and the general upgrading of the Chinese economy, is enduring in part because of its clear top-down values and long-term strategy. China's programs of "mass innovation, popular entrepreneurship," "targeted poverty alleviation, "and "innovation-driven development," as well as the 2017 government's report to the 19th National Congress of the Communist Party of China, have all laid the foundation for continued growth. These strategies have also determined the quality of economic growth in China and are poised to lead to more bottom-up investment opportunities wellsuited for impact investors. The main goal of this "new era" of economic transformation is to shift quickly from high-speed to high-quality growth while building a modern economic system. For this to be possible, however, China needs to go through a structural transformation based on scientific, technological, and social innovations.

Impact Investing is a new way to combine public welfare and finance, consistent with the United Nations' Sustainable Development Goals (SDGs) and the principles of sustainable development. Because government and non-governmental organizations (NGOs) programs can only go so far toward meeting the USD $1.5 to $3 trillion dollars needed per year to achieve the SDGs, the private sector has a major role to play. Yet social problems can only be solved by the private sector if they are turned into profitable business opportunities. Accordingly, Impact Investing is emerging as a viable pathway toward achieving high-quality development.

The demand for investments that combine a financial return with desired social or environmental impact is growing. The remaining question is how China can facilitate and channel Impact Investments, using its unique value proposition. While some developing countries lack global recognition in the investor community, China has the capability and knowledge to attract impact investments. Given the recent upsurge of Chinese innovation and entrepreneurship, in addition to China's "new era" policy push that further involves the private sector in sustainable development and caring for the public good, there should be no shortage of both Chinese and international investors and financiers eager to respond to this call.

Even though China is primed to become an Impact Investing powerhouse, it currently lacks a proper and reasonable "business model" for Impact Investing. The overall goal of this chapter is to provide a critical and fresh perspective on the development of the Impact Investing industry in China over the last 10 years, summarizing the main challenges and lessons learned. Further, the chapter discusses the key drivers behind the growth of Impact Investing in China, and considers what future interventions could aid its success, including incentive mechanisms, such as the establishment of efficient markets, as well as how to address investment gaps and redirecting capital.

This study is based on a literature review as well as semi-structured interviews with relevant impact investors (see Appendix 22.1 for a list of interviewees), along with Impact Investment case studies from the industrial sector. The chapter also includes a secondary data analysis looking into the unmet capital needs for sustainable development and Impact Investing in China.

This chapter contributes to the emerging literature and academic research on the development of Impact Investing in China. It also connects the discipline of Impact Investing to a broader and more holistic framework of Chinese impact-seeking enterprises and investment strategies. In addition to Impact Investing—defined in the narrowest sense—the chapter considers venture philanthropy organizations (VPOs) and base of the pyramid (BoP) typologies as complementary drivers for the development of Impact Investing in China. Unlike prior studies that focused on geographies which had already established themselves as leading international investment destinations—such as Singapore, London, or Dubai—the findings of this study are based on a broad sample of Chinese firms.

The rest of the chapter is organized as follows. The first section draws from the literature review and introduces Impact Investment in the context of China's emerging market economy. The second section reviews the practice of Impact Investing in China, explaining how Chinese firms are applying the concept of Impact Investing to business, and their efforts to maintain profits while simultaneously fulfilling other goals like poverty alleviation and fostering sustainable development. Third, this paper discusses the challenges associated with implementing Impact Investing and concludes by providing suggestions for further improvements to the Impact Investing field in China. The conclusion offers prospects for further research.

LITERATURE REVIEW: DEFINING THE SPECTRUM OF IMPACT INVESTING

Impact investing seeks to provide capital to develop and grow companies, like traditional investing, but differentiates itself by utilizing a double bottom line inclusive of financial and social returns (Allman and Nogales 2015). This chapter also explores two other typologies of impact investment being applied in China: venture philanthropy and BoP. All three strategies can be translated into specific investment opportunities that generate sustainable impact, and thus they are helpful tools for closing the annual funding gap between capital supply and demand in the Chinese impact investment market.

Impact Investing

Ever since the United Nations' 2030 Agenda for Sustainable Development launched in 2015, there has been a change in the global paradigm. The 17 SDGs and their related 169 precise targets acted as a trigger for governments, corporations, and academia worldwide. The SDGs motivated these entities to consider their individual roles—how the public, private, and research sectors each had unique responsibilities and capabilities to contribute—as well as to reimagine the collective system and how these sectors could work together to transform strategic decision-making, business processes, and operations (Hill 2011).

As the practice of philanthropy has gained traction in China, buzzwords such as "impact investing," "venture philanthropy," and "social venture capital" have emerged. All of these belong to a broader umbrella concept called "Impact Investing," and in China these terms are often used interchangeably. Impact investing pursues both financial return and measurable social impact, being placed in between the two extremes of charitable giving (which emphasizes social value), and traditional investing (which emphasizes only economic value). As such, any investing that pursues and measures financial return and social impact should be considered Impact Investing (Zhou 2017). In China, the primary vehicles that generate the expansion and sustainability of social impacts are venture philanthropy and charitable donations. These two typologies are located in between the two extremes of the profit-impact investment spectrum.

Impact investing was initially driven by philanthropic capital, so it is still often confused with grants and donations. Impact Investing simultaneously pursues both goals of financial and social returns. Impact investors believe that adherence to this investment philosophy will ultimately increase returns, while minimizing risks (Allman and Nogales 2015) and ensuring greater sustainability. According to the Monitor Institute, impact investors can be defined as financiers who actively place capital in businesses and funds that generate social and/or environmental good and return at least the nominal principal to the investor (Monitor Institute 2009).

Some fascinating developments have taken place in this emerging sector, many of them funded by a new generation of Impact Investment companies. New research from Fidelity Charitable suggests that the proportion of donors engaging in Impact Investing is headed for a substantial growth, as new generations of Americans build their wealth and develop an affinity for social goals in their investments (Fidelity Charitable 2019).

In practice, Impact Investing firms are "hybrids"—they attract greater investment through values-alignment and by providing incentives for mainstream companies to pursue social welfare objectives while maintaining a profitable approach (Kim et al. 2019). The practice of Impact Investing specifically means that these "hybrid" organizations pursue a combination of financial and social goals by constructing investment portfolios that jointly optimize financial and social outcomes (Hong and Kostovetsky 2012).

Impact Investing can use different instruments (e.g. debt and equity) and be applied by multiple types of entities, ranging from individuals and charitable organizations to private for-profit investment funds. Impact Investing can help address the world's most pressing challenges by directing money to core solutions areas, such as sustainable agriculture and food production, energy efficiency, universal access to basic services (including housing, health care, and education), or microfinance.

Venture Philanthropy

As China's wealth grew, so did its philanthropic activity. The Chinese government is increasingly convinced of philanthropy's potential to contribute to society and is considering joining hands with private philanthropists to cope with the growing social and environmental concerns resulting from China's rapid development.

Venture philanthropy is defined as the application of venture capital methodologies to philanthropic endeavors. In venture philanthropy, funding and resources are invested in search of a social return, usually as donations or charity by entrepreneurs, venture capitalists, trust funds, and corporations (Pepin 2005). In contrast to traditional charitable grants awarded to nonprofit organizations by a community, private, or corporate foundation, venture philanthropists, with their philosophy of high-engagement, regard charitable giving as a long-term investment. In China, many firms engage in philanthropic activities because they provide a benefit to society, while also relieving the increasing pressures of private fortune accumulation. This dual benefit is particularly present in developing countries such as China, where governments and local communities are powerful stakeholders (Gao 2011; Gao and Hafsi 2015).

Venture philanthropy is a growing global movement that adapts existing tools of venture capital for social benefit (John 2015). As a sector, venture philanthropy contains a diverse mix of players, including neo-philanthropists, traditional foundations, the private equity community, and even governments working with social entrepreneurs, social enterprises, and other investees. These venture philanthropists are creating new forms of social finance and new ways of increasing and measuring the impact of their investees' work.

VPOs help social enterprises achieve social impact and economic sustainability. Based on the case study of VPO Danone Communities, Leborgne-Bonassié et al. (2019) found that VPOs provided social entrepreneurs with financial and nonfinancial support to tackle social challenges, and they acquired knowledge and improved their reputation in turn. This is exemplified by Van Slyke and Newman's (2006) case study of Tom Cousins, a social entrepreneur who used his own philanthropic investments to leverage additional resources via extensive public-private partnerships. Cousins did this with the sole intent of redeveloping a region facing disinvestment and poverty.

There is a strong correlation between an investor's attitude toward charitable giving and their likelihood of becoming an impact investor. Especially in China, giving back to society is an important way to maintain cohesiveness, especially in face of rising social and environmental challenges. Both philanthropy and Impact Investing can solve social problems, but Impact Investing is more sustainable than pure philanthropy, because the world cannot grant its way out of poverty or solve the climate-related problems without transforming the private sector. Hence, it is important to encourage the migration from venture philanthropy to Impact Investing and social entrepreneurship.

Base of the Pyramid

The established definition for BoP is traditionally applied to emerging markets and includes the poorest people in a society. BoP defines a group that is almost always the largest in the wealth pyramid, the impoverished. The BoP approach proposes combined solutions for business development and poverty alleviation. This strategy uses business to lift billions of people out of poverty and desperation. By reducing inequality, BoP can avert social decay, political chaos, terrorism, and environmental meltdown, as these outcomes are aggravated by the widening wealth gap between rich and poor countries (Jagtap et al. 2014; Zhang and Tong 2012).

Poverty eradication is a challenge faced by all. Countries all over the world have taken measures to reduce poverty, and some have achieved remarkable results. China's success in poverty alleviation benefited from a series of policies and institutional reforms (Liu et al. 2020). Supporting poor households to develop their industries has been the main strategy adopted by the Chinese government.

Policymakers and academics are increasingly paying attention to market-based approaches to alleviating poverty, especially those that combine business development with poverty alleviation (Prahalad 2004). The objective of Impact Investing is to promote inclusiveness and opportunities for all, especially the vulnerable and marginalized at the bottom of the pyramid. Impact investors financially support the ventures of social entrepreneurs, who seek to positively impact the BoP by improving their livelihoods, and/or creating targeted social and environmental benefits. In short, the poor can be better served by Impact Investments (Ashta 2012).

The concept of BoP is highly aligned with Impact Investing. The poorest among us are certainly a population that impact investors hope to benefit, with positive environmental impacts via products and services that serve those in poverty or extreme poverty. Compared to mainstream venture capital, impact investors tend to be more accommodating with investment yields, as well as more flexible with the payback period. In China, these enterprises, mostly small and medium-sized, are mostly concentrated in the business sectors of housing, education, environment, and health, all of which directly touch people's daily lives, and especially those in the BoP.

THE PRACTICE OF IMPACT INVESTING IN CHINA: AN OVERVIEW

This section describes the context and practice of Impact Investing in China, and draws on a literature review, along with semi-structured interviews with impact investors. It also draws from case studies across agriculture, manufacturing, and the digital economy.

A New Investment Community

Impact Investing is still a relatively new concept in China. For many social enterprises and foundations, Impact Investing is still a vague concept. For some, there are misunderstandings of the sector's investment philosophy, which is mistaken for being either primarily commercial or purely philanthropic. Others do not know they are highly successful impact investors even though they routinely invest in robust social impact projects, whereas some institutions and projects claim to do Impact Investing without actually practicing it.

Aside from international development organizations, such as the International Finance Corporation (IFC), and multilateral development banks like the Asian Development Bank (ADB), there are only a handful of self-identifying social and/or environmental impact investors in China. Those that exist can be coupled in three main categories of actors: (i) private foundations and nonpublic funds, (ii) venture capital businesses (private equity, commercial venture capital, and enterprises with social responsibility), and (iii) government-backed enterprises. While these three types of actors have different missions, time frames for investing, financial hurdle rates, and impact goals, they are equally committed to promoting the development of the China's Impact Investing market (Table 22.1).

The largest investors are development finance institutions (DFIs), such as large foundations (including the Bill and Melinda Gates Foundation), commercial banks, investment funds, and high-net-worth individuals. Each tries to achieve a positive social impact on society, the environment, or sustainable development through social finance and banking.

TABLE 22.1 Brief Summary of Major Impact Investors in China.

Institution	Foundation year	Sponsor	Total amount invested (in millions of USD)
China Social Entrepreneur Foundation (友成企业家扶贫基金会)	2007	Three entrepreneurs	--
Leping Foundation (乐平公益基金会)	2008	Beijing Fuping School (富平学校)	--
LGT Venture philanthropy	2008	LGT Foundation	0.3
SA Capital	2008	SA Capital	0.5
SOW Foundation (心苗基金)	2009	HongKong SOW Foundation	0.1
Lanshan Fund (岚山基金)	2011	Private equity	50
Changsi Fund (创思)	2012	Schoenfeld Foundation	--
China Impact Fund	2012	World Resource Institute	--
Xin Hu Education Fund (新湖■育基金)	2012	Xin Hu Group	--
Tsing Capital (青云创投)	2002	Tsing Capital	--
Avantage Ventures (浩盈优世基金)	2012	Avantage Ventures	20

Source: Foundations' documentation and websites.

851

After the first international public finance forum and social Impact Investment summit, held in Shenzhen in 2017, the China Venture Capital Yearbook has begun to publish an important set of statistics. Table 22.2 depicts China's Top 20 Impact Investing institutions in 2018.

In recent years, a model of "managed social innovation"[1] has been emerging in China, with local governments taking the lead in generating and implementing new citizen-oriented products, processes, and services. The central government has embraced local innovative activities. In some metropolitan areas, local governments have also begun to sponsor nonprofit incubators and social innovation hubs in order to directly promote the establishment and growth of social nonprofits. A study on managing social innovation showcases a government sponsored Venture Philanthropy in Shanghai and examines several components of Shanghai's leadership in social entrepreneurship (Jing and Gong 2012).

These new impact-driven innovations are often defined by charity. In the private sector, social enterprises and nonprofits are increasingly combining e-commerce and digitalization with charity. For example, Buy42.com[2] offers employment opportunities to people with disabilities—a new public service model in China. Buy42.com is defined by its creation of shared value, going beyond profit. This corporate philanthropy strategy recognizes that societal needs, not only conventional economic needs, can shape markets.

Donation is another traditional form of philanthropy, in which charitable capital is injected into organizations to keep them operating, often with the promise of no financial return. Although not consistent with the mainstream concept of Impact Investing, charity is necessary in a Chinese context, even though the proportion of donations as investment vehicles is very low.

Venture philanthropy and Impact Investment are aligned in Chinese culture because both typologies pay significant attention to how investments can create and grow enterprises. But venture philanthropy is significantly less appealing for financial returns than Impact Investing.

True long-term, sustainable, and competitive economic value is created when businesses align with societal needs. A business needs a successful

---

[1] Social innovation involves the formation of new institutions, new policies, and new forms of social interaction that serve social needs, primarily developed and diffused through non-government social organizations.

[2] Buy42.com is a new website and service that asks people to donate their second-hand clothes. Buy42 then works on these donated clothes to create fashionable vintage. The company earns only a percentage of the money made from the resale of clothes to run the website and pay the company's staff. The rest of the income is donated to the low-income poor through charities.

TABLE 22.2 China's Top 20 Impact Investing Institutions, 2018.

Investor	Type
Shenzhen Capital Group Company, Ltd. ("SCGC") (深创投)	Government-backed enterprise
NewMargin Venture Capital Co., Ltd. (永宣创投)	Government-backed enterprise
China Venture Capital (中国风投)	Government-backed enterprise
ADDOR CAPITAL (毅达资本)	Government-backed enterprise
Soft Bank China (软银中国)	Global investment bank
Qiming Venture Partners (启明创投)	Venture capital
Sequoia China (红杉资本中国基金)	Venture capital
Stone VC (基石创投))	Venture capital
CDH Investments (鼎晖投资)	Venture capital
Matrix Partners China (经纬中国)	Venture capital
Oriental Fortune Capital Investment Management Co., Ltd. (OFC) (东方富海)	Venture capital
Northern Light Venture Capital (北极光创投)	Venture capital
IDG Capital	Venture capital
Fortune Capital (达晨财智)	Venture capital
Legend Capital (君联资本)	Venture capital
Hillhouse Capital (高瓴资本)	Venture capital
Hony Capital (弘毅投资)	Venture capital
Warburg Pincus (华平投资)	Venture capital
Granite Global Ventures (纪源资本)	Venture capital
DT Capital Partners (德同资本)	Venture capital

Source: China Venture Capital Research Institute (2018).

community, not only to generate demand for its goods or services but also because successful communities provide access to critical public assets and a stable economic environment. Communities need sustainable business that ensure their future welfare while fulfilling daily needs. By adopting a shared value mindset and a business model that is attractive to impact investors, a company's competitiveness and the well-being of its community stakeholders are more closely intertwined.

Motivations for the Practice of Impact Investing in China

As an ancient society that has increasingly realized business ventures that integrate stakeholder beyond just shareholder value, China is particularly well suited for social Impact Investing. Impact Investing took root when the country realized that by themselves, NGOs, governments, and enterprises cannot solve all of China's existing problems. Upon this realization, national social entrepreneurs began to emerge.

It is important to note, however, that many entrepreneurs in China do not realize they are social entrepreneurs. They just do what they think is right, practice a mission, and create innovative solutions to environmental and social problems. Their efforts, along with those of venture philanthropists, mainly focus on achieving poverty alleviation targets and fulfilling social responsibilities, to promote green and sustainable social development in China.

Impact Investing is now playing an increasingly important role in the field of social governance in China. Beyond cultural factors, there are several reasons Chinese firms are willingly participating in Impact Investing. The first is market imperfections; several problems cannot be solved by the market alone. If everyone pursues high profits, thereby ignoring social needs that do not necessarily bring high returns, social problems outside the public scope of intervention will not be addressed. The second reason why Impact Investing is ripe to grow in China is the breakthrough realization that the Chinese government cannot solve all social problems, nor can the nonprofit sector. NGOs are mostly charitable entities, which need to be continuously funded by donations, so their influence is limited, and their sustainability is often threatened by inconsistent funding.

In contrast, social enterprises are committed to solving social problems, but are endowed with commercial features, such as high efficiency, efficacy, and the flexibility to participate in the social management and development process actively and effectively. Compared to traditional investment practices, Impact Investing puts higher requirements on entrepreneurs, not only in terms of excellent entrepreneurship skills and dedicated innovation abilities but also in terms of upholding the original intentions of solving social problems in the face of financial pressures.

Several businesses are currently engaging with Impact Investing in China. The China Overseas Group, a leading property developer and construction contractor in mainland China and Hong Kong SAR, has been exploring new business models to better balance urban and rural development. China Overseas Group worked with other enterprises across their supply chain to solve social problems and reduce production, supply, and marketing costs, all while gaining a better corporate image and boosting economic returns. For example, starting in 2008 the China Resources Group has been developing "Hope Towns," which establish a complete rural ecological chain. In Hope Towns, villagers can access basic infrastructures, production facilities, and develop their production skills, as well as establish sustainable economic and administrative organizations. The agricultural products and light industrial products produced in Hope Towns are made available by the retail network of the China Resources Group (e.g. Vanguard Supermarket). In this case, Impact Investing solves social development problems and increases the competitiveness of their supply chains. Overall, these examples show how Impact Investing can generate positive social change.

Targeted Poverty Alleviation Needs Social Capital

With the introduction of President Xi Jinping's "Targeted Poverty Alleviation," and the goal to end absolute poverty by 2020, a huge scale of capital has been invested by the Chinese central government. From 2010 to 2017, the volume of special funds invested in poverty alleviation increased from RMB 22.27 billion to RMB 86.10 billion (Table 22.3). However, the marginal effect of this public investment on poverty reduction has been declining, largely because of declining efficiencies in capital utilization resulting from the market mechanisms adopted.

As social forces for change, venture philanthropy and Impact Investing have become central to China's poverty-alleviation practice. However, compared to the Chinese government, market and social forces are not fully participating in the poverty alleviation process. The market has failed to play a decisive role in the allocation of anti-poverty resources. Moreover, many social entities still regard poverty-relief work as a political task, without specific rules and targets, relevant norms and guarantees, or sufficient quantitative assessment indicators (Li and Wei 2016).

TABLE 22.3 Special Fund for Poverty Alleviation, Chinese Central Government (2010–2019).

Year	Government special fund for poverty alleviation (billion RMB)	Poor population (in millions)	Headcount ratio (%)	Marginal effect of funding on poverty alleviation (million people per 1 billion RMB)
2010	22.27	165.67	17.20	–
2011	27.20	122.38	12.70	8.78
2012	33.21	98.99	10.20	3.90
2013	39.40	82.49	8.50	2.66
2014	43.29	70.17	7.20	3.17
2015	46.75	55.75	5.70	4.17
2016	67.00	43.35	4.50	0.61
2017	86.10	30.46	3.10	0.68
2018	106.00	6.60	1.69	0.17
2019	126.09	5.51	0.56	0.04

Source: National Bureau of Statistics (2019).

To maximize its anti-poverty capacity, China mobilized other social forces to participate in the process of poverty alleviation (Huang 2016). Due to government direction, the private sector now has a major role in reducing poverty in rural areas—through the creation of jobs, generating and paying taxes, and providing direct assistance to local vulnerable populations.

At the same time, social organizations also play an active role in poverty alleviation, and their investments can yield significant results. Social organizations are generally made up of high-level professional groups with ample financial resources, communication networks, and organizational capacity. For example, foundations such as the China Women Foundation and the China Red Cross launched poverty alleviation projects to aid poverty-stricken areas to alleviate poverty (Li and Wei 2016). Investors like Alibaba, an Internet giant in China, have taken several poverty alleviation measures to support the development of poor regions, with measures such as subsidized rural credits, access to new agricultural technologies, labor force training, and support of new business (Li et al. 2016). These measures positively impacted developing rural e-commerce ecosystems and contributed to poverty alleviation. Local firms also take action to alleviate poverty, but their efforts are mostly part of Corporate Social Responsibility (CSR) engagements, rather than Impact Investment per se.

In addition to corporate initiatives, several development programs in infrastructure and public services were implemented by local governments in poor areas, which helped these communities improve their immediate environments (Yan 2016). In Longnan, one of the poorest regions in China, several actions have been taken jointly by local governments and Alibaba to nurture, support, and regulate the development of the local rural e-commerce ecosystem, efforts that managed to alleviate poverty (Li et al. 2019).

Therefore, targeted poverty alleviation is an important area for Impact Investing in China. Investors and corporations can work through market mechanisms to improve the efficiency of capital utilization and positively impact poverty reduction.

THE MATURING MARKET FOR IMPACT INVESTING IN CHINA

In China, activities related to Impact Investing are on the rise. This increasing interest can be seen in the amount of initiatives promoting and raising awareness about Impact Investing in the mainstream investment community and public sphere, as well as the amount of contact between projects and investors. In 2018, the Chinese Social Enterprise and Social Investment Forum was held in Shenzhen, Guangdong Province. Ma Weihua, former president of China Merchants Bank, and now the rotating chairman of the China Alliance of Social Value Investment, and the chairman of the board of directors of the China Global Philanthropy Institute, led the Impact Investment Chinese delegation to Seoul, South Korea, to participate in the "Asian-Pacific Region Impact Investment Seminar and the Korea NAB Inauguration Conference," co-organized by the Global Social Impact Investment Steering Group (GSG), the British Council, and the United Nations Economic and Social Commission for Asia and the Pacific. This initiative will speed up the acceptance of impact investments by the mainstream investment market in China. Mr. Ma has the innovative leadership and takes Impact Investing as the focus to promote a new change in the public sector. His influence can bring social enterprises and Impact Investment into the mainstream investment market. This elevated Impact investing to a higher level of importance.

While interest in the sector may be growing rapidly, China's Impact Investing scene is still in its earliest stages. A few initiatives are gaining early traction and establishing a presence on the ground, but there are few completed Impact Investing transactions, not to mention successful exits. However, in the past two years, both the government and private investors have gradually turned their attention to Impact Investing and have committed themselves to help possible impact investors target the right social and environmental enterprises and sectors. Therefore, many private enterprises, including social enterprises, have become key actors in the Impact Investment space and are utilizing and benefiting from its diversified forms of intervention that span the impact investment spectrum, from socially responsible investment (SRI) to venture philanthropy and BoP. Global investment banks and private wealth funds also play a major role in funding impact-oriented businesses.

Impact investors consider serving the poor as an opportunity. For example, the private equity company Ehong Capital primarily invests in companies focused on "food, healthcare and low-carbon" solutions. When it was established, Ehong did not pursue or advertise Impact Investing, but its investment philosophy and standards were similar to those advocated by impact investors. In the following 10 years, Ehong has been committed to investing in high-quality projects in green agriculture, low-carbon environmental protection, health care for the elderly, and knowledge sharing, among other fields. Another firm, Granite Global Ventures, is a venture capital firm that invests in market-based solutions and entrepreneurs who are addressing the needs of low-income families in developing countries, while at the same time providing an attractive financial return.

One sector where Impact Investing has found traction in China is rural renewable energy technology. Solar-related technologies have been considered effective solutions to improve the lives of billions of poor around the globe. Zhou et al. (2012) explored how solar thermal technology was diffused in rural China where groups of BoP lived. Using case studies, Zhou et al. (2012) studied how solar firms in China promoted their products to BoP customers. They also found that the key success factor behind the diffusion of solar products in BoP markets a synergic innovation between the technological innovation and solar company's BoP-oriented business models—which can achieve both impact and financial success for investors, sometimes via IPOs or acquisitions.

Impact investments are frequently categorized by the targeted impacts they seek and are increasingly viewed as a tool to encourage investors and enterprises to simultaneously pursue financial and social outcomes. But such activity remains a niche practice relative to the rest of the investment industry (Economist 2017). In China in particular, impact investing still needs to be verified and validated by the market. In the future, a platform for Impact Investing will be formed and Impact Investing projects, products, and derivatives developed.

Challenges to Impact Investment in China

As mentioned, Impact Investing in China is still in its infancy. It is a relatively new concept for many social enterprises and foundations and is not very well understood. As the cases mentioned above and numerous examples from across the globe show, impact-oriented investing begins by avoiding causing any negative impacts to the community and the environment. But Impact Investing seeks to go further and deliver positive impacts and enact changes that promote true sustainable development. Today, most Chinese investors do not know about impact investment projects, and they craft their investment philosophies for strictly commercial or solely charitable purposes. While any investment needs to demonstrate its potential to generate—and this holds true for impact investments—Chinese impact investors need to clarify how investing for impact can be synonymous with making profit. Today the industry suffers from misperception, as social entrepreneurs often say Impact Investing is not all that appealing, because highlighting the word "impact" makes people think they will lose profits.

Research on the practice of Chinese firms for the past few years reveals that firms lack three core elements for the successful execution of Impact Investing: a lack of a clear strategic plan, systematic and organization-wide management, and lack of balance and focus (Mahoney 2013). In reality, it is not easy for a company to balance profit and impact. A clear strategic plan for Impact Investing also avoids problems down the road. Although it is generally agreed that social enterprises put social goals ahead of profits, in the actual interaction with social investors, the balance between profits and the influence of social goals can be blurred. Furthermore, while Impact Investing is dedicated to fostering social enterprises that seek innovative and efficient solutions to social problems, not all social problems easily translate into business opportunities.

Even in developed countries, the scarcity of high-quality hybrid investment options with consequential and measurable social benefits is frequently cited as a limitation to this industry's growth (Brest and Born 2013; McCreless 2017).

In parallel with having a clear strategy, organizations that already promote Impact Investing can do a better job at marketing the industry's potential benefits. Impact Investing gives investors a unique competitive advantage and helps them identify potential risks and capture new business opportunities. The public also lacks correct knowledge concerning the scope of influence of impact investment and social entrepreneurship, which are often misinterpreted as charity. Time and effort need to be taken to address different stakeholders in China to explain to them what Impact Investing is about and what it can deliver to China, including government officials.

Furthermore, there are practical challenges regarding expected asset performance, timing of exit, fund placement timing, resource allocation, and operational expenses, as well as supply-side constraints (e.g. lack of impact advisors serving this segment of the market, a lack of transaction platforms, lack of access to products). Impact investors themselves face huge challenges in China, which include perceptions about their impact on investment performance and perceived legal restrictions. Lacking policy support, social enterprises are put at a disadvantage vis-à-vis traditional for-profit enterprise.

An increasing number of institutions are now involved in investing in social enterprises and in Impact Investing. However, the legal status of most Impact Investment institutions in China is still dominated by the nature of charitable foundations, and their investment modalities are still dominated by donations. There are few Impact Investment models using equity and bonds, and venture capital is often a poor fit given its focus on financial returns.

Additionally, the lack of unified impact evaluation standards leads to difficulties in proving the credibility and value of companies' social and environmental impacts, which plays into difficulty in getting fair valuations. Because of the lack of recognition of corporate social value and impact measurement in China, impact investors are scarce, and some excellent social firms have to sacrifice social value to meet financing needs along the development process.

Impact Investing requires skillful thinking to integrate multiple, highly distinct types of investment options and outcomes. The field of impact investment needs more outstanding entrepreneurs with both social responsibility and entrepreneurship skills. Impact Investing fund managers need to be compensated with different incentive packages than those in conventional private equity funds, compensated by the financial performance of the fund.

DISCUSSION

The theory of change behind Impact Investing is based on the belief that entrepreneurship and market mechanisms can solve the social and environmental problems efficiently and effectively. For many years, the excesses of greed and profit-seeking in global financial markets have ignored social values. Yet social value does not have to be pursued at the expense of financial returns. If organizations seek only social benefits instead of return on investment, they often compromise their development and struggle to scale, ultimately failing to yield economic sustainability. By rewarding companies that dually focus on impact and profits, Impact Investing is a promising solution to the so-called grand challenges of sustainable development.

Impact Investing allocates economic resources efficiently to social entrepreneurs for innovative activities that realize the growth of social value. Compared to traditional enterprises, the advantage of social enterprises lies in their organizational characteristics. They are suitable to enter social public sectors and help the government efficiently solve complex social and environmental problems. The ideal social enterprise model orients entrepreneurs toward solving social problems, striving to reduce the marginal cost of beneficial products and services through continuous innovation. The result is that their company benefits the public as much as possible, creates social value, and generates financial returns.

Given the need for China to create sustainable economic growth over the decades to come, Impact Investing has an important role to play. Impact Investing should gain traction in the country, and several trends indicate that it will. Going forward, however, China's Impact Investing industry needs to rely more on the market to solve social problems. China needs to learn more from other countries about how to promote a favorable investment environment, with the government playing a central role, as both recipient of investment and investor.

Furthermore, in China, further research and study is necessary to identify priority sectors for intervention interest. These sectors should undergo market studies and in-depth research to facilitate a deeper understanding of the targeted field. Only at this point should investment due diligence factors, such as competitive environment, investment opportunity, and team competitiveness, be taken into comprehensive consideration.

For example, Ehong Capital identified pensions, education, low-carbon environmental protection, and green agriculture as their investment preferences, mainly based on the following four aspects: market demand and size, policy concerns, alignment with Ehong's areas of expertise and competitive advantage, and investor preference. Lvkang Medical Care cooperates with the local government. The marginal cost of its services was greatly reduced to bring professional services to as many middle- and low-income disabled and semi-disabled elderly as possible, while achieving appropriate profits. Qiangying Duck Group, through a series of innovative activities, such as duck seedling variety innovation, incubation technology innovation, breeding technology, and mode innovation, have reduced the marginal cost of products, so that they do not only realize appropriate profits but also create employment and entrepreneurial opportunities for local poor farmers.

Recommendations

The Chinese investment market has a large financial capacity and it is very resourceful. Thus, attracting only a small part of its capital into the field of Impact Investment could create substantial value. Public policy can help foster the participation of more capital by developing policies that encourage more investment into Chinese impact companies, both domestically and internationally. So far, the Chinese government and regulators have mainly promoted Impact Investment through scattered initiatives.

China's Impact Investment industry needs to rely more on the market and social forces to play a positive role in solving social problems. In the future, the Chinese central government should provide specific supporting policies to improve financial and regulatory incentive mechanisms to attract more enterprises, cooperatives, and other social forces into Impact Investing. Policies relating to foreign investments in Chinese startups need further clarity.

To create an optimal environment for Impact Investing, the Chinese central government should also vigorously carry forward the best of traditional Chinese culture and bring greater awareness to Impact Investing, while also appropriately incentivizing the investment community to participate. Only by promoting the recognition of social value domestically in China's capital market can more mainstream investment institutions be introduced to the field of Impact Investment.

For businesses and institutions already engaging in Impact Investing in China, recommendations include setting clear and shared goals, prioritizing long-term planning, strengthening corporate governance, and better allocating resources toward activities that are tightly connected with the core of the business. Impact investors and social entrepreneurs could also do a better job at marketing its potential benefits. The business case for Impact Investing should be more widely disseminated to a larger set of institutional investors in order to facilitate the integration of nonfinancial elements into the overall investment strategy and portfolio.

Measuring and monitoring the performance in all stages of the investment cycle is fundamental, as investors and investees must be kept abreast of progress. But China seems to be taking a longer time to adopt impact measurements. This phenomenon can be caused by lack of understanding about the importance of measuring impacts, lack of motivation, and lack of budget or resources to do it. Future research could help identify the unique constrains faced in China, examine how impact investors incorporate risk into their decision-making, and which key metrics and criteria affect their decision-making.

CONCLUSION

This chapter presents an account of the complexities of Impact Investing in China. While China already is a major investor with a global reach, it is still in an embryonic stage of developing its Impact Investing industry. In this respect, China is expected to become a major world player in Impact Investing in the future, due to: (i) the alignment of the concept of Impact Investment with the spirit of the 19th Communist Party of China's National Congress; (ii) Impact Investing conforming to the five concepts at the heart of China's national development strategy: innovation, coordination, openness, green (sustainable), and sharing (among the community); (iii) China's urgency to solve its social and environmental problems; and (iv) its huge market space of 1.4 billion inhabitants.

Impact Investing presents itself not only as a momentary "trendy" investment opportunity, but also as a long-term investment strategy that can help create more stable and sustainable economies for decades to come. All forms of Impact Investing currently practiced in China (e.g. venture philanthropy, BoP) have the potential to become attractive alternatives for investors that are willing to divert from the single pursuit of profit to a more impact-oriented approach. If Impact Investing becomes widespread, then this economic force could help boost incomes, reduce poverty, and related effects.

Research on the practices of Chinese Impact Investing firms reveal the following shortcomings: lack of a clear strategic plan, lack of a systematic and organization-wide management, and lack of balance and focus (Wong 2013). The first challenge in China is to better identify portfolios of investments that simultaneously optimize across financial and social outcomes. Up to now, most Chinese Impact Investing funds rely on an intuitive approach to create portfolios that generate both impact and revenue. But intuition is often fallible when it comes to achieving outcomes, and especially impacts. Chinese Impact Investors must also develop robust answers to questions such as: To what extent do Impact Investing decisions efficiently achieve both social and financial outcomes? How might these decisions be made more efficient, thereby increasing overall value creation?

Beyond domestic investors, the potential for cross-boundary Impact Investing is especially significant in developing countries and emerging markets such as China (OECD 2016). Many mature overseas impact investors, such as the LGT Foundation and the Ford Foundation, have begun to pay attention to China's social service market in particular. Compared to domestic impact investors and foundations in China, international impact investors and funds have clearer and more specific positioning and tend to choose investment projects in the fields they are familiar with.

Further, a national platform for capturing, channeling, and promoting impact investment projects has not yet been established. A Chinese nationwide Impact Investing network similar to the Global Impact Investing Network (GIIN), that gathers investors, research institutions, and public authorities to establish industry norms, would help raise awareness and create traction for all parties in the Chinese Impact Investing ecosystem.

ACKNOWLEDGMENTS

I would like to thank Professor Yang Danhui at the Institute of Industrial Economics, China Academy of Social Science, for the expert advice and extraordinary support. My thanks also go to the China Enterprise Confederation for arranging the interviews. In addition, I would like to acknowledge the kind assistance of reviewers and the book editors Elsa De Morais Sarmento and R. Paul Herman, who inspired and encouraged me.

REFERENCES

Allman, K., and Nogales, X.E.D. (2015). *Introduction to Impact Investment* (K. Allman and X.E.D. Nogales, eds.). Hoboken, NJ: John Wiley & Sons.

Ashta, A. (2012). Co-Creation for Impact Investment in Microfinance. *Strategic Change* 21(1–2):71–81.

Brest, P., and Born, K. (2013). When Can Impact Investing Create Real Impact? *Stanford Social Innovation Review* 11(4):22–31.

Economist (2017). Impact investing inches from niche to mainstream. (5 January). https://www.economist.com/finance-and-economics/2017/01/05/impact-investing-inches-from-niche-to-mainstream (accessed 22 March 2020).

Fidelity Charitable (2019). The Fidelity Charitable 2019 Giving Report. https://www.fidelitycharitable.org/content/dam/fc-public/docs/insights/2019-giving-report.pdf (accessed 22 March 2020).

Gao, Y. (2011). Philanthropic Disaster Relief Giving as a Response to Institutional Pressure: Evidence from China. *Journal Business Research* 64(12): 1377–1382.

Gao, Y., and Hafsi, T. (2015). Government Intervention, Peers' Giving and Corporate Philanthropy: Evidence from Chinese Private SMEs. *Journal of Business Ethics* 132 433–447.

Hill, C. (2011). *International Business: Competing in the Global Market Place*. New York: McGraw-Hill Irwin.

Hong, H., and Kostovetsky, L. (2012). Red and Blue Investing: Values and Finance. *Journal of Financial Economics* 103(1):1–19.

Huang, C. W. (2016). Research on China's Path of Development-Oriented Poverty Reduction: Review and Prospect. *China Agricultural University Journal of Social Sciences* 33: 5–17.

Jagtap, S., Larsson A., and Hiort V. (2014). How Design Process for the Base of the Pyramid Differs from That for the Top of the Pyramid. *Design Studies* 35(5): 527–558.

Jing, Y., and Gong, T. (2012). Managed Social Innovation: The Case of Government-Sponsored Venture Philanthropy in Shanghai. *Australian Journal of Public Administration* 71: 233–245.

John, R. (2015). Venture Philanthropy: Venturing into Entrepreneurial Philanthropy. In *The World That Changes the World* (W. Cheng and S. Mohamed, eds.). San Francisco: Jossey-Bass.

Kim, I., Wan, H., Wang, B. et al. (2019). Institutional Investors and Corporate Environmental, Social, and Governance Policies: Evidence from Toxics Release Data. *Management Science* 65(10): 4901–4926.

Leborgne-Bonassié, M, Coletti, M., and Sansone, G. (2019). What Do Venture Philanthropy Organizations Seek in Social Enterprises? *Business Strategy Development* 2: 349–357.

Li, L., Du, K., Zhang, W, and Mao, J.-Y. (2019). Poverty Alleviation Through Government-Led e-commerce Development in Rural China: An Activity Theory Perspective. *Info Systems Journal* 29: 914–952.

Li, Y., Li, Y., and Su, B. (2016). Realizing Targeted Poverty Alleviation in China: People's Voices, Implementation Challenges and Policy Implications, *China Agricultural Economic Review* 8: 443–454.

Li, P. L., and Wei, H. K. (2016). *Annual Report on Poverty Reduction of China 2016.* Beijing: Social Sciences Academic Press.

Liu, M., Feng, X., Wang, S., and Qiu, H. (2020). China's Poverty Alleviation Over the Last 40 Years: Successes and Challenges. *Australian Journal of Agricultural and Resource Economics* 64: 209–228.

McCreless, M. (2017). Toward the Efficient Impact Frontier. *Stanford Social Innovation Review* 15(1): 49–53.

Mahoney, L. (2013). Sustainability and Inclusiveness Primer: Challenges of Impact Investing in China. https://knowledge.ckgsb.edu.cn/2013/09/09/ china-business-strategy/challenges-of-impact-investing-in-china/amp/ (accessed 22 March 2020).

Monitor Institute (2009). Investing for Social and Environmental Impact: A Design for Catalyzing and Emerging Industry. https://www2.deloitte .com/content/dam/Deloitte/global/Documents/Financial-Services/gx-fsi-monitor-Investing-for-Social-and-Environmental-Impact-2009.pdf (accessed 22 March 2020).

National Bureau of Statistics (NBS) (2018). *Poverty Monitoring Report of Rural China 2018.* China Statistics Press. Beijing.

OECD (2016). Development Co-operation Report 2016: The Sustainable Development Goals as Business Opportunities. Paris.

Pepin, J. (2005). Venture Capitalists and Entrepreneurs Become Venture Philanthropists. *International Journal of Nonprofit and Voluntary Sector Marketing* 10: 165–173.

Prahalad, C. K. (2004). *The Fortune at the Bottom of the Pyramid: Eradicating Poverty Through Profits.* Upper Saddle River, NJ: Wharton School Publishing.

Van Slyke, D. M., and Newman, H. K. (2006). Venture Philanthropy and Social Entrepreneurship in Community Redevelopment. *Nonprofit Management and Leadership* 16: 345–368.

Venture Capital Research Institute. (2018). *The Yearbook of China Venture Capital.* Beijing: China Development Press.

Wong A. (2013). Sustainability and Inclusiveness Primer: Challenges of Impact Investing in China. https://knowledge.ckgsb.edu.cn/2013/09/09/china-business-strategy/challenges-of-impact-investing-in-china/ (accessed 22 March 2020).

Yan, K. (2016). *Poverty Alleviation in China: A Theoretical and Empirical Study.* Berling: Springer.

Zhang, L., and Tong, Y. (2012). Why companies go BoP: An exploratory study in Chinese context. Technology Management for Emerging Technologies (PICMET). Proceedings of PICMET '12: IEEE.

Zhou, J. (2017). The Development of Impact Investing and Implications for China. Master's thesis, MIT Sloan School of Management. https://dspace.mit .edu/bitstream/handle/1721.1/111448/1003321342-MIT.pdf?sequence=1& isAllowed=y (accessed 22 March 2020).

Zhou J., Tong Y., and Liu, X. (2012). Diffusion of solar thermal in China's BoP market. Technology Management for Emerging Technologies (PICMET). Proceedings of PICMET '12: IEEE.

APPENDIX 22.1: LIST OF INTERVIEWEES

Dr. Lin Lei, Professor of Information Systems and Technology Management, China Academy of Science, and the author of *Intrapreneurship* (Beijing: China Machine Press, 2018)

Dr. Teng Binsheng, Dean and Professor of Strategy and Innovation Management, Cheung Kong Graduate School of Business

Zhang Wenbin, Secretary, Department of Managerial Innovation, China Enterprise Confederation

Qiu Chaomin, President, Partner Venture Capital of China

Tao Xin, Investment Manager, Partner Venture Capital of China

CHAPTER 23

Impact Investing Through Corporate Social Responsibility: The Indian Experience

Tanvi Kiran, PhD and Shivam Dhawan, MA

Abstract

The Corporate Social Responsibility (CSR) provisions of the Companies Act of 2013 were thoughtfully designed by the Indian government to achieve harmony between businesses' economic goals and society's social welfare concerns. This study shall comprehensively present a detailed picture of impact investment projects undertaken by the corporate sector under the mandated CSR provisions in areas with the potential of creating positive social, economic, and environmental impacts on the Indian society. The study attempts to provide a new dimension to the existing body of literature, by examining the magnitude, nature, the type, and the extent of the CSR expenditure in the focal areas of impact investment, through the analysis of CSR expenditure data of over 19,000 Indian companies during a period of four financial years (2014–15 to 2017–18). The findings reveal that "education and skill development" emerged as the most popular impact investment area, while "social empowerment" received the least corporate attention in terms of CSR expenditure. The share of non-public sector companies in the total CSR expenditure outweighed public sector undertakings. Furthermore, the distribution of CSR expenditure is somewhat asymmetrical across different regions of India. The study also offers policy relevant recommendations for the effective compliance of the CSR mandate, which can generate powerful socioeconomic developmental impacts in the country.

Keywords

Corporate Social Responsibility; CSR; CSR Mandate; Effective Compliance; Impact Investment; Impact Investing; Socioeconomic Development; India

INTRODUCTION

This chapter examines the pattern and extent of impact investment projects created by Indian companies under the purview of the Companies Act of 2013 (Government of India 2013). These provisions mandate firms to spend a certain proportion of their investments on social and community development initiatives, thereby making the companies a major stakeholder to bridge the social welfare gap in India. This chapter provides new insights into the existing body of literature by focusing specifically on corporate social responsibility (CSR) investments, its magnitude, nature, type, and extent, as a channel to achieve socioeconomic, developmental, and environmental impacts in Indian economy.

The concept of Impact Investing has gained a lot of attention in the Indian economy, especially after the enactment of Companies Act of 2013, and CSR in particular is regarded as a potent tool to achieve the goals enshrined in the concept of Impact Investing, especially in the context of India, which despite being an emerging economy faces sizable socioeconomic inequalities (Dev 2017) and still struggles to achieve holistic social and community development.

The concept of CSR encompasses a wide range of activities undertaken by companies that sustainably integrate their social welfare concerns with their business operations, becoming accountable for their impacts at the community at large. Scholars argue that profit-making corporations have a moral and social responsibility to give something back to society in the form of welfare and development initiatives, which is generally done on a voluntary basis (Moore 1999). A major policy document by the European Union and the Organization for Economic Co-operation and Development (European Union and OECD 2016) underlined the need for providing favorable conditions to social enterprises to select the most suitable strategy to support pilot projects of social interest.

India made a game-changing decision by enacting the Companies Act of 2013 (Manchiraju and Rajgopal 2017), becoming the first country to make it mandatory for large and profitable businesses to undertake CSR investments on a predefined list of activities,[1] by following the self-governing principle of "comply or explain." This states that if a company is not able to spend the mandated CSR amount in a given year, it needs to disclose the reasons for it (Varottil 2018). In this context, the mandated CSR expenditure becomes analogous to Impact Investing, a powerful blend of attaining reasonably good economic returns while addressing environmental and social challenges (Jackson 2013). Thus, through their mandated CSR commitments, private business enterprises can achieve positive social impacts alongside increased financial performance and enhanced brand reputation in the context of the Indian economy (Bayoud and Kavanagh 2012).

Against this backdrop, the specific objectives of the present chapter are: (i) to study the trends in the total amount spent on CSR development activities in India; (ii) to examine the distribution of CSR expenditure across the six identified impact investment areas and to identify the preferred and the least attractive areas for investment; (iii) to examine the geographical distribution of CSR expenditure in India, so as to identify possible concentration areas, if any; and (iv) to compare public and private sectors CSR spending of impact investment projects in India.

The chapter is organized as follows. The next section details the data and metrics employed. Then this chapter provides an overview of the CSR model in India and the focal areas of impact investments under CSR, respectively, with findings presented. Then this chapter offers key observations and recommendations.

---

[1] The advised list of CSR activities and projects in India range from initiatives in education, health care, nutrition, natural resources, environment, sanitation, rural development, welfare of elderly, women and child, and so on.

DATA AND METHODS

This chapter involves the analysis of data concerning CSR expenditure of over 19,000 Indian companies that fall under the provisions of India's Companies Act of 2013. The data originates from the publicly available data repository (National CSR Portal) of the Indian Ministry of Corporate Affairs, encompassing a period of four financial years (2014–15 to 2017–18).[2] The study makes use of four parameters to examine CSR expenditure channeling in India, the magnitude, nature, type, and geographical breakdown (named "extent") of impact investments as seen in Table 23.1.

OVERVIEW OF THE CORPORATE SOCIAL RESPONSIBILITY MODEL IN INDIA

In India, the concept of CSR has a legal status since the inclusion of Clause 135 in the Companies Act of 2013, passed by the Indian Parliament and entering into force in April 2014. The CSR rules and provisions are applicable to all Indian and foreign business enterprises operating in India with a net profit upwards of INR 0.05 billion, or a net worth above INR 5 billion, or an annual turnover above INR 10 billion.

The new rules, effective from the fiscal year 2014–15, require these companies to set up a CSR committee and to spend at least 2% of their average net profit of the preceding three years on the list of CSR activities. As mentioned above, companies that do not comply must disclose their reasons. The contravention of the provisions of the CSR carries legal penalization (Kalaiselvi and Karthika 2020). The Indian CSR model is depicted in Figure 23.1.

FOCAL AREAS OF IMPACT INVESTMENT UNDER CSR

The CSR provisions of the Companies Act of 2013 have made it obligatory for the concerned companies to invest at least 2% of their average net profit on the list of activities that have far-reaching implications with regard to the development and welfare of the society at large (Singh and Verma 2014).

Schedule VII of the Companies Act specifies the list of activities eligible for investment under CSR (Mitra and Schmidpeter 2017). Since most

---

[2]The data pertaining to these four financial years was continuously accessed in the month of April 2019.

TABLE 23.1 Description of the Parameters, Methods and Metrics Used in the Study.

No.	Parameters	Methods and Metrics
1	Total CSR spent on developmental activities ↑ **(Magnitude of CSR)**	Total annual expenditure on CSR development activities, expressed in billion Indian National Rupees (INR)
2	Impact investment area break-up of CSR expenditure in India ↑ **(Nature of CSR)**	The nature of CSR expenditure across the six identified "Impact Investment Areas" shall be studied by making use of expenditure data values in absolute terms and by calculating the percentage share of each of the impact investment category/subcategories in the total CSR expenditure for that year. These areas are Education and Skill Development; Environment and Related Areas; Social Empowerment; Health, Nutrition, Water, and Sanitation; Specialized Mission Projects; Miscellaneous Areas.
3	Geographical distribution of CSR expenditure in India ↑ **(Extent of CSR)**	Indian states are categorized and grouped into six geographical regions. The annual share of CSR expenditure made by companies in each of the regions in the total CSR expenditure is calculated to facilitate comparisons across different geographical regions.
4	CSR spending of public sector undertakings and non-public sector undertakings ↑ **(Type of CSR)**	CSR expenditure, both in absolute terms and the percentage shares of public and nonpublic (private and foreign) undertakings, are calculated and compared across the four financial years.

Source: Authors' elaboration.

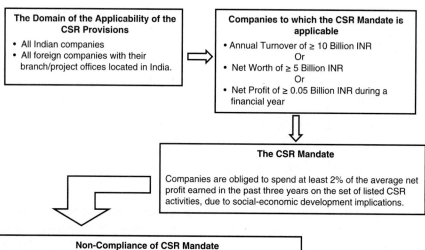

FIGURE 23.1   The Corporate Social Responsibility Model in the Indian Context. *Source*: Authors' formulation based on the Companies Act of 2013 (Government of India 2013).

activities focus on the socioeconomic improvement of the disadvantaged and at-risk sections of the society, for the present study, each was labeled as a focal area for Impact Investing, able to generate beneficial outcomes. Focal areas and activities of a similar nature were grouped together for the purpose of this study, to facilitate comparisons and benchmarking at a later stage of the study.

This study follows the formal classification for the six main areas under analysis: Education and Skill Development; Environment and Related Areas; Social Empowerment; Health, Nutrition, Water, and Sanitation; Specialized Mission Projects; Miscellaneous Areas.

Impact Investment Area 1: Education and Skill Development

Under the CSR provisions, investment in "Education and Skill Development" projects involve spending in the multitude of activities related to the following subcategories:

- Education: creation of classrooms (both traditional and digital), providing scholarships and career counseling to students, setting up science and technology laboratories, capacity building, student and teacher training, education awareness programs, and more
- Livelihood Enhancement Projects: reduction of poverty through the creation of sustainable employment opportunities; for example, creation of agriculture-based projects that provide alternative job options, capacity building, and social inclusion services
- Special Education: special needs education and learning instructions to mentally and physically challenged children and adults so they can reach their fullest potential
- Vocational Skills: nonacademic skill enhancement technical training to the persons in order to equip them for a specific occupation, vocation, and job

Impact Investment Area 2: Environment and Related Areas

- Agroforestry: Agro-based activities such as growing of trees, plantations, along with livestock (dairy, poultry, and more) for sustainable agricultural development. A study by Kumbamu (2017) underlined the importance of building social and solidarity economies (SSE) to create socioecological and economic value in the field of agriculture to enhance farmers' bargaining power within the community. The CSR-compliant companies can participate and invest in similar initiatives to boost sustainable growth in agroforestry sector.
- Animal Welfare: activities for the welfare and care of the animals such as providing shelters, hospitals, mobile clinics, organizing adoption and rehoming drives for the animals, and more
- Conservation of Natural Resources and Environment Sustainability: restoration of mined-out lands, harvesting of water, development of green belts, afforestation drives, protecting the biodiversity, recycling of plastic, installation of solar panels, and economically and ecologically sustainable management of nonrenewable resources and more

Impact Investment Area 3: Social Empowerment

The category of "Social Empowerment" has a very broad base and includes a diverse set of areas. CSR expenditure in each of these areas shall have a huge impact in creating autonomy, social justice, and welfare for socially disadvantaged groups (marginalized sections, women, senior citizens, and orphaned children) in the context of the Indian economy.

- Gender equality: includes corporate investment in those projects and activities that aim to provide equal access to opportunities (such as literacy, health, professional skills, and more) to both men and women so that all can realize their development potential
- Senior citizens welfare: setting up special homes and shelters for the elderly, counseling and recreational activities, specialized hospitals, mobile dispensaries, and provision of affordable medical services
- Welfare of orphaned children: constructing orphanages, imparting vocational skills, provision of technology-driven educational infrastructure (laptops, computers, tablets, and more), creation of specialized schools to facilitate social inclusion
- Reduction of socioeconomic inequalities: training and empowerment of rural youth for self-employment activities, technical assistance to marginal farmers on new methods of farming, infrastructures (such as rural electrification through renewable energy resources), construction of hostels, shelters for economically and socially disadvantaged section of Indian society (Scheduled Castes, Scheduled Tribes, and Other Backward Classes), and more
- Women empowerment: creation of special schools for girls, technical training to women, funds for startups exclusively managed by women entrepreneurs, arranging capacity building and training workshops for women-headed self-help groups (Datta and Gailey 2012), setting up homes, shelters and hostels for women, and more

Impact Investment Area 4: Health, Nutrition, Water, and Sanitation

- Health care: health awareness camps on life-threatening diseases (AIDS, cancer, leprosy, and more), drug and alcohol abuse rehabilitation centers, health care technology incubators, blood donation drives, medical transportation, online and mobile phone–based medical consultation, and more
- Nutrition: awareness workshops on child development and malnutrition, research and development of affordable consumer goods, nutrition and wellness initiatives for lactating mothers and their children to

target the reduction of maternal, neonatal, and infant mortality rates, and more

- Water: installation and renovation of tube wells, hand pumps, wells, mobile water dispensers, rainwater harvesting projects, raising awareness regarding the use of safe drinking water
- Sanitation: behavior change initiatives and awareness programs for social communities on open defecation, construction of environmentally friendly mobile toilets and zero-water urinals, especially in slum areas, wastewater treatment projects, creation of ecofriendly products for human waste management system, setting up cost-effective sanitary-pad vending machines, and more

Impact Investment Area 5: Specialized Mission Projects

- Prime Minister National Relief Fund: provide urgent assistance to the families whose lives have been adversely affected by natural disasters/calamities like earthquakes, cyclones, and floods, and victims of riots
- Swachh Bharat Kosh:[3] investments made through CSR under this specialized fund are used for the provision of sanitation services such as construction of toilets (especially for girls) in rural, urban areas, and schools
- Clean Ganga Fund: created by the Indian government to address the issue of declining water quality in the sacred Ganga, or Ganges, river (Trivedi 2010). Companies can directly contribute toward the fund or carry out certain activities like collection of floating debris, solid waste management, planting trees, spreading awareness, or facilitating ground-breaking technologies in this regard.
- Other Central Government Funds: specific central government funds that focus on construction and maintenance of roads, bridges, rural electrification, building affordable homes for poor, and more

Impact Investment Area 6: Miscellaneous Areas

- Heritage, Art, and Culture: sponsorship of art and cultural events, refurbishment of antiquities, museums, scholarships for art and culture, and more

---

[3]Swachh Bharat Kosh is a Hindi term, which in English can be translated as Clean India Fund.

- Sports: conducting and sponsoring sporting events in rural areas, infrastructure and training facilities, and scholarships
- Rural and Slum Development Projects: creating a wide range of services in the rural and slum areas: water, sanitation, education, health care to adopting the entire village itself (Pradhan and Ranjan 2011)
- Welfare of Armed Forces: organizing and sponsoring events as well as undertaking welfare initiatives for armed forces, war widows and their dependents

FINDINGS

Parameter 1: Magnitude of Impact Investment: Total CSR Spent on Developmental Activities

The total amount spent by the companies falling under the domain of the CSR provisions on different socioeconomic development activities is depicted in Figure 23.2.

The amount spent on the CSR developmental activities has decreased by approximately 16% from INR 100.7 billion in the year 2014–15 to INR 83.7 billion during 2017–18. The reasons behind this fall in CSR expenditure may be attributed to companies' noncompliance of their CSR commitments (Goel and Ramanathan 2014). As per the existing literature, companies may sometimes be genuinely not able to comply due to multiple reasons, such as unfavorable market conditions, turnover losses in a given year(s), delay in the formulation and registration of investment projects (Kapoor and Dhamija 2017). All these factors combined might have resulted in a decline of CSR expenditure.

A brief glimpse of the CSR investments to all six Impact Investment categories has been presented in Figures 23.3a and 23.3b. These figures shall frequently be referred to while describing the sectoral details of CSR investments in India (parameter 2), which is discussed in detail below.

Parameter 2: Nature of Impact Investment: Sectoral Breakup of CSR Expenditure in India

The share of each of the six identified social impact areas and their subcategories in the total CSR expenditure for each year from 2014–15 to 2017–18 has been calculated using the data from the CSR expenditure database. The findings are detailed below.

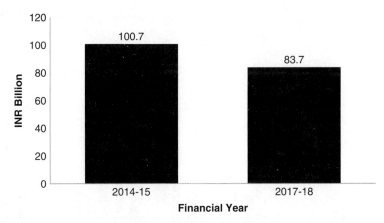

FIGURE 23.2 Total Amount of CSR Investments (2014–15 and 2017–18). *Source*: Authors' calculations using the database on CSR expenditure (accessed in April 2019), Ministry of Corporate Affairs, Government of India.

CSR Spent in Impact Investment Area 1: Education and Skill Development

Figures 23.4a and 23.4b show that the share of education and livelihood enhancement projects in the total CSR expenditure has continuously increased from 25.7% to 32.3% and from 2.8% to 5.0%, respectively, from 2014–15 to 2017–18. The percentage shares of special education and vocational skills have also witnessed a marginal increment during the same time period with some fluctuations during the intervening period. In absolute terms, the total CSR expenditure in "Education and Skill Development" has reported an increment from INR 31.9 billion to INR 34.9 billion, thereby resulting in a considerable improvement in its respective share from 31.7% to 41.7% from 2014–15 to 2017–18 as seen in Figures 23.3a and 23.3b. This growth pertains to the preference given by CSR companies to the education sector.

The analysis of the sub-categories within this impact investment area reveals that investment in education has been a preferred area of investment, whereas special education has attracted the lowest CSR expenditure during the four financial years.

CSR Spent in Impact Investment Area 2: Environment and Related Areas

Keeping in mind its importance for sustainable development (Busch, Lehmann, and Hoffmann 2012), the investment in environment has been

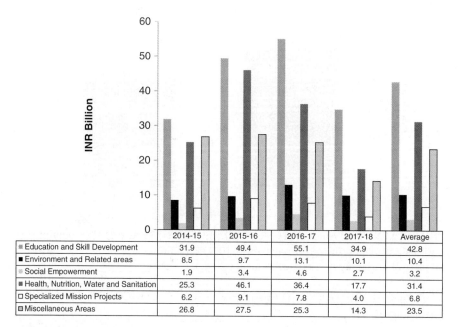

	2014-15	2015-16	2016-17	2017-18	Average
▨ Education and Skill Development	31.9	49.4	55.1	34.9	42.8
▪ Environment and Related areas	8.5	9.7	13.1	10.1	10.4
▨ Social Empowerment	1.9	3.4	4.6	2.7	3.2
▪ Health, Nutrition, Water and Sanitation	25.3	46.1	36.4	17.7	31.4
▫ Specialized Mission Projects	6.2	9.1	7.8	4.0	6.8
▫ Miscellaneous Areas	26.8	27.5	25.3	14.3	23.5

FIGURE 23.3a   CSR Allocations to All Six Impact Investment Categories. *Source*: Authors' calculations using the database on CSR Expenditure (accessed in April 2019), Ministry of Corporate Affairs, Government of India.

one of the focal areas under the CSR mandate. Except for the investment in agroforestry, the share of projects and activities related to animal welfare, conservation of natural resources, and environmental sustainability witnessed an increment in 2017–18 as compared to 2014–15 as shown in Figures 23.5a and 23.5b. There has been an approximate four-fold rise in the expenditure share of CSR activities related to natural resources conservation, from 0.4% in 2014–15 to 1.7% in 2017–18. On an average during the period, the expenditure in the overall "environment and related areas" has accounted for a sizeable share (9.1%) in the total CSR expenditure with projects on environmental sustainability occupying a dominant share of 7.7% within this impact investment category, as depicted in Figure 23.3b.

CSR Spent in Impact Investment Area 3: Social Empowerment

Business firms investing in projects that target social empowerment can go a long way in creating a sense of self- sufficiency, autonomy, and social inclusion for socially disadvantaged groups (Utting 2007), especially in

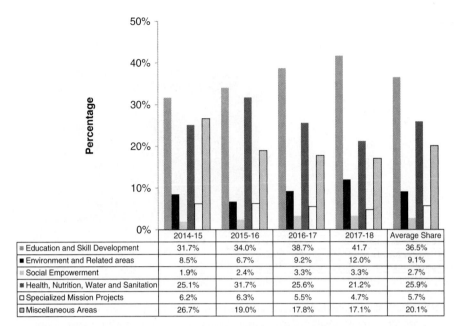

	2014-15	2015-16	2016-17	2017-18	Average Share
▨ Education and Skill Development	31.7%	34.0%	38.7%	41.7	36.5%
▪ Environment and Related areas	8.5%	6.7%	9.2%	12.0%	9.1%
▨ Social Empowerment	1.9%	2.4%	3.3%	3.3%	2.7%
▪ Health, Nutrition, Water and Sanitation	25.1%	31.7%	25.6%	21.2%	25.9%
▫ Specialized Mission Projects	6.2%	6.3%	5.5%	4.7%	5.7%
▨ Miscellaneous Areas	26.7%	19.0%	17.8%	17.1%	20.1%

FIGURE 23.3b   Percentage of all CSR Impact Investments. *Source*: Authors'
calculations using the database on CSR Expenditure (accessed in April 2019), Ministry of
Corporate Affairs, Government of India.

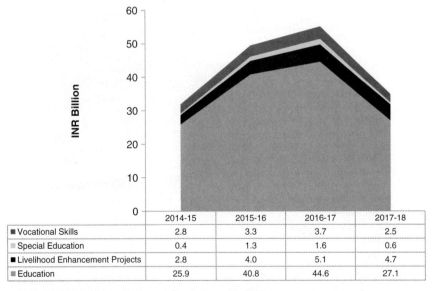

	2014-15	2015-16	2016-17	2017-18
▪ Vocational Skills	2.8	3.3	3.7	2.5
▨ Special Education	0.4	1.3	1.6	0.6
▪ Livelihood Enhancement Projects	2.8	4.0	5.1	4.7
▨ Education	25.9	40.8	44.6	27.1

FIGURE 23.4a   CSR Allocations to Education and Skill Development. *Source*:
Authors' calculations using the database on CSR Expenditure (accessed in April 2019),
Ministry of Corporate Affairs, Government of India.

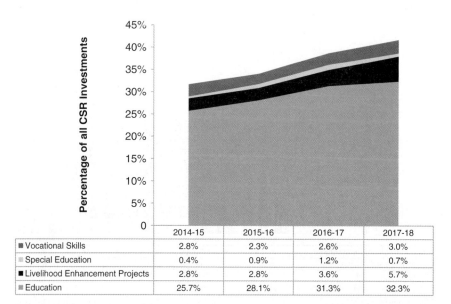

	2014-15	2015-16	2016-17	2017-18
■ Vocational Skills	2.8%	2.3%	2.6%	3.0%
▨ Special Education	0.4%	0.9%	1.2%	0.7%
■ Livelihood Enhancement Projects	2.8%	2.8%	3.6%	5.7%
▨ Education	25.7%	28.1%	31.3%	32.3%

FIGURE 23.4b   Percentage of all CSR Investments to Education and Skill Development. *Source*: Authors' calculations using the database on CSR Expenditure (accessed in April 2019), Ministry of Corporate Affairs, Government of India.

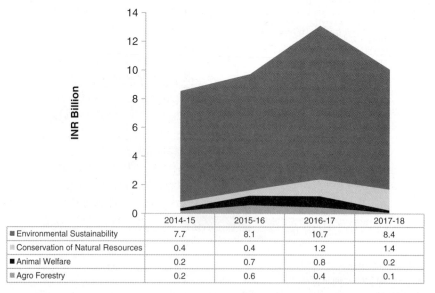

	2014-15	2015-16	2016-17	2017-18
■ Environmental Sustainability	7.7	8.1	10.7	8.4
▨ Conservation of Natural Resources	0.4	0.4	1.2	1.4
■ Animal Welfare	0.2	0.7	0.8	0.2
▨ Agro Forestry	0.2	0.6	0.4	0.1

FIGURE 23.5a   CSR Allocations to Environment and Related Areas. *Source*: Authors' calculations using the database on CSR Expenditure (accessed in April 2019), Ministry of Corporate Affairs, Government of India.

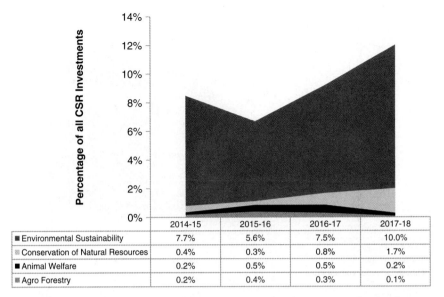

	2014-15	2015-16	2016-17	2017-18
■ Environmental Sustainability	7.7%	5.6%	7.5%	10.0%
▩ Conservation of Natural Resources	0.4%	0.3%	0.8%	1.7%
■ Animal Welfare	0.2%	0.5%	0.5%	0.2%
▩ Agro Forestry	0.2%	0.4%	0.3%	0.1%

FIGURE 23.5b Percentage of all CSR Investments to Environment and Related Areas. *Source*: Authors' calculations using the database on CSR Expenditure (accessed in April 2019), Ministry of Corporate Affairs, Government of India.

the context of Indian society. As shown in Figure 23.3b, the projects and activities related to "Social Empowerment" attracted on an average of only 2.7% of the total CSR expenditure during the period under study. Business companies invested mostly in ventures aimed at women's empowerment and projects targeting socioeconomic inequalities, whereas CSR activities targeting the welfare of senior citizens and orphans got little attention from companies, as reflected by their low CSR expenditure shares, as reflected in Figures 23.6a and 23.6b. Further, the share of CSR activities related to women empowerment witnessed an increasing trend (from 0.7% to 1.1%), while gender equality registered a declining trend (from 0.5% to 0.1%) in 2017–18, as compared to 2014–15. This observation indicates that in terms of the share of CSR expenditure, the two closely related categories (women empowerment and gender equality) witnessed an opposite trend.

CSR Spent in Impact Investment Area 4: Health, Nutrition, Water, and Sanitation

On average during this period, approximately one-fourth of the total CSR expenditure (25.9%) has been allocated to investment projects in Health,

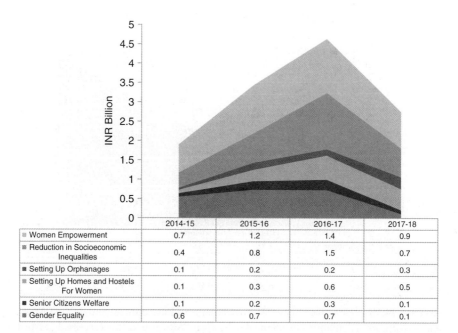

	2014-15	2015-16	2016-17	2017-18
▪ Women Empowerment	0.7	1.2	1.4	0.9
▪ Reduction in Socioeconomic Inequalities	0.4	0.8	1.5	0.7
▪ Setting Up Orphanages	0.1	0.2	0.2	0.3
▪ Setting Up Homes and Hostels For Women	0.1	0.3	0.6	0.5
▪ Senior Citizens Welfare	0.1	0.2	0.3	0.1
▪ Gender Equality	0.6	0.7	0.7	0.1

FIGURE 23.6a   CSR Allocations to Social Empowerment. *Source*: Authors' calculations using the database on CSR Expenditure (accessed in April 2019), Ministry of Corporate Affairs, Government of India.

Nutrition, Water, and Sanitation,[4] as reflected in Figure 23.3b. This reflects a positive trend specifically in India, where large numbers of people lack adequate access to health care services (Radwan 2005). Projects targeting the eradication of poverty, hunger, and malnutrition have witnessed considerable increase from 2.7% to 5% over time, with a declining trend seen in initiatives related to sanitation and health care, the latter still occupying the greatest average share in this focal area during the four-year time period, as shown in Figures 23.7a and 23.7b.

CSR Spent in Impact Investment Area 5: Specialized Mission Projects

Figure 23.8b reveals that the share of "Prime Minister's National Relief Fund"[5] in the total CSR expenditure has been continuously falling from

---

[4] As per the CSR investment areas notified by the India's Companies Act, 2013, the investment in "Health, Nutrition, Water and Sanitation" follows similar lines as the "WASH" initiative (Water, Sanitation, and Hygiene) by UNICEF.
[5] As stated earlier this fund provides urgent assistance to the families whose lives have been adversely affected by natural disasters/calamities.

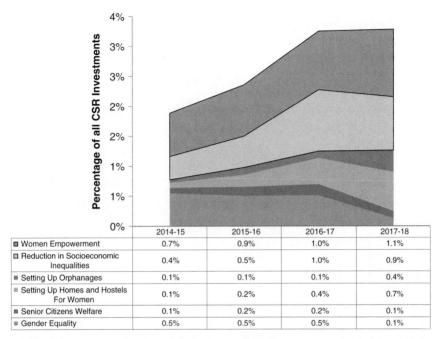

	2014-15	2015-16	2016-17	2017-18
Women Empowerment	0.7%	0.9%	1.0%	1.1%
Reduction in Socioeconomic Inequalities	0.4%	0.5%	1.0%	0.9%
Setting Up Orphanages	0.1%	0.1%	0.1%	0.4%
Setting Up Homes and Hostels For Women	0.1%	0.2%	0.4%	0.7%
Senior Citizens Welfare	0.1%	0.2%	0.2%	0.1%
Gender Equality	0.5%	0.5%	0.5%	0.1%

FIGURE 23.6b   Percentage of all CSR Investments to Social Empowerment. *Source*: Authors' calculations using the database on CSR Expenditure (accessed in April 2019), Ministry of Corporate Affairs, Government of India.

2.3% to 0.7% from 2014–15 to 2017–18, whereas the share of "Swachh Bharat Kosh" has increased from 1.1% to 1.4%. The rise in CSR contributions toward "Swachh Bharat Kosh" reflects that CSR mandate has been able to leverage the corporate efforts toward achieving the development goals of clean India and improved sanitation (Lawania and Kapoor 2018).The CSR investments in Clean Ganga Fund and other central government funds have declined overall during the given time period with some fluctuations in between, as seen in Figure 23.8. This is not a good sign because it indicates reduced corporate responsibility toward controlling and managing the pollution levels in the river Ganga, which despite having historical and religious relevance (Sanghi 2014) is extremely important for providing livelihoods to a sizable Indian population. Figure 23.8b further indicates that since other central government funds include multiple schemes targeting diverse development activities, its average CSR percentage share is highest when compared with three other specialized mission projects.

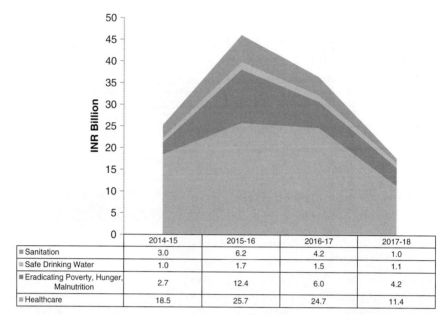

	2014-15	2015-16	2016-17	2017-18
▦ Sanitation	3.0	6.2	4.2	1.0
▦ Safe Drinking Water	1.0	1.7	1.5	1.1
▦ Eradicating Poverty, Hunger, Malnutrition	2.7	12.4	6.0	4.2
▦ Healthcare	18.5	25.7	24.7	11.4

FIGURE 23.7a   CSR Allocations to Health, Nutrition, Water, and Sanitation. *Source*: Authors' calculations using the database on CSR Expenditure (accessed in April 2019), Ministry of Corporate Affairs, Government of India.

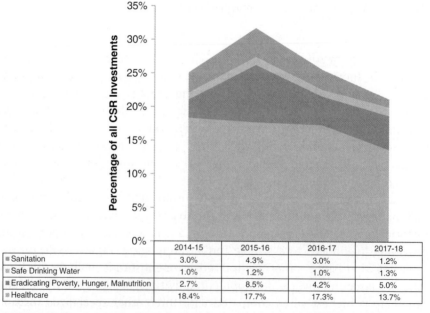

	2014-15	2015-16	2016-17	2017-18
▦ Sanitation	3.0%	4.3%	3.0%	1.2%
▦ Safe Drinking Water	1.0%	1.2%	1.0%	1.3%
▦ Eradicating Poverty, Hunger, Malnutrition	2.7%	8.5%	4.2%	5.0%
▦ Healthcare	18.4%	17.7%	17.3%	13.7%

FIGURE 23.7b   Percentage of all CSR Investments to Health, Nutrition, Water, and Sanitation. *Source*: Authors' calculations using the database on CSR Expenditure (accessed in April 2019), Ministry of Corporate Affairs, Government of India.

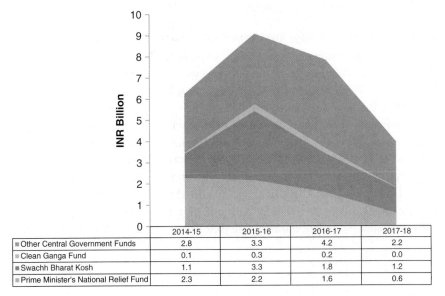

	2014-15	2015-16	2016-17	2017-18
■ Other Central Government Funds	2.8	3.3	4.2	2.2
■ Clean Ganga Fund	0.1	0.3	0.2	0.0
■ Swachh Bharat Kosh	1.1	3.3	1.8	1.2
■ Prime Minister's National Relief Fund	2.3	2.2	1.6	0.6

FIGURE 23.8a CSR Allocations to Specialized Mission Projects. *Source*: Authors' calculations using the database on CSR Expenditure (accessed in April 2019), Ministry of Corporate Affairs, Government of India.

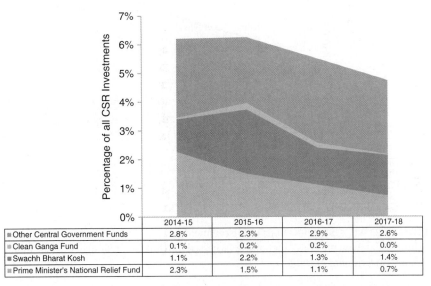

	2014-15	2015-16	2016-17	2017-18
■ Other Central Government Funds	2.8%	2.3%	2.9%	2.6%
■ Clean Ganga Fund	0.1%	0.2%	0.2%	0.0%
■ Swachh Bharat Kosh	1.1%	2.2%	1.3%	1.4%
■ Prime Minister's National Relief Fund	2.3%	1.5%	1.1%	0.7%

FIGURE 23.8b Percentage of all CSR Investments to Specialized Mission Projects. *Source*: Authors' calculations using the database on CSR Expenditure (accessed in April 2019), Ministry of Corporate Affairs, Government of India.

CSR Spent in Impact Investment Area 6: Miscellaneous Areas

Figure 23.3a reveals that the total CSR expenditure incurred in "Miscellaneous Areas" has decreased from INR 26.8 billion to INR 14.3 billion from 2014–15 to 2017–18. However, as seen in Figures 23.9a and 23.9b, the shares of CSR initiatives in heritage, art, and culture; sports; and welfare of armed forces have been witnessing an upward trend during the four financial years. Further, it can be deduced that the average percentage share of rural development projects is highest, while the share of CSR initiative for the welfare of armed forces is found to be the lowest. The share of rural development projects has also increased from 10.5% to 12.7% from 2014–15 to 2017–18, whereas the share of slum area development has recorded a sizable downward trend from 1% to a paltry 0.1% during the same period.[6] This reflects a positive trend, considering that the corporate sector is undertaking

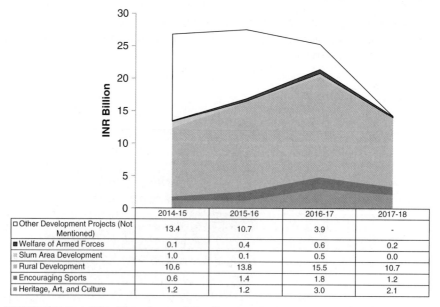

	2014-15	2015-16	2016-17	2017-18
▫ Other Development Projects (Not Mentioned)	13.4	10.7	3.9	-
▪ Welfare of Armed Forces	0.1	0.4	0.6	0.2
▨ Slum Area Development	1.0	0.1	0.5	0.0
▨ Rural Development	10.6	13.8	15.5	10.7
▪ Encouraging Sports	0.6	1.4	1.8	1.2
▨ Heritage, Art, and Culture	1.2	1.2	3.0	2.1

FIGURE 23.9a   CSR Allocations to Miscellaneous Areas. *Source*: Authors' calculations using the database on CSR Expenditure (accessed in April 2019), Ministry of Corporate Affairs, Government of India.

---

[6]When the share of slum development expenditure is compared with itself, then there is a sizable reduction of 90% (from 1% in 2014–15 to 0.1% in 2017–18).

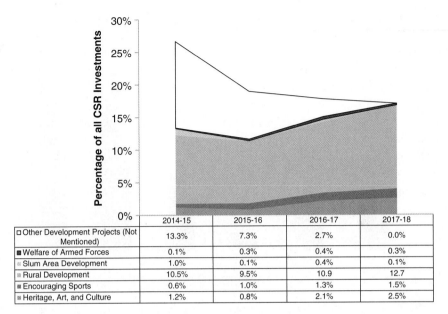

	2014-15	2015-16	2016-17	2017-18
□ Other Development Projects (Not Mentioned)	13.3%	7.3%	2.7%	0.0%
■ Welfare of Armed Forces	0.1%	0.3%	0.4%	0.3%
▨ Slum Area Development	1.0%	0.1%	0.4%	0.1%
▨ Rural Development	10.5%	9.5%	10.9	12.7
▨ Encouraging Sports	0.6%	1.0%	1.3%	1.5%
▨ Heritage, Art, and Culture	1.2%	0.8%	2.1%	2.5%

FIGURE 23.9b   Percentage of all CSR Investments to Miscellaneous Areas. *Source*: Authors' calculations using the database on CSR Expenditure (accessed in April 2019), Ministry of Corporate Affairs, Government of India.

development initiatives in rural India, where a considerable portion of population resides in a rural setting (Bliss 2019).

Parameter 3: Extent of Impact Investment in Terms of Geographical Distribution of CSR Expenditure in India

In the context of the present study, the Indian states have been divided into seven regions for the examination of the geographical distribution of CSR expenditure. As per the Indian government's report on the composite development index of states, which is based on 10 important socioeconomic components (Rajan et al. 2013), it was found that majority of the Indian states comprising the central and eastern regions were "least developed," northern and northeastern were "less developed," major western region states were "relatively developed," and the southern region had a mixed bag of states ranging from least to relatively developed states. There exist interregional disparities as far as level of development is concerned, as evidenced from the report.

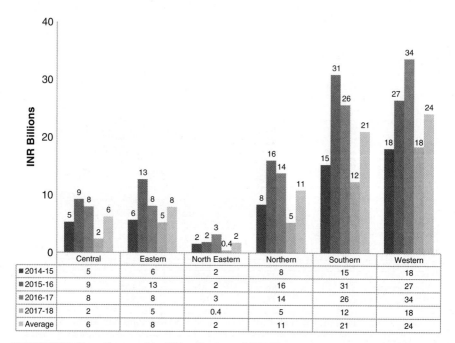

	Central	Eastern	North Eastern	Northern	Southern	Western
■ 2014-15	5	6	2	8	15	18
■ 2015-16	9	13	2	16	31	27
■ 2016-17	8	8	3	14	26	34
■ 2017-18	2	5	0.4	5	12	18
Average	6	8	2	11	21	24

FIGURE 23.10a   Geographical Distribution of CSR Investments.   *Source*: Authors' calculations using the database on CSR Expenditure (accessed in April 2019), Ministry of Corporate Affairs, Government of India.

Note: The INR values have been rounded off to the nearest integer.

As shown in Figures 23.10a and 23.10b, the western region has emerged as the preferred region for CSR commitments by business companies, closely followed by the southern region, as reflected in their respective CSR allocations and average percentage shares (35% > 29%). On the other hand, the northeastern and central Indian states attracted the lowest development projects and initiatives during the four financial years (2% < 8%). Therefore, it can be deduced that the geographical distribution of the CSR expenditure on development projects is skewed toward the more developed regions in comparison to the less developed ones.

Parameter 4: Type of Impact Investment in Terms of CSR Spending by Public Sector and Non-Public Sector Undertakings

Both the eligible public sector companies (run by the central and state government) and non-public sector undertakings (private business firms and

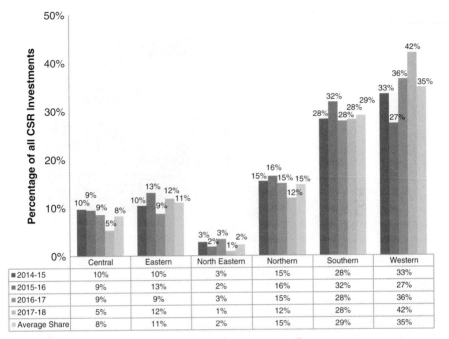

FIGURE 23.10b Percentage of CSR Investments by Geographical Regions of India.
Source: Authors' calculations using the database on CSR Expenditure (accessed in April 2019), Ministry of Corporate Affairs, Government of India.

Note: The percentage values have been rounded off to the nearest integer.

foreign companies) have been mandatorily contributing toward development projects under the CSR provisions of the Companies Act. Figures 23.11a and 23.11b depict that the share of public sector companies in the total CSR expenditure has been increasing, while a complete opposite pattern is shown by the non-public sector companies from 2014–15 to 2017–18. The CSR expenditure incurred by non-public sector undertakings has traditionally been relatively higher than the public sector undertakings, as indicated by their average relative shares from 2014–15 to 2017–18. This indicates that though the average share of the non-public companies has been higher, the public sector companies registered faster growth of CSR activities from 2014–15 to 2017–18. It further reflects that more and more public sector companies are being covered in the CSR mandate, as signaled by its rising share from 28% in 2014–15 to 45.9% in 2017–18, which is a good sign, as both public and private sector firms are contributing toward developmental projects in India.

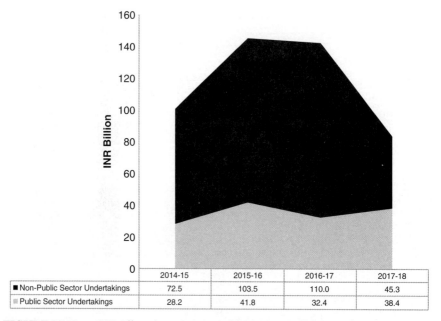

	2014-15	2015-16	2016-17	2017-18
■ Non-Public Sector Undertakings	72.5	103.5	110.0	45.3
▨ Public Sector Undertakings	28.2	41.8	32.4	38.4

FIGURE 23.11a   CSR Allocations Among Public Sector and Non-Public Sector Undertakings in India. *Source*: Authors' calculations using the database on CSR Expenditure (accessed in April 2019), Ministry of Corporate Affairs, Government of India.

DISCUSSION

This chapter analyzed the magnitude, nature, extent, and type of impact investments made by CSR companies in areas which have the potential of creating positive social, economic, and environmental effects on the Indian society. It used four parameters to present a detailed picture of "Impact Investments" created through the CSR channel in India, as depicted in Figure 23.12.

During this period of four financial years (2014–15 to 2017–18), the average amount spent by companies on CSR initiatives reached INR 118 billion, which is approximately 0.1% of gross domestic product (GDP).[7] In relative terms, this amount might appear to be small, but concerning the limited fiscal capacity of the hugely populated country, this amount spent through CSR

---

[7] As per the Handbook of Indian Economy (Reserve Bank of India 2019) the GDP of India at constant prices was INR 131798.57 billion. The average amount of CSR expenditure (INR 118 billion) during 2014–15 to 2017–18 therefore approximates 0.09% of GDP.

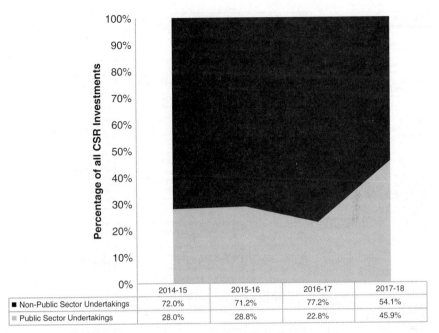

	2014-15	2015-16	2016-17	2017-18
■ Non-Public Sector Undertakings	72.0%	71.2%	77.2%	54.1%
▩ Public Sector Undertakings	28.0%	28.8%	22.8%	45.9%

FIGURE 23.11b   Percentage of CSR Allocations Among Public Sector and Non-Public Sector Undertakings in India. *Source*: Authors' calculations using the database on CSR Expenditure (accessed in April 2019), Ministry of Corporate Affairs, Government of India.

actions can go a long way in helping fulfill the development needs of India, where approximately one-fifth of the population lives below the poverty line, with a greater sharing of responsibility between the government and private players (Panagariya and More 2014).

It is very difficult to achieve the developmental demands of a country like India, which is immensely populated. Nonetheless, as far as the nature of CSR investment is concerned, the CSR activity finds its presence in all the six focal areas of impact investment, but some have been given more preference than the others by CSR companies. To begin with, the findings reveal that "Education and Skill Development" have emerged as a popular impact investment area. This is probably because the companies are aware that the investments in education, vocational, and technical skills can harness the demographic potential of India (Chopra and Marriya 2014) by creating a literate, skilled and trained labor force. They are aware this can then serve as an important factor of production, capable of viable economic returns to companies. Heath, nutrition, water, and sanitation have been identified as the

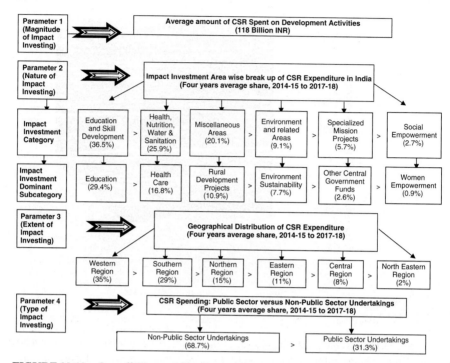

FIGURE 23.12   Overall Picture of Impact Investment Through CSR Channel in India (2014–15 to 2017–18). *Source*: Authors' calculations using the database on CSR Expenditure (accessed in April 2019), Ministry of Corporate Affairs, Government of India.

second most preferred intervention area for CSR-compliant companies, with health care attracting the highest investment projects in this category. The reasons behind such preferences are beyond the scope of the present study; nonetheless, as evidenced by the existing literature, the two areas of education and health are crucial in the Indian context, where a sizeable proportion of people are illiterate (Venkatanarayana 2015) and lack access to basic health care (Barik and Thorat 2015).

A considerable CSR expenditure has been incurred in the "Miscellaneous Projects" category, where companies have mostly invested in rural development projects, such as construction of roads, bridges, shelters, and civic amenities in rural areas. Since the majority of Indians reside in rural setups having large developmental needs, CSR investments in this area can be viewed to create powerful socioeconomic impacts. Furthermore, the "Social Empowerment" category has received the least attention in terms of CSR expenditure commitments, and most investments in this category have been in the projects targeting "Women Empowerment." The higher share of CSR investments for projects targeting empowerment of women is considered to be a positive outcome, as it can lead to huge improvements in social, economic, and psychological development of women, especially in India, where males still occupy a higher percentage of the formal labor force (Deshpande, Goel, and Khanna 2018) and continue to earn relatively higher wages across different sectors. Another important observation is that although "Social Empowerment" has been a laggard impact investment category, its share in the total CSR expenditure has shown an increasing trend from 2014–15 to 2017–18 as seen in Figure 23.3b. This is indicative of the fact that even though the pace is slow, companies have shown their willingness to spend more in this particular focal area, capable of creating social inclusiveness and reduction of socioeconomic inequalities in India.

As far as the geographical outreach of CSR investments is concerned, an asymmetry in the distribution of CSR expenditure has been observed, wherein the relatively developed region (western) attracted most of the investment projects, while comparatively less developed regions (northeastern and the central Indian states) have garnered the lowest investments in terms of average CSR expenditure. As per a report published by Shree Gurukripa Institute of Finance and Development (2017), the CSR funds have been geographically concentrated in the western Indian states, which, as previously discussed, are relatively more developed than the remaining regions. There is a dearth of studies about the causes of asymmetrical geographical distribution of CSR investments in the Indian context, and future research should be done in this area.

It has been observed that both private and foreign companies located in India have contributed in a sizeable manner toward the CSR commitments. However, the share of non-public sector companies in the total CSR expenditure has outweighed the share of public sector undertakings. A possible explanation for this is the existence of a few profit-making public sector enterprises in contrast to large number of successful private sector companies operating in India (Nagaraj 2015). That is why the share of CSR investments by the non-public sector has been reported to be higher owing to existence of relatively large percentage of private sector companies which fall under the statutory provisions of the CSR Act. Despite its relatively lower share, public sector companies have registered faster growth of CSR activities from 2014–15 to 2017–18, which is a positive sign in the Indian context, as both sectors are spending (though in different proportions and growing at different pace) in the focal areas capable of creating beneficial outcomes.

Through the CSR mandate of "comply or explain," the Indian government has made private business companies an important participant in the holistic development process of the country. They are now responsible for a social conduct and accountable for the correct provisioning of public goods and services. Critics of this policy consider that making it obligatory for corporations to spend a minimum amount on development activities is merely an attempt of the government to outsource its traditional social welfare responsibility to private players (Sarkar and Sarkar 2015). However, in the light of the findings of the present study, it is clear that through these CSR commitments, a significant volume of funds was spent in critical impact investment areas of education, skill development, livelihood enhancement projects, rural development, health care, and environmental sustainability initiatives, by both private and public companies.

Thus, the CSR mandate has been a positive endeavor by the Indian government. The corporate sector has reacted positively and acted as a major stakeholder, undertaking investments in critical areas able to generate powerful socioeconomic developmental impacts in the country, while continuing to ensure financial gains and improving its corporate reputation.

KEY RECOMMENDATIONS

In light of the key observations of the study, specific recommendations have been drawn. First, the CSR expenditure in the focal areas capable of generating impact investments ought to be more directly related to the different region's developmental needs. It is therefore suggested that CSR provisions of the Statutory Act are amended so that concerned companies are more motivated to spend a higher portion of their prescribed commitments in the regions and Indian states that are relatively less developed.

Second, some focal areas have received more attention and preferential treatment in terms of relatively large CSR investments (e.g. Education and Health) than the other focal areas. It is therefore suggested that the focal areas where CSR investment is lower are identified by authorities and acted upon. A digital platform could be put in place to allow for more transparent coordination among different companies, so that investments in other important focal areas of impact investments are also achieved.

Third, to motivate companies to invest more in sectors and geographical regions with less CSR activities (such as the focal area of "Social Empowerment"), it is suggested that the government considers incentives (e.g. in the form of tax benefits) for those companies that specifically undertake impact investment projects in those focal areas and regions.

Fourth, some development projects cannot be undertaken by a single company due to the high volume of costs. In that event, an institutional mechanism should be set up by the government, so that the companies can jointly pool resources to undertake bigger impact investment projects, by entering into formal partnerships and consortiums.

Fifth, the government should set up more effective legal mechanisms and stricter CSR disclosure norms, amounting to stern punishment (e.g. fines or prosecution) in case of the contravention of the provisions of the CSR mandate.

Last, the CSR mandate in India can be regarded as a potent tool to achieve the large development demands of the Indian population, as it mandates the corporate to be socially responsible and accountable by investing in focal areas of impact investments. However, except for the data available on CSR investments described in this chapter, no other standardized tools exist to date to measure tangibly the social and financial outcomes generated from these CSR initiatives. The prime objective of the CSR mandate is to achieve harmony in a sustained manner between society's welfare concerns and corporate business interests. Therefore, rigorous measurement tools to assess the impact generated in each of the investment categories (focal areas) are needed if the long-term sustainability of the goals enshrined in the Indian CSR mandate are to be taken seriously.

REFERENCES

Barik, D., and Thorat, A. (2015). Issues of Unequal Access to Public Health in India. *Frontiers in Public Health* 3: 245.

Bayoud, N. S., and Kavanagh, M. (2012). Corporate Social Responsibility Disclosure: Evidence from Libyan Managers. *Global Journal of Business Research* 6(5): 73–83.

Bliss, S. (2019). India: Population and Urbanization. *Geography Bulletin* 51(2): 78.

Busch, T., Lehmann, N., and Hoffmann, V. H. (2012). Corporate social responsibility, negative externalities, and financial risk: The case of climate change. Amsterdam: Tinbergen Institute, Discussion Paper (No. 12-102/IV/DSF40).

Chopra, A., and Marriya, S. (2014). Corporate Social Responsibility and Education in India. *Issues and Ideas in Education* 1(1): 13–22.

Datta, P. B., and Gailey, R. (2012). Empowering Women Through Social Entrepreneurship: Case Study of a Women's Cooperative in India. *Entrepreneurship Theory and Practice* 36(3): 569–587.

Deshpande, A., Goel, D., and Khanna, S. (2018). Bad Karma or Discrimination? Male–Female Wage Gaps Among Salaried Workers in India. *World Development* 102: 331–344.

Dev, S. M. (2017). The Problem of Inequality. *Review of Development and Change* 22(1): 1–43.

Goel, M., and Ramanathan, P. E. (2014). Business Ethics and Corporate Social Responsibility: Is There a Dividing Line? *Procedia Economics and Finance* 11(1): 49–59.

Government of India (2013). The Companies Act, 2013. Ministry of Corporate Affairs. https://www.mca.gov.in/Ministry/pdf/CompaniesAct2013.pdf (accessed March 2020).

Government of India. (n.d.). Database on CSR expenditure. Ministry of Corporate Affairs. https://www.csr.gov.in/ (accessed March 2020).

Jackson, E. T. (2013). Interrogating the Theory of Change: Evaluating Impact Investing Where It Matters Most. *Journal of Sustainable Finance & Investment* 3(2): 95–110.

Kalaiselvi, S., and Karthika, P. (2020). Corporate Social Responsibility in India. *Our Heritage* 68 (30): 2515–2525.

Kapoor, G. K., and Dhamija, S. (2017). Mandatory CSR Spending-Indian Experience. *Emerging Economy Studies* 3(1): 98–112.

Kumbamu, A. (2017). Building Sustainable Social and Solidarity Economies: Place-Based and Network-Based Strategies of Alternative Development Organizations in India. *Community Development* 49(1): 18–33.

Lawania, B. D., and Kapoor, S. (2018). Leveraging Corporate Social Responsibility for the Advancement of Development Goals in India: Sanitation and Cleanliness Movement in India. *Australasian Accounting, Business and Finance Journal* 12(2): 46–70.

Manchiraju, H., and Rajgopal, S. (2017). Does Corporate Social Responsibility (CSR) Create Shareholder Value? Evidence from the Indian Companies Act 2013. *Journal of Accounting Research* 55(5): 1257–1300.

Mitra, N., and Schmidpeter R. (2017). *Corporate Social Responsibility in India*. *Cham*: Springer.

Moore, G. (1999). Corporate Moral Agency: Review and Implications. *Journal of Business Ethics* 21(4): 329–343.

European Union and OECD (2016). Policy brief on scaling the impact of social enterprises: Policies for social entrepreneurship.

Panagariya, A., and More, V. (2014). Poverty by Social, Religious and Economic Groups in India and Its Largest States. *Indian Growth and Development Review* 7(2): 202–230

Pradhan, S., and Ranjan, A. (2011). Corporate Social Responsibility in Rural Development Sector: Evidences from India. *School of Doctoral Studies (European Union) Journal* 2: 139–147.

Radwan, I. (2005). India: Private Health Services for the Poor. *Health, Nutrition and Population (HNP) discussion paper.* Washington, DC: World Bank.

Rajan, R., Pandey, T. K., Jayal, N. G., Ramaswami, B., and Gupta, S. (2013). *Report of the committee for evolving a composite development index of states.* Ministry of Finance, Government of India.

Reserve Bank of India (2019). Handbook of statistics on Indian economy. https://www.rbi.org.in/Scripts/AnnualPublications.aspx?head=Handbook%20of%20Statistics%20on%20Indian%20Economy (accessed March 2020).

Sanghi, R. (2014). *Our National River Ganga.* Springer Publications. Switzerland.

Sarkar, J., and Sarkar, S. (2015). Corporate Social Responsibility in India: An Effort to Bridge the Welfare Gap. *Review of Market Integration* 7(1): 1–36.

Shree Gurukripa Institute of Finance and Management (2017). Corporate social responsibility outlook report. *Chennai.*

Singh, A., and Verma, P. (2014). CSR@ 2%: A New Model of Corporate Social Responsibility in India. *International Journal of Academic Research in Business and Social Sciences* 4(10): 455–464.

Trivedi, R. C. (2010). Water Quality of the Ganga River: An Overview. *Aquatic Ecosystem Health & Management* 13(4): 347–351.

Utting, P. (2007). CSR and Equality. *Third World Quarterly* 28(4): 697–712.

Varottil U. (2018). Analyzing the CSR spending requirements under Indian company law. In *Globalization of Corporate Social Responsibility and Its Impact on Corporate Governance* (Du Plessis J., Varottil U., Veldman J., eds.), pp. 231–253. Cham: Springer.

Venkatanarayana, M. (2015). When Will India Achieve Universal Adult Literacy? *Journal of Educational Planning and Administration* 29(2): 177–204.

CHAPTER 24

What Drives Impact Investors? Benchmarking Developed and Developing Countries

Robin Kipfer, MSci

Abstract

During the last decade, the Impact Investing industry has experienced significant growth. But what drives traditional investors into becoming impact investors? And to what extent do extrinsic and intrinsic drivers for the transition into impact investors differ between countries? Based on semi-structured interviews with 19 impact investors in India and in Finland, this inductive-exploratory study sheds light on the drivers for Impact Investing. The findings provide evidence that extrinsic drivers differ significantly between a country such as India, where impact investors have traditionally focused on private equity and private debt investments, and a country such as Finland, where a majority of impact investments are done through outcome-based instruments, such as impact bonds. The engagement of public entities and the influence of capital providers are the two extrinsic drivers that emerged more consistently from the interviews. It was also found that impact investors share similar intrinsic drivers, regardless of their profile and geography. They are all driven by the desire to address a social or environmental issue in a financially sustainable way. Furthermore, unlike philanthropy, financial returns gained through Impact Investing have allowed the redeployment of capital and hence have further enhanced societal and environmental impact. Understanding the particular characteristics of Impact Investing markets in Finland and in India and what drives and shapes impact investor's practices in these two distinct markets can be useful to better foster the development of Impact Investing around the world.

Keywords

Finance; Impact investing; Social impact; Impact investors; Private equity; Social Impact Bonds; Motivations; Incentives; Drivers; Values

INTRODUCTION

While Impact Investing is quickly gathering momentum worldwide, understanding the principles and incentives that drive impact investors in different markets is essential to allow impact investments to penetrate the mainstream industry and perform to their best capacity. Given the nature and magnitude of today's most pressing social and environmental problems, public finances and philanthropic donations have proven to be clearly insufficient to address their scope and size (Cohen 2018). Furthermore, Impact Investing has proven to benefit all parties: it helps governments to address social issues, it generates double-bottom-line returns for investors, and it contributes actively to social sector improvements (Acevedo and Wu 2018; Cohen 2018). This has led to a quick growth of interest and activities related to impact investments (Höchstädter and Scheck 2015).

However, despite the rapid growth of the Impact Investing market globally, impact investors' intrinsic and extrinsic drivers to enter the industry have not yet been studied in depth. While it is known that impact investors challenge the traditional dichotomy between investing to maximize financial returns and donating for ethical reasons, traditional investors' drivers to become impact investors are still not totally clear.[1] Moreover, not much is yet known about how market structures evolve and how incentive structures can be designed to attract more actors to the Impact Investing industry. As their practices evolve and set themselves apart (Daggers and Nicholls 2016), examining how impact investors respond to intrinsic and extrinsic drivers is crucial.

To address this gap, 18 impact investors from India and Finland were interviewed through a blended exploratory-inductive study. Two very distinct countries were chosen for this benchmarking, at different sides of the Impact Investing spectrum. India and Finland stand at opposite ends in terms of economic development, as well as Impact Investing market features. On the one hand, due to its high social and environmental needs and its strong capital market, India is typically known as the largest Impact Investing market in the world, especially concerning private debt and private equity investments (Pandit and Tamhane 2017). On the other hand, Finland, a member of the European Union (EU), is known to be one of the most developed and innovative countries in the world (Helliwell, Layard, and Sachs 2018). Finland holds to praise its seven social impact bonds (SIBs),[2] including the largest one in Europe, as well as the first Environmental Impact Bond.

Based on a literature review and on the empirical data collection from these two different Impact Investing markets, this chapter aims to uncover the importance of impact investor's extrinsic (e.g. market regulations and market infrastructures) and intrinsic drivers (e.g. investors values and approaches) and to ascertain to what extent they can differ.

The findings reveal that impact investors share similar intrinsic drivers across markets—setting apart who operates in the Impact Investing industry. Those interviewed all believe that social and environmental issues should be addressed in a financially sustainable way. By earning a financial return alongside the measurable social and environmental benefits, impact investors can redeploy the capital and thus generate further societal and environmental returns. Nonetheless, the way they act and the financing instruments they

---

[1]Fewer than five studies that consider drivers for impact investments could be found in the literature. A few of them mention personal values and motivations (e.g. Roundy et al. [2017], Toniic [2018], and Barclays [2018]), and even fewer discuss market-based incentives (e.g. Bauer and Hollmann [2018], GIIN [2011]). However, it seems that a study covering both motivations and incentives and comparing them in two different markets has never been conducted. See Chapter 1, "Impact Investing: Innovation or Rebranding?" by Haifa Ben Abid.

[2]See Chapter 14, "Social Impact Bonds: Promises and Results" by Maria Basilio.

use are typically determined by extrinsic drivers such as the specificities of the markets they operate in.

The remainder of this paper is structured as follows. The next section provides a review of the literature setting the theoretical foundation for the empirical research. It focuses on financial instruments used and on the extrinsic as well as intrinsic drivers for impact investments. Then, the methodological choices are described. The findings obtained from the empirical research are presented and discussed in the two following sections. Finally, limitations and suggestions for future research on this topic are discussed, and the chapter ends with concluding remarks.

METHODOLOGY

This section describes and motivates the research design as well as the methodology used to collect and analyze data in this study.

Research Design

Due to the current dearth of literature on drivers and incentives for Impact Investing (Höchstädter and Scheck 2015), this study followed a blended inductive-exploratory research design,[3] with guiding research questions shaping the approach to data collection and analysis (Saunders and Lewis 2014). A key element of the research design is the research strategy (Saunders, Lewis, and Thornhill 2009). Qualitative methods[4] were employed to explore a few cases in depth during the data collection, through interviews (Patton 2002).

Data Collection and Analysis

Data was collected in two countries, India and Finland. These two were chosen for several reasons. First, according to Eisenhardt (1989), comparing two opposite cases in the same research enables to investigate and contrast

---

[3] According to Eisenhardt (1989), an exploratory methodology is appropriate for studies that explore a new phenomenon with only limited existing literature.

[4] Qualitative research seeks to understand relationships and influences between different phenomena, rather than the phenomena itself (Gioia, Corley, and Hamilton 2012). This research strategy seems to be particularly well suited for understanding how the external and internal drivers affect impact investors practices.

patterns that go beyond initial impression and, hence, allow triangulation and the drawing of more reliable conclusions. Second, Finland and India stand at opposite extremes in terms of economic development, poverty, and Impact Investing activities. While India is known to be a test bed for Impact Investing activities and one of the largest equity and debt Impact Investing markets (Pandit and Tamhane 2017), Finland boasts seven Impact Bonds, including the largest one in Europe, and is one of the leaders in outcome-based funding (GSG 2018b).

The empirical research relies on 18 semi-structured interviews[5] (lasting from 30 minutes to one hour) with impact investors in India and Finland, originating from venture capital funds, a non-banking financial company, independent public funds, a financial advisory company, a foundation, a philanthropic investment fund, an institutional investor, and an asset management company.

The interviewees were selected using a combination of intensity sampling[6] and snowball sampling[7] strategies. The tables in Appendix 24.1 provide a general overview of the group of impact investors interviewed. For each country, they are listed from 1 to 9.

As suggested by the literature (Eisenhardt 1989; Patton 2002), carefully designing the interview guide[8] is essential to ensure the quality of the content of the interviews. The guiding protocol for interviews was divided into three sections: (i) background questions and personal motivations, (ii) external context and incentives, and (iii) concluding remarks and future trends. In addition, to test the clarity and simplicity of the questions, two pilot interviews were conducted on neutral participants from India and Finland, prior to the first interview, as recommended by Saunders and Lewis (2014).

---

[5]Semi-structured and in-depth interviews have proven to be especially appropriate in exploratory research since these allow examining experiences, values, and perspectives of the interviewees (Patton 2002; Saunders and Lewis 2014).

[6]Intensity sampling is used to select information-rich cases that manifest the phenomenon intensely (Patton 2002). In this research, it allowed selecting impact investors from a wide range of investors profiles (such as venture capital investors, institutional investors, etc.).

[7]In a snowball sampling, information-rich cases are identified first and then, in turn, they point out to other interesting cases. This strategy makes sense when information-rich cases are hard to access (Patton 2002). In Finland, two interviewees (Finland-5 and Finland-7) were selected using this strategy.

[8]This means that topics and questions to be covered are developed in advance in an outline form, although the sequences and wordings can be defined during the interview (Eisenhardt 1989).

Although no direct formula exists for transforming data into findings (Patton 2002), open coding procedure[9] is commonly used for inductive research (Miles and Huberman 1994) and was thus adopted in this research. Data was manipulated through several stages, such as categorization and integration, for sense-making.

A convenient way to analyze multiple case studies is to look for within-group similarities before carrying out cross-case analysis (Eisenhardt 1989). Given the distinct nature of the Impact Investing industry in India and in Finland, and to ensure a robust comparison, a similar analysis was followed for each country independently, ahead of the comparison of results among them. Furthermore, this strategy enabled better understanding of the implications of the findings for each country, and for the Impact Investing community, and to formulate recommendations on how to drive new impact investors and increase the attractiveness of these markets.

LITERATURE REVIEW

Based on the literature review, this section discusses different Impact Investing instruments and drivers and contrasts their specificities in India and Finland.

Financial Instruments Commonly Used for Impact Investments

Many impact investments are done through private equity, private debt funding, and impact bonds (Finkelman and Huntington 2017). Private equity investments are typically best suited to fast-growing companies with good exit opportunities operating in rapidly moving markets (Social Impact Investment Taskforce 2014). The second vehicle, private debt, usually targets established businesses with predictable cash flows (Finkelman and Huntington 2017). SIBs are often found in stable areas with solid evidence backing outcome metrics and used for preventive intervention whose costs can be offset by potential savings (Gandhi 2019; Wendt 2018). Table 24.1 summarizes the key characteristics of the three instruments mentioned above.

---

[9]This procedure is also named "categorization process" by Spiggle (1994).

TABLE 24.1 Common Financial Instruments for Impact Investments.

Instrument	Features (+ Pros, – Cons)	Best suited to
Private equity	*Purchase of equity stake provides capital for growth and implicit company valuation* + Variations on dividend and voting rights + Strong upside potential and ability for investors to assert control – Difficult to value early stage businesses, no guaranteed return, exit opportunities limited – Typically, smaller investments – Usually riskier than debt, but with higher returns	Fast-growing companies with capable leaders Companies with large growth potential and good exit opportunities Companies offering for-profit solutions
Private debt	*Company issues bonds to investors* + Variations on interest rate, duration, and security + Steady income for investors – Limited ability to assert control – Bigger investment size than private equity but smaller than bank debt – Returns typically smaller than equity, because technically lower risk	Established companies with large, stable, and predictable cash flows Businesses with clear investment plans and predictable outcomes Companies offering for-profit solutions

TABLE 24.1 *(continued)*

Instrument	Features (+ Pros, − Cons)	Best suited to
Impact bonds (SIBs)	*Results-based instrument that leverages private or commercial capital toward sustainable development* + Investors only fully repaid if the program is successful + Promotes a results-based culture + Drives private capital to public projects + Flexibility in the way financing is used − Difficulty to structure, align all the actors (free rider, principal-agent problems) − Difficulty to define clear, measurable metrics − Although the project usually lasts several years, expected results and ground structure are determined at the beginning and are not adjustable over time − Incurs administrative costs to administer − Outcome payers have limited control and may not be directly involved with the project design and management	Projects targeting priority areas for both the public and private sectors Interventions whose costs can be offset by the potential cost savings Business sectors and projects with solid evidence, backed by credible outcome metrics

Source: Adapted from Finkelman and Huntington (2017), Wendt (2018), Social Impact Investment Taskforce (2014), Gandhi (2019).

Drivers for Impact Investments

In the context of Impact Investing, investors must have the intention to generate a positive impact on the environment or on the society through their investments (Global Impact Investing Network n.d.; O'Donohoe et al. 2010). The literature discusses at least two approaches to understand the roots of this behavior, as well as the reasons that drive individuals to become impact investors. According to the first approach, drivers can originate from the market (extrinsic elements such as market regulations and market infrastructures) (Global Impact Investing Network 2011; Clark, Emerson, and Thornley 2014). According to the second one, they can also arise from the investor (intrinsic elements such as investors' values and approaches) (Roundy et al. 2017; Global Impact Investing Network 2018).

Extrinsic Drivers for Impact Investments

Market-based drivers refer to factors that influence market participants' behaviors by modifying economic variables (such as taxes, prices, regulations) (Prahl and Hofmann 2016), enhancing the enabling environment (e.g. saving and interest rates, capacity for impact investments), and providing market infrastructures (Bauer and Hollmann 2018). Usually, these are typically associated with the government and public policy, although in some cases private actors can also initiate them (for example, by altering market price, or lobbying) (Prahl and Hofmann 2016). Research on the role of policymakers and other public entities as catalyzers of Impact Investing highlighted the importance of the public sector to fully unleash the potential of Impact Investing (e.g. Acevedo and Wu [10]2018; GSG 2018b; Clark et al. 2014; Global Impact Investing Network 2018; Wood 2014).

In addition to developing a supportive regulatory system and providing market infrastructures, public entities can enhance the Impact Investing industry by offering incentives to impact investors (GSG 2018a;

---

[10]In their study, Acevedo and Wu (2018) evaluated how public policy and other elements of the Impact Investing ecosystem (such as government financial conditions, the history of financial markets, the establishment of research, and educational institutions for Impact Investing) contribute to the development of the Impact Investing industry. The paper concluded that all have a role in the creation of an enabling environment for impact investments.

Global Impact Investing Network 2018; Wood 2014). As claimed by Clark et al. (2014, p. 13), "By nature, impact investors represent a marriage of public and private interests. They seamlessly integrate a commitment to improving public welfare with the power and efficiency of capital markets. Policymakers...are natural partners for impact investors." The Global Impact Investing Network (Global Impact Investing Network 2018, p. 18) also highlighted that government policies can drive traditional investors to become impact investors (or deter them). Namely, the provision of credit enhancement (such as guarantees and first-loss capital), tax incentives and other subsidies, and co-investment by a government agency were the three most helpful policies cited by the respondents of the survey (Global Impact Investing Network 2018).

Furthermore, although governments are essential for the creation of an enabling environment, many other aspects of the Impact Investing ecosystem also affect impact investors' practices (Acevedo and Wu 2018).[11] In order to drive impact investors, market-based incentives for impact should take place along the investment chain (Bauer and Hollmann 2018). This means that incentives should target not only the management of capital (such as venture capital funds), but also entities located upstream and downstream, such as capital providers (e.g. Limited Partners), development organizations, social enterprises, and the government itself—in other words, organizations that provide capital, those that manage it, and those that receive it (Bauer and Hollmann 2018). Currently, it seems that market-based drivers have not directly targeted organizations providing capital, and, hence, these entities are often not driven to impact investments (Global Impact Investing Network 2011; Bauer and Hollmann 2018).

In several countries, impact investors are already reportedly being driven by market-based initiatives (GSG 2018b; Clark et al. 2014; Wood 2014). In the United Kingdom, for instance, investors investing in qualified impact sectors can enjoy up to 30% reduction on their income tax bill for the year (GSG 2018b). Similarly, in the United States, a recent legislative initiative promoted the B Corp label,[12] with the aim of facilitating investments in financially sustainable businesses with a clear social mission. This highlights the role of the public sector in building capacity and setting standards for impact investments (Wood 2014).

---

[11] Ibid.

[12] The B Corp label, or Benefit Corporations label, is an official designation for businesses that meet a specific set of criteria regarding their impact performance as well as corporate structure (Wood 2014).

Intrinsic Drivers for Impact Investments

Impact investors can also be driven by intrinsic elements, such as personal values, motivations, and investment approaches (Roundy et al. 2017; Global Impact Investing Network 2018). A few existing studies analyzed these factors and showed that impact investors are all motivated by the aim to make a positive difference (Roundy et al. 2017; Barclays 2018). Interestingly, Barclays (2018) found a positive correlation between the propensity to become an impact investor and other life-related decisions such as creating a family. Along similar lines, Roundy et al. (2017) highlighted that the approach impact investors have to new investment is often tied to the investor personal life. For example, an impact investor who has children is more likely to look for investment opportunities related to education. As argued by Roundy et al. (2017, p. 501), "If [impact investors] were not driven by such values, then they would invest in asset classes that focus on producing solely financial returns." However, it also seems that the level of priority they assign to impact is affected by several elements (personal as well as external ones) and hence, vary between impact investors[13] (Balandina-Jaquier 2016; Barber, Morser, and Yasuda 2019).

Returns on investments and motivations for impact

Investment returns are a very common and debatable topic within the Impact Investing community (O'Donohoe et al. 2010; Roundy et al. 2017). In order to understand what drives impact investors, it is essential to consider the potential gains (financial, social, environmental) (Bauer and Hollmann 2018). Even if there is still need for more research on the need of Impact Investing to give up financial returns or another form of flexibility for the sake of social impact (Barclays 2018), there is mounting evidence highlighting a positive correlation between impact and financial performance (Global Impact Investing Network 2018; O'Donohoe et al. 2010).

When discussing impact investment returns, it is necessary to go beyond financial results. As stated by Barclays (2018, p. 31), "investors don't just earn financial returns from holding investments; they may also receive emotional returns." Furthermore, these emotional returns may occur when scrutinizing investment opportunities (before the investment), when monitoring the investment (during), as well as when tracking its impact (after)

---

[13]In order to assess the depth of this issue, Barber, Morser, and Yasuda (2019) analyzed what they named as the "willingness-to-pay for impact" and found significant differences among impact investors.

TABLE 24.2   Finance First and Impact First Investments.

	"Finance First" Investments	"Impact First" Investments
Type of investors	Foundations, commercial investors, venture capital funds, institutional investors (pension funds)	Foundations, high-net-worth individuals, large corporations, sovereign wealth funds, nonprofit organizations
Typical strategies	Focus on less challenging social issues and lower impact opportunities Integrate ESG factors into research and decision processes	Often focus on tougher social issues, pilot innovative and unknown models Seek to harness market mechanisms to generate positive impact
Financial objectives	Expect risk-adjusted market return or market-beating return	Ready to give up some financial return in order to maximize the impact Accept higher financial risk
Impact objectives	Target tangible impact Look for opportunities in which impact directly drives profit	Prioritize impact maximization over financial return Motivation to make a difference on specific issues and to use the market as a means to achieve it

Source: Adapted from Balandina-Jaquier (2016) and Höchstädter and Scheck (2015).

(Roundy et al. 2017). However, as analyzed by Barber, Morser, and Yasuda (2019), impact investors' willingness-to-pay for nonpecuniary earnings varies across impact investor types and is affected by several attributes such as regulatory and political pressure, the organization's mission orientation, and geographical location.

In the literature, some authors, such as Balandina-Jaquier (2016), Höchstädter and Scheck (2015), and the Global Impact Investing Network (2009), imply that the variation in willingness-to-pay for impact has to do with assigning a higher priority to one of the two main objectives for investments (impact versus financial returns). As such, they segmented impact investors into two groups: "financial first" and "impact first." Table 24.2 summarizes these key points.

From the above literature review, only a few studies have directly focused on the analysis of drivers for impact investments, and even fewer discuss both extrinsic drivers as well as intrinsic drivers for impact investors. Furthermore, although it is known that returns expectations and impact investment practices can differ between developing and developed countries (O'Donohoe et al. 2010; Bauer and Hollmann 2018), it remains unclear if drivers differ as well. This literature gap will be addressed next.

FINDINGS

Based on the results from the 18 interviews, this section seeks to shed some light on the intrinsic as well as extrinsic drivers for impact investors in India and in Finland. In order to better understand impact investors' practices in both countries, it starts with a short overview of the two Impact Investing markets.

Country Context and Impact Investing Activities

Before exploring what drives impact investors to enter the Impact Investing industry in India and in Finland, it is important to acknowledge specificities of the two country contexts as well as the characteristics of the two Impact Investing markets.

India

In India, in alignment with the literature, the interviewees highlighted several characteristics of the external environment that affect Impact Investing practices. First, impact investors explained how the size as well as the socioeconomic diversity of the Indian population results in an impressive variety of issues. Interviewees claimed that in India, societal and environmental problems are "affecting so many different socioeconomic classes" (Interviewee India-5), "obvious and everywhere" (Interviewee India-8), "vivid" (Interviewee India-9), and "multidimensional" (Interviewee India-1), which highlights the range that can be addressed by Impact Investing.

Furthermore, Indian impact investors also underlined that during the last decade, individuals realized the business potential hidden behind all these national and local socioeconomic problems; this was behind the recent growth of the Indian Impact Investing market. The following quotations illustrate this idea:

> In India, problems are really obvious and everywhere. Even if you just go down the road, you will find people having at least 10 different kinds of problems which can very easily be solved. And recently, people really started to realize that solving these problems is actually a big business also.
>
> (Interviewee India-8)

> You know, I think the reason is simply the size of India's population. There are so many people with totally different interests and most of them still lack basic services. Also, as an entrepreneur or investor, if you can capture just a specific niche segment in India which means, let's say, 100 to 200 million potential customers... there are a lot of low-hanging fruits emerging from all the social and environmental issues, which you can really target as an impact investor.
>
> (Interviewee India-5)

Interviewees also claimed that in India, the social and environmental issues often affect basic needs and services and thus are costly in the short term. For this reason, they require fast actions and easy-to-implement solutions from social entrepreneurs to impact investors.

With regard to Impact Investing activities in India, the interviews confirmed that the market is dominated by private equity and debt impact investments. During the interview, a majority of impact investors described the Indian Impact Investing context by using expressions such as "financially sustainable companies" and "for-profit start-ups," highlighting the fact that for them, Impact Investing means primarily private equity and debt investments.

Finland

In Finland, instead of discussing the socioeconomic diversity and the size of the population, interviewees underlined high tax rates, the strong welfare model, and the key role of the public sector. Similarly, it was explained that most of the social and environmental problems are expected to be addressed by public entities in first instance. The following quote illustrates the Finnish context:

> Here, people pay a very high percentage of tax and, hence, they expect a lot from the public sector. Especially for issues related to the average well-being of the society. . . . Child welfare, unemployment, refugees, etc. are followed very closely by the society. Hence, governments have to be very careful.
>
> (Interviewee Finland-7)

It is also interesting to mention that in Finland, impact investments are not necessarily used to finance short-term projects that tackle basic needs and services, as it is the case in India. On the contrary, impact bonds are typically developed for preventive purposes, to improve the future quality of life and save money in the long term. For example, it was said that preventing issues such as alcohol abuse, type 2 diabetes, and children in custody care could save the Finnish government several billion euros every year (Interviewee Finland-1). The following quotations from the interviews in Finland highlight this long-term approach:

> I think that at the moment, there is kind of a growing concern that social problems are increasing much faster than municipalities' and governments' financial resources to tackle them. For this reason, instead of putting more money to manage the problems once there, we should definitely focus on preventing them. And these SIBs enable long-term financial prevention perfectly.
>
> (Interviewee Finland-9)

> From what I have seen in Finland, social impact bonds are not used to solve an issue directly but more to increase savings in the long term. So, even if you have to pay and invest at the beginning, you can then achieve very huge savings in the long term.
>
> (Interviewee Finland-2)

Concerning Impact Investing activities, while in India impact investors use mostly private equity and debt vehicles, in Finland the interviews underlined that impact investments are typically made through more complicated and specific instruments such as SIBs. Impact investors explained that results-based instruments are particularly wellsuited for countries with strong public sector and high tax rates, since they enable public entities to pay only for successful initiatives with proven results. The following quote, from an employee of an independent public fund, illustrates this finding:

> Actually, one of the reasons why we have used and still focus on social impact bonds in Finland is that we really want to change the way how taxpayer's money is used. You know, structuring and financing the SIBs is not the issue for us. The big issue is that we want to change the way how the government spent our tax money, and also want to make sure that the public sector is buying more and more results instead of just budgeting for different kinds of activities.
>
> (Interviewee Finland-1)

Extrinsic Drivers for Impact Investments

As mentioned in the previous section, the specificities of the external environment influence the way impact investors operate, which is why Impact Investing practices differ between emerging and developed countries. Based on the literature review and on the interviews' findings, the following section sheds some light on what kind of extrinsic drivers shape impact investors' practices in Indian and Finnish markets. Although a broad range of extrinsic drivers exist (from factors that affect economic variables to the enhancement of market infrastructures), this section only discusses drivers related to public policies and to capital providers. These are the primary two drivers that emerged more consistently in the interviews.

Public Policy

First, in both countries, impact investors highlighted the key role and the influence that the public sector has on their investment practices. In India, public entities recently realized that due to the size of the country and to the political system, it is impossible to tackle all the social and environmental problems without the support of private actors and private finance. For this reason, the government has been strongly promoting Impact Investing through many initiatives, such as educational events, and indirectly by enhancing the social entrepreneurship ecosystem through financial incentives, for instance.

In Finland, interviewees also underlined the crucial role and influence of the Finnish government. Due to peculiar structure of impact bonds, which typically involve both private as well as public actors, the majority of impact investors agreed that the Impact Investing industry would not have reached its current state (or would maybe never have started) without the strong involvement and support from the Finnish government. The following quotes exemplify what respondents replied when asked about the role of the government in the Finnish Impact Investing industry:

> Of course, the government and municipalities play a crucial role in Finland. First, they have been the end payer of most of those impact bonds. So, they have totally accepted the idea of paying the return at the end, if everything goes well. Secondly, if [Finnish innovation fund] Sitra has done such an amazing job to promote Impact Investing, it is because Sitra is contracted by the government to do this. So yeah, without that, there would not be any of those SIBs today.
>
> (Interviewee Finland-4)

> I think most of the encouragements for Impact Investing come from the government in Finland....Actually, without the government playing this central role in SIBs, I guess we would never have been involved in outcome funding and other kind of impact investments.
>
> (Interviewee Finland-5)

Hence, it seems clear that impact investors are, to some extent, driven by government and public entities initiatives. In India, these have focused on the private equity and debt side of Impact Investing, whereas in Finland, outcome-based funding vehicles have been prioritized.

The Importance of Capital Providers

Second, interviewees from Finland as well as from India highlighted how important capital providers, such as institutional investors, are to drive traditional investors to become impact investors. These entities stand at the top of the investment chain, and thus they have a strong influence on the way other entities approach investment opportunities.

In India, the interviewees claimed that thanks to the long history of the Indian financial market as well as to the high number of foreign investors, a strong track record of successful exits has been built over the years. For this reason, capital providers are now typically asking for impact investments, which has been creating a growing demand to be fulfilled and, in turn, attracting more impact investors. The following quotes illustrate this:

I think that there is a clear growing demand from their side for more ethical investments which focus on ESG [Environmental, Social, and Governance] issues and look at impact. So, I think LPs [Limited Partners] are very important to take the market forward and can clearly accelerate its development.

(Interviewee India-6)

Actually, I started working about eleven years ago in a traditional venture capital fund. It is only a few years ago, when we felt the growing demand from the LPs, that we decided to raise capital for an Impact Investing fund. We needed new employees to manage this fund and this is when I got the opportunity to change to the Impact Investing industry.

(Interviewee India-9)

In Finland, a few interviewees underlined how problematic it is for institutional investors to notice that Impact Investing practices are sometimes seen as investments that require concessionary financial returns. According to these investors, SIBs focused too much on developing the impact side of the equation (impact metrics) rather than on financial returns. In consequence, capital providers (restricted by a fiduciary duty) are often not eager to make impact investments. The following responses highlight this problem:

I think it all started the wrong way in Finland. We started emphasizing the impact side, that it needed to be measured very accurately, saying that it had to be impact first and returns later. And now, you know, when you go to an institutional investor and ask them about Impact Investing, these people are usually not interested. Yes, they say that they would like to have an impact. But also that their fiduciary duty is to make money, and that they cannot sacrifice returns.

(Interviewee Finland-4)

I believe that in Finland, institutional investors are hungry for impact. However, as long as they don't see any success stories from impact investments, they can't take the risk to invest in something they don't know.

(Interviewee Finland-6)

In a few words, extrinsic drivers for impact investments are essential as they dictate the way impact investors operate. Because impact investments typically occur in the middle of public and private interests, public actors play a crucial role for traditional investors to become impact investors. Furthermore, capital providers also strongly affect the way investors and impact investors approach investment opportunities.

Intrinsic Drivers for Impact Investments

As discussed in the literature review, impact investors can also be driven by intrinsic elements, such as personal values and motivations. The findings from the interviews confirmed this idea and showed that overall, impact investors are driven by personal values that focus on positive societal or environmental change, this evidenced in both countries.

Findings underlined that it is really the desire to perform well while simultaneously doing good that determine the stakeholders found in the Impact Investing industry. Interviewees claimed that if they were only driven by social values, they would focus on traditional philanthropy rather than on impact investments. Similarly, if the motivation was purely financial, they would work in a traditional investment company looking for financial returns only. The following quotes are examples of what respondents replied when asked what motivated them to join the Impact Investing industry:

> There is a spectrum of investors. And when you look at it you can see three different groups. If you look at the leftmost side, one can come and say: "I want only impact, I don't care about financial return." On the opposite, on the rightmost side, an investor can say: "I want high financial returns no matter the way." But if you look between, in the middle, that is where you are looking at both, where you are trying to kind of understand what the best way is to maximize both financial return and impact. And you know, that is what really fascinates most of us.
>
> (Interviewee India-2)

> I think that for me, the most important thing is that I had a clear idea of what I wanted to achieve, of the positives changes I wanted to achieve in our society. And then I saw the Impact Investing, the idea to use private capital as a tool to be able to achieve those changes which would be good for the population, good for the environment, and sustainable in the long run.
>
> (Interviewee Finland-1)

Furthermore, many underlined the importance of working with organizations addressing social and environmental issues in a financially sustainable way. During the interviews in India and Finland, it became clear that impact investors believe that market-based solutions can efficiently tackle social and environmental issues. For instance, interviewees said that a majority of impact businesses are high-growth businesses bringing high returns mostly because of the impact aspect they have. In Finland, several interviewees also highlighted that using longer-term instruments (e.g. SIBs) allows making larger sustainable gains. The concepts of "sustainable and future benefits" (Interviewee Finland-6) as well as "slow but never-ending returns" (Interviewee Finland-7) were used to describe this approach.

Finally, interviewees from both countries highlighted that for them, Impact Investing drives special emotions and positive feelings. While some claimed that impact investments are a perfect way to give back to the society, others explained that they see Impact Investing as a more exciting and future-oriented strategy than traditional investments, which requires combining several skill sets (such as financial analysis with strategic advice). Several expressions from Indian interviewees, such as "creating something new" (Interviewee India-1), "a new challenging field" (Interviewee India-3), and even "revolutionizing the way venture capital funds invest" (Interviewee India-9), as well as the following quote from Finland, illustrate this idea:

> In my opinion, Impact Investing is also a sort of, let's say, future-oriented practice. In my life, I have always been attracted by innovations and things which are not fully known yet. If you go to the traditional investment markets for example, yes, you can make money. But you don't really decide how you invest. You often just follow the rules of the markets. And this is different in Impact Investing and in SIBs, where you can basically build any sort of new Impact Investing vehicles.
>
> (Interviewee Finland-6)

In summary, impact investors are all driven by similar intrinsic values and motivations, regardless of their investors' profile and geography. In addition to earning financial returns, impact investors also carefully look for opportunities that generate a positive societal and environmental impact. Above all, they appreciate witnessing the sustainable impact their investments have on society and the environment. Results-based instruments allow them to gain financial returns, but also to make long-term savings by focusing on preventing social problems from developing. Similarly, financial returns earned through other traditional instruments, such as private equity, allow them to reinvest capital over time and increase the impact generated.

DISCUSSION

Despite the fast-growing interest in Impact Investing, academic research on impact investors remains limited, and several key issues have not been examined yet. It is still unknown to what extent extrinsic and intrinsic drivers for impact investors differ between countries, as well as what determines those divergences. To address this gap, a blended inductive-exploratory study was conducted in India and in Finland.

The findings show that impact investors, regardless of their profile and country of origin, share similar intrinsic drivers. However, extrinsic drivers differ significantly between an emerging country, such as India, and a developed one, such as Finland. Based on the results above and the literature review, this section discusses the drivers and the reasons behind the country differences.

First, with regard to the extrinsic drivers for impact investors, the results of the study are aligned with the existing literature (e.g. Acevedo and Wu 2018; GSG 2018a; Bauer and Hollmann 2018; Wood 2014). They indicate that in both countries, the public sector (namely the government) plays a crucial role in catalyzing the Impact Investing economy and in incentivizing the entry of new players by supporting elements of its enabling environment. In Finland, public entities have strongly (and successfully) promoted outcome-based instruments, such as SIBs. These efforts are directly reflected in the Finnish Impact Investing scene, where most impact investments occurred through those types of vehicles. On the other hand, in India, where the government has focused on developing an enabling environment for private equity and debt impact investments, impact investors have primarily been using those instruments. However, while existing research underlined the importance of public actions and policies to drive impact investors, the results of this study highlight that those initiatives also shape the way impact investors behave and the kind of financing instruments they use.

The findings also showed that capital providers have a strong influence on the way impact investors approach new investment opportunities (acting as capital managers). In other words, if the demand from capital providers for impact investments increases, the number of funds for Impact Investing should also increase. However, if capital providers are not eager to make impact investments, then capital managers do not have another choice than to invest traditionally. Barber, Morser, and Yasuda (2019) found that capital providers' willingness-to-pay for impact was in several cases negatively affected by, for example, policies restricting financial returns. Interestingly, in Finland, capital providers claimed to be "hungry for impact" (Interviewee Finland-6), but also asked for more support from financial authorities to get involved in Impact Investing activities. Hence, the findings of this further highlight the need to have market-based drivers (such as policies and regulation) that target capital providers as well, and not merely capital managers.

Second, with regards to the intrinsic drivers for impact investors, the interviews in India, as well as in Finland, confirmed that in both countries impact investors share similar values that aim to positively impact society and the environment, that they all aspire to a better world. The results show that impact investors earn more than financial returns; they also earn emotional returns. Moreover, by enabling them to redeploy capital, impact investments allow earning sustainable emotional and financial returns, as opposed to philanthropy through single-time donations.

The existing literature already discussed ethical values and other intrinsic elements as drives of impact investors (e.g. Roundy et al. 2017; Global Impact Investing Network 2018). It is often disaggregated into two categories, "impact first" and "finance first" impact investors, based on the priority they assign to the two main objectives of their investments. Furthermore, Barber, Morse, and Yasuda (2019) underlined that the prioritization given to each of these two is actually more of a reflection of the investor's willingness-to-pay for impact, which in turn affects his or her capital allocation decisions. The present study, on the other hand, found that in both countries all impact investors enjoy working with financially sustainable organizations and believe that a majority of these are excellent investment opportunities from a financial perspective as well, bringing high returns mostly because of the impact aspect they have. In other words, they believe that the financial and impact performance of the investments are positively correlated and come hand in hand. Although this does not put into question the fact that different impact investors may have different willingness-to-pay for impact, it infers that segregating impact investments into impact first and finance first investments might not necessarily be needed when analyzing what drives impact investors. Taking the Impact Investing perspective, it might not matter that much for its ultimate results, whether the investor is primarily or initially driven by the impact or by the financial results of an investment. This study found no proof of investment decisions resulting in meaningful difference.

Finally, the results of this study confirmed that although impact investors are all driven by values that aspire to a better world, the willingness-to-pay for impact varies considerably, depending on the regulatory environment in which they operate, on their investor profile, and on the involvement of the public sector. However, while Barber, Morse, and Yasuda (2019) found that the willingness-to-pay for impact was higher in Europe than in Asia, no similar trend clearly emerged from the results of this study. It underlines that in Finland, impact investors especially enjoyed the long-term emotional and financial earnings derived from impact investments, whereas in India they tended to focus more on shorter term earnings. Factors such as the political environment, the specificities of the instruments used for impact investments in each country, and the nature of the social and environmental problems might be determinant factors behind these differences.

CONCLUSION

The main goal of this study was to examine whether drivers for impact investors differ across geographies, and what could explain those divergences. To fulfill this aim, an empirical research based on personal interviews with 19 experienced impact investors in India and in Finland was conducted. The results highlighted that extrinsic drivers differ between a country such as India, where impact investors have focused on private equity and private debt investments, and a country such as Finland, where impact investments are primarily done through outcome-based instruments, such as impact bonds. However, the findings also show that intrinsic drivers do not vary substantially across geographies.

The results reveal that extrinsic drivers, and especially the specificities of the market they operate in, can act as determinants of impact investors' operations, as well as the financing instruments they use. In the two countries, the key role of the public sector was highlighted. However, public entities' activities differ between countries, and thus, extrinsic drivers for impact investors diverge as well. While in Finland public entities are active participants of the Impact Investing industry and thus have set the standards and required market infrastructures, in India, public actors have taken a less active role and focused more on building capacity for impact investments.

Despite the country differences, impact investors share similar intrinsic drivers in the Impact Investing industry of these two countries. They all believe that in the long term, societal or environmental problems should be tackled in a financially sustainable way. By earning a financial return on their investments, impact investors can re-deploy the capital over time and further increase the impact they generate. Hence, it is really the belief about the existence of a positive correlation between financial and impact performances that drives impact investors. Although their willingness-to-pay for impact may vary, the present study found no proof of this affecting impact investor's decisions.

This study has limitations, which also serve as directions for future research. Overall, generalizing the results is strongly restricted due to the size and specificities of the samples. While analyzing drivers in India and Finland enabled us to contrast two very distinct but enticing Impact Investing markets, the findings can hardly be generalizable, due to the unique and distinct nature of these countries. The influence of historical, structural, and economic contexts should be more carefully scrutinized in future studies. Furthermore, comparing the two countries was especially complex since the samples consisted of impact investors with very different profiles. Comparing what drives, for example, a Finnish impact investor working in an independent public fund with an Indian impact investor working in a venture capital fund turned out to be extremely challenging.

In conclusion, gaining a better understanding of impact investors' intrinsic and extrinsic drivers to enter and operate in the Impact Investing industry enables the design of better incentives, by adapting market settings, regulatory environments, and public policies to better suit their needs. Furthermore, this seems to be essential to allow impact investments to penetrate the mainstream financial industry, as well as to perform to their best capacity.

REFERENCES

Acevedo, J. D. R., and Wu, M. (2018). A Proposed Framework to Analyze the Impact Investing Ecosystem in a Cross-Country Perspective. *Review of European Studies* 10(4): 87–113.

Balandina-Jaquier, J. (2016). *Catalyzing Wealth For Change: Guide to Impact Investing*. Guide Extract, Part I: an introduction to impact investing, pp. 1–37. https://cdn.shopify.com/s/files/1/1302/3227/files/GuideExtract_Part_I.pdf. (accessed 4 November 2019).

Barber, B. M., Morse, A., and Yasuda, A. (2019). *Impact Investing*. Working paper series, issue 26582, National Bureau of Economic Research.

Barclays, (2018). Investor motivations for impact: A behavioral examination. Wealth Management (July). https://www.barclays.co.uk/content/dam/

documents/wealth-management/investments/impact-investing-product/investor-motivations-for-impact.pdf. (accessed 18 December 2019).

Bauer, S., and Hollmann, D. (2018). *Nudging the investment ecosystem by incentivizing impact.* Deutsche Gesellschaft für Internationale Zusammenarbeit (GIZ) (June). https://www.roots-of-impact.org/wp-content/uploads/2018/07/Intellecap-GIZ-Incentivizing-Impact-2018.pdf. (accessed 20 November 2019).

Clark, C., Emerson, J., and Thornley, B. (2014). *The Impact Investor: Lessons in Leadership and Strategy for Collaborative Capitalism.* Hoboken, NJ: John Wiley & Sons.

Cohen, R. (2018). *On Impact: A Guide to the Impact Revolution.* https://www.onimpactnow.org/. (accessed 20 November 2019).

Daggers, J., and Nicholls, A. (2016). *The Landscape of Social Impact Investment Research: Trends and Opportunities.* Oxford University and SAID Business School (March). https://www.scrt.scot/wp-content/uploads/2016/04/Landscape-of-social-impact-investment-research.pdf. (accessed 23 November 2019).

Eisenhardt, K. M. (1989). Building Theories from Case Study Research. *Academy of Management Review* 14(4): 532–550.

Finkelman, J., and Huntington, K. (2017). *Impact Investing: History & Opportunity.* Athena Capital Advisors (January). http://gsgii.org/reports/impact-investing-history-and-opportunity/. (accessed 18 December 2019).

Gandhi, V. (2019). *To DIB or not to DIB.* India Development Review, Opinion. (21 February). https://idronline.org/to-dib-or-not-to-dib/?fbclid=IwAR0CvSDGilp6XntF3WJlntjLM-fuY8RnwepFjOPZqC5JamCj9JAezyi8X0w. (accessed 20 December 2019).

Gioia, D. A., Corley, K. G., and Hamilton, A. L. (2012). Seeking Qualitative Rigor in Inductive Research: Notes on the Gioia Methodology. *Organizational Research Methods* 16(1): 15–31.

Global Impact Investing Network (GIIN) (n.d.) What you need to know about Impact Investing. About Impact Investing. https://thegiin.org/impact-investing/need-to-know/#what-is-impact-investing. (accessed 19 November 2019).

Global Impact Investing Network (GIIN) (2009). *Investing for Social & Environmental Impact: A Design for Catalyzing an Emerging Industry.* Monitor Institute (January).

Global Impact Investing Network (GIIN) (2011). *Impact-Based Incentive Structures.* Issue Brief (December).

Global Impact Investing Network (GIIN) (2018). *Annual Impact Investor Survey,* 8th ed.

Global Steering Group for Impact Investment (GSG) (2018a). *The Impact Principle: Widening Participation and Deepening Practice for Impact Investment at Scale.* Working Group Report (October).

Global Steering Group for Impact Investment (GSG) (2018b). *Catalyzing an Impact Investment Ecosystem: A Policymaker's Toolkit.* Working Group Report (October).

Helliwell, J., Layard, R., and Sachs, J. (2018). *World Happiness Report 2018.* New York: Sustainable Development Solutions Network.

Höchstädter, A. K., and Scheck, B. (2015). What's in a Name: An Analysis of Impact Investing Understandings by Academics and Practitioners. *Journal of Business Ethics* 132(2): 449–475.

Miles, M. B., and Huberman, A.M. (1994). *Qualitative Data Analysis: An Expanded Sourcebook.* Thousand Oaks, CA: Sage.

O'Donohoe, N., Leijonhufvud, C., and Saltuk, Y. (2010). *Impact Investments, An emerging asset class.* J.P. Morgan Global Research (November).

Pandit, V., and Tamhane, T. (2017). *Impact Investing: Purpose-driven finance finds its place in India.* McKinsey & Company, Private Equity and Principal Investors Practice (September).

Patton, M. Q. (2002). *Qualitative Research & Evaluation Methods.* 3rd ed. Thousand Oaks, CA: Sage.

Prahl, A., and Hofmann, E. (2016). *Market-Based Climate Policy Instruments.* Climate Policy Info Hub, 27th June 2016.

Roundy, P., Holzhauer, H., Dai, Y. (2017). Finance of Philanthropy? Exploring the Motivations and Criteria of Impact Investors. *Social Responsibility Journal,* 13(3): 491-512.

Saunders, M., and Lewis, P. (2014). *Doing Research in Business and Management: An Essential Guide to Planning Your Project.* Upper Saddle River, NJ: Financial Times Prentice Hall.

Saunders, M., Lewis, P., and Thornhill, A. (2009). *Research Methods for Business Students.* 5th ed. Upper Saddle River, NJ: Financial Times Prentice Hall.

Social Impact Investment Taskforce (2014). *Impact Investment: The Invisible Heart of Markets.* Social Impact Investment Taskforce report (15 September).

Spiggle, S. (1994). Analysis and Interpretation of Qualitative Data in Consumer Research. *Journal of Consumer Research* 21(3): 491–503.

Toniic (2018). *Powered Ascent report: Insights from the frontier of impact investing,*

2018. Toniic, Power Ascent Report (July).

Wendt, K. (2018). What Vehicles for Impact Investments Are Available and What Asset Classes Are Preferred? In K. Wendt, *Positive Impact Investing: A Sustainable Bridge Between Strategy, Innovation, Change and* Learning. Springer International Publishing, Sustainable *Finance*, pp. 9–10.

Wood, D. (2014). *The Role of Government in Impact Investing*. Shelterforce (26 March). https://shelterforce.org/2014/03/26/the_role_of_government_ in_impact_investing/. (accessed 24 February 2020).

APPENDIX 24.1: EXPERTS INTERVIEWED

Interviewee	Company Profile	Position
India-1	Non-banking financial company	Head of Investor Relations and Products
India-2	Philanthropic investment fund	Investment partner
India-3	Foundation	Country Director
India-4	Financial advisory company	Chief Executive Officer
India-5	Venture capital fund	Founder and Managing Director
India-6	Venture capital fund	Founder
India-7	Venture capital fund	Senior Manager
India-8	Venture capital fund	Investment Associate
India-9	Venture capital fund	Director, Equity Investments

Interviewee	Company	Position
Finland-1	Independent public fund	Project Director, Impact Investing
Finland-2	Independent Public fund	Director, Venture Capital and Private Equity Funds
Finland-3	Independent public fund	Chief Investment Officer
Finland-4	Institutional investor	Chief Executive Officer
Finland-5	Asset management company	Director, Product Development
Finland-6	Venture capital fund	Director, Development
Finland-7	Venture capital fund	Chief Executive Officer
Finland-8	Venture capital fund	Partner
Finland-9	Venture capital fund	Founding Partner

Understanding the Demand for Impact Investments: Insights from the Italian Market

Alessandro Rizzello, PhD, Elisabetta Scognamiglio, PhD, Ludovica Testa, LM, and Lorenzo Liotta, LLM

Abstract

Over the last decade, the popularity of Impact Investing increased in research and practice. Academic studies and practitioners' reports focusing on Impact Investing have so far primarily focused on the supply side of investors allocating capital in this growing industry. However, much remains to be learned about the demand side of impact investments, the ventures that create the impact and the profit streams—their industries, their needs, their goals for impact capital, and how impact can be added to all types of investees. In order to address this gap of scholarly attention, this chapter seeks to answer the following research questions: (i) which business sectors and industries are more impact investment ready: (ii) what is the level of impact readiness, and its integration in businesses' organizations and growth strategies; and (iii) what is their approach toward impact issues, in

929

terms of intentionality, and importantly, how to measure their impact. The study is based on a survey of more than 300 Italian startups. The findings highlight the degree of impact investment readiness or startups belonging to 22 different business sectors. Results reveal, among other things, a high score of readiness for respondents belonging to business sectors, not traditionally impact-oriented, such as artificial intelligence, smart mobility, health care, and agritech, and provide useful insights to enhance how impact investors and impact investees can align their goals and expectations for financial value creation and impact value creation across all asset classes, including private debt and private equity.

Keywords

Impact Investing; Sustainable Finance; Startups; Startup Ventures; Social Ventures; Intentionality; Measurability; Investment Readiness; Social Impact; Impact Measurement; Italy; Private Debt; Private Equity; Artificial Intelligence

INTRODUCTION

One of the most pressing questions facing local as well as global communities around the world is how to put resources to work in innovative ways to address major social challenges, ranging from extreme poverty to climate change (Utting 2018). In such a context, entrepreneurs are engaging in efforts to solve these challenges through ventures based on sustainable business models, which often require substantial capital for their early-stage operations. On the other hand, public services and civil society initiatives are often too constrained by tightened public finances or by institutional inertia (Sachs et al. 2019).

A growing demand for capital for sustainability purposes has mobilized massive amounts of new private capital into sustainable entrepreneurial organizations, providing new tools and asset classes for investors. Within this area, sustainable finance (SF) practices, consistent with social and environmental standards, were developed by balancing financial goals with sustainable development outcomes (Weber 2019). By adopting a new paradigm that embraces social and environmental impact with financial investment, social impact investing (SII), one of the fastest growing sustainable-finance sectors, has contributed to increase the diversity of capital provided for accomplishing the Sustainable Development Goals (SDG). The concept of SII diverts from the traditional view whereby social and environmental issues can only be addressed by philanthropic actions, while refundable investments are limited solely to commercial sectors providing exclusively financial returns (Agrawal and Hockerts 2019). SII investment logic includes the expectation that, in addition to a social return, capital is repayable to the investor with a financial return—which could be above, below, or at market rates. In this sense, SII provides an opportunity to simultaneously achieve social or environmental outcomes while also achieving financial returns (Chowdhry et al. 2018). This concept differs from socially responsible investment (SRI), aimed at essentially avoiding social or environmental harm while still pursuing profit. SII diverts also from program-related investments (PRI) and mission-related investments (MRI), which have the specific aim of complementing the grantmaking of private foundations and endowments.

In 2019, Impact Investing reached a market size of over USD $502 billion, according to the Global Impact Investing Network (GIIN) (Mudaliar et al. 2020). The strength of Impact Investing industry is considered as one of the main contributors to the fulfillment of the United Nations SDGs (Trabacchi and Buchner 2019).

A flourishing Impact Investing ecosystem is founded upon three main pillars: demand, supply, and intermediaries of impact capital. The demand includes all organizations seeking impact capital, such as traditional nonprofits and charities, social enterprises that blend impact and profit, social-purpose and mission-driven businesses, for-profit impact enterprises, and for-profits integrating impact. The supply side encompasses asset owners and allocators of capital, including pension funds, high-net-worth individuals and families, family foundations, endowments, foundations, community development funds, banks, and other financial institutions (Block et al. 2018; Logue et al. 2017). All these actors are characterized by the willingness to evaluate a balance and blend of financial performance and social and environmental returns. Many impact investors identify their investment opportunities considering selection criteria based on environmental, social, and governance (ESG) criteria (Viviani and Maurel 2019; Brandstetter and Lehner 2015). Finally, government and other actors, such as regulatory authorities or advisory firms, play a pivotal role as market builders through policies, rules, and regulations, and market interventions.

Two main types of instruments receive the largest capital allocation: private debt and private equity (GIIN 2018). Impact investments are directed at organizations positioned at different stages of their business life cycle, ranging from seed to growth stage (Xu et al. 2020) . It has been estimated that Impact Investments in startups through private equity and debt consistently represent 20% to 40% of total impact investments, making them popular Impact Investing asset classes (GIIN 2018).[1]

Over the last decade, the popularity of the Impact Investing concept also increased in academia, as one of the main topics within the sustainable-finance and impact-investing research (Balkin 2016; Lehner 2016; Rizzello et al. 2016). Academic studies and practitioners' reports focusing on Impact Investing to date have helped to educate the supply side of the Impact Investing market by exploring impact investors' motivations and strategies (e.g. Joy et al. 2011; Lyon and Owen 2019; Nicholls et al. 2015). However, much remains to be learned about the demand side in Impact Investing, specifically related to the startup ventures segment, one of the main class of investees. Furthermore, in academia, the reduced research investigating demand for Impact Investing has limited its focus to *mission-centered* enterprises, such as social enterprises, non-governmental organizations (NGO), or benefit corporations.[2] Thus, academic research has not focused enough on for-profit organizations, for instance, which—independently from the formal adoption of an "impact oriented" legal framework—integrate impact by positively addressing some of the most pressing social or environmental issues.

This study seeks to address this gap of scholarly attention. This research departed initially from the request of an institutional impact investor to ItaliaCamp,[3] which felt the need to identify the most suitable business sectors for Impact Investing, that is, those with the highest levels of readiness for impact investments within the startup segment.[4] To answer this question, three criteria were identified to structure this research: (i) the degree of knowledge and

---

[1]To see how one group of impact investors, known as TONIIC, invests across asset classes, view this 2019 report: https://toniic.com/t100-focus-the-frontier-of-sdg-investing/.

[2]See for example, Shortens and Boenigk (2017); Leborgne-Bonassié et al. (2019); Phillips and Johnson (2019); Joy et al. (2011). According to the Benefit Corporation (https://benefitcorp.net/), a benefit corporation is a "traditional corporation with modified obligations committing it to higher standards of purpose, accountability and transparency" with the purpose of committing to "creating public benefit and sustainable value in addition to generating profit."

[3]An Italian institutional impact company specialized in impact finance and impact reporting.

[4]The study is part of a broader research project commissioned by an Italian institutional investor directed to understand the impact finance demand deriving from Italian innovative ventures.

intentionality with respect to impact, (ii) how a startup venture approaches social impact evaluation, and (iii) how likely are startup ventures to modify some aspects of their business or organizations in order to improve impact investment readiness with the purpose to apply for new investment capital seeking impact.

In order to achieve these objectives, this study performed an inductive analysis through an online survey involving 574 Italian startups, identified through internal desk research, and extracted from the ItaliaCamp startup database.

Considering the above-mentioned research analysis criteria, the survey was structured to explore three main areas of investigation. First, it explored how startups integrate impact in their business strategy. Second, how they conducted any evaluation of social impact. Third, the survey intended to understand the level of readiness of startup ventures in terms of organizational and strategic adjustments if deemed necessary to receive impact investments.

This chapter is organized as follows. The next section describes methodology; the following section provides an overview of relevant concepts around the themes of startup financing and Impact Investing. Then the results of the survey for this particular set of startups are described. The last two sections provide final remarks and considerations for the Impact Investing industry.

METHODOLOGY

The investigation started from a broader research project, upon the request of an institutional impact investment wholesaler, aiming to identify the business sectors more suitable for an impact investor among the startup segment. In order to achieve this objective, a survey was architected, built, and conducted with more than 500 startups, identified through a dataset review.

The startups involved in the survey were sourced from the ItaliaCamp startup database, which included all small innovative startups engaged by ItaliaCamp since 2012. All the companies that started operating from 2015[5] were identified, making up a total of 574 innovative startups. At the end of 2019, the total number of innovative startups was of 10.882. Thus, the startups

---

[5]This requirement of five years in operation (number of years since its formal creation) is in line with the definition of startup given by the Startup Act in Italy. For more details, see https://www.mise.gov.it/images/stories/documenti/Slides%20innovative%20 startups%20and%20SMEs%2007_2019.pdf.

extracted from this database represent 5.3% of the total of Italian innovative startups. Next, an online survey was sent to all the startup ventures listed in the database, and yielded 302 responses, or a 53% reply ratio.

The structured questionnaire was composed of 28 questions,[6] structured into four main thematic sections: (i) startup demography characteristics, (ii) social impact focus, (iii) social impact evaluation focus, (iv) propensity to improve impact investment readiness (e.g. by introducing changes in business and organization). The questionnaire and the different sections of the survey are detailed in Appendix 25.1.

STARTUP VENTURE FINANCING AND IMPACT INVESTING: AN OVERVIEW

This section provides a brief review of the literature, focusing on the different components of the questionnaire, introducing definitions, and providing the background for the analysis of results.

Generally, impact investments in startup ventures are made by adopting a sustainable venture capital (SVC) approach and are made by funds or funds of funds, but in some cases also by international organizations and public venture capital funds (Liu 2019). All these actors tend to include startups with high potential to deliver triple-bottom-line outcomes in their portfolios. In other words, startups offering innovative solutions for addressing social or environmental challenges (e.g. in agriculture and sustainable "bio" products, smart grid and renewables, water sanitation and waste management, smart mobility, green building, or biotech medical devices) are desired targets for capital allocated by impact investors in the startup segment.

Traditional venture capital investments into startup companies take into consideration specific financial needs of these types of investees (Davila et al. 2003). Startup investment decision-making processes consider the goodness

---

[6]The survey was implemented using Wufoo, an online form builder. Data was then exported to a data file compatible with Excel and finally analyzed with R software. The online survey was delivered on 24 July 2019 with answers collected during the following eight weeks, from 24 July to 18 September 2019. With the purpose of increasing the response rate, two reminder emails were sent to encourage participants who had not yet responded. The timing for answers closed on 18 September 2019. The survey was sent to the 90% of the sample by email, accompanied by a cover letter explaining the reasons and the objective of the project. The remaining 10% was covered by one-on-one survey submissions conducted by the authors.

of fit between opportunity and personal investment criteria and involves various stages before it is consummated. Investors first screen businesses that meet their investment parameters, by excluding, for example, startups with poor management, poor profit potential for their level of risk, or that provided insufficient information. The concept of "investment readiness" is generally used to assess the level investability of investees and is based on an analysis that includes a series of parameters shared and accepted in literature (for an overview see Gumpert 2003; Mason and Kwok 2010).

In the Impact Investing academic landscape, researchers have poorly explored factors enabling Impact Investing readiness in startups. Existing evidence is fragmented, and furthermore, studies focus on a single class of investees at a time, such as venture philanthropy in social enterprises (Leborgne-Bonassié et al. 2019), investments into startups with a social mission (Cacciolatti et al. 2020), or investments into sustainability-focused startups (Antarciuc et al. 2018).

More empirical insights on the demand side for Impact Investing could help fill this gap, by providing a useful contribution for both investors and academics, by exploring the basic elements that impact investors normally consider during their investments in startups, and this could make a better match between what investors are looking for and the demand of impact capital from startups.

By considering the literature on the essential pillars characterizing Impact Investing, it is possible to identify three main basic drivers lying at the base of the readiness for impact investments, besides those normally considered in the traditional financial due diligence.[7] These specific drivers underlying the readiness for impact investments are: (i) intentionality (with social and environmental impact being intentionally integrated in the entrepreneurial mission); (ii) measurement of impact; and (iii) impact management and reporting. These are three key dimensions analyzed in this study, detailed in the sections below.

Intentionality

In Impact Investing, the concept of impact evolved from a static approach to a growing awareness that revolves fundamentally around change. The

---

[7]Generally, a due diligence process of early stage investments will involve a better understanding of the market (i.e. market research), the current stage of their business, and the startup team (i.e. personal interactions), plus reference checks, which provide additional insights into all three of these areas.

potential impact (and its measurement) derived from a company's operation represents one of the basic elements considered in an impact investment due diligence.

It is useful to disentangle the impact that investors have on the companies they invest in, from the impact generated by investees, which represents the change in social or environmental variables derived directly from the business—including its products, operations, and management. In this context, the intentionality of impact, universally recognized in all definitions of Impact Investing, has to be understood as the intentionality to generate a financial and a social or environmental return, both measurable, through businesses or organizations able to deliver a measurable social or environmental net-positive change.

In startup ventures, it is also possible to observe different levels of focus and alignment toward impact as a goal. Independently of the adoption of an "impact-oriented" legal corporate framework, the ways impact is generated by a startup may range between an indirect and a direct consciousness of achievement of impact. In other terms, if a startup explicitly embraces impact in its mission, it may be considered an "impactful" startup.[8] For these reasons, the distinguishing element characterizing impact is intentionality, intended as an explicit ex-ante declaration of a corporate impact mission, and the proactive search for activities that can deliver social value.

Measurability

According to the OECD (2019), two main conditions are crucial to succeed in the impact space: defining impact goals and reporting on their progress. By having a deliberate focus on achieving positive social or environmental outcomes, Impact Investing necessarily implies the thorough measurement (quantitatively, qualitatively, or both) of social and environmental returns, alongside financial returns. Preparing for impact is necessary not only to define intended impacts (ex-ante and ex-post) at the start of the investment cycle but also to verify whether these were effectively achieved. Measurability, therefore, constitutes a fundamental feature of Impact Investing, starting from the monitoring phase, which should be used as a management tool by the investees.

Impact investors can use a panoply of methods, quantitative and qualitative (e.g. theory of change at various points in the investment

---

[8]Startups able to achieve social or environmental impact given their business models—by contributing, for example, to one or more of the 17 SDGs—may be included in this category.

process) to communicate with investees about their intended impact, underlying assumptions, and potential strategies for achieving intended impact (Reisman et al. 2018). This has given rise to a multitude of tools for and approaches to measuring impact across sectors, such as the Impact Reporting and Investment Standards (IRIS) or Social Return on Investment (SROI) (Social Impact Investment Taskforce 2014).

Propensity to Improve Impact Investment Readiness

The assessment of the potential to achieve impact as well as of the capabilities of investees to manage and measure predefined impact targets is crucial. Demand for impact capital by startup ventures requires not only a robust financial business model, but also a well-defined theory of change, useful to identify areas where assumptions and additionality are weaker, with a view to testing the overall business model, as well as the adoption of evidence-based metrics and reporting mechanisms (Antarciuc et al. 2018). While companies traditionally know how to report their financial accounts, there is not a single adopted framework when it comes to impact reporting, which is case specific (Lall 2017). As a result, several tools have emerged to account for the impact performance beyond strictly financials of impact investments (Dufour 2019).

FINDINGS

The findings of the survey are described next, following the sequence of the survey's sections.

Startup Ventures Demography Characteristics

The first set of questions of the survey questionnaire served to identify the main characteristics of the respondents (see Appendix 25.1), such as business sector[9] and dimension (e.g. average number of employees and annual

---

[9]The institutional investor who initially asked for the study indicated a set of business sectors to be included in the research: Agritech/Foodtech, Artificial Intelligence, Blockchain, Deep Tech, Design/Made in Italy, EcoIndustries, Fintech, Health Care, Smart Mobility, New Materials, Social Impact, Space. If the business sector of respondents were different from this list, respondents were requested to specify.

TABLE 25.1   Startups by Business Sectors.

Sectors Specified in the Survey	Other Sectors Pointed Out by Respondents
Agritech/Foodtech	Biotechnology
Artificial Intelligence	Circular Economy
Blockchain	Ecommerce
Deep Tech	Education
Design/Made in Italy	Green Building
EcoIndustry	Human Resources Tech
Fintech	Marketplace/Dropshipping
Health care	Productivity
Smart Mobility	Smart Factory
New Materials	Smart Home
Social Impact	Smart Working
Space	Travel and Consulting
	Urban Farming

Source: Authors based on survey data.

revenues). Beyond the 12 business sectors already specified in the survey,[10] a total of 13 additional business sectors were cited, listed in the column "Other Sectors Pointed out by Respondents" of Table 25.1.

The respondent startups display a considerable degree of homogeneity concerning their business size and revenue. They have a small average number of employees, as well as early-stage annual revenues. As to startup size, 75% of the respondents have less than 10 employees (90% have less than 20 employees), while 80% declare an average annual revenue lower than EUR € 500,000. A total of 82% of respondents are innovative startup ventures regularly registered in the special section of the formal Italian Business Register dedicated to innovative startups.

Figure 25.1 shows that only 10% self-report belonging to the "Social Impact" sector and that almost a quarter of all of startups belong to the

---

[10]A total of 3 of the 12 sectors specifically listed in the survey due to the institutional investor request (Blockchain, Design/Made in Italy and Space) did not receive any counts in the survey.

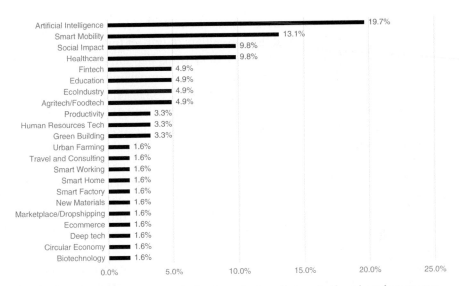

FIGURE 25.1   Startup Ventures by Business Sector. *Source:* Authors based on survey data.

Artificial Intelligence and Smart Mobility sectors.[11] The analysis in this chapter will be presented in these two categories: 10% social impact sector and 90% nonidentifying with formal social impact. This second analysis will allow us to reach the goal of our research: to explore the impact readiness of startup ventures that are not "impact oriented" by definition or self-identification.

For the ventures' funding, almost three in four (72%) respondents claimed having already received funding: primarily reporting, equity (65.5%), debt (13.5%), and grants (21%). Those companies having already received investments obtained them mostly from private investors (61.5%), followed by public investors (23.5%), and only 15% from institutional investors.

Social Impact

The second section of the survey explores startup ventures' degree of awareness and knowledge toward social impact. It was necessary to inquire about the degree of intentionality in the achievement of impact among startups'

---

[11]For the definitions, see: https://ec.europa.eu/environment/enveco/eco_industry/pdf/main_report.pdf.

business model (see Appendix 25.1), as social and environmental impact intentionality represent one of the core pillars of Impact Investing.

Question B1 showed that the 94% of startups had already heard about social impact—and that 45% of those considered impact directly and intentionally in their missions. Almost one in three (32%) reported generating impact indirectly through its products or services, and 18% operating in a business that was already oriented toward impact (Question B2).

When asked why impact was useful to consider for their organization, 33% mentioned the interest to attract investments, to increase reputation (19%), to communicate with stakeholders (17%), to better define strategic orientation (17%), and to assess their companies' performance (10%) (Question B4). The impact areas where startups considered they had generated most of their effects were Innovation, Health and Wellness, Environmental, and Sustainability (Question B3).

Contemplating the subset of startups that are *not considered impact oriented* (90% of the companies, that is, all those not self-reporting as belonging to the social sector), results show that 95% stated having a good awareness of social impact issues (Question B1). Furthermore, still among this subset, 40% of respondents declared they considered impact intentionally in their missions, and that 30% embraced impact "indirectly" as it was already embedded in their products or services (Question B2) (Figure 25.2).

Questions B.3 and B.4 investigated, respectively, the impact areas where startups declared achieving most effects and their underlying motivations for considering impact in their organization. The impact areas where firms stated

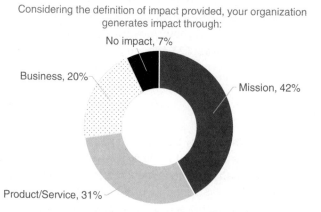

FIGURE 25.2   Impact Intentionality. *Source:* Authors based on the survey.

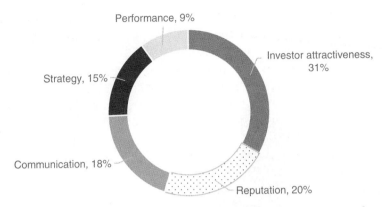

Performance, 9%

Investor attractiveness, 31%

Strategy, 15%

Communication, 18%

Reputation, 20%

FIGURE 25.3 Motivations for Integrating Impact. Note: 7% did not reply, so figure does not total 100%. *Source:* Authors based on the survey.

they generated most of their effects were Innovation, Health and Wellness, Environmental, and Sustainability.

Investor Attractiveness (31%) and Reputation (20%) were the two main reasons for considering impact that an organization could generate, as shown in Figure 25.3. Most startups thus consider themselves as having a good knowledge and awareness of social impact definition and issues.

Evaluation of Social Impact

The third section of the survey relates to impact measurement practices of surveyed companies. Question C.1 shows that the 20% of companies did not consider impact measurement in their activities, 30% are starting to consider impact measurement through qualitative assessments, only 8% are assessing in a quantitative way, 23% integrate impact in their strategy planning, and 20% monitor periodically impact objective defined previous in strategy plans.

Among startups that did measure their impact, 90% used internal resources and 10% external evaluators. The main reasons why impact was not being measured related to the lack of expertise (42%) or because startups did not consider it a strategic priority (25%).

Considering how impact is conducted and perceived in companies for the subset of *startups not reporting an impact orientation,* results for Question C1 show that only 22% of respondents did not adopt some form of impact measurement (Figure 25.4). The remaining 78% included some form of impact in their reporting systems, ranging from qualitative (33%) to

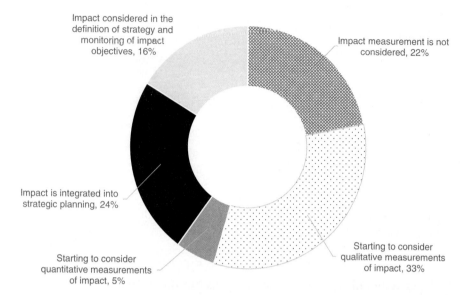

FIGURE 25.4   Impact Measurement Practices. *Source:* Authors based on the survey.

quantitative methods (5%). For a quarter of companies (24%), impact was integrated directly into the company's strategic planning.

Overall, 56% of startups adopted some sort of qualitative measurement framework, by integrating impact in their strategies (23.5%) or qualitative reports (32.5%). It is interesting to note that 22% of respondents, self-reporting as *not impact-oriented business sectors*, also introduced quantitative methods to evaluate themselves (5.5%) and regularly monitor impact goals of their strategy (16.5%).

Results derived from the sub-population of *respondents belonging to Social Impact business sectors* (Figure 25.5), confirmed these actors integrated impact as part of their mission and strategy, having chosen quantitative methods for these assessments (33%), a higher percentage than seen for the overall population of interviewees (5%).

Moreover, it is interesting to note how respondents *not belonging to impact-oriented business sectors* evaluated their impact practices. Only 8% of respondents interacted with external evaluators.

Further, combining these results with those derived from Questions C2 and C3, two additional findings emerged: respondents adopting qualitative frameworks in their evaluations of impact opted for internal resources (89%). On the other hand, companies that adopted more structured approach to impact measurement (through a strategic integration of impact goals, and

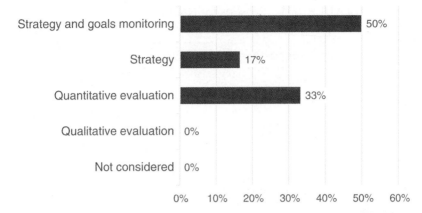

FIGURE 25.5 Impact Measurability Practices Within the Self-Reported Social Impact Business Sector. *Source:* Authors based on survey data.

TABLE 25.2 Approaches to the Evaluation of Impact.

Approach to Measurability	External Evaluators	Internal Resources
Qualitative evaluation	11%	89%
Quantitative evaluation	0%	100%
Strategy integration	0%	100%
Strategy integration and goals monitoring	22%	78%

Source: Authors based on survey data.

performance monitoring and evaluation), used external evaluators more frequently (Table 25.2).

Among the reasons pointed out for lack of greater engagement with impact measurement was lack of expertise (42%), while 17% named complexity, and 8% the cost and time-consuming nature of these activities. For the remaining 33%, impact considerations had little interest or was given no priority in their companies (Table 25.3).

Propensity to Improve Impact Investment Readiness

The fourth section of the survey (Section D of Appendix 25.1) explores how startups approached Impact Investing in their organizations. Question D1

TABLE 25.3   Reasons for Not Engaging
Further with Impact

Reasons for Not Approaching Impact	
Lack of expertise	42%
Complexity	17%
Onerous	8%
Lack of interest	8%
No priority	25%

Source: Authors based on the survey.

shows that 15% of respondent had already received an impact investment from private investors (44%), public investors (33%), and institutional investors (23%) as shown from the answers to Question D2.

Considering only the respondents, which from Question D1 replied they had never received an impact investment, 82% affirmed to be impact investment ready (Question D4). Questions D5 and D6 confirm respondents consider being well informed about the theme of Impact Investing. Indeed, 33% stated they knew an impact fund or more and all of them indicated at least one name.

Finally, Questions D7 and D8 are useful to understand if respondents would be willing to integrate in their business model assessments of the impact attained by their companies (Question D7), and the allocation of more human and financial resources to impact management if requested by an investor (Question D8). Overall, 90% responded they were willing to introduce evaluation practices concerning the impact attained by their organization if requested by an investor, while 88% stated they would be willing to invest more in human and financial resources if requested by an investor.

Considering just the subset of *startups not-impact oriented*: 15% had already received an impact investment. Among this 15%, about half (51%) of startups received these investments from a private investor, 37% from a public investor, and 12% from an institutional investor (Questions D1 and D2).

Relatively to Question D4, 81% affirmed to be impact investment ready (totaling agreeing, agreeing to a great extent, and totally agreeing), while only 4% considering themselves as not impact ready (Figure 25.6).

Questions D5 and D6 show that 27% of startups not *impact-oriented* know about impact funds, with all indicating at least one name. Question D7, as

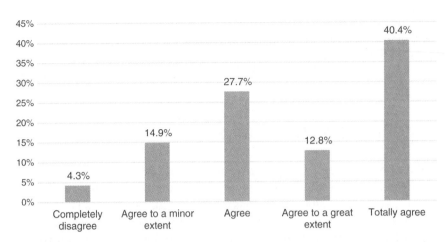

FIGURE 25.6   Impact Investment Readiness. *Source:* Authors based on survey data.

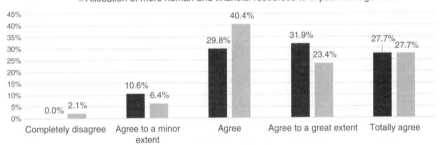

FIGURE 25.7   Propensity to Improve Impact Investment Readiness. *Source:* Authors based on survey data.

shown in Figure 25.7, reveals 90% of startups stated their openness to introduce some form of impact measurement in the management of their organizations (with 60% totally agreeing or agreeing to a great extent), if the opportunity to receive impact investments arose. Only 10% were poorly oriented toward integrating impact in their activities, showing scarce interest toward such source of financing.

Concerning the willingness to dedicate financial or human resources to integrating impact management (Question D8), 92% of respondents declared being ready (agreeing to totally agreeing), to consider in its business model introducing evaluations of the impact attained the organization, if requested by an investor. This result is in line with the findings related to Question

D7, where the 10% of respondents who had already mentioned not being yet ready to integrate impact in their business models. Overall, the willingness to deploy more human and financial resources to impact measurement is higher than the first option of only integrating these practices in companies' business strategies.

IMPACT INVESTMENT READINESS SCORING

To measure the overall Impact Investment Readiness of the analyzed startups of this survey—that is, the aggregated result of all Questions B.2, C.1, D.4, D.7, and D.8—a global score was implemented,[12] segmented by business sectors. Each question was considered as representative of a particular feature of the concept of "impact readiness." Each answer received a specific score, as reported in Appendix 25.3, in order to harmonize the results across demographics.

Questions with four options were also classified with a four-point scale (1, 2, 3, 4); questions with five options were classified with a five-point scale (0, 1, 2, 3, 4). Then, for each sector, the frequency of each answer was investigated in order to define the correspondent score.

In order to compare results between different sectors, scores were divided into three different levels, corresponding to different degrees of readiness, identified by High (for scoring 16.5 points or more), Medium (for the interval scoring included between 12.8 and 16.4 points), and Low (for scoring 12.7 points or less).

This analysis showed that business sectors with a higher level of readiness are E-Commerce, Travel and Consulting, Social Impact, Human Resources Tech, Health Care, Circular Economy, Education, Fintech, and Smart Home sectors (see Appendix 25.1 for details of each business sector). Startups working in these sectors consider social impact as an important item of company strategy, and they also try to monitor and evaluate it. Furthermore, these organizations also declared being interested in modifying their business model or being ready to invest more in human or financial resources in order to attract impact investors.

It is also interesting to observe that the Education and Circular Economy sectors, traditionally thought to be able to attract impact investments more easily, scored lower than E-commerce or Travel and Consulting—sectors usually unrelated to Impact Investing. Furthermore, if the scores of these five

---

[12]B2 (Intentionality), C1 (Measurability), D4 (Readiness), D7 (Propensity Business Model), D8 (Propensity Impact Management).

questions are considered separately (as in Appendix 25.3), it can be observed that the main difference between higher level of readiness and lower relates to Questions C1 and D4. This means that the more sensitive issues influencing the level of readiness for startups are intentionality and the measurability, two aspects very closely related.

Next, in order to weight these results with the share of firms in each sector of the dataset, the distribution of respondent startups by sectors was considered. So, the scores depicted above were weighted by the share of startups belonging to each sector, in order to provide a clearer picture of investment readiness.

As described in the previous paragraph, readiness was classified Low, Medium, and High, with results shown in Table 25.4. Results, summarized in Table 25.5, indicate this time that Artificial Intelligence, Social Impact, Smart Mobility, Health Care, and Education now display a higher (weighted) degree of readiness. By comparing these results with those reported in Table 25.5, there are visible differences, deriving from the weight of each sector in the population of respondents. Sectors as Education display Medium scores, demonstrating a good propensity enforced by a higher number of survey respondents. The scores for Artificial Intelligence changed substantially, demonstrating how the number of respondents influence the final score.

Sectors such as Smart Mobility, Health Care, Education, and Fintech are more consistent, having similar (Medium and High) scores in both total and average score methodologies. These sectors can be considered the most impact investment ready.

These results constitute only preliminary evidence that needs to be further researched and corroborated, in particular:

- Because the number of startups in each sector of the dataset influences results. Sectors such as Education, Fintech, Human Resources Tech, Circular Economy, E-commerce, Smart Home, and Travel and Consulting, even if showing a higher readiness total score, included a lower number of respondents (2% of the total dataset). This evidence needs to be further researched using other types of business datasets to test and validate the present results.
- Differences by sector and type of company. The dataset only includes startups that are by definition small organizations. Thus, these results cannot go further, requiring a more extensive analysis from other types of studies focusing on other typologies of firms.

TABLE 25.4   Total Scores: Measurement of Impact Investment Readiness.

Sector	Total Score	Readiness
Social Impact	20.000	High
E-commerce	19.000	High
Travel and Consulting	19.000	High
Health Care	18.000	High
Education	18.000	High
Fintech	18.000	High
Circular Economy	18.000	High
Agritech/Foodtech	17.000	High
EcoIndustries	17.000	High
Human Resources Tech	17.000	High
Smart Home	17.000	High
Smart Mobility	15.000	Medium
Green Building	13.000	Medium
Artificial Intelligence	12.000	Low
Biotechnology	12.000	Low
Deep Tech	12.000	Low
Urban Farming	12.000	Low
Productivity	11.000	Low
Marketplace/Drop-shipping	11.000	Low
New Materials	11.000	Low
Smart Working	11.000	Low
Smart Factory	9.000	Low

Source: Authors based on survey data.

CONCLUSION

The analysis performed in this chapter highlights the degree of impact investment readiness of Italian startup ventures present in the dataset of ItaliaCamp, an Italian impact company, by also performing an analysis by business sectors. The dataset included 302 startups characterized by a small firm size and annual revenue in 22 business sectors. Throughout the

TABLE 25.5 Average Scores: Measurement of Impact Investment Readiness.

Sector	Average Score	Average Readiness
Artificial Intelligence	2.361	High
Smart Mobility	1.967	High
Social Impact	1.967	High
Health Care	1.770	High
Education	0.885	Medium
Fintech	0.885	Medium
Agritech/Foodtech	0.836	Low
EcoIndustries	0.836	Low
Human Resources Tech	0.557	Low
Green Building	0.426	Low
Productivity	0.361	Low
E-commerce	0.311	Low
Travel and Consulting	0.311	Low
Circular Economy	0.295	Low
Smart Home	0.279	Low
Urban Farming	0.213	Low
Biotechnology	0.197	Low
Deep Tech	0.197	Low
Marketplace/Dropshipping	0.180	Low
New Materials	0.180	Low
Smart Working	0.180	Low
Smart Factory	0.148	Low

Source: Authors based on survey data.

analysis, findings distinguish between *impact-oriented* business sectors from those *not impact-oriented*.

In order to explore the impact investment readiness, three main drivers were considered: first, the degree of awareness and knowledge of Impact Investing basics; second, the approach toward the integration of impact, both in terms of intentionality and quality of impact measurement; and, third, the openness degree to improve impact investment readiness. All these factors were later added to create a score for impact investment readiness. Data and readiness scores were later disaggregated by business sectors and weighted by the number of companies belonging to those sectors, to identify sectors with a higher degree of impact investment readiness.

Regarding both the awareness and knowledge about Impact Investing and the approach toward impact (intentionality and measurement), the results reveal a high score also for respondents belonging to business sectors not traditionally impact-oriented, such as Artificial Intelligence, Smart Mobility, Health Care, and Agritech.

As to the approach toward the evaluation of impact, the data shows a higher prevalence of the adoption of qualitative impact assessment methods (and ex-post evaluations), mostly conducted in-house by the companies, as well as planned at the strategic level by considering specific evaluation criteria/target. Respondents who displayed a low preference for integrating impact in their businesses revealed this was due to a low relevance given to this theme within their companies.

Furthermore, the findings reveal that for nonimpact types of businesses, there is a considerably high degree of willingness toward improving impact investment readiness—by introducing significant changes in their organizations' business models, along with the allocation of more human and financial resources to impact assessments.

Finally, business sectors scoring a high degree of impact investment readiness (by average) are Artificial Intelligence (2.36), Smart Mobility (1.97), and Health Care (1.77), which feature both that they have a significant number of respondents belonging to them and that have a good level of readiness.

Even if some economic sectors were less well represented in this database, that is, in the population of startups analyzed by this survey, these results still have interesting insights, especially for future research on this topic.

Barriers to improving impact investment readiness remain, mainly due to the scarcity of financial resources these startups face to dedicate to the measurement and management activities required by Impact Investing. These challenges are known to be faced to a great extent by companies with this type of profile, startups with a smaller company size and, consequently, lower annual revenues. At the same time, these considerations suggest this class of investees needs to enhance the introduction of tools and services oriented toward the enhancement of impact investment readiness.

The empowerment given by a higher level of readiness, granted by the adoption of dedicated resources to integrate impact, could in fact be a major driver for startup ventures presenting high level of willingness to improve their business or organizations by adopting the necessary changes to receive impact investments (but facing a scarcity of human and financial resources). These insights can also be useful for Impact Investing market builders, seeking to grow the market of investable ventures seeking to deliver impact.

This analysis also opens up future avenues of research focusing on the Impact Investing market. The demand side of Impact Investing deserves further theoretical and empirical explorations. Factors enabling impact investment readiness should provide robust conceptual frameworks to advance the industry, which have until now been only considered from practitioners' studies. Furthermore, future research investigating the Impact Investing market should include all investees, and not only those organizations that are mission oriented or nonprofits.

The Impact Investing industry is growing and evolving. Even though standardized frameworks and metrics are still formalizing, the industry has enormous potential to contribute toward a holistic transformation that gradually integrates sustainability issues into all investment paradigms.

ACKNOWLEDGMENTS

We would like to thank all startups that participated in this survey because they allowed us to elaborate the results of this work.

REFERENCES

Agrawal, A., and Hockerts, K. (2019). Impact Investing: Review and Research Agenda. *Journal of Small Business & Entrepreneurship* 31:1–29 https://doi.org/10.1080/08276331.2018.1551457.

Antarciuc, E., Zhu, Q., Almarri, J., et al. (2018). Sustainable Venture Capital Investments: An Enabler Investigation. *Sustainability* 10(4): 1189–1204.

Balkin, J. (2016). *Investing with Impact: Why Finance Is a Force for Good.* New York: Routledge.

Block, J., Colombo, M., Cumming, D., et al. (2018). New Players in Entrepreneurial Finance and Why They Are There. *Small Business Economics* 50(2): 239–250.

Brandstetter, L., and Lehner, O. (2015). Opening the Market for Impact Investments: The Need for Adapted Portfolio Tools. *Entrepreneurship Research Journal* 5(2): 87–107. https://doi.org/10.1515/erj-2015-0003.

Cacciolatti, L., Rosli, A., Ruiz-Alba, J., et al. (2020). Strategic Alliances and Firm Performance in Startups with a Social Mission. *Journal of Business Research,* 106: 106–117. https://doi.org/10.1016/j.jbusres.2019.08.047.

Chowdhry, B., Davies, S., and Waters, B. (2018). Investing for Impact. *Review of Financial Studies* 32(3): 864–904.

Davila, A., Foster, G., and Gupta, M. (2003). Venture Capital Financing and the Growth of Startup Firms. *Journal of Business Venturing,* 18(6): 689–708.

Dufour, B. (2019). Social Impact Measurement: What Can Impact Investment Practices and the Policy Evaluation Paradigm Learn from Each Other? *Research in International Business and Finance* 47: 18–30.

GIIN (2018). Annual Impact Investor Survey 2018. Global Impact Investing Network. https://thegiin.org/research/publication/annualsurvey2018 (accessed 10 February 2020).

Gumpert, D. E. (2003). *Burn Your Business Plan! What Investors Really Want from Entrepreneurs.* Needham, MA: Lauson Publishing Co.

Joy, I., de Las Casas, L., Rickey, B., et al. (2011). Understanding the demand for and supply of social finance. https://www.nesta.org.uk/report/understanding-the-demand-for-and-supply-of-social-finance/ (accessed 22 February 2020).

Lall, S. (2017). Measuring to Improve Versus Measuring to Prove: Understanding the Adoption of Social Performance Measurement Practices in Nascent Social Enterprises. *VOLUNTAS: International Journal of Voluntary and Nonprofit Organizations* 28(6): 2633–2657.

Leborgne-Bonassié, M., Coletti, M., and Sansone, G. (2019). What Do Venture Philanthropy Organizations Seek in Social Enterprises? *Business Strategy & Development* 2(4): 349–357.

Lehner, O. M. (2016). *Routledge Handbook of Social and Sustainable Finance.* London: Routledge.

Liu, C. (2019). Financing social enterprises: A systematic approach. In *Handbook of Research on Value Creation for Small and Micro Social Enterprises* (C. Maher, ed.), pp. 126–150. Hershey, PA: IGI Global.

Logue, D., McAllister, G., and Schweitzer, J. (2017). Social Entrepreneurship and Impact Investing Report. Report prepared for innovationXchange, Department of Foreign Affairs, and Trade by the University of Technology Sydney. https://www.uts.edu.au/node/273516/social-entrepreneurship-and-impact-investing-report (accessed 10 February 2020).

Lyon, F. and Owen, R. (2019). Financing Social Enterprises and the Demand for Social Investment. *Strategic Change* 28(1): 47–57.

Mason, C., and Kwok, J. (2010). Investment Readiness Programs and Access to Finance: A Critical Review of Design Issues. *Local Economy* 25(4): 269–292.

Mudaliar, A., Bass, R., Dithrich, H., et al. (2020). Sizing the Impact Investing Market. https://thegiin.org/research/publication/impinv-market-size (accessed 22 Feb. 2020).

Nicholls, A., Paton, R., and Emerson, J. (2015). *Social Finance*. Oxford, UK: Oxford University Press.

OECD (2019). *Social Impact Investment 2019: The Impact Imperative for Sustainable Development. Paris: OECD Publishing.* https://doi.org/10.1787/9789264311299-en.

Phillips, S., and Johnson, B. (2019). Inching to Impact: The Demand Side of Social Impact Investing. *Journal of Business Ethics* 160:1–15. https://doi.org/10.1007/s10551-019-04241-5.

Reisman, J., Olazabal, V., and Hoffman, S. (2018). Putting the "Impact" in Impact Investing: The Rising Demand for Data and Evidence of Social Outcomes. *American Journal of Evaluation* 39(3): 389–395.

Rizzello, A., Migliazza, M., Caré, R., et al. (2016). Social Impact Investing: A model and research agenda. In *Routledge Handbook of Social and Sustainable Finance* (O.M. Lehner, ed.), pp. 102–124. London: Routledge.

Sachs, J., Schmidt-Traub, G., Mazzucato, M., et al. (2019). Six Transformations to Achieve the Sustainable Development Goals. *Nature Sustainability* 2(9): 805–814.

Schrötgens, J., and Boenigk, S. (2017). Social Impact Investment Behavior in the Nonprofit Sector: First Insights from an Online Survey Experiment. *VOLUNTAS: International Journal of Voluntary and Nonprofit Organizations* 28(6): 2658–2682.

Social Impact Investments Taskforce (SIIT) (2014). Measuring impact. Subject paper of the Impact Measurement Working Group of the Social Impact Investment Taskforce established under the UK's Presidency of the G8. https://www.thinknpc.org/wp-content/uploads/2018/07/IMWG_Measuring -Impact1.pdf (accessed 3 May 2020).

Trabacchi, C., and Buchner, B. (2019). Unlocking global investments for SDGs and tackling climate change. In: *Achieving the Sustainable Development Goals Through Sustainable Food Systems* (R. Valentini, J. Sievenpiper, M. Antonelli, and K. Dembska. eds.), pp. 157–170. Zurich, Switzerland: Springer. Cham.

Utting, P. (2018). Achieving the Sustainable Development Goals through Social and Solidarity Economy: Incremental versus Transformative Change. http://www.unrisd.org/80256B3C005BCCF9/(httpAuxPages)/DCE7DAC6D 248B0C1C1258279004DE587/$file/UNTFSSE—WP-KH-SSE-SDGs-Utting-April2018.pdf (accessed 20 Feb. 2020).

Viviani, J., and Maurel, C. (2019). Performance of Impact Investing: A Value Creation Approach. *Research in International Business and Finance* 47: 31–39.

Weber, O. (2019) Sustainable finance and the SDGs. In *Achieving the Sustainable Development Goals: Global Governance Challenges* (S. Dalby, S. Horton, R. Mahon, and D. Thomaz, eds.), pp. 225–256. New York: Routledge.

Xu, B., Costa-Climent, R., Wang, Y., et al. (2020). Financial Support for Micro and Small Enterprises: Economic Benefit or Social Responsibility? *Journal of Business Research* (article in press). https://doi.org/10.1016/j.jbusres.2020 .01.071.

APPENDIX 25.1: QUESTIONNAIRES

Section A. Business Demography Characteristics

The first section of the survey investigated the main characteristics of startups, such as business sector, legal form, dimension, amount, and type of investment received. It included a total of 13 questions, 12 being multiple-choice answers (see below for more details). Information derived from these questions was useful to describe the sample and to allow the analysis of the impact investment readiness of startups by business sector, distinguishing social sectors from others.

TABLE 25.6 Questionnaire, Business Demography Section.

Demography Characteristics		
A.1	What is the name of your organization?	*Open-endend question*
A.2	In which italian region does your organization operate?	*Multiple choice about Italian regions and abroad options*
A.3	When was startup established?	*Multiple choice about last 5 years*
A.4	In which of the following market sectors does orgaization operate?	Agritech/Foodtech
		Artificial Intelligence
		Blockchain
		Deep Tech
		Design/Made in Italy
		EcoIndustries
		Fintech
		Health Care
		Mobility
		New Materials
		Social Impact
		Space
		Other (specify)
A.5	Is your organization an innovative startup regularly registered in the special section of the Business Register dedicated to innovative startups?	Yes
		No
A.6	What is the legal form of your organization?	SRL
		SPA
		Cooperative
		Social Enterprise
		B-corp
		Other (specify)

TABLE 25.6 (*continued*)

Demography Characteristics		
A.7	How many people are employed in your organization?	1–10
		11–20
		21–50
		51–100
		101–150
		Over 250
A.8	What is the average revenue achieved in 2018?	< 0.1 €/Mln
		0.1 €/Mln – 0.5 €/Mln
		0.5 €/Mln – 1 €/Mln
		1 €/Mln – 2 €/Mln
		2 €/Mln – 5 €/Mln
		5 €/Mln – 10 €/Mln
		10 €/Mln – 2 €/Mln
		Over 50 €/Mln
A.9	What is the corporate composition of your organization?	Single shareholder
		Participated by private entities
		Participated by public entities
		Participated by institutional investors (asset management companies, mutual funds, pension funds)
A.10	Have you ever received investments?	Yes
		No
		No, but I'm in fundraising
A.11	Which type?	Equity
		Debt
		Grants

TABLE 25.6 *(continued)*

Demography Characteristics	
A.12 What amount?	0 - 0.05 €/Mln
	0.05 €/Mln - 0.1 €/Mln
	0.1 €/Mln - 0.25 €/Mln
	0.25 €/Mln - 0.5 €/Mln
	0.5 €/Mln - 1 €/Mln
	1 €/Mln - 1.5 €/Mln
	Over 1.5 €/Mln
A.13 From which type of investor?	Private investors
	Public investors
	Institutional investors (asset management companies, mutual funds, pension funds)
	Other (specify)

Source: Authors.

Section B. Social Impact

TABLE 25.7 Questionnaire, Section on Social Impact.

B_Social Impact	
B.1 Have you ever heard of social impact as an effect generated by an organization?	Yes No
B.2 **"The impact is the positive change that the organization wants to intentionally generate for the territories and communities on which it acts in a long period of time in line with business objectives. We define impact that change that turns out to be measurable, additional and, above all, intentional."** Considering the definition of impact you can say that . . .	Your organization directly and intentionally generates impact because it is an integral part of its strategic mission
	Your organization indirectly generates impact through its product/service
	Your organization indirectly generates impact because it operates in a business that is already oriented toward impact (e.g. green, water sanitation, social inclusion, smart mobility, etc)

(continued)

TABLE 25.7 *(continued)*

B_Social Impact		
		Your organization is not geared to generating impact, either directly or indirectly
B.3	In which areas does your organization generate the most effects?	Health and wellness
		Education
		Development and territorial enhancement
		Social inclusion
		Environmental sustainability
		Innovation
B.4	Why do you think it is useful to consider the impact generated by an organization?	To assess my performance
		To communicate with my stakeholders
		To increase my reputation
		To attract new investments also for social impact purposes
		To better define my strategic orientation

Source: Authors.

Section C. Approach to the Evaluation of Impact

The third section of the survey explores if and how startups consider the evaluation of the impact achieved in their business models. Indeed, the measurability of the impact achieved by the investees represents one essential pillar in Impact Investing due diligence, besides the classical risk/return of financial assessments.

TABLE 25.8 Questionnaire, Section on Impact Evaluation.

C_Evaluation of Social Impact		
C.1	Considering the activities your organization develops, you	. . . don't consider impact in the management or evaluation of your performance
		. . . are starting to consider impact measurement, through your first qualitative evaluative assessments
		. . . are starting to consider impact measurement, through your first quantitative evaluative assessments
		. . . integrate impact in your strategic planning
		. . . consider impact when defining of your strategy and periodically monitor impact objectives previously set
C.2	How do you measure impact?	Using internal resources
		Using external evaluators
		Other (specify)
C.3	Why is impact not measured?	Lack of expertise
		Lack of interest
		It is too complex
		It is expensive
		Other (specify)

Source: Authors.

Section D. Propensity to Improve Impact Investment Readiness

The fourth section of the survey was dedicated to the exploration of impact investment readiness perception of startups and their propension to improve it by introducing adaptations in their business, organizations, or strategies, if necessary, to receive impact investments.

TABLE 25.9 Questionnaire, Section on Propensity to Improve Impact Investment Readiness.

D_Impact Investing		
D.1	Considering that the term "impact finance" means "the use of financial resources directed to organizations and businesses capable of generating financial returns and, at the same time, social and/or environmental returns," have you ever received impact investments?	Yes No
D.2	From whom did you receive impact investment?	Private investors Public investors Institutional investors (asset management companies, mutual funds, pension funds) Other (specify)
D.3	What was the amount of the impact investment?	0 – 0.05 €/Mln 0.05 €/Mln – 0.1 €/Mln 0.1 €/Mln – 0.25 €/Mln 0.25 €/Mln – 0.5 €/Mln 0.5 €/Mln – 1 €/Mln 1 €/Mln – 1.5 €/Mln Over 1.5 €/Mln
D.4	I consider that my organization can be a recipient of impact investments, i.e. financial resources directed explicitly to organizations and businesses capable of generating financial returns and, at the same time, social and/or environmental returns.	Completely disagree Agree to a minor extent Agree Agree to a great extent Totally agree

TABLE 25.9   *(continued)*

D_Impact Investing		
D.5	Do you know investors and/or intermediaries in impact finance?	Yes No
D.6	If yes, which ones?	*Open-endend question*
D.7	I would consider in my business model introducing evaluations of the impact attained by my organization, if requested by an investor.	Completely disagree Agree to a minor extent Agree Agree to a great extent Totally agree
D.8	I would be willing to allocate human and financial resources to impact management (the management of actions and risks to achieve the pre-established social/environmental impact objectives), if requested by a potential impact investor.	Completely disagree Agree to a minor extent Agree Agree to a great extent Totally agree

APPENDIX 25.2:   SCORING RESULTS

TABLE 25.10 Scoring Results.

Questions Sector	Answers	B2 Intentionality	C1 Measurability	D4 Readiness	D7 Propensity Business Model	D8 Propensity Impact Management	Total Score	Readiness	Average Score	Average Readiness	Range: Average Score	Range: Total Score
Artificial Intelligence	19.7%	3	3	2	2	2	12.000	L	2.3607	H	0.1475 0.8852 L	9.0000 12.6667 L
Smart Mobility	13.1%	4	1	4	3	3	15.000	M	1.9672	H	0.8853 1.6231 M	12.6668 16.3334 M
Health Care	9.8%	4	4	4	4	2	18.000	H	1.7705	H	1.6232 2.3607 H	16.3335 20.0000 H
Agritech/Foodtech	4.9%	2	3	4	4	4	17.000	H	0.8361	L		
EcoIndustries	4.9%	2	3	4	4	4	17.000	H	0.8361	L		
Education	4.9%	3	4	3	4	4	18.000	H	0.8852	M		
Fintech	4.9%	3	3	4	4	4	18.000	H	0.8852	M		
Green Building	3.3%	1	1	4	3	4	13.000	M	0.4262	L		
Human Resources Tech	3.3%	3	4	3	3	4	17.000	H	0.5574	L		
Productivity	3.3%	1	0	4	3	3	11.000	L	0.3607	L		
Biotechnology	1.6%	3	1	2	3	3	12.000	L	0.1967	L		
Circular Economy	1.6%	3	4	4	4	3	18.000	H	0.2951	L		
Deep Tech	1.6%	4	1		4	3	12.000	L	0.1967	L		
Ecommerce	1.6%	4	3	4	4	4	19.000	H	0.3115	L		
Marketplace/Dropshipping	1.6%	3	1	3	2	2	11.000	L	0.1803	L		
New Materials	1.6%	4	3	1	2	1	11.000	L	0.1803	L		
Smart Factory	1.6%	3	0	2	2	2	9.000	L	0.1475	L		
Smart Home	1.6%	4	1	4	4	4	17.000	H	0.2787	L		
Smart Working	1.6%	3	1	3	2	2	11.000	L	0.1803	L		
Travel and Consulting	1.6%	4	4	4	4	3	19.000	H	0.3115	L		
Urban Farming	1.6%	4	1	3	2	2	12.000	L	0.2131	L		
Social Impact	9.8%	4	4	4	4	4	20.000	H	2	H		

Source: Authors.

APPENDIX 25.3:   DETAILED SCORING FRAMEWORKS

TABLE 25.11   Scoring Details.

Question		Answer	Score
B.2	"The impact is the positive change that the organization wants to intentionally generate for the territories and communities on which it acts in a long period of time in line with business objectives. We define impact that change that turns out to be measurable, additional and, above all, intentional." Considering the definition of impact you can say that . . .	Your organization directly and intentionally generates impact because it is an integral part of its strategic mission	4
		Your organization indirectly generates impact through its product/service	3
		Your organization indirectly generates impact because it operates in a business that is already oriented towards impact (e.g. green, water sanitation, social inclusion, smart mobility, etc)	2
		Your organization is not geared to generating impact, either directly or indirectly	1
C.1	Considering the activities your organization develops, you	. . . don't consider impact in the management or evaluation of your performance	0
		. . . are starting to consider impact measurement, through your first qualitative evaluative assessments	1
		. . . are starting to consider impact measurement, through your first quantitative evaluative assessments	2
		. . . integrate impact in your strategic planning	3
		. . . consider impact when defining of your strategy and periodically monitor impact objectives previously set	4

(continued)

TABLE 25.11   (*continued*)

Question		Answer	Score
D.4	I consider that my organization can be a recipient of impact investments, i.e. financial resources directed explicitly to organizations and businesses capable of generating financial returns and, at the same time, social and/or environmental returns.	Completely disagree	0
		Agree to a minor extent	1
		Agree	2
		Agree to a great extent	3
		Totally agree	4
D.7	I would consider in my business model introducing evaluations of the impact attained by my organization, if requested by an investor.	Completely disagree	0
		Agree to a minor extent	1
		Agree	2
		Agree to a great extent	3
		Totally agree	4
D.8	I would be willing to allocate human and financial resources to impact management (the management of actions and risks to achieve the pre-established social/environmental impact objectives), if requested by a potential impact investor.	Completely disagree	0
		Agree to a minor extent	1
		Agree	2
		Agree to a great extent	3
		Totally agree	4

Source: Authors.

CHAPTER 26

The Importance of Scale in Social Enterprises: The Indian Case

Vikram Raman, CA, MBA

Abstract

When social enterprises achieve scale, it helps build a stronger case for the larger Impact Investing ecosystem. But many social enterprises struggle to scale. Most are micro, small, and medium enterprises and when compared to larger firms, social enterprises face a different set of challenges when it comes to scaling up their businesses, particularly in the context of developing economies. The primary goal of this chapter is to demonstrate the importance of *scale* from the viewpoint of social enterprises, which are at the core of the Impact Investing movement. While it is difficult for all types of businesses to scale, social enterprises have earned a reputation for being less aggressive in pursuing profits due to their more inclusive approach. It is imperative, however, that they diligently pursue scale. But on the path toward enhancing growth and achieving higher levels of operation and scale, social enterprises need to get the fundamentals right. Just as important as attaining growth is the vital aspect of how that growth is achieved and managed. As social enterprises become larger and more profitable, they can easily deviate from their original inclusive business models and impact objectives. This chapter presents a lively account of factors that can support scale-building for early-stage social enterprises in an emerging market context, with a focus on India, combined with a checklist to address key scale-related challenges. This chapter is based on a desk review, along with in-depth interviews and discussions with founders and senior management representatives of selected social enterprises and illustrated with examples from the author's experience with Indian social enterprises that have achieved significant scale.

Keywords

Social Enterprise; Scale; Scaling Up; Scalability; Scale Factors; Sustainability; Impact Investing; Social Impact; Value; Capital; Ideal Investor; India

INTRODUCTION

A significant number of social enterprises struggle to scale. To enable a social enterprise to enhance its growth and reach higher levels of operation, it is necessary to get the fundamentals right. While the general perception is that social enterprises are not as aggressive in pursuing profits as traditional businesses due to their more inclusive approach, it is imperative that they diligently pursue scale. There are two main reasons for this. Firstly, the social or environmental impact sought by a social enterprise is typically a function of its scale. Most of these inclusive businesses seek to impact millions of underserved people or serve several low-income communities.[1] Secondly, financial sustainability is necessary to ensure that a social enterprise continues to function and grow. Without sustainable sources of revenues and a positive EBITDA (earnings before interest, tax, depreciation, and amortization), a company will struggle to remain operational in the long run. It is very difficult to run a business sustainably without reaching a certain level of scale that is consistently above the break-even threshold.

---

[1]"Social enterprise as poverty reducing strategy for women" by Fotheringham and Saunders (2014) examines the viability of the social enterprise as a poverty reducing strategy for women. It states that women may be the primary gender employed in the social service sector, and that close to 70% of the 1 billion people facing extreme poverty in 2015 were women.

Social enterprises are widely considered to include a broad spectrum of types (Dees 1996), which straddle and integrate boundaries between for-profit and nonprofit sectors (Emerson and Twersky 1996). This chapter focuses primarily on social enterprises that are for-profit entities, and which pursue both financial returns and fiscal sustainability, along with specific impact objectives that could be social and/or environmental. According to the *European Journal of Sustainable Development*, "Scalability refers to the ability of a business to grow without losing customers, diminishing quality or changing the core value proposition of the organization" (Mathaisel 2015, p. 1). This applies to all business enterprises in general, commercial as well as social.

There are a host of internal and external factors that shape and influence the extent to which early-stage social enterprises can scale. A social enterprise needs to be fully cognizant of its internal dynamics, as well as that of its market, in order to build effective and resilient pathways to scale. Social enterprises also need to attract external capital to be able to scale. There are different types of capital available, ranging from debt and plain-vanilla equity to mezzanine and innovative investment structures. Not all of these forms of capital are readily available to social enterprises, however, and the ideal form of capital is based upon various elements including the current stage of business, the end-use of financing, future growth prospects, and the risk perception of the business. Each type of capital brings associated benefits and constraints, which uniquely and critically shape the scalability of a social enterprise. This chapter illustrates various classes of equity investors linked to the growth phase and examines which actors can serve as ideal investors for social enterprises.

Equally important to achieving scale is how such scale is achieved. As a social enterprise becomes larger and profitable, it can deviate from its original inclusive business model and its impact objectives. Its business practices might change to become much more commercial than originally envisaged. While it is natural for businesses including social enterprises to adapt and evolve as they grow, it is vital to continue to pursue impact objectives and seek to achieve higher levels of impact at scale. Scale needs to be achieved responsibly, without compromising core values and ethics, or else it can lead to serious ramifications that threaten the very continuity of the social enterprise.

Achieving scale for social enterprises helps build a stronger case for the larger Impact Investing ecosystem. The primary goal of this chapter is to emphasize the importance of scale from the viewpoint of social enterprises, which are at the core of the Impact Investing movement. This chapter presents an overview of factors that drive scale, typically for early-stage social enterprises in an emerging market context, with a focus on India. It provides specific examples of Indian social enterprises that have achieved significant scale and delves into their main drivers of growth. These case studies describe social enterprises' growth stories and highlight inflection points that helped them scale faster, along with salient lessons learned along the way. They illustrate that it is indeed possible for social enterprises to achieve substantial levels of impact and financial sustainability, as long as sustainable growth strategies are executed effectively. This chapter also provides a reference checklist for social enterprises that can assist them in identifying and addressing key scale-related challenges. It is essential that social enterprises periodically review their operations to assess performance in light of recognized challenges, as well identify red flags and develop proactive and preventative alert systems.

This chapter was compiled on the basis of an extensive desk review, as well as examples cited from the author's experience in Impact Investing. In-depth interviews and discussions were held with founders and senior management representatives of select social enterprises, which are featured in the two case studies (see Appendix 26.1 for the list of interviewees).

This chapter is divided into seven remaining sections. The next section focuses on requirements for achieving scale. The following section concerns partnering with the ideal investor. The next section deals with scaling responsibly and highlights a social enterprise in India that faced serious issues linked to the way it pursued growth. This is followed by a section that highlights case studies of Indian social enterprises that achieved significant scale and takes into account underlying causes. The next section describes metrics tracked by social enterprises and impact investors and shows how scale can be important to impact investors. The section following this presents a checklist to assess scaling performance. Pursuant to these sections, the last section offers concluding remarks.

SOCIAL ENTERPRISES AND REQUIREMENTS FOR ACHIEVING SCALE

According to the Organization for Economic Cooperation and Development (OECD), "small 'green entrepreneurs,' driven by financial profit combined with environmental consciousness, can drive a bottom-up transformation and job creation, by developing new business models and pioneering green business practices that influence mass markets and eventually are adopted by the wider business community" (OECD 2013, p. 37). This section describes the characteristics and contributions of social enterprises as well as a host of internal and external factors that influence the ability of social enterprises to scale.

SOCIAL ENTERPRISES: CHARACTERISTICS AND SOCIAL AND ECONOMIC CONTRIBUTIONS

According to the Social Enterprise Alliance,[2] a social enterprise "is an organization specifically set up to address a social or environmental problem through a market-driven approach."[3] Dart, Clow, and Armstrong (2010) categorize social enterprises as "organizations which deliberately cultivate both social and economic value." Another possible frame for defining social enterprises offered by the same authors is that they are organizations "which have social and economic value creation as central to their organizational strategy" (Dart, Clow, and Armstrong 2010). Similarly, a *Forbes* article entitled "2019's Top 5 Most Innovative and Impactful Social Enterprises" (Bullock 2019) stated that "social enterprises practice a hybrid model that uses business solutions to make a positive impact in the world...they are still for-profit companies, but they make money by solving social problems." What these definitions have in common is that at the root of social entrepreneurship initiatives is the goal of fulfilling unmet social needs—inverting or transcending traditional norms of profit maximization and wealth creation (Arena, Azzone, and Bengo 2014, p. 3).

Because of the diversity of social enterprises, it can be challenging to empirically map their business demographics, characteristics, and activities (Dart, Clow, and Armstrong 2010). Most social enterprises generally belong to the category of micro, small, and medium enterprises (MSME). India has over 36 million MSMEs, which contributed to 37.5% of India's gross domestic product (GDP) as of 2016 (British Council 2016, p. 4). Compared to larger firms, they face a different set of challenges when it comes to scaling up their businesses. Key challenges include lack of access to finance, inadequate human resources, and insufficient working capital, among others. In addition to financial capacity, several hurdles commonly experienced by startups are also relevant to social enterprises, including defining and validating the

---

[2]Social Enterprise Alliance is the national membership organization and key catalyst for the rapidly growing social enterprise movement in the United States.

[3]Available at https://socialenterprise.us/about/social-enterprise/.

business concept, maintaining customer focus, and building a management team (Picken 2017). Moreover, there is a large productivity gap between large firms and SMEs, particularly in many emerging and developing economies (OECD 2018, p. 7). Hence, "scale" in the context of social enterprises is significantly influenced by size, age, stage of business, and region of operations.

A study by the British Council (2016, p. 3) highlighted access to capital as the key barrier to social enterprises, as 57% of social enterprises face this constraint. Other significant barriers identified were lack of grant funding, maintaining cash flows, lack of awareness among banks and support organizations, and shortage of managerial skills and recruiting staff. Many social enterprises are at an early stage of their business. As of 2012, it was estimated that more than 89% of Indian social enterprises were less than 10 years old and 88% of them were in pilot, startup, or early-growth stage (Beggin and O'Neill 2015, p. 4).

In several countries, the economic share of the social and solidarity sector in terms of GDP and employment has risen steadily in recent years, including after the 2009 crisis. In the United Kingdom (UK), 41% of social enterprises created jobs compared to 22% of SMEs in 2015 (Villeneuve-Smith and Temple 2015, p. 5). In France, the social economy represented 10% of the GDP in 2014, and in Belgium, employment in social enterprises increased by 12% during the period 2008 to 2014 and accounted for 17% of total private employment in 2015 (European Union 2016). In India, it is estimated that around 2 million social enterprises existed in 2016, two-thirds of which had the objective of creating direct employment, including in disadvantaged groups. On average, among the 258 social enterprises surveyed in the British Council's study, social enterprises employed 19 people, 17 of which were full-time[4] (British Council 2016, p. 2).

The main characteristics and economic and social contributions of social enterprises are described in Table 26.1.

FACTORS THAT INFLUENCE A SOCIAL ENTERPRISES ABILITY TO SCALE

Most social enterprises struggle to scale. In order for a social enterprise to enhance its growth and reach higher levels of operation, it is necessary for it to get the fundamentals right. Their growth prospects and path forward are shaped and influenced by several factors, both internal and external.

---

[4]Survey data was collected between September 2015 and January 2016.

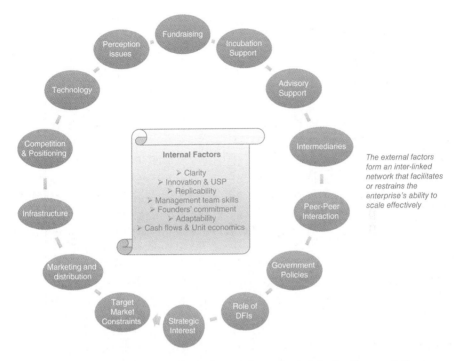

FIGURE 26.1   Internal and External Factors That Influence Scale. *Source*: Author.

Figure 26.1 summarizes these crucial factors into one diagram, with the core internal factors being supported by a linked external ecosystem. Each of these are described below in further detail.

INTERNAL FACTORS THAT INFLUENCE SCALING

Below, the range of internal factors that affect scaling are described in detail.

Business Model Clarity

A company's depth of understanding about the unique needs and priorities of its end customers is directly linked to the strength of its business model. Strong business models cannot be built without adequately studying "target customers" needs and current gaps. Furthermore, a business model that clearly outlines a specific focus area is easier to relate to, compared to one that tries to address too many aspects. It is imperative to build a strong

TABLE 26.1 Social Enterprises Characteristics and Economic and Social Contribution.

Characteristics	Economic and Social Contributions
Attracting critical funding toward sectors with significant gaps	The growth of social enterprises has encouraged further flow of capital, primarily into emerging economies, to help address specific gaps. The United Nations (UN) Sustainable Development Goals (SDGs) outlines a list of 17 goals to be achieved by 2030. Several funds, financial institutions, and corporates globally are aligning themselves to address the SDGs and invest in social enterprises. Impact Investing, a concept formally coined only in 2007, has grown to over USD $500 billion as per a report by the Global Impact Investing Network (GIIN) (Mudaliar and Dithrich 2019, p. 6). As per an article in Bloomberg, sustainable investing—where investment strategy is aligned toward combining environmental, social, and governance (ESG) factors while not compromising financial returns—today covers USD $30 trillion in assets (Chasan 2019a).
Creation of employment opportunities	Globally, MSMEs play a critical role in job creation. In India alone, as per a 2019 job survey of the MSME sector by the Confederation of Indian Industries (CII), MSMEs created 13.5 to 14.9 million jobs per annum (Confederation of Indian Industry 2019, p. 9) between 2015 and 2018.
Making businesses more inclusive	One of the key objectives of a social enterprise is to make its business inclusive by providing access to quality goods and services to underserved segments. A significant portion of their target markets includes people in lower and lower-middle income segments. People in this income strata seek affordable yet quality products and services, representing a USD $5 trillion consumer market (International Finance Corporation 2014, p. 2).
Promotion of women-owned businesses	Gender equality and female empowerment are important impact investment themes today. Several social enterprises enable women to be economically independent. For instance, microfinance institutions (MFIs) serve borrowers that are typically women from low-income families. Empowering these women with better livelihood opportunities uplifts entire families out of poverty.

(continued)

TABLE 26.1 (continued)

Characteristics	Economic and Social Contributions
Supply chain strengthening to underserved segments	By providing access to goods and services to underserved segments, social enterprises connect and benefit several stakeholders along the supply chain.[5]
Instilling a sense of pride in local communities	Social enterprises provide an avenue for showcasing products and talent of local communities and create a sense of ownership and pride.[6]
Measurement of Impact	Social enterprises seek to objectively measure and quantify the social or environmental impact and outcomes of their activities. This includes capturing the number of people served, sector-specific metrics (e.g. number of women gaining access to financial inclusion, number of additional light-hours for school-aged children), and general metrics (e.g. increased savings, livelihood impact for low-income end users).

Source: Author.

[5]For example, smallholder farmers lack bulk storage facilities for their fruits and vegetables and try to sell their produce immediately after harvest at the prevailing market prices, generally influenced by middlemen. Any produce that cannot be brought to the market in time is left to perish. As per the Food and Agriculture Organization of the United Nations, it is estimated that 45% of fruits and vegetables perish every year due to lack of appropriate storage and cold chain. If cold chain facilities are in place at scale and accessible to smallholder farmers, they can store their produce longer until they obtain the right price or have their goods transported to the market where demand is higher (and be willing to pay a premium).

[6]Several artisanal product companies, such as Industree (Mother Earth) or Jaipur Living, have supported thousands of local rural artisans in sustaining their livelihoods by providing market linkages to their products.

foundation to serve as the basis for further expansion; social enterprises need solid business model fundamentals backed by market research and clear assumptions.[7]

Replicability

It is important to establish upfront whether a business is scalable. There are business models that inherently operate on and maintain a relatively low-level scale, such as enterprises that meet specific local community needs (e.g. improving educational outcomes of primary school children in a particular rural district). For all others, their products or services offered and their general business models must have the ability and replicability across regions to be scalable at a larger level, which means they must address needs that are present across a larger region or set of demographics. Replication can occur by opening new branches or social franchising, as articulated by the OECD (OECD 2016, p. 7). A social enterprise can build a local presence in a new area and customize its offerings to local needs. It can also adopt the strategy of expansion through franchises, promoting local ownership while ensuring adherence to established quality systems and processes, and by maintaining strong oversight. Either strategy could enable a social enterprise to rapidly replicate a successful business model in other regions.

It is crucial to avoid undue complexity and embrace simplicity, focus, and clarity. With respect to Company A cited as an example, each unit of the hospital is easily replicable to other locations as each hospital has low capital expenditure compared to conventional hospitals; they have only 20–25 beds each and are supported by consistent processes. These factors

---

[7]This can be exemplified through two social enterprises from India, anonymized as Company A and Company B. Company A had a clear focus on providing high-quality yet affordable prenatal, maternal, and postnatal medical services for lower-income strata. They built their hospital model with low capital expenditure along with a strong emphasis on best practices and processes. Company B had a focus on making rural India more inclusive by offering a range of products and services. Company B continued to periodically change their offerings, and eventually the business model became quite fuzzy. None of the offerings of Company B achieved any meaningful scale and reach. Company A has been successful in scaling its business by expanding its hospitals 15 times in the last 12 years and has been profitable for many years as a result of the niche focus of its business model, whereas Company B's revenues have plateaued and it struggled to achieve sustainability. Other factors also contributed to Company A's relative and absolute success; however, if the very foundation (i.e. business model) remains unclear, it is highly unlikely that the social enterprise will achieve meaningful scale.

enabled them to expand their hospitals by a factor of 15. Further, in the case of Ziqitza Healthcare Limited (ZHL), a social enterprise that provides access to emergency medical services to millions of people in India, operations have grown from 10 ambulances at inception to over 3,000 ambulances in about 15 years. Addressing a strong unmet need across India, they have ensured that their services are replicable through uniformity of service, strong operations know-how, well-trained paramedics, and best-in-class call center technology. These factors held constant as they expanded from one state to another in India, before emerging as a Pan-India player that now has global ambitions. The ZHL case is further elaborated in Case Study 26.1.

Innovation and Differentiation

A critical question to ask is "What is the unique selling proposition (USP) of the business?" In attempting to answer this, a social enterprise must identify, emphasize, and build on its unique differentiating factors. These will help it stand out in a crowd of enterprises. Businesses that embrace innovation and have a clear USP are often more successful at scaling, at attracting more capital, and at better addressing their target market's needs.

In the case of KisanKraft Limited (Case Study 26.2), a social enterprise in India that provides farm mechanization for small and marginal farmers, they sought to differentiate their products from smaller and regional players in a crowded market. They worked closely with their bulk manufacturers in China to ensure that their products were designed to keep in mind their usability in the Indian market, with very close attention given to every single component. They also tied up with several dealers across India and set up dedicated service teams that served to bolster confidence in KisanKraft's products, which created an excellent support network to help increase sales. Further, the company also created separate product lines, distinguishing between premium and low-cost offerings. These helped establish KisanKraft as a strong, well-differentiated brand and helped scale revenues more than 270 times in just 12 years, reaching over 2.5 million farmers.

Milk Mantra[8] is a social enterprise based in the state of Odisha in India that collects milk from over 43,000 low-income dairy farmers, processes it, and sells it under the brand "Milky Moo." They have achieved significant scale for a relatively young dairy company that was set up only in 2009, in a

---

[8]From the outset, this company had the objective of serving local dairy farmers and providing them fair, transparent pricing for their milk. They have implemented this at scale using their Ethical Milk Sourcing program benefiting 43,000 farmers.

market dominated by established public sector enterprises. The key driver for Milk Mantra has been innovation—as per a Business Standard article (Behera 2014), they focused on their packaging using innovative technology to increase the shelf life of their milk compared to other brands. They also launched multiple value-added products to diversify their product portfolio, including a first of its kind curcumin-fortified milkshake. Further, they developed an ethical milk sourcing program that ensures transparent payment to dairy farmers based on scientifically measured fat-content and other parameters for their milk. These initiatives have helped position Milky Moo as a premium brand and helped them expand operations across several states in eastern India, supported by a host of investors (Roy 2017), including impact investors and traditional private equity firms.

Strong Management Team with Compelling Execution Capability

It is crucial to have the right leadership and internal capabilities to execute a business plan, even if the plan is impeccably designed and theoretically sound. A management team with complementary skill sets is an extremely valuable asset. It is necessary to establish depth in management capacities for all critical functions and strengthen hiring for areas that are indispensable to growth. In Case Study 26.1, the management team at ZHL had strong complementary skill sets across marketing, finance, operations, technology, legal, and public affairs—which helped the company address various challenges and opportunities along its growth journey. Financial planning and reporting, market analysis and social marketing, employment leadership and management, and creating and sharing a blueprint for measuring social impact are considered to be vital skills essential for social entrepreneurs to successfully scale up their businesses (OECD 2016, p. 13).

Dedicated Founders Without Dilution of Focus

Founders must be wholly dedicated to impact. A social enterprise needs the complete backing of its founders, particularly as several early-stage companies tend to have lean management teams and are dependent on the founders' commitment and vision. One consideration is whether a key founder is managing multiple ventures simultaneously, which can negatively affect management and become a severe impediment to scale. Additionally, founders should be open to ceding certain levels of control and delegating important tasks as they seek to build and expand their teams. Delegation serves talent attraction and retention,[9] which is vital to an organization's success and scale. For example, an impact investment firm had to write off its investment in an Indian social enterprise that managed a wholesale pharmacy distribution business because the founders did not stay true to their commitment of backing an expansion into lower-income segments, which was the main criteria for the impact investment firm. The founders of this social enterprise also had divergent interests in real estate and shifted their focus away from running the social enterprise effectively. Consequently, the social enterprise had to be shut down and several investors incurred losses.

Adaptability of the Business to Changing Market Conditions

Market dynamics are constantly changing, and it is vital to be nimble. It is necessary to periodically revisit key assumptions in a business model and ask if they are still relevant. Have customers' preferences altered due to unforeseen factors? Is there a significant change in the cost of inputs or the availability of labor? What is the impact of competition? Is there a new avenue for growth, such as a government tender that could present a public-private partnership (PPP) contract opportunity that would fuel growth and reach? These are some of the questions that the management needs to consistently apply to their business model and approach. Entrepreneurs need to avoid having a static or tunnel-vision view, and instead consider multiple scenarios. The success of ZHL (Case Study 26.1) would not have been possible if the company had not been ready to seize the growth opportunity presented by PPP tenders floated by several state governments in India. Through expanding into this new channel, ZHL demonstrated that it was prepared to adapt its business by transitioning from a capital-intensive business model to an asset-light one.

Cash Flows and Unit Economics

For a business model to be sustainable in the longer run, it must create sources of revenue that generate sufficient—and ideally substantial—operating cash flows. It is necessary to build in reasonable and realistic

---

[9]See Chapter 5, "Leadership by Results for Impact Investors and Investees," by Rajen Makhijani.

growth and margin assumptions; a successful business should be able to generate positive margins as it scales and not rely exclusively on financing cash flows (external infusion of funds) for growth. Also, there need to be adequate controls in place to ensure that there are no cash leakages. Further, it is vital to constantly consider unit economics that are central to the business.[10] For instance, when ZHL (Case Study 26.1) bid for several state government tenders for running statewide ambulances, they had to submit financial bids based on an estimated operating fee per ambulance call served.[11] ZHL had to make the operating fee low enough to be competitive but high enough to ensure that if they won the tender, they would not end up losing money by running the ambulances; they had to have a positive margin per ambulance dispatch to cover all running costs and manage operations sustainably. ZHL was successful in setting a fee that was both profitable but also competitive as compared to several other bids submitted to each tender.

EXTERNAL FACTORS THAT INFLUENCE SCALING

Appropriate Funding Options

The one external factor that *severely* restricts the ability to scale, even if most other key parameters are in place, is access to funding, and more specifically, the lack of it. Securing access to capital is an especially momentous barrier for early-stage social enterprises. Due to the perception of early-stage enterprises as high-risk investments, they face inherent challenges to attracting sufficient funds and the appropriate type of capital, compared to their more mature counterparts. According to the International Finance Corporation (IFC, World Bank Group), it is estimated that the unmet credit needs of formal MSMEs in developing countries is USD $5.2 trillion (IFC 2017, p. 27). If this figure is taken along with the needs of informal MSMEs, it rises to a staggering USD $8.1 trillion.

Debt is generally more readily available to mature enterprises with stronger balance sheets. This is changing, however, with the advent of

---

[10]Unit economics refers to revenues, costs, and margins of a business model calculated on a per-unit basis (the unit could be one unit of product or service offered, or could be calculated per office, region, or vertical). Unit economics reveal the profitability of each unit (i.e. if there is a positive contribution margin on each unit).

[11]This is the fee that the state government would pay the successful service provider under that tender per ambulance trip made and is the primary source of revenues for the service provider under the tender.

various Fintech companies that are primarily focused on lending to MSMEs. In India, entities such as Capital Float, Neogrowth, Kinara Capital, and Mintifi are among those offering a range of credit products suited to smaller enterprises. Drip Capital specializes in offering advances against trade receivables of exporters. All of these are using advanced technology and applying AI-based algorithms, in addition to leveraging the increasing availability of smartphones.

To secure the capital they need, social entrepreneurs need to be clear about both how much they need, which depends on the stage of business, and also what type of capital is required. Equity capital is the costliest over time and involves dilution. Debt is generally cheaper though riskier. Most banks tend to turn down debt requests because of a lack of hard assets or insufficient collateral, or simply because a business does not have a long enough track record. Hence, before reaching out to external sources of funding, entrepreneurs should consider investing their personal money into the business, which doubly serves as a show of commitment. Only after personal funds are expended should a founding team seek capital from other external sources. According to an article in Yourstory.com,[12] access to capital is the number one challenge faced by social enterprises (Dutta 2019). According to the already cited report on the State of Social Enterprises in India by the British Council, 57% of social enterprises opine that access to external capital—debt and equity—is a major barrier to growth. When looking for an equity investor, suitability must be assessed (refer to the section "Partnering with the Ideal Investor for Financing" for more details). On a positive note, Impact Investing has been attracting more capital, particularly in India. According to a report by McKinsey & Company, Impact Investing in India has grown at 14% per annum from 2010 to 2016 and attracted USD $1.1 billion in funding in 2016 alone (Pandit and Tamhane 2017, p. 13).

Need for Incubation Support

Most social enterprises are early stage in nature and lack the resources and direction to reach a robust level of operations. In this stage, an incubator's support becomes critical and could well be the difference between achieving initial scale or shutting down. As per a World Economic Forum (WEF) article based on the findings of the Failure Institute, about 83% of social enterprises in Mexico lasted less than 3 years and only 5.2% lasted more than 10 years (Gasca 2017). This reflects the state of social enterprises across the globe—if

---

[12]Yourstory.com is a media platform that showcases stories of entrepreneurs.

they do not get the right level of support upfront, their chances of survival, let alone their ability to achieve scale, diminish significantly. In India, incubators and seed-stage investors such as Villgro (along with the Menterra Fund), Ankur Capital, and Unitus Ventures offer much-needed support to social enterprises at the critical seed stage. These investors do not just provide funding but work closely with the entrepreneurs to help shape the business model, bring advisors on board, provide access to shared resources, as well as help raise further capital to grow. They work like an extended management or founder team and are deeply invested as the growth and viability of their social enterprises validate their own purpose and success. For instance, Villgro, an incubator based in Chennai, India, has invested INR 573 million in several ventures that have gone on to raise INR 1.8 billion in additional capital and have impacted 19 million lives as a consequence of the incubation support they provided (Villgro Innovations Foundation 2018 p. 24).

Peer-to-Peer Interaction

Interaction with other social entrepreneurs is a great avenue to share best practices, understand ground realities across sectors and markets, hear about success stories, and gain learnings from mistakes. Forums such as Sankalp (organized by the Aavishkaar Intellecap Group) and Unconvention (pioneered by Villgro) in India present excellent platforms to facilitate such interaction. Furthermore, several impact investors make it a point to periodically bring together their portfolio companies for collective brainstorming sessions. For instance, Acumen held an India Chief Executive Officer (CEO) Summit in 2015 to bring together the top hierarchies from its India portfolio companies to jointly discuss operational challenges to achieving sustainable growth. Apart from bringing the portfolio CEOs under one roof, the event also helped provide vital insights from industry leaders of reputed companies such as Bain, GE India, and Infosys. Such initiatives offer a lot of value-add and serve to help social enterprises in their journey toward sustainability and greater scale.

Encouraging Government Policies and Initiatives

While several governments have provided tax breaks and support to technology startups, as well as large greenfield projects (setting up Special Economic Zones or SEZs), the social enterprise ecosystem has been largely ignored by governments. There are some positive signs, however. The Indian government has recently, as part of the 2019 Budget, announced its intent to set up a Social Stock Exchange to list social enterprises and facilitate greater access to capital. Going by the experience of the Social Stock Exchange in the United Kingdom (UK) and of Impact Investment Exchange Asia (IIX) in Singapore, this would not be an easy task. In an article in Quartz India, Professor Durreen Shahnaz, founder of IIX, cautions that while setting up a social stock exchange platform is a positive step, social enterprises need to become investment ready before listing. Besides, investors need to see strong deal flow to be attracted to such platforms, and there must be a board ecosystem that supports both social enterprises and investors (Shahnaz 2019). Another reform initiative of the government of India is to increase the availability of corporate social responsibility (CSR) funding through a CSR rule that mandates that corporates meeting certain turnover and profitability criteria must commit at least 2% of their net profits toward social causes. While this has had an impact on funding for nonprofit organizations, there are reports of misuse, and besides, the rule does not permit channeling these CSR commitments toward financing for-profit social enterprises or impact investment vehicles.

Target Market Constraints

Social enterprises typically seek to target low-income groups and the vast "bottom-of-the-pyramid" segment. According to the already cited report by the International Finance Corporation, the bottom of the economic pyramid represents a household income of USD $5 trillion globally (IFC 2014, p. 2). Furthermore, the informal or unorganized workforce constitutes a significant part, if not the majority, of several emerging economies. As per an article in Development and Cooperation[13] (D+C), it is estimated that the informal market in India employs about 90% of the employable labor force and constitutes close to 50% (Ghatak 2017) of India's gross national product (GNP). Any product or service targeted at the informal market needs to be priced attractively to be within their reach. This could exert a lot of margin pressure on social enterprises and on their ability to scale. Hence, it is important to understand these constraints beforehand, and anticipate how they impact growth prospects. If there is not much leeway to increase the selling price, running operations efficiently in a cost-effective manner is critical.

---

[13] An EU-based international development affairs website.

Marketing and Distribution

One of the main challenges social enterprises face is having low awareness in their target markets; enterprises' target customers do not know they exist. To address this, an enterprise needs to invest in a well-thought-out marketing strategy that resonates well with their target audience and utilizes cost-effective approaches. Ideally, the communication is in the local vernacular and would include roadshows, village fairs, door-to-door campaigns, and meetings in community centers to better explain the benefits of products or services.

Another aspect that needs to be carefully considered is the distribution channel—enterprises need to choose between direct sales and relying on partnerships with other regional players. Selecting the right distribution channel is a critical decision and needs to be evaluated based on internal strengths and weaknesses, as well as the merits of aligning with a potential partner. For instance, several manufacturers of solar lanterns use MFIs as distribution partners to sell their products in rural hinterlands where they do not have a direct presence, but where MFI partners are established because of their existing loan portfolios.

Infrastructure

Closely intertwined with government policies and target market constraints is the factor of infrastructure development. Many target markets, especially when serviced at scale, are widely dispersed. Given that "bottom-of-the-pyramid" populations are often co-located in areas with poor connectivity, substandard roads and last-mile infrastructure often increase difficulties and compound the lack of access for social enterprises as well as the customers that need their services or products. That lack of infrastructure can present opportunities, however. Limited electricity access impairs the productivity of rural communities and entrepreneurs—forcing people to look for alternatives, such as affordable solar energy. Bangladesh, for instance, has witnessed favorable government policies backed by global development agencies, which has enabled the large-scale adoption of solar home systems (SHS). The country now has one of the largest installations of SHS in the world with more than 4 million units, providing electricity to 20 million people and several villages with better economic opportunities (Hutt 2020). Cold-chain infrastructure is another critical necessity that enables companies to preserve and sell fruits and vegetables with minimal waste.

Today, it is estimated that one-third of food produced globally is lost or wasted (Food and Agriculture Organization 2019). Good warehouse infrastructure and efficient logistics are essential to prevent food loss in transit. Social enterprises such as Lawrencedale Agro Processing India (LEAF) maintain a fleet of refrigerated transfer trucks and regional distribution centers with state-of-the-art cold rooms to offer integrated cold chain support to farmers across southern India.

Advisory Support

Social enterprises benefit immensely from having the right advisory support with skill sets that are complementary to the management. Advisors help fine-tune the business, ask relevant questions, and help provide overall guidance on the path toward scale. In addition to providing capital, several investors now provide relationships to a pool of advisors and consultants that can play a constructive role. For instance, the Grassroots Business Fund (GBF), a USD $50 million mezzanine impact fund, had their portfolio CFO to spend a considerable amount of time helping GBF portfolio companies in India set up better financial controls, cash management, and budgeting. Initiatives such as AlphaSights leverage digital connectivity to provide enterprises with access to consultants and experts from a vetted pool across regions with a range of expertise at affordable rates.

Intermediaries

Intermediaries like investment banks, consultants, and impact ecosystem builders provide much needed support to social enterprises. For example, Unitus Capital, a boutique investment bank that helps raise capital for social enterprises in Asia, has raised well over USD $1 billion (Unitus Capital 2017) for a range of social enterprises since 2008, particularly in the sector of financial inclusion. Intermediaries such as Unitus Capital and Intellecap work closely with entrepreneurs and manage the entire capital raise process from building a pitch deck, to constructing a financial model, managing outreach to investors, leading negotiations, and closing the deal. Organizations such as Impact Investment Exchange Asia (IIX), based in Singapore, serve as impact ecosystem builders. IIX is focused on building the impact ecosystem in Southeast Asia and Bangladesh, providing multiple services including advisory, research, networking platforms, capital raising support, and seed funding.

There are now several intermediaries with platforms dedicated to advertising and sourcing the talent needs of social enterprises. For example, Shortlist Professionals based in Mumbai, India, leverages the use of technology to screen candidates using interactive online assessments to better match clients' needs. Entities such as Aasaanjobs and Babajob (since acquired by Quikr, a technology unicorn in India) focus on the vast blue-collar job segment in India, providing an end-to-end recruitment marketplace connecting several jobseekers.

Further, even though they are not intermediaries, entities such as the GIIN and the Global Steering Group for Impact Investment (GSG) serve as catalysts to help increase awareness of Impact Investing, strengthen advocacy, and spur investment activity in this space.

Level of Competition and Positioning

Increased competition among social enterprises within a particular social sector or geography is generally an indicator of a higher level of interest in that area, and augurs well for scale opportunities. It helps facilitate greater fund flows, attract more talent, serve more clients, and forces enterprise participants to achieve greater efficiency. A good example of such high competition in an impact ecosystem is that of the microfinance sector in India. What was a fledgling sector more than a decade ago has seen remarkable growth at a compound annual growth rate of 23% over the last 10 years (Economic Times Bureau 2019a), and at 42.9% between April and June of 2019 to reach a staggering INR 1.91 trillion (~USD $27 billion), distributed across 92.7 million loan accounts (Press Trust of India 2019). Today there are more than 200 active MFIs in India, several of which are operating profitably, and many have become publicly listed entities with successful initial public offerings (IPOs). While the growth in India has been remarkable, the MFI growth story is truly global—according to the Microfinance Barometer 2019, the global MFI credit portfolio stands at USD $124 billion at the end of 2018 and has grown annually at 11.5% from 2012 through 2018 (Convergences 2019, p. 2).

Technology

The advent of technology has been a true game-changer in several spheres of life, including how companies operate around the world. Technology facilitates faster knowledge transfer and helps social enterprises to strengthen their networks and coordinate better (OECD 2016, p. 16). Social enterprises that embrace relevant technology effectively can potentially achieve rapid scale. Mobile phone and smartphone penetration, in particular, has created several linkages that were not previously possible. MSMEs that are struggling to raise capital now have access to Fintech companies that can assess financial and operational information online and process loans within a matter of hours. India has the second largest mobile handset market in the world, with more than 800 million mobile phone users including over 500 million smartphone users (Economic Times Bureau 2019b). The penetration of smartphones increases the reach for many Fintech companies; so, it is not a surprise that India has the second largest number of Fintech startups globally, at over 2,000 (Mitter, 2019). Furthermore, the MSME digital lending industry in India is projected to grow to between USD $80 and 100 billion by 2023 (Omidyar Network and BCG 2016, p. 1).

Perception Issues

There is a general perception that investments in social enterprises do not generate attractive financial returns, or that there is an inherent conflict between achieving social and environmental impacts and securing financial returns. As the Impact Investing field is still nascent, this is something that a social entrepreneur is very likely to face when interacting with the public at large, or more specifically with an investor audience. Social entrepreneurs need to be able to convince investors that their businesses can achieve attractive returns with scale. Financial returns and impact go hand in hand—as a business grows, it becomes more sustainable and impacts more clients and stakeholders.

Increased awareness of the UN SDGs among the investor community could combat this perception. A recent UBS white paper (UBS 2019) highlights key challenges investors face regarding alignment with the SDGs and suggests certain measures to be adopted. According to the report, key challenges—and potential solutions—relate to: (i) low public awareness of the SDGs, calling for measures to increase awareness; (ii) confusion regarding the terms "sustainability" or "sustainable investing," establishing the need to advocate for standardization of various terms used; and (iii) inconsistent application of sustainability factors hampering the ability of investors to contribute more, in this case recommending alignment of investment solutions with investors' specific sustainability interests.

On a positive note, it is encouraging that customers are now clearly demanding products that are sourced from companies with high performance across environmental, social, and governance (ESG) factors. In a

2014 study (Nielsen 2014, p. 2), which surveyed 30,000 respondents across 60 countries, the consumer research firm Nielsen found that 55% of participants are willing to pay extra for products and services from companies that are committed to positive social and environmental impact. It also found that 67% of respondents would prefer to work for a socially responsible company. Additionally, other studies indicate that Millennials are more committed to backing social and sustainable investments than other strata of the population—52% of Millennial investors see the social responsibility of their investments as important selection criteria compared to 30% of World War II–era investors (Spectrem Group 2018). As Millennials come to possess more wealth, there will be greater impetus for sustainable investing and social enterprises.

Role of Development Financial Institutions

Development financial institutions (DFIs), which can be multilateral as well as bilateral institutions, have been consistently investing in and committing increasing amounts of capital to impact investment funds globally. According to a report by GIIN and Dalberg, DFIs have committed over USD $7.5 billion (GIIN and Dalberg 2015, p. 12) to Impact Investing in India alone, directly or indirectly through other funds. DFIs are also looking at innovative ways to increase their direct investment footprint in Impact Investing. For instance, CDC (originally called the Colonial Development Corporation, the world's first DFI), the UK government–backed DFI, has set up Catalyst Strategies (CDC Group 2019a) through which it seeks to invest in nascent and frontier markets as well as new inclusive trial models. As part of these strategies, the British government established a GBP £40 million Impact Acceleration Facility to facilitate CDC's existing commercial investees to collaborate with social enterprises and help create synergies and unlock the social enterprises' potential. Further, the CDC, along with the Dutch Good Growth Fund, has been instrumental in setting up Afghanistan's first private equity fund.

Apart from indirectly investing in social enterprises through their investment commitments to impact investment funds, DFIs are also a vital source of direct capital to social enterprises that are relatively mature. Several DFIs have invested directly in social enterprises across impact sectors, such as in financial inclusion (particularly MFIs) in India as well as in off-grid ventures globally. For instance, the International Finance Corporation (IFC) invested over USD $150 million (IFC 2015) in equity and debt in Bandhan, an MFI in India. IFC remained Bandhan's largest shareholder as the MFI scaled, completed its transformation into a bank, and had a very successful public listing in 2018. Several MFIs in India have achieved successful IPOs on the backing of investments from DFIs and large private equity investors. These investments and initiatives by DFIs help increase the flow of funding to social enterprises and help them achieve scale.

Growing Strategic Interest

The Impact Investing industry and social enterprises are witnessing increased interest from strategic players (i.e. well-established business conglomerates). One such sector that has received substantial strategic interest recently is the Access to Clean Energy space, addressing the needs of SDG7. According to a report released by Wood Mackenzie and Energy 4 Impact, corporate investments in off-grid energy access companies exceeded USD $500 million out of a total disclosed funding of USD $1.7 billion in 2018 (Wood Mackenzie Power and Renewables and Energy 4 Impact 2019, p. 9). This is about 20% higher than the previous year, which attracted USD $417 million in strategic investments and was over 27 times greater than commitments made in 2013. Most of this interest is fueled by European oil and gas majors (e.g. Shell) and energy utility companies (such as ENGIE), but the trend is becoming more global with investments from several Japanese majors as well. Some specific examples of strategic investment in off-grid solar ventures include a minority investment by Shell in d.light (d.light 2019); a USD $50 million investment round led by Mitsubishi Corporation in BBOXX (BBOXX 2019) and acquisitions of FENIX International and Simpa Networks by ENGIE. Such investments by strategic players help provide capital at scale to social enterprises and also facilitate much-needed exits for earlier-stage investors, as indicated in an articled featured in Greentech Media (Pyper and Merchant 2017).

Further, strategic interest is also growing for early-stage energy access ventures. SOLshare is a social enterprise based in Bangladesh that provides an innovative peer-to-peer electricity trading (with remote monitoring support) between homes that have SHS and those that do not. As per an article published in a Singapore-based entrepreneur-focused web portal called e27, SOLshare raised USD $1.6 million (Akhaya 2018) in a Series A funding round led by Innogy New Ventures (part of the German utility firm Innogy), EDP[14]

---

[14]Electricidade de Portugal (EDP), a Portuguese utility firm.

and IIX Growth Fund. Schneider Electric, a global leader in energy automation and efficiency, recently announced the launch of its third impact fund, a EUR €20.9 million fund (Schneider Electric 2019) with the backing of Norfund (Norwegian DFI), Electrifi (a facility funded by the European Union to promote energy access in emerging markets), and Amundi (Europe's largest asset manager). Schneider Electric's impact fund will invest in startups that work toward providing access to energy in Asia-Pacific. This is part of Schneider Electric's Access to Energy program that was launched in 2009 and that has already brought access to energy to over 24 million people in 10 years.

PARTNERING WITH THE IDEAL INVESTOR FOR FINANCING

This section touches on the importance of having the right kind of capital and investor to back a social enterprise, as capital and investor parameters can significantly influence the level of scale that is achieved by a social enterprise. For a social enterprise to scale, it is essential to attract external capital at some point of the business life cycle. It is crucial to identify the right type of investor, a decision that is based on the type of capital required, the stage of the business, the end-purpose budget items that require funding, and the period for which the capital is required.

Nonprofits can exist and scale on the backing of consistent grant infusions, but for-profit social enterprises need strong revenues and operating cash flows to profit, and financing (external) cash flows if profit is not materializing. Broadly speaking, there are four main types of external funding available (Figure 26.2).

While the purpose of this chapter is restricted to for-profit social enterprises, there are investors who are equipped with the ability to support a range of organizations, including for-profit social enterprises and nonprofit entities. For instance, Omidyar Network—a philanthropic investment network that has committed more than USD $1 billion globally to impact investments and grants—supports various types of for-profit social enterprises in addition to nonprofits (Omidyar Network 2016).

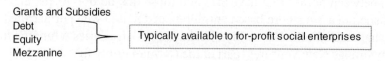

FIGURE 26.2 Types of Capital Available for Social Enterprises. *Source*: Author.

A social enterprise should bear the following points in mind when raising external capital. First, do not raise short-term debt to procure a long-term asset. Fundamentally, short-term debt should never be used to fund a long-term end-use (such as an asset with high gestation period) as it would result in a severe asset-liability mismatch and strain on liquidity. Second, avoid very high leverage. A debt-to-equity ratio that is higher than industry levels would serve as a warning sign that the social enterprise's financials are stressed. High leverage exerts constant pressure on cash reserves and can prove to be an impediment to further capital raising plans. Third, ensure that the type of capital sought and the external investor are best suited for the venture's mission, proposed end-use of funds, and expansion plans. The social enterprise must not raise more capital than is necessary, along with a little buffer.

Debt

Among the types of capital available to for-profit entities, debt is generally the cheapest. However, due to various reasons debt is not easy to raise. Firstly, banks typically extend debt only on the backing of hard assets, or by using founders' personal guarantees as collateral. Secondly, many lenders look for a profitable track record before they are willing to extend meaningful amounts of capital. Thirdly, government-mandated priority sector lending targets typically do not have a wide reach, and sanctioned debt often gets concentrated among a narrow group of borrowers.

The use of debt can well be viewed as a double-edged sword. Increasing reliance on debt for growth implies a constant pressure on cash reserves through debt servicing (interest and repayments). MSME lenders in India typically charge in the range of 16% to 24% per year to compensate for the increased risk due to lack of hard collateral. Such loans are explicitly not cheap, but they can address immediate liquidity needs (MAPE Advisory Group and MXV Consulting 2017, p. 33).

According to a report by Omidyar Network and BCG (2016, p. 1), about 40% of India's MSME lending is done through the informal sector, where interest rates are at least twice as high as the formal market. The social enterprise or MSME needs to plan appropriately to take on only as much debt as it can reasonably confidently service without default. Additionally, there needs to be clarity on whether the need for debt is long-term or for working capital (short-term). Enterprises should not take on debt, especially if interest rates are high, to pay for a long-term asset or end use.

Equity

Equity is the best suited long-term financing option. But it presents some disadvantages:

- *Dilution:* The founders need to give up a portion of their company's ownership, depending on the valuation and the amount of capital sought. Investor stakes range from small minority (5–10%) to significant minority (generally up to a third), to majority (over 50%).
- *Returns:* Equity return expectations are typically much higher than that of debt investors. It is generally in the vicinity of 25% and upwards in local currency terms. Hence, it is considered the costliest form of capital.
- *Long-term:* Equity investors usually look at a long-term investment horizon, typically in the range of 5–7 years. Hence, social enterprises should seek to have quality working relationships with their investors. It is imperative to choose the right long-term partner to ride with the company.
- *Covenants:* While debt investments also have covenants, the rights and covenants relating to equity investors are quite exhaustive. Some common covenants include affirmative voting rights, board rights, liquidation preference (in the case of preferred shares), and exit rights (such as drag along, tag along, and buy-back). Founders are also bound by lock-in and noncompete clauses.

Table 26.2 summarizes different classes of equity investors based on a social enterprise's stage of capital raise. This could serve as a useful reference to social enterprises as they seek various classes of equity investors and can provide a sense of what to expect depending on their stage or scale of business.

Having the right equity investor on board can make a world of a difference to a social enterprise's scale potential (Table 26.3). Investment amounts can vary significantly

Mezzanine

This type of capital combines elements of debt and equity. Covenants and rights associated with this investment structure are closely related to equity terms but will typically kick in only after the instrument has been fully converted into equity. The Grassroots Business Fund's (GBF) investments in

TABLE 26.2 Classes of Equity Investors Relevant to Social Enterprises.

Type	Who	Stage of Business/Scale	Investment[15] (USD $)	Investment Period	Primary Benefits
Incubation/Seed	Incubators and Accelerators[15]	Proof of concept (based on initial pilot results) up to Seed stage	$50 to $250 thousand	3–5 years, sometimes longer	• First external round • Support services (business plan, advisors, shared resources)
Angel/Pre-Series A	High-Net-Worth Individuals and Angel networks	Seed stage to Pre-Series A	$50 thousand to $1 million	3–5 years, sometimes longer	• Core team growth • Set up sales networks • Refining products
Series A	Institutional investors (including impact investment funds)	Initial growth phase	$1 to $5 million	5–7 years	• Optimize product or service • Achieve scale in a particular target market
Series B	Institutional investors (including DFIs and Impact Investment Funds)	Evidence of scale, need capital to build business toward high growth	$5 to $20 million	5 years	• Further expand market reach to new regions • Increased marketing to create greater awareness • Exit for Angels, early investors
Series C onwards	Commercial investors and DFIs	High growth phase, capital to expand business further	Upwards of $20 million	3–5 years	• Rapid expansion • Acquire smaller companies • Partial or full exit for Series A holders
Strategic	Corporates and Buy-out funds	Can be at any stage, more common to invest at a mature stage	Wide range, depending on stage of entry	Long term bet, aimed at a controlling stake or acquisition	• Sharing of best practices • Business synergies • Exit for financial investors
Pre-IPO	Commercial investors and DFIs	At a high scale, usually the last funding round before an IPO	$50 to $100 million, sometimes smaller	Short term (1–2 years before IPO)	• Provide enough cash reserves until public listing

Source: Author.

[15]While investment amounts can vary significantly, these are allocation ranges applicable to funding of social enterprises.

TABLE 26.3   Characteristics of an Ideal Equity Investor for a Social Enterprise.

Characteristic	Description
The right amount of capital and dilution	Too much capital upfront means more dilution and potentially leads to a high level of experimentation, and consuming cash much faster than anticipated; conversely, too little capital means a constant firefight with limited resources. Hence, it is important to find an investor who provides the right balance suited to the current stage of the social enterprise.
Alignment	Investors generally take a long-term view, so it is important to have the right partner for the long-term and ideally a partner who provides sufficient freedom to founders. In this context, many impact investment funds take a patient capital approach (i.e. by seeking to build their portfolio companies over a long time frame, bearing high risk, holding founders accountable to performance, and not exerting undue pressure for an untimely exit). Another basic parameter to consider is mission alignment—are the social enterprise's mission, founders' interests, and investors' expectations well-aligned?
Adds value beyond just capital	This is perhaps the most important criteria in investor selection. What are the benefits of partnering with one investor versus another? What benefits does a particular investor bring to the table beyond just opening their purse strings or providing an attractive valuation? How will partnering with this particular investor enable the business to scale better? Some key value-adds provided by ideal investors are: • **Access to advisory networks and mentorship:** Support that addresses the gaps of the social enterprise. For instance, Acumen has a strong advisory board that is representative of multiple regions and sectors. Their board actively participates in investment decisions and also lends its time and support to Acumen's portfolio companies (social enterprises) in their field of expertise or region. Advisors' and mentors' inputs on how to address gaps in critical functions such as human resources or finance can help social enterprises scale better. • **Strategic and board-level support:** Equity investors typically take active roles in the boards of their portfolio companies, as directors or observers (i.e. those who participate in board meetings but without any voting rights). They weigh in on the strategic direction of the social enterprise and provide inputs, concerns, and recommendations relating to performance and growth prospects.

- **Technical Assistance:** Many impact investors set aside a dedicated amount of their capital to support their social enterprise investees, in addition to the investment capital provided. Examples of such technical assistance are well-captured in a report by the GIIN (2017). Acumen provides capacity-building support across three themes: governance, operations, and finance, which address key operational areas including sales, talent, technology, and impact. ResponsAbility, a Swiss impact asset manager that has invested over USD $10 billion since its inception in 2003, set up its first dedicated Technical Assistance Facility (TAF) in 2009. Further, as evidenced by a Climate Policy Initiative (Tonkonogy and Hallmeyer 2018, p. 47), GBF raised a USD $11.5 million donor-funded TAF to provide business advisory services (BAS) to its investees in addition to its investment fund.

- **Access to shared resources:** Social enterprises, especially those at an early stage, lack internal resources to effectively execute their growth plans. Impact accelerators and incubators such as Villgro offer seed-stage and early-stage social enterprises access to shared resources such as office space, legal counsel, human resources, product development and design, financial management, and so on. Such support is vital to grow a social enterprise's business from incubation to pre-Series A or Series A stage. Some later stage impact investors such as GBF also provide access to resources such as a Portfolio CFO and Portfolio Change Manager who work across the portfolio with several social enterprises, helping streamline their financial controls and execution strategies.

- **Sharing of best practices and networks:** An ideal investor would look for opportunities to create synergies across the portfolio of social enterprises and share best practices relevant to the industry. For instance, within an impact investor's portfolio, a social enterprise providing access to affordable and safe medicines could leverage the network of another company that is managing a chain of hospitals. The investor could play an active role in bringing the two social enterprises together and helping them partner. Such initiatives create a win-win situation that encourages scale. Investors also should provide access to their networks and help their investees with linkages to relevant experts, policymakers, co-investors, corporate partners, etc.—these are generally extremely valuable for social entrepreneurs who do not come with strong networks.

(continued)

993

TABLE 26.3 (continued)

Characteristic	Description
	• **Improved brand recognition:** Social enterprises gain recognition by being part of a reputed investor's portfolio. All impact investors typically publish press releases that speak of their investment in a particular social enterprise. Many investors also run active blogs that highlight the achievements of social enterprises in their portfolio. Further, some investors actively promote their investee social enterprises in Impact Investing events such as Sankalp, SOCAP, Skoll World Forum, and Unconvention. These practices help social enterprises increase their visibility, share their growth stories and challenges, and receive feedback from a wide audience.
Access to further funding	Does the investor have limited ability to invest in further rounds; lack the ability to syndicate capital; or lack attracting co-investors from their network, despite positive business performance? A best practice is to assess how far along the investor can commit early on, as the need for the next funding round almost always arises earlier than anticipated—regardless of whether the enterprise's need for funding is driven by good performance (scaling up fast and needed to meet expansion needs) or otherwise (using too much money due to higher operating expenses and negative margins). Enterprises can gauge this in part by researching investors, as impact investors generally report how much further funding their portfolios of social enterprises have attracted. For instance, Aavishkaar estimates that for every USD $1 invested, its investees (social enterprises) have gone on to raise a further USD $4.37 in additional investments as of 31 March 2018 (Aavishkaar 2018, p. 6). Unitus Ventures, which invests in seed-stage and early-stage social enterprises, has assessed that its investees have raised an additional 3.9x capital as of 31 December 2018 (Unitus Ventures 2018, p. 2). These metrics serve as an important indicator of the long-term scale potential of social enterprises.
Level of involvement	Some investors are very hands-on in their approach, while others are more distant, diving deeper only when the situation warrants it. There needs to be abundant clarity on this aspect before signing up for funding. Some active investors wear multiple hats by participating in steering committees in turnaround situations, helping build financial models for investees, facilitating capital raises for them, and also getting involved in key hiring decisions. Sometimes, just asking the right question at the right time is very helpful (e.g. "Why has attrition increased in this region?" or "Why have sales plateaued despite reducing prices?"). Not all entrepreneurs would be comfortable with that level of engagement, but this approach helps early-stage companies identify gaps.

994

Source: Author.

India, for instance, are structured as compulsorily convertible debentures. As long as they remain debentures, the investees pay a fixed interest coupon, but once they are converted into equity, the investor's equity rights kick in and the founders have a right to buy back portions of GBF's stake (based on agreed upon performance criteria). Convertible Notes and SAFE notes (Simple Agreement for Future Equity), instruments, which are very popular among technology startups today, could help social enterprises raise capital without overdiluting ownership in the early stages of growth.

Innovative Structures

There are now many new forms of blended capital structures in the funding ecosystem, two of which are described in the subsequent paragraphs.

Pay-for-success contracts, such as social impact bonds and development impact bonds, enable enterprises that aim to achieve specific impact objectives to secure funding through financial structures that pool capital together from philanthropists, foundations, governments, and for-profit investors. These contracts reward upfront funders—investors that bear the financial risk and costs of a project—based on the level of impact-related success achieved, and typically have social enterprises as key implementers of the expected impact, and are subject to rigorous verification and validation by third parties.

The second is the Women's Livelihood Bond (WLB), an initiative of IIX, which has pooled USD $8 million from various investors in a blended finance structure to provide critical debt funding to social enterprises in South East Asia that are furthering financial inclusion among women. WLB1 offers a 5.65% return to investors and is expected to impact around 385,000 women (IIX Foundation 2017, p. 8 and 30). IIX has gone on to raise an additional USD $12 million as part of WLB2 (IIX Foundation 2020).

Venture debt is another funding option that could be considered. This is typically offered as a funding top-up to companies that have just completed an equity round. Companies could use the venture debt proceeds to meet immediate working capital needs while the equity funding component could be deployed for longer-term expansion needs. Companies that are experiencing significant revenue traction and have raised multiple equity rounds generally find it relatively easier to raise venture debt, the parameters of which may create difficulties for most social enterprises to qualify.

SCALING RESPONSIBLY

This section serves to briefly discuss the potential perils of scaling too fast as witnessed in the world of technology startups and assesses how these perils relate to social enterprises. Further, this section examines a case study that exemplifies how ineffectual and irresponsible management during the growth stage affects social enterprises.

With greater scale comes stronger financial performance and wider impact. However, if scale is not managed properly, or if it is achieved irresponsibly, it can be detrimental. Several technology startups, such as WeWork, have grown significantly in a short span of time and with the backing of considerable amounts of funding and overpriced valuations. The substantial correction in WeWork's valuation and deferment of its IPO plans indicate the perils of "blitzscaling,"[16] where technology ventures scaled rapidly to secure market leadership, and either won pole position or lost big. Because it worked in the case of companies like Amazon and Google does not mean others would be successful emulating the same approach. In fact, investors are clued in to the odds; those who have been at the forefront of the blitzscale approach are prepared to take losses on several of their portfolio companies, as long as they have a few "home runs" and exits that provide returns at many multiples of the initial capital invested. Besides, several "successful" highly scaled ventures are still incurring massive losses and are nowhere near running profitably, such as Uber.

Social enterprises, generally speaking, are outside the purview of blitzscaling, as the Impact Investing ecosystem does not have the backing of mega-large funds (such as the USD $100 billion Vision Fund). This is largely because the investment requirement per round for social enterprises is typically much lower than that of large e-commerce ventures. The biggest impact investment fund to date is the USD $2 billion Rise Fund (Mittelman 2017), founded by TPG in 2016.[17] However, the investor appetite has been increasing, as demonstrated by other large impact funds being set up recently. For instance, LeapFrog Investments' third fund raised more than USD $700 million (Businesswire 2019), and KKR[18] raised in excess of USD $1 billion for its Global Impact Fund (Chasan 2019b).

---

[16]Sullivan (2016), in a *Harvard Business Review* article called "Blitzscaling."
[17]They have gone on to raise an additional USD $1.8 billion out of a targeted USD $2.5 billion second fund (Mendonça 2020).
[18]KKR is a global investment firm that manages multiple alternative asset classes.

Further, many social enterprises still follow a brick-and-mortar model, even though technology is playing an increasingly important role. The growth models and metrics that are applied to technology startups in many cases do not apply to social enterprises. While scaling, technology ventures aim to grow in two main parameters: the number of users (including repeat users) and the gross merchandise value (GMV).[19] While user growth is important for social enterprises and technology ventures alike, GMV is often misleading as it is very different from net revenues (Parik 2016) and is not relevant to most social enterprises.

Also, social enterprise customer bases, and their aspirations, are different from those of commercial e-commerce ventures. Take the example of MFIs. Many MFIs are among the largest for-profit social enterprises today. MFIs have achieved significant scale in meeting the requirements of their vast customer base, which comprise individuals and self-help groups from low-income communities borrowing small amounts of money to start businesses and otherwise enhance their livelihood. The average MFI loan in India is only about INR 33,500 (Equifax and SIDBI[20] 2019, p. 6) or approximately USD 450. This customer base is materially distinct from tech-savvy urban consumers that have much larger disposable incomes and form the backbone of e-commerce ventures.

Even if social enterprises are usually safe from the perils of blitzscaling, there are countless instances of impact-oriented companies scaling irresponsibly. The case of SKS Microfinance in India is often cited as an example in this regard. SKS, founded in 1997, was the first Indian MFI to be publicly listed and became the world's largest MFI. Its IPO was touted as a great success when it happened in 2010, raising over USD $350 million and providing very attractive exits to its equity investors (Chandran and Narayanan 2010). However, soon after the IPO, a spate of suicides among microfinance borrowers in the state of Andhra Pradesh (AP) highlighted several coercive practices being employed by MFIs in India, including SKS, in their loan disbursement and collection process. The Andhra Pradesh government acted quickly through its AP Microfinance Ordinance that sought to protect the end-borrowers and prevented MFIs from recovering their outstanding loans (India Microfinance 2010). This led to significant write-offs across loan books, and many MFIs had to shut down operations entirely because of their dependence on operations in the state of AP. SKS, which had close to 30% portfolio exposure in AP, had to bear massive losses for several consecutive quarters. SKS also suffered

---

[19]GMV is a metric commonly used by e-commerce companies that measures the value of merchandise transacted during a given period. This is different from revenues earned by the e-commerce companies, which typically earn only a commission on the GMV.
[20]Small Industries Development Bank of India.

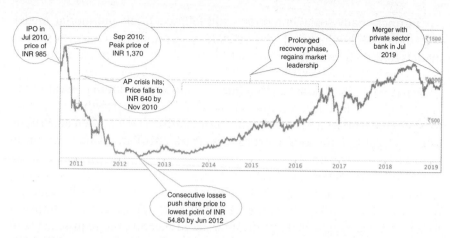

FIGURE 26.3 SKS Stock Performance Post-IPO. *Source*: Author based on data sourced from Moneycontrol.com (Moneycontrol.com 2019).

the exodus of several senior management members, including its founder, Vikram Akula. Just before the IPO, SKS had grown its business at a CAGR of 122% (Shah and Jain 2013) over four years from 2007, and its net nonperforming assets (NPA) were just 0.16% of its loan book. In the immediate aftermath of the AP crisis, SKS's share price dropped from its peak price of INR 1,370 in September 2010 to INR 640 by November 2010, as reflected in the chart in Figure 26.3.[21] The price continued to drop steeply in subsequent years until it bottomed out at INR 54.80 in June 2012, an erosion of 96% from its peak price.

Eventually, however, the company restructured its operations. SKS rebranded itself as Bharat Financial Inclusion Limited and diversified its loan base across India. In its second attempt to scale, the company scaled responsibly and successfully reassumed market leadership in India with a market capitalization of INR 126 billion (USD $1.78 billion) in December 2019. Bharat Financial Inclusion also merged its operations with a private sector bank. The road to recovery was long and one that was built on the learnings of the downturn of its business in Andhra Pradesh. In the aftermath, the company strengthened its corporate governance measures, as well as its lending and recovery practices, and loan officers were sensitized with better training in order to achieve scale responsibly.

The following Figure 26.3 illustrates the various phases of SKS after its IPO in 2010.

Learnings inferred from the SKS case that are relevant to social enterprises in their journey toward scale are listed in Table 26.4.

---

[21] Based on data sourced from www.moneycontrol.com.

TABLE 26.4 Responsible Scaling Learnings Relevant to Social Enterprises.

Learnings	Description	Scale-related factors
Prioritize ethics and governance	Social enterprises cannot compromise on ethics and strong governance principles, irrespective of a growth phase. While scale and sustainability are important, pursuing them without the vital building blocks of ethics, governance, and accountability does not yield positive results in the long run.	Internal factors: Founders' commitment Management team's compliance with ethics and governance principles
Avoid mission drift	A social enterprise is inherently a double- or triple-bottom-line organization, which needs to account for financial as well as social and/or environmental objectives. Financial performance and social impact often go hand in hand with scale. However, a singular pursuit of profits and financial results at the expense of impact-oriented objectives can lead to what is referred to as mission drift. As a result, multiple stakeholders (including low-income communities, local government agencies, affiliates, and impact investors) are likely to become unhappy with the company's performance, despite positive financial returns. This could also lead to negative publicity and media, which has to be managed carefully.	Internal factors: Founders' commitment Clarity of the business model External factors: Target market constraints Perception issues Government policy
Protect consumers' interests	A social enterprise must always be focused on its end consumers. It must endeavor to understand whether its business practices are counterproductive, or if they are beneficial to its consumers. All employees need to adhere to the rule book and basic principles of conduct and ensure that consumer grievances are taken seriously. If there are oppressive practices in place, they should be condemned immediately and responsible officials need to be held accountable, and policies changed for the better.	Internal factors: Founders' commitment Management team's compliance with ethics and governance principles

(continued)

TABLE 26.4 *(continued)*

Learnings	Description	Scale-related factors
		External factors: Target market constraints Perception issues Advisory support
Avoid or limit concentration risk	The Indian MFIs that were severely adversely affected by the AP Microfinance Ordinance had a high concentration of assets (loan receivables) in one region (in this case, the State of AP). To run a business successfully at scale, assets should ideally be diversified across regions, products, and varied consumer groups. This learning was implemented by MFIs in their second round of growth, as they built more diverse client bases across multiple states and product categories.	Internal factors: Clarity of the business model Replicability Adaptability Management team skills External factors: Target market constraints Government policy Perception issues Competition and positioning

Restructuring involves protracted efforts

After a severe downturn, it is possible to restructure operations and come out successfully, as in the case of SKS. But it is a prolonged and testing process and calls for excellent strategy execution. Besides, there is no guarantee for success—many companies do not survive harsh downturns, especially if further capital backing becomes scarce.

Internal factors:

Founders' commitment
Management team skills
Adaptability

External factors:

Fundraising
Target market constraints
Government policy
Competition and
positioning
Marketing

Source: Author.

CASE STUDIES

The following case studies concern social enterprises in India that have achieved significant scale in a relatively short time span. The case studies demonstrate the effect of scale on social impact as well as financial sustainability, and they substantiate how both of these parameters grow hand in hand with scale. These companies have adopted inclusive business models with a clear focus on providing affordable, quality goods and services to underserved segments in India. In the process, they positively impacted millions of lives without compromising on financial returns.

The data presented in these case studies are based on extensive discussions with founders and senior management representatives of the social enterprises, as well as on information presented on their corporate websites.

Case Study: Ziqitza Healthcare Limited (ZHL)

Founded in Mumbai in 2005, Ziqitza Healthcare Limited (ZHL) operates in India in the sector of health care. At the time of ZHL's founding, the overwhelming majority of ambulances in India had no life-saving equipment on board. Most ambulances only had stretchers, and some had oxygen cylinders, but they did not stock other equipment (cardiac support, defibrillators, etc.) considered standard in emerging medical services (EMS) worldwide. In fact, many ambulances were just used as hearses. There was also no dedicated line for requesting an ambulance at that time.

The founders of ZHL, who all came from corporate backgrounds and had personal experiences of poor ambulance support in India, decided to launch a service modeled on internationally reputed emergency medical services, such as the London Ambulance Service. They studied their model in depth, looking at the call center technology and overall operations, and then launched ZHL—Dial 1298 for an Ambulance to serve the city of Mumbai.

ZHL aims to offer high-quality EMS ambulances that are accessible to everyone, irrespective of income and ability to pay. ZHL leveraged its independence; by not being affiliated with any particular hospital, the caller was able to decide which hospital they were taken to. Based on research

---

and initial operational insights in the city of Mumbai, they concluded that low-income callers were typically using their ambulances to head to a public hospital, whereas middle- and higher-income callers sought private hospitals. On the basis of this data, they decided that anyone using their ambulances to reach public hospitals would pay a maximum of 50% of the regular fare charged to deliver to a private hospital—and sometimes, the entire fee was waived. This way, ZHL initiated an innovative cross-subsidy model in the field of EMS services.

Box 26.1 ZHL's Growth Story and Inflection Points

Growth Story

Financial performance: ZHL grew significantly from a topline of less than USD $50,000 in 2005, to annual revenues in excess of USD $60 million in fiscal year 2019. The company has been running profitably for many consecutive years, with a median EBITDA (earnings before interest, tax, depreciation, and amortization) margin of about 9% (on revenues).

Impact: As of December 2019, the company served over 23 million people, with more than 3,000 ambulances across 16 states. This includes serving 7.6 million pregnant women and over 19,000 babies delivered with Pan-India operations.

Inflection Points[22]

The company's growth story received a stimulating boost through the following inflection points:

Early backing of investors: ZHL received significant investor support during the first three years of its operations. In 2007, Acumen Fund invested in a Series A round, and in 2008, the company raised a Series B from multiple investors including a strategic investor (EMSC from

(continued)

---

[22]Inflection points or turning points are moments in the company's history that changed the growth trajectory or helped strengthen the company's operations.

(continued)

the United States) and other investors (including Acumen and large Indian financial institutions). This helped with the initial buildup of operations.

PPP contracts: ZHL bid and successfully won contracts with several state governments in India to operate their ambulances for a fee (based on predetermined parameters). These PPP contracts, which started in 2009 and 2010, helped the company to expand its operations and scale significantly without having to make capital expenditures on ambulances and medical equipment. Further, under these PPP contracts, the ambulance services were offered absolutely free of cost to end users—enabling several million people, many of whom were from low-income communities, to gain access to quality emergency medical care.

Source: Based on discussions with Ravi Krishna, co-founder of Ziqitza Healthcare Limited.

Figure 26.4 shows Ziqitza Healthcare's growth in operational, financial, and impact terms.

For "Cumulative People served" refers to numbers on the right Y-axis.

When ZHL launched operations in India, millions of people, particularly in low-income communities and rural hinterlands, did not have access to emergency medical services. ZHL realized that in order to be able to reach the vast underserved segments of population, they had to scale their model on a cost-effective and asset-light basis. In other words, ZHL had to avoid capital expenditure spending, specifically by not acquiring ambulances or purchasing expensive life-saving medical equipment. It was able to do so through partnerships with the public sector. ZHL's rapid scale was achieved on a truly inclusive basis—as their revenues increased by over 2,200 times in 14 years, they never deviated from their main focus of providing access to underserved and low-income segments. In the process, ZHL served over 23 million people, and the scale of their operations paired with an asset-light business model ensured healthy profitability levels (median of 9% EBITDA margin over the last 9 years). ZHL's performance (see Table 26.5) highlights the fact that social enterprises can scale effectively without compromising social impact or financial sustainability.

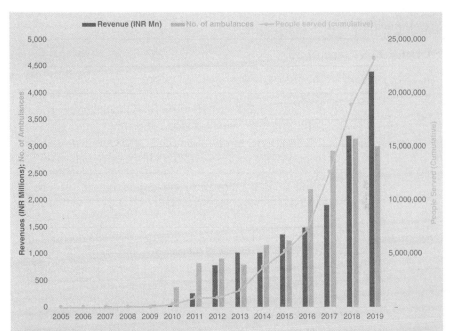

FIGURE 26.4 ZHL Growth Chart. *Source*: Ziqitza Healthcare Limited, information shared by co-founder, Ravi Krishna.

For "Revenues (INR millions)" and "number of ambulances," refer to numbers on the left Y-axis. For example, in 2014, revenues were around INR 1,000 million and number of ambulances was about 1,200.

TABLE 26.5 Critical Factors for ZHL's Scaling.

Strong fundamentals and replicability	ZHL ticked several boxes regarding fundamentals: (i) strong founders and management team; (ii) clear and focused business model; (iii) compelling understanding of the market and end-users' needs, (iv) robust operations (including well-trained paramedic teams offering uniform, high-quality service, while using world-class technology for managing call centers), (v) uncompromising commitment to ethics and transparency; and (vi) a clear intent to scale sustainably over time. These factors ensured that ZHL's business model was highly replicable as the company expanded further.

(continued)

(*continued*)

TABLE 26.5   (*continued*)

Investor support	The company was open to having external investors that were very involved in ZHL's growth, management, and operations. Most investors had board rights and actively participated by helping shape the company strategy, providing critical feedback on financials, taking part in key hiring decisions, and offering multiple network linkages (advisors, consultants, etc.). Having a mix of investors (strategic, impact investor, and large domestic institutions) helped the company gain varied perspectives and usher in best practices.
Adaptability	ZHL was always looking for partnerships and avenues for expanding operations. When it became clear that the expansion model based on owned ambulances would be extremely capital-intensive at scale, the company was quick to seize the opportunities that came through PPP contracts with state governments. They realized that such tenders would be floated by governments across India, and so ZHL actively participated in and won several tenders, while advocating strongly for open and transparent bidding processes. The PPP contracts enabled the company to achieve massive scale and impact over time, which could not have been accomplished if the company had not prioritized adaptability.

Source: Based on discussions with ZHL's co-founder, Ravi Krishna.

Case Study: KisanKraft Limited

Founded in 2005, KisanKraft Limited ("KisanKraft") operates in the agricultural sector. More than 86% of India's farm landholdings are less than 2 hectares in size, and the average landholding is just 1.08 hectares—a figure that has been reducing further over time (Mukherjee 2018). These trends in farming and land ownership have it be that large tractors and equipment that are commonly used on larger farmlands are unsuitable for the majority of India's farms. An additional market trend affecting Indian farms, especially small ones, is a shortage of labor because the rural work-force is increasingly migrating to urban settings to take up low-skill jobs.

Ravindra Agrawal, the founder and managing director of KisanKraft, used to be a software professional based in the United States with Microsoft. He hails from a rural family, and during one of his trips in India he witnessed first-hand that a bulk of Indian farmers were unable to use farm equipment due to their small farm sizes. He also realized that much of the garden equipment he used back in the United States could help smallholder farmers improve their productivity. This led to the inception of KisanKraft, a company that develops and sells a wide range of farm equipment specifically designed with small farm uses and constraints in mind.

KisanKraft innovated in several small and meaningful ways to ensure its products received wide acceptance. The company developed a wide range of products (more than 16) and SKUs (more than 300) to meet every requirement of small and marginal farmers. The products were tested to ensure that they met the standards and rigor of heavy agricultural use. Unlike garden equipment, farm equipment needed to be sturdy enough to be used for many hours a day daily throughout the farming and harvesting season. Additionally, KisanKraft encouraged farmers to lend their equipment to other farmers when not in use in order to earn extra income. KisanKraft had to ensure that its products were within an affordable price range for small farmers, while simultaneously ensuring high quality. They were able to achieve this by carefully identifying and working closely with select Chinese manufacturers that were already producing similar machinery for garden equipment companies. This helped KisanKraft keep manufacturing costs low, and constant super-vision helped ensure high product quality that adhered to their desired specifications.

The company spent extensive time educating farmers about the benefits of using their products by offering thousands of field demon-strations and exhibitions every year. They also deployed branded trucks loaded with KisanKraft equipment to be used as mobile display and demo units. KisanKraft had its products tested and certified by approved testing institutes and agricultural universities to obtain approval under government subsidy schemes. Farmers could avail themselves of these subsidies upon purchase, thereby reducing their input cost even further.

Box 26.2 KisanKraft's Growth Story and Inflection Points

Growth story:

Financial performance: KisanKraft grew its revenues from zero in fiscal year 2005–2006, to INR 507 million in 2013–2014, and then to INR 1445 million in 2018–2019. The company has been growing at a compounded annual growth rate (CAGR) of 41.50% over the last 10 years (60% from fiscal year 2007) and has been profitable every year since 2008. They have a Pan-India presence, backed by a 100,000-square-foot central warehouse, 85 exclusive showrooms, and 15 regional offices.

Impact: KisanKraft products have benefited the lives of over 2.5 million small and marginal farmers across India. The company also has 375 direct employees and works with more than 3,000 dealers.

Inflection points:

Regional Offices: In 2012, the company started setting up regional offices for faster delivery of machinery and after-sales service support to its dealers.

Due diligence: In 2013 and 2014, the company invited big four accounting firms to scrutinize its accounts, assets, and operational processes to help identify strengths and weaknesses, and more particularly the pressing pain points of the business. They realized that sales processes and inventory controls had to be streamlined further and immediately set in place corrective measures. The company was growing rapidly, and without the findings of this due diligence exercise, some critical functional gaps may have been overlooked to the company's peril.

Central warehouse: By 2014, KisanKraft set up a fully functional, state-of-the-art central warehouse with 100,000 square feet of capacity in the outskirts of Bangalore to cater to nationwide distribution needs. Their previous warehouse was much smaller, which made it difficult to meet growth requirements. The new central warehouse provided stronger inventory control and enabled KisanKraft to continue its scale journey without facing major inventory shortages and issues.

Assembly line: In 2014, the company realized it needed to set up a domestic assembly line for certain types of products in order to take advantage of the benefits of in-house manufacturing such as differential pricing and better customization. Moving to domestic assembly line production positioned KisanKraft to secure advantages from the Indian government's Make in India program, and subsequently substantially increase domestic manufacturing over time.

Source: Author, based on discussions with Managing Director Ravindra Agrawal and CEO Ankit Chitalia of KisanKraft.

Figure 26.5 captures KisanKraft's growth story and its increasing impact with scale.

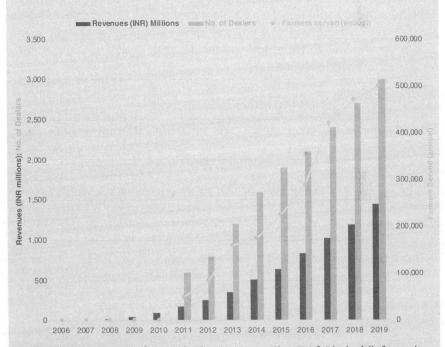

FIGURE 26.5   KisanKraft Growth Chart.   *Source*: KisanKraft Limited (information shared by Managing Director Ravindra Agrawal and CEO Ankit Chitalia).

"Revenues (INR millions)" and "number of dealers" are depicted in the left Y-axis. "Farmers served" refers to numbers of farmers and is depicted on the right Y-axis. For instance, in 2017, revenues were just over INR 1,000 million and the number of dealers was about 2,400.

Number of dealers and farmers served are reflected only from 2011 onwards.

Farmers served annually is a best estimate, as calculated by KisanKraft, based on number of products sold (they do not sell directly to farmers).

(continued)

(continued)

KisanKraft's key barrier to scale stemmed from the fact that they had to cater to a vast segment of smallholder farmers for whom affordability, quality, and usability of products in small plot sizes were critical factors (factors that helped KisanKraft scale are highlighted in Table 26.6). They outperformed several small local players that provided very few products and offered limited sales and service support. KisanKraft realized that in order to effectively address the requirements of smallholder farmers, they had to offer a wide range of products, as well as become a Pan-India player—which would only be possible if they scaled. They achieved scale by focusing on what farmers need, establishing strong networks with dealers, adopting clear and affordable pricing for their products, and committing to strong service support.

TABLE 26.6   Factors That Helped KisanKraft Scale.

Dealer support	KisanKraft's founder Ravindra understood early on that given the significant number of small and marginal farmers widely dispersed across India, it would be impractical to sell directly to the farmers. Thus, all sales were made only to registered dealers. In order to ensure dealers had consistent support, KisanKraft excelled in after-sales service with dedicated service teams and a high service-to-sales staff ratio.
Innovation and differentiation	KisanKraft's focus on the needs of small and marginal farmers, and their understanding of how various farm products are put to use, facilitated their close attention to detail on every single product component. This quality-first ethos and innovative approach to overall product design have been applied to every single product sold by KisanKraft. They also launched a dedicated low-cost brand to complement KisanKraft's relatively premium product offerings. The company's commitment to innovation and differentiation based on end-consumers' needs strengthened its sales across product categories.

TABLE 26.6	(*continued*)
Advance payments	KisanKraft knew that customer credit was often misused, and so the company spent a lot of time and effort to institute a framework that would realize the full value of their sales. Since the beginning, they insisted on receiving the full cashless payment (direct to bank) for their products in advance of delivery initiation. With this approach, KisanKraft eliminated a major pain point in managing credit.
Inventory planning and spares	As the company was dealing with a wide range of products and multiple SKUs, several of which were in high demand, it became imperative to assess inventory requirements efficiently and proactively. To ensure their customers always have the parts they need, KisanKraft insists on maintaining high levels of spares because the farm equipment is subjected to heavy usage and the need for spares constantly arises.

Source: Author, based on discussions with Managing Director Ravindra Agrawal and CEO Ankit Chitalia of KisanKraft.

By adhering to this business model, KisanKraft's revenues grew by 272 times since FY2007 to FY2019 at an annual growth rate of about 60%. KisanKraft served over 2.5 million farmers over the same time period and served their needs without conceding profitability—ensuring sustained profitability at a net profit level for several years of operations. Remarkably, the company was able to do this without raising external equity capital (it is primarily promoter-funded). KisanKraft stayed true to their vision of improving the livelihoods of small and marginal farmers and becoming market leaders in farm mechanization—and they did so by pursuing scale. KisanKraft is well on course to achieving their target of building a network of 10,000 dealers and impacting 5 million farmers within the next 3 years.

SCALING METRICS

The scale of a social enterprise is a vital characteristic for investors of all sizes and stages of investment to measure and track. As social enterprises in an investor's portfolio scale and perform better, their portfolio's health and quality improve along with the potential for higher financial returns. Investors typically track various scale indicators of the social enterprises they back. Social enterprises are also measured by a range of core impact metrics, such as those developed by the GIIN called IRIS+.[23] These metrics are comprehensive and organized by various categories including sector, SDGs, dimension of impact (scale, depth, etc.), impact focus (environmental or social), investment lens (gender, SME, etc.), and financial factors.

As much as possible, scaling indicators should reflect impact on the specific relevant populations and categories that are targeted or affected by the business's operation, such as women, the youth, or the vulnerable.[24] Beyond the guidance provided by IRIS for a multitude of indicators across several sectors, below are some of the impact metrics commonly used to measure and infer scale:

Internal to the social enterprise:

- Number and range (diversification) of products sold[25]
  - (a) Can be disaggregated by product type, income group, or region
- Number of direct jobs created
  - (a) Can be disaggregated by gender, age, ethnicity, race
- Sector-specific metrics
  - (a) Such as MWh (megawatt hours) or GWh (gigawatt hours) of clean energy produced[26]

Financial metrics:

- Average revenue growth
  - (a) Can be disaggregated by income group or region
- Salaries and wages paid
  - (a) Can be disaggregated by gender, age, or educational level
- Months of cash available to meet scale needs
- Additional capital raised

---

[23] Available at https://iris.thegiin.org/metrics/.

[24] The Criterion Institute has a publication with relevant guidance in this context: http://criterioninstitute.org/resources/files/2012/08/The-Landscape-of-Gender-Metrics.pdf.

[25] For instance, KisanKraft tracks the number of products sold on a per-SKU (Stock Keeping Unit) basis because they have over 300 SKUs across product lines. This can be a proxy for the level of company diversification.

[26] For instance, d.light estimates that its products have helped generate 221 GWh of renewable energy.

(a) Expressed in multiples of original capital invested
- Number or percentage of investees that are profitable at a portfolio level
- Taxes paid

External (stemming from the company's operations)

- Number of people impacted[27]
  (a) Can be disaggregated by income group, region, gender, ethnicity, or race
- Number of indirect jobs created in the external value chain
  (a) Can be disaggregated by income group, region, gender, ethnicity, or race
- Increase in number of low-income end-users and their incremental savings
- With respect to financial inclusion, important metrics include, for instance, the number of women with access to financial products, and increase in their earnings.
- With respect to clean energy, metrics tracked include the number of people using clean energy products, number of people gaining access to reliable clean energy for the first time, the number of people using clean energy products for income generation, tons of CO_2 saved, and the number of kerosene lamps replaced.[28]

These types of metrics should be tracked and presented in impact investors' annual reports and impact reports. A positive performance on the above parameters can be helpful in marketing the social enterprise and the impact investor to a wider audience. It is also a vital source of information when an impact investor is looking to raise further funding.

Further, most impact investors undertake semi-annual valuation exercises for each social enterprise in their portfolio, as well as on a combined basis at the fund level. Increases in the scale of investees, evident from higher revenues and better profitability results (e.g. EBITDA or net profit),

---

[27] Such as the number of people served by ambulances operated by ZHL, or the number of farmers served by KisanKraft.

[28] d.light estimates that as of March 2020, its products have empowered 100 million lives, including 26 million school-aged children having access to solar lighting, saved 23 million tons of CO_2, and US \$4.1 billion saved in energy-related expenses.

typically result in higher valuations. These are vital to impact investors to showcase, as they have their own investor base to report to.

Another very important benchmark that impact investors track is the number of exits (sale of investors' stake in the social enterprise) and the realization from each exit. An incubator, seed-stage, or early-stage impact investor typically sells their stake to a larger or later-stage investor or DFI during a Series B or Series C capital raise. Acumen, for instance, had a successful exit at 2.4 times the capital invested (Acumen and Open Capital Advisors 2019, p. 16) from d.light in 2018, when the social enterprise raised a USD $40 million Series E round of funding from Inspired Evolution and DFIs including FMO, Swedfund, and Norfund (Sunkara 2018). Later stage investors would typically exit when the company is acquired by a strategic investor or when the company goes public. Accordingly, a successful exit is only possible if the social enterprise is scaling well. Conversely, if a social enterprise fails to scale and performs poorly compared to its peers, it typically results in lower valuations and potential write-offs of capital invested.[29]

A McKinsey report assessed 48 exits that took place in India between 2010 and 2015, and estimates that the median internal rate of return (IRR) enjoyed by impact investors is 10% (Pandit and Tamhane 2017, p. 25). About 58% of the exits met or exceeded the average expected market rate of 7%. The top tercile of exits witnessed an IRR of 34%, and were typically performed by investors who committed about USD $1.4 million on average per deal (indicative of early or Series A stage impact investors who invested early and benefited from the scale effect when investees exited).

DFIs are the largest backers of Impact Investing funds, as they seek to invest in emerging economies and help combat poverty. For instance, according to a GIIN report, in Indonesia alone, DFIs contributed to USD $3.6 billion in impact capital between 2007 and 2017 compared to just USD $148.8 million by private impact investors (GIIN and Intellecap 2018). In addition to financial returns (IRR targets), DFIs have their own set of impact parameters that assess the performance of their impact investments. Typically, most DFIs seek to measure jobs created (directly and indirectly in the supply chain), taxes paid by their investees, and sector-specific metrics. For instance, Norfund estimated that in 2018, its portfolio created 304,000 jobs, produced 17.4 terawatt hours (TWh) of clean energy, paid NOK[30] 13.9 billion in taxes, and lent NOK 274 billion to investees' clients (Norfund 2019). These figures are

---

[29] Impact investors measure their exits in cash multiples of invested capital (MOIC) or IRR.
[30] Norwegian krone.

calculated for each investee, and an increase of such figures over previous results indicates that an investee is scaling.

There is always an underlying expectation of positive financial return[31] (Norfund 2019). This means that profitability is a precondition and DFIs will not back investments that are not projected to be sustainable. Hence, it becomes imperative that impact investments and social enterprises scale to garner increased support from DFIs. Having a DFI as an investment partner also results in additionality (i.e. mobilization of private sector capital that might not have been possible without the DFI's investment). For instance, the CDC estimates that additional capital in excess of USD $570 million was mobilized alongside their own investments in 2018 (CDC Group 2019b, p. 47).

CHECKLIST FOR SOCIAL ENTERPRISES LOOKING FOR SCALE

Table 26.7 describes the essential elements of a scaling checklist, derived from the evidence presented in the preceding sections of this chapter. This checklist can be employed by social enterprises to address how they fare against respective scale-related challenges. Weights can be assigned to the checklist based on the social enterprise's own assessment of which challenges are most critical. This could help social enterprises develop an internal scoring system, assign targets that need to be achieved within certain timelines, and assess how these scores vary over time. The Table can also provide an alert system, to highlight areas where the social enterprise is falling short. For instance, under the Talent checklist line, if salaries are noted as "not current," it would trigger an alert or a red flag that could help a company code such challenges as high priority and address them in a timely manner. Table 26.8 provides a checklist to assess scale-related performance.

This checklist should be reviewed periodically (at least quarterly or semi-annually) to gauge the social enterprise's performance as it scales, enabling it to promptly address any red flags that may arise. It is vital to assess areas of weakness and red flags that emerge from aspects of the enterprise. For each red flag identified, it is imperative to:

- *Fully understand its underlying causes.* Analyze in detail all the reasons for red flags. For instance, if gross profit margins have reduced

---

[31]Norfund achieved an IRR of 9% since 1997, CDC has an average annual return on assets of 6% since 2012.

TABLE 26.7 Scale-Related Performance Requirements.

Scale Challenge	Description	Scale-Related Factors	Weighted score (example)
Business model building	This is the most central element. If the business fundamentals (mission, values, goals, well-defined product or service, and growth strategy) are not clear and strong, the organization will struggle as it seeks to scale up.	Internal factors: (i) Clarity of the business model (ii) Replicability (iii) Innovation and differentiation (iv) Founders' commitment External factors: (i) Need for incubation and advisory support (ii) Target market constraints	25
Meeting impact targets	The social enterprise has to demonstrate rigor with respect to its impact obligations as it scales. According to the 2015 JP Morgan and GIIN Impact Investor Survey, over the past three years investors consistently pointed to a shortage of high-quality investment opportunities with a track record (JP Morgan and GIIN 2015). As a result, investors tend to avoid investing in social enterprises with limited capacity to measure impact.	Internal factors: (i) Business model inclusiveness (ii) Corporate governance (iii) Clarity of the business model External factors: (i) Marketing and communication (ii) Target market constraints	20

Talent hiring and retention	It is important to have the right parameters in place that make it conducive to hire and retain talent and maintain a well-balanced ideal team. To successfully scale up, critical skills need to be in place between the social entrepreneur and the management team, including financial planning, market analysis, social marketing, employment leadership, and the ability to measure social impact (OECD 2016, p. 13).	Internal factors: (i) Committed founders (ii) Management execution skills	10
Capital raising	Raising the *right amount* of capital at the relevant stage of business, ensuring that the *type of capital* is well-aligned with the end-use of financing.	Internal factors: (i) Cash flows (ii) Differentiation External factors: (i) Appropriate funding options (ii) Level of competition and positioning (iii) Strategic interest/role of DFIs (at a later stage)	15

TABLE 26.7 *(continued)*

Scale Challenge	Description	Scale-Related Factors	Weighted score (example)
Profitability	Achieving rapid revenue growth without a well-defined path to profitability leads to high levels of cash burn. It is thus vital to target reaching profitability on a steady-state basis.	Internal factors: (i) Unit economics (ii) Business (financial) model (iii) Cash flows External factors: (i) Technology (ii) Government policy	15
Sustaining growth	Once a reasonable level of scale is achieved, it is imperative to sustain growth in order to achieve a compelling competitive position in the market.	Internal factors: (i) Cash flows and controls (ii) Positive unit economics (iii) Adaptability (iv) Advisory support (v) Replicability External factors: (i) Appropriate funding options	15
			Total 100

Source: Author.

TABLE 26.8 Checklist to Assess Scale-Related Performance.

Scale Challenge	Checklist (Positive parameters)
Business model building	Long-term view with clear vision and mission statements
	Simplicity and clarity of revenue drivers, operating costs, and target market(s)
	Key business model assumptions related to scale are clearly listed
	Scenario analysis (various scenarios, typically base case, best case, and worst case, along with resultant outcomes)
	Unique selling point of the product or service is clear
	Incubator support is available
	Advisor(s) or Advisory Board are in place
Meeting impact targets	Higher number of beneficiaries impacted, through increasing business scale and reach
	Impact assessment carried out using reliable research methods, with periodic monitoring
	Independent third-party verification and audits conducted
	ESG performance report published on a regular basis (at least annually)
	Strong corporate governance and compliance mechanisms in place
Talent hiring and retention	Employee stock option (ESOP) pool allocation (this is useful to retain managerial talent and compensate for lower than market salaries)
	100% dedication to the venture by founders
	Strong middle management team in place
	Staff health and safety are prioritized
	Gender pay parity is implemented across management levels
	Salaries are current (not overdue)
	Reward mechanisms are based on performance
	Comprehensive annual leave policy adopted
	Attrition levels are within industry averages

TABLE 26.8   *(continued)*

Scale Challenge	Checklist (Positive parameters)
Capital raising	Fundraising timelines and milestones are identified well in advance
	Sufficient runway exists (at least 6 months of cash before further capital infusion)
	Valuations are within industry benchmarks (higher valuation indicates greater differentiation advantage)
	Adequate room for further equity dilution (space for further equity rounds)
	Clearly identified end-use of funds
	Access to working capital (working capital needs are immediate)
	Encouraging investor response (receiving multiple term sheets is indicative of being a sought-after business)
	Funding traction in the relevant sector (multiple investments imply high investor interest in the sector)
	Access to intermediaries (engaging investment banks and legal advisors can help raise capital efficiently)
Networks	Membership in relevant industry organizations and forums
	Channels available for knowledge transfer and communication of ideas for social enterprises across the sector
	Ability to enter partnerships with other aligned social enterprises—could lead to synergies such as access to finance, shared resources, exploring new ideas, and scaling impact
Profitability	EBITDA profitability achieved (consistent EBITDA profitability and revenue growth suggest strong business fundamentals)
	Healthy gross profit margins (to ensure that products or services are not offered at negative variable margins)
	Net profit margins and returns are in line with, or higher than, market benchmarks, reflecting efficiencies of scale
	Profitability ratios do not fluctuate significantly over time (if highly varied, would indicate instability in the business)
	Unit-level cash positive results achieved
	Robust accounting system, cash controls, and Management Information Systems (MIS) are in place; leveraging technology applied as much as possible.
	Frequent checks and balances, regular audits (this helps improve transparency)
	Favorable regulatory and taxation policies

TABLE 26.8   (*continued*)

Scale Challenge	Checklist (Positive parameters)
Sustaining growth beyond initial traction	Strong operating cash flows and unit economics (the business can sustain growth on its own)
	Adequate cash reserves backed by investors with deep pockets (investors who can participate in multiple rounds)
	Well-balanced and experienced board of directors serving as an able guide to the management in furthering growth
	Business growth reflects adaptability (awareness of market developments, actively seeks expansion opportunities)
	Strong control systems and processes established to minimize or prevent leakages

Source: Author.

significantly although revenues have increased, understand if this is as a result of price reductions due to seasonal promotions or due to operating costs escalating beyond control (say, an increase in raw material prices or supply chain costs). Then list each of these out and objectively quantify their financial impact on gross margins.

- *List remedial measures.* For each salient reason identified above, identify feasible remedial measures. For instance, with respect to increase in raw material costs, remedial measures could be to negotiate with existing suppliers or to expand the supplier base further. Feasible targets would serve to substantiate such measures. For instance, if the raw material price increase was 20% in one quarter, a short-term target could be to reduce this to 10%.

- *Identify the stakeholders responsible to implement such remedial measures.* This is a very important step, because if measures are identified but no one is assigned the specific responsibility of implementation, there is a lack of accountability. Someone, under whose purview such cause and remedial measures reside, needs to own the implementation. Such a person must have the relevant skill sets and the requisite authority to execute the measures. With respect to raw material price reductions, the procurement head or supply chain manager would be expected to take ownership.

- *Assign timelines for resolution.* Set appropriate timelines for implementing the measures, in consultation with the person responsible for implementation. Based on the inputs from the procurement manager, it could be agreed that raw material prices would be reduced by 10% within the current quarter and would be on par with previous prices in six months' time.

- *Follow up on resolution execution.* Once targets and timelines have been duly assigned, they need to be reviewed on a frequent basis to ensure that the right level of efforts are being invested to resolve the reasons behind the red flags. If results are not forthcoming as anticipated (for instance, if the raw material prices are not down by 10% in the current quarter in the above example), it needs to be assessed if it was on account of lack of efforts or if the targets and timelines need to be revised. Ideally, the measures identified are implemented within agreed timelines, unless there are some exceptional circumstances. Otherwise, the process could lead to multiple target revisions and timeline extensions.

CONCLUSION

Scaling a business is not an easy endeavor in general, let alone for social enterprises. A social enterprise by its own nature pursues both impact and financial returns. And scale is vital to ensure it achieves its impact objectives on a financially sustainable basis.

If social enterprises have fundamental internal factors in place—including having a strong and replicable model, differentiation, dedicated founders, and a well-balanced management team with good execution capabilities—they can successfully achieve sustainable growth over time. Their trajectory is also significantly affected by a host of external factors that are evolving rapidly within the Impact Investing ecosystem globally. These include an expanding number of funding options, which are increasing as the Impact Investing industry grows globally, and support by a multitude of investors, with encouraging government policies—all of which accelerate the adoption of ESG and CSR and the development of infrastructure, especially in developing countries. The role of advisors and intermediaries is another critical external factor that determines social enterprises' ability to raise capital and scale their businesses. In addition, technology is expected to be a game-changer for social enterprises to reach more underserved segments globally. The growth of smartphone penetration in several emerging economies and the advent of mobile money and payments systems enable several MSMEs to gain better access to capital, as well as reach a wider range of consumers.

The compounded effect of these various factors shapes the growth and scale of social enterprises. For instance, in the case of the company ZHL, despite having committed founders, strong management, operational skills, and great technology, the factor that had the most significant influence on its scaling was favorable government policies that offered the opportunity to scale across India on an asset-light basis. However, the fact that they had strong internal factors meant that the company was well prepared to take advantage of changing market dynamics resulting from public policies. Further, ZHL emphasized adherence to ethics, transparency, and good governance while working with several Indian state governments, while simultaneously ensuring that its operations were carried out profitably.

When looking to scale, a social enterprise must carefully assess its funding needs and available financing options. Due care must be taken to ensure that the tenure of capital raised matches the timing of the proposed end-use. When raising equity, the social enterprise must be ready for a long-term partnership and be fully aware of the investor's mission, financial return and exit expectations, impact criteria, and value-adds beyond capital infusion. Over time, a scaling social enterprise should demonstrate stronger financial capabilities by displaying sufficient revenues and profitability through a compelling financial performance, coupled with increasing evidence-based impact, which together attract larger investors and more capital for its growth and expansion. Case studies of Ziqitza Healthcare Ltd and KisanKraft Ltd indicate that significant scale combined with strong financial performance and compelling impact can be achieved without having to raise multiple rounds of financing (KisanKraft is primarily promoter-funded and ZHL raised only two rounds of equity financing), as long as there is a strong execution and good business fundamentals.

But as a social enterprise grows and becomes a more mature entity with stronger financials, it must stay loyal to its inclusive nature and impact objectives. It needs to scale responsibly and have a permanent focus on its end-consumers' perspectives and interests, so as not to compromise its ESG ethos and values. A continued emphasis on maintaining the highest level of ethics and transparency is needed throughout decision-making processes over time. If these elements are compromised, it can lead to a severe downturn in business followed by prolonged and expensive restructuring efforts. To stay on track, social enterprises must periodically assess their performance and how they are measuring up to various scale-related challenges. They must have adequate systems in place to identify and report red flags on a timely basis along with appropriate remedial measures.

The success of the social enterprises is critical for the Impact Investing community as a whole. Impact investors, irrespective of the stage at which they invest, will explore suitable exit options from social enterprises in their portfolio if and when it is appropriate. A successful exit only materializes if the underlying social enterprises achieve scale, hence, scale of social enterprises becomes a crucial building block that helps impact investors achieve successful exits, and in turn attracts more capital into the Impact Investing ecosystem. The time is right for many more social enterprises to emerge, grow, and flourish. The Impact Investing world is likely to witness an increasing number of social enterprises achieve scale across sectors and regions, and offer convincing returns and exits to investors, while at the same time significantly increasing their social and environmental impact.

ACKNOWLEDGMENTS

The author wishes to thank Mr. Ravi Krishna (co-founder of Ziqitza Healthcare Limited) for his valuable inputs relating to the case study on Ziqitza Healthcare Limited, and Mr. Ravindra Agrawal (Managing Director of KisanKraft Limited) and Mr. Ankit Chitalia (CEO of KisanKraft Limited) for their valuable contribution relating to the case study on KisanKraft Limited. The author also extends his gratitude to this book's co-editors, Elsa de Morais Sarmento and R. Paul Herman, for their valuable support and feedback that have helped shape this chapter.

REFERENCES

Aavishkaar (2018). *Aavishkaar Impact Report* 2018. www.aavishkaar.in/images/download/publications/Aavishkaar%20Impact%20Report%202017.pdf (accessed March 2020).

Acumen and Open Capital Advisors (2019). Lighting the way: Roadmap to exits in Off-grid Energy. acumen.org/energy-exits-report/ (accessed March 2020).

Akhaya, T. (2018). SOLshare raises Series A from Singapore's IIX Growth Fund (28 September). https://e27.co/singapores-iix-growth-fund-funded-bangladesh-based-solshare-bring-p2p-solar-energy-grid-rural-homes-20180928/.

Arena, M., Azzone, G., and Bengo, I. (2014). Performance Measurement for Social Enterprises. *Voluntas* 26 (10). doi.org/10.1007/s11266-013-9436-8.

BBOXX (2019). *BBOXX official press release (28 August)*.

Beggin, M., and O'Neill, K. (2015). The Social Enterprise Review. www
.northeastern.edu/sei/wp-content/uploads/2015/02/Spring_2015_SE_
Review_Final.pdf (accessed March 2020).

Behera, N. (2014). Cashing in on cows, Milk Mantra style, Business Standard News (15 September). https://www.business-standard.com/article/
companies/cashing-in-on-cows-milk-mantra-style-114091400779_1.html.

British Council (2016). The state of social enterprise in India. www.britishcouncil
.org/sites/default/files/bc-report-ch4-india-digital_0.pdf (accessed March
2020).

Bullock, L. (2019). 2019's Top 5 Most Innovative and Impactful Social Enterprises, Forbes (5 March). www.forbes.com/sites/lilachbullock/2019/
03/05/2019s-top-5-most-innovative-and-impactful-social-enterprises/#
69c12c41774a (accessed March 2020).

Businesswire (2019). LeapFrog breaks Impact Investing record, with $700 Mn
Emerging Markets Fund (10 May). www.businesswire.com/news/home/
20190509006034/en/LeapFrog-Breaks-Impact-Investing-Record-700M-
Emerging (accessed March 2020).

CDC Group (2019a). Our approach to innovating with catalytic capital
(30 September). www.cdcgroup.com/en/news-insight/news/our-approach-
to-innovating-with-catalytic-capital/ (accessed March 2020).

CDC Group (2019b). Making a Difference. *Annual Review* 2018. assets
.cdcgroup.com/wp-content/uploads/2019/07/29142246/22218_CDC_
Annual-Review_2018_190723.pdf (accessed March 2020).

Chandran. R., and Narayanan, P. (2010). SKS IPO success heralds more
microfinance offers. Livemint (3 August). www.livemint.com/Money/
Xg59geiz0yVLS5ha8xitWJ/SKS-IPO-success-heralds-more-microfinance-
offers.html (accessed March 2020).

Chasan, E. (2019a). Global Sustainable Investments Rise 34 Percent to $30.7 Tril-
lion, Bloomberg (3 April).

Chasan, E. (2019b). *KKR tops $1 Billion fundraising goal for Global Impact Fund,*
Bloomberg (8 August).

Confederation of Indian Industry (2019). Survey on jobs creation and outlook
in MSME Sector. cii.in/PublicationDetail.aspx?enc=azchajyTg8MAuG
5mcLNdVYNizYXF+oWjad8kMdhn0x4LdsMxG21+fLemPVcqYYO61RkH
wnKBDJsiFTHSV7TAT1R9PbO7ybRV11ekxRnQAl49Cb83gM/3Mtc7ma2
o1wCvw0iX/38zDWahf5g6ke1nTKDOykZl/dYVmOSlaOqsBmTLU7APU
ureAXvI9RfkyeHz (accessed March 2020).

Convergences (2019). *Microfinance Barometer* 2019. www.convergences.org/wp-content/uploads/2019/09/Microfinance-Barometer-2019_web-1.pdf (accessed March 2020).

Dart, R., Clow, E., and Armstrong, A. (2010). Meaningful Difficulties in the Mapping of Social Enterprises. *Social Enterprise Journal.* 6: 186–193. doi.10.1108/17508611011088797.

d.light (2019). d.light official Press release (6 November).

Dutta, R. (2019). *Five key challenges faced by social entrepreneurs in India (4 June).*

Economic Times Bureau (2019a). India's microfinance sector remained strong despite slowdown: ICICI Securities (11 October)

Economic Times Bureau (2019b). Overall India handset market growth to fall in 2020 (24 December). https://economictimes.indiatimes.com/tech/hardware/overall-india-handset-market-growth-to-fall-in-2020/articleshow/72950192.cms?from=mdr.

Emerson, J., and Twersky, F. (1996). *New Social Entrepreneurs: The Success, Challenge, and Lessons of Non-Profit Enterprise Creation.* San Francisco: Roberts Foundation.

Equifax and SIDBI (2019). Microfinance Pulse Vol III (October 2019) www.sidbi.in/files/article/articlefiles/3rd%20edition%20-%20Microfinance%20Pulse%20Report.pdf (accessed March 2020).

European Union (2016). *Social Enterprises and Their Eco-Systems: Developments in Europe.* European Commission, Luxembourg: Publications Office of the European Union.

Food and Agriculture Organization (2019). The state of food and agriculture. United Nations. www.fao.org/state-of-food-agriculture/en/ (accessed March 2020).

Fotheringham, S., and Saunders, C. (2014). Social Enterprise as Poverty Reducing Strategy for Women, *Social Enterprise Journal* 10(3): 176–199.

Gasca, L. (2017). Three reasons why social enterprises fail and what we can learn from them (8 June). https://www.weforum.org/agenda/2017/06/3-reasons-why-social-enterprises-fail-and-what-we-can-learn-from-them/ (accessed March 2020).

Ghatak, A.R. (2017). India's informal economy (14 September). https://www.dandc.eu/en/article/indias-informal-sector-backbone-economy (accessed March 2020).

GIIN (2017). Beyond Investment: The Power of Capacity-Building Support. https://thegiin.org/assets/GIIN_issuebrief_capacitybuilding_finalwebfile_101217.pdf (accessed March 2020).

GIIN and Dalberg (2015). The landscape for impact investing in South Asia. https://thegiin.org/assets/documents/pub/South%20Asia%20 Landscape%20Study%202015/1_Full%20South%20Asia%20Report.pdf (accessed March 2020).

GIIN and Intellecap (2018). The landscape for Impact Investing in Southeast Asia https://thegiin.org/assets/Indonesia_GIIN_SEAL_report_webfile .pdf (accessed March 2020).

Hutt, R. (2020). Life for millions in Bangladesh is being transformed thanks to this simple solution (13 January). https://www.weforum.org/agenda /2020/01/bangladesh-solar-power-energy-grid-rural-life/#:~:text=Life%20 for%20millions%20in%20Bangladesh,lives%20of%20 million%20people .&text=The%20world's%20progress%20on%20transitioning,Here's%20how %20to%20fix%20it.

IIX Foundation (2017). Blueprint paper: IIX Women's Livelihood Bond™ – Changing Finance, Financing Change. https://iixglobal.com/ wp-content/uploads/2019/02/IIX-Foundation_WLB-Final-Blueprint-Paper_FEB-2019.pdf (accessed March 2020).

IIX Foundation (2020). IIX Women's Livelihood Bond 2 Successfully Closes (15 January).

India Microfinance (2010). Andhra Pradesh Micro Finance Institutions (regulation of money lending) Ordinance (15 October).

International Finance Corporation (2014). Shared prosperity through inclusive business: How successful companies reach the base of the pyramid (1 November).

International Finance Corporation (2015). IFC plays pivotal role in Microfinance Institution Bandhan's transformation into India's newest bank (23 August).

International Finance Corporation (2017). MSME Finance Gap: Assessment of the Shortfalls and Opportunities in Financing Micro, Small and Medium Enterprises in Emerging Markets. https://openknowledge.worldbank.org/ handle/10986/28881 (accessed March 2020).

MAPE Advisory Group and MXV Consulting (2017). Fintech India: The changing landscape of SME lending. http://mapegroup.com/pdf/fintech-india-changing-landscape-sme-lending.pdf (accessed March 2020).

Mathaisel, D. F. (2015). Is Scalability Necessary for Economic Sustainability? *European Journal of Sustainable Development*, 4(2): 275. 10.14207/ejsd .2015.v4n2p275.

Mendonça, E. (2020). TPG's Rise Fund II moves closer to target amid rise of Impact Investing, PE News (20 January). https://www.penews.com/articles/ tpgs-rise-fund-moves-closer-to-target-20200120 (accessed March 2020).

Mittelman, M. (2017). TPG Seals Record $2 Billion for Rise Impact Fund. Bloomberg Quint (3 October). www.bloombergquint.com/markets/tpg-seals-record-2-billion-for-rise-impact-fund-co-led-by-bono   (accessed March 2020).

Moneycontrol (2019). Stock chart - Bharat Financial Inclusion Ltd. www.moneycontrol.com/stock-charts/bharatfinancialinclusion/charts/SM11# SM11 (accessed March 2020).

Mudaliar, A., and Dithrich, H. (2019). GIIN - Sizing the Impact Investing Market. https://thegiin.org/assets/Sizing%20the%20Impact%20Investing%20Market _webfile.pdf (accessed March 2020).

Mukherjee, S. (2018). Indian farm size shrank further by 6% in 5 years to 2015–16. Business Standard (2 October) (accessed March 2020).

Nielsen (2014). Doing Well by Doing Good. Increasingly, consumers care about corporate social responsibility, but does concern convert to consumption? www.nielsen.com/wp-content/uploads/sites/3/2019/04/global-corporate-social-responsibility-report-june-2014.pdf (accessed March 2020).

Norfund (2019). 2018 Report on Operations. www.norfund.no/app/uploads/ 2020/01/VIrksomhetsrapporten_final-2018.pdf (accessed March 2020).

OECD (2013). Green entrepreneurship, eco-innovation and SMEs, OECD Working Paper on SMEs and Entrepreneurship. CFE/SME(2011)9/FINAL (accessed March 2020).

OECD (2016). Policy brief on scaling the impact of social enterprises. https://www.oecd.org/employment/leed/Policy-brief-Scaling-up-social-enterprises-EN.pdf (accessed March 2020).

OECD (2018). Enabling SMEs to scale up. https://www.oecd.org/cfe/smes/ ministerial/documents/2018-SME-Ministerial-Conference-Plenary-Session-1.pdf (accessed March 2020).

Omidyar Network (2016). Across the Returns Continuum. www.omidyar.com/ sites/default/files/file_archive/Across%20the%20Returns%20Continuum .pdf (accessed March 2020).

Omidyar Network and BCG (2016). Credit disrupted: Digital MSME lending in India. www.omidyar.com/sites/default/files/file_archive/18-11-21_Report_ Credit_Disrupted_Digital_FINAL.pdf (accessed March 2020).

Parik, N. (2016). Why GMV is a false indicator of your startup's success (14 June). https://yourstory.com/2016/06/gmv-e_commerce-startup-success/.

Pandit, V., and Tamhane, T. (2017). Impact Investing: Purpose-driven finance finds its place in India. Mc Kinsey & Company. https://thegiin.org/assets/ Impact-investing-finds-its-place-in-India.pdf (accessed March 2020).

Picken, Joseph. (2017). From startup to scalable enterprise: Laying the foundation. *Business Horizons (July)*. 10.1016/j.bushor.2017.05.002.

Press Trust of India (2019). Microfinance industry grew by 42.9% in Q1 in FY'20 (29 August).

Pyper, J., and Merchant, E. F. (2017). Engie's Fenix acquisition gives a major boost to energy access efforts. Greentech Media. (23 October). https://www.greentechmedia.com/articles/read/engies-fenix-acquisition-boost-energy-access (accessed March 2020).

Roy, D. (2017). Milk Mantra raises Series D round. VC Circle (17 January). https://www.vccircle.com/milk-mantra-raises-series-d-round-neev-fund-existing-investors/ (accessed March 2020).

Schneider Electric (2019). Schneider Electric announces the creation of its third impact fund Schneider Energy Access Asia. Schneider Electric (2 October). https://www.se.com/ww/en/about-us/press/news/corporate-2019/schneider-energy-access-asia.jsp (accessed March 2020).

Shah, M., and Jain, S. (2013). SKS Microfinance's IPO subscribed 13.69 times, Business Standard (21 January).

Shahnaz, D. (2019). The highs and lows of creating the world's first social stock exchange. Quartz India (17 October).

Spectrem Group (2018). Spectrem Group Press Release - New Spectrem Group Report Unveils Unique Generational Preferences and Proclivities of Millennials and Generation X Investors and Ways Advisors Can Best Engage with Them (17 January). https://spectrem.com/Content/press-release-millennials-report-release-011718.aspx.

Sullivan, T. (2016). Blitzscaling. Harvard Business Review (1 April). https://hbr.org/2016/04/blitzscaling (accessed March 2020).

Sunkara, K. (2018). Solar products maker d.light raises $41 mn from African investment firm, others (17 December).

Tonkonogy, B., and Hallmeyer, K. (2018). *Designing Technical Assistance Facilities for Adaptation and Resilience Companies*. Climate Policy Initiative. https://www.climatepolicyinitiative.org/wp-content/uploads/2018/05/Designing-Technical-Assistance-Activities-for-Adaptation-and-Resilience-Companies.pdf.

UBS (2019). Awareness, Simplification and Contribution: Core requirements needed to actually achieve the United Nations' Sustainable Development Goals (21 January). www.ubs.com/global/en/wealth-management/chief-investment-office/investment-opportunities/sustainable-investing/2019/wef-2019.html (accessed March 2020).

Unitus Capital (2017). Unitus Capital blog archives (4 April). http://unituscapital
.com/blog/26/THANKS_A_BILLION_UNITUS_CAPITAL_CROSSES_1_
BN_IN_CAPITAL_RAISED_FOR_OUR_AMAZING_CLIENTS_July_24_2
(accessed March 2020).

Unitus Ventures (2018). *Annual Impact Report* 2018. https://unitus.vc/annual-
impact-report-2018/ (accessed March 2020).

Villgro Innovations Foundation (2018). Impact Report 2018. www.villgro.org/
wp-content/uploads/2019/05/Villgro_Impact-Report_Digital.pdf (accessed
March 2020).

Villeneuve-Smith, F., and Temple, N. (2015). Leading the World in Social Enterprises, State of Social Enterprise Survey 2015. Social Enterprise UK Publishing. https://www.socialenterprise.org.uk/wp-content/uploads/2019/05/
FINALVERSIONStateofSocialEnterpriseReport2015-2.pdf (accessed March
2020).

Wood Mackenzie Power and Renewables and Energy 4 Impact (2019). Strategic
Investments in Off-grid Energy Access: Scaling the Utility of the Future at the
Last Mile. https://www.energy4impact.org/file/2086/download?token=9-
hw5RF1 (accessed March 2020).

APPENDIX 26.1: EXPERTS INTERVIEWED

Interviewees	Profile of the company	Position
Ravi Krishna	Ziqitza Healthcare Limited (Social enterprise)	Co-Founder
Ravindra Agrawal	KisanKraft Limited (Social enterprise)	Co-Founder and Managing Director
Ankit Chitalia	KisanKraft Limited (Social enterprise)	Chief Executive Officer

The Role of the Entrepreneurial University and Engaged Scholarship in Impact Investing Capacity Building

Richard T Harrison, PhD and Suwen Chen, MBA, MSci

Abstract

If the university of the nineteenth century was governed primarily by a teaching and education mission and that of the twentieth century by a research mission, the university of the twenty-first century will be driven by a prosocial engagement mission in which Impact Investing could be the accelerator of this epic transformation. Universities are increasingly being required to be more socially and environmentally responsible in creating a sustainable and resilient society, in the context of the triple bottom line, United Nations Sustainable Development Goals (SDGs), and Net-Zero. This chapter reviews the changing nature of the contemporary university, in which the tension between rigor and relevance is increasingly being resolved in favor of relevance as engaged scholarship, evidence-based research, and practitioner-led Mode

2–type research become more prominent. Using the "Entrepreneurial University" as a framing construct, we explore the emerging role and potential of the university in building capacity for Impact Investing through both its teaching and research functions and, in particular, through the demonstration effect of its activity as an impact investor itself. Drawing on a series of mini-case studies and organizational vignettes, both the great potential of and certain limitations to the Entrepreneurial University are recognized across multiple aspects of Impact Investing, which is seen as an extension to its role in supporting regional economic growth, social responsibility, and sustainable development.

Keywords

Entrepreneurial University; Academic Capitalism; Academic Entrepreneurship; Entrepreneurial Education; Impact Investing; Social Entrepreneurship

INTRODUCTION

The role of universities in supporting the developing field of Impact Investing is potentially significant, but also to a considerable extent underdeveloped. Universities are long-term institutions that can play a unique role in field-building, developing talent, and connecting finance to other expertise. This is reflected in a number of developments. First, over the past decade, there has been a substantial shift in student attitudes and expectations. For example, the Deloitte Millennial Survey (2017) shows that the Millennial generation is more interested than ever in the power of business to solve social problems and needs to be equipped for this new task. The IBM Global Student Survey (2010) had previously highlighted this, identifying globalization, the environment, and sustainability as the key challenges, but concluding that fewer than 4 out of 10 student respondents believed that their education prepared them to address the realities of a shared planet.

Second, and in part at least in response to this, there have been increasing calls for universities to reorient themselves toward a scholarship of engagement (Van de Ven 2007), a participative form of research for obtaining the views of key stakeholders to understand a complex problem, hence producing knowledge that is more penetrating and useful than when researchers work alone. This is a reaction to a diagnosis of the current state of research characterized by a gap between theory and practice (from both sides), which reflects the knowledge production problem that academia values the production of knowledge over its dissemination and implementation. As a perspective, an engaged scholarship has four characteristics. First, it is a *form of inquiry*, where researchers involve others and leverage their different perspectives to learn about a problem domain, Second, it is a *relationship*, involving negotiation, mutual respect, and collaboration to produce a learning community. Third, it involves *studying complex problems* with and/or for practitioners and other stakeholders, Fourth, it is an *identity* of how scholars view their relationships with their communities and their subject matter (Harrison 2018).

Third, this engaged scholarship does not exist in a vacuum. In terms of knowledge production, for example, it parallels the earlier distinction (Gibbons et al. 1994) between Mode 1 research—traditional individual-led discipline-based cognitive research that is applied later (if at all) by others than those producing it—and Mode 2 research—interactive problem-oriented transdisciplinary knowledge production where this knowledge is validated in use. This involves a virtuous circle whereby issues arise from practice and are defined in conversation with those in practice, from which the data are generated, and academics, working alongside Schön's (1983) reflective practitioners, develop the frameworks for sensemaking. In terms of knowledge dissemination, on the other hand, the engaged scholarship tradition has much in common with evidence-based management movement (Rousseau 2005), which applies the scientific method to use the best available evidence for evaluating practice.

In an engaged institution, an ideal education lies between the two poles of experience and purpose, of thought and action, of self-realization and social responsibility. To put it simply, "an education is meaningful when it liberates the spirit and feeds the soul and at the same time, prepares us to make good decisions, contribute to public life, and live as responsible citizens" (Ramaley 2005). More specifically, the scholarship of engagement means connecting to our most pressing social, civic, and ethical problems, where campuses become viewed by both students and professors not as isolated islands but as staging grounds for action. At a deeper level, however, what is also needed is not just more programs, but a larger purpose, a larger sense of mission: "the scholarship of engagement also means creating a special climate in which the academic and civic cultures communicate more continuously and more creatively with each other, helping to enlarge what anthropologist Clifford Geertz describes as the universe of human discourse and enriching the quality of life for all of us" (Poston and Boyer 1992).

The core argument of this chapter can be summarized as follows. The rise of Impact Investing presents opportunities and challenges to contemporary universities and could help to shape and establish what constitutes the identity of a "university" in the twenty-first century. If the university of the nineteenth century was governed primarily by a teaching and education mission and that of the twentieth century by a research mission, the university of the twenty-first century will be driven by a prosocial engagement mission in which Impact Investing could be the accelerator of this epic transformation.

This study is based on a literature review and semi-structured interviews, featuring a series of mini-case studies and organizational vignettes. More specifically, besides desk research, two one-hour Skype interviews were conducted with the co-founder and executive director of Intentional Endowments Network, and Chief Executive Officer (CEO) of Net Impact to get their first-hand knowledge and experience.

The remainder of this chapter will explore the implications of this scholarship of engagement for enhancing the contribution of the university to the development of Impact Investing as part of the wider "third mission" of the sector, both in general terms and with respect to specific case illustrations of good practice.

THE ENTREPRENEURIAL UNIVERSITY

The term "Entrepreneurial University" can be traced back to Etzkowitz (1983), who used the term to describe those universities that developed and implemented a range of activities beyond the traditional core of teaching and research, to contribute to regional development and increase their incomes. Very quickly, this idea became associated with a very particular set of activities based around university technology transfer (Dill 1995), innovation (Clark 1998; Van Vught 1999), and academic entrepreneurship (Shane 2004; Siegel and Wright 2015). While much of this literature enthusiastically promoted this new role of the university, there were also concerns raised about the extent to which marketization and the rise of "academic capitalism" would compromise in the longer term the fundamental mission of the university (Slaughter and Leslie 1997).

However, there is no one-size-fits-all definition of the Entrepreneurial University, and a clear-cut definition is also unlikely to be achievable considering that the diversity of entrepreneurial approaches is one of the concept's most essential characteristics (Fayolle and Redford 2015).[1] Notwithstanding

---

[1] See Table 27.1 for a summary of various definitions.

the concerns raised, it is clear that the increasing importance of knowledge in the technical and social dimensions of today's world provides greater relevance to the Entrepreneurial University (Table 27.1). In this context, universities transcend their traditional focus on teaching and basic research to carry out technology transfer, marketing ideas, patent registrations, undertake consultancy, continuing education, and professional development, and incorporate spin-off companies that contribute to industrial innovation, economic growth, and job creation. They do so as anchors for and drivers of the knowledge economy and increasingly are seen as the focal point of indigenous bottom-up economic development, especially at local and regional scales (Goddard and Vallance 2011). Increasingly, these "third streams" activities are being added to a number of new activities to support the development of a prosocial orientation in the sector, including support for Impact Investing. However, not all universities do or can make the same contribution to economic development. As the OECD (2007) demonstrated in a 14-country, five-continent study, the economic impact of the university sector was a function of the historically formed industrial character of the regional and national economy, the extent to which higher education was formally incorporated into economic development policy, and the institutional makeup of the higher education system itself.

Recent literature suggests that universities can be entrepreneurial in two ways. First, *academic entrepreneurship* emphasizes the commercialization of research findings and knowledge generated (Klofsten and Jones-Evans 2000; Roessner, Bond, Okubo, and Planting 2013). This allowed universities to connect its third mission to research by becoming knowledge hubs (Youtie and Shapira 2008), a process that is not without criticism given the challenges and opportunities arising from technology transfer (Powell and Smith-Dor 2003). Second, the university's teaching function can be linked to its third mission through *entrepreneurial education* (Gibb and Hannon 2006; Gibb and Haskins 2018), resulting in the building of entrepreneurial capability (Altmann and Ebersberger 2013).

Given this, we argue that the Entrepreneurial University can and should go beyond its institutional form and multifaceted process and orientation. A change or evolution of the mission accordingly can lead to the creation of new institutional frameworks and entities within the university, and the development of new activities, relationships, and positions internally and externally. For the purpose of this chapter, we set the discussion of Impact Investing within the European guiding framework for Entrepreneurial Universities (i.e. HEInnovate) published by OECD and the European Commission, which includes the principal attributes and key parameters of

TABLE 27.1 Definitions of an Entrepreneurial University.

Year	Author	Definition
1983	Etzkowitz	An Entrepreneurial University is a university that is "considering new sources of funds like patents, research funded by contracts and entry into a partnership with private enterprises."
1995	Chrisman, Hynes, and Fraser	An Entrepreneurial University involves "the creation of new business ventures by university professors, technicians, or students."
1998	Röpke	An Entrepreneurial University has three different meanings: the university itself, the members of the university faculty, and the interaction of the university with the environment.
1999	Subotzky	An Entrepreneurial University is characterized by closer university-business partnerships, by greater faculty responsibility for accessing external sources' of funding and by a managerial ethos in institutional governance, leadership, and planning
2002	Kirby	An Entrepreneurial University has the ability to innovate, recognize, and create opportunities, work in teams, take risks, and respond to challenges.
2003	Etzkowitz	An Entrepreneurial University is a natural incubator, providing support structures for teachers and students to initiate new ventures: intellectual, commercial, and conjoint.
2006	Guerrero-Cano, Kirby, and Urbano	An Entrepreneurial University has the ability to innovate, recognize, and create opportunities, work in teams, take risks and respond to challenges (Kirby 2002), on its own, seeks to work out a substantial shift in organizational character so as to arrive at a more promising posture for the future (Clark 1998). In other words, a natural incubator that provides support structures for teachers and students to initiate new ventures: intellectual, commercial, and conjoint (Etzkowitz 2003).
2012	OECD	An Entrepreneurial University has eight pillars: leadership and governance, organizational capacity, people and incentives, entrepreneurship development in teaching and learning, pathways for entrepreneurs, university–business/external relationships for knowledge exchange, Entrepreneurial University as an internationalized institution, and measuring the impact of the Entrepreneurial University.
2017	Etzkowitz	An Entrepreneurial University enhances the research university by joining a reverse linear dynamic moving from problems in industry and society, seeking solutions in academia, to the classic forward linear model, producing serendipitous innovations from the meandering stream of basic research.

Source: Adapted from Guerrero-Cano, Kirby, and Urbano (2006) with more recent developments.

higher-education institutions. As a self-assessment tool, this aims to help universities to determine their strengths and weaknesses in the context of effectively contributing to their local and national environments.

THE ROLE OF AN ENTREPRENEURIAL UNIVERSITY

Local and Regional Economic Growth

Activities facilitated by institutions can be viewed as the driving force to boost economic growth and prosperity (Guerrero, Cunningham, and Urbano 2015), and universities are no exceptions. An Entrepreneurial University based on the principles of engaged scholarship could contribute even more as it provides new alternatives to identify entrepreneurial opportunities (Guerrero and Urbano 2010) and the creation of "entrepreneurial capital" (Erikson 2002). Previous studies have evidenced the economic impact of university teaching, research, or entrepreneurial activities by adopting different theoretical approaches and methodologies (Drucker and Goldstein 2007; Goddard and Vallance 2011). Guerrero, Cunningham, and Urbano (2015) conducted an exploratory study using data collected from 2005 to 2007 for 147 universities located in the United Kingdom. Their analysis demonstrates positive and significant economic results of teaching, research, and entrepreneurial activities through the development of various types of capital (e.g. human capital, knowledge capital, social capital, and entrepreneurial capital). More specifically, according to this research, "the higher economic impact of the United Kingdom's Entrepreneurial Universities (the Russell Group) is explained by entrepreneurial spin-offs," while for the rest of the country's universities, "the highest economic impact is associated with knowledge transfer (knowledge capital)." The unique roles that an Entrepreneurial University plays in the sphere of Impact Investing generate "impact capital," which has a multiplier effect on economic contribution and regional development. A conceptual framework (see Figure 27.1) is proposed to illustrate the economic impact of an Entrepreneurial University through the Theory of Change.[2]

Social Responsibility and Sustainable Development

While the critical role of universities in contemporary society has been widely acknowledged, most literature emphases its economic contribution

---

[2]A Theory of Change explains the process of change by outlining causal linkages in an intervention (i.e. its shorter-term, intermediate, and longer-term outcomes).

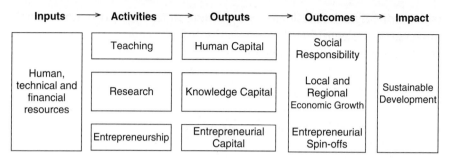

FIGURE 27.1   A Conceptualization of the Theory of Change of an Entrepreneurial University. *Source*: Adapted from Guerrero, Cunningham, and Urbano (2015).

(Leisyte and Horta 2011; Audretsch 2012; Pinheiro, Langa, and Pausits 2015), perceiving universities as commoditized knowledge producers, economic entities, shapers of human capital, and actors in networks (Boucher, Conway and Van Der Meer 2003). However, an Entrepreneurial University is not merely an engine for economic growth. Instead, it is required to take part in more social and environmental responsibilities and contribute to sustainable development on the assumption that it is a shared responsibility to foster a better environment and create a fairer society. As highlighted by UNESCO's Chief for Higher Education, Peter Wells, "Perhaps never before in recent history has the role of higher education been so intricately tied to the economic, social and environmental fabric of the modern world" (Wells 2017). The societal challenges we are facing nowadays demand broader roles of Entrepreneurial Universities and call for a renewed understanding of them. That these roles increasingly reach beyond the traditional academic roles of teaching and research and the more recent economic mission is clear: not only are universities "the most important site of interconnectivity in what is now a knowledge society," they are "a key institution for the formation of cultural and technological citizenship" and "a site of public debate, thus reversing the decline of the public sphere" (Delanty 2001).

It is within this context that some new concepts have been raised by various scholars as a response, such as "responsible research and innovation" in higher education (Monsonís-Payá, García-Melón, and Lozano 2017), a university ecology (Wright 2016), and "civic university" (Goddard, Hazelkorn, Kempton, and Vallance 2016). The notion that a university actively and continually negotiates its relationships with myriad of governing, economic, and civil organizations reflects the complexity of the contemporary role of universities in creating a sustainable and resilient society. The civil society and ecology models also offer valuable insights into how individuals could participate in developing responsible research and innovation (RRI) in higher education. This "seeks to bring issues related to research and innovation into the open, to anticipate their consequences, and to involve society in discussing how science and technology can help create the kind of world and society we want for generations to come" (RRI Tools 2019).

Drawing upon the research on a university's societal engagement, from a narrow focus on economic functions to its broad social and environmental roles, we argue that while academic capitalism and commercialization were probably the dominant motif of the last quarter of the twentieth century, social responsibility and sustainable development have become the emerging motif for the Entrepreneurial University in the first quarter of the twenty-first century. This has at least two implications. First, it means a university needs to manage entrepreneurship to ensure its positive social and environmental impact (e.g. financial inclusion, poverty alleviation, supporting vulnerable groups, and social sectors). The ability to discover novel solutions to enable more efficient use of resources and services and to address market and government failures is one of the key features of an Entrepreneurial University, which helps to establish an enterprising environment to repurpose the utilization of existing and new research and knowledge. Despite the common (mis)perception that most entrepreneurship produces positive changes, it could generate negative effects if used in the wrong way, and there is a long tradition of research highlighting the "dark side" of entrepreneurship and its consequences for individuals and society (Kets de Vries 1985; Baumol 1996; Shepherd 2019). Therefore, entrepreneurship needs to be managed appropriately by universities to ensure it benefits social welfare in both financial and nonfinancial aspects.

The second implication is that a university itself is required to be more socially and environmentally responsible in the context of the triple bottom line, United Nations Sustainable Development Goals (SDGs), and Net-Zero. For example, in October 2019, Times Higher Education, a leading commentator on and analyst of the sector, announced that they would include all 17 SDGs in their 2020 University Impact Rankings (Ross 2019). Similarly, the Aspen Institute is a key catalyst to drive the change toward sustainable business education. For instance, between 2001 to 2012, they ranked the top sustainable Masters in Business Administration (MBAs) globally in Beyond Grey Pinstripes, an independent, biennial survey specifically targeted to assess how academic institutions prepare their students for tomorrow (Arevalo and Mitchell 2017).

As a robust and active network of "more than 160 leaders from colleges, universities, and other endowed nonprofits and their stakeholders, financial industry practitioners and academic experts," the Intentional Endowments Network (IEN) highlights which college endowments are being invested impactfully. It also connects and shares ideas and best practices on sustainable investing and student-managed funds through the SIILK (Sustainable & Impact Investing Learning & Knowledge) Network (Chin and Dyer 2018). It was mentioned in their 2019 Impact Report that based on a survey from 774 US colleges, universities, and affiliated foundations (with USD \$630 billion in total endowment assets), there was an 8% increase in assets that are managed with environmental, social, and governance (ESG) considerations from 2016 to 2018 (Ashley and Dinerman 2019). When interviewed about the role of contemporary universities, the co-founder of IEN[3] mentioned that besides financial capital, "universities have a unique resource—social capital, and they can leverage their influence as both investors and communities. People look up to them as holders of knowledge and credible public service institutions—trust and credibility are especially valuable nowadays. University's educational role is also important, so they have to walk the talk."

Net Impact's[4] CEO was also interviewed in the context of this work and reiterated the importance of engaged scholarship as well. He said that "rather than staying in the comfort zone and marginalizing students' need," universities must "respond fast to the exponential growth of Impact Investing and sustainability movement in general" and "put the students at the center of curriculum design and career training." Otherwise, students will "have to retool themselves to fill the gap between what they have learned in the ivory tower and what are required in the real world." Net Impact has made annual ratings of the best places and classes to learn about sustainability and has highlighted the curricula related to Impact Investing and related areas in 200 universities around the world (Net Impact 2019).

THREE MISSIONS OF AN ENTREPRENEURIAL UNIVERSITY IN IMPACT INVESTING

This brief profiling and analysis of the Entrepreneurial University allow us to position it within the context of Impact Investing for further analysis. The evolving relationship between capital markets and social well-being is a topic

---

[3] Interview with Georges Dyer, co-founder and executive director of Intentional Endowments Network, 7 February 2020.
[4] Interview with Peter Lupoff, chief executive officer of Net Impact, 7 February 2020.

attracting much global attention and research interest. The Global Social Impact Investment Steering Group, a task force set up by the G8 in 2015, claims that the twentieth-century risk-and-return approach to investing will be replaced by a new model built on risk, return, and impact. The European Union (EU) has also been proactively supporting the SDGs and the Paris Climate Agreement by advocating Sustainable Finance since 2015 and put together the Action Plan in 2018 (Eur-lex 2018).

Impact Investing is at the frontier of sustainable finance and has experienced significant growth in the most recent five years, topping USD $502 billion in early 2019 (Mudaliar and Dithrich 2019). J.P. Morgan and the Rockefeller Foundation have conducted research and argue that Impact Investing will be "one of the most powerful changes in the asset management industry" and estimated that up to USD $1 trillion could be devoted to impact investments by 2020. While practitioners secure new deals and develop new tools, academics are still in the initial stages of establishing Impact Investing as a field of inquiry (Daggers and Nicholls 2016). To keep up with the rapid development of practice in the real world, there is an urgent call for related teaching, research, and entrepreneurial activities, which can make a distinctive contribution to the field of Impact Investing.

Audretsch (2012) claims that Entrepreneurial Universities have a greater responsibility than only producing and transferring knowledge; an Entrepreneurial University should lead to the creation of entrepreneurial thinking, actions, and institutions. Under this scenario, Entrepreneurial Universities have emerged as central actors playing an active role in promoting innovation, teaching, knowledge transfer, and entrepreneurship (Urbano and Guerrero 2013). Besides its traditional function in teaching and research, the "third mission" of the university, the need for entrepreneurial strategy without jeopardizing the teaching and research quality, is becoming unprecedentedly important. Impact Investing as an emerging field is a ripe ground for the Entrepreneurial University to play multiple roles through its research, curriculum development, extracurricular engagement activities, and direct action (see Table 27.2 for a summary of some current university initiatives related to Impact Investing).

The Entrepreneurial University can support Impact Investing in all the above mentioned three missions, and each mission can be linked to the seven pillars and their key parameters under the OECD Guiding Framework. However, not all the parameters equally support Impact Investing, and some of the more directly related ones have been illustrated in Table 27.3. The seventh feature of "measuring the impact of the Entrepreneurial University" should be integrated into every activity and therefore is not listed separately.

TABLE 27.2   Examples of Universities Involved in Areas Related to Impact Investing.

Main Focus	University	Initiatives Related to Impact Investing
Teaching	Duke University, Durham, NC	CASE: Center for the Advancement of Social Entrepreneurship; Impact Investing Program
	INSEAD, France	Research, curriculum, and partnerships
	Nanyang Technological University, Singapore	Social impact club and Impact Investing panel
Research	Carleton University, Canada	Carleton Centre for Community Innovation
	Georgetown University, Washington, DC	Beeck Center for Social Impact and Innovation
	Heidelberg University, Germany	Centre for Social Investment (CSI)
	National University of Singapore, Singapore	Asia Centre for Social Entrepreneurship and Philanthropy (ACSEP)
	Politecnico di Milano, Italy	International Research Centre for Social and Impact Innovation (TIRESIA)
	University of Cape Town, South Africa	Research Base; Partnership; Social Impact Bonds
	University of New South Wales, Swinburne University of Technology, The University of Western Australia, Australia	Centre for Social Impact
	University of Oxford, UK	Skoll Centre for Social Entrepreneurship; Training and programs

TABLE 27.2   (*continued*)

Main Focus	University	Initiatives Related to Impact Investing
Entrepreneurship	Cambridge University, UK	Commitment to addressing climate change in its £3bn endowment fund
	Glasgow Caledonian University, UK	Ashoka U Changemaker Campus
	Harvard University, Cambridge, MA	IRI: The Initiative for Responsible Investment
	University of Chicago, Booth Business School	Training, competition, internship/partnership, awards/scholarship
	University of Edinburgh, UK	Investment of £1.5 million in Big Issue Invest; Support for social enterprises; Courses and competitions
	University of Northampton, UK	Investment in 2 Social Enterprise Investment Fund II (including £200,000 in the Big Issue Invest "Corporate Social Venture" Fund); Ashoka U Changemaker Campus
	University of Pennsylvania, Philadelphia	Wharton Social Impact Initiative
	University of St Gallen and Insper Business School, Switzerland, Brazil	Multidisciplinary and Cross-cultural Collaboration in Impact Investing: Meeting Point/Centre for Expertise; Industry Knowledge Platform; Front-line Experience

Source: Authors based on desk review.

What is clear from this scheme/approach is that academic initiatives related to Impact Investing are widespread. In the following paragraphs, we present several examples to elaborate on how Entrepreneurial Universities can play a role in various aspects of Impact Investing across continents through teaching, research, and entrepreneurship.

TABLE 27.3   OECD's Guiding Framework for Entrepreneurial Universities in the Field of Impact Investing.

#	Pillars	Key Parameters
A	Leadership and Governance	The university: a) has a model for coordinating and integrating Impact Investing related activities and events at all levels across the university. b) is a driving force for entrepreneurship development in the broader regional, social, and community environment.
B	Organizational Capacity, People, and Incentives	The university: a) has mechanisms in place for breaking down traditional boundaries and fostering new relationships in the area of Impact Investing, bringing internal stakeholders together (staff and students), and building synergies between them. b) has clear incentives and rewards for staff who actively support the university's Impact Investing agenda. c) gives status and recognition to other stakeholders who contribute to the university's Impact Investing agenda.
C	Entrepreneurship development in teaching and learning	The university: a) takes an entrepreneurial approach to teach Impact Investing related content in all departments, promoting diversity and innovation in teaching and learning. b) encourages collaborations and engagement with external stakeholders in the field of Impact Investing, which is a key component of teaching and learning development. c) integrates research results on Impact Investing in education and training.

TABLE 27.3 *(continued)*

#	Pillars	Key Parameters
D	Pathways for entrepreneurs	The university: a) raises awareness of the value of developing entrepreneurial abilities amongst staff and students in the area of Impact Investing. b) provides support for individuals and groups to move from entrepreneurial ideas to action. c) makes the resource of mentoring by academic and Impact Investing industry personnel available. d) facilitates access to private financing for its potential entrepreneurs. e) provides access to business incubation facilities.
E	University–business/external relationships for knowledge exchange	The university: a) is committed to collaboration and knowledge exchange with industry, society, and the public about Impact Investing. b) demonstrates active involvement in partnerships and relationships with various stakeholders in Impact Investing. c) has strong links with incubators, science parks, and other external initiatives, creating opportunities for dynamic knowledge exchange in Impact Investing. d) links research, education, and industry (wider community) activities together to affect the whole knowledge ecosystem Impact Investing.

Source: Adapted from the OECD Entrepreneurial Universities Framework (2012).

*A university can assess itself on a scale of 0-10 for each parameter, and then use the Guiding Framework and accompanying material as a way of working on areas where improvement is considered a priority.

Duke University (US)

The Center for the Advancement of Social Entrepreneurship (CASE) at Duke University's Fuqua School of Business was founded in 2001 and was one of the first MBA centers focused on the role of enterprise in solving social problems. Ten years later, in 2011, a signature initiative on Impact Investing was created with the approval of the CASE advisory board and the dean's office. In the same year, a new initiative alongside a new global advisory board was announced at the Social Capital Markets (SOCAP) Conference with a significant project grant from the Rockefeller Foundation. One year later, USD $1 million was raised, and another USD $10 million was raised 24 months afterwards, in partnership with others inside and outside of Duke (Drexler and Noble 2014).

Since 2001, Duke University has received funding from more than 20 partners, including foundations, financial institutions, investor networks, as well as individuals. Their collaboration network expands across the entire spectrum of Impact Investing, from mainstream investment banks and funds to business angel investors, to technological and social innovators on the front lines working on almost every continent. More than 850 Fuqua MBA students are taught about Impact Investing, and over 600 practitioners at global meetings are convened to help the establishment of a database, including 8,000 impact enterprises. They have also advised policymakers at the White House regarding how to make advancements in this field.

Building upon previous successes and its core research capabilities, CASE newly launched another signature program, the Social Entrepreneurship Accelerator at Duke (SEAD), as part of the US Agency for International Development (USAID), to help entrepreneurs specialized in global health to scale their impact. This is achieved through partnership with internal colleagues at Duke (e.g. the Duke Global Health Institute, Duke Medicine, and the International Partnership on Innovative Healthcare Delivery), and external experts globally (e.g. Investors' Circle, and the USAID mission in East Africa). Academics, practitioners, entrepreneurs, investors, and policymakers are engaged to help ask and answer questions on how to scale up global health outcomes and share their insights and experience in both enterprise development and investing. Duke University has also gone one step further by leveraging its role as employer—it has operated a test program employee benefit to educate and partially fund energy efficiency improvements for administrators, faculty, and staff.

The University of St Gallen and Insper Business School (Switzerland and Brazil)

In 2012, Impact Investing Latin America (IILA) Knowledge Platform was launched as a joint initiative between the University of St Gallen in Switzerland through its hub office in São Paulo and Insper Business School in Brazil. The platform aims to facilitate the development of Impact Investing in Brazil. Initial projects included impact measurement, hybrid investment models, and business support for impact entrepreneurs, which were fine-tuned after the 2nd Impact Investing Conference, held in August 2013 in São Paulo. Several major challenges were highlighted by academics, entrepreneurs, and investors to promote Impact Investing in Brazil: unavailability of investment data; lack of legal framework and transparency; absence of standardization and necessary knowledge to make investment decisions; conservation of individual project information; and reluctance to share, collaborate, and innovate (Drexler and Noble 2014).

To address those issues, the student body was utilized as the initial central component of the interdisciplinary platform. After the platform was launched, a continuously increasing number of students from different areas of studies have approached them to join front-line projects in Latin America. Over 20 students from different backgrounds are currently conducting their Master's or PhD theses in the area of Impact Investing. IILA also provides a neutral, not-for-profit research-oriented space that goes beyond academic circles and has implemented an initiative for impact measurement for public policy, called Insper Metricis. Cooperation between the two universities relies on a steering committee that spans both universities' Impact Investing initiatives following the platform's three fundamental values: partnership with local partners, prioritization of front-line research, and systematic engagement among different stakeholders.

The success of the platform has encouraged other organizations to join, such as the Centre for Organization Studies of the School of Business and Economics of the University of São Paulo (FEA-USP). Their aim is to develop a scheme to assess the impact of projects supported by a development bank in the area of family farming; the Humanistic Management Center (Switzerland) as a sounding board for the IILA Knowledge Platform; the BMW Foundation for potential projects in the area of intrapreneurship and for engaging privately owned foundations; and Oikos, a student association for sustainable economics and management.

University of Edinburgh (United Kingdom)

The University of Edinburgh has been proactively supporting social entrepreneurship and Impact Investing in terms of financial support, incubation, visa endorsement, mentoring, training, and pitch competition, to name but a few. For instance, the Sustainable Business Initiative (SBI) is based within its business school, which is a signatory of the Principles for Responsible Management Education (PRME), the first organized relationship among the United Nations and management-related academic institutions, business schools, and universities. SBI hosts frequent talks, events, career fairs and delivers the Masterclass of Advance Sustainability Programme.

In addition to its annual Start-up Festival Week and regular Entrepreneurship Club activities, the university has a Make Your Mark Event. This is a 48-hour challenge for its undergraduate students to create a business that has a positive social impact by tackling inequality (e.g. homelessness, child labor, gender equality, access to clean water, isolation and loneliness in an aging society, financial literacy, fuel poverty, and sustainable energy). All of these provide an opportunity of idea exchange and inspiration, as well as a platform of networking and collaboration among students, faculty, practitioners, investors, policymakers, and other stakeholders.

Moreover, the University of Edinburgh makes direct investments into funds and social enterprises to demonstrate its commitment. The University of Edinburgh was the first university in Europe to become a member of Principles for Responsible Investment, which is a UN-backed initiative aimed at making the global financial system more sustainable. Since 2017, it has invested £1.5 million into a new partnership with the Big Issue Group (Social Enterprise Investment Fund II) that seeks to dismantle poverty and create the opportunity for people and communities across the United Kingdom. Social Enterprise Investment Fund II (SEIF II) "invests in social enterprises and charities that are finding innovative solutions to tackle some of the toughest social problems…including homelessness, social and financial exclusion, and youth unemployment." It is the largest financial investment in social enterprise ever made by a UK university, and this latest investment is "part of Edinburgh's continuing commitment to making a significant, sustainable, and socially responsible contribution to Scotland, the UK, and the world" (University of Edinburgh 2017).

In 2018, the university started to invest £10,000 per year for five years into a social enterprise named Prosper Social Finance, UK's first student-run socially responsible investment fund. At its core, Prosper challenges the traditional perceptions of finance and aims to make investment more compassionate and approachable. They are achieving this goal through four channels: first, creating a responsible investment portfolio underpinned by ESG criteria and Prosper 's values; second, generating positive social and environmental impact by investing all profits from investment into local charities or social enterprises; third, providing training and workshops to empower students with the necessary knowledge and skills, thus making finance more inclusive and accessible; and last but not least, building a community to raise people's awareness and promote collective actions toward a more sustainable world (e.g. Zero Waste Campus Campaign).

University of Cape Town (South Africa)

The University of Cape Town in South Africa established the Bertha Centre for Social Innovation and Entrepreneurship in 2011 as the first academic center in Africa dedicated to social innovation, primarily focusing on education innovation, inclusive health innovation, and policy and scaling. In order to develop a local impact-focused, social investment market in Sub-Saharan Africa, they have built the Innovative Finance Initiative to operate independently and partner with investors around the globe.

A good example of their attempt to conduct practical research with a tangible outcome is their work in social impact bonds (SIB).[5] Based on the belief that outcome-based contracts facilitated by SIBs present great opportunity in Africa, and the notion that South Africa is an excellent testing ground for the funding concept given its sophisticated financial market and strong imperative to improve cross-sector service delivery, they have identified the South African National Treasury as an essential gatekeeper in government's capability to structure the bonds and have been working closely with them from the start of the research. An advisory board was created to include both public stakeholders and potential private funders. The Bertha Centre has also been working with provincial governments most likely to commission the SIBs to explore topics that are the most attractive (e.g. early childhood development, education, business development services, and health). In addition, efforts were made to involve service providers in their research through information sessions, roundtables, and individual meetings as outcome-based financing tools may seem threatening to them.

As a result, the initial feasibility study on SIBs in business development services in South Africa was published in 2014. Bertha Centre now has several

---

[5]See Chapter 14, "Social Impact Bonds: Promises and Results," by Maria Basilio.

ongoing projects funded by the government and private parties relating to outcome-based payments and is preparing an Innovation Fund for the near future (Drexler and Noble 2014).

National University of Singapore (Singapore)

As a thriving global financial hub with a liberal investment landscape, Singapore is well poised to lead socially responsible investment in the region with international nonprofit organizations and development finance institutions running their regional operations from Singapore. It has also become a hub for impact funds, such as Blue Orchard, Bamboo Capital, and Insitor Impact Asia Fund, to help investors direct resources into social enterprises (Prakash and Teo 2019).

In the meantime, the social enterprise movement in Singapore has grown rapidly, led by several organizations, such as the Singapore Centre for Social Enterprise (raiSE) and the Asia Centre for Social Entrepreneurship and Planning (ACSEP). Founded in 2011, ACSEP, a research center situated at the National University of Singapore, primarily focused on rigorous and multidisciplinary research on Asian social entrepreneurship and philanthropy in order to build capacity in the social sector. Through the support and collaboration with various stakeholders and partners and the adoption of a "two-pronged approach" to education and research, they "hope to influence thinking and inspire social innovation that enables a more vibrant, inclusive, and equitable future for all" (Asia Centre for Social Entrepreneurship and Philanthropy [ACSEP] 2020). The programs delivered by ACSEP include impact assessment and social performance management, strategic philanthropy and effective giving, social innovation and social entrepreneurship, and 200 years of philanthropy in Singapore.

FROM TOP-DOWN TO BOTTOM-UP

Besides the more formalized top-down approach through the establishment of research centers and the design of new curricula, there are also bottom-up initiatives to facilitate and boost the development in this area. Universities can lead as part of a multisector approach to global problem solving, including in finance and capital markets. The multi-form student-led Impact Investing club is a case in point, which has become a trend across a number of universities in the United States.

For example, the Impact Investing club at the University of Michigan started in 2017 with a research division but has since grown tremendously to three divisions: research, consulting, and microfinance. They have an Impact Microfinance Fund, which aims to provide micro-loans to social entrepreneurs local to the Ann Arbor/Detroit communities that face capital barriers to drive revitalization and new opportunities and are hosting the 2nd Annual Michigan Impact Investing Symposium in April 2020. Similarly, Darden's Impact Investing Club (DIIC) is a student-run venture fund, which operates independently and is responsible for its own affairs and activities. It does not belong to any part of the university, although most members are University of Virginia students and employees. DIIC supports and partners with innovative for-profit enterprises to generate both financial and social/environmental returns.

Harvard students are even more enthusiastic, as both the Business School (HBS) and Kennedy School have their own Impact Investing clubs. While the HBS Impact Investing club equips their members with the necessary knowledge and skills as successful impact investors across a full spectrum of investing—from established ESG investing in public equities to venture-stage start-ups—the HKS Impact Investing club gives more emphasis on building the body of knowledge and foster relationships between the students, the broader community, and the Impact Investing sector.

Financial institutions have been actively engaging and partnering with universities in various ways. For instance, each year since 2011, in order to help address critical environmental, social, and governance issues, Morgan Stanley's Institute for Sustainable Investing and Northwestern University's Kellogg School of Management invite graduate students from all over the world to submit their ideas of investment vehicles and innovative financing. In 2019, "365 students from 80 graduate schools submitted investment prospectuses targeting sustainability and impact challenges in 31 countries. The growth in overall proposals submitted and the breadth of the problems they aim to address underscores that a new generation of investment leaders view finance as a critical tool for helping solve global challenges" (Morgan Stanley 2020).

Another example is the MBA Impact Investing Network and Training (MIINT), a "year-long experiential program designed to give students at business and graduate schools a hands-on education in Impact Investing" (Wharton School 2020). This is a collaboration between Wharton Social Impact and Bridges Impact Foundation, during which students would assess early-stage impact venture capital deals, and therefore learn about how to integrate social/environmental impact into the entire investment process.

RECOGNITION OF THE BOUNDARY OF A UNIVERSITY'S INTERVENTION

In exploring the actual and potential intervention of the universities in promoting and supporting the development of Impact Investing, we recognize that while Entrepreneurial Universities present great potential in multiple aspects of Impact Investing and regional economic development, as well as decarbonization, poverty reduction, gender empowerment, financial inclusion, and so forth, it also needs to be aware of the hazard that may come alongside the privileges conferred by an academic institution. Specifically, "where is the appropriate boundary of a university center in terms of the market building" is a question that should be asked and carefully thought about despite the pride of being a "do tank," not just a "think tank." This role of educator, neutral convener, and source of credible knowledge is based on operating within the sphere of a university. If a university strays too far outside that realm, does it risk its legitimacy and neutrality? How could a university achieve an optimal balance among its three missions, are there best practices or each must find its own unique way? One of the ways to circumvent and mitigate these risks is through partnerships with other public and private organizations, as illustrated in previous examples.

The rise of Impact Investing offers both new opportunities and challenges for the university. How it responds will, in large measure, shape what it means to be a "university" in the twenty-first century. As we have already argued in this chapter, the nature and role of the university are changing. The university of the nineteenth century was governed primarily by a teaching and education mission and that of the twentieth century by a research mission. The university of the twenty-first century, however, is increasingly being driven by a prosocial engagement mission in which the development, analysis, and evaluation of its own Impact Investing activities and that of others will play an important role.

CONCLUSION

Impact Investing is an exciting yet complex field that has attracted some of the brightest and best minds in the areas of philanthropy, finance, social entrepreneurship, nonprofit management, and policymaking. Using the Entrepreneurial University as a framing construct, this chapter has explored the emerging role and potential of the university in building capacity for Impact Investing through both its teaching and research functions and, in particular, through the demonstration effect of its activity as an impact investor itself. Drawing on a series of mini-case studies and organizational vignettes, we recognize both the great potential of the Entrepreneurial University across multiple aspects of Impact Investing, which we see as an extension to its role in regional economic growth, social responsibility, and sustainable development.

However, the road toward a socially responsible Entrepreneurial University is not all rosy, and there are certain challenges today and tomorrow. In particular, this chapter highlights the importance of mission-lock in an Entrepreneurial University, as some of the previously mentioned activities may conflict with universities' own values and sit in opposition to the values of social investment. The changing nature of contemporary universities is one in which the tension between rigor and relevance is increasingly being resolved in favor of relevance as engaged scholarship, evidence-based research, and practitioner-led Mode 2 type research become more prevalent. But as universities broaden the range of their engagement and impact activities—for example, through company-sponsored consultancy projects—they potentially face goal and aspiration conflicts with their external clients. At its best, these may be high-profile benchmark projects, successful in competing for funding with other types of institutions. However, they may also be designed to produce a report in favor of the sponsor.

In the spirit of engaged scholarship, we recognize that often significant differences remain as to the definition and understanding of Impact Investing in the academic and practitioner communities (Höchstädter and Scheck 2015). Accordingly, we advocate that in this rapidly emerging area, academics ought to work together with practitioners who are eager to learn, open for collaboration, and willing to exchange and share practices and insights within an enlarged Impact Investing community. Only through a joint effort of both private and public sectors through partnerships (e.g. exchange platform, academics, and practitioners' symposium, Impact Investing fund competition, training, and career fairs) can an enabling ecosystem for Impact Investing be created and promoted. In a broader sense, we believe these arguments are equally applicable and crucial to constructing meaningful business education in the twenty-first century, which can catalyze both the social and financial innovation required to tackle the growing global challenges.

REFERENCES

Altmann, A., and Ebersberger, B. (2013). *Universities in Change: Managing Higher Education Institutions in the Age of Globalization*. New York: Springer.

Arevalo, J., and Mitchell, S. (2017). *Handbook of Sustainability in Management Education*. Cheltenham, UK: Edward Elgar Publishing Limited, p. 420.

Ashley, G., and Dinerman, D. (2020). *Endowments Investing for a Thriving, Sustainable Economy: Impact Report 2019*. Intentional Endowment Network. https://d3n8a8pro7vhmx.cloudfront.net/intentionalendowments/pages/5253/attachments/original/1582043409/IEN_Impact_Report_2019_FINAL.pdf?1582043409 (accessed 12 March 2020).

Asia Centre for Social Entrepreneurship & Philanthropy (ACSEP). (2020). *About ACSEP: Asia Centre for Social Entrepreneurship & Philanthropy (ACSEP)*. https://bschool.nus.edu.sg/acsep/aboutus/thought-leadership/ (accessed 12 March 2020).

Audretsch, D. (2012). From the Entrepreneurial University to the University for the Entrepreneurial Society. *Journal of Technology Transfer* 39(3): 313–321.

Baumol, W. (1996). Entrepreneurship: Productive, Unproductive, and Destructive. *Journal of Business Venturing* 11(1): 3–22.

Boucher, G., Conway, C., and Van Der Meer, E. (2003). Tiers of Engagement by Universities in Their Region's Development. *Regional Studies* 37(9): 887–897.

Chin, S., and Dyer, G. (2020). *IEN_Student Managed SRI Fund Toolkit*. Intentional Endowment Network. https://d3n8a8pro7vhmx.cloudfront.net/intentionalendowments/pages/51/attachments/original/1558553881/IEN_Student-ManagedSRIFund_toolkit_%283%29.pdf?1558553881 (Accessed 12 March 2020).

Clark, B. (1998). *Creating Entrepreneurial Universities*. Oxford: Pergamon.

Daggers, J., and Nicholls, A. (2016). *The Landscape of Social Impact Investment Research: Trends and Opportunities*. Eureka. http://eureka.sbs.ox.ac.uk/7019/1/Landscape-of-social-impact-investment-research.pdf (accessed 12 March 2020).

Delanty, G. (2001). *Challenging Knowledge: The University in the Knowledge Society*. Maidenhead: Society for Research into Higher Education and Open University Press.

Dill, D. (1995). University-Industry Entrepreneurship: The Organization and Management of American University Technology Transfer Units. *Higher Education* 29(4): 369–384.

Deloitte. (2017). The 2017 Deloitte Millennial Survey. https://www2.deloitte.com/content/dam/Deloitte/global/Documents/About-Deloitte/gx-deloitte-millennial-survey-2017-executive-summary.pdf (Accessed 12 March 2020).

Diexler, M., and Noble, A. (2014). *From Ideas to Practice, Pilots to Strategy II Practical Solutions and Actionable Insights on How to Do Impact Investing*. Weforum.org. http://www3.weforum.org/docs/WEF_ImpactInvesting_Report_FromIdeastoPractice_II.pdf (accessed 12 March 2020).

Drucker, J., and Goldstein, H. (2007). Assessing the Regional Economic Development Impacts of Universities: A Review of Current Approaches. *International Regional Science Review* 30(1): 20–46.

Erikson, T. (2002). Entrepreneurial Capital: The Emerging Venture's Most Important Asset and Competitive Advantage. *Journal of Business Venturing* 17(3): 275–290.

Etzkowitz, H. (1983). Entrepreneurial Scientists and Entrepreneurial Universities in American Academic Science. *Minerva*, 21(2-3), pp.198–233.

Etzkowitz, H. (2003). Research Groups as "Quasi-Firms": The Invention of the Entrepreneurial University. *Research Policy*, 32(1), pp.109–121.

Etzkowitz, H. (2017). Innovation Lodestar: The Entrepreneurial University in a Stellar Knowledge Firmament. *Technological Forecasting and Social Change* 123: 122–129.

Eur-lex. (2018). *Action Plan: Financing Sustainable Growth*. https://eur-lex.europa.eu/legal-content/EN/TXT/?uri=CELEX:52018DC0097 (accessed 12 March 2020).

Fayolle, A., and Redford, D. (2015). Introduction: Towards more entrepreneurial universities—myth or reality? In A. Fayolle and D. Redford (eds.), *Handbook on the Entrepreneurial University*. Cheltenham: Edward Elgar Publishing Limited.

Foss, L., and Gibson, D. (2015). The Entrepreneurial University: Context and institutional change. In *Routledge Studies in Innovation, Organizations and Technology*. New York: Routledge, p. 2.

From Ideas to Practice, Pilots to Strategy II. (2018). *Essential Steps to Building a University Impact Investing Programme: The Case of Duke University*. http://reports.weforum.org/impact-investing-from-ideas-to-practice-pilots-to-strategy-ii/5-growing-the-impact-investing-sector-what-universities-can-do/5-1-essential-steps-to-building-a-university-impact-investing-programme-the-case-of-duke-university/ (accessed 12 March 2020).

Gibb, A., and Hannon, P. (2006). Towards the Entrepreneurial University. *International Journal of Entrepreneurship Education* 4: 73–110.

Gibb, A., and Haskins, G. (2018). Key issues in the development of the entrepreneurial university of the future: Challenges, opportunities and responses. In R. Harrison and C. Leitch, ed., *Research Handbook on Entrepreneurship and Leadership*. London: Routledge, pp. 431–462.

Gibbons, M., Trow, M., Scott, P., Schwartzman, S., Nowotny, H., and Limoges, C. (1994). The New Production of Knowledge: The Dynamics of Science and Research in Contemporary Societies. *Contemporary Sociology* 24(6): 751. https://doi.org/10.2307/2076669.

Goddard, J., and Vallance, P. (2011). Universities and regional development. In A. Pike, P. Rodríguez, and J. Tomaney (eds.), *Handbook of Local and Regional Development*. London: Routledge.

Goddard, J., Hazelkorn, E., Kempton, L., and Vallance, P. (2016). *The Civic University*. Northampton, MA: Edward Elgar Pub.

Guerrero, M., Cunningham, J., and Urbano, D. (2015). Economic Impact of Entrepreneurial Universities' Activities: An Exploratory Study of the United Kingdom. *Research Policy* 44(3): 748–764.

Guerrero, M., and Urbano, D. (2010). The Development of an Entrepreneurial University. *Journal of Technology Transfer* 37(1): 43–74.

Guerrero-Cano, M., Kirby, D., and Urbano, D. (2006). A Literature Review on Entrepreneurial Universities: An Institutional Approach. *3rd Conference of Pre-communications to Congresses. Business Economic Department. Autonomous University of Barcelona*, p. 5.

Harrison, R., and Leitch, C. (eds.) (2018). *Research Handbook on Entrepreneurship and Leadership*. London: Routledge, pp. 431–462.

Höchstädter, A., and Scheck, B. (2015). What's in a Name: An Analysis of Impact Investing Understandings by Academics and Practitioners. *Journal of Business Ethics* 132(2): 449–475.

IBM. (2010). IBM Study: Education Lags in Preparing Students for Globalization and Sustainability. https://www-03.ibm.com/press/us/en/pressrelease/31937.wss (accessed 12 March 2020).

Jayaram, G. (2019). *Impact Investing Panel*. https://blogs.ntu.edu.sg/ (accessed 12 March 2020).

Kets de Vries, F. (1985). The Dark Side of Entrepreneurship. *Harvard Business Review* 63(6): 160–167.

Kirby, A. (2002). *Entrepreneurship*. Maidenhead: McGraw-Hill.

Klofsten, M., and Jones-Evan, D. (2000). Comparing Academic Entrepreneurship in Europa: The Case of Sweden and Ireland. *Small Business Economics* 14(4): 299–309.

Leisyte, L., and Horta, H. (2011). Introduction to a Special Issue: Academic Knowledge Production, Diffusion and Commercialization: Policies, Practices and Perspectives. *Science and Public Policy* 38(6): 422–424.

Lesjak, D. (2018). Improving Higher Education (Institutions) with the Matrix of Managerial and Financial Objectives. *Procedia: Social and Behavioral Sciences* 238: 249–258.

Monsonís-Payá, I., García-Melón, M., and Lozano, J. (2017). Indicators for Responsible Research and Innovation: A Methodological Proposal for Context-Based Weighting. *Sustainability* 9(12): 2168.

Morgan Stanley. (2020). The Challenge: Mobilizing Finance to Improve the World. https://www.morganstanley.com/ideas/kellogg-morgan-stanley-sustainable-investing-challenge-2019-finalists (accessed 12 March 2020).

Moss, G. (2018). *Cambridge University Throws Weight Behind Impact Investing.* https://www.ipe.com/countries/uk/cambridge-university-throws-weight-behind-impact-investing/www.ipe.com/countries/uk/cambridge-university-throws-weight-behind-impact-investing/10025406.fullarticle (accessed 12 March 2020).

Mudaliar, A., and Dithrich, H. (2019). *Sizing the Impact Investing Market.* https://thegiin.org/assets/Sizing%20the%20Impact%20Investing%20Market_webfile.pdf (accessed 12 March 2020).

Net Impact. (2019). *Guide to Business Schools for Social and Environmental Impact.* https://www.netimpact.org/sites/default/files/2017-2018-guide-to-b-schools-r1-2.pdf (accessed 12 March 2020).

OECD (2007). Higher Education and Regions: Globally Competitive, Locally Engaged. Paris, 2012. *OECD Entrepreneurial Universities Framework.* https://www.oecd.org/site/cfecpr/EC-OECD%20Entrepreneurial%20Universities%20Framework.pdf (accessed 12 March 2020).

Pinheiro, R., Langa, P., and Pausits, A. (2015). The Institutionalization of Universities' Third Mission: Introduction to the Special Issue. *European Journal of Higher Education* 5(3): 227–232.

Poston, L., and Boyer, E. (1992). Scholarship Reconsidered: Priorities of the Professoriate. *Academe* 78(4): 43.

Powell, W., and Smith-Dor, L. (2003). Networks and Economic life. *Journal of Economic Sociology* 4(3): 61–105.

Prakash, R., and Teo, K. (2019). *Singapore's Role in Social Investing in Asia: AVPN.* https://avpn.asia/blog/singapores-role-social-investing-asia/ (accessed 12 March 2020).

Ramaley, A. (2005). Scholarship for the public good: Living in Pasteur's quadrant. In A. Kezar, T. Chambers, and J. Burkhardt (eds.), *Higher Education for the Public Good.* San Francisco: Jossey Bass, p. 180.

Roessner, D., Bond, J., Okubo, S., and Planting, M. (2013). The Economic Impact of Licensed Commercialized Inventions Originating in University Research. *Research Policy* 42(1): 23–34.

Ross, D. (2019). *We're Including All 17 SDGs in the 2020 University Impact Rankings.* Times Higher Education. https://www.timeshighereducation .com/blog/were-including-all-17-sdgs-2020-university-impact-rankings (accessed 12 March 2020).

Rousseau, D. M. (2005). Evidence-based management in health care. In C. Korunka and P. Hoffmann (eds.), *Change and Quality in Human Service Work,* pp. 33–46. Munich: Hampp.

RRI Tools (2019. *About RRI: RRI Tools.* https://www.rri-tools.eu/about-rri (accessed 12 March 2020).

Schön, D. (1983). *The Reflective Practitioner: How Professionals Think in Action.* London: Temple Smith.

Shane, S. (2005). *Academic Entrepreneurship.* Cheltenham: Edward Elgar.

Shepherd, D. (2019). Researching the Dark Side, Downside, and Destructive Side of Entrepreneurship: It Is the Compassionate Thing to Do! *Academy of Management Discoveries* 5(3): 217–220.

Siegel, D., and Wright, M. (2015). Academic Entrepreneurship: Time for a Rethink? *British Journal of Management* 26(4): 582–595.

Slaughter, S., and Leslie, L. (1999). *Academic Capitalism.* Baltimore: Johns Hopkins University Press.

Taucean, I., Strauti, A., and Tion, M. (2018). Roadmap to Entrepreneurial University: Case Study. *Procedia: Social and Behavioral Sciences* 238: 582–589.

University of Edinburgh. (2017). *University Investment Will Be a Force for Social Good.* https://www.ed.ac.uk/news/2017/ps1m-investment-will-be-force-for-social-good (accessed 12 March 2020).

Urbano, D., and Guerrero, M. (2013). Entrepreneurial Universities: Socio-Economic Impacts of Academic Entrepreneurship in a European Region. *Economic Development Quarterly,* 27(1): 40–55.

Van de Ven, A. (2007). *Engaged Scholarship.* Oxford: Oxford University Press.

Van Vught, F. (1999). Innovative Universities. *Tertiary Education and Management* 5(4): 347–354.

Wells, J. (2017). UNESCO's introduction: The role of higher education institutions today. In: F. Grau, J. Goddard, B. Hall, E. Hazelkorn and R. Tandon, ed., *Higher Education in the World. Towards a Socially Responsible University: Balancing the Global with the Local.* Global University Network for Innovation (GUNI).

Wharton School. 2020. *Pitching for Impact: Results from the 8th Annual MIINT Competition: The Wharton School.* https://www.wharton.upenn.edu/story/pitching-for-impact-results-from-the-8th-annual-miint-competition/ (accessed 12 March 2020).

Wright, S. (2016). Universities in a Knowledge Economy or Ecology? Policy, Contestation and Abjection. *Critical Policy Studies*, 10(1): 59–78.

Youtie, J., and Shapira, P. (2008). Building an Innovation Hub: A Case Study of the Transformation of University Roles in Regional Technological and Economic Development. *Research Policy*, 37(8): 1188–1204.

A Road Map for Implementing Impact Investing: The Case of Multinational Companies

Filipa Pires de Almeida, MSc and Marta Bicho, PhD

Abstract

Impact Investing aims to create impact by responding to social and environmental issues while also generating financial returns. Impact Investing is rapidly growing as an investment strategy as companies find advantages in aligning business value creation with purposeful investment. The goal of this chapter is to understand how companies have been implementing Impact Investing strategies and to suggest best practices. Three multinational companies—General Electric Company, IKEA, and Unilever—were selected for an in-depth qualitative study using secondary data. These three companies were chosen because they already embraced Impact Investing strategies: aligning their core business, values, mission, and purpose with the generation of both impact (social and environmental returns) and profits. Each company's investment profile was analyzed in detail in order to identify the design, positive outcomes, and challenges of their unique Impact Investing strategies. Based on the evidential basis of this study, this chapter offers a road map for Impact Investing that can serve as a guide to preparing, implementing, and monitoring Impact Investing strategies. The road map comprises three anchors, *Underlying Conditions, Underlying Resources,* and *Impact Investing. Underlying Conditions* explains all the desirable elements a company should have in order to start the process of Impact Investing, while *Underlying Resources* comprises the possible tools and means to promote good planning and implementation. Finally, the third anchor *Impact Investing* suggests steps toward the implementation and compliance of a successful Impact Investing strategy. This chapter concludes with a menu of best practices drawn from the experiences of these multinational companies.

Keywords

Impact investing; Multinationals; Corporate Strategy; Corporate Social Responsibility; Sustainable Organizations; Responsible Business; Sustainability; Impact; General Electric; IKEA; Unilever

INTRODUCTION

Addressing social and environmental challenges is one of the biggest business opportunities of our times. Since no company can survive in a society that fails (van Tulder 2018), companies that are able to tackle social and environmental issues with profitable services and products can keep themselves ahead of the market, and by creating these competitive advantages they maintain profits and market leadership (van Tulder 2018).

While in the past, the responsibility for solving social problems was mostly ceded to governments and non-governmental organizations (NGOs) (Porter and Kramer 2011), today's increasing social inequities make up real risks for the private sector. By tackling social problems through core business operations, companies can grow their markets and keep their competitive edge (Porter and Kramer 2011; van Tulder 2018). Moreover, whereas in previous decades social enterprises were driven by their morals and values, in recent years companies have recognized that generating impact is good business. As such, companies are taking a central role toward contributing to world challenges (van Tulder 2018). Investing with a clear intention of creating social or environmental value is now perceived as one of the most profitable opportunities of our times. This kind of investment is known as

Impact Investing, which refers to investments that aim to generate positive outcomes regarding social or environmental value, in addition to financial profits (Daggers and Nicholls 2016; Global Impact Investing Network 2019).

While there are multiple actors in the Impact Investing ecosystem—including capital providers, companies, data providers, impact certification organizations—this study focuses on companies, and particularly companies that want to reform their traditional business models for greater social or environmental good. This study aims to shed light on how businesses can leverage higher profits by investing their capital in projects that are a benefit for their core business *and* society at large. This chapter draws on evidence from three multinational companies that have already embraced Impact Investing strategies: General Electric (GE), IKEA, and Unilever.

The analysis of these companies' Impact Investing strategies investigated: (i) the alignment of a company's investments with their stated strategy, purpose, and mission; (ii) the process of implementing Impact Investing instruments; (iii) how a company prioritized or chose well-suited Impact Investing instruments from the total list of options; and finally, (iv) impact measurement and financial returns. This chapter also reports the positive outcomes and challenges that arose from these three companies' Impact Investing processes, which contributes to the broader literature and understanding of the successes and challenges of implementing Impact Investing strategies in a corporate context.

The next section describes the methodology of the study. The following section is devoted to the theoretical concept of Impact Investing, and the next section is dedicated to company profiles. The following three sections contain the main findings, including the road map for Impact Investing and best practices for Impact Investing, which were built on the data and evidence presented in this chapter. The final section offers final remarks and concludes the chapter.

METHODOLOGY

The research question underlying this study is: *How are multinational companies implementing Impact Investing strategies?* The goal is to further understand the processes underlying the implementation of Impact Investing in a multinational corporate context, using case studies and secondary data to draw out best practices.

This study is qualitative,[1] and analyzes secondary data from three multinational companies, General Electric (GE), IKEA, and Unilever. The qualitative approach was chosen due to lack of comparable data resulting from the novelty of the subject (Ormiston et al. 2015). Additionally, a qualitative review enabled a deeper and more interpretative understanding of the implementation and challenges of Impact Investing strategies and instruments. The study relies on secondary data, mainly from published reports by the companies under analysis, as well as reports published by reputed consulting companies or higher education institutes. Data was collected between 2012 and 2020.

GE, IKEA, and Unilever were chosen because they already embraced Impact Investing strategies and were aligning their core business, values, mission, and purpose, with the generation of both impact (social and environmental returns) and profits. This choice was based on the following criteria, presented in order of importance: (i) the chosen companies are established firms with long-term visions and external openness, and they show a past track record of clear values, cultural beliefs, and leadership; (ii) given their status as multinational companies, the chosen companies have significant market power and consequently higher levels of influence on the economic ecosystem, as well on stakeholders along their value chain; (iii) they are part of the United Nations (UN) Global Compact, which is the world's largest corporate initiative aligned with the sustainable agenda;[2] and (iv) data availability, as multinationals they are required to make their reports publicly available and have relatively transparent information about their impact-driven initiatives.

Data analysis comprised the following steps: (i) an extensive desk review related to Impact Investing for the selected companies; (ii) identifying and selecting the key Impact Investing instruments[3] used by each company; and (iii) identifying the positive outcomes and challenges of the Impact Investing process for each company. This analysis attempted to discern the underlying

---

[1] Qualitative research is described as an "approach for exploring and understanding the meaning of individuals or groups" (Creswell 2014, p. 32). In contrast, quantitative research is related with metrics or numbers (Creswell 2014). Qualitative approaches can produce deep insights about complex issues resulting in more in-depth understanding of research issues.

[2] These companies participate in the United Nations' Global Compact. Unilever has participated since 2000, IKEA since 2004, and General Electric since 2008.

[3] Impact Investing instruments selected are based on the Impact Investing spectrum proposed by the European Venture Philanthropy Association (EVPA) (EVPA 2019; Sampaio 2014; Wendt 2018; OECD 2019; Wyman 2016), since EVPA's framework mapped the most relevant Impact Investing instruments.

reasons behind why impact investments were made, to determine the alignment of investments with each company's purpose, and to detail the Impact Investing implementation process undertaken by each company, as well as their subsequent measurement of impact and financial returns.

IMPACT INVESTING

Corporate social responsibility (CSR) is a common term used to describe companies' socially responsible behavior, such as initiatives or activities related to social or environmental issues, the main purpose of which is often protecting the company's image and financial interests (Bice 2017; Erhemjamts, Li, and Venkateswaran 2013; Nikolaeva and Bicho 2011). However, there has been an increasing quest for companies to go beyond reputationally driven socially responsible conduct and to instead integrate measurable impact purposes into their core business while still earning a profit (Porter and Kramer 2011; van Tulder, 2018; Ioannou and Serafeim 2019; Eccles, Ioannou and Serafeim 2014). One way of doing this is for companies to practice Impact Investing within their own business models (Allman 2015).

There is a general agreement that Impact Investing entails more than investing with good intentions (Burand 2015, p. 57). The principles of Impact Investing encompass the creation of financial and social results, along with managing the inherent risks of an investment (GIIN 2019). Through Impact Investing, companies are able to address market failures and create social value, while creating financial and business value. This is highlighted in the scholarship on strategic management and the shared value theory (Porter and Kramer 2011). Companies considering new investments, projects, or a new stream of innovations can consider investing according to the principles of Impact Investing in order to produce societal results alongside financial gains.

This study abides by the definition of Impact Investing used by the Global Impact Investing Network (GIIN 2019), which states that Impact Investing refers to "investments made with the intention to generate positive, measurable social and environmental impact alongside a financial return." Impact Investing draws on two relatively distinct characteristics, the first being the creation of social impact and the second being the generation of financial returns (Allma 2015; Höchstädter and Scheck 2015). In this context, social impact refers to measurable positive outcomes in people's lives that are derived from the actions and activities of a business, as well as through the use of a business's products and services (Daggers and Nicholls

2016; Ebrahim and Rangan 2014), whereas financial returns result from the successful sale of beneficial goods or services that are produced by a business (Buran 2015). In this way, financial and impact-oriented success are deeply coupled.

Impact Investing's financial returns differentiate it from grant funding and philanthropy, while its generation of extra-financial impact distinguishes it from traditional investment (Höchstädter and Scheck 2015). As such, in the investment spectrum, Impact Investing is placed between the focused impact of philanthropy (traditional[4] and strategic philanthropy) and the financial focus of conventional commercial investing[5] (Schrötgens and Boenigk 2017). Figure 28.1 depicts this description, shedding light on some of the main instruments employed by impact investors, as well as

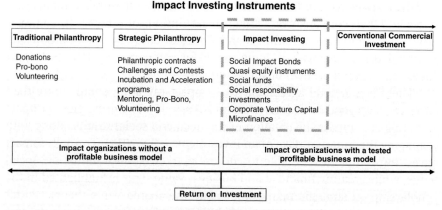

FIGURE 28.1   Map of Traditional Philanthropy, Strategic Philanthropy, Impact Investing, and Conventional Commercial Investment. *Source*: EVPA (2019), Sampaio (2014), Wendt (2018), OECD (2019), and Wyman (2016), adapted by the authors.

---

[4]Traditional philanthropy relates to investments in organizations that do not require returns of investment (European Venture Philanthropy Association [EVPA] 2019; OECD 2019; Wyman 2016). Some examples of traditional philanthropy instruments are donations, pro-bono, and volunteering. Strategic philanthropy includes tools such as philanthropic contracts, challenges, contests, incubation, and acceleration programs, mentoring, pro bono, and volunteering instruments. They always require an outcome and a measured impact, but not necessarily financial returns.

[5]Conventional commercial investment refers to investments in organizations with a profitable business model that only require financial returns measurement and monitoring (EVPA 2019; Sampaio 2014; OECD 2019; Wyman 2016). Impact Investing requires direct evidence of financial and impact results socially or environmentally.

the variety of investments traditionally used by investors.[6] The different Impact Investing instruments used by GE, IKEA, and Unilever will be described in comparison to the strategic philanthropy instruments employed by each company. Such strategic philanthropy instruments were typically a company's first step on their Impact Investing journey, or they were used to complement ongoing Impact Investing initiatives (Rockefeller 2020).

Traditional philanthropy within a corporation relates to internal investments made without expectation of future revenue or returns (European Venture Philanthropy Association [EVPA] 2019; OECD 2019; Wyman 2016). Some examples of traditional corporate philanthropy instruments are donations, pro-bono services, and volunteering. Strategic philanthropy also includes tools and instruments such as offering philanthropic contracts, hosting challenges and contests, managing incubation and acceleration programs, supplying mentorship, offering pro-bono services, and enabling staff volunteerism. Strategic philanthropy always requires an outcome and a measured impact, but not necessarily financial returns. In contrast, conventional commercial investment refers to investments made in organizations with a profitable business model that only require measurement and monitoring of financial returns (EVPA 2019; Sampaio 2014; OECD 2019; Wyman 2016). Impact Investing instruments require both direct financial and impact results.

Table 28.1 describes the most important Impact Investing and strategic philanthropy instruments included in this study. Cited Impact Investing instruments are social impact bonds,[7] quasi-equity instruments, social funds, social responsibility investments, corporate venture capital, and microfinance. Cited strategic philanthropy instruments are also represented below, since they can be a preliminary step for the subsequent adoption of Impact Investing practices (Rockefeller 2020).

COMPANY PROFILES

This section describes the profile of the three selected multinationals, General Electric (GE), IKEA and Unilever, as well as their most frequently used instruments for Impact Investing. Table 28.2 displays each company's organizational profile, including their mission, number of countries in which they are present, sectors of operation, number of employees, and revenues, as of April 13, 2020.

---

[6]There are several Impact Investing tools and instruments (Molecke and Pinkse 2017).
[7]See also Chapter 14, "Social Impact Bonds: Promises and Results," by Maria Basílio.

TABLE 28.1 Impact Investing and Strategic Philanthropy Instruments.

	Aim/Definition
Strategic Philanthropy Instruments	
Philanthropic Contracts	A contract made with a social purpose organization (SPO) that implies the existence of an agreement where intended impact goals are defined beforehand, which are to be measured and monitored through time (EVPA 2018; Scarlata and Alemany 2010).
Challenges and Contests	A competition to attain financial and technical support, among other benefits (EVPA 2018).
Incubation and Acceleration Programs	A program through which an organization supports very early stage social enterprises by providing them with business development support, mentoring, infrastructure, and access to relevant networks, in order to make them investment-ready (EVPA 2018).
Mentoring, Pro-bono, and Volunteering Activities	Professionals who provide specific skilled support to an organization without the payment of a fee (EVPA 2018).
Investment with Impact	
Social Impact Bonds	A financing mechanism aimed at funding preventive interventions relying on an outcome-based contract. Characterized by contracts between governments (or any public entity) and social entities, which use private investment to develop, coordinate, or expand effective programs (EVPA 2018).
Quasi-Equity Instruments	Contracts through which venture philanthropists provide funding to SPOs, and in return acquire ownership rights on part of the SPOs' businesses (EVPA 2018).
Social Funds	A vehicle created to enable pooled investment by a number of investors into impact-driven companies and other holdings, usually managed by a dedicated organization (EVPA 2018).
Social Responsibility Investment	Proactive practices, such as Impact Investing, shareholder advocacy, and community investing (EVPA 2018).
Corporate Venture Capital	Supports the acquisition of firms with a social impact that aligns with the core business of the company (Wyman 2016).
Microfinance	Organizations that offer loans and other financial services in relatively small amounts (Battilana and Lee 2014).

Source: Authors.

TABLE 28.2 Organizational Profile of General Electric, IKEA, and Unilever.

	Mission	Number of Employees	Sectors	Presence number of countries	Revenues in million EUR €2018
General Electric	*To invent the next industrial era, to build, move, power, and cure the world.*	300,000	Leader in energy, health, transportation, and infrastructure	130	110,000
IKEA	*To create a better everyday life for many people.*	208,000	Retail, manufacturing, food services, largest producer of wooden furniture	38	38,800
Unilever	*To add vitality to life. We meet everyday needs for nutrition, hygiene, and personal care with brands that help people feel good, look good, and get more out of life.*	161,000	Consumer goods: food and beverages, cleaning agents, beauty products, and personal care products	190	51,000

Source: IKEA (2020), Panmore (2020), Unilever (2020c).

General Electric

GE has a long-term commitment to sustainability, entrenched throughout its sectors of operation. GE delivers innovative solutions to essential energy, health care, and transportation infrastructure (General Electric 2019). Even though impact is not deeply and widely rooted in GE's strategy, products, and innovation's strategies, the company intends to produce positive social and environmental impact.

	Strategic Philanthropy				Impact Investing			
	Philanthropic contracts	Challenges/ Contests	Incubation/ Acceleration programs	Mentoring / Pro-Bono / Volunteering	Social funds	Social responsibility investments	Corporate Venture Capital	Microfinance
General Electric		Eco-magination challenge	Eco-magination challenge	Eco-magination challenge			Ecomagination challenge GE Business Innovations	
IKEA	IKEA Social Entrepreneurship IKEA Social Initiative Disha	IKEA challenges	IKEA Social entrepreneurs	IKEA Social Entrepreneurship IKEA Social entrepreneurs IKEA challenges Disha	Ingka Investments	Ingka Investments	IKEA Social Entrepreneurship IKEA challenges Ingka Investments	IKEA Social Entrepreneurship
Unilever	Dove self-esteem project Vaseline Healing project Lifebuoy with Amref Health Africa Girl Guide superheroes Enhancing Livelihoods Fund		Business incubator Indonesia Toilet Accelerator	Hindustan Unilever's Project Shakti Kabisig program Academies of Shine Toilet Accelerator Jaza Duka Mastercard Business incubator Indonesia Enhancing Livelihoods Fun	The Ocean Fund		Knorr Sustainability Partnership Fund Toilet Accelerator Loop	Microcredit in Ghana Hindustan Unilever's Project Shakti Academies of Shine Enhancing Livelihoods Fund

FIGURE 28.2 Impact Investing Instruments of General Electric, IKEA, and Unilever. *Source*: Authors.

GE's sustainability[8] strategy is based on its environmental, social, and governance (ESG) standards, as part of the company's oversight of business strategy and risk management. GE's main concerns involve integrity and compliance, human rights, and climate change and energy (General Electric 2019e). The company has operationalized ethical supply chain programs, female empowerment strategies, and climate change mitigation innovation strategies. GE also develops donation programs through the GE Foundation,[9] which supports in-kind and capital investments, and promotes national development programs through its energy, health care, and mobility expertise (General Electric 2019c).

The pressure to develop cleaner energy options is pushing this giant toward greater sustainability. Sustainability became a visible part of GE's efforts in 2005, with the launch of Ecomagination Challenge (extensively

---

[8]Sustainability is the "development that meets the needs of the present without compromising the ability of future generations to meet their own needs" (Brundtland 1987). There are three pillars of sustainability—social, environmental, and economic factors.

[9]The GE Foundation is dedicated to GE Philanthropic efforts, see for instance: https:// www.ge.com/sustainability/philanthropy.

TABLE 28.3 Evolution of the Ecomagination Project.

	2005	2010	2015	2017
Number of Products	*baseline*	23	Not Disclosed	Not Disclosed
Total cumulative revenue (in million EUR €)	*baseline*	77,000	180,000	245,000

Source: General Electric (2019b).

represented in the GE Impact Investing instrument spectrum in Figure 28.2), which aims to conciliate clean energy solutions with business performance. The results of GE's Ecomagination challenge are visible in the company's growth of new products and revenues (Table 28.3).

GE Ecomagination and GE Business Innovations are the programs that gave birth to Impact Investing strategies within GE, as described and detailed in Figure 28.2.

IKEA

IKEA initiated its sustainability strategy in the early 2000s, when the company began working on some of the societal problems identified in its internal production line and external supply chain, such as child labor, poverty, resources degradation, and inequality of opportunity.[10] Since then, IKEA has been refining its sustainability policy and aligning it with their core business, which has enabled IKEA to solve environmental and social problems while reinforcing its competitive edge.

In 2012, IKEA launched the "People & Planet Positive" strategy, which is now aligned with the United Nations Sustainable Development Goals (SDGs). IKEA considers this strategy to be a responsibility and a business opportunity. This program strives to transform IKEA's business and make it more impactful by improving "life at home" for people across the world (IKEA 2019c). The "People & Planet Positive" strategy allowed IKEA to incorporate sustainability goals in its decision-making process and in its value chain strategy, in close cooperation with every co-worker, customer, and partner.

---

[10] In 2000, IKEA launched the IWAY program, a code of conduct for suppliers and social programs.

Since 2015, all IKEA's cotton, fish, and seafood come from more sustainable sources (IKEA 2019b). By 2020, IKEA aims to acquire all its wood from sustainable sources (IKEA 2019b), and to completely phase out single-use plastics from its stores worldwide (IKEA 2018a). The IKEA Group is also committed to producing the same amount of renewable energy as it consumes in its operations by 2020. The company is also transitioning to a low carbon business and is investing heavily in renewable energy and improved energy efficiency. By 2030, IKEA aims to have a circular business[11] built on clean renewable energy and regenerative resources[12] (IKEA 2018c).

IKEA's Impact Investing strategy is in line with its overall sustainable strategy and business model. As evidenced in Figure 28.2, its Impact Investing portfolio is broad and diversified, with instruments spanning social bonds, social responsibility investments, corporate venture capital, and microfinance, some of which are aimed toward IKEA's social entrepreneurship program and others to Ingka Investments (INGKA 2019).

Unilever

Unilever's sustainability strategy is central to its business model. Through its program "Unilever Sustainable Living Plan," launched in 2010, the company aims to build a business with greater profits, a reduced environmental footprint, and increased social impact. Specifically, the goals of this sustainability strategy are to help more than a billion people improve their health and well-being, to halve the environmental footprint of Unilever products, to source all agricultural raw materials sustainably, and to enhance the livelihoods of stakeholders across Unilever's value chain.

Unilever's Research and Development (R&D) Department is devoted to sustainability; as stated by the company: "innovation is at the heart of Unilever's ambition to grow sustainably. Science, technology and product development are central to our plans to keep providing consumers with great brands that improve their lives while having a positive impact on the environment and society" (Unilever 2020a). The company invests approximately EUR €1 billion each year in R&D (Unilever 2020a), and its R&D workforce of around 6,000 people are involved in shaping Unilever's impact

---

[11] A circular business is based on the concept of the circular economy which is "one that is restorative by design, and which aims to keep products, components, and materials at their highest utility and value, at all times" (Webster 2015, p. 16).
[12] This means designing products from the beginning to be repurposed, repaired, reused, resold, and recycled, generating as little waste as possible.

strategy (Unilever 2019g). Unilever's impact investments in R&D have already brought about positive results in terms of consumer satisfaction, sales, and overall business outcomes (Unilever 2019b). This is perceivable by Unilever's 28 sustainable living brands, which, according to its company Sustainable Living Plan, have been supporting positive change for people and the planet. These sustainable living brands include Dove, Lipton, and Hellmann's (Unilever 2020b), and they have continuously outperformed the average growth rate of Unilever.[13]

Unilever's investment in projects that generate social and environmental impact is not based on the traditional model of charitable philanthropy. It is instead aligned with Unilever's business priorities and strategy—these impact investments grow Unilever's profits while supporting the Unilever Sustainable Living Plan and its five transformational change areas: climate change and forests; sustainable agriculture; land use and livelihoods; health and well-being; and women's empowerment.

The company also created the Unilever Foundation in 2012. The foundation works with other organizations worldwide to provide a combination of direct funding, expertise, products, and employee support to address country-specific needs. Unilever's corporate community investments totaled EUR €77.9 million in 2018 (Unilever 2019h). The overwhelming majority (94%) was categorized as direct community investments or commercial initiatives designed to deliver impact while growing Unilever's brands, while only 6% were charitable donations. The allocation strategy behind Unilever's community investments demonstrates that the company has graduated from the status quo of creating positive impact through charitable donations and traditional philanthropy—instead, Unilever is a model exemplar for corporate Impact Investing. Unilever's community investments vary in type, with 76% being cash contributions, 19% in-kind donations, and 1% employees' time (Unilever 2019).[14] The company uses several Impact Investing instruments to attain both positive impact and business results, like the Ocean Fund and Academies of Shine, described further in Figure 28.2.

Figure 28.2 lists the Impact Investments instruments used by each of the three multinational companies. As mentioned before, some strategic philanthropy instruments are also touched on. More detail can be found in Appendix 28.2.

---

[13]These sustainable living brands are growing 69% faster than the rest of the business and delivering 75% of the company's growth (Unilever 2020).

[14]More details at https://www.unilever.com/sustainable-living/enhancing-livelihoods/inclusive-business/creating-and-sharing-wealth/.

FINDINGS ON IMPACT INVESTING STRATEGIES

This section describes the findings on General Electric, IKEA, and Unilever's Impact Investing strategies, making use of some examples presented in Table 28.2. Tables 28.4, 28.5, and 28.6 highlight the positive and challenging outcomes of these companies' corporate strategies. Individual data points collected on companies' impact investing strategies were categorized and classified as either a *positive outcome* (e.g. development of new products, workforce motivation, partnerships development, good management practices, positive business results, etc.) or a *challenge* (e.g. difficulties companies identified in the process because their dimension, misalignment of investment strategy, core business, etc.).

In the case of GE, the Ecomagination Challenge delivered some positive outcomes (Table 28.4). GE managed to innovate in new ways and created partnerships with startups. Start-up partnerships facilitated the development of new products, which resulted in EUR €245 billion in cumulative, incremental revenue from 2005 through 2017.[15] GE focused on the creation of sustainable innovations, while its reputation and the range of partners kept growing considerably. However, not everything went smoothly. Aligning and integrating a small project like Ecomagination (with so many intervening stakeholders) with a huge multinational like GE was not always easy. Specifically, it was a challenge for GE to ensure that Ecomagination was being developed according to the company's core objectives and strategies. Using a new project with no track record inside of GE as the impetus for revising the company's existing practices toward a new vision of social and environmental impact proved challenging. Moreover, Ecomagination's processes were at times difficult to manage since some partners were not aligned on expected outcomes.

For IKEA, the implementation of Impact Investing projects changed their internal business processes and brought stronger innovation, brand reinforcement, higher sales of higher-quality products, as well as a more reliable supply chain. IKEA's values-driven culture and its focus on impact were fundamental to its ability to implement a profitable business model that solved social problems. The company's challenges related to the mainstreaming of these Impact Investing strategies across different geographies and maintaining standards when dealing with small-scale partners. Furthermore, IKEA found it challenging to make its "measurement and comply" processes straightforward enough to be successful across all of its programs.

---

[15]See Table 28.3.

TABLE 28.4   Positive Outcomes and Challenges of GE's Impact Investment Process.

GE Ecomagination Challenge (EC) Instrument	
Positive Outcomes	Challenges
Ecomagination strategy resulted in many good outcomes: 22 investments and commercial partnerships, one acquisition, and seed funding for 10 start-ups and innovators. GE was also able to bring innovative energy ideas to the market (General Electric 2019b).	It was difficult for the company to find space for accommodating actions toward positive impact while still driving its business further in a competitive way—exemplified by the belief "that a big company couldn't improve the environment while also improving the bottom line," Ann Condon, GE's Director of Resources and Environmental Strategies (General Electric 2017).
Submissions on the Ecomagination challenge[16] came from a wide range of innovation sources—startup entrepreneurs, research institutes, universities, and governments. It ended up bringing an incredible diversity of ideas.	GE found it difficult to build relationships with such a large roster unusual partners. Many of EC's external partners were not from the energy sector, even if they had projects in the green energy sector. Thus, to implement EC, GE had to develop a new network of partnerships. This was especially true for the "Powering the Grid" challenge.[17]
GE heavily invested in cleaner technology solutions through EC, which returned EUR €245 billion in cumulative revenue until 2017. The company also reduced greenhouse gas emissions by 42% since 2004.[18]	It was a challenge to adjusting internal working processes to match small scale projects. Most of the EC ideas were preliminary in nature, and extremely small in comparison to GE's massive energy business. Many of them were not business ready; they could not plug into GE's energy business as planned. This made choosing winning projects difficult.

[16] More information about Ecomagination is available in Appendix 28.1.
[17] More information at https://www.gegridsolutions.com/press/Ecomagination/press.htm.
[18] More information at https://www.ge.com/reports/5-ways-companies-can-weave-sustainability-dna/.

TABLE 28.4 *(continued)*

GE Ecomagination Challenge (EC) Instrument	
Positive Outcomes	**Challenges**
Ecomagination gave GE the opportunity to invest in a much wider variety of startups, which had the chance to get structured and receive feedback even if they were not the winners. Many non-winners got other types of funding from non-GE sources.	No single set of criteria was used to evaluate each submission, so judges were a bit lost in the process. They were also overwhelmed by the quantity of projects submitted. This also made it difficult for judges to evaluate EC submissions properly.
EC gave visibility to GE, mainly from the *people's choice award*, an engagement opportunity for the public to choose their favorite project, which ended up having substantial coverage.	Interaction with VC partners was complex, mainly because they had a different vision. They wanted good investment opportunities with an exit strategy, which in many cases diverged GE's business vision that was also concerned with good impact results.
Some of the relationships formed through the challenge accelerated growth of some GE's businesses, adding several hundred million euros in revenue (see Table 28.1).	The impact measurement on GE's business performance was difficult, mainly to get an agreement on the criteria to be used.
	GE did not know what to expect in terms of results from this program, since nothing like this had been done before, so resource allocation to the project was a considerable challenge.
	In order for EC to pay off, some of the nascent ventures needed to gain scale or accelerate growth, but many were in their earliest stages, so it was difficult to produce immediate positive results.
	It was difficult to deal with so many new ideas at the same time, especially because so many had a high probability of failing.
	The program was discontinued in 2017. The reasons for that are still to be publicly clarified, but the GE's overall performance had been declining dramatically. A plausible explanation would be that the company had to abandon the program because of financial constraints (Yahoo Finance 2019).

Source: Author's elaboration, based on the desk review and particularly Chesbrough (2012).

TABLE 28.5 Positive Outcomes and Challenges of IKEA's Impact Investment Process.

Positive outcomes	Challenges
IKEA generated substantial innovation along its value chain, including the launch of IKEA Social entrepreneurs, TaskRabbit, and ThisAbles (see Figure 28.2 and Appendix 28.2 for more information).	IKEA found it difficult to simplify processes for future partnership developments and for further replication across geographies. This is exemplified by ThisAbles, which began in Israel but needed a further boost to be replicated.
Sustainable sourcing impact investments minimized IKEA's production risks and fostered increasingly reliable sources of products and resources through values-driven partnerships.	Impact measurement is a current practice in IKEA (as seen in the IKEA Sustainability Report FY2018), but the act of regularly updating their social, environmental, and business impact metrics given several burgeoning impact initiatives across different products and geographic markets placed significant burdens on the company.
Investments led to higher-quality and better-crafted products (e.g. handcrafted products from the White Nile project).	It was challenging to manage a heterogenous network of small-scale suppliers and entrepreneurs, with very different scales, given IKEA's massive supply needs. This was especially true for their Social Entrepreneurs program (mentioned as an IKEA Impact Investing instrument in Figure X.2).
IKEA's focus on environmental and social benefits reinforced their brand and increased sales.	IKEA struggled to promote a consistent culture (e.g. sustainability related) of strong values in different geographies and operations. It is an area where IKEA outperforms other corporations, but it also demands continuous effort.

TABLE 28.5 *(continued)*

Positive outcomes	Challenges
Their commitment to impact reinforced a positive company culture and boosted employee motivation, as seen on the witness Global citizens blog (IKEA Foundation 2019b).	In order to evaluate whether investments generated impact benefits and/or financial payoffs, it required IKEA to undertake rigorous planning and execution to measure social, environmental, and business results.
Some impact projects gave IKEA a bigger platform to reach more of the public, including potential customers (e.g. ThisAbles project).	Showing how social and financial objectives can reinforce each other was a challenge for IKEA. The company found it difficult to represent itself as a recognized leader in the sector, not only for its success, but also for its sustainable policy: "We are committed to succeeding—to secure the success of our business while contributing to a sustainable future" (IKEA, 2018).
After impact interventions and increasing internal mission alignment—to create a better everyday life for people—target markets experienced a clear improvement in measured results.	
Investments had a clear alignment with the SDG agenda, and IKEA set clear goals for each SDG, as seen in IKEA Sustainability Report FY2018 (IKEA 2018c).	
Investments reinforced business performance, through profitable ventures like TaskRabbit, as well as projects that incentivized risk management across the value chain.	

Source: Author's elaboration, based on the desk review and IKEA Foundation (2019b) and IKEA (2018c).

TABLE 28.6 Positive Outcomes and Challenges of Unilever's Impact Investment Process.

Positive outcomes	Challenges
Innovation along the value chain, through investments like Loop or the Knorr Sustainability partnership fund.	Managing a considerable budget and a wide network of partnerships, small projects, and partners, in different regions with a variety of programs.
Improvement of its reputation as one of the world's most sustainable brands, recognized by consumers (Forbes 2018).	Measuring impact of a wide range of projects and aligning impact projects with the business strategy and mission of the company was a big challenge. Unilever had external impact evaluations done (e.g. by Price Waterhouse Coopers, known as PWC); however, the effort of aligning all the projects alongside a common purpose required considerable effort (Unilever 2019a).
Reinforcement of Unilever's long-term growth and business sustainability, as well as profits over time.[19]	Process simplification for project replication across geographies (e.g. Hindustan Unilever Project Shakti was a good example with Guddi Baji in Pakistan, but further actions could be taken to guarantee replication for other projects like Jaza Duka Mastercard; see Appendix 28.1).[20]
Minimization of risks concerning suppliers and the value chain through smallholders and agriculture activities support (e.g. Microcredit in Ghana, Knorr Sustainable Partnership Fund).	Continuous promotion of an impact-oriented corporate culture and a strategic model based on impact results and value creation for society and consumers. Unilever's strategic and sustainability alignment was clear, and this benefited its business results, but the permanent adoption of this culture among the company's collaborators is a constant work in progress.

[19] Unilever in 2018 has 26 Sustainable Living brands (up from 18 in 2016), including six top brands—Dove, Lipton, Dirt is Good, Rexona, Hellmann's, and Knorr—as well as their B Corp certified brands, such as Ben and Jerry's, and the recently acquired Seventh Generation and Pukka Herbs. Over the last four years, Unilever's Sustainable Living brands outperformed the company's average growth rate.

[20] All these projects are mentioned in Figure 28.3 and can be further explored in the Appendix of this chapter.

TABLE 28.6 *(continued)*

Positive outcomes	Challenges
Increased trust with all its stakeholders, including suppliers (which partner with Unilever on multiple programs), consumers, and collaborators.	
Development of products that serve the bottom of the pyramid, taking advantage of this huge section of the population as Unilever's biggest sales channel (e.g. Hindustan Unilever's Project Shakti project). Such users become Unilever's indirect sales force.[21]	
Clear alignment with the SDG agenda, seen in Unilever Sustainable Living Plan.[22]	
Minimization of production risks, more reliable resource sources and products through strengthened partnerships (e.g. Enhancing Livelihood Fund and Knorr Sustainable Partnership Fund).[23]	

Source: Author's elaboration based on the desk review from Forbes (2018) and Unilever (2019a).

---

[21] Further information on these projects is available in this chapter's Appendix.
[22] More information at https://www.unilever.com/Images/uslp-performance-summary-2018_tcm244-536032_en.pdf.
[23] More information about this program is available in the Appendix 28.1.

For Unilever, innovation, reputation, and an outstanding business performance are the main positive outcomes of its Impact Investing strategy. The company was able to draw several positive outcomes from its partnerships, as well as enlarge its client base. However, the large size of the company and its widespread operations made it difficult to work with relatively small partners. Other noteworthy challenges included replicating projects across borders and maintaining a uniform level of impact measurement across such a diversified portfolio, as clarified in Table 28.6.

Given the outcomes described above and all the information gathered from these companies' investment strategies, it is evident there are common elements that jointly produce success. These seem to indicate a pattern other companies can follow to implement Impact Investing successfully. These are identified below, in three sections: Underlying Conditions, Resources, and Impact Investing Strategies.

Findings: Underlying Conditions

First, a successful Impact Investing project appears to originate from the identification of a challenge in the value chain, deriving from central operations or the supply chain. External pressure to resolve social or environmental issues often results in an opportunity for value creation. Take, for example, IKEA's need to solve child labor issues in its value chain and its lack of products for handicapped people (ThisAbles); or Unilever's investment in supply chain security (e.g. Enhancing Livelihood Fund and Knorr Sustainable Partnership Fund); or GE's investment in new ideas for innovative clean energy given their current dependence on fossil fuels.

Second, IKEA and Unilever in particular display a strong culture of engagement with clients and employers, as well as other stakeholders. Their strong cultures were incorporated into daily corporate practices, and company's values were integrated into strategic planning and intended impact objectives. Culture and values influence behaviors and are key drivers for the success of corporate Impact Investing. In the case of GE, the integration of a values-driven culture is not so expressive, which might be a factor behind the early end of Ecomagination.

Third, the involvement of executive leadership seemed to be crucial to the companies' strategic impact initiatives and investment strategies. Both Unilever and IKEA have exemplified a top-down strategy with strong bottom adherence. Fourthly, all three companies display openness to partnerships, which seems critical and one of the main success factors of their investments' strategies. Last, IKEA and Unilever have stronger long-term visions, and show a clear alignment with impact as a business enhancer. Both companies established long-term ambitious objectives. For example, IKEA intends to become a circular business in 2030, and Unilever aims to help more than 1 billion people improve their health and well-being. These goals guide companies to establish objectives for Impact Investing, as well as successfully implement and monitor impact projects. GE demonstrates a greater focus on business and profit objectives in the shorter-term, even though sustainability is a stated focus and integral part of GE's overall strategy.

Findings: Resources

There are also common elements related to the resources each company resorted to, which include workforce talent, the level of team commitment toward Impact Investing, the choice of instruments, as well as the correct implementation processes. IKEA and Unilever rooted their business and sustainability strategy in annual in-depth studies, based on evidence from stakeholders and the general public. Information about their markets and value chains were carefully researched. The mass of evidence they collected points to a total commitment by these companies to the creation of value and impact throughout their attempts to solve social and environmental issues. GE heavily researched the development of new technologies, but there is less evidence of their impact focus.

Another strength of IKEA and Unilever is their allocation of human resource talent to Impact Investing. Their staffing commitment toward Impact Investing strategies and their alignment with core strategy and operations are evident. This level of involvement was not evident in GE.

These three companies were clear about the objectives they wanted to reach with their investments. Clarity is key to defining the path toward implementing Impact Investment strategies, identifying the best instruments to use, and establishing fruitful partnerships.

Findings: Impact Investing Strategies

Concerning the implementation of Impact Investing strategies, it is noteworthy that all three companies interwove their company's mission with business performance, investments, and impact considerations. This is a similar pattern across GE, IKEA, and Unilever's investment strategies—where these elements reinforce each other and are a source of reputation, motivation, and business performance.

IKEA and Unilever show a very similar approach. They relied on strong leadership and culture throughout the process of implementing Impact Investing strategies and established successful strategies with clear positive spillovers for business performance. By comparison, GE's approach is distinct. Despite its revenues, GE's implementation process presents some structural deficiencies, such as the absence of a strong impact culture and possible misalignment between company leadership and the mission and impact objectives of its Impact Investing strategies, as well as an overall lack of impact performance measurement (as evidenced in Table 28.3 and Appendix 28.1 and 28.2).

In the three cases under analysis, results were measured and monitored. However, their approaches were distinct, with each company selecting its own impact measurement frameworks. For instance, GE measured the number of new products developed and the revenues they made from Ecomagination (see Table 28.3), while Unilever reported on its Sustainable Living Brands.[24] IKEA set clear goals and key performance indicators (KPI) to attain the SDGs (IKEA 2018c) and also reported on the impact of its social entrepreneurship program.[25] IKEA's financial reporting on some of its more impactful investments is not very thorough, however, as evidenced by its social entrepreneurship program.

A ROAD MAP FOR IMPACT INVESTING

A road map for Impact Investing was developed based on the analysis of the Impact Investing strategies used by these three multinational companies. The road map aims to serve as a guiding tool for the preparation, implementation, and monitoring of Impact Investing strategies. The road map is comprised of three anchors: (i) Underlying Conditions, (ii) Underlying Resources, and (iii) Impact Investing (Figure 28.3). The *Underlying Conditions* section presents all the desirable elements a company should have to begin the process of Impact Investing. *Underlying Resources* includes the tools and means needed to promote a good planning and implementation plan. *Impact Investing* describes some of the steps a company needs to go through to implement a successful and compliant Impact Investing strategy.

---

[24]See the results of this program on the Section: "Company Profile."
[25]More information at https://www.ikeasocialentrepreneurship.org/.

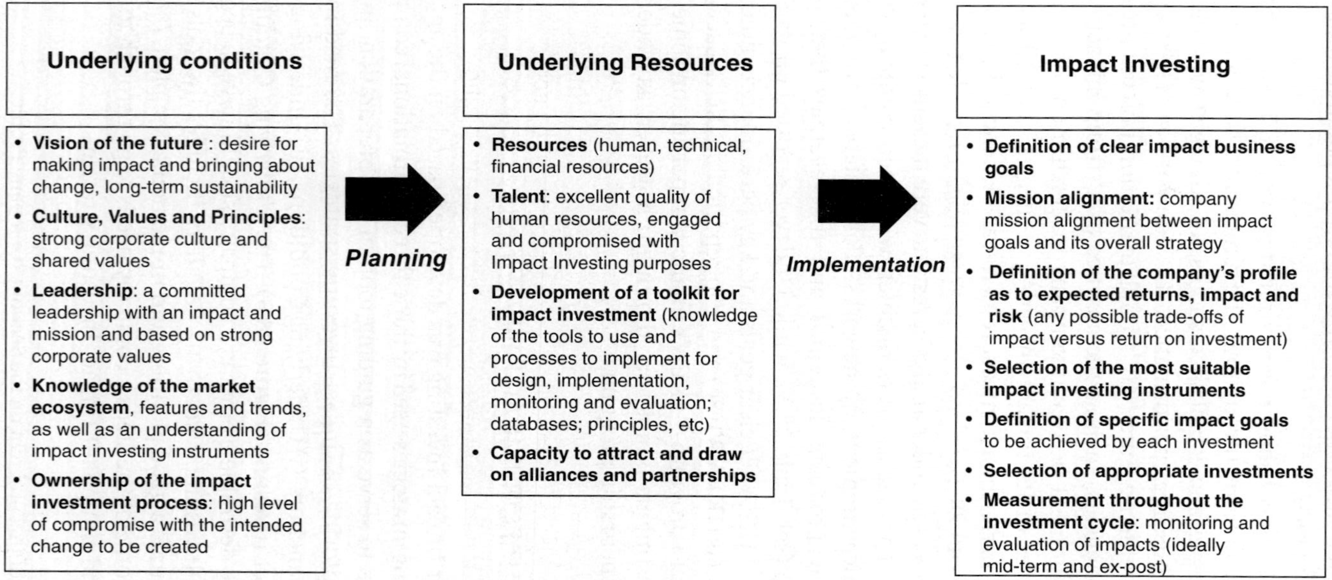

FIGURE 28.3 A Road Map for Impact Investing. *Source:* Authors.

Impact Investing

- **Definition of clear impact business goals**
- **Mission alignment:** company mission alignment between impact goals and its overall strategy
- **Definition of the company's profile as to expected returns, impact and risk** (any possible trade-offs of impact versus return on investment)
- **Selection of the most suitable impact investing instruments**
- **Definition of specific impact goals** to be achieved by each investment
- **Selection of appropriate investments**
- **Measurement throughout the investment cycle:** monitoring and evaluation of impacts (ideally mid-term and ex-post)

Implementation

Underlying Resources

- **Resources** (human, technical, financial resources)
- **Talent:** excellent quality of human resources, engaged and compromised with Impact Investing purposes
- **Development of a toolkit for impact investment** (knowledge of the tools to use and processes to implement for design, implementation, monitoring and evaluation; databases; principles, etc)
- **Capacity to attract and draw on alliances and partnerships**

Planning

Underlying conditions

- **Vision of the future** : desire for making impact and bringing about change, long-term sustainability
- **Culture, Values and Principles:** strong corporate culture and shared values
- **Leadership:** a committed leadership with an impact and mission and based on strong corporate values
- **Knowledge of the market ecosystem**, features and trends, as well as an understanding of impact investing instruments
- **Ownership of the impact investment process:** high level of compromise with the intended change to be created

There are six *Underlying Conditions:* (i) a long-term vision of the future of a company's sustainability and impact; (ii) culture, values, and principles—since no company can implement a successful Impact Investing strategy in the long run if it's not embedded in their culture; (iii) leadership—since Impact Investing is aided by consistent top-down support; (iv) ownership of the Impact Investing process, which is crucial for remaining nimble and adaptive throughout implementation; (v) openness to outside alliances, since partners are central for most Impact Investing instruments; and (vi) existence of a challenge that ignites the entire Impact Investing process.

The framework highlights five *Underlying Resources:* (i) human, technical, and financial resources that companies need to implement an Impact Investing process; (ii) talent that is committed to Impact Investing and the company's impact strategy; (iii) knowledge of the market ecosystem; (iv) development of an Impact Investing strategy; and (v) capacity to attract and operationalize partnerships, since partnerships are the basis of nearly every successful Impact Investing strategy.

The *Impact Investing* block details seven guidelines companies can follow to make the Impact Investing process viable and successful: (i) define how the company's mission is in alignment with its investment strategy and impact objectives; (ii) define the company's profile in terms of expected return and risk; (iii) define the business goals the company wishes to deliver; (iv) select the most suitable Impact Investing instruments, according to their Impact Investing strategy; (v) define clear impact metrics to be achieved; (vi) select the appropriate investments and projects; and (vii) measure, monitor, and evaluate the company's Impact Investing strategy throughout its implementation.

Further information related to this section, including detailed data on companies, can be found in Appendix 28.1.

Best Practices

This section highlights best practices that emerged in the exploration of the Impact Investing processes of the three multinational companies. A corporate mindset is crucial to successfully implement an Impact Investing strategy.

Companies must set clear goals for Impact Investing that reflect their determination to invest in projects that generate both impact and profit. Further, Impact Investing strategies must be aligned with a company's core business strategy and long-term vision, and impact projects should be treated as business enhancers, not lost profits. All three cases studies make evident that the success of Impact Investing projects depends on the alignment between the core operations of a business and their intended positive impacts.

It is essential to master the delicate balance between prioritizing the company's mission and its financial performance. As seen in the cases reported (especially in IKEA and Unilever), companies ought to entrench their impact missions in their business models and everyday corporate culture.

While grassroots support is helpful, for the three companies studied, top-down support for Impact Investing strategies made the difference. Leadership needs to be actively involved and act as a catalytic force for action. Whenever possible, Impact Investing strategies should originate at the board level and C-level.[26]

Impact Investing principles should be an intrinsic part of company culture. These values should be fully incorporated into the daily decisions of the workforce on all levels. When a company decides which impact outcomes to prioritize and work toward, companies should conscientiously explain and uplift key values to their employees, either through formal or informal trainings, performance measurement mechanisms, or other means.

GE, IKEA, and Unilever developed a deep knowledge about Impact Investing instruments. They tackled the complexity of this sector by considering their desired level of involvement and the number of resources they had available to devote to the Impact Investing process. For example, acceleration programs are better suited for companies that are more open to risk and are willing to invest in external innovation with more uncertain returns. Corporate venture capital, social responsibility investments, and microfinance, however, can be better options for companies that value a higher focus on solely financial return.

Best practices also point to the importance of setting impact goals early, as well as developing plans for ongoing measurement. As showed by Unilever's measurement of its Sustainable Living Brands, it is fundamental to set clear impact and business goals from the outset. Furthermore, it is fundamental to

---

[26]C-level executives play a strategic role within an organization. C stands for "Chief," so a C-level executive is the top level of the company, such as Chief Financial Officer and Chief Marketing Officer.

evaluate the success of impact investments, and to keep the monitoring process oriented toward success. Impact can be measured by the company, or by a third party. Setting goals, monitoring progress, and assessing results help companies keep track of impact performance (as the case of Unilever Sustainable Living Brands, which showed high performance). Reliable success metrics and positive results work as a huge motivation trigger. In case of negative performance assessments, clear feedback can uncover the underlying reasons for underperformance, and inform necessary adjustments.

Being open to partnerships and investing in ideas have broad support from the larger stakeholder community and a wise strategy (as shown by IKEA's Social Entrepreneurship program, Unilever's partnerships with small farmers, and GE's Ecomagination Challenge). These partnerships brought companies' new ideas, resources, and profits they could not have generated by themselves.

CONCLUSION

This chapter offers a step forward toward understanding the often-challenging process of integrating impact into the core business strategy of a corporation (Scheyvens et al. 2016). It investigates how three multinational companies managed to implement Impact Investing strategies and suggests a road map for this implementation. This chapter's findings are relevant for companies increasingly engaged in developing and implementing strategies to address societal challenges and create social impact.

The three companies analyzed—IKEA, Unilever, and GE—all implemented Impact Investing strategies with some degree of success. These three made use of social and environmental challenges identified in their value chains, turning potential problems into opportunities to invest with impact into markets they were highly familiar with. IKEA and Unilever utilized sustained Impact Investing strategies that were aligned with each company's wider mission, core business, leadership, and culture. Even though GE had some degree of success with its Impact Investing projects, the relatively weak connection between their chosen impact instrument and the company's core operations, paired with comparatively passive leadership and culture, may have led to the discontinuation of GE's impact program after a decade of success. Progressive leadership of the Impact Investing process alongside cultural engagement from employees was shown to be a pivotal success factor.

A road map for Impact Investing was proposed based on the case studies from GE, IKEA, and Unilever, and it includes three main anchors:

(i) Underlying Conditions, (ii) Underlying Resources, and (iii) Impact Investing. The *Underlying Conditions* includes the desirable elements a company should have before they start the process of Impact Investing. *Underlying Resources* covers the instruments and tools needed to promote a successful planning and implementation process. *Impact Investing* comprises the steps a company should follow in order to successfully implement an Impact Investing strategy. This road map can be used by companies as a tool to develop or validate their Impact Investing strategies.

Limitations

This research presented in this chapter has several limitations. First, it includes case studies only from three multinational companies. Thus, the findings are only applicable to the Impact Investing instruments used by the selected companies. Furthermore, the data underlying the analysis is secondary data. Thus, opportunities for future research include interviewing the leaders of these companies, in addition to third parties or stakeholders, as well as expanding the analyzed universe to cover additional companies with a diversity of geographic scopes, target impacts, and market share.

ACKNOWLEDGMENTS

The authors express their gratitude to the editors, Elsa de Morais Sarmento and R. Paul Herman, for their support and feedback. The first author would like to acknowledge the financial support from the Center for Responsible Business & Leadership (CRB) at the Católica Lisbon School of Business & Economics (grant CUBE-CRB-BGCT/2). The second author acknowledges the financial support from Fundação para a Ciência e a Tecnologia (FCT) (grant UIDB/00315/2020).

REFERENCES

Allman, K. A., ed. (2015). *Impact Investment: A Practical Guide to Investment Process and Social Impact Analysis*. Hoboken, NJ: John Wiley & Sons.

Battilana, J., and Lee, M. (2014). Advancing Research on Hybrid Organizing: Insights from the Study of Social Enterprises. *Academy of Management Annals* 8 (1): 397–441.

Bice, S. (2017). Corporate Social Responsibility as Institution: A Social Mechanisms Framework. *Journal of Business Ethics* 143 (1): 17–34.

Brundtland, G. H. (1987). Report of the World Commission on environment and development: our common future. https://sustainabledevelopment.un .org/content/documents/5987our-common-future.pdf (accessed February 24, 2020).

Burand, D. (2015). Resolving Impact Investment Disputes: When Doing Good Goes Bad. *Washington University Journal of Law & Policy* 48: 55–87.

Chesbrough, H. (2012). GE's Ecomagination Challenge: An Experiment in Open Innovation. *University of California Berkeley. Berkeley Haas Case Series* 54 (3): 140–154.

Creswell, J. W. (2014). *Research Design: Qualitative, Quantitative, and Mixed Methods Approaches*. London: Sage Publications.

Daggers, J., and Nicholls, A. (2016). The Landscape of Social Impact Investment Research: Trends and Opportunities. http://eureka.sbs.ox.ac.uk/7019/ 1/Landscape-of-social-impact-investment-research.pdf (accessed 29 March 2019).

Ebrahim, A., and Rangan, V. K. (2014). What Impact? A Framework for Measuring the Scale and Scope of Social Performance. *California Management Review* 56 (3): 118–141.

Eccles, R. G., Ioannou, I., and Serafeim, G. (2014). The Impact of Corporate Sustainability on Organizational Processes and Performance. *Management Science* 60 (11): 2835–2857.

Erhemjamts, O., Li, Q., and Venkateswaran, A. (2013). Corporate Social Responsibility and Its Impact on Firms' Investment Policy, Organizational Structure, and Performance. *Journal of Business Ethics* 118 (2): 395–412.

European Venture Philanthropy Association (EVPA) (2018). VP/SI glossary. https://evpa.eu.com/uploads/documents/Glossary-2017.pdf (accessed April 1, 2019).

European Venture Philanthropy Association (EVPA) (2019). Investing for impact – EVPA impact strategy paper. https://evpa.eu.com/knowledge-centre/publications/investing-for-impact-evpa-impact-strategy-paper (accessed January 29, 2020).

Forbes (2018). *The world's most reputable companies* 2018. http://www.forbes .com/sites/vickyvalet/2018/03/15/the-worlds-most-reputable-companies-2018/#750abbf226d5 (accessed April 15, 2019).

General Electric (2017). Reports. http://www.ge.com/reports/5-ways-companies-can-weave-sustainability-dna/ (accessed April 11, 2019).

General Electric (2018). Disaster and Humanitarian Relief Highlights. http://www.ge.com/sustainability/sites/default/files/GEA33650_Disaster_and_Humanitarian_Relief_Factsheet_R7.pdf (accessed April 1, 2019).

General Electric (2019a). Careers. www.ge.com/careers/culture (accessed April 10, 2019).

General Electric (2019b). Global Impact 2012. http://www.ge.com/globalimpact2012/ecomagination.html#!report=alternative-fuelvehicles (accessed April 10, 2019).

General Electric (2019c). Sustainability: Myanmar. https://www.ge.com/sustainability/sites/default/files/GEA18004_Myanmar.pdf (accessed April 10, 2019).

General Electric (2019d). Sustainability. https://www.ge.com/sustainability/ehs/ (accessed April 10, 2019).

General Electric (2019e). Sustainability. https://www.ge.com/sustainability/ (accessed April 10, 2019).

Global Impact Investment Network (2019). What You Need to Know About Impact Investment. https://thegiin.org/impact-investing/need-to-know/#what-is-impact-investing (accessed April 5, 2019).

Höchstädter, A. K., and Scheck, B. (2015). What's in a Name: An Analysis of Impact Investing Understandings by Academics and Practitioners. *Journal of Business Ethics* 132 (2): 449–475.

IKEA (2018a). IKEA Facts and Figures 2018. https://highlights.ikea.com/2018/facts-and-figures/for-a-more-sustainable-future/ (accessed April 5, 2019).

IKEA (2018b). IKEA Life at Home 2018. https://lifeathome.ikea.com/home/ (accessed April 13, 2019).

IKEA (2018c). IKEA Sustainability Report 2018. https://preview.thenewsmarket.com/Previews/IKEA/DocumentAssets/535135.pdf/ (accessed April 5, 2019).

IKEA (2019a). People and Planet Positive. https://www.ikea.com/ms/en_US/pdf/people_planet_positive/IKEA_Sustainability_Strategy_People_Planet_Positive_v3.pdf (accessed April 4, 2019).

IKEA (2019b). Sustainable Growth. https://www.ikea.com/gb/en/this-is-ikea/about-the-ikea-group/sustainable-growth/ (accessed April 13, 2019).

IKEA (2019c). We Are Building the IKEA of the Future. https://www.ikea.com/gb/en/this-is-ikea/about-the-ikea-group/sustainable-growth/ (accessed April 5, 2019).

IKEA (2020). Welcome Inside Our Company. https://www.ikea.com/ms/en_US/this-is-ikea/company-information/ (accessed February 28, 2020).

IKEA Foundation (2019a). Funding Decisions. https://www.ikeafoundation.org/about-us-ikea-foundation/funding/ (accessed 13 April 2019).

IKEA Foundation (2019b). Witness Program. https://blog.ikeafoundation.org/about-this-blog/ (accessed April 4, 2019).

INGKA (2019). Investing for Our Future. https://annualreport.ingka.com/investing-for-our-future/ (accessed April 4, 2019).

Ioannou, I., and Serafeim, G. (2019). Corporate Sustainability: A Strategy?, https://www.hbs.edu/faculty/Publication%20Files/19-065_16deb9d6-4461-4d2f-8bbe-2c74b5beffb8.pdf (accessed February 3 2019).

Molecke, G., and Pinkse, J. (2017). Accountability for Social Impact: A Bricolage Perspective on Impact Measurement in Social Enterprises. *Journal of Business Venturing* 32 (5): 550–568.

Nikolaeva, R., and Bicho, M. (2011). The Role of Institutional and Reputational Factors in the Voluntary Adoption of Corporate Social Responsibility Reporting Standards. *Journal of the Academy of Marketing Science* 39 (1): 136–157.

Ormiston, J., Charlton, K., Donald, M. S., et al. (2015). Overcoming the Challenges of Impact Investing: Insights from Leading Investors. *Journal of Social Entrepreneurship* 6 (3): 352–378.

Panmore (2020). General Electric's (GE) Vision Statement and Mission Statement. http://panmore.com/general-electric-ge-vision-statement-mission-statement (accessed February 28, 2020).

Porter, M., and Kramer, M. (2011). Creating Shared Value. *Harvard Business Review* 89 (1, 2): 62–77.

Rockefeller (2020). Impact Investing: Strategy and Action. https://www.rockpa.org/wp-content/uploads/2017/10/RPA_PRM_Impact_Investing_Strategy_Action_WEB.pdf (accessed April 5, 2020).

Sampaio, P. (2014). Filantropia de Impacto. Laboratório de Investimento Social Nota de Investigação #6.

Scarlata, M., and Alemany, L. (2010). Deal Structuring in Philanthropic Venture Capital Investments: Financing Instrument, Valuation, and Covenants. *Journal of Business Ethics* 95(2): 121–145.

Scheyvens, R., Banks, G., and Hughes, E. (2016). The Private Sector and the SDGs: The Need to Move Beyond Business as Usual. *Sustainable Development* 24 (6): 371–382.

Schrötgens, J., and Boenigk, S. (2017). Social Impact Investment Behavior in the Nonprofit Sector: First Insights from an Online Survey Experiment. *Voluntas: International Journal of Voluntary and Nonprofit Organizations* 28 (6): 2658–2682.

Unilever (2012). Unilever Launches Global Foundation. https://www.unilever.com/news/press-releases/2012/12-01-27-Unilever-launches-Global-Foundation.html/ (accessed April 4, 2019).

Unilever (2019a). *Sustainable Living.* Independent Assurance. https://www.unilever.com/sustainable-living/our-approach-to-reporting/independent-assurance/ (accessed April 10, 2019).

Unilever (2019b). Unilever Sustainable Living Plan Performance Summary 2018. https://www.unilever.com/ performance-summary-2018_tcm244-536032_en.pdf (accessed April 10, 2019).

Unilever (2019c). About Unilever. https://www.unilever.com/about/who-we-are/about-Unilever/ (accessed April 5, 2019).

Unilever (2019d). Creating and Sharing Wealth. https://www.unilever.com/sustainable-living/enhancing-livelihoods/inclusive-business/creating-and-sharing-wealth/ (accessed April 10, 2019).

Unilever (2019e). *Global Challenges.* Local Actions. https://www.unilever.com/Images/global-challenges-local-actions_tcm13-5100_tcm244-409749_1_en.pdf (accessed April 4, 2019).

Unilever (2019f). Knorr Sustainability Partnership Fund. https://www.unilever.com/about/suppliers-centre/sustainable-sourcing-suppliers/knorr-sustainability-partnership/knorr-sustainability-partnership-fund/ (accessed April 13, 2019).

Unilever (2019g). Research and Development. https://www.unilever.com/careers/our-teams/research-development.html (accessed April 14, 2019).

Unilever (2019h). Sustainable living: Enhancing livelihoods. https://www.unilever.com/sustainable-living/enhancing-livelihoods/inclusive-business/creating-and-sharing-wealth/ (accessed April 5, 2019).

Unilever (2019i). Sustainable Living: Healthy Handwashing Habits for Life. https://www.unilever.com/sustainable-living/improving-health-and-well-being/health-and-hygiene/healthy-handwashing-habits-for-life/ (accessed April 13, 2019).

Unilever (2019j). Sustainable Living: Our sustainability governance. https://www.unilever.com/sustainable-living/our-strategy/our-sustainability-governance/ accessed April 4, 2019).

Unilever (2019k). Sustainable Living. https://www.unilever.com/sustainable-living/overview/ (accessed April 4, 2019).

Unilever (2019l). Values and Principles. https://www.unilever.com/about/who-we-are/our-values-and-principles/ (accessed April 2019).

Unilever (2020a). Innovation in Unilever. https://www.unilever.com/about/innovation/innovation-in-unilever/ (accessed February 24, 2020).

Unilever (2020b). Unilever's Purpose-Led Brands Outperform. https://www.unilever.com/news/press-releases/2019/unilevers-purpose-led-brands-outperform.html/ (accessed February 24, 2020).

Unilever (2020c). Unilever's Sustainable Living Plan Continues to Fuel Growth. https://www.unilever.com/news/press-releases/2018/unilevers-sustainable-living-plan-continues-to-fuel-growth.html (accessed January 28, 2020).

van Tulder, R. (2018). Business and the Sustainable Development Goals: A Framework for Effective Corporate Involvement. https://www.rsm.nl/fileadmin/Images_NEW/Positive_Change/Business_and_Sustainable_Development_Goals_-_Positive_Change_0_Rob_van_Tulder.pdf (accessed April 5, 2019).

Webster, K. (2015). *The Circular Economy: A Wealth of Flows*. Isle of Wight: Ellen MacArthur Foundation.

Wendt, K., ed. (2018). *Positive Impact Investing: A Sustainable Bridge Between Strategy, Innovation, Change and Learning*. Cham: Springer Nature.

Wyman, O. (2016). Corporate Social Investment: Gaining Traction. https://www.oliverwyman.com/content/dam/oliver-wyman/global/en/2016/feb/OW_Corporate_Social_Investment_Final.pdf (accessed January 26, 2020).

Yahoo Finance (2019). General Electric. https://finance.yahoo.com/quote/GE/history?period1=1271286000andperiod2=1555282800andinterval=1dandfilter=historyandfrequency=1d (accessed April 1, 2019).

APPENDIX 28.1: IMPACT INVESTMENT PROFILES

Following are nonexhaustive detailed findings on the companies' Impact Investment profiles and behavior, which set the basis for the proposed road map for Impact Investing.

UNDERLYING CONDITIONS

Vision of the Future

GE

"GE remains committed to preparing for and responding to future natural disasters and humanitarian crises, diligently maximizing the impact of our financial, technological and human resources" (General Electric 2019e). The company demonstrates not only that it is innovation driven, but also that it develops all strategy on the basis of producing more efficient, sustainable, and business-strong solutions.

IKEA

"Customers and co-workers are at the heart of our transformation, and there will be significant opportunities for our co-workers in the future. We are committed to going on this journey together with our co-workers in a way that is aligned with our culture and values, so they feel informed and supported every step of the way" (IKEA 2019c).
"To create a better everyday life for the many people, this is the IKEA vision. . . . This makes it possible for us to make long-term investments for the future" (IKEA 2019a).

UNILEVER

"As a business we keep one eye on the future, adapting and evolving to stay one step ahead" (Unilever 2019a).
"A sustainable future for smallholders is one in which their incomes and living standards rise.
And our future success will depend on theirs. We rely on smallholders for a sustainable supply of some of our most important ingredients, including tea, palm oil, vegetables, cocoa, and vanilla.
By strengthening our connections to smallholders and helping them flourish, we will make our supply of sustainably sourced ingredients more secure and more transparent. That can reinforce the trust that our consumers have in our brands and help us continue to grow" (Unilever 2019d).
"We're also committed to continuously improving the way we manage our impacts and our longer-term goal of developing a sustainable business."

Culture, Values, and Principles

GE

There is no evidence that GE culture is clearly associated with a value-driven approach and focused on impact.
"What matters most is the human capital. We need great ideas, innovation, and leadership to stay current and relevant."
David Joyce, President and CEO, GE Aviation (General Electric 2019a)

IKEA

"We are a values-driven business with a culture based on strong values.[27]
We believe that the IKEA culture—how we work and what we value—is fundamental to achieving our vision.... It is not only what we do, but how we do it that matters. We always do our best to maintain the highest ethical standards and to be a good partner in society.
Our culture and values shape the way we do business and create a powerful desire to do the right thing.
We put the focus on our co-workers and provide a framework and guidance for our priorities.... We stay close to our vision and culture and get even closer to our customers.
We want to be an IKEA where customers meet passionate, knowledgeable, and service-minded co-workers, who understand life at home and help make dreams a reality.
We will rely on our culture of entrepreneurship, always moving forward and not waiting for perfection. We will work together to achieve continuous improvements"[28]
By August 2017, 95% of IKEA co-workers stated that "sustainability is a natural part of the everyday work."[14]

---

[27] Togetherness and enthusiasm; desire for renewal; cost-consciousness; accepting responsibility; humbleness and willpower; simplicity; leadership by example; daring to be different; and striving to meet reality.
[28] An example of this strong culture is the IWitness Global Citizens program. This program gives IKEA co–workers a chance to see first–hand how the money raised through IKEA good cause campaigns contributes to a better life for children in the world's poorest communities. Co–workers visit various projects run by IKEA Foundation partners and share their experiences on IKEA Foundations' Global Citizens blog.

UNILEVER

"Our values define how we do business and interact with our colleagues, partners, customers and consumers. Our four core values are integrity, responsibility, respect and pioneering. As we expand into new markets, recruit new talent, and face new challenges, these guide our people in the decisions and actions they take every day" (Unilever 2019l).

When Paul Polman became chief executive of the soap-to-ice-cream-maker in 2009 (joining from a Swiss rival, Nestlé), the Dutchman spent a night in Lever's rooftop bed as part of a total immersion in the history of his new firm. It helped persuade him, a year later, to launch a "Sustainable Living Plan," the name for his attempt to make Unilever the preeminent example of how to do capitalism responsibly, just as it had once done under Lever (Economist 2014).

Leadership

GE

GE does not show a clear commitment to impact leadership. GE holds its leaders *accountable* for creating a culture of compliance in which employees understand their responsibilities and feel comfortable raising concerns without fear of retaliation (General Electric, 2019).

IKEA

IKEA has developed its blueprints in a top-down manner. When the company hired Steve Howard as its Chief Sustainability Officer, in 2011, it appointed him to its seven-person executive management group. This group, which included the heads of all the operating divisions, was setting the company's vision and developing its strategy. Their work has facilitated the simultaneous pursuit of aggressive growth and bold sustainability plans. The sustainability agenda thus crafted at the top is being executed throughout the company.

UNILEVER

The Unilever Leadership Executive (ULE), led by the Chief Executive Officer (Alan Jope), is responsible for managing profit and loss and delivering growth. It monitors implementation and delivery of the Unilever Sustainable Living Planet.

At ULE level, sustainability and corporate responsibility are championed and led by the Chief Marketing and Communications Officer (Keith Weed) (Unilever 2019j), but the whole board embeds the sustainability purpose of the company, since there is no other vision or strategy for Unilever besides sustainability: "Our brands give us a unique opportunity to create positive change, to grow our business, and to achieve our purpose of making sustainable living commonplace" (Unilever 2020b).

Ownership (of the company on the impact purpose)

GE

"We are committed to Environment, Health & Safety excellence to protect our people, our communities and GE. We hold ourselves to the same high expectations and standards everywhere we work, and we assess the EHS impacts of our businesses globally before, during and after operations" (General Electric 2019d).

IKEA

Sustainability is an integrated part of the way IKEA is doing business, and it is seen as a precondition for doing business (IKEA Foundation 2019a)

UNILEVER

Unilever Sustainable Living Plan is the global Unilever strategy for sustainability and business growth and for each of the nine pillars of the USLP, Unilever sets out the strategy, targets, and performance and how they are taking action to drive value for business and society.

Openness to Outside Alliances

GE

GE used an open innovation strategy through Ecomagination, showing its openness to external ideas, alliances, partnerships, and investments. The process was co-developed between partners.

IKEA

IKEA develops almost all its investments on the basis of partnerships.

UNILEVER

"We do not believe . . . companies such as ours can make a difference without working in partnership with others. That is why, as a multi-local multinational, we tackle global concerns with local actions and work in partnership with local agencies, governments, and non-governmental organizations" (Unilever 2019e).

"These partnerships with governments and NGOs enable us to have a greater impact and reach those most in need, playing a key role in contributing to the SDGs" (Unilever 2019i).

Existence of a Challenge (the company discovered a problem that needed to be solved)

GE

General Electric felt the need to innovate and promote more sustainable solutions. This is the reason why the company applied all its energies and a good number of resources on the Ecomagination challenge.

IKEA

IKEA ThisAbles project is a great example on how the company developed an investment strategy from a big challenge from one of its niche consumers: people with disabilities.

TaskRabbit is also another good example of how a failure on an extension of the sales process led the company to partner with another entity and support the launch and growth of an important product line for many markets.

UNILEVER

Unilever sustainability strategy emerged out of its studies on the consumer behavior and future business growth perspectives. The specific examples used on this case study show clearly how many impact initiatives come out of a need to solve a challenge.

For example, the remoteness of some villages in Indonesia has forced Unilever to develop innovative ways to distribute the products, helping social entrepreneurs (Unilever 2019f). Likewise, the lack of sanitation conditions led it to create an accelerator in sanitation industry.

UNDERLYING RESOURCES

Resources: Human, Technical, and Financial

GE

GE innovation department relied on experimenting with new products with impact as seen in Ecomagination, which devoted efforts and resources on these investments.

IKEA

IKEA is devoting its efforts and resources on the development of a sustainable policy and new sustainable products, cooperating with different partners to develop new impactful solutions (IKEA 2018c).

UNILEVER

Unilever has a very good innovation department and invests its innovation budget on the development of new impactful solutions, as referred previously in this chapter. The company is devoting its R&D workforce of around 6,000 people to work for its impact purposes (Unilever 2019g).

Talent and Human Resources Compromised with Impact Investing Purposes

GE

"We work with the highest integrity, compliance culture and respect for human rights while also reducing the impact of our technology and environmental footprint" (General Electric 2018).

IKEA

IKEA strategy is committed to sustainability.
Sustainability—environmental, economic, and social well-being for today and tomorrow—is becoming an integrated part of our business and is one of the strategic cornerstones in the IKEA Group direction. "Growing IKEA Together."
"We are working with social entrepreneurs and engaging actively in local communities to be an inclusive business. We continually develop our approach to vulnerable groups within the IKEA value chain" (IKEA 2019c).

UNILEVER

"We want our business to grow but we recognize that growth at the expense of people or the environment is both unacceptable and commercially unsustainable. Sustainable growth is the only acceptable model for our business. Our Unilever Sustainable Living Plan (USLP) is central to our business model. It sets out how we are growing our business, whilst reducing our environmental footprint and increasing our positive social impact" (Unilever 2019c).

Knowledge

GE

GE Research leverages its multidisciplinary core capabilities to design and develop advanced solutions to complex, challenging problems. They have more than 1,000 experts, 350 projects, and 400 publications per year, which demonstrates its clear bet on knowledge. GE's focus on research for positive social and environmental impact is not as strong as the other two cases.

IKEA

Every year, Ikea Group and INGKA Holding publish a research report on how people live in and relate to a specific aspect of their homes. Since 2014 it has dealt with morning routines, food and kitchens, and disagreements at home, as well as sense of comfort at home.

For example, they concluded, "64% of people globally would rather live in a small home in a great location as opposed to a large home in a less than ideal location, and 23% of people feel they have to leave the home to find alone time" (IKEA 2018b).

On the basis of this research, IKEA can develop innovations and new strategies, not only for products but also for client relationship management, helping it to sell more, with more purpose and with the commitment to improve the life of its clients and consumers.

UNILEVER

More than 6,000 people work within R&D in a variety of purposeful and impactful roles. "Our scientists explore and develop the technologies of the future, whilst our product developers use this science and technology to develop and bring to market Unilever's next generation innovations. In unity, this team goes beyond to combine the search for breakthrough technologies with the constant drive to respond to competitors, move into new markets, and strengthen our brands with purpose."

"At Unilever, R&D works hand-in-hand with marketing to creating fantastic innovations. Our science and technologies are used to unlock the benefits of the products that reach 2 million consumers each day. We truly make a difference," David Blanchard, Chief R&D Officer (Unilever 2019g).

Development of a Strategy for Impact Investing

GE

Ecomagination challenge was clearly planned by GE. They decide to invest through acceleration and venture capital in new ideas with the objective to develop innovative new products in the company.

IKEA

IKEA investment strategy emerged from the business objectives to have high-quality products, with strong environmental and social impact. They knew from the beginning that investing in their social entrepreneurs' program could be a good strategy of using microfinance and venture capital at the service of the impact and business objectives on their mind.

UNILEVER

Paul Polman created the Sustainable Living Brands strategy with the purposeful objective to invest in sustainable and socially driven brands. For that, Unilever established objectives and started to set different investing instruments (microfinance, socially responsible investments, social funds, etc.) according to the reality they were founding along the process.

Capacity to Attract and Draw on Alliances and Partnerships

GE

Explained in the table "Openness to Outside Alliances" in the Underlying Conditions section.

IKEA

Explained in the table "Openness to Outside Alliances" in the Underlying Conditions section.

UNILEVER

Explained in the table "Openness to Outside Alliances" in the Underlying Conditions section.

IMPACT INVESTING

Mission Alignment
GE
Deep alignment between the company's mission and GE Ecomagination objectives: "One aspect of our Ecomagination business strategy focuses on reducing the impact of electricity generation and use for our customers and ourselves, through a wide range of technologies" (General Electric 2017).
IKEA
IKEA shows a deep alignment between its mission and investments made; they are either more impact oriented or more return oriented. To improve people's lives, they invest in new high-quality products from small entrepreneurs or they invest in new lines of products to serve niche clients (ThisAbles).
UNILEVER
"Unilever is committed to address the unmet social needs and the business can play a unique role in helping to solve them," Keith Weed, Chief Marketing and Communications Officer, Unilever (Unilever 2012). "Whatever the brand, wherever it is bought, we're working to ensure that it plays a part in helping fulfil our purpose as a business—making sustainable living commonplace" (Unilever 2019c).

Company's Risk and Return Profile
GE
Ecomagination was clearly designed to promote innovation and impact, but return was a precondition to success.
IKEA
IKEA has different kinds of investments, spanning from returned-focused to impact-focused investments.
UNILEVER
Unilever has different kinds of investments, spanning from returned-focused to impact-focused investments. Unilever considers impact to come along with business success, but some impact investments do not necessarily imply a direct financial return.

Definition of Business Goals

GE

Business goals were clearly predetermined alongside Ecomagination. They wanted to innovate and have powerful products for the market.

IKEA

IKEA never forgets its business central activity in any of its investments. Krister Mattsson, Head of Ingka Investments, is a clear example of this posture (referring to investments in the forest industry): "Here we're not only supporting the clean energy transition and responsible forest management, we also balance our financial exposure. Energy and wood are very important resources to us, and our product margins go down if the prices for either increase, so our investments provide us with some protection. We think of it as long-term macro-hedging, as well as sustainable investments" (INGKA 2019).

UNILEVER

"We aim to double the size of our business while reducing our environmental impact and deliver increased social value," Keith Weed, Chief Marketing & Communications Officer (PSI 2012). "Together with our partners, we will deliver life-saving solutions as we work toward achieving these ambitious goals" (Unilever 2012).

As a major firm in the global consumer goods market, Unilever utilizes its corporate responsibility strategy as a supporting approach to maintaining industry position and business sustainability.

"An effective corporate social responsibility strategy adds to Unilever's efforts for a sustainable business in the consumer goods industry. Stakeholders' interests are satisfied through appropriate approaches that ensure holistic corporate citizenship and responsibility fulfillment" (Panmore 2017).

Selection ot the Most Suitable Instruments

GE

Explained in the table "Development of a Strategy for Impact Investing" in the Underlying Resources section and alongside other tables of this appendix.

IKEA

Explained in the table "Development of a Strategy for Impact Investing" in the Underlying Resources section and alongside other tables of this appendix.

UNILEVER

Explained in the table "Development of a Strategy for Impact Investing" in the Underlying Resources section and alongside other tables of this appendix.

Definition of Impact Goals

GE

No clear evidence on the alignment between impact investing and goals setting. But we know GE acts always with the aim to produce better technologies with business, consumer, and impact-positive results.

IKEA

All IKEA financing instruments are dependent on partners providing annual program reports demonstrating that funds have been used properly and according to original intentions (IKEA Foundation 2019a).

All investments require development of a detailed program proposal, focused on creating a baseline, setting program objectives, and establishing key performance indicators that will be used to measure annual progress and ultimate program achievement.

The DISHA project, for example, was from the beginning intended to: "Touch the lives of 1 million women over a period of three years and establish a model for broad-based replication. It was designed to provide women and girls with the skills and knowledge that will help them secure employment or start their own businesses and support the Government of India's flagship skill development initiatives through policy, research and development support services" (United Nations 2017).

UNILEVER

Unilever not only measures impact but also defines goals to be attained per investment.

For example, in a smallholder community project in Madagascar: "the partnership aims to reach 50,000 people in 10,000 households in the Sava Region by 2019, by increasing access to fair financial services, providing community education on health, hygiene and child protection, as well as helping farmers improve their agricultural and business skills" (Unilever 2019k).

Selection of Appropriate Investments

GE

The selection of the appropriate investments is a direct consequence of the business and impact goals defined by the company and the challenge in the value chain identified. In the case of GE, the Ecomagination challenge of a consequence of the need to innovate, open the company to new ideas and bring trends of the future as a competitive advantage for the company. Opening a challenge and investing in the best ideas was a clear strategy for GE to follow.

IKEA

The selection of the appropriate investments is a direct consequence of the business and impact goals defined by the company and the challenge in the value chain identified. In the case of ThisAbles, for example, the challenge founded (no adequate furniture to disabled people) showed the company that having an open source model for innovation and investing internally in these ideas could be a perfect new way to invest successfully in this niche market.

UNILEVER

The selection of the appropriate investments is a direct consequence of the business and impact goals defined by the company and the challenge in the value chain identified. For Unilever, the challenges found in the value chain helped the company to understand that supporting and financing smallholder's farmers and investing in their ideas could be a good chance to mitigate risk and develop competitive advantage. These are common strategies in the Knorr Sustainability Fund, Enhancing Livelihoods Fund, and the Toilette accelerator.

Measurement and Compliance

GE

In the case of Ecomagination, results were deeply measured and monitored. The company could realize the revenues it made out of the project and evaluate the program balance in detail.

IKEA

Results are deeply measured and monitored.

For example, IKEA Foundation partners have to demonstrate every year "that funds have been used properly and according to original intentions. Concept notes are developed by the partners in close consultation with the IKEA Foundation's administration. The Board decides whether the proposed programs are within the Foundation's charter and in line with our expectations for financial and operational efficiency as well as reflecting IKEA core values" (IKEA Foundation 2019a).

UNILEVER

Unilever measures the results of its actions and investments. For example, its smallholder's program was able to impact 746,000 smallholders, enabling them to access initiatives aiming to improve their agricultural practices by 2018.

In 2017, their Sustainable Living brands grew 50% faster than the rest of the business (Unilever 2019b).

In the Knorr Sustainability Partnership Fund, annual sustainability and revenue results are measured through defined KPIs and gains and shared between Unilever and the farmers (investees) (Unilever 2019f).

"Independent external assurance helps us to drive continuous improvement in performance and in the quality, rigor and credibility of our data. We need accurate and robust data on our sustainability performance to help us make decisions, monitor performance, and report progress to our stakeholders" (Yahoo Finance 2019).

APPENDIX 28.2: IMPACT INVESTING INSTRUMENTS

Below is a nonexhaustive mapping of these companies' investment and strategic philanthropy instruments. Only the most relevant were selected for the purposes of this study. (Social impact bonds and quasi-equity instruments were not used, because they were not part of these companies' portfolios.)

1. General Electric
    1.1. Ecomagination Challenge
    1.2. Business Innovations
2. IKEA
    2.1. IKEA Social Initiative
    2.2. Disha
    2.3. IKEA Social Entrepreneurship
    2.4. IKEA Social Entrepreneurs
    2.5. IKEA Challenges
    2.6. Ingka Investments
3. Unilever
    3.1. Microcredit in Ghana
    3.2. Hindustan Unilever's Project Shakti
    3.3. Business Incubator in Indonesia
    3.4. Toilet Accelerator, Toilet Board Coalition
    3.5. Knorr Sustainability Partnership Fund
    3.6. Dove Self-Esteem Project
    3.7. Kabisig Program
    3.8. Academies of Shine
    3.9. Lifebuoy with Amref Health Africa
    3.10. Girl Guide Superheroes
    3.11. Vaseline Healing Project
    3.12. Enhancing Livelihoods Fund
    3.13. Loop
    3.14. The Ocean Fund
    3.15. Jaza Duka Mastercard in Kenya

1. General Electric's instruments

1.1 Ecomagination Challenge

The Ecomagination Challenge was launched in 2005 in partnership with many venture capital firms[29] and was a key part of GE's business strategy to accelerate the development and deployment of clean energy technology and drive a global energy transformation. It was a contest where every company, individual, or entity could submit their ideas and get capital, mentoring, and acceleration from GE, with institutional and collaborator support.

The company used this strategy of open innovation to build more efficient machines that produce cleaner energy, reduce greenhouse gas emissions, use clean water and cut its use, and are profitable.[30] Nowadays, these technologies have gone from expensive pilots to mainstream services, and they have been accelerating fast.[31]

Main objectives of the Ecomagination Challenge[32] include: (i) innovation on clean and sustainable solutions; (ii) solving environmental and sustainability challenges in a profitable, business-viable way, among others.

These projects allowed for reduction of greenhouse gas emissions and promoted better use of water. GE invested a total of USD $20 billion in cleaner technology solutions through EC that have returned US $270 billion in revenue. The company had reduced greenhouse gas emissions by 42 percent since 2004.

1.2. Business Innovations

GE Business Innovations is a program that includes GE Ventures, Licensing, Business Creation, and New Market Development. GE invests in promising startups, commercializes GE's IP, creates companies, and advances initiatives that seed the future of their businesses and communities.[33]

AirXos is a recent investment in a drone system that potentially can utilize unmanned aircraft to deliver packages to consumers, transport organs

---

[29]Kleiner Perkins, RockPort Capital, KPCB, Foundation Capital, Emerald Technology Ventures, and Carbon Trust. Today GE's partners include Masdar, Walmart, Total, MWH, Goldman Sachs, BHP Billiton, Intel, and Statoil, among others.

[30]https://www.ge.com/reports/ecomagination-ten-years-later-proving-efficiency-economics-go-hand-hand/.

[31]https://www.ge.com/reports/5-ways-companies-can-weave-sustainability-dna/.

[32]*GE's ecomagination Challenge: AN EXPERIMENT IN OPEN INNOVATION, Henry Chesbrough.*

[33]https://www.ge.com/businessinnovations.

between hospitals, conduct search missions in remote areas, inspect bridges and highways, and perhaps transport people.

2. IKEA's instruments

2.1. IKEA Social Initiative[34]

By mid-1990s, IKEA and many other companies became acutely aware of widespread child labor in South Asia. This was the starting point for IKEA's fight against child labor in the supply chain and promotion of child rights around the world.

Among other initiatives, the company developed a strategic philanthropy initiative, the IKEA Social Initiative, established in 2005. The main partners are the two leading global child-right organizations: UNICEF and Save the Children,[35] as well as other like Clinton Health Access Initiative.[36] The IKEA Social Initiative invests in a range of programs with a holistic approach to create a substantial and lasting change in the lives of children and women;[37] improving their health, enabling access to a quality education for children, and empowering women to create a better future for themselves and their communities.

IKEA Social Initiative has committed more than USD $180 million in cash and in-kind donations to UNICEF's programs to save and improve the lives of children and their families.

UNICEF representatives note how IKEA's commitment to the project is clear and long lasting: what makes IKEA Social Initiative a true partner is the company's deep commitment to social responsibility and their direct engagement with issues affecting children. They have truly joined with UNICEF to tackle issues like child labor at their root causes.[38]

IKEA's contributions come more than just in money: IKEA Social Initiative support includes donations of 344,000 quilts after the 2005 Pakistan earthquake in Kashmir; early childhood development kits for Iraq, and cash and in-kind support to the 2004 tsunami-affected countries of India, Sri Lanka, Pakistan, and the Maldives. IKEA Social Initiative donated 18,000 tables for use in schools and health centers in Liberia and Burundi, thousands of much needed quilts to tsunami survivors in Indonesia and Sri

---

[34]https://business.un.org/en/documents/8372.
[35]As a first step, IKEA worked with Save the Children to help formulate a child labor code of conduct, "The IKEA Way on Preventing Child Labor."
[36]https://www.ikea.com/in/en/people-and-planet/ikea-foundation-pub7720149a.
[37]https://business.un.org/en/documents/8372.
[38]https://www.unicef.org/french/people/ikea.html.

Lanka, 45,000 baby blankets for survivors of the Pakistan earthquake, and 5,000 bed sheets, 20,000 bath towels, 10,242 sleeping bags, 7,000 school bags, and 30,000 bowls to survivors of the China earthquake.

2.2. Disha

Disha is a partnership between India Development Foundation, UNDP, and Xyntéo, supported by IKEA Foundation. It was launched in 2005 and aims at supporting one million underprivileged women in India to learn marketable skills and connect them with income opportunities. The project strives to enable women to become economically self-sufficient so that they, their families, and future generations can have better opportunities in life.

It is a people-centered approach, outcome-oriented monitoring, and enables women to secure employment or start their own enterprise.

Besides its investment of USD $12,253,883, IKEA is also giving technical support to the project.[39]

2.3. IKEA Social Entrepreneurship

The IKEA Social Entrepreneurship initiative was founded in the Netherlands in 2018 to support and accelerate the movement of social entrepreneurship within and outside IKEA's value chain. It aims to support a significant positive impact on society and the environment through its activities. These projects are in start-up phase and IKEA plans to do financial support (grants, loans, and equity investments), nonfinancial support in the form of skills and mentorship programs (co-worker engagement program), and by using their IKEA channels and other marketplace.[40]

The authors want to further understand if this project aims to consolidate IKEA Social Entrepreneurs program gradually.

2.4. IKEA Social Entrepreneurs[41]

Started in 2012, before IKEA Social Entrepreneurship. IKEA has now several ongoing partnerships with social entrepreneurs. Through this collaboration with social entrepreneurs, IKEA wants to support positive economic and

---

[39]http://www.in.undp.org/content/india/en/home/sustainable-development/successstories/press-release--undp-partners-with-larsen-and-toubro-infotech-and.html and http://www.in.undp.org/content/india/en/home/operations/projects/poverty_reduction/creating-employment-and-entrepreneurship-opportunities-for-women.html.
[40]https://evpa.eu.com/members/ikea-social-entrepreneurship.
[41]https://www.ikea.com/gb/en/this-is-ikea/people-planet/people-communities/social-entrepreneurs/.

social development across the world—long-term sustainable change in a way that charity by itself cannot.

In 2018, they were supporting 58 social entrepreneurs and impact projects, with EUR 12 million, in 14 countries,[42] including:

- Syrian women in refugee camps in Jordan, in cooperation with the Jordan River Foundation (year 2016)
    - The program emerges from the urgent need to get people into work and into society. Today more than 100 artisans are part of the initiative, a number that will double during 2019 and that is expected to reach 400 by the end of 2020. The idea is to help women in refugee camps to create new expressions based on their skills and traditions so they can begin their own business, and spur local entrepreneurship.
    - Products include textiles, handwoven rugs, and other decorative items designed for export and the local market in Jordan. IKEA designers were involved in the project.
    - IKEA began its initiative in 2016 when it opened production facilities in Amman, near Jordanian refugee camps.
- Refugees in Austin, Texas
    - The idea is to create opportunities for refugees to rebuild their lives—internationally, but also locally. Open Arms in Austin, Texas, started as a small, local initiative that worked with only one IKEA store. The ambition was to empower refugee women through fair-wage employment, consisting of turning leftover IKEA fabric into new products.
    - Today, Open Arms has become a successful enterprise, going from 2,000 products per year to 20,000. The program in Austin has become a model for IKEA. Nearly 20 stores are now working with upcycled collections, and more than 100 stores carry larger, international collections co-created with social entrepreneurs. They are all driven by the same ethical values and objectives—to make it possible for refugee women to stand on their own, to integrate and provide for themselves and their families.

---

[42]Including India, Thailand, Uganda, Sweden, Denmark, Belgium, Netherlands, Croatia, Romania, Jordan, United States, and Canada.

- White Nile Project[43]
  - Uganda is the biggest coffee exporting country in Africa, yet the average size of a coffee farm is less than 0.25 hectare—just a quarter the size of a football field. It is not easy to run a profitable farm with such small resources. To help support the economic independence of farmers, as well as more sustainable farming practices, IKEA has teamed up with a regional coffee project. As a result, they are now introducing the first ever single-origin coffee to the IKEA Swedish Food Market: 100% Arabica beans from the White Nile region, a special coffee with a unique taste, created in cooperation with thousands of small-scale farmers.
  - The project started out almost 20 years ago, in an attempt to promote the cultivation of high-quality Arabica coffee in a region known as the producer of less favored beans. By supporting the initiative, IKEA contributes to the economic empowerment of farmers and their families.
  - By making a long-term commitment to the White Nile farmers growing Arabica beans, IKEA is entering a partnership where everyone is a winner. The special PÅTÅR coffee is not a charity project—it is a business opportunity.
- Handmade rugs with India and Bangladesh[44]
  - Handmade rugs are co-created with weavers in India and Bangladesh, who are empowered to run their business and are experts on how to make the most of different weaving techniques to achieve a unique design.
  - During the last years, since the 2010 launch of the program, the initiative has dramatically improved the working conditions for the weavers in the region.
  - IKEA launched inclusively a new loom that enables weavers to adopt a more ergonomic working position and requires less muscle power to operate, making it easier for more women to weave rugs. IKEA made sure that the new loom technology cannot be patented, making it freely available to anyone who wishes to use and develop it.

---

[43] https://www.ikea.com/es/en/news/a-coffee-with-a-mission-pub124e0a71.
[44] https://www.ikea.com/ms/en_US/pdf/reports-downloads/IKEA_BEHIND_Handmade_rugs.pdf.

- As result of the project, more women are becoming weavers. More than 500 people were trained through IKEA weaving schools. Approximately 5,500 weavers and 4,500 other workers are involved in the initiative.[45]
- The ambition is to improve the rug and carpet industry in India and Bangladesh as a whole. It is a long-term commitment without an end date.

Through these partnerships IKEA has access to limited edition collections of handmade and fair products that are sold in selected stores around the world and the profits serve to nourishing this program more. Developing the business with a social mission creates life-changing opportunities for families and communities, which in turn leads to better health care, education, gender empowerment, and reduced poverty. These partnerships are a new business model, where everyone wins.

As they gain access to a global marketplace, the social entrepreneurs are able to provide local artisans with employment on their own terms, making it possible for them to provide for their families without leaving their villages. All partners thus benefit from the collaboration. Through the partnership, the social entrepreneurs learn about design, production, sustainability, work environment, export, and more. In exchange, IKEA gains access to artisans skilled in traditional handicrafts.

2.5. IKEA Challenges

IKEA is developing open innovation processes where it is partnering and opening contests in order to innovate in its production line, while bringing social impact.[46] One example:

- ThisAbles project[47]
  - The ThisAbles project started with a hackathon that brought together engineers and people with disabilities to work on ideas at an IKEA store.[48]

---

[45] https://www.ikea.com/ms/en_AU/pdf/reports-downloads/IKEA_BEHIND_
Handmade_rugs.pdf.
[46] https://www.dezeen.com/2018/02/10/ikea-hacks-10-best/.
[47] https://thisables.com/en/about/.
[48] https://thisables.com/en/.

- As part of IKEA's vision to "create a better everyday life for as many people as possible," IKEA Israel joined forces with the nonprofit organizations Milbat and Access Israel, which specialize in creating solutions for populations with special needs and disabilities. As part of this challenge/contest, partners and some innovators jointly developed a new and revolutionary line of products that bridge some of the gaps between existing IKEA products and the special needs of people belonging to these populations.

2.6. Ingka Investments

Ingka Investments aligns IKEA investments with its business needs and wants to make a positive difference in the societies where it invests. They invest in renewal energies, forests, fast-moving startups on retail development, customer fulfilment, digitalization, innovation, circular economy, and so on. Investments include bonds, venture capital, listed shares, and alternative investments (such as infrastructure funds), all of them aligned with IKEA vision, business idea, culture, and values.[49]

According to Krister Mattsson, Head of Ingka Investments, "Here we are not only supporting the clean energy transition and responsible forest management, we also balance our financial exposure. Energy and wood are very important resources to us, and our product margins go down if the prices for either increase, so our investments provide us with some protection. We think of it as long-term macro-hedging, as well as sustainable investments."

The primary aim of Ingka Investment portfolio is to invest in and acquire companies that will benefit the core IKEA retail business, usually through adding a competence or a service that complements their offer. Ingka Investments invests, develops, and manages financial assets to support the growth of the IKEA retail business and to safeguard the future financial strength of Ingka Group. Some examples are:

- TaskRabbit[50]
  - During 2017, Ingka Group acquired TaskRabbit, an online, on-demand task management network that helps people manage their everyday lives at home by connecting them to trusted Taskers who can help get it done.[51]

---

[49] https://www.ingka.com/what-we-do/ingka-investments/.
[50] https://www.taskrabbit.com/.
[51] https://www.ikea.com/ms/en_US/pdf/sustainability_summary/INGKAGroup_SustainabilitySummaryReport_FY18.pdf.

- TaskRabbit exists to make life easier for its users (it offers IKEA customers additional ways to access flexible and affordable service solutions), but it's also about giving anyone the opportunity to be able to do the work that suits them, whenever they want. Taskers choose their own schedules and can work around whatever else they have planned. For some it can be a full-time job, and for others it can be a way of earning money while studying.[52]
- As Taskers can work more, IKEA can sell more furniture, and customers get the convenience.
- Ingka Group and TaskRabbit planned to continue to grow together during FY19, looking at opportunities for expanding into more markets. Following a successful launch in Canada, there is a blueprint for quicker, more efficient rollouts, and the future of the partnership looks bright.
- Morssinkhof Rymoplast
  - MR is a plastics recycling company based in the Netherlands, a family-run business that has been operating for over 50 years and is one of the leaders on this industry. In February 2017, Ingka Investments made a minority shareholding investment and took the opportunity to invest in its future.
  - With the European strategy for plastics in a circular economy in place it's likely that recycled plastics products will become even more desirable, and both companies see a big opportunity on this partnership in order to invest in MR production capacity and allow IKEA a new line of recycled plastic production.[53]

3. Unilever's instruments

3.1. Microcredit in Ghana

To reach remote villages in Ghana, Unilever and UNICEF have teamed up with a local bank to provide microcredit facilities to enable village women to buy products on credit for onward sale. Over 400 women are involved, giving them a useful source of income and Unilever access to villages that it would otherwise be difficult to reach.[54]

---

[52]https://www.ikea.com/ms/en_US/pdf/sustainability_summary/INGKAGroup_SustainabilitySummaryReport_FY18.pdf.

[53]https://www.ikea.com/ms/en_CA/pdf/yearly_summary/INGKAGroup_SustainabilitySummaryReport_FY18.pdf.

[54]https://www.unilever.com/Images/global-challenges-local-actions_tcm13-5100_tcm244-409749_1_en.pdf.

3.2. Hindustan Unilever's Project Shakti

Hindustan Project Shakti means "empowerment." Instead of using its customary wholesaler-to-retailer distribution model to reach remote villages, Unilever in India recruits village women, provides them with access to microfinance loans, and trains them in selling soaps, detergents, and other products door to door. More than 65,000 women entrepreneurs participate, nearly doubling their household incomes on average, while increasing rural access to hygiene products and thus contributing to public health.

Shakti entrepreneurs distribute Unilever's brands in many thousands of villages across India. The company provides training on basic accounting, sales, health and hygiene, and relevant IT skills.[55]

They are conducting evaluations and building impact-measurement tools in order to gain and share insights.

They asked agency Kantar Public to look at the impact of Shakti in four states (Karnataka, Maharashtra, Bihar, and Uttar Pradesh). Completed in 2017, the analysis showed that the opportunity to earn an income was the biggest motivation in prompting women to join the initiative, and that most of them had not been employed before. They felt that Shakti enhanced their monthly income, leading to an increase in spending capacity, and also improved their financial decision-making abilities. It also found that the program helped women to increase their confidence, self-esteem, negotiating skills, communication, and engagement capabilities, and supported the development of the entrepreneurial mindset needed to run a business.[56]

These social gains have been met by business gains for the company. As of 2012 Project Shakti had achieved more than US $100 million in sales. Its success has led Unilever to roll out similar programs in other parts of the world. A similar project to Shakti is Guddi Baji (literally "The Good Sister), building knowledge, confidence, and sales in Pakistan.

3.3. Business incubator Indonesia[57]

In Indonesia, 90% of all businesses are small or medium-sized and are responsible for generating over half the country's income. They are a major engine for growth in the local economy, so the Indonesian government is keen to find

---

[55] https://www.unilever.com/sustainable-living/enhancing-livelihoods/opportunities-for-women/expanding-opportunities-in-our-retail-value-chain/.

[56] https://hbr.org/2015/01/the-truth-about-csr; https://www.unilever.com/sustainable-living/enhancing-livelihoods/inclusive-business/connecting-with-smallholder-farmers-to-enhance-livelihoods/#244-419633.

[57] https://www.unilever.com/Images/global-challenges-local-actions_tcm244-409749_en.pdf.

new ways of encouraging more entrepreneurs to start businesses. Unilever Indonesia works with over 2,000 small and medium-sized suppliers and distributors, so is an appropriate partner to work with the country on its initiative to encourage unemployed youths to become entrepreneurs. For example, in Jakarta they trained young entrepreneurs in food hygiene to sell traditional hot cooked meals made with Unilever products. Unilever Indonesia is now establishing a business incubator to provide training and business advice for entrepreneurs.

3.4. Toilet Accelerator, Toilet Board Coalition (TBC)[58],[59]

Initiated in 2014 and formalized in 2015 as a business-led partnership and platform, the TBC has the ambition to address the global sanitation crisis by accelerating the Sanitation Economy. The TBC is enabling private sector engagement; connecting large and small companies; and ensuring close collaboration between private, public, and nonprofit sectors with the common goal to achieve Sustainable Development Goal 6, universal access to sanitation.

The TBC runs the Toilet Accelerator, the world's first accelerator program dedicated to sanitation entrepreneurs in low-income markets. The members of the Toilet Board Coalition believe that accelerating the sanitation economy will deliver significant impact to business and society, mainly in these societies where sanitation problems are huge.

In 2017, it supported Samagra, a social enterprise that refurbishes run-down community toilets in India, and which received mentoring from our Domestos Global Brand Director (Unilever). For a small monthly fee, Samagra enables families to use clean, safe toilets and other related services.

In 2018, the TBC team added additional metrics related to the cohort businesses' investability and therefore prospect to reach scale and thus optimize societal impact. These metrics address the health of the organization, operational indicators, investment indicators, and overall impact. The focus of implementing the metrics is to develop a baseline of all organizations that have gone through the TBC accelerator program. This baseline will allow the TBC to assess growth on a quarterly basis for all current cohort members, and biannually for alumni cohort members who continue to work with the TBC.[60]

---

[58] https://www.unilever.com/sustainable-living/improving-health-and-well-being/health-and-hygiene/toilets-for-a-better-tomorrow/.

[59] https://medium.com/@TheToiletBoard/the-toilet-accelerator-samagra-story-a9a979 8a5a7b.

[60] http://www.toiletboard.org/accelerator.

3.5. Knorr Sustainability Partnership Fund[61]

The aim of this fund is to support farmers on complex sustainable agriculture projects which they may be unable to tackle alone. Knorr invests 50% of any agreed project budget, matched by an equivalent investment from the farmer side. This will enable farmers to try out new ideas and accelerate implementation of sustainable agricultural practices.

Each year Unilever co-invests 1 million euros with their suppliers and farmers in knowledge and equipment to accelerate the implementation of sustainable practices. Financial benefits resulting from the project have to be shared equally between the parties investing and a full report of the project, as well as sustainability achievements must be shared with Knorr at the end of the project.

3.6. Dove Self-Esteem Project[62]

Since 2005, the Dove Self-Esteem Project has helped more than 35 million young people build self-esteem and positive body confidence through our educational programs (confidence-building workshops for classrooms and educational activities for mentors and youth leaders). In 2018 alone, the program reached 6.3 million young people—a 12% increase from 2017. This is the biggest reach in a single year to date. Unilever's ambition is to help 40 million young people by 2020.[63] The program is run in cooperation with the World Association of Girl Guides and Girl Scouts since 2013, in order to get the message across to more young women.

The positive impact of the school self-esteem programs has been proved by academic studies[64] and Unilever also concluded that when women learn about Dove's Self-Esteem Project, their perception of Dove shifts and they are more likely to buy Unilever products.

---

[61] https://www.unilever.com/about/suppliers-centre/sustainable-sourcing-suppliers/ knorr-sustainability-partnership/knorr-sustainability-partnership-fund/.

[62] Effectiveness of a brief school-based body image intervention Dove Confident Me: Single Session when delivered by teachers and researchers: Results from a cluster randomised controlled trial. *Behaviour Research and Therapy* 74(2015): 94–104. https://www.research gate.net/publication/282593257_Effectiveness_of_a_brief_school-based_body_image _intervention_'Dove_Confident_Me_Single_Session'_when_delivered_by_teachers_and _researchers_Results_from_a_cluster_randomised_controlled_trial.

[63] https://www.unilever.com/sustainable-living/improving-health-and-well-being/ health-and-hygiene/building-body-confidence-and-self-esteem/.

[64] *Behavior Research and Therapy Journal* (2015).

3.7. Kasibig program

The Kabisig program brings store owners together with Unilever's distributors at Kabisig Summits, where they learn skills such as stock control, financial management, sales techniques, and customer service. Over 2015−2018, around 180,000 store owners have benefited from the Summits. Since it began at scale in 2016, Kabisig has enhanced the skills and training of over 165,000 women store owners and helped about 24,000 people set up new businesses. At the same time, Unilever's sales volume in participating Super!Stores has grown by 7% to 12% higher than stores that have not been through the program.

3.8. Academies of Shine[65]

In Brazil, the Brilhante laundry brand found that 70% of women want to start their own business because it is seen as one of the best chances for women to provide for their children and pay for their education. But Unilever also learned that only 7% of women feel they have the confidence and skills to do so. Fear of failure is a major cause of this hesitation.

To combat this, Unilever set up Escola Brilhante (Academy of Shine) in a partnership with local players who run the operations. It is an online women's entrepreneurship program that includes a microfinance helpline. Women can learn business skills and build their confidence in as little as five minutes a day through free courses. By 2018, Escola Brilhante supported over 140,000 women. After the program, 98% say they will start their own business—up from 74% before they started.

3.9. Lifebuoy with Amref Health Africa[66]

In Kenya, the company has partnered with Amref Health Africa, launching a program in 2017 in Migori County, one of the areas with the highest level of neonatal mortality in the country. Through community health workers, support groups, and health centers, the program educated new mothers over a period of six months on the importance of handwashing with soap, raising awareness of the risks of transmitting diseases to their newborn via contaminated hands.

New mothers who took part in the program were more likely to wash their hands with soap than the control group during three occasions: after

---

[65]https://www.unilever.com/sustainable-living/enhancing-livelihoods/opportunities-for-women/enhancing-entrepreneurial-life-skills-through-our-brands/.
[66]https://www.unilever.com/sustainable-living/improving-health-and-well-being/health-and-hygiene/healthy-handwashing-habits-for-life/.

changing nappies (26% vs. 2%), before breastfeeding (42% vs. 3%), and after visiting the toilet (39% vs. 10%). In addition, 90% of the new mothers reached talked about the program to their friends, family, and neighbors, highlighting a positive ripple effect.

3.10. Girl Guide Superheroes[67]

Through a partnership with World Association of Girl Guides and Girl Scouts (WAGGGS), 100,000 Girl Guides and Scouts in India became handwashing heroes by promoting this lifesaving habit within their local communities.

Each handwashing hero is trained on the importance of using soap while washing hands before eating and after using the toilet, with materials featuring the School of Five superhero Sparkle as a Girl Guide. They are also equipped with the necessary skills to share these learnings with others, encouraging the practice of using soap at critical occasions to spread across communities, protecting people from illnesses and infections. In total, WAGGGS reached more than 3 million children and their families through an adapted version of Lifebuoy's School of 5.

3.11. Vaseline Healing Project[68]

Since 2015, Unilever has helped to heal the skin of over 4 million people across 74 countries, through donations of Vaseline® products, as well as through relief missions to provide skin care treatment and training for local health workers. In 2018, they supported communities in Indonesia following an earthquake, tsunami, and volcano eruptions. In Bangladesh, they helped Rohingya refugees. And in Jordan, they sponsored a series of doctors on three-month placements, rotating around different Syrian refugee camps.

3.12. Enhancing Livelihoods Fund

Unilever developed the Enhancing Livelihoods Fund (ELF) in 2015 in partnership with Oxfam and the Ford Foundation to enable investment in innovative projects in the supply chain. These projects aim to improve the agricultural practices, skills, and livelihoods of smallholder farming communities, with a specific focus on empowering women and training. The fund provides a mix of loans, guarantees, and grants. It aims to incentivize investment in new processes that make a difference to communities while improving sustainability and crop yields.

---

[67] https://www.unilever.com/sustainable-living/improving-health-and-well-being/health-and-hygiene/healthy-handwashing-habits-for-life/.
[68] https://www.unilever.com/sustainable-living/improving-health-and-well-being/health-and-hygiene/ready-to-respond-to-disasters-and-emergencies/.

By 2018 they had enabled around 746,000 smallholder farmers to access initiatives aiming to improve their agricultural practices. Unilever also provides in kind materials and tools that are deeply helpful for farmers, with this and other programs and partnerships.

One of the projects inside ELF is the Comoros project (launched in 2017), that works with the supplier, Firmenich, to ensure a better representation of women in the supply chain and to help them to get a higher and more stable income. The 250 women involved are receiving training in sustainable agricultural practices. They are also building their knowledge in areas such as literacy and numeracy, entrepreneurship, and family planning. Access to a health insurance scheme and income diversification activities are other key elements of the initiative.[69] Other projects working with coconut sugar, palm oil, and tea[70] production are being financed by this Unilever program.

3.13. Loop™

In January 2019, Unilever announced the participation in Loop™, an innovative waste-free shopping and delivery model for reusable packaging innovations and refillable product formats. Products are shipped directly to consumers and are then returned and refilled.[71]

3.14. The Ocean Fund

In October 2018 at the Ocean Conference in Bali, Unilever announced its participation in the Ocean Fund. Managed by Circulate Capital, this cross-value chain investment fund is designed to accelerate the growth of waste collection and waste management in South and Southeast Asia. Unilever, PepsiCo, Proctor & Gamble, Dow Chemical Company, Danone, and Coca-Cola have joined forces to invest USD $100 million in the fund. The fund is being formed as a social and environmental impact investment fund for the primary purpose of reducing pollution and ocean plastic and combating environmental deterioration by providing risk-tolerant financing and related assistance to investments.[72]

---

[69] https://www.unilever.com/sustainable-living/enhancing-livelihoods/inclusive-business/connecting-with-smallholder-farmers-to-enhance-livelihoods/.

[70] 40 Partnerships and programs supporting sustainable tea. https://www.unilever.com/sustainable-living/reducing-environmental-impact/sustainable-sourcing/sustainable-tea-leading-the-industry/.

[71] https://www.unilever.com/sustainable-living/reducing-environmental-impact/waste-and-packaging/rethinking-plastic-packaging/.

[72] https://www.unilever.com/sustainable-living/reducing-environmental-impact/waste-and-packaging/rethinking-plastic-packaging/.

3.15. Jaza Duka Mastercard in Kenya[73]

In 2017, Unilever began a strategic partnership with Mastercard in Kenya. Together, they launched the Jaza Duka initiative, which uses a combination of innovative technology, targeted training, and the strength of the company's relationships with its distribution network to free retailers from the constraints of cash. ("Jaza Duka" translates as "fill up your store.")

By digitizing the processes of buying supplies and selling goods, small-scale retailers can build the credentials they need to access short-term working capital loans from Kenya Commercial Bank (KCB). The initiative combines distribution data from Unilever and analysis by Mastercard, on how much inventory a store has bought from Unilever over time. The results from the analysis are used to provide a microcredit eligibility recommendation to Kenya Commercial Bank (KCB). This solves the problem that banks usually require formal credit history or collateral, resulting in entrepreneurs borrowing from informal lenders at high interest rates and trapping them in a cycle of debt.[74]

This gives to these entrepreneurs better control of their inventory, so they can keep their shelves full and meet consumer demand. They are also able to access training and essential financial tools to help grow their sales and incomes. Retailers increased sales by 20% on average within the first six months. Unilever believes it could help them to have real impact. If they can support small retail entrepreneurs to grow beyond their current financial limitations and bring its sustainable products to more consumers, it could help transform economies in emerging markets and drive Unilever's growth.

---

[73]https://www.unilever.com/sustainable-living/enhancing-livelihoods/inclusive-business/empowering-small-scale-retailers-for-growth/.

[74]https://newsroom.mastercard.com/press-releases/mastercard-and-unilever-break-down-barriers-to-growth-for-micro-entrepreneurs-with-first-of-its-kind-digital-lending-platform/.

Impact Investing and European Wealth Managers: Why Impact Investing Will Go Mainstream and Evolve to Suit European Investors

Trang Fernandez-Leenknecht, CAIA, LLM

Abstract

Capital markets and private market participants have a role to play in solving global challenges. Several countries, European Union (EU) and non-EU Member States, have tackled the topic and addressed the need for capital to be channeled into Impact Investment. However, harmonized, large-scale regulations are necessary for a consistent implementation and diffusion to a mainstream scale of Impact Investing across Europe. Two approaches can be implemented: (i) clients becoming oriented and advised on a routine basis, if suitable, to Impact Investing, and (ii) wealth managers investing part of their assets under management into Impact Investing. The European Commission's (EC) Action Plan "Financing Sustainable Growth" aims at integrating Sustainable and Impact Investing at every stage of the wealth management chain. This constitutes a formidable opportunity to leverage and democratize Impact Investing in all European and non-European investors. With the EC's Action Plan on Sustainable Finance, financial intermediaries will need to ask every client about their sustainability investing preferences within the framework of the Markets in Financial Instruments Directive II (MiFID II) and the Insurance Distribution Directive (IDD) product suitability assessment. MiFID II and IDD, underpinned by the EC Action Plan, may play a key role in contributing to the European effort of combining "impact at scale" with "capital at scale" by driving more capital toward solutions focused on generating significant positive effects for people and the planet.

Keywords

Markets in Financial Instruments Directive, MiFID; Insurance Distribution Directive; Suitability; Financial Advice; Investment Advice; Financial Intermediaries; Impact Investing; Impact Reporting; Private Investors; Pension Fund; Wealth Management; Retail; Disclosure Regulation; European Securities and Markets Authority; European Union; European Regulation; European Union; France; Switzerland

INTRODUCTION

The world's biggest problems are also the world's biggest business opportunities.

Peter H. Diamandis[1]

Worldwide, sustainable investment assets—which include assets in impact investments—have grown 34% to USD $30.7 trillion from 2016 to 2018 (Global Sustainable Investment Alliance 2018). With a share of 11% of the global amounts, Europe accounts for the largest concentration of impact investment assets globally, which amounts in 2018 to USD $228.1 billion

---

[1] Peter H. Diamandis is the founder of the X Prize and co-founder and executive chairman of Singularity University.

(L'Impact Invest Lab 2018). The United Nations (UN) Sustainable Development Goals (SDGs) and the Paris Agreement on Climate Change[2] (European Commission 2018b and European Commission 2018c, p. 1) have undoubtedly been a driver of the increased interest in investing for positive impact (WWF and PWC 2019). However, there is still work to do when the amount allocated to sustainable investments is compared with the total value of assets under management worldwide—which totaled USD $74.3 trillion in 2018 (Fages et al. 2019). There is still also considerable room for improvement in the product offer range for retail investors (Global Impact Investors Network[3] 2020) and the advice provided to end clients in particular (Eurosif 2018).

Capital and private market participants no doubt have a role to play in solving global challenges. Sustainable Investing, which includes Impact Investing, is destined to become part of the way both institutional and retail clients invest their money. Capital markets are key in helping to reorient capital flows toward investments in sectors and activities contributing to the sustainability of the economy (European Commission 2018a). These topics have been gaining traction amongst mainstream institutional investors in Europe, suggesting a wide potential for further reshaping the retail investment landscape. The wealth management sector will have to evolve—given the growing pressure from investors and policymakers—to employ public markets to "democratize" access to Impact Investing by providing liquidity and transparency, and most importantly, scale. Several initiatives exist, built either with a top-down approach through governmental actions or a bottom-up approach by the private sector.

Both European Union (EU) and non-EU Member countries have tackled this topic and addressed the need for capital to be channeled into more sustainable types of investments. However, harmonized large-scale regulations are necessary for a consistent and effective implementation of Impact Investing, and its ultimate diffusion to mainstream scale across Europe. Two approaches can be implemented: (i) clients being advised on a routine basis and oriented, if suitable, to Impact Investing; and (ii) wealth managers being required through regulation to invest parts of assets under management into Impact Investing.

According to the European Investment Bank,[4] Europe has to close an overall investment gap of yearly EUR €270 billion in transport, energy and

---

[2] Regulation (EU) 2019/2089 (European Union 2019).
[3] Hereafter referred to as GIIN.
[4] European Investment Bank (2016).

resource management infrastructure including water and waste.[5] The European Commission (EC) estimates that extra yearly investment of around EUR €180 billion is needed to achieve EU climate and energy targets by 2030[6] (European Commission 2018a, Action 1.1).

In order to foster investments in sustainable projects and set an example, the EU has pledged to make at least 20% of its budget directly climate-relevant (European Commission 2015). In 2017, the European Fund for Strategic Investments (EFSI) mobilized almost 30% of investments into energy, environment, and resource efficiency projects and social infrastructure. Until 2020, the EFSI will raise investment targets to at least 40% of EUR €500 billion (European Commission 2018a). Yet, some investors are still confused regarding what constitutes a sustainable investment. Hence, further steps are still needed to clarify frameworks and channel more investment into sustainable sectors.

At a supranational level, since 2016 the EU introduced a series of regulatory measures in the area of sustainable finance. Most of these measures, mainly the implementation of processes aimed at introducing voluntary market standards and mandatory legal obligations, were designed under the umbrella of the EC Action Plan entitled "Financing Sustainable Growth,"[7] released in March 2018. In this plan, the EC asserted its goal to reorient capital flows toward more sustainable investments, increase transparency and long-term finance, and mitigate the impacts that climate change (as well as broader social and environmental issues) can have on financial systems (Swiss Sustainable Finance 2019b).

The Markets in Financial Instruments Directive II (MiFID II[8]) and its corresponding Insurance Distribution Directive (IDD[9]) in the insurance industry regulate investment fund and insurance product distribution. Since January and July 2018, respectively, the MiFID II and IDD aim to strengthen the level of consumer protection in financial services and increase transparency in the industry across EU member States. Although both directives differ in some provisions, MiFID II and IDD will be equally addressed in the following paragraphs with respect to the implementation requirements in the context of the EC Action Plan.

---

[5]European Commission 2018a, Action 1.1. Estimated yearly average investment gap until 2020.
[6]Estimated yearly average investment gap for the period 2021 to 2030.
[7]Hereafter referred to as the Action Plan.
[8]European Commission (2014). Directive 2014/65/EU.
[9]European Union (2016a). Directive (EU) 2016/97.

The primary effects of MiFID II include the need for retail investors to seek advice in order to have access to any financial instrument deemed to be *complex*. In fact, the Impact Investing community faces several growth challenges, in particular relating to the distribution to retail investors. Most impact investment opportunities have historically been developed based on small-scale project finance such as activities in micro-finance, affordable housing, and access to energy in developing economies. Strategies for impact investments addressed activities and entities that faced a financing gap and were initially focused on projects at growth stages and ventures, rather than mature businesses,[10] and mostly concentrated in illiquid assets,[11] hence not suitable to the retail market (2i 2019, p. 22).

Further, the secondary effects of MiFID II depend on the reactions and adaptations of market players. Proper implementation of the framework as per MiFID II regulation may give room for opportunities in Impact Investing as "Policy and regulation can catalyze industry growth by establishing incentives for impact investments and creating a supportive regulatory environment for investors and businesses generating impact" (GIIN 2018b). Investment fund distribution is likely to change via the primary and secondary effects of MiFID II.

This chapter addresses if and how the MiFID II can effectively contribute to the European and global effort of combining "impact at scale" with "capital at scale" (Rust S. 2019), by driving more capital toward solutions focused on generating significant positive effects for people and the planet.

This chapter was compiled on the basis of an extensive desk and legal review and the author's combined legal, financial, and practical experience as an advisor for private clients in the banking sector and philanthropic and impact investing projects, and as an institutional and private investor. It also contains real-life examples cited from the author's experience.

The next section addresses the impetus of the EC to introduce mandatory and voluntary measures in the area of sustainable finance, within the context of the EC's Action Plan on sustainable finance. It also examines the MiFID II as a new regulation and its impact on financial advisory of end clients, as well as how it may support the integration and generalizing of Impact Investing in the retail market. The third section sets out how MiFID II

---

[10]The entry of large-scale, for-profit asset managers in the sector has shown a transfer of the approach to mature including listed companies and activities. Due to their size, the new entrants have quickly represented a significant part of total assets under management. With reference to the GIIN (2018a), p. 28.

[11]The majority of respondents use private equity (78%) and private debt (71%). With reference to the GIIN (2018b), p. 27.

could ignite a greater diffusion of Impact Investing, even in countries where sustainability-promoting standards and/or regulations are already in place. The final section concludes by summarizing what MiFID II achieved so far and what is still yet to be accomplished for Impact Investing to be suitable for every European investor.

MIFID II: A GROWTH-DRIVER FOR IMPACT INVESTING

The Action Plan of the European Union

According to Eurosif, the leading European association for the promotion and advancement of sustainable and responsible investment, Europe has seen[12] an increase in demand by retail investors by over 800%, a fantastic potential of a pool of growth that needs to be mobilized (Eurosif 2018, p. 76). Yet retail clients hardly have the opportunity to invest according to sustainability preferences. Current national legislations, strongly shaped by MiFID regulations, contain no specific requirements to entrench sustainability in investment preferences by financial advisers. As a result, sustainability preferences are not even discussed with many retail investors, which is reflected by a lower demand of sustainable oriented products. Investment advisers have consequently fewer incentives to supply to these considerations and asset managers to design suitable products. In addition, sustainability-focused vehicles are perceived by many investment professionals as presenting an inopportune tradeoff with returns—despite numerous studies pointing to the opposite—and retail investors are not given the tools to understand the real impact of these financial products.

The EC has expressed its determination to lead the global work in this area and support sustainability-conscious investors to choose suitable projects and companies (European Commission 2018d). It proposed a roadmap to lay out the right conditions and incentives for investors to fund projects whose main scope targets low-carbon and energy-efficient infrastructure. The EC Action Plan (2018) leaned on MiFID II directs firms to "ask about their clients' preferences (such as Environmental, Social, and Governance factors) and take them into account when assessing the range of financial instruments and insurance products to be recommended, i.e. in the product selection process and suitability assessment" (European Commission 2018a, section 2.4). The retail sector has the potential to become

---

[12]In the period 2015–2018.

one of the bedrocks of sustainable finance (Eurosif 2018, p. 76), and Impact Investing could benefit from its scaling-up effect thanks to the potential of being distributed to retail investors.

The Action Plan outlines 10 reforms in three areas:

- Reorientation of capital flows toward sustainable investments
- Management of financial risks stemming from climate change, environmental degradation, and social issues
- Enhancement of transparency and long-termism in financial and economic activity

Within the framework of MiFID II and IDD regulations, the EC Action Plan on sustainable finance aims at giving sustainability the impetus, frame, and standards that have previously been missing in the end-client market in the EU.

Suitability and Appropriateness Tests

The key aspect that MiFID II and IDD touch upon regarding investor protection is clients' evaluation for product and portfolio *suitability* and *appropriateness*. The directives require investment firms and insurance distributors to assess whether product or portfolio strategies align with clients' profiles by the provision of any type of investment advice and portfolio management.

The suitability test in the MiFID II framework constitutes one of the most important requirements for the distribution of investment products at the European level, which includes sustainable and impact investments. This assessment of product-to-client suitability requires that investment firms providing investment advice (independent or not) to effect suitable recommendations to their clients, and for firms providing portfolio management to make suitable investment decisions on behalf of their clients within the directions of investment mandates. Under Article 25(2) of MiFID II,[13] and Articles 54 and 55 of the MiFID II Delegated Regulation,[14] intermediaries

---

[13] EU Directive 2014/65 (European Commission 2014), respectively, for insurance product suitability and appropriateness tests, under article 30(1) IDD (European Union 2016a).

[14] Delegated Regulation (EU) 2017/565 (European Commission 2016). Delegated Acts are instruments used to amend or supplement existing laws, such as to add new rules considered nonessential (whereas implementing acts introduce measures to ensure that laws are implemented in a consistent way across the EU countries). See https://ec.europa.eu/info/law/law-making-process/adopting-eu-law/implementing-and-delegated-acts_en (accessed 20 May 2020).

are required to assess clients' investment objectives and risk tolerance when offering financial instruments (European Commission 2014; European Commission 2016).

Amendment of Delegated Regulation under the MIFID II[15] in the context of the EC Action Plan (European Commission 2018b)—not adopted yet—will require investment firms to ask their clients about sustainability preferences and consider these preferences when advising them, as part of the product selection process and the suitability assessment.

In order to raise firms' and supervisors' attention and awareness, pending changes to the legal framework, the European Securities and Markets Authority (ESMA), the technical advising body in the implementation of MiFID II,[16] has included "good practices" in its final guidelines on certain aspects of the MiFID II suitability requirements (ESMA 2018a). ESMA has been making focused amendments pursuant to changes in the MIFID II Delegated Regulation on the topic of sustainability and monitors legislative proposals[17] under the EC Action Plan (ESMA 2018b). The guidelines principally address situations where services are provided to retail clients (ESMA 2018a). It can be noted, however, that the EC Action Plan suggests that firms "should" collect sustainability preferences, thereby creating a more stringent requirement than a "good practice" for firms to consider nonfinancial elements.

Assessing "Complex" Suitable Products

Suitability test is the process of collecting information about a client, and the subsequent assessment by the firm that a given investment product is suitable for them. Prior to the provision of investment advisory and portfolio management services, information must be given on the characteristics of each financial product offered (ex-ante information)[18] (European Commission 2014,

---

[15]Respectively IDD Delegated Regulation (draft) that aims at establishing sustainability considerations and preferences in the client advisory process in the insurance sector (European Commission 2018c, p. 3).

[16]European Securities and Markets Authority, MiFID II. https://www.esma.europa.eu/policy-rules/mifid-ii-and-mifir (accessed 19 May 2020).

[17]In May 2018, the EC adopted a package of measures implementing several key actions announced in its Action Plan on sustainable finance. The package includes: 1. Taxonomy, 2. Disclosure and Duties, 3. Benchmarks, 4. Sustainability Preferences (consultation). For more information see https://ec.europa.eu/info/business-economy-euro/banking-and-finance/sustainable-finance_de#committments.

[18]Article 50(2), (European Commission 2016).

art. 24(4)). The impacts of suitability are wide-reaching, meaning advisers must show not only whether the product was suitable, but also whether there were better alternatives (European Commission 2016, art. 53(1)). They cannot just state that the definitions of suitability have been met, but *how* suitability is met. Investment firms must prepare a report explaining how the advice provided meets the client's investment objectives, risk profile, ability to withstand losses, and preferences. Reports to clients must specify the type and complexity of the financial service and the nature of the investment service (ex-post information).[19]

The statement of suitability must be sent either just before the transaction is carried out or immediately after the client becomes bound. The suitability requirements apply to institutional and individual investors. These obligations are intended to protect investors and have been detailed and strengthened by requiring investment advisors and managers to consider their clients' risk tolerance and ability to bear losses.

In the case of investment services being provided without advice—such as execution-only services or when the service is performed on the client's initiative—the requirement of *appropriateness* applies in lieu of suitability (European Commission 2014, art. 25(2)(3)).[20] Investment firms must assess if the complex financial instrument and/or service is appropriate[21] for the individual *retail* clients (e.g. relevant knowledge and experience), whereas institutional clients are not subject to appropriateness requirements because they are deemed qualified investors.

MiFID II suitability requirements provide an opportunity to improve client servicing and advisory services as financial intermediaries have needed to adjust their processes or consider changes to business models altogether. Well ahead of client product advisory phase, the Action 7 of the EC Action Plan (European Commission 2018a) requires that institutional investors and asset managers implement sustainability considerations. As per these requirements, firms and managers must explain how, in the investment decision-making process, sustainability shall be incorporated when investment advice is provided. In its guidelines, ESMA reminds firms that the suitability assessment is not limited to recommendations to buy a financial instrument but includes a recommendation to buy, hold, or sell

---

[19]Recital 77 MiFID II Delegated Regulation (European Commission 2016).
[20]See also articles 55 and 56 MiFID II Delegated Regulation (European Commission 2016).
[21]The appropriateness test also applies when the client wants to invest in noncomplex financial instruments (for example, shares traded on regulated markets, bonds, debt instruments, investment funds, or money market instruments).

an instrument, or *not to do so*[22] (ESMA 2018a, p. 50). Thus, suitability is at the heart of the entire investment process, from fund creation through to distribution.

Integrating Impact Investing into Investment Funds

The EC[23] defines "investment funds" as investment products created with the unique purpose of collecting investors' capital. That capital is collectively invested through a portfolio of financial securities such as stocks, bonds, and other instruments. Investment funds play a major role in streamlining the accumulation of personal savings, whether for retirement or for major investments. They are also important in making institutional and personal savings available to the economy, such as loans to companies and projects, which contribute to growth and jobs.

According to the Global Impact Investing Network (GIIN), Impact Investments are defined as investments made with the intention to generate positive, measurable social and environmental impact alongside a financial return. Investments referred to as "Impact Investing" characterize the approach of investing in funds or projects with declared impact goals (Mougeot 2019), such as social (e.g. affordable housing, microfinance) or environmental (e.g. energy efficiency, waste reduction) goals. Impact Investing is the only investment category explicitly designed to generate an impact in the real economy[24] (2i 2019, section 1.2). "Within the sustainable investment universe, impact investment is one investment approach that is based on specifically assessing and reporting on the impacts of an investment" (European Commission 2017, section 3.4).

Capital deployments in the Impact Investing category traditionally tend to solve a lack of access to finance, such as microfinance and seed capital investments. They tend to be made via investment vehicles that qualify as complex products, such as private equity, infrastructure, debt, and private

---

[22] Art. 16(2) and 25(2) MiFID II (European Commission 2014) as well as recital 87 and Art. 21 MiFID II Delegated Regulation (European Commission 2016).

[23] See European Commission on Investment funds at https://ec.europa.eu/info/business-economy-euro/growth-and-investment/investment-funds_en.

[24] In its Final Report 2018 on Sustainable Finance (HLEG Final Report), the High Level Expert Group noted that most ESG-related products today have not been designed to influence the decisions of players in the real economy, such as that investee companies align their investment plans with climate goals (European Union 2018, p. 10). The products are primarily designed to marginally include financial risks relating to ESG factors, e.g. by reducing the exposure to risky activities while increasing the exposure to green activities (ex. green funds, low carbon ETFs).

capital (2i 2019, p. 23). These asset classes are usually reserved to qualified and experienced investors as they require protection reinforcement.

The majority of impact investors are banks, pension funds, financial advisors, wealth managers, family foundations, government investors, and development finance institutions.[25] Yet, impact project holders and social enterprises demand innovative and flexible funding structures that institutional investors are often hesitant to provide. Efforts are needed, in particular from financial institutions, in order to bring impact into mainstream capital markets and integrate impact into core financial products. The accessibility and availability of such products will need to be improved by developing and providing products suitable for a broader spectrum of investors— including retail investors.

Interest in impact-focused financial products has never been stronger than today, as demonstrated in numerous surveys and academic research.[26] Many retail investors are concerned about sustainability and want to leverage their exposure in order to generate positive change in the real economy (2i 2019, p. 9 and annex 1). A great many researches have shown that specific segments of society, specifically the so-called Millennial generation and women, wish their values to be reflected in the companies they spend their money with and that they entrust their money to. Major financial institutions are currently adopting impact-related objectives, and impact-related claims and pledges[27] are multiplying (2i 2019, p. 4) alongside stronger regulatory requirements at the EU level. With significant investors and large fund providers groups recently getting involved and setting up impact investment funds, Impact Investing has become the growing methodology mobilizing private and public capital to address social challenges.

Within this context, MiFID II aims to strengthen the level of investor protection and increase transparency across the investment fund distribution. MiFID II within the EC Action Plan integrates sustainability factors into the investment process and the suitability assessment.[28] The EC draft

---

[25]More information at https://thegiin.org/impact-investing/need-to-know/.

[26]Morgan Stanley: Sustainable Signals (https://www.morganstanley.com/pub/content/dam/msdotcom/ideas/sustainable-signals/pdf/Sustainable_Signals_Whitepaper.pdf), Natixis: Mind Shift (https://www.im.natixis.com/us/resources/mind-shift-getting-past-the-screens-of-responsible-investing), Bauer et al. (2018).

[27]Such as Climate Action 100+, the Katowice Pledge, the UNEP Responsible Banking Principles, ISO 14097, and the Science Based Target Initiative for Financial Institutions.

[28]In addition to the suitability test, MiFID's sustainability governance includes the target market assessment (e.g. retail investors) and the introduction of sustainability-related disclosure requirements for financial institutions.

legislation[29] talks about "environmental, social and governance (ESG) preferences" or "sustainability preferences" and assumes end investors are exclusively interested in increasing their portfolio in ESG- or sustainability-oriented positions (Swiss Sustainable Finance 2019b; Waygood 2019). However, there is a much wider spectrum of preferences that the MiFID II suitability test needs to consider (Eurosif 2018, pp. 34, 37–38), among others, the whole range of sustainable-minded investment approaches, including negative screening, stewardship, and Impact Investing[30] (Eurosif 2018, p. 41; Mougeot 2019). Hence, the definition of investment preferences within the framework of MiFID II should be client-led, undertaken at the level of each individual client on a case-by-case basis with the assistance of advisers or tools to inform about the possible options, and not predetermined by a narrower version of what sustainable investment might mean.

If executed tactfully, regulations such as MiFID II can help integrate Impact Investing into investment funds, which would aggregate and deploy capital into securities and projects generating positive social and environmental impacts on a massive scale. Alternatively, direct investments can be selected in the form of "green bonds" or other instruments—that is, funding projects with positive environmental benefits, or in companies committed to improving certain impact issues. This could enable retail investors to find financial products that match their impact-related expectations and to enhance the larger diffusion of such products on the mass market (2i 2019, p. 4).[31]

---

[29] EC Delegated Act amending Delegated Regulation (EU) 2017/565 as regards the integration of Environmental, Social, and Governance (ESG) considerations and preferences into the investment advice and portfolio management (European Commission 2018b). In the context of product governance, ESMA proposed requiring manufacturers and distributors to consider clients' ESG preferences within the target market of investment products and within the mandatory product review process.

[30] The EC Staff Working Document on Sustainable Products in a Circular Economy and the Draft Disclosure Regulation identify "financial products which have as an objective a positive impact for the environment and society." "The Action Plan proposes to widen the scope of the EU Ecolabel to financial products because consumers are increasingly interested in investing in products with a positive sustainability impact."

[31] In this context, the Ecolabel scheme is one of the first concrete tools that the EC plans to launch to help achieve this objective. For more information see European Commission's Sustainable Finance: EU and global commitments, https://ec.europa.eu/info/business-economy-euro/banking-and-finance/sustainable-finance_de#committments.

DEVELOPING IMPACT INVESTING TO SUIT THE RETAIL MARKET

Currently, when investment advice is given, clients' preferences regarding sustainability and Impact Investing are not sufficiently considered. As a matter of fact, financial advisors are not incentivized to ask clients whether they have any sustainability preferences (Waygood 2019). Moreover, evidence shows that upstream fund manufacturers and asset managers still do not systematically consider sustainability factors and risks in the investment process (European Commission 2018a, section 3.2). Hence, end investors may not receive the full information they need, should they want to consider sustainability-related issues in their investment decisions. As a result, investors are not sufficiently informed of the risks of *not* considering sustainability when assessing the performance of their investments over time. In order to improve the investment decision-making process, transparency toward end investors needs to be increased.

In addition to the mandatory reporting obligation according to MiFID II, the EC has introduced in the implementation of its Action Plan new disclosure regulations for investment products[32] (European Union 2019). These disclosure regulations would identify "financial products which have as an objective a positive impact for the environment and society" (2i 2019, p. 10). Specific disclosure requirements associated with impact-related claims apply to investment vehicles, and impose: (i) "a description of the environmental or social characteristics or the sustainable investment objective; (ii) information on the methodologies used to assess, measure and monitor the environmental or social characteristics or the impact of the sustainable investments selected for the financial product, including its data sources, screening criteria for the underlying assets and the relevant sustainability indicators used to measure the environmental or social characteristics or the overall sustainable impact of the financial product" (European Union 2019, art. 10).

The Disclosure Regulation entered into force on December 20, 2019.[33] This is the farthest-reaching sustainable finance initiative adopted by the EU to date, as it affects existing mandatory obligations under the 12 most significant financial normative frameworks, including MiFID II[34]

---

[32] Regulation (EU) 2019/2088 (European Union 2019).

[33] Application expected in 15 months from the date of entry in force.

[34] In addition to MiFID II, these are: Capital Requirements Directive (CRD), Insurance Distribution Directive (IDD), Institutions for Occupational Retirement Provision Directive II (IORP II), and Solvency II.

(Swiss Sustainable Finance 2019b, p. 4). The MiFID II suitability requirements will create a clear incentive for both fund manufacturers and distributors to consider what disclosures they can reasonably make around sustainability factors.

In addition, the EC Action Plan has led to 28 initiatives involving the adoption of voluntary, nonlegislative market standards alongside mandatory legal obligations. The most important and urgent task facing the Action Plan is to create a shared understanding of what "sustainable" means.[35] A unified phraseology would create a unified EU classification system—or taxonomy—alongside clear guidance on qualifying activities[36] and detailed information[37] on the relevant sectors and activities, based on screening criteria, thresholds, and metrics (European Commission 2018a). On 15 April 2020, the European Council adopted its position with respect to the Taxonomy regulation,[38] which should be established by the end of 2020 or 2021 (depending on the activities concerned) for a full application by end of 2021 or 2022 (European Commission 2020a).

Particularly useful for retail investors who would like to express their investment preferences on sustainable activities are labeling[39] schemes for sustainable financial products. The choices by retail investors could be indeed facilitated by being integrated in various tools, such as comparison websites or financial planning services. Thus, the need to create standards (European Commission 2018a) for green financial products (EU Green Bond

---

[35] Action 1 of the EC Action Plan (European Commission 2018a).

[36] These are climate change mitigation; climate change adaptation; sustainable use and protection of water and marine resources; transition to a circular economy including waste prevention and recycling; pollution prevention and control; and protection and restoration of biodiversity and ecosystems.

[37] See Art. 13 Proposal for a regulation of a framework to facilitate sustainable investment (European Commission 2018d). The relevant documents in this context are: "OECD Guidelines for Multinational Enterprises" (OECD 2011) and "UN's Guiding Principles on Business and Human Rights" (United Nations 2011), including the principles and rights set out in the eight fundamental conventions identified in the International Labor Organization's (ILO) "Declaration on Fundamental Rights and Principles at Work and the International Bill of Human Rights" (ILO 1998).

[38] Proposal for a regulation on the establishment of a framework to facilitate sustainable investment (European Commission 2018d) and the report by the European Technical Expert Group on Sustainable Finance, that contains recommendations relating to the EU Taxonomy, as well as an implementation guidance for companies and financial institutions (European Technical Expert Group on Sustainable Finance 2020).

[39] The EC has been exploring the use of the EU Ecolabel for retail financial products, which could become applicable once the EU sustainability taxonomy is adopted.

Standard)[40] and labels (EU Ecolabel)[41] has been supported by numerous surveys[42] showing that retail investors increasingly want their investments to consider sustainability considerations. Financial industry impact matrixes may help to get the larger picture of the current situation and what tools can help to sustain a wind of change. In a study by the Worldwide Fund (WWF) and with reference to expert interviews and experience (WWF and PWC 2019, para. 6.10), a quantitative impact rating for different impact frameworks and regulations has been drawn up based on the Sustainable Finance Regulation for the different areas in the investment industry, with 1 being the weakest impact, and 5 the strongest. The MiFID II would be rated as high (5) in specific areas where strategic changes were required, such as investment strategy, and rated just below (4) for investment advice, portfolio management and discretionary mandates, and general disclosure requirements in retail and private banking.

GENERALIZING IMPACT INVESTING TO A MAINSTREAM SCALE

Impact Investing should not remain the preserve of high-net-worth individuals or institutional investors (traditionally deemed "qualified" investors). The low penetration of Impact Investing can be partly explained by the lack of knowledge of both client advisers and the public. However, it does not stem from a lack of client interest, as over 65% of retail investors consider environmental and social objectives to be important factors in their investment decisions (European Union 2018, p. 25; Walker et al. 2019, p. 127). Pursuant to the EC, integrating sustainability into investment advice should be a priority lane for financial firms, as firms can play a central role in reorienting the financial system toward Impact Investing.

---

[40]Within the framework of the Prospectus Regulation, the EC has specified in the second quarter of 2019 the content of the prospectus for green bond issuances to provide potential investors with additional information.

[41]The Taxonomy agreement constitutes a turning point for the EU Ecolabel, as it provides for disclosure of key indicators for financial products.

[42]Vigeo Eiris and the FIR (2017), Natixis Investment Managers (2017) and Schroders (2017). According to Natixis, "The real disconnect between the two (institutional and individual) populations may be based more on semantics than impact on investment performance" while "the key to bridging the gulf between the sentiment of individual investors and the skepticism of professional investors may be using more exact language about ESG."

As stated in the previous section, advice provided to retail investors does not sufficiently consider preferences for sustainable and impact investments (European Commission 2018a, section 2.4). Financial intermediaries providing advice and portfolio management services must be required to ask for their clients' preferences in terms of sustainability factors and take them into consideration when selecting products and assessing their suitability. However, increasing accessibility of impact investments to a much broader set of individuals and institutions requires providing greater clarity and standardization to facilitate measurable social and environmental impact alongside financial returns.

The industry must develop investable and accessible products that result in demonstrable impact. While Impact Investing can now be found in common investment vehicles—such as exchange-traded funds (ETFs) or bond securities—and span a variety of asset classes suitable for various investor profiles—from conservative to more risk tolerant investors—the Impact Investing sector remains more popular with institutional investors and is still failing to make a real breakthrough to individual investors.

The multi-stakeholder think tank 2i Investing Initiative set out the key takeaways[43] in its research on the suitability assessment test in Europe regarding the engagement of individual investors in the context of environmental impact (2i 2019, p. 10). In order to enable retail investors to include impact in their investment decisions, the 2i Investing Initiative recommends that financial professionals:

- Leverage the power of retail investors as shareholders and investors to support and reorient investments in the real economy from unsustainable to sustainable activities.

- Enable retail investors to express their sustainability investment objectives[44] and identify suitable financial products (e.g. Ecolabel) that align with these objectives.

- Aid retail investors' identification of suitable financial products, hence preventing greenwashing by avoiding mis-selling of unsuitable products to sustainability-minded retail investment customers.

---

[43] 2i's report triggered, via the High Level Expert Group on Sustainable Finance (HLEG), the reform of MIFID and IDD introduced by the EC regulatory package on sustainable finance (amendment of delegated acts).
[44] Draft Delegated Acts: MiFID II (European Commission 2018b) and IDD (European Commission 2018c).

The lack of advisers' knowledge in this area has been recognized as an obstacle. Many advisors do not have sufficient knowledge of ESG and Impact Investing, which leads to the topic not even being raised to the clients. In order to promote and enhance advisors' systematic provision of advice about impact-focused investment products, advisors should be offered training programs that equip them with material content on the different products and the underlying concepts.

Beyond increasing familiarity among investors and advisors, there must be a broader culture change in the investment industry, specifically about the long-term risks of ignoring sustainability (Eurosif 2018, p. 32). When reorienting capital flows toward sustainability-led investments, the allocation of capital requires a comprehensive shift in how triggering changes in the real economy (as strategies in mitigating[45] ESG-related risks have proven to be ineffective). For this purpose, "sustainable impact investment" products will need to be developed (2i 2019, p. 6). During the COP 21, the secretary-general of the OECD warned, "If we want to get serious about unlocking green investment, we need to get serious about systematically integrating climate risks into our understanding of fiduciary duty" (Gurría 2015).

Historically, the definition of fiduciary duty (i.e. legal obligation of investors to act in the best interest of beneficiaries) for financial institutions has been concerned mainly with managing financial risk and generating financial performance. Going forward, investment advisors need to be persuaded that a *blended approach* (Eurosif 2017) to investment is legitimate,[46] that is, a new definition of fiduciary duty that equally prioritizes financial and nonfinancial objectives, such as social or environmental impact.

THE IMPACT REPORT: A PROTECTION TOOL FOR THE INVESTOR

In addition to the EC's reforms to the MiFID II regime, as well as the inclusion of clients' sustainability preferences in suitability assessments and reporting, impact reports should be established on a mandatory, routine basis. In *Handbook on Sustainable Investments* (Paetzold 2017, Chapter 13) by Swiss Sustainable Finance, Impact Investing is characterized by two elements: the intention to have a positive social or environmental impact through the project

---

[45]Those strategies are usually designed to marginally integrate financial risks related to ESG factors by reducing the exposure to risky activities.
[46]See below France's 90%/10% "solidarity" funds.

core business or activities, and secondly the investment's impact must be measurable and replicable. An impact report helps investors to assess the second, and measure and replicate their impact results.[47] Regular impact reporting supports a better understanding of what Impact Investing entails, as well as its positive externalities.

An impact report can be compared to a portfolio statement, which is an overview of the financial situation of a client's portfolio, which the client uses to follow the key performance indicators and the evolution of performance of every investment position. The impact report holds the same objective, but instead of looking at the portfolio from a financial point of view, it shows the evolution of impact objectives and measures chosen metrics that track the portfolio's social and environmental impacts. For example, an impact report can include the portfolio's greenhouse gas (GHG) emissions, which can be compared to a benchmark or broader index. Impact reports can also map progress with respect to the UN SDGs. Impact reports provide credible and comparable impact data that is essential for investment decision-making.

In line with the purpose of MiFID II, an impact report meets the call for greater transparency and communication in favor of investors and product suitability (or appropriateness) assessments. An impact report in these terms would also better ensure the portfolio's compliance to the MiFID II requirements. Furthermore, transparent communication from advisors to clients about portfolio impact would help clients better understand the Impact Investing approach, its vehicles, and the range of impacts their investments can generate. It also enhances confidence in Impact Investing by mitigating the risks of greenwashing. In sum, by responding to MiFID's objective of investor protection, impact reports could prove to be a major asset in promoting Impact Investing. Unfortunately, few media, investor, or academic articles in the matter have been supporting the interesting features of an impact report in terms of client decision-making and MiFID II requirements.

OVERVIEW IN SELECTED COUNTRIES

Europe has been witnessing a rapid expansion of sustainable and impact investments, partly driven by regulation. As in 2019, several European

---

[47]Impact investing requires measuring effects (direct and indirect) achieved through impact investment, often distinguishing it from other categories of Responsible Investment (RI) (e.g. ESG Integration and ESG-screened funds), whose requirements for impact metrics vary by investor type.

jurisdictions[48] have adopted a sustainable finance action plan in one form or another (Eurosif 2018, p. 84 and ss). This section focuses on two country examples, France and Switzerland, an EU and a non-EU member state, respectively; both countries established themselves as pioneers in the area of sustainable finance well before the EC Action Plan.

France has introduced compelling policy identifying investment approaches to tackle entrenched social and economic problems. France's "solidarity" funds are systematic channels that are used to deploy and fuel capital into impact investment–type funds (Finansol 2019). As an international financial center closely linked to other European financial locations, Switzerland is also feeling the effects of EU regulations. In Switzerland, however, the main players in the industry have been considering voluntary recommendations more feasible than regulatory measures (Swiss Sustainable Finance 2018a). The Swiss pension sector has developed practices to incentivize institutions and their employees to account for sustainability.

The case studies presented next show that prior availability of sustainability-promoting standards and regulations have sustained a smooth and large integration of impact-related investments[49] (Eurosif 2018, Figure 17 and European Data Table, p. 83), starting with a top-down approach through governmental actions or a bottom-up approach by the private sector and growing to include mass markets. In this context, several of the initiatives introduced by the EC Action Plan are amendments that build on or are inspired[50] by existing regulatory frameworks, such as MiFID II and IDD. In fact, the stated key goal of these EU initiatives is to integrate sustainability factors into existing processes, rather than create new ones.

It remains to be seen how these two countries, and EU and non-EU countries in general, will apply the new EU regulations on sustainable investing

---

[48] In addition to France and Switzerland, Belgium, Denmark, Italy, Norway, Poland, Spain, Sweden, the Netherlands, and the United Kingdom have regulations in place.

[49] According to the European Data Table (Eurosif 2018, p. 83), in 2017 the top three countries with highest assets under management in Impact Investing are Italy, the UK, and Switzerland. In the case of France, obviously a growing market, some data are showing some decrease, going against the global tendency. Explanations to that are two-fold: some asset owners that manage internally part of their assets are not considered; more importantly, new standards on the French market have led to stricter definitions, which have strongly impacted the figures as a result (Eurosif 2018, p. 61).

[50] Such as the article 173-VI of the Ecological and Energy Transition Act in France (Gouvernement Français 2019c). Much in line with the French article 173, the Disclosure Regulation (European Union 2019) sets disclosure parameters on a European scale for asset managers and investors with regard to their approach of fiduciary duty (Eurosif 2018, p. 34)

and how the Impact Investing market will react in the long term. In every case, these trends are a clear signal that sustainability criteria will be an integral part of financial regulations in the near future.

FRANCE: INNOVATIVE "90/10 SOLIDARITY" PRODUCTS

France is a major player in Impact Investing among the EU member states, introducing compelling policies at the national level since 2001. Over the years France's regulators have built an understanding and capacity in Impact Investing, and as the market developed, impact became embedded in French regulatory frameworks and culture of its financial industry.[51] Today, the country displays a model of joint work among various stakeholders, which "systemizes" the reorientation of financial assets into impact by requiring wealth managers to allocate a minimum amount of assets under management into "solidarity" investments. Initiatives by industry bodies have sustained momentum and ensured quality as the market grows. In France, three main channels provide access to so-called Social Impact Investments:[52] (i) distributors such as banks[53] or mutual insurance; (ii) direct subscriptions in company capital;[54] and (iii) business and employee savings.[55]

Business and employee savings are the largest channel, and account for over 60% of solidarity savings (Tiberghien 2020). Solidarity funds known as "90/10" funds (representing 90% and 10%, adding up to 100%) are required to invest between 5% and 10% of their assets in approved organizations, defined as "solidarity-based enterprises of social utility." This rule, which is specific to employee savings funds, has in practice been applied to all other solidarity mutual funds by fund managers in order to promote homogeneous rules

---

[51] In particular article 173-VI of the Ecological and Energy Transition Act (Gouvernement Français 2019c) that requires the mandatory disclosure on ESG and climate-related policies and sets responsibilities of asset owners (mainly French pension funds) (Eurosif 2018, pp. 90–91).

[52] According to the definition by the French "Comité Consultatif Français sur l'Investissement à Impact Social" in 2014.

[53] However, the most common retail products in France, such as Livret A and life insurance, either do not offer, or have very limited access to, "solidarity" investments, according to Finasol.org.

[54] The number of companies calling for funding is limited, however—about 30, according to Finasol.org.

[55] In French "Plans d'Epargne Entreprise (PEE)," by law Employee Savings Schemes must present at least one "solidarity" fund to employees as beneficiaries of Employee Savings Schemes.

management, increase product legibility across all investors, and present more attractive products (Finansol 2019, para. 1.1). The development of solidarity funds continues to be regularly encouraged by public authorities, notably thanks to the Law of Modernization of the Economy of 2008.

The purpose of solidarity funds is to finance solidarity-based activities through solidarity-based enterprises and solidarity financing bodies (Finansol 2019, section 1.1). Solidarity financing bodies are intermediaries whose activity consists in proposing and implementing financing tools with the aim of having a social or environmental impact or both (Finansol 2019, section 1.2). Solidarity funds provide medium- and long-term resources to actors who act directly in targeted sectors such as social housing, employment, and environmental protection. In 2014, French solidarity finance enabled the creation or consolidation of 43,000 nonrelocatable jobs, and more than 5,000 people in poor housing were rehoused (Novafi March 2020). Policymakers made solidarity-based investments mandatory for wealth managers, who are required to reserve capital for "solidarity" investees while presenting "solidarity" adapted products to their investors.[56] This tension between law and market forces has led the industry to be more accessible with new products suited to the needs and preferences of the full spectrum of investors (from retail to institutional), and to develop advanced blended finance vehicles and products.

With EUR €9.3 billion as of 31 December 2018, assets under management of "90/10" funds have increased six-fold in nine years (Finansol 2019, section 2.3.1). The success of these funds has drawn interest from other countries, such as the United Kingdom and Australia. Finansol, the industry association in solidarity finance, has set a target of 1% of households' financial wealth to be in solidarity savings by 2025[57] (Tiberghien 2020).

France has developed a solid experience with "solidarity finance," mainly on social impact, and plans to pursue efforts through Impact Investing in both private equity and listed universe (Eurosif 2018, p. 92). The sustainable investment market is largely dominated by institutional investors, where insurance companies are the main players as asset owners. Retail investors are mainly exposed through corporate saving plans (Eurosif 2018, p. 61).

---

[56] For example, providing stable financial support to social economy organizations poses a real challenge for the managers of the funds concerned, because they have a permanent liquidity constraint, to cope with possible withdrawals.

[57] From 0.25% in 31 December 2018. See Finansol.org, «Quels impacts pour la société ? La finance solidaire, une réponse fiable et concrète pour financer les défis majeurs d'aujourd'hui…». https://www.finansol.org/quels-impacts-pour-la-societe/ (accessed 25 May 2020).

Since May 2019, the Action Plan for Business Growth and Transformation, the so-called PACTE Law[58] (Gouvernement Français 2019b), closely connected to the sustainable development objectives supported by the European Commission, aims to promote the transformation of French companies, according to the principles of social and environmental responsibility in particular.[59] PACTE Article 77 introduces EU legislation such as MiFID II (Caceis 2019). PACTE also includes some important points regarding retail investors. It makes it mandatory to offer responsible products in saving plans and life insurance. As a result, mandatory offering should mechanically push retail investors to choose responsible products. The challenge of training advisors to responsible products remains (Eurosif 2018, p. 92).

With the introduction of MiFID II suitability requirements within the framework of the EC Action Plan, the primary impact for EU wealth managers and EU investment advisers will be that their end clients' sustainability preferences will need to have been considered: (i) when fund shares are sold to EU end clients on an advised basis, or (ii) when they are selected for inclusion in an EU end client's portfolio (Baker McKenzie 2019). The MiFID suitability test is intended to be a systematic process, going beyond product governance in general, given that it will need to be undertaken at the level of each EU individual client on a case-by-case basis. Combining the obligations imposed by solidarity funds and MiFID II could help to raise the degree of integration of Impact Investing in France, as well as the wide dissemination of impact-focused investments, thanks to a higher awareness.

SWITZERLAND: FROM INSTITUTIONAL TO INDIVIDUAL PENSION INVESTORS

Switzerland is not part of the EU and therefore not legally bound to directly follow the new provision impelled by the EC Action Plan and MiFID II. However, Europe is an essential partner for the Swiss financial sector. The CEO of Swiss Sustainable Finance, Sabine Döbeli, has urged, "With the EU Action Plan on Sustainable Finance, discussions are brought to a new level

---

[58] Plan d'Action pour la Croissance et la Transformation des Entreprises. Loi no. 2019-486 du 22 mai 2019 (Gouvernement Français 2019a).

[59] There is no specific sanction for failing to take into account "social and environmental issues." Nevertheless, if certain conditions for failing to consider "social and environmental issues" are met, the law could give rise *in principle* to civil liability for the company and even individual liability for its managers.

and the requirements will influence many Swiss financial players. While we can build on broad Swiss know-how in sustainable finance, we have to make sure that Swiss frameworks reflect international trends" (WWF and PWC 2019, p. 8). The vast majority of Swiss retail investors' savings are accumulated in the so-called "2nd pillar" pension scheme. This capitalization-based system[60] constitutes what is probably the most influential group of asset owners in the Swiss financial market[61] (WWF and InRate 2019, p. 8). As such, financial service providers in this 2nd pillar economy have a key role to play in advancing Switzerland's sustainable finance industry—as they function as a bridge between capital and the real economy as well as powerful multipliers.

The objectives of the EC Action Plan are highly relevant for both public and private pension funds, although there are currently no binding regulations for Sustainable and Impact Investing with regards to pension plans in Switzerland (WWF and PWC 2019, p. 3). In the EU, the EC has created the necessary framework conditions for this to happen in the EU pension sector[62] by incorporating sustainability standards into the Institutions for Occupational Retirement Provision Directive II (IORP II)[63] (Pensions Europe 2018; Eurosif 2018, p. 31). The Swiss pension sector must also develop practices to incentivize institutions and their employees to account for sustainability factors by default, and to integrate advisory on sustainable investments similar to MiFID II suitability test.

The significance of these 2nd pillar funds cannot be underestimated as they represented 133% of Swiss gross domestic product (GDP) in 2018 (Thinking Ahead Institute 2018). The Swiss 2nd pillar accumulates funds amounting to around CHF 910 billion[64] (WWF and InRate 2019, p. 8), of

---

[60] Swiss financial security in retirement rests on three pillars: state, occupational, and private (but facultative) retirement provision. The three pillars complement each other and provide the best possible financial security.

[61] Pension funds and insurance companies are driving sustainable investment and investing directly in equity and indirectly through investment funds. Together, pension funds and insurance companies hold 39.10% of listed equities.

[62] IORP II has not yet kickstarted within the framework of the EU Action Plan on Sustainable Finance, but the aim was for sustainability to be integrated within this financial regulation beforehand. Since January 2019, IORP II has required all pension funds in the EU to integrate ESG factors and to report on them regularly.

[63] Directive 2016/2341 (European Union 2016b).

[64] Which covers only independent pension funds and does not take into account the assets of insurance companies.

which around CHF 650 billion are in supplementary plans[65] (Swisscanto 2019). Certain pension plans are based on self-determination and freedom of choice, that is, individual members and/or affiliated corporate investors may select their own strategy profile based on their personal risk profile and investment preference. Pension funds are sensing the mounting public pressure from governments, regulators, and individuals to address the impact of their investment activity (WWF and PWC 2019, section 1.3). Surveys show that an increasing number of individual investors in Switzerland want their pension assets to be aligned with their personal values (Fernandez-Leenknecht 2017).

In 2018, Switzerland's asset owner segment (including pension funds) has seen a substantial development in sustainable investments to CHF 455.01 billion, which accounts for 65%[66] of Switzerland's total sustainable investment market of CHF 716.6 billion (Swiss Sustainable Finance 2019a, p. 8). Despite an annual[67] growth of 35% to CHF 16.3 billion, Impact Investing[68] still has room for improvement in Switzerland as it amounts to a market share of only 2% of all sustainable assets (Swiss Sustainable Finance 2019a, p. 30).

The Swiss and European markets are strongly interconnected. In anticipation of MiFID II,[69] Switzerland and non-EU countries serving EU clients in general have adapted to EU standards in order to maintain or obtain access to the EU market ("EU passport"),[70] (Betsche 2019). The Swiss Financial Services Act (FinSA) and the Financial Institutions Act (FinIA) entered in force in January 2020. Swiss banks and wealth managers must take care to comply with the new EU standards when offering financial products to EU customers. While MiFID II does not apply to Switzerland directly, many financial intermediaries and pension funds have nevertheless been implementing MiFID II, because they want to continue servicing EU-based clients or have

---

[65]Supplementary schemes have higher flexibility than base schemes in terms of investment and plan guidelines.

[66]In comparison, private investors constitute 14% to the Swiss sustainable investment market, and their share has been continuously declining (SSF 2018, p. 66).

[67]From 2017 to 2018.

[68]In total, 94 products were defined as impact investments by 22 asset managers with individual volumes of asset under management ranged from around CHF 13 million to CHF 2.9 billion. However, the market shows a certain level of concentration, with three managers contributing to 53% to the overall volume of impact investments in Switzerland.

[69]And the Markets in Financial Instruments Regulation (MiFIR), Regulation (EU)No 600/2014.

[70]FinSA and FinIA do not, however, provide for any information on sustainability risks from financial advisers; the euro compatibility of the law could thus be questioned from this angle.

EU branches or subsidiaries, but also in order to implement a standardized advisory process to all their client bases (Swiss Sustainable Finance 2019b, p. 5). The primary impacts for financial managers and investment advisers in Switzerland (and other non-EU countries) are that the sustainability preferences of their EU client's must be considered if: (i) fund shares are sold to (EU) investors on an advised basis, or (ii) they are selected for inclusion in an EU investor's portfolio (Banker McKenzie 2019). Being less prescriptive[71] than its EU counterpart, Swiss firms will likely have to refer to the MiFID II's provisions where the detail in the Swiss FinIA/FinSA is absent.

CONSIDERATIONS FOR THE FUTURE

A larger integration of Impact Investing into all portfolios has proven to be insufficient in Europe, mainly because of the lack of legislative and economic incentives, and even in countries with long-standing experience in sustainable and Impact Investing. The compelling, large-scale reform under the EC Action Plan on sustainable finance may become the trigger to a potential paradigm shift in the financial markets. Sweeping regulatory change, such as the mandatory standards imposed by MiFID II,[72] will affect the entire value chain. The "market will have to embrace the integration of sustainability considerations into every step of the investment process"[73] (WWF and PWC 2019, p. 19), from the increasing move to transparency, to embedding sustainability in client advice, to product design and impact reporting of the portfolio.

The pace of change must accelerate. As recently demonstrated during Climate Week 2019, when activists and protestors around the globe filled the streets calling for bold action on climate, the general public has reached a cultural tipping point. Impact Investing needs to be top of mind for every financial adviser and pension trustee when making investment allocation decisions and advising their clients. In the EU, the growth potential for Impact Investing in the retail market is huge, the fund industry should adapt and integrate impact into a greater share of the savings needs of the 89% of EU

---

[71]For example, financial service providers may still render financial services, even when the performance of appropriateness and/or suitability tests have failed or the financial service provider has reached the conclusion that the service rendered is not appropriate and/or suitable due to insufficient information provided by the client prior to the transaction.

[72]And the corresponding IDD in the insurance sector.

[73]Statement by Dr. Jan Amrit Poser, Chief Strategist and Head Sustainability of Bank J. Safra Sarasin.

households, who have no investment funds but mainly cash (Deloitte 2015, p. 12).

MiFID II is in force since 2018 and financial institutions in EU and non-EU territories (that need to apply MiFID II) have been applying the suitability test. The updated MiFID II Delegated Acts in accordance with the EC Action Plan on sustainable finance have not yet been adopted. Proposals must be followed by a 3- to 6-month objection period, and then a 12-month delay before they are enacted. The new Delegated Acts are expected to be introduced after the application of the Disclosure Regulation,[74] most likely by the end of 2020 (Commission Delegated Regulation 2018).

Investment fund distribution will change as the primary and secondary effects of MiFID II come into play. The primary effects encompass the need for client advisors to ask every client their sustainability preferences and assess the suitable investment products during the suitability test. The practical outcome for asset managers (and fund manufacturers) will likely be an additional phase of due diligence assessing the sustainability profile of their funds (Baker McKenzie 2019), which will be transferred down to the end investors, along with the costs of this additional phase of research and analysis. In this context, a key area of focus will be the access to high-quality, reliable data on the sustainability profile of investments, as well as the production of credible impact reporting. For this purpose, the market for wide-ranging data will need to develop into more widespread and mature businesses, as these data providers are themselves frequently unregulated (WWF and PWC 2019, pp. 20–21). Similarly, impact assessment methodologies ought to be used more consistently across the board, and greater awareness is needed on the reliable use of impact metrics and benchmarks across sectors and regions

Questions also remain around how firms will be able to effectively assess and gather information about securities in smaller unrated or non-EU companies. Buying sustainability and impact data from data providers will become increasingly important, if not vital, for financial institutions to keep up with regulatory requirements (WWF and PWC 2019, pp. 20–21) and maintain competitivity in EU markets. The issue of a lack of data is expected to diminish over time with the establishment of a clear EU framework and taxonomy. This consolidation is already in motion. Impact Investing recently gained greater attention when the International Finance Corporation (IFC)'s "Operating Principles for Impact Management" (IFC 2019) were published

---

[74]See notes 59 and 60.

October 4, 2019. With the IFC weighing in with concrete principles, the cumulative standards of the GIIN, and EU regulations overall, the industry may see stricter definitions and categorizations of Impact Investing in the coming years. The resulting broadening of the impact investment universe will provide investors with more opportunities.

The secondary effects of MiFID II's implementation depend upon the reactions and adaptations of market players. As the complexity of properly implementing and enforcing MiFID regulation increases, it will likely translate into additional steps and longer investment and decision-making processes. The amended rules require a transaction to meet the investment objectives of the client related to financial returns and nonfinancial objectives—in addition to the client's risk tolerance and any preferences, provided a proper client profiling and data collection. Standardized distribution and product classification procedures in Impact Investing—similar to "traditional" non-sustainable investment products—must be implemented, and segmented if need be. Procedure simplification could avoid prohibitive additional costs and any greenwashing risks while promoting a larger range of investment product types and a diversification in investment approaches.

While requirements to account for certain nonfinancial factors are not new (see the section above on the overview in selected countries), several European jurisdictions have adopted a sustainable finance action plan in one form or another (Eurosif 2018, p. 84);[75] the mandatory aspect of integrating sustainability and impact preferences into the investment process in a routine, large-scale level represents a potentially ground-breaking change. In accordance with the EC Action Plan, MiFID II suitability requirements can become the instrument for a large-scale awareness of Impact Investing at the European level.

In this regard, the GIIN's recommendations for a broader recognition and implementation of Impact Investing focus on three main axes (GIIN 2018b):

(i) Investor Identity
- Defining clearly the characteristics of an impact investor
- Setting a new the paradigm of investment behavior and expectations
- Bolstering education and training of professionals in finance and business

---

[75] In addition to France and Switzerland, Belgium, Denmark, Italy, Norway, Poland, Spain, Sweden, the Netherlands, and the United Kingdom have regulations in place.

(ii) Investment Products

- Improving the accessibility of impact investments by accommodating the capital needs of various types of investees
- Expanding the universe of impact investments by increasing products suitable for the full spectrum of investors (from retail to institutional)
- Developing tools and services to support the incorporation of impact into investors' routine analysis allocation, and deal-making activities (e.g. the services provided by investment banks, rating agencies, and data providers)

(iii) Policy and Regulation

- Going beyond the mere recognition of the vital importance of impact-focused investments by establishing clear and strong incentives
- Catalyzing industry growth by creating a supportive regulatory environment for investors and businesses generating impact

The EC Action Plan and MiFID II may breathe life into these recommendations and play a key role in contributing to the European effort of combining "impact at scale" with "capital at scale"—driving more capital toward solutions that focus on generating significant positive effects for people and the planet. This will support the current, latent demand for impact investments into a higher volume of activity while maintaining the integrity of practice and driving talented human capital into the industry. Greater awareness and distribution of impact-focused investments can result in a virtuous circle that roots the concepts and practices of Impact Investing deeper into society as a whole.

Retail banking has a critical role to play in financing Impact Investing projects, given their unique position as facilitators of capital flows through their lending, investment, and advisory processes (WWF and PWC 2019, section 6). As such, retail banks should ramp up their efforts to help retail clients to transition to more sustainable investments and impact-focused investments. Similarly, private banking can ask their wealthier clients about their impact preferences and take them into account when considering the range of financial products they offer. In this regard, environmental and social factors must be taken into consideration in the product classification process, and banks must develop different methodologies for assessing suitability to these norms.

However, the most significant problem—especially for individual clients—is the lack of definition of clear characteristics for Impact Investing. A unified taxonomy is essential for the widespread expansion of Impact Investing. It is hard for clients to understand what they are investing in, given the sheer number of different categories and definitions of Impact Investing available in the marketplace. The lack of common reporting standards and metrics continues to spark serious concerns around the credibility of Impact Investing and may hinder the development of the sector as a whole. The Taxonomy Regulation (European Commission 2020a) is due to become fully applicable starting by the end of 2022. Interestingly, MiFID II may prove to be the right tool at the right time: the medium-term investment choice made by retail investors is very often bank deposits, which are unlikely to yield real inflation-based returns in what has been a persistently low interest rate environment. Impact Investing may represent a welcome alternative for both client advisors and end clients. Even if some see impact investments as generating less return than nonsustainable counterparts (in other words, expectations are "market-like" returns) (Eurosif 2018, p. 76), multiple reports and researchers have demonstrated the benefits of sustainable investments in terms of both financial performance and risk management. Thus, in addition to the inclusion of considerations other than market forces (e.g. the desire to have a positive impact on society), financially material sustainable-based information in investment processes have led to better-informed investment decisions and better risk-adjusted returns in the long run[76] (Swiss Sustainable Finance 2018, International Monetary Fund 2019, p. 87).

CONCLUSION AND NEXT STEPS

Going forward, governments and policymakers must go beyond their comfort zones. "Strongly supporting the transition" (EC Sustainable Finance 2019) has proven so far to be insufficient for triggering and implementing a real move for change. Sheer incorporation of ESG factors is insufficient, and ESMA recently clarified that sustainability preferences will not take precedence over other suitability criteria. The *preferences* merely contribute to the assessment, after suitability has been addressed in accordance with

---

[76]The IMF (International Monetary Fund) found the performance of sustainable funds is comparable to that of conventional equity funds.

the criteria of knowledge and experience, financial situation, and investment objectives.

In December 2019, the European Green Deal was enacted by the EC in a response to environmental challenges, such as the eradication of GHG emissions by 2050[77] (European Commission 2019). This new framework will enable the facilitation of "public and private investments needed for the transition to a climate-neutral, green, competitive and inclusive economy" (European Commission 2020b). ESMA launched a common supervisory action with National Competent Authorities (NCA) on the application of MiFID II suitability rules across the EU, which will be conducted during 2020. This action will allow ESMA and the NCAs, among other, to measure intermediaries' progress in implementing the rules (ESMA 2020). The EC is now expected to undertake a wider review of how a range of regulations[78]—including MiFID II and IDD—regulate retail distribution issues such as product disclosure, investor protection, and client suitability. The review will consider which rules do and do not work, and which areas overlap, contradict each other, or are superfluous.

Impact Investing is all about the real economy in the current society but integrates considerations of the common good and our future generations. It is about how an individual or entity decides to allocate its capital in a way that makes its activity, business and production, or services futureproof. It is not only risk-sensitive, but also focuses on finding novel solutions and opportunities to existing and expected future problems. Moreover, the current COVID-19 pandemic crisis and its massive consequences on the world's economy have had many forecasting that more sustainability-oriented finance will be necessary to ensure future viability to safeguard the global system in the long term.

---

[77]The "Green Deal" by the EC presents an initial roadmap of the key policies and measures needed to be achieved by Europe. It will be updated as needs evolve. It is an integral part of the EC's strategy to implement the United Nation's 2030 Agenda (United Nations 2015). The European Green Deal Investment Plan presented on 14 January 2020 aims at mobilizing at least EUR €1 trillion of sustainable investments over the next decade.

[78]Financial services and products offered to clients in the EU will be impacted by the additional sustainability-related requirements. New rules of existing elements of EU financial market legislation are the following: Directive 2009/65/EC (UCITS); Regulation (EU) No 1286/2014 (PRIIP), Directive 2009/138/EC (Solvency II); Directive 2011/61/EU (AIFMD); Directive 2014/65/EU (MiFID II); Directive (EU) 2016/97 (IDD); Directive (EU) 2016/2341 (IORP); Regulation (EU) No 345/2013 (European venture capital funds); Regulation (EU) No 346/2013 (European social entrepreneurship funds), and Regulation (EU) 2015/760 (European long-term investment funds).

Given that MiFID II in the context of the EC Action Plan on sustainable finance is in the earliest stages of implementation amid a dire global financial crisis, the effective impact of MiFID on the financial sector and their end clients remains to be seen, along with whether these regulations can make Impact Investing suitable for every European investor. Already, MiFID II alongside the EC Action Plan is forcing debate and conversation, which is spurring change to happen.

ACKNOWLEDGMENTS

With gratitude for the kind contribution of Marine Delmarche, and Elsa de Morais Sarmento and R. Paul Herman, editors of this book.

REFERENCES

2i Investing Initiative (2019). Impact washing gets a free ride, An Analysis of the Draft EU ecolabel criteria for financial products. https://2degrees-investing.org/wp-content/uploads/2019/06/2019-Paper-Impact-washing.pdf (accessed 10 January 20).

Baker McKenzie (2019). *ESG Regulatory Reform, Impact on Asset Managers* (31 July). London, UK. https://www.bakermckenzie.com/-/media/images/insight/publications/2019/07/esg-regulatory-reforms/esg-reforms--implications-for-asset-managers.pdf?la=en (accessed 10 March 2020).

Bauer, R., Ruof, T., and Smeets, P. (2020). Get Real! Individuals Prefer More Sustainable Investments (February 21). https://papers.ssrn.com/sol3/papers.cfm?abstract_id=3287430. (accessed 10 March 2020).

Betsche, M. (2019). Nachhaltiges Finanzwesen in der EU und die Schweiz, SGA-ASPE Schweizerische Gesellschaft für Aussenpolitik (January), p. 3. https://www.sga-aspe.ch/nachhaltiges-finanzwesen-in-der-eu-und-die-schweiz-2/ (accessed 6 March 2020).

Caceis Investor Services (2019). France's innovative PACTE law with a European ambition. Spotlight (28 October). https://www.caceis.com/whats-new/news/spotlight/article/frances-innovative-pacte-law-with-a-european-ambition/detail.html (accessed 15 May 2020).

Deloitte (2015). MiFID II: What will be its impact on the investment fund distribution landscape? https://www2.deloitte.com/content/dam/Deloitte/dk/Documents/finance/MIFID2.pdf (accessed 10 March 2020).

European Commission (2014). Directive 2014/65/EU of the European Parliament and of the Council of 15 May 2014 on markets in financial instruments and amending Directive 2002/92/EC and Directive 2011/61/EU Text with EEA relevance, OJ L 173, 12.6.2014, pp. 349–496.

European Commission (2015). Climate Action. https://ec.europa.eu/clima/policies/budget_en (accessed 16 February 2020). https://ec.europa.eu/info/business-economy-euro/banking-and-finance/sustainable-finance_en (accessed 10 March 2020).

European Commission (2016). Commission Delegated Regulation (EU) 2017/565 of 25 April 2016 supplementing Directive 2014/65/EU of the European Parliament and of the Council as regards organizational requirements and operating conditions for investment firms and defined terms for the purposes of that Directive (Text with EEA relevance), C/2016/2398, OJ L 87, 31.3.2017, pp. 1–83

European Commission (2017). Defining "green" in the context of green finance. *Final report (October)*.

European Commission (2018a). *Communication from the Commission to the European Parliament, the European Council, the Council, the European Central Bank, the European Economic and Social Committee and the Committee of the Regions, Action Plan: Financing Sustainable Growth, COM/2018/097 final* (8 March).

European Commission (2018b). Commission Delegated Regulation (EU) .../... of XXX amending Delegated Regulation (EU) 2017/565 as regards the integration of Environmental, Social and Governance (ESG) considerations and preferences into the investment advice and portfolio management. https://ec.europa.eu/finance/docs/level-2-measures/mifid-delegated-act-2018_en.pdf (accessed 6 March 2020).

European Commission (2018c). Commission Delegated Regulation (EU) .../...of XXX amending Regulation (EU) 2017/2359 as regards the integration of Environmental, Social and Governance (ESG) considerations and preferences into the investment advice for insurance-based investment products. https://ec.europa.eu/finance/docs/level-2-measures/idd-delegated-act-2018_en.pdf (accessed 6 March 2020).

European Commission (2018d). Proposal for a regulation of the European Parliament and of the Council on the establishment of a framework to facilitate sustainable investment. COM/2018/353 final, *2018/0178(COD) (Text with EEA relevance)* (24 May).

European Commission (2019). The European Green Deal. Communication from the Commission to the European Parliament, the European

Council, the Council, the European Economic and Social Committee and the Committee of the Regions, Brussels, COM (2019) 640 final (11 December). https://ec.europa.eu/info/sites/info/files/european-green-deal-communication_en.pdf (accessed 18 March 2020).

European Commission (2020a). EU taxonomy for sustainable activities. (First published 18 June 2019; last update 17 April 2020). https://ec.europa.eu/info/publications/sustainable-finance-teg-taxonomy_en (accessed 15 May 2020).

European Commission (2020b). Financing the green transition: The European Green Deal Investment Plan and Just Transition Mechanism. Press release (14 January). https://ec.europa.eu/commission/presscorner/detail/en/ip_20_17 (accessed 18 March 2020).

European Commission (n.d.). Investment funds, EU laws and initiatives relating to collective investment funds. https://ec.europa.eu/info/business-economy-euro/growth-and-investment/investment-funds_en (accessed 19 May 2020).

European Investment Bank (2016). Projects Directorate and the Economics Department of the EIB, *Restoring EU competitiveness (2016 updated version).*

European Securities and Markets Authority (2020). ESMA launches a Common Supervisory Action with NCAs on MiFID II suitability rules (5 February). https://www.esma.europa.eu/press-news/esma-news/esma-launches-common-supervisory-action-ncas-mifid-ii-suitability-rules (accessed 13 March 2020).

European Securities and Markets Authority (2018a). Final Report Guidelines on certain aspects of the MiFID II suitability requirements (28 May). *ESMA35-43-869.*

European Securities and Markets Authority (2018b). ESMA publishes final Guidelines on MiFID II suitability requirements. *Press Release* (28 May).

European Securities and Markets Authority (n.d.). MiFID II. https://www.esma.europa.eu/policy-rules/mifid-ii-and-mifir (accessed 19 May 2020b).

European Union (2019). Regulation (EU) 2019/2088 of the European Parliament and of the Council of 27 November 2019 on sustainability-related disclosures in the financial services sector (Text with EEA relevance), PE/87/2019/REV/1, OJ L 317, 9.12.2019, pp. 1–16 (9 December).

European Union (2018). Financing a sustainable European economy. Final Report 2018 by the High-Level Expert Group on Sustainable Finance, *Secretariat provided by the European Commission* (31 January).

European Union (2016a). Directive (EU) 2016/97 of the European Parliament and of the Council of 20 January 2016 on insurance distribution (recast) Text with EEA relevance, *OJ L, pp.* 19–59 (26 February).

European Union (2016b). Directive (EU) 2016/2341 of the European Parliament and of the Council of 14 December 2016 on the activities and supervision of institutions for occupational retirement provision (IORPs) (Text with EEA relevance) OJ L 354, 23.12.2016, pp. *37–85* (23 December).

European Union (2014). Directive 2014/65/EU of the European Parliament and of the Council of 15 May 2014 on markets in financial instruments and amending Directive 2002/92/EC and Directive 2011/61/EU Text with EEA relevance, *OJ L 173, pp.* 349–496 (12 June).

Eurosif (2017). The European Commission launches a fiduciary duty consultation (13 November). http://www.eurosif.org/the-european-commission-launches-a-fiduciary-duty-consultation/ (accessed 6 March 2020).

Eurosif (2018). European SRI Study.

European Technical Expert Group on Sustainable Finance (2020). Technical Report – Taxonomy: Final report of the Technical Expert Group on Sustainable Finance (9 March).

Fages, R., Heredia, L., Carrubba, J., et al. (2019). Global Asset Management 2019: Will These '20s Roar? *Boston Consulting Group* (3 July).

Fernandez-Leenknecht, T. (2017). *Planification financière durable 2.0. Point de Mire*, La Tribune Indépendante des Entrepreneurs de la Finance, Prévoyance Professionnelle. Printemps No. 68.

Finansol (2019). Synthèse de l'Etude sur les Fonds "90-10."

GIIN (2018a). Annual Impact Investor Survey 2018, the 8th edition. *Global Impact Investing Network.*

GIIN (2018b). *The future of impact investing, the future of the world.* IPE Investment and Pensions Europe (May). Global Impact Investing Network. https://www.ipe.com/the-future-of-impact-investing-the-future-of-the-world/10024466.article (accessed 25 February 2020).

Global Sustainable Investment Alliance (2018). *Global Sustainable Investment Review* 2018.

Gouvernement Français (2019a). Loi no. 2019-486 du 22 mai 2019 relative à la croissance et la transformation des entreprises. *Legifrance (23 May).*

Gouvernement Français (2019b). PACTE, the Action Plan for Business Growth and Transformation. https://www.gouvernement.fr/en/pacte-the-action-plan-for-business-growth-and-transformation (accessed 15 May 2020).

Gouvernement Français (2019c). Loi no. 2015-992 du 17 août 2015 relative à la transition énergétique pour la croissance verte (1), JORF no. 0189 du 18 août

2015 page 14263, texte no. 1. NOR: DEVX1413992L. *Legifrance* (18 August). https://www.legifrance.gouv.fr/eli/loi/2015/8/17/DEVX1413992L/jo/texte.

Gurría, A. (2015). Rethinking fiduciary duty for a more sustainable planet. Open remarks to the OECD-UNEP COP21 side event on Governance of Institutional Investments (10 December 2015). OECD. Paris. https://oecd.org/pensions/private-pensions/rethinking-fiduciary-duty-for-a-more-sustainable-planet.htm (accessed 15 May 2020).

IFC (2019). *Operating Principles for Impact Management*. International Financial Corporation. World Bank Group.

ILO (1998). Declaration on Fundamental Principles and Rights at Work. International Labor Organization. https://www.ilo.org/actrav/areas/WCMS_DOC_ATR_ARE_DECL_EN/lang--en/index.htm (accessed 10 March 2020).

International Monetary Fund (2019). Global Financial Stability Report, *Lower for Longer (October)*.

L'Impact Invest Lab (2018). État des lieux du marché française de l'investissement à impact social.

Moloney, N., Ferran, E., and Payne, J. (2015). *The Oxford Handbook of Financial Regulation*. Oxford, UK: Oxford University Press.

Mougeot, M. (2019). Responsible pension plans? It's about time! Mercer (27 March). https://www.mercer.ch/our-thinking/responsible-retirement-plan-investments.html (accessed 25 February 2020).

Natixis Investment Mangers (2017). Mind Shift: Getting past the screens of responsible investing. *Investor Insights Series* (13 June).

Novafi (2016). Quelles sont les différences entre les fonds solidaires et les fonds ISR? (17 May). novafi.fr/fiches_pratiques/differences-fonds-solidaires-fonds-isr (accessed 7 March 2020).

OECD (2011). *OECD Guidelines for Multinational Enterprises*. Paris. https://www.oecd.org/daf/inv/mne/48004323.pdf (accessed 10 March 2020).

Paetzold, F. (2017). *Handbook on Sustainable Investments: Background Information and Practical Examples for Institutional Asset Owners*. Swiss Sustainable Finance, CFA Institute Research Foundation. CFA Society Switzerland.

Pensions Europe (2018). Sustainable finance action plan is important for pension funds. *Press release (8 March)*.

Rust, S. (2019). Industry body sets out "core characteristics" of impact investing. IPE Investment and Pensions Europe, May Magazine (5 April). https://www.ipe.com/industry-body-sets-out-core-characteristics-of-impact-investing-/10030493.article.

Schroders (2017). Global perspectives on sustainable investing. *Global Investor Study* (28 September).

Swisscanto (2019). Swiss Pension Fund Study.

Swiss Sustainable Finance (2016). Performance of Sustainable Investments (July). https://www.sustainablefinance.ch/upload/cms/user/2016_06_30_sustainableInvestment_Performance.pdf (accessed 21 May 2020).

Swiss Sustainable Finance (2018). Market Study.

Swiss Sustainable Finance (2019a). Market Study.

Swiss Sustainable Finance (2019b). Focus: Action Plan.

Thinking Ahead Institute (2018). *Global Pension Assets Study*. Willis Tower Watson.

Tiberghien, F. (2020). L'impact investing: innover. Coursera. https://de.coursera.org/lecture/impactinvestinginnover/frederic-tiberghien-finansol-uXBcf (accessed 7 April 2020).

United Nations (2011). *Guiding Principles on Business and Human Rights Implementing the United Nations "Protect, Respect and Remedy" Framework*. United Nations Human Rights.

United Nations (2015). Transforming our world: The 2030 Agenda for Sustainable Development. UN General Assembly (21 October). https://sustainabledevelopment.un.org/content/documents/21252030%20Agenda%20for%20Sustainable%20Development%20web.pdf (accessed 25 February 2020).

Vigeo Eiris and the Forum pour l'Investissement Responsible (FIR) (2017). The French and SRI: Results of the 8th National Survey. Ipsos, Press release (22 September).

Walker, J., Pekmezovic, A., and Walker, G. (2019). *Sustainable Development Goals: Harnessing Business to Achieve the SDGs Through Finance, Technology and Law Reform*. Hoboken, NJ: John Wiley & Sons.

Waygood, S. (2019). Why EU legislation could herald a boom in ESG investing. Responsible Investor (17 June). https://www.responsible-investor.com/articles/steve-waygood-why-eu-legislation-could-herald-a-boom-in-esg-investing (accessed 25 February 2020).

WWF and InRate (2019). *Swiss Pension Funds and Responsible Investment: Pension Funds Rating* 2018/2019.

WWF and PWC (2019). Paradigm shift in financial markets. PWC (19 March). https://www.pwc.ch/en/publications/2019/paradigm-shift-in-financial-market-EN-web.pdf (accessed 10 March 2020).

CHAPTER 30

Fintech for Impact: How Can Financial Innovation Advance Inclusion?

Frederic de Mariz, PhD

Abstract

Over the past decade, the financial sector has been an engine of innovation with new financial instruments, such as green bonds or social impact bonds, and new business models, enabled by technology. Fintech refers to business models that provide financial services and are mostly enabled by technology. The rising Fintech sector creates a major disruption and brings the promise of enhanced financial inclusion. Inclusion of individuals and small enterprises has made considerable progress over the past two decades. Yet more than 1.6 billion adults globally still do not have access to financial services. This chapter reviews the main benefits of financial inclusion and the contribution of Fintech to this policy agenda. This chapter then emphasizes the quality dimension of financial inclusion, on top of access. Financial inclusion is the largest recipient of Impact Investing capital, either in the form of equity—public or private—or debt, from a wide range of investors, both institutional and retail. By combining the latest academic research and case studies, this chapter analyzes how

Fintech—including peer-to-peer payments in China, transfers in Kenya, digital banking in Brazil, e-commerce in Argentina, and other examples of financial innovation—can expand inclusion. The intent and metrics pursued by Fintech are focused on access and customer satisfaction and can meaningfully help fight poverty, reduce inequalities, and accelerate the attainment of Sustainable Development Goal (SDG) 1 (no poverty) and SDG-10 (reduced inequalities). There are still challenges to overcome, particularly high levels of informality, subpar quality in financial services, regulatory challenges, and low levels of financial education.

Keywords

Fintech; Financial Inclusion; Impact Investing; Sustainable Development Goals; SDG; Innovation; Financial Inclusion; Inclusion; Financial Technology; Financial Services; Technology; Innovation; Banking; Electronic Payments; Payment Systems; Quality

INTRODUCTION

Over the past decade, the financial sector has been an engine of innovation with new financial instruments, such as green bonds or social impact bonds, and new business models, enabled by technology. Fintech refers to business models that provide financial services and are mostly enabled by technology. The rising Fintech sector creates a major disruption and brings the promise of enhanced financial inclusion.

Financial inclusion is a public policy objective that fosters development through access to financial services for all. The definition of financial inclusion includes three dimensions: (i) access, (ii) usage, and (iii) quality of financial services. Inclusion of individuals and small enterprises has made considerable progress over the past two decades, but it has also reached excesses in some situations. Yet more than 1.6 billion adults globally still do not have access to financial services. Regulatory changes, technological innovation, and disruptive business models have helped the expansion of financial services.

Can the revolution that is currently taking place in payments and Fintech foster more inclusion? Under which conditions is financial inclusion desirable and impactful? Are investments in Fintech necessarily impact investments? How can institutional investors finance Fintech across asset classes and multiple Sustainable Development Goals (SDG)?

Financial inclusion is the largest recipient of Impact Investing capital, either in the form of equity—public or private—or debt. Examples ranging from digital banking in Brazil, to payments in China, or remittances in Kenya underline the importance of the quality dimension, which is the key element to bridge the gap between access to and usage of financial services.

By combining the latest academic research, case studies, and professional experience in emerging markets, this analysis expands considerably the traditional focus on microcredit. Through the lens of Fintech—including payments, lending platforms, insurtech (for insurance-technology), and other examples of financial innovation—this chapter highlights the practical opportunities of financial inclusion. There are still challenges to overcome, particularly high levels of informality, subpar quality in financial services, regulatory challenges, and low levels of financial education.

The next section describes the acceleration of financial innovation with business models enabled by technology that act as catalysts for financial inclusion. The following section analyses the many benefits but also limitations and shortcomings of financial inclusion, which have turned it into a key policy objective. The following section then emphasizes the role of payments as an entry point for financial inclusion. The chapter continues with a detailed analysis of the quality dimension of financial inclusion, which is essential to translate access into usage of financial services. In a final section before the conclusion, the chapter underlines the points of attention to policymakers in order to unlock the potential for financial inclusion to attract Impact Investing capital and attain SDG.

THE PROMISE OF FINTECH: INNOVATION WITH A PURPOSE

Can Fintech enhance financial inclusion?
The evolution of the financial system is inherently based on innovation, but recent years have shown an acceleration in this trend, and technology bears the promise of a radical transformation in the sector. New business models and companies are challenging incumbents. Fintech is growing rapidly, driven by three factors: high margins in select financial products attracting new players, lower costs of technology and the ubiquity of cell phones, and a stronger support for innovation by regulators. Fintech has created high hopes.

In this fast-changing environment, regulators face the difficult task of fostering enough innovation while avoiding jumps that could jeopardize the health of the financial system and harm customers. Regulators globally have embraced the challenge of Fintech, favoring new business models in the financial sector, which can increase contestability and improve both the access to and the quality of financial services. The example of Europe sheds light on the key principles that are guiding regulators nowadays and influencing policymakers globally. Recent directives have moved the focal point on the customer, under the principle that banking data should belong to citizens. Directives from the European Commission on transparency, portability, and interoperability are putting more emphasis on customers' rights and protection. By contrast, the previous consensus implied that data belonged to financial intermediaries in exchange for the classic functions they performed, such as deposit taking. Regulators globally are encouraging the innovation of open banking and target the right balance between higher market contestability and financial soundness.

However, if innovation is only meant to generate new business ventures, we may be missing a unique opportunity. Fintech bears the promise of more inclusion, more efficient macroeconomic policies, and a better allocation of capital to unlock opportunities, advancing Sustainable Development Goals—SDG-1 (no poverty), SDG-5 (gender equality), and SDG-10 (reduced inequalities)—with a potential to support most of the other goals. This is a unique opportunity for societies to build a more open and inclusive system, which can serve to foster development and alleviate poverty and allow citizens and businesses to deploy their full potential. Like the advent of the Internet, financial technology may reinforce the existing divide in societies or bear the promise of a more inclusive society. Analyzing Fintech with an Impact Investing lens touches on diverse and interconnected segments of knowledge such as finance, macroeconomy, and public policy.

Financial inclusion has become a key policy objective in most emerging economies but is also topical in developed markets. There is a large literature offering support for a link between financial inclusion and development, while excessive or inappropriate inclusion can also bring risks. The World Bank estimates that more than 1.6 billion people and more than 200 million businesses lack financial services worldwide (World Bank 2016). Additionally, hundreds of millions are underserved and are not able to reach their full productive potential for lack of financials access. Access to and usage of financial services have traditionally improved, thanks to deeper branch networks and innovations, such as banking correspondents in Brazil and the creation of group lending in Bangladesh, both in the 1970s. Over the past two decades, technology and regulations are forces that have boosted inclusion. While access has improved, it is far from ubiquitous.

There are several definitions of financial inclusion. For the World Bank, "financial inclusion means that individuals and businesses have access to useful and affordable financial products and services that meet their needs—transactions, payments, savings, credit and insurance—delivered in a responsible and sustainable way." The Center for Financial Inclusion (CFI) states that financial inclusion allows everyone to have "access to a full suite of quality financial services at affordable prices, with convenience, dignity, and consumer protection, delivered by a range of providers in a stable, competitive market to financially capable clients" (Kelly and Rhyne 2015). The definitions illustrate that being financially included is different from—and much more complex than—being banked: having a bank account at a formal bank institution, including banks, cooperatives, and credit unions. Mas (2009) notes that financial inclusion consists in having access to a wide range of financial services, not just credit. Financial inclusion considers all economic agents, either individuals or corporates, with a special attention for the more vulnerable and excluded segments, such as the poorer segments of the population in emerging markets and small- and medium-sized businesses. Importantly, the reverse concept of financial exclusion is a growing concern in developed economies, such as the United States (Burhouse and Osaki 2014). The World Bank (2013) notes that 20% of the US adult population is underbanked, which the authors define as having a bank account but using financial service from another alternative (i.e. a non-FDIC[1] insured financial provider). This chapter uses the definition that comprises the three dimensions of access, usage, and quality (Roa 2015; Banco Central do Brasil 2015) and stresses the quality dimension of inclusion. Claessens (2006) explains: "access refers to supply, whereas use is the intersection of the supply and demand schedules." Quality is the catalyst that converts the potential access to actual usage.

Electronic payments are an entry door for inclusion, including payments with credit, debit, prepaid cards, and other electronic means such as online and mobile payments. The growing use of electronic payments can open the door to a wider range of financial services, including—but not limited to—credit. The rise in electronic payments brings various development-related benefits to a country, while cash usage is associated with informality. Reaching a higher level of electronic payments is a positive achievement but is not sufficient to guarantee inclusion.

Research shows that asymmetries of information can be detrimental to the market as a whole. The credit market is imperfect in a sense that there

---

[1] Federal Deposit Insurance Corporation.

may not be a price that clears the supply and demand for credit, if banks simply refuse to lend for lack of information (Akerlof 1970; Stiglitz and Weiss 1981, 1992) and credit market conditions amplify and propagate the effects of real monetary shocks, under a phenomenon described as the financial accelerator (Bernanke, Gertler, and Gilchrist 1994). Bernanke, Lown, and Friedman (1991) explain that borrowers who face relatively high agency costs in credit markets will bear the brunt of economic downturns. Agency costs stem from the situation where a principal (the lender) cannot without cost acquire information on the agent (the borrower). Credit is different from other goods, due to the central role of information, and sunk costs from information gathering act as barriers to entry for borrowers (Greenwald and Stiglitz 2003).

Stiglitz (1989) stressed the importance of asymmetries of information in the credit market, explaining that screening and monitoring of clients are two essential functions of financial institutions. Loans are different from other goods and markets, since they are not contemporaneous: money is repaid in the future, loans are heterogeneous, and they bear information problems. Stiglitz and Weiss (1992) developed a theory of credit rationing. According to the model, charging a higher interest rate can reduce profits for a lender, as the interest rate (price of money) does not play its normal clearing function. The authors advance two reasons for the negative correlation: an adverse selection and an incentive effect. Pinheiro and Moura (2003) argue that asymmetries of information lead some borrowers to be "informationally captured" and credit bureaus can reduce those asymmetries. Investors are therefore correct to focus their attention on financial market infrastructure companies, such as information repositories. Companies like Experian and Equifax dominate the Brazilian market of credit bureaus and should experience enhanced quality of the credit scores they produce on the back of a 2019 regulation that incorporates positive credit information into scores (De Mariz 2020).

Fintech is an industry composed of companies that use technology to make financial systems and the delivery of financial services more efficient. Fintech is an essential tool to boost financial inclusion. Not surprisingly, microfinance and financial services have been the largest recipient of investments, representing 24% of total Impact Investing compared with 15% for the second sector, energy (GIIN 2019).[2] One can approach financial innovation via new financial instruments, such as social impact bonds (De Mariz and Savoia, 2018) or Green Bonds (Deschryver and De Mariz 2020). The second approach, which is the focus in this chapter, consists in analyzing financial

---

[2]Global Impact Investing Network.

innovation in business models, enabled by technology and that disrupt the status quo, allowing for a fairer and more open financial sector. Financial innovation represents a unique opportunity for Impact Investing across asset classes. Impact Investing is defined as providing capital to businesses that meet four objectives: they pursue a financial return, aim for a social or environmental impact, express intention in that social aim, and measure the impact (GIIN 2019).

Overall, innovation in financial services is accelerating. As an example, there were 550 active Fintech firms in Brazil as of 2019, according to Brazilian venture capital fund Distrito, and 231 had been created between 2016 and 2018. The two largest categories are payments (21%) and lending (16%). Thirty percent offer solutions that are Business-to-Consumer (B2C), 54% are Business-to-Business (B2B), and the rest are mixed models. Meanwhile, incumbents are also investing heavily to enhance their platforms and service offering, either via internal projects or via inorganic growth. Latin America's largest private bank, Itaú, has been an important seed investor in Fintech via its incubator and co-work venture called Cubo and has launched its own 100% digital bank called Iti.

For banks, financial innovation and digitalization provide opportunities for cost savings and revenue gains, as well as transforming the customer experience. Traditional banks are innovating in order to boost efficiency gains, which are meant to offset some of the margin pressure stemming from competition. Physical branch reduction and rationalization bring meaningful cost savings for banks, while many processes are migrated to digital platforms. Digital channels (mobile and internet) are now the main transaction channel for the largest Brazilian banks, accounting for approximately 70% of total transactions and rising, according to the Brazilian Central Bank (De Mariz 2016).

On top of cost savings, the mobile distribution channel generates revenue opportunities. Brazilian banks originate an increasing percentage of personal loans via mobile, including payroll-deducted consumer loans. Banks have also been exploring cross-selling opportunities—for example, proposing foreign exchange or travel insurance when clients activate the international feature on their credit cards. Brazilian banks also offer loan renegotiation options on their mobile apps. Going forward, banks note that there is additional revenue potential with the upcoming inclusion of fee-generating services such as insurance products on the mobile platform. Moreover, mobile banking is becoming more important for building customer relationships—as a channel that can potentially engage with users 24/7, enhance the customer experience as well as customer loyalty.

With the use of financial services from nontraditional providers set to rise sharply, banks have responded to threats from Fintech competitors via partnerships. In many cases, Fintech ventures are not disrupting existing players but searching for opportunities to collaborate, as incumbents bring the benefits of deeper pockets and proximity with the regulators. Fintech firms benefit from low client acquisition cost, and target low- to middle-income clients, offering niche solutions and often a smarter customer online experience. In many cases, Fintech firms are not necessarily implementing a disruptive technology but rather building on existing tracks laid by incumbents.

In the payment sector, for example, many new acquiring companies emulate the existing ecosystem but propose a faster technology, better antifraud intelligence, and lower prices to their retail clients. Plastic cards are often dematerialized to be supported by smartphones, removing the need for plastic. The acceptance of near-field communication (NFC) and quick response (QR) codes is picking up in Latin America, with heavy investments being made by Big Tech companies such as e-commerce giant Mercado Libre throughout Latin America or digital banks such as Agibank in Brazil. Peer-to-peer payments are picking up, following the outstanding success of Chinese platforms WeChat and Alipay and Indian platform Paytm. Brazil is scheduled to implement Peer-to-Peer (P2P) payments in November 2020, thanks to a new switch developed and controlled by the Brazilian Central Bank. For P2P, the main barrier to overcome is often interoperability across systems and software.

Similarly, the distributed ledger technology (DLT), broadly referred to as blockchain, is a meaningful innovation that can impact the financial sector. DLT has the potential to meaningfully impact traditional businesses, such as exchanges, especially post-trade, due to higher transparency, faster settlement, and lower costs. Ancillary services—the traditional recurring revenues of exchanges—could be impacted, such as listing, registration, collateral management, and custody. By contrast, DLT should not disrupt trading or clearing activities, as DLT may be too slow, and its decentralized nature removes the benefits of netting. Exchanges are likely to lead innovation, including Nasdaq or the Chilean Stock Exchange. In fact, DLT is particularly useful and disruptive in businesses based on a centralized authentication and approval system, involving the ownership of some asset, and that present a delay in settlement due to technological inefficiency. Public notaries and custodians (as we know them today) may not exist in the future of financial services. Cryptocurrencies, which also rely on DLT, have attracted much attention, but their volatile nature and lack of institutional support make them still marginal in the financial sector.

Through innovation such as blockchain, some services will be made redundant and pricing will evolve. The enthusiasm around DLT and Fintech has come mostly from developed markets, with initial public offerings, initial coin offerings, and private placements.

WHAT ARE THE BENEFITS AND LIMITS OF FINANCIAL INCLUSION?

Why is financial inclusion so important?

The case for inclusion is both political and economic. Several political currents suggest that inclusive societies can be seen as fair and allow people to fulfill their human and economic potential (Rawls 1971, 1988). John Rawls builds his theory of justice in contrast to the utilitarian view and defines a hypothetical initial state, where the wealth of the economy has not been shared, and all participants in a society agree on the essential basic treatment that should be offered to each of them. This "veil of ignorance" defines the basic level of inclusion and comfort that an individual would accept in a given society. Rawls underlines that his theory of justice is political in essence, and not metaphysical or based on a religious or philosophical prerequisite. His theory can be defined as an implementation of the game theory to a view of justice. Authors have also linked the emergence of a middle class, loosely linked to inclusion, to benefits in terms of institutions and adoption of democracy. Pressman (2007) detailed in a reference article his views on the middle class, and its contribution to "economic growth, as well as social and political stability." Chun et al. (2016) find empirical support for the hypothesis that a rising middle class would have led to democratization around the globe.

The economic arguments can be divided into three broad groups. Levine (1997), in a seminal paper, showed that the previous literature focused more on the relationship between money and growth, while he analyzed the channel between financial development and economic growth. According to him, the financial system is a "real" sector and does not respond passively to economic growth. He suggested a "positive, first-order relationship between financial development and economic growth."

The first and most studied set of arguments links financial inclusion with higher economic growth and a reduction in poverty (Beck and Demirgüç-Kunt 2008; Cull, Demirgüç-Kunt, and Lyman 2012; Demirgüç-Kunt and Singer 2017). The literature "suggests that under normal circumstances, the degree of financial intermediation is not only positively correlated with growth and employment, but it is generally believed to causally impact growth" (Cull, Ehrbeck, and Holle 2014, p. 6) due to lower transaction costs and better distribution of capital and risk across the economy. Financial inclusion can favor disadvantaged and poor people by allowing them to increase their income and the probability of being employed (Bruhn and Love 2014). A transaction or deposit account can be the stepping-stone to full financial inclusion, providing a pathway to a broader range of financial services provided through stronger and more diverse financial institutions.

Emerging evidence indicates that access to financial services through formal accounts can enable individuals and firms to smooth consumption, manage risk, and invest in education, health, and enterprises. Authors investigated the effect of access to finance on job growth in 50,000 firms across 70 developing countries and found that "increased access to finance results in increased job growth," especially "among micro, small, and medium enterprises" (Ayyagari et al. 2016, p. 4, 27). Despite the still relatively small, albeit growing, number of randomized control evaluations (RCT), consensus is that financial services do have a positive impact on a variety of microeconomic indicators related with development, including self-employment business activities, household consumption, and well-being (CGAP 2015; Bauchet et al. 2011; Angelucci, Karlan, and Zinman 2013). Controlling for other relevant variables, almost 30% of the variation across countries in rates of poverty reduction can be attributed to cross-country variation in financial development (Beck, Demirgüç-Kunt, and Levine 2007). Additional research also found that financially included women fare better than men in terms of increasing their individual income (Gonzalez, Righetti, and Di Serio 2014).

The second argument links financial inclusion with a reduction in inequalities. Indeed, higher financial inclusion disproportionately impacts the poorer segments of the population more and therefore can contribute to reduce inequality, which has been demonstrated to have positive effects on society. In fact, research suggests that equal societies reach higher growth rates and achieve higher income levels and more stable growth (Easterly 2001). Easterly finds that a "higher share of income for the middle class and lower ethnic divisions are empirically associated with higher income and higher growth" (Easterly 2001, p. 1). The middle-class consensus leads to "more education, better health, better infrastructure, better economic policies, less political instability, less civil war and ethnic minorities at risk, more social 'modernization' and more democracy" (Easterly 2001, p. 1). The reflection on inequalities has experienced a renewed focus with historic analyses on the distribution of income and wealth (Piketty 2014).

The third argument links higher financial inclusion with a better efficiency of policymaking and stability. With higher access to financial services, levels of formality increase in the economy and more people fall within the reach of government policies. Authors highlight a relationship between financial inclusion and sought-after policy outcomes, such as women empowerment, health, education, gender equality, and peace (Han and Melecky 2013; Klapper, El-Zoghbi, and Hess 2016). Broad access to bank deposits can have a positive effect on financial stability. Klapper and Singer (2014) note that by moving away from cash payments to digital to distribute government wages and cash transfers such as pensions, "governments can cut costs and reduce leakage." By including a larger part of the population into the formal financial system, governments increase the potential impact of economic policymaking (Cull, Ehrbeck, and Holle 2014). Wider inclusion and lower levels of informality also make monetary policy more effective.

As a result of this growing body of research, financial inclusion has become in the past decade a growing focus of public policy. At the G20 Summit in Seoul in 2010, financial inclusion was recognized as one of the main pillars of the global development agenda. The World Bank Group also launched an initiative to reach Universal Financial Access (UFA) by 2020. The Maya Declaration, launched in 2011 in Riviera Maya, Mexico, is an important international framework for including the unbanked in order to "unlock their full economic and social potential while contributing to reduced income disparities, inclusive development and overall national financial stability" (Alliance for Financial Inclusion 2014).

Bankarization—the access to banking and financial services—has made considerable progress, yet also has its limits; bankarization is not inclusion. There is a rich literature on microcredit, developed and democratized ever since Muhammad Yunus won the Nobel Prize for Peace in 2006 thanks to his visionary action for poor women in Bangladesh. Microcredit has spread to many countries, and innovative business models—through correspondents, for example—have increased access. Correspondents, sometimes called agents, perform a limited number of financial services following domestic regulations and are a major example of branchless banking (Christopoulos, Gonzalez Farias, and Azevedo Marques 2015). Those services typically include payments of bills (such as utilities and phone), cell phone top-ups, and deposits. Brazil counts roughly 300,000 banking correspondents, which compares with 22,000 full banking branches. In India, the government and Reserve Bank of India have taken "initiatives to spread banking services such as expanding the number of rural bank branches, allowing the banking correspondent model and adoption of technology" (Gwalani and Parkhi 2014, p. 372).

However, research also shows that financial inclusion has not always met its claimed objectives. In particular, the risks of excessive or inadequate financial inclusion have led policymakers not just to focus on access and usage, but also to add two other dimensions to financial inclusion: depth and capabilities. As discussed earlier, depth allows entities to offer a wide variety of financial services and to shy away from the focus on credit. Capabilities, in turn, put the emphasis on the abilities of consumers to select, identify, and use services that are tailored to their needs. In some cases, evidence does not support a statistically relevant relationship between financial inclusion and poverty reduction. In an influential paper, Angelucci, Karlan, and Zinman (2013) highlight that data from Mexican microcredit did not show a statistically relevant correlation between access to microcredit and higher revenues or financial resilience of borrowers. Other authors analyze some causes of overindebtedness, and underline the responsibility of microlenders—for example, in the Bolivian microfinance crisis (Rhyne 2001). Authors add that the "emerging field of behavioral economics has identified biases that can lead borrowers to take on more debt than is good for them." In some more extreme cases, high growth in microcredit has led to multiple lending, defined as borrowers taking credit from multiple sources at once, excessive leverage for households, leading to massive consumer defaults, and tragic incidents in some instances, as in the case of India in 2010 (De Mariz, Reille, and Rozas 2011). Morocco, Bosnia, and Pakistan have also experienced episodes of massive consumer delinquencies in microcredit, and authors have recommended that microfinance institutions improved their marketing and underwriting, designing "products that better match client needs and cognitive abilities," improving credit reporting, and developing "early warning systems" (CGAP 2011). Countercyclical policies can also bear risks when using credit to support consumption (Bonomo, Brito, and Martins 2014).

Adding to the literature linking financial development and growth, Cermeño and Roa (2013, p. 4) note that "traditional economic models derived from Arrow-Debreu do not incorporate frictions and market imperfections," such as asymmetries of information and therefore do not include financial institutions in the drivers of growth. In fact, those models consider capital accumulation and technological change as drivers of growth. The authors present another stream of thinking, which shows that financial institutions thrive due to information and transaction costs and that under-developed financial systems lead to credit rationing (Levine 2005; La Porta et al. 2000). Moreover, research shows an endogenous relationship between the depth of the financial system and growth instability. Sahay et al. (2015) flag that "financial inclusion increases economic growth up to a point" and that "financial stability risks increase when access to credit is expanded without proper supervision." On the flip side, the authors interpret that "in contrast to credit access, increasing other types of access to financial services does not impact financial stability adversely" (Sahay 2015, p. 4). If credit seems to have a bell-shaped impact on growth, other financial services such as savings or payments have a linear relationship.

Kenya is the leader in Africa for mobile banking and a success story for financial inclusion, with cell phone penetration being much higher than bank branches. Telecom companies led and benefited most from this market shift. In Kenya, the example of M-Pesa shows how a society leapfrogged the regular brick-and-mortar banking infrastructure to build a digital banking platform, initially focused on payments. Kenyan telecom operator Safaricom launched in 2007 its mobile banking service called M-Pesa, especially in the rural areas where banking services are typically nonexistent. Experiments with mobile banking in Africa show the potential that new technology offers for savings and transfers, since M-Pesa was allowed to increase meaningfully financial inclusion in Kenya (De Mariz 2013), where two-thirds of the adult population report using mobile payments. There are two main reasons for this success: regulations and market structure.

Kenyan regulators did not impose an excessive burden on operators. Mobile banking is inseparable from the adoption of agents or banking correspondents, who were regulated in 2008. Mobile banking in Kenya was initially designed for fund transfers: funds deposited at agents were deposited at regulated banks by Safaricom, strictly segregated, and users could transfer funds and make payments via their cell phones. Systemic risk was deemed not meaningful because Kenyan telecom operator Safaricom was not conducting banking activities, such as lending. Money laundering concerns were mitigated by a cap on transfer amounts (approximately USD $800 per day) and by keeping participants' details (Know-Your-Customer policy, or KYC). Building on that strong foundation, Safaricom launched a lending product, M-Shwari. With M-Shwari, clients can borrow as little as USD $1, for a month (renewable once), at ~140% p.a., and the credit decision is immediate.

Regulations were important, but the market structure was also conducive to mobile banking for five reasons. First, Safaricom was a state-controlled company and 40% owned by Vodafone, which gave comfort to the Central Bank of Kenya. Second, Safaricom was the dominant player in telecom (85% of the market share), which helped avoid issues of interoperability as the payment transfer system was at first a closed loop. Third, mobile banking rarely adds net new customers to telecom operators but rather penetrates the existing customer base of the telecom company, according to CGAP. As such, the large market share of Safaricom helped deploy the new product. Fourth, about one-fifth of the telecom resellers of Safaricom were exclusive. This exclusive relationship was key to train and incentivize the workforce to sell a new product. Finally, other players such as banks, or acquirers, did not contest or block the venture of Safaricom either through lobbying with regulators or through competing services. This helped the fast and nationwide deployment of mobile banking. The special regulatory situation and market structure explain the fast and broad adoptions of electronic payments and transfers in Kenya.

According to the World Bank, "not all financial products are equally effective in reaching development goals, such as reductions in poverty and inequality," as "current evidence suggests that the biggest impacts come from savings accounts—provided that they are inexpensive and serve a specific purpose—and digital payments" (Demirgüç-Kunt, Klapper, and Singer 2017, p. 19). While 40% of the population worldwide still does not have an account, transaction accounts "can act as a gateway for individuals to adopt other relevant financial services they need to smooth their consumption and manage income shocks" (World Bank 2016, p. 5).

WITHIN FINTECH, ELECTRONIC PAYMENTS ARE AN ENTRY POINT FOR FINANCIAL INCLUSION

How can electronic payments boost the overall growth in inclusion?

Electronic payments include online transfers; card-based instruments such as debit, credit, or prepaid cards; and e-money (World Bank 2016). Electronic payments, also referred to as digital payments, are often opposed to cash usage and payments by checks. An essential goal of electronic payments is to reduce transaction friction, with better convenience and cost for users. "The practical applicability of the neoclassical modeling approach is now challenged by at least two alternative theoretical paradigms" (Merton and Bodie 2004, p. 6). First, "New Institutional Economics, focuses explicitly on transaction costs, taxes, computational limitations, and other frictions." The other paradigm: "Behavioral Economics, introduces nonrational and

TABLE 30.1 The Size of Electronic Payments Globally: Global Payments by Micro-, Small-, and Medium-Sized Retailers (Estimated Values, 2015).

	Total payments (USD $ in trillions)	Of which electronic (USD $ in trillions)	Percent of electronic (%)
Global	34.0	15.0	44
High-income OECD	11.1	7.9	71
Latin America & the Caribbean	3.5	1.5	43
Middle East & North Africa	1.3	0.4	30
Sub-Saharan Africa	1.5	0.4	25
Eastern Europe and Central Asia	3.1	1.3	46
East Asia & Pacific	9.5	2.7	31
South Asia	4.0	0.8	20

Source: World Bank (2016, p. 6).

systematically uninformed behavior by agents" (Merton and Bodie 2004, p. 6). Humphrey, Pulley, and Vesala (1996) analyze 12 European countries and estimate a reduction in operating costs of €32 billion, or 0.38% of GDP, between 1987 and 1999, driven by the 36% increase in electronic payments and 32% increase in ATM in the total segment of payments. According to Banco Central do Brasil (2007), fully migrating to electronic payments would generate a cost saving of 0.7% of Brazilian GDP, using 2005 data, or approximately BRL R$15 billion.

Furthermore, electronic payments represent a very large market, as seen in Table 30.1. The World Bank (2016) estimates the "global market opportunity for expanding the adoption of electronic payments by merchants is large, estimated at USD $19 trillion of payments made and accepted in cash and checks by micro, small and medium retailers (MSMRs) in 2015" (World Bank 2016, p. 11). Latin America represents USD $3.5 trillion, of which just 46% is already electronic. This compares with an average of 71% for high-income OECD[3] countries. The authors add that B2B transactions (Business to Business) represent a large opportunity, and that new models are emerging for online payments.

---

[3] Organization for Economic Co-operation and Development.

In Brazil, D'Erasmo (2013) shows that a lower cost of financial services leads to higher levels of formalization and higher levels of credit, giving support to policies that incentivize higher degrees of competition. Innovation and Fintech have the potential to bring meaningful efficiency gains for the participants of the payment ecosystem, and to end users in particular.

Payments have been the focus of policymakers, considering all kinds of connections between the different potential parties (GBP, or Government, Business, People). For example, Government-to-People (G2P) payments have largely benefited from a move to electronic channels, because this slashes the costs associated with the disbursement of benefits and wages. The World Bank calls for leveraging on "government payment programs to promote financial inclusion," as "the large volume of payments issued by governments, as well as the nature of some specific programs like social spending programs, represents an opportunity to promote or facilitate financial inclusion on a large scale" (World Bank, 2012, p. 3).

In Brazil, the Bolsa Familia, the largest conditional redistribution program in the developing world, is a case study in G2P transfers, as the program delivers financial assistance to nearly a third of the total population, and 99% of the recipients receive digital payments into a card or bank account, representing a public policy success (World Bank 2012, 2015a and 2015b). The program "seeks to reduce poverty and inequality" and "break the intergenerational transmission of poverty by conditioning these transfers on beneficiary compliance with human capital requirements," such as "school attendance, vaccines, pre-natal visits" (Lindert et al. 2007, p. 2). There are over 32,000 retail locations where benefits can be withdrawn, and 65% of benefits are received at lottery locations. G2P payments reduce the administrative cost of the program for the government and offer an entry point into the financial system for recipients. According to the World Bank, moving to electronic payment and consolidating four programs into one "improved efficiency by reducing administrative costs" from 14.7% to 2.6% of the value of the grants disbursed (Lindert et al. 2007, pp. 112, 113). However, while electronic G2P payments bring efficiency to the system, they are not always associated to an effective inclusion of people: 88% withdraw all the money right away in Brazil, and the use of bank accounts for cash management purposes is still limited. The poorer the household, the more likely they are to withdraw their full transfer at once.

Globally, although the number of accounts has grown, the number of active users has lagged. In Colombia, the Daviplata program launched by privately owned bank Davivienda met partially the results initially expected.

Daviplata is responsible for the electronic transfer and disbursement of payments by the Colombian central government to public servants, military, and retirees. Research has shown that a large part of the transfers is withdrawn in full by recipients, thereby limiting the benefits of constituting savings and inclusion at large. By contrast, another Colombian experiment in People to Government (P2G) and Business to Government (B2G) has shown clear success. The Colombian banking sector and a private clearing house (ACH Colombia) have developed over the past decade an online payment instrument, which is embedded in government and business websites and allows "businesses and consumers to authorize electronic payments directly from their bank accounts to government agencies and to other businesses" (Better than Cash Alliance 2015, p. 1). In the period of five years up to 2013, the authors find that the number of "payments made this way had increased by more than tenfold to almost a million a month" (Better Than Cash Alliance 2015, p. 1). The online tool is known as Secure Online Payments (Pagos Seguros en Línea, PSE) and is a private sector innovation that was supported by the Colombian government.

In Mexico, the success of a G2P program had two simultaneous dimensions: a move toward electronic payments and toward centralized payments. In 2012, "97% of pension payments were made by electronic transfers" (Babatz 2013, p. 23). The unification and digitalization of payments to government employees, retirees, and social transfers was a wide success. By digitizing and centralizing its payments, the Mexican government has "saved USD $1.27 billion per year," equivalent to "3.3% of all its total expenditure on wages, pensions and social transfers" (Babatz 2013, p. 37). Savings came in the form of float revenues, with no more anticipation in payment, lower transaction fees, less leakage, and fewer operational errors.

The payment sector has been a focus of innovation for government, and is the main target of Fintech. From the Fintech perspective, payments present the triple advantage of having high operating margins for newcomers, requiring less capital investment (compared to credit, for example), and gathering valuable data on customers (which can generate other types of revenues). Payments are a logical entry product for Fintechs. In fact, before resorting to credit, customers need to have a transaction account, build a transaction history, and provide evidence of their ability to save over time. The Big Techs—companies outside of the financial sector—can leverage their large clients base of recurrent users and extract information from the wealth of data that they process, in order to offer credit or asset management services. Those companies include social media, urban mobility, or e-commerce. Fintechs have targeted poorly served niches. In Brazil,

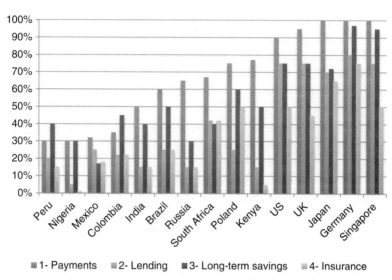

FIGURE 30.1   Metrics of Adoption and Degree of Financial Products. *Source*: World Bank Group, 2015a, adapted by author.

Pagseguro targets the lower-income small- and medium-sized businesses, and has developed product innovation with simpler and more affordable point-of-sale equipment. Pagseguro now counts 3 million merchants as clients and publicly listed on the NYSE in 2018.

A higher adoption of financial services is associated with higher levels of development (Figure 30.1). While payments are a typical entry point for service providers to acquire clients, other financial services are paramount for individuals and businesses, especially savings, insurance, and credit.

The main focus of Fintech so far has been on payments. However, lending has seen the emergence of new models, using technology to better assess client risk or to develop more agile distribution channels (De Mariz 2016). Credit bureaus and financial market infrastructure companies play a key role to facilitate credit growth. The growing power and sophistication of computers has led to the rise of scoring systems based on big data. Importantly, banks have developed the understanding of their clients not just based on negative credit history, but more and more on positive data. Positive data coming from deposit, transfers, payments in general and credit amortization have allowed banks to define a more accurate portrait of their clients, thereby refining the pricing of risk at the individual level. Recent research has meaningfully expanded the body of data that can be predictive for credit concession to include simple transactions and behavioral data.

Credit bureaus, such as Equifax globally, and collateral registries such as CERC in Brazil, are looking into nontraditional datasets to predict credit behavior or collateral to guarantee operations. Likewise, Morocco is the first country in North Africa to launch an electronic national registry of movable assets. Implemented in 2020 with the support of the IFC, it will ease access to finance for micro, small, and medium-sized enterprises, especially those owned by youth and women, because it enables them to use collateral as guarantees for loans to start or grow their business. Meanwhile, the mixed success of peer-to-peer credit platforms reinforces the classical functions of screening and monitoring performed by financial intermediaries, in line with Diamond (1984), who explained that banks perform a necessary function of delegated monitoring of borrowers.

Wealth accumulation and savings are another essential financial service. Women's World Banking (2014) notes that for poor women, access to a safe place to save and build assets is as important as access to loans. In poorer communities, saving mechanisms are often informal and unreliable. Poorer segments tend to save at home, by buying excess inventory for their businesses, or livestock. They also rely on neighborhood savings clubs. The small amounts are often seen as the main barrier for consumers to bring their savings to a bank branch, especially as the time spent to deposit the cash is a real disincentive. Mas (2009) notes that the cash-in and cash-out capabilities offered by financial institutions or cooperatives must be easy, cost-efficient, and convenient for consumers to be willing to save with official mechanisms. For the rising middle-class, online brokerage companies, such as XP in Brazil, offer open platforms with superior user experience, digital capabilities, and a larger investment offering than closed-architecture banks, expanding the base of domestic capital in Brazil and diversifying sources of capital for companies.

Insurance is also an important channel for financial inclusion protecting consumers against unforeseen hardship. Banco Compartamos in Mexico is one of the largest micro-insurers globally and includes life micro-insurance coverage of MXN $15,000 pesos in every credit operation. In a Brazilian context, Gonzalez, Vidal, and Christopoulos (2013) note that micro-insurance represents a very large untapped market, which requires regulatory adjustment. Ventures such as Minuto Seguros offer a better insurance distribution experience with an open platform offering access to several carriers and a fully digitalized process. In the health segment, Fintech Vitality in South Africa leverages technology to change the distribution of policies, pricing of risk, and after-sale service in the health insurance segment.

THE DRIVERS OF FINANCIAL INCLUSION: THE QUALITY DIMENSION

What drives the adoption of electronic payments and higher levels of financial inclusion?

Research over the past 20 years has advanced the understanding of the drivers of payments, focusing on mainly two, the access and usage dimensions. This section reviews the recent literature and then emphasizes a third, the quality dimension.

One stream of research underlines the relative costs of cash versus card usage (Von Kalckreuth, Schmidt, and Stix 2014). The proximity of banking services, such as the density of point of service (POS) and the ownership of plastic cards, has a positive relationship with electronic payments. All-in costs, including fees borne by the cardholder and the cost for the merchant, have a strong correlation with the usage of electronic payments. A seminal paper by Humphrey, Pulley, and Vesala (1996) analyzed the determinants of the choice of payment instruments, after comparing datasets from 13 industrialized countries between 1987 and 1993, showing that the movement toward electronic payments is "uniform and unmistakable" across countries and can lead to a meaningful reduction in social cost (Humphrey, Pulley, and Vesala 1996, p. 936). Mantel (2000) highlights the role of sociodemographic and technological factors on the propensity to use electronic payment systems or the probability of them being used. Klee (2006) relates the use of payment instruments with household characteristics using survey data for the United States and finds that debit card use increases with income and education. Schuh, Shy, and Stavins (2010) find that reward programs generate an "implicit monetary transfer to credit card users from non-card (or cash) users," moreover, "because credit card spending and rewards are positively correlated with household income, the payment instrument transfer also induces a regressive transfer from low-income to high-income households" (Schuh, Shy, and Stavins 2010, p. i).

Another stream emphasizes the role of consumer preferences and transaction characteristics. Bounie and Francois (2006) find that transaction size is determinant, as well as the type of product and spending place. O'Brien (2015) uses a dataset from the Federal Reserve 2012 Diary of Consumer Payment Choice, which includes all the "recorded financial transactions of approximately 2,500 individuals who participated in the diary during their variously assigned three consecutive-day periods within the month of October 2012," showing that "cash continues to play a large role as a payment instrument especially in lower value transactions for all demographic groups" (O'Brien 2015, p. 1). Research based on a decade of data from acquiring companies in Brazil showed that macroeconomic variables such as consumption and employment are key determinants of plastic card usage, but so are behavioral explanations, such as customer perception that they can better control their personal finances when paying in cash and a distrust against banks (De Mariz 2017).

Research on payments in developing countries tends to be scarce and patchy, due to smaller data samples and currency volatility. Research shows that "about 30% of transactions in Uruguay are made using either credit cards, debit cards, bank transfers or direct debit. The figure is 51% in Turkey and 73% in Chile, countries with similar level of income per capita" (Lluberas and Saldain 2015). Using the World Bank's Global Findex database on 37 African countries, Zins and Weill (2016) found that "being a man, richer, more educated and older favor financial inclusion with a higher influence of education and income" (Zins and Weill 2016, p. 46). Importantly, they also show that "mobile banking is driven by the same determinants as traditional banking" (p. 46), suggesting that mobile banking is not a more inclusive channel.

A large part of this research is written by central banks, for whom understanding the issuance and monitoring of currency in circulation is essential. Interestingly, the Bank of England, one of the most open to financial innovation, expects cash to remain important in the future (Fish and Whymark). In the case of the UK, money in circulation represents close to 4% of GDP, with coins representing 3% of total money and banknotes the remaining 97%. Money is used for hoarding and for transactional purposes. Studies in the UK showed that 18% of people hoarded cash "to provide comfort against potential emergencies" (Fish and Whymark, p. 223). Baumol (1952) applied a principle of "inventory control analysis" to the theory of money. He analyzed the transaction demand for cash that is dictated by rational behavior, which corresponds to holding a cash balance that can "do the job at minimum cost" (Baumol 1952, p. 545). The model considers the interest rate on money and the broker fee for cash withdrawal as the two drivers of the demand for cash. Inventory models such as Baumol's highlight the function of cash as a means of payment. Other authors have added other dimensions to cash demand, such as a precautionary motivation, speculation and hoarding.

Precaution is a driver for the still high propensity to keep cash and shy away from electronic payments. Cusbert and Rohling (2013) studied the effect of the financial crisis of 2008 on the demand for cash in Australia, finding that "the demand for currency increased abnormally quickly in late 2008, resulting in an additional USD $5 billion (or 12 percent) of Australian banknotes on issue by the end of that year," which is "consistent with the disproportionate rise in demand for high-denomination banknotes." This raise was associated with "precautionary motives by people concerned about the liquidity or solvency of financial institutions and by financial institutions as a contingency" (Cusbert and Rohling 2013, p. i). The demand for money due to precautionary reasons according to Keynes has a different meaning and consists in the demand for money used to make unexpected expenditures. Keynes defines the precautionary cash balances as those held "to provide for contingencies requiring sudden expenditures and for unforeseen opportunities of advantageous purchases, and also to hold an asset of which the value is fixed in terms of money to meet a subsequent liability in terms of money" (Keynes 1936, p. 196). In Keynesian economics, precautionary demand is one of the determinants of demand for money (and credit), the others being transactions demand and speculative demand. The precautionary demand for money refers to real balances held for use in a contingency. As receipts and payments cannot be perfectly foreseen, people hold precautionary balances to minimize the potential loss arising from a contingency. The precautionary demand is dependent on the size of income, the availability of credit, and the rate of interest. High-denomination bank notes are usually used for store of value, which is confirmed by the fact that 60% of the US dollars in circulation are held outside of the United States, where they have limited acceptance. The theory on the demand for cash highlights the main benefits of cash, such as the convenience, universal acceptance, anonymity, or seigniorage revenues for the issuer of banknotes and coins. On the flip side, cash usage bears costs, from reduced fiscal revenues driven by higher informality, the cost and inconvenience of withdrawing cash from automated teller machines (ATM) and bank branches, security concerns (against thefts), and the cost of printing, handling, and management.

While the existing literature has focused on the dimensions of access and usage, this section now underlines the importance of quality services. Within the quality dimension, several characteristics are essential drivers of inclusion. Thus, what are the characteristics of good quality payment systems? What best practices can be shared when establishing new payment systems and regulations? If citizens have access to the payment capability, why would they not use them? What constrains their usage?

The three main reasons for being unbanked include the costs associated with bank accounts, distances traveled to reach a bank or financial agent, and the various requirements involved in opening a financial account (Allen,

Demirgüç-Kunt, and Klapper 2012). World Bank (2013) shows that 34% of firms in developing economies have a bank loan, versus 51% in developed markets. The World Bank (2016) estimates that "200 million enterprises in developing economies are still constrained in terms of financing, even though small and medium enterprises generate the greatest number of new jobs, employ the largest number of people in aggregate" (World Bank 2016, p. 4). Being financially excluded is also linked to income level: the richest 20% of adults in developing countries are more than twice as likely to have a formal account as the poorest 20%. Regulations relating to banking correspondents, simplified financial services, mandatory free basic financial offering, investments into branch opening, and mobile banking have helped increase meaningfully the convenience for citizens to be banked. Those who have access but choose not to use services pose less of a problem for policymakers. Among survey participants without an account in the 2014 Findex survey, only 4% said they do not need one (Demirgüç-Kunt et al. 2015).

The financial capability of the customer has become an increasingly central aspect of the thinking about financial inclusion. Authors define financial capabilities for customers who "have knowledge, skills, and behaviors that enable them to make sound financial decisions" (Kelly and Rhyne 2015). Financial education is multifaceted: it does not necessarily precede an uptake of financial services but rather goes hand in hand with experimenting new financial solutions and improving one's financial capability.

Quality has often been related to the financial education of the customer. In the case of payments, there are six dimensions to the concept of quality: cost, benefit, ease of use, speed, security, and privacy. Those dimensions taken together explain why and how users decide to adopt electronic payments. Electronic payments will favor financial inclusion only if participants address the question of quality. Measures that promote electronic payments include simplified accounts, innovative solutions such as mobile banking, and the formalization of the economy with mandatory salary payments on accounts, leveraging Fintech solutions. Assessing the quality dimension of payments can mostly be approached via surveys (De Mariz 2017). In the list of benefits of cash usage, Brazilian customers spontaneously quote the convenience and discounts offered in cash payments as the two main attributes. The main barriers to access and usage of accounts are the high fees, low-income levels, informality, and poor perception on banks. Low usage is due to economic but also to attitudinal reasons (World Bank 2016; Banco Central do Brasil 2013; Schuh and Stavins 2010). Electronic payments bring transparency, security, privacy,

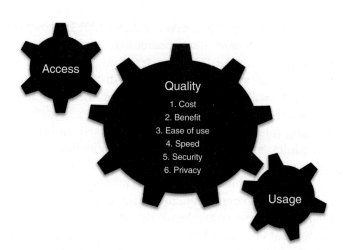

FIGURE 30.2   The Six Characteristics of Quality Applied to Payments. *Source*: Author.

speed, and cost savings. Other authors note that advantages of cash include anonymity, convenience, universal acceptance, and instantaneous settlement (Mas 2015).

Contrary to the traditional representation that financial inclusion is based on a tripod of overlapping access, usage, and quality, this chapter presents quality as the catalyst between the two other dimensions (Figure 30.2). Most of the comments on the quality dimension have focused on the customer abilities, relating to the theme of financial education. Rather than focus on the payment mode, a user-centric methodology should be used, starting from the benefit that the user is looking for and analyzing which method of payment can be most appropriate. There are six characteristics of the quality dimension of payments.

Within the quality dimension, there are six characteristics that drive the adoption of electronic payments. This approach considers both the merchant and the cardholder, while most of the literature considers only one side of the equation. Cost includes explicit costs, such as Merchant Discount Rate (MDR), cash management, safekeeping expenses, and fees for the cardholder. Benefits include client data intelligence for merchants, rewards, and the possibility for cardholders to establish a credit history. Surveys show mixed views on whether cash or cards help better control personal finances and spending. Ease of use correspond to the wide acceptance, ease to swipe and process, convenience of carrying cards versus cash. New tools to capture transactions are growing such as NFC and QR codes. Cards can be more suitable for recurring payments and online purchases. Speed is essential not just to approve the transaction but also to settle it. Cash presents the advantage of immediate settlement but needs to be transported to a bank to earn interest and be safe. Security of transactions include the ability to track transaction information, confirm, revoke, cancel transactions in case of errors or frauds, and maintain audit trails to provide transparency and fight criminal activities. Related to that legitimate desire for transparency, privacy concerns consist of avoiding undue use of payment information and maintaining due anonymity.

CAN FINTECH ENABLE MORE IMPACT INVESTING AND SUPPORT SDGS?

If innovation is only meant to generate new business ventures, we may be missing a unique opportunity.

Fintech offers the promise of advancing several SDGs, including SDG-1 (no poverty) and SDG-10 (reduced inequalities), with a potential to support most of the other goals, especially SDG-5 (gender equality). This is a unique opportunity for societies to build more open and inclusive social systems, to foster development and alleviate poverty and allow citizens and businesses to deploy their full potential. So what is the role of regulators to advance Fintech and attract more capital in the segment?

Before looking at the potential of Fintech to attract impact capital, this section analyzes the challenges of Fintech for regulators and policymakers.

Fintech creates unique challenges to regulators, whether because of the pace of innovation, their disruptive nature, fast growth, the technicality of business models, or cross-border dematerialization. On the one hand, sandboxes are meant to foster a much welcome innovation. On the other hand, improperly designed innovation can put populations at risk, as in the well-documented cases over microcredit indebtedness. As argued in the previous section, regulators should not focus exclusively on access, which often brings the false impression of successful policies. To promote effective usage, quality is essential. Also, it should not be the role of regulators to single out winning solutions or technologies. Moreover, Fintech, with its reliance on data, can bring new threats for customers, shedding a new light on customer protection and cyber-risk. In many cases, Fintech grows outside of the traditional banking sector, forcing regulators and supervisors to consider the essence of financial services and not just the form, adopting a functional perspective (Merton 1995).

There are four key challenges for regulators: (i) reducing informality; (ii) enabling innovation; (iii) fostering financial inclusion; and (iv) collaboration. Policies can make electronic payments more attractive for users versus cash, such as offering incentives to cardholders to use plastic cards and receiving tax rebates for fiscal receipts. Recognizing the threat of informality, some countries, such as Colombia and Argentina, allow merchants to offer discounts for sales paid with electronic payments. Argentine retailers that accept card payment can claim a tax discount for the cost of the terminal. Similar policies in Korea have led card payments to increase from 5% of personal consumption expenditures to more than 50% in 2009. Cash is unlikely to disappear in the short-term, but its relevance will decrease. Different means will likely coexist, such as checks, prepaid cards (in particular for food and transportation), automatic debit (for recurring bills), or invoices (*boletos* are popular in Brazil).

Innovation is a decisive challenge for regulators, as regulators try to strike the proper balance between risk and innovation (Santana 2014). For innovations, such as payments via mobile money or crypto currencies, the "end game is to make grids safer, [...] more convenient, [...] more contestable, [...] and much cheaper than current systems, especially for micro-transactions" (Mas 2015, p. 1). Risks related to innovation can also include other themes that are relevant to policymaking such as consumer protection. Regulators have developed simplified regulatory requirements to allow smaller or emerging financial institutions and users to adopt financial services while complying with a minimum set of rules. Regulators have acknowledged that some "categories of institutions may be regulated differently from banks as long as they do not hold, collectively, a significant proportion of deposits in a financial system" (Bank of International Settlements 2015, p. 1). The literature also highlights the need to coordinate different regulatory bodies. For example, Borio (2014), in his analysis of financial stability, stresses the need to consider the monetary, prudential, and fiscal policies together. While regulators focus on the four above mentioned objectives or formalization, innovation, inclusion, and collaboration, what role can impact investors play to define metrics or targets for Fintechs?

As fintech attracts more impact capital, is Fintech enabling more impact metrics and tracking? Do investors into Fintech require more impact metrics?

Fintech has the possibility to reduce informality and boost inclusion, which is critical to attain SDGs. Along with the traditional financial disclosure, Fintech companies have focused most of their impact reporting efforts on data collection about access and customer satisfaction. Only few companies report disaggregated data with a gender lens, company size, region, or sector. In fact, recent initial public offerings of Fintech companies have focused on the number of clients and on "net promoter" scores, which are a proxy for customer satisfaction and ultimately for the quality dimension of their services. Financial access, known as one of the main bottlenecks for firm's growth and development is particularly relevant if it impacts customers who were previously excluded from the financial system. A wider access through a democratization of services can yield more concrete impacts and better development results in particular in more vulnerable populations or smaller sized companies.

In fact, despite the frameworks and methodologies already widely available, few companies have developed a full goal and indicator framework aligned with SDGs. "Creating useful ratings for impact requires ways of understanding and measuring impact that are standard enough to compare, while being specific enough (e.g. sector-specific) to be meaningful," according to the Global Impact Investing Network (GIIN 2018, p. 55).

Access and inclusion are the key focus—and a key achievement—of selected Fintech companies. For instance, Brazilian payment company Pagseguro stated in a 2018 financial report that 75% of its clients did not accept electronic payments previously and were therefore informal. Likewise, Brazilian insurtech Minuto Seguros states that 66% of its clients never used insurance previously and were therefore included into this financial vertical thanks to the digital platform.

CONCLUSION

Financial inclusion has made considerable progress, and the recent growth in Fintech has led to the inclusion of millions of formerly excluded or underserved citizens. Fintech ventures can meaningfully help fight poverty, reduce inequalities, and accelerate the attainment of SDGs 1, 5, and 10.

Payments offer an entry door into financial inclusion for the more than 1.6 billion people that do not currently have a transactional account globally. Measures that promote payments include simplified accounts, innovative solutions such as mobile banking, and the formalization of the economy with mandatory salary payments on accounts. Analyzing the quality dimension of financial services—and not just access to—is essential to avoid excesses and ensure that services meet the needs of the different categories of users. The chapter provided a detailed approach and lists the six dimensions of quality payments, consisting in cost, benefit, ease of use, speed, security, and privacy.

Beyond the business aspects, the examples provided by P2P payment platforms in China, digital banking and SME payment platforms in Brazil, transfers in Mexico and Kenya show the opportunities brought about by financial inclusion to vulnerable and poor populations and their potential to foster economic growth and development. Inclusion is unmistakably linked to positive development impact, even though it has sometimes led to excesses in the cases of multiple lending in microfinance.

Financial services are the largest recipient of Impact Investing, and Fintech will continue to attract meaningful investments in public equities, private equity, and debt from a wide range of investors, both institutional and retail, due to their strong growth. The intent and metrics pursued by Fintech focus on access and customer satisfaction, a proxy of quality.

Despite the strong contribution of Fintech businesses to financial inclusion, it would be a simplification to state that Fintech investors are mostly impact investors. The Global Impact Investing Network (GIIN) estimates that over 1,340 organizations currently manage USD $502 billion in Impact Investing assets worldwide. In fact, the definition of Impact Investing combines four essential and necessary attributes: (i) a financial return, (ii) a social return, (iii) the intention to create a social impact, and (iv) the explicit measurement of impact. As Fintechs continue to grow and gain relevance against traditional financial institutions, it is natural to expect that they attract more impact investors.

In turn, those impact investors may demand more disclosure and reporting on the actual impact of those companies, beyond financial returns. With their focus on unattended or poorly attended segments of the populations, Fintechs can make a decisive contribution to SDG-1 (no poverty) and SDG-10 (reduced inequalities).

REFERENCES

Akerlof, G. A. (1970). The Market for "Lemons": Quality Uncertainty and the Market Mechanism. *Quarterly Journal of Economics* 488–500.

Allen, F., Demirgüç-Kunt, A., Klapper, L., et al. (2012). The foundations of financial inclusion: Understanding ownership and use of formal accounts. World Bank, Policy Research Paper 6290.

Alliance for Financial Inclusion (2014). *The 2014 Maya Declaration Progress Report: Measurable Goals with Optimal Impact.*

Angelucci, M., Karlan, D., and Zinman, J. (2013). Win some lose some? Evidence from a randomized microcredit program placement experiment by Compartamos Banco. National Bureau of Economic Research, Paper No. w19119.

Ayyagari, M., Juarros, P., Martinez Peria, M. S., et al. (2016). Access to finance and job growth: Firm-level evidence across developing countries. Policy Research Working Paper 6704, World Bank.

Babatz, G. (2013). Sustained effort, saving billions: Lessons from the Mexican government's shift to electronic payments. Better Than Cash Alliance Case Study. http://betterthancash.org.

Banco Central do Brasil (2007). *Custo e Eficiencia na Utilização de Instrumentos de Pagamento de Varejo.* Reforma do sistema de pagamentos de varejo.

Banco Central do Brasil (2013), O Brasileiro e sua Relação com o Dinheiro.

Banco Central do Brasil (2015). Relatório de inclusão financeira.

Bauchet, J., Marshall, C., Starita, L., et al. (2011). Latest findings from randomized evaluations of microfinance. Washington D.C: CGAP, Access to Finance Forum.

Baumol, W. J. (1952). The Transactions Demand for Cash: An Inventory Theoretic Approach. *Quarterly Journal of Economics* 66 (4): 545–556.

Beck, T., Demirgüç-Kunt, A., and Levine, R. (2007). Finance, Inequality and the Poor. *Journal of Economic Growth* 12(1): 27–49.

Beck, T., and Demirgüç-Kunt, A. (2008). Access to Finance: An Unfinished Agenda. *World Bank Economic Review* 22(3): 383–396.

Bernanke, B. S., Lown, C. S., and Friedman, B. M. (1991). The Credit Crunch. *Brookings Papers on Economic Activity* 1991(2): 205–247.

Bernanke, B., Gertler, M., and Gilchrist, S. (1994). The financial accelerator and the flight to quality. National Bureau of Economic Research, Working Paper no. w4789.

Bank of International Settlements (2015). Guidance on the application of the Core Principles for Effective Banking Supervision to the regulation and supervision of institutions relevant to financial inclusion. https://www.bis .org/bcbs/publ/d383.pdf.

Better Than Cash Alliance (2015). Colombia's Online E-Payments Platform: Private Sector Innovation Inspired by Government Vision, BTCA Case Study No. 3.

Bonomo, M., Brito, R. D., and Martins, B. (2014). Macroeconomic and Financial Consequences of the Post-Crisis Government-Driven Credit Expansion in Brazil. Brasilia: Banco Central do Brasil, Working Papers 378.

Borio, C. E. (2014). Monetary policy and financial stability: what role in prevention and recovery? BIS Working Papers No.440.

Bounie, D., and François, A. (2006). Cash, check or bank card? The effects of transaction characteristics on the use of payment instruments. Telecom Paris

Economics and Social Sciences Working Paper No. ESS-06-05. http://dx.doi .org/10.2139/ssrn.891791.

Bruhn, M., and Love, I. (2014). The Real Impact of Improved Access to Finance: Evidence from Mexico. *Journal of Finance* 69(3):1347–1376.

Burhouse, S., and Osaki, Y. (2014). FDIC National survey of unbanked and under-banked households. Federal Deposit Insurance Corporation. https://www .fdic.gov/householdsurvey/2017/2017report.pdf.

Cermeño, R., and Roa, M. J. (2013). Desarrollo financiero, crecimiento y volatilidad: Revisión de la literatura reciente. Centro de Estudios Monetarios Latinoamericanos, CEMLA, Working Paper no. 9.

CGAP (2011). Too Much Microcredit? A Survey of the Evidence on Over-Indebtedness. https://www.cgap.org/sites/default/files/CGAP-Occasional -Paper-Too-Much-Microcredit-A-Survey-of-the-Evidence-on-Overindebted ness-Sep-2011.pdf.

CGAP (2015). On the Road to Financial Inclusion 2020. Center for Financial Inclusion.

Christopoulos, T. P., Gonzalez Farias, L. E., and de Azevedo Marques, T. C. (2015). Evaluating Banking Agents: A Case of Brazilian Banking Correspondents. *DLSU Business & Economics Review* 24(2).

Chun, N., Hasan, R., Rahman, M. H., et al. (2016). The Role of Middle Class in Democratic Diffusion. *International Review of Economics & Finance* 42: 536–548.

Claessens, S. (2006). Access to Financial Services: A Review of the Issues and Public Policy Objectives. *World Bank Research Observer* 21(2), 207–240.

Cull, R., Demirgüç-Kunt, A., and Lyman, T. (2012). Financial Inclusion and Stability: What Does Research Show? https://www.cgap.org/sites/default/ files/CGAP-Brief-Financial-Inclusion-and-Stability-What-Does-Research-Show-May-2012.pdf.

Cull, R., Ehrbeck, T., and Holle, N. (2014). Financial inclusion and development: Recent impact evidence. Focus Note, 92.

Cusbert, T., and Rohling, T. (2013). Currency demand during the global financial crisis: Evidence from Australia. Reserve Bank of Australia, RDP 2013-01.

D'Erasmo, P. (2013). Access to Credit and the Size of the Formal Sector in Brazil. IDB Working Paper No. IDB-WP-404. http://dx.doi.org/10.2139/ssrn .2330184.

De Mariz (2020). Using Data for Financial Inclusion: The Case of Credit Bureaus in Brazil, *Journal of International Affairs*. https://jia.sipa.columbia.edu/ online-articles/using-data-financial-inclusion-case-credit-bureaus-brazil.

De Mariz, F. (2016). How is Fintech shaping the future of financial institutions? UBS Research.

De Mariz, F. (2017). The Brazil payment industry at a crossroads. UBS Research.

De Mariz, R. (2013). New payment systems are changing the customer experience. UBS Research.

De Mariz, F., Reille, X., and Rozas, D. (2011). Discovering Limits. Global Microfinance Valuation Survey 2011. Washington, DC: CGAP.

De Mariz, F., and Savoia, J., (2018). Financial Innovation with a Social Purpose: The Growth of Social Impact Bonds. In Sabri Boubaker, Douglas J. Cumming, and Duc Khuong Nguyen (eds.), Research Handbook of Investing in the Triple Bottom Line: Finance, Society and the Environment. Cheltenham, UK: Edward Elgar Publishing, 2018.

Demirgüç-Kunt, A., Klapper, L. F., Singer, D., et al. (2015). The Global Findex Database 2014: Measuring financial inclusion around the world. World Bank Group. http://documents1.worldbank.org/curated/en/187761468179367706/pdf/WPS7255.pdf.

Demirgüç-Kunt, A., Klapper, L., and Singer, D. (2017). Financial inclusion and inclusive growth: A review of recent empirical evidence. World Bank Group. http://documents1.worldbank.org/curated/en/403611493134249446/pdf/WPS8040.pdf.

Deschryver, P., and De Mariz, F. (2020). What Future for the Green Bond Market? How Can Policymakers, Companies and Investors Unlock the Potential of the Green Bond Market? *Journal of Risk and Financial Management* 13(3): 61 https://doi.org/10.3390/jrfm13030061.

Diamond, D. W. (1984). Financial Intermediation and Delegated Monitoring. *Review of Economic Studies* 51(3), 393–414.

Easterly, W. (2001), The Middle Class Consensus and Economic Development, *Journal of Economic Growth* 6: 317. doi:10.1023/A:1012786330095.

Fish, T., and Whymark, R. (2015). How has cash usage evolved in recent decades? What might drive demand in the future? Bank of England, *Quarterly Bulletin 2015 Q3*, 216–227. https://www.bankofengland.co.uk/-/media/boe/files/quarterly-bulletin/2015/how-has-cash-usage-evolved-in-recent-decades-what-might-drive-demand-in-the-future.pdf?la=en&hash=4AA04C755C1B8BBDC70CE55CAD488E348FEDDAC5.

GIIN (2018), Roadmap for the Future of Impact Investing: Reshaping Financial Markets, GIIN Research. https://thegiin.org/assets/GIIN_Roadmap%20for%20the%20Future%20of%20Impact%20Investing.pdf.

GIIN (2019). Global Impact Investor Survey 2019. GIIN Research. https://thegiin .org/assets/GIIN_2019%20Annual%20Impact%20Investor%20Survey_ webfile.pdf.

Gonzalez, L. E., Vidal, V., and Christopoulos, T. P. (2013). Microinsurance: Opportunities and Restrictions in an Emerging Market. *Revista PRETEXTO* 14(2): 20–39.

Gonzalez, L. E., Righetti, C., and Di Serio, L. C. (2014). The Impact of Microcredit on Income: The Case of Banco Real in Brazil. *Revista de Economia Contemporânea* 18(3): 453–476.

Greenwald, B., and Stiglitz, J. E. (2003). *Towards a New Paradigm in Monetary Economics*. Cambridge, UK: Cambridge University Press.

Gwalani, H., and Parkhi, S. (2014). Financial Inclusion: Building a Success Model in the Indian Context. *Procedia-Social and Behavioral Sciences* 133: 372–378.

Han, R., and Melecky, M. (2013). Financial inclusion for financial stability: Access to bank deposits and the growth of deposits in the global financial crisis. World Bank: Policy Research Working Paper 6577.

Humphrey, D. B., Pulley, L. B., and Vesala, J. M. (1996). Cash, Paper, and Electronic Payments: A Cross-Country Analysis. *Journal of Money, Credit and Banking* 28(4), 914–939.

Kelly, S., and Rhyne, E. (2015). By the numbers: Benchmarking progress toward financial inclusion. Center for Financial Inclusion. Accion.

Keynes, J. M. (1936). *The General Theory of Employment, Interest, and Money*. New York: Harcourt, Brace & World.

Klapper, L., and Singer, D. (2014). The opportunities of digitizing payments. A report by the World Bank Development Research Group, the Better Than Cash Alliance, and the Bill & Melinda Gates Foundation to the G20 Global Partnership for Financial Inclusion. Working Paper 90305.

Klapper, L., El-Zoghbi, M., and Hess, J. (2016). Achieving the Sustainable Development Goals. CGAP, UNSGSA.

Klee, E. (2006). Families' use of payment instruments during a decade of change in the US payment system. Federal Reserve System.

La Porta, R., Lopez-de-Silanes, F., Shleifer, A., et al. (2000). Investor Protection and Corporate Governance. *Journal of Financial Economics* 58(1), 3–27.

Levine, R. (1997). Financial Development and Economic Growth: Views and Agenda. *Journal of Economic Literature* 35(2): 688–726.

Levine (2005). Finance and Growth: Theory and Evidence. *Handbook of Economic Growth, 1*: 865–934.

Lindert, K., Linder, A., Hobbs, J., et al. (2007). The nuts and bolts of Brazil's Bolsa Família Program: implementing conditional cash transfers in a decentralized context. Social Protection Discussion Paper 39853, vol. 709.

Lluberas, R., and Saldain, J. (2015). Paper or Plastic? Payment Instrument Choice in Uruguay. *Revista de Economía* 22(1): 35.

Mantel, B. (2000). Why do consumers pay bills electronically? An empirical analysis.

Mas, I. (2009). The Economics of Branchless Banking. *Innovations* 4(2): 57–75. DOI: 10.1162/itgg.2009.4.2.57.

Mas, I. (2015). Strains of Digital Money. *SSRN Electronic Journal.* DOI: 10.2139/ssrn.1728125.

Merton, R. C. (1995). A Functional Perspective of Financial Intermediation. *Financial Management* 24(2): 23–41.

Merton, R. C., and Bodie, Z. (1995). A Conceptual Framework for Analyzing the Financial System. The Global Financial System: *A Functional Perspective*, 3–31.

O'Brien, S. (2015). Consumer Preferences and the Use of Cash. San Francisco Federal Reserve, 2015.

Pinheiro, A. C., and Moura, A. (2003). 10 Segmentation and the Use of Information in Brazilian Credit Markets. *Credit Reporting Systems and the International Economy*, 335.

Piketty, T. (2013). Le capital au XXIe siècle. Le Seuil.

Pressman, S. (2007). The Decline of the Middle Class: An International Perspective. *Journal of Economic Issues* 41(1): 181–200.

Rawls, J. (1988). La théorie de la justice comme équité: une théorie politique et non pas métaphysique. In Individu et justice sociale, pp. 277–318. Le Seuil (programme ReLIRE).

Rawls, J. (1971). *A Theory of Justice.* Cambridge, MA: Harvard University Press.

Rhyne, E. (2001). *Mainstreaming Microfinance: How Lending to the Poor Began, Grew, and Came of Age in Bolivia* (No. 332.1 R4.). Bloomfield, CT: Kumarian Press.

Roa, M. J. (2015). Financial inclusion in Latin America and the Caribbean: Access, *Usage and Quality. Research Paper* 19.

Sahay, R., Cihak, M., N'Diaye, P., et al. (2015). Financial inclusion: Can it meet multiple macroeconomic goals? *International Monetary Fund, Working Paper no.* 15/17.

Santana, M. H. (2014). Mercados de capitais no Brasil. In *Conference at FEA-USP*, Sao Paulo.

Schuh, S. D., Shy, O., and Stavins, J. (2010). Who gains and who loses from credit card payments? Theory and calibrations. Federal Reserve Bank of Boston, Public Policy Discussions Papers No.10-03.

Schuh, S. D., and Stavins, J. (2010). Why Are (Some) Consumers (Finally) Writing Fewer Checks? The Role of Payment Characteristics. *Journal of Banking & Finance 34*(8): 1745–1758.

Stiglitz, J. E. (1989). Financial Markets and Development. *Oxford Review of Economic Policy 5*(4): 55–68.

Stiglitz, J. E., and Weiss, A. (1981). Credit Rationing in Markets with Imperfect Information. *American Economic Review 71*(3): 393–410.

Stiglitz, J. E., and Weiss, A. (1992). Asymmetric Information in Credit Markets and Its Implications for Macro-Economics. *Oxford Economic Papers 44*(4): 694–724.

Von Kalckreuth, U., Schmidt, T., and Stix, H. (2014). Choosing and Using Payment Instruments: Evidence from German Microdata. *Empirical Economics 26*(3): 1019–1055.

Women's World Banking (2014). Savings: A Gateway to Financial Inclusion.

World Bank Group (2016). Innovation in Electronic Payment Adoption: The Case of Small Retailers. World Bank Publications.

World Bank Group (2015a). Innovative Digital Payment Mechanisms Supporting Financial Inclusion: Stocktaking Report. Payment System Development Group.

World Bank Group (2015b). Payments Aspects of Financial Inclusion, Committee on Payments and Market Infrastructures, World Bank Publications.

World Bank Group (2013). Global Financial Development Report 2014: Financial Inclusion, vol. 2. World Bank Publications.

World Bank Group (2012). General Guidelines for the Development of Government Payment Systems, Financial Infrastructure Series. World Bank Publications.

Zins, A., and Weill, L. (2016). The Determinants of Financial Inclusion in Africa. *Review of Development Finance 6*(1), 46–57.

Index